car also had a more modern body, similar to what would finally appear as the 1903 Ford (and Cadillac). As before, its two-cylinder horizontal engine was located beneath the seat. Wire wheels and flaring leather fenders were again used, but because of a difference in suspension, the car sat higher than the second experimental vehicle.

Also during the year, it is believed that a handful of runabouts (figures range up to one dozen) were produced sporadically by Detroit Automobile. A photo of what is believed to be one of these runabouts appears here, but cannot be substantiated. The car has many similarities to Ford's forth experimental car, but whether the Detroit Automobile models came first, or were based on the fourth model, is an open question.

Approximately 20 years ago, the late James Bradley, then head of the automotive collection at the Detroit Public Library, identified this vehicle as possibly being one of the handful of runabouts produced in 1901 by the Detroit Automobile Co. Similarities between this and Ford's fourth experimental car would suggest a close tie between the two vehicles, though it would be hard to determine which of the cars actually came first. On Nov. 30, Detroit Automobile Co. was again reorganized, and became the Henry Ford Co.

Although building a race car was a consuming interest of Ford during this year, he did finish work on his fourth experimental vehicle. Although sitting higher than the second car, this design sported a more modern runabout body, not unlike that which would appear on both the 1903 Fords and Cadillacs. It too used a two-cylinder horizontally opposed engine located under the seat, and it had curved leather fenders. The body was of wood, finished in black, with either silver or gold leaf trim. The car still exists in the Henry Ford Museum in Dearborn.

The high point of Ford's year occurred on Oct. 10 at Grosse Point, Mich., when Ford matched his experimental racer against Alexander Winton's well known race car. A third car, driven by William Murray of Pittsburgh, Pa., was also supposed to be in the race, but was withdrawn because of mechanical troubles. Actually, it was overheated bearings on the Winton which caused the car to slow down and allowed Ford to catch up after the fifth mile, and take the lead on mile eight. Ford's car bears the number "4" so possibly there was supposed to be even another car in the race. Ford's prizes were $1,000 plus a glass punch bowl, but it appears that the cash was never awarded by the race committee.

The year 1901 was not necessarily a banner one in the annals of Ford history, but by year end the early racing world was thoroughly startled by the exploits of one Mr. Henry Ford. As mentioned in the last chapter, the year opened with the dissolving of the Detroit Automobile Co. by its principal founders. That should have left Ford without a job. But, it did not.

Several of the stockholders of the original company felt there was still hope for Ford produced cars, and noted that the few which had been built (figures now ranged from seven to twelve according to news reports of the day) had sold easily and had a good reputation. In view of that, these men reorganized Detroit Automobile Co., reduced the size of the plant, and re-hired Ford as superintendent. He was given the job with the understanding that he was to build what he felt would do the company the most good.

Whether or not these instructions were the smartest or the best is open to discussion. Ford did build what he felt was the best vehicle for the moment—but it was a race car. Maybe Henry seriously felt that the publicity gained from winning races would help the company in the long run. Maybe he wanted to take some of the publicity away from Alexander Winton and his Winton cars, which were winning nearly every race that they entered. Or, maybe he just felt like going racing.

Whatever the reason, Ford's major interest during this time was a rather light racing machine of 1,600 pounds which resembled a fenderless low-slung runabout of the day. Fitted with wire wheels, a small front-mounted radiator covered with a hood, and sporting a right-hand steering wheel and two-passenger seat, the car really did not look much like the racing machines of the day. Under the seat, however, was a different animal. Ford again looked to his two-cylinder horizontal engine design for power. But this one had a huge square bore and stroke of seven inches, which displaced 540 cubic inches. This developed 26 horsepower at the then high figure of 900 RPM.

If Ford had a desire to beat Winton with this car, it was probably rooted in some jealousy and in some ruffled feathers. After all, in 1899 Winton had produced over 100 cars, following only Columbia and Locomobile in production, to be America's third largest car builder. And, during this time, Ford was still playing with his second vehicle. Also, it was recalled by Alexander Winton that during this time a young mechanic had come to his Cleveland, Ohio, factory seeking a machinists job. That man, Henry Ford, had been turned down because it was felt that he lacked experience. Yes, it is certain that Ford wanted to beat Winton. But not all of the race hinged on personalities. If Ford could win against the best known racing car and driver of the time, the resulting publicity would certainly help to sell Ford-designed cars.

On Oct. 10, 1901, Ford had a chance to beat Winton. The race, staged at the Grosse Pointe Race Track north of Detroit, consisted of only two cars—Ford's and Winton's. Ford and Alexander Winton both drove their own cars, with Ford receiving some early advice from Tom Cooper, a noted bicycle racer, and from Edward Huff, who would act as Ford's riding mechanic. The 10-mile event saw Winton leading at first, but Ford catching up after the half-way mark, as the Winton began to suffer from overheated bearings. Ford took over at the eight-mile mark, and crossed the line well ahead of Winton. The Ford ran at an average speed of 43.5 MPH, though Henry claimed the car would actually go a mile a minute.

Following the win at Grosse Pointe, Ford's backers were so enthusiastic that they decided to reorganize the company once again. Subsequently, Detroit Automobile Co. was once again disbanded, and on Nov. 30 a new operation called the Henry Ford Co. was organized in its place. To Ford's dismay, however, the backers insisted that Ford was to concentrate on production-type cars, and if he wanted to build racing cars, he must do so on his own time and with his own funds. To say the least, Ford was not happy about this.

Overshadowed by Ford's racing activity, however, were some interesting production cars that did come from Detroit Automobile Co. One was Ford's fourth hand-built car, which appeared to be a much more sturdy version of his second vehicle. As he did with his racer, he used a steering wheel rather than a tiller. The

Henry Ford's first racing car is seen in action at Grosse Pointe in this old painting. Shown, again with a mustache, are Henry behind the wheel, and riding mechanic Edward "Spider" Huff. Huff is braced on the running board to counter-balance the car on the corners. Ford won the 10-mile race against the favored Winton at an average speed of 43.5 MPH. However, he later claimed that the vehicle was capable of going over a mile a minute. Later still, in November, the car did set a mark of 69.2 MPH in the flying mile. The opposed two-cylinder engine had a square bore and stroke of seven inches and displaced 540 cubic inches.

CRESTLINE

90 YEARS OF FORD

George H. Dammann

Motorbooks International
Publishers & Wholesalers ®

Motorbooks International books are also available at discounts in bulk quantity for industrial or sales-promotional use. For details write to Special Sales Manager at the Publisher's address

Library of Congress Cataloging-in-Publication Data Available

Dammann, George H.
    90 years of Ford / George H. Dammann.
        p.   cm. — (Motorbooks International Crestline series)
    New ed. of: Illustrated history of Ford, 1903-1970.
        ISBN 0-87938-682-7
    1. Ford automobile—History.   I. Dammann, George H. Illustrated history of Ford, 1903-1970.   II. Title.   III. Title: Ninety years of Ford.   IV. Series: Crestline series.
TL215.F7D347   1993
629.222′2—dc20   93-30070

Printed and bound in United States of America

FOREWORD

Over two decades ago, a small Illinois publisher took an ultimate risk, and came out with an entirely different book on Fords. In effect the book was an experiment. This was in the late 1960s, an era when very few automotive history books were successful. Those few that did manage to pay their own way were usually filled with miles of text, with an occasional picture to score a point. Yes, the famed Floyd Clymer had published many low-cost soft cover books, but these were mainly collections of old advertisements or test reports on new cars. Peterson Publishing Co., Popular Mechanics, and a few others had come out with 75-cent soft cover pictorial publications, but these were more extended magazines than actual books, and few dealt with antique cars.

In 1968, probably due to a photo-journalism background, I had an idea for a total pictorial history, that would tell its story not in ponderous columns of type, but with short chapter leads, followed by captioned photos. Hopefully, it would show every production model produced by a manufacturer from inception to present day. To make reference easy, it would be in chronological order, with a chapter for each year, and the models appearing in a definite sequence in each chapter. It was a novel idea—too novel for most large publishers. Hence, Crestline Publishing wound up taking a total succeed-or-die chance. The results, of course, are obvious today. Crestline—now a part of Motorbooks International—has 30 titles on the market, all in its own rather unique format. The company for years has enjoyed a reputation of being one of the top publishers of fine, high quality automotive and agricultural history books. Obviously, this could not have occurred had not our readers shown their loyalty and support over the years, as each new title appeared. To all of you— Thank You!

But, back in early 1970, when *ILLUSTRATED HISTORY OF FORD* first appeared in print, no one could have dreamed that 23 years later the book would still be on the market, still be among the better selling automotive books, and would enjoy the reputation as being one of the longest running automotive books ever published. Least of all believing this was the author, who after four other similar books on Lincoln, Chevrolet, Buick, and Chrysler, wanted to do a complete rewrite of the original Ford edition. As mentioned, this book was in effect an experiment or a prototype. Its edges were too rough, its information too thin, its layout a bit clumsy. Everyone had learned from this volume, and the experience allowed us to produce better and succeedingly better Crestliners. Now it was time to make a really good book out of the Ford volume.

Alas, such was not to be the case. Every time work was started on Ford, it became sidetracked for something else—new automotive titles; a cross-country move; a new agricultural series, more new titles, etc. Finally, 23 years after the first Ford book appeared under the George Dammann signature, the new model arrived. Even Henry's Model T hadn't stayed on the market that long!

On the other hand, the delay did improve the book in one major way. Throughout the years, especially in the early years, many people knew we were collecting material for the new volume. And, during these years, a vast amount of research and photographic material was supplied that served to greatly enhance the value of the volume as a research tool.

Initially, the photos used in the first volume came from three major sources, via three of the finest people I have ever worked with. They were the late Henry E. Edmunds, former director of the Ford Archives at the Henry Ford Museum in Dearborn; the late James J. Bradley, then head of the Automotive History Dept. of the Detroit Public Library (and a very good friend), and John Mayberry, now retired as manager of the Photographic Department, Ford Graphics, at Ford Motor Co., Dearborn. Mr. Edmunds supplied most of the photos of the Model T and Model A cars, and some of the early 1930s material. Mr. Bradley came in with the vast remainder of the 1930s material and carried the book through the mid-1950s, and Mr. Mayberry supplied virtually all of the later year pictures.

However, as the new research progressed, it was decided to try to use as many different pictures from various sources as we could. Many of the archival photos were getting quite well known, having appeared in numerous publications over the years. Some have even been in print ever since they were first released by Ford, in their initial intent of being new-model publicity photos. Although there is certainly nothing wrong with reusing this material, and many of these original publicity photos have been used within these pages, we were hoping for a fresh approach wherever possible.

Here, once again James Bradley came into the picture, opening up a complete collection of *FORDFAX* and *FORD TIMES* magazines, plus digging deep for material that was outside of the mainstream of normal research. John Mayberry also again was a tremendous help. While working with him on Crestline's *FORD TRUCKS SINCE 1905,*— (by James K. Wagner), he brought forth a substantial collection of publicity photos that had never been published. And John's assistant, Hal Stopchinski, former Librarian of the Photo Media

Department, Ford Motor Co., opened his "private" collection of publicity photos, going back into the formative years of Ford. Over the years Hal had selected these as much for their aesthetic beauty as for their portrayal of the vehicles involved. Also contributing greatly to this project was another very good friend. He is James Wren, who heads the Patent Library at the Motor Vehicle Manufacturers Assn. Jim somehow always managed to come up with the right material at the right time, no matter how obscure the subject might have been.

Within this time frame, I also "lucked" into some very lucrative finds. Thomas C. Thomas, a fellow Model T enthusiast, had just taken over as Editor of the *MODEL T TIMES*, the club publication of the Model T Club International. In cleaning out the old files, he came up with a vast amount of Model T photos. About this time, a struggling Texas magazine called *SPOKE WHEEL*, contracted with me for a few articles on Fords, and rather than paying in cash, divested itself of a large collection of Model A and 1930s Ford photos.

Many of Crestline's other authors also came in with substantial donations from their own private collections. Among these were the late Don Butler of Detroit; Walter McCall of Windsor and Thomas McPherson of Toronto, Ontario; Dennis Casteele of Lansing, Mich.; James Moloney of Santa Barbara, Cal.; Donald Narus of Parma, Ohio; Fred Crismon of Bittberg, Germany, and Charles Wendel of Atkins, Iowa. Also providing material of varying amounts were the late Hugo Pfau, then under contract to Crestline; William Bomgardiner of Hershey, Pa., then editor of *ANTIQUE AUTO-*

MOBILE, Rev. Paul A. Wobus of Concordia, Mo.; Roaring 20s Autos, then of Wall, N.J.; Louis Halverson, director of the Automotive Section of the Philadelphia Free Library; Howard & Shelby Applegate of Annville, Pa., and Henry Paulman Jr., chairman of Paulman Publications of Chicago.

And, of course, much credit must go to Ford Motor Co., via its various branches, for allowing us to reproduce the catalog and brochure illustrations that appear throughout this book, and in effect, constitute a majority of photos used in the last 20 chapters. Without the cooperation of the Ford Motor Company itself, this book could not have been finished.

At the same time, it should be noted that although cooperation was received from Ford, this book has neither the authorization nor the backing of Ford Motor Co. In no way is it intended to be a promotional piece for Ford Motor Co., nor do any of the views or comments herein reflect either the thoughts or feelings of the Ford Motor Co. or its personnel. In this light, as author, I take full responsibility for any and all opinions and comments found within these pages. This book was compiled with the sole intent of displaying the majority of Ford automobiles in the most comprehensive and interesting way possible, for both present and future research into the vehicles produced by this major manufacturer. For the sake of our many readers, I hope I have succeeded.

George H. Dammann

At the unlikely time of 4 a.m. on June 4, 1896, an intense 33 year old engineer cranked up a strange looking contraption outside a workshop behind his Detroit home. Hopping onto the sputtering machine, he drove down an alley and onto Bagley Ave. A few blocks further and the machine coughed to a stop. The man made a few adjustments, restarted the engine, and ran the vehicle back home. Once there, he caught only a brief nap before leaving for his regular job at the Edison Illuminating Co.

The tall, thin man was Henry Ford, and this run marked the first actual road test of the first Ford car. In later weeks during the summer, he and his wife Clara and son Edsel would climb into the sputtering little 500-pound vehicle, and drive out into the Dearborn country-side to either the Ford or the Bryant farms at the then amazing speed of almost 20 MPH.

Thus was laid the groundwork for what was to become one of the mightiest automotive empires in the world. However, at this time it was doubtful if the young engineer had any thoughts about empires or even producing cars on a commercial basis. More than likely Mr. Ford had enough to think about just keeping his fruit of three years work and experimentation running over the rough roads to his parents' or in-laws' farms. Besides, at this point, auto building was simply a hobby to be engaged in while working at his regular job of engineer at Edison's Detroit plant. Ironically too, in later years Ford and Edison would become fast friends — traveling and camping companions — though in this current time frame surely Ford would have been awed simply by the presence of Thomas A. Edison. Who was this man named Ford who at this interval in life would have such a marvelous future still in front of him? Henry Ford was born on his parents' Dearborn farm on July 30, 1863. Although he was a life-time advocate of farming and rural life, he did not consider agriculture a suitable occupation for himself. Thus, at about the age of 16, he moved into nearby Detroit to take on a series of machine shop jobs where he could be closer to the machinery that he loved. Married in 1888 to a Dearborn farmer's daughter by the name of Clara Bryant, he chose to remain in Detroit with his bride, still seeking his fortune in and around machine shops and the machinery that they contained.

The year 1891 was a banner one of sorts for the Fords. It was then that he took his first really good job, being hired as an engineer for the Edison Illuminating Co. Then, on Nov. 6, his only child — Edsel — was born. The decent job and young family gave stability to Henry Ford, allowing enough income for his continuous tink-ering with a new-fangled toy called a gasoline engine.

Over the next few years, Ford continued to work on variations of gasoline engines which he kept reading about in engineering magazines. Finally, on Christmas eve, 1893, his first home-designed and built engine coughed its way to life in the family's kitchen sink. At this time, though he may have dreamed about building a self-propelled vehicle some day, Ford was content to continue his experiments with gasoline engines of various designs. Finally, early in 1896, he decided the time was ripe to build his own horseless carriage. Part of this decision may have come from his friend, Charles B. King, who had been working on a horseless carriage of his own design. In fact, when King tested his vehicle on March 6, 1896, it is believed that Henry Ford was one of his helpers following behind on a bicycle. By this time, of course, Henry's car also would have been well along in its production, but not yet far enough to join his friend King.

It is also safe to assume that Ford had read with interest the accounts of America's first automobile race, sponsored by the Chicago Times-Herald. This famous race was won by a Duryea, which was one of America's first production cars. King himself had intended to enter this race, but did not get his car finished on time. Instead, he attended as a member of the Mueller-Benz team, and piloted that car to second place. It is also known that King helped Ford design and obtain parts for his first engine. Yet there seems to be no record indicating that the Ford and King vehicles were ever operated at the same time in the same place. King himself went on to start his own engine business, which he later sold to Ransome E. Olds. After working at Olds (later Oldsmobile and Reo), he joined with Jonathan Maxwell to form the Northern Mfg. Co. in 1902. He remained with this company, which produced the Northern car, until 1908, when he left to study and observe engineering in Europe. Returning to Detroit in 1910, he designed his own car, which he was able to put into production in 1911. King cars were manufactured in Detroit from 1911 to 1923, when the bankrupt company was purchased and moved to Buffalo, N.Y. A few Kings were produced there in 1923 and 1924 before the company folded forever. It is reported that the last batch of Kings were shipped to England for sales there as 1925 models.

Throughout the summer of 1896, Ford continued to run, improve, and play with his car, which he now referred to as a Quadricycle. By the fall of that year, however, he was envisioning a more improved vehicle, using ideas that could not be incorporated into the Quadricycle. In line with these ideas was the problem of money for further experiments and the question of what to do with the first car. Both problems were quickly solved when a person by the name of Charles Ainsley offered $200 for the Quadricycle. In practical-ity, the first Ford had now been sold.

Ironically, the car survived various owners, and at a later date Ford was able to buy it back and restore it to its original shape. It is now an important part of the Ford display at the Henry Ford Museum in Dearborn. Here visitors are able to see the hand-built two-cylinder engine with open connecting rods, the large open flywheel, belt and chain drives, and other now-primitive but then unique engineering ideas to spring from the fertile mind of Henry Ford.

One of the most photographed and best known early vehicles is the first Ford, built in 1896 by Henry Ford and first run at 4 a.m. on June 4 of that year. The two-cylinder car used a belt clutch, operated by the right-hand lever. Low was engaged by pulling the lever back, neutral was in the center, while high was engaged with the lever forward, as shown. Top speed in low was about 10 MPH, while high was just double that. At this point, Ford did not name the car after himself, but referred to it as a "Quadricycle."

This 3/4-view of the Quadricycle shows it after such refinements as an oil lamp, bell, and seat had been added by Ford so that he could take his family for rides. One old photo shows that Ford had a small seat installed behind the dashboard at one time for Edsel to ride in, but apparently this seat did not last long. Initially, the Detroit press was quite interested in the car, but after its first few appearances, this interest died away.

In one of the few photos showing Henry Ford with a mustache, the 33-year old engineer poses with his Quadricycle. The mustache did not last nearly as long as the car — later photographs, made only a month or two after this, show Ford as being clean shaven. Attached to the front of the car is a battery powered door bell which Ford felt was necessary to warn people from in front of the vehicle The Quadricycle had no reverse, and originally had no brakes. Later Ford devised a type of transmission brake that worked sufficiently well for the speeds at which the car was driven. A few months after this photo was made, Ford sold the car in order to have money and space to work on his second vehicle. Happily, about 10 years later, he was able to repurchase the Quadricycle, still in good running order, and preserve it for posterity.

Henry Ford, now $200 richer from the sale of his Quadricycle, took the money and invested it wisely — he purchased tools, parts, and raw materials for what would become his second vehicle. No doubt a good portion of the design for the second car was already in his mind when he sold the Quadricycle, but the vehicle did not materialize as quickly as he had hoped. Work on the car probably stared in the fall of 1896, but it wasn't until mid-1898 that the car finally made its debut. Both in appearance and performance, the second model was much advanced over the Quadricycle.

Weighing 875 pounds and sporting a leather dash and leather fenders and running board, the second vehicle had such niceties as a covering over its two-cylinder engine, full springing for all four wheels, oil lamps, fully padded carriage seat, and even a carpeted floor. The front wheels, steered by tiller, were about three-fourths the size of the rear wheels. Final drive from the transmission was by chain to the rear axle.

Shortly after Ford brought out his second car, a very wealthy Detroit businessman named William H. Murphy asked for, and was given, a lengthy demonstration ride by Ford. The trip, quite long for its day, wound from Detroit through Farmington and Pontiac and back to Detroit. Murphy apparently was so pleased with both the performance and Ford that he lost little time in proposing that he and some of his equally wealthy cronies become involved in a new venture to produce such vehicles. The new company, to be located at 1343 Cass Ave., was to be known as the Detroit Automobile Co. and have Henry Ford as its superintendent. The new company was formed on July 24, 1899, shortly after Ford resigned from Detroit Edison.

Although Ford had the talent to build cars in his back shed, it seems that a much more difficult project faced him as he tried to set up a new manufacturing facility. Among the problems he complained of were incompetent help, supplied parts that were poorly manufactured, indecisions as to what kind of vehicles to produce, and not being given the opportunity to experiment with his new ideas.

Meanwhile, the company had announced prematurely that it would soon unveil an entire spectrum of models, including "a Trap, a Phaeton, a Touring Cart, Runabout, Physician's Stanhope, and a Heavy Delivery Vehicle." Surprisingly, it was the delivery vehicle that materialized first.

The high, open-front truck weighed 1,200 pounds, was fitted with rubber tired wood-spoke wagon-type wheels, and had an opposed two-cylinder engine mounted beneath the cargo floor. Coach lamps, plate glass side panes, a grab rail around the leather dash, and an oil headlamp gave it a look of class — which could have been enhanced even further had fenders been attached. Still, despite its neat looks, its performance reportedly left much to be desired, and it is believed that only one model was built.

On the automotive side, reports vary. Some say that by the end of 1899, one and one-half cars had been completed, while others say that toward the end of the first and only full year, as many as a dozen runabouts had been produced. Whatever the production, it was far short of the ambitious predictions first made for the company and its models. Finally, after 1-1/2 years of operation and the loss of $86,000 (definitely a large sum in 1900) the company was officially dissolved in January, 1901.

The hand-built, four-stroke, two-cylinder engine of the Quadricycle developed about four horsepower from its bore of 2-1/2 inches and its stroke of six inches. The chain drive ran from the belt-powered transmission to the right rear wheel, while a moveable pulley on the belt took the place of a clutch. The engine was started by reaching over the cylinders and spinning the flywheel in neutral until the ignition caught.

1898-1900

Henry Ford's second car appeared in 1898 after about 18 months work. The pretty little runabout sported a black polished wood body, and had black leather fenders and dash and a black upholstered seat. Steering was still by tiller, but workable brakes had been devised. The car performed very well, so much so that a demonstration run from Detroit to Farmington, Pontiac, and back to Detroit resulted in Ford being called on to head the newly created Detroit Automobile Co.

The Detroit Automobile Co. was formed on July 24, 1898, after William Murphy, a wealthy Detroit businessman, was taken on an impressive all-day tour by Ford in his second vehicle. The new company originally planned to offer a selection of six or more different automotive styles, plus this heavy-looking delivery truck. However, after almost a year, only this one truck and a few runabouts had been produced. Actually, no photographic evidence exists to substantiate the claim that any runabouts had been built, or what they looked like. But, old records do indicate that anywhere from one and one-half to a half-dozen such cars were actually produced. The truck, though modern looking for its time, was reported to be far from perfect, and its fate is unknown. After a loss of $86,000, the backers decided that further investment was futile and the company was dissolved in January, 1901. Lack of fenders gives the truck a slightly stark look, but this is offset by such styling niceties as plate glass side windows, curved dash with a surrounding grab rail, side coach lamps, front headlight, solid rubber tires, and plated hub caps.

The year 1902 should have been the first for the Ford Company. It was, but it was the wrong company. As the new year rolled in, the month-old Henry Ford Co. was already in rough waters. Even though Henry had been given one-sixth of the company's stock and the position of chief engineer, it seemed he still couldn't get production into gear. Stockholders' friction was growing as no cars materialized and as Henry reneged on his promise not to engage in race car design, but to concentrate instead on production vehicles.

True, Henry did finish an experimental runabout which he had begun in 1901, and possibly a few other copies of this car were produced and sold. As opposed to his fourth experimental model and the Detroit Automobile runabouts, this car almost seemed to be a regression, with its tiller steering, fenderless wire wheels, and low sloping dash. However, its engine appeared to be an improvement over the other models. Again located under the seat, the two-cylinder horizontally opposed engine had a bore and stroke of 4x5 inches, a displacement of 125.7 cubic inches, and produced 12 horsepower. Hooked to a revised two-speed planetary transmission, the car could scoot along at a comfortable 25 MPH.

Despite this car, trouble for Henry Ford walked in the door at the start of the year. The trouble was in the form of Henry M. Leland, a perfectionist engineer of wide acclaim in Detroit, who was head of his own Leland & Faulconer Co., a large and diverse engineering firm known for its precision products. Mr. Leland was brought into the Henry Ford Co. to act as a consultant. The directors who hired him hoped that his appearance would force Ford to move faster on production and start to turn out the runabouts that never seemed to materialize.

The appearance of Leland had a totally different effect, in fact, it destroyed the company. Leland and Ford could not get along. A master craftsman, Leland liked little that he saw at the Henry Ford Co. He was critical of Ford's designs, didn't like the workmanship of the employees, and had no qualms about stating his dislikes to the directors. To say the least, Ford must have been furious.

By March, Ford had taken all that he was able, and on March 10, after only three months with the firm bearing his name, he resigned and forced another reorganization of the company. When Ford resigned, he traded his stock for $900, the designs for a new race car, and the sole use of his name. This forced the directors to disband the Henry Ford Co., and as a result, the Detroit Automobile Co. again emerged. Although Ford no longer had anything to do with Detroit Automobile, it is interesting to note that on Aug. 10, the directors again went to Henry Leland for advise. Rather than disband the company as some thought would happen, Leland reworked somewhat the designs for the Detroit Automobile runabout, engineered the formation of a new company, and provided the firm with a new Leland & Faulconer single-cylinder engine which had been turned down by Oldsmobile. The new company was reorganized under the name Cadillac Automobile Co., named for the French explorer who had founded Detroit. Leland's first model was unveiled on Oct. 7, 1902, as a 1903 model. It bore a very strong resemblance not only to the earlier Detroit runabouts, but also to the production product that Ford would bring out in 1903.

The subsequent history of Cadillac is a different story, as is that of Leland. At this point, however, no one could have dreamed that Henry Ford and Henry Leland would once again face each other. Yet that very event took place almost 20 years later, when Leland's fledgling Lincoln Motor Car Co. became embroiled in a huge financial disaster. At that point, the now-millionaire Henry Ford stepped in to salvage the company and add it to his kingdom. One must always wonder if Ford felt the same satisfaction in taking over the Lincoln company that he felt in beating Alexander Winton—after all, both had at one time turned down both he and his ideas.

But Lincolns and Cadillacs were not on Henry's mind at this time. With his few dollars and new-found freedom, he set to work in earnest designing his next race cars. Although he was working on two cars simultaneously, only one would receive any honors this year. That was the famous "999," named after a record-breaking New York Central locomotive. The other car, first known as the "Arrow," would have to wait two years for its turn in the spotlight.

During the cars' construction, Tom Cooper, the bicycle racer who had helped with Ford's first race car, came back into the picture with both interest in and finances for the project. Ford and Cooper designed the two cars, with Ford creating the huge 4-cylinder engines with their 7-1/4x7 inch bore and stroke, and 1,156 cubic inch displacement. Also engaged in the project was Edward Huff, Ford's riding mechanic, and a young bicycle racing friend of Cooper's by the name of Barney Oldfield. Although Ford and Cooper devoted long hours and a great deal of money on the racers, the pair could never get them to run properly—if at all. Finally, in disgust, Ford sold the cars and his interest in them to Cooper for $350 apiece plus $100 extra for assorted parts. Cooper took the lot to his Toledo, Ohio, shop and there, after some experimentation, the problem was found to be simply one of carburetion. Despite their falling out financially, Ford and Cooper remained friends, and Ford continued to maintain a healthy interest in the two racers.

Meanwhile, Ford was again thinking of production cars. Possibly his failures with the racers helped in this respect. Thus, on August 20, Ford sat down with Alexander Malcomson and discussed the formation of a new company to build Ford-designed runabouts based quite heavily on the old Detroit Auto designs. This

Designed while he was still with Detroit Automobile in 1901, Ford began to work on this car while with the short-lived Henry Ford Co. He then took the designs with him when he left. It apparently was this vehicle that Henry Leland did not like when he (Leland) was hired as a consultant by the directors of the Henry Ford Co. Leland's presence at the company caused Ford to quit, taking with him his name, some automotive and race car designs, and $900. This little runabout, which was driven extensively by Ford, used a two-cylinder horizontally opposed engine of 125.7 cubic inches, and a planetary transmission. It could cruise along nicely at a comfortable 25 MPH.

time, Ford went to work in earnest designing a saleable runabout, and by October, a work force was hired and final touches were being put on the new Ford automobile. In November, the Ford & Malcomson Co. was formed, and in December a plant on Mack Ave. in Detroit was rented for production of the new car.

Meanwhile, the team of Cooper, Oldfield and Huff had modified the race cars and had entered the one called 999 in the Manufacturer's Challenge Cup race at Grosse Pointe. This race, held on Oct. 25, once again pitted the world renown Winton racer against a Ford-designed machine, plus two other cars. It was Oldfield's first race, but the fearless ex-bicycle racer turned mechanic now proved why he would soon be considered the world's champion driver. Following Oldfield's victory, Ford lost no time in cashing in on the fame of "999." Cooper, apparently not really caring who got the credit, allowed Ford to pose with the car for several photos, and didn't seem to mind that the news reports almost totally ignored the fact that it was Cooper's car, not Ford's that had won the race. But, Ford needed the publicity—Cooper did not.

Henry Ford poses with Barney Oldfield at the controls of the racer "999" following its victory in the Manufacturers'' Cup Race at Grosse Pointe, Mich., on Oct. 25. This was the second time that a Ford-designed car had raced a famous Winton racer and won. Although Ford had sold his interests in the car to Tom Cooper, he was allowed to pose with the vehicle and take credit for its design and construction. Today, few people have heard of Cooper, and it is widely believed that "999" was Ford's car. The chassis was a composite of white ash and steel, providing a wheelbase of nine feet, four inches. The front wheels were 34 inches in diameter, while the rears were 36 inches.

Although this and the other racer on this page are both billed as "999" and both show Barney Oldfield at the wheel, there are enough differences between the cars to make one think they are actually photos of both of the racers that Ford and Cooper built. Note that even though the cars look quite similar, the radiators are totally different, and this model seems to have some sort of lubricating or fuel monitoring attachment over the heads—no, it is not overhead valves. Since Oldfield drove both cars, and both were referred to as "999" on occasion, it is possible that these are the two cars that were built. Years later, one of the cars was wrecked at Milwaukee, while the other wound up in Los Angeles, where it was eventually found and restored by a Ford dealer. It is this restoration that is on display at the Henry Ford Museum in Dearborn.

The Ford Motor Co. was officially incorporated on June 16, 1903, and the first cars to bear the Ford name made their official appearance in July. Between Jan. 1 and June 16, however, the principals in the new company had been busy setting up shop, putting the finishing touches on and test running the new car, and attending to all of the other thousand and one things that were necessary to form a new company from scratch. And, for the first time in several years, Ford did not get involved in racing.

The new factory on Mack Ave. in Detroit was part of Alexander Malcomson's holdings. Malcomson was the big money behind this new Ford venture, and at first the company was to be called Ford & Malcomson. For some reason, this company was dissolved and for a short time the name Fordmobile Co. was considered. In fact, early ads for the car list both the car and the company as "Fordmobile." By late spring, the name Ford Motor Co. evolved, and ended once and for all the switching of corporate names.

When the first Fords appeared they were quite similar to the first Cadillacs, which had been introduced on Oct. 17, 1902. It was quite obvious that both Leland and Ford had leaned heavily on the original Detroit Automobile designs when they redesigned their respective models. The main difference between the two cars was that the Cadillac had a single cylinder engine supplied by Leland & Faulconer, while the Ford used a two-cylinder engine supplied by the Dodge Brothers. On the other hand, the finish on the Cadillac was supposedly far superior to that of the Ford, even though the bodies were made by the same company.

Both cars had the same initial list price of $750, and though the Cadillac had only one cylinder, its engine was more powerful than the one used by Ford. Shortly after its introduction, however, the Ford price was raised $100 while Cadillac's remained the same. Thus, at the outset at least, a Ford cost more than a Cadillac.

Designated the Model A, the first Fords had an opposed two-cylinder engine located under the seat. Having a cast iron block, the square-designed engine ran a bore and stroke of four inches even, displaced 100.4 inches, and produced eight horsepower. Early models used a Scheibler carburetor, while later ones used a Holley. These engines, though designed in major part by Ford, could not be built at the Ford plant because there simply was not the manufacturing space or expertise for such a project. Instead, one of the largest and busiest production machine shops in Detroit was contacted. That was the Dodge Bros. Co.—the same brothers who would later use their profits from Ford to found their own Dodge Bros. Motor Co.

At the time, however, the Dodges were skeptical of Ford, despite his backing by Malcomson. They finally agreed to supply 650 engines, transmissions, and chassis at $250 each, plus a covering bonus of 100 shares of stock in the new company. The engines and chassis were to be paid for cash on the line.

Only one body style was offered, a two place runabout. However, a detachable tonneau was available, and cars sold with this unit were usually referred to as 4-passenger models. The C.R. Wilson Carriage Co. of Detroit was contracted to build the bodies. This was one of the largest wagon or buggy body builders in Detroit, and was the same company that was supplying similar bodies to Cadillac. The cost of the 2-passenger bodies was $52 each plus an added $16 for the upholstered seat. The wheels and axles came from yet another supplies, while the white 28x3 clincher-type tires came from the Hartford Rubber Works. These tires were smooth and carried 70 pounds of air.

Although the plant was busy turning out Model As for the remainder of the year, there was no clear-cut production figures for the first six months. Ford records indicate that a total of 670 Model As were built, but this number includes those cars produced in the first months of 1904 as well as in 1903.

As mentioned earlier, Ford himself did no racing this year. However, it is fairly safe to assume that he kept his eye on the two "999" cars owned by Tom Cooper and raced by Barney Oldfield. During the year, Oldfield made some heroic runs, including breaking the mile-a-minute mark at Indianapolis on June 20, and a month later doing that mile in 55.8 seconds. He also won a tremendous victory on Memorial Day in Yonkers, N.Y., by beating the far-favored Peerless.

Then came Winton. Alexander Winton, having been burned on other occasions since he had lost to Ford first and Oldfield/Ford second, took a page from Henry's own book. He designed his own huge engined racer, and made Oldfield an offer he could not resist to be his official driver. Oldfield and Cooper parted as friends. But ironically, again at Grosse Pointe, Mich., there was a rematch of the Winton car, with Oldfield at the wheel, and the "999" with Cooper at the tiller. And, in a total upset, Cooper and the "999" won two out of the three scheduled races.

Although it is not known for a fact, it is safe to assume that Ford was on hand for these races, and again got the urge to set some speed marks. Contacting Cooper, who really didn't need both "999" racers, Ford bought one of the cars back and rehired Edward "Spider" Huff as his riding mechanic. Now his eye was not on Winton, but on the land speed record, which at the time was 77.13 MPH, set the year before by a French Mors. By year end, Ford was ready to again go racing.

Toward the end of the year, another interesting event took place—one which in the long run would give vast amounts of publicity to Ford and his company, and eventually would result in the downfall of what at that time was the country's largest automotive combine. That event was the filing of a suit against Ford by George B. Selden and Electric Vehicle Co. for Ford's refusal to join the Assn. of Licensed Automobile Manu-

The first real production car to bear the Ford name was the Model A, which was introduced in July of 1903. It sold for $850 in basic trim, with the headlights, horn, and brass dash rail shown here being aftermarket accessories. Weighing 1,250 pounds, the car had a top speed of 30 MPH. Finish was in red, with black fenders and black leather upholstery. Barely visible on the rear deck is the gas filler cap, with the gas tank located under the rear compartment. Although this model, in the Henry Ford Museum, has black treaded tires, the original tires were smooth white rubber with no tread.

Thirty years after he watched the introduction of the first car to bear his name, Henry Ford and his son Edsel take a run in the company's restored Model A. This scene occurred in 1933, during the company's 30th anniversary party. The seated Fords give an idea of the size of this car. The wheelbase was 72 inches and the tires were 28x3 clinchers. Following Ford's 75th anniversary in 1978, a survey was made to see how many 1903/04 Model As still existed. The amazing tally was that 82 exist world wide, 68 of these being in the U.S., with eight of these being in Michigan and six in Pennsylvania. Figures vary over the number of Model As actually built during the car's one-year run. Ford accepts the official tally of 607, while other sources, based on Dodge engine records, list a total of 1,708.

facturers (ALAM). The suit, filed on Oct. 22, demanded that Ford pay a royalty of 1.25% of gross receipts to ALAM in order to build an internal combustion automobile under license based on patents held by Selden and controlled by Electric Vehicle Co. of Hartford, Conn. Electric Vehicle was the parent company of Columbia, which in 1903 was one of America's largest automobile producers.

Ironically, in the spring, Ford had approached ALAM and applied for membership, with full intention of paying royalties. ALAM at that point inspected Ford's factory on Mack Ave. and declared that Ford was not an automobile manufacturer in any sense of the word, but simply was an assembler of parts produced by others. Ford fumed, and proceeded to market his cars without the blessings of ALAM.

Probably one of the pivotal points in Ford's decision to market cars without the ALAM license came about with the appointment of a major distributor for Ford cars in New York and Philadelphia. That distributor was John Wanamaker, head of a well-known chain of department stores, who appears to have been delighted to join Ford in the battle against the Selden Trust. Wanamaker ran many ads in the major city newspapers guaranteeing that his stores would stand behind any Ford buyer and protect them against trouble from the trust. This was in response to a threat by ALAM that it would not only sue makers of unlicensed cars, but would file suit against the buyers as well. Threats of this type, combined with the anti-trust mood of the day, made Ford a hero in many eyes, and gave the little company far more publicity than it really deserved.

For those wanting a 4-passenger car, Ford offered a detachable tonneau for $100 extra, and then listed the car as its 4-place model at $950. Rear compartment passengers entered through the back door and had their choice of sitting forward or sideward. The bodies were supplied by the C.R. Wilson Carriage Co. of Detroit and were almost identical to the bodies supplied for the very similar Cadillac which Leland was producing at the reorganized Detroit Automobile Co. which had been founded in part by Ford. In this era, the detachable tonneau concept was very popular, allowing car owners the option of having either a 2-place runabout or a 4-place tourer.

The chassis of the Model A was neither exceptional nor unique for the era, but pretty much followed established engineering practices. The rectangular box-like affair in front is the tubular radiator with its coils surrounded by cooling fins. The 8 horsepower engine is located amidships, under the seat, and runs a 2-speed planetary transmission with foot controls, not unlike what Ford would later use on the Model T. Braking was by foot-operated bands on the transmission. Chain drive ran from the transmission to the open differential. The Dodge Bros. produced engine, transmission and chassis.

Although the Ford Motor Co. was not incorporated until June 16, 1903, Henry Ford must have been quite certain that something big was going to happen with his name. In February of 1903, he ran ads in some trade papers listing the "Fordmobile" to be manufactured by the Fordmobile Co. of Detroit. The silhouette pictures of the cars looked quite similar to those that actually did appear in July, but the ads listed no specifics about the cars except to describe the dimensions (5x9 inches) of the transmission, It is interesting to note that the tonneau version listed and priced two accessory tops, which may or may not have been available in 1903. However, such tops did exist in 1904. As can be seen, the actual Ford cars were priced $100 higher than the "Fordmobiles" shown here.

When George B. Selden filed his patent for a "Road Engine" in 1877, he did not have a workable vehicle. In fact, through delaying tactics and changes, Selden managed to keep the patent alive but not granted until Nov. 5, 1895, when the Patent Office issued No. 549,160 in his favor. With this in hand, he sold the rights to Electric Vehicle Co. of Hartford, Conn., parent of the highly respected Columbia cars. Electric Vehicle and a few other Selden license holders then formed Assn. of Licensed Automobile Manufacturers (ALAM) to guard their rights and file suit against any auto manufacturer or importer who was not operating under a Selden license. The basis for Selden's patent was this model on file with the Patent Office. It wasn't until the Ford suit came into being that Selden was forced to build a full-size workable example of his road wagon.

One wonders if the makers of this early pedal car were impressed by the "999" designation of the Ford/Cooper/Oldfield racing car, or the famous New York Central locomotive No. 999, which hit a record speed of 112.5 MPH. Since the car had a basic appearance of a 1903/04 Ford, it is probable that it was named after the racer, which by the end of 1903 had become one of the most famous vehicles on the American racing scene. The design of this toy also indicates how quickly the public accepted and recognized the Model A as a symbol of an actual motor car, known widely enough to be copied into a child's plaything. The manufacturer of the pedal car is unknown.

For a small and still relatively insignificant company and its intense general manager, 1904 was a mighty busy time. During this year Ford took legal action against the country's major automotive syndicate; broke the world's land speed record; started a subsidiary branch in Canada, and launched three new models. The new models were the AC, which was a more powerful version of the A; the C, which had a hooded front, and the B, a large car with a new Ford-designed 4-cylinder engine. However, none of these models appeared until September, and today would probably be considered 1905 vehicles.

Chronologically, the first big event of the year occurred on Jan. 8, when Ford, again accompanied by his friend and racing mechanic Edward "Spider" Huff, took the "999" out onto the ice of frozen Lake St. Claire, just outside Detroit. With Ford at the wheel and Huff hanging on the side of the engine to hold open the carburetor, the monster car bounded over the incredibly rough ice at a reported 36 seconds for the measured mile, or just about 100 MPH on the nose. However, the run wasn't official, and when the AAA timers were there to officially clock the race on Jan. 12, the machine managed only 39.4 seconds through the traps, or 91.37 MPH. Still, this was enough to set the existing land speed record, which by then had been 84.73 MPH. And, of course, this caused Ford to gain a wealth of publicity.

Ford was no person to waste this publicity, and he quickly steered it toward the new 4-cylinder engine that was being developed for the new Model B which would appear in September. Despite the fact that the record breaker was the old "999," there were many who thought the car was a totally new vehicle. Part of this was due to an appearance change, caused by the removal of the radiator, plus the fact that Ford called the car the "Arrow" rather than "999."

Following the record run, Ford retired the car. Tom Cooper, meanwhile, kept racing the second "999" until it was totally wrecked at Milwaukee later in the year. At this time, he repurchased the "Arrow/999" from Ford, rebuilt it into track trim, and proceeded to race it at least through the 1905 or 1906 seasons. About 1912 the car was finally retired from racing, restored by a San Francisco Ford dealer, and subsequently donated to the Ford Museum at Dearborn, where it remains on display.

Ironically, Ford's land speed record lasted only 15 days. On Jan. 20, at Ormond Beach, Fla., William K. Vanderbilt ran the measured mile in 30 seconds flat, astounding the world with the fact that a man could travel at 120 miles an hour and survive.

Although Henry Ford did no further racing this year, the company did build at least one race car, and turned it over to Frank Kulick, a company mechanic. The car was little more than two frame rails between wire wheels, containing a pair of modified Model A engines coupled together and connected directly to the rear axle by a chain drive and clutch. This car and its driver set light-car records for one; three; four, and five miles in 1904; won a multitude of races in 1905 and 1906, and set world records for one; eight, and 24-hour distances in 1907. Following a serious accident by Kulick in 1907, Ford decided to retire from active racing.

While all of the racing provided a bright spot in the year, a gloomy area was being provided by the Selden Trust. Despite the trust's initial response that Ford was only an assembler, not a manufacturer of cars, the volume that was flowing from the factory definitely made the ALAM people take notice. By Sept. 30, when the new models were introduced, Ford had turned out a reported 1,708 cars. And, ALAM certainly wasn't happy about losing its 1.25% of these gross receipts, even if they were generated by an assembler. Although no license infringement had yet been proven, both sides were gearing for battle, and had taken their fight into the press, where Ford was slowly and steadily emerging as the underdog hero fighting the greedy automotive cartel. Both sides also used a tremendous amount of advertising to state their respective cases, with Ford being helped tremendously in this battle by John Wanamaker and his stores.

Ford and his team did not seem too worried about the threat of a suit from ALAM. In fact, they either seemed to be enjoying it, or ignored it altogether. Thus, when a small group of Canadians from Windsor (across the river from Detroit) were interested in starting their own automobile company, they went to Detroit to ask advice of Mr. Ford. Apparently both sides liked what they saw, and in a relatively short time work was begun on organizing Ford's first foreign operation. On Aug. 17, Ford Motor Co. of Canada was organized with exclusive rights to produce and sell Ford products in all parts of the British Empire, exclusive of Great Britain itself. For this, the parent U.S. company received 51% of the Canadian company's stock. It didn't take long for the Canadian group to get into operation, and in October, Model As were rolling from the plant, having been assembled from parts sent over from Ford's U.S. assembly plant. Later in the month, Ford of Canada began buying its runabout and tonneau bodies from the William Gray & Sons Co. of Chatham, Ontario, while continuing to receive all running gear components from the U.S.

Helping tremendously in the new company was the fact that the little Model As were selling well. In fact, after the first nine months of operation, the company showed a profit of $98,851 on the sales of 658 cars. Ford and his crew were busy at their drawing boards trying to come up with new models to entice the public.

However, for the most part, the Model A remained the chief product throughout 1904, with no changes of note. Its engine remained the 2-cylinder opposed model of four-inch square bore and stroke, that provided eight horsepower from its 100.4 cubic inches. This engine plus most of the running gear, were still supplied by the Dodge Brothers.

Then, in September, the Model A was phased out and two new models appeared. They were the Model AC, which was really the Model A with a more powerful engine, and the Model C, which was a much more modern looking car with a hooded front. Both cars had a 78-inch wheelbase as opposed to the 72-inch wheelbase of the Model A. However, both models used the Model A's 2-speed planetary transmission with its foot-pedal shift controlling the two forward and one reverse speeds. The transmission used a cone clutch and chain drive to the rear axle. Brakes were by bands on the differential.

Under the seat of both the AC and the C was a new 2-cylinder opposed engine. Similar in design to the Model A engine, the new block had a bore and stroke of a square 4.25 inches. This displaced 120.5 cubic inches and produced 10 horsepower. This engine also was built by the Dodge Bros. under contract to Ford.

The biggest change in direction came with the new Model B, but it is unclear exactly when this car was first introduced. At the very latest, it appeared with the Models AC and C, although several examples may have been around in the late spring or early summer. Whatever, the Model B was a radical departure from Ford's initial concept of light cars and low prices for the general public.

Whereas the Models A, AC and C all weighed approximately 1,250 pounds, the Model B tipped the scales at 1,700. Also, its big 4-door touring body rode on a wheelbase of 92 inches. And, under the front-mounted hood lived Ford's first 4-cylinder engine. This in-line model used a bore and stroke of 4.25x5 inches, thereby being able to use the Model AC's pistons. It displaced 283.5 cubic inches and produced 24 horsepower. As did the 2-cylinder engine, this model also used a Holley carburetor. The engine was mounted longitudinally and used a torque-tube drive shaft. It also used a cone clutch and a planetary transmission of two forward speeds, controlled by foot pedals. However, its top speed of 40 MPH mandated larger brakes. These were to be found on the two rear wheels, being Ford's first use of drum brakes. Priced at $2,000, this was not a car for the working man, and many believe it was Malcomson and his moneyed group, not Ford, who insisted on the design of this model.

Because of conflicting records in these early years, it is impossible to tell how many of each model were made—in fact, even the total figures conflict. It has been reported that the company sold 658 Model As in the first nine months, and actual production for this period was 670. Other records show that by Sept. 30 of this year, total production reached 1,708, but these obviously were not all Model As. Ford reported 1904 calendar year production of 1,695, and has accepted the figure of 1,900 for the combined production of Models A and AC. Although no production figures can be ascertained for the Model B, many sources tend to feel that it hovered somewhere around the 150 mark for calendar year 1904.

Throughout most of 1904, the unchanged Model A remained the sole product of the Ford plant. Fresh from the factory, the car looked like this, minus any of the accessories that a dealer would install. In this form, it weighed 1,250 pounds and sold for $850, though some ads show the price at $800. The most common accessories were a top for an extra $50, and kerosene or gas lamps. As can be seen by the flywheel, the cast iron 2-cylinder opposed engine resided under the seat. The transmission was a 2-speed planetary type, operated by foot pedals.

Considered a separate model, even though the tonneau could be removed, was the Model A Runabout with tonneau. Selling for $950 (or $900 according to some ads), this car offered 4-passenger seating via a rear-entrance tonneau that bolted to the rear deck. Production figures on the Model A vary greatly, with sources quoting the total 1903/04 production as anywhere from 670 to 1,708. Years ago Ford used to lean toward the higher figures, but today tends to accept the 670 total as being more realistic. Shown in a 1904 tonneau model is George Brown, a Dodge Bros. employee who later became a chief test driver for Dodge. At this point, the engine and most of the running gear was being built under contract for Ford by the Dodge Bros. company.

1904

THE FORD

Boosted into Popular Favor by the Knocks of the Trust

You can't frighten a grown up man with a toy pistol; neither can you scare a man who wants the best car made from buying the Ford. The mechanical genius of Mr. Henry Ford enabled The Ford Motor Co. to produce a two cylinder car so perfect in construction and so low in price that it has sounded the death knell of the Trust.

The cheapest two cylinder Tonneau car sold by the Trust is $1,500, so the Ford saves you $600.

Price with Tonneau, $900.   As a Runabout, $800.

We agree to assume all responsibility in any action the Trust may take regarding alleged infringement of the Selden Patent to prevent you from buying the Ford—"The Car of Satisfaction."

Parked in front of the Atlas Automobile Co., Ford's dealer in western Pennsylvania, is the new Model AC runabout, which was introduced in September, and today would probably be considered a 1905 model. Priced at $850, the same as the Model A, the AC is shown here fitted with accessory kerosene lights and a horn, but no top. The Model AC was simply a stretched Model A with a new 2-cylinder opposed engine of 120.5 cubic inches, which produced 10 horsepower and gave the car much more pep and speed than the original Model A.

All dressed up in accessories of the day is this restored Model C runabout, wearing the optional top, kerosene cowl laps, and gas headlamps. Both the Model AC and C used the same cast iron 2-cylinder engine located under the seat. Built by the Dodge Bros., but designed by Ford, this engine had a square bore and stroke of 4.5 inches, and produced 10 horsepower. This gave both the AC and C a claimed top speed of 38 MPH. This car has the wrong tires. All 1904 Fords used white tires without tread, supplied by the Hartford Rubber Works. These tires were 28x3 clincher types, running 70 pounds of pressure.

As with the Model A, the tonneau version of the Model AC was considered a separate 4-passenger car, and not a runabout with an accessory tonneau. Again as with the Model A, the Model AC 4-passenger version was priced officially at $950, though this magazine ad from "The Horseless Age" notes a price of only $900. This is one of the ads that Ford used to toss barbs at the Selden Patent Trust, which was pressing its suit for royalties on Ford cars. Of the most accepted production figures, Ford claims a combined total of 1,900 Model A and AC cars built, which would put AC production at 1,230 if the 670 figure for the Model A is accepted.

Of much more modern appearance than the Model AC was the new Model C, which also was introduced in September. The car used the same 78-inch wheelbase of the Model AC, but was fitted with a hooded front, which brought its appearance more in line with the automotive trends of the day. Under this hood lived the gas tank, whereas on the Model A and AC, the tank was located under the rear deck. Both the Models AC and C sold for the same price of $850 in runabout form as shown here. However, the kerosene lamps and horn would have been extra, as would the interesting and unusual wheels, with what appears to be an early type of demountable rims. Note the tires are the smooth white rubber models supplied by the Hartford Rubber Works.

As was the case with the Models A and AC, the Model C Runabout With Tonneau was considered a separate model. The detachable rear unit added $100 to the basic cost of the car and provided well-padded and comfortable leather seats for two additional passengers. Entrance was via a rear door. Though the seats were comfortable, leg room was cramped due to the slope of the runabout's rear deck. Visible here is the chain drive which connected the differential with the 2-forward speed planetary transmission. Note that there are no brake drums. Braking was accomplished by bands on the differential.

Early 1904 ads had only the two Model A variations to talk about, and often listed prices $50 cheaper for each model than the company officially promoted. This ad also bragged about the 92 MPH world record set by Henry Ford, while a box just under the prices guaranteed that the Ford company would assume all responsibility if any action was taken against any owner by the Selden Patent Trust. In the hopes of scaring buyers away from non-member companies, the Selden people had threatened to sue not only the non-member manufacturers for patent infringement, but also to bring suit against anyone who purchased a non-licensed car.

A total departure from Ford's concept of light cars and low prices was the new Model B, which had a 4-cylinder in-line engine under the hood and was able to reach a speed of 40 MPH. It is believed the car was designed to quiet Malcomson and his money group, who felt the company should aim for the luxury market. This, of course, was in direct opposition to Ford's belief in low priced cars for the mass market. Available only as a 4-passenger touring, the Model B weighed 1,700 pounds and cost $2,000. Its engine displaced 283.5 cubic inches and developed 24 horsepower. It also used a 2-speed planetary transmission, but had shaft drive and used drum brakes on the rear wheels.

It was this series of drawings and a small scale model that George B. Selden, a New York patent attorney, used to press his royalty claims against all manufacturers of gasoline-powered motor vehicles. Using these 1895 patents, a group calling itself the Assn. of Licensed Automobile Manufacturers (ALAM) attempted to levy a 1.25% royalty on all automobile manufacturers, with the sum based on total gross receipts of the company. Ford had at first applied for membership in ALAM, but was turned down by the group on the grounds that his company simply assembled cars, and was not a manufacturer. But, when Ford sales reached a noticeable level, ALAM decided it was time to press for royalties. Now it was Ford's turn at refusal, and he decided to fight the group rather than join.

No. 549,160.

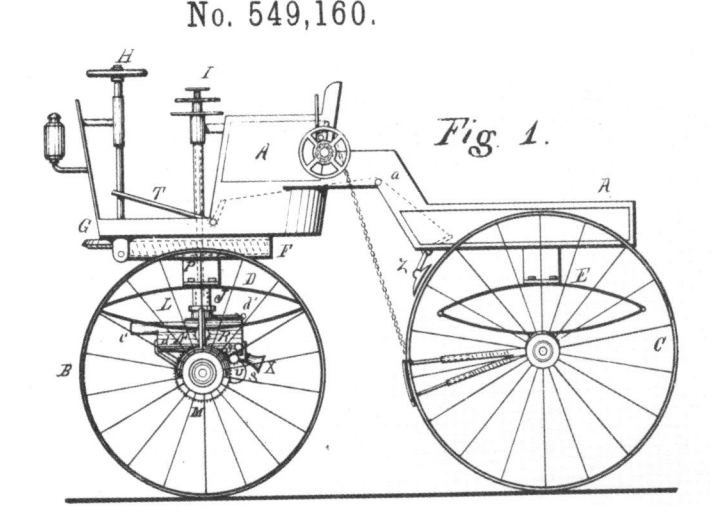

Fig. 1.

1904

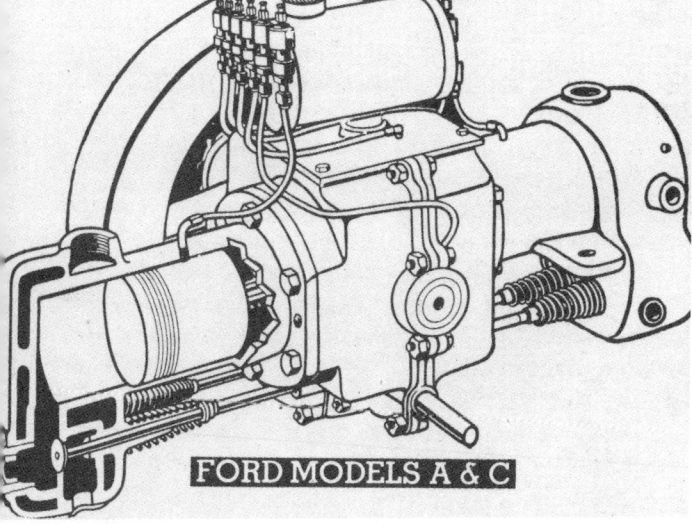

FORD MODELS A & C

Designed in major part by Henry Ford, but produced by the Dodge Bros. under contract, the Model A used an 8 HP engine consisting of a cast iron block containing horizontally opposed cylinders and L-head valve design. Bore and stroke were a square four inches, while the displacement was 100.4 cubic inches. The crankcase split vertically, with the crankshaft running horizontally to the large flywheel. A series of six visible manually adjusted oilers crowned the engine and provided lubrication for pistons, crankshaft, and connecting rods.

Prior to its record run, the rebuilt "999" sits in a powerhouse that was "borrowed" for some needed repairs. Because Ford referred to this car as the "Arrow," confusion has existed as to whether it was a totally new vehicle or a rebuild of one of the 999 racers that had been built and run by Ford and Tom Cooper. After Ford's record breaking run, Cooper again bought the car and raced it at least through 1905 or 1906.

A close-up of Ford's world record breaking Arrow or 999 racer shows the modifications made to the former 999. The torpedo-shaped unit above the block is a gas tank, which used gravity flow through a 2.25-inch pipe to feed the four huge cylinders. The radiator has been removed and a single water supply tank is mounted on the front. Since the one-mile plus entrance runs were relatively short and the weather was very cold, neither a large fuel supply nor cooling system were considered necessary. A small shield ahead of the steering wheel was Ford's only concession to relief from the icy wind. Huff's ride was not counted on at first, but the ice proved to be so rough that Ford was unable to operate a foot throttle, and needed someone to hold open the carburetor throats.

With Henry Ford at the wheel and mechanic and friend Edward "Spider" Huff holding open the carburetor, a rebuilt "999" racer appears here set to break the world speed record on the ice of frozen Lake St. Claire, near Detroit. The first action occurred on Jan. 8, when the team ran the one-mile course unofficially at 36 seconds, or just about an even 100 MPH. However, when the official AAA timers were set up on Jan. 12, the car was able to make the run in only 39.4 seconds, or 91.37 MPH. Still, this was enough to break the old record and give Ford plenty of new material for publicity and advertising. At the time of the run the ice was so rough that it bounced the car so badly that Ford could not hold his foot on the accelerator. So, in desperation, Huff crawled forward and held the throttle open by hand.

After breaking the world speed record, Ford did no further racing in 1904. However, he did authorize the building of one track racer, and turned it over to Frank Kulick, a company mechanic and driver who had shown some prowess in racing. The car was essentially two modified AC or A engines set between two light frame rails and supported by four rather fragile looking wire wheels. Kulick took several light-car records in 1904, and went on to win a multitude of races in 1905 and 1906, culminating in setting three world records in 1907.

After little more than two years in the automotive business, the Ford plant was forced to move to larger quarters this year. Actually, work on the plant had been started early in 1904 when it became apparent that the old Mack Ave. facility would never be large enough for the ambitious plans of Ford and his management. Consequently, a new 3-story cement block building was contracted for on the corners of Piquette and Beaubein Avenues in Detroit. Called the Piquette Ave. plant, the new structure was more than 10 times larger than the old Mack Ave. plant. It contained not only special assembly and painting rooms, but also space for experimental work above the second floor executive offices.

At this point too, Ford and James Couzens, a Malcomson assistant who had been working closely with Ford, recognized that unless more actual manufacturing was done by the company, profits and production would always be dependent upon outside firms—in this case, primarily the Dodge Bros. Thus, the pair set up the Ford Mfg. Co. in late 1905 to take over the manufacture of engines and running gear. The new company would operate totally outside of the original Ford Motor Co., but would be 100% dependent on the primary company for its business, management, and direction.

In line with the move to the new plant, the Model AC was dropped, and only the Models C and B were continued. Then, in February, the new Model F was introduced as what essentially was a larger and more powerful version of the Model C. The Model C continued to be available in runabout and runabout-with-tonneau styles, while the Model B was available only as a 4-passenger touring car. The new Model F also came as a 4-passenger touring car, but its 2-passenger model was known as a "Doctor's Coupe." In addition, it is possible that a few Model AC runabouts also were left over and sold as 1905 cars.

About the only change in the Model C was that its running gear was now painted in a light yellow, which greatly complimented the red body finish. The car continued to use its 10 HP 2-cylinder engine that was rated at 120.5 cubic inches, but its bore and stroke was now listed as 4.25x4.5 rather than the square 4.25 bore and stroke of 1904. Its wheelbase remained at 78 inches, and its tires continued to be 28x3 white clinchers supplied by Hartford Rubber Works.

The relatively new and not too popular Model B touring car also went unchanged, It sported Ford's first production 4-cylinder longitudinally-mounted engine under its hood, and used torque-tube rather than chain drive. It utilized a cast iron block, with a bore and stroke of 4.25x4 inches, which displaced 283.5 cubic inches and developed 24 horsepower. It used a planetary transmission similar to that in both the Models C and F, with two speeds forward and one reverse. Transmission control was by foot pedals on all models. Many historians will argue that the Models C and B should rightfully

be considered 1905 models only, and thus be regarded as having only 1905 as their sole year of life. Because of the early introductory date, coupled with the fact that model-year designations had not been firmly established, this book treats the cars as 1904 and 1905 models, with no 1906 carryover.

Thus, the only true 1905 Ford this year is the Model F. Not unlike the Model C, the Model F used a 2-cylinder under-seat engine. But this block had a bore and stroke of 4.5x4 inches, displaced 127 cubic inches, and claimed 16 horsepower. As did all Ford engines, it used a Holley carburetor, cone clutch, and 2-speed planetary transmission. Like the Model C, it had chain drive and band brakes on the differential. Its wheels were 30 inches, as opposed to the 28-inch variety on the Model C or the 32-inch stock on the Model B. Interestingly, some material of Hartford Rubber Works, which supplied all Ford tires, lists all three models as having 28-inch wheels. The wheels on the Model F were painted a cream color to match the running gear, which provided a nice contrast to the dark green bodies.

Production figures remain muddled for this year, with Ford claiming a total production of 1,599. However, it is not clear if this figure stands for all three models or only the Model F.

Whether it is a new 1905 model or a carry-over 1904 remains in dispute. Regardless of how it is considered, the Model C Touring car with detachable tonneau appeared for the last time this year. It continued to use its 2-cylinder cast iron engine with opposed cylinders, which was located under the drivers seat. However, this year the engine is listed as having a bore and stroke of 4.25x4.5 inches, while in 1904 the Model C reportedly had a square 4.25-inch bore and stroke. The 10 horsepower engine gave enough power for a 38 MPH top speed. Known for light and simple construction and economy of maintenance, the popular Model C sold for $950 this year, with the cowl lights being extra. It weighed about 1,250 pounds and had a 78-inch wheelbase.

Decked out with a host of extra cost items is this Model C runabout, which in 1905 was priced at $800. This unit wears the folding top and side curtains, brass kerosene lamps, horn, and a very interesting set of demountable rims with a 9-bolt pattern. The white tires without tread were standard and were supplied by Hartford Rubber Works. As noted before, this car could be transformed into a 4-passenger model simply by adding the detachable tonneau. When brought to full upright position, the top could be fitted with a front panel, containing a transparent section, for all-weather protection.

Considered by some to be the only really new 1905 Ford is the Model F, which was introduced in February of this year. Filling a size and price slot between the Models C and B, the 1,400 pound car rode on an 84-inch wheelbase and cost $1,000, not counting the lamps and horn shown here. As did the Model C, the Model F also used an under-seat 2-cylinder opposed engine, and put the gas tank under the hood. It also used a 2-speed planetary transmission, with chain drive from the transmission to the differential. The side-entrance tonneau was not detachable as on the Model C, but was permanent as on the Model B.

The only Ford this year to have more than two cylinders was the Model B, which shared only the transmission with other models. It had Ford's only 4-cylinder engine, and this was mounted longitudinally under the hood. It also sported shaft drive and drum brakes on the rear wheels. Available only in 4-passenger touring car form, and riding on a 94-inch wheelbase, the relatively large car weighed 1,700 pounds and sold for $2,000. As with the Model C, the Model B is often considered a 1905 vehicle only, and not a 1904 carry-over. As with the Model C, 1905 was also the final year for this car.

On the Selden scene, nothing of any dramatic nature transpired, as lawyers on both sides dragged in routine evidence, most of a highly technical nature. Finally the court ordered George Selden to produce a working model of his car. This was probably at the Ford Company's insistence that there were plenty of running Fords on the roads, but not a Selden in sight. The Selden, completed about mid-year, was supposed to reflect only the engineering as shown on the original patents, and contain no parts or concepts except those in existence in 1895. Contrary to these orders, several more recent innovations were incorporated into the display vehicle, much to the chagrin of Ford's lawyers. Still, the Selden ran very poorly, and did little to impress anyone of the merits of the long on-going case.

On the racing scene, Ford once more had his eye on the world's speed record. Part of this interest may have been prompted by the new Model K which was going to be introduced late in 1905, but which will be treated as a 1906 model. This car was to hold a brand new 6-cylinder engine that in production form would displace over 400 cubic inches and develop 40 horsepower. Ford, who was no slouch at publicity stunts, probably figured that a record breaking run in a racer equipped with the new Model K engine would do wonders in promoting interest in the new car. This was despite that fact that the Model K was a vehicle that Ford himself really did not like. It was one that had been forced upon him by the Malcomson interests, who wanted to produce luxury automobiles in which they could ride in pride.

Installing the new Model K engine in a set of light frame rails, Ford designed a light racer not unlike an oversized version of the one Frank Kulick was using around the country. However, unlike Kulick's racer, the new Model K machine was a total failure. Its first run in New Jersey in August was far from successful, and later tries at Ormond Beach, Fla., would prove to be even worse. Undaunted, Ford took the car back to Detroit, and set upon ways to modify the Model K engine. He and Frank Kulick would reappear with the machine in 1906.

1905

The new Model F was featured in many of the 1905 ads, such as this one, which even lists the rare Delivery Car. But, though Ford posted its Model F price at $1,000, the cost in this ad is shown at $1,200. It has been reported that there was also a 2-passenger Doctor's Coupe available in the Model F line for $1,250, but photographic evidence of this car has been impossible to find. All Model F cars were finished in dark green with cream wheels and running gear, though in this ad it appears that the running gear is a dark color.

The Selden vs. Ford patent case had this year settled down to rather boring and highly technical engineering presentations by both sides. But, the one big event concerned the court's demand that Selden build a full-size operating automobile based on the patent drawings he had submitted prior to the patent being granted in 1895. Although the court ordered Selden to adhere strictly to the patent drawings and not include any designs or items that were not available in 1895, the builders strayed from this rule in several instances. This fact, in the succeeding years of the trial, would provide Ford's lawyers with excellent ammunition regarding the fact that as filed, Selden's vehicle could not have operated as a successful self-propelled machine. Despite using improved components, the first Selden example is reported to have run very poorly, with almost constant stalls and breakdowns. Note that the driver's seat bears the numerals "1877," which is the year that Selden claimed he first designed the vehicle.

Even though the car was now a year old, Frank Kulick continued to set records and thrill spectators with his unusual little racer. Essentially two modified (the company literature claimed they were stock) Model C engines working in unison provided the power. Four rather fragile looking wheels gave the support, and two ultra-light frame rails held the whole thing together. Still, the little car managed to beat such racing giants as the Fiats and Renaults, and broke both the 1-mile and 5-mile records on several occasions during the year.

Although it is definitely a 1904 car, the Model AC was certainly carried over into the 1905 calendar year as a run-off vehicle. In its 1905 ads, Ford claimed the Model AC "is the result of 13 years of actual experience in building gasoline automobiles." This apparently alluded to Ford's experimenting with gasoline engines in 1892. Ford also promoted the fact that the 10 horsepower cast iron engine had its cylinder head and water jacket cast in one piece, with no removable heads of packed (gasket) joints.

In August of 1905, Henry Ford was ready to make another attempt at the world's land speed record. At this point, he was probably prompted mainly by a desire to reclaim the record. But he also saw the potential win as an excellent way to promote the new luxury Model K that the company was planning to introduce in 1906. His racer, called the "Model K," featured a 6-cylinder engine, but not necessarily of the same form that would appear in the passenger car. At the first record attempt at Cape May, N.J., the engine developed only 60 horsepower, and its performance was such that Fiat, Darracq, and the American Christie all beat him with little trouble. Shortly after, at Atlantic City, it was the Christie that again beat Ford, leading Henry to take the car back to Detroit for more modifications. The car would reappear at Ormond Beach, Fla., in January, 1906, with a 100 horsepower version of the 6-cylinder engine. This photo, incidentally, was taken at Ormond Beach at that time. Note that the car did not use a radiator as such. Leading the engine was a large brass water tank, with the actual cooling taking place in the 14 cooling coils that completely surrounded the engine.

To a corporate historian, 1906 is probably one of the most important in the annals of Ford Motor Co. For it was in this year that Henry Ford assumed the presidency, and then quickly moved to oust Alexander Malcomson and buy his shares of stock. Now Henry Ford had full and total control of the company bearing his name.

All of this corporate action occurred in July, beginning with the death of John S. Gray on July 6. Gray, who was Malcomson's uncle, had been a major financial backer of the company, and as such had been elected president when the company was formed. But in the succeeding few years since the initial papers were drawn, some very rough edges had sprouted, and by 1905 the company management was almost divided into two camps. There were those who favored Ford's ideas, and those who backed Malcomson. The difference was basically one of overall aims. Ford still felt that the best future for the company was in the design of a good but relatively low cost car for the masses, with profits figured on volume. Malcomson leaned heavily toward the concept of low volume, high profit luxury cars, one or more of which he could be proud to own.

It was undoubtedly Malcomson and his contingent that pushed through the 4-cylinder Model B, which Henry did not like, and demanded production of the 6-cylinder Model K, which Henry is supposed to have despised. Meanwhile, a former Malcomson employee, James Couzens, had now thoroughly swung his allegiance to Ford. He was the one who had helped Henry set up the Ford Mfg. Co. as a separate entity to build components for the Ford Motor Co. Couzens, who had a brilliant mind for business, was destined to become one of the most powerful key men in the later Ford empire. At this point, he felt it was Ford's idea that bore merit.

With Ford in control as president, and Ford Mfg. Co. able to siphon off any or all profits from Ford Motor Co., Malcomson certainly must have known he was between a rock and a hard place. Thus, within a week, he had sold his interest to Ford, and Henry was fully in command.

But being in command didn't necessarily give Henry the cars he wanted. For this year at least, he was stuck with the Model K. But he also had the new Model N, which was more along his idea of what a low-price car should be, and the carry-over Model F, which was Ford's last 2-cylinder design.

As noted in Ford's 1906 catalog, the Model F was held through the 1906 production simply because demand for the 2-cylinder car was so strong that the company could not let it drop. This year it was available only as a 5-passenger touring car of 1,400 pounds, priced at $1,100 to $1,200. The elusive Doctor's Coupe model mentioned in 1905, but not substantiated, was not mentioned this year. Finished in dark green with yellow running gear, the car could be fitted with several types of full tops, with a variety of brass cowl and headlamps of both gas and kerosene fuel, and with seldom-seen demountable rims. It retained its 84-inch wheelbase.

Under its front seat lived Ford's last 2-cylinder engine, while the 9-gallon gas tank was hidden under the hood. Interestingly, an original catalog in the author's collection puts the bore and stroke at 4.5x4 inches, and sets the horsepower at 12, while other specification sheets of the day show the bore and stroke as being 4.25x4.5, with horsepower set at 10. A top speed of 35 MPH was claimed. Apparently for the first time, standard equipment included cowl-mounted oil lamps, steering post mounted horn, and tools.

Introduced in January was the new 4-cylinder Model N, which was available only as a 2-passenger runabout. Finished in maroon and sporting a nicely styled boat-tail rear deck, the little car weighed only 1,050 pounds and rode on the same 84-inch wheelbase as did the Model F. Priced at $500, equipment included cowl lamps and a horn. But, a top was $50 extra for one in leather, or $30 for one in rubber-coated canvas. (Again, one catalog shows a list price of $500, while other sheets show a price of $800.)

Under the hood lived a newly designed 4-cylinder engine of 3.75x3-3/8 inch bore and stroke, rated at 149

Taken directly from a 1906 catalog is this plate of the new Model K Touring car. This illustration, which appears in two different 1906 Ford catalogs, shows a multitude of features that differ from those normally accepted for the Model K. Note the totally different body styling, front fenders, high narrow radiator, and small side vent panel on the hood. In addition, these catalogs list the Model K as having a 114-inch wheelbase, while all later material shows a 120-inch wheelbase. Despite many claims that the Model K was not changed during its 3-year run, it seems that a few early models may have been run off looking like this illustration, whereas the majority of production featured the 120-inch wheelbase and more modern looking body. When or if such a change was made cannot be substantiated, but further information along this line would be appreciated. In all other specifications, the catalogs agree, and even the price of $2,500 and the weight of 2,400 pounds remains the same. Since these brochures do not mention the Model K runabout which was introduced sometime later in the year, it is possible the change in wheelbase and bodies was made at that time.

cubic inches and developing 15 to 18 horsepower. Ford claimed the car would get 20 miles to a gallon, have a top speed of 40 MPH, and run as slow as 3 MPH in high gear without stalling. The transmission was noted to be an improved type of 2-speed planetary with an improved clutch. Driving brakes operated on the rear wheel hubs (drum brakes) controlled by the side lever, while the emergency brake, controlled by a foot pedal, was on the driveshaft. The tires were 28x2.5 inches, made by Firestone, though some charts show the Model N to use 30x3 tires.

The most expensive Ford this year was the Model K, which had been introduced in late 1905, but was considered a 1906 model. Priced at $2,500 and carrying styling similar to other luxury cars of the day, the large machine was a far cry from the economical cars for the masses that Ford had set his sights upon. Having a 114 or a 120-inch wheelbase and weighing 2,400 pounds, the car was available first as a 5-passenger touring car, and then as a 2-passenger runabout. These were finished in Royal Blue, with black leather upholstery, and came equipped with kerosene cowl lamps and horn. Tops and windshields were available from the aftermarket.

Under the long hood lurked Ford's first 6-cylinder engine, a rather giant unit with the cylinders cast singly and running a 4.5x4.25 inch bore and stroke, which displaced 405 cubic inches and developed 40 horsepower. Ford claimed the car would average 16 miles per gallon, have a top speed of 50 MPH, and could idle down to 4 MPH in high gear. When the runabout was introduced, Ford guaranteed a top speed of 60 MPH. The transmission was a 2-speed planetary, which turned out to be the car's weak point, as it apparently was not engineered for the power or weight of the car. Brakes operated on the rear wheels via the side lever, while the emergency operated on the driveshaft from a foot pedal. Wheel sizes are up for grabs, as is the actual wheelbase. One catalog on file shows the wheels to be 32 inches with 4-inch clincher tires, while a second shows 30x4 clinchers on the front and 36x4 on the rear. Also, one catalog notes the wheelbase as 120 inches, two others show the wheelbase as 114 inches, and another sheet lists both figures. Possibly the shorter wheelbase was used on the runabout, though this is only speculation.

If wheelbases and tire sizes prove to be confusing, it is nothing compared to getting into production figures. According to most accepted records, production totalled either 2,798 or 8,729, with Ford Motor Co. accepting both figures but commenting on neither. If the higher figure is used, it means that Ford was the largest automotive producer in 1906. If the smaller figure is used, it puts Ford in second place, being beaten by Cadillac, and just nosing ahead of Rambler by a scant 33 cars.

On the racing scene, Ford still had an eye on the world speed record as the year began, and thus once again took the Model K racer to Ormond Beach, Fla., for speed

trials. Only this time, he had Frank Kulick to do the driving, and the supposedly stock Model K engine had its horsepower raised to 100. Still, the results were comparable to 1905, with the team missing one race, getting stuck in the sand in another, and being beaten by a French Darracq in a third. The Model K went back to Detroit and Kulick went back to his rather odd little 4-cylinder Model C racer, with which he was still setting records around the country.

Substantiating the fact that at least some Model K production did resemble the catalog illustrations is this original photo, made about 1908. At first it was thought that the car had a custom touring body, but comparison with the catalog pictures tends to confirm that it is indeed one of the early models. Its only accessories appear to be the large tool box on the running board and the unusual 12-lug demountable rims. It also appears that a box of some type has been mounted between the springs, but it is not known if this was an accessory or a home-made item.

LEFT SIDE MOTOR. MODEL K

Taken from the 1906 catalog is this illustration of the left side of the new 6-cylinder Model K engine. Note that each cylinder is cast separately, in what is sometimes referred to as a "jug" type of engine. As did all Fords, the K used a Holley carburetor. Note that this plate also gives a good view of the high and narrow radiator, which does not appear on any other K models except those in the early catalog. With its 4.5x4.25 inch bore and stroke, the Model K engine produced 40 horsepower and was rated at 405 cubic inches displacement.

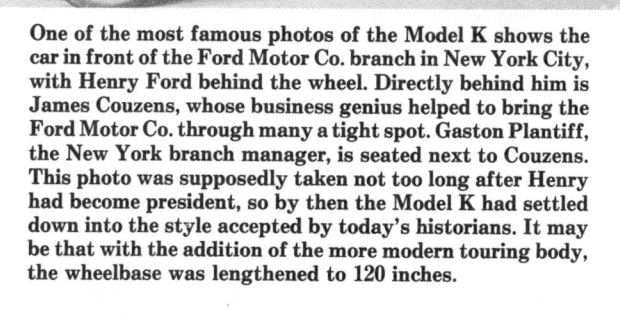

One of the most famous photos of the Model K shows the car in front of the Ford Motor Co. branch in New York City, with Henry Ford behind the wheel. Directly behind him is James Couzens, whose business genius helped to bring the Ford Motor Co. through many a tight spot. Gaston Plantiff, the New York branch manager, is seated next to Couzens. This photo was supposedly taken not too long after Henry had become president, so by then the Model K had settled down into the style accepted by today's historians. It may be that with the addition of the more modern touring body, the wheelbase was lengthened to 120 inches.

At least one of the earlier type Model K tourers was restored, and exists somewhere today. This photo, made at the 1967 Illinois State Fair, shows the car after it was named Grand Champion of the Antique Auto & Sports Car section of the fair. The car claimed a total of 98 of a possible 100 points. Its owner at the time was Durward Fagan of Palos Heights, Ill. Besides the Model K designation, these cars were also referred to as 6-40 Models, alluding to six cylinders and 40 horsepower.

Because of the fender lines, it was first thought that this was the Model K Touring car with the rear doors removed. Closer study shows that it is the runabout with a 2-passenger rear seat on the rear deck, and a set of very unusual fenders and running boards. Note the tremendous Aermore exhaust whistle on the side and the tool box suspended below the runningboard. The leather blowout boots on the front tire were just part of the joys of motoring in this era.

Introduced well after the Model K Tourer was the Model K runabout, a 2-passenger vehicle shown here fitted with a single "mother-in-law" seat on the rear deck. Almost an afterthought vehicle, the car did not appear in any of the early catalogs. Comparing the seating positions of the runabout with the touring car, it seems possible that the 2-passenger model retained the 114-inch wheelbase throughout its life. All mechanical components of this car were identical to those of the touring car model, but a top speed of 60 MPH was guaranteed for the runabout. Note the difference in the design of the fenders of this model compared with the other runabout shown here, or with the touring cars. No explanation can be offered.

1906

Coming closer to the popular light car that Henry Ford envisioned was the cute little Model N, which sold for $500 or $600, depending on which list is used. Weighing only 800 pounds and riding on an 84-inch wheelbase, the little 4-cylinder car nevertheless quickly developed a reputation for dependability and performance, with its top speed being 45 MPH. This photo has caused arguments over the years. It is often identified as having Clara Ford driving and Mrs. Harold Wills as a passenger. However, some others claim the driver is a Miss Marquette while the passenger is a Mrs. Clarkson, who was the switchboard operator at the Piquette Ave. plant.

This hood-off view shows the location of the newly designed 4-cylinder engine used in the Model N. Having a 3.75x3-3/8 inch bore and stroke, the engine displaced 149 cubic inches and developed 15 horsepower. This was enough to run the car at 40 to 45 MPH. Ignition was by two sets of dry cells, while the carburetor was a Holley. The gasoline tank, located under the seat, fed by gravity. It held 10 gallons, which was supposed to be good for 200 miles. Note that the springs are full elliptic in the rear, and half-elliptic in the front.

A 15 year old Edsel Ford plays in the snow with some friends in a new Model N runabout. Cowl lamps were standard equipment, but the top was an accessory. The transmission was a planetary type, with two forward speeds and one reverse. The car used a disc clutch and shaft drive, and had drum brakes on the rear wheels. It was finished in a deep maroon.

The only hold-over in the Ford line was the Model F. It was also Ford's only 2-cylinder car and the only one to have the engine located under the seat. With the rapid development going on in automotive design, the one year old Model F was already an archaic vehicle by most standards. Still, Ford claimed it was continued in production because of the great demand for this style car—although others claim the only reason it was offered in 1906 was to get rid of an over-abundance of 1905 cars. Although no changes were made to the 1,400-pound car, its price increased from $1,000 to $1,200 and then dropped to $1,100 during the 1906 season. The 128 cubic inch engine produced either 10 or 12 horsepower, depending on which specification sheet is used, and the car claimed a top speed of 35 MPH. The cowl lamps and horn were included in the price, but the gas headlamps on this model were accessories. The car was photographed by the author at Greenfield Village's Old Car Festival in the mid-1970s. At that time it was owned by Karl Coffman of Tiffin, Ohio.

Approximately 200 Model N engines await installation in their chassis at the Piquette Ave. plant. Note how the engines are standing on their combination fan and flywheels. Apparently this heavy wheel was strong enough to support the full weight of the block. The engines appear to be fully assembled, and are complete with manifold and carburetor.

The right side of the Model N engine housed the valve system, which was not covered. This made for relatively easy adjustment of the valves, but dust and grime on the stems, springs, and push rods added up to a high wear factor. Unlike the Model K, which had separately cast cylinders, the Model N combined two cylinders in each block. The carburetor is a Holley, while the ignition was of the jump-spark system, using dry cell batteries and a Splitdorf 4-unit coil. Surprisingly, the engine used an aluminum crankcase, with cast iron cylinders. The large flywheel at the front of the engine also contained the fan blades, which doubled as spokes for the flywheel.

RIGHT SIDE MOTOR, MODEL N

This view of the assembly room at the Piquette Ave. plant, taken in November, 1906, shows a double row of Model N chassis awaiting final assembly. Note that these cars have not yet received their rear axles or drive assemblies. In the days before the assembly line, parts were brought to the cars, and the vehicles were assembled piece by piece by teams of workers, almost in the manner that one would build a model car today.

If nothing else, this was the year that Henry Ford really began his lifetime goal of building the "Universal Car." This was to be a dependable vehicle that the average working man could buy, run, and maintain. The Model T was still almost two years away from introduction, but in 1907 the tried and tested Model N and the new Models S and R set the stage for the overwhelming acceptance of the Model T.

Whereas 1906 might be considered one of corporate importance, 1907 was one of automotive refinement. True, two new models were introduced, but in reality they were simply refined versions of the Model N. What was going on was some interesting designing and experimentation for the still dreamed of Model T, and some in-fighting in the Selden Patent case. Also, during the year the Ford Mfg. Co. was dissolved and its operations absorbed into the Ford Motor Co. The short-lived firm had served its purpose in helping to force the 1906 resignation of Malcomson and several of his backers, and its continuation was now just a paperwork complication that served no real purpose.

As 1907 began, Ford really had only two models on the market. These were the huge Model K and the well accepted Model N. The 2-cylinder Model F was dropped somewhere during 1906, although it continued to appear in most Ford advertising for the year. As occurred in 1906, buyers were staying away from the Model K in droves, but the Model N was a total success. Reportedly, it outsold the Model K by a 10-to-1 margin or better.

The Model K apparently settled down to one wheelbase this year, that of 120 inches for both the touring car and the roadster. Its engine remained the unchanged unit of 4.5-inch square bore and stroke which produced 40 horsepower and gave the touring a top speed of 50 MPH and the roadster a guaranteed speed of 60 MPH. Wheels again seem to have varied on the Model K, but the most accepted listing shows 34x4 clincher rims for the touring car and 36x4 for the roadster. The touring car was finished in what was now called Touring Blue, but how this differed from the 1906 Royal Blue is not known. The roadsters were now finished in Roadster Red, but it is not known when this color was introduced, as some early sheets describe the roadsters as being finished in a light gray. If anything changed on the Model K, it was the price. The huge car was now up to $2,800, which was exactly four times the cost of the Model S.

The other unchanged car was the Model N, a nifty little 2-passenger runabout that weighed but 1,050 pounds and held Ford's first really successful 4-cylinder engine. With a bore and stroke of 3.75x3-3/8, it had its cylinders cast in two blocks of two each. The cylinders were of cast iron, while the crankcase was of cast aluminum. Tires were now 28x3 Firestones, with the old 28x2.5 versions having been dropped in 1906. About the only change in the Model N was the addition of a second color early in the year. Now buyers could have a choice of maroon or dark green with black running gear. The

price seems to have settled down to an agreed $600, but the cowl lamps and horn were no longer included in this figure.

In early February, the Model N was joined by the Model R, which essentially was nothing more than a deluxe version of the N. The car used the same 84-inch wheelbase chassis, was powered by the same 15 horse engine, and had the same 2-speed planetary transmission, multiple disc clutch, and shaft drive as the Model N. Its wheels, however, were a slightly larger 30x3.

What was different was the body, which offered a slightly larger 2-passenger runabout style, with full fenders and running boards. The rear deck was not pointed in a boattail as was the Model N, but had what was referred to as a "beetle back." This more rounded stern could accommodate a spare wheel and tire, and represented Ford's first use of a factory-installed spare. As with the Model N, the car was claimed to have a top speed in excess of 45 MPH, and a low-end non-stall speed in high gear of 4 MPH.

Selling for $750, the Model R was available in either Brewster Green or Carmine Red. Unlike the Model N, the R's price included two oil cowl lamps, an oil rear light, and a bulb horn mounted on the steering wheel. The weight of the Model R varies between specification sheets, with some showing the same 1,050 pounds as the Model N (unlikely) and others showing 1,400 pounds. Production of this car in 1907 was 2,500 and apparently the factory could not keep up with the orders. Factory capacity and outside supply, especially by the suppliers of body parts and wheels, could not be increased, even though many more Model Rs could have been sold if they could have been built.

Partially in order to solve the parts problem, the Model S was introduced later in the year. Essentially the Model S was an interim car, placed between the spartan Model N and the quick-selling Model R, whose further production was halted by lack of certain body parts. Thus, the Model S used the same chassis, engine, and running gear of the Models N and R, but used the Model N's 28-inch wheels. From the Model R it took the flared fenders, running boards, lamp, and horn, but the body was the standard unit used on the Model N, including the pointed boattail back. However, the Model S did have its own unique seats, which were larger and of higher back than those on the Model N, but not as large as the Model R. A Ford brochure of the day stated, "So the Model S may be said to combine the choicest features of those two wonderfully popular models (N and R) at a cost of $50 less than the Model R."

At first the Model S was introduced only as a 2-passenger runabout at $700, but shortly after introduction, a 3-passenger roadster was added at $750. This later model was simply the runabout with the rear deck removed and replaced with a finished platform containing a single small seat. To differentiate the Model S from the N and R, it was offered in two different colors, either red with yellow running gear, or Roadster Green with yellow running gear.

In retrospect, one wonders now if the Model S would have ever materialized had not Ford been faced with a supply problem of wheels and seats. Regardless, the S did help to alleviate that problem. Total production was either 6,775 or 14,877 (or somewhere in between) depending on whose figures are used. Regardless of which figures are taken, Ford this year was the undisputed king of the production hill, with its closest rival being Buick, with a reported 4,641 cars built.

While all of this production activity was going on, the lawyers on the Selden Patent case were also busy. By the start of the year, all the evidence from both sides had been submitted to the court, and both sides felt that it was now time to take their case to the press as well. Among the chief guns that Ford used was its ridicule of the crude cart that Selden had been ordered to build. The court wanted proof that Selden's claimed vehicle could indeed be operated before it would rule on the validity of the patent. Such a machine was built and demonstrated in 1906, but its performance was anything but inspiring.

Meanwhile, the Ford company also built a rather interesting vehicle and powered it with a crude engine resembling one patented by the Englishman Lenoir in 1860. This was an attempt to refute Selden's claim of originality based on his supposed 1877 construction of his first wagon. The Ford people mounted the Lenoir-type engine in a 1903 Model A chassis and tested the vehicle in Detroit in late May. In its test run, and during another in July, the car not only ran relatively well, but reached a speed of 12 MPH, as opposed to the Selden wagon which could barely move beyond a fast walk. Ford's attorneys immediately claimed that

Large and sporty, and virtually never seen, was the Model K roadster, or 6-40 Roadster, as it was now called. The numbers, of course, referred to six cylinders and 40 horsepower. Priced at $2,800 and weighing 2,000 pounds, the car utilized a 120-inch wheelbase, though there is some contention that the roadster still retained the 114-inch chassis. The top, lights and windshield on this model were all accessories. The car is equipped with the single "mother-in-law" seat in the rear, but some sheets state that a 2-place rear seat (as shown in the 1906 chapter) was also available. The car supposedly was finished only in Roadster Red, but other sources, including this photograph, indicate that gray or off-white was also an available color. Ford claimed a top speed of 60 MPH for this model.

because the much earlier Lenoir engine proved more successful than the later Selden engine, the entire Selden patent should be re-examined and/or denied.

While this was going on, however, the Assn. of Licensed Automobile Manufacturers (ALAM) which held the rights to the Selden patent, decided to build their own car. Recognizing the failings of Selden's vehicle and stewing at the ridicule the car was receiving from the press, the New York financiers who controlled ALAM decided to build a vehicle that would work. Thus, Henry Cave, an engineer at Electric Vehicle Co. (one of ALAM's top firms) was chosen for the construction job. Cave constructed a vehicle which sort of resembled Selden's own unit, but which contained a great many mechanical advantages over the first car.

In June, both of the Selden vehicles were taken to a race track in Guttenberg, N.J., (directly across the Hudson River from New York City) and were demonstrated for the press. No one had much to say about the first Selden wagon, but the ALAM vehicle drew much interest from the news media, especially when it held its own in a race around the track against a Ford Model K. Ford's attorneys immediately yelled foul, claiming that the car had so many advanced ideas, and incorporated so many design elements that were impossible to obtain in 1877, that the vehicle proved absolutely nothing. ALAM, of course, took the opposite view, noting that if Ford could put an 1860 Lenoir-type engine in a 1903 chassis, they too could take a few design liberties. And thus, the trial dragged on throughout yet another year.

On the racing scene, Ford did not try for any world records, and possibly as a consequence wound up taking one. Following the dismal performances of the Model K racer, Ford turned the machine over to Frank Kulick to use in his racing exploits. Somewhere along the line, the car received a new name of No. 666, and was fitted with a new V-shaped radiator of conventional tube design, replacing the wrap-around cooling tubes of the first model. There are some who claim that the No. 666 was a totally new car and not a rebuild of the first Model K racer, but the author was unable to either substantiate or disprove this contention.

Regardless of whether it was a new or a rebuilt car, Frank Kulick entered the vehicle in a few races and then took it to the Detroit Fair Grounds for a 24-hour endurance contest. With him as co-driver was Bert Lorimer. Between the two, the car raised the world's 24-hour record to 1,135 miles at an average speed of 47.2 MPH. The old record had been an average of 33 MPH for a 24-hour total of 826 miles.

However, the glory of Frank Kulick and No. 666 were not long lived. In September, while running at the Michigan State Fair, the car went out of control and crashed through the fence. Kulick was trapped beneath the overturned vehicle and suffered severe injuries. Ford chose not to rebuild the car, and for a time, lost interest in racing.

1908

In the annals of automotive history, 1908 stands out as one of the major high points. Because it was this year, after approximately two years of top secret planning and design, that the new Model T would be unveiled. With a combination of positive elements behind it (a car-hungry public; an affordable price; an excellent design, and a good company name) the Model T was destined for success. But, at this time, no one could have ever dreamed of just how successful this car would be.

Introduced on Oct. 8, 1908, the new Model T was actually a 1909 model, and there are those who will rightfully argue that no mention of the car should be made in a chronological chapter dealing with 1908 vehicles. There are also those who will argue that the first 800 Model Ts came with two foot pedals and two hand levers, rather than the three pedals and one lever of all the other Ts. Therefore, they will say, these 800 should be considered true 1908 models while all the rest should be considered 1909 or later. The author personally feels that all of the first Model Ts are 1909 models, but that the introduction in 1908 was so significant in the automotive world that it should be treated in its calendar year, rather than in the model year.

Compared with the other Ford offerings of 1908, the new Model T was a thoroughly unique vehicle. It had a brand new engine of 20 horsepower. Its bore and stroke was 3.75x4 inches and it displaced 176.7 cubic inches. What was totally different about this engine was that all four cylinders were cast in one block, and the cylinder head was removable. Considering the foundry techniques of the day in regard to mass production, this in itself was a remarkable piece of work. A low tension magneto, containing 16 V-shaped magnets, was built into the flywheel. Lubrication was by a well-designed splash/gravity system, and cooling was by water pump. However, during the 1909 season, after the first 2,500 cars, the pump was done away with and the much simpler (and cheaper) thermosyphon cooling system was employed.

The transmission remained a 2-speed planetary. On the first 800 cars, there were two levers, one for reverse and one for the parking brake, and two foot pedals. On later models, only one lever handled the parking brake, neutral, and high speed, while the three pedals were for low speed, reverse, and the driving brake. All of the pedals operated their respective bands within the transmission, thus doing away with the typical plate or cone type of clutch. The transmission terminated in a ball-and-socket joint that connected to the drive shaft. All transmission parts, including the clutch and brake bands, ran in a constant oil bath.

The bare chassis, which with running gear weighed about 900 pounds, was of 100-inch wheelbase. The axles were attached to transverse springs, which tended to give the car a rolling type of motion on rough roads. Still, this style suspension would be retained right through the last T in 1927. The rear axle housing was stamped metal rather than cast iron, while the front axle was a forged unit of I-beam design.

It is interesting to note that in this era of open cars, Ford not only offered a touring and a roadster, but also came in with a closed coupe and two rather pretentious vehicles—a town car and a landaulet. Of course, few of the closed vehicles were sold. The tourings were available only in red; the roadster (often referred to as a runabout) came in gray, and the closed cars were finished in dark green. However, there are reports that these colors could be switched if a dealer had enough pull with the factory. Leading the car was a highly polished brass radiator and a relatively short aluminum hood without louvers. Compared to other cars of the era, it was a very nice and contemporary looking vehicle. Compared to other cars in its price class ($850 for the touring) it was totally in a world apart, unmatched by anything being produced anywhere.

Despite the fact that the new Model T always takes the headlines in any narrative about the 1908 Fords, the fact is that there were nine months of non-Model T activity preceding the big day. During this time, Ford continued with its previous alphabetized models, contracted for a new plant to be built in Highland Park, Mich., and continued to butt heads with the Seldenites at ALAM.

Foremost on the list of available cars throughout most of 1908 was the Model K series, which still consisted of the almost never seen 3 or 4-passenger roadster, and the touring car. That the Model K was unchanged from previous years is no surprise. In fact, it is unlikely that any of these large but unprofitable cars were actually built in 1908, and those that were sold as 1908 vehicles were almost certainly left over 1907 models (some even contend 1906 leftovers). The big 120-inch wheelbase cars were still officially priced at $2,800 for either model, but since many were forced upon dealers, the actual sales prices were often much lower, as the dealers tried to get them off the floor.

As before, the Model K continued to use its 6-cylinder jug-type engine with each cylinder cast individually. Its bore and stroke remained 4.5x4.25 inches, it continued to be rated at 40 horsepower, and its top speed was reported to be 60 MPH for the roadster and 50 for the touring.

The basic little Model N was continued as an unchanged runabout, but something new was added to the line. The new car was a landaulet, designed for the taxi trade. The interesting little car, of very limited production, made quite a handful for the 84-inch wheelbase chassis, and when loaded, probably gave the little 15 horsepower 4-cylinder engine a severe headache. It is believed that these bodies were supplied by the C.R. Wilson Co., which over the years had supplied many other Ford bodies and body components. Although the basic Model N runabout sold for $600 this year, it is not known what price was asked for the landaulet.

Although this photo was made in 1906, it gives a good view of the back of the unchanged Model N. Note the sharp point of the "boattail" rear deck, as opposed to the rounded deck on the Model R. This compartment could be used for the storage of tools, cleaning cloths, extra gas and oil, etc. But, unlike the Model R rear deck, it was too small for a spare wheel. Although the car was equipped with kerosene cowl lamps, a rear light was deemed unnecessary. From the position of the clutch lever, it appears that the car was in high gear when this photo was made. But that doesn't mean that the engine was running.

The Assn. of Licensed Automobile Manufacturers (ALAM) was a unit formed by New York financiers to control Selden's patent and insure that royalties were paid. Through these patents, the company controlled many of the member firms, including Electric Vehicle Co. of Hartford, Conn. This company built the prestigious Columbia, which at one time had been America's best-selling and best-known car. Seeing the dismal performance of the Selden wagon set ALAM to build their own copy of the Selden. Constructed at the Columbia plant by Electric Vehicle engineers, the car bore a rough resemblance to the original Selden, but its performance was on par with most cars of 1907. At a race track in Guttenberg, N.J., the car performed very well, and even held its own against a Ford Model K. Ford's attorneys immediately yelled "foul," pointing out that many of the parts used in this car could not have been obtained or built with the technology available in 1877.

In order to dispute Selden's claims that his patent represented the first workable gasoline-powered vehicle, the Ford company built this funny looking little thing. What made it remarkable, however, was that it used a copy of an engine patent in 1860 by an Englishmen named Lenoir. Whereas Selden's vehicle, supposedly built of 1877 patent plans, could barely reach 4 MPH, this Lenoir-powered car putted along at an easy 12 MPH. The engine was set in an old Model A chassis, fitted with a cobbled Model A body and Model C hood. Here, Henry Ford poses in the car in front of the Ford Motor Company's New York City office at 1723 Broadway.

Just as Henry Ford posed in his Lenoir-Ford, George B. Selden posed in his copy of the motor wagon which he claimed to have invented. The court had ordered Selden to build an "exact copy" of the patent drawings to prove that such a vehicle was feasible. However, Ford's lawyers claimed that many of the items used in this particular car were totally different than those shown on the patent drawings. The model could barely run at 4 MPH.

By September, when it was obvious that no further Model R body parts or wheels could be obtained, Ford came up with a unique solution. It introduced the Model S as an interim vehicle between the Models N and R. The car used the same chassis and running gear of both models, had Model R fenders and running boards, but reverted to the Model N 28-inch wheels, and had its own exclusive 2-passenger seat mounted on the Model N boattail body. Priced at $700, it first came out only as a 2-passenger runabout It was finished in either red or Roadster Green, both colors using yellow running gear and wheels.

Although this photo is often credited as being taken in 1906 at the Piquette Ave. plant, it actually could not have been made until the fall of 1907. The car at the center is the new Model S 3-passenger roadster, not yet fitted with its rear seat, but already sporting the "casket handles" on the front seat backs. These were for the rear passenger to use when getting in or out, or just to stay in place on rough roads. This gives a good look at the different back used on this model as opposed to the turtle decks (both boattail and beetle-back) used on the 2-passenger versions. Here also can be seen the unique curved cowl that was used only on the Model S roadster. At this time, each semi-completed car would be driven outside of the plant and be personally run-in and tuned by a mechanic. After this, it would be returned to the building for the installation of such things as hoods, cowl lamps, rear seats, and whatever.

A view of the back yard of the Piquette Ave. plant, taken in 1907, shows a virtual bottle-neck of Model R and S chassis awaiting installation of the respective bodies. Behind these rolling chassis is the run-in area where the semi-completed cars were tuned and the engines given their initial break-in times. Behind that is the plant itself. It is interesting to note that only one lone Model K is partly visible at the top left corner.

Shortly after the Model S runabout was introduced, Ford came up with the Model S roadster. Selling at $750, this was essentially the runabout with a flat rear end and a single "mother-in-law" seat behind the main seat. The roadster also had a new and exclusive cowl, somewhat like that found on the Model K roadster. On this restored vehicle, the cowl lamps would have been included with the price, but the top and acetylene headlamps were extra. Note that the top gave no protection whatsoever to the rear seat passenger. When this car was photographed in 1968 it belonged to Warren LaBarre of Portland, Ore.

This is the shipping room of the Piquette Ave. plant. Taken in the fall of 1907, this photo shows a group of Model S 3-passenger roadsters being readied for shipment to various dealers. From here, the cars would be rolled out onto a loading dock and placed aboard rail cars for shipment to their final destinations. Note that a couple of the cars in the rear are equipped with factory-installed tops. Usually these tops were dealer installed.

A DAYS OUTPUT

This catalog illustration of the popular little Model N shows it outfitted with extra-cost lamps and top. In its $600 form, the car was sold as a virtually bare vehicle, but still, its price brought it within reach of many who otherwise could not afford a car. The three pedals on the floor did not operate as they do on a Model T. Instead, one pedal was for the rear hub brakes, one was for the transmission parking brake, and the third was for reverse. The large lever on the side controlled the transmission. Pulled all the way back, the car was in low range. In the center was neutral, and pushing it all the way forward put the car in high gear, where it would have a 45 MPH top speed.

The beautiful looking Model K Touring Car shared the $2,800 price tag with its roadster kin. However, this price did not include the top or the acetylene headlamps shown here, but the horn and kerosene cowl lamps were included. Despite its excellent engine, the Model K had a reputation for transmission troubles. Also, buyers of luxury cars in this price range were still not impressed by the Ford name when they could get much more prestigious makes for the same price. Sales of the Model N and R were so good, and those of the Model K so bad that Ford forced its dealers to take one Model K for every 10 N or R models that they ordered. The car was now finished in Touring Blue, but it is not known how this differed from the Royal Blue of 1906.

When viewed from the front, the Model N was a rather stark looking little car, yet it was a hit with the buyers. Tire size had now been increased to 28x3 Firestones, though some charts still show the 1907 N using the same 28x2.5 tires of the 1906 models. Buyers now had a choice of colors--either all maroon or dark green with black running gear. When photographed in the early 1970s, this car was owned by Gary Porter of Renton, Wash.

New for the year was the Model R, introduced in February and priced at $750. The car used the same chassis and running gear as the Model N, but sported such refinements as full fenders and running boards, a wider and deeper seat, 30x3-inch wheels and tires, and kerosene cowl lamps and horn included in the price. Ford was taken by surprise at the car's popularity. Subcontractors had only been given enough orders to produce 2,500 special components for the car, and by mid-summer it was obvious that sales would well exceed this amount. Model Rs were available either in Brewster Green or Carmine Red.

This catalog illustration of the Model R shows the "beetle-back" styling used on the car, as opposed to the "boattail" styling used on the Model N. Under this rear deck lived Ford's first use of a spare wheel, making on-the-road tire changes less of a chore. The beetle-back body was one of the components that Ford could not obtain once the initial 2,500 units had been delivered. This illustration also shows an interesting little nickel plated railing around the rear deck. It is not known if this was a dealer installed accessory, or if it was a planned stock item that was never put into production. As with the Model N, the side lever controlled the two forward speeds and neutral.

Both the Models R and S lines were continued also, unchanged from 1908. They shared the same chassis, engine, and running gear of the Model N. The Model R, which was Ford's prestige 4-cylinder car, continued to be available only as a 2-passenger runabout for $750. It was the only one of the three 4-cylinder models to use 30x3 inch wheels and tires, and was the only one factory "ironed" to receive a top. According to the 1908 catalog, this "ironing" was done because 95% of all Model R customers ordered a top with the car. Most of these tops were dealer supplied and installed, but some were added right at the factory.

Falling between the Models N and R in appointments was the interim Model S, still available either as a 2-passenger runabout for $700 or as a 3-passenger roadster for $750. Also, some lists indicate that a 2-passenger rear seat was available for the Model S, making it into a 4-passenger car. However, this seat may have been an after-market item. As in 1908, the Model N and S series continued to use 28x3-inch wheels and tires. The Model S was the only 4-cylinder Ford to use a curved steel cowl, whereas both the N and the R used a flat dashboard between the engine and passenger areas.

As before, the Model N was available in all maroon or in dark green with black running gear. The Model R came in Brewster Green or Carmine Red; the Model S had red or green as its primary color while its running gear was yellow, and the big Model K used Touring Blue for that model and Roadster Red or gray for the roadster.

On the corporate side, it was already noted that the Piquette Ave. plant was becoming too small for the planned production of new models. Thus, contracts were let for a new plant in Highland Park, Mich. The old Piquette Ave. plant would be retained until 1911, when it was sold to another famous automaker of the era, by the name of Studebaker.

In other action, Ford continued to be embroiled in the Selden Patent Case, but little was done this year as Selden's attorneys appeared to be playing a game of wait and delay. Meanwhile, others had taken action similar to Ford, and had filed suit against ALAM. One of these was the Allen-Kingston Co. of Kingston, N.Y., which won its restraint of trade suit against Selden on grounds not unlike those presented by Ford. However, Allen-Kingston was a very small operation which started building cars in 1908 and closed up shop somewhere around 1910. The Selden people probably weren't too worried about this case. The other move against Selden, however, involved the Velie Motor Co. of Moline, Ill., which started up its business this year. The fact that Velie was closely tied into the giant John Deere Co. may have given the ALAM attorneys more than a few sleepless nights.

As to production for the year, again the figures conflict greatly, with two sets being accepted by different quarters. One list shows a total of 6,015, not counting the Model T production, while another accepted figure shows 10,202, including the Model T production, which is believed to be either 800 or 2,500. If the larger figure is used, Ford remained the nation's largest auto producer. However, if the smaller figure is used, Ford ranked third, falling behind Buick's 8,820 and Studebaker's 8,132.

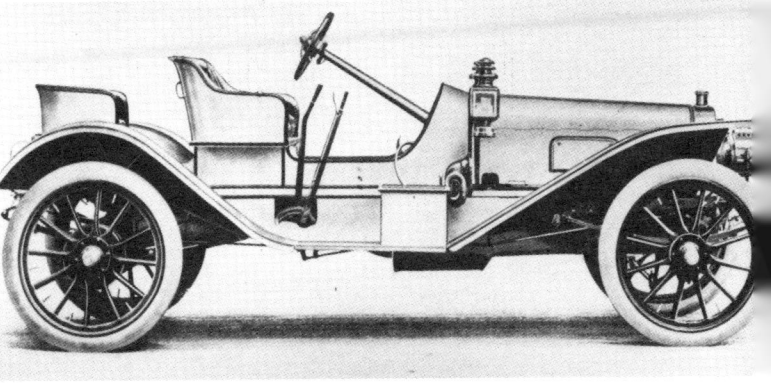

The large and sporty looking Model K or 6-40 Roadster appeared for the last time this year, if it appeared at all. Of the two Model K styles, this was by far the least popular, and it is pretty certain that whatever few were sold in 1908 were actually 1907 or even 1906 models re-titled as 1908 machines. There was absolutely no change in the car this year, and even its stated price remained the same $2,800. It is known that these cars could be fitted with a 2-passenger rear seat, rather than the single seat shown here, but it is not known if the 2-passenger rear seat was a factory option or an after-market accessory. All Model K roadsters were supposed to have been finished in a bright red, yet most catalog illustrations, such as this, portray the car in what appears to be a light gray or ivory.

The big Model K Touring Car was forced on dealers for the last time this year. Even its 40 HP 6-cylinder engine with separately cast cylinders had become an obsolete design by now, and its transmission troubles were well known. Dealers supposedly were forced to take one Model K for every 10 4-cylinder cars they ordered, and thus many of these big blue machines were sold for far less than their stated $2,800 price. This car is equipped with the relatively expensive acetylene headlamps. Its weight was still rated at 1-ton.

The little Model N remained in production almost until the Model T was announced. A popular car, it provided basic transportation for the low cost of $600. At this price, it was fitted with open fenders and step plates, but no lights. Still, it did have a nicely designed rear deck which could hold small supplies or packages, and its proven 4-cylinder engine gave it enough pep to carry two people at 45 MPH. Buyers even had a choice of colors--maroon or dark green. This photo was taken at the Ford farm near Dearborn.

Ford's only new model for the year--not counting the Model Ts--was a rather strange creature called a Landaulet. Although designated a Model N, the car used fenders more akin to the Model R. The low-production car was probably never intended to compete in the luxury market, but seems aimed for the taxi or car-for-hire field. Its tonneau held two or possibly three passengers, while another could enjoy all of the elements while seated next to the driver. The door windows could be lowered, but it is not known if the front glass was moveable. Although landau irons are fastened to the side, it is not known if these were strictly decorative or if the rear portion of the top could be folded. Judging by the severe lines of the rear quarters, it would seem that the irons were only decorative. It is believed that these bodies were supplied by the C.R. Wilson Co. of Detroit, and that they were finished in either black or dark green. What remains unknown are the price, weight, or production total of the landaulet.

Still falling between the spartan Model N and the classier Model R was the $700 Model S Runabout. The 2-passenger car came in either red or Roadster Green, with yellow running gear. The car used its own unique seat, larger than that on the Model N, smaller than the one on the Model R. The body of the 2-passenger Model S was the same as that used on the Model N, and the car also used the N's 28-inch wheels as opposed to the 30 inchers on the Model R.

This pair of well-suited men looks happy after winning some early racing event in their Model R. Continued unchanged from the previous year, the $750 car still used the rounded "beetle back" which could hold a spare wheel. Cowl lamps and horn were standard in the price, but the acetylene head lights were extra. Note the trophy perched on the cowl, and the fact that the participants were dressed in suits, white shirts, and ties—not really the normal racing gear. As before, Model Rs were available in either red or Brewster Green.

Despite the fact that the Model S Runabout shared its body with the Model N, the Model S Roadster had a body uniquely its own. Of 3-passenger configuration, this car was the only 4-cylinder Ford to use a cowl behind the dashboard, and the only one to use the rather racy fenders with small running boards. Under the single rear seat lived a comparatively spacious tool and storage box, hinged at the front with access from the rear. Selling for $750, complete with cowl lamps, the car weighed approximately 1,400 pounds. It could squeeze 45 MPH from its 15 horsepower 4-cylinder engine. This restored model lives at the Henry Ford Museum in Dearborn.

The first of more than 15 million was this new Model T Touring Car, introduced in October of 1908, but considered a 1909 model. Since the car is of such great significance to the motoring world, and since only the first 800 cars built in 1908 had the 2-lever control, this book will list them under the 1908 section, and leave it to others to argue whether the 2-lever models are 1909 registry or indeed true 1908 vehicles. The touring car was priced at an amazing $850, weighed approximately 1,200 pounds, and could cruise all day long at up to 45 MPH. Compared with other cars of its era, it was an excellent bargain.

Touring Car with Top

When fitted with its accessory top, the new Model T was just the thing for taking all-day trips, an idea only dreamed of a few years earlier. The car was finished in bright red, set off by the brass radiator, and brass cowl and tail lamps and horn, which were included in the price. The gas headlamps and top were extras, but it is doubtful that too many cars were sold without these items. The top could be fitted with side curtains, and a front shield with large celluloid panels, but at this point, no provision was made for a glass windshield.

Except for the lack of a curved cowl, the new Model T Roadster followed the styling of the popular Model S, and came equipped with a single mother-in-law seat on the rear deck. Underneath this seat was a fairly ample storage box. Priced at $825, the roadster was the least expensive Model T. It was finished in light gray, with the upholstery being in No. 1 machine-buffed leather. Although a top was not included with the roadster, it was fitted for top iron installation. This top, however, would enclose only the front seat passengers.

1908

Model T Coupe
4 cylinder. 20 h. p. Inside driven
$950.00 f.o.b. Detroit

Whether Ford was hoping to attract a luxury trade, or was looking for the livery trade is unknown. However, the initial Model T line did offer two high-styled vehicles not usually associated with owners who drove their own cars. These were the Landaulet, shown here, and the town car. Priced at $950, the landaulet was a style usually found in taxis of the day. In fact, a Ford option for this car was a factory-installed taxi-meter. The car was finished in dark green with a black top, fitted with decorative landau irons. Since this was rated as a 5-passenger vehicle, the tonneau must have been spacious enough for three passengers.

Ford's first enclosed production car was the new Model T Coupe, priced at $950. Ford himself was not too keen on this style, once stating that "a person would have to be out of his mind to travel surrounded by so much glass." Remember, this was an era of plate glass, which could shatter into horrible shards in the event of an accident or roll-over. The door and quarter windows could be lowered, but it is not known if either the windshield or the rear window were moveable. The left door was functional, but must have been almost impossible to use, being blocked by the steering column and both control levers. Like the other two closed models, the coupe was finished in dark green. Because many physicians preferred cars of this type for making house calls, this style of body was often referred to as a "Doctor's Coupe." Yes, in this era, doctors still visited the patients at home.

Model T Town Car
4 cylinder. 20 h. p. 5 passenger
$1000.00 f. o. b. Detroit

Pride of the new Ford Model T line was the Town Car, a $1,000 vehicle designed to be either chauffeur driven, or (more likely) used in the livery service. Production figures for the 2-lever varieties are not available, but it is obvious that sales of this model were quite limited. As with the landaulet, this vehicle was classed as a 5-passenger model.

Model T Chassis.—Left

HIGH PRICED QUALITY IN A LOW PRICED CAR

Considering the other makes on the market, the new Model T offered quite a bargain to prospective buyers, and did much to hasten America's ownership of a family car. The stripped chassis weighed about 900 pounds. Ford loved to brag about its use of vanadium steel, a relatively new high-strength steel that was used throughout the car. Catalogs of the day point out that no cars, even those in the $5,000 range, could be made of better steel than what was used in the Model T.

1909

This was the first full production year of the first generation of what would become a world famous family of Model Ts. Public acceptance was excellent, and the company kept cranking out new models just as fast as its facilities would allow. At first the pace was slow, so that between its introduction date and Jan. 1, 1909, only 309 cars had been built, all with two levers. However, in 1909 proper, things began to move, and by the end of April, car number 2,500 had been turned out. And, by Dec. 31, a total of 14,161 Model T Fords had been built. Now Ford was certainly a force to be reckoned with. Serial numbers for Ford's fiscal year, which was Oct. 1, 1908 to Sept. 30, 1909, run from 1 to 11,000.

Confusing this issue are statistics that show Ford's 1909 production to be a seemingly impossible 17,771, which would have ranked it in first place. However, it would seem that a more realistic 1909 production tally would be that of 13,825, which puts Ford in second place, only a scant 800 cars away from Buick and well ahead of Studebaker.

During this run, all Ts did not come from the same mold. Ford made changes as they appeared necessary, as flaws crept in, and as component supplies changed. But two major change breaks occurred which almost cast the 1909 Model T into three distinct cars. The first, of course, was the switch from the 2-lever control to a single clutch-brake-high gear lever, and a pedal for reverse. This occurred after construction of the first 800 cars, though many sources put this figure at 850. Then, following car 2,500, a whole multitude of changes occurred—enough in fact to warrant a completely new section in the parts manual for "those cars built after No. 2,500."

Basically, the major specifications remained the same. The engines were cast of gray iron, had removable cylinder heads, and used 3.75-inch pistons with a 4-inch stroke. Displacing 176.7 cubic inches, this engine developed 22 horsepower at 1600 rpm. There were three main bearings, but babbitt was not used in the upper half, only on the lower units.

After engine No. 2500, the gear-driven water pump was discarded and a thermosyphon cooling system became standard. This involved adding more water jacket space in the front of the block and eliminating the gear-driven pump. This, of course, mandated a totally new block casting. With this new design, the oil filler was moved from the left front to the right side. Internally, the engines had new pistons and connecting rods, new and longer crankshafts, a new crankcase and transmission cover, new-design heads, and a newly designed timer. Also, the cars started with either a Buffalo or two different models of Kingston carburetors. Later, Holley units were also added to the list.

As mentioned, the transmission control for reverse went from a side lever to a foot pedal after car number 800 (or 850, depending on which list is used). In addition to this major change, the transmission also received newly designed triple gears, clutch drum, main shaft, and rear bearing. The drive shaft was also modified during the year, the ring gear changed a couple of times, and various axle changes were made.

The chassis remained unchanged in its 100-inch wheelbase and 10-foot 8-inch overall chassis length. Its normal tread was 56 inches, but through 1916, a 60-inch "southern" tread could be ordered. This was necessary because of the rutted roads in the south, the ruts being caused by both tobacco and cotton wagons which all used a 60-inch tread. Tires were 30x3 in the front and 30x3.5 on the rear.

Even the body styles went through several changes, but these cannot be as distinctly defined as the before and after 2,500 figure of the engines. Several body sources were used, with most bodies being all wood or light metal sheeting over a wood frame. Some of the touring bodies came from the Pontiac Body Co. of Pontiac, Mich. These were aluminum paneled jobs, and were supplied until September, 1909. Ford also gave a large touring car contract to a brand new body company that had started in Detroit. This was the Fisher Bros. Body Co., started by seven brothers, some of whom had worked for the C.R. Wilson Co., another major body supplier to Ford. Yes, that is the same Fisher outfit that today is the Fisher Body Division of General Motors.

Colors remained the same as on the first Model Ts, except that touring cars now could be ordered in either red or Brewster Green. All closed cars were done in Brewster Green, and after June, when red was no longer available, all touring cars were done in the dark green also. Contrary to popular belief, black was not available at all this year.

At the start of the year, such frills as windshields and tops were not offered by the factory, but the addition of tops to the list of factory accessories was quick in coming. As the year progressed, management took note of the fact that more and more cars were being ordered with tops, windshields, and carbide lamps. As a result of this, these items were slowly priced into the cars, and by the end of 1909, could almost be called standard equipment. By 1910, they were standard.

Upholstery and door panels were done in No. 1 grade leather, almost always black. Generally, the diamond pattern tufts were buttoned in place, but some sources used a sewn pattern. Also, some doors had side pockets, others did not, again depending on the supplier. Some buyers complained that the rear seats of their touring cars were more narrow than others. Again, even the body dimensions were not always the same.

With production consistently running behind orders, Ford really didn't need any more publicity. But, a welter of publicity was to be his simply for entering one race and beating four other cars. This event was a New York to Seattle race, promoted by Robert Guggenheim of mining fame, to promote the Alaska-Yukon-Pacific Exposition in Seattle. The race was to be run over a set 4,100 mile route, with 30 checkpoints, and only Chicago and Cheyenne designated as parts depots. As evidence of road conditions of the day, it was stated that any driver who used railroad tracks for travel would be disqualified.

At first, 14 cars entered, but when the starting time came around, only five were on the line. They included two factory Fords, an Acme made in Reading, Pa., from 1903 to 1911; a Shawmut, made in Stoneham, Mass., from 1906 to 1909, and an Italian Itala. Driving one of the Fords (called No.1) was the company's top racing driver Frank Kulick, now recovered from his injuries suffered in the Michigan Fair Grounds crash of No. 666. With him was H.B. Harper, the company's advertising manager. Ford No. 2 was piloted by J.C. Smith and Bert Scott, two Ford employees who had volunteered for the job.

The Fords led almost the entire race. From New York to St. Louis was a Sunday drive. But west from there, all the way to Cheyenne, the days were nothing but pouring rain and the so-called roads were nothing but troughs of sticky gumbo. Over a week was spent negotiating this leg. At Cheyenne, the Itala gave up, and the race was now a hot contest between the Fords and the Shawmut. Kulick reached American Falls, Idaho, 12 hours ahead of the others, but then disaster struck. A series of bad directions had him lost in the wilds of Washington, and he arrived at Seattle almost a day behind Ford No. 2.

At the finish, an exhausted team of Smith and Scott were welcomed by Henry Ford himself. They had crossed the continent in 22 days and 55 minutes, averaging 7.75 MPH, which gives an indication of the roads

of the day. The Shawmut came in 17 hours later, Kulick about 24 hours later, and the Acme followed by about a week.

With all of this glory going on, one would expect a dark cloud somewhere. And it came in the form of the Selden case. After a thorough inspection of all three patent model cars, the two Seldens and the Lenoir-Ford, and a thorough study of the records, the presiding judge ruled in favor of the ALAM. According to the judge, who apparently was not all that versed in mechanics, "No fundamental difference appeared between the 2-cycle external compression Selden motor and the 4-cycle internal combustion used by Ford. Apparently he felt that if the thing ran, it was covered under the patent.

Ford's attorneys immediately called for an appeal. However, due to a packed court calendar, a new hearing could not be set until 1911, and so the case dragged on and on again. Meanwhile, with the case being tried in the newspapers far more often than in the courts, Ford was emerging as a folk hero. Here was a farm boy who through his own ingenuity had built up a corporation that was bringing a well-built and affordable car to the average working man. ALAM, meanwhile, was portrayed as a group of greedy New York financiers who were trying to skim money from every car purchase while hiding behind what appeared to be a fraudulent patent claim. Publicity-wise, Henry was clearly the underdog and the hero.

By far Ford's most popular model was the Touring Car, which was priced at $850 and weighed approximately 1,200 pounds. During the 1909 fiscal year, which went from Oct. 1, 1908 to Sept. 30, 1909, Ford produced a total of 7,728 touring cars. Because all records were kept on a fiscal year basis at this time, it is difficult to try to ascertain either model-year or calendar-year figures. For this chapter, all quoted production figures will be for the fiscal year. This restored model resides in the automotive section of the Henry Ford Museum at Greenfield Village, Dearborn.

After one year of service, this Illinois Model T Touring Car still looked quite fresh, when photographed in Aurora in 1910. But the mud-caked wheels attest to the midwestern roads of the era. At the start of the year, most touring cars were shipped without lights, windshields, or tops. But, as the year progressed, more and more orders stipulated these "accessories," and by year-end, most touring cars left the factory with the extra-cost items already installed. The carbide generator on the running board produced the gas needed for the John Brown headlamps.

On the early models, before a practical accessory windshield was developed, buyers of the accessory top could order a front panel along with the side curtains. This would quite effectively keep the car's occupants protected from bad weather, but must have done wonders for visibility. It's a good thing in this era that speeds were low and traffic light. These clear panels were made of a heavy gauge celluloid, which would tend to yellow and crack after several years of use. This year, touring car buyers had their choice of red or dark green until June, when red was dropped and dark green became the only color available.

1909

Ford's second most popular car was the 3-passenger Runabout with its quaint little single rear seat perched on the tool and storage box. A total of 2,351 were produced, with prices at the start of the year being $825. This, of course, did not include the top or windshield or the John Brown headlights shown here. This model, sometimes called the Roadster, began the year being finished in light gray. Later on, dark green was added as an option, and then it appears that light gray was dropped, thus making the entire Ford line available in only dark green.

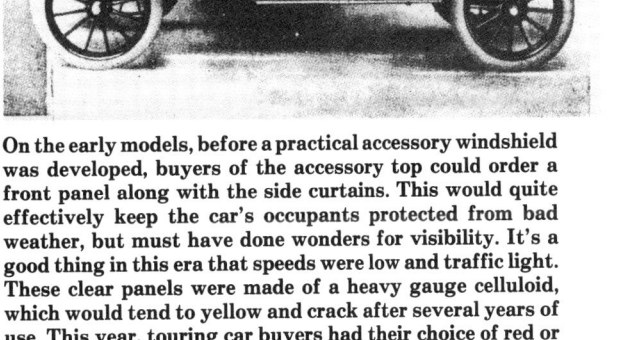

Designed primarily for doctors and other professional people who still made house or business calls was the 2-passenger Coupe, which was priced at $950. A decidedly unpopular body style, the coupe drew only 47 orders this year. Beveled plate glass was used in all of the windows. The door windows could be lowered by adjustable straps, but it is not known if any other windows could be opened. Both doors were hinged at the rear and opened from the forward edge. However, because of the steering column and brake lever being in the way, it is doubtful if much use was made of the left-hand door.

Ford's other prestige vehicle, probably more at home in the livery trade, was the Landaulet, which sold for $950. The car was identical to the town car, but had a totally open front, which apparently was more acceptable to the taxi trade than was the town car style. Whether it was its design or its $50 lower price tag, sales of the landaulet were 298, or 62 more than the town car. In this unusual photo, Dutee W. Flint, a Ford dealer at Providence, R.I., is standing on the fender to demonstrate the strength of the vanadium steel used in the car, and to prove its overall sturdy construction. There are conflicting reports over whether or not the rear quarters of the landaulet and town car could be lowered or whether the landau irons were strictly decorative. The slightly concaved look of the rear quarter in this photo would indicate that the irons might have been functional and that the rear section could be lowered on balmy days.

Appearing exactly as it left the factory was the Town Car, Ford's most expensive and pretentious car. Costing $1,000 as shown, the car was probably far more popular as a taxi or livery vehicle than as a prestige town car. Confusion exists on the seating, with some information putting this as a 5-passenger car, while other lists note that it was a 7-passenger vehicle, which means it would have had two jump or opera seats in the tonneau. However, the car was not all that large, and to hold seven passengers seems like a tight squeeze. A surprising total of 236 were built this year.

A mystery car of sorts is the Tourabout, a strange little 4-passenger car which Ford researchers claim came out in 1910. Other information tends to show that it was a mid-year introduction that simply did not make the 1909 catalogs. Despite the fact that the car does not show up on the 1909 production lists, there are even those who would argue that the $950 sport-type body was built only in 1909 and that those sold in 1910 were run-offs from the previous year. Substantiating the mid-year model contention is a restored model, shown at many AACA meets in the late 1960s, that bears the original engine with serial number 2550. Sources say that when fitted with a full top covering all four passengers, the car was called a Tourister. But, if fitted with only a half top over the front seat only (like a roadster's) the car was known as a Tourabout. That being the case, what was it called when it had no top?

Ford No. 2, now totally restored and pretty, was the winner of Robert Guggenheim's New York to Seattle race. Held to promote the Alaska-Yukon-Pacific Exposition which was being held at Seattle, the race first drew many entrants. However, though several rule changes and the threat of a suit from the Selden contingent, the final starting line consisted of only six cars, two of them being Fords. Driving No. 1 Ford was Frank Kulick, Ford's well known factory racing driver. Car No. 2, shown here, was probably intended to be a back-up vehicle, not a winner. It was driven by two unknown factory volunteers, J.C. Smith and Bert Scott. As it turned out, Car No. 2 won the race in 22 days and 55 minutes, about 24 hours ahead of Kulick. In 1959, to celebrate the 50th anniversary of the Model T, No. 2 was completely restored and retraced its race route. Only now it traveled over much better roads.

Among his many accomplishments, Henry Ford is often credited with popularizing the left-hand location of the steering wheel. Whether or not he can take credit for this is open to discussion, but certainly his use of the left-hand position on such a volume selling car as the Model T had a fair share to do with the U.S. acceptance of left hand drive. By 1909, the country had more or less accepted the keep-to-the-right form of driving that we now take for granted. But steering location appeared to be at the whim of each manufacturer (the 1913 Duck even had the steering wheel in the back seat). Ford explained his choice of the left hand location with this illustration from the 1909 catalog. Here it is shown that with left-hand control, both passenger and driver can get out from the curb side, whereas right-hand control means they must exit into the muddy street and the traffic. Also, the catalog points out, when passing another vehicle going in the opposite direction, a left-hand position allows the driver better visibility of the on-coming vehicle.

Displaying a well-deserved look of disgust and disappointment is driver Frank Kulick, behind the wheel of New York to Seattle Ford racer No. 1. As was to be expected, Kulick and his co-driver, H.B. Harper, Ford's advertising manager, led most of the race. But a few bad directions in Washington had the pair hopelessly lost in the backwoods of that state. As a result, Ford racer No. 2 came in almost a day ahead of Kulick. Still, the feat of both Fords covering the 4,100-mile route provided all of the publicity anyone could want for the new Model T, and it was an ecstatic Henry Ford who greeted the cars in Seattle.

1910

With its new Model T line only a little more than a year old, Ford entered 1910 with virtually no changes. Only one new model graced the 1910 catalog, and that was the Tourabout, which some contend was really a mid-year 1909 model. With the coming of 1910, the car took full status as a cataloged vehicle, and thus is officially accepted as a 1910 vehicle.

Essentially the Tourabout was the roadster fitted with a 2-passenger rear seat rather than the single mother-in-law seat on the roadster. Some information indicates that the Tourabout used the roadster's front seat in the rear also, and though this cannot be substantiated, it does seem logical. Both models had substantial cargo boxes located under their seats, and both the Tourabout and roadster rear seats could be replaced with a small metal rail, probably for tying down small packages. Most illustrations show the Tourabout with a full top to protect all passengers, but it also was available with just a roadster top covering only the front seat occupants.

An interesting note is that this year all Fords were finished in dark green, with supposedly no exceptions. Yet, most photographs of Tourabout models show the car in what appears to be a gray finish, lending weight to the argument that though these cars were called 1910 models, most were built in 1909 before the green-only policy went into effect.

During the course of the year, it was stated that both the landaulet and the coupe would be dropped. It appears that the landaulet was discontinued early in the year, but the coupe remained through 1911 and possibly even 1912. It is possible that the information regarding the coupe's demise came about via a body change made this year. Whereas the 1909 coupes had their doors hinged at the rear, opening from the leading edge, this year's coupe bodies had forward hinged doors, latching at the B-pillar. Whether this represented just a change in design, or resulted from a change in coupe body suppliers, is not known.

During the year, running changes occurred as improved designs or less expensive methods of construction were found. Among these was the standardization of windshields, tops, and side curtains on all models. Now there was a dealer delete for those buyers who insisted they did not want such items, while the majority of buyers were happy to find they did not have to add the weather protection as extra-cost items.

This year all bodies were of all-wood construction, with the metal or aluminum paneled bodies of the previous year not being used. Because of the very high finish obtained by countless coats of hand rubbed paint and varnish, the panels appear to be metal, but actually are beautifully finished wood. Another new item this year was a Stewart speedometer, which accompanied the John Brown carbide headlamps and kerosene cowl lamps and the brass Rubes bulb horn as standard items. On many of the early cars, the windshield was manufac-

tured by the G.A. Metzger Co. of New York City, while the dash-mounted coil box was by Heintz. As the year progressed, other suppliers were found for these units. Also during the year, the ribbing pattern on the running boards changed its design.

Surprisingly, the more expensive cars (coupe, town car, landaulet) did not come with speedometer or carbide lamps, only cowl lights. The package of speedometer, headlamps, and carbide generator cost $80 extra. This was probably due to the fact that these models were considered "city cars," and thus would not need the bright lighting or speed monitoring of the open cars, which were much more likely to be used in the open country and occasionally on dark rural roads.

On the mechanical side, the rear axle was modified; the steering wheel spider (spokes) was slightly larger, and the spring shackles were modified slightly. Early models had Buffalo carburetors, but these were later dropped in favor of Holley or Kingston units.

Despite Ford's intent to keep the car as economical as possible, prices did rise $100 on the touring car, $75 on the roadster, $200 on the town car, and $100 on the coupe. The rise on the open cars could be attributed to the inclusion of the top and headlamps in the price, but there is no answer as to why the closed models increased.

Although Ford's production figures do vary, it appears that during the fiscal year (Oct. 1, 1909 to Sept. 30, 1910) a total of 19,050 Model Ts left the factory. If these can all be counted as 1910 production, then we have a total of 18,942 finished vehicles and 108 bare chassis shipped to dealers. Of this number, the touring cars accounted for the most sales, with 16,890 being produced. This number also includes the handful of Tourabouts that were built. During this period, engine numbers ran from 11,101 to 31,900, indicating a total of 20,799 engines built. Other sources show these figures to run from 11,146 to 31,532, giving a total of 20,386. Calendar year engine numbers for 1910 reportedly ran from 14162 to 34901, showing production of 20,739, but this would include 1911 cars produced in the late fall of 1910. Other lists show calendar year vehicle production of 32,053, which seems impossibly high. Regardless, either Ford or Buick was the largest car producer again this year.

On the corporate side, the major news was the total move into the new plant on Woodward Ave., in Highland Park, Mich. Completed on the first day of 1910, the move put Ford into the largest factory complex of its kind in the world, devoted strictly to the manufacture of automobiles. The factory, which employed some 16,000 workers, drew the attention and subsequent visits of industrial giants the world over. At the time it was the largest factory under one roof in all of Michigan, and because of its vast expanse of windows, was often referred to as the "Crystal Palace."

On the Selden scene, all activities this year were of a confidential nature as lawyers on both sides regrouped

1910

Although the basic Touring Car was unchanged this year, several items that had been extra-cost accessories were now standard. These included the top and windshield, John Brown Model 15 carbide headlights, carbide generator, and Stewart speedometer. Also new was the basic cost, now up to $950. This year, all Fords were finished in Brewster Green, with black pin striping, though some sources say red pin striping was also available. No other color options are listed.

and laid plans for the coming appeal that Ford had instigated.

If things were quiet in the lawyers' offices, they were not on the race tracks. Once again Frank Kulick was proving that a well-designed Ford could do wonders in his hands. This time his mount was a specially built 2-seater with a modified Model T engine and a V-shaped radiator. Capable of speeds over 85 MPH, the car won numerous major races in all parts of the country, bringing a wealth of publicity to Ford and a wealth of prizes to Kulick.

A final bit of Detroit action, not directly related to Ford but one that would have tremendous importance in the future, was the purchase of the B.F. Everitt Co. by Walter O. Briggs. Everitt had been supplying bodies and trim parts to Ford and several other auto manufacturers for a couple of years, but was having trouble meeting its production schedules. Briggs had joined the company in 1904, and was responsible for getting a lucrative upholstery and trim contract from Ford. In 1910, the Everitt Co. became the Briggs Mfg. Co., and soon landed a contract for 10,000 Model T body components (or complete bodies, depending on how the records are interpreted). Briggs, by this contract, became a major supplier to Ford, a role that would become larger and larger right through the 1930s.

Mrs. Bess McKay, the first woman driver in Mercer County, Pa., poses in her new Ford. With the top down and the windshield folded in half, the dark green Fords could hold their own with cars priced thousands of dollars more. The public obviously thought so too, as a total of 16,890 Touring Cars and Tourabouts were build during the 1910 fiscal year. Of the quoted figure, most were Touring Cars, as Tourabout production is believed to have been fairly low. This is the only year that touring car bodies were made of all-wood construction. In 1909 some were all-wood, while others were aluminum or steel paneled. In 1911, a return was made to steel paneling, but not on all bodies. The Touring Car weighed 1,200 pounds, had a 100-inch wheelbase, and was 134.5 inches long overall. Tires were 30x3 in the front, 30x3.5 in the rear.

Mud and dust were not the only detriments to early motoring. Weak bridges also caused their share of headaches, as attested to by this trio of early motorists. The car is the new Tourabout, now in its only official year. However, many will claim the model was introduced as a late 1909 car, and other records tend to show Tourabout sales into the 1911 season. Substantiating those who set 1909 as the real date for the Tourabout is the gray paint scheme on this model. Yet, in 1910, all Fords were dark green. The Tourabout essentially was the Runabout with a 2-passenger rear seat and a top covering all four passengers. It is claimed that the car could also be ordered with a top covering only the front passengers, similar to a runabout top. Priced at $950, the same as the Touring Car, the Tourabout's production figures are lost among those of the Touring Car. But, it is believed they are fairly low. This car is also referred to as the Tourister in some material.

Ford's second most popular car was the Runabout, of which 1,486 were built during the fiscal year. Priced at $900, the car came completely equipped with John Brown carbide headlights and carbide generator mounted on the running board, and John Brown kerosene cowl lamps and taillight. Also included was the top, which protected only the front seat passengers, leaving the lone occupant of the rear seat at the mercy of the weather. Below the rear seat was a relatively large storage box, and the seat itself could be removed. The bulb horn, which was standard equipment, was produced by the Rubes Co.

1910

By today's standards, the Coupe continued to look like a telephone booth on wheels. This year the car received a major change in that the doors were now hinged at the leading edges rather than at the B-pillar as in 1909. Whether this resulted from a design change or from a switch in body suppliers is not known. Despite the change of latch location, it seems that the left hand door would still have been impossible to use because of the steering wheel and clutch/brake lever. Taking honors as Ford's first fully enclosed car, the Coupe cost $1,050 and drew a total of 187 orders. Of these, most would have been professional people such as doctors, or women and elderly men who didn't appreciate the rigors of an open car in inclement weather. It is interesting to note that only cowl lights were provided, with the headlights being extra. It is probable that these closed models were considered "city cars" and as such did not need headlights, as opposed to the open models, which often went to buyers who lived in rural or suburban areas.

Ford's most expensive model continued to be the Town Car, which was priced at $1,200 this year. Designed primarily for the taxi trade, rather than the prestige car buyer, the rather attractive vehicle drew a total of 377 orders this year. As with the Coupe, the Town Car came minus headlamps or speedometer, which were $80 extra. Again, these were probably deemed unnecessary for cars that would be operated almost exclusively on lighted city streets. Missing from this year's sales list was the Landaulet, which was essentially a town car without a windshield or top over the driver's position. Still, records indicate that two landaulets were constructed and sold at $1,100 each. On both the town car and landaulet models, the landau irons were functional, and the rear portion of the passenger's compartment could be folded down.

An interesting vehicle is this Town Car, seen here operating as a taxi in Winnipeg, Canada. The body is very similar to the accompanying catalog illustration. But, the rear door is larger than that on the cataloged car, and features a rear fender cut-out. This could possibly be a Canadian sourced production body, or it could be one of the after-market bodies that were quite popular in this era.

Charles T. Fisher, one of the seven Fisher brothers who would form the Fisher Body Co., sits in the right front seat of a new Ford touring car body. Ford knew the Fishers from their days at the C.R. Wilson Co., one of the major body suppliers for Ford. Thus, when the Fishers started their own body company, Ford was one of their first customers. Note that this body is totally made of wood. On some cars, the flat panels would be covered with thin sheet metal, while on others, a multitude of lacquer coats would produce a deep, metal-like finish. Completing a body to this stage was the easy part. Applying the lacquer finish could take four or more weeks of tedious hand brushing and sanding, over and over.

1911

From a relatively quiet 1910, the year 1911 was about as action packed as one could want. In just about every category imaginable, Ford made news, changes, or advances. The Selden case was won; production leaped; prices went down; new models were introduced; a bevy of mechanical changes took place; a primitive production line was instituted; a new factory was begun in England—and the list went on and on. For sure, 1911 was not a quiet one.

From the overall automotive scene, the largest news of the year occurred on Jan. 9, when the U.S. Appeals Court overturned the earlier district court ruling in favor of the Selden contingent. The Assn. of Licensed Automobile Manufacturers (ALAM) had used their same argument that the Selden patent covered all vehicles powered by a liquid hydrocarbon engine. The district court judge, who had only a poor grasp of mechanical things, agreed by stating that he saw "no fundamental differences between a 2-cycle external compression engine as patented by Selden, and the 4-cycle internal combustion engine used by Ford."

In the Appellate Court, Presiding Judge Noyes appeared to have a far better knowledge of physics and mechanics, and took an active interest in the actual designs and workings of the engines. In his final ruling, Judge Noyes said that the Selden patent was indeed valid, but that the specific type of engine used in Selden's machine was so different from the design used in Ford cars, that no infringement of patent existed on Ford's part. Thus, the famous Selden case, which had been in and out of courts since 1903, was finally resolved. The result was that neither Ford nor any other automobile manufacturer had to pay royalties to the ALAM. With this decision, there was little reason for the ALAM members to remain in the organization, and within a year, ALAM slipped from existence.

Just about coinciding with the Selden settlement,

Ford's lowest price model was the 3-passenger Runabout or Roadster, also called the Commercial Roadster. Priced at $680, it followed the lines of other Model T styles, and did not use the curved fenders or low body of the new sport-type roadsters. The rear seat and storage box were readily removable, either for hauling packages between the fender aprons, or for the addition of some sort of cargo box. The John Brown headlights and running board carbide generator were included in the price, as was the top and windshield. John Brown Co. also supplied the brass kerosene cowl and taillamps, which were slightly different than those used in 1910.

though strictly coincidental, were the major change made to the Model T. These changes included new steel panelling; new radiator; new wheels; new fenders; new engine; new axles, and a new color, not to mention two new models. Of course, all of these changes did not occur in January, or the resulting car simply could have been considered a brand new model. However, the majority of the running changes seem to have occurred during the mid-winter production.

This, of course, makes any thought of model-year identification impossible. For example, the new steel panelled bodies, finished in Royal Blue, were introduced in January. This leads some to contend that the "blue" Fords are the true 1911 models. But the two new styles, the Torpedo Roadster and its companion Open Roadster, actually went into production on Oct. 26. These are usually thought of as 1911 models, though a few will argue for the 1910 date, based on calendar production. Also, the switch from Brewster Green to Royal Blue occurred in October, and the blue finish was used on some of the all-wood bodies, in addition to the composite metal and wood units of 1911 vintage.

With the exception of the two new additions, body styles remained what they had been, but the landaulet was definitely gone. Reports conflict on the Tourabout also. The unusual and not popular car was not listed in the 1911 catalogs, nor does it show on the production figures. Yet Ray Miller of Model T fame has documented two such cars as having been built well into the 1911 calendar year. Possibly these were left over bodies built at special request, or more likely, re-engined and re-numbered to fit into the 1911 pattern. But why then do they not appear on the production lists?

Major axle changes also took place, with the front axle having new 2-piece spindles, and the rear axle now having a cast iron center section and 6-inch hub flanges. The wheels, though retaining their 24-inch diameter and still wearing 30x3 tires on the front and 30x3.5 on the rear, now had thicker spokes. Later in the year they would also gain tapered bearings to fit the new tapered axles.

On the outside, one of the most noticeable changes was in the front fender design. The trailing edge of the new fenders now swept in towards the hood, giving the fender a much more solid appearance. The rear fenders too gained a new design, with a sweep in toward the body, which did away with the old apron design. The running boards again changed slightly and the rear windows of the touring and roadster tops went from a small oval to a much larger rectangle sometime during the year.

Within the car, the steering wheel grew to 15 inches in diameter. Coil boxes cannot be help in determining age, as this year these items were supplied by Heintz, Kingston, and Jacobson-Brandon, and apparently were installed as stocks arrived from the three different suppliers. The speedometer remained a Stewart, while the horn remained a Rubes, but the windshield was now produced by the Rands Mfg. Co.

Under the hood, a few needed changes also took place. The new blocks incorporated babbitt upper bearings for the three mains; had cover plates over the valve springs, and had a new crankcase with a separate inspection plate which allowed taking up of the bearings without dropping the entire crankcase. In addition, the newly designed transmission case had a larger access hole for getting at the bands, which frequently needed adjusting or replacing. Carburetors remained either Kingstons or Holleys.

The previously mentioned Torpedo and Open Roadsters (or runabouts, as some material calls them) were Ford's attempt at a totally sporty car. The cars used the same 100-inch wheelbase chassis as other models, but their low profile gave them a longer appearance. This lowness was accomplished by removing the gas tank from under the seat, thus allowing the seat and body to be fitted closer to the chassis. The seat was also moved further back than that on the touring car or roadster, a move which resulted in a longer and lower steering column. The gas tank was increased in size to 16.5 gallons (all others had 10-gallon tanks) and located behind the seat, in a manner common to most of the "sport-type" cars of the day. Both oval and rectangular tanks were used throughout the production, possibly as supplies arrived. The Torpedo Roadster was also the first open Ford to be fitted with front doors, and a had the first body which blended into the dashboard. Ahead of the body, the hood was 24 inches long, as opposed to the 22-inch aluminum hoods used on all other models. Still, no hood louvers were used. Also unique to these models were the curved fenders, which were totally different than those of any other Ford car.

With all of this going on, one would expect prices to rise. They did just the opposite. The ever-popular touring car dropped $170 to $780, while the standard runabout dropped $220, down to a new price of $680. It and the new Open Roadster (runabout) shared the same spot as Ford's lowest priced models. Even the town car, still Ford's most expensive model, dropped $240 to a new low of $960, and thus Ford had no models listed for over $1,000. *Note: One exception to this is a listing which shows the landaulet still posted at $1,100, but since none were built in 1911, it seems that this listing was released in error by the Ford factory.

On the racing scene, Frank Kulick started out the year by winning virtually everything at the Mardi Gras races in New Orleans. He then moved on to the midwest, where he spent the spring and summer beating everything in sight and taking top honors at the major races at Chicago, Milwaukee, and Detroit. In September he reached his high point at Detroit, by beating the famed Bob Burman and his world famous Blitzen Benz. After watching this race, Henry Ford is reported to have put a $1,000 bill into Kulick's hand, asking only that he quit the race track circuit. Kulick did, but remained a competitor in such things as ice racing and hill climbs

through 1912.

On the corporate side, the new Highland Park plant had settled down to a hitch-free routine, which meant the cars could be turned out with the greatest of ease and economy. The dealer network was now over the 5,000 mark, the Canadian plant was operating at a profit, and the new manufacturing facility was being opened at Manchester, England.

With all of this activity, it would seem that a solid record would exist of the number of cars turned out. No such luck. A tally of models built during the fiscal year of Oct. 1, 1910 to Sept. 30, 1911, shows 34,858, including sales of 248 stripped chassis. Of these, of course, the touring car accounted for the most builds, having 26,405 to its credit. Yet, the serial numbers for this period run from 31533 to 70749, indicating engine production of 39,216. For the calendar year, engine numbers ran from 34901 to 88900, showing production of 53,999 engines for that period. These engine number figures have sometimes been quoted as total production figures, but it is well known that more engines are built than are cars to accept them, considering the need for replacements, short blocks, and outright engine sales to outside sources. And still another list for the fiscal year shows car and motor numbers running from 31,901 to 69,876, for a total production of 37,975. And, a final list for the calendar year, puts Ford's production at 69,762. Regardless, Ford was still far ahead of the field, with its closest competitor being Studebaker, which together with its companion E.M.F. line, listed a questionably high production of 26,827. Ford was now the undisputed major car producer in the country, and was determined to remain in that spot.

Although trucks per se are not covered in this book, car/ truck combinations such as the Commercial Roadster probably have their rightful place. With the rear seat box removed, this owner has added a cargo box to the rear and can now go about whatever business he was in at the time. Probably he converted the car back to its 3-passenger configuration whenever needed. Since the Tourabout is simply the Roadster with a 2-passenger rear seat, it is surprising that it was dropped after only one year. Actually, there are at least two 1911 Tourabouts registered, with serial numbers that show they were produced well into the 1911 production year, yet Ford's records show none being built. Oddly, however, though the Tourabout is not mentioned in the catalogs, it was given a 1911 list price of $725 with a 4-place top. Instead of the John Brown lighting system, this car uses a pre-charged gas cylinder, possibly by Prest-O-Lite. Whether this system was an option or a switch in suppliers is not known.

This winter scene on one of Detroit's boulevards has two happy ladies enjoying an outing in one of the new Open Roadsters (or Runabouts). Appearing this year only, the car shared the line's low price of $680 with the Commercial Roadster. Essentially, the Open Roadster was the new Torpedo Roadster without doors or forward body panels. Gas tanks appear to have varied. This model uses a rectangular tank, while others are shown with cylindrical tanks. The brass brace, running from the center hinge on the windshield to the running board was necessary on these models to support the heavy glass in its folded configuration. A total of 7,845 roadsters were built this year, but there are no break-downs as to how many were commercial types and how many were the new sport models.

Probably the best looking Ford yet was the new Torpedo Roadster (Runabout) which was priced at $725 fully equipped. This was the first Ford open car to use doors in the front, and the first to have a body panel between the dashboard and the door posts. In order to lower the body and seats, the gas tank was moved to the back, in a style common to sport-type cars of the day. The tank was of 16.5-gallon capacity as opposed to the 10-gallon tanks used on other models. Apparently the supply of these tanks was not consistent, as these cars appear with cylindrical, rectangular, and elliptical tanks. The fenders were exclusive only to the Open and Torpedo Roadsters, and were not used on any other Ford products.

A commercial variation on the new Open Roadster (Runabout) were these Fire Chief's Roadsters which appear to have been marketed in limited quantities. The car is the standard model, less windshield and top, but fitted with a large brass bell, front bumpers, and a cargo box on the rear. Finished in bright red, the cars apparently were aimed at major city markets such as New York or Chicago. Also obvious are the use of demountable rims, which allowed the carrying of a spare tire, barely visible on the right running board. Although all open cars were sold with windshields, tops, and headlights as standard equipment, these items could be omitted as a delete option. When ordered in stripped form, the cars were $80 less than the posted prices. The cost of the Fire Chief's Roadster is not known.

From the rear, the Torpedo Runabout shows off its sporty exterior gas tank. This view also gives a good look at the exclusive fenders with the front ones flaring directly into the frame rails and the rear ones equipped with their own special aprons. The doors were hinged at the front, but it seems unlikely that the driver could use his door for exit, as the steering wheel would have effectively blocked anyone from using the left entry. Both the Open and Torpedo Roadsters had 24-inch long hoods, as compared to the 22-inch hoods of all other models. Although it is doubtful that few buyers did so, the torpedoes could be ordered without windshield, top, or lights for $645. When photographed in the 1960s, this beautifully restored car belonged to Roy Collins of Brunswick, Ohio.

The Touring Car exemplifies the most popular Ford of the year. Priced at only $780 fully equipped, this model enjoyed a fiscal year run of 26,405 copies. Bodies this year were of composite construction, using sheet metal panels over a wooden frame, as opposed to the all-wood bodies of 1910. The relatively new Fisher Body Co. of Detroit was a large supplier of bodies to Ford this year. The car sported new rear fenders, which flowed into the lower body sides. The top had a large rectangular rear window, which during 1911 production replaced the small oval units. Most Model Ts used the standard 56-inch tread, but those destined for delivery to rural areas in the southern states could be fitted with 60-inch tread axles to fit the ruts caused by the cotton and tobacco wagons, which traditionally had 5-foot wheel spacing.

This photo probably should appear in the 1912 section, even though it is of a 1911 Touring Car. But this vehicle is fitted with the new Fore-Doors, which were sold by Ford dealers to owners of 1911 and early 1912 Touring Cars. The doors and forward panels helped give the formerly door-less models a more modern appearance by bringing them into line with the late-entry 1912 Fore-Door Touring Cars. Somewhere along the line, this car has lost both its top and its carbide generator, but it did gain the new doors.

New fenders identify this as the 1911 Coupe. With this exception, the almost ludicrous body remained unchanged from 1910. Priced at $840 this year, a reduction of $210, the car still remained the least popular Model T, with only 45 being built in the calendar year. As before, standard equipment included two kerosene-fired John Brown cowl lights and a kerosene taillight, but no headlights. As mentioned earlier, this was probably because coupes and town cars were considered "city vehicles" as opposed to the more practical open cars which were popular in rural and suburban areas. And, in most cities of this era only marker lights or carriage lamps were required for night operation. Fueling this car must have been fun, as the 10-gallon gas tank was located under the driver's seat.

Down in price to $960, the Town Car still was Ford's most expensive model. Yet, for a car of this type, it was fairly popular. A total of 315 were built, most of which probably went into the taxi and livery business. Although records show that none were built this year, some lists continue to show the open-front Landaulet being available at $1,100. Possibly such a car would have been built to special order had any orders materialized. It appears that at least two different styles of town car were on the market this year, probably representing the differences in construction of at least two different suppliers. This is one version, shown in the 1911 catalog, which illustrates a rear door ending at the fenderline. A second variation is similar to the Canadian taxi in the 1910 chapter, with a wider rear door having a cut-out above the fender. Since these bodies were supplied by outside builders, it is not surprising that differences such as this should appear.

Although Fords were not the most popular vehicles for funeral car or ambulance bodies, at least a few of the 248 stripped chassis sold this year went to such specialty body manufacturers. It is known that this car was delivered to the Livingston Funeral Home of Hastings, Neb., but it is not known who built the body. Possibly the work was done by a local carriage maker. The article accompanying the photo stated that the body could be easily removed and replaced with a standard passenger car body. When Ford sold stripped chassis, the units included fenders and aprons, radiator, dash board, and hood. The body shown here was obviously of all-wood construction, and featured some of the beautiful carved panels and decorative posts that were so common on funeral vehicles in this era. Unlike most funeral cars of the time, this one was not finished in black, but appears to have been done in either white or light gray with gold leaf trim.

1912

Two main styling events marked the 1912 year, but neither occurred until well into the model or sales year, so in effect, we have two distinctive styles of cars for this period. If one considers the 1912 models to follow Ford's fiscal year beginning Oct. 1, 1911, then the first series of cars to come from the factories were virtually identical to the 1911 models.

Then, either in January or April (again, reports conflict) the cars went through a styling revision, which was most noticeable on the touring car and the Torpedo Roadster. Most apparent in the change was the inclusion of front or "fore" doors on the touring cars and the town cars. At this time also, the touring car received a newly styled body of much smoother line, while the Torpedo Runabout received a more stodgy body that did much to ruin its interesting and sporty lines of 1911 and early 1912. Concurrent with the introduction of the Fore-Door Touring was the marketing of special cowl panels and front doors so that owners of 1911 and early 1912 touring cars could bring their vehicles up to more modern appearances. Such conversion packages may also have been available for the town car owners. But, because access was blocked on the driver's side anyway, only the doors on the passenger's side were functional.

In addition to the new door treatment, the touring car sides lost the former seat protrusion, and now were of smooth line from sill to sill. Sadly, such smoothing of the style did not occur on the Torpedo Roadster. Instead, the car received a much higher seat and body, had the same flat cowl and vertical windshield of the plain roadster, and now shared common front fenders with all other models while having its distinctive rear fenders used on the plain or "Commercial Roadster" as well. However, unlike those on the touring car, the doors of the Torpedo were not detachable, and both were functional. The rear deck of the Torpedo continued to hold a 16-gallon gas tank as opposed to the 10-gallon under-seat units of all other Fords. This deck also provided a home for a relatively large storage box.

The Open Runabout was dropped, but it is not clear whether it was dropped at the start of the 1912 season, or if a few trickled out as 1912 models before the new style bodies were introduced at mid-year. With the new models came a name change, and the regular 3-passenger roadster was now called the Commercial Roadster, with promotion given to the fact that its removable third seat could easily be replaced with a cargo box. For the first time also, the removable seat was called a "rumble seat."

Supposedly, the coupe was also dropped, and it does not appear in 1912 literature or on the price lists. Yet, production lists show a total of 19 coupes built during the fiscal year. It is very probable that they were simply a continuation of the 1911 models, or the final run-off of contracted bodies. It is not known if they were sold as 1912 or 1911 cars—probably the bill of sale would have determined the year by the chassis number.

And, though Ford made no mention of the change, the town car apparently received a newly designed body, or possibly a new body supplier. In addition to receiving its own exclusive forward panels (door on the right, panel on the left) the car now had a newly designed driver's seat, new tonneau with an upswept beltline to a higher rear panel, new flat roofline, and new rear doors with a pronounced forward-pointing reverse scallop on the lower sill. Also, the tonneau now was equipped with two extra folding seats, so that the car literally became a 7-passenger vehicle—albeit, a very cramped vehicle when carrying seven passengers. It is not known whether or not all of the 802 town cars built this year were equipped with this body, or if some had either of the two former style bodies.

On all models, rubber floor mats were used in the front, but the new touring cars had fiber or cocoa mats in the rear. Likewise, on the new touring cars, the rear doors were hinged at the leading edge, rather than at the trailing edges as on former models. Another change was made in the running board design, and both the kerosene cowl lamps and the carbide headlamps could be either E&J or John Brown models. Early 1912 cars were all finished in dark blue, but there are indications that the second generation of 1912 cars could also be ordered in black.

In an unusual move, Ford experimented with a production Depot Hack, quietly introducing this style in April. The body, which sort of combined a touring car with a pickup truck, was designed and built by the Indianapolis Wagon Body Co., a firm that later became the very well known Martin Parry Co. It is not known how many such hacks were contracted for at first, but apparently Henry Ford himself cancelled the contract after only 16 were built. The reason for the cancellation apparently was that installation of the body required modifications to the Model T chassis and steering column, and Ford did not want anyone modifying his chassis units—at least not before the units were sold. Although the Depot Hack contract went down the drain, Martin Parry Co. built commercial bodies for Ford for many years, including many depot hacks that were sold on the aftermarket by Ford and other dealers. It appears that most of the 16 hacks that were built under Ford's contract were sold in Indiana or Illinois, and at least one authenticated example of this style exists in restored form today.

On the price scale, Ford again lowered the boom, reducing all prices across the board. The ever-popular touring car dropped $90 to a new low of $690, while the Torpedo dropped $135 to list at $590, which was the same price as the Commercial Roadster. The smallest decrease occurred with the town car, which went down only $60 to a list of $900 even. The coupe and the Open Roadster, though shown on some lists, are not priced, nor was the Depot Hack.

Mechanically, little happened in 1912, as Ford seemed content with its 22 horsepower engine of 3.75x4 inch bore and stroke and 176.7 cubic inches. The planetary transmission still was pedal operated (and would be through 1927) and consisted of high and low plus reverse. Apparently a running change occurred with the heads, which were raised slightly and given a slightly different combustion chamber configuration, which altered the compression ratio slightly but made no difference in the horsepower or displacement. On some engines, a unique combination of oil filler and timer cover was used, but apparently this unit did not work well and was dropped in favor of the former styles. Ford's own production of some components seems to have become bogged down in spots due to the rate at which vehicles were being turned out. Thus Ford turned to the Dodge Bros. to manufacture some of the flywheel magnetos. Dodge was still a major supplier of Ford's transmission and running gear parts, but had been phased out of the engine program over the years. Carburetors seem to have settled down to Holleys exclusively by year-end, although both Holley and Kingston units were used at the start of the season.

As always, production figures have to be compared against existing major lists. A tally of all vehicles built during the fiscal year shows 68,773 units rolling out the door. This includes 2,133 stripped chassis shipped to outside body builders, and 1,845 of the new Delivery Car, which is not covered here because it is well documented in Crestline's "Ford Trucks Since 1905" by James K. Wagner. This again conflicts with the fiscal year production lists showing the serial numbers going from 70750 on Oct. 1, 1911, to 157424 on Sept. 30, 1912, or a total of 86,674 engines and chassis. Two lists show calendar year production beginning at 88,901, but one list shows the end figure at 171,300 for a total production of 82,399, while the other list ends at 183,563 for a total production of 94,662. However, the later list may pertain to engines only, as it is unclear whether chassis are included. And, a final listing, too often accepted as gospel, puts production at a highly unlikely 170,211. Regardless, Ford was by far the nation's largest auto maker, well above second place Willys-Overland with its combined production of 28,572. Assisting in this production was Ford's new plant in Kansas City, which opened in 1911 but only entered its first full year of production in 1912.

On the racing scene, this was to be Ford's last official involvement until the 1930s. Frank Kulick and his modified Model T did some exhibition races, including outrunning an iceboat on Lake St. Clair, and winning several hill climbs, but he was kept out of track racing by Henry Ford, who felt the sport had become too fast and too dangerous. In his sole attempt at a world speed record, again on frozen Lake St. Clair, he failed to beat the 141 MPH set at Daytona Beach by Bob Burman in 1911. Following a relatively uneventful year, Ford quietly slipped out of sponsored auto racing.

It is not clear if the Open Roadster was built in 1912 or ended with the start of Ford's fiscal year. Promotional catalogs and production lists ignore the car, yet it was featured in some Ford literature of 1912. If it was produced as a 1912 vehicle, it would have used the identical styling of the 1911 model, and would have appeared only in the early months of the 1912 season. Its price probably would have been in the $600 range. The car is shown stuck axle deep in a spring thaw in a Ford booklet of the time. The caption warned drivers of the consequence of "being too polite on a narrow road, unless you know the consistency of the roadside mud." Note the rear-mounted tool box. This was an item introduced on the 1912 Torpedo, and did not appear on the 1911 models. Likewise, the large cylindrical 16-gallon gas tank was sometimes used in 1911 along with rectangular and elliptical units, but was used almost exclusively in 1912.

Ford's new style Torpedo Roadster (Runabout) lost much of the appeal that it had as a 1911 and early 1912 model. Priced at $590, the same as the Commercial Roadster, the model apparently did not fare too well on the sales charts, and was redesigned for 1913. Since its production is combined with that of the Commercial Roadster, it is impossible to tell how many of the 13,376 roadster units were Torpedoes. The new body now used a standard dashboard and windshield, but had its own exclusive 2-passenger seat of slightly lower proportions than used on other models. It also used the same front fenders as used on all other Model Ts, and shared its rear fenders with the second generation of Commercial Roadsters. All fuel tanks were now cylindrical 16-gallon units mounted on the rear platform.

1912

All buttoned up for a winter run is this late 1912 Torpedo Roadster (Runabout) which was introduced in either January or April of 1912, depending on which records one wants to use. Prior to the building of this version, the 1912 Torpedo Roadster looked identical to the much more sporty 1911 model. New for the year was the tool or storage box. By the looks of the tire pump by the front wheel, the box had better have contained tools. According to a notation on the back, this photo was taken at Kirkland, Ill., in 1914.

An early 1912 version of the 3-place Runabout is this restored model, owned by C.E. Bailey of Cabot, Ark., when photographed in the late 1960s. This model is shown with its third seat removed, and replaced by a small parcel tray. Note that the rear fenders follow the design of the 1911 models. The second generation 3-passenger roadster took the name Commercial Roadster, but early literature simply refers to this car as a 3-passenger Runabout (Roadster).

The second generation 1912 3-place Commercial Roadster shared its rounded rear fenders with the Torpedo Roadster. This was the only 1912 model Ford that was not fitted with dash panels and removable doors. For the first time, Ford used the terminology "removable rumble seat" to describe the rear seat. With this removed, a flat floor space 3.5-foot square could be used for cargo, or as a base for any number of commercial bodies. The Commercial Roadster had the same $590 price as the Torpedo and its production is tallied in with that of the Torpedo, the lists simply showing 13,376 roadsters being built during the calendar year.

With its rear seat removed and a cargo box inserted in its place, the Commercial Roadster made a neat little pickup truck—and one that could be converted back into a car on Sunday. This model does not have John Brown headlights, but it might be wearing the E&J models which were also supplied this year. Rather than using a carbide/water generator, it is fitted with a pressurized tank of gas on the running board. The top folded back very neatly, but would have blocked some of the cargo space.

The first generation of 1912 Touring Cars appeared virtually identical to the 1911 models, but in January (some contend April) the second generation arrived. These cars had a totally new composite body of sheet steel over a wood frame. The seats no longer extended past the lower body, but instead the panels now formed one smooth surface from seat rail to sill. All 1912 second generation cars were equipped with the new "fore doors," which consisted of removable cowl panels and a functional door for the front passenger, and a dummy door on the driver's side. The non-operating driver's "door" was simply because the steering column and wheel and clutch/brake lever made it impossible for the driver to exit on the left side. Many owners were not overly impressed with the new fore-doors, and used them only in inclement weather. This nicely restored car was photographed by the author in the early 1970s at the Old Car Festival at Greenfield Village. At that time it belonged to William Nickle of Saginaw, Mich.

Photographed with its proud owners when only six weeks old was this second generation 1912 Touring Car. This photo gives a good view of the "fore doors" which consisted of the cowl panel and a functional door on the right, a dummy on the left. Not only did the new body style incorporate front doors, it also saw the rear door hinging change from forward to rear latches. By far Ford's most popular model, the Touring Car accounted for 50,598 sales during calendar year 1912. Its price of $690 included the forward panels, cowl lamps, taillight, and carbide headlights by either John Brown or E&J, and a full top with side curtains. The gas generator on the running board produced acetylene gas for the headlights by dripping water from the upper tank onto powered calcium carbide in the lower container.

1912

An accessory that was just starting to come into vogue in this era, at least on low cost cars, was wire wheel sets. True, some of the more expensive sporty cars already came equipped with such wheels, but it was a rare Model T buyer who would invest in such a high priced accessory, especially since the car already came with four perfectly good wood spoke wheels. In addition to providing a smoother ride and totally changing the car's appearance, the wire wheels provided one other major advantage. It meant that a spare wheel could now be carried. In an era when frequent tire repairs had to be painfully made at the side of the road, the concept of easily putting on an inflated tire with just a few bolts was enticing indeed. The two major manufacturers of wire wheels were Houck and Buffalo. When this car was photographed at Santa Barbara, it was owned by Norm Siefert.

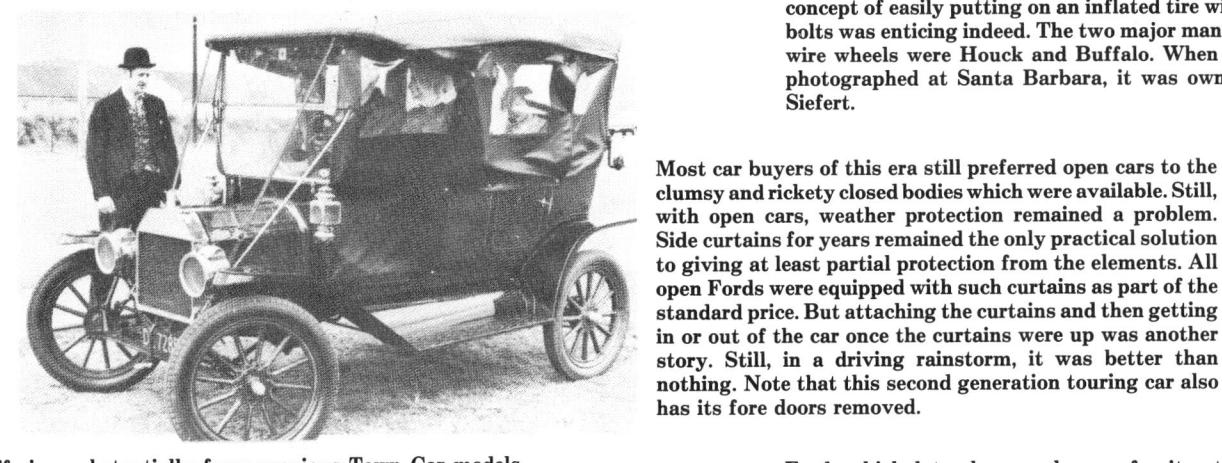

Most car buyers of this era still preferred open cars to the clumsy and rickety closed bodies which were available. Still, with open cars, weather protection remained a problem. Side curtains for years remained the only practical solution to giving at least partial protection from the elements. All open Fords were equipped with such curtains as part of the standard price. But attaching the curtains and then getting in or out of the car once the curtains were up was another story. Still, in a driving rainstorm, it was better than nothing. Note that this second generation touring car also has its fore doors removed.

Differing substantially from previous Town Car models, this year's version appears to have a totally new body and/or a new body source. Priced at $900 and keyed primarily to the livery and taxi trade, the Town Car this year accounted for 802 units. For the first time, standard equipment included the John Brown headlights and carbide generator, and a Steward speedometer. Comparing this body with the 1911 version, one finds a more solidly framed windshield; new flat roofline; front panels and a door on the right; new driver's seat, and totally new tonneau styling. Also, this year's version was equipped with two extra folding seats in the tonneau, thus becoming Ford's first production 7-passenger car. A thoughtful touch was the grab handle on the B-pillar, to assist passengers in climbing into the relatively high vehicle. The landau irons continued to be functional, as the rear quarter section could be lowered. Note how the new rear fender design blends nicely into the apron and lower rear panel.

Ford, which later became known for its station wagon models, made its first experiment into the depot hack field this year—depot hacks being regarded as the grandparents of all station wagon concepts. A contract was signed with the Indianapolis Wagon Co. to produce an unknown number of depot hack bodies for installation on the Ford chassis, with these units to be sold as complete vehicles by Ford dealers. This was opposed to the usual method of a dealer or customer buying a stripped chassis and then having a local body builder supply whatever style hack was desired. The all-wood hacks were fitted with a cargo-type body, which could hold a removable rear seat. The top fit over the driver's seat only, similar to the Commercial Roadster. The chassis were shipped to Indianapolis for the body work, and then the completed hack was shipped to a local dealer. The car shown in this original photo is one of two sold to the Coleman Ford Agency, in Rosedale, Ind. The only trouble with the plan was that the wagon company had to modify the chassis to fit the body, and when Henry Ford learned of the modifications, he cancelled the contract.

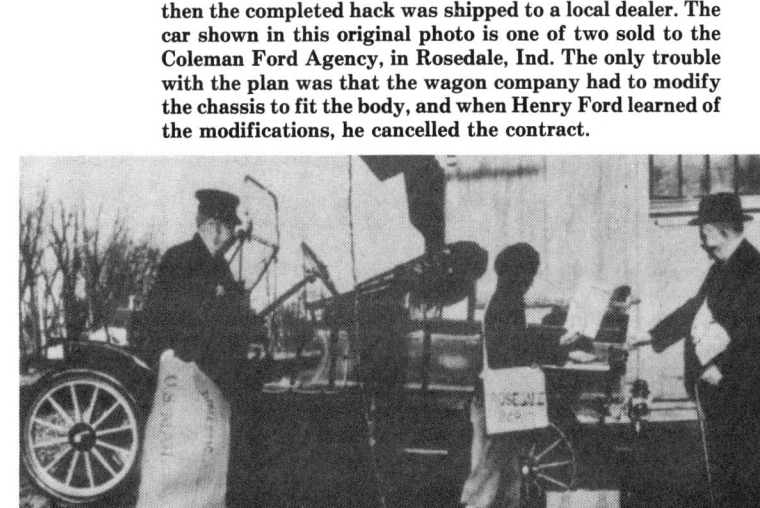

Despite the fact that only 16 Depot Hacks were built by Indianapolis Wagon Body Co. before Henry Ford cancelled the order, one still remains in restored condition. In the mid-1960s it was owned by James Soules of Decature, Ill. Of the 16 units produced, it is believed that all were sold in Indiana and Illinois. As its name implies, depot hacks were originally used as taxis specializing in carrying passengers and luggage from the railroad station to their homes or hotels. Indianapolis Wagon Body later became the large Martin Parry Co., which made huge volumes of commercial truck bodies for all makes, including Ford, throughout the pre-World War II era.

Although trucks will not be covered in this book, having been very well documented in James K. Wagner's *FORD TRUCKS SINCE 1905*, published by Crestline, Ford's new Delivery Van was such a significant vehicle that it bears mentioning here. This marked the first time that Ford considered the Model T for more than just carrying passengers. Thus, it contracted for the construction of special delivery van bodies to be sold as complete units by dealers, rather than have the dealers contact an aftermarket body builder. Priced at $700 complete, the vans drew the attention of all sorts of retailers from the mom/pop grocer shown here to the giant John Wanamaker department store chain. Ford thought it had a winner with this one, when a total of 1,845 were sold early in the fiscal year. The all-wood body was equipped with two swing-out doors in the back, and roll-up side curtains for the open front entrances. During 1910 and 1911, a group of 250 similar Ford trucks were operated as a test fleet by various Bell Telephone companies, and the success of these units prompted Ford to introduce its Delivery Van as an official model. In the days when home delivery of virtually everything was taken for granted, a huge market existed for dependable light vehicles such as this. However, potential buyers found the $700 price to be cost prohibitive, and after an initial good run, sales dropped off significantly, to the point where the little truck was dropped in 1913.

In one of its last officially Ford-sponsored events, Frank Kulick and his modified Model T get set to try for a new world speed record on frozen Lake St. Clair, near Detroit. This was the place where Henry had set a world speed record many years before, but Kulick wasn't that lucky. His speed was reportedly far less than the 141 MPH mark set in 1911 by Bob Burman at Daytona Beach. Note the tire chains on the car's rear wheels. The run must have provided quite a ride for Kulick and his unidentified riding mechanic.

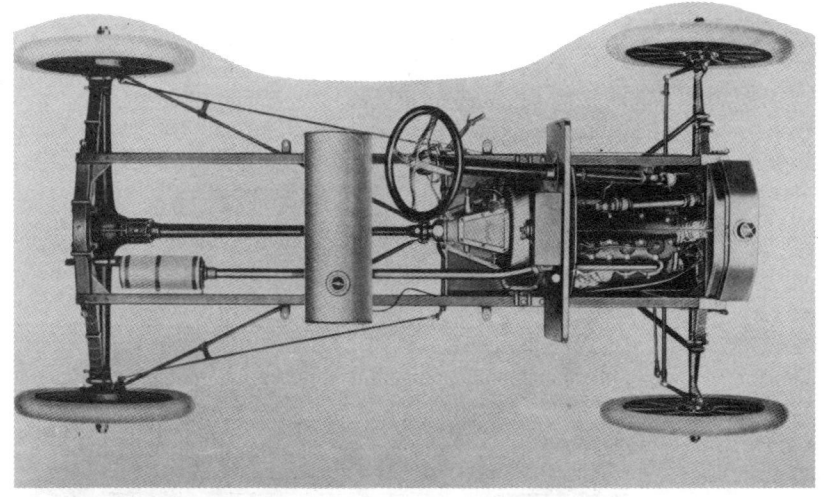

Although this stripped chassis photo appeared in numerous Ford catalogs, this was not the form in which chassis were sold to outside buyers. All of the 2,133 stripped chassis that were sold during the 1912 fiscal year include hoods, front and rear fenders, and running boards and aprons. Such things as seats, floor, and the body itself would be the responsibility of whatever company was building the body. In this type of sale, the buyer bought simply the chassis, and any modifications made after the sale were the owner's responsibility. Ford didn't like the Indianapolis Wagon contract because that company was making the modifications, and then giving the cars back to Ford dealers for sale, thus putting the responsibility for the modifications back on Ford. Had Indianapolis bought the chassis outright, there probably would have been no problem.

Once again the "unchanging" Model T changed. The changes, which were most apparent in the body styles, occurred in September, 1912, and were hailed by Ford as the new 1913 models. Of course, some will look at the introduction date and contend that the two major styles, Touring Car and Runabout, were actually third generation 1912 models, crediting that year with having three distinct body styles. For the sake of consistency, this book considers these later cars the true 1913 models.

Only three styles were built this year, and only two of these changed. They were the Touring Car and Roadster, which both received new bodies, and the Town Car, which appears to have settled in on the new body adopted on the 1912 models. The former Torpedo Roadster (Runabout) and Commercial Roadster were gone, now being combined into the single Runabout (again, sometimes referred to as a Torpedo Roadster).

The most noticeable changes on both of these models were the new folding windshields, with the pronounced slope of the lower portion, and the new overall body lines which now gave a smoother contour from cowl to seat back. The Touring Car now had three non-detachable doors, and a stamped panel on the driver's side resembling a door frame. The Roadster had a single door on the right, but again, the driver's side had a door frame stamping. On the Touring Car, the rear doors were again hinged at the rear, thus being forward opening. Apparently these doors had a problem with opening—they would do just that constantly on rough roads. So, during the 1913 year at least, three major body bracing changes were made to stiffen the sides and alleviate this problem. On the Roadster, a removable "turtle deck" now covered the rear quarter, and provided parcel space under its hinged lid.

The doors on the 1913 models were of rectangular design, with squared corners. They extended all the way to the splash aprons. This was the only year Ford used such a door design, as the 1914 models would revert to the smaller doors with rounded corners. A note here might avoid confusion: American built touring cars and roadsters consistently used a dummy door on the driver's side. However, Canadian-built models of these cars had functional doors on both sides. This was not because Canadians found it any easier to snake between the steering wheel and post and clutch/brake lever, but because Canadian production also went to British possessions, which mandated right-hand drive. At this time, Canada was the only part of the British Empire to use left-hand steering, with all of the remaining sectors opting for the right-hand drive of the mother country. And, a dummy door on the left would be rather awkward if the drive was on the right.

In an everlasting program to cut costs, much of the brass on this year's cars was now of black-painted steel. This included the headlights; cowl and taillamps; steering wheel spider; horn, and carbide generator. Only the headlight bezels and horn rim were of brass, as was the radiator. Another cost saver was the substitution of leatherette door and interior panels in place of the real leather used up to this time. The finish on all cars was dark blue with gray pinstriping. There is a strong contention that black was also available, but such an option does not show in the Ford literature. The same holds true for Brewster Green.

Mechanically, only a few changes were made. The ever-troublesome rear end unit was again modified, and the new differential, though similar, was more sturdy and was equipped with a hex-head filler plug. Frame modifications were made during the year as a new rear cross member was devised which eliminated the old cast body mounting brackets.

Under the hood, the camshaft was modified to give a slightly greater overlap, resulting in smoother running, but slightly less power. Again too, the cylinder head was modified slightly, once more resulting in a bit lower compression. Compression ratios had started at 4.5:1 on the early Ts, had a slight but unrecorded drop in 1912, and were now down to 4:1. Displacement dropped slightly to 176.6 cubic inches. Horsepower at 1600 rpm was rated at 20 brake or 22.4 NACC. Early models had Holley carburetors, but during the run a switch was

One of the best known historical Ford photographs depicts two major innovations that occurred in 1913. These were the introduction of the new Ford Runabout with its smoother sides and turtle back, and the start of Ford's first real assembly line. The new roadster model would set the pace for this style right into the mid-1920s, while the automotive assembly line would reshape the methods of automotive production world wide from this point on. Here, in the first semi-experimental body drop at the Highland Park plant, a Ford chassis is receiving its new Runabout body, which had been assembled on the upper floor. Other chassis assemblies, constructed on the ground floor, are slowly moving down the line for their respective bodies. Since only runabouts and touring cars were produced on the line (the Town Cars being hand assembled) the body drop was still a relatively simple operation. Yet, for the era, it was a startling innovation which drew the attention of most of the manufacturing world, not just the automotive sector.

made back to Kingston units. The primary supplier of coil boxes this year seems to have been the K-W Co. of Cleveland, although Heintz and Kingston boxes were also used.

Prices, in line with Ford's desire to produce the best light car for the least money, continued to drop. The start of the fiscal/model year saw the Touring Car priced at $600; the Roadster at $525, and the Town Car at $800. Further reduction throughout the year would reduce these prices by another $25 to $50.

All this, of course, sent the production figures to new heights, though the figures continue to remain confused. A tally of fiscal or model year production shows the ever-popular Touring Car having a run of 125,715; the Roadster 33,129; the Town Car 1,415, and the Delivery Car (produced only early in the year) 513, in addition to 8,438 stripped chassis. This gives a total of 170,210 rolling vehicles produced from Oct. 1, 1912 to Sept. 30, 1913. Other lists show chassis serial numbers running from 150,001 to 332,500, which would indicate 182,499 cars built, while Ford's own list compiled in 1918, shows only 168,200 cars.

Engine numbers are no help either. A new engine series, built at Detroit, had block numbers running from B-1 to B-12247. The old run, according to one list, ran from 169452 to 370147, indicating 200,695 engines in this series, while another list for the same dates shows the numbers starting at 157425 and ending with 248735, indicating only 91,310 engines. The 1913 calendar year list shows engine numbers going from 183564 to 408347, or 224,783 engines built in 1913, which would include a substantial amount of early 1914 engines.

On the corporate side, April 1 was a banner day for Ford—in fact, for the entire U.S. automotive industry.

For it was on this date, after much experimentation, that Ford's first assembly line became operational. Starting first by manufacturing only the magnetos, the new line concept was greatly expanded and experimented with throughout the year. Per car production time by the end of 1913 had dropped from 14 to 9.5 hours to 1.5 hours, and the Highland Park plant was now capable of rolling 1,000 chassis out of the door during each shift. Later in the year, production got an even greater boost when a new factory at Cleveland, Ohio, became operational.

Yes, its the wrong color, but this spiffy restoration represents what could be done to dress up the pragmatic Ford Runabout in the mid-teens. The wire wheels would have provided a smoother ride and more sporty appearance, and also offered easy tire changing as opposed to roadside flat fixing—at least for the first flat. The rear-mounted spare is a novelty on this year's Ford, but would be incorporated into the car's overall design in coming years. By mounting the spare in this position, it also acted as a rear bumper. With the exception of the paint job and the running board luggage rack, the car is in stock form.

Naturalist John Burroughs is shown driving his new Touring Car, already mud splattered, which was a gift from his friend Henry Ford. A newly designed body, with two functional doors on the right, but only an operational rear door on the left, was of much smoother line than previous models. The jaunty sloping windshield also set the new models apart from their predecessors. By far Ford's most popular model, the Touring Car had a calendar year run of 126,715. It weighed 1,200 pounds, started the model year priced at $600, and by mid-summer of 1913 was being advertised at $550. Neither head nor cowl or taillights can be used as a means of identification, as they came from several different suppliers, including John Brown, E&J, Victor, or Corcoran.

Ford's new Runabout set the style that would continue basically unchanged until the mid-1920s. Not too different from the previous year's Torpedo Roadster in overall style, the totally new body featured a solid left panel with an embossed door design and a functional door on the right. The removable "turtle back or turtle deck" had a small lid and provided space for storage of tools, small parcels, etc. This was the only year that the turtle deck would have squared rear corners. All succeeding models would have rounded corners. Priced at $525 and weighing about 1,100 pounds, the popular little car had a calendar year run of 33,129, all finished in dark blue. A new innovation on this year's open cars was the sloping lower portion of the windshield.

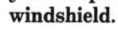

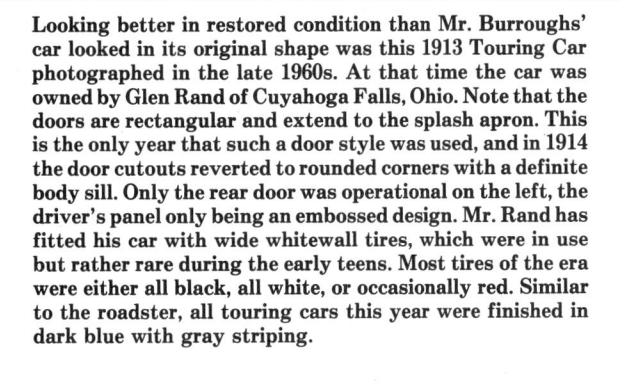

Looking better in restored condition than Mr. Burroughs' car looked in its original shape was this 1913 Touring Car photographed in the late 1960s. At that time the car was owned by Glen Rand of Cuyahoga Falls, Ohio. Note that the doors are rectangular and extend to the splash apron. This is the only year that such a door style was used, and in 1914 the door cutouts reverted to rounded corners with a definite body sill. Only the rear door was operational on the left, the driver's panel only being an embossed design. Mr. Rand has fitted his car with wide whitewall tires, which were in use but rather rare during the early teens. Most tires of the era were either all black, all white, or occasionally red. Similar to the roadster, all touring cars this year were finished in dark blue with gray striping.

The catalog illustration of the Town Car is similar to the one used in the 1912 brochures, and even shows the little bills on the leading edges of the front fenders, which did not appear on the 1913 models. Use of the old 1912 illustration may be why the lamps and horn are shown in brass rather than paint. The car also is shown with all-white tires, which were common in this era, but loosing in favor to the less expensive black rubber. Like the open models, Town Cars were finished in dark blue with gray striping. This is the last year that there would be a break between the driver's compartment and the tonneau, as the 1914 models would have a newly designed town car body with smooth sides. Ford this year more realistically called this a 6-passenger car.

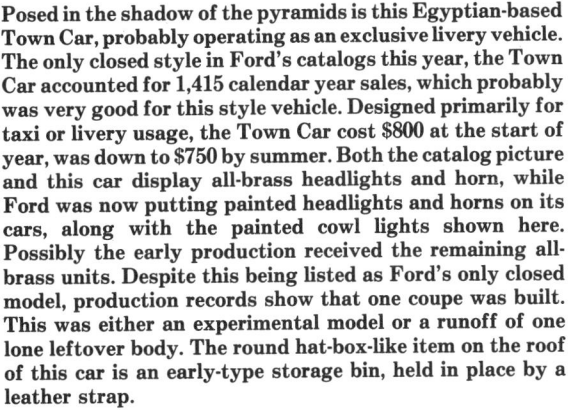

Posed in the shadow of the pyramids is this Egyptian-based Town Car, probably operating as an exclusive livery vehicle. The only closed style in Ford's catalogs this year, the Town Car accounted for 1,415 calendar year sales, which probably was very good for this style vehicle. Designed primarily for taxi or livery usage, the Town Car cost $800 at the start of year, was down to $750 by summer. Both the catalog picture and this car display all-brass headlights and horn, while Ford was now putting painted headlights and horns on its cars, along with the painted cowl lights shown here. Possibly the early production received the remaining all-brass units. Despite this being listed as Ford's only closed model, production records show that one coupe was built. This was either an experimental model or a runoff of one lone leftover body. The round hat-box-like item on the roof of this car is an early-type storage bin, held in place by a leather strap.

Although the term Commercial Roadster was dropped, Ford salesmen were quick to point out that the new Runabout featured a removable turtle deck, and this could be replaced with a pickup bed for weekday work. It seems unlikely, however, that anyone expected the type of conversion seen here. A funeral director in Cutbank, Mont. who probably could not afford an expensive production hearse, has utilized his roadster for funeral work. But, since the casket was too long to fit lengthwise in the pickup bed, it was simply carried laterally across the sides. One hopes the road to the cemetery was not too bumpy.

1913

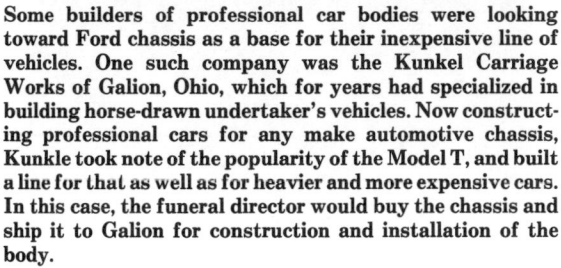

No. 155 Casket Body on Ford Chassis

One of Edsel Ford's toys was this modified roadster, whose styling is more like that of the 1911 Open Roadster than the new model. Among the design innovations are a new low and rounded cowl, the standard slanting windshield, bill-less front fenders, and a rear-mounted gas tank of rather large proportions. Note that the steering wheel has been reversed, a practice common in those days to give the driver more leg room. Edsel took the car on a lengthy trip through northern Michigan. It was one of a multitude of Fords and Lincolns that throughout his life, Edsel would have modified for his own personal use.

Some builders of professional car bodies were looking toward Ford chassis as a base for their inexpensive line of vehicles. One such company was the Kunkel Carriage Works of Galion, Ohio, which for years had specialized in building horse-drawn undertaker's vehicles. Now constructing professional cars for any make automotive chassis, Kunkle took note of the popularity of the Model T, and built a line for that as well as for heavier and more expensive cars. In this case, the funeral director would buy the chassis and ship it to Galion for construction and installation of the body.

In addition to the almost 8,500 commercial bodies of all kinds that were placed on Ford chassis this year, there were other conversions being made to the total cars. One such was this rail inspection car, which utilized a perfectly stock Touring Car. Only flanged wheels have been installed in place of the normal ones, and the steering wheel has been removed. A couple of tool or flare boxes on the running board completed the conversion. With Fords becoming more and more popular, and proving their dependability over other similar priced cars, conversions of all kinds escalated, with the end results being limited only by the imagination of the builders.

Although commercial buses will not be covered in this book, this Omnibus body by the McKay Carriage Co. of Grove City, Pa., actually falls between bus and livery vehicle and probably can best be described as a jitney-type vehicle. Ford chassis were becoming very popular with all sorts of body builders, and a total of 8,438 such rolling units were shipped during the calendar year. In addition, Ford produced 625 Delivery Cars during the year, but dropped the style in mid-season, thus giving this market to the independent builders.

Commercial Roadsters weren't the only Fords that went into business. Already the public was finding the Model T the perfect vehicle to convert into anything that the imagination could dream up. Here, N.C. Billy, a traveling butcher from Balfour, N.D., has fitted his Touring Car with a homemade meat market. Ice was stored in the large top bins, while the other two shelves held meat and butcher tools. The rear partition served as a cutting board when lowered. Rather than install a roadster top, Mr. Billy left the touring car top intact, fastening the rear arms to the meat body. Here too can be seen how the windshield overhung the new door panels.

Holding true to form, the "unchanging" Model T changed again this year, again receiving new bodies for all three models, new lower prices, and a new color—black! The latter change was probably the most important overall, as it set the pace for Ford colors, or lack of them, until 1925, and set the stage for Henry Ford's alleged famous saying that "You can have any color you want, as long as its black."

The reason for the black-only concept was two-fold. First, as mass production increased, it was much more simple to stock one color paint only, and not have to worry about various colors or shadings. And, even more important, black japan was the only fast drying paint at this time. All colors required numerous coats, usually as many as 14, which had to dry, be hand sanded, and repainted with each application. To properly finish a body, considering the drying time between each coat, took upward to two weeks, or even longer if humid weather slowed the drying process. By using the relatively quick drying japan black, the bodies could be finished in 1/10th the time. Thus, it was not until a relatively fast drying nitrocellulose lacquer was developed in 1923, that cars could be painted in colors quickly enough to match high-volume production lines. Even then, Ford would not consider colors until 1925, and then only on closed bodies.

And, Ford's first high production line went into total operation this year. On Jan. 14 the experimentation at Highland Park ended and the world's first moving assembly line for automobiles went into operation on a full-time basis. Almost concurrent with the start of this line was Ford's announcement that it would pay a minimum wage of $5 a day, which was more than double its previous pay scale or that paid by other Detroit industries, both in or out of the automotive field. Ford quickly became "the place to work," and drew worldwide attention to itself for its policy of putting a share of its profits back into the hands of its workers. Even the capitalist-hating Lenin had to compliment Ford for his humanitarian efforts.

Again, Ford continued with only three styles, the Touring Car, Runabout, and Town Car, but all three received new bodies. All styles still had the large flat rectangular dash board or cowl (for the last time) but newer and smoother side panels were evident. These panels included a new door design, with rounded corners and sills that ended above the apron. The rear doors on the touring car were still hinged at the rear, but the door handle was now located on the inner panel, rather than at the top of door. Door handles were located on the inside only, not on the exterior. Leatherette was used more extensively within the car, to the extent that models built toward the end of the year had total leatherette interiors, as opposed to the earlier models which still used real leather seat cushions. The windshields of the open cars were redesigned, although in their fully raised position, they looked identical to the 1913 versions. Only now, the upper portion swung inward rather than outward when lowered, and hung down inside of the car instead of resting on the lower portion.

Fenders on all models remained flat-topped, but now had slightly different reinforcing rods and embossing. About mid-year a change was made from the bill-less types of 1913 to a small forward bill or beak, similar to the 1912 style. Lights and lamps were still supplied by John Brown or E&J, although Victor or Corcoran units were put on some cars. Wheels continued to be 24 inches in diameter and took 30x3 tires in the front

An early model of the Touring Car is this restored vehicle, owned by John Mahaffey Jr. of Orlando, Fla. Calling attention to the fact are the front fenders, which have no bills and resemble those of the 1913 cars. Notice that the top did not attach to the windshield, but sat about an inch higher. The space between the top and the windshield was covered by a cloth flap, which was a part of the top. Although a Florida car, this one does not appear to have the 60-inch "Southern" tread which was still available. All other Model Ts used a 56-inch tread. Smooth white tires were still in vogue in this era.

Sporting its newly revised body is this restored Touring Car. This car wears the billed front fenders which appeared about mid-way in the run. By far the most popular Ford, the Touring Car had a 10-month production run of 165,832. It sold for $550 at the start of the season, was down to $500 by the summer of 1914. When photographed in the mid-1970s, this car was owned by Charles Burge of Sylvania, Ohio. The spare tires on the running board are just that. Because Ford still did not use demountable rims, any tire repairs had to be made on the spot, by worrying the tire and tube from the clincher rim while the wheel remained on the car.

The upper half of the windshield hanging inside the car, rather than resting on the outward side of the lower half, identifies this as a 1914 Runabout. The small bill at the ends of the front fenders identify it as a mid-year or later model. The expression on the gent's face seems to indicate that he really doesn't care what the car is at this moment. The Runabout, often called a Roadster, was priced at $500 in October, 1913, was down to $450 in mid-summer. During the 10-month production span, ending Aug. 1, a total of 35,017 Runabouts were built.

and 30x3.5 on the rear. Under the hood, the only major change was a cast iron intake manifold, rather than the aluminum one used previously. Both Kingston and Holley carburetors were used, and sometime during the year the coil boxes were modified, going from wood to metal. These boxes were still located on the firewall inside the car. The troublesome rear end again was modified, as a running change, sometime about mid-year.

The Town Car, which accounted for 1,699 sales, received a totally new body, with an integral cowl, smooth sides, and rounded doors fitting flush into the panels. The front doors were both functional, and the windshield was now a two-piece affair which could be opened. Removable glass partitions could be inserted between the front seat edges and the drip rail, providing more weather protection for the driver. The car was still called a 6-passenger model in the catalogs, but was referred to as a 7-passenger vehicle on other lists.

Prices again were down, with the Touring Car starting at $550 and dropping to $500 during the year; the Runabout starting at $500 and going down to $450, and the Town Car starting at $750 and dropping to $700.

Production figures are into their usual guessing game. But actual production found during the fiscal year is complicated by the fact that Ford cut short this year, running it only from Oct. 1, 1913, to July 31, 1914. During this time, records show a total of 165,832 Touring Cars, 35,017 Runabouts, and 1,699 Town Cars being built. Also shown was a total of only 119 stripped chassis being delivered, which seems very low considering 8,438 such units were sold in 1913. Tallying these figures gives a fiscal year production of 202,667. For the calendar year 1914, which would include many 1915 models, Ford claimed production of over 2500,000. This recorded its first quarter-million year, and in fact, the first such year in the entire industry. Ford later tempered this figure by saying 248,307 cars had actually been built in the calendar year. Engine numbers for the fiscal year ran from 370148 to 570790, which indicated production of 200,642, if all had gone into new cars. Calendar year numbers, broken down on a monthly basis on another list, show the starting number to be 370401, with the Dec. 31 number being 611100, or a total of 230,788.

On the corporate side, the Dodge Bros., who had been major suppliers of powertrain equipment since 1903, introduced their new Dodge Bros. car in November. The vehicle was a heavier one than the Model T, and in effect offered a step-up to Model T buyers who wanted something better on the next round. Ford, who had been at odds with the Dodge brothers on several occasions, saw this as the final straw, and in December, terminated all Dodge contracts. In a more happy vein, Ford this year opened new plants in both Houston and Dallas, Texas, and put the finishing touches on its first French plant in Bordeaux—just in time for the start of World War I.

Most changed of all three models was the Town Car, which now had a totally revised body. Among the changes were an integral cowl bending in to meet the firewall, and smooth sides containing flush mounted doors of modern design. The front doors were hinged at the leading edges, and both were operational. This was probably because some Town Car buyers specified right-hand drive. Also new on this model was the 2-piece windshield, with the upper portion able to swing inward. The large glass partitions reaching from the driver's seat to the roof were removable. Still popular for taxi and livery work, the Town Car had a run of 1,699 during the 10-month fiscal year. It sold for $750 in October, was down to $700 by summer.

With its top up and its wheels painted a contrasting color, this Runabout was indeed a cute little car. Note that these fenders do not have the bills on the end, indicating an early production model. All windshields were basically similar, folding rearward, but did reflect the differences of the three suppliers. They were Diamond Mfg. Co.; Rand Mfg. Co., and Vanguard Mfg. Co. Although all cars were now available in black only, wheels could still be ordered in either black or dark blue, but not in the light shade shown here.

Many stripped chassis were converted to different uses, but this is really an extreme. Hood and cowl say the vehicle is a 1913/14 chassis unit, but electric headlights say that the photo was taken after 1915. Used, and probably home-built at Nome, Alaska, the conversion represents one of dozens of attempts to use motor vehicles on snow and ice. The large single toboggan at the front provided hard but positive steering, while the two smaller side skis seem to act as outriggers, probably to keep the single rear wheels from digging in too deeply. Later attempts along this line would use tracked arrangements on the rear for better traction.

Although Ford quickly gave up the idea of producing its own depot hacks, the concept of such vehicles was very strong in this era. One manufacturer of these vehicles was the Seaman Co, of Milwaukee, Wis. Versatile vehicles, used primarily to haul luggage, passengers, and small parcels to and from the train station, these cars could quickly be converted from cargo to passenger carriers. It is shown here in its cargo carrying form. Within minutes, a rear and center seat could be installed, making it a 6-passenger car. Roll-up side curtains provided weather protection. This was one of only 119 stripped chassis reported sold this year. However, the author has reservations about this figure, in view of the fact that 8,438 chassis were sold in 1913, and 13,459 such units would be sold in 1915.

Again Ford went through a change, only this time the changes were quite noticeable. It would be a dull person indeed who could not tell a 1915 Model T from a 1914—or would it? Sure, two new models appeared; a new cowl style graced the three regular models; electric headlights became standard, and a host of mechanical innovations were made. But since all of these changes were scattered over what could be considered the 1915 model year (fiscal year, Aug. 1, 1914 to July 31, 1915), it really is quite difficult to tell if a car is a 1915, 1916, or possibly even a late 1914.

The two new models were the Sedan and the Coupelet, marking a return to the closed car field. Some sources indicate both were introduced in November, 1914, as 1915 models, while some contend that they appeared as early as April, 1914, and might thus be considered mid-year 1914 fare. Since they carried the new curved cowlings and louvered hoods of the 1915 models, this book will consider them in that year. Even more puzzling are the Runabout and Touring Car, which were officially introduced at Highland Park in January, 1915, but reportedly only trickled into production while the 1914 styles were run right up to April, 1915.

The new Sedan was of the "centerdoor" style, and often was referred to as a Centerdoor Sedan. Its rather high aluminum paneled body contained two folding seats in front and one plush rear seat. It had but one door on each side, entering into the rear compartment. The driver and front seat passenger then squirmed into their spartan seats via a small center aisle. All six windows could be lowered via adjustable straps, and the windshield was not only split in the middle, but the upper portion consisted of two panes, one which swung inward and the other which could be swung outward to act as a type of visor. Selling for $975 initially, the price soon dropped to $740 by mid-1915. Being Ford's least popular car, it had a run of only 989.

Ford's other new style was the Coupelet, which can be considered the company's first true convertible. A 2-passenger style, the Coupelet featured two functional doors with a sedan-type windshield, adjustable side windows, and a full convertible top that fit snugly around the upper windshield frame, and into which the doors would pocket. Unlike the sedan, which had its own exclusive rear fenders, the Coupelet used the same rear fenders as all other Ts, and shared the turtle deck style with the Runabout, although the deck of the Coupelet was larger. Priced at $750 and weighing 1,540 pounds, the relatively heavy Coupelet had a run of only 2,417.

Both the Sedan and the Coupelet carried the new louvered hood and cowl design which would be adopted by the open cars and the Town Car when these vehicles finally came into production. In line with the new cowl was a reduction in size of the firewall, which now conformed to the shape of the hood and provided only a slight break between hood and cowl. Early cars continued to use a bulb horn, but located under the hood;

mid-season had hand-operated Klaxon horns, and late models had electric-driven units. Electric lights began to appear for the first time during the run, and these required a new magneto with larger magnets, plus a new coil. The electric system did not use a storage battery and thus the lights would burn only when the engine was running—very dim when idling or running slow, very bright when running fast. In addition to the new electric headlights, E&J or John Brown kerosene tail and cowl lights were still supplied.

The open cars received another new windshield, this one being fully upright. Again, the upper portion folded inward. Upholstery in all open cars and in the front of the Town Car was now totally in leatherette, with natural leather being a thing of the past. Closed cars used cloth upholstery. Speedometers were supplied during the first half of the year, and were either by Steward or Sears Cross. At mid-year, these were deleted from the standard equipment list.

Mechanically, there were also changes. The troublesome rear axle was redesigned again, this time going through its final change. The center section was now cast iron, with the axle tubes pressed into the center. The aluminum transmission cover was redesigned and now had a flat steel inspection plate; the driveshaft now had a one-piece design at the forward end; the foot pedals lost their embossed letters, and the spark and throttle ends were now of pressed steel. On cars with electric lights, a new stoplight switch was included.

Under the aluminum hood, the engine had another reduction in compression, but this apparently did not affect horsepower or performance. The lowering probably was accomplished by newly designed connecting rods of medium weight. As mentioned, because of the new electric lights, the magneto coils had to be enlarged and the magnets increased in size. The spark coil boxes, still located on the passenger side of the firewall, were now all identical, regardless of the supplier. Again, carburetors could be either Kingstons or Holleys.

Prices on the cars continued to drop, with the year end figures being about $50 less on all models. At the start of the year, the ever-popular Touring Car was priced at $490; the Runabout at $440; the town Car at a surprisingly low $690; the new Sedan at $975, and the Coupelet at $750. By year-end, the Sedan would drop to $750 and the Coupelet to $600.

Production, figured by counting individual body style builds between Aug. 1, 1914, and July 31, 1915, was 308,162, which includes 13,459 stripped chassis, but does not include any figure for the Town Car, which may have been incorporated into the chassis figure. Engine serial numbers, starting January, 1915, and running through July, 1915, go from 670000 to 856513, for a total of 199,972, while calendar year engine numbers run from 656064 to 1028313, for a total of 372,249 engines. Another list of engine numbers has these figures going from 611101 on Jan. 1 to 1029200 on Dec. 31, for a total of 418,099 blocks. You choose!

Just as activity was taking place within the car ranks, so too was it on the corporate side. Despite there being no immediate lack of space at Highland Park, Ford was looking well into the future. With unlimited production projections in mind, the company purchased 1,000 acres along the Rouge River just south of Detroit, in what then was Springwells Township. That, of course, would subsequently become the River Rouge plant. In September, the 1-millionth Ford rolled off the line almost unnoticed. It was delivered to Stanley Roberts, a Ford dealer at Toledo, Ohio, who used it in promotional displays at county fairs. Following this, he turned it into a racing car, in which form it was subsequently wrecked and destroyed. Considering the conflicting production figures found for each year, one wonders however, how the 1-millionth car was ever determined.

Ford now proudly claimed to have 25 assembly plants producing Model Ts in all parts of the country. This did not include its smallest plant, which turned out only 18 to 25 cars a day. This low-production plant was at the Panama-Pacific Exposition in San Francisco, and was the major part of Ford's display there. Operating only three or four hours a day, the display was a miniature assembly line which would produce completed full-size cars as an amazed public looked on.

And finally, on Dec. 10, almost out of the fiscal year, Ford somehow figured that it produced its 1-millionth Model T, as opposed to the 1-millionth Ford built in September.

Down in price and going lower, Ford's Runabout started the calendar year at $440 (with the old style rear fenders) and finished it at $400 or less with the new fenders, hood, and cowl. Weighing 1,380 pounds, the Runabout enjoyed 47,116 sales between Aug. 1, 1914, and July 31, 1915, which is as close as a model year can be approximated. The owners of this restored car have sanded down the wheels and varnished them in their natural oak. The author did the same thing on the three Model Ts that he owned over the years. However, no 1915 Fords came from the factory with natural wheels. All were painted solid black, or on special order, could be had in dark blue.

A rear view of the Runabout shows off the new curved rear fenders that graced all Model T during the 1915 run. Actually, even though the new style open cars were introduced at Highland Park in January, 1915, it wasn't until April that the full transition to the new fenders, cowls, hoods, or windshields was made across the country. This beautifully restored car was owned by Lee Park of Akron, Ohio, when photographed in 1966. Mr. Park could verify a June, 1915, manufacture date. The Runabouts (often called Roadsters) now had all upholstery in leatherette, with leatherette covered cardboard on the door and kick panels.

FORD MOTOR CAR

Despite the fact that the new style Model T open cars were introduced at Highland Park in January, it wasn't until April that all of the 1914-style components had been used up and the "true" 1915 styles appeared. Thus, there were many sales of such transitional vehicles as this Touring Car, shown wearing the new louvered hood, Klaxon horn, and billed front fenders, but still using the old body and cowl, slanted windshield, and flat rear fenders. The owner of this vehicle splurged on a set of Buffalo wire wheels, which allowed him to carry a spare alongside the dummy front door. But, by the looks of the activities under the hood, some spare engine parts might have been in order. And look at the expression on the man in the rear. Is he hoping a friendly horse will come along, or just wishing he was back on his front porch?

1915

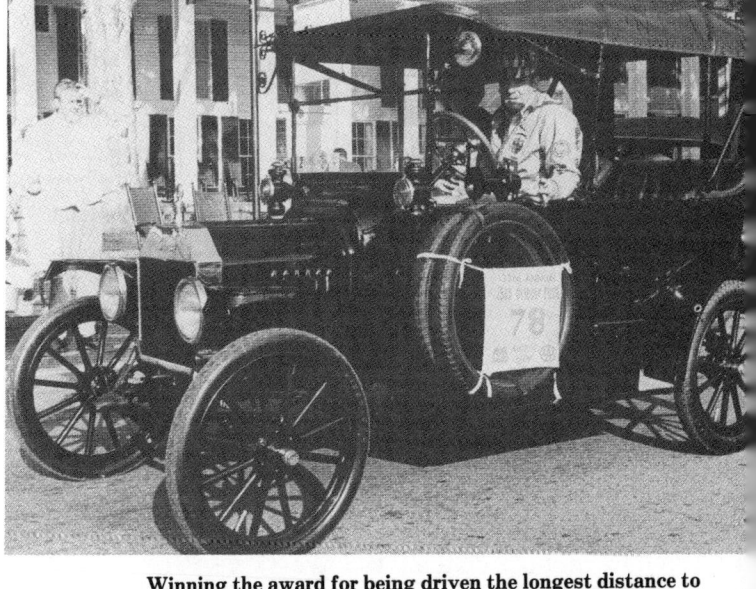

The popularity of the Touring Car is attested to by the fact that almost a quarter million of this style alone were built during the Aug. 1 to July 31 fiscal year. The exact total of 244,181 certainly surpassed any automotive production worldwide, and was more than double the total production of General Motors. Selling for $490 at the start of the 1915 season, the 1,500-pound Touring Car dropped in price by about $50 the following summer. This original photo gives a good view of the new cowl and vertical windshield, with its adjacent kerosene lamps to augment the new-fangled electric headlights. This was the first windshield that did not require extra bracing.

Winning the award for being driven the longest distance to the 1968 Glidden Tour was this beautiul Touring Car restoration owned by Lewis Lamp of Winchester, Va. The top was essentially unchanged from the previous year, but the interiors of all open cars were now upholstered in leatherette rather than real leather, and the door and kick panels were of leatherette covered cardboard. The rear panel on the touring tops could be rolled to allow for flow-through ventilation. Mr. Lamp's car carries two spare tires against the dummy front door, but since the car still has its clincher wheels, changing these tires with the wheels in place was a rather nasty job.

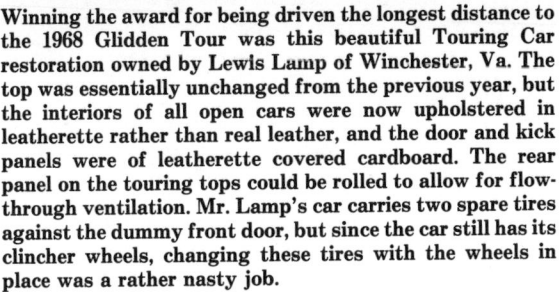

Ford's first true convertible, one that could be made as completely weather-tight as a closed car, was the new Coupelet. Priced at $750 on its introduction in November, 1914, the 1,540-pound car later dropped in price to about $600. Probably its being priced at almost double the runabout caused its lack of buyer interest, and only 2,417 were sold between its introduction and July 31. Considered a closed car by Ford, the Coupelet had a cloth interior, as opposed to the leatherette used in the open models. Both of its doors were functional, were hinged on the trailing edges, and had outside stirrup-type door handles. The fenders were the same as used on all other 1915 Model Ts. Klaxon horns were not used on these cars. Early models had a bulb horn located under the hood, while later models had Ford's first electric-driven horn, also located under the aluminum hood.

From the rear, the Touring Car presented a rather big blank of steel, especially when the top was removed. Even though electric headlights were now fitted, kerosene tail and cowl lights by either J. Brown or E&J were still supplied. On many later models, the kerosene taillight was fitted with an electric bulb socket so that it would normally operate as an electric light, or could be used as a kerosene lamp in an emergency.

Bundled up for cold weather, these two early Michigan motorists enjoy the top-down experience of their new Coupelet. The windshield of this model lived in a fixed frame similar to that of the sedan. The upper portion consisted of two plates of glass. The outer pane could swing outward and act as a form of visor, while the inner one swung inward for ventilation. The door glass was adjustable via cloth straps with notches, and the panes could be lowered almost level with the sills. When down, the top bulked a bit more than the runabout top.

A rear view of the new Coupelet shows that the rear deck differed substantially from the turtle deck used on the Runabout. Not only was this deck larger, but its sides were more vertical. It provided a good amount of storage space for the era. This is an early version of the Coupelet, built before the introduction of electric lights. Since the electric lights required a different magneto with larger coils and magnets, cars not designed for the new lights could not be easily converted from carbide to electric. A highlight of the Coupelet was the use of attractive functional landau irons. This year's Coupelet top had blank quarters, which apparently restricted visibility. The 1916 models would have small quarter windows.

Ford's real Sedans looked just like this restored model, which was owned by Marion Ocheltree of Sacramento, Cal., when photographed in 1963. Marking Ford's first entry into the total closed car field, the vehicle drew much interest but few sales, and only 989 were sold between the November, 1914, introduction and July 31. At first, the 1,730-pound car was priced at $975, but by summer the price had dropped to $750. Finished with a cloth interior, the car featured two rather severe folding seats in the front and a plush rear seat. It was considered a 4-passenger vehicle. Both doors were functional and led into the rear area. Front seat passengers had to wiggle through a narrow aisle to their positions. Early models had the gas tank under the rear seat, but this provided poor gravity flow to the engine, especially when going uphill. Sometime during the 1915 run, the gas tank was relocated under the driver's seat. The windshield was similar to that on the Coupelet, with both the upper and lower halves being able to swing inward, while a second upper pane could be swung out in a visor-like manner.

Often pictured as the first Ford Sedan, or as the 1915 Sedan, this experimental car was photographed in Ford's Highland Park plant while designs were underway for the real sedan. The car, which had been in the experimental stage since 1910, bears many items totally different than those found on production models. Most noticeable is the hood, which had nine louvers as opposed to the six on production models, and the curved front fenders, which were not used on any Fords until the 1917 models. It also has carbide headlights of the full-brass type, which went away in 1913, and lacks any cowl lights. The windshield and side windows seem right, but the large rectangular rear window with rounded corners never materialized. The almost ridiculous side-mounted coach lamps were never available, even as an accessory, while the tool box on the running board definitely was an accessory, and a popular one at that. But, because early Ford publicity used this photo as an example of its new Sedan, the car has been accepted over the years as the "true" 1915 version.

The Town Car body remained little changed, accepting the new cowl relatively easily, but keeping its own exclusive windshield. Unlike the new Sedan, which used its own rear fenders, the Town Car shared its fenders with all other Model Ts. Oddly, production figures apparently were not kept of the Town Car, and it is not known if its number was incorporated into the total for the bare chassis. Priced far below the Sedan or Coupelet, the Town Car cost only $690 at the start of the season, then dropped another $50 during the year. When photographed at the Old Car Festival at Greenfield Village in the mid-1970s, this restored version was owned by Jack Harper of Ann Arbor, Mich. Its cloth upholstered rear seat would indicate that it was destined for livery or private use, not taxi work.

Many outside body builders such as York, Mifflinburg, and Cantrell found a ready market for their depot hack bodies mounted on Ford chassis. These companies probably accounted for a fair portion of the 13,459 chassis that were sold by Ford dealers this year. The price for the chassis started at $410 in August, but was down to $360 by the following July. Not only did the major body builders get into the depot hack business, but many a small-town cabinet shop also found a ready market for locally produced models, as long as the price was competitive. This 6-passenger model could either be a York or a locally built body.

Ford once again advertised a taxi version of the Town Car, but it seems that there was no difference in the price between the regular offering and the cab model. Apparently the main difference between the two models was in the upholstery, with the taxi version using leatherette for both the front and rear seats, while the regular model used a cloth rear seat. Although this model appears to have a single-pane windshield, this really was made of two panes, with the upper one able to swing inward for ventilation.

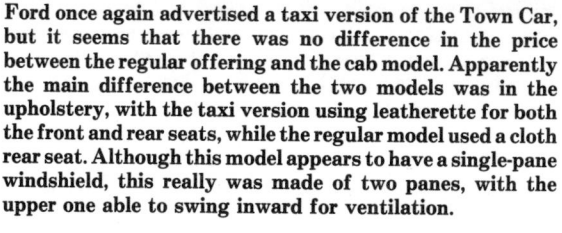

Camping in style could occur even in 1915, if the camper equipped his Runabout with the Automobile Telescope Apartment, manufactured by Gustav DeBretteville. After traveling all day, an owner need only stop at a suitable place and set up camp. First he would pull the entire rear section out to three times its length. This part would be supported by built-in braces which swung to the ground. The back contained a double bed, curtained windows, and rear tent flap. When the back was extended, a full kitchen telescoped from the forward left side, while the right side became a dressing room. And, all of this cost only $100. It was claimed that upon returning home after a weekend in the woods, the whole unit could be detached in 15 minutes, and the car be returned to its normal service.

Many a Ford buyer wished for a bit more weather protection than the stock open car offered. One company which was happy to accommodate this desire was the Fouts & Hunter Carriage Mfg. Co. of Terre Haute, Ind. Advertised as "especially suited to physicians," the top consisted of a rigid frame and windshield that would replace the standard runabout top and windshield. More sturdy side curtains filled in the quarters, while those on the door also had a rigid frame and would open with the door. Despite Ford's insistence on calling this model a Runabout, most outside ads such as this referred to the car as a Roadster.

Modifications to existing Fords did not always come from outside manufacturers. Even Ford constantly stressed the fact that its Runabout could quickly be converted into a commercial vehicle by simply removing the turtle deck and replacing it with a commercial body. But this interesting bit of Ford instruction tells Touring Car owners how they too can have a removable body for week-day commercial use and weekend family touring. The instructions told the owner to simply hacksaw through the door sills, remove the rear body bolts, and slip the rear portion rearward, with the top and rear seat still in place. Then a commercial or pickup body could be installed. Reverse the operation on a Saturday night, and the family had a car again.

For the younger set, which considered Ford bodies too stodgy but liked the Ford price and dependability, an entire plethora of companies sprang up offering speedster bodies for the Model T. One of the most popular speedster conversions was made by the Ames Co. of Owensboro, Ky., which produced the Ames car from 1912 to 1915, and then switched to manufacturing coupe, sedan, and speedster bodies for various chassis, but primarily for Ford. Regular equipment in the kit included the special body, hood, radiator shell, seats, gas tank, and tool box. The wheels were not supplied, but could be obtained from several manufacturers of wire wheels, such as Houck, Buffalo, or Pasco. Other major speedster suppliers in this era were Ospeco Mfg. Co. of Detroit, Universal, and Candler.

Of more sedate yet sporty line was the Gentlemen's Streamline Roadster body kit available from Auto Sheet Metal Works of Chicago. This kit also consisted of a new set of fenders and a drop-on body and cowl, and contained a small folding windshield and folding top. A spare wheel could be carried behind the oval gas tank. In addition to the speedsters shown here, literally dozens of other manufacturers of all sizes produced their own variations of this style. The intent is not to show them all, but just to present a sample of what was available.

Auto Sheet Metal Works of Chicago was the producer of this Model 89, streamline Speed Roadster for the 1915 Model T. The kit included new front and rear fenders and step plate, a new tapered dash, V-radiator, round or oval gas tank, two rear-mounted oil tanks, five wire wheels, one being rear-mounted as a spare, and a front bumper. Auto Sheet Metal claimed that it was the originator of the Ford Speedster body kit.

Convert your Ford Car into a Classy Roadster

See page 15 for another style made by us.

Far removed from speedster conversions was this rear attachment which supposedly could quickly convert any farmer's touring car into a farm tractor. Produced by American Truck and Tractor Co. of Detroit, this too was one of many ideas to put the family car to work during the week. For this unit, the rear fenders had to be removed. Other types used smaller rear wheels and kept the fenders in place. All of these types were basically the same, using reduction gears in place of the rear wheels, with these gears powering the lugged traction wheels. Almost all manufacturers of these units claimed that the equipment could be installed or removed in only a few minutes. Defeating this idea was the Ford's marginal thermosyphon cooling system, which had all it could do just to keep a car running on the road without boiling.

Not only did the Fouts & Hunter Carriage Mfg. Co. of Terre Haute, Ind., produce a cozy cabin for the Runabout, it also built what it described as a Limousine Top for Ford Touring Cars. Similar to the Runabout version, this model featured a rigid frame with a solid top, to which the semi-rigid quarter panels were attached. As with the Runabout, the door curtains on this version swung open with the doors. The cross bars on the celluloid windows were for added rigidity. It is not known if this unit used its own windshield, as did the Runabout version, or if it incorporated the Ford windshield.

The Millspaugh & Irish Co. of Indianapolis was a large body manufacturing concern which specialized in all types of taxi, livery, and professional car bodies for all kinds of chassis, and even had a line of quasi-luxury type bodies for inexpensive chassis. One such unit was this centerdoor sedan body for those who wanted a totally different style than that being built by Ford. The rather large body used no cowl, but ran its firewall right up to its own slanted 7-louver hood. A plush rear seat and folding forward seats gave 5-passenger capacity, while roller shades in all side windows provided privacy. The body also held one of Ford's first examples of electric cowl lamps. Standard Ford fenders were used. A variation of this body had a rear door and removable seats. It was designed for funeral homes, and could double as a hearse when necessary.

Although commercial vehicles will not be covered in this book, early professional cars and ambulances formed sort of a gray area between cars and trucks. Therefore, a few will be included, with the criteria being that the chassis be from an automobile, and not a heavy-duty frame designed for truck use. Representative of most 1915 Model T professional car bodies is this Motor Hearse built by the Pfeiffer Auto & Carriage Works of Omaha, Neb. Built specifically for a C.E. Johnson of Wanneta, Neb., it was finished in a light gray with gold trimming.

Very ornate for a hearse on a Ford chassis was this carved unit by the Columbia Body Co. of Detroit. Only the Ford fenders and headlights appear stock, with Columbia supplying its own radiator and cowl in addition to the very unusual cab and carved wood body. The use of wheels with 5-lug demountable rims is an unusual but very practical touch, while the all-white tires must have given the car a very distinctive look. The large coach lights almost look like those on the experimental Centerdoor Sedan.

The 1916 Model Ts can be considered the last of the "old time" styles, and as such were changed very little over the 1915 products. Ford had some big styling ideas in mind, but these would have to wait for the 1917 models to emerge. For this year, at least, the major changes consisted of switching the hood from pressed aluminum to pressed steel, and the transmission cover from cast aluminum to cast iron. Both of these moves were more in line with cost savings than improved engineering. Other cost savers included the removal of the speedometer as a standard item (a move actually made in mid-1915) and the deletion of all brass trim on the lights and horn. Only the little brass radiator and thimble-like hubcaps provided brightness on the 1916 cars.

Later in the year, the touring cars had a minor change when the seat frames were switched from wood to steel. Over the years this would provide a more rigid seat, as the normal flexing of the body would eventually cause the old wood frames to loosen and work out of shape. Later too, crown fenders appeared on some 1916 cars, but this appears to be more of a running change, as "new" 1917-style rear fenders came into use when the old flat stock ran out. All 1916 cars should have the flat-topped front fenders with the small bill at the leading edge.

Also on the cost saving side was a move that probably did much to hasten the improvement of south-eastern and Gulf state roads. This was the announcement that from mid-summer on, no further orders would be filled for 60-inch tread cars. Usually known as "Southern Specials," these 60-inch tread vehicles were appreciated in the tobacco and cotton growing rural southern regions, because the tread matched the 60-inch wheel spacing used on the heavy cargo wagons. Thus, the cars could easily run in the wagon ruts. With the standard 56-inch tread, a driver always had the dilemma of having two wheels in a rut and two outside. But, the 60-inchers required special axles, wider fenders, and longer fender brackets, and special tie rods and axle housings. And, these specialties did not fit in with Ford's plans for volume mass production.

Only one real styling change took place, and that occurred on the Coupelet, which now sported a pair of opera windows in the rear quarter of the folding top. Apparently, these windows were supposed to assist a driver in backing the car into a parking space, but the panes are so small that it is doubtful if they served anything but an ornamental purpose.

The line of models remained the same as in 1915, but with prices down and production up. Using fiscal year figures, Aug. 1, 1915 to July 31, 1916, shows that the Touring Car dropped another $50 top a new low of $440, while its production soared to 363,024. Likewise, the Runabout also was down $50 in price to $390, while its production more than doubled, going up to 98,633. The Town Car (taxi) received the same $50 reduction, down

to $640 and enjoyed a run of 1,972. The largest price drop occurred with the year-old Sedan, which decreased $235, going from $975 to $740, while its production almost doubled, rising to 1,859. The Coupelet also was enjoying more popularity, with its production up to 3,532, while its price was down $160 to a new $590 tag. Even the bare chassis price dropped $50, now selling at $360, which was only $30 less than the complete Roadster. However, the stripped chassis was the only sales unit not to show an increase, with its total deliveries being only 11,742 as opposed to over 13,000 in 1915. Also in the production list was a special military contract for 20,700 ambulances to be used in war-torn Europe.

Tallying these figures gives a fiscal year production of 501,462, which heralded Ford's first half-million fiscal year. For the same period, engine numbers ran from 856514 to 1362989, showing engine production of 506,475, which pretty well matches the chassis figure. For the first time, there are no widely conflicting production lists.

Under the car, except for the new transmission cover, there were no changes to speak of. On the wheels, however, a running change took place sometime during the year. This was a conversion to Firestone non-skid pattern tires as original equipment. Firestone had actually had these tires available as a dealer-installed item since 1909, but Ford preferred the white smooth-tread tires until this year. With the new tires, recommended tire pressure was reduced from 70 pounds to 55. Tire size remained the same 30x3 on the front, 30x3.5 on the rear. Clincher rims were still used, though both wire spoke wheels and after-market wheels with demountable rims were available from most dealers.

Totally correct in its lack of bass trim is this restored Touring Car, which was owned by Charles Boyd Sr. of Louisville, Ky., when photographed in the mid-1970s. Today, many restorers try to brighten the car's image by adding such 1915 trim as brass headlight bezels and cowl lamp rims. Accounting for far more than half of Ford's total production this year, the Touring Car had a run of 363,024 between Aug. 1, 1915, and July 30, 1916. Weighing 1,500 pounds, the car began the year at $440, and dropped down into the $300s by the following summer. Despite the electric headlights, standard equipment still included two kerosene cowl lights and one taillight. The taillight was identical to the cowl lights, except that its lens was red rather than clear glass.

Production of the 2-passenger Runabout was more than doubled this year, as 98,633 copies went out the door during the 1916 fiscal year. Weighing 1,395 pounds, it began the year priced at $390, the first time a Ford had gone under the $400 mark. By the following summer, its price ranged around $350. Ford insisted on calling this a Runabout, although almost everyone referred to it as a roadster. This unit, operating in a northern climate, has been equipped with a hood cover to keep the engine warm. No such consideration was made for the driver. An early model, this car has the smooth white tires that were finally phased out this year in favor of black Firestones with non-skid tread on the rear wheels.

Ford always touted the Runabout as a perfect vehicle for working people, because it could quickly be converted from a car to a light truck and back again. But this year, another concept was being promoted for businesses requiring delivery services. It was the cargo trailer, which could be hooked behind a runabout in even less time than it would take to remove the turtle deck and insert a cargo box. The unit shown here was built by the Erie Trailer Co. of Erie, Pa., and could be equipped with rail sides as shown or with a cargo box. Apparently Ford dealers encouraged the use of trailers, and many even stocked them as part of their accessory line.

FORD MOTOR CARS

Still enjoying a small but steady market as a taxi, the Town Car saw its production top off at 1,972 this year. Initially priced at $640, it would end the season at just about $600. Some references call this a 6-passenger car, others rate it as 7-passenger, depending on how many could squeeze into the rear seat, and auxiliary folding seats. It is unclear whether a cloth interior and rear seat were available this year, or if the entire vehicle was panelled and upholstered in leatherette. Despite economies, roller shades were still provided on the rear door windows. Note that although his car has the 1916 lights and lamps, with no brass trim, it is still equipped with the early 1915 bulb horn rather than the Klaxon.

It appears that the 3-piece windshield of 1915 was not used on the closed cars this year, but when the deletion was made cannot be ascertained. The windshield shown on this model is a very standard 2-pane unit, with the lower half being able to swing inward and the upper half swinging outward. The inward swinging second upper pane is not evident. Ford's heaviest and most expensive car, the Sedan weighed 1,730 pounds. It was priced at $740, which was $235 below the 1915 opening price. Even at that, by late season was down almost $100 more. Still, the style remained Ford's least popular model, with only 1,859 being built. Significant of the running changes, even in Ford's advertising material such as this illustration, the 1916 style headlamps are shown, along with 1915 cowl lamps.

The only significant styling change this year occurred on the Coupelet, which now sported small opera windows in its top quarters. These were supposed to eliminate a blind spot when backing up, but probably did little except to improve the appearance slightly by breaking the large expanse of leatherette. As was the case with the Sedan, the Coupelet also appears to have lost its unusual 3-piece windshield in favor of a rather standard 2-pane unit. Enjoying almost twice the sales of the Sedan, the Coupelet had a run of 3,532. It weighed 1,540 pounds, began the year at a greatly reduced price of $590, and finished at just about $500. Unlike the Touring Car or Runabout, the left front door on the Coupelet was functional, opening from its leading edge. The door contained full windows, regulated by adjustable straps. These windows snugged against the top rails when raised, thereby making a fully weather-tight vehicle similar to today's convertibles. Despite having the 1916 top, this car still carries the 1915 style lights.

An unusual vehicle, bearing no resemblance to anything on the market, was this coupe, parked next to an equally strange sedan. The scene was supposedly made at one of Henry Ford's farms near Dearborn, and the car reportedly is a custom-bodied 1916 chassis fitted out for Henry Ford himself. The relatively high coupe body is of almost archaic style, even for 1916. An interesting feature is that the car not only has electric headlights, but also has an electric tail and cowl lights rather than the standard kerosene variety. The sedan also appears to be fitted with a different body, and does not appear to be stock above the beltline. Whatever they are, these are not production Fords.

For some reason, Ford's sales of stripped chassis this year was down by almost 2,000 units, with only 11,742 being sold to outside body builders. Weighing 1,060 pounds, and priced at $360 including fenders, electric headlights, and kerosene tail and cowl lights, the bare chassis provided the foundation for any number of special bodies. In the professional car field, they were used for inexpensive hearses, such as this carved casket wagon built by the G.A. Schnable & Sons Co. of Pittsburgh, Pa. A relatively new manufacturer, Schnable started in business in 1914 and assembled its own chassis for its expensive line of funeral cars. However, for its low priced vehicles, it found the Ford chassis to be a very acceptable unit.

All Souls Hospital of Morristown, N.J., was the recipient of this ambulance by an unknown builder on a lengthened Ford chassis. The unusual body styling features a very open driver's compartment, large openings near the rear, and a totally open back. All of these could be protected from the weather by roll-up side curtains. Although they did not look like this, Ford also received a contract to build 20,700 ambulances for the military, apparently both for use stateside and in Europe, where World War I was raging. Despite the large number ordered, it has been impossible to find a photograph of such an ambulance on a 1916 chassis, leading to the question of whether this order came in within the time frame of the 1916 model year, or if it was after Aug. 1, 1916, which would have put it in the 1917 model year and on the 1917 style chassis.

1917

In August, 1916, the public was given a look at the "totally new" Model T, which Ford's dealers had been hinting about for several months. Well, though far from being "totally new," the 1917 Ford did have a new and more modern look, was priced still lower than its 1916 kin, and drew even more sales than the previous year, despite the fact that the country was at war and that some production materials were hard to find.

In reality, the new T was nothing more than the 1915/16 vehicles with some minor engine differences, and new front end sheetmetal. Gone were the little brass radiators and box-like hoods. A new and taller radiator with a painted shell now met a taller and more graceful hood with six full-length vertical louvers on the rear half of the lower panels. This hood blended into a slightly revised cowl, which in turn fitted into all of the standard bodies of the previous year except that of the Sedan. On that model, a new design produced a body almost identical to previous models, but one that was slightly higher, and could accept standard rear fenders rather than requiring special rear fenders as did the 1915/16 styles. In addition to the new hood and radiator shell, new curved and crowned front fenders joined the crowned rear fenders that had been added as a running change late in 1916.

Many reports seem to indicate that the demise of the brass radiator was due to the metal shortages imposed by World War I. Actually, it appears that the move was rooted in both cost saving and a desire to modernize the cars by making them look more like their contemporaries. To the average motorist, who probably detested having to polish the brass radiator constantly, the move meant better appearance and less maintenance. Now, the only bright spots on the car were the small hubcaps, now nickel plated instead of brass, and the nickel radiator cap. Everything else was painted black.

Under the hood, the cast iron nozzle for the water hose had to be made longer to reach the new and higher radiator. To assist cooling, the cylinder head was made larger, while the compression ratio was again lowered, going down to 3.98:1 from the 4:1. The displacement still remained 176.7 cubic inches and brake horsepower was still rated at 20 at 1600 rpm. As before, carburetors were either Holleys or Kingstons.

All body styles remained the same, though this was the last year for the Coupelet and supposedly for the Town Car. However, the latter model's production dribbled right into 1919. Whereas Ford and the world were amazed at total production exceeding a half-million in 1916, this year the Touring Car alone accounted for over a half-million sales. In fact, during the fiscal year from Aug. 1, 1916 to July 30, 1917, a total of 568,128 Touring Cars were delivered, all priced at a new low of $360. The Runabout, Ford's second most popular car, also saw record sales, with 107,240 of the 2-seaters going to dealers. This model was now priced at an amazing $345, fully equipped, which included electric headlights, kerosene tail and cowl lights, horn, tools, and top boot.

Holding steady in the production game was the Town Car, now priced at $595. A total of 2,328 went into the taxi and livery business. Possibly the new low prices or growing customer acceptance of closed cars caused both the Sedan and the Coupelet to increase sales almost five-fold. The Sedan, with its new and less expensive body, now listed at $645. Though still Ford's most expensive model, its sales figures this year reached 7,361. Meanwhile, Ford's original convertible, the Coupelet, had sales of 7,343, with its price being $505.

Apparently because of the war and the need for light commercial chassis, Ford's sales of bare chassis shot up dramatically, reaching 41,165 for the $325 foundation package. Also on the books this year was another military contract for ambulances, this one totalling 1,452.

All of this added up to an amazing production of 735,017, not counting the new truck chassis which were introduced on July 27, and are not a subject of this book. Engine numbers during this fiscal period ran from 1352990 to 2113501, for a total of 750,511 engine assemblies. Although other lists show slightly different numbers, all are very close to these figures, with little of the wide variance of former years. During this period, the 2-millionth Model T rolled off the line, with its birth date being listed as June 14, 1917.

In a final change late in the year, the hand-operated Klaxon horn was replaced with a new electric driven unit. This had been tried and discarded in 1915, but was back again in improved form. Also made as a running change was the use of tapered roller bearings on the front wheel hubs, replacing the former ball bearings.

The new curved front fenders and newly designed radiator and hood are very evident in this side view of the 2-passenger Runabout. By using a taller radiator and a full radiator shell, a taller hood could be used, which blended in nicely with the slightly revised cowl. Remaining Ford's second most popular car, the Runabout reached an enjoyable sales total of 170,240. Still Ford's lightest and least expensive car, it weighed 1,385 pounds and cost only $345, fully equipped with electric headlights, oil tail and cowl lights, and a top complete with side curtains. Note the use of Firestone non-skid tires on the rear wheels, while the front ones remained smooth. According to this illustration, white tires were still a standard item, though most material would suggest that black tires were normal. Again, the switch from white to black tires was a running change, made only as supplies ran out at the respective assembly points.

It appears that somewhere along the line, the Runabout tops received a new rear panel, equipped with three small back windows in place of the larger single pane. It is not known if this back panel actually was introduced in 1917, but other runabout illustrations for this year show similar panels, whereas cars shown prior to 1917 seem to have the single-pane panels. The rear panel could be rolled up, similar to the side curtains, for flow-through ventilation, even with the top raised. The kerosene taillight is similar in shape to the cowl lights, but has a red main lens, and also has a small clear lens on the right side to illuminate the license. The demountable rims on this car are either from a 1919 or later model, or were aftermarket accessories by either Hayes or Kelsey. Ford did not offer these rims as a factory option until 1919.

Touring the Yosemite National Park in 1917 was made a bit easier by equipping this Runabout with one of several different kind of camping bodies that were sold as aftermarket items. These adventure-seeking tourists have also equipped their Runabout with demountable rims, and have added a large and very necessary tool box to the right running board. Note that this top also uses the 3-pane back panel. The license plate is interesting, in that it seems to be some sort of U.S. government plate, and not state issue.

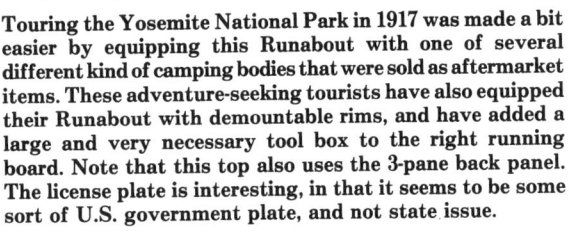

Providing transportation for the Merel Perry family of Flint, Mich., was this Touring Car, fitted with a running board luggage rack and a carrier for an extra tire. But, not having demountable rims, the tire would still have been a miserable chore to work onto the clincher rims. The car wears the side-mounted Klaxon horn, and also has a tiny outside rearview mirror, a relatively rare accessory in 1917. By far Ford's most popular model, the Touring Car drew an amazing 568,128 orders between Aug. 1, 1916, and July 30, 1917. Weighing 1,480 pounds, it was priced at $360, complete with lights, tools, top, top boot, and Klaxon horn. However, a speedometer was now an accessory.

For those who wanted to couple good weather protection with the low cost of a touring car, several aftermarket firms could supply tops or side curtains which were supposed to be superior to those that came with the car. One such supplier was the Brackbill Co., which offered patent side panels of glass with metal framing. These fit on the rear quarter, behind the door, and in the B-pillar space between the front and rear doors. A similar set of panels then fit onto the door sills, and would open with the doors. Lacking windshield wipers, defrosters, or any of the other comfort items taken for granted today, the Model T was still not a very pleasant car to drive in wet, cold, or sloppy weather.

A question arises over whether or not this was the final year for the Town Car. The taxi-oriented vehicle definitely appeared in 1917, but some later pieces indicate that it was phased out as a style after July 30, 1917. Yet, production records carry the car for another two years, even though it does not appear in the catalogs. Having a run of 2,328, the $595 vehicle seems to have had only one change from the previous year. That involves the windshield's upper pane, which now swung out, rather than inward. This, and the front end sheetmetal changes shared by all Model Ts, appears to be the only ways to differentiate between the 1916 and 1917 models. And at that, the windshield might have been a running change, and not a model-year improvement. Once again, buyers had a choice of having the rear compartment done in cloth or leatherette, while the front compartment was always in leatherette.

The Sedan, with its very high body, took full advantage of the new higher hood line, and did not appear quite so grotesquely out of proportion as did the earlier versions. Actually, the Sedan was the only Ford to receive a new body this year, though it is almost impossible to tell the new version from the old. However, the new Sedan was slightly higher and had a better fit on the frame, thus allowing the standard rear fenders to be used. No longer would the Sedan require its own exclusive rear fenders. The interior was done completely in cloth, with a carpeted rear floor, and a rubber mat in the front. Roller shades were provided on the rear quarter windows and over the large oval rear window. Weighing 1,745 pounds and costing $645, this was Ford's heaviest and most costly car. Still, its production was more than four times that of 1916, with a total of 7,361 being sold between Aug. 1, 1916, and July 30, 1917.

Appearing for the last time was the Coupelet with a convertible top. A Coupelet would be on the books for 1918, but it would be a different and more modern style. Once again on this model, the landau irons were functional and the top could be lowered. When in the raised position as seen here, the top fit snugly against the window edges and latched with the windshield frame. The door windows were adjustable via riser straps, and could be regulated to a multitude of different positions from full up to lowering flush with the sill. Weighing 1,580 pounds, the Coupelet was priced at $505. Its sales were 7,343, almost even with those of the Sedan. Some will argue that the new style Coupelet was a late-1917 entry, basing these assertions on the car's build date. This point will not be argued, but for the sake of simplicity, the new style Coupelet will be considered a 1918 style, and the convertible type will be classed as the only 1917 model. As before, the windshield was fitted into a fixed frame similar to that used on the Sedan. The upper half would swing outward, while the lower pane could be swung inward. Both doors were functional on this car, as opposed to the Runabout, where only the right door was operable.

In the previous chapter, it was mentioned that records show a production of 20,700 ambulances being built for the military in 1916, yet not one single photograph of a 1916 chassis in military dress could be found. What does crop up are numerous photos of these light military trucks, all in 1917 sheet metal, and sporting a body not unlike those used on the depot hacks of the era. Possibly these are the "ambulances" found in the 1916 production figures. A body of this type could be used for virtually any light duty service imaginable, from troop transport (with removable seats installed), to ambulance work (with stretcher racks), to light delivery usages. It is interesting that this vehicle does not have a windshield, but instead utilized a front curtain, seen here rolled up on the firewall. This year, Ford shipped a total of 41,165 bare chassis, each weighing 1,060 pounds and costing $325. This price included fenders and running boards, and lights and horn. However, the hood ended at the firewall, and no cowl was provided.

1917

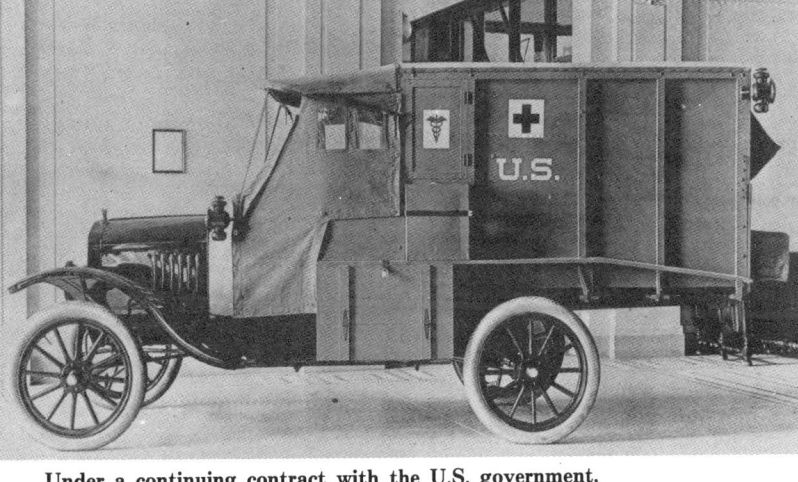

Ford still promoted the use of its Runabout for commercial purposes, and encouraged its dealers to stock various kinds of popular rear boxes to replace the turtle decks. One such unit is shown here. Produced by the Field Co., the slip-in body was available in either 52 or 60-inch lengths. The all-wood body featured flared sideboards and a drop-down tailgate. When doing this catalog piece, the artist drew a rather stylized top and rear panel, with a strange back window unlike anything supplied by Ford.

Under a continuing contract with the U.S. government, Ford built an additional 1,425 ambulances for the military during this fiscal year. These were equipped with special bodies, not unlike large packing crates, with open front compartments and no windshields. Side curtains and a canvas front panel provided weather protection. Rear fenders were not included as the Army Medical Corps preferred the board-like splatter shield to a curved fender. This was probably because the flat area could be used to carry additional equipment. It is not known what type of supplies were carried in the large storage box ahead of the rear wheel.

An interesting illustration is this one of a special Centerdoor Sedan body available for installation on a bare Ford chassis. Not only is the body interesting, but so too is the phantom illustration of the chassis, which shows 1917 fenders, a 1916 radiator and hood, and 1914 headlights. The body was built by the Robbins Body Corp. of Indianapolis, and was available to any Ford dealer who wanted to handle it as an aftermarket item. Lower and far more plush than Ford's sedan offering, the body had much more comfortable front seats, velvet curtains for the rear quarter windows, and roller shades for both the door windows and the back glass. Robbins was a fairly large body company that used most of its talents in providing relatively luxurious bodies for such cars as Jewett, Paige, Marmon, Cole, Stutz, and Willys-Knight. The company became part of Graham-Paige in 1927.

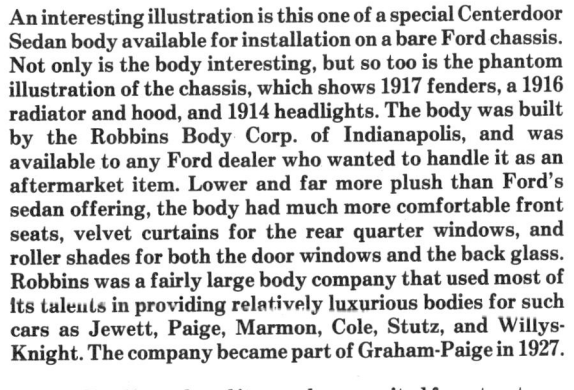

Although Ford introduced its own long-awaited farm tractor this year, there were at least 45 different companies offering tractor conversion kits for Fords in 1917. Most were similar to the unit shown here, built by the Geneva Tractor Co. of Ohio. These conversions were supposed to be quickly detachable so that a farmer could return his car to family use in only a matter of minutes. With this unit, the running boards and rear fenders of the Runabout were removed, the wheels were replaced with a gear train, and the studded steel tractor wheels with their own separate axle were installed. This does not sound like a "couple of minutes" work. A major factor against almost all of these conversions was the fact that the Ford's cooling system was barely able to keep from boiling in normal operation, and any steady hard pulling such as found in field work would surely have resulted in extreme overheating

An April, 1917, issue of the *CALIFORNIA CULTIVATOR* shows this ambitious tractor conversion by the Smith For-A-Tractor Co. of Chicago. Not only did Smith units feature low-geared steel tractor wheels, as did all other converters, this well-engineered unit also had its own full-length frame which attached to the car at the front axle, thus taking most of the stress away from the car's frame. Also, the kit included a much larger radiator, which permanently replaced the regular Ford radiator, and help to keep the engine from boiling. Costing $255, the kit apparently was popular with smaller farmers who wanted to mechanize, but who could not afford a full-size tractor. Smith claimed that as of April, 20,000 such kits had been sold and another 50,000 were to be built during the year. The company was a division of the Smith Form-A-Truck Co., one of the largest converters of Ford cars and light trucks into heavy-duty transporters.

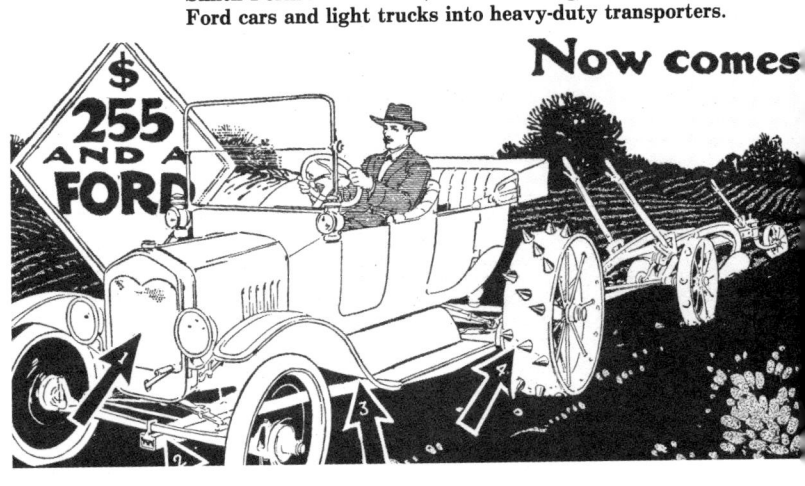

Now comes

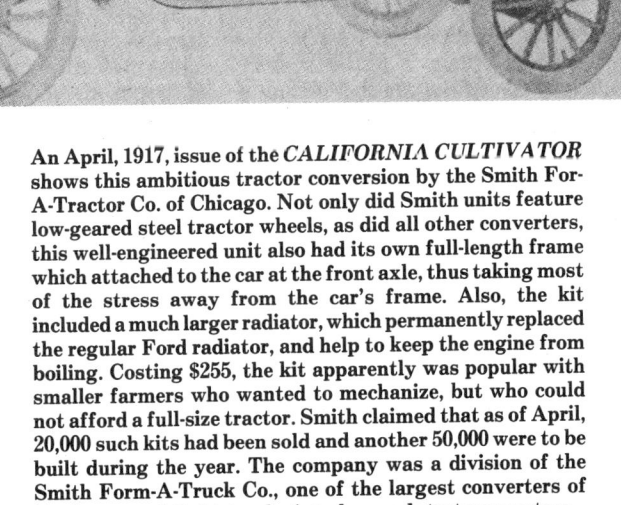

Virtually no changes occurred this year, but two new cars appeared, and two were supposedly dropped, though one of these supposed non-existent cars appears to have remained in very healthy production.

The two new models were the Coupe, which replaced the Coupelet, and Ford's first official 1-ton truck chassis. Disappearing were the Coupelet, and also the Town Car, though the latter move is open to dispute. True, the 1918 catalogs did not show a Town Car and very little was mentioned about the style in Ford's 1918 material, but production figures show that 2,142 of these vehicles were built during fiscal year 1918, which was almost equal to the 1917 production, so it is assumed that the style remained a relatively healthy product during the year.

The new Coupe also poses a puzzle. Some contend that there was an early issue, and that the car was really a mid-1917 model. Giving weight to this argument are early catalog renderings of the new Coupe, which do not match the actual photographs of the car, nor do they resemble later catalog renderings. This early model is identical to the later version below the sill line, but carries an arched roof and leatherette rear quarters that did not appear on the photographed examples. It is not known what this car actually was. It could have been an early version which was quickly and quietly changed,

either through a switch of body suppliers or simply a manufacturing change, or it could have simply been an incorrect artist's rendering, possibly made of an experimental model before the actual car went into production (much like the well publicized pictures of the experimental 1915 sedan).

The real Coupe ended Ford's "first convertible," in that its top was fixed and constructed similar to the Sedan's top structure. However, when the door windows and quarter windows were lowered, the center posts and door frame posts could be removed, thus creating Ford's first true "hardtop" styling. It appears that this feature occurred only on the 1918 Coupes, and was discontinued about the same time that the 1919 models were introduced. The lower portion of the new Coupe body was quite similar to that of the old Coupelet, and the doors remained rear-hinged, with both doors being functional. It also appears that the turtle deck was unchanged from that of the Coupelet.

For the first time in years, there were no price reductions this year, and initial car costs were the same as in 1917. However, as World War I caused material shortages and price increases, so too did Ford's prices rise. Thus, the Runabout, again the lowest priced of the line, climbed from $345 to $500; the Touring Car went from $360 to $525; the Sedan climbed from $645 to $875, and the new Coupe went from $505 to $750. Even the price of a bare chassis went up, starting at $325 on Aug. 1, 1917, and ending at $475 one fiscal year later. Again, the chassis was only $25 less than a complete Roadster.

As the war caused prices to rise, it also caused production to go down, both because of material shortages and because a substantial amount of Ford's production facilities was converted to the manufacture of military-related items, ranging from helmets and gas masks to caissons and field kitchens, to ambulances and trucks, to howitzers and patrol boats. In fact, the world's first assembly line for boats was created when Ford utilized

Because of the heavy involvement in war production, the number of cars turned out by Ford was down this year. The Touring Car suffered the most from this lack of production space and manpower, and only 432,519 units rolled off the line, representing a decrease of 135,609 from fiscal 1917. The war economy also caused an increase in prices throughout the year, with the Touring Car starting at $360 in August, 1917, and ending at $525 by July 1918. And, if this wasn't bad enough, prospective civilian buyers had to compete with the military for deliveries, as literally thousands of Touring Cars were bought by both the American forces and the British war units for use on the European front. As this typical example proves, virtually no changes were made in the car except for the painting of military information on the sides. It is not known if these cars were painted in military olive drab or if they were left in their standard black paint. Note that the upper portion of the windshield still folds down inside the car. Although the 1,480-pound Touring Car was virtually unchanged from the 1917 version, on the domestic market it was advertised as a "totally new" vehicle, with promotions calling attention to the crowned fenders, high "streamlined" hood, and large painted radiator shell.

The Runabout, commonly called the Roadster, was still Ford's lightest and least expensive car. During the year, its weight remained a constant 1,385 pounds, but its price traveled from $345 in August, to $435 in February, to $500 in July, 1918. Also suffering from tight production brought on by World War I, the Runabout dropped to 73,559 units produced, a decrease of 33,681 from fiscal 1917. Standard equipment still included the electric headlights and kerosene tail and cowl lights, plus top, side curtains, and top boot.

a large building at the still uncompleted River Rouge complex to manufacture the high-speed patrol craft known as Eagle Boats.

But all this hampered car production, and thus only 432,519 Touring Cars left the plant, which was still almost five times more than the total production of then-famous Willys-Overland, which at this time was Ford's closest rival in the sales race. The Runabout (or Roadster) was also down, with 73,599 builds recorded during the Aug. 1, 1917, to July 30, 1918 fiscal year. However, production of the Sedan again increased almost five-fold as people were becoming more used to the relative comfort of closed cars. Also, roads were improving to a point where closed cars would not be shaken apart by the bumps and ruts found on most city streets and all rural roads only a few years prior. Sedan production reached a record 35,697 cars, while the new Coupe style attracted 14,771 buyers. Also, the not-listed Town Car shows up on the production lists with a total of 2,142 builds, while bare chassis production was listed at 37,648 units. In addition, the military accounted for another 2,136 ambulance units and 399 special trucks, while the new 1-ton truck chassis (which will not be discussed in this book) had sales of 41,105 units.

Tallying these figures gives a total of 596,336 for the fiscal year, or 639,976 if the military and truck chassis are added in. Also, foreign production was reported at 24,000 units, which would put the total world Ford figure at 663,976 vehicles for the period. In the U.S., engine numbers began at 2113502 on Aug. 1, 1917, and closed with 2756251 on July 27, 1918, for total engine production of 642,749, a figure which comes remarkably close to that of chassis production.

What is this car? This original Ford promotion illustration shows a very nice looking Coupe with a body identical to that on the new 1918 model, but with a roof and rear quarters totally unlike the real issue. Note that the all-leatherette roof is arched nicely over the seat area, with the leatherette continuing down the rather wide quarter panels. As with the "real" Coupe, this one too has the removable door post and B-pillar and three hinges on the doors. Because of this illustration, some believe that it represents an early Coupe, or a mid-1917 model. However, no production data can be found to substantiate such a claim, and no photographic evidence shows such a car. Possibly it is only an artist's rendering made from a pre-production model or from designer drawings, or possibly it is body from an outside supplier that was considered but turned down by Ford.

Ford continued to extol the virtues of its Runabout as the perfect vehicle for salesmen and those businesses needing a light delivery vehicle. Usually the turtle back was replaced with an open pickup body, but some businesses added weatherproof boxes for their wares. One company producing such boxes was the Columbia Body Co., which really specialized in depot hack, taxi, and light delivery bodies. The box simply slid into the space vacated by the turtle deck. The Bull Durham Co. of North Carolina supplied a fleet of such cars to its tobacco salesmen. The cars are equipped with aftermarket demountable rims of five lugs, probably Kelsey products, but no spare is evident. Note that Ford continued the rear top panel with its three small panes. With a body of this type installed, the top could not be lowered.

The "real" 1918 Ford Coupe featured a relatively flat roof and more narrow quarter panels sheathed in metal. With all windows up, it was a practical and weather-tight car. When the windows were all lowered, the B-pillar and upper door posts could be removed, thus creating what can be considered Ford's first "hardtop" styling. Because of the removable pillars, the rear-hinged doors had to have their hinges on the lower section only. Surprisingly, three hinges were used rather than the expected two. The new Coupe weighed 1,685 pounds. It began its life priced at $505, but by the end of the model year was up to $750. Relatively popular for a new closed style, the car drew 14,771 orders during the calendar year.

1918

As mentioned, when all four windows of the new Coupe were lowered, the B-pillars and door posts could be removed and stored under the seat. Apparently this was not a popular styling item, and in 1919 the coupes appeared with fixed posts and pillars, and thus the "hardtop" concept had only a one-year run with Ford. However, many other car manufacturers used similar removable posts in both coupes and sedans for several years in this era. The Coupe was also the only Ford not to have its gas tank under the driver's seat. Instead, the tank was located in the turtle deck. This was a strange location, considering that it greatly reduced the usable storage space in the compartment, plus it made it very difficult to convert the car to a commercial application, such as one could easily do with the removable deck on the Runabout.

Appearing for the last time, though not even listed in the 1918 catalogs, was the Town Car. Still, the vehicle attained a production total of 2,142, which was almost as many as built in 1917. Used almost exclusively by the taxi and livery trade, the car continued to be classed as a 6-passenger vehicle in some references, and as a 7-passenger in others. It began the year priced at $595, but does not appear on the mid-year price lists, even though there surely were sales made through the entire 1918 season. Ford probably let the low-production Town Car slide off the books because its sales did not fit the mass production policy of the company. Besides, several other independent body companies were producing similar or better taxi bodies for the Model T, and pricing them within a very competitive range.

With World War I still raging, Ford was devoting a great deal of its manufacturing and manpower to military production, turning out a wide variety of material ranging from helmets to howitzers and from gas masks to field kitchens to high-speed patrol boats. On the automotive side, another 2,136 ambulances identical to the 1917 production were turned out, and another order was filled for 399 Delivery Cars for the U.S. Army. These unusual vehicles resembled the depot hack type unit shown in the 1917 section, and were equipped with full canvas tops and side curtains, including a rather bulky storm apron to protect the driver and passenger. Despite Ford having put into production its new 1-ton truck chassis this year, the Delivery Cars were built on the passenger car chassis, and were probably intended for light garrison work, not for field activities.

Enjoying its best sales year ever, the Sedan drew a total of 35,697 orders. This 5-fold increase came about despite Ford's overall decrease in production caused by World War I, and apparently was caused by the public's desire for more comfortable riding conditions than offered by the open touring cars and roadsters. Weighing 1,715 pounds, the Sedan started the model year being priced at $645, but increased to $875 by the end of the season. The cars shown in this section have the Firestone non-skid 30x3.5 tires on the rear and smooth 30x3 tires on the front. These look white in the illustrations, but were actually a gray color, and are listed as "black" in the Firestone book.

Ford's new 1-ton truck chassis, not illustrated in this book, drew 41,105 orders this year, but these did not seem to cut into sales of the bare car chassis, which saw 37,648 deliveries. Priced at $325 as shown at the beginning of the year, the chassis also increased, going up to $475 by year end. When delivered to outside body builders, the chassis included electric headlights, front fenders, and running boards. The rear fenders could be purchased extra. The hood rested on the firewall hood former, as the cowl was now an integral part of the body, and thus not included. Builders of car bodies formed their own cowls, while truck and depot hack builders usually used a flat dash panel butting against the firewall.

NEW YORK DOUBLE TARIFF TAXI

With the reported demise of the Town Car, several companies quickly came in with their own taxi and livery bodies to fill the void. One of these was the large Columbia Body Co. of Columbia, Pa., which offered several variations of this style. The most elaborate of its styles was the Landaulet Limousine, designed primarily for the private livery trade, which included funeral homes and limousine services. Some sales probably went to those people who preferred a Ford for private chauffeur-driven use, though such buyers would be few and far between. As did Ford's Town Car, this model featured functional landau irons and a folding rear section. The tonneau was completely upholstered in a type of velour.

Filling a space between the very utilitarian New York Taxi and the Landuaulet Limousine was Columbia's Detroit Double Tariff Taxi. This body had an operational door on the right front, but only a decorative panel similar to the Touring Car or Runabout on the left. It could be ordered with either a full 2-passenger front seat, or a single place seat with finished luggage area, such as found on the New York model. The relatively large rear compartment was rated at 5-passenger capacity when two rearward facing folding seats were used. The driver's compartment was upholstered in imitation Spanish leather, while the rear could be ordered in the same material, or in a type of broadcloth. This car also has the demountable rims and front bumper, but again, it is not known if these were part of the package.

In addition to its light truck and taxi bodies, the Columbia Body Co. was also well known for its depot hack bodies, which could be fitted to any number of different chassis, but were extremely popular Ford additions. Called the Combination Passenger & Merchandise Body, this unit contained a 2-passenger driver's seat, and three removable seats with space for another five or six passengers. With any or all of the rear seats removed, the vehicle converted into a handy delivery truck. Two low doors on the right were operational, but only a passenger door was provided on the left. A swing-down tailgate made package loading easy, while full roll-up side curtains provided a degree of weather protection. This same body could also have been mounted on Maxwell or Chevrolet chassis.

Produced expressly for the New York City market was Columbia's New York Double Tariff Taxi. It is not known if the package included the Kelsey demountable rims and accessory front bumper shown here, or if these were add-on items. The New York style vehicle had only a single-place driver's seat, while the area normally filled by the passenger seat was used to carry luggage. This doorless area was finished in black rubber and leatherette, and fitted with varnished wood slats to prevent the luggage from rubbing on the material. A small removable door was fitted to the driver's side.

The Mifflinburg Body Co. of Mifflinburg, Pa., was another major supplier of depot hack bodies for Ford chassis. This is the Suburban Body No. 130-A, which featured a nicely framed windshield and carried seating for six to eight passengers. Its low sides were augmented by a guard bar along the rear seats, while the seats themselves were provided with padded armrests. As was typical for this type of body, two doors were provided on the right, but only one on the left. A swing-down tailgate and roll-up side curtains completed the package. Depot hacks were sort of an in-between vehicle, not quite taxi, not quite truck, but which could provide both functions. As their name implied, their primary intended usage was to transport rail passengers from the station to in-town destinations or to resort hotels. The development of this vehicle eventually led to the design of the modern station wagon.

Another Mifflinburg offering was the Country Club Model 135-A, which was similar to the Suburban body, but had higher sides and more utility-type seats. Its wood framed windshield consisted of two panes, a lower one fixed in place, and a swing-out upper unit. Leatherette covered the top, while side curtains could be rolled up in bad weather.

About this time, two well-known body companies merged. They were the Martin Body Co. and the Parry Mfg. Co., which joined forces to form the Martin-Parry Body Co., with headquarters at York, Pa. Noted primarily for excellent truck bodies, the company also could not resist the growing demand for depot hack styles, and soon began offering their own models. The premier version of this line was called the Park Auto Body, Model 229-A. As did the Mifflinburg Suburban, the Park offered three sets of well-upholstered seats with padded arm rests, and relatively low sides. Its side curtains were made in three separate sections, covering each area between the pillars. It too used a swing-out upper windshield pane.

FORD MOTOR CARS

Prior to its merger with the Martin Body Co., the Parry Mfg. Co. was producing a fine line of truck bodies at its plant at Indianapolis, Ind. One of its products, for a Ford passenger chassis, was this Combination Passenger & Commercial Body, Model 204. More of a jitney than a depot hack, it was fitted with two sets of seats running lengthwise, which could provide seating space for eight passengers. The swing-down tailgate came complete with a folding step. When freight hauling was in order, the padded leather seats could be folded out of the way. Padded side rails provided back support, armrests, and cargo sides, while roll-up side curtains provided weather protection for the rear compartment only.

Virtually identical to the 1917 issue was the new lot of 2,136 ambulances that Ford produced for the U.S. military this year. Most of the shipment went to the Army, which found them to be very practical and dependable vehicles, both stateside and overseas in Europe. Although other body builders were involved, the major supplier of these special ambulance bodies appears to have been the J.G. Brill Co. of Philadelphia, which was really more famous as a producer of electric street railway cars than of ambulance units. It is not clear whether the chassis were shipped to Philadelphia for installation of the bodies at Brill's own plant, or if this work was done at one of Ford's assembly plants. Since the ambulances were listed as a separate contract, it seems likely the final assembly was done by Ford. Otherwise, the chassis would have simply been included in the overall bare chassis total.

Although the 1919 model cars didn't look that much different than the 1918 models, this year saw some significant changes in the Model T which were sure to delight potential owners. The two major innovations concerned a new electrical system with an electric starter, meaning that owners no longer had to crank balky engines; and demountable rims, meaning that a flat tire no longer required messy flat fixing at the side of the road. Other changes included a slightly new styling for the Coupe, the final demise of the Town Car, another new rear end, new engine castings, a new radiator shell and mounting, and new wheel bearing seals.

Probably the most significant advance was the introduction of a new electric system with self-start. At first available only as an option on closed cars (Coupe and Sedan) the system included an electric starter, generator, storage battery, and head and taillights. Often, on cars with the new electric system, the kerosene cowl lights were eliminated, though this was by customer option, and not a rule.

In order to accommodate the new electric system, a totally new engine block and transmission case had to be designed, with mountings for the generator and starter and openings for these to operate. The flywheel also had to be fitted with a ring gear for the starter to engage, and the timing gear cover had to be redesigned so that the 6-volt generator could be driven from a gear mounted on the camshaft. Because the timing gears now had the additional pressure of the generator upon them, the gear cut was changed from straight to helical to reduce noise and backlash and provide more strength. Eventually, as these gears became plentiful, Ford recommended them as replacements for all timing gears, regardless of the age of the engine.

Inside those cars equipped with the new electric system was an ammeter, a combination ignition and light switch, and a floor-mounted starter button. In addition, an inside choke and carburetor control was located on the dash, augmenting the choke wire that protruded through the radiator shell. Despite all of the changes involved in the new electric system, the unit was used for starting and lighting only. Ignition was still by the flywheel-located magneto, with independent coils for each cylinder, and a rotating commutator or timer. Subsequently, a dash-mounted switch would be included allowing a driver to switch back and forth from magneto to generator ignition, but throughout the life of the Model T, magneto ignition remained standard on all cars.

Obviously, with the number of engine changes required for the new electric system, plus the reluctance of many rural buyers to want the expense of such a system, the changeover was gradual in its acceptance. For the start of the year, only the closed cars could be fitted with the electric system, and then it was a $75 option. By mid-season, it appears that the closed cars all came with the new system, unless a buyer specifically refused it. At this point, the open cars could be fitted with the new engines and systems, again as a $75 option. And, as supplies of the old blocks and transmission covers became used up, all cars were fitted with the new castings, whether they were to have an electric system or not.

The other major development included Ford's offerings of demountable rims as a $25 option. These rims, usually made by Hayes or Kelsey, had been available as aftermarket items for some years, but were never standardized nor sanctioned by the company. Now Ford settled on a 4-lug bolt pattern for the rims, named both Kelsey and Hayes as suppliers, and eventually began to manufacture its own rims. These new rims meant that spare tires could be carried, which could easily be slipped onto a wheel. A flat on the former clincher rims meant that the tube had to be worried out of the tire while both were still on the car, a repair made, and the tire pumped back up, all at the side of the road. Since only one spare was envisioned, two different size tires were no longer practical, and Ford settled on 30x3.5 as the all-around tire size. This also spelled the end of smooth tread for the front tires and non-skid for the rear. Now all cars were fitted with Firestone non-skid all around.

Again the rear axle housing was modified, this time gaining a new gasket and oil seals. Information varies on the new Timken tapered roller bearings for the front wheels. Some sources would indicate that this change occurred during the 1917 model year, others indicate that it came about during late 1918 or 1919. Also on the front ends were new radius rods, tie rods, and spring perches. Ford was now manufacturing some of its own carburetors, and so these units could either be by Kingston, Holley, or Ford. During the year, new lighter weight connecting rods appeared, and a new brush-type timer was tried, found unsuccessful, and discarded in favor of the old roller-type. Despite all of the changes to the engine, the displacement remained 176.7 cubic inches, and its output remained 20 brake horsepower at 1600 rpm, with the bore and stroke still being 3.75x4 inches.

In the body department, only two minor changes occurred. The first affected only the Coupe, and consisted of the removable B-pillars and door posts now being made permanent, thus ending the "hardtop" look possible on the early versions of this car. However, it is not known when during the 1919 model year this change occurred, nor if the fixed pillars can be construed as a model year identification. Definitely, there were no fixed pillar models in 1918, but early 1919 models may have had the removable pillars.

The other styling change concerned the radiator, which was now spring mounted rather than resting on leather or rubber pads as it had in 1918. The new mountings meant that new shells had to be designed which would accommodate the springs. These shells are identical in appearance with earlier shells, but because of the mountings, cannot be interchanged.

With the end of World war I, a depressed economy resulted in production falling to its lowest point in years, while prices either remained constant or even took a slight downturn. Highest production once again was enjoyed by the Touring Car, but its total was only 286,935, which was 145,584 below the 1918 figure, and just about half of the 1917 mark. The Runabout also crashed heavily, with only 48,867 leaving the factory between Aug. 1, 1918, and July 30, 1919. Down to a lesser degree from the previous year were the Sedan with 24,980 units, and the Coupe with 11,528. Also shown on the list are 17 Town Cars, which may have been run-off 1918 models or might have been special government orders, as were the 2,227 ambulances built for the government. Car chassis, as opposed to the 1-ton truck chassis, accounted for another 47,125 units, while the truck chassis were up to 70,816.

All of this gives a model or fiscal year total of 419,452, not counting the military or truck chassis. Engine numbers ran from 2756252 on Aug. 1, 1918, to 3277851 on July 31, 1919, indicating production of 521,599 engines, of which at least 73,043 went into trucks or to military vehicles. Also, on April 2, the 3-millionth Model T left the plant.

Within the corporation, the decrease in production did nothing to stifle enthusiasm at Ford's top level. During the year, the entire corporation was reorganized through a complicated maneuver which formed new corporations, absorbed the old facilities, and then reformed the whole thing into a totally new Ford Motor Co.

Anyone on the outside would have never noticed the difference. Who did notice the difference, however, were the former stockholders, who were all bought out during the changeovers, leaving the Ford family 100% owners of the corporation.

Completing all of the corporate dealings, Ford now turned his attention to the River Rouge plant, which had barely begun to materialize when World War I interrupted the proceedings. Now the old Eagle Boat production facility was turned into a body plant, and foundations were laid for blast furnaces, coke ovens, power plant, and manufacturing facilities. It was Henry's dream to have a facility where every phase of automotive production, from basic raw material to completed automobile, would be done on one site. The River Rouge complex, which eventually would become the world's largest single-industry manufacturing facility, came very close to fulfilling that dream.

During this year too, Ford signed a body contract with the Edward G. Budd Mfg. Co. for production of bodies that its own plants were unable to produce. Budd would eventually become Ford's largest supplier of bodies and body parts. Also during the year, Ford began to manufacture its own plate glass, and greatly stepped up the production of its own carburetors. And lastly, with peace finally returning to Europe, a new branch factory for cars was opened in Copenhagen, Denmark, while a new tractor factory started up in Cork, Ireland. The Copenhagen factory was destined to become quite successful, while the Cork facility often was thought of as a thorn in the side, despite Ford's affinity for both the Irish and the English.

If catalog illustrations are meant to enhance the appeal of a car, Ford missed by a mile on this plate of its Touring Car. True enough in perspective, the photo/drawing makes the car look high and dumpy. Still, this remained Ford's best selling car, with the sales figures finishing the model year at 286,935. Priced at $525 at the beginning of the 1919 fiscal year (Aug. 1, 1918) the car increased slightly in price. At mid-year, the availability of demountable rims added $25 to the price, and later still, an optional electric starting system would add another $75. However, few Touring Cars of 1919 received the self starter option.

Surprisingly, with its top raised, the Touring Car seems to have better lines than with it folded. Top, top boot, and kerosene tail and cowl lamps continued to be standard equipment, as were the electric headlights. Both the Touring Car and the Runabout continued to use the interesting back panel with its three small celluloid panes. Open cars continued to use a 2-piece windshield, with the upper half folding inwardly down. As before, the two right doors were functional, but only the left rear door operated, with the driver's unit being simply an embossed design on the side metal. The Touring Car's weight was now listed at 1,500 pounds.

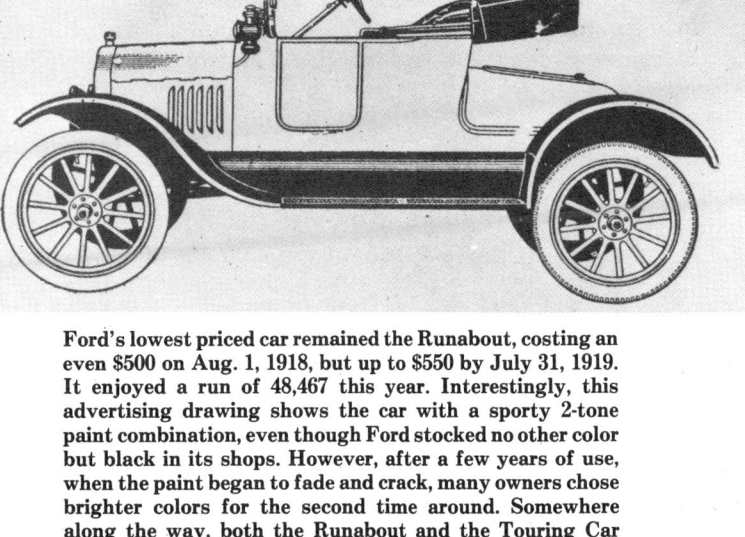

Ford's lowest priced car remained the Runabout, costing an even $500 on Aug. 1, 1918, but up to $550 by July 31, 1919. It enjoyed a run of 48,467 this year. Interestingly, this advertising drawing shows the car with a sporty 2-tone paint combination, even though Ford stocked no other color but black in its shops. However, after a few years of use, when the paint began to fade and crack, many owners chose brighter colors for the second time around. Somewhere along the way, both the Runabout and the Touring Car gained weight, with the Runabout now listing at 1,390 pounds, or five pounds more than in 1918. The Touring Car gained 20 pounds, but there is no indication where this extra weight came from.

Although Ford's 1-ton truck chassis was gaining greatly in popularity, builders of relatively light vehicles still turned to the Runabout as a good base. The builders of this interesting chemical/hose body have simply inserted their complete and compact unit in place of the turtle deck, mounted a large fire extinguisher on the running board, and painted the whole thing red and gold. And, there it is—instant fire truck. And, it was probably at a price that even the smallest village could afford. Since the Runabout's left door was only an embossed design, there was no reason not to hang the ladder and pike poles on that side.

Wearing the new demountable rims that became available for closed Fords early in the model year is this Coupe, which also has been fitted with the new electric starting and lighting system. The new electrics added $75 to the car's base price and 150 pounds to its total weight. Without the extras, the Coupe weighed 1,680 and cost $650, though most buyers went with the $750 package, which included the electrics and the standard 4-lug demountable rims. The Coupe no longer featured removable door or B-pillars, but for some reason, many of the early models retained the three hinges on the lower part of the door's trailing edge. Coupes built near the end of the so-called model year appear to have been fitted with the three hinges spread the length of the door, with the uppermost one being quite high on the B-pillar. It is not certain if the demise of the removable pillars occurred at the start of the model year, or if this was a running change made within the 1919 model time frame. During the model year, a total of 11,528 Coupes were built.

The Runabout was still thought of as a quasi-commercial vehicle, and Ford constantly encouraged its conversion to light truck duties. This concept certainly filtered down to the dealership levels, where service cars of this kind were often mounted on Runabout chassis with the turtle decks removed. Here a nicely lettered box with brass or nickel plated side rails has been installed, along with a huge tool box on the running board. The top boot, when installed, kept the folded top in a neater bundle, but probably few owners bothered with the boot once the vehicle became a couple of years old. Firestone non-skid tires have been used on all four wheels, but this car/truck retains its old clincher rims.

Lack of cowl lamps might indicate that the owner of this Sedan had opted for the new electric starting and lighting system, and wanted his car to have the modern "all electric" look, unencumbered by kerosene lamps. Priced at $850 with the electrics, the Sedan weighed 1,875 pounds. Demountable rims would have add another $25, but for some reason this owner felt he had no use of these items. Total production of the Sedan was down to 24,980 units during this off-sales year.

Again, as was the case with the Runabout, an advertising illustration of this year's Sedan showed the car in a sporty light tone, and not in the universal black, which was the only color in Ford's plants. This drawing shows the car in stock form, without the demountable rims which were introduced early in the season. Roller shades continued to be standard equipment on the rear quarter and oval back windows. Often called a "Centerdoor Sedan," this style was rapidly gaining in popularity as more and more buyers desired the comforts of a closed car to the wind-blown ride of touring cars and roadsters. Aiding in this selection was the slowly improving road system, which allowed higher speeds and longer trips over smoother roads, all conducive to families desiring more comfort when riding.

Yes, the Town Car officially ended its run with the 1918 models, and even here there are those who will argue that 1917 was the last of the bred. Yet, production figures show that 17 Town Cars were built during the 1919 fiscal year, which began on Aug. 1, 1918. Probably all of these cars were built in the early part of the year, and looked exactly like the 1918 models. Thoughts vary on what these cars were, with the two most logical ideas being that they were simply run-off 1918 models that strayed over the fiscal/model year, or that they were special vehicles built under a government contract. Whatever, they were the swan song of one of Ford's more interesting early body styles.

Taking advantage of the new 4-lug demountable wheels which became available throughout the entire line late in the season was the Columbia Body Corp. of Columbia, Pa. This Suburban or depot hack body gives an idea of how the side curtains could provide weather protection and convenience at the same time. With Columbia's system, special framed panels would open with the doors. These panels contained wire brackets that held the door units in place. Unlike the roll-up curtains used on the rear opening, the door units had to be stored flat, usually in special bins within the roof structure. Another Columbia feature was the fact that the upper portions of the celluloid windows could be unsnapped for ventilation. Ford turned out a total of 47,125 bare chassis this fiscal/model year. Costing $475, the majority of the 1,060-pound chassis went to body builders such as Columbia.

Throughout the life of the Model T there were those companies which supplied speedster kits to convert the car into a racy looking sport model. One such conversion this year was the Cyclone body from Michigan, which sold for under $70. The kit consisted of a body and cowl, twin bucket seats with upholstery, an 18-gallon cylindrical gas tank, sloping hood, four special fenders, two special running boards, and a large tool box. Painted in primer lead, the kit could also be had in a choice of red, yellow, blue, or black for an extra $10. Not included, but pictured were the radiator shell, horn, spare tire carriers, and demountable rims. It is interesting that a set of wheels with 5-lug demountable rims cost $12.50 in either black or natural finish from an aftermarket supplier, while Ford wanted $25 extra for a factory supplied 4-lug set.

Another speedster kit, also from Michigan, was the Greyhound, which cost $68 complete, with buyers having a choice of all gray, light blue with white trim, or red with black trim. The kit consisted of a special cowl, twin bucket seats with removable upholstery, an 18-gallon oval gas tank, a 5-gallon cylindrical auxiliary gas tank, and special fenders and short running boards. Available at extra cost were the special radiator shell and hood, and the streamlined headlight shells that flared into the fenders. The upholstery was done in red leatherette in a diamond pattern, with black binding. The total body weighed 225 pounds.

$68.75

$68.00

Greyhound
Speedster Body

If there was destined to be a year of few changes, model year 1920 would be deserving of the title. There were changes, true, but few and far between, and what changes there were seemed to defy any model year breaks, but just occurred almost at whim.

For example, some historians claim that this was the year that electric starting became standard on closed cars, and optional on open ones. True, but the options occurred during the 1919 model year and carried into 1920, and the last half of the 1919 model season saw so few closed cars ordered without self starting that it is almost academic to refer to these units as anything but standard. The same holds true for demountable rims, which first came out in 1919 and then became virtually standard on all cars, although technically these were an option right through the 1925 season.

There is the contention that the Touring Car received a new body, albeit little different than former bodies. Well, sometime during the year the open cars did receive a new oval gas tank under the front seat, which eventually would allow for lower seating, and late in the year a new rear quarter panel was designed for the Touring Car, but this appears so late in the 1920 season that it really constitutes a 1921 change.

Inside the cars there was a new "dash panel," consisting of ammeter, light and ignition switch, and choke control, but this also appeared on all 1919 cars with self starters. One item that was totally new for 1920 was the steering wheel, with the spider now of pressed steel, the wheel itself now made of hard rubber composition rather than wood, and the diameter being 16 inches rather than the former 15 inches.

Under the hood, virtually all engines now bore the new castings set up for generator and starter. On those cars not equipped with these electrics, plates covered the access holes. But again, this was a change that began with the 1919 models, as was the switch to lighter connecting rods. A new style Ford carburetor was introduced, but many cars still were fitted with Kingston carburetors and some still had Holleys.

The Coupe again changed, but only in the fact that its three door hinges were now spread evenly up the door, with one on the upper post, one at the beltline, and one just above the base curve. Again, this appears to have been a running change made early in the season, but one that should not really be considered a model year determination.

Another running change consisted of switching the running board brackets from forged to pressed steel, while under the car a switch was made from a cast iron

Yes, its a 1920 Runabout, and yes, the color is wrong. But the author's contention during the 15 years that he owned the car was, "Its my car and I like it yellow!" Besides, Fords might have been "black only" when they left the factory, but after a few years of paint fading and chipping, many were repainted in brighter hues, such as this yellow and black combination with natural wheels. The car was one of 63,514 Runabouts turned out this year with self starter and demountable rims. Another 31,889 were built with clincher rims and magneto electrics only. With the full electric system, an owner had his option of running on either magneto or the electrical system once the car was started. Contrary to most Ts, which seem to run better on the electrical system, this particular car ran much better when switched over to its magneto. The package of rims and self starting added $100 more to the Runabout's base price of $550. However, during the year, prices began to tumble, and by mid-summer, 1920, were $100 or more lower than at the start of the model year.

All Runabouts continued to be fitted with the removable turtle deck. When in place, this proved to be a handy storage spot for small articles. The lid was fitted with two latches on the trailing edge, and a piano hinge across the back. New to these cars was the spare tire, now made possible by the addition of factory-installed demountable rims. In addition to providing an extra ready-to-roll tire, the spare did double duty as a rear bumper. Full electrics meant that the car was provided with a small taillight on the spare's cross brace. But the addition of the kerosene light package provided both tail and cowl lights. An interesting original accessory was the combination spotlight and rearview mirror mounted on the windshield post. The left-hand step plate is for decoration only, as the driver's side had only an embossed door design. Its weight of only 1,540 pounds meant that the Runabout was a peppy little car, and a real fun vehicle to drive. Without the electrics and rims, the car weighed 1,390 pounds, and thus was Ford's lightest vehicle.

pinion bearing spool on the rear axle to a pressed steel unit. Also, a new pressed steel fan was designed and began to find its way under the hood as supplies of the old riveted models ran out.

The car models remained the Touring Car, Runabout, Coupe, and Sedan, but in all cases, prices were up about $50 per car from the opening 1919 prices. However, as the year progressed, cost cutting went into effect, and by the end of what can be considered the model year, prices once again were down by $100 or more per model.

Again for the sake of order, this chapter will consider the model year 1920 to be the same as Ford's fiscal year 1920, which stretched from Aug. 1, 1919, to July 30, 1920. Within this frame, the Touring Car was again the most popular model, accounting for 367,785 units with starter and demountable rims, and 165,929 units without these options, for a grand total of 533,714 builds. Second in popularity, but slipping drastically in the sales race, was the Runabout, which had a run of 63,514 with starter and rims, and 31,899 without the accessories, for a total of 95,403 units. Creeping up on the Runabout in sales was the Sedan, now listed with electrics and rims as standard, as was the Coupe. The Sedan drew 81,616 orders while the Coupe drew 60,215. In addition, there were 16,919 bare chassis built with electrics and rims,

and 18,173 without. This gives a grand total for the year of 806,040 vehicles, not counting 135,000 truck chassis. Engine numbers on Aug. 1, 1919, began at 3277852 and ended July 31, 1920, at 4233351, for a total of 955,499 engines built during the model year. Also, the 4-millionth Model T was built on May 11, 1920.

On the corporate side, the entire world was watching Ford's building activities at the River Rouge plant. Taking much attention was the new steel making facility, including the blast furnaces, the first to be totally owned by an auto manufacturer. In addition to the furnace, power plant, and building construction, Ford was also widening and dredging the ship channel so that lake freighters could deliver raw material virtually at his door step. And, to carry that raw material from the ships to the respective processing areas, a 24-mile railroad was being constructed within the vast complex.

Of interest is the note that the Ford catalog now listed 15 foreign branches, all headed by its foreign department in New York City. Among these were eight in Canada, plus London and Manchester, England; Sao Paulo, Brazil; Cadiz, Spain; Bordeau, France; Buenos Aires, Argentina, and Copenhagen, Denmark.

Well bundled up against the weather, this quintet is out for a winter drive in their new Touring Car. The lack of cowl lights would indicate that the car has the optional $75 self starting and battery electric system, but the vehicle does not have the optional demountable rims which would have added another $25 to the cost. With the full package of electrics and rims, the Touring Car was priced at $675 and weighed 1,650 pounds. In this form, it drew 367,785 orders, thus being Ford's most popular package. With the rims and electrics deleted, it cost $100 less and weighed 150 pounds less, and drew 165,929 orders. When looking at the small difference in price today, one wonders what kind of person would put up with hand cranking and roadside tire repair just to save $100. But remember, in most sections of the country in 1920, that $100 represented a month's salary or more for the average working man.

It is fairly safe to assume that of the 65,514 buyers who ordered their Runabouts with self starters and demountable rims, the majority were private individuals who purchased their cars for pleasure usage. Conversely, probably the majority of those 31,889 buyers of the basic car were those who would convert the Runabout to its commercial role. One such vehicle was part of a fleet owned by the Bruce Wigle Plumbing & Heating Co. of Detroit. Wigle installed what appears to be its own combination tool box and storage body, complete with pipe racks on the left side. The lower body unit, which butted against the cab portion, covered the frame rails and provided a floor for the turtle deck or whatever cargo box was added. The kerosene tail and cowl lamps were standard on cars without the electric system, optional on others. Note how the load of tools and fittings has settled this model well back on its haunches. Although the top would fold back on the cars, in this particular case it had to remain up because the rear box unit would not allow the arms to swing rearward.

Ford's most popular package on its Touring Car is shown in this well restored model from Tacoma, Wash. It included the full electrical system and demountable rims, and also the kerosene tail and cowl lamps, which were optional when the full electric system was ordered. Notice that Ford did away with its 3-pane rear panel, and now used only a single celluloid pane. It is believed that this was a running change, determined by suppliers and remaining stock, and not necessarily a 1920 model-year change-over. Although priced at $675 at the start of the model year, prices began to go down, and by mid-season were $100 lower per car.

The Coupe still featured forward latched doors, but sometime during the early part of the model year the hinges were moved. Now the uppermost hinge was located at the top of the door pillar, whereas in most of 1919 all three hinges were below the sill line. This change made for a much more sturdy door attachment. On the original Coupe design, the door posts and B-pillar were removable, so a hinge would have been impossible in the upper area. In 1919, when the removable pillars were deleted, the hinges sill remained below the sill level for some time. Since there is no clear evidence of when this change was made, the movement of these hinges should not be taken as a model-year designation. Ford's least popular car, the Coupe accounted for 60,215 orders, all fitted with electric starting and demountable rims. Weighing 1,760 pounds, it cost $850 at the start of the season, was down at least $100 by early spring. Note that the spare tire carrier does not have a spare tire, as this was an extra cost item.

People tend to forget what the well-equipped traveling salesman looked like in the mid- and far-western states in this era. Before the days of superhighways (or even paved roads) and convenient truck stops and motels, wide-ranging salesmen who chose to travel by auto had to be ready for just about anything. This included cooking and boiling water by the roadside, and sleeping in the car or in a tent in some convenient pasture. Running board luggage racks, usually on the left side, were a common place to carry luggage and utensils, while it is assumed that the more important sales presentations and samples were carried on the rear seat. Rover probably provided both company and protection. For the first time this year, kerosene tail and cowl lights were omitted as standard equipment on all closed cars, and on all open cars equipped with the full electric system. However, these items were available as options.

Coming into vogue in this era were disc wheels. Rather ugly by today's standards, the discs held a certain amount of aesthetic appeal during the decade or so from the late teens to the late twenties. Early in this time frame, they also provided a very practical aspect, in that they allowed a spare to be carried, rather than requiring a person to repair a flat roadside on a clincher rim. However, Ford's new demountable rims, or a wide variety of aftermarket demountables, would have served the same purpose. This owner has equipped his Centerdoor Sedan with a set of rather rare Globe disc wheels, which included the rear-mounted spare here being put to good use. As people (especially city people) began to appreciate the comforts of a closed car to the wind-blown joys of open models, orders for the Sedan kept increasing this year. In 1920, a total of 81,616 left the factory. All were fitted with full electrics and demountable rims, and weighed 1,875 pounds. The Sedan started the year at $975, but its price later declined to about $800 at mid-season.

Utilizing one of the 18,173 bare chassis turned out with clincher rims and no auxiliary electric system was this vehicle, shown wearing a depot hack body by York Body Co. In basic form, the chassis weighed 1,060 pounds and cost $525 at the beginning of the season, though the price was as low as $360 by mid-1920. Designated the York Suburban, Model 803, this body included seats upholstered in tan imitation Spanish leather. The middle seat was a 2-piece affair, and either half could be removed separately. The rear seat also was removable. Full roll-up side curtains provided weather protection.

No, this is not an armored car. It is one of 35,092 stripped Ford chassis units that were sold this year. Wearing its delivery clothes, the chassis has been fitted with a collapsible canvas and wire cab produced by York Body Co. of York, Pa. The company designed the cab strictly for transporters of such chassis. Weighing only 46.5 pounds, the cab could be folded up and carried like a suitcase when the driver finished his delivery. It was used primarily by dealerships delivering chassis to body builders, or by factory teams driving these units from assembly plants to nearby dealers or body companies. Any long distance movement of chassis would have been by rail. Notice that this chassis was ordered without rear fenders, but does have the demountable rims and probably the self-starting electric system. If so, it would have been one of 16,919 sold in this form for $620 at the start of the season. The bare chassis, with rims and electrics, weighed 1,210 pounds.

Almost any auto accessory catalog worth reading in this era would contain one or more ads for speedster bodies that could be placed on a Ford chassis. Some of these bodies were quite lavish, while others could best be described as downright crude. All were shown wearing far more equipment than came with the basic kit. This Arrow conversion, for example, is listed at $69. That included body, hood, seats, radiator shell and windshield. The top and wire wheels were extra. Stock Ford headlights, fenders, aprons, and running boards were retained. Although somewhat popular with the younger set in their day, few of these speedsters have survived, mainly due to the relatively poor construction found in most of the kits.

Although one York Suburban offers contrary evidence, it can be safely assumed that the majority of the 16,919 chassis sold with self-starting and demountable rims went to the builders of depot hacks and taxi and livery vehicles, while the remaining basic chassis went to truck body builders. This fully equipped hack also supports a York body, known as Suburban Model 808. Appearing to be slightly more deluxe than the Model 803, it has a protective bar between the C and D-pillars for the third seat passengers, and utilizes 3-panel rather than 4-panel designs on the sides. The rear and center seats were removable and the tailgate was of the swing-down type. Of 3-door design, it followed the open cars' practice of not having a functional door for the driver.

Although foreign-built Fords will not be detailed in this book, occasionally one pops up that is so interesting that it is hard to ignore. One unit fitting this description is this French taxi, constructed by the E. Tengal Co. of Seine, France, on one of the bare chassis supplied to overseas customers by both the U.S. and Canadian Ford plants. Appearing right after the war, and replacing the unavailable Town Car, this vehicle features the open front in vogue with French taxi operators of that era. The blank rear quarters are solid, and cannot be lowered. The taxi-meter appears to be hooked to a thin ring gear on the rear wheel. Bulb horn and European cowl lights complete the interesting picture.

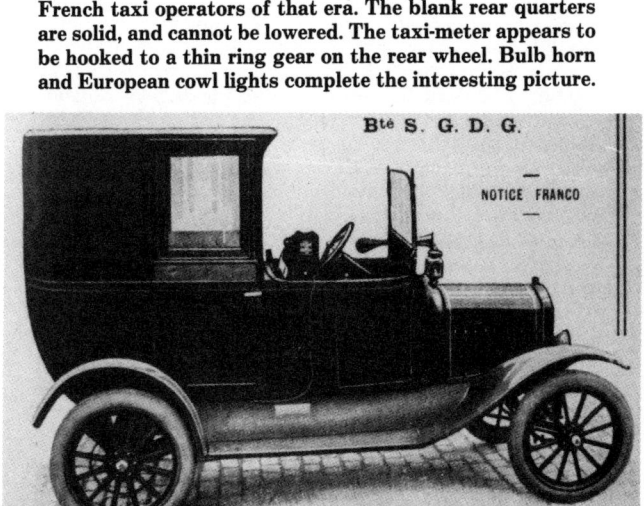

Following a trend established the previous year, the so-called 1921 Model Ts came on the scene also showing virtually no change from the 1920 models. Granted, during the course of the year a few changes did occur both to the running gear and to the touring car body, but all of these were really running changes and cannot be construed as determining a definite 1921 model.

In the body department, the only change was a slightly new cowl stamping and a new rear quarter panel, both appearing on the Touring Car only. All other body styles remained identical to the 1920 production. The new quarter panels were now a 1-piece stamping, and as such, a vertical bead was no longer evident behind the rear fender. Some contend that this change accompanied the switch to oval gas tanks and lower seats, and occurred with the 1920 models. Other sources indicate that there was no relation between the gas tank/seat change and the quarter panel design, and that each occurred as supplies of the former design ran out.

Another interesting occurred during the year as more and more states began to place anti-glare requirements on car headlights. Ford, which had used clear lenses up until now, met these requirements by supplying headlight lenses with dark green glass visors cast into the lens. However, for some reason, these lenses proved to be unpopular, and within the year a switch was made to the now-familiar "H" design corrugated Ford lens. The green visored lenses are very rare today, and should be used on 1921 model cars only.

Under the hood, a new engine block casting appeared. These blocks featured a 1-piece valve tappet cover, which was less expensive to manufacture, but proved to allow more oil leakage than the previous 2-piece covers. Also, another light-weight connecting rod was designed, magneto retaining wires were omitted; the front motor mount was changed, and a new pressed steel muffler was designed. Both Kingston and Ford carburetors were used.

Again, the seemingly always troublesome rear end was redesigned, with this version having a new pinion bearing housing of pressed steel, featuring exposed mounting bolts. And, in cars destined for mountain country, a new 10-tooth pinion gear was offered as an option. This, of course, increased power, but it also reduced the car's top speed. And, as mentioned, these were all running changes, and none can be used to accurately determine the model year.

Within the ranks, all models remained the same as in 1920, but prices had dropped substantially between the August, 1919, and the August, 1920, dates, and would go down even further during the 1921 model year. Thus, the base price of the Touring Car began at $440, and slid to $415, while the Runabout started at $395 and slid to $370. With demountable rims and electric starting, these prices went up by $95 on each model, but even this was $5 less for these options than the 1920 cost. Prices for the Sedan and the Coupe were $795 and $745 respectively, with a $50 reduction during the year. As before, Sedans and Coupes came with electric starting and demountable rims as standard equipment.

On the production scene, the figures became muddled again, this time because Ford switched from an Aug. 1 to July 31 fiscal year to a combined calendar and fiscal year. For this reason, 1921 production figures run an 18-month stretch from Aug. 1, 1920, to Dec. 31, 1921. Then, on Jan. 1, 1922, the 1922 production takes over. As can be imagined, some late 1920 and early 1922 vehicles appear in the 1921 production, but as there was virtually no change between any of these cars, the difference is really academic. Those collectors who wish to pinpoint the exact date of a specific vehicle normally can do so via engine numbers, which can be traced to a specific month.

Accordingly, the Touring Car remained the most popular with 732,270 examples. Of these, 647,300 were fully equipped and 84,970 were without starters or demountable rims. The Runabout had 197,663 examples, of which 171,745 had rims and electrics, while 25,918 did not. The Sedan enjoyed 179,734 sales, creeping up on the Runabout, while the Coupe saw 129,159 examples roll off the lines. In addition, a total of 36,792 bare automobile chassis left the plant, 23,436 with electric and rims, 13,356 without. The total for the 18-month period was a striking 1,275,618, not counting 118,583 1-ton truck chassis or 42,860 foreign builds. Engine serial numbers began at 4233352 on Aug. 2, 1920, and ended at 5568071 on Dec. 31, showing a total of 1,334,719 engines turned out during this period. Also occurring in this period was the production of the 5-millionth Model T on May 18, 1921.

On the corporate side, a dismal business picture faced all U.S. manufacturers in the summer of 1920. Ford was particularly hard hit, as a result of buying out its stockholders and financing its huge River Rouge complex. Part of the price decreases were to stimulate sales and keep the cars moving. Later in the year, Ford dealers across the nation literally had dozens of unwanted cars crammed down their throats and were forced to pay for them upon delivery. This was done in order to keep the company's cash flow moving. But, this decision, plus a few minor plant shutdowns and other austerity moves, kept the finances rolling and Ford ended up the year in a very stable position. In fact, Ford produced more than 55% of all cars built in America in 1921, despite a few temporary financial setbacks.

And, even though the dealers may have had some ruffled feathers over the heavy-handed way Ford forced them to accept unsold and unwanted cars, the formal complaints were minimal. After all, no dealer in his right mind wanted to take a chance on loosing the contract to represent Ford in any given community.

"Fully equipped except speedometer," was how the 1920-21 catalog described the Runabout. However, with the kerosene cowl lights now deleted also, "full equipment" consisted of top with boot and side curtains, and a basic tool kit. Electric headlights were standard, and worked off the magneto. But unless the self-starting package was ordered for an extra $70, only a kerosene taillight would be provided. This car also lacks the demountable rims, which added another $25 to the price. In basic form as shown here, the car would have cost $395 in mid-summer, 1920, and dropped to $370 by June, 1921. In this form, it weighed 1,390 pounds and had a run of 25,918 units between Aug, 1, 1920, and Dec. 31, 1921.

During the 18-month model year from Aug. 1, 1920, to Dec. 31, 1921, the fully equipped (starter and rims) Touring Car saw a remarkable production of 647,300 units, which was almost eight times the production of the basic Touring Car. When so fitted, the vehicle weighed 1,650 pounds and cost $535 at the beginning of the model year. By the end of the year, this price had dropped to $510. Notice that again, a 3-pane back curtain is evident, while other illustrations show single-pane curtains. Not visible in either photo is the new rear quarter panel, which provided a smooth curve from the back panel to the door line. Previous quarters were made in two pieces, and had a vertical bead just aft of the rear fenders. When fitted with the demountable rims, all tires were of equal 30x3.5, while cars turned out with clincher rims continued to use 30x3 tires on the front and 30x3.5 on the rear.

Fitted out with the self-starting electric system and demountable rims, the Runabout drew 171,745 orders during the 18-month 1921 model year. This was almost seven times the number of basic models ordered. Obviously, owners were beginning to appreciate the joy of being able to start the car (most times) without cranking, or of changing a tire without going through a messy roadside patch/repair ritual. When equipped with the electrics and rims package, the Runabout weighed 1,540 pounds and cost $490 in September, 1920, and $465 about 17 months later. Although most owners used a rear mount for the spare rims, which also doubled as a rear bumper, this motorist has chosen to carry his rims on the running board, adjacent to the dummy driver's door. When photographed during the 1969 Glidden Tour, this car was owned by Robert Haverstick of Dauphin, Pa. Note how the rear quarter curtains wrapped around from the back panel to the main top iron. This year it appears that Ford used both styles of rear panels, either with three celluloid panes, or with a single pane, on both Runabouts and Touring Cars.

Ford's most popular model this year appeared in two major forms. It came as the basic Touring Car with magneto-powered lights, crank starting, and clincher rims, or as an "optionally" equipped car with self-starting and demountable rims. In its most basic form, it began the 1921 model year costing $440, but was down to $415 by Dec. 31, 1921. In basic form, it weighed 1,500 pounds even, and during the 18-month model year saw 84,970 copies move out the door. Although usually sold as a package, demountable rims could be ordered without the car having a self-starter option. When ordered separate, they cost $25 above the base price.

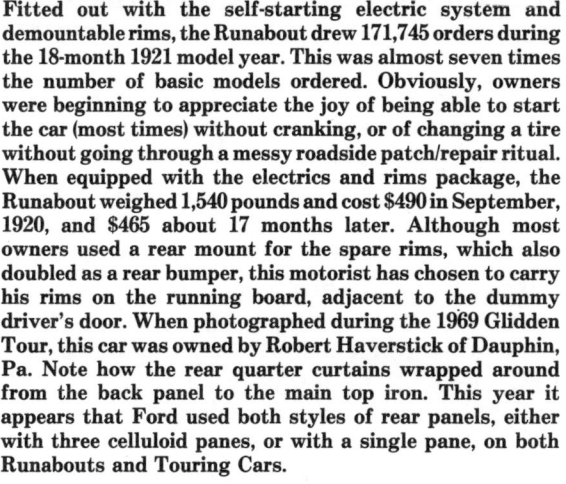

Remaining as Ford's poorest selling model, but gaining rapidly in popularity was the Coupe, which came complete with electric starting and demountable rims. Enjoying an 18-month run of 129,159, the 1,760-pound car began the model year priced at $745, but was down to $695 by season's end. Closed cars were fitted with spare tire racks, but not the spare rim or tire, which were still extra cost items above the package. Both the door and quarter windows could be lowered to sill level, while the upper part of the windshield swung outward and the lower portion swung inward. Braided welting of beige and brown was used around the seat back, entire headliner, and door edges.

Ford photographers crammed five large people into this Sedan to show how much of a load the car could carry. But, by the way the car has settled on its rear springs, it looks like maximum capacity was attained. One hopes they weren't planning to climb any serious hills. Actually, this picture has often been used to illustrate 1920 as well as 1921 Centerdoors, and could even have been used for 1919, because there was no visible change between this year's sedan and previous models. However, a big change occurred in the car's popularity, which escalated to the point where 179,734 examples were built during the 18-month season. All weighed 1,875 pounds, but the early models cost $795, while toward the end of the season the price was down to $760. The Sedan continued to use its square gas tank under the driver's seat, while the right front seat was a folding type, and could be swung up against the dash for easier entry or exit. Roller shades on the rear quarter and oval back window were standard equipment, as was decorative braided welting around the rear seat back, the complete headliner, and down the length of both the B and C-pillars.

When viewed from directly head on or from the rear, the Sedan was a rather funny looking car. But when seen from this angle, climbing a set of steps at a Portland, Ore., high school, it looked absolutely ridiculous. In this era, dealers of all makes would use stunts such as climbing steps, embankments, or hills to prove the power of their respective cars. The only thing missing in this picture is the appreciative awed audience that usually was on hand to view this kind of entertainment. This dealer has equipped his car with a double tire carrier, so that two rims could be carried rather than the usual single rim. Because of the under-seat position of the gas tank, stunts like this sometimes failed, because the gas supply would be lower than the carburetor, and thus starve the engine into stalling.

Another company offering speedster bodies appeared this year. It was the Bub Body Corp. of Schleisingerville, Wis. It began supplying dealers with nice looking all-steel speedster kits such as this. Contained in the kit was a special grille and hood, a 1-piece cowl and body split horizontally into upper and lower sections, four cycle-type fenders, and a side-mounted spare tire carrier. The wheels were not disc-type, but were decorative steel covers that fit over the outside of regular Ford wheels. The top, apparently hung on a wire frame, could be stored in the rear compartment. Both sloping windshield and oversized steering wheel added a sporty flair to the car. Note the tiny single taillight perched atop the left rear fender.

In this era, all sorts of public conveyances were rolling around towns and cities of all sizes. A type of vehicle that would not gain a foothold in the U.S. was the Jitney or Jitney Bus. Even though this conveyance concept would become popular in many countries, and is still often seen in today's so-called "developing or third-world" countries, the American public never really took to this type of livery. Still, in 1921, several body manufacturers created such styles for both Ford car chassis and the 1-ton truck chassis. One such offering for the light or car chassis was produced by the Atlas Co. Of 10-passenger configuration, it featured longitudinal seating, with its high sides acting as seat backs. Roll-up curtains protected the passengers but did little to keep the driver from the weather.

American Body Co. was another manufacture to offer Jitney bodies for both the light car chassis and the 1-ton chassis. This is the light version, known as American Model 200 Combination Jitney & Freight Body. The very thinly padded seats could be folded up to provide more floor space for cargo when passengers were scarce. During the 18-month 1921 season, Ford turned out 23,436 chassis with electric starters and demountable rims, and another 13,356 in basic form such as found on the two Jitneys shown here. The base chassis weighed 1,060 pounds, while the outfitted model weighed 1,210 pounds. The chassis also went through a slight price decrease during the model year, starting at $360 in base form and dropping to $345. As with the cars, the electric and rim package added $95 to the base price.

As the general public began its unending love affair with the car, promoters of all kinds of products began creating all sorts of silly things to roll around America's streets. There were cars that looked like typewriters, like radios, candy bars, sausages, milk bottles, loaves of bread—you name it, and somebody figured a way to put it on wheels. Among the more interesting ideas were the shoe cars which popped up in many cities, all usually built by some local company. These usually advertised either a local shoe store or repair shop, or a specific brand of heels or soles. This particular model was turned out on a much modified Coupe body by the Little Auto Body Co. of Denver, Col., for a local shoe emporium. It appears that the turtle deck was left alone, while only cosmetic wrapping was added to the body. The hood and shell, however, were subject to their own form of torture. A local roller rink in Sarasota, Fl., still uses a parade vehicle of this type, only made up to look like a large shoe skate.

It seems that no book on Ford could be complete without this photo of a sort of rolling church created by a Brooklyn, N.Y., minister. Apparently he felt more inclined to go chasing after his congregation rather than wait for them to appear at his door. Built on the standard car chassis, the church supposedly contained a pulpit and a small organ, in addition to being fitted with stained glass windows and a folding steeple. The swing-out windshield is a novel takeoff on the factory design. Records do not indicate how large a congregation the church would hold, but for sure, there were no bingo games in the basement.

1922

For the third straight year, Model T production whirled along with nary a change to ascertain one model year from another. Historically, a multitude of important events took place this year, but they were all on the corporate side, and had no effect whatever regarding the car on the street—except to put many more of them there at still lower prices.

All four models remained the same this year as last, with the only real styling change involving the Sedan. On this model, the former window regulator straps were replaced by metal brackets on the window edges which engaged locking brackets on the window frame. Oddly, these brackets were used only on the forward quarter windows and the door glass, while the rear quarter windows retained the adjusting straps. Also, this was a running change, occurring only on the later-built models. The author's own 1922 Sedan used the adjustment straps all around.

Another styling item occurring on the Sedan actually began in late 1921. This involved the use of metal overlays on the window framing, which supposedly was an improvement because the former wood frames would eventually loose their black paint. However, in later years many restorers (including the author) more concerned with appearance than authenticity, would remove this metal and sand and varnish the wood frames. The same holds true with the wood spoke wheels. Many Model Ts of this era (including those owned by the author) sport varnished natural wood spokes, whereas the original wheels were always painted black.

Mechanically, all blocks in 1922 appear to have the -piece valve tappet cover, which started to appear on the 1921 models. This, plus a change in the attachment of the spark advance rod at the base of the steering column, were about the only mechanical moves made during the year.

In August, 1922, the new 1923 Touring Car appeared, which confuses the daylights out of the production figures, since these were now listed on a Jan. 1 to Dec. 31 basis. Then, apparently sometime in September, the new 1923 Runabouts began to trickle out, while the really new closed car, a 4-door Sedan, appeared in October. During this fall period, or maybe even earlier, production may have ceased temporarily on the "Centerdoor" Sedan and on the old style Coupe. The production figures are mixed in the 1922 models and therefore no real compilation of "true" 1922 model production can be made.

Using the calendar year figures only, which of course will include 50% of the 1923 Touring Car production, gives a tally of 594,403 units for that model. The Runabout figures show a tally of 165,355 builds, while Coupe production shows 198,382, marking the first time in Ford's history that a closed 2-door outsold the open version. The "Centerdoor" Sedan, which is a true 1922 figure, shows that 146,060 of this model were produced. Also in the figures, but not really affected by the model year, were some 38,541 light or car chassis sold to independent body builders. This shows a total production of 1,142,742, not counting 4,826 of the 1923 4-door Sedans or the 154,039 1-ton truck chassis built during the calendar year. With this kind of production occurring, it is no wonder that the 6-millionth Model T was produced on May 18, 1922.

Engine serial numbers for this period run from 5638072 to 6953071, showing that some 1,314,999 blocks left the factory. Another often-used list for the 1922 year shows total car builds at 1,173,745, but no model breakdown can be found to ascertain these figures.

Helping to achieve this popularity, of course, was Ford's continuous reduction in prices, attributable to the high degree of mechanization and cost analysis in the Ford plants. Thus, the basic Touring Car, still with clincher rims and magneto electrics only, began its model year at $355, was down to $348 at the start of the fiscal year, and by the time the new 1923 version was on the books, was priced at $298. This was an astounding price for a brand new full-size 5-passenger Touring Car! The Runabout fared even better in price, though not in production. Its price tags began the model year at $325, dropped to $319 at mid-season, and bottomed out at $269 when the new model appeared in the fall of 1922. This, of course, was for the basic car. With electric starting and demountable rims, the cost was $95 higher.

In the closed car field, the "Centerdoor" Sedan began the season at $660 fully equipped with starter, lights, and rims, was down to $645 at mid-winter, and trickled the last few models out of the showrooms at $595 or less, depending on dealer discounts. The Coupe also experienced the same drop, going from $595 to $580 to $530. Even the light chassis in basic form went from $295 to $235. It is interesting to note that at the start of the season, the stripped chassis sold for more than a complete Runabout did at the end of the year, and that even at year-end, the basic Runabout was only $34 more expensive than the basic chassis unit.

All of this phenomenal production, price, and sales activity was certainly noticed by the industrial world. Never, up to this time, had any corporation turned out the manufacturing records being achieved by Ford. For the first time in history, a single manufacturer would turn out over 1-million vehicles in a year, and then proceed to repeat this feat year after year from this point on.

Greatly assisting in this production achievement was Ford's inclination to do as much of its manufacturing "in house" as possible, rather than to rely on outside suppliers. In line with this concept, its huge new iron foundry became operational (actually in November, 1921) and all 1922 Ford blocks were now produced at the River Rouge plant. Also, noting the increased acceptance of the full electrical system with its storage battery, Ford began to produce its own batteries at the Highland Park plant. And, the first assembly plant began to operate under license in Japan.

But the biggest and best move (in historical perspective) occurred early in the calendar year, when on Feb. 4, 1922, discussions were completed and Ford agreed to purchase the ailing Lincoln Motor Car plant for $8-million and settlement of outstanding debts. The Lincoln car, which had been on the market for only one year, was the child of Henry M. Leland, who had been instrumental in the formation of the Cadillac Co., which rose from the ashes of the old Henry Ford Motor Co. in 1903. It was Leland's criticism of Henry Ford and his ideas which had in-part caused Ford to leave the company in its early days. This was the move which set the stage for reorganization and subsequent change of name to the Cadillac Motor Car Co.

Leland had been with Cadillac for years, but an eventual fight with William C. Durant, president of General Motors, over military production caused Leland to resign and to form a new company to produce Liberty aircraft engines. Leland, a super-patriot, had wanted General Motors to jump into war production even before the U.S. became engaged in the conflict. Durant, who shared many pacifist ideas with Henry Ford, was reluctant to enter this field of manufacture. After a heated argument, Leland left Cadillac, and once again started off on his own.

But, such was the reputation of the 74-year old Leland in America's automotive and engineering circles, that he had no trouble in finding backing for a new and ultra-modern factory building in Detroit. Nor did he have trouble landing a substantial government contract to build Liberty aircraft engines. Searching for a name for his new venture, Leland settled on that of his boyhood hero, Abraham Lincoln, and thus the Lincoln Motor Co. was formed.

The well-equipped Runabout this year looked no different than it did in the previous year, but its basic price told an amazing story. In plain form, without the electric starter and demountable rim package shown here, the car began the 1922 season (in August, 1921) at $325. It was down to $320 by mid-season, and finished out its model year at an unbelievable $269—for a brand new full-size car! In such basic form it drew only 31,923 orders, but when equipped with the electric/rims package, its sales shot up to 133,433. The starter and necessary generator and battery added $70 to the factory price, the rims an additional $25, while both together added 120 extra pounds to the basic 1,390-pound car.

However, the company that was born in a war economy soon found itself dying in peacetime. The company had produced only 6,500 Liberty engines before the war ended and the government cancelled the engine contract. Faced with huge debts on the brand new plant and its equipment, and having a trained work force of 6,000, Leland had to do something and do it quickly. The logical move was to re-enter the automotive scene. This he did, with announcements of a new luxury car, to be the finest design on the American road.

The complete history of the formation of Lincoln is found in *THE CARS OF LINCOLN MERCURY*, by George H. Dammann and James K. Wagner, published by Crestline/Motorbooks International. Therefore, these activities will not be detailed here. Suffice to say, that by 1922 Lincoln cars were on the market, but the company was in such a financial mess that it looked almost beyond salvage. Ford stepped into the picture, probably took note of the company's excellent plant and crew of skilled workmen, greatly admired the engineering that had gone into the new Lincolns, and certainly was impressed by the fact that the company's assets were listed at over $14-million, while its sales price was slightly more than $8-million. And, despite many press releases stating how Ford and Leland were long-time friends (possible, but probably not true) one can only picture the delight that Ford must have felt in taking over Leland's factory, in view of the way he had criticized the Ford operations 20 years earlier.

Although Leland was offered a position in the reorganized Lincoln company, the 79-year old engineer apparently had had enough, and after a short time, resigned and retired from the Detroit automotive circles. And, to his credit, Henry Ford did not lower the standards of Lincoln products, as many feared he would do. Instead, he allowed the company to operate as a semi-autonomous structure within the Ford framework, and continue to produce the fine line of luxury cars for which it is still known.

As before, Ford continued to extol the virtues of the Runabout as a light commercial vehicle, pointing out that the turtle deck could be installed for weekend or pleasure use, and then substituted with a commercial body for week-long business errands. In line with this, several commercial body companies produced a wide variety of slip-on units for the Runabout. One such was the Galion Co. of Ohio, which produced this Model 100 Steel Slip-On Pickup body. Although the Runabout was virtually unchanged in 1922, late in the model year a larger turtle deck began to appear.

Having the most production and the shortest run in actual time produced was the Touring Car, which for the 1922 model year was unchanged from the 1921 version. By August, however, the new 1923 model Touring Car was introduced, and this "true" 1922 version was dropped. But, because Ford's production figures were kept on a Jan. 1 to Dec. 31 basis, it is impossible to tell how many of the 594,403 Touring Cars produced this year were 1922 or 1923 styles. Of the amount built, 514,333 were equipped with self-starters and demountable rims, while 80,070 were in basic form. With the starter/rim package the car weighed 1,620 pounds and was priced at $450 at the start of the season. This tag went down to $443 by January, and was as low as $393 when the new model appeared in August, 1922. When photographed in 1970, this example belonged to Paul Cressman of Akron, Ohio.

Although the Runabout was usually promoted for its commercial applications, many ingenious people, especially in rural areas, found multiple uses for their Touring Cars also. Besides the numerous tractor conversions, at least this one owner has found a way to power his circular saw with his tourer. One simply removes the rear fender, jacks up the back, and throws a belt over the wheel. Even though the package of self-starter and demountable rims outsold basic cars by almost seven to one, there were still 80,070 buyers who opted to save the $95 that these "luxuries" cost and took the car with clincher rims and magneto ignition and lighting. In this form, the car began its 1922 season at $355, was down to $350 by January, and was priced at $298 when the new models appeared in August. This well-used example wears the kerosene cowl lights that were usually fitted to cars without the full electric system. It also has a spare tire that would have to be worried onto a clincher rim in case of a blowout, and has been fitted with the very popular aftermarket running board tool box. As ever, the left front door of the Touring Car did not exist, but was only an embossed design in the side panel. Therefore, entry was not hindered by this mounting of the spare tire. Even though the weather appears cold, the raised hood sides would indicate that engine cooling was still a problem when sawing wood for any length of time.

Although most light chassis went for commercial and depot hack bodies, at least a handful found their way to custom body builders who supplied alternative units for buyers who wanted Ford dependability but a more luxurious body. An extreme in this area was this creation by the Bub Body Corp. of Schleisingerville, Wis. Called the Bub Sport Cab, the total package included a nickeled radiator shell with grille, and complete hood, body, and fenders. The standard Model T headlights are the only original exterior item. The special disc wheels are painted to match the hood. The cab portion, with its heavy visor and dummy landau irons, was covered in black Fabricoid. The body and cowl were sheet steel and could be painted to the owner's color choice, or could also be covered in Fabricoid. It does not appear that the Bub Sport Cab was supplied as a kit, but rather as a finished product only, available through select Ford dealers. Bub also was known for its speedster conversions.

The lure of a roadside produce vendor was as strong in the early 1920s as it is today, especially when the motorist was convinced the peaches were just picked from the neighboring upstate New York orchard. Once Ford's least popular model, the Coupe no longer fit that role. Buyers, especially those in urban areas, began to appreciate the full weather protection of closed bodies. Coupe sales this year reached 198,382, which put this model's sales 33,026 above those of the Runabout. All Coupes came complete with self starters and demountable rims, but the visor shown on this car was an accessory that was rapidly gaining in popularity. Prices for the 1,760-pound model began at $595 in August, 1921, were down to $580 at mid-season, and bottomed at $530 in September, which would put the car into the 1923 model year.

1922

Probably the majority of the 15,228 basic Model T chassis that went to body builders wound up carrying commercial or business bodies. On these, a paid driver could be expected to crank his own engine and fix his own flat tires. However, this Mifflinburg Model 130-A Suburban Body was put on a basic chassis, probably to save the $95 cost of a starting system and demountable rims. The basic chassis, which weighed 1,060 pounds, began the season priced at $295, was down to $285 by mid-year, and by mid-summer of 1922 was down to $235, which was only $34 less than the basic Runabout.

Although the Sedan this year had its wooden window frames sheathed in metal, many restorers (including the author) later removed this metal and sanded and varnished the wood sills. This certainly did nothing to increase the authenticity of the restoration, but it greatly enhanced the visual appearance of the car. During the year, changes were made to both the door handles and the window adjustment system. Early cars, such as the author's shown here, retained the bail or stirrup-type handles and the strap-type window regulators. On some later cars, the door handles became the "T" or bar-type, and the front quarter and door windows were regulated by notched metal strips within the frame, into which a latching device on the window frame would fit. These were running changes. The growing popularity of closed cars brought production of the Sedan to a record 198,382 between Jan. 1 and Dec. 31, 1922. Weighing 1,950 pounds and thus being Ford's heaviest vehicle, the Sedan began its model year priced at $660, was down to $645 by January, and closed the model year at $595. All came complete with self starters and demountable rims, but the visor, hand operated windshield wiper, rear view mirror, cowl lights, tool box, and step plates on the author's car are all accessories. The author owned this quaint vehicle for over 20 years, using it extensively in both Illinois and Florida. The mud flaps are an anachronism, but the oil drip pan is a necessity.

Another Mifflinburg design, also on a basic chassis, was this Suburban model with the high solid armrests. A more deluxe version than the Model 130-A, it features fully framed windshields, operational front door on the driver's side, and probably more finely upholstered seats. Mifflinburg bodies came out of Mifflinburg, Pa., and were built in a wide variety of styles, each slightly different than the other. All used basically the same concept of seating eight passengers, having the center and rear seats easily removable, being fitted with swing-down tailgates, and having roll-up side curtains for weather protection.

FORD MOTOR CARS

Of the 38,541 chassis sold this year, 23,313 were fitted with Ford's $95 electric starting/demountable rims package. It is safe to assume that most of these chassis went for professional car, depot hack, and livery use, plus a handful of custom car bodies. The remaining batch of basic chassis probably went into the commercial car and light truck field. This is still another Mifflinburg design. Called Country Club Model 131-A, it utilizes relatively high armrests of open design, which are actually part of the body framing. Its roof rails are also a different design than other Mifflinburg bodies, as are its side curtains. Note that the roll-up curtains for the passenger/cargo area fit outside of the body when lowered, while those for the driver fit inside the body structure. A deluxe body, this one also features a functional driver's door and fully framed windshield glass. Fully equipped bare chassis were first priced at $390, but by the end of the model year were down to $330.

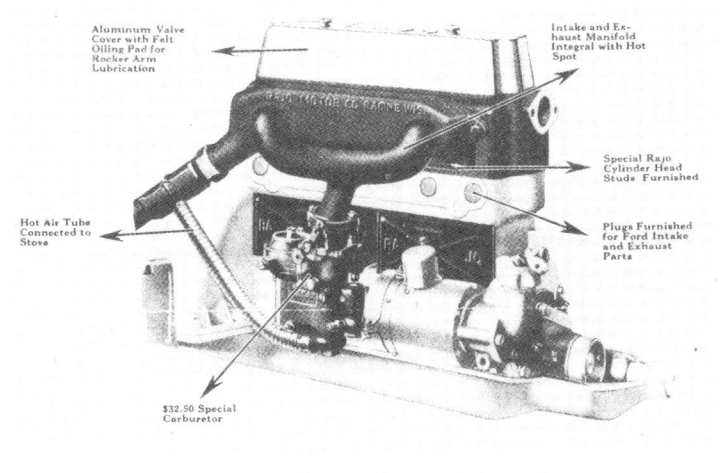

One has to wonder about the interaction of various body builders in this era. A good example is this Suburban body on a basic Model T chassis. Built by the Waterloo Body Corp. of Waterloo, N.Y., it is almost a carbon copy of the Mifflinburg design shown here. The main differences seem to be a use of dark paneling inside the light colored wood framing, and a non-framed plate glass windshield. The high arm rests are identical in design to the Mifflinburg unit, though the C-pillar has been moved forward. Otherwise, the bodies certainly seem to have come from the same set of prints.

WATCH THE FORDS GO BY

As Model Ts took over the country's roads, many owners were looking for more power and performance than provided by the stock 20 HP engine. Filling this gap were several companies, such as Frontenac (run by the Chevrolet brothers, of all things) and the Rajo Motor Co. of Racine, Wis. A complete Rajo conversion consisted of a special head, complete with valves and manifolds, an aluminum valve cover, special plugs for the old exhaust and intake ports, and a special carburetor. Not a cheap conversion, the carburetor alone cost $32.50, which was about 10% of the cost of a complete new Model T. The total conversion was $85 including the carburetor. With this modified engine, Rajo guaranteed speeds from a smooth 5 MPH to 60 MPH tops, with no modifications to the gearing.

One of the more proficient suppliers of replacement speedster bodies for Model Ts was the Ames Body Co. of Owensboro, Ky. This company had built its own cars from 1910 to 1915. At that point, it found more profit in supplying bodies for other chassis. Though relatively inexpensive, the Ames bodies enjoyed a degree of popularity due to their better than average construction and the fact that they could be bought almost piece by piece. This Ames restoration lacks the company's cycle fenders, but does wear a set of relatively expensive wire wheels. The body and hood were of stamped sheet metal, and were fitted with interesting little adjustable ventilators, more often used on stoves and ovens of the day. The seats were pressed steel, fitted with removable cushions. Gas tank and storage box were also Ames items, but not supplied with the kit. Ames appears to have made body kits of various kinds at least through the mid or late 1920s, when the company switched to manufacturing upholstered furniture.

Speedster body builders were still quite evident, turning out all types of units for Model Ts, ranging from the very fine to the downright stupid. One of the nicest looking kits on the market was the Mercury Speedster, of which a few restored examples exist. This particular model wears Buffalo wire wheels with knock-off hubs, has functional non-mufflered outside exhaust, and a Frontenac-modified engine. The basic Mercury kit included the nickel radiator shell, special hood and body, upholstered seat, nickel framed windshield, and cycle fenders. Lights, Moto-meter, and step plates were accessories.

Was there really a model-year 1923? That is a question that has caused more confusion among Model T buffs than any one single contention. One would think that with all of the material available on Fords, one could pull out a catalog or a file, point to a specific date or item, and say here is or is not a 1923 car. Wrong!

The whole confusing issue of 1923 began in August, 1922, when the "new" 1923 Touring Car was shown. This had essentially the same radiator, hood, and body as the 1922 model, but was fitted with a new sloping windshield and a newly designed "one-man" top, plus lower seats, which actually started appearing throughout the 1922 season. Some contend (as does the author) that this was a 1923 style, while others call it a mid-1922.

Then, in September, the "new" Runabout appeared. This also had a slanted windshield and new top, but again used the same 1922 body. This too should be considered a 1923 model. But now Ford issued its 1923 catalog. In it were shown the "new" Touring, but the "old" Runabout, and the old style Coupe and Centerdoor Sedan, which the company once claimed were discontinued at mid-1922.

Again, more confusion as the new "Fordor" sedan enters the picture in November, 1922. This, of course, is a 1923 model. But Ford directives to its dealers state that the company will not be able to supply sufficient numbers of this car to the public, and that the dealers should continue to sell the 2-door or Centerdoor Sedan. Since the true "Tudor" Sedan would not come out until June, 1923, and as a 1924 model, this meant that the Centerdoor Sedan was planned for 1923 sales, despite later contention that there was no such thing as a 1923 Centerdoor.

Exactly the same holds true with the Coupe, with its forward opening doors. This was not supposed to have been built in 1923, yet it apparently was continued well into the 1923 calendar year. Then, in June of 1923, comes a new Ford catalog showing all of the new style cars usually thought of as 1923 models. But, Ford regards them as 1924 vehicles.

Adding to this are the calendar year production notes, which show 96,410 2-door sedans built between Jan. 1 and Dec. 31, 1923. Were these all the new Tudors, or were some of them Centerdoors? If they were all Tudors, then by Ford's accounting, they should be considered 1924 models. Even worse is the Coupe production, listed at 313,273. This is a big bunch of cars to have floating free, without specific designation. Were they the new style coupes, and thus actually 1924 models, or the old style, or a combination of both?

Author's Note: In the original *ILLUSTRATED HISTORY OF FORD,* the stand was taken that the 1923 model-year cars were identical to the 1924 models. At the time, I certainly had enough backing on this. However, further research and the availability of more

material which developed over the subsequent 20 years have, in fact, changed my mind. Today, my contention is that only the slanted windshield Touring Cars and Runabouts constitute true 1923 models, while the Centerdoor Sedan and old-style Coupe represent closed car offerings for 1923, even though they are identical to the 1922 models. The only real 1923 closed car is the 4-door sedan (Fordor) which appeared in November, 1922. In June of 1923, an entire new series of Model Ts was introduced, and we will follow Ford's contention that they were all 1924 models. As to the production tallies, we assume they are correct for the open cars and the Fordor, but really have no idea as to which vehicles are represented by the figures for the Coupe or the 2-door Sedan. These may have been the old models, the new 1924 styles, or a combination of both as noted above.

Then, the only "totally new" 1923 car was the 4-door Sedan, for which Ford coined the word "Fordor" which was used almost to the present day. The body consisted of aluminum panels over a wooden frame, similar to the construction of the Centerdoor, but there the similarity ended. Three inches longer than the Centerdoor, the new Fordor looked far longer, lower, and more modern, even though it was only one inch lower than the Centerdoor. For the first time, crank-up windows were used in the doors, in place of adjustable straps or sill ratchets. The lower section of the windshield was stationary, but the upper portion could still be opened. A ventilator in the cowl was a replacement for the hinged lower windshield. The gas tank remained under the front seat.

Since visors were coming into vogue, the new sedan had one as standard equipment. It also had a large rectangular rear window in place of the Centerdoor's archaic oval. Upholstery was in brown broadcloth with dark brown striping. Roller shades were provided on the rear and rear quarter windows. These were of a silk material, harmonizing with the upholstery.

Ford apparently anticipated a rash of orders for the new Fordor, despite its price of $750, and thus in a late 1922 directive to its dealers, instructed them to downplay the car's modern lines and attractive features, and instead try to maximize the good points of the Centerdoor. The company also pointed out that production problems were anticipated, and deliveries would not be made as quickly as hoped for. This prediction is born out in the 1922 production figures, which show that only 4,286 Fordors were turned out between October and Dec. 31, 1922. However, 1923 calendar year production was shows 144,444 Fordors being built, but it is not known how many were of 1924 stock.

All of the 1923 models, as considered here, retained the old low radiator and hood, and the sloping cowl. Even the early examples of the Fordor used the low hood design, with the high hoods (often thought of as 1923 models) not appearing until June, 1923, and then being considered 1924 models by Ford. All early cars used

1923

wooden fire walls, but sometime around the early part of calendar 1923, these were changed to sheet metal stampings. However, this was a running change spread over all models as supplies of the wooden firewalls ran out.

Overall production figures for the calendar year are fantastic, as Ford sales rose again to unbelievable heights. But, as pointed out, these figures really have little meaning on a model-year basis, and thus serve to show only how many cars of each style were produced during calendar year 1923. These cannot be taken to show how many model-year 1923 cars were made, as the 1924 models, which came out in June, 1923, really constitute a major portion of this production.

As always, Touring Car sales accounted for the largest number, with 929,092 of the 3-door tourers leaving the factory. Of these, 792,651 had electric starting and demountable rims, while 136,441 retained the clincher rims and magneto lights and ignition. The second most popular style was the Coupe, registering 313,273 units, though it is not known how many of these are the old or the new body. Coming in third place was the Runabout, with total production at 295,592. Of these, 238,638 had full electrics and demountable rims, while only 56,954 chose not to go with the $85 option. As mentioned, the Fordor Sedan accounted for 144,444 units, but it is not known how many were 1924 style. The largest confusion occurs with what is listed simply as 2-door sedans. Registering 96,410 builds, it is not known what portion, if any, are Centerdoors, or if all are in fact 1924 Tudors. Light chassis accounted for another 52,317 units, of which only 9,443 were in basic form, while the remaining 42,874 had demountable rims and self starters. All told, this gives a calendar year figure of 1,831,128 vehicles having been built by Ford, not counting truck production. This was a record not to be broken until the 1960s.

If one looks to engine serial numbers to help straighten out the model-year confusion, little help is forthcoming. One list, which takes production from Aug. 1, 1922, to July 31, 1923 (possibly a "normal" model year) shows the numbers running from 6334197 to 8122674, for a total of 1,788,477 blocks turned out in this time. A somewhat conflicting list notes Sept. 22, 1922, as "the start of the 1923 model year," and begins this period with block No. 6543607. This list ceases with June 30, 1923, and notes the "start of the 1924 model year" referring to block No. 7927374 as the final 1923 engine. This shows production of 1,383,767 engines destined for 1923 model year cars and trucks. This seems like a low figure, especially when compared with the calendar-year engine serials which run from 6953027 to 9008371, for a total of 2,055,344 blocks built from Jan. 1 to Dec. 31, 1923.

With this production, it is no wonder that three milestone cars were turned out during calendar 1923. On Jan. 12, the 7-millionth Ford appeared. This was followed by the 8-millionth on July 11, 1923, while the 9-millionth snuck in just under the wire on Dec. 26, 1923. Of course, both the 8 and 9-millionth were actually 1924 models, according to Ford's accounting.

Prices for the year seemed to remain fairly steady, with a possible up or down swing of only a couple of dollars, usually at dealer option. Thus, the basic Touring Car was priced at $298, while the Runabout was $269. The price for the optional electric starting and demountable rims package was now down to $85 on these two models. The Centerdoor Sedan remained at $595, and the Coupe stayed at $530. The only really "high priced" vehicle was the new 4-door Sedan (Fordor) which started out at $750, but soon dropped to $725, where it apparently remained throughout the 1923 model year. The bare chassis was unusual in its price structure, in that in basic form it cost $235, while it brought $330 when equipped with self starter and demountable rims. This was a $95 increase for this package, while on the open cars, the same option cost only $85 more.

Being really a transitional vehicle, few examples exist of what this author considers the "true" 1923 Runabout. The car would have used the 1922 body, cowl and hood, and low radiator with no apron on its shell. It would have the new slanted windshield and the new style top, and could either have the early type of turtle deck, such as this restored model, or if a late version, might have the larger 1924-style turtle deck. Cowl lights might have been installed on this model if it was one of 56,954 Runabouts built this year without the self-starting electric system. Varnished wheels and balloon tires give non-authentic appeal. Throughout the calendar year 1923, the Runabout maintained a price of $270 to $265 when ordered without the electrics/rims package. The 238,638 that were ordered fully equipped sold from a early high of $365 to a low of $350 for the new "1924" style. All weighed 1,540 pounds complete or 1,390 in basic form.

Displaying its new 1923 style top and windshield, but the low hood-line, this restored Runabout is a good example of the continuing commercial application of this body style. Fitted with later model varnished spoke wheels and balloon tires, the cute little vehicle is probably a real eye catcher at local meets. The carrying position of the spare is not unusual when runabouts were put to commercial use. Since these bodies still had only one functional door on the right, there was no reason not to carry the spare in this position. Note how the line of the new style top drops downward at the rear. This was a new design used on both the Runabout and Touring Car tops this year, and supposedly was of modern line.

Although this book will follow Ford's contention that all of the "new" style vehicles that came out after June, 1923, were 1924 models, many restorers and owners still feel that these cars are "late" 1923 models, and thus deserve to be included in the 1923 section. The difference between the two styles can be readily seen in this artist's rendition, which appeared in a Ford catalog issued in mid-1923. The body remained the same, but the cowl required less slant due to a higher radiator and shell and hood line. Totally new was the apron below the radiator, which hid the former exposed mounting bolts. The new and much larger turtle deck is also evident. Reports indicate that some of these decks began to appear on the "early" or "true" 1923 Runabouts.

Lack of radiator valence, low hood, and slanting windshield all point to this as being one of the "transitional" 1923 Touring Cars, built between the introduction of this model in August, 1922, and the introduction of the 1924 models in June, 1923. At the time this photo was taken, the car belonged to Jerry Pulliam of Mobile, Ala. Like many other restorers, Jerry caved in to the temptation of decking his car with numerous accessories of the era, including spring-type snubbers on the front axle, front and rear bumpers, cowl lights, step plates, and a hand operated windshield wiper. Fitted with full electrics and demountable rims, the car would have cost $393 throughout most of its production run. In basic form, with magneto ignition and lights, and clincher rims, it was priced at $298.

Again, although this book for the sake of clarity will consider all of those Model Ts built after June, 1923, to be 1924 models (as did Ford itself), this late issue is being shown because many restorers today want to consider these cars late-1923 vehicles. This car features the top with the down turned rear section, indicating it was built late in the 1923 calendar year, as the first 100,000 of the new style Touring Cars used tops with the lower edge running in a straight line to the rear panel. Fitted with demountable rims and a full electric system, Touring Cars were priced at $380. Without the electrics and rims, they cost $295. The weight remained 1,500 pounds in base form, or 1,650 with the full package. It is impossible to tell how many of each model were built because the production figures were kept on a calendar year basis. However, from Jan 1 until Dec. 31, 1923, a total of 792,651 fully equipped Touring Cars were built, while another 136,441 were turned out in basic form.

As far as can be ascertained, the 1922-style Coupe, with its front latching doors, is the only "true" 1923 Coupe. The more modern version with rear latching doors is really a 1924 model, though many of today's owners will quickly argue that their car was built in 1923 and thus is a 1923 model. For the sake of clarity (as such) these cars are treated in the 1924 chapter. Thus, the old style Coupe continued with its $530 price tag and 12,760-pound weight. This model has been fitted with a new type of accessory glass visor, an item which would become standard on the 1924 style. Calendar year production for the Coupe stood at 313,273, but it is not known how many of these were this style, or how many were the new version. The accessory wire wheels provide this car with a sporty, if not unusual appearance. With demountable rims being standard equipment on both Coupes and Sedans, the owner of this model obviously wanted the wires for appearance and ride comfort, not for the convenience of tire changing. Also installed on this car and just barely visible beneath the headlights, are a pair of strap-type shock absorbers. These units attached to the frame horns. They featured a spring loaded drum on the frames, with the strap ends attaching to the outward ends of the front axle. Jouncy side-to-side movement was retarded by the spring action, which certainly must have improved the ride of the top heavy coupe.

Ford's only really new style for the 1923 model year was the 4-door Sedan, known by its Ford-coined name of "Fordor." Introduced in November, 1922, the model was first bothered by start-up production problems, and only 4,286 were turned out before year-end. In calendar year 1923, however, a total of 144,444 were built, but it is not known how many had the true 1923 style hood of this model, or how many were built after June in the new 1924 style. The car looked much longer and lower than the Centerdoor, even though it was only three inches longer (all aft of the rear axle) and only one inch lower. All four doors were functional, and all contained crank-up window controls, though the rear quarter windows still used adjustment straps. First priced at $750, its cost dropped to $725 sometime early in calendar 1923. The spare tire, which also doubled as a rear bumper, would have been an extra cost item, although the tire carrier was standard equipment. When photographed in 1964, this car belonged to Robert Sturble of Johnson City, N.Y. From the front visor to the large rectangular rear window, this model had it all over the Centerdoor in modern looks and convenience.

What car is this in the 1923 chapter? Twenty years ago the author would have squawked like a duck at the thought of putting the Centerdoor Sedan in the 1923 section. After all, everything pointed to the car's demise at the end of the 1922 season. Today, however, information would indicate that this is really the only 2-door Sedan that belongs in the 1923 chapter, and the more modern late-1923 Tudor is really a 1924 model. After the Fordor was introduced in November, 1922, company directives to the dealers broadly hinted that deliveries of this model would be very slow, and dealers should instead sell the virtues of the 2-door sedan, which at the time was the Centerdoor. Thus, still priced at $595 and weighing 1,875 pounds, the Centerdoor appears to have been sold well into the 1923 calendar year, which would have been more than two-thirds of the 1923 model year. But, since production figures were computed from Jan. 1 to Dec. 31, 1923, it is not known how many of 96,410 2-door units listed were Centerdoors, or whether most or all were the new style Tudor.

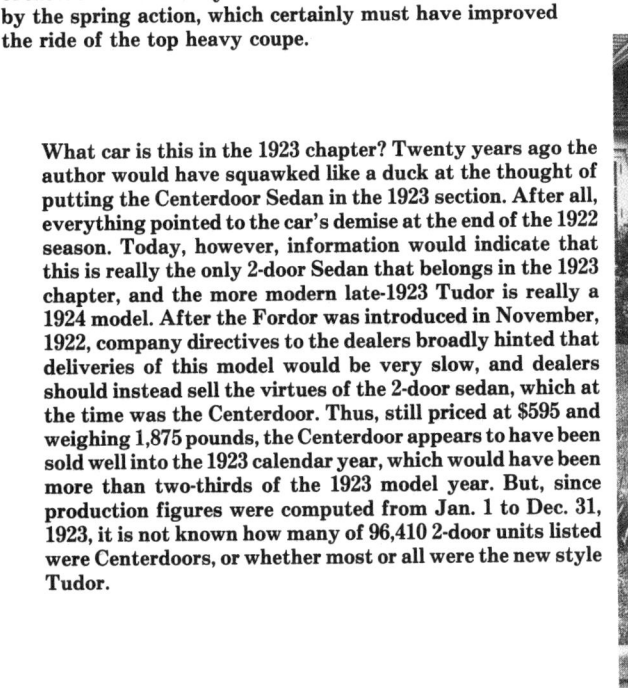
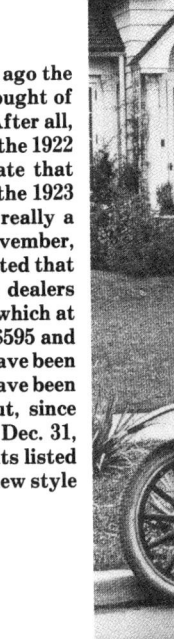

This small photo is one of the few showing the Centerdoor Sedan with accessory wire wheels. It also appears to have the same type glass visor as shown on the wire wheeled Coupe. Possibly they were outfitted by the same accessory dealer? This car was listed as a "late 1922 model," and thus could qualify as one of the 1923 Centerdoor Sedans to be handled by Ford dealers who were unable to get sufficient stocks of 1923 Fordors. It is not known when the Centerdoor finally faded from the 1923 model year, but probably well before the more modern Tudor appeared in June, 1923. Designating the late 1922 and 1923 Centerdoors from earlier models were the window adjustment latches in the door and front window frames. The rear quarter windows continued to be adjusted by straps, as were all of the windows in Sedans built before mid-1922.

1923

Henry Ford, always a fan of auto racing, here sits behind the wheel of the Barber-Warnock-Fronty Special. Entered by the Barber-Warnock Ford dealership of Indianapolis in the 1923 Indy 500, the Frontenac-modified Ford was driven by Lora Corum to a 5th place finish, completing the 200 laps at 82.5 MPH. Slightly to the left of Ford, though unidentified, appears to be Louis Chevrolet, who with his brothers was now busy turning out the highly regarded Frontenac racing conversions for Ford engines. To the right of Ford, chomping on his cigar, is Barney Oldfield, who had last raced at Indy in 1916. This was Ford's second year at the track. In 1922, a Jack Curtner entered his own Fronty-Ford and placed 14th, being flagged on lap 160. Also, the Chevrolet Brothers Mfg. Co., which built the Fronty-Fords, entered their own version. With Glenn Howard at the wheel, that entry developed engine trouble and finally quit after 165 laps, thus gaining 18th place.

All wrapped up for bad weather is this depot hack with what appears to be a body by J.T. Cantrell of Huntington, N.Y. This gives a good indication of the limited visibility enjoyed by the driver and passengers when the side curtains were rolled down. Especially amusing must have been the distortion caused by those little wrinkled celluloid windows. But, judging by the icy looking road, the poor visibility was a good trade-off against winter blasts. This calendar year, Ford turned out a total of 52,317 light chassis, of which 42,874 were equipped with self starters and demountable rims, as shown here. These would have cost $330 and weighed 1,210 pounds, with the rear fenders at extra cost. The other 9,443 chassis would have been in base form, with magneto electrics and clincher rims. These, probably all used for light truck chassis, cost $235 and weighed 1,060 pounds.

A family version of a snowmobile is this model, which uses only the chassis and cowl from a Touring Car or Runabout, and adds its own wood-frame body. One wonders why the builder didn't simply use a normal chassis-cowl unit, unless this vehicle was made from a wrecked passenger car. Information credits it as being a 1923 model, but if so, its windshield has been changed back to the 1922 style. A relatively high machine, entry required step plates just ahead of the tracks. The running gear is credited to the Snowmobile Co. The vehicle was on display at the Hemp Antique Museum at Rochester, Minn.

Snowmobile conversions for Fords flicked in and out of the market ever since the first Model T chugged across the countryside. One of the more successful converters of this type of machine, and the one that coined the word "Snowmobile" was the Snowmobile Co. of Rochester, N.H. Operating through Ford agencies, the company would sell kits, parts, or completed vehicles. This is one of their pickup conversions, utilizing a standard Runabout as its base. Power was applied through the forward rear axle, while the rearward one provided tension on the tracks. The vehicle would run at an average speed of 18 MPH. Snowmobile Co. claimed the tracks gave 40 times the traction of an ordinary rear wheel, while the forward skis provided 60 times the bearing surface. When warm weather returned, the ski equipment and tracks could be easily removed, and the car returned to its normal shape.

1923 MODEL T SNOWMOBILE

Ford's confusing ritual with its model changes continued through the 1924 model year, but at least in this instance, by the time the 1923 calendar year was nearing its close, the 1924 model year Fords were pretty well established. As previewed in the previous chapter, a major styling change occurred throughout the entire line in June, 1923. For once, the changes were not made on a running basis as earlier style supplies ran out, but seem to have been well planned so that all old style items ran out and were replaced by the new designs all within the June, 1923 framework.

Of course, the problem now is what to call these new styles. Ford apparently wanted to refer to all of them as 1924 models, even though their production began in June, 1923. Today, however, many owners of Model Ts built from June until the end of December, 1923, want to register their cars as 1923 models, not 1924. In this book, we are not seeking an argument. But, simply for the sake of categorizing these cars into one model year, they will all be considered 1924 models, rather than early and late 1923.

Among the significant sheet metal changes to occur in June were higher radiators and shells with correspondingly higher hoods and more smoothly shaped cowls. A major change, insofar as quick identification goes, involves a small apron or valence of stamped metal under the radiator. Fitted with a hole for the crank, this small item greatly improved the front appearance by hiding the mounting bolts and giving the radiator and shell a more complete look. Complimenting the new apron were slightly restyled front fenders with a small lip or valence.

The Touring Car and Runabout continued to use their former bodies, but with the new cowl. All Runabouts were now fitted with the new and larger turtle deck that had begun to appear during the early part of calendar 1923. Likewise, both open cars used their new one-man tops with the more enveloping rear quarters. Rear windows continued to vary, probably between suppliers. The majority of tops appeared to have two almost square rear windows, while a few had the old style with three vertical rectangles, and some touring cars had rear curtains with two small oval celluloid windows.

Except for the new front styling, the Fordor was unchanged, but somewhere about June, 1923, it was joined by its companion "Tudor." This totally new model technically replaced the Centerdoor, although in reality both Fordor and Tudor could be considered Centerdoor replacements.

The new Tudor had its doors hinged at the cowl, opening from the B-pillar, in a style that has become traditional for all 2-door models today. As with the Fordor, the lower portion of the windshield would not open, but a ventilator was provided in the cowl. A visor was used over the windshield, though it seems this might not have been a standard item on the first Tudors, coming into usage on Coupes and Tudors only toward the end of the 1923 calendar year.

Inside, the car was upholstered in brown boadcloth with mahogany striping, while the headliner was in a plain brown cloth. The right seat folded forward for access to the rear, but the gas tank remained under the stationary driver's seat. Crank type window regulators

One of the more famous photos of Henry Ford shows him in a reflective mood, standing between the 10-millionth Model T and his original Quadricycle, no doubt contemplating what a distance separated the two vehicles. The 10-millionth car, which rolled off the line on June 4, 1924, was no different than any of the 773,102 Touring Cars which were brought to life during calendar year 1924. As did 673,579 of this model, the car had demountable rims and the electric starting and lighting package, which would have put its price at $380 at the beginning of the season, or $375 when this car came out. It weighed 1,650 pounds. Also available was the basic Touring Car. Accounting for 99,523 sales, mostly in rural areas, and without electric starting or demountable rims, this version would have cost $295 early in the year, and $5 less at mid-season. It weighed 1,500 pounds in this form. The 10-millionth car was shipped to New York, and from there the famed Ford racing driver Frank Kulick drove it to San Francisco. He went via the Lincoln Highway, which was about the only continuous coast-to-coast highway at the time. Enroute, the car was seen by millions of people, as special showings were set up at select dealerships across the country.

were used in the doors, and silk curtains were provided for the rear and rear quarter windows. The rear quarter windows were fixed in place and could not be opened.

Last to appear in the new style list was the Coupe, with conflicting information showing the car being introduced anywhere from early summer to late fall, 1923. From hood to B-pillar, the Coupe looked identical to the other two closed cars. For the first time, its doors were hinged at the front, and its cowl had a ventilator door. Behind the B-pillar was a totally new Coupe design containing an integral trunk with a hinged deck, which provided the most storage space of any of the Ford styles. Also, behind the seat was a small recessed parcel shelf.

As before, self starting and demountable rims were standard on the closed models, but still optional as an $85 factory accessory package on the open cars. Also, on open cars, the new style cowl did not contain a ventilator door as did the closed models. All closed cars were now fitted with interior dome lights, but such a novelty was never considered for the open models. However, several accessory interior or dash lights were available for both open and closed models. Other accessories coming in strongly now included rearview mirrors, hand-operated windshield wipers, speedometers, Moto-meters, and an endless array of accessories to improve the performance of the engine—a few of which actually worked.

Mechanically, almost everything remained the same, with a few innovations coming into the picture as running changes throughout model year 1924. Among

these were new pistons of slightly lighter weight and having a reinforcing ridge around the base of the apron; a new and shorter front camshaft bearing; a new oil line inside the engine, and a new oil deflecting ridge inside the transmission case.

In the pricing department, there was little change during the year, with the only real mark-down occurring with the Fordor, which had begun its 1923 life at $750, quickly dropped to $725, and started the 1924 model year at $685. By the time the 1924 calendar year ended, it was down to $660. The two totally new closed cars, the Tudor and the Coupe, retained their prices fairly well, with the Tudor introduced at $590 and its year-end price being $580, while the Coupe was introduced at $525 and finished the year at $520. The open cars also varied very little, with the basic Touring Car and Runabout (with clincher rims and magneto lights and ignition) starting the model year at $295 and $265 respectively and each dropping by only $5 by year end. Similarly, the fully equipped Touring Car and Runabout were introduced in June, 1923, at $380, and $350 respectively, and ended their 1924 model year at $375 and $345.

Production figures are again virtually meaningless insofar as model year builds are concerned, because the calendar year computation takes in only the last half of the 1924 model year and the first half of what normally would be thought of as 1925 vehicle. Still, for the period from Jan. 1 to Dec. 31, 1924, the figures indicate a total production of 773,102 Touring Cars, which was a drop of over 150,000 units this year. Of these, 99,523 were still ordered with clincher rims and

The new higher radiator and hood line featured on all Fords this year, plus the new and larger turtle deck of the Runabout, are both evident in this factory publicity photo of the 1924 Model T. The Runabout, now more and more often called a Roadster, was available as shown here with full electric starting and lighting system and demountable rims for $350. In basic form, still fitted with clincher rims and magneto electrics, it cost only $265 at the start of the season. Both versions would drop another $5 in price by year-end. Now Ford's third best selling car, although its lowest priced model, the Runabout accounted for 43,317 sales in basic form, and 220,955 as a fully equipped car. It weighed 1,390 pounds in base form, and 1,540 when equipped.

All bundled up for bad weather is this Runabout, which is showing off its new "one man" top. As always, the car came complete with side curtains, but the new increased envelopment of the top and rear quarters made the curtains smaller than on the old models. The left side curtain contained a small flap on its lower rear corner for the driver to make hand signals. The right curtain would open with the door, but because there still was no door on the left side, that curtain fastened directly to the quarter curtain. Neither of the open cars used the new vent door in the cowl, as did the closed models.

magneto starting, while the remaining 673,579 were fully equipped. Runabout production also was down, with only 264,272 being produced, a drop of 30,000. Of these, 220,955 were fully equipped, while 43,317 still went out with the old rims and lack of electric starting. As before, the Runabout took third place after the Coupe.

Second in production and first among the three closed cars was the Coupe, which recorded 327,584 units, which was 14,000 above the 1923 figure. The totally new Tudor came in with 223,203 vehicles, and the Fordor registered 84,733 units, which was a surprising drop of 60,000 sales. Most of these lost sales, however, may have been picked up by the Tudor. Light (car) chassis sales were 47,001, of which only 3,921 were without the demountable rims or self starting.

The recorded production for the calendar year resulted in a total of 1,720,795 vehicles, not counting the 1-ton trucks, which was 110,333 below the 1923 calendar year. For this same period, engine numbers ran from 9008372 to 10994033, for a total of 1,985,661 blocks. For an approximate model year, beginning July 2, 1923, and running to July 31, 1924, gives block numbers ranging from 7927375 to 10266471, which would show a block production of 2,339,096 for the 13-month period that could approximate the model year. However, this figure seems high, although another list shows block production from Aug. 1, 1923, to July 31, 1924, ranging from 8122675 to 10266471, for 2,143,796 blocks built in the 12-month model year. And still another often accepted list shows 1924 vehicle production to be 1,749,827, but this may have included some foreign production.

Despite the sales drop, Ford's profits remained high and its expansion at both the River Rouge and satellite plants continued. Among the new corporate developments this year was the launching of the *HENRY FORD II* and the *BENSON FORD*, two huge lake freighters which went into service carrying raw materials from various ports to Ford's new River Rouge complex. Launched at Loraine, Ohio, and Ecorse, Mich., respectively, the ships were the largest diesel-driven freighters on the Great Lakes. They formed the base of what was to become the "Ford Navy," of cargo ships carrying items such as iron ore, coal, lumber, and other raw products to Ford's plants.

During the year also, the 10-millionth Model T was produced on June 4, 1924. A Touring Car, the vehicle was promptly lettered and shipped to New York, from where it was then driven to San Francisco over the Lincoln Highway, which was then the only completed coast-to-coast highway in the U.S. Today, this route would be basically the same as U.S. 30 and I-80.

Although profit was not a problem, in the corporate offices the decline in production did not go unnoticed, especially since other manufacturers, including an upstart General Motors make named Chevrolet, were pricing more modern and comfortable vehicles not too many hundred dollars above Ford's untouchable low prices. With the lower production and increasing competition in mind, Ford began a two-pronged attack. First there was an immediate and massive advertising campaign, including installment buying plans. Secondly, there was a secret but full-scale redesigning project which would result in the much more modern looking 1926 models. But for the coming 1925 season, ads and salesmanship would have to help hold the line.

Far less famous than its 10-millionth cousin is this 1924 Touring Car, whose only claim to fame is that it is wearing a special top manufactured by the Buob & Scheu Co. of Cincinnati. This top differed from the standard Ford fare in that all three door panels were attached to the door frames, and opened with the doors. The curtains were braced with wire rods, and formed a much more sturdy package for winter or inclement weather than did the regular Ford curtains, while the large celluloid panels gave much better visibility.

As always, the Runabout had its commercial applications. But in this case, the addition of a plumber's tool body seems a permanent fixture, and not a body that would be slid out for weekend pleasure driving. Because of the high body with its attached signboard, the top could no longer be lowered. Since there was no door on the left, neither the pipe rack nor the tool box on the running board would interfere with entry or exit. Many of the basic Runabouts went for such commercial applications, but since this model has demountable rims which were $20 extra, it probably also has the $65 electric package, which included the electric starting system and Ford battery and generator.

According to production records, the new Coupe was Ford's second most popular car, after the Touring Car. A total of 327,584 were reported built. But, because production records ran from Jan. 1 to Dec. 31, 1924, it is not known how many of these vehicles are considered 1924 or 1925 models. Regardless, since both models were identical, at least in this case, the argument is more or less academic. Featuring a totally new body, the Coupe entered the season at $525, and as did the open models, dropped $5 by mid-season. It weighed 1,760 pounds, and came complete with demountable rims and electric starting and lights. Early models did not have a visor as standard equipment, but offered this item as a $3 accessory. About mid-season the visor was included in the total price.

This photo gives a good look at the totally new coupe body, with its large integral trunk and its doors hinged at the A-pillar. This was Ford's first model to have an integral storage or cargo area, reached via a relatively large hinged deck panel. The rear bumper was an accessory, as Ford felt that the spare tire itself constituted enough protection for the back. Unusual on this car are the 5-lug demountable rims and what appears to be balloon tires. Ford began to offer balloon tires and varnished spoked wheels as accessory items in 1925, but they would be of the 4-lug variety. Also, 6-lug rims were used on the rear of the 1-ton truck chassis, but no reference can be found to 5-lug rims. Since this is an original photo, not a restored car, it is possible that the wheels and rims are a dealer-installed aftermarket item, as are the bumpers.

A totally new design for Ford was the Tudor Sedan, a companion to the Fordor and essentially a replacement for the old Centerdoor design. Entering the Ford picture in June, 1923, the style proved to be a popular one, and during calendar year 1924, accounted for 223,203 sales. It is not known how many of the 1923 calendar year production of 96,410 were the new Tudor model or how many of these were the old Centerdoor style. Priced at $590 initially, the Tudor dropped $10 by September. It weighed 1,875 pounds, and came complete with a full electric system and demountable rims. As did the Coupe, early models appeared without a visor, this item being installed by the dealer as a $3 accessory. Later in the season the visor would be a standard item on all closed cars. The right front seat folded for easy entry to the rear, but the left seat was stationary, as its base portion continued to cover the gas tank.

Although the body itself was a carryover from the Fordor introduced in November, 1922, as a 1923 style, the "new" 1924 Fordor did include the same frontal changes as enjoyed by the rest of the line. Sometime during the year, as a running change, the doors became all-steel, as opposed to the earlier doors which were constructed of aluminum panels over wooden frames. The new doors, assembled of steel stampings, were lighter, stronger, and of course, much cheaper than the old hand-assembled units. Still, the Fordor listed at 1,950 pounds, being Ford's heaviest car. Its price began the season at $685, later dropped to $660 complete. Interior light, roller shades on the rear and quarter windows, and brown broadcloth upholstery with dark brown striping and beige headliner completed the picture. Calendar year production reached 84,733. Note the open cowl vent, and the standard visor. Barely visible was a new accessory gaining great popularity–an inside rearview mirror.

Flags fluttering, this Fordor found itself in an unexpected role. It became the executive inspection car for the Detroit, Toledo & Ironton Railroad. No great conversion was necessary here. Simply remove the fenders and steering gear, add spacers and flanged wheels, install two flag holders and railroad lights on the rear, and the car was in business. Ford had purchased the bankrupt and failing D.T.&I. railroad in 1920, seeing in it another conveyance to move raw materials into the River Rouge plant. Through greatly improved management, upgraded roadbeds, and the purchase of much needed new equipment, the railroad was turned into a very solvent business—to the extent that it was purchased by the Pennsylvania Railroad in 1929 at a tremendous profit to Ford. Note the unusual cowl light, drilled through the A-pillar rather than installed on the cowl.

Built by the Derham Body Co. of Rosemont, Pa., for a Philadelphia customer who "appreciates the advantages of a small but dependable Town Car," this Model T reportedly cost over $5,000 when completed. Derham, who never was a low-buck body builder, lengthened the Ford chassis by 11.5 inches to a new 111.5-inch length in order to accommodate the longer tonneau section. The extended running boards were covered with white rubber and bound in brass, and were fitted with positions for dual sidemounts (being the first acknowledged Ford to wear these attractive fixtures). The new flared fenders, ala pre-1914, were of shiny black grain-dash leather, hand stitched over heavy wire frames. The radiator shell remained stock Ford, but the hood was lengthened eight inches and flared into a custom cowl. The entire car, including the open chauffeur's compartment, was upholstered in Radel's Blue Turkish Velvet, with blue broadcloth on the headliner and panels. The tonneau or coupe section was finished in blue-black with a black leather functional landau quarter, while the section forward of the B-pillar was in black. Special 6-lug wheels were in Primrose Pink with black striping, set off by whitewall tires. Because the gas tank was relocated aft of the rear axle, between the frame horns, some form of fuel pump was required. As an attention to detail, it was noted that the black leather of the upper bodyworks had all of the leather grail running parallel to the ground.

In this era, "Meritas" bodies enjoyed a kind of popularity. A French design, these bodies consisted of a canvas-type material stretched over a wooden frame. The advantages were supposedly light weight, less rattles, weather and rust resistance, and luxury appeal. Needless to say, though several custom companies produced "Meritas" bodies, few found their way onto Ford chassis. One that did was this example that appeared at the National Automobile Show at the Hotel Commodore in New York City. Produced by the Mengel Body Co. of Louisville, Ky., the full custom included a new radiator shell, higher custom hood, drum headlights, totally different fenders and running boards, disc wheels, trunk with spare tire carrier, and front and rear bumpers, in addition to a totally custom 4-door body with blanked rear quarter panels and dummy landau irons. Little information can be found about the products of the Mengel Body Co.

As usual, a good number of bare light chassis produced during calendar year 1924 became bases for various types of depot hack bodies that were being produced by a wide selection of established body builders, plus numerous carpenter and cabinet shops in many smaller cities. This is one of the mass produced units available through Ford dealers. Built by the Springfield Body Co. of Springfield, Mass., it differs from many of the other types by having a central aisle between the two removable center seats. Most other styles used a small aisle on the right of this seat. Called Body No. 364, this deluxe unit also featured a full-length forward quarter window and fully-framed swing-out windshield.

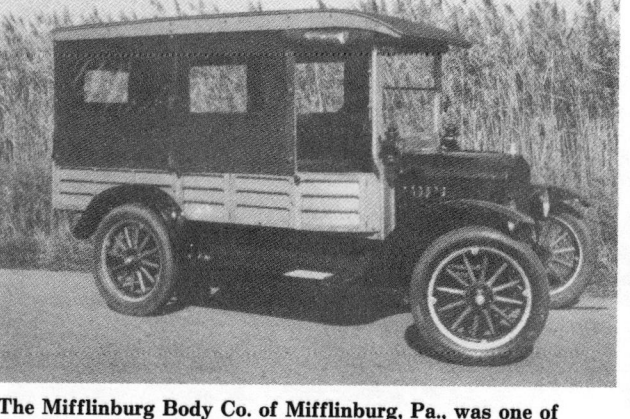

The Mifflinburg Body Co. of Mifflinburg, Pa., was one of the larger producers of depot hack bodies, available in all price ranges. This was one of the company's more economical models, with a non-framed plate glass windshield. The relatively basic side curtains contained large celluloid panels, as compared to some of the tiny panels on other curtains. This car wears the kerosene cowl lights which were still used by some owners, and which are dearly loved by today's restorers. Though certified as a 1924 chassis by Roaring 20s Autos of Wall, N.J., in 1971, this vehicle wears the optional varnished wood spoke wheels and balloon tires that did not become available through Ford dealers until the 1925 model year.

The Cantrell Suburban body for light Ford chassis was built by J.T. Cantrell & Co. of Huntington, N.Y. A comparatively expensive body, it featured a metal-framed windshield with a swing-out upper glass, plus armrests for the passengers. Using snob-appeal in its ads, Cantrell pointed out that its Suburbans made excellent auxiliary vehicles, and could be used in bad weather or when owners desired not to subject their limousines or touring cars to the elements. Weather protection was of roll-up side curtains, which probably were far less "snug" than implied in the advertising. Of the 47,901 light chassis produced this year, only 3,921 were of the basic variety with clincher rims and magneto ignition, showing that even owners of light commercial vehicles and depot hacks appreciated the convenience of electric starting and changeable tires. In basic form, the chassis first cost $230, while the fully-equipped version cost $295. Both dropped $5 in price by mid-season.

In later years, military production would make a substantial contribution to Ford's overall manufacturing program, but in this era, sales to the military were few and far between, and usually of an experimental nature. One such vehicle to put on a coat of olive drab was this scout car type of vehicle which apparently was constructed on a light chassis. The hood, radiator shell, fenders and running boards seem to be the only standard items on the car, with the fenders being well filled by the Chevrolet-like disc wheels and 6.20x21 tires. These probably gave better ground clearance and better flotation in soft ground than did the standard Ford 30x3.5 tires. Oddly, the spare was carried on the right side, which would have made access awkward, as front seat passengers would have to climb over the steering wheel and clutch lever. A half-tarp provided protection for the legs of both driver and passenger, but the upper bodies were left to the elements.

Another Model T experiment conducted by the Army's Ordinance Dept. in 1924 involved this car, fitted with an unidentified speedster body with a rumble seat. This marks one of the first recorded uses of a rumble seat by a Ford. Complete with pioneer tools on the apron, this car also wears the Chevrolet-like 6.20x21 disc wheels, and also carries its spare on the right side. Although Ford saw no need to equip his cars with bumpers, the military obviously saw the advantages of these accessories, and equipped all of their experimental scout and field cars with them.

1924

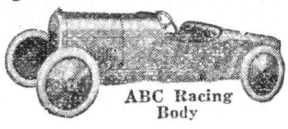

A Trim Looking Job

ONE of our good friends, Mr. W. E. Kraf[...] Box 149, Memphis, Tennessee, sends us th[...] picture of a speedster job which he has built an[...] which, in our opinion, is a very snappy, pleasi[...] looking product.

Says Mr. Krafft: "I am a constant reader [...] your magazine and certainly enjoy your ma[...]

articles. I have just completed this little rac[...] I have not concentrated my best efforts on t[...] motor, yet, but I expect to have a fast wag[...] when I do. I am going to use Fronty equipme[...] At the present time it is more of a speeds[...] than a racer."

There is an aristocratic look to this prod[...] of the south and its lines suggest real speed p[...] sibilities.

The day of the backyard-built speedster was far from over. These ads from a 1924 issue of *FORD OWNER & DEALER* indicate that a very healthy market was still available to those dealers who wanted to stock such bodies. As can be noted, the styles ranged from simple open-wheel racing type bodies to rather attractive roadsters. Also to be noted is the fact that not one illustration shows standard Ford wheels. The discs shown could either be complete wheels or simply metal pans that fitted over the standard spoke wheels, and supposedly gave a more "modern" appearance to the car.

1925

Among some automotive circles, it was rumored that a "new" Model T was to make its appearance. Adding fuel to these rumors was the growing popularity of competitive makes, which though not knocking down Ford's empire by any means, were certainly nibbling away at prospective sales. Among these competitive aces was Chevrolet, which true or not, claimed a half-million sales for 1925. This was slightly more than a quarter of Ford's annual car production, but it was still 500,000 more non-Ford vehicles on the road. Hudson was also in there with its popular and inexpensive Essex, which recorded sales of almost a quarter-million, while Willys, Buick and Dodge each had over 200,000 sales to "Ford buyers who now wanted something better." The house had not yet fallen, but writing was seen on the walls.

But, if these indications were obvious to many both within and outside of Ford's compound, Henry himself did not seem too concerned. True, a "new" Model T was on the drawing boards, but there seemed no hurry to bring it out. It would come out, but in July, 1925, and listed as a 1926 model. For the 1925 model year, which can be roughly figured to run from July 24, 1924, to July, 1925, the cars were virtually unchanged from the 1924 models.

Only one new model emerged during this time, and probably should not even be included in this book. It was strictly a commercial vehicle, and actually did not appear until March, 1925. This was the new Roadster Pickup, which essentially was the Runabout with a factory-installed pickup bed in place of the old turtle deck. For some reason, Ford kept its pickup production separate from that of the Runabout, and it is covered in this book only because it really is more car than truck, utilizing all automobile components as opposed to one-ton TT components.

The other major change in this year's vehicles involved an accessory, not a standard item. That was the availability of varnished-spoke wheels and demountable rims for balloon 4:40x21 tires. The varnished wheels and balloon tires could either be purchased as a package, or independently. Using only 32-pounds pressure, as opposed to the 80-pounds in the old 3.0 or 3.5x30 tires, the new balloons gave a much improved ride. Along with the introduction of these tires was a new 5-to-1 steering ratio, which first became available only when the balloon tire option was ordered. Later, this ratio became optional on all models, and later still it became standard. It is also believed that the initially optional hand-operated windshield wiper went through the same transition from option early in the year to standard fare by model year end. Some references mention the availability of nickel-plated radiator shells, but it now appears that this was caused by confusion with the 1926 closed models, which came out in July, 1925, with nickeled shells.

Mechanically, virtually every change was on a run-

ning basis, as previous supplies ran out. Some of these changes may have occurred on 1924 cars, some on 1925, and a few late enough to fall into the 1926 year. Among these modifications were new "quick-change" transmission bands with removable ears; lighter weight connecting rods; a longer oil pan; a new oiler tube and funnel, and new metal body sills for the open cars, again reducing the amount of wood used in the bodies.

For once, prices remained the same for the entire model year, with the basic Runabout listing at $260. This would be the lowest price ever recorded for a brand-new full-size American car, albeit one that had to be cranked. With electric starting and demountable rims, it cost $85 more. The Touring Car also enjoyed a low price advantage, with the basic model going for $290, while the equipped car cost $375. Some material would indicate that this was the last year that any Ford could be purchased without starter or demountable rims, but other Ford information would indicate that such "basic" vehicles could still be obtained via special factory order through 1926. If so, the starter and rims were probably a "delete" option.

New on the open car scene was the aforementioned Roadster Pickup, which sold for $281 in basic form or $366 fully equipped. The light chassis, complete with front end sheet metal, was priced at $225 in basic form, or $290 equipped. In the closed car ranks, the popular Coupe was priced at $520, the Tudor at $580, and the Fordor at $660.

As pointed out in previous chapters, production figures really are meaningless insofar as model-year cars go, because the production was tallied on a Jan. 1 to Dec. 31 basis, while the model-year cars are considered to be those built between July 1, 1924, and June 30, 1925. Still, for want of any other figures, these are presented for comparison with other years and with other makes.

As always, the Touring Car fared the best with sales of 691,212, of which 64,399 were still ordered with magneto ignition and clincher rims. Also, this was a drop of 81,890 from the 1924 figures, and 1924 represented a drop of over 150,000 from 1923. Clearly, the Touring Car, though still the most popular model in America, was beginning to loose its appeal to closed vehicles.

Second in the production tally was the Coupe, which recorded 343,969 builds. This was 16,385 above the 1924 figure and over 30,000 above the 1923 total. In third place was the Runabout, with 298,642 units produced. Of these, 34,206 were still in basic form, while the rest were fully equipped. Surprisingly, Runabout production was up by over 34,000 units, and this did not even include the Roadster Pickup, which accounted for 33,795 more units leaving the factory. At this point there seems no logical explanation for the rise in Runabout production as opposed to the fall in Touring Car sales.

Also down in production were the two sedans, with

the Tudor dropping to 195,001 sales, for a loss of over 28,000, and the Fordor recording only 81,050 builds, for a loss of 3,683. The Fordor's loss doesn't look like too much until one remembers that the 1924 production reflected a whopping drop of 60,000 units from the 1923 figures.

Engine numbers more accurately reflect the model year production as these ran from Aug. 1, 1924, to July 27, 1925. These show the blocks starting with number 10266472 and ending at 12218728, for total production of 1,952,256 engines. Of course, not all of these were car blocks, as many went into the 1-ton trucks and others were for routine replacement. This figure was only 30,000 below the model year 1924 mark, compared with the calendar year body production which was 17,153 below the 1924 mark. As mentioned, these figures were far from being considered a disaster, but those in charge did not like the trend, and action would be taken in 1926.

Despite the downturn, Ford did manage to turn out its 11-millionth car in January, 1925, and its 12-millionth model in June, 1925.

On the corporate side, activities were as fast paced as ever. Overseas, new plants were opened in Yokohama, Japan; Asnieres, France, and Geelong (Melbourne), Australia. In the U.S., new assembly plants were opened in Louisville, Ky., and St. Paul, Min., while a new engineering facility began operations at Dearborn.

Insofar as Henry Ford went, it seems like this was his year to play with airplanes. On Jan. 25, 1925, Ford airport was opened in Dearborn, and in April, Ford Airlines inaugurated its first scheduled commercial flights between Dearborn, Chicago, and Cleveland. The planes were Stout Model 2-ATs, built at Ford Airport. In August, 1925, Ford bought the Stout Co., making it a division of Ford Motor Co.

Probably more interesting than this year's Model T issue, the single-engine Stout 2-AT is credited with being the first all-metal commercial aircraft to be built and flown on scheduled flights in the U.S. Called the "Pullman," the plane was designed by William B. Stout, who later designed Ford's famous tri-motor. The original 2-AT used a single 400 HP Liberty motor, carried a pilot and four to six passengers, depending on weight. It could cruise at 116 MPH at 10,000 feet, with a range of 500 miles. The famous Ford Tri-motor was born when Stout redesigned the Pullman, added three 200-HP Wright Whirlwind engines in place of the single Liberty, and came up with one of the most famous early airliners of all times.

Ford's only new vehicle for 1925 really shouldn't even be in this book. Also, it barely makes it into the 1925 chapter. The new kid was the Roadster Pickup, which was essentially the Runabout with a factory installed pickup bed rather than a turtle deck. Since Crestline/Motorbooks International has published James K. Wagner's excellent book on Ford's commercial vehicles, only those early units which are really more car than truck will be included in this volume. And, of course, that lets in the new pickup. As was the Runabout, the Roadster Pickup was available in either basic form, for $281, or with electric starter and battery and demountable rims, as shown here, for $366. Introduced in March, 1925, it recorded 33,795 calendar-year sales, but most of these would be of the 1926 variation. It is not known how many were built in 1925 form between its March birth and the end of the Model year in July. Interestingly, the Runabout sold for $260 in basic form, which included the turtle deck. For another $25, a slip-in pickup bed could be purchased from a Ford dealer. Thus, for $285 a buyer could have a car with both turtle deck and pickup bed, while the plain pickup (same bed) cost $281. It would seem that the extra $4 would be a much better investment, but apparently many buyers did not see it that way.

This Detroit produce hauler shows how the new Roadster Pickup looked in working trim. Actually, the official name of this vehicle was "Runabout With Pickup Body," but its popular title quickly became "Roadster Pickup" or just plain "Pickup." The all-steel, slide-in body was 56 inches long, 40.75 inches wide, and 13 inches deep, and came complete with an adjustable swing-down tailgate. When purchased as a Pickup, rather than as a Runabout, it was equipped with a 9-leaf rear spring, which certainly would have helped in carrying such loads as shown here. The top was the same as used on the Runabout, and could be lowered, though doing such would drastically reduce the cargo area because of the folded top's overhang.

Retaining its title as Ford's most popular model was the Touring Car. However, its production this year was down to 691,212, which was a drop of 81,890 from the 1924 figures, and 232,000 from the 1923 calendar year production. Again, since Ford's production totals were kept on a calendar-year basis, which would take in half of the 1925 model year and half of the 1926 year, it is really impossible to tell how well the 1925 touring Car actually fared. Of the amount built, 64,399 were still in basic form, without electric starter or demountable rims. They cost $290 as opposed to a fully equipped version which went for $375.

Although most restorers like their cars to look older, not newer in years, Charles Van Ooteghem of Sterling Heights, Mich., almost turned his 1925 Touring Car into what at a quick glance would pass for a 1926 version. The car sports wire wheels that gained a fair amount of popularity in the 1926-27 era, plus has accessory bumpers, and a non-Ford paint color. This was the last year that the Touring Car would have only three doors. When the new 1926 models arrived, both the Touring and the Runabout would have driver doors for the first time since 1911.

Looking as if he would much rather have been somewhere else, this mid-1920s traveler was caught in some unnamed western stream. The assortment of luggage, 1925 Illinois license plate, and far-western scenery all indicate that this was no Sunday drive. Although travel conditions in the U.S. were getting better, and many states now claimed hundreds of miles of paved roads, there were still large gaps in the map where the long-distance traveler would have to fend for himself. The luggage stored against the spare tire would indicate that the turtle deck was probably filled with such necessities as extra gas, oil, grease, and an assortment of tools and spare parts.

Showing off Ford's new optional balloon tires is this little Runabout, which in any comparative form, was Ford's lowest priced car. In fact, in basic form, with hand cranking and clincher rims, it sold for $260, which was the lowest price ever recorded for a brand new full-size American car. However, the owner of this factory fresh model probably paid the extra $65 for the electric starter and accompanying battery, generator, and electric wiring. Regular demountable rims with 30x3.5 tires cost an additional $20, while the new balloon tires (4.4x21) cost $25 extra. The new tires used only 32 pounds of pressure, as opposed to the 70 or 80 pounds used in the standard tires. Of the 298,642 Runabouts built during calendar year 1925, a total of 34,206 were still sold in basic form, with the remaining 264,436 being fully equipped. Note that the demountable rim package included a spare tire carrier, but not the spare tire.

Mamma and children take a stroll in a Michigan woods after driving there in their new $520 Coupe. Despite the limited seating of coupes and roadsters, it is surprising how popular these two styles were in this era, even among families with children. Calendar year production of the Coupe was 343,969, which placed the car as Ford's second most popular style. This figure was 16,385 above the 1924 calendar year production and over 30,000 above the 1923 total, clearly indicating a preference for this body style. It weighed 1,760 pounds.

From the side, the Coupe displayed less of the "telephone booth on wheels" appearance that it had in previous years. This model shows two new accessories available this year—the 4.40x21 balloon tires and varnished spoke wheels. Although many restorers (including the author) have converted the plain black spoke wheels of early Ts to the much more attractive varnished wood, no Model T prior to 1925 should be fitted with anything but black spokes, except of course for aftermarket discs, wires, or demountables.

Ford's new ad campaign tried to show family situations involving the enjoyment of a Ford car, such as Mamma taking child and friend to the park for the afternoon. With sales slipping to such upcoming makes as Chevrolet and Essex, Ford no longer could complacently rely on its long-established reputation. Still, Fordor production sagged to 81,050 for the calendar year. Officially, the 1,950-pound car was listed at $660, but this ad, from a July, 1924, issue of *GOOD HOUSEKEEPING* (the start of the 1925 season) lists the car at $685 f.o.b. Detroit. Likewise, it lists the Tudor $10 higher than the factory list, and the Coupe $5 higher. Still, the closed cars offered quite a bit for the money, including electric starter and lighting; along with a Ford battery; lockable doors; floor rugs; dome light; revolving-type window lifts; visor; ventilator on the cowl, and at dealer option, rearview mirror and hand-operated windshield wiper. Considering the price, upholstery in two-tone broadcloth was surprisingly good and durable.

Enjoying its share of popularity was the 2-door Sedan, or Tudor. The word had no reference to the British "Tudor" but simply was a logical accompanying name to the coined "Fordor." Calendar year production for this model totalled 195,001, with no possibility of telling how many were in 1925 guise or how many were 1926 models. Priced at $580, the car weighed 1,875 pounds, complete with electric starting and demountable rims of the 3.5x30 size. Balloon tires and larger rims were a $25 option.

Straying from his automotive interests, Henry Ford this year began to play with airplanes. On Jan. 15, 1925, the Ford Airport was opened at Dearborn, and in April, Ford Airlines inaugurated scheduled commercial flights between Chicago, Cleveland, and Dearborn. The planes used were Stout 2-AT models, designed and built at Ford Airport by William B. Stout. So impressed was Ford by the plane's performance, that in August, 1925, he bought the company, making it a division of Ford Motor Co. The initial 2-ATs used 400 HP Liberty engines and could carry a pilot plus four to six passengers. In 1926 the 3-AT was developed, which was the first of Ford's famous line of Tri-motors.

1925

Chugging around Dearborn's Greenfield Village as a tourist attraction was this 1925 T fitted with accessory wire wheels and wearing an older version York body. Working a full day, each and every summer day, the little hack proved the continuing reliance of the Model T design. In addition to providing a historic atmosphere, it also gave thousands of tourists their only chance to ride in a real Model T. York bodies were produced in York, Pa., and were a relatively popular commercial grade hack body.

During calendar year 1925, Ford turned out a total of 59,973 light chassis for the depot hack light truck trade. Despite the downturn in car production, at least this figure showed an increase, being over 12,000 above the calendar 1924 total. Surprisingly, of these 6,523 were in basic form, which was not quite double the amount of basic chassis turned out the year before. Fully equipped, as was this model, the chassis cost $290 and weighed 1,210. This version is wearing a Springfield No. 364 body, and has its side curtains down for inclement weather. A rather deluxe body, this model featured four functional doors, all hinged on the B-pillar, plus a forward quarter window and fully framed, swing-out windshield. The curtains carried moderate size celluloid panes. The design of the forward roof and its visor adds a nice touch to this body style.

In 1924 there was a Derham custom on a Ford chassis. This year, Fleetwood came up with this interesting 5-passenger special-order sedan, mounted on a modified Model T chassis. Built, of all things, in centerdoor style, the car carried not only a special body, but also custom radiator and shell, hood, fenders, running boards, lights, and wheels. The windshield was a sloping 2-piece unit, equipped with visor and windshield wiper. All six side windows could be lowered via "Perfect" rotary window regulators. The doors were hinged on the C-pillar, latching at the front. The front seats were bucket types, with the driver's being stationary, and the passenger's being of the folding type, able to store against the dash when not in use. Upholstery throughout was in a patent wool cloth with a distinctive pattern called Wiese's Gray Snakeskin. Finish was in Fleetwood Light Blue, with a black upper structure, moldings, fenders, and aprons. The wheels were in Fleetwood Blue also, with gold striping. Nickel plating was used on the radiator shell, lights and wheel hubs. Fleetwood referred to this style as its "Clear Vision Body," noting that the door placement allowed a very thin A-pillar which would not obstruct the driver's vision.

More in line with Ford prices, but far removed from the Fleetwood custom, was this custom coupe offered by the Columbia Body Co. of Detroit. Priced at $525, completely assembled and including the Ford chassis with electric starting and demountable rims, the car was designed for salesmen or professional people, with emphasis on funeral directors. The 2-passenger car had a relatively large storage area behind the seats, accessible from either inside the car or from the rear via the deck lid. The doors, hinged at the rear, were equipped with rotary window regulators, but it is not known if the quarter windows used straps or rotary regulators. The rear and rear quarter panels were covered in a black leatherette, as was the top and visor. When offered to the funeral trade, the car was called a "Special First Call Car." Remember, these were the days when most funerals were held in the home of the deceased, and in all but a few cases, the entire job of body preparation (which took quite a bit of equipment) had to be done on the premises. Therefore, a funeral director had to have a vehicle large enough to carry his equipment with him, in a vehicle that still gave a presentable appearance in front of someone's home. In the other market, regular traveling salesmen must have appreciated the large and easily accessible storage area combined with the Ford's dependability.

1926

In a last ditch effort to keep ahead of competition while steadfastly retaining a "recognizable" Model T, Ford came up with one of its most extensive redesign projects ever staged since the introduction of the Model T in the first place.

With the exception of the Fordor, all models had brand new, longer, lower all-steel bodies. Closed cars had nickeled radiator shells and choices of colors. Open cars got operational doors on the driver's side. Later, all got optional wire wheels and optional "sport packages." Initially, sales soared. But, they soon began to decline again as potential buyers discovered that the critics had been right all along when they described the car as "the same tired old horse under a new blanket."

Even Ford himself, in a directive to dealers mailed about June, 1925, urged them not to tell the people that this was a "NEW" car. He noted that the word "NEW" would imply redesigned chassis, engine and running gear, while in reality, these were essentially the same as they had been since 1908. This fact, the letter pointed out, should be used as a strong selling point—that the car was still the same dependable and economical machine that it had always been.

What was totally new was its appearance. Even the least changed model, the Fordor, benefitted from the new radiator shell, longer hood with a whole collection of louvers, and smoother cowl line. The new fenders also helped, being larger and wider. They now extended closer to the ground both front and rear, and blended more fully with the wider running boards. All models became lower by 1.5 inches because of the new chassis height. Aside from this, the Fordor retained its old 1923 body, and was the only model to keep its fuel tank under the driver's seat.

Both the Coupe and the Tudor had totally new bodies, sharing the A-pillar and cowl unit. These A-pillars now held a 1-piece plate glass windshield, hinged at the top and opening forward. In these and the open cars, the gas tank was now located under the cowl, within the passenger compartment, but with the filler neck situated under a small door where the old cowl vent was located on previous closed models. On the Fordor only, this door was still an operational vent.

The rear deck of the Coupe was now full-width and integral, with the fenders bolted directly to the sides. The rear deck compartment was wider, longer, and deeper, and now extended over the rear frame horns. Its lid was connected at the top by concealed hinges, while an automatic catch held it open. The seats in both the Coupe and the Tudor were 2.5 inches lower than previously, and the Coupe now had a larger package shelf behind its seat. The Tudor, meanwhile gained two newly styled front seats, both of which would tilt out of the way.

In height, the Tudor was now four inches lower from its top to the road, while the Coupe and both open cars were 4.5 inches lower. The Coupe, Tudor, and Touring Car were all 3.5 inches longer, while the Runabout grew 7.75 inches.

Although both the Touring Car and the Runabout had brand new bodies, it was the Runabout that changed the most. The car now had two operational doors, and though its body was still divided into two sections (coupe or seating compartment and rear or turtle deck) the deck was no longer an easily removable bolt-on unit. Now it was virtually an integral part of the car. Similar to the deck of the Coupe, it was full-width and had the fenders bolted directly to its sides. The double-panel lid was similar in design to that of the Coupe, and gave access to a much larger and deeper storage compartment, described as both waterproof and dustproof.

The Touring Car also got a new body, with its doors and lowered height being its main claim to fame. Like the Runabout, the Touring Car now had a functional door for the driver, plus its rear doors were now forward hinged. Thus, the rear doors on the Fordor were the only doors on any Ford that still opened to the front.

Upholstery on the open cars continued to be in patented Ford Leather Cloth, black of course, while new upholstery material was used in the closed cars. In the Fordor, this was of gray material with a red stripe and gray floor carpeting with red flecks. Gray silk roller shades were provided on the rear and rear quarter windows. The Coupe and Tudor used a similar material but the design had a green stripe and green fleck in the carpet. These cars had gray silk roller shades on the rear windows only.

The big news for many was that for the first time colors were available. At first the open cars came in black only, with the Coupe and Tudor in green and the Fordor in maroon. By mid-summer, all closed cars could be ordered in either green or maroon, and not too long after this, gray was added to the list of options. At this time, open cars became available in gunmetal blue or brown. All models continued to use black fenders and aprons, while the open models used a black radiator shell. Later, the nickel shell became an extra-cost option on the open cars. All cars also gained the prestige of having nickel headlight rims.

Wheels are a bit of a puzzle. Reports indicate that early in the season, open cars still came with the old 30x3.5 clincher rims unless the extra-cost demountable rims were ordered. Likewise, the 30x3.5 demountable rims were standard on the closed cars unless the 21x4.5 demountable balloon tires were ordered. Supposedly all cars had black wood spoke wheels unless varnished spokes were ordered, and these supposedly were available only with the balloon tires. The puzzle comes with reports that it wasn't until January, 1926, that the optional wire wheels became available. Yet, an early Ford catalog, issued about June or July, 1925, clearly shows the open cars with the optional "sport package" consisting of wire wheels among other things, and a later full-line catalog shows all models fitted with the "sport package" including wire wheels. The question is whether there were such wheels available as a factory option before January, 1926. These wheels, incidentally, were only available in Casino Red for the maroon cars; vermillion or light green for the green cars, and yellow or black for the black cars. As more colors materialized during the year, the wheel colors became optional to the buyers.

Despite all of these changes, the "new" Ford really was the same tired old horse. The new bodies and fenders weighed more, so therefore new and larger brakes had to be installed. The rear wheel brakes, operated by the hand lever, increased from 8 to 11 inches in diameter, and the width went from 1-5/32 to 1.5 inches. The transmission brake band, operated by the right foot pedal, was increased in width from 1-1/8 to 1.75 inches. Also, the left and right pedals themselves changed and were now further apart, wider, and had flanges on the outer ends.

But, despite the fact that attention was paid to making the cars stop better, no thought was given to making them perform better. Virtually nothing was changed on the running gear, except for the relocation of the coil box. Thus, the comparatively underpowered Ford was now even more listless with its heavier outer structure. What might have been a snappy little performer 10 years earlier was now relegated to the back row in the performance department of the mid-1920s. True, for average usage, the car was probably fast enough to keep up with most other light cars. But no one in his right mind would race his stock Ford against a Chevrolet, Whippet, or Essex, and expect to win. And even in 1926, few Americans wanted to have the slowest car on the block, no matter how dependable or economical or world famous that car might be. The big problem was to convince Henry Ford of the merits of this argument.

But as the model year first began, there was sufficient interest in the "new" car, and few concessions were made to sales. As the year wore on, however, and sales began to slip, price adjustments and "free" accessories made their way into the dealerships. Oddly, while the closed cars received a mid-season reduction in prices, the open cars were given a price increase, probably to help offset the reduction on the closed models. Also, during the year, the special order open models without demountable rims, starters, or generators were dropped completely. These cars had been priced at $290 for the

Touring Car; $260 for the Runabout; $281 for the Roadster Pickup, and $225 for the bare chassis. Production figures were not kept on these basic models, but it is safe to assume they were minuscule or they would not have been dropped.

In the fully equipped ranks, the Touring Car started out at $375 but rose to $380 by mid-season, while the Runabout began at $345 and went up to $360. The Roadster Pickup went from $366 to $380, and the bare chassis rose from $290 to $300. In the closed car ranks, the Fordor dropped from $660 to $545, while the Tudor went from $580 to $495 and the Coupe declined from $520 to $485.

For a change, production figures reflect the model-year production, running from July 27, 1925, to July 30, 1926. These, then, would overlap with the previous year's figures, which ran from Jan. 1, to Dec. 31, 1925, and included over 50% of the 1926 production. But, for the model year, Ford turned out 1,502,018 cars in 1926 trim. Of these, the most popular remained the Touring Car, with 364,409 units produced, closely followed by the Runabout, with 342,575 units. Running not too far behind the Runabout was the Coupe with 288,342 copies. The Tudor claimed 270,331 builds, while the Fordor remained the least popular with 102,732. Two units that arguably might not belong in this book are the Roadster Pickup with 75,406 units and the bare light chassis with 58,223 examples delivered.

Engine serial numbers for this period began with 12218729 and ended with 14049029, for a total of 1,830,300 blocks, which included truck engines and replacement units. For the 1926 calendar year, these numbers ran from 12990077 to 14619254, for a total of 1,629,177 blocks.

Although the overall impact of the new Ford was not that strong, in other endeavors, Ford was making headlines. In the aviation field, Ford's airlines began to carry the nation's first commercial airmail, and also began to use the nation's first radio navigation system. Development of the new tri-motor by Ford's Stout Metal Airplane division was delayed by a mysterious fire in the plane's hanger at Ford Airport, but work picked up again, and on June 11, 1926, the first Tri-Motor made its initial flight. Called the Model 4-AT-A, the craft was quickly certified by the CAA, and production began. Powered by three Wright J-4 Whirlwind engines, and priced at $65,000, the plane could carry 11 passengers plus pilot and mechanic or co-pilot. A total of 14 were built this year.

On the corporate side, the year saw the opening of two new major factories, one at Chester, Pa., and the other at Ploetzensee, Germany. Ford was now operating 60 plants in the U.S. and 28 overseas.

1926

Ford widely advertised its Runabout as America's lowest priced full size car, costing but $260. Although some Runabouts were probably sold at that figure, by now the vast majority of buyers wanted self starting, a full electric system, and demountable rims with balloon tires. These all upped the f.o.b. Detroit price to $345 at the start of the model year, and to $360 by mid-season. Still priced $150 below a comparable Chevrolet Roadster, now its main competitor, the Ford Runabout was still able to pull 342,575 orders during the model year. The totally new body styling is most evident in the large rear section, which promised "dust and waterproof" storage for packages. Open cars continued to use a 2-piece ventilating windshield with the old 50-cent hand wiper now a complimentary dealer item. Newly designed side curtains now opened with BOTH doors, since drivers of open cars finally had operating doors on the left side. The car weighed 1,655 pounds.

Adding confusion to the reports that it wasn't until January, 1926, that wire wheels became available as an option is this early catalog, issued in the late spring of 1925, which shows all models with wire wheel options. Also confusing is the fact that Ford showed its open cars all decked out in what appeared to be a "sport package," leading to the belief that such "packages" were available. Actually, these so-called sport models were simply a collection of dealer installed accessories. On the early open cars, black was the only color available, and the radiator shells were also painted black. Later, open models could be ordered in Gunmetal Blue or Phoenix (light) Brown, and nickel plated radiator shells could be purchased as an option. Shown from the early catalog is this "sport" model, wearing the new pneumatic windshield wiper at $3.50; a fawn top boot at $5; Gipsy side curtains at $3 a pair; nickeled bumpers at $15 a pair, wire wheels at $35 for a set of five, and an automatic stop light at $2.50.

Making good use of the new operational front door of the Touring Car, this lass is prepared to take family or friends for a spin. Still Ford's most popular car, the Touring drew 364,409 orders during the model year. Prices, including balloon tires, demountable rims, self starter and full electric system, began at $375 but rose to $380 at mid-season. A totally restyled vehicle, the new all-steel body of the Touring Car was 3.5 inches longer than its 1925 offering, though its wheelbase remained 100 inches. Likewise, the new suspension combined with the body design resulted in the car being 4.5 inches lower from its raised top to the road. In base form, the Touring weighed 1,633 pounds, while fully equipped it went at 1,738 pounds.

A mid-season factory photo shows the Touring Car with two popular options, wire wheels at $35 a set, and a colored body, either in Gunmetal (light) Blue or Phoenix (light) Brown. For the first half of the season, open cars were available in black only, but once the new color choices became available, black took a definite drop in popularity. Still, fenders and aprons of all cars were done in black, while the radiator shells and windshield posts of open cars were also finished in black, as were the interiors. The upholstery on these cars was in black artificial leather with a pebble grain finish. Side curtains now had four operating door panels, making entry much easier in wet or cold weather. Note that all doors are now forward hinged.

Although it is doubtful that too many were sold, Ford continued to advertise its basic open cars, noting that the Touring Car could still be obtained at $290 complete. Of course, complete did not include the balloon tires or demountable rims shown in the accompanying illustration, nor did it include an electric starter, generator, or full electric system. This was the final year for such basic models. By 1927 all cars had self starters and demountable rims or wire wheels. By mid-season, in fact, the basic Ford was no longer advertised, and possibly not available.

Ford's most popular closed car was the Coupe, which drew 288,342 orders. The 1,860-pound car was priced at $520 at the start of the season, but dropped to $485 at mid-year as Ford tried to enhance sales through price reductions. At first available only in dark green, the car could also be ordered in maroon or gray after mid-year. Sporting a totally new body, the Coupe now offered an integral trunk with vast (for the era) storage space. This compartment now extended over the rear frame horns, and was full-body width, having the rear fenders bolted directly to the sides. The new dust and waterproof deck lid was connected by concealed hinges and featured an automatic locking bar to hold it open. Also new was the 1-piece windshield, hinged at the top. When captured during a show years ago, this nicely restored car belonged to Donald Pendock of Newaygo, Mich.

Shown partially restored in the author's barn in Illinois during the early 1970s is this 1926 Tudor, the third Model T in the author's roster of cars. The visor is still awaiting installation, but at this point the interior has been redone—though not in the original gray with green stripe material that was impossible to find at that time. With the gas tank now under the cowl, both front seats were of the tilting type, making access to the rear seat possible from either side. Previously, all access to the rear had to be from the right side, as the driver's seat was over the gas tank and could not move. The new tank location also made it possible to adjust the driver's seat for leg room, although in a Model T that was always limited for the 6-foot 3-inch frame of the author.

At first the popular Tudor was available only in the same dark green, called Channel Green, as used on the Coupe. Then, by mid-season, it too was offered in maroon or gray. Weighing 1,972 pounds, the Tudor began the year at $580, but dropped to $495 at mid-season as Ford attempted to stem its diminishing sales. Still, model-year production of the Tudor reached 270,331. As did all models except the Fordor, the totally new Tudor featured its gas tank under the cowl, with the filler located under the small vent-like door. Both the Coupe and Tudor shared the same 1-piece windshield, hinged at the top, and the same A-pillars. The padded visor with its four visible support ribs, was standard on all closed cars. The new body was 4 inches lower and 3.5 inches longer than the 1925 version, while the seats were 2.5 inches lower from the top to the floor.

The only model to have a holdover body was the Fordor. Still, the new lower suspension did bring the car down 1.5 inches from the previous model. Weighing 2,004 pounds, it was the only Ford to exceed the one-ton mark. Initially priced at $660, its cost dropped to $545 at mid-season as sales lagged. Model year production was 102,732, making it the least popular of all models. At the start of the year, it was available in maroon only, but at mid-season it picked up the same dark green as used on the other closed cars, and also the newly introduced gray. Seating remained the same as in the previous models, but the interior was now finished in gray upholstery with a fine red stripe, while the carpets were in gray with red flecks. The headliner was in solid gray, and the shades on the rear and rear quarter windows were of gray silk. When photographed years ago, this fine example belonged to William Hanson of Rockville, Md.

The interior of the Fordor Sedan remained the same as it had in previous years, except that its upholstery was now gray with red stripes rather than beige with brown striping. The red striping was selected to match the maroon finish, which initially was the only color available on the Fordor. Likewise, upholstery in both the Coupe and Tudor was gray with green stripes to match the dark green finish of those cars. What is not clear is whether the upholstery colors were changed to match the exterior finish when all closed cars could be ordered in any of three different exterior shades. All Fordors were equipped with a dome light and silk roller shades on the rear and rear quarter windows, while the Coupe and Tudor simply had a dash light and a single silk roller shade on the rear window. All closed cars now had windshield wipers and rearview mirrors as standard equipment, but a rear brake-activated stop light was still a $2.50 accessory.

Wire wheels were a definite improvement to open cars, but didn't seem to do much for the already top heavy looking Fordor. Still, as the year progressed, more and more buyers were opting for the $35 accessory wheels, which were considered far more modern in appearance than the wood spokes. Also available this year were wood spoke wheels in natural finish, which at the time did not draw too much attention, but which are greatly admired by today's collectors. Since the Fordor retained its old body, it continued to be the only closed car to have a 2-piece windshield, and was the only Ford car not to have its gas tank in the cowl. The tank continued to live under the driver's seat, and thus the cowl door ahead of the windshield remained a functional vent. When photographed in the 1970s, this well restored model belonged to Thomas Beckwith of Canton, Ohio. Its only concession to owner preference is the non-standard pinstriping on the body sides.

Still more car than truck was the cute little Roadster Pickup, officially called "Runabout With Pickup Body." Priced at $365 at the start of the season, it too went up in cost to $380 as open car prices were raised to help offset the decrease in closed car costs. At the start of the year, this model also could be ordered in basic form, without demountable rims or electric starter package, for $280. Weighing 1,736, the little truck had a run of 75,406. Although the new Runabout rear made conversion to the truck a much more difficult job than with the old body style, as shown here, buyers could purchase the Runabout, and then for $25 additional, get the pickup bed. As with the Runabout, rear fenders now bolted directly to the bed. The pickup was available in dark green only, with black not being an available color.

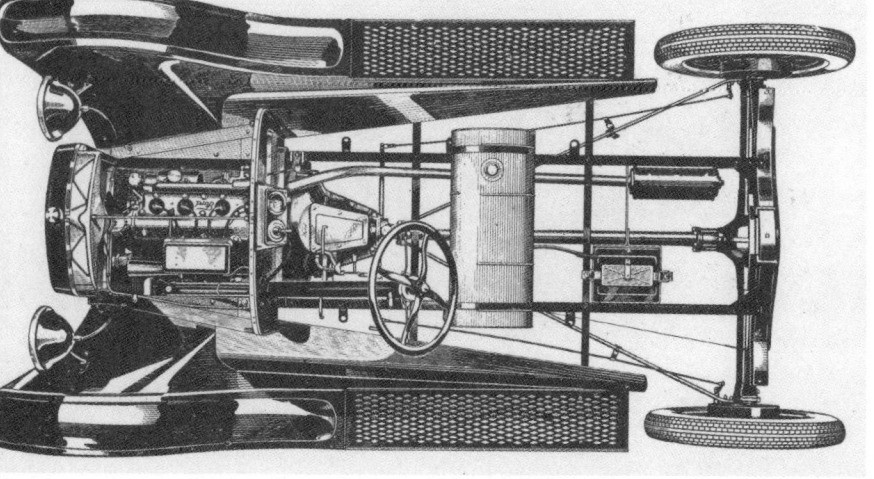

Still a major sales item in Ford's roster was the bare Commercial Chassis, which this year enjoyed a run of 58,223. As did other open models, the chassis too had a slight mid-year price increase, going from $290 to $300. In the early part of the season, it too was available in bare form for $225, but it is doubtful if very many were sold this way. This model is the fully equipped version, as proven by the rear-mounted battery box; dash-mounted ammeter; electric horn below the coil box, and generator and cut-out to the right of the block. Bare chassis were sold in the form shown here, except that they would have their hoods installed. Builders of depot hack bodies and light commercial delivery cars were the principal buyers of bare chassis, though a few really did go to custom body houses for special body units sometimes costing as much as 10 times or more the price of the bare chassis.

One of the multitude of buyers of bare Ford chassis was the Springfield Body Co. of Springfield, Mass. One of its products this year was the No. C-34 body, which was identical to the Suburban Body No. 6, produced by the Mifflinburg Body Co. of Mifflinburg, Pa. Of 3-door design, this body did not provide a front door on the driver's side. It's unusual 3-pane windshield, with swing-out upper portion and swing-in lower part, was typical of both Springfield and Mifflinburg. The company supplied similar bodies adaptable to such makes as Chevrolet, Star, Essex, and just about any other light chassis that might be available.

Although snowmobile conversions of this type were no longer all that unusual on Ford chassis, most of these units were now built from the 1-ton truck chassis rather than the light commercial version. But this model, produced by the Snow Flyer Corp. of New Holstein, Wis., not only used the light commercial chassis, but also the Runabout's forward section. In order to accommodate the double-trucked Ford axles, the chassis had to be greatly extended. A new pickup bed and fenders also had to be formed. On such conversions, the front axle of the double truck usually provided the motive power, while the rear axle was simply an idler unit. The company also made a conversion based on an unmodified Runabout. In this case, an auxiliary chassis was used at the rear instead of a frame extension. Such conversions cost between $165 and $250, plus extra cost items such as a Ruckstell Axle for $59; a Surlock Differential for $13.50, and a 44-tooth ring and 10-tooth pinion gear set for $20. The company also produced similar conversions for Chevrolet roadsters and light trucks.

Yes, some of the light commercial chassis actually were fitted with custom bodies. But not all of these were of the super expensive variety. This attractive convertible coupe body was produced by the Rex Co. to fill a need for a true convertible as yet to be offered by Ford. The top operated by functional landau irons, leaving the upright door frames in position. It is not known if these frames were removable with the top lowered. Wind-up windows were fitted in the doors, while the 1-piece windshield was hinged at the top, swinging outward from the cowl. It appears that Rex used its own cowl, matching it to the Ford hood and firewall. A nice 2-tone paint job completes the picture. The car is shown with the optional varnished wood spoke wheels, but probably could be ordered with wire wheels as well.

1926

First flown on June 11, 1926, was Ford's first tri-motor airplane, known as the 4-AT-A. Built by Stout Metal Airplane Division, located at Ford Airport in Dearborn, the plane incorporated three Wright J-4 Whirlwind engines. *Jane's* book of world aircraft claims that the plane could carry 11 passengers plus pilot and co-pilot, while other references state that it had eight-passenger capacity. Once certification was made by the CAA, production began on the $65,000 craft, and by year-end, a total of 14 had been delivered to various airlines. At this point, the plane was still an open cockpit affair, but later models would enclose the pilot and co-pilot within the cabin.

Modified Model Ts were running at small dirt track races all over the U.S., and were even active in some of the major events, even though the company was giving them no official backing. For example, in 1924, the three Fronty-Fords entered at Indianapolis were still running at the end of the race, placing 14th, 16th and 17th. In 1925, however, only one Fronty-Ford was entered, and after 33 laps it was retired due to transmission troubles. This year, the Chevrolet Bros., who produced the Frontenac conversions, entered the only Ford in the race. A novel front-wheel drive machine, it completed only 23 laps before a broken connecting rod forced it out. Not to be outdone on the other side of the Atlantic, a German racer by the name of Gustav Munz won his class at the then-famed Eiffel Cup race in his heavily modified Model T. Shown here rounding a tight turn on the dirt track, the car used a modified French head and a 5-speed sliding gear transmission, not really stock components. The wheels and axles with front brake drums are interesting also, but at least the radiator shell appears to be stock.

Louis and Arthur Chevrolet, who gave their names to the car that became Ford's most competitive rival, had walked out of the Chevrolet Motor Co. in a fit of rage in 1913. They quickly moved to Indianapolis, where they founded the Frontenac Motor Co., after learning that their own name remained the property of the Chevrolet Motor Co. For several years, the brothers built only racing cars, trading on their reputations as top-flight racing drivers and engineers. By 1921 the brothers had a chance to enter into car production. But, the well designed but expensive Frontenac came onto a rather depressed market and within two years was into bankruptcy. A good part of this failure was due to stock manipulations of New York and Indiana investors, with the unwitting Chevrolets caught in the middle. By 1925 the Frontenac company was dead, and the brothers picked up their own name and formed the Chevrolet Bros. Mfg. Co. of Indianapolis. Apparently by this time, General Motors had lost the restriction on the use of the Chevrolet name, or had grown too large to give a darn. Continuing to market under the Frontenac name, the Chevrolets specialized in manufacturing a 16-valve cylinder head with dual camshafts, which could be bolted directly to a standard Ford block. The complete kit included special encased timing gears and chains, valve covers, intake manifold, and exhaust headers. Described as the "Latest in speed equipment by America's foremost racing engineers," the heads were supposed to be excellent in their operation but far too expensive for the average race car owner to afford. These "Fronty-Fords" remained on the scene for several years, then this company also faded from the automotive world, and today is all but forgotten.

FRONTENAC 16 VALVE HEAD COVERS REMOVED

After 19 years and more than 15 million vehicles, the Model T line ended officially on May 25, 1927. Henry Ford had agonized long and hard over the demise of his beloved T, but sales figures and corporate profits could not be denied. The car that was designed to be every-man's vehicle in 1908 really had no place in the 1927 market. The upstart Chevrolet, which hadn't even been a dream when the Model T was conceived, this year broke the million vehicle mark. Other makes such as Essex, Whippet, Oakland, Buick and Dodge had also long enticed Ford owners with their "next step up" sales tactics.

Ford's big problem, however, was that it had no new model ready for production. The procrastination of the company's conservative elements (especially Henry's) led to a situation where ideas were being considered, but the long road from drawing boards to assembly line had yet to be traveled. Ford solved this problem in a simple and ingenious way, yet a way that hurt the company in the long run. On May 26, the plants simply shut down. Model T production ended not with a slow dying trickle, but with the slamming of the doors. Suddenly, thousands of Ford employees, from assembly line workers to salesmen to office clerks to middle management, found themselves on indefinite layoff.

Many marginal dealers would find it impossible to survive the succeeding months, while others drastically cut costs and had to live on used car sales, parts replacement, and mechanical work. Many skilled employees were forced to look for work in competing auto plants. And many potential buyers decided not to wait for the new Fords, but to go with other makes instead. And, it would be six months before a new Ford product would see the light of day.

Meanwhile, Henry and Edsel Ford and a small staff of engineers and designers worked in total secrecy to develop the new car, while the public patiently or impatiently awaited the results. Henry took personal charge of the chassis, engine, and running gear, while Edsel, who also served as president of the Lincoln division, was in charge of styling. But that is getting ahead of the story.

For 1927, what Fords were produced were virtual carbon copies of the 1926 offerings. A few changes did occur, however. For example, the wire wheels, which were still considered a $35 extra cost item, were so popular that most cars were equipped with them. Because of this, the wood spoke wheels became a credit

option. Also, even here, the standard black wood spoke wheels were seldom seen except on the pickup and bare chassis, while the varnished wood spoke wheels were the ones most often ordered when the wires were not wanted.

By February the wood spoke wheels had been dropped from the standard equipment picture on all closed cars, with these models coming out with black wires as standard, or colored wheels at a slightly higher price. Now only the open cars had the wood spokes as an option. On the wire wheels, available colors remained English Vermillion, red, light green, and yellow.

Colors also became available on all models, and no longer were open cars restricted to only Gunmetal Blue or Phoenix Brown. Now any model could be ordered in any of the six available colors. It appears that black was available only as an option on the Pickup, which normally was finished in Commercial (dark) Green, and on the bare chassis. Fenders and aprons remained in black on all vehicles regardless of the body color selected. This was commonplace throughout the entire automotive industry of the day.

Pricewise, there was no change from the costs set at mid-season in 1926. Thus the Runabout cost $360; the Touring was $380; the Coupe was $485; the Tudor $495, and the Fordor $545. The Pickup was $380 in factory form, which did not include the Runabout's rear deck. However, the pickup bed could still be ordered separately for $25 and added to the Runabout, thus giving a buyer the option of having either a car or a truck with just a few hours work for conversion. Missing from the price roster this year were the basic touring and runabout models. Now all cars came with complete electric systems and demountable rims or wire wheels, whether the buyer like it or not. Actually, so few people were interested in saving the cost of these items that the factory felt it was not worth offering this option.

Sport packages continued to be offered for the open cars, but these were not true factory packages, but instead were accessory collections sold at the dealer level on an item-by-item basis. Catalog illustrations of these sporty open cars loaded with the accessories have led

At day's end on May 26, 1927, with only a small ceremony, the last Model T rolled off the line at Dearborn, thus ending an era begun in 1908. The car, a rather plain Touring, was lettered "The Fifteen Millionth Ford," and was subsequently posed with two other major milestones. These were the first Model T and Henry's first car, the Quadricycle. However, one puzzle arises. If the car were truly the 15-millionth, then it was not the last Ford, having been followed by at least 7,033 others. Or, if it was truly the last Model T off the line, then it was Ford number 15,007,033. Whatever, the car was good for publicity purposes and it did represent the end of one of the most dynamic and productive automotive endeavors the world has ever seen. Oddly, Ford's concept of a car that every working man could afford was not lost on the world, and over the decades has materialized in some very unexpected places. Even Hitler in 1938, when introducing Dr. Porsche's revolutionary Volkswagen, gained tremendous support when he promised production of a vehicle that every German family could afford. Too bad he didn't stick with cars rather than turning to tanks, guns, and other war machines.

to the belief that such cars were actually separate "sport" models, when in fact no definitive information has ever been found to show that Ford intentionally packaged these items into sub-models.

On the production scene, the short year painted a dismal picture for sales, and again caused a conflict in numbers. Some sources contend that 356,188 cars were built during the calendar year, which would seem high if the model-year figures of 478,588 are accepted. Using these latter figures, it appears that a total of 95,778 Runabouts were produced, making this the most popular style of the year. Following close behind was the Touring Car, with 81,181 builds, while the only other open vehicle, the Roadster Pickup (officially called Runabout With Pickup Body) accounted for 28,143 units. In the closed car line, the Tudor became the most popular model for the first time, with 78,105 builds. Unseated from its popularity position was the Coupe, registering 69,939 units, while the Fordor remained the least popular with 22,930 units being produced. Also on the books were 19,280 light chassis deliveries. These figures represent the fiscal year production, which ran from Aug. 2, 1926, through the last day of production on May 25, 1927, which is about as close to model year figures that one can get.

Within this period, engine serial numbers ran from 14049030 to 15006625, showing a total of 957,595 blocks turned out, of which 41,318 went into 1-ton truck production. This would indicate a seemingly over-high figure of 916,277 blocks. For the 1927 calendar year alone, the block numbers ran from 14619255 to 15076231, showing 457,026 blocks built within that time. Actually, although manufacture of completed cars ended on May 25, engine production never fully ceased. In fact, some reports would indicate that Ford continued

to produce Model T blocks at the rate of up to 12,000 per month right through 1931, and then slackened back to about 100 a month as demand for the now-outdated engines slowly diminished. Even at that, right up into 1941, production of 10 or more Model T engines a month was recorded. The last Model T block turned out was No. 15176888, built on Aug. 4, 1941. This means that a total of 170,263 blocks were built AFTER the Model T was officially terminated.

Almost all will agree that over the years, a grand total of 15,007,033 Model Ts were built. This fact was not lost on Volkswagen, when on Feb. 17, 1972, it produced Beetle No. 15,007,034 and thus became the first manufacturer to exceed Ford for a single-model run. Still, even at that, other less accepted reports would put the Model T's production at 15,456,781, or 15,766,539 . . . . and so the confusion remains.

While this was going on, another major Ford-related event was taking place in Detroit. This involved Ford's two major body builders, the Murray Corp. of America and the Briggs Mfg. Co. As happened with engine production, the demise of the Model T did not mean the closing of these companies. Both continued on their merry way producing Model T sheet metal and body components, albeit on far lesser scale, for the replacement market. However, both companies saw that a merger of the similarly operating firms might produce better cost savings and higher profits. Ford, who had already planned to have the firms build the majority of his new Model A bodies, did not see it that way. He wanted the companies to remain independent of each other, competitively bid against each other, and thus keep his body costs at the lowest possible price. Ford fought against the merger and won. Thus, the two companies continued as independent firms, producing millions of Model A bodies, but competing against each other in order to do so.

The tie bar running in front of the radiator marks this as a very late 1927 Runabout. Added to help prevent fender shake and rattle, the rod also provided a handy place to mount the headlights. A running change made during the 1927 model year, the bar cannot be used as an identification guide because such units were installed at various assembly plants only as earlier stocks of lights and fenders ran out. Now Ford's most popular car, the Runabout enjoyed 95,778 sales at $360 per copy, with black wood-spoke wheels. It weighed 1,655 pounds. Buyers now had a choice of any of six available body colors, but all fenders and aprons were still done in black, as were the standard wheels.

A few accessory items really spruces up the Runabout. Shown here are the wire wheels at $35 a set; the triangular "Gipsy" (no, not Gypsy) side curtains at $3 a set, and a top boot at $5. The owner also went for the extra-cost nickeled radiator shell, but left off the attractive double-bar bumpers at $15 a set. The dark color on this Runabout would indicate that it was finished in either dark green or maroon, as black was no longer an option. For an additional $25, small businessmen could still obtain a pickup bed that within an hour or so of work would replace the Runabout's rear deck. However, this conversion was not as easy as it had been on the pre-1926 models.

1927

This Touring Car displays the fender tie bar, marking it as a late production, probably built at the very end of 1926 or in the 1927 calendar year. In relatively standard form, its only extra-cost accessory is the nickeled radiator shell, rather than the painted shell which was supposed to be standard on open cars. However, there are strong indications that open cars may have had nickeled radiators installed as standard equipment late in the year as a sales incentive. Black wood-spoke wheels also would have been standard fare, but again, it appears many open cars were equipped with wires as a matter of course. No longer Ford's top selling car, the Touring now slipped behind the Runabout in popularity, with only 81,181 being produced during this short-run year. The car listed at $380 and weighed 1,738 pounds.

Displaying a wide range of accessories, open cars of this kind are often thought of as "sport models," although such a designation was never made by Ford. Not only does this Touring Car have a set of matching-color wire wheels, it also has the $15 set of nickeled bumpers, the set of glass wind wings that cost $6.50, and the fawn colored top boot that cost $5. The nickeled radiator shell might have been an extra cost item, or might have been a no-charge factory installation put on as a sales incentive. The dark colors on both of the Touring Cars shown here would indicate that they were finished in either maroon or dark green. This car also carries Ford's relatively new combination tail and stop light. This listed at $2.50 installed, and included a special switch hooked to the brake pedal. In this era, it still was not mandatory to have stop lights in many states.

Lack of fender tie bar and varnished wood spoke wheels would indicate that this Coupe was built before February, 1927, when all closed cars began to receive wire wheels as standard equipment. The addition of both bumpers and varnished wheels greatly enhances the appearance of this model, which was probably finished in Channel (dark) Green, the most popular Coupe color. Priced at $485 and weighing 1,860 pounds, the popular little 2-seater drew 69,939 orders in this short year. Notice the lady's hat is perched on the storage shelf located behind the front seat. Ford made good mention of the "substantial" size of this shelf for carrying purses, small parcels, and even hats.

Although this illustration is from an early 1926 catalog, it well illustrates the appearance of those Coupes produced after Feb. 14, 1927, when wire wheels became standard on all closed cars. At this point, the so-called archaic wood-spoke wheels became a special order option at no extra charge. Added cost items on this model were the bumpers, combined stop and taillight, and the rearview mirror, which cost fifty cents. Ford liked to advertise the spacious 19 cubic foot capacity of the Coupe's rear compartment, and the fact that the double paneled deck lid made the compartment virtually water and dust proof. The only disadvantage to this compartment was that the spare blocked easy access. It appears that this car also has been fitted with Ford's new automatic vacuum windshield wiper, which was a $3.50 accessory installed. The vacuum was drawn from the manifold.

The most popular closed car in Ford's line this year turned out to be the Tudor, a body style that henceforth would retain the production title. Having a run of 78,105, the practical little car cost $495 and weighed 1,972 pounds. Tie bar and wire wheels identify this as a late model. This drawing gives a detailed look at the standard closed car visors, which consisted of leatherette stretched over a metal frame consisting of an outside perimeter with two inside braces. These visors seem to vary, with some being padded so that the bracing does not show, and others having the leatherette stretched directly over the visible frame, as seen here. All Coupes and Tudors were equipped with gray silk roller shades on the rear windows.

It could be a 1926 or it could be a 1927 model, because at the start of the year there was absolutely no difference in the basic Fordor. All came equipped with nickeled radiator shells and black wood-spoke wheels as standard equipment, had gray upholstery with either red or green striping, and had gray silk roller shades on both the rear and rear quarter windows. The shades' little pull-cords are visible in this car. Ford's most expensive model, the Fordor cost $545. At 2,004 pounds it was not only the heaviest Ford, but also the only one to weigh over one ton. It also was the lowest production car, having a run of only 22,930.

Although all closed Fords were equipped with wire wheels after Feb. 14, 1927, it appears that these wheels were becoming standard fare on the Fordor as early as October, 1926. But, because the Fordor was a hold-over body, and was over three inches higher than other closed models, the openness of the wire wheels did nothing for its aesthetic appearance. Actually, the more solid looking wood-spoke wheels turned out to be much more attractive on this model than did the rather spindly wires. The Fordor remained the only Ford car to have its gas tank under the driver's seat. However, because the cowl was not filled with gas tank as on the other models, this allowed the gas filler door of the other models to remain an operational cowl vent on the Fordor. This year, certain colors were not restricted to specific models, and thus the Fordor could be ordered in a light color such as Gunmetal Blue or Phoenix Brown or gray, such as shown here.

Still more car than truck was the Roadster Pickup, officially known as Runabout With Pickup Bed. The vehicle was simply a factory assembled pickup version of the Runabout, which sold for $380 and weighed 1,736 pounds. It was produced in Commercial (dark) Green with black fenders, apron, radiator shell, and wood-spoke wheels. It could also be obtained in all black at a special order option, but no longer was it available in basic style. Now all models had self starters, full electrics, and demountable rims. The top was the same as used on the Runabout, and included full side curtains but no boot. The driver's door, which is functional, has been made useless on this model by the spare rim carrier attached to the running board. A total of 28,143 of these cute little trucks were turned out this year. Also available was the pickup bed for $25, which could be installed on any runabout. It is not known how many beds were sold in addition to complete trucks.

A good market remained for the sale of bare chassis to builders of depot hacks, light commercial vehicles, taxis, etc. Even in this shortened model year, Ford sold a total of 19,280 light chassis for $300 each. These chassis were all fitted with full electric systems, starters, and demountable rims, as the basic bare chassis was no longer available. This late model (note the tie bar) has a few extras not normally sold with the bare chassis, however. These include the nickeled radiator shell, varnished wood-spoke wheels, and front bumper. The manufacturer of this body is not known. Often such bodies were built by a local cabinet shop which also would turn out a handful of light truck and hack bodies each year in addition to its carpentry work.

If this body looks familiar its because it appeared in the 1926 chapter as a Springfield Model C-34, produced in Springfield, Mass. This year the same illustration appears in Mifflinburg's catalog as a Model 634. In the previous Mifflinburg catalog, it was listed as a Suburban Model 6, while in this year's Springfield catalog it appears as a Model 6 Suburban. (And some people think car models are confusing?) Also, the same body, with the same background but a different windshield and front end airbrushed on, appears in a Star advertisement in 1927, and in Chevrolet brochures in 1925 and 1926. Some of this may be attributed to the printer and plate maker, who in this case was one and the same for all companies. But unless both Springfield and Mifflinburg were actually producing identical bodies, it seems unlikely that the printer could have gotten away with such simple airbrushing changes. Other similarities have been noted between other bodies from Mifflinburg, Pa., and Springfield, Mass., but so far no definite tie has been established between the two companies.

It seems unlikely that the Model T could just go away without at least one example being snapped up by the Detroit, Toledo & Ironton Railroad Co., headquartered at Dearborn. This railroad was a pet of Henry Ford, having been resurrected virtually from the grave to serve his Dearborn empire and River Rouge plant. The car appears to be a late model Fordor, wearing the old high body, but equipped with the new tie bracket which fitted between the fender braces and made a perfect place to mount the headlamps. It appears that the 12-spoke wheels are simply modifications of the standard wood-spoke wheels, but the front axle is definitely not from Ford's parts supply. Fenders and aprons have been omitted, but the running boards have been left in place,. Standard caboose lights have been added to the rear. The steering wheel is missing, but it is not known if the post was left in place for mounting the throttle and spark levers.

Although the day of the open speedster was rapidly drawing to a close, and offerings of speedster conversion kits had decreased rapidly, it is safe to assume that a handful of these sporty but uncomfortable little vehicles were still being produced in backyard shops across the country. It is unknown if this particular car was converted from an actual marketed kit, or whether it was just a restorer's dream. Regardless, the beautifully constructed car serves as an illustration of a type of vehicle that attained moderate popularity among the youthful set for a span running approximately from the late teens to the mid-twenties.

It seems unbelievable today, but when Ford chased the last Model T from the factory on May 26, 1927, there was absolutely nothing to take its place. On that rainy afternoon, Henry Ford is reported to have turned to Eugene Farkas, the company's chief designer, and said, "Well Gene, we have to do it now." What he referred to, of course, was that everyone had better get down and start designing a new car so that the company would have something to market in 1928!

At this point, Ford was really burdened by an unimaginable set of circumstances. It seems impossible that these could occur in one of the world's largest industrial empires. But, believe it or not, there was no true engineering or development department; there was no true styling department save for a small group at Lincoln headed by Edsel Ford; there was no true marketing plans for the future, and there was no definite idea of what the new model was supposed to be.

Up until now, Henry Ford and his contingent of ultraconservative backers had resisted most innovations that would have improved the Model T. Edsel Ford had definite ideas of what the modern car should consist of, but most of his ideas had been put to use on the expensive and luxurious Lincoln, of which company he was president. Some experiments had been carried out on an "X" type of 4 and 8-cylinder engine, but the design proved unworkable. Henry Ford would not even consider a 6-cylinder engine, mainly because it would cast him in the role of a "follower" rather than as a leader in his field. And so the crew got busy.

About the only thing that required little discussion was the chassis. Both Henry and Edsel were in agreement on the size, design, and 103.5-inch wheelbase length. From there, Henry took charge primarily of the engine, transmission, and running gear, while Edsel's role was mainly to design a set of bodies that would be strong, comfortable, appealing, and economical to produce. Both men succeeded in their respective roles, but not without the expected problems that would materialize. There are internal reports of many 16 to 18 hour days for the entire crew, and 7-day weeks were the norm.

Finally, after expenditures of between $100 and $200-million for retooling (Henry used to say somewhere in the neighborhood of $100-million, others compute it at over $200-million) the big day was at hand. On Dec. 2, 1927, the new Model A was unveiled to a public whose enthusiasm would be totally unheard of in today's world. The press heralded the event as one of the greatest of the century, and people flocked in droves to see the new car wherever it was displayed.

And a totally new car it was. Designated the Model A in order to divorce it entirely from the old Ford alphabetical sequence which had culminated in the Model T, the new car was capable of jackrabbit low speed performance; 60 to 65 MPH top end; had a selection of seven colors for its six advertised body styles (actually only five were available), and looked as good as anything on the road in its price class—and a lot better than most.

True, it still had a 4-cylinder engine, but this was of totally new design. It also had a sliding gear 3-speed transmission (like real cars), a conventional clutch, and 4-wheel brakes. Ironically, all of these would give troubles in the immediate future. It was first advertised to be available in six body styles, a Tudor, a Fordor, two Coupes, a Roadster, and a Phaeton.

However, because of start-up problems, the Fordor would not appear for another six months. Among the claimed innovations was the extensive use of electric welding in the body construction, which was a relatively new concept in 1927. Also, the bodies were finished in a baked enamel, which not only gave buyers a car with a very trouble-free finish, but also allowed for much faster production methods. In all, a total of 40 different kinds of steel were used in the car, with the type of steel being determined by the need for tensile strength, flexibility, hardness, etc. However, once the initial introduction of the car was over, the company had to sit down and solve a multitude of problems. Foremost were the corporate problems. These involved getting all 34 assembly plants in the U.S. and Canada geared for the new cars. It was one thing to convert the River Rouge plant, quite another to get all the satellites running. Also, there was the dealer network to contend with. Many marginal dealers had either folded or taken on other makes because they could not stand to be without cars throughout most of 1927. Even now, dealers who had survived this far were folding because they could not get deliveries of the new Fords. By February of 1928, it was reported that only seven of Ford's 35 North American plants (including River Rouge) were actually producing cars, and that many Ford dealers still had not received even one Model A to put on display, let alone to sell.

And what of the cars that were out there?

First, a look under the hood showed a 4-cylinder engine that to the average person might still look a bit like the Model T block. But it was anything but that. Having a bore and stroke of 3-7/8x4.25 inches, it displaced 200.5 cubic inches and developed 40 brake horsepower at 2200 rpm. It had three main bearings and mechanical valve lifters.

Initial models were fitted with Zenith or Holley double venturi carburetors. The cooling system was a modified thermo-syphon, fitted with a pump impeller. The unit drove a 3-speed sliding gear transmission through a multiple-disc clutch. Both clutch and transmission were scaled copies of those used on the current Lincolns. Initially, the electrical current had been supplied by a 5-brush "Powerhouse" generator, while the starter was developed by Ford but produced by Abell. By May, both of these units had been found to be unworkable and the generator was replaced by a con-

1928

ventional 3-brush unit, while the starters became Bendix units. The double venturi carburetors were also replaced by single throat models during the year, and the entire 4-point engine mounting system was changed to a "floating" 3-point system before the year ended.

At this time also, the ever-troublesome dry multiple-plate clutch was discarded in favor of a conventional single plate clutch, and subsequently, most earlier cars had their clutch assemblies replaced when work became necessary. Initially, the engines also had a 5-bearing cam shaft, but by late 1928, this was changed to a 3-bearing shaft. This move involved another redesign of the block.

Also of interest were the problems that developed with the chassis and running gear. The first cars had a 4-point engine mounting, but as mentioned above, a new 3-point mounting was developed and put into production in early fall of 1928. This mounting involved the redesign of the front cross member and the engine mounting brackets.

On the running gear, the main problem involved the brakes. The first models were issued with an equalizer brake system that worked on all four wheels. In use, the rear brakes were activated first by pressure on the pedal, and the front brakes then became activated as more pressure was applied. The emergency brake, mounted on the far left, only locked the brakes into place, and did not act independently. Several state safety agencies objected to the single action of these brakes, and Pennsylvania went as far as to prohibit the sale of Model As because of what it considered unsafe braking. Ford was forced into a crash program to redesign the braking system. The result was to leave the service system alone, but add an independently operating emergency system, with the lever in the center, adjacent to the shift lever. Thus, only the first few Fords sold have the left hand brake lever. These also probably had the red steering wheels, made of a red rubber substance. During the year this too was changed, and became a black wheel of a rubber composite.

Other changes during the year involved minor modifications to just about everything, including wheels, axles, wiring, steering, lights—you name it, as usage brought problems to light, they were changed in running order, much as had been done with the Model Ts. Thus, a comparison of a Model A built in December, 1927, will show a great many variations, both large and small, from one built in October or November of 1928.

In the body department was where Ford really excelled. Though start-up problems occurred here also, most went unnoticed. Stylewise, the cars were a total hit, with lines coming close to those of scaled down Lincolns, and seven colors for buyers to choose from. The colors included light and dark blue, light and dark beige, gun metal gray, light gray, and black.

Initially, six body styles were advertised, but start-up problems on the Fordor held that style back for almost six months. Thus, the first offerings were the Phaeton (touring car), Roadster, Standard Coupe, Sport Coupe, and Tudor Sedan. In April, a Business Coupe appeared, which was really a variation of the Sport Coupe. And in May, the long-awaited Fordor finally saw the light. Lastly, in July, a Special Coupe, another variation on the coupe theme, appeared, bringing to eight the total models available in 1928.

Of these, the only two open cars were the Phaeton for 5-passengers and the 2-passenger Roadster, which came in two variations—a Business model with a trunk deck, or a Sport model with a rumble seat. Tops and side curtains on both were in black artificial leather, but initial copies of the Roadster had brown whipcord tops an curtains. Neither model used outside door handles this year. It appears that the Phaetons were produced totally by Ford, whereas body parts for the Roadsters were supplied by both Budd and Briggs.

The Coupes were all based on the same theme, and differed mainly in top structure and interior fittings. The Sport Coupe had a rumble seat, while the others had rumble seat options. The Standard Coupe was built with a metal superstructure, whereas the Sport Coupe had a choice of a whipcord or leather top in convertible style, complete with dummy landau irons. The Special Coupe succeeded the Standard Coupe in July, bringing with it a steel top with the rear portion covered in leather. The Business Coupe was a less-dressed version of the Sport Coupe, and fitted with a trunk deck rather than a rumble seat.

The Tudor Sedan, which was destined to become the most popular Model A, was among the introductory models, and was the only real family car available until the Fordor showed up in May. The nicely styled car had a steel rear quarter, leatherette top, and was fitted with the impressive visor worn by all Fords this year. Its late-arriving 4-door companion, meanwhile, had a top completely covered in brown leatherette. Also, the Tudor had what is known as "coupe-pillar" design on the front, whereby the body had a forward curve and exposed A-pillars. The Fordor had its body sides running flush from the cowl. Of 2-window design, all of the Fordors were built by Briggs.

Production was tallied on a calendar year basis, but seems to cause little confusion, as Ford's model years appear to have reverted to a calendar year basis also, or at least came close to it. Of course, for 1928, the 1927 production must also be included, as this was simply the start-up for the 1928 models.

Of all models, the $550 Tudor was the most popular, with 1,948 built in 1927 and 208,562 in 1928 for a total model run of 210,510. Next in popularity was the late entry Fordor at $585. Once Briggs got rolling, it managed to turn out 82,349.

Of the coupes, the attractive Sport Coupe at $550 proved to be the most popular with 734 built in 1927 and 79,099 coming out in 1928 for a model-year total of 79,833 (a second list shows 82,879). The Business

Coupe, which was a variation of the Sport Coupe, started out with a $495 price tag and a production of 629 in 1927. In 1928, a total of 70,784 were built, but this tally includes the Special Coupe which was introduced in July, giving this combined style a total production of 71,413.

Of the open cars, the Roadster was the most popular, with its $385 price tag probably contributing to its strong sales appeal. In all, 269 were built in 1927 and 81,937 in 1928, for a total of 82,206. Of these, 51,807 had the optional $35 rumble seats, while 30,399 were built in "businessman's style" with a trunk compartment. Lastly, the Phaeton at $395 drew 221 builds in 1927 and 47,255 in 1928 for a model-year total of 47,476.

Engine numbers began with No. 1 on Oct. 20, 1927, and ran through No. 5275 by year end, and to No. 810122 on Dec. 31 for the 1928 total. This compares to 611,488 automobiles produced during that time, plus another 63,515 trucks and 42,711 light commercial chassis for a grand 1928 model/calendar year total of 713,528 including 1927 production.

Included in this list are a few vehicles which constantly cause contention with historians. They are the Town Car, the Station Wagon, and the Taxicab. Many historians, including Crestline's own James K. Wagner, contend that these vehicles were issued so late in the year that they should be considered 1929 models only. That might hold true for the Station Wagon, of which only five were built at the end of 1928. But the Town Car showed a production of 89, while the Taxicab had 264 models credited to its list. Therefore, these vehicles are included in the 1928 section. And, since there was absolutely no definitive model year changes between 1928 and 1929, it does seem that the early models could be titled in either year.

As mentioned earlier, trucks in themselves will not appear in this book, the subject having been thoroughly detailed by James Wagner in Crestline's *FORD TRUCKS SINCE 1905*. However, in cases where the light commercial vehicles were far more car than truck, and where the vast majority of components were from the car lists, not the truck bins, these little vehicles will be included at the end of each chapter, at least through the 1950s. Such vehicles will not be covered in their total depth, but simply with random and/or representative samplings.

First Pictures of the New Ford Car

Get complete details TODAY at Ford salesrooms

FORD MOTOR COMPANY
Detroit, Michigan

One of Ford's introductory ads for the new Model A shows all six body styles that were supposed to be available to dealers in December of 1927. Of course this didn't happen. The Fordor suffered numerous start-up problems and didn't appear until May, while in April another new coupe joined the pack. But because start-up was far more troublesome than anticipated, many smaller dealers didn't even get a sample car to show to their customers until early spring. Thus, ads such as this were the only views the public had of the new Fords. Among the beautifully designed components of the new cars were the wire wheels, which had amazing strength and flexibility, and still prove to be strong and sturdy today after over 65 years of use.

Low car on the totem pole, insofar as price went, was the Business Roadster, which entered its life at $385, but was up to $480 by mid-season. Designated the Model 40-A, the car weighed 2,050 pounds and thus was the lightest of all Model As. Only 269 were built in 1927, but production jumped to 51,807 for 1928. Sporting a relatively large rear compartment, the car not only found favor with professional people of all kinds, but also with municipalities where low initial cost and ease of upkeep were primary considerations. This particular unit was assigned to the fire chief of River Rouge, Mich., where the new 40 horsepower engine probably insured that he arrived at a fire scene long before the other equipment.

Ford did not list the rumble seat or sport version of its Roadster as an independent model, yet it kept production figures separate for this variation. Thus, it is known that 30,130 Roadsters had rumble seats, making total Roadster production 81,937. Prices for this model began at $420, but crept up to the $480 mark by mid-season. Both Budd and Briggs produced body components for the Roadster, but these components were shipped to the various Ford plants for assembly, painting, and trim, as opposed to closed car bodies which were shipped as complete units. The rumble seat was a rather odd innovation which rose from virtual obscurity to relative popularity and back to total obscurity all within the decade from 1929 to 1939. Note that the 1928 Roadsters did not use exterior door handles. To open a door, one had to reach inside for the latch release. The top material, with matching side curtains, was of a drab whipcord with imitation Spanish leather edging.

Going under the name of Standard Business Coupe, the Model 45-A was a cute little car first priced at $495. However, during the year, the 2,225-pound vehicle rose to $550. Not to be confused with the later issue Business Coupe, the Standard Business Coupe used full rear quarter windows and a steel-backed rear quarter. Production began in 1927 with 629 rolling off the line, followed by 79,099 later in the year. However, this figure is shared with Standard Coupe models with rumble seats, and Special Coupe models which replaced the Standard version in July. In many Ford ads and literature, this car was simply referred to as the "Coupe." In addition to its large luggage area, it sported a package shelf behind the seat.

Formerly called a Touring Car, but now more pretentiously known as a Phaeton, the Model 35-A represented Ford's only other open car. Initially priced at $395, the car climbed only to $460 by mid-year and thus became the least expensive Ford. The attractions of an open touring car were beginning to wane, and as a result, only 47,476 were built. Of these 221 were turned out in 1927. This attractive model has been fitted with dual sidemounts. This year the welled fenders and sidemount attachments were dealer-installed items, but beginning in 1929, these became factory installations. The trunk, windwings, spare-mounted mirrors, and spare covers could all be bought through dealership sources. As with the Roadster, outside door handles were deemed unnecessary this year. The 2,140-pound car initially had only a hand-operated windshield wiper, but in May this was changed to an electric model. The material for the top and side curtains was not the same as used on the Roadsters, but appears to have been a rubber coated fabric. Upholstery was in smooth artificial black leather, while the door panels were of grained black cardboard and the floor mats were of black rubber.

There is some conflict as to whether the Standard Coupe was considered a sub-model in the coupe family, or whether it was simply the Coupe with a $35 accessory rumble seat. Often the reference is to "Standard Coupe" with the rumble seat or "Standard Business Coupe," when fitted with a trunk deck. Note that all coupe bodies used what was called a "coupe pillar" design for the forward or A-pillar. With this design, the pillar forms a forward flaring body line beyond the cowl, resulting in a distinctive break at the cowl. All Model 45-A Coupes used a gray interior cloth with thin blue lines. The rumble seat material was in a black grained imitation leather. Production of this model ceased in July, 1928, with the introduction of the Special Coupe.

Until the Fordor finally arrived, Ford's most expensive car was the Sport Coupe, Model 50-A, which was priced at $550. Looking like a cabriolet, the car featured a solid top covered in tan whipcord and fitted with dummy landau irons. Available only in rumble seat style, the very attractive car weighed 2,265 pounds. It proved to be Ford's most popular coupe style, with a total of 79,833 being built, of which 734 were produced in 1927. The interiors were done in a brown striped material, with brown cardboard cowl covers. Early models had brown carpeting, but at mid-year, black rubber floor mats became standard. Also available was a blue and gray checkered material with gray cardboard cowl covers.

The last coupe model to arrive was the Special Coupe, which in July succeeded the Standard Coupe. It was given the designation Model 49-A, but surprisingly, separate production figures were not made, and its totals are included with the Standard Coupe. Actually, the car was simply the standard version, but with an imitation leather top that wrapped around the rear panel. Priced the same as the Sport Coupe ($550) the car came primarily with a trunk deck, but a dealer-installed rumble seat could be ordered for $35 extra. The interior of the Special Coupe was in plain brown cloth, with brown cloth door panels, equipped with pockets. The top material was the same black artificial leather used on the Fordor. All Standard and Special Coupe models were fitted with silk roller shades on the rear window, with brown being used on the Specials and gray on the Standard models. Early Special coupes had brown carpeting, but after a few months the floor covering reverted to black rubber mats.

Arriving in April or May, was the Business Coupe, Model 54-A. Designed for the salesman or professional person who wanted a bit more style than found in the Standard Business Coupe, this car used the same body as did the Sport Coupe, but lacked the landau irons and had a luggage compartment in place of the rumble seat. Priced at $525, it enjoyed a 1928 run of 37,343. The car used the same blue and gray checked material that was available on the Sport Coupe, but it appears the brown cloth interior was not available. Instead, upholstery could be in brown imitation Spanish leather, with the same material used on the door panels. The top also differed from the Sport Coupe, in that it was in black artificial leather rather than whipcord. Although landau irons were not included, they became a popular dealer-installed accessory on this model.

Ford's most popular car, this year and for years to come, was the Tudor Sedan, of which 1,948 copies were built in 1927 and 208,562 were turned out in 1928, for a model-year presentation of 210,510. Initially priced at $495, the cute little car slowly rose to $550. It weighed 2,340 pounds. The interiors were available in two types of gray cloth with gray headlinings and door panels, or a blue striped cloth with plain blue panels and liner. Initially brown carpets were supplied, but these reverted to black rubber floor mats late in the season. Blue silk roller shades were fitted over the rear window. Unlike the Fordor, the Tudor also used the "coupe pillar" design at the cowl. Note the hood louvers on this very early model. The upper louver line was parallel with the aprons, but this caused a conflict with the horizontal hood and cowl line. Since the louvers were all the same size, it appeared that the upper line ran downhill toward the rear. This was solved by making each louver a bit larger than the one ahead, with the end result being that both upper and lower horizontal lines were parallel with their respective major lines.

Finally appearing in May was the long awaited Fordor, with its Briggs-built body. This was the only Model A not to use the distinctive A-pillar design, but instead had its body run flush against its special cowl. Designated the Model 60-A, the 2,386-pound car was priced between $570 and $585. Partially due to its late start, the Fordor claimed only 82,349 copies in 1928. Built only in 2-window style, it featured a top completely covered in brown imitation Spanish leather. Early models used a steel-framed glass visor, but this was soon replaced by the standard leather covered visor seen here. This model sports a vent door on the cowl side, but this would disappear as a running change during the year. Interiors were done only in brown cloth, with the rear doors having pockets, but no pockets were provided in the front. Brown carpeting was first used front and rear, but later the front carpet gave way to black rubber floor mats.

Appearing late in the year, in fact so late that some contend it is a 1929 model only, was the unusual Briggs-built Town Car. This ultra-pretentious Ford had an equally pretentious price tag of $1,200. A total of 89 of these models left the plant, sporting Ford's first cowl lights. The car made heavy usage of the Fordor's body and styling, but the interior was richly appointed in a brown mohair, while the chauffeur's compartment was done in natural black leather. A removable leather top could be fitted over the chauffeur's compartment and the front doors contained roll-up windows. The top and rear quarters were covered in black natural leather. The divider window between compartments was of the sliding type.

Another car of contention is the Taxicab, which again some say should be considered a 1929 introduction. Still, since a total of 264 were produced in the 1928 model year, it seems safe to assume that at least the first of these would be considered 1928 models. Produced by Briggs, and designated a Model 135-A, this car had Ford's first 3-window sedan style, and carried a reversion back to the "coupe pillar" design of the A-pillars. Priced at $800, the car featured a glass partition between compartments and had a jump seat in the rear for a fourth passenger. However, there was no passenger seat in the front, as this area was fitted for the taxi meter and luggage carrying only. Normally, the rear compartment would be finished in gray imitation leather, with the front being done in a similar black material. It appears that this body style could also be ordered as a chauffeur-driven sedan, with the partition. In this form, the rear area would be finished in gray velour, while the front would still be in black imitation leather, but with a full front seat.

The practice of car/truck conversions continued with the Model A, but no longer with the direct sanction of Ford. Still, a multitude of aftermarket companies, most working through Ford dealers, began to dream up various ideas for turning Ford cars into something they were not. One such conversion was this slide-in cargo box produced by the large York-Hoover Body Co. of York, Pa. a major builder of truck and depot hack bodies. The unit, shown here on the Business coupe, would fit onto or into any of Ford's current coupe styles. Since installation required removal of both the deck lid and the rear body panel, let alone the spare tire carrier, this was not as quick a conversion as had been the old runabout/pickup conversion of Model T days. With this unit, a welled fender would be necessary for a sidemounted spare.

Arriving in November, 1928, almost in time to be considered only a 1929 model, was the Deluxe delivery. This cute little truck was based on the Tudor Sedan body and used the nickeled radiator shell and headlamps of the passenger car line rather than the painted features of the truck line. Priced at $595, the truck could be ordered in any of the passenger car colors, or with an added-cost 2-tone paint scheme as shown here. Its features included a single rear cargo door with a rear window, folding passenger and driver seats, and a left-hand sidemounted spare. A screened partition separated the cargo area from the driver. The interior was finished in Spanish brown imitation leather for the seats and "steel craft" paneling, a type of heavy-duty cardboard.

Ford continued to produce a Roadster Pickup, but no longer was it convertible from car to truck use. Designated the Model 76-A, the vehicle was now totally a truck, carrying a price of $445 to $465. The cab, which almost looked like a cut-off roadster, featured a non-folding top, which could easily be removed entirely. The pickup bed was interesting, as it was the exact same bed that had been used on the Model T pickups. The 4.5x21 inch tires were standard on all Model As, but required sidemounts on the commercial vehicles if the owner wanted to carry the optional spare. As was the case with the Roadster and Phaeton, the Roadster Pickup also did not have exterior door handles. Its interior was finished in black imitation leather, with black cardboard panels.

Not showing up until August, 1928, was Ford's first Closed Cab Pickup, priced at $445, the same as the open cab model. Despite its new front end, the Closed Cab Pickup not only used the pickup bed from Model T days, but its entire cab was a direct carryover, including the visor with its four prominent ribs. Designated the Model 82-A, the truck used all of the passenger car's components, differing mainly in the use of painted radiator and headlight shells. Unless specially ordered at extra cost, all commercial Fords were finished in dark green with black fenders, running boards, and shells. All-black was a no-cost special order option, and any of the passenger car colors were available at extra cost.

Also appearing in August of 1928 was the Panel Delivery, which listed at $575. Designated the Model 79-A, this truck had its components produced by Budd, with final assembly at various plants. Its cargo space was 57 inches long by 50 inches wide, with a floor to ceiling height of 46.5 inches. Features included double rear cargo doors with windows, two folding seats upholstered in imitation brown Spanish leather, a sidemount spare on the left, and a hand-operated windshield wiper. Some reports show that the knocked-down bodies were available directly to dealers, for dealership installation, rather than from assembly plant orders.

Just as Ford introduced the Model A to the automotive world, it also brought out a new tri-motor to the aviation world, albeit with far less flair. Called the 5-AT, the new model used more powerful Pratt & Whitney Wasp engines of 420 horsepower, which gave the craft a top speed of 122 MPH. Passenger capacity was also increased, and varied from 13 to 17, depending on which interior version was ordered. Lift was increased via larger wings which now had a span of 77 feet as opposed to 74 feet. This led to a greater load capacity, now rated at 3,640-pound payload for a gross weight of 13,500 pounds. The 5-AT was rated at an 18,500-foot cruising ceiling and had a 560-mile range. This year too, Ford airlines became Stout Airlines, but its Cleveland-Detroit-Chicago run remained the same.

The "true" Model A Station Wagon did not appear until the 1929 season, but still, five were built this year. The vehicle was the first attempt by a car manufacturer to build its own version of this style. In a switch of roles, the body components were manufactured at Ford's plant at Iron Mountain, Mich., and shipped to Murray in Detroit for final assembly. Murray also appears to have manufactured the metal components used on the wagons.

1929

Ford hit a milestone year in 1928 with the introduction of the Model A. Now, in 1929, it could capitalize on that mark and pass another milestone—that of once again being the major car manufacturer in the world.

Finally, after numerous agonizing start-up problems during the 1928 year, production was finally running at a smooth pace, and cars in sufficient number were being shipped to the dealer network. The public had accepted the Model A with enthusiasm to a point where many dealers must have thought they were back in the heyday of the Model T. True, Chevrolet had introduced a new 6-cylinder engine, and this was taking some of the edge from the Model A, but overall, Ford had its own way in the marketplace.

As could almost be expected after the major change over from Model T to Model A and the difficulty of getting all plants into production, Ford made virtually no change to the 1929 line, save for the running improvements that were made as weak points became apparent. Therefore, it is virtually impossible to look at a later model 1928 and a 1929 car and tell the difference without knowing the serial number. The only major exceptions to this rule lie with the open cars, which now sported outside door handles, and with those models that were not available in 1928, such as the Station Wagon, Cabriolet, and the virtual profusion of 4-door offerings that materialized.

On the mechanical side, a few changes were made during the year, but these were all of the running variety and cannot be used for definitive dating. Actually, the only positive dating involves the engine serial numbers, which started with 810123 on the first of January, 1929, and ended with 2742695 on Dec. 31. During this period, the 1-millionth engine was built during February's run, while the 2-millionth came out in July.

All of these blocks were the 4-cylinder cast iron units of 3-7/8x4.25 bore and stroke that displaced 200.5 cubic inches and developed 40 brake horsepower at 2200 rpm. Beginning with the January production, all engines had new light-weight aluminum pistons and solid skirts, and the oil dip stick now ended in a small round finger hole rather than the larger oval grip.

Under the hood, the shroud between the radiator and the fan was eliminated, not so much to improve air flow, but more to improve profits, as economy appears to be the only reason for this change. In the spring, a new breather cap appeared, as did a new rear main bearing cap. By now, Model A engines were gaining a reputation for being oil burners, and to help reduce this burning, new oil return pipes and holes were made in the valve chamber to reduce the oil level in the chamber itself. In July, the valve guide bushing was reduced a quarter-inch in length to help reduce valve sticking, and a new breather pipe with upward sloping baffles was devised in a effort to reduce oil blow-by.

The overheating problem was tackled in the fall by redesigning the cylinder head and gasket to allow more water flow through the block, while in an unrelated move, a new oil pump with a cast body and ribbed shank was designed. And so the running changes went, with many minor ones being made in addition to the major moves listed here. Similar minor moves were also made on the chassis and running gear, again, not as definitive model-year changes, but simply as improvements or economies when the company recognized both need and solution.

In the body department is where the major changes took place. Ford jumped from eight major styles in 1928 to 17 major styles in 1929, and this did not include the coupe's business/sport variations nor the Taxi or Town Car. Oddly, after the problems of getting the Fordor on the market, Ford now had a total of eight different 4-door models to choose from. Among these were Standard and Town Sedan models bearing the names of their builders, which were either Briggs or Murray. As General Motors would do later with the Fisher Body name, Ford took a leaf from the sales book of Lincoln and other prestige car builders, and capitalized on the fact that certain bodies were being "exclusively" produced by these two well-known body builders.

Also among the new models was the Cabriolet, which was Ford's first return to a true convertible styling since the Coupelet of 1914-1917. The car featured fixed full-length A-pillars which blended into the body at the cowl and held a swing-out windshield. Roll-up windows were provided in the doors, while the top folded in now-conventional convertible fashion, using functional landau irons for support when raised. The body was totally built by Briggs and shipped in finished form to the assembly points.

Also totally new on the scene was the Station Wagon, of which five were built in the 1928 year. Representing the first production wagon by a major auto manufacturer, as opposed to similar bodies installed on bare chassis by outside suppliers, the car drew a surprising amount of 4,954 orders. An interesting manufacturing process was instigated with the wagon. All of the wood parts were produced by Ford's own plant at Iron Mountain, Mich., from local lumber. But, rather than do the assembly at Iron Mountain, the components were shipped to the Murray Corp. at Detroit for the actual building. And later, when it was apparent that Murray could not keep up with these orders, the contract was extended to the Baker-Raulang Co. of Cleveland. The latter company, incidentally, was formed by a 1915 merger of the Baker Electric Co. and the Rauch & Lang Electric Co. of Cleveland and Chicoppe Falls, Mass. Both of these companies had been major producers of electric cars since the early automotive years, but had now added production and custom body building to their manufacturing processes as the demand for their luxurious but out-dated electric vehicles diminished with each passing year.

Being seen a bit more on Fords this year was the use

of sidemounted spares. Whereas sidemounts were strictly dealer installed options in 1928, cars could now be ordered direct from the assembly point with either left, right, or twin mounts.

Production this year soared, with 1,5558,667 Model As leaving the plants, and another 156,433 Model AA trucks being produced. Included in the automotive figure are chassis for 130,608 light trucks, which were essentially the cars with commercial bodies. Most popular of all the styles was the Tudor Sedan, available in only one model. Its production totalled out at 523,922. Not even coming close to this was the second place slot, which was occupied by the Roadster (all varieties) with 191,529 builds, with the Standard Coupe coming in third with 178,982, and the Fordor Sedan grouping being fourth with a total of 146,097. Because of the profusion of models, a total production run down will no longer be made in the text, but will appear for each model in the captions.

In other activities, Ford finally got out of the railroad business, selling the Detroit, Toledo & Ironton Railroad to the Pennsylvania Railroad for over seven times what had been paid for it nine years earlier. Of course, the railroad was a far cry from what it had been in 1920, and was now regarded as one of the most modern and well equipped intermediate rail lines in the country.

Outside door handles identify this as the 1929 Business Roadster rather than the 1928 model. Otherwise, there was virtually no difference between the two years. Still designated the Model 40-A, the 2,161-pound car cost $450 in base form, which did not include the practical wind wings shown here. Nickel plated bars between the top and the leading edge of the trunk deck kept the top from rubbing on the paint when folded. Roadsters were available in five colors this year: gray, beige, green, blue, and black. All were equipped with electric windshield wipers, which had been an added cost item in 1928. Both Briggs and Budd continued to supply roadster components, with final assembly being done at Ford's own plants.

Aluminum fender steps identify this as the Sport Roadster, which was equipped with a rumble seat and a $485 price tag. This year Ford turned out a total of 191,529 roadsters, but did not differentiate how many were rumble seat or business models. In fact, Ford rarely used the designations "Business" or "Sport," but simply would list the "Sport" model as "Roadster with rumble seat." Roadster tops and side curtains continued to be of black artificial leather, but the top boot was a beige whipcord. An unusual accessory on this particular model is the aftermarket trunk, which fits behind the rear mounted spare. Usually when such trunks were added, a welled fender and sidemount spare would be used.

Totally new for the year was the Cabriolet, Model 68-A, which made its debut at the 1929 New York Auto show. However, production did not begin until March, with all bodies coming from the Briggs plant in finished form. Priced at $670, the Cabriolet was one of the more expensive Fords, but not necessarily the most popular. Even though this model represented the 2-millionth Model A in July, its total sales peaked at either 15,548 or 16,421, depending on which production lists are used. In fact, in September, Ford cancelled orders for an additional 5,000 such units, preferring to hold back until the 1930 line appeared. The car was Ford's first return to the true convertible style since the 1914-1917 Coupelet. The top folded back from the rigid windshield frame, and when up, was kept in place by the functional landau irons. Roll-up windows provided weather protection, nesting in the B-pillars. These could be removed when the top was lowered. This year the Cabriolet came in only one color: Cigarette Cream with a brown upper body. It was available only in rumble seat style, and was among the deluxe models that sported Ford's first use of cowl lights.

Although the Phaeton today is one of the most sought after Model A styles, in 1929 it represented the low end of the pole, being neither desirable nor practical. In only a few short years, automotive design, higher road speeds, and a desire for enclosed comfort, had taken the touring car style from the most popular to one of the least ordered types of vehicle. Still wearing Model 35-A designation, the 2,203-pound car was priced at $460, complete with side curtains and top of black artificial leather. A load of accessories adorn this version, including the quail radiator ornament, wire grille guard, dual sidemounts, wind wings, step plates, cowl lights, and luggage rack with trunk. It is doubtful if too many Phaetons actually achieved this level of trim in 1929. Phaeton production reached 49,818. The same five colors available for roadsters were also available on the Phaetons. This particular model was done in beige with brown trim and orange wheels. All fenders on all models were in black, as were the aprons.

Proving that the Standard Coupe was available in rumble seat trim is this cute little model, photographed at Hershey, Pa., in the early 1970s. Although not cataloged as 4-passenger car, the buyer could have a factory-produced, dealer-installed rumble seat added to his Standard Coupe for about $35. Although on some models the rumble seat would have caused a change in designation, it appears that on the Standard Coupe such a move was considered no more than an accessory addition. Proving to be a very popular style, a variation of the Model 45 was carried through the entire Model A run. However, this would be the last year for the archaic "coupe pillar" or exposed A-pillar design. Beginning with the 1930 models, all body styles would have the sides flush with the cowl. Note that this car is equipped with aftermarket sealed beam headlights, probably of post-war vintage. Though not authentic for a 1929 car, these lights certainly are an asset if the vehicle is used after dark.

Having only a 6-month run was the Special Coupe, Model 49-A. Just as it had replaced the Standard Coupe in July of 1928, it was this year replaced by the Standard Coupe in July. The difference between the two cars appears to be simply one of top treatment, with the Special Coupe having a top and rear panel of artificial leather, similar to the Fordor. Priced at $550, the car came equipped with trunk deck only, although dealer-installed rumble seats were supposedly available. Production reached 178,982, with approximately half of this being Special Coupe models and half Standard Coupes.

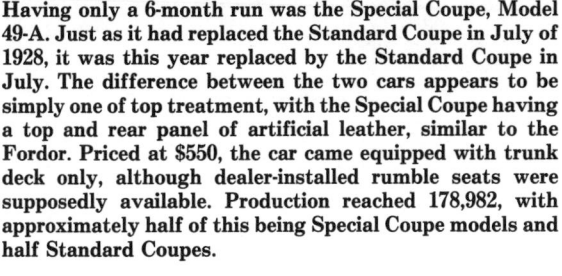

After July, the Special Coupe became the Standard Coupe, or just plain Coupe, with model designation 45-A. Still priced at $550, it appears that a switch from the leather-trimmed Special to the steel-backed Standard was one of internal Ford economics, and not due to lack of sales. With production totalling 178,982, this coupe variation was the third most popular car in Ford's stable, falling in just behind the roadsters. Cataloged only in trunk version, the car was available with an interior done either in brown check cloth or blue-gray artificial leather, whereas the Special model was finished only in brown cloth with a hairline stripe. When photographed at Long Beach in 1980, this well restored car belonged to Eugene Show of San Diego. It sports aftermarket wind wings, running board trim, and step plates. Production of the 2,256-pound car was solely at Ford's own plants.

New oval quarter windows differentiate the 1929 Business Coupe from its 1928 version, although some records would indicate that not all Business Coupes had the windows in 1929. Known as the Model 54-A, the car was a variation of the Sport Coupe, but unlike its sporty relative, would not be carried into the 1930 model year. Costing $525 and weighing 2,216 pounds, the car had a top of black artificial leather stretched over a light convertible-like frame, as opposed to the full steel tops of the other coupes. A total of 37,644 were produced this year, all by Ford. This was just about the same as the 1928 production. The Spanish brown artificial leather interior was again available, and was joined in September by the same blue-gray artificial leather interior used in the Standard Coupe. For those who preferred cloth interiors, a gray with white stripe was available. All coupes had package shelves behind the seat, and all used either brown or gray cowl cardboard. The Business Coupe came only with a trunk space, but again, dealer installed rumble seats could be purchased for about $35.

By far Ford's most popular car, the practical Tudor Sedan accounted for 523,922 orders this year, a mark that would never again be achieved by any Model A. Designated the Model 55-A and virtually unchanged from 1928, the car cost $525 and weighed 2,348 pounds. Two-tone variations, with the belt molding and back panel painted in a contrasting color to the rest of the body, were very popular this year. The roof, of black rubberized artificial leather, ended at the steel rear panel. The visor was done in the same material as the roof. Although three interior variations were available in 1928, only two interiors were offered this year. They were a brown checked cloth or a blue hairline stripe cloth, with plain matching headliners.

Looking almost like the new Cabriolet was the Sport Coupe, Model 50-A, which was unchanged from 1928. Priced at $550 and weighing 2,250 pounds, the car was offered this year in a choice of top materials. There was whipcord or three variations of natural leather: Dark brown, light brown, or 2-tone brown. The brown hairline cloth interior which was dropped in September of 1928 was reinstated, and was joined by a new brown check cloth. The blue check interior was no longer available. Production almost doubled from the previous year, topping out at 134,292. A quick identification between the Sport Coupe and the Cabriolet was the visor. The coupe had one, the Cabriolet did not.

Built only by Briggs, the Fordor Sedan, Model 60-A continued to have a top and rear quarters completely covered in beige imitation leather. It was priced at $625 and weighed 2,419 pounds. All models this year featured the "military" type of visor, with the steel framed glass version having been phased out in mid-1928. Also gone this year was the left hand cowl vent, which was probably deleted in an economy move. The Fordor came in three variations, with total production being 146,097 for all three models. On the Model 60-A the only interior available was a brown hairline stripe cloth, which was a carry-over from the 1928 cars. Some information would suggest that the brown-top models were discontinued at mid-season, being totally replaced by the black and steel topped versions, but this cannot be ascertained.

New for the year was the Model 60-B Fordor Sedan, built only by Briggs. The car was identical in every way to the Model 60-A, except that its top and rear quarters were finished in black pebble grain artificial leather, and it was available only with an interior done in brown checked material. All of these Fordors featured full bench seats front and rear, without armrests. Interior refinements included a dome light and silk roller shades on the rear window. All Model As used horns furnished by the Spartan Co.

The third variation of the Briggs-built Fordor Sedan to appear this year was the Model 60-C. Again, this version was identical to the two leather-topped styles, but it used a top of rubberized fabric which blended into a steel rear section. Also, on this car, the interior was finished in plain brown wool, although some sources say that the brown check seat material also became available. Barely visible on the car is the new flying quail radiator cap that became very popular in this era, either as an extra-cost accessory or as a dealer-supplied incentive. Despite wide acceptance of the Model 60 styles, Ford did not carry this design into the 1930 year.

This may or may not be the new 2-window Fordor Sedan, Model 170-A. This advertising piece by Ford does not identify the car, and it could very well be the black-topped Model 60-B. The difference between the new 170-A and the 60 Series was barely evident from the exterior, with the exception of the top portion. On the 170-A this was of all metal, from windshield to rear beltline, and apparently the rear quarter was larger. Built only by Briggs, the style appears to have been based on the all-steel 3-window Fordor which was a larger body than the wood and metal composite Model 60 Fordor line. Brought into production in late summer (reports indicate late July) with virtually no dealer announcement, the car could possibly be Briggs' bid for a replacement of the Model 60 line, which was to be terminated at year end. This year the 170-A was available only with brown checked seats and plain brown headliner and door panels. Since no cut-off date is shown for the Model 60 cars, it is possible that the 170-A succeeded at least some of these cars before the end of the year. No separate production figures were kept on this car, and it is grouped with the 146,097 listed for all Briggs-built 2-window Fordors.

Introduced in January, 1929, were the new 3-window Town Sedans, produced by both Briggs and the Murray Corp. Priced at $695 for either model and weighing the same 2,517 pounds, the cars appeared the same at a quick glance, but turned out to be quite different in reality. In fact, two different model numbers were used to differentiate between the two. Model 155-A was the Murray version shown here, while the Briggs unit was Model 155-B. Visually, the main difference between the two was in the windows. These had a low arched effect in the Murray cars, and a squared-off line in the Briggs version. Both models wore Ford's new cowl lights, and both had deluxe interiors in a choice of brown or green mohair with matching headliners of napped cotton. In addition, the Murray bodies could also be ordered in gray check cloth.

A more squared window line identifies this as the Briggs version of the new Town Sedan. Designated the Model 155-B, the car was similar to the Murray version, but very few parts were interchangeable. A total of 84,970 Town Sedans were built this year by both companies, but no tally was kept as to how many each company produced. Records indicate that a Briggs Town Sedan body cost Ford $229.71 delivered to Dearborn, while the similar Murray body cost $237.98. All Town Sedans had rather plush interiors which included side arm rests, a center pull-down arm rest in the rear seat, and a robe cord across the back of the front seat.

Since only five pilot models had been produced at the end of 1928, the new Ford Station Wagon can be considered a true 1929 vehicle. In fact, it was introduced in January as part of the new Model A line. Hailed as the first assembly line wagon and designated the Model 150-A, the car sold for $695. It was classed with Ford's commercial vehicles but used all of the automotive components such as bright radiator shell and headlights. The hood and cowl were finished only in Manilla Brown. The wood portions were produced at Ford's plant at Iron Mountain, Mich., and sent to Murray for assembly. When Murray was unable to keep up with production, the Baker-Raulang Co. of Cleveland also came into the picture. In all, a total of 4,959 wagons were produced for the 1929 season. Side curtains, which snapped onto exterior clips surrounding the windows were used for weather protection. The left hand sidemount was standard, as was the cutout on the driver's door to clear the tire. The body was of hard maple with birch paneling. The wagon was classed as an 8-passenger vehicle, with the rear and middle seats being removable for cargo hauling. The drop-down tailgate had chain supports.

Differing from the Town Sedan only in its level of trim was the new 3-window Standard Fordor or Standard Sedan, which was introduced along with the Town Sedan in January, 1929. As with the Town Sedan, Ford used different designations for the two builders. Thus, the Murray version was the Model 165-A, while the Briggs offering, shown here, was the Model 165-B. The standard models can be quickly identified from the Town Sedan by the lack of cowl lights, which really was the only external difference between the two styles. The interior was a different story, with the Standard model being available only with seats in brown checked cloth with plain brown cloth for the door panels and headliner. Later, Briggs bodies were available in seats in brown hairline stripe, but this was not an option on Murray bodies. Either version was priced at $625, the same as the 2-window models. The cars weighed 2,497 pounds. Production on the Standard models reached a combined 53,941, indicating that more buyers were willing to pay a bit more to get a bit more.

Again Ford offered its unusual Town Car, priced at $1,200. It was designed for those who could afford chauffeured cars but wanted a smaller car than the typical huge limousines of the day. The concept had merit, but not practicality. Still, a surprising 913 were turned out by Briggs. All featured interiors done in English Bedford Cord or French Broadcloth, with the chauffeur's compartment done in real black leather. A canopy top would fit between the windshield header and the B-pillar. The divider window was of the sliding type. Weighing 2,525 pounds, this was the heaviest model of the year, and also the most expensive. Some lists show its 1929 price at $1,400.

Production of Ford's special Taxicab model soared this year, reaching 4,576. Designated the Model 135-A, the car used its own exclusive body built by Briggs, and was the only 4-door model to use the exposed A-pillars of "coupe pillar" design. Priced in the neighborhood of $800, the car had a single driver's seat, backed by a full partition which curved forward into the front area normally reserved for passengers. Within this curve was a rearward facing jump seat which gave the tonneau a 4-passenger capacity, albeit a crowded capacity. Forward of this curved bulkhead was the Taximeter unit and a storage area for luggage. This beautifully restored version is one of the few remaining examples of this car. When photographed years ago it belonged to Harold Dye of Lilburn, Ga. One of the problems facing the sales of the Taxicab was its seating capacity. Most big-city operators wanted 5-passenger cabs, and in fact, New York City law required 5-passenger capacity. And, in smaller towns where capacity wasn't that critical, any much cheaper sedan could serve almost as well as the special cab.

Appearing to be more car than truck was the Deluxe Delivery Car, which was officially introduced on Jan. 24, but did not get into production until February. Designated the Model 130-A and priced at $595, the lines followed those of the Tudor sedan. In fact, it could be ordered in the same color combinations as the Tudor. A single rear door with left-hand hinges gave access to the rear, which was paneled in "steel craft" cardboard. The driver and passenger seats were finished in brown imitation Spanish leather. The cargo floor was 35 inches long and 43 inches high. For an extra $10, it could be fitted with a full shelf which essentially provided two cargo spaces, each approximately 20 inches high. Unlike the regular commercial vehicles, the Deluxe Delivery used bright headlights and radiator shell and automotive running boards.

Quite rare even in its day, and highly prized today, is the Open Pickup, Model 78-A which remained unchanged from 1928. Still using its bed from the Model T era, the cute little truck featured a soft top which utilized snap-on side curtains for weather protection. The standard finish was dark green with black radiator, lights, fenders, aprons, and wheels. The interior was done in black imitation leather with black cardboard door and cowl panels. Initially priced at $445, the Open Pickup dropped to $430 by year end, and as such was the lowest priced complete vehicle on Ford's roster. Unlike the open cars, the Open Pickup did not get outside door handles.

A comparison between the Deluxe Delivery Car and the regular light Panel Delivery shows that the latter was much more of a truck, even though it was based on essentially the same chassis as the cars. Cataloged as the Model 79-A, the truck used a body that was virtually a carry-over from the Model T days. True to the commercial vehicle format, the Panel Delivery used a black painted radiator shell and headlights, and commercial untrimmed running boards. Prices for this particular vehicle varied from $575 to $615 throughout the year. As were most commercial vehicles, this one was finished in a dark green, now called Rock Moss Green, but could also be special ordered in black.

1929

Far more popular than the Open Cab Pickup was the Closed Cab Pickup, which also used a cab and bed style directly from the Model T era. These units continued to be supplied by Briggs, stamped from dies cut for the 1925 vehicles. Priced at $495, Closed Cab Pickups used the old Model T visor with visible ribs, and came complete with outside rearview mirror. Production of all pickups this year reached 77,917, but there is no way to tell how many were open or closed cab models. However, it is safe to assume that the majority had closed cabs. In addition, it appears that this style was carried into 1930, with another 20,780 pickups of both types being built in this style between Jan. 1 and May 30, 1930, when the new 1930 style was phased in for these particular truck styles.

Even though Ford was now producing its own station wagon, the aftermarket body builders continued to supply their own versions of these bodies for mounting on Ford's light commercial chassis. There were a variety of reasons for this, but mainly the outside builders continued to supply these bodies for many different makes of chassis, none of which had depot hacks of their own. Thus, with relatively little conversion, these bodies could also be made to fit Ford chassis, so there was little reason not to continue this market. Also, there were those who felt that the outside sourced body might be better than one built by Ford. And, there was the problem of supply. At the start, at least, Ford was slow in meeting its station wagon orders, whereas the aftermarket units were readily available. This particular body, wearing a Ford visor, was produced by the Mifflinburg Body Co. of Pennsylvania. Designated Model 32-F Suburban, it featured three deluxe upholstered leather seats, with the rear two being removable. Its load space was 69 inches long, or 10 inches longer than Ford's own wagon.

Standard Commercial Body Co. of Michigan was never a large factor in the station wagon field, but they did include such styles in their extensive listing of ready-to-fit truck bodies. Designated the Model F-293 Suburban by Standard, this rather lengthy body offered a load space 68 inches long, as opposed to Ford's 59-inch cargo floor. Both rear and center seats were removable and a drop-down tailgate was standard. Clip-on side curtains were used on the doors, while roll-up curtains covered the rear sections. Surprisingly, this heavily retouched illustration does not show the chassis with a sidemount. Possibly it is on the right, or, since the bright radiator shell would indicate that this was a passenger car chassis, a sidemount and welled fender was not included in the price.

One of the most unusual vehicles ever to grace a modified Ford passenger car chassis is this snowmobile hearse, used by the M.J. Managan Funeral Home of Dunsieth, N.D. Apparently the funeral coach was not convertible back to wheeled status, but was used strictly for snowy weather services, which in North Dakota probably occupied a fair portion of the year. Converted by the Gleason Garage of Bottineau, N.D., the vehicle appears to be the only one of its kind ever constructed for this unique occupation. Based on the Tudor Sedan, vestiges of the original body can be seen at the A-pillar and at the body break just ahead of the Managan nameplate. The top appears to be canvas stretched truck-like over the heavy top bows. The rectangular unit on the windshield is an electric heating coil, used as an early type of defroster.

Ford's aviation endeavors really shifted into high gear this year. After completing a total of 78 4-ATs, production switched to the new 5-AT in late 1928. The plane used three 420-horsepower Pratt & Whitney Wasp engines and could carry up to 15 passengers. Sought not only by the commercial airline industry, but the military as well, and enjoying a reputation which was the envy of most other aircraft manufacturers, the Tri-motor actually reached a one-a-day production schedule in May, an unheard-of rate for the aviation industry. This model, owned by the U.S. Navy, is equipped with a set of wheel skirts to help reduce the drag of the exposed landing gear. Eventually, Ford Tri-motors would see service in virtually every country in the world, and would remain in commercial service long after much newer planes were scrapped and forgotten. In fact, a handful of Tri-motors are still in use, carrying passengers on short excursions at major antique car and aircraft meets.

The new Model A line appeared in January, and those who expected a rehash of the 28/29 line were in for a huge surprise. True, the "new" Model A bore all of the family resemblance of the old style, but still the designers achieved wonders while keeping within the parameters of the original concept.

Radiator shell, hood, cowl, A-pillars, fenders, and wheels were all new for the year. The radiator shell was now higher and more narrow, as was the food, which flowed nicely into the new cowl. The cowl itself was both higher and wider, and now incorporated the A-pillars on all models, ending forever the archaic "coupe pillar" design. Headlights were larger and more rounded and the fenders were more full and flowing, giving the car a much heavier and solid appearance.

On all models, the belt molding trim began at the radiator shell and traveled the entire length of the car, wrapping completely around the bodies on the 4-passenger styles, and around the superstructure on the coupes. Even the wheels were new, now being 19-inches and wearing 4.75 tires, as opposed to the 21-inch wheels with 4.50 tires used on the 28/29 models. The new wheels both lowered the car and helped to give it a more solid look.

Within the model framework, three new DeLuxe

Ford's third most popular car, and its most popular open model was the standard Roadster, Model 40-B (Std). However, in base form it did not look like this trimmed version shown in a dealer's introductory display. Whereas this model features dual sidemounts and the $35 dealer installed rumble seat, the $435 factory versions had a trunk deck and a single rear-mounted spare wheel, with the tire being an extra cost option. Still, production of the Standard Roadster reached 112,901, or more than 10 times that of its deluxe version. The folding windshield and automatic windshield wiper were now stock items on all open cars, as were folding wind wings. Since the deluxe version of the roadster didn't appear until August, it seems logical that many dealers would have given a sporty look to the standard models in the early months of the year in order to enhance sales.

models were created initially. They were a roadster, coupe, and Fordor, all identified by their deluxe interiors, bright cowl molding and attractive cowl lights which matched the headlights in design. In June, a DeLuxe Phaeton was introduced, but it was nothing like the standard Phaeton. This new model was a 2-door affair, with seating much like a modern convertible, with full front and rear seats. Then, in November, barely in time to escape being classed as a 1931 model, came the last of the new DeLuxe line. That was the Victoria, which was basically a sporty looking close-coupled 2-door sedan. Built by both Briggs and Murray, this car had the distinction of having Ford's first bustle back trunk, but with access from the inside only. It also marked the first use of a slanted windshield on a Model A.

Windshields were also a factor on the Roadsters and Phaetons. These models had totally redesigned windshields with all metal being either stainless steel or chrome. These windshields now could be folded flat across the cowl for full open driving. Windwings, which were now included as a standard item, would fold flat against the windshield when it was folded, providing a very sporty picture. On the DeLuxe versions this sport look was even more enhanced by the use of a lefthand sidemount, with dual sidemounts being optionally available on special order.

In the Fordor field, there was a shifting of models, but no startling developments as all of the 1929 styles were modified into 1930 trim. The exception is the Model 60 series of 60-A; 60-B, and 60-C styles, which were discontinued. Following on this path shortly after introduction was the Standard 2-window Sedan, Model 170-B, which was phased out in March to be replaced by a DeLuxe version of the same body.

The super-popular Tudor, with a slightly longer body

Although Ford officially had no commercial version of the Standard Roadster this year, it did encourage its dealers to install various commercial bodies for those buyers who still wanted a car/light truck conversion. Even relatively large body companies such as the Mifflinburg firm found enough sales in these slip-in units to manufacture and advertise a full line. This is the Mifflinburg Slip-On Pickup body, which could be fitted to either the Standard Roadster or the Business Coupe. Installation simply involved removing the trunk deck, and sliding in and bolting down the pickup bed, in less than an hour's work. Buyers who were considering this type of conversion had to order a left hand sidemount rather than a rear spare. In stock form the Standard Roadster weighed 2,147 pounds and was 12 feet, 11 inches long overall.

but otherwise unchanged, continued to draw the lion's share of orders. Initial plans were to offer the car in both standard and deluxe trim, but the deluxe versions never occurred. A Model A DeLuxe Tudor almost didn't make it at all, not being introduced until mid-season of 1931, and then having only a 6-month run. Ford either felt that sales of the Tudor were so good that the incentive of a deluxe model was not needed, or it assumed that buyers of the Tudor were pragmatic family people who would not spend money for fancy trimmings.

As much as the exterior of the car was changed, the running gear portion was left alone. Sometime in March new rear engine supports were designed and a larger oil return pipe was installed on the rear main bearing to speed the return flow of oil in cold weather. Also, the metal wire conduit which carried the wires from the generator to the terminal block was changed to a pliable loom because the conduit was found to chaff the wires and cause short circuits. And in May, another new crankcase breather pipe was installed in an attempt to lessen oil blow-by. Aside from these earth shaking changes, nothing appears to have been done to either engine or running gear that could be considered a major innovation. Ford was again operating under the theory that if something isn't broken, don't fix it.

Engine numbers for this period start with 2742696 on Jan. 1, 1930, and run through 4237500 on Dec. 31, showing total engine production of 1,494,804 for the calendar/model year. This compares to total vehicle production of 1,045,004, which was still in the million

ballpark, but a substantial drop of 513,663 from the 1,558,667 produced in 1929. Of course, the depression economy which began in October, 1929, with the Wall St. crash, did little to enhance the sales of cars, and all makers were feeling the pinch. In comparison to other manufacturers, Ford was well in the game, producing almost twice the number turned out by Chevrolet, and nearly 10 times that of the next closest rivals, Buick and Hudson.

Of the cars produced, the Tudor accounted for over one-third of the total production, listing 376,271 units for the year. Running in second place was the Standard Coupe, with 226,027, while the Standard Roadster still commanded third place with 112,901. The only other model to have over 100,000 units was the 3-window Town Sedan, a deluxe trimmed car which accounted for 104,953 sales. At the low end of the scale was the Taxicab, which supposedly wasn't even offered in 1930, but which shows on the list as having 10 produced. Also on the puzzling side is the Town Car, which also does not show a carry-over into 1930, yet which registers 63 units as having been built.

On the price lists, all models were down somewhat from the 1929 levels, with posted prices being anywhere from $10 to $50 lower than the comparable previous year's model.

On the corporate side, two new assembly plants were opened in California. The first was a new facility at Long Beach, while the other was a plant at Richmond to replace the older facility at San Francisco.

Initially, sales of the Standard Roadster were very good, but by late spring open car buyers were becoming scarce. To help boost sales, Ford came out with the Deluxe Roadster, Model 40-B (Dl). Costing $495 and available only with a rumble seat, this car was quickly identified by its cowl lights and its tan fabric top as opposed to the black artificial leather top used on the Standard version. In addition, its seats were in 2-tone tan genuine leather, while the Standard model had black artificial leather upholstery. The Deluxe version also had brown carpeting instead of a rubber floor mat, and its door and cowl panels were in tan leather rather than black cardboard. The rumble seat was in matching tan, but artificial leather was used here rather than the genuine variety. The Deluxe Roadster also used a special low windshield and wind wings, which were not interchangeable with the standard model.

Except for a few accessories which could have been dealer or restorer installed, this Standard Phaeton appears just as it would have in 1930. Designated the Model 35-B, the 2,235-pound car was priced at $440. Still, the appeal of open cars was slipping mightily with each passing year, and as a result only 16,479 were built in 1930. Available in five solid and two 2-tone color combinations, the Phaeton used the same black artificial leather top and side curtains as did the Standard Roadster. The interior too was done in the same material of black artificial leather for the seats and black grained cardboard for the panels. The accessories on this version include cowl lights, quail radiator cap, right-hand windshield wiper, and swing-out signal arms just below the folding windshield stanchions. The Standard Phaeton was Ford's shortest car, being only 12 feet 7.5 inches from bumper to bumper, as opposed to 13 feet for most others.

Sharing virtually nothing with the Standard Phaeton except its name was the Deluxe Phaeton, Model 180-A. Introduced in June, 1930, the $645 car was aimed at those who wanted a sporty, semi-luxurious open car, sort of like today's sports car. The Deluxe Phaeton featured its own exclusive 2-door body of 4-passenger configuration. Two folding seats occupied the front, while a single bench seat with arm rests filled in the back. All were upholstered in the same beige genuine leather that would be used in the later-arriving Deluxe Roadster. The windshield was low-cut as compared to those of the Standard Phaeton and Roadster, and the wind wings were styled to match. Although shown in black in the promotional photo, the car could be ordered in a choice of 11 colors. Never intended for high production, the rather expensive car drew only 3,945 orders this year.

Shown with its top up and side curtains installed is this Deluxe Phaeton. The top and curtains were of a tan fabric interlined with rubber. When not in use, the curtains lived in their own compartment behind the rear seat back. Both the left-hand sidemount and the folding trunk rack were standard items on this car, while a right-hand spare was an often-seen extra-cost option. A specially designed trunk that would fit on the luggage rack was a dealer accessory. These trunks were manufactured exclusively for Ford by the Abel & Bach Co. of Milwaukee. The rear quarter of the body was slightly depressed to allow the top to fold with a minimum of bulking, giving an almost straight line appearance rearward from the windshield when the top was folded. The Deluxe Phaeton weighed 2,285 pounds.

Except for changes to meet the new cowl structure, the Cabriolet was essentially a direct carry-over from the 1929 version. Representing a true convertible, with roll-up door windows and weather-tight interior, the 2,273-pound car was designated 68-B. Priced at $645, it was designed for those who wanted a sporty open car with the option of a weatherproof coupe. Available only in rumble seat form, the car proved to be quite popular, with 25,868 being produced. All left the Briggs plant in "knocked-down" form, with final assembly being done at the respective Ford assembly plants. In standard trim, the car came with a rear-mounted spare. The windshield would swing outward for ventilation, and the upper door posts were removable.

Shown with an optional left sidemount and its top raised is this well restored Cabriolet. When sidemounts were installed, the cars were usually equipped with a rear luggage rack and aftermarket trunk. Three interior changes appear to have been made on the Cabriolet this year. The first 5,000 models were upholstered in a gray checked cloth, similar to that used in the 1929 models. Then, in late February, a tan bedford cloth was used. And, in July when the adjustable front seat came into being, it seems a switch was made to a brown bedford cloth. In all cases, panels were done in matching broadcloth, while all rumble seats were done in brown artificial leather, regardless of the material used in the front compartment. The top was done in the same tan cloth with rubber lining as used on the Deluxe Phaeton and Roadster models. The chrome-plated landau bars were functional, and supported the top when it was raised.

The windshield visor and lack of cowl lights are the only two quick identification points that differentiate the Sport Coupe from the Cabriolet. Also, the Sport Coupe used the full-framed doors of the regular coupe, sported a convertible-type top that would not fold, and had dummy landau irons. Designated the Model 50-B and costing $530, the car was available in rumble seat form only. In standard form, it wore a rear-mounted spare, but single or dual sidemounts could be ordered when a rear luggage rack was desired, as on this model. A relatively middle of the road car insofar as production went, the Sport Coupe listed 69,167 builds this year. As did on the other coupes, an adjustable front seat became standard at mid-season.

What did rumble seat passengers do when it rained? Well, most of them got wet. But a very few owners availed themselves of such aftermarket contraptions as this wire-frame canvas covered unit which could be installed to protect the otherwise exposed passengers. Built by an unknown supplier, this unit is shown installed on a well restored Sport Coupe during a California parade in the early 1960s. This year, the Sport Coupe was available in either brown hairline cloth or gray checked cloth upholstery in the front, while the rumble seat was in black artificial leather. The top was upholstered in gray artificial leather, although some examples appear to have been finished in the same tan material as used on the Cabriolet. The rear mounted spare was standard, but the bumper cross-bar was an accessory.

With windshield open, a businessman makes his rounds in the new Standard Coupe, Model 45-B(Std). The second most popular car in Ford's 1930 book, the Standard Coupe drew 226,027 orders. The car cost $500 and weighed 2,257 pounds. Although resembling the 1929 version, the coupe sported a totally new body which had a roofline 1.5 inches lower than the previous model. In order to keep the headroom approximately the same, the seats were also lowered about 1.5 inches from the former model. Usually fitted with a trunk deck, the car could carry 14 cubic feet of material in the rear, plus offering space on the package shelf behind the seat. Mifflinburg and other aftermarket companies offered the same pickup and commercial bed conversions for this car as they did for the Standard Roadster. When those were in use, a sidemounted spare would be ordered. Such a sidemount would also have made it easier to load the trunk, but oddly, few Standard Coupes are pictured with anything but rear-mounted spares.

It is not known how many Standard Coupes were fitted with rumble seats, as these units could be quickly installed at the dealership level for about $35 extra. Buyers had a choice of brown or gray checked cloth for the seat and matching cloth panels and headliner. In February, an interior of black artificial leather also became optional, apparently aimed at fleet and salesmen's cars, where the interiors would be subject to hard wear. When installed, the rumble seat was upholstered in black artificial leather. Doors were paneled in matching broadcloth and were equipped with relatively large storage or map pockets. Matching silk roller shades were fitted to the rear windows, while black rubber floor mats were standard.

About a month after the Standard Coupe was introduced, the Deluxe Coupe, model 45-B(Dl), came out. Priced at $550, the car offered a choice of nine different body colors, as opposed to seven for the standard version. It also was fitted with cowl lights. The primary difference between the two coupe classes was in the upholstery and interior trim. The Deluxe version was done in either brown mohair or brown bedford with seat buttons, as opposed to the pleated upholstery in the Standard models. Initially brown bedford cloth was used for the doors and headliner also, but this was changed to brown broadcloth at mid-year. A dome light was also standard on this model. Far less popular than the Standard version, the Deluxe Coupe drew only 28,937 orders, probably reflecting the fact that most buyers of this class of car could not see the $50 extra for a slightly fancier interior.

As was the case with the Standard Coupe, the Deluxe Coupe came as a trunk version only, unless the extra-cost rumble seat was ordered. The rumble seat could be either dealer or factory installed and cost about $50 extra for the Deluxe type. This differed from the Standard model only in its upholstery material, with the seat being done in a brown crushed-grain artificial leather, rather than in the black of the Standard models. Also, the side panels were in cardboard with a similar brown crush-grain finish as opposed to the standard black cardboard. The left sidemount on this car would have been far more practical on a trunk equipped model, where the spare often made it difficult to load heavy objects into the trunk. All coupes this year were just a hair shy of being 13 feet overall from bumper to bumper.

This new Tudor sports an option that received much publicity but little actual use in this era. It is wearing a set of Goodyear Airwheels, which were supposed to smooth the bumps, provide a much better ride, and increase gas mileage. The low pressure 9.00x13 wheels were not unlike the "flotation" tires in use today on equipment designed to operate on soft ground. Despite their claims, the tires gave the car a wallowing ride and made steering difficult. Goodyear was just one of several major companies to introduce these oversized tires, but none met with any success. The positive side to the story is that such experimentation caused the auto manufacturers to consider more practical tires, resulting in all cars in general going to smaller wheels and lower pressure tires during the succeeding decade.

By far Ford's most popular car continued to be the Tudor Sedan, Model 55-B, which sold for $490 and probably represented Ford's best buy for the dollar. Despite the fact that some lists show a deluxe version available, it appears that the Tudor this year was produced only in standard trim. With sales topping out at 376,271, it appears that there was no need for Ford to come up with a deluxe version as a buyer incentive. Sporting a totally new body, the Tudor this year weighed 2,372 pounds, with the gain probably due to the 2.25-inch added length in the rear portion of the body. Buyers had their choice of seven exterior colors and three interior schemes. The later were upholstery in a blue hairline stripe, brown check, or gray checked cloth, with matching plain cloth headliners and panels. As on all closed Fords, the windshield could swing out for ventilation.

Shown here with a military paint job but otherwise perfectly stock is the Standard Fordor Sedan, also officially known as the 3-window Fordor. Priced at $625, it bore model 165-C when built by Murray and Model 165-D when built by Briggs. A total of 41,133 were built, but it is not possible to determine how many came from each factory. This is the Briggs version, identifiable by the straight line upper window edge. Despite the similarities in design, there were virtually no parts or panels that were interchangeable between the Murray and Briggs versions. Because the Murray body cost Ford almost $8 more than the Briggs body, some price lists show the Murray bodied sedans listing at $10 more than the Briggs. Both bodies were virtually unchanged from the 1929 production. Civilian buyers had their choice of seven exterior colors and seats in either gray or brown check with plain matching panels and headliner. In 1930, the U.S. military began to upgrade its fleet of World War I vintage vehicles, and as result, placed large orders with Ford for various kinds of cars and light trucks, including many sedans which did duty as officers' transportation.

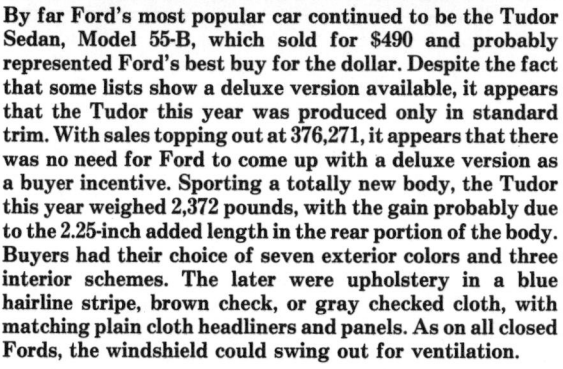

The Briggs bodied Town Sedan, Model 155-D, differed externally from the Standard 3-window Sedan only in its use of cowl lights. The main difference between the Town Sedan and the 3-window, besides a $50 bill, was in the deluxe interior. More than twice as popular as the Standard Sedan, the Town Sedan commanded 104,935 orders, shared between Briggs and Murray. The straight upper window line from A-pillar to rear quarter panel identifies this as a Briggs production. Both Briggs and Murray versions weighed 2,495 pounds. Town Sedans featured a dome light and silk roller shades not only on the rear window, but also on the quarter windows. The body would run into the early 1931 model year, until replaced by the slant-windshield version at mid-year.

The arched top window lines bear proof that this is the Murray bodied version of the 3-window Town Sedan. Except for the accessory step plates, this well restored model looks as if it just rolled from the dealer's floor. All Town sedans sported deluxe interiors with buttoned upholstery on the seats, side and center arm rests for the rear seat, a rear dome light, matching silk roller shades on the rear and quarter windows, and assist straps for the rear passengers. Buyers had their choice of four interiors: brown or green mohair with matching panels and matching cotton headliner; brown bedford cord throughout, or brown bedford cord seats with brown broadcloth panels and brown cotton headliner. In all cases, brown carpeting was used. Regardless of which interior was selected, all four doors were equipped with storage pockets. The rear quarter windows could not be lowered on these models.

The last model to enter Ford's 1930 roster was the Victoria, Model 190-A. It was introduced in November, 1930, barely in time to be considered a 1930 car. Weighing 2,375 pounds and costing 4580, the car accounted for 6,306 units before the 1931 season. The Victoria style, which would evolve into the 5-passenger coupe, has the distinction of being the first closed Model A to use the new visorless slanted windshield design. Built by both Murray and Briggs, these cars too have few interchangeable body parts, though the differences between the two manufacturers are not as great as on the 3-window sedans. The rather stubby looking car featured a top and rear quarter covered in gray artificial leather of the same type as used on the Sport Coupe. Considered part of the Deluxe line, it had such features as mohair upholstery, silk roller shades on both the rear and quarter windows, sun visors, door pockets, and cowl lights. A small luggage area was found by pulling forward on the rear seat back.

The 2-window Fordor, produced only by Briggs, was first introduced only in Standard trim, as the Model 170-B(Std). Weighing 2,488 and priced at $590, its production was curtailed at the end of March, after only 5,279 were built. At that point, the car re-entered the roster as the Deluxe 2-window Fordor, Model 170-B(Dl), priced at $650. As shown here, only the cowl lights spell the exterior difference between the Deluxe and the earlier Standard models. In Deluxe guise, a total of 12,584 were produced. As with the Town Sedan, the primary difference between the two models was the interior, with buyers of the Deluxe version having a choice of brown mohair seats and arm rests and matching panels and a brown cotton headliner, or brown bedford cord seats and arm rests with brown broadcloth panels, or an interior entirely in brown bedford cord. All of the special interior features of the Town Sedan were found on the 2-window Deluxe models.

1930

Taxicab Details

Dimensions

Width of Doors	26⅛"
Height of Body	49¼"
Height of Car—Road to Top	71¾"
Width of Rear Seat	48¼"
Size of Auxiliary Seat	16" x 16"
Depth of Rear Seat	18"
Length with Bumpers	155 ½"
Length of Body	98"
Weight	2500 lbs.

Comfort

Rear seat will accommodate three passengers and an auxiliary seat with back to driver will accommodate another. Upholstery in grey velour and imitation leather. Driver's seat is fully enclosed. It is separated from passengers' compartment by metal and glass partition.

Upper section of partition, windshield, rear door and rear quarter windows all are of shatterproof glass.

PRICE (F. O. B. DETROIT). $725.00

Freight and Handling	Delivered Price

FORDFAX

Although most Ford sales lists for 1930 omit the Town Car, records indicate that Briggs turned out a total of 63 such units on 1930 chassis. This particular model, was advertised by Theodore Luce Inc., the Lincoln agency in New York City, on March 22, 1930. It shows the car with dual sidemounts and whitewall tires, in addition to a uniformed chauffeur. Although no price is listed for this year, it seems probable that it was still in the $1,200 to $1,400 range. The Town Car was probably kept in production only because it could be adapted to the 1930 cowl with little effort. Also, since 1929 production of this model had reached 913, Ford may have felt that there was some future for the car. Still, the fact that it doesn't appear on most dealer lists this year is a puzzle, and may indicate that the 63 produced were simply run-off of bodies on hand. As before, the car carried a deluxe trimmed rear compartment, with the front done in black natural leather.

That Ford initially planned to offer the Taxi in 1930 is evident from this notice in Fordfax of January, 1930. The fact that only 10 such cars were produced in 1930 before the style was dropped at the end of January is also known. Why Ford decided to leave the taxi market is also a puzzle, as a total of 4,576 were sold in 1929. Had production continued, the car would have used the Standard Sedan body of either Briggs or Murray, with only interior conversion necessary. It appears the interior would have followed that of the 1929 style, with one jump seat facing rearward, and one 3-passenger rear bench seat facing forward. The driver was completely enclosed by a glass and steel partition, and had a single-place leather seat. The rear was upholstered in gray velour. It interesting to note that all glass was shatterproof, not just the windshield.

Only a builder's plaque identifies this beautiful restoration as having been assembled in Cleveland by Baker-Raulang. Otherwise, the bodies were virtually identical, regardless of which of the three companies did the final assembly. Note how the side curtains fasten on the Ford wagons, as opposed to the roll-up type of curtains used by other body manufacturers. Ford installed a series of snaps around the perimeter of each window, to match the snaps on the curtains. With this arrangement, the curtains would easily open with the doors. When photographed in the mid-1970s, this wagon was owned by Clyde Roberts of Dover, N.H.

Considered a commercial vehicle, the Station Wagon, Model 150-B, did not receive its 1930 face lift until June. Apparently those built between January and June used the 1929 Ford commercial styling that was carried over into 1930. When the new wagon did appear in its 1930 guise, it was slightly changed from previous models. Among the differences were lack of visor, a more noticeable curve in the roofline just above and behind the A-pillar, and the forward curve at the bottom of the exposed A-pillar. As before, color options were not available, with Manilla Brown being the only finish used on the hood and cowl, and black covering the fenders, wheels, and all other metal parts. Costing $640 and weighing 2,482 pounds, the wagons saw production drop to 3,510. And, of these, 1,570 still wore the 1929-style sheet metal. As before, the basic wood patterns were cut at Ford's plant at Iron Mountain, Mich., with assembly now being done at Detroit by both Murray and Briggs, and in Cleveland by Baker-Raulang. The left sidemount was standard.

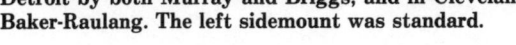

Introduced late in the 1930 season was the Model 225-A Special Delivery, conceived and built for Ford by the Baker-Raulang Co. of Cleveland. Using the stock Station Wagon as a base, the 2-door truck was really a variation of the wagon body. One of the first off the line went to work in Dearborn for the Department of Commerce, serving as a radio test vehicle. It is posed here in front of one of the famed Tri-motors. As did the wagon, the Special Delivery used a varnished wood body, with a varnished wood interior. Seats were in black artificial leather, while a heavier black artificial leather was used for the roof. The large varnished birch side panel provided an excellent billboard for the owner's identification. Introduced in December, 1930, only 19 were built before the 1931 changeover. They cost about $600.

1930

One of the more rare vehicles produced this year was the Briggs-built Town Car Delivery, Model 295-A. Although some records would indicate that this was a 1931 vehicle only, not being introduced until January, 1931, other evidence shows that Briggs did indeed build at least three of these models in 1930. These used the vertical windshield design shown here as opposed to the slant windshield of the 1931 versions. Based on the Town Car, the delivery version featured a cab interior in black artificial leather, and a rear compartment finished in birch plywood. A removable top, identical to that used on the Town Car, covered the front compartment in bad weather, while roll-up windows in the doors made the whole unit weather tight. Dome lights were provided in both the front and rear compartment, and coach lamps, cowl lights, rearview mirror, and sidemounted spare were all standard features. A partition with a full-length sliding door divides the two compartments. The body was all aluminum, handcrafted over special dies.

Although car styling changed in January, 1930, the commercial vehicles went right on wearing their 1928/29 sheetmetal. Finally, by mid-May, the new passenger car styling caught up with the light commercial chassis, and all of the light trucks began to look like the cars, except for the painted grille shells and headlights. Still one of the cutest trucks in the line, despite its rapidly dropping popularity, was the Open Cab Pickup. Only 3,429 of the 2,073-pound units were built. All had modified cabs to meet the new cowlings, but all continued to use the old Model 78-A pickup bed that Briggs had continuously cranked out since 1925. As did the Roadster and Phaeton, the new Open Cab Pickup also had a windshield that would fold flat across the cowl. On this model, owners could lower the top, or even remove it fairly easily. Surprisingly, side curtains were now considered an extra-cost item.

The Closed Cab Pickup proved to be a much more popular light truck than did its open companion, and a total of 86,383 left the factory. All were priced at $435. Designated the Model 82-B, it featured an entirely new cab similar in line to Ford's popular coupe models. But it still used the old Briggs-supplied 78-A pickup bed. Visor, rearview mirror and sidemount were all standard items. The top was covered in a black rubber fabric, while the interior was in black embossed cardboard with a black imitation leather seat. As on the closed cars, the windshield swung outward for ventilation.

After years of excellent sales, both the depression and advanced aircraft engineering were beginning to take their toll on the famed Tri-motor. Production went into a gradual decline and by 1933 ceased altogether. By now the company was producing the 7-AT with one Wasp and two Wasp Junior engines. Of 13-passenger capacity, this plane was suffering not as much from design deficiencies as from the economic conditions which had hit the infant airline industry far harder than it had other businesses. Ford now found itself repowering and rebuilding some of its earlier planes, such as this 4-AT, into more modern and powerful craft. But though temporarily helpful, such activities were not enough to keep the aviation division on a healthy level, and thus, Ford's aircraft production slowly passed on.

1931

As the new year dawned, things did not look all that good for the total automotive industry, nor for Ford in particular. The depression was deepening and car sales were so far off that many of the lesser makes were facing the last years of their lives. Even the industry giants such as Ford and General Motors were finding the going rough. After all, out of work people did not go out and buy new cars, and those who did have jobs were not inclined to fritter away their cash in the face of what could be next week's or next month's layoff.

In a situation of this sort, one would expect the overall automotive scene to pull in its horns, turn a deaf ear to costly engineering and design changes, and offer virtually nothing except puttsy little dull cars that could be produced with a minimum of cost and change. One would expect that to happen—but it did not. Instead, the industry overall began a period of design and engineering innovation that had not been realized up until this time, and really, has never been matched since. The year 1930 ushered in a decade of automotive change that has yet to be equaled by any other decade since, when measured in terms of new innovations and inventions, save possibly the current decade of computerization and chip technology.

The reason for this flamboyance in the face of disaster was simple. If the car companies were to survive, they had to sell cars. And in order to sell cars in this economic atmosphere, they had to provide something special— possibly an early version of the dream machine. And thus, in this decade, would come the multi-cylinder engines, the performance charts, the longer wheelbases, skirted fenders, well styled and comfortable bodies, vivid colors, and even some of the most beautiful and expensive custom bodies ever to grace automotive chassis. True, the average person who could be convinced to buy a new car probably still went for the rather drab blue or gray 2-door sedan. But at least he bought a new car, and it was probably thoughts or dreams of the more flamboyant machines that sparked the buying interest in the first place.

And where did Ford stand as this decade came into view? In 1931, its position was not the best. True, almost 4-million Model As were scurrying over the highways of virtually every country in the world, and the design had proven to be one of the most reliable and trouble free automobiles ever developed. But the design was not that much different than the introductory models of 1928, and in the interim other companies had moved ahead with their own products.

Chevrolet, now Ford's tooth-and-nail competitor, had introduced its 6-cylinder engine in 1929, and now came out with an entirely redesigned car of very attractive line and a 5.5-inch longer wheelbase. Plymouth, which had just gone through a $2.5-million styling renovation, still had a 4-cylinder engine, but its engineering advances had moved the car into the third sales spot nationally, and it was nibbling heavily at Ford's market.

Meanwhile, people were beginning to wonder if Henry Ford was going to repeat the mistake he had made with the Model T, and keep pushing a tired old design far beyond its limit. Adding weight to this fear was the fact that Ford was still reluctant to make definite model year changes. Other companies in the automotive industry had learned the advantage of changing the car with each year. But Ford still preferred to make its changes on a running basis, as needed, and as a result, the 1931 issue was little different than the 1930. Ford had some new competitive ideas in mind, but they were not to be seen in 1931, and true to form, they were not being broadcast to the public either.

Granted, there were a few minor changes on the Model A to differentiate the 1931 style from the 1930 issue. The most obvious change was in the radiator shell, which now had stamped and painted inserts at both top and bottom. Less noticeable were the new running boards and 1-piece splash aprons. Later, the Ford script on the shell was changed slightly. But actually, all of these were running changes and not definite model year indicators. For example, the new radiator shell actually appeared on the Victoria in November, yet did not reach all of the Model A assembly plants until late March, 1931. And, the new aprons did not reach all of the plants until September.

Under the hood there also was little change. Some reports would indicate that the Zenith carburetor was changed slightly, while use of the Holley carburetor remained constant. In March, the exhaust manifold design was changed slightly, but otherwise everything remained the same and the 4-cylinder engine continued to displace 200.5 cubic inches and crank out 40 brake horsepower at 2200 rpm. Engine numbers ran from 4237501 on Jan. 1 to 4830806 at the end of November, when it appears that production was halted. However, production of the Model A engine resumed again in January of 1932, as the Model A was carried into that year until the true 1932 cars came out in March. The 1932 production numbers ran from 4830807 to 4849340, being differentiated from the 1932 Model B engines which began with number 5000000.

The tabulation shows that only 593,305 engines were turned out during calendar year 1931, plus another 18,533 came out in early 1932, which probably should still be counted as part of the 1931 model year. This compares with model year production of 488,059 cars, including station wagons but excluding light commercial chassis or Model AA trucks. Of all of this production, the only model to achieve sales of over 100,000 was the Standard Tudor, which registered 148,425 builds. Once again the Standard Coupe came in second place, but this time with only 79,816 sales. Third place was taken by the Town Sedan with 55,469 units, while the standard Roadster, which had occupied third place in 1930 this year barely made the production charts with only 5,449 builds. Conversely, the Deluxe Roadster made up the gap by coming in fourth with 52,997 sales.

With the exception of the Standard 2-window Fordor, which was dropped in March, 1930, all of the other previous styles were on hand going into 1931. Then, in May, a new series of 3-window Sedans was introduced, replacing the old style 3-window and Town Sedans. Built by both Murray and Briggs, the cars featured totally new bodies, with modern slanted windshields and no visors. Other styling changes included a new roof line and door design, and rear quarter windows that could be lowered. To avoid the previous parts hassle caused by Briggs and Murray building different style bodies, Ford specified that all bodies must be identical, and therefore it is virtually impossible to tell whether the new slant window sedan was Briggs or Murray sourced.

The first two slant window designs came out as a Standard and a Deluxe version of the 3-window style, but shortly thereafter, a 2-window town Sedan was introduced. This model used the same basic body pattern as did the 3-window models, but had blank rear quarters and was available in Deluxe trim only. At the same time, the Cabriolet body was also redesigned slightly, and this model also gained a slant windshield. It is interesting to note that although all of the slant windshield cars were given their initial introductions in March, it wasn't until May that deliveries of the new styles actually replaced their former models.

Lastly, at the end of May came Ford's final Model A offering. Considered by some to represent the epitome of Model A styling, the new car was called the Convertible Sedan, though in reality it was neither a sedan nor a true convertible. In appearance, it looked more like the Victoria or even the Deluxe Phaeton, having a close-coupled 4-passenger body of 2-door configuration. Its top really can be considered only semi-convertible, in that the canvas portion rode up or down on two permanent side rails which also incorporated the A, B, and C-pillars. These provided an all-steel framing for both doors and quarter windows. Definitely a member of Ford's luxury series, the Convertible Sedan had an interior finished in genuine leather seats and imitation leather panels, with full carpeting front and rear. Both front seats folded and the driver's seat was adjustable. Luxury touches included pockets in both doors and ashtrays and arm rests for the rear seat. Priced at $640, this was the most expensive Model A, and probably as a result, its production only reached 4,864.

As mentioned earlier, because of production problems in bringing the new 1932 models out, Model A production was carried into March of 1932, giving the make an essential 14-month model year. During this year, the 20-millionth Ford was produced and two new plants were opened in Europe, at Dagenham, England, and Cologne, Germany. And, despite the very dismal economic picture world-wide, there was a degree of optimism within Ford, and surprisingly, within most of the American automotive scene. The car business might have been a mighty ill at this time, but at least the giants weren't ready for the grave.

Once Ford's most popular open car, the Standard Roadster, Model 40-B(Std) this year recorded only 5,499 sales. However, a large part of its lost production was picked up by the new Deluxe Roadster, which had been introduced in mid year, 1930, to help boost the sagging interest. The Standard Roadster continued to use its own tall windshield and wind wings, and came equipped with rear spare and trunk compartment, though an optional rumble seat could be added at the dealer level for about $50. Priced at $430 and weighing 2,155 pounds, this not only was the lightest and lowest priced Model A of the year, it was the all-time low for a brand new Model A car. The price included wind wings, top boot, automatic windshield wiper, and a rear spare wheel, but not the spare tire, which was an extra-cost accessory. As was the case with many of the lower priced Model As, the new double indented radiator shell did not arrive until mid-spring. Total Model A Standard Roadster production was 392,135 for the 4-year run.

Soaring in sales, as compared with its plain-jane standard sister was the Deluxe Roadster, Model 40-B(Dl), which had been introduced in the summer of 1930. Sales accounted for 52,997, or roughly 10 times the number of Standard models. However, since the model was built for only about 18 months, its total sales for the period were only 64,315. Weighing 2,230 pounds, the Deluxe Roadster cost $475, or only $45 more than the Standard model. For this, buyers got a rumble seat, cowl lights, genuine leather front seat in beige, rumble seat in matching artificial leather, brown floor carpet, and a special low windshield and wind wings. This was quite a luxury package for $45, and it is easy to see why the standard car's sales took a nosedive in the face of this competition. However, this year the sidemounted spare was not offered as a no-cost option, but had to be ordered as an extra-cost accessory. The rear-mounted spare was normal equipment.

Although production of the Standard Roadster had dropped considerably, there still were enough of these cute little cars in commercial use to warrant aftermarket supplies of slide-in cargo bodies. This advertising drawing, taken from a real vehicle, shows a closed box-type of body, probably with double swinging rear doors, that would have been perfect for light cargo such as carried by a traveling garden seed purveyor. Other types of slide-in bodies were the pickup bed variety, and taller boxes that would meet the top-line of the car. When companies or traveling salesmen selected open roadsters, they were usually tempted by price, not comfort, and the $60 difference between this car and a comparable coupe was often enough to determine the selection, especially in warmer parts of the country.

Unchanged from the previous model was the Standard Phaeton, Model 35-B. Once Ford's most popular style, the Phaeton was rapidly going the way of all open cars, and as a result, sales were down to only 4,076. This was less than one-tenth of those of 1928 or 1929. For the four year Model A span, Phaeton production was 117,849. The car was down in price too, listing at $435, or only $5 more than the Roadster. It weighed 2,212 pounds. As before, the interior was upholstered in pleated black artificial leather, with black cardboard panels. The top and side curtains were in a black long-grained artificial leather. The windshield would fold across the cowl.

Unlike the situation with the Roadster, Ford's most popular coupe model was the Standard version, Model 45-B(Std), which sold for $490. Outselling the Deluxe type by three to one, the car had wide appeal with salesmen and fleet car buyers who wanted a bit more comfort than found in the Standard Roadster. In base form, the car was equipped with a rear spare and trunk deck. However, it could be ordered with a rumble seat, or be fitted with any of the wide range of aftermarket slide-in bodies that were available to the roadster. Total sales for the year were 79,816, giving this type of car a grand total of 556,238 for the four year run, not counting another 74,987 sales of the Business Coupe style.

Showing off its new radiator shell and cowl lights is this Deluxe Coupe, Model 45-B(Dl). The small step plate on top of the rear fender says that this model was equipped with the optional rumble seat, which at the $525 base price, did not come with the car. What buyers did get this year, in addition to the cowl lights, was a choice of three different interiors: Either all brown mohair; brown mohair panels with a brown bedford cloth seat, or all tan broadcloth. Headliners were in either brown or tan napped cotton to match the seats. On Standard Coupes, buyers had their choice of a black artificial leather interior (usually used on fleet cars) or a gray or brown checked cloth seat with matching plain panels and headliner. On Deluxe models, the optional rumble seat would be finished in brown artificial leather, while Standard models would get a rumble seat finished in black artificial leather. The Deluxe Coupe weighed 2,265 pounds, while the Standard went in at 2,257 pounds.

About the same time that Goodyear introduced its Airwheels, General Tire Co. came out with its own version of these Mickey Mouse tires. Known as Streamline Jumbos, the Generals were sold by both tire stores and participating Ford dealers. A set included both tires and special pressed steel wheels and hubcaps. Based on the same concept as today's flotation tires, the low-pressure doughnuts were supposed to provide a smoother and safer ride. However, cost plus hard steering plus odd appearance combined to keep the tires from achieving any lasting popularity. They are shown on a rumble seat equipped Deluxe Coupe, but could be fitted to any model Ford. Normally, Model As took 4.75x19 inch tires.

Looking a bit on the tired side is this Sport Coupe, photographed in the late 1930s. Designated the Model 50-B, the car came in Deluxe trim only, with a rumble seat as standard fare. It used the same lower body as the Standard Coupe, but had its own unique superstructure not unlike that of the Cabriolet. However, on this car the top would not fold and the landau irons were strictly decorative. Costing $500 and weighing 2,283 pounds, the car drew only 19,700 orders this year. However, during its total run, it accounted for 88,867 units with the 1930/31 body and 214,125 with the previous 1928/29 body. The top continued to be in the same 2-tone gray artificial leather used in 1930, but two new interiors joined the gray checked cloth seat and plain gray panels of the previous year. These were a cloth interior of brown checked seat and plain brown panels and an artificial leather interior of black seat and gray panels. The rumble seat again was done in black artificial leather with black cardboard panels.

When announcement was made of the new slant windshield sedans in March, it was decided to give the Cabriolet the new windshield treatment also. However, production was held back until all of the vertical windshield models were sold, so therefore the new style Cabriolet did not materialize until May or June. The new windshield resulted in a new model number of 68-C, but otherwise did not change the $595 price or the 2,273-pound weight. Briggs built a total of 11,801 cabriolet bodies this year, but no breakdown was made as to how many had vertical or slant windshields. The windshields on these cars would swing out as on all the other closed models, rather than folding across the cowl as on the Roadster or Phaeton. This car is in basic form, with a rear-mounted spare. Initially introduced by Briggs in 1929, the Cabriolet style accounted for 54,090 units during its 3-year run.

Initial versions of the Cabriolet, Model 68-B, looked like this well-restored unit. With the top up, the attractive car looked like the Sport Coupe, but without the visor. The difference, however, was that the Cabriolet's landau irons were functional and the top would fold down. Costing $595, the car came in Deluxe form only and only with a rumble seat. However, the dual sidemounts and rear-mounted trunk and rack on this model were at extra cost, as were the chromed tire covers with rearview mirrors, and the Chevy-like stone guard. The tops on the Cabriolet were done in tan canvas interlined with rubber, and the rumble seats were always in black artificial leather. Buyers had an interior choice of brown bedford cord seat with brown broadcloth panels, or brown crushed grain genuine leather with similar artificial leather on the panels.

Today one of the most desired body styles, the Deluxe Phaeton really attracted little interest during its 2-year life span. Its first year's production was only 3,946, while this year only 2,229 were built, thus ranking it with the Town Car, Convertible Sedan, and Taxi as the rarest of all Model As. Priced at $580 and available in Deluxe trim only, the Model 180-A bore no resemblance at all to its namesake, the Standard Phaeton. The car featured genuine leather seats with matching artificial leather panels and brown carpeting. The folding trunk rack and left sidemount were standard, while dual sidemounts were a common accessory. As did the Phaeton and Roadster, this car had a folding windshield that would lay flat across the cowl. The rear quarters were slightly scalloped, so that when folded the top would be part of an almost horizontal line running the length of the car.

With its top raised and side curtains in place, the Deluxe Phaeton was not nearly as appealing looking as when it was totally open. The top and curtains were of a tan canvas interlined with rubber, the same as used on the Cabriolet and Convertible Sedan. The side curtains snapped into place, and would open with the doors, being supported by heavy internal wires. The flap just above the door handle is to allow for hand signals. Heavy celluloid was used in the window portions, but this tended to turn yellow after a few years of use. Almost a total body onto its own, the Deluxe Phaeton shared very few parts with any other Ford. It may have been dropped before the end of the model year, after a total production run of only 6,175 for the 18 or so months that it was in production.

Enjoying its only full year of production was the Victoria, Model 190-A, which had been introduced in November, 1930, as a 1930 car but carrying Ford's first double embossed radiator shell. This shell would be the primary identity mark for most (not all) of the 1931 models. Still, some cars were produced well into mid-spring with the previous smooth shell design. Available with either a steel or a leatherette top, the Victoria was priced at $580 and weighed 2,375 pounds. Both Murray and Briggs built the bodies, with production reaching a surprising 33,906 this year. In all, Victoria production reached 40,212 for the total 14-month run. When photographed at Hershey in the mid-1970s, this car belonged to Willard Prentice of Maryland. It had the tan leatherette top and wears the standard rear-mounted spare.

The last totally new Model A to be introduced to the public was the Convertible Sedan, Model 400-A. First shown at the end of May, the car was built by both Murray and Briggs, though it is impossible to ascertain how many were produced by each company. In the short time left before the Model A run ended, a total of 4,864 were built in this country, and another 229 were assembled outside the U.S., primarily in Canada and Argentina. Priced at $640 and weighing 2,335 pounds, the Convertible Sedan was really neither a sedan nor a true convertible. The top did go down, but on rollers set in a fixed roof rail which connected with the door framing and formed the C-pillar. As to seating arrangement, the car was relatively close coupled, and was similar in design to the Victoria or the Deluxe Phaeton. It was a very close relative to the true 5-passenger convertibles that would materialize later in the decade. Available only in Deluxe trim, the car came complete with left sidemount and folding trunk rack. Its interior was finished in genuine deep tan crushed leather, with matching panels in artificial leather. The top was in tan canvas-like fabric interlined with rubber, complete with a matching boot in tan fabric.

In April, a switch was made to only steel tops on the Victoria. The former leatherette models were no longer built, and buyers no longer had a choice of top treatment. In addition to the brown mohair or brown bedford cloth interiors, a new tan broadcloth interior was made available in April, but shortly after this, the bedford cloth was dropped as an option. Although a rear spare was standard on the Victoria, many buyers went for the much more attractive and practical package of left sidemount and folding rear trunk rack. The Victoria was the first Ford sedan-style to offer an enclosed luggage compartment. It was located in the bustle back, accessible by pulling the rear seat back forward. When photographed, this car was owned by Charles Davis of Palm Harbor, Fla.

The only body style to record over 100,000 units this year was the ever-popular Tudor, or Standard Tudor, to differentiate it from the very late arriving Deluxe Tudor. A tremendous family car, and dollar-for-dollar probably one of the best automotive buys on the market, the Model 55-B(Std) was priced at $490. Production this year reached only 148,425 which was less than half of the 1930 builds. But still, by far, it led the sales race within the Ford model line. Certainly the most popular of all Model As, the style had a total production of 1,259,128 over its 4-year life span, and was the only Model A to exceed 1-million units built. Pictured in a Detroit parking lot in this original 1931 photo, the car still wears its dealer stickers on the windshield and sports absolutely no accessories whatsoever. In this depression-ridden time slot, fewer and fewer American were able to scrape up the money for a major purchase such as this, and thus, accessories were something that could be attached later, if at all. The Tudor weighed 2,462 pounds.

Produced for only the first half of the model year was the Series 165 Standard Sedan, which had been introduced by both Murray and Briggs in 1929. This is the Murray version, the Model 165-C, which sold for $590. It was identifiable by the slight arches in the upper window frames. Although the bodies were very similar in appearance, there was virtually no interchange of parts between the Murray and Briggs designs—a situation which must have led to many exasperated moments in parts rooms and supply depots. Ford would put an end to the idea of outside suppliers building their own versions of the same body style, and from July on, virtually all bodies would have interchangeable parts, regardless of the source.

Introduced in June of 1931 in an effort to boost sagging sales was the Deluxe Tudor, Model 55-B(Dl). The move may have helped somewhat, as 21,948 were sold in the six months remaining in the model year. Priced at $525, or only $35 above the Standard model, the Deluxe version offered cowl lights, interior dome light, adjustable driver's seat, carpeting, rear seat arm rest, and deluxe upholstery in four choices: Brown mohair throughout; tan broadcloth throughout; brown bedford cloth seats with brown broadcloth panels, or green mohair throughout. Standard Tudors had interiors of either brown or gray checked seat cloth with plain brown or gray panels. However, after the Deluxe model arrived, a commercial interior was available on the Standard models. It consisted of an artificial leather in dark brown sharkskin. This well-dressed model from Des Moines wears the accessory sidemount and rear-mounted trunk and rack.

The Briggs version of the Standard Fordor was designated the Model 165-D. It was quickly identified by the straight-line design of the upper window frames. Despite its profusion of Deluxe models, this year Ford utilized a relatively high percentage of its advertising space in the promotion of Standard cars and the less flamboyant models. Again, however, sales of the Standard Fordor lagged well behind those of the Deluxe versions, and only 18,127 of this model were built. Production is believed to have been divided relatively even between Briggs and Murray. Overall, during its 3-year run, the Standard Fordor accounted for 113,201 sales, or roughly half of the fancier version. This year, the Standard Fordor came with only one interior scheme. It consisted of brown checked cloth seats with plain brown panels and a brown cotton headliner. Standard Fordors weighed 2,462 pounds, regardless of the builder.

The arched design of the upper window line quickly identifies this as the Murray-built Town sedan, Model 155-C, which was simply a fancy version of the Standard Fordor. Priced at $630, the Town Sedans were more than three times as popular as the Standard Fordor, accounting for 55,469 sales this year and ranking the car in third place in the by-model sales position. First introduced in 1929, the Town Sedan versions accounted for 245,374 units produced during the 3-year life span, with production believed to be about evenly divided between Briggs and Murray.

The Briggs version of the Town sedan was known as the Model 155-D. In regular form, all Town Sedans used rear-mounted spares, though sidemounts were available for those buyers who wished to install a trunk or rack on the rear. Priced at only $40 more than the Standard Fordor, the Town Sedan offered three interior choices: Brown mohair throughout; green mohair throughout, or brown bedford cloth seats with brown broadcloth panels. Buyers also received rear arm rests on both sides plus a folding center arm rest, silk roller shades on both the rear and rear quarter windows, a rear dome light, rear assist straps, spacious pockets on all four doors, a robe rail, and as usual, the exterior cowl lights. By late spring, however, sales of all the 4-door cars were beginning to slump, and a crash effort was made to get an entirely new series of bodies on the market. Thus, both the Standard Sedans and the Town Sedans were terminated between April and June.

Sharing the fate of the 3-window sedans was the Deluxe Fordor, Model 170-B(Dl) which also would be phased out of production in the late spring. Built only by Briggs, and introduced only in the spring of 1930 as a replacement for the Standard 2-window Sedan, the car shared many body parts with the Briggs-built 3-window versions, but none with the Murray designs. Production figures on the car vary. All lists show production of 12,854 for the 1930 model year, but one reliable lists puts the 1931 production at 3,251, while another equally reliable list puts it at only 740. Why this difference arises is not known, nor could it be determined which list is correct. The Deluxe Sedan was priced at $630, the same as the Town Sedans, and offered most of the same Deluxe trimmings. However, the green mohair interior was not available in this model, and buyers had a choice of only all brown mohair or brown bedford cord seats with brown broadcloth panels. The folding trunk rack and left sidemount was a relatively common accessory package.

Introduced in May or June was the new line of slant windshield sedans produced by both Murray and Briggs. But unlike the old sedan line in which each manufacturer came up with its own version, Ford now mandated that both companies produce identical bodies with interchangeable parts. Because of this, it is virtually impossible to tell if the slant windshield cars were sourced from Murray or Briggs. Lowest priced of the new models was the Standard 3-window Sedan, Model 160-A, which replaced the former Models 165-C and D. Despite the similarity of the price, weight, and styling, these were totally new bodies, not just simply the old units with new A-pillars. Sadly, production of these bodies was incorporated into the 18,127 Standard Sedans turned out this year.

Replacing the Models 155-C and D Town Sedan was the new Town Sedan, Model 160-B, which used the same body as the Standard Sedan but with a more luxurious interior. The car was priced at the same $630 as the former Town Sedan, and its production totals are mixed in with the 55,469 figure attributed to all variations of Town Sedans built this year. Notice that the totally new body used the arched upper window frames of the former Murray design rather than the straight line treatment of the Briggs models. The new slanting windshield and visorless windshield header were considered very stylish and European looking. They were designed to offset inroads by the larger Chevrolets.

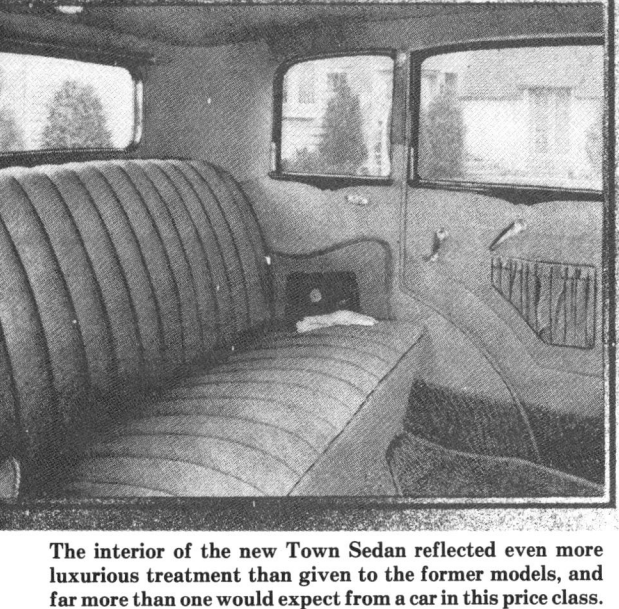

The interior of the new Town Sedan reflected even more luxurious treatment than given to the former models, and far more than one would expect from a car in this price class. Buyers of both the Town and the Deluxe Sedans had their choice of four different interiors. These were: Brown mohair throughout; brown bedford cord seats with brown broadcloth panels; tan broadcloth throughout, and deep brown shark-grained genuine leather seats and matching artificial leather throughout. Roller shades no longer appeared on the quarter windows because these could now be lowered partially for ventilation. The shade still appeared over the rear window, just behind the oval dome light. Side arm rests were found in the rear, while large pockets graced each door. Window moldings were in a grained mahogany finish.

In mid-April, the 20-millionth Ford rolled out of the River Rouge plant with Henry Ford at the wheel. The car was one of the new slant windshield versions of the Town Sedan, which had gone into production only a few days earlier. The Town Sedan was the first of the new 4-doors to go into production, starting in mid-April, even though pilot models had been shown in March. The Standard Sedan followed in late May, with the Deluxe Fordor not appearing until mid-June. Confusing this issue are production charts which show these cars being built in March, which is about when the retooling for the new bodies began and production of the old styles ceased. After a tour of major showrooms, the 20-millionth Ford was returned to the relatively new Henry Ford Museum in Dearborn.

Whitewall tires were an option rarely seen in the depression year, but they sure spruce up a restored vehicle such as this Station Wagon. Still wearing Model No. 150-B, the wagon suffered its share from the falling market, and only 2,848 were built, including those that were converted to campers and delivery vehicles. With production down, Briggs apparently bowed out of the scene, leaving assembly of these cars to Murray and Baker-Raulang. All wood parts were still cut and processed at Ford's own Iron Mountain facility in upper Michigan. Priced at $625, the wagon weighed 2,505 pounds. Its interior was in black artificial leather seats with black cardboard panels. This year Murray shipped its wagon bodies totally assembled to the various Ford plants. However, since the Cleveland, Ohio, plant of Baker-Raulang did not have the machinery to form the metal cowls, bodies from this source were shipped without front sheet metal to their final assembly plants, where the bodies were fitted to the Murray-built cowls.

Last of the new slant window 4-door models to appear was the Deluxe Sedan, which essentially was the basic body of the other slant windshield sedans, but fitted with blank quarters rather than quarter windows in the rear. Designated the Model 160-C, this car now was built by both Briggs and Murray, whereas the original version was produced only by Briggs. A solution to the production puzzle described in the early Deluxe Fordor may involve this car. Since one list shows a total of only 740 models built, while the other shows a total of 3,251, it might be possible that the 740 figure was the production of the Model 170-B for 1931, while the 3,251 was the total production of all Deluxe sedans for the year. This would indicate 2,511 of the Deluxe sedans were built in slant windshield form—but this is just a guess!

Available through Ford dealers was this camping variation of the Special Delivery, Model 225-A. The car uses the 2-door body of the Special Delivery, including the full-length rear doors, but instead of blank panels, it is fitted with grille-covered openings, with roll-up side curtains inside. Called the Traveler's Wagon, it was developed by Ford's designers and put on the market in 1931. Its primary market was supposed to be South America, where it would serve as a type of early camper for persons making long journeys in the primitive back country. The rear portion contained a double folding cot, stove, and storage cabinets for thermos bottles. A 10-gallon water tank was filled through the cap on the roof, and nested between the roof bows. Only 10 were built, apparently all on special order. Of these, only one came out of the Buenos Aires plant. The bodies were built in Cleveland by Baker-Raulang, and shipped complete, minus cowls, to assembly plants closest to the ordering agency.

1931

Finished in natural maple and based on the Station Wagon concept, the Special Delivery, Model 225-A, was a pretty if not unusual looking little truck. Also known as the "Natural Wood Panel Delivery," it was built only at Cleveland by the Baker-Raulang Co., with the cowls apparently coming from Murray. Costing $615, the little truck had a surprisingly nice run of 841 this year, with another 40 being produced in early 1932 on run-off Model A chassis. Though based on the regular wagon, the Special Delivery was of 2-door configuration, used vertical double rear doors rather than a horizontal tailgate, and had roll-up windows in the front doors, as did the Traveler's Wagon. Operating in the vicinity of White Plains, N.Y., this unit is typical of the types of businesses Ford aimed for with the Special Delivery.

New for the year, in fact, not introduced until late May, was the Deluxe Pickup, Model 66-A. Derived from Ford's somewhat popular 1-ton Model AA Service car, the Deluxe Pickup used all passenger car components forward of its cab, and had its own special bed with stainless steel rails. Briggs apparently developed the body as a special vehicle for General Electric dealers, but then offered it as a luxury model through Ford dealers. A total of 293 were built before year end. Apparently a buyer had a choice of a Briggs-built soft-top cab as shown here, or could order a special Budd-built cab with an all-metal roof. A very unusual feature of the Deluxe Pickup was its box, which blended into the cab sides.

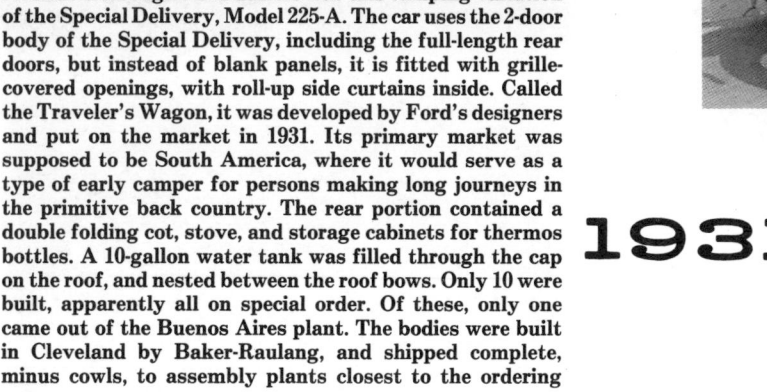

Also using passenger car components forward of the cowl was the Deluxe Delivery, which continued to wear the tag of Model 130-B. As did the Town Car and the Special Delivery, this little truck also used the passenger car chassis as its base. It was produced by both Budd and Briggs and enjoyed a relatively high sales ranking, probably due in part to its $540 price tag. This year a total of 9,529 were built, with another 392 turned out early in the 1932 calendar year, on Model A chassis. Apparently the only change in this model, besides the new radiator shell, was new latching device on the large single rear door.

Ironically, though the country was going through its worst depression year thus far, Ford continued to offer interesting commercial vehicles that epitomized flagrant luxury. Thus, the $1,150 Town Car Delivery represented the most expensive model in Ford's light vehicle line. Still designated the Model 295-A, the truck now sported a new slant windshield and a new all-aluminum body from the B-pillar rearward. Briggs continued to produce this vehicle, but with such a high price tag, low numbers could be expected. They were—only 190 were built. Another five were turned out in 1932, apparently placed on run-off Model A chassis early in the year. As before, coach lamps and dual covered spares were standard equipment.

A variation of the Deluxe Delivery appeared in mid-May. It was the Drop-Floor Delivery, Model 225-A. It was developed by Ford's Chicago branch in March, but not put into production until two months later. Looking pretty spiffy in Deluxe trim, this model featured a body with a cargo floor that dropped to hub level behind the rear axle. The body had to be modified to meet this drop, and the door also had to be re-engineered so that a walk-in type of rear entrance could be made. However, because of this door, bumpers could not be used, and so the bodies turned out to be quite damage prone. Not a popular model, Briggs built only 77 in the remainder of 1931, and turned out another 12 in early 1932. It was priced at $560, only $20 more than its companion Deluxe Delivery, but this price did not include the beautiful stainless steel spare wheel cover.

Ford entered the year with its old pickup bed holdover from the 1925 Model T, but in May a new bed finally appeared from the Briggs plant. It was this unit which offered 22.2 cubic feet of cargo space, as opposed to the old bed of 16.8 cubic feet. Known as the Model 78-B, the bed was available either as a separate item that could be installed on the buyers' own Ford chassis unit, or could be purchased as a complete truck as shown here. Interestingly, Briggs developed its own rear fenders for this unit. These fit nothing else in the Ford line, even though they appear quite similar to regular Ford fenders. Shortly after this body was introduced, a canopy top was offered. This consisted of four heavy corner posts, an all-steel top, and roll-up storm curtains for front, rear, and sides.

A comparison of the plain Panel Delivery body with the Deluxe Delivery shows a world of difference between the two. Basically, the Deluxe version was built to be seen, while the standard unit was built to work. Carried over from 1930 and designated the Model 79-B, this body was built by Murray. A total of 8,282 were built this year, with some of this production extending into the early part of 1932. The interior consisted of two folding seats in black artificial leather, and steel panel linings halfway up the cargo area. As was the case with the Deluxe Delivery, the Panel Delivery also received a drop-floor variation in late spring, but it appears these were no more popular on this truck than they were on the fancy model.

Ford's light truck operations will be touched on only lightly here, and only because so many passenger car components were used in the chassis and running gear. The base for a multitude of bodies for virtually every trade imaginable was the Commercial Chassis, which cost $340 without the cab shown here. Although no photos could be found of a 1931 commercial vehicle with an open cab, dealer listings show that both open and closed cabs were still available this year. However, the open cabs were very rare, with only 2,637 being produced as opposed to 95,529 closed cabs. As in the past, Ford commercial units used painted headlights and radiator shells, but otherwise differed very little from passenger car chassis. The attractive sidemount was standard on all light models. However, it was there not for appearance, but for the very practical reason that there was no other convenient place to store the spare.

Built in 1932, but using a 1931 Model A chassis and engine as its base, was this futuristic looking car called the Arrow Plane. The design and construction was by Hill Auto Body Co. of Cincinnati, Ohio, a relatively complete body repair shop which delved in and out of custom car, boat, and airplane building right up until World War II. Using a rear engine configuration, the basic idea was the brainchild of Lyman Voelpel of Chicago, who it seems initially had ideas of producing the car on a volume basis. The production ideas never materialized, and the Arrow Plane remained a one-off vehicle. However, it did serve as a base for a 6-vehicle fleet of futuristic cars built in 1933 by Hill for the McQuay-Norris Co. (see 1933 chapter). The Arrow Plane looked very similar to the "Cars of Tomorrow," that were displayed at the 1939 World's Fair by General Motors. It is believed that this car still exists, with Florida listed as its last known home.

The last half of 1931 was slowly slipping away, and the Ford organization overall was beginning to worry at a serious level. The depression economy was bad and cars were hard to sell. Fords in general were selling, but not at the pace they should. Chevrolet had taken over the number one sales spot in 1927 and 1928. That was understandable, because of the start-up delays of going from the Model T to the Model A. But now Chevrolet was once again number one, and upstart Plymouth was gaining ground in third place. Both of these cars were longer, better riding, better looking, and had more cylinders than Ford. A change was needed and fast. But so far, only very vague hints of a new car had come from Ford.

Both public and dealers were wondering the same thing. Had "Old Henry" put himself in a trap once again by having an outmoded design on the lines and nothing on the drawing boards? For the public it was an academic question. For dealers, it was a matter of life itself. Some were still recuperating from the losses suffered in the 1928 changeover. Thus, poor 1931 sales, plus a very stagnant economy added up to one thing: Many dealers could not afford another major shutdown while an untried car was put into production.

But that is exactly what did happen. On Dec. 7, just 10 years before another day of infamy, Ford created its own disaster and shut down the plants. Introduction of the new Ford was to be made early in 1932, but this didn't happen. As the New Year came about, nothing was being built in Ford factories. Again, Ford's labor force, from mill donkey to highly trained professional, was out of work. Again dealers were living on used cars, parts, and what few commercial vehicles they could sell. Both commercial vehicle and engine production was carried on at some plants, and some sources would hint that a few Model A cars trickled out of some of the assembly plants as late as March, 1932, but for all practical purposes, Ford production had dropped to point zero. It was 1927/28 all over again!

The problem was similar to the Model T changeover, but not quite as bad. At least this time Ford knew what it was going to produce. The difficulty was that not enough time had been allowed for the transition, and virtually no time had been given to test the new vehicles, or more importantly, to prove that the new engine was feasible.

Finally, on March 9, the first new Ford drove out of Dearborn, and by the end of the month every dealer in the country had at least one "top secret" model to show to the customers. The big introductory day finally arrived on April 2, and the public finally got a look at Henry's latest mechanical masterpiece.

What they found was a car that looked like a nicely modified Model A, one with a slightly longer wheelbase, smoother lines, modern touches, and overall in keeping with what the next generation of Ford should look like. BUT—what was that thing under the hood?

Staring at buyers was Ford's answer to the new 6-cylinder cars that Chevrolet, Plymouth, and other lesser volume makes were producing. Count them—it had eight cylinders, arranged in a neat compact "V" design that up until now had been the hallmark only of luxury cars. Ford's thinking (and again he proved to be right) was that none of the low price car makers would be able to up him on this. If he had come out with a Six, it would have been just another 6-cylinder car. If the other makers now came out with a V-8, they would just be playing copycat. And no one in the low price market was going to come out with the next step, which was a V-12.

But the V-8 engine that drew all of the attention was also the culprit in the long delay of getting the new cars on the market. Developed in less than a year in a top secret crash program, the new engine posed and developed so many engineering and manufacturing problems that certainly many people must have doubted Ford's sanity. True, V-8 engines had been about for years, and one of the finest was currently being manufactured by Ford's own Lincoln plant. But these were high price units, requiring much hand labor by highly paid skilled craftsmen. No one had yet designed a V-8 crankcase that could be manufactured quickly or cheaply enough to power a low price car.

But Ford did—finally. To detail the problems encountered in design and production engineering could fill easily 100 pages with technical information far beyond the scope of this book. Suffice to say that the start-up was horrendous. And even at introduction, many within Ford's ranks wondered if the new block would last the year. Many did not!

What greeted the public was a bright green V-8 engine of 221 cubic inches which could produce 65 horsepower at 3400 rpm. The pistons were set at a 90-degree angle, with the valves being of L-head configuration. The bore and stroke was 3-1/16x3.75, with a compression ratio of 5.5:1. The pistons were of aluminum and had three rings. Living in the valley was a new single barrel carburetor, produced either by Ford or by a new supplier, the Detroit Lubricator Co. At the front of the engine, a combination coil and distributor was driven directly from the camshaft, while a crankshaft pulley drove the dual water pumps and Ford's own new generator with attached fan. The whole package was designated the Model 18.

Wisely anticipating production problems, possible latent operational difficulties, and a certain degree of buyer resistance against the extravagance of an 8-cylinder engine (all of which did occur, incidentally) Ford hedged its bet, and for the first time since the Model T appeared, offered a second engine option. This was the Model B, which was essentially an update of the Model A engine. Having four cylinders and a bore and stroke of 3-7/8x4.25 inches, the "new" mill displaced the same 200.5 cubic inches as did the old Model A, but developed 50 brake horsepower at 2500 rpm. It was equipped with either a newly designed Zenith or a Holley carburetor.

Buyers had their choice of engines, but the cars looked the same. The only exterior differentiating marks between the two blocks were that V-8 powered cars bore a small emblem on the cross bar and had exclusive V-8 hubcaps. And, both buyer resistance and production problems did materialize. As a result, the V-8 cars outsold the 4-cylinder ones by a 2.5-to-1 margin, but this was a far lower V-8 interest than Ford had expected. True, by 1933, V-8 sales would be more than 40 times those of the Model B, and by 1934 Model B sales would be so poor that the engine choice would be terminated before mid-year. But in 1932, a dubious public, horror stories regarding performance and longevity, and continuing production problems kept V-8 sales far lower than anticipated. In fact, of the 254,694 cars sold, only 178,749 had V-8 engines. And many of these (especially the early ones) had to be returned for new pistons (sometimes several sets); new bearings; new heads, and in extreme cases, new engines. The year was not trouble free.

Giving virtually no trouble was the rest of the car. Both running gear and body design were well thought out, and were really next generation progression of already proven components. Although Ford wanted a totally new car for his new V-8, such was not to be, at least not this year. Thus, the chassis was essentially a modification of the Model A unit, now having a 106-inch wheelbase rather than 103.5, but still based on the ladder-frame principle. The new X-frame that was supposed to support the V-8 would not appear until 1933. Supporting the chassis were new Ford-built wire wheels with 5.25x18 inch tires as opposed to the former 4.75x19.

Riding on this new chassis was a series of 14 bodies, all styled under the direction of Edsel Ford. Those who expected wildly futuristic designs were disappointed, and would have wait for the Chrysler Airflow. What did grace the showroom floors were, like the chassis, well proportioned second generation versions of the previous Model A bodies, graced by a new radiator shell with a real grille, new sweeping but open fenders, and a new multi-louvered hood. But the headlights still perched on the tie bar, the exterior horn still nested by the left fender, and the spare tire still graced either the rear panel or the left front fender. But the cars looked new. And, they were new.

In the world of production figures, as could be expected, the Tudor Sedan led the pack, with combined standard and deluxe production reaching 76,766 for the V-8 models, and 40,630 for the Model B versions, for a grand total of 117,396. The Tudor was the only style to exceed the 100,000 figure in production. Coupes in general came in second with 70,720 units not counting the sport styles, while the Fordor Sedans in general were third with 34,926 total units. As could be expected, the open cars were at the low end of the scale, with the Model B Convertible Sedan making the worst showing

with only 41 orders, though its V-8 version did account for a healthy 842 more.

For those who like to count engine numbers, production of V-8 engines officially began with No. 1 in March and ended with No. 212,238. However, at the end of April, the first 4,250 blocks had to be rebuilt by dealers, and until well into the year, an unknown number had to be either rebuilt or replaced. As before, all engine production was done at River Rouge, with the completed units shipped to the various assembly plants. When the initial rash of problems began to develop, such as the pistons cracking, the repairs were made at the dealership level.

The relatively trouble-free Model B engine actually went into production on Nov. 29, 1931, using No. 5000000 for the opening number to differentiate the block from Model A numbers. By 1931 year end, numbers had reached 5001863, and by the end of 1932, they stood at 5179579. Even in appearance, this engine could not be mistaken for the Model A, having a redesigned cylinder head, its own fuel pump (it now had to fetch from a rear tank rather than a cowl supply), new water pump, redesigned oil pan, and inside, new crank and camshafts and connecting rods.

By mid-year, most of Ford's troubles had been solved and the overall system was running smoothly—as were the cars. After the initial start-up pain, time could now be found to do the rest of the job. This involved coming out with a totally new car for Henry's totally new engine. That would occur in 1933.

Ford's lowest price and lightest car continued to be the Standard Roadster, Type 40(Std), which cost $460 and weighed 2,203 pounds. A practical car for fleet usage where price was considered over comfort, the cars found many homes in corporations and municipalities. This particular model became the fire chief's transportation in Piedmont, Cal. It was one of 520 turned out in V-8 form. Ford also produced another 948 with Model B 4-cylinder power. All bodies were built by Briggs and were upholstered in black-brown artificial leather with matching cardboard panels. Initially the top was in black rubberized fabric, but sometime after May a switch was made to a rubber-lined black and white fabric with matching boot and side curtains. At the same time, the folding wind wings no longer were supplied as standard equipment, but became an option. A trunk deck was standard, but a rumble seat could be ordered.

All set for bad weather is this Briggs-bodied deluxe Roadster, Type 40(Dl). One of 6,893 built with a V-8, it was joined by 3,719 in 4-cylinder form. Including all four variations, Briggs turned out a total of 12,080 roadster bodies this year. All featured the fold-down windshield of Model A days, and all were built with a trunk deck unless a rumble seat was ordered. In Deluxe trim the car cost $500 as a V-8 or $50 less as a Four. It weighed 2,308 as a V-8 or approximately 200 pounds less as a Four. Besides the cowl lights, Deluxe trim included a genuine leather front seat with matching genuine leather panels, and a matching rumble seat (if ordered) but in artificial leather. Tan rubber floor mats were used in all models. Also, the top on this model was in a drab interlined fabric throughout the production span, and windshield wings remained regular equipment. A spare was also standard, but single or dual sidemounts with or without covers could be special ordered.

Initially introduced as a Deluxe model, the Sport Coupe was downgraded to a Standard model shortly after its introduction. Figures would indicate that few if any were ever sold in Deluxe version. A carry-over from the Model A, the Briggs-built body was essentially a soft-top coupe with full door framing and a convertible-like roof that could not be lowered. It was the only Ford to sport the beautiful decorative landau irons. Designated the Type B-50, it recorded a dismal production of only 1,982 in V-8 form and 739 as a Model B. As a V-8 it cost $535 and weighed 2,375 pounds, while as a Four it was $50 and 200 pounds less. A rumble seat was standard, and the top had a removable back panel so rear passengers could converse with those in the front. The top was covered in a tan artificial leather, while the rumble seat was in black-brown artificial leather. Three different interiors were used, but these came via production changes, and were not at buyers' choice. From inception until June, the interior was totally done in a brown cloth with diagonal design. In June and July a brown checked material was used throughout, and models built after July had a brown stripe cloth throughout. It appears that production stopped in the fall, and the style was not revised for the 1933 models.

Far more comfortable than the Roadster was the Briggs-built Cabriolet, available only in Deluxe trim. Designated the Type B-68, the car cost $610 as a V-8 or $560 as a Four. It weighed 2,398 pounds as a V-8. On this model, the V-8 engine was by far the favorite choice, accounting for 5,499 sales as opposed to 427 in 4-cylinder form. Thus, Briggs built a total of 5,926. All came with the rumble seat and rear spare as standard equipment. Styling included a fixed-frame windshield and roll-up windows, making a totally weather tight package when the top was raised. The top material was the same as used on the Deluxe Roadster. Cabriolet buyers had a choice of either a genuine leather or a cloth interior, while the rumble seat was always in brown artificial leather. In leather, the seats were in genuine brown colonial grain, but the panels were in matching artificial leather. In the cloth style, the seat was in brown bedford cord with plain brown cloth panels.

Shown as a working car in 1954 is this snow-covered 4-cylinder Model B 5-window Coupe, Type B-54. It is wearing aftermarket sealed beam headlights from the late 1930s and an original left sidemount. This car has the standard trunk deck, but rumble seats were optional. A relatively popular car, it was produced by Briggs, Murray, and Ford, with all bodies being identical, regardless of source. As a V-8 it cost $490 and drew 28,904 orders, while as a Four it cost $440 and accounted for 20,342 sales. Its V-8 weight was 2,398 pounds. Initially buyers had a choice of four cloth and one extra-cost leather interiors. The cloth interiors were: Thorn brown mohair throughout; brown check seats with plain tan panels; brown stripe seats with plain brown panels, and brown diagonal dash seats with plain tan panels. This latter interior was dropped in June. When ordered along with the cloth interior, the rumble seat would be finished in black-brown artificial leather. The rear window of these cars could be lowered, regardless of whether the rear was fitted with a rumble seat or a trunk deck.

Although Ford lists do not show a deluxe version of the 5-window Coupe, there are enough such examples running around to conclude that this must have been a fairly popular dealer-level conversion. Such conversions probably would have been done almost exclusively on the V-8, and would have involved the addition of cowl lamps and rumble seat, and possibly the extra-cost genuine leather interior with the rumble seat done in matching artificial leather. With this package, carpets were used in both the interior and the rumble seat rather than the brown rubber floor mats. This interior remained available until the end of August, when a cost cutting plan changed the genuine leather interior to one of artificial leather, and the floor carpets were done away with. However, some lists indicate that the genuine leather interior was still available even after the artificial version was introduced.

Ford did not have an official deluxe version of its 5-window Coupe, but it did have its 3-window Coupe, available only in Deluxe trim. Designated the type B-520, and produced by Murray, the car enjoyed impressive sales of 20,506 as a V-8, but only 968 in 4-cylinder form. As a V-8 it cost $575 and weighed 2,493 pounds, with the Model B version being $50 and 200 pounds less. A relatively unique style, this was the only Ford to have a glove box in the dashboard, and the only one to have forward latching doors. Because of the latter feature, sidemounts could not be installed because they would block the door swing. Officially called the Deluxe Coupe, this car initially offered buyers a choice of one leather and three cloth interiors. The cloth packages were: Rose beige mohair throughout, brown bedford cord seats with brown mohair panels, and tan pinstripe cloth throughout. The genuine leather interior could first be ordered as standard equipment, but after July this became an extra-cost option. Normally, the car was equipped with a trunk deck, but a rumble seat could be ordered at extra cost. When fitted to a cloth-trimmed car, it was finished in brown artificial leather, but when fitted to a leather-trimmed model, it came in a drab artificial leather to match the interior.

Destined to be dropped at the end of the year was the Convertible Sedan, Type B-400. Produced only by Murray, the unusual car drew only 842 orders as a V-8, and with 41 sales, represented the poorest selling Model B. It continued to use the interesting top developed in its Model A days, which rode on fixed rails. This design provided fully framed windows and doors and a solid base for the top when raised, but gave little of the open car feeling when the top was lowered. Priced at $650 and weighing 2,480 pounds as a V-8, it was $50 less as a Model B. Buyers had a choice of a cloth interior in brown bedford cord seats with brown plain broadcloth panels, or a rust brown genuine leather interior with matching panels in artificial leather.

With the top raised, the convertible Sedan was a compact looking car with lines quite similar to the Victoria or the old Deluxe Phaeton. The top was of drab rubberized fabric similar to that used on the other deluxe open cars. Normally a rear-mounted spare was supplied, but when a folding luggage rack or a trunk was desired, single or double sidemounts were required. On this model, however, the sidemounts tended to produce an even more stubby appearance. A canvas boot protected the top when it was lowered, but because of its overall design, the top had a tendency to bulk in the down position. Both front seats would fold forward to allow access to the rear. This and the Deluxe Coupe were the only "closed" Fords to have chromed windshield frames. Ford considered this a "closed car."

Supposedly one of Edsel Ford's favorite body designs, the Victoria, Type B-190, drew a healthy 72,41 orders as a V-8, but only 521 in 4-cylinder style. Often referred to by its nickname "Vicky," it sold for $600 and weighed 2,483 in V-8 guise. Built by Murray, and available in Deluxe trim only, the Victoria featured an integral luggage area located in the bustle behind the rear seat, with access from the inside only. Normally, the car would wear a rear-mounted spare. Sidemounts were available but seemed to have the same effect as they did on the Convertible Sedan—they made the car look stubby. Three cloth interiors were available on these cars: Rose beige mohair throughout; brown bedford cord seats with brown plain broadcloth panels, or tan pinstripe cloth throughout. Note the front mounted horn peeking out. At the start of the year these were supplied by Sparks-Withington, but apparently that company was unable to meet production, and a switch was made back to the Spartan Co. for the rest of the year.

Except for the cowl lights and the V-8 emblems on the cross bar and hub caps, the Deluxe Tudor V-8 did not look that much different than the Model B Standard Tudor. Production figures indicate that the public felt the same, and saw little sense to paying $50 more for a slightly better interior and cowl light. Thus, only 18,836 V-8 and 4,077 4-cylinder Tudors were turned out in Deluxe trim, less than one-quarter the number of Standard models. Still, the combined production of all four styles gave Briggs a fine order of 117,376 bodies, with this style being the only 1933 Ford to exceed 100,000 units. Buyers had an interior choice of rose beige mohair or tan pinstripe throughout, or brown bedford cord seats with plain brown panels. Initially, a no-cost option was an interior of copra-color genuine leather throughout, but after July this interior was changed to an extra-cost option. On all Deluxe models, the rear seats were fitted with assist straps, ash trays, and rear seat arm rests. All Tudors were equipped with roller shades on the rear windows, with many of these having tassels left over from Model A production.

As before, Ford's most popular car continued to be the Tudor Sedan, Type B-55. With its body built by Briggs, the car this year was available in four major types, a Standard Four or V-8, and Deluxe versions of these two. This is the Standard Model B, showing off its 4-cylinder engine. In this form, the car turned out to be the most popular Model B, accounting for 36,553 sales, and selling for $450. As a Standard Tudor V-8, it drew 57,930 orders and sold for $500. The Four weighed 2,378 pounds. Initially buyers had an interior choice of brown mohair throughout or brown diagonal texture seats with plain tan panels. However, the later trim was dropped in June and was replaced by a brown check seat material. This trim was available only in June and July, and by August had been replaced by a brown striped seat material with plain brown cloth panels. Also in August, an extra-cost interior of copra color artificial leather was made available, primarily for use in fleet cars. Horns on these cars were Spartan models, very similar to those used on the Model A.

The lowest price and lowest production 4-door model was the Phaeton, available in both Standard and Deluxe form, and either as a V-8 or a Four. The Standard V-8 version appears here. Designated the Type B-35, it sold for $495 in this form or $445 as a Four. Ford was attempting to sell the model to local and state police forces, hence the "gang busters" promotional photo. This model is equipped with a 2-piece bullet-proof windshield and bullet deflectors on both front and rear bumpers in line with the tires. Also attached to the front are red flasher lights and siren, while gun racks were installed in the rear compartment. In more domesticated form, the car attracted 483 buyers who wanted the V-8 model and 593 who preferred the Four, with combined production being just 1,076. Initially wind wings were included in the price, but shortly after introduction, these became extra-cost items. As with the Standard Roadster, early cars had tops and curtains of black rubberized fabric, but by May this was changed to black and white cloth interlined with rubber. A top boot was not supplied with the Standard model. The interior was done in black-brown artificial leather with matching cardboard panels.

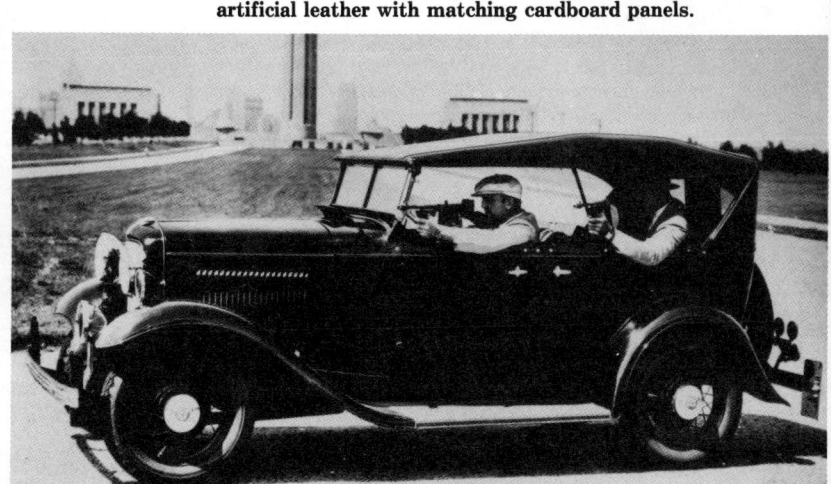

Showing off its folding windshield with the wind wings also folded is the Deluxe Phaeton. No longer a special body as it had been in Model A times, the Deluxe version was now simply a fancy edition of the Standard Phaeton. Only slightly more popular in this guise, Ford sold 923 with V-8 engines, but only 281 with Fours. Thus, Briggs built a combined total of only 2,280 of this attractive model. Deluxe versions sold for $545 as a V-8 and $495 as a Four. The extra $50 above the Standard's price gave buyers an interior done in genuine beige leather seats with matching panels in artificial leather; cowl lights; wind wings, and a top and curtains done in beige canvas interlined with rubber, including a matching canvas top boot.

This year Ford had only one Fordor style, the Type B-160, though when its Standard and Deluxe and V-8 and 4-cylinder variations are added in, the car fell into four separate slots. Still, possibly because of the $90 price difference, its sales were approximately one-third of the Tudor's. As a result, in the Standard vein, sales peaked at 9,310 for the $590 V-8 and 4,116 for the $550 Four. The V-8 weighed 2,538 pounds. Buyers had several interior choices, but only brown mohair was carried throughout the year. Brown diagonal dash cloth was an option through June, when it was replaced by brown check cloth, which was available for only two months. At the end of July, brown stripe cloth was substituted for the brown check, and in August an interior of beige artificial leather became available, probably as an extra-cost option.

The Briggs bodied Fordor Sedan was a nice looking car for its time, especially in its Deluxe trim and sporting V-8 hubcaps. Priced at $645 in this form, it sold over twice as many units as it did in comparable Standard guise, with 18,880 going to market. Its 4-cylinder relation, however, did not do well in Deluxe trim, and only 2,620 were sold. Deluxe buyers received three interior options, which included rose beige mohair, brown bedford cord, or tan pinstripe. For the first few months a interior of genuine leather seats and matching artificial panels was available at no charge, but after July this became a special extra-cost option. Assist straps, robe rails, and rear arm rests were part of the Deluxe package. On all Fordors, the rear quarter windows could be lowered. All models used a rear roller shade and had dual sun visors for front seat passengers.

Featuring a totally new body of larger proportions than that of the Model A was the Station Wagon, Type B-150. Promoted primarily with the 4-cylinder engine, it did have the V-8 as an option, though less than one third of the buyers took the more expensive block. Thus, 1.032 were sold for $600 in 4-cylinder form, while only 351 went for the $650 with price the V-8. Baker-Raulang produced all of the bodies at its Cleveland plant, but it is not certain if that company also built the cowl and windshield assembly, or if these continued to be supplied by Murray. Side curtains still provided weather protection. When not in use, they lived in special racks between the roof slats. A right-hand sidemount held the spare. Seats were finished in black-brown artificial leather and consisted of two bucket seats in front and bench seats in the center and rear, both of which were easily removable. At mid-year cowl lamps became standard equipment, as did stainless steel headlights, but it does not appear that these changes constituted a deluxe model, but rather were an appearance improvement.

Ford certainly was aware of the lack of interest in open cab trucks, so its reasons for bringing out a new version of the Open Cab Pickup is a mystery. Adding to the puzzle is the fact that the open model didn't appear until late May, after the regular pickup was well established, and then had just about the same $435 price tag as the closed version. Available only in 4-cylinder form and designated Type B-76, it used a newly designed cab and a new pickup bed, both by Murray (though some sources attribute these to Briggs). The top and side curtains were of a black rubberized fabric similar to that used on the early Standard Phaetons and Roadsters, while the seat was in black-brown artificial leather. Only 593 were built. Available colors were brown, red, green, orange, or white, but not black. Oddly, the top was non-collapsible, but could be easily removed.

Cute as a button in its white shoes is this restored Pickup, Type B-82, with its body supplied by Murray (though one source credits Briggs). Sometimes called a Closed Cab Pickup to differentiate it from the open version, the truck was available only with a 4-cylinder engine. Priced at $435 complete, it enjoyed 14,259 sales. The newly designed pickup bed, also produced by Murray, was now almost 70 inches long and 46 inches wide. On all of the new commercial cabs, the windshield would swing open, but the rear window was fixed in place. Pickups, both open and closed, used the same type of artificial leather seat covering and had their panels covered in black painted masonite. The floor mat was in tan (not black) rubber. The right hand mounting of the spare was standard, and dual sidemounts were possible but virtually never seen.

Ford no longer had its Town Car or Special Delivery models, but it did have one fancy panel truck left. It was the Deluxe Panel delivery, which shared its designation of Type B-79 with the plain Delivery. Fitted with such passenger car components as grille, headlights, and cowl lights, it was priced at $540 as a 4-cylinder model and $590 as a V-8. However, only 69 models were turned out with the V-8, while the remaining 2,550 had the Four. Seating consisted of two bucket seats with folding backs, with the passenger seat being removable. These were done in the same brown-black artificial leather as most other commercial Fords. Masonite panels covered the walls, while the cargo floor was of hard maple with metal skid rails. Budd produced 2,619 of the Deluxe versions, and another 3,503 of the Standard Panel Delivery, of which only 46 had V-8 engines.

A very limited production vehicle was the Sedan Delivery, priced at $520 in 4-cylinder form. The little truck used the Tudor body shell converted to delivery use by the LeBaron Division of Briggs Mfg. Co. The conversion consisted of adding a single door in the back panel, blanking in the quarter windows, installing a wood floor and masonite panels in the rear, and providing a left sidemount. Deluxe touches of cowl lights and stainless steel headlights were standard equipment. Designed primarily to fill fleet contracts from Morton Salt and Jewel Tea, both submitted by the Chicago branch, the truck also found a few additional buyers. However, sales reached only 344 for the 4-cylinder model and only 58 for the V-8 version.

1932

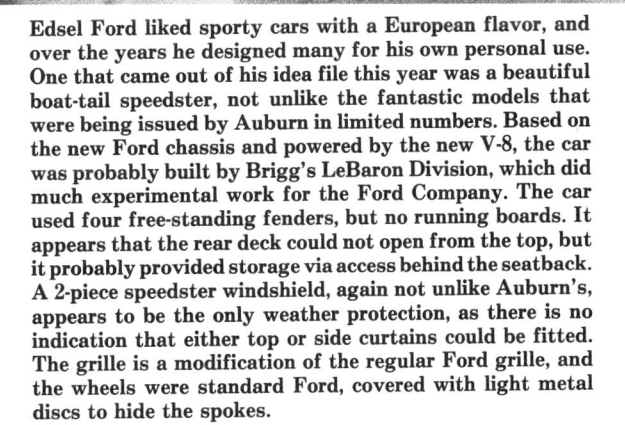

Although the Detroit, Toledo & Ironton Railroad had been sold by Ford to the Pennsylvania Railroad in 1929, the line still continued to use Ford sedans for its inspection cars. This year's version was a Standard Fordor Model B, fitted with special wheels for riding the rails. Totally different than previous versions which used standard railroad wheels, these hybrid units had their flanges behind the special rubber tires. Unlike some vehicles of this type which could switch easily from road to rail, these rubber tires were simply for comfort on the rails, and because of the large flanges, could not be used on the road. Railroad marker lights, trunk, and compressed air horn seem to have completed the conversion. Why the fenders were removed is anybody's guess, as it appears that there would have been enough clearance for the unique wheels even with the fenders.

Ford had no Town Car this year—pity. That didn't bother the British, as they simply designed their own. Constructed by Windovers Ltd., this low-production vehicle used the British assembled V-8 chassis for a base and came out with a very respectable Town Car style. An unusual touch was the treatment of the front doors, with the door post extending all the way up the B-pillar to the drip rail, even though there was no forward pillar or top window frame. Possibly this was done to give the front windows better support when they were raised. Note that the upper-most hinge on both doors is just slightly below the drip rail, but because of the forward latching, the rear door hinges all have to be grouped in the upper half of the door.

Just as the Americans took a liking to Ford's new V-8 (once the bugs were chased out), so too did the Europeans, and there are many examples of custom European body work on the new Ford chassis. Representing the German school of design is this attractive Cabriolet, with a limited production body built by the Karl Deutsch Co. Similar in styling to Ford's own Convertible Sedan, the car used a completely convertible top rather than the unusual arrangement that ran in rails. The large chromed landau bars were functional, and stiffened the top when it was raised. Dual windshield wipers and small spot light add an interesting touch, but it is not known if the large driving light above the bumper was original equipment.

Edsel Ford liked sporty cars with a European flavor, and over the years he designed many for his own personal use. One that came out of his idea file this year was a beautiful boat-tail speedster, not unlike the fantastic models that were being issued by Auburn in limited numbers. Based on the new Ford chassis and powered by the new V-8, the car was probably built by Brigg's LeBaron Division, which did much experimental work for the Ford Company. The car used four free-standing fenders, but no running boards. It appears that the rear deck could not open from the top, but it probably provided storage via access behind the seatback. A 2-piece speedster windshield, again not unlike Auburn's, appears to be the only weather protection, as there is no indication that either top or side curtains could be fitted. The grille is a modification of the regular Ford grille, and the wheels were standard Ford, covered with light metal discs to hide the spokes.

The Italians took an interest in the new Ford, just as did the rest of Europe. In a small shop (at that time) a relatively young designer by the name of Pinin Farina took a new Ford chassis and constructed his own idea of a cabriolet body. Bearing a surprising similarity to the 1933 Ford styling, the car features forward raked louvers and forward opening doors with the leading edge matching the line set by both windshield and hood. It appears that the original grille and headlight bar was used, but the fenders were reworked somewhat. Bumpers and wheels were original, and the hubcaps attest to the V-8 under the long hood. It is not known if Farina built the car to a customer's order, if it was a speculation vehicle, or if he simply constructed it for his own use.

Today, one seldom thinks of the 1933 Fords as "30th Anniversary" models. But that is exactly what they were. And, to celebrate this role, Ford designers, together with representatives engineers from LeBaron, Murphy, Briggs, and Budd, got together right after the 1932 models went into production, and began work on the anniversary models.

Actually, there is speculation that the V-8 engine possibly should have been held back one year so that the entire package of new car, new chassis, and new engine could be presented in one big anniversary promotion. But badly slipping sales forced the crash program for the V-8, and the somewhat redesigned Model A bodies that appeared in 1932 might have been a part of that same rush to get something new on the market.

Now for 1933 there was new everything—new chassis, new bodies, and virtually a new V-8. Finally, Ford had a really competitive package, and none too soon. For the past two years the company had gone from high profits, to no profits, to deep losses. Ford needed some strong medicine, or the illness would be terminal.

Again, Henry and son Edsel delved into their separate areas of expertise. Henry concentrated on the new chassis and improvements to the V-8. Edsel took responsibility for the new styling. And both succeeded to a marvelous degree.

Designated the Model 40 to differentiate it from anything yet developed, the new car was available with both the V-8 engine, which was still called the Model 18, and the 4-cylinder block, which was still referred to as the Model B. Thus, it is not improper to refer to these cars by the old Model B or Model 18 designations, or the Model 40 handle.

Providing a base for the car was a brand new chassis of "X" frame configuration which was specifically designed to accommodate the weight and stresses of the V-8 engine. Ford's traditional use of transverse springing was combined with well engineered radius rods and Houdaille shock absorbers to give the cars an exceptional meld of flexibility and roadability.

Enhancing the ride, in addition to the appearance, was the new wheelbase of 112 inches, which was a half-foot step up from 1932 and 8.5 inches longer than the Model A. Wheels were again made smaller, while the tires got wider. Ford continued to make the well designed wire wheels, but they now wore 5.5x17 tires, a factor which brought the chassis lower to the ground and visually brought the wheels into better proportion with the body. Overall the cars were 183 inches long, which was a 17.5-inch increase in length from the previous year.

Brakes transmission, and running gear, including axles, remained basically the same as in 1932, but with slight variations to fit the new chassis. Many of these parts are interchangeable from 1932 through 1934.

Under the hood, the engine was changed somewhat from the first examples of 1932, but many of the modifications were running changes (many of which were dire necessities early in 1932). This year, however,

the blocks did get new aluminum heads in place of the cast iron units. With this change, compression was raised from 5.5:1 to 6.3:1, a move which increased the brake horsepower output to 75 at 3800 rpm. The new heads, incidentally, used the same 21-stud pattern so that the block castings did not have to be changed.

With the new heads came a slightly different design of the aluminum pistons, with more oil ring holes. These pistons were all supplied by three different companies: Aluminum Industries; Aluminum Co. of America (ALCOA), and Bohn Aluminum Co. Water pumps too were changed slightly, with the main difference being that the new pumps were lubricated with oil rather than grease. For the owner, this meant periodic lubrication of the dual pumps with an oil can rather than a grease gun. And during the year, cars destined for the southern states were often (but not always) fitted with a new 6-blade cooling fan.

Carburetors were the same as in 1932, and were made either by Ford or by Detroit Lubricator Co. The fuel pump also remained unchanged, and continued to be supplied by A.C. Air cleaners were supplied by either Burgess or Holley, even though the latter company no longer supplied carburetors to Ford.

Throughout 1932, a multitude of improvements had been made to the V-8, so by the time the 1933 models arrived, buyer resistance to this plant had just about evaporated. As a result, interest in the Model B 4-cylinder engine was minimal, with only 7,560 buyers opting for the little block as opposed to 304,948 taking the V-8. As could be expected, only a few changes were made to the Model B, and none involved major engineering. As a running change, the 2-blade fan was replaced with a 4-blade unit, so all the 1933 cars had the new fans. The Zenith carburetor also had some minor modifications, and a new oil bath air cleaner by United Specialties was made available as an extra-cost item shortly before the 1933 cars came out.

Engine numbers for the Model B this year began at 5179580 and went to 5263534 for a total of 83,954 4-cylinder blocks. Many of these went into commercial vehicles, where the more economical engine was still a definite factor. V-8 numbers went from 212239 to 561592, for a total of 249,353 blocks turned out.

Despite the initial attention given here to the mechanics, it was the totally new bodies that enhanced the public this year. Longer, lower, more flowing, fitted with valanced fenders and a beautiful V-grille, plus rakish front latching doors, the styling epitomized the artistic talents of Edsel Ford and his small band of designers. Well in keeping with other cars of the day, the smooth flowing lines were neither ultra-modern nor stodgily conservative, but appear to be right in tune with what was to be expected for a low priced car of the era.

The interiors too were totally new, and were equipped with a wood grained dash panel that featured Ford's first overall use of a glove box. Also, the instrument cluster now was directly in front of the driver, rather than being centered on the dash. Centered on the dash now was Ford's first standard ashtray and lighter, with these flanked by the choke and throttle controls. Also centered at the very top of the dash was the new crank-out windshield opener. A single windshield wiper was still standard, but dual sun visors were now installed on all closed cars.

Including the station wagon, which was usually considered a commercial vehicle, Ford came out with 15 different models this year, including the Standard and Deluxe variations of similar body styles. New for the year was a 3-window Coupe in Standard trim and a 5-window Coupe in Deluxe trim, while the Convertible Sedan was gone. As in previous years, the Tudor Sedan was the most popular, and was the only model to not only have production go over the 100,000 mark, it was the only single model to achieve such status. Its Standard version alone sold 106,387, while the Deluxe variation sold 48,233, and this does not include the additional 2,996 in 4-cylinder form.

As had been the case for the past few years, Ford left the major portion of its body building to outside firms, primarily the Murray Corp. of America and Briggs Mfg. Co. However, a major strike occurred at Briggs in the fall of 1932, and as a result, retooling for the new Ford bodies could not be made within the allotted time frame. Since the Ford contract was so large, no other body companies could successfully come in to fill the void. Murray was already close to saturation, as was Budd. Fisher had its total interest in General Motors, and some of the smaller companies, and the semi-custom shops, did not have the production capabilities to manufacture in the quantity, quality, or price range that Ford required.

The Briggs strike was finally ended, but as a result, Ford did not get its new models out before the fall introductory dates. In fact, it wasn't until Feb. 9, 1933, that the cars were finally shown. Again, Ford was late on stage, and a multitude of sales were lost to Chevrolet, Plymouth, and even Dodge, just on the fact alone that several months of "1933" cars had gone by while Ford continued producing 1932 models.

Ford still strongly felt that it was ahead of the game producing just chassis and letting competing body companies supply the major portion of the body line, but there were those within the company who would have preferred that Ford once again handled its own total package. They wouldn't get their way for several more years, but still, the Briggs strike and resultant production delays certainly added fuel to their arguments of "total" production.

As mentioned in the first paragraph, seldom does one think of the 1933 models as being 30th anniversary styles, or even as being part of Ford's celebration of its first 30 years in the automotive business. But Ford did celebrate, and it did let the country know that 30 years had indeed passed since the first real Ford saw the light of day.

Among the celebration activities were the production of the 21-millionth Ford, and of far more importance to automotive and history buffs world wide—the official opening of Greenfield Village. Henry Ford's major contribution to the preservation of Americana, Greenfield Village and its accompanying Edison Institute, have since become one of the great tourist meccas in the eastern part of the U.S., attracting thousands of visitors from all parts of the world each year.

No, the Standard Roadster really didn't look like this in showroom condition. But it did provide a base for this Cote Motors racer which was one of 11 Fords entered in the 1933 revival of the Elgin Road Races. Ford swept the field, winning the first seven positions. In its more sedate form, the $475 Standard Roadster wore full fenders and running boards, had a single painted horn, and weighed 2,422 pounds. This light weight quickly made it a favorite for racing conversions such as this, as the V-8 engine provided more pep-per-pound than on any other model. A trunk deck constituted regular equipment, but a rumble seat was available as an extra cost option, as was virtually all other "Deluxe" equipment if one wanted to build a Deluxe model from a Standard base. Few apparently wanted to do this, and as a result, only 126 Standard Roadsters were sold in V-8 form, while another 107 buyers saved $50 by taking the 4-cylinder engine.

Far more popular than the Standard Roadster was the Deluxe version, which sold for $510 as a V-8 or $460 as a Four. Bodies for all roadsters were built by Murray and were designated Type 710. Ford built 4,223 with V-8 engines, but only 101 with the Four. In Deluxe trim, all had rumble seats, genuine leather front seats, dual chromed horns and cowl lights, top boot, cigar lighter, and ash tray. This was quite a bargain at the $35 difference between Standard and Deluxe versions, and by the looks of the production records, most buyers felt the same way. The roadsters still featured bolt-on windshield frames, painted on Standard models, chromed on the Deluxe, but these could no longer be lowered. Side curtains still provided protection, and clipped onto the door sills. The wind wings were still accessories, but would once more become regular items with the 1934 models. With all of the extra equipment, the V-8 Deluxe Roadster weighed 2,461 pounds.

Available only in Deluxe trim was the Cabriolet, Type 760. More comfortable and popular than the roadster, it accounted for 7,852 units with a V-8, but only 24 with the 4-cylinder engine. Built by Murray, the car sold for $585 and weighed 2,545 pounds. Its main differences from the roadsters were the use of an integral windshield frame, roll-up windows, and a folding top that fit flush with both windows and windshield when raised. Built only as a rumble seat model, it had a front seat of genuine copra-color leather, with the rumble seat in matching artificial leather. The front seat could also be ordered in brown bedford cord, with matching panels. The top was in beige canvas interlined with rubber. It used a concealed rumble seat latch, located behind the driver's seat. The rear panel was zippered and could be removed without lowering the top, thereby allowing flow-through ventilation or conversation with rumble seat passengers.

Twice as popular as the 3-window Coupe was the Briggs-built 5-window Coupe. Total production of this body reached 45,217 in all four variations, as opposed to 22,692 for the 3-window. Most popular of all four varieties was the V-8 Standard model shown here, which drew 31,791 orders. It cost $490 and weighed 2,534 pounds. Priced at $440 was the Standard 5-window Coupe with the 4-cylinder engine. It became one of the more popular Fours, with 2,148 being sold. All 5-window Coupes had a trunk deck as stock equipment, but could be ordered with a rumble seat. Both 3 and 5-window Standard Coupes initially gave buyers a choice of either a brown mohair or tan pinstripe interior. However, in April two extra cost interiors were offered. They consisted of either a copra genuine leather or a similar imitation leather seat with matching panels. To be a perfect restoration, this model should have black fenders and aprons, as no fenders were painted in body color this year.

Substantially less popular in Deluxe trim than in Standard was the Briggs 5-window Coupe. Costing $540 in V-8 power, the Deluxe model recorded only 11,244 sales, with another 28 being powered by the Four. Both Standard and Deluxe 5-window Coupes were known as the Type 770. Exterior differences between the two included a chromed windshield frame, dual horns and cowl lights, and a left taillight. Interiors could be in either rose beige mohair; brown bedford cord, or brown stripe broadcloth. In April a genuine leather interior was offered as an extra-cost option, but the imitation leather interior found on the Standard Coupe was not available in the Deluxe models. When the optional rumble seat was ordered, it was finished in a copra-color imitation leather matching the interior leathers. On all coupes, the rear window could be lowered for ventilation, but the quarter windows on the 5-window model were fixed in place.

Along with its open 2-door models, Murray also produced the sportily attractive 3-window Coupe, Type 720. Not as popular as the 5-window model, it nevertheless was available in both Standard and Deluxe versions and with either a Four or a V-8, thereby giving buyers a choice of four different varieties. The V-8 Deluxe, shown here, cost $540 and weighed 2,538 pounds. A total of 15,894 were sold in this form, while another 24 had the Four. In Standard trim, with a trunk deck and lacking all of the other Deluxe features, the car cost $590 as a V-8 and weighed 2,534 pounds. In this guise, sales amounted to 6,585, with another 189 built with the Four. Both Standard and Deluxe models had the trunk deck as regular equipment, with rumble seats being an extra cost option.

Totally changed from the previous models was the new Victoria, Type 740. Built by Murray, the close-coupled 4-passenger car was available in Deluxe trim only, and weighed 2,595 pounds. Not especially popular, it claimed only 4,193 sales in V-8 form, and only 25 as a Four. Essentially a variation of the Tudor, the car had a nicely sloping rear deck with a surprisingly large luggage area, accessible only from the inside. Buyers had a choice of the same three interiors as used in the Deluxe Coupe and Sedan. Tilting bucket seats were used in the front, with a bench seat in the rear. Rear passengers had a silk roller shade on the back window, assist straps, and side arm rests. The rear quarter windows could be lowered.

The most popular model by a long mile was the Standard Tudor, Type 700, which was built by Briggs. It was the only single model to have a sales record in excess of 100,000, with the final tally being 106,387 in V-8 form alone. Another 2,911 had the 4-cylinder engine. Thus, in that shape, it was also the most popular Four. Weighing 2,621 pounds, it had a V-8 price of $500 even. Its seating arrangement was similar to that of the Victoria, but no luggage space was provided behind the rear seat. A single painted horn and painted windshield frame was a quick sign of a Standard model. Interiors were in brown mohair or a pinstripe broadcloth. In April, probably at the request of fleet buyers, an interior of artificial leather seats and panels was provided. This was the same material that was available on the coupe models.

The Murray-built Phaeton was also available in four variations, either Standard or Deluxe and with either a V-8 or a Four. Surprisingly, it was the only model to draw more orders as a Four than a V-8. In standard trim, the 4-cylinder engines were found in 457 units, while the V-8 went into only 232. In the Deluxe range, however, the story was different. Here, 1,483 had the V-8 while only 241 had the Four. The V-8 cost $495 in Standard trim and weighed 2,520 pounds, while in Deluxe form it cost $545 and weighed 2,529 pounds. On this Deluxe model, the wind wings were still an option, as was the top boot. In 1934 they would be included in the Deluxe package. Canvas side curtains still provided weather protection. They lived in their own envelope behind the rear seat. Deluxe models were upholstered in beige genuine leather, while standard units used a black-brown imitation leather throughout. This was the only Ford 4-door to have its doors hinged at the B-pillar, and the only one to have a rearward opening door. All other body styles had all doors latching at the leading edge in "suicide" fashion.

A massive economy run, co-sponsored by White Star Gas and Ford took place this year and involved a fleet of 30 Deluxe Tudors. Running two round trips a day between Kalamazoo and Detroit, the cars logged 10,000 miles in the 12-day span, averaging 21.9 miles-per-gallon. Other long-distance economy promotions staged by Ford this year included a 40,000 mile run around New England; 10,000 miles around New York's Catskill Mountains; seven days running between Washington, D.C., and Mt. Vernon, and 10,000 miles in the Mojave Desert. Having less than half the popularity of its Standard version, the Deluxe Tudor still listed 48,233 sales as a V-8, and thus was the most popular Deluxe style also. The Deluxe also saw 85 orders with the 4-cylinder engine. The V-8 price was $550 while its weight was 2,625 pounds. Among the features on the Deluxe model were ash trays for the rear passengers; a front cigar lighter; arm rests on the front doors and for the rear passengers, and a right-hand sun visor. As did the Standard version, this model also could be ordered with a leather interior after April, with genuine leather being used. The black fenders, common to all 1933 Fords, are quite obvious in this photo.

Definitely lacking the sales appeal of the Tudor was the new Standard Fordor. Shown here in pre-production form, this experimental version wears the commercial type fenders without valences, which were first considered for 1933 production. Some information would indicate that a few very early passenger cars were released with these fenders and running boards, and it is known that some of the early station wagons were so fitted. Possibly because of the strike at the Briggs plant, it appears that all production of the 4-door sedans this year was done by Murray. In Standard form, the car drew 19,602 orders with the V-8 and 682 with the Four. In V-8 guise it cost $560 and weighed 2,675 pounds. Some early models may also have been turned out with plain rear spares, but early in the year the Standard cars had canvas tire covers. By spring they were wearing the same metal spare covers as were the Deluxe models. Because of the new fender line, sidemounts were relegated strictly to station wagons and commercial vehicles.

The highest priced Ford this year, not counting the station wagon, was the Deluxe Fordor, Type 730. In V-8 form it was priced at $610 and weighed 2,684 pounds. As with the Standard version, Murray took over production. Ford put out 45,443 in V-8 power but only 179 with the Four. Total Fordor production of all variations totalled 65,906. The Deluxe Fordor carried all of the features common to other Deluxe models and used the same interior fabrics. After April, it also could be ordered with an interior in genuine copra drab (beige) leather. On all Fordors, the quarter windows could be opened partially for ventilation.

Having a totally new body this year was Ford's most expensive passenger car, the Station Wagon, Type 860. Priced at $640, it weighed 2,635 pounds with the V-8. Production reached 1,654 in V-8 form and 359 with the Four. For some reason, the Cleveland-based Baker-Raulang Co. this year lost the wagon contract, and Murray again took over the final assembly. The wood was still cut and trimmed at Ford's own Iron Mountain plant. Amusingly, the wagon wore Deluxe cowl lights, had the painted horn of Standard models, and was usually considered a commercial vehicle. Seats were in black-brown artificial leather. The front and rear seat were now full bench types, while the center seat was divided in the middle for access to the rear. Essentially, it consisted of two single seats. Again, the center and rear seats were easily removable. Side curtains still provided weather protection. They were of tan fabric with celluloid panels. The wagon was available only in brown hood and cowl, with varnished wood sides and interior, and black fenders.

Although Ford this year was not promoting any direct commercialization of its coupes or roadsters, it certainly didn't mind when a fleet buyer such as the Wm. Wrigley Jr. Co. converted the new Victoria into sedan delivery use. Under an arrangement with the Chicago branch, Wrigley purchased an unknown number of Victorias; made a cargo compartment of the rear area, and blanked in the quarter windows with Wrigley chewing gum advertising. Dual spotlights and Vogue Tyres complete the pretty picture. Note that the tires are double whitewalled, both inside and out. Imagine the expression on the salesmen's faces when they learned they were lucky enough to be assigned one of these cuties.

A sedan Delivery was still being built based on the Tudor shell, but the work was no longer being done under the auspices of Ford. The LeBaron division of Briggs Mfg. Co. had been unable to interest Ford in continuing the Tudor-based little truck, so they offered it directly to dealers on a special order basis. It retailed for $587 in Standard trim or $637 in Deluxe. Unlike the former Sedan Delivery which was all truck, the LeBaron version could be converted back to a Tudor, albeit one with a large cargo door in the rear. But, the blank side panels would snap out, restoring the windows. The rear seat would quickly slide into place, and even the door handle on the special cargo door would detach to help hide the panel truck look. Now the only evidence of commercial usage was the cargo door outline and the high-mounted spare, which no longer was an asset to the vehicle's overall line. It is probable that most of these vehicles were finished in the artificial leather interior.

The LeBaron Division of Briggs Mfg. Co. is more famous for its fine custom and semi-custom bodies on luxury passenger car chassis than it is for work on Ford units. However, like all custom body shops of this era, it was finding customers scarce, and therefore looked to almost any endeavor that would bring work into the plant. One such project involved the creation of these 7-passenger Sedan-Limousine bodies for the Ford passenger car chassis. In a novel move, LeBaron based the vehicle on its own Sedan Delivery body shell, with doors modified from standard production units. An unusual touch was the high-rise upper rear door line, which allowed passengers a bit more headroom when entering or leaving the car. The interior was either in bedford cord or wool broadcloth. Custom touches included a trunk rack, special bumpers, and Martin 7.00x16 whitewalls on Cleve-Weld chromed spoke wheels. The Sedan version, shown here, sold for $975, while the Limousine, which included a partition with a sliding glass window between compartments, sold for $1,040. Designed primarily for the livery trade, the cars were not sold direct to Ford dealers, but went through New Era Motors of New York City, which acted as distribution agents. Marketing by New Era was by both direct fleet sales or by way of authorized Ford agencies.

This year Ford had only one commercial vehicle that used passenger car sheet metal and trim. It was the Sedan Delivery, Type 850, which sold for $570 as a V-8 or $520 as a Four. All other commercial vehicles, including the pickups, this year used the carry-over 1932 styling that was relegated to the commercial line, and thus fall beyond the scope of this book. The Sedan Delivery had its own body shell, built by the LeBaron division of Briggs Mfg. Co., the same builder that was busy converting Tudors into another type of sedan delivery. However, this model was total truck, offering a far larger cargo area on its extended body. Also, its single rear door was larger, while its front doors were smaller, being interchangeable with those of the Fordor. Slightly more popular in 4-cylinder form than as a V-8, this model saw 1,914 orders with the little engine and 1,752 with the Eight. The passenger compartment had two folding bucket seats in artificial leather, that gave access to the cargo area without going around to the back. Once again, the Chicago branch was one of the major markets for this vehicle.

Once LeBaron developed the Sedan-Limousine, it didn't take New Era long to see the taxi potential of this body. Using the same exact shell of the limousine model (a modification of the Sedan Delivery shell) the cab differed primarily in its interior arrangements. A partition separated the two compartments, and the rear area contained two jump seats, giving 5-passenger capacity in the rear, plus one more in the front. The old Model A Taxi could hold only four paying passengers. Upholstery was in genuine leather. Extra touches included the use of disc wheels with General Jumbo low-pressure tires; full safety glass in all windows; trunk rack; special heater; fender/running board rub-rail; special bumpers, and lighted taxi sign. These cars were marketed as New Eras, not Fords, and as such carried the "New Era" name boldly across the grille and on the special hubcaps. Priced at $995, all sales were through New Era, either direct or to authorized Ford agents. Of interest are the posted fares on the door, which state 15-cents for the first quarter mile, and 5-cents per quarter thereafter.

The LeBaron-New Era production wasn't the only Ford taxi on the streets this year. Probably impressed by the overall design of the Model 40, the York-Hoover Body Corp. came out with its own cab version. Designated the York-Hoover Model F-40-33, it was designed to be a drop-on unit for the Ford passenger car chassis, mating to the special station wagon cowl and windshield header. The body bore a definite resemblance to Ford's own production, even though the entire unit was built in York's own shops. Unlike New Era, York-Hoover used Ford's stock wheels, but then went and produced its own hood with two large horizontal louvers. Both the LeBaron and the York-Hoover models used a heavy stainless steel rub strip starting at the front wheel opening and continuing along the running board to the leading edge of the rear fender. The body was upholstered in genuine leather, used shatterproof glass throughout, and had its own rear-seat heater. The interior contained a partition between compartments, which was fitted with two rearward facing jump seats. The top was covered in imitation leather. Some models were produced with a removable top section over the driver so that the cab could be converted to town car style.

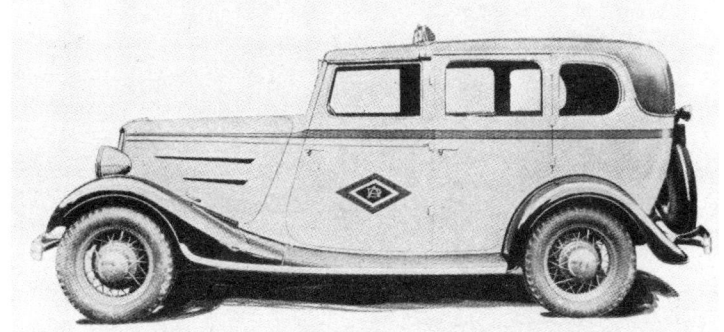

Looking very much like a hearse or ambulance, but intended for passenger car use only, was this limited sales package from the LeBaron Division of Briggs. Just as it had designed a car/truck conversion package for the Tudor Sedan, it also designed a similar truck/car package for the Sedan Delivery. Priced as an option at $115 above the regular Sedan Delivery price, the package consisted of large glass panels for the cargo area; metal side boards that could be inserted over these panels, and a fully upholstered rear seat. The rear cargo door was equipped with a detachable handle so that it could be removed when the vehicle was used as a 2-door sedan. Access to the rear seat was via the front doors only. The standard tilting passenger seats were used in the front. Leg room for the rear passengers must have been marvelous. It is believed that very few such convertible Sedan Deliveries were built, and it is doubtful if any survive today.

With the depression economy still very evident, many professional car builders were turning to lighter chassis as a way to produce more economical vehicles. Usually ignored by this industry up until now, such chassis as Ford and Chevrolet were finding more and more buyers as alternatives to Cadillac and Packard prices. One company banking heavily on the lower priced chassis was the A.J. Miller Co. of Bellefontaine, Ohio, one of the major builders of professional cars. Miller turned out this fleet of ambulances for an unknown customer, fitting a nicely designed beavertail body to a stretched Model 40 chassis. The huge windshields are fitted with dual wipers and spotlights, while a 3-unit rotating red beacon rests on the roof. Rear access could be made either by the side or the rear door. A spare tire was not part of the deal.

Looking quite like its funeral car version was this standard ambulance body without the relatively new beavertail design. Compare the back panel of this car with the other Miller ambulances shown here. Built for the Manhasset-Lakeville Fire Dept. Rescue Squad of Manhasset, N.Y., this car uses cut glass quarter windows, but plain windows in the doors. The same large windshield is used as on the beavertail models, but only a single wiper is supplied. The A.J. Miller Co. used all of its own components, including cowl, and refrained from the front-latching front doors found on most Fords.

Another A.J. Miller offering was the "B. Franklin" funeral car, which utilized the same body shell as found on the standard ambulances. Having a wheelbase of 136 inches, these cars provided local funeral homes with an economic alternative to high priced chassis. This body was adaptable to many light chassis, including Chevrolet and Dodge. Standard Ford fenders, hood, and grille were used, but the bodies required heavier springs. The large object visible through the quarter window is a flower tray, which mounted over the coffin and allowed the funeral arrangements to be carried in the same car as the deceased, thus avoiding the expense of a separate flower car.

Running on a stretched wheelbase of 148 inches is this Professional Service Car produced by the Shop of Siebert of Toledo, Ohio. This was Siebert's first year in the professional car field, but it would be a factor in stretched Fords from this point on. Later it would produce its own extension components, but in 1933 it is believed that kits supplied by the W.G. Reeves Co. were used. Reeves had continued to provide such conversion kits since early in the Model T days. The Cleve-Weld chromed wheels and low pressure tires were probably added not only for looks but to help support the added weight of the body. Looking like oversized panel trucks, professional service cars were used to transport bodies, coffins, and equipment prior to the actual funeral service. In this era, when most funerals were still conducted from the home of the deceased, transportation of the necessary items had to be done in a subtle yet dignified manner, and thus the use of such plain but attractive vehicles was warranted. Inside, they usually had plain paneling, either in attractively finished plywood or masonite.

1933

The Hill Auto Body Co. of Cincinnati was at it again this year. After building the one-off Arrow Plane in 1931, Hill landed a contract from the McQuay-Norris Co. of St. Louis to produce a fleet of six ultra-modern streamliners that could be used by their salesmen, and that would attract attention to their products when the cars were parked outside auto parts stores. McQuay-Norris produced a full line of pistons, rings, and replacement engine and chassis parts. Although commissioned in 1932, the six streamliners used stock 1933 Ford passenger car engines and chassis in normal configuration. Unlike the rear-engine Arrow Plane, the streamliners had their engines under a compartment in the front, and seating, steering and controls were the same as they would have been in a normal car. The six vehicles, which apparently were never given an official name, were on the road up until World War II, traveling in the southern states in the winter and up north in the summer. Apparently to impress the boys at the auto stores, each car carried a total of 15 gauges mounted in a mahogany panel, which reported every conceivable engine function. Seating configuration was similar to that of the old centerdoors, with entry to the rear compartment, and a narrow aisle leading to the two forward bucket seats. The rear compartment carried the salesmen's samples. Hill Auto Body & Metal Co. remained in business until 1960, but it does not appear that any other streamliners were ever built by the company.

Using the new Ford V-8 engines and various other Ford components was the Dymaxion, produced by Buckminster Fuller, a relatively well-known automotive design and engineer. Planned as an ultra-modern "super car," the vehicle weighed 1,850 pounds, was capable of 120 MPH, and could cruise at 40 miles-per-gallon. A total of three were built, all using frames of duraluminum, with balsa wood bracing and thin aluminum skin. Aviation design was used to such a degree that the cars even had rear steering, which probably led to their downfall—one of the cars went out of control during a test and killed two officials of Gulf Oil Co. The cars were built in the old Locomobile plant at Bridgeport, Conn. Fuller never could get the backing nor the interest necessary to put the cars into production, even though one of the surviving three was bought by Leopold Stokowski, then leader of the Philadelphia Symphony Orchestra. Fuller, incidentally, is best known for his invention of the geodesic dome, which is now used in thousands of architectural applications world wide.

The Detroit, Toledo and Ironton Railroad wasn't the only line to use Ford cars for railroad work. The Chicago, Burlington & Quincy Railroad (now the Burlington Northern) also found the new sedans to be excellent for both rail inspection teams and executive travel. Not a C.B.&Q. shop job, these units were built by Fairmont Railway Motors, and probably were marketed to other lines as well. The extent of this production is not known. The unusual wheels probably represent the last known use of demountable rims on a Ford car. Rail flanges rode inside the tires, and it appears that the wheels and flanges would have to be removed in order to make this car suitable for street driving. The steering wheel would indicate that both rail and road operation was possible. The welled right front fender is from the light commercial chassis, while the dual chromed air horns are strictly aftermarket.

Although most Europeans were totally taken in with the new Ford V-8, the Russians obviously were not impressed. In fact, they simply kept turning out limited numbers of their Model A copy at the Molotov plant in Gorki. Henry Ford had helped the Russians set up this facility in 1930, under an arrangement that the author has never been able to understand. It appears that production could reach as high as 200 cars or trucks a day, though it is doubtful if such peaks were ever attained. Called the GAZ-A, the car was virtually identical to the American Model A. It appears to have remained in production until 1935 when it was replaced by another 4-cylinder car looking like a cross between a 1933 Ford and a Citroen. In 1939 a copy of Ford's V-8 materialized, along with another new styling exercise that again leaned heavily on older Ford designs. But World War II cut short production of that model.

On Dec. 6, 1933, Ford staged one of its largest introductions of "NEW" models that it had ever put on. Suppliers were invited to set up their own displays, newsmen and automotive writers were welcomed, and participating dealers were brought in and given gifts of cigars and actually served beer (remember, Henry Ford hated both smoking and alcohol). And, surprisingly, the "preview" worked. Ford gathered major headlines in the nation's press and automotive journals.

Why Ford gave major attention to the 1934 models is still a question, because actually the cars looked little different than the 1933 versions. Even the major change, a slightly redesigned grille and straight-line hood louvers, was really not a 1934 design, but a running change that started with the September, 1933 models. True, fenders and aprons were now painted in body color rather than black, and the Standard line was reduced by a couple of models, and there was a new hubcap and grille emblem design. But for all practical purposes, it takes a very sharp eye and memory to tell a 1933 from a 1934 Ford.

Mechanically though, some significant changes had taken place. Under the hood was a much improved V-8, with its horsepower raised from 75 to 85 at 3800 rpm (some say 90 HP). Although the engine still had a 3-1/16x3.75 inch bore and stroke and displaced 221 cubic inches, some major changes allowed for the increase in horses. Foremost among these was the replacement of the Detroit Lubricator carburetor with a new Stromberg unit fitted with a newly designed A.C. air cleaner for easier breathing. Beneath the new downdraft carburetor was a totally new intake manifold. The resulting package produced a smoother running and more powerful engine.

Also of major significance was a new crankshaft. This was Ford's first use of a fully counterbalanced, cast alloy crankshaft, which contributed to a substantial reduction in vibration. Also changed on the new engine were the pistons, which now had open skirts. Other advances included a unitized valve assembly, new thermostats, and a new fuel pump.

Engine numbers on the new blocks began with 561593 on January first, and ended with 1352202 on Dec. 31. However, since many of the above mentioned changes were made on a running basis, some or all of these changes possibly can be found on late 1933 blocks.

In the 4-cylinder world, nothing changed except that production was terminated in August. Engine numbers ran from 5263535 to 5292536, showing that a total of 29,001 4-cylinder blocks were turned out this year, with only 1,912 of these going into passenger cars. The remainder either went into commercial vehicles or were used as replacement blocks. However, the total lack of interest shown by the public in the new Fords when fitted with 4-cylinder engines quickly convinced the company that it was silly to continue this engine any longer. The V-8 had won true acceptance.

Other mechanical changes to the cars included a new "gas saver" rear axle ratio, available only as an option; a new steering ratio for easier parking; revised springs and shock absorbers, and a new size battery, this one measuring the same 10.5 by 7.25 inches in size, but being eight inches high as opposed to the old 7.5 inches. Also on the electrics was a new 2-step cutout regulator, while at mid-year a new starter switch was added as a running change.

Inside the cars, a new dash panel greeted the drivers. Similar in layout to the 1933 issue, it deleted the machine-turned instrument panel, and now had the instruments mounted in an embossed platform featuring the same woodgrain applique as the rest of the dash. Totally new was the wiring for the new radios that were available as dealer installed accessories. When in place, the radio itself lived behind the instrument cluster, just above the clutch pedal. On the right firewall was room for Ford's new accessory heater. New woodgraining applique design, new stitching on the door panels, and some new materials completed the interior picture.

Within the body framework, all basic shells were continued unchanged, but three Standard models were supposedly dropped from the roles. They were the 3-window Coupe; Roadster, and Phaeton, now supposedly all available only in Deluxe trim. The coupe did not appear, but production records indicate that four roadsters were actually built in Standard form. However, the Phaeton shows a rather healthy 750 units produced in Standard trim, despite this not being listed as an available model.

Supposedly available only in Deluxe form this year was the Roadster, Type 710. Still, records show four were built in Standard style, which meant they had trunk decks rather than rumble seats and lacked the Deluxe trim such as cowl lights, twin chromed horns, and chromed windshield frames. Of the 5,070 Deluxe Roadsters built this year, all but 32 had V-8 engines. Now priced at $525, the 2,461-pound car continued to feature an all-leather interior, with the rumble seat done in matching artificial leather. Snap-on side curtains still provided weather protection. The greyhound hood ornament was a popular accessory in this era, being a direct copy of those used on Lincolns. Wind wings are a puzzle, as some information would indicate that they were standard equipment on all roadsters this year, while other information shows them as extra-cost accessories. Possibly their standardization was a mid-year sales incentive decision. Since no Standard Roadsters were shown in Ford's official listing, the four that were built must have been for a special order, possibly to appease a good fleet customer.

Overall, production figures must have pleased even the most cantankerous bean counter in Ford's offices, as a combination of better economic conditions and public acceptance of the new block boosted sales to levels not enjoyed since the advent of the V-8. In all, 514,975 Fords left the factory. Of these, 513,063 were V-8s, while the remaining 1,912 had the Four. Of all styles, three had sales over 100,000. They were the two Tudor varieties, which together recorded 246,566 units, of which 124,870 were in Standard trim and 121,696 were in Deluxe form. And, this figure does not include the 197 with 4-cylinder power. Also in the 100,000 club was the Deluxe Fordor, with 102,268 builds to its credit.

The only body to undergo any serious modification was the Murray-built Victoria. The car, which had featured Ford's first usable luggage space on a sedan model, now offered the same space but with access from the outside. On the previous model, the space was reached by pulling down the back of the rear seat. Now only a releasing lever lived behind the rear seat. When pulled, it opened a latch on a large back panel. Pulling rearward on the spare tire opened this panel, allowing the luggage to be inserted over the spare. An interesting feature of this new access was the accordion-pleated canvas bellows that connected the panel to the sides, protecting the luggage when the panel was closed. This interesting trunk arrangement was used just this one year, and only on the 20,083 Victorias that Murray built.

Another interesting activity this year concerns a car that never made it. With the economic situation as bad as it was, Ford decided that a smaller and cheaper car,

possibly one more akin to the Model T concept, might be warranted. As a result, shortly after the 1932 models were on the market, engineers and designers began work on a new mini-Ford that would be a companion car to the Model 40 Series, which was also in the planning stages.

The mini-Ford was to have a 105-inch wheelbase, and be a scaled down version in almost all respects to the Model 40. Interestingly, even though the Model B 4-cylinder engine was available in the Model 40 cars, the mini-Ford was to have a scaled down version of the V-8, not the Four. To be known as the Model 44, the top secret car was only a month or so away from actual production in mid-1933, and was to have been introduced as a 1934 model. However, it appeared that the overall economy was picking up, and with the depression somewhat on the run, Ford became convinced that such a small car would not find a ready market, especially since the price would not have been that much lower than a comparable Model 40. The major portion of the design program was salvaged by the overseas operations, however, and the car essentially became the new French Ford.

All of this activity resulted in one historic note. That was the production of the 1-millionth V-8 car. This occurred on June 20, 1934, as a Deluxe Fordor with a special paint job was moved off the lines under the watchful eyes of both Henry and Edsel. After the usual photographs and publicity activities, the car was shipped to Chicago and put on display at Ford's exhibit at the World's Fair, which was in progress in the Windy City.

Companion to the roadster, but three times as popular, was the Cabriolet. Also available only in Deluxe trim, the car cost $590 as a V-8. In this form, a total of 14,496 were built, while only 12 buyers opted for the Four. Featuring roll-up windows and a fully weather-tight interior, the 2,545-pound car came with a standard rumble seat, and was not available in trunk form. In this photo, the spare tire cover is missing. Normally, this was a standard piece of equipment, as were chromed dual horns, chromed windshield frame, cowl lights, and step plates on the right taillight and fender for the rumble seat passengers. All interiors were done in genuine leather, but a color change was made in May. Early models were in a copra color, while those built after May had their interiors done in a taupe shade. The top material was the same as used on the roadster, and was a drab canvas interlined with rubber. A bedford cord interior could also be ordered, but regardless of the interior, the rumble seats were always done in artificial leather. Once again, the Murray Corp. was the sole contractor for the Cabriolet and Roadster bodies. On all open cars equipped with rumble seats, the rumble seat latch was located behind the front seat.

Prettying up the driveway of its home in Glen Ellyn, Ill., is this Standard 5-window Coupe, which the author owned for several years. Far more popular than the Deluxe version, the Standard 5-window had a run of 47,623 in V-8 power, but only 20 with the Four. All versions used a trunk deck as standard equipment, but rumble seats could be ordered at extra cost. Brown mohair or tan pinstripe cloth interiors were standard, but leather interiors, either in genuine leather or artificial, could be ordered at extra cost. As with the Cabriolet, during May a switch was made from copra to taupe color for both the real and artificial leather interiors. Single horn, painted windshield frame, and lack of cowl lights were the identifying factors for Standard Coupes. As before, the Murray Corp. built all coupe bodies.

Despite there being only a $40 difference between the Deluxe and Standard 5-window Coupes, the Deluxe version had only half the sales of the cheaper Standard, which sold for $515. Thus, the $555 Deluxe model had 26,879 sales as a V-8, but only three with the 4-cylinder engine. The owner of this model opted for the extra-cost rumble seat, plus the concaved bumper guards which appeared in Ford dealerships during the year. Also added was the greyhound hood ornament, which originally was a $10 accessory. Buyers had a choice of rose beige mohair or brown stripe broadcloth interiors, unless the extra-cost leather or artificial leather was chosen. On the leather interior, the same color change occurred in May as did on all models. Designated the Type 770, the 5-window Coupe drew 745,525 orders in all forms.

The only Ford to really change this year was the Murray-built Victoria, Type 740. The close-coupled 2-door sedan had always featured a small luggage compartment behind the rear seat, but access was always through the interior. Now the car had a new rear, with a swing-out back panel which gave access to the luggage area from the outside. The deck latch resided behind the rear seat back, and after unlatching, the panel was opened by pulling on the spare tire. Pleated bellows and a sliding guide protected the luggage and kept the deck from opening too far, but also made loading the luggage a bit clumsy. Because of this deck, the Victorias required special non-interchangeable rear bumpers and longer taillight arms. This was the only time Ford ever used such a design on a car, and the idea would disappear at the end of the model run. The Victoria concept was not carried into 1935. Available in Deluxe trim only, the 2,595-pound Victoria cost $610. Murray built 20,083, all in V-8 power as the Four was not offered in this style. Adding a bit of confusion to the Victoria is the fact that the swing-out trunk panel was not introduced until May, and thus those models built prior to May would have had the same solid back as found on the 1933 issue. Interiors were the same as for all Deluxe models, with genuine leather being an extra-cost option. Artificial leather was not available in the Victoria.

Enjoying only one-third the popularity of the 5-window Coupe was the Murray-built 3-window Coupe. Available in Deluxe form only, and priced at the same $555 as the Deluxe 5-window, the Type 720 3-window had only 26,348 orders in V-8 form and seven with the Four. Built with the trunk deck as normal fare, the 3-window could also be ordered with the extra-cost rumble seat. All coupes, whether equipped with rumble seat or trunk, had a lowering mechanism for the rear window. This allowed conversation with rumble seat passengers when in that form, or was excellent for flow-through ventilation in any form. Despite its better looks, the 3-window Coupe was less practical than its 5-window companion. On the 5-window, the larger superstructure and extra windows made for easier parking and also provided a very handy parcel shelf behind the front seat. Interior options were the same for both Deluxe models. Note the hood latch just ahead of the cowl. All 1934 and some very late 1933 Fords had two latches, one forward and one aft, while most 1933 models had just one latch at the center.

Ford's most popular model was the Standard Tudor, Type 700. Sales reached 124,870 in V-8 form and 185 as a Four. Coupled with the 121,708 in Deluxe trim, a total of 246,763 of these bodies left the Briggs plant this year. Priced at $535, the 2,621-pound car proved to be the ideal family vehicle for thousands of Americans looking for cheap but dependable transportation. Appearing in March was a new seat tilting design which prevented the passenger seat from hitting the dash when moved forward. Interiors were in the same material as used in the Standard Coupe, with both genuine and imitation leather being available at extra cost.

1934

Taking second place in the sales race was the Deluxe Tudor, priced at $575 and weighing 2,625 pounds. Briggs supplied a total of 121,708. Of these, all but 12 subsequently were equipped with V-8s. Deluxe trim included the dual cowl lights and horns, chromed windshield frame, cigar lighter, ash tray, arm rests both front and rear, a sun visor for the passenger, and Deluxe interior materials, with genuine leather being a cost option. New for the year was optional wiring to accommodate the new Ford dealer-installed radios. These usually had their dials and controls in the ash tray area, but a second version arrived during the year which occupied the area normally taken by the glove box. As before, no provision was made for carrying luggage or parcels. These items either had to go inside, or the buyer had to invest in an aftermarket luggage carrier and trunk.

Ford's sportiest 4-door car was the Phaeton. Surprisingly, in Standard form, it was also Ford's lowest price model, selling for just $510, while the Deluxe version went for $550. Designated the Type 750, it featured a body by Murray. Although some records would indicate that a Standard version was not available this year, production lists show that 750 were turned out in Standard form. Of these, 377 had the 4-cylinder engine, while only 373 had the V-8. In Deluxe trim the story was different, however. Here, of the 3,540 that were built, 3,128 had the V-8 while 412 retained the Four. Still, it is puzzling why such a sporty car would have such a high percentage of 4-cylinder installations. Also puzzling is the upturn in total sales for this model. This year, Murray produced a total of 4,290 Phaetons of all types, as opposed to 2,413 built in 1933. The car used the same chromed windshield frame as did the roadster. On this, the window would swing out from the bottom, being held in open positions by slide arms on each side.

Production of the Fordor Sedans returned to Briggs this year, and apparently provided a windfall for the company, as sales of this model soared. In all, a total of 125,451 Fordor shells were turned out, as opposed to 65,906 in 1933. Of that amount, the Deluxe Fordor with V-8 claimed 102,268, making this model the third best selling Ford in the book, falling into place just behind the Standard and Deluxe Tudors. In addition, 384 Deluxe Fordors were turned out with 4-cylinder engines. As shown here, the Deluxe model cost $625 and weighed 2,684 pounds. In its Standard version, the V-8 model claimed 22,394 sales, while another 405 buyers went with the Four. Of interest on this body was the new ventilation system in the front windows. When the window crank was moved a half-turn, the window would go back about one inch, allowing a bit more than a half-inch ventilation space between the glass and the frame. Further turning of the crank would lower the window in a conventional manner. Upholstery material in the Fordors matched that of other Standard and Deluxe models, and included the optional use of imitation or real leather in the Standard models and genuine leather in the Deluxe. As was the case with all Deluxe Fords, the cars could be wired for radios this year, but these radios were still a luxurious option that were purchased by very few. All Fordors were designated Type 730.

Even from the rear, the Deluxe Phaeton was a beautiful piece of automotive design, especially when fitted with a folding luggage rack. Of all Ford's models, this was the only one to have its rear doors latching at the rear. All other models used forward latching doors in every application, but Murray took exception on this model and hinged all doors at the centerpost. Because the Standard version is not listed, it is assumed that it used an artificial leather interior similar to the 1933 model. The Deluxe versions were done in genuine leather, and had the same May color change as did the other open cars. As was the case with the Roadster, wind wings were first classed as an option, but later in the year probably became standard items.

Wearing its totally awkward looking spare wheel is the Station Wagon, Type 860. The 2,635-pound car was the most expensive Ford, listing at $660. Constructed of basswood, birch, and maple cut and trimmed at Ford's own Iron Mountain plant, the body received its final finishing at the Murray Corp. Sales were up this year and Ford built 2,905 for V-8 chassis and another 95 that would wear 4-cylinder engines. The wagons were not classed as either Standard or Deluxe, but actually were considered part of the commercial line. As such, they had a combination of trim items, such as painted single horns but bright cowl lights, and painted windshield frames. The upholstery was in the same black-brown imitation leather as used in 1933. Still built without body windows, the wagons used canvas side curtains with very large celluloid panels for weather protection. Because decent weather resistant varnish had yet to be developed, wagons required almost annual sanding and re-varnishing if they were to be kept good looking.

Marketed under the New Era name were these 7-passenger vehicles with stretched wheelbases, wearing bodies built by the LeBaron division of Briggs Mfg. Co. In producing these cars, LeBaron used the basic shell of its Sedan Delivery, modified into 4-door passenger car configuration. New Era would provide these vehicles with sedan, limousine, or taxi interiors, in all varieties of plushness, ranging from spartan leather interiors on bus-types such as this, to quite fancy velours for the livery trade. This particular example was used by a Greyhound affiliate on low passenger runs where high passenger capacity buses were not necessary. Of course this vehicle certainly had to have the accessory greyhound radiator cap. The raised rear door line provided slightly easier access to the rear. Note the roof-top luggage box and the fact that heavy duty bumpers have been substituted for the standard Ford units. New Era of New York City ceased marketing under its own name at the end of the 1934 season.

In the waning days of the custom body business, it was not unusual for the major shops to swap bodies or use each other's products to satisfy the whims of a customer. One such case is this creation from the Derham Body Co. of Rosemont, Pa. Using a 119-inch wheelbase stretched chassis fitted with a LeBaron 7-passenger special sedan body, Derham took full credit for the finished limousine for a Philadelphia customer. The uncovered spare and rear luggage rack make this vehicle look more like a taxi than a prestige custom. In fact, the New Era taxis, which used the same LeBaron bodies, really had more style and appeal than did this model. However, in true Derham form, the interior was probably flawless, and of ultra-fine material.

In one of the stranger moves in automotive design, the Derham Co. was able to buy several dozen Model A Town Car bodies that had never been installed on chassis in 1930. Enos Derham, president of the Rosemont, Pa., firm, modified these bodies, blended them with the 1934 sheet metal, and came up with a string of very acceptable low-price town cars. Although several of these semi-custom vehicles were fitted out with plush interiors and sold to private customers, it is believed the major portion of the production wound up in the Philadelphia and New York livery business. The front doors had roll-up windows, and the driver's compartment could be made weather tight by a disappearing top that lived behind the B-pillar header when not in use. A sliding glass partition divided the two compartments. The front compartment was upholstered in genuine black leather, while the rear was in the customer's choice of fabric. The Town Car could be ordered with the tonneau in either three or 5-passenger seating.

Derham wasn't the only company to eye lower price chassis during this twilight of the custom body business. All body shops were fighting for their lives, and were turning to all sorts of manufacturing, from wheelbarrows to steel cabinets to truck components, in order to stay in business. But, most still found the time to turn out a few custom bodies for the handful of customers who were left to appreciate such vehicles. Though most of these creations were built to order, both Derham and Brewster still built limited numbers of cars on speculation. Brewster & Co. of New York City and Springfield, Mass., had once been part of Rolls Royce of America. This year it decided to produce a line of special town cars with the distinctive heart shaped Brewster grille, cow-catcher like bumpers, and radically flared fenders. The expensive versions were to be built on Packard and Buick chassis, the lower cost ones on Ford chassis. Both limousine and open front town car styles, such as this Ford chassied creation, were available. Oddly, Brewster refused to market the makes through their respective dealers, but instead sold them as "Brewsters" only through the few prestige car dealers that remained authorized Brewster agents. Reports vary, showing anywhere from 100 to 300 Ford chassied Brewsters having been built between 1934 and 1935 when Brewster finally folded.

The A.J. Miller Co. of Bellefontaine, Ohio, continued to utilize both Ford and Chevrolet chassis for their lower priced professional cars, especially for such work vehicles as service cars, which seldom participated in actual funeral processions. Sometimes in this era production may have exceeded sales, and older chassis were fitted with current bodies. A case in point is this long wheelbase service car delivered to the Tom Bartlett Funeral Home in mid-1934. Though probably titled as a 1934 vehicle, its base appears to be a 1933 Standard chassis. What appears to be a carved panel on the side is actually an embossed metal plate set into a large window-like frame in the body. Service cars had a tendency to look like large, fancy panel trucks.

The well-known Rollston Co. of New York City, a major supplier to Duesenberg, Packard, and other prestige makes, also turned to Ford this year. Again settling on an open front town car style, Rollston came up with this version, which featured relatively large rear doors and large blank quarter panels. As was the case with other town cars of this era, the front compartment could be made totally weathertight when necessary. The top and rear panels were covered in fine-grain leather. Note how the cowl lights have been relocated to the front fenders. Because of its concentration on the popular Packard prestige chassis, Rollston was able to keep producing custom bodies right up until the start of World War II. At that point, it began to make stainless steel kitchen equipment for the navy, and continues in that role today. Throughout the 1930s, Rollston supplied seats, windshields, and window components to many of the other custom body firms.

Displaying a beavertail rear end that became quite popular in this era is this Miller-Ford. Built by the A.J. Miller Co. of Bellefontaine, Ohio, in limousine style, the rather plain car made use of chromed Cleve-Weld spoke wheels for eye appeal and to help support the weight of the rather heavy body. Shown in basic form in this delivery photo, the long wheelbase car probably would be fitted with window curtains or drapes before actual usage. The clamps visible through the windows on the C-pillar and rear quarter probably will hold flower trays. These allowed the floral arrangements to be seen through the windows during the actual procession.

No one was snobbish during these days of tight dollars. Thus the LeBaron Division of Briggs, which was famous for its custom car bodies, saw nothing wrong with devoting the major portion of its facilities to building New Era car bodies and Ford Sedan Delivery trucks. The only true commercial Ford to use passenger car front end components, the Sedan Delivery provided LeBaron with a nice sum of 9,811 builds this year. Of this amount, 9,328 had the V-8, while only 483 had the Four. Designated the Type 850, the truck was essentially a stretched Tudor body, but fitted with more narrow Fordor front doors. The cargo compartment continued to be lined in Masonite, while seats were upholstered in dark brown imitation leather. The cowl and dashboard were also in passenger car styling, rather than using the truck components. The Sedan Delivery used the chromed windshield frame and cowl lights of Deluxe models, but the single horn of the Standard cars.

Drag racing had still not become a factor on the overall racing scene when this photo was made in the summer of 1951. But racing against the clock on California and Nevada dry lake beds was a big sport for western hot rod clubs. Essentially, this was a type of drag race, but running just one car at a time. The other variation, as seen here, involved flying starts, and/or two-way runs. Regardless of the type of race, a vast number of 1933/34 Ford coupes and open models were used up in such activities. The light, flexible, and well styled cars were a natural for the back yard hot rod builder, while speed parts for the popular V-8 were both plentiful and relatively inexpensive.

Here's one of the reasons that the 1933 and 1934 roadsters are so scarce today. From the first introduction of the car until well into the 1950s, these sleek machines were the all-time favorites of both hot rodders and auto racers. The author remembers many a stock car race in the late 1940s and early 1950s when a 30-car field might include one Chevy, one Dodge or Plymouth, and 26 or 27 Fords, mostly from 1933 to 1941 vintage. Even the famous Wilbur Shaw piloted a Ford, running this model in the 1934 Gilmore Gold Cup Race at the Los Angeles airport. Dirt track racing was notorious for throwing rocks and debris through the radiator cores, so this car was equipped with an extra stone guard, which looks suspiciously like one from a 1932 Chevrolet. Despite the lack of fenders, these racers were considered stock cars and not open-wheel racers. Ford's easily maintained and peppy V-8 coupled with the roadster's fenderless weight of just about 2,000 pounds, made these about the quickest cars on the circuit.

One of the ultimate hot rods was created by none other than Edsel Ford himself. After building his first boattail speedster in 1932, Edsel and designer E.T. Gregorie came up with another version in 1934. The car used a low-slung 2-passenger body of boattail configuration, small racing windshields, and enveloping individual fenders for each wheel. The front fenders turned with the wheels, while the rear ones matched the spring action of the axle. Initially the car had a mesh grille vaguely similar to the production Fords, with the low-set headlights blended into the catwalks. In 1940 Edsel redesigned the front of the car slightly, adding the lower grille with its horizontal bars, and the upper V-grille. At this point, the original wheel discs were removed to once again display the stock Ford wire wheels. After Edsel's death in 1943, the car found its way to California. In 1958 it was purchased by Earl Pallasch, shown with the vehicle in 1970. He brought it to his home in DeLand, Fla., where it might still be residing today.

1935

For the first time in 25 years, Ford introduced its new line of cars at the prestigious New York Auto Show. The event occurred on Dec. 27, and the Ford display spread over all three floors of the show, catching the attention of both the press and the public. In an era when such shows drew far more interest and attention than they do today, such a display was a major turnabout in Ford's promotional concepts. Heretofore Ford had set introduction dates at its own convenience, rather than be concerned with what the rest of the industry was doing. But from this point on, more emphasis would be placed on annual changes and fall/winter introductions.

And Ford had good reason to show its cars this year. Although the 1933/34 cars had been well accepted, they were no match for the appeal of the totally new 1935 models. Essentially, the only carryovers from 1934 were the 112-inch wheelbase and the V-8 engine. But even here, the wheelbase was part of a totally new chassis design, while the engine received further modifications, once more making it an even better power plant.

The new Ford reflected the heavier, more rounded styling of the era. It had a longer hood; fully skirted fenders; bullet headlamps; a more spacious and rounded body, and front doors which once again hinged at the forward edge. Some models had a new sloping back similar to the old Victoria, while others had Ford's first true integral trunk.

Although the wheelbase remained 112 inches, the car was slightly more than 6.5 inches longer than the previous model. This was the result of a totally new frame, which placed the engine and transmission further forward. This movement allowed the passenger compartment to be located fully between the axles, rather than have rear seat passengers riding over the axle, a design innovation which greatly increased ride comfort and allowed for wider seats.

In line with the new frame, spring revisions were made both in the springs themselves and in the mounting bases; new self-adjusting mechanical brakes appeared; there was new transverse steering, and the cars had a new and almost 2-inch wider tread, this now being 55.5 inches at the front and 58.25 at the rear. The wheels were still wire spoke (for the final year) but were reduced one inch, now fitting the new 6.00x16 tires. This, along with the spring and frame modifications, helped to bring the car closer to the ground, again, giving a more sleek look.

Under the hood, the engine still was rated at 85 horses at 3800 rpm, but was now located 8.5 inches further forward than in 1934. A minor casting change along with a new valve cover provided much improved engine ventilating, a new crankshaft bearing appeared on some engines, and a new optional head was developed for high altitude areas. The dual throat downdraft Stromberg carburetor was retained, but it too underwent some refinement to improve idling. Also, two new types of air cleaners were introduced as options. One was made

by United and the other by Donaldson. In all, the engine changes were far from being major, but they did add up to a smoother running, longer lived, and better idling engine.

Block numbers started in January with 1352203 and ended in December with 2503757, for a total of 1,151,554 V-8 engines turned out this year.

Coupling this engine to the wheels was a brand new clutch of larger diameter and semi-centrifugal design; a new and longer driveshaft, and a slightly revised rear axle and differential.

Body styles also increased, with a total of 13 styles now being available over last year's 12 (not counting the quasi-commercial station wagon or sedan delivery). Although the Victoria was gone, two new "Touring Sedans" were now on the list. Produced in Deluxe trim only, these were available in either Tudor or Fordor form. Essentially they were the regular Briggs-built bodies, but included Ford's first true integral trunk found on a 5-passenger car. Unlike the 1934 Victoria, which simply had a hinged panel to achieve access to the area behind the rear seat, these cars had a full trunk deck, pronounced bustle back, and lined storage area. The one failing was that access was from the top, as the rear mounted spare prevented a full trunk door. This deck location, combined with the spare tire, made loading or unloading the trunk quite difficult, especially for women or short men. Loading was sometimes described as "dropping the packages down a well."

In the open car market, the Standard Phaeton was gone. But actually, many promotional pieces indicated that it was gone in 1934, even though it did have a healthy production schedule. Replacing it on the model charts, but not in physical form, was the new Convertible Sedan. This was Ford's first open 4-door to have roll-up windows and a totally weather-tight interior. In effect, it was the Cabriolet in 4-door configuration. Though beautiful, it was Ford's most expensive car this year, and its $750 price tag probably was one of the factors which kept its sales down to 4,234—the lowest of any model on the list. And this is despite the fact that the Convertible Sedan was selected as the Official Pace Car for this year's Indianapolis 500.

As before, the Murray Corp. continued to build all of the coupe and open bodies, while Briggs Mfg. supplied all of the Tudor and Fordor bodies, plus the Sedan Delivery. The Station Wagon continued to be a joint project of Ford's own Iron Mountain, Mich., lumber plant and the Murray Corp., while the popular pickups continued to be made by Budd. However, because the pickups no longer used the facial sheetmetal of the passenger car line, they are not covered in this book (see *Ford Trucks Since 1905* by James K. Wagner).

For the first time in the 1930s, Ford outsold all of its competition to take over first place again (though Chevrolet tends to dispute the figures). Yet, Ford did turn out 819,795 cars during this model year, compared

One of Ford's sportiest cars, but far from being its best selling, was the Roadster, Type 710. Available in Deluxe form only, the rumble seat equipped car cost $550 and weighed 2,597 pounds. Its Murray-built body was finished in gray-brown genuine leather front seat, with the rumble seat finished in matching artificial leather. Early models used artificial leather for the door and kick panels, but after January, these too were of genuine leather. A total of 4,896 were built. A running change occurred early in the year involving the rumble seat lock. Early models continued to use an internal latch and smooth deck, similar to the 1934 models, but as supplies ran out, an exterior lock with T-handle was installed. Side curtains continued to live in their own pouch behind the seat, while a new tool box now resided under the front seat cushion.

Less than half as popular as its 5-window cousin was the 3-window Coupe, Type 720. Like the Cabriolet and Roadster, it was also available only in Deluxe trim. However, unlike the open cars, a rumble seat was not standard on this model, but had to be purchased as an option. Murray built a total of 31,513 this year. Each cost $570 and weighed 2,647 pounds with the trunk compartment, not a rumble seat. As was the case with the other rumble seat models, the interior latch for either trunk deck or rumble seat lid was changed to an exterior T-handle. But on this coupe, the move was a running change, made near the end of November, 1934. Therefore, early versions of this car could have smooth rear decks. The rounded doors used on this model were totally unique, and would not interchange with any other body style. Mohair, broadcloth, and leather interiors were available, but when ordered, the rumble seat was always in imitation leather of a gray-brown hue.

to the 554,457 built by Chevrolet. However, Chevrolet buffs will point to the calendar year production of 1,066,197 and contend that Chevrolet, not Ford, was still the leader. The fact remains that the depression was slowly being shaken off, more and more people were buying new cars (even the sport models) and—in truth—this year Ford did have a better looking car than did Chevrolet!

Of the total built, the Standard Tudor was once again the wide favorite, with 237,833 sales to its credit. At $510 it was also Ford's lowest priced car, and represented quite a bargain when compared to anything else on the market. True, Chevrolet's Standard Coach at $485 was cheaper, but it did not take on the styling of the new Deluxe Chevrolets, and really looked like something left over from the early 1930s—which it was. The only other Ford to exceed 100,000 in sales turned out to be the Deluxe Fordor Touring Sedan, the new kid with the bustle back. By year end, it had seen its sales go up to 105,157, indicating that people did appreciate the added trunk space.

All these sales added up to the production of the 2-millionth V-8 engine on June 13, while on Oct. 31, Ford built its millionth car of 1935 (although this was into the 1936 model year and was a 1936 car). Also of future importance was Ford's opening of the first soybean plastics plant at Dearborn, the first such plant to be owned by an automobile manufacturer. In later years, Henry Ford conducted many experiments with plastics produced by this facility.

Companion to the Roadster was the Cabriolet, which also was available only in Deluxe trim and only as a rumble seat model. Designated the Type 760, the Murray-built car cost $625 and weighed 2,687 pounds. The major distinction between the Cabriolet and the Roadster was the fact that the Cabriolet had roll-up windows and a snug fitting top, similar to today's convertibles. In addition to the same leather interior as on the Roadster, the Cabriolet could be ordered with a cloth interior in taupe bedford cord. Both cars used the same top material of a drab fabric interlined with rubber. As was the case with the Roadster, the rumble seat latch went from a hidden interior unit to an exterior T-handle. However, this change occurred with Job One, not as a running move. Apparently Murray worked on a round-number contract on this model, as an even 17,000 were built.

Accessory wheel discs totally change the appearance of this Standard 5-window Coupe, but the painted grille and single painted horn still show that it is not a Deluxe model. Designated the Type 770, the car had twice the sales in Standard trim than in Deluxe, probably owing to the fact that it was a very popular model for fleet and business purposes. Murray built a total of 78,477 in Standard form. Each sold for $520 and weighed 2,620 pounds. A rumble seat was an option, but it would be safe to assume most came through with trunk decks. The same T-handle addition was made to the rear decks of the 5-window Coupes as occurred on other models. In this case, models built after December had T-handles. The wheel discs on this car simply covered the spokes and were supposed to add an even more modern appearance to the car by covering the "archaic" wire spoke wheels. Such discs were made by several different manufacturers, and were a popular aftermarket item.

1935

Chrome plating of the grille, dual horns, and windshield frame immediately say that this is the Deluxe version of the 5-window Coupe. In this trim form, Murray turned out 33,065, so that the total 5-window Coupe production this year reached 111,542. This was a healthy figure for any single body style. Priced at $560 and weighing 2,643 pounds, the Deluxe version offered such luxuries as a dome light, ash tray, and passenger sun visor. Upholstery was in mohair or broadcloth, as opposed to the bedford cord or brown check cloth in the Standard models. All versions had rear windows that could be lowered, whether in trunk or rumble seat form.

New for the year was the Briggs bodied Tudor Touring Sedan, available only in Deluxe trim. Designated the Type 700, the same as the other Tudors, it was priced at the same $595 as the plain Deluxe Tudor. In addition to providing substantially more space and outside access for the luggage, the bustle back added visually to the car's appearance. Besides the new trunk, another interesting item on the Touring Sedans was the stainless steel running board molding. This item was found only on these sedans and on the Convertible Sedan, and was not used on any other model. Oddly, the Tudor Touring was available in the same type bedford cord as the regular model, but not in the broadcloth version. Instead, a Deluxe interior in taupe worsted suede was available. This was the same material that later would be used as an option in the Standard Tudor.

Ford's lowest priced and by far highest production model was the plain-Jane Standard Tudor, Type 730. Costing only $510, it saw production reach 237,833 in Standard form alone. No doubt due to the still erratic economic times, people preferred the painted grille, single painted horn, and lower cost interior to the $85 extra price that Deluxe trimming would have cost. Including the Deluxe versions, Briggs turned out a total of 322,525 of these Tudor bodies this year. Although there was no access from the outside, this year all Briggs Tudor and Fordor cars did have a small luggage compartment in the rear. Access was made by pulling down the rear seat back, in a manner similar to the 1933 Victoria. Unlike the coupe models, the Standard Tudor still was equipped with a dome light and ashtray, and rear seat passengers had arm rests.

For an extra $85 buyers who opted for the Deluxe Tudor received a brighter looking face, arm rests for the front seat passengers, and a higher quality of upholstery. Still, the tight money of the day played a factor here, and only 84,692 buyers went for the Deluxe version. This was about one-third the number that ordered the Standard. Priced at $595, the Deluxe model weighed 2,737 pounds. Deluxe interiors were either in taupe mohair or broadcloth, with a genuine leather interior being available at extra cost. Standard interiors were at first only in light brown bedford cord, but in August a darker brown bedford cord and a worsted suede became available. Also, Standard buyers could opt for the extra-cost leather interior, but in artificial not genuine leather. All models used tan rubber front floor mats, but Deluxe models had brown carpeting in the rear, while Standard models used a matching rubber floor mat.

1935

Among the most sporty yet least popular models this year was the beautiful Phaeton, Type 750. One of only two 4-door models built by Murray, the $580 car drew only 6,073 orders. Available only in Deluxe trim, the car featured an interior entirely in gray-brown genuine leather. As was the case with the Roadster, initial door panels were turned out in matching artificial leather, but after January these were covered in genuine leather. The top and side curtains were in the same drab material interlined with rubber as was used on all other open cars. Wind wings were standard equipment, and the side curtains lived in the storage area behind the rear seat. All top bows and rear window frames were chrome plated, as was the windshield frame. Unlike the previous models where all doors were hinged on the center post, the Phaeton now had all doors open from the rear edge.

The highest price and lowest production style in Ford's line this year was the Convertible Sedan, Type 740, which joined the touring sedans as Ford's new styles of the year. Companion to the Phaeton as the Cabriolet was to the Roadster, the Murray-built Convertible Sedan was another attempt at providing closed car comfort with the option of touring car openness. All four doors had roll-up windows surrounded by chromed frames, which would nestle into the top when raised. A removable center post slipped into place between the windows. Available only in Deluxe trim, the car was most often seen with a genuine leather interior similar to that in the Phaeton. However, it could be ordered upholstered in bedford cord. As in Briggs-built sedans, this Murray vehicle also had a storage space behind the rear seat. Costing $750, the car was by far the highest priced of this year's Fords, a fact which probably contributed to only 4,234 having been sold, despite its very attractive lines. It weighed 2,827 pounds.

By far the most popular of the slant-back Fordor Sedans was the Deluxe version, seen here in British trim, with left-hand drive and a strange set of mandatory marker lights on top of the front fenders. Otherwise, it is identical to its U.S. counterparts. This car sold for $655 according to some lists, and $635 according to others. Regardless, its sales were well above those of the Standard version, topping out at 75,807. This meant that Briggs produced a total of 124,983 slant-back models for the year, not counting the Touring Sedans. The same interiors were available on this model as on the Deluxe Tudor. The Standard version had only a light brown bedford cord available until February, when a brown mohair was also offered. All closed cars this year were equipped with a rear roller shade.

When seen from the rear, it is impossible to tell whether this accessory laden Fordor is a Deluxe or Standard model. If it is a Standard, it is one of 49,176 built by Briggs this year. Priced at $575, it came in only second best to its Deluxe companion. This is a surprise when considering the wide margin in difference between the sales of the Deluxe and Standard Tudors. Among the accessories on this example are the chrome wheel rings, spotlight, greyhound hood ornament, wind wings, and the very practical folding luggage rack which could augment the rather limited luggage space behind the rear seat. On all Fords this year, the metal spare tire cover was standard equipment.

Ford's only other single model to exceed 100,000 in sales, besides the Standard Tudor, was the brand new Fordor Touring Sedan, which enjoyed a run of 105,157. Available only in Deluxe trim, the car sold for $655 and weighed 2,787 pounds. It bore the same Type 730 number as the other Briggs-built Fordors. As did the Tudor Touring Sedan, the Fordor version also featured a stainless steel molding along the running board. Although the optional genuine leather interior was the same as on the Deluxe Fordor, the Touring Sedan's cloth interiors were of a different material. On this model, buyers had a choice of taupe bedford cord or taupe worsted suede. All used tan floor mats in front with brown carpeting in the rear. For some strange reason, the Fordor Touring Sedans used a left hand taillight which was about half again as long as the right one. All other cars except this model had matched taillights.

Loading up the new trunk of the touring models was not the easiest thing in the world, especially if a short person was combined with an extra-heavy piece of luggage. Of course, in Ford's promotional pictures, a rather tall man has no trouble with a light suitcase. Still, in comparison to trunkless models, the outside access was far less trouble than lowering the seat back to get at a rather limited space. As mentioned in a preceding caption, the taillights on these models were mismatched, and the left one would fit no other model. All Deluxe cars featured dual taillights, while Standard models had only a single unit on the left. However, a right hand light could be bought as a dealer-installed option, and many were. On all models, the gas filler cap was located on the left taillight arm.

The LeBaron Division of Briggs Mfg. continued to modify its parent's Tudor production into what was now titled the "Convertible Delivery Car." Essentially, it was the Standard Tudor with the back converted into a cargo area via masonite panels, and removable blank panels set in the quarter window areas. The rear was furnished with a full size door, cut to match the standard rear glass, with hinges on the left so that the door would open from the curb side. Because Ford did not make welled fenders this year, the spare had to be carried on this door, a factor which really improved its appearance. Apparently most of the production went to large fleet buyers such as National Cash Register, which is credited with requesting the design. It is not known if this car was available to dealers on an individual order basis, or if it was for fleet sales only. Ford does not list the model on its production rolls or price sheets, so it is possible that it was a fleet-only conversion by LeBaron. Supposedly, it took only a couple of minutes to convert this car to a 5-passenger sedan by removing the window panels and installing a rear seat.

Something new was added to the Station Wagon this year, in the form of an all-new body. Finally, it got roll-up windows, at least in the front doors. The rear doors and quarter windows and the rear window still relied on side curtains for protection. Continuing to be roughly classed as a commercial vehicle, this year the wagon nevertheless used all Deluxe passenger car trimmings on the front end. The wood was still cut and trimmed at Ford's Iron Mountain plant, with final assembly by Murray in Detroit. The interior was done in gray-brown artificial leather seats, with natural wood paneling and tan rubber floor mats. Priced at $670, it was the second most expensive Ford after the Convertible Sedan, and at 2,896 pounds, it was Ford's heaviest passenger vehicle. A total of 4,536 were built, all reflecting the totally new body with center-latching doors and vertical body/cowl line. Because of the all new body, the nomenclature was changed to Type 790.

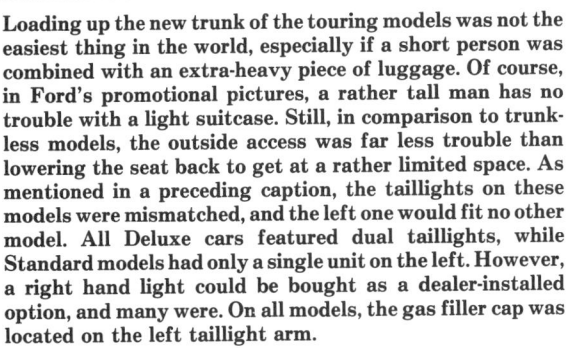

Ford's "real" Sedan Delivery this year was the Type 780, produced by Briggs, of which 8,308 examples were sold. The vehicle used all passenger car sheetmetal, and was trimmed in Standard fashion, with painted grille and single painted horn. Similar in appearance to the Convertible Delivery Car, it nonetheless had a much longer cargo area and was designed specifically as a delivery truck, not a sedan conversion. Priced at $585, it had two front bucket seats in gray-black imitation leather; a cargo area paneled in masonite; steel skids on the floor, and an internal storage area against the right wall for the spare.

It is hard to tell whether the respectable James Cunningham, Son & Co. of Rochester, N.Y., borrowed a page from Brewster's book, or came up with this idea on its own. Long known for fine professional cars, military vehicles, and flawless luxury cars, Cunningham had just as rough a time in the depression as did any company. It had ceased making its luxury chassis and military contracts were scarce. Now its main link to life was the professional car line, plus an occasional custom body. Suddenly, this year Cunningham introduced its own Town Car version, to be sold as Cunninghams and through Cunningham hearse and ambulance dealers. The car bore far more Ford resemblance than did the Brewster, but also was about $1,000 cheaper, selling for $2,600. It appears that this model was carried onto the 1936 chassis as well, but was dropped when the 1937 streamliners arrived.

Stretched vehicles of this type had always been a specialty of the Shop of Siebert of Toledo, so it is no wonder that the new Ford chassis appeared under that company's colors. Built from Deluxe Fordor Touring models, these cars were sectioned at the B-pillar and received new 6-passenger center sections of Siebert's own design, which blended into the Ford sheetmetal design. Although artificial leather covers the top of this version, other units utilized a full-length luggage rack across the roof. Such vehicles were used by low density bus lines; as touring coaches for bands and entertainment troupes; hotel livery, and in metropolitan areas, as airport buses, with the latter role becoming more and more important with succeeding years.

Fighting gamely for its life, the Brewster Co. continued to offer its beautiful Town Car on a Ford chassis for $3,500. Now located totally at Springfield, Mass., the company apparently no longer used the unusual heart-shaped Brewster grille this year, but instead blended the regular Ford grille into its own special hood. Brewster also used its own custom fenders and "cow catcher" bumper, in addition to the flawless town car body. Sadly, the market for cars of this type was all but gone, and after a series of valiant attempts to keep going, Brewster finally closed its doors in August, 1936. Because the Ford grille is so evident on these later models, some historians contend the cars should be called "Fords with Brewster Bodies." However, Brewster continued to market these cars under its own name, through select quality car dealerships, primarily in New York City and Boston.

The bus version of Siebert's stretch had such special features as marker lights; heavy-duty wheels; special firm suspension, and a roof-long luggage rack that also doubled as a cantilever brace to prevent center sag. In an era when bus travel was far more extensive than it is today, many small bus lines formed a network of routes across the country, linking scores of small towns that otherwise would have had no public transportation. To supply these lines with relatively economical vehicles, several companies such as Siebert specialized in these conversions. The wheelbase on the Siebert version was 190 inches.

Although the Siebert stretches were interesting vehicles, the company's main line since 1853 had been in the building of hearses and ambulances, making the transformation from horse drawn units to motorized vehicles relatively early in its career. During the 1930s, the company took on the relatively inexpensive Ford chassis as a base for its professional cars, looking toward the market that could not afford the high priced luxury chassis. In this field, its most popular model was its Limousine Hearse, priced at just $1,370. The car was based on a stretched Standard Tudor, with all work past the B-pillar being done in Siebert's own shop.

The ambulance version of the stretched Siebert Ford was priced at $1,470, probably because of the additional equipment needed even in the most basic car. The 2-tone paint job was an extra-cost option, but the leaded glass quarter windows were standard. Siebert continued to use Ford's stock wire wheels, having determined that they were certainly strong enough for this type of work. Siebert would market its vehicles through participating Ford dealers, or through the sales network of National Hearse & Ambulance Co., also located in Toledo. The ambulance was Siebert's second most popular model.

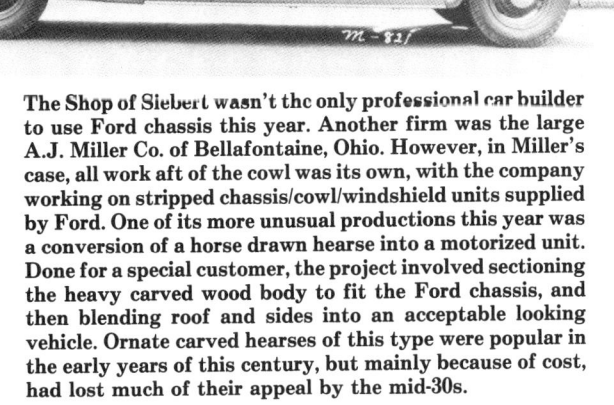

The least expensive vehicle in the professional car line of Shop of Siebert was the Service Car, which in effect was little more than a very nice looking panel truck designed for use by the funeral trade. Using the same basic body as the ambulance and hearse, the service car had blank panels in place of windows, and a masonite or velvet covered interior, depending on buyers' choice. Priced at $1,300, it was aimed not at the small funeral director, but at the large homes with expensive equipment, who wanted a low-cost but good looking errand vehicle.

The Shop of Siebert wasn't the only professional car builder to use Ford chassis this year. Another firm was the large A.J. Miller Co. of Bellafontaine, Ohio. However, in Miller's case, all work aft of the cowl was its own, with the company working on stripped chassis/cowl/windshield units supplied by Ford. One of its more unusual productions this year was a conversion of a horse drawn hearse into a motorized unit. Done for a special customer, the project involved sectioning the heavy carved wood body to fit the Ford chassis, and then blending roof and sides into an acceptable looking vehicle. Ornate carved hearses of this type were popular in the early years of this century, but mainly because of cost, had lost much of their appeal by the mid-30s.

Much more conventional than the carved conversion is this Limousine Hearse produced by the A.J. Miller Co. on the new Ford chassis. The car features the "beaver tail" rear design so popular in this era, which was merely a back sweep of the lower rear body line. In building these cars, Miller would design a relatively standard body shell which could be easily converted to any one of several different makes of chassis. The chassis manufacturer, in this case Ford, would then supply the forward section, cowl, and fenders, while Miller would make the frame extension and fit the unit into a workable vehicle. Miller would probably work on any chassis that a buyer ordered, but it seems that Chrysler, Packard, and Pontiac were among its favorites, along with Ford.

An unlikely combination of personalities this year put together the largest racing team ever seen on the Indianapolis 500 track. Not only did Ford supply the pace car and satellite vehicles, but it also had four special racers on the track. Early in the year Preston Tucker (of later Tucker car fame) and Harry Miller, the noted race car builder, proposed to Ford that they design a series of race cars that could sweep the field. A 10-car team was proposed, to be driven by the best racers in the land. The cars were to be a new front wheel drive design, and powered with a highly modified version of the Ford engine. Edsel was all for the project, but Henry procrastinated. When he finally gave his approval, so much time had slipped by that the Tucker-Miller firm had only 79 days to go from scratch to finished cars. By working 100 or more hours a week, the shop managed to get half of the cars ready for the race. The engine and newly designed front end worked perfectly, while the sleek low-slung bodies drew everyone's admiration. But because of a design oversight in the steering column, the vehicles were difficult to control once the race got underway. A few of the top name drivers quit the team, saying the cars were unsafe. Ted Horn managed to qualify in 26th starting position, while three other Fords also made the line-up. Another qualified as an alternate, while two others failed to make the grade and the remaining three could not be completed on time. Horn lasted the longest, but went out after 134 laps, still claiming 16th place. Three of the four Fords were forced out by steering problems. Henry Ford was so embarrassed over the performance that he ordered all the cars locked up in a warehouse, where they remained for over two years before being sold to non-Ford interests. This marked the end of Ford's racing activities until interest could be regenerated in the mid-1950s.

One of the more intriguing Ford customs this year came from the shops of Figoni in Paris, France. Utilizing a stock Ford chassis and fenders, Figoni fitted a close-coupled 5-passenger coupe body to the stock cowl. The top was solid and could not be removed, and though very attractive, provided little visibility for rear seat passengers. The trunk appears to be an attached unit, not integral with the body. The hood is stock Ford, but with the three horizontal bars removed. The wheels are custom. Overall, the car is unmistakably Ford.

William B. Stout, designer of the Ford Tri-Motor, had kept himself busy during the span between his last tri-motor design and 1935. Among his innovative designs were a novel rail car and a modern city bus which was built by Gar Wood. This year, he attempted to form his own automobile company, to produce the ultra-modern Scarab. Essentially, the car used all Ford running gear, but had its own special chassis, with the engine in the rear, and its own unique body based on Stout's tubular space frame concept. An ad in *Fortune Magazine* mentioned production of about 100 cars a year, to be sold at $5,000 each, which was a pretty hefty sum for a car in 1935. Despite some excellent backing from both Dow Chemical and the Wrigley family, the company finally went into bankruptcy in 1937 after a half-dozen or so Scarabs were actually delivered. In all cases, the owners seemed pleased with their vehicles, and (similar to Tucker in 1947) had Stout really been able to get into serious production, he might have had a marvelous vehicle on the road.

It may have been ugly, but it was based on all Ford components, and it represents the final effort of the American-Coleman Co. of Littleton, Colorado, to move into actual auto production. Designed by Harleigh Holmes, this vehicle was the fifth in a series of attempts to produce a totally novel car for the American-Coleman Co. This same company today produces 4-wheel drive truck conversions; front-drive axles, and tow tractors for airports. It is not known if American-Coleman wanted to actually produce the car, or simply wanted the patent rights to market to other companies. Among the many innovations on this vehicle was an exterior frame, seen here forming the outer edges of the fenders and running board, and an arched front axle that went across the top of the engine. This allowed the engine to sit four inches lower and several inches further forward, for better balance and weight distribution. It was reported that Coleman was considering production of this car at $1,000 each, but apparently nothing ever came of the plan.

After the drastic change year of 1935, no one really expected the 1936 Fords to change much. And really, they did not, although the totally new styling of the front end coupled with new wheels and fenders, gave them an unmistakably different look from their predecessors. Under the hood some more needed changes took place, to provide a still better running car, and in the dealers' books, a few more options were given to buyers, including the appearance of a few more body styles. By mid-year, a total of 17 different body variations were available, as opposed to 14 in 1935.

The most significant changes, of course, were in the sheet metal parts exclusive of the bodies. Both front and rear fenders were redesigned, and now had a more plump appearance. The grille became wider, and now consisted only of vertical bars set in a thin stainless steel frame. The horns moved from the outside to new positions behind the catwalks, and were hidden by their own small circular grilles with vertical bars. The hood louvers were redesigned slightly, and set off by three horizontal stainless bars, rather than four.

It is interesting to note that all of these changes involved "bolt-on" items rather than major modifications. As a result, the entire front end of the 1936 Ford could be transplanted onto the nose of a 1935 car. Capitalizing on this, Ford sold "conversion kits" at the dealership level. The kits cost about $215, plus another $70 for installation, and included new front fenders, hoods, grille shells, and headlights. Thus, it is possible to find a 1935 Ford wearing the sheet metal of a 1936 model, a fact that could possibly drive some restorers and antique car judges a bit wild.

In line with 1935 practice, a quick visual distinction could be made between Standard and Deluxe models. The latter had stainless steel grille bars, chromed horn covers, and a chromed windshield frame, while on the Standard jobs, all of these were painted in body color. Also, Standard models continued to have only one sun visor and a less plush interior.

Under the hood there were several changes. Many cars received a new block with main bearing inserts, while others used the 1935 style block with cast babbitt bearings. The new block went into production at about the same time the 1936 models were introduced. However, it appears that the old style block was also supplied throughout the model year, with production of that design not ending until September, 1936.

Early 1936 engines also had new aluminum pistons, but it appears that by mid-year a return was made to steel pistons. Regardless, all were of a new domed design, which increased compression slightly. These pistons were designed to work in conjunction with the new cast aluminum heads which were introduced on a limited basis in mid-1935. By the 1936 production, these heads had become regular fare. A mid-year change involved a completely redesigned oil pump, with the new unit having a 4-inch diameter screen assembly in place of the former pickup tube. In line with the new pump

was a new oil pan, with no oil sump, and having the drain plug on the bottom rather than on the side.

Early engines also continued to use the dual downdraft Stromberg carburetor of 1935, but from January on, all cars had a new Stromberg No. 97 carburetor that actually began to appear on select engines at the start of the model year. Further changes included a new and larger radiator with better flow for improved cooling (overheating was always a Ford shortcoming) and in the transmission new helical gears for all speeds, not just second and high.

Block numbers started with 2503758 on January first and ended with 3216674 on Dec. 31, for a total of only 712,916 engines produced this year. This was a decrease of 438,638 blocks from what was produced during calendar year 1935.

Also very apparent on the new Fords were the wheels. Gone were the pretty but now archaic and expensive wire spoke wheels. In their place were new, more modern, and cheaper to manufacture artillery spoke wheels made of pressed steel. The new wheels used the same 16-inch diameter as before, but the width was increased to four inches. The standard tire was 6:00x16, but near the end of the model year a cost savings switch was made to 5:50x16 tires. New for the year was an 18-inch diameter "farmers wheel," designed for use in areas where poor road conditions demanded higher clearance. Also, sets of all-chrome wheels were available as an option at $47.50 a set until spring, when new stainless steel full wheel covers were offered by dealers. Both the chromed wheels and the wheel covers were factory supplied accessories, not aftermarket items, though similar units were also available from numerous auto parts stores.

In the body department, virtually no immediate changes took place, although Ford publicity would have buyers think the car was a totally new vehicle, not a 1935 model with a new face. Actual 1935 production ended on Sept. 9 of that year, and the changeover to the 1936 styling was completed in a little over a week. However, introduction of the new models did not begin until mid-October, after all dealers had been assured of at least one new model with which to awe the public.

As before, Murray built all of the open cars and coupe models while Briggs Mfg. Co. built all of the Fordor and Tudor bodies. Briggs production equalled 66% of Ford's bodies, with Murray producing 22% and Budd 11%. Budd's production, incidentally, was all for commercial chassis, and consisted mainly of pickup bodies. Of the new models to appear this year, two actually were simply Standard versions of styles that had only been available in Deluxe trim in 1935. These were the Standard Tudor Touring Sedan and the Standard Fordor Touring Sedan. The two really new models didn't appear until mid-way in the model year. These were the Club Cabriolet, which came out in March, and the Convertible Touring Sedan, which came out in April. Both had bodies built by the Murray Corp.

Most significant of the two was the Club Cabriolet, which really set the stage for the modern convertible coupe. The car was essentially the Cabriolet, with a rear passenger area with bench seat, rather than a rumble seat. In addition to the enclosed rear passenger area, the car featured a trunk deck with a substantial luggage compartment.

The new Convertible Touring Sedan was essentially the former Convertible Sedan, but with an integral trunk with exterior access. But unlike the trunks on the Tudor and Fordor Touring Sedans, Murray gave this style a full-size swing-up trunk deck. In order to do this, the spare had to be moved from the rear, and since Ford had no welled fenders available, the spare had to be moved inside. Thus, the main claim to fame of this model is the fact that it was the first modern Ford car to utilize an inside spare. Included with this design was a new locking device to make raising the deck lid easier and holding it in place when opened, and new "stubby" taillights that were unlike any others in use by Ford.

Of the 17 body styles available, only five came in Standard trim. They were the Tudor Sedans in both plain and touring styles; the Fordor Sedans in plain and touring versions, and the 5-window Coupe.

All cars continued to have basic wiring for radios, which were becoming more and more popular. Installed at dealer level, Ford now offered two different radio styles, either priced at $45. Other popular dealer supplied accessories were folding trunk racks at under $10, and dual windshield wipers at $3. These wipers consisted of a non-motorized right hand wiper connected to the left wiper by a thin rod. Late in the year motorized right hand wipers became standard on all Deluxe models. Factory-installed options included a rumble seat for any coupe model for about $25 extra, and all-leather interiors for any model. And, this year too, there was the popular Pines trim, which consisted of three heavy chromed

horizontal bars that swept around the grille and hood sides. These were available from both Ford dealers and aftermarket suppliers.

The overall popularity contest was once again won by the Standard Tudor Sedan, which was now up $10 in price to $520. It had a run of 174,700. However, some of this production may have included the touring model, as no figures can be found for the Standard version of that car. Running in close second was the Deluxe Fordor Touring Sedan, which was priced at $650. This car showed sales of 159,825, but again, some of this might be attributed to the Standard version of this car, since no Standard model figures can be found. Third on the list, and the only other model to break 100,000, was the Deluxe Tudor Touring Sedan, with 125,303 builds to its credit. It is interesting to note that between the Tudor and Fordor Touring Sedans there were a total of 285,128 bodies produced, showing that the American public had taken a very quick liking to the innovation of having accessible trunk space on their cars. On the overall sales side, however, Ford was disappointed to see Chevrolet once again in the lead. Chevrolet's sales tallied 931,012 for the model year, as opposed to Ford's 711,385. Although Chevrolet's Deluxe line changed very little, part of its sales increase was due to its standard models now having the styling of the better cars rather than the carry-over 1934 styling that they had in the previous year. As was the case with Ford, Chevrolet's most popular model was the 2-door sedan, but its production was 220,844 compared with Ford's 174,700.

Ford's least popular model this year was the Roadster, available in Deluxe trim only. Produced by Murray, it sold only 3,862 copies. At 2,561 pounds, it was also Ford's lightest car, but its price of $560 put in at mid-range in the cost column. Side curtains still provided weather protection, but the wind wings were standard equipment. The interior top bows were chrome plated on cars built in the first half of the year, but after April these bows were painted. Interiors were finished in brown genuine leather with matching artificial leather used in the rumble seat. There were no trunk versions available. White wall tires this year were a $12 additional charge.

Enjoying almost four times the popularity of the Deluxe Roadster was the Murray-built Cabriolet, which saw production reach 14,068. Designated the Type 760, this was not a cheap car. It sold for $625 in Deluxe trim only. There was no Standard model nor any trunk-back versions. The interior finishing was the same as on the Roadster, but the primary difference between the two cars lies in the fact that the Cabriolet had roll-up windows in the doors, a coupe-type of windshield frame, and its top would make a snug weather-tight compartment when raised. Of course, the rumble seat passengers got all the weather they could want, whether the top was up or down. As before, the Cabriolet could be ordered with a cloth interior as a no-cost option. This year the cloth was a taupe bedford cord until January, when a switch was made to taupe napped cotton. In June another switch was made, this time to a plain drab cloth.

Ford's newest body style was the Club Cabriolet, which was introduced in March as a companion (not a replacement) to the regular Cabriolet. Built by Murray, the car essentially set the stage for the modern convertible. It used two folding-back bench seats in the front, with a more narrow bench seat in the rear, and a substantial trunk area aft of the top. Although rear seat passengers found scant leg room and poor visibility, at least they were inside when the rain began—and, there was room for luggage. The Club Cabriolet could quickly be identified from the regular model by the length of its top. No cheapie by any means, its tag of $675 made it one of the more expensive Fords. It wore the same Type 760 designation as the regular Cabriolet, and weighed 2,661 pounds, or 12 pounds more than the regular model. Although the windshield posts and frame were the same as on the coupes, the windshields of the Cabriolets would not open.

Murray's 3-window Coupe body was unchanged, and therefore continued to offer its unique rounded door frames, exclusive to this car only. Considered more of a sport or prestige car than its 5-window counterpart, it was available in Deluxe form only. But still, a rumble seat was a $25 extra-cost option. With trunk deck, it sold for $570, which made it a bit more costly than the 5-window Deluxe Coupe. Possibly because of this, its sales reached only 31,513 as opposed to a total of 108,472 total sales of 5-window models. However, the 3-window version did outsell the Deluxe form of the 5-window car. On this model, the rear window could be lowered for ventilation or conversation with rumble seat passengers, whereas on the 5-window style the rear window now was set in place. As an extra-cost option, the interior could be finished in brown genuine leather. Otherwise upholstery was in taupe mohair or two different shades of brown broadcloth.

Although the Standard 5-window Coupe far outsold the 3-window variety, the Deluxe 5-window Coupe, Type 770, did not. Sales of the $555 Murray-built car reached only 29,938. As was the case with all closed coupes, the rumble seat was a $25 accessory, while a trunk deck, hinged at the top edge, was the regular fitting. Whereas the optional leather interior of the Standard model was in imitation leather, the extra-cost upholstery on this model was in genuine brown leather. Otherwise a taupe mohair interior was offered with brown broadcloth being a no-cost option until November when a switch was made to a gray-brown broadcloth for the option. Since a major portion of this style in both trim levels were produced in trunk form, Murray or Ford probably felt that it was not necessary to have a rear window that could be lowered, as was the case with the 3-window style.

Grilles painted in body color identify this as the Standard 5-window Coupe. Ford's lowest price model, it listed for $510. The most popular car in Murray's production schedule, it accounted for 78,534 units, all with a trunk deck as regular equipment, but with a rumble seat available. Designated the Type 770, it was a popular car with both business fleets and salesmen, let alone those who wanted dependable transportation at the lowest possible price. A brown imitation leather interior could be ordered at extra cost. Regular interiors consisted of tan bedford cord until June, and dark brown bedford cord from June until the end of the run. Also, in May and June, a 2-tone brown mohair interior was available, while a 2-tone taupe mohair interior was a no-cost option in June and July.

Once again, the most popular Ford was the Tudor Sedan, Type 700, with its body by Briggs Mfg. Co. Priced at only $520, the car drew 174,770 orders. As before, it had a small luggage area behind its sloped back, with access via the rear seat back. Two nicely upholstered folding-back bucket seats occupied the front, while a single bench seat with arm rests was used in the rear. The normal interior on this car was tan bedford cord, while an imitation leather scheme was an extra-cost option. No-cost optional cloth interiors of 2-tone brown mohair became available in May and June; a 2-tone tan mohair scheme came in June and July, and a dark brown bedford cord was available from July on.

Although the Touring or trunk-back design was relegated only to the Deluxe line at the start of the year, Standard Tudor Touring Sedans were introduced in December, probably in an attempt to give a boost to the rather sluggish sales picture. Identified by the same body color grilles and single taillights of other Standard models, these cars featured the same handy bustle back trunk as found on the Deluxe cars, but with Standard interior trim. Priced at $545, the cars weighed 2,718 pounds. Even on Standard models, the spare tire cover was a regular piece of equipment, but it lacked the chrome or stainless trim rings that brightened the covers of Deluxe models. Interiors on the touring models were the same as on the regular Standard Tudor. For some reason, separate production figures were not kept on the Standard Tudor Touring, and it is not known if its tallies are included in the 174,770 Standard Tudors, or in the 125,303 Deluxe Touring Tudor models that were registered this year.

Apparently the least popular of the four varieties of Tudors available this year was the Deluxe Tudor Sedan. Briggs turned out only 20,519 of this model, listed at $565 in basic form as seen here. This year the combination of all Tudor and Fordor bodies built by Briggs amounted to 66% of the total bodies bought by Ford. Amazingly, Briggs had its production costs so low that it was able to turn out a complete Tudor body shell for under $40, while a completed Deluxe body with full upholstery and trim was produced for under $200. Despite these low costs, it appears that many in the Ford complex were unhappy that outside contractors were relied on for all body building and that Briggs had the lion's share of this business in its Tudor and Fordor bodies. At this time, Briggs was also building bodies for Chrysler and Packard. In addition to its being almost at the saturation point in body contracts, the company was the scene of almost constant labor strikes.

With production reaching 125,303, the Deluxe Tudor Touring Sedan certainly proved that people liked the concept of accessible luggage space. Priced at $590, the car had its own exclusive spot until December, when a Standard version of this model was turned loose. Since no production records were kept on the Standard version, it is possible that the production mentioned here was shared between two trim levels. When photographed years ago, this beautifully restored model was owned by John Lischke of Marietta, Georgia. It is equipped with the odd accessory right hand windshield wiper that cost $3. This unit did not have its own motor, but was actuated by a rod connected to the left wiper. Late in the year, it seems that motorized right hand wipers became a feature of Deluxe models. Also on this car are the contrasting-color wheels at $5 a set and the chrome wheel rings at $7 a set. The rub rail on the running board appears to be from 1935 stock, or is an aftermarket item.

Although they are among the most sought after models today, in 1936 the Phaeton was well down on the popularity scale. Only 5,555 were built this year. One of three open 4-doors produced by Murray, the car retailed for $590 and weighed 2,641 pounds. Designated the Type 750, it was available only in Deluxe form and with an interior in genuine brown leather. Wind wings and chromed windshield post and frame were similar to those on the roadster. Top bows were chromed until April, when they were changed to a paint finish. The top material was the same as used on all other open cars, and was the same drab canvas interlined with rubber as used in 1935. The chromed grille side panels appear on all factory photos of this car, and apparently were exclusive to this model.

Appearing in April was Ford's second new style of the year, the Convertible Touring Sedan. Also built by Murray, the car was simply the Convertible Sedan with a new bustle-back trunk built into the rear end. Unlike the Briggs-built Touring Sedans, however, the trunk on this model featured a full length deck, and incorporated Ford's first modern usage of an internal storage area for the spare tire. The trunk hinged at the top and locked at the bottom with dual latches. Despite its rather large capacity, usable storage space in the trunk was drastically reduced by the spare tire which occupied most of the floor area. Also unique to this car were the stubby taillights which fitted on the trunk deck rather than on the fenders. But moving the taillights meant that the gas filler pipe, which ran through the left taillight pod on all other models, stuck rather prominently out of the left fender on this model. Murray did not keep separate production figures on this model, so there is no way to tell how many of the 5,601 convertible sedans built this year had trunk backs. The new model was $20 higher than the slant-back version, and thus at $780, became Ford's most expensive style. The same cloth or leather interiors used on the slant-back style were available on the trunk model, but in June the all-leather interior was dropped in favor of a combination leather and cloth scheme, in which the seats were in natural brown leather, but the panels were in bedford cord. This trim package was subsequently dropped in August, and the last few models were turned out once again in all-leather. What is not clear is whether the new trunk-back model joined or succeeded the slant-back version. Obviously both were on the market at the same time, but the available slant-back models might just have been run-off, as production was concentrated solely on the new trunk-back style.

Only slightly more popular than the Phaeton was the Convertible Sedan, also by Murray. A total of 5,601 were built, but it is not known how many were in the early slant-back form, or how many were of the trunk-back version that was introduced in April. Priced at $760, the slant-back model featured hidden luggage space behind the rear seat. The car differed from the Phaeton in that all four doors had roll-up windows and the top, when raised, would create a weather-tight interior. Available only in Deluxe trim, the car had an interior in genuine brown leather, although for some reason (probably cost) the front seat back was in matching artificial leather. The car also was available with a cloth interior in taupe bedford cord. The top boot was of drab canvas, which matched the rubber interlined drab canvas used on the top.

Apparently the least popular of the 4-door sedans was the Standard Fordor, of which only 31,505 were built. Still designated the Type 730, the car was part of the family of four 4-door models turned out by Briggs. It cost $580 and weighed 2,699 pounds. Although the body was identical to the 1935 fare, one change did occur. That involved the rear quarter windows, which now pivoted outward for ventilation, rather than rolling down. This was definitely a cost-saving move, as a pivot hinge is certainly much cheaper to produce than a roll-up window assembly. As before, Standard models had only single taillights on the left. However, a right-hand taillight was a relatively popular dealer-installed accessory. It is interesting to note that in the Tudor family, the Standard model far outsold the Deluxe versions, while in the Fordor tribe just the opposite was true.

Not introduced until December was the Standard Fordor Touring Sedan, which was simply a low-trim version of the Deluxe model. By bringing in this car as a sales incentive later in the year, Ford had four 4-door variations to offer customers. Priced at $605, the car offered a $45 reduction from the Deluxe model. However, Briggs did not differentiate between Standard or Deluxe production on this model, and therefore it is not known how many of the 159,825 touring bodies were in Standard trim. As with other Fords, Standard models had the grille and horn grilles painted in body color; wore only a left taillight, and had a less plush interior. Interiors on both Standard Fordors were tan bedford cord. Optional no-cost cloth interiors were offered in 2-tone brown mohair in May; 2-tone tan mohair in June, and dark brown bedford cord from July onward. In addition, an extra-cost interior in brown imitation leather was available throughout the year. Floor mats were in gray rubber this year.

Until December, the only Fordor Touring Sedan available was in Deluxe trim like this model. In this form it cost $650 and weighed 2,816 pounds. However, in December a standard version was introduced, but since no separate production records were kept on the latter version, it is not known how many of the 159,825 Fordor Touring Sedan bodies were in Deluxe trim. As on all Deluxe models, the pressed steel spare tire cover had a stainless steel trim ring. This plus dual taillights identified the car from the rear as a Deluxe vehicle. New for the year were the pivoting quarter windows, with full chromed framing. The trunks on all touring models were lined in black cardboard, with three different embossing styles used throughout the year. This was the last year that the small top-loading trunk deck would appear, and the last year for exterior spare tires on any models.

In May, the 3-millionth V-8 rolled from the Dearborn assembly line under the watchful eye of Edsel Ford. It was a Deluxe Fordor, one of 42,867 of this style Briggs-bodied car turned out this year. Note that being a late-model Deluxe, the car is equipped with twin windshield wipers. Priced at $625, the 2,746-pound car carried the same Type 730 designation as did all of the other 4-door variations. Normal interiors on the Deluxe Fordors were either taupe mohair or taupe bedford cord. Early models had a brown broadcloth option but this was dropped after November, when it was replaced by a gray-brown broadcloth option. In January a brown boucle material also became available, while a genuine brown leather interior was available at extra cost throughout the year. In all models, a gray rubber floor mat was used in the front, while brown carpeting occupied the rear floor. However, early models used tan rubber floor mats until the supply of those units was finished.

Still considered part of the commercial line, but still wearing the trim of the Deluxe passenger cars was the Station Wagon, Type 790. The wagon was Ford's only vehicle to exceed 3,000 pounds, weighing 3,020. It listed for $670, and saw its popularity rise as 7,044 were sold this year. As before, the wood was cut and trimmed at Ford's Iron Mountain plant, with final assembly done by the Murray Corp. Ford still stressed the fact that roll-up windows were included in the front doors, but didn't brag too much about side curtains being necessary for the rest of the windows. These curtains now featured very large isinglass panes. When not in use they stored between the roof ribs. Besides the overall front end change, the wagons were differentiated from the 1935 issue by having seats done in brown imitation leather with gray floor mats, rather than gray-brown seats and tan mats. In April, the wagons began to be equipped with rear bumpers, which formerly were available only as an accessory.

Although Ford did not offer a taxi cab model, it did offer hard wearing leather interiors as an extra-cost option in all of its models. These interiors were favored by fleet customers and salesmen, and in the 4-door models, made great taxi interiors. Artificial leather was used on the Standard lines, while in the Deluxe line the seats were in genuine leather while the panels and headliner were in imitation leather. Therefore, take one 4-door Ford with the optional interior, add an aftermarket taxi meter that fit into the glove box, apply a special paint job, and instant cab is the result. One such unit was this Deluxe version owned by a cab fleet in Van Nuys, Cal.

Ford's new Sedan Delivery reflected all of the frontal changes made to the passenger cars, while the Briggs-built body remained unchanged. This was Ford's smallest commercial vehicle this year, as the strange little Convertible Delivery car by LeBaron was not offered in 1935. Designated the Type 780, the pretty little trucks saw production reach 7,592 in Standard trim. This nice restoration wears the original round rearview mirrors of the era, and has a set of front signal lights which appear to be of post war vintage. Almost all signal lights of this era used lenses cut out with directional arrows, rather than just large lenses. Not visible is the new indented rear bumper on these trucks, which allowed the driver to get closer to the body for easier loading. The horns lived behind the little round grilles below the headlights. On Standard models, one horn by Schwarze was used, while Deluxe models had two Spartons.

Produced in limited quantity this year was the attractive Deluxe Sedan Delivery, which was the Standard version dressed up in all of the Deluxe passenger car trim. In addition, this example wears such dealer accessories as a spotlight, outside chromed rearview mirror, whitewall tires, and beauty rings on the wheels. A total of 209 were produced in this form, with few if any going into farm use as shown in this promotional photo. This model wears only one windshield wiper, which could mean that it is an early version, since all Deluxe models received dual wipers later in the season. This view gives a look at the single left-hinged cargo door used on these Briggs-supplied bodies. Spare tires on these units lived in their own recessed compartment on the right side of the cargo area.

Ford no longer offered the Convertible Delivery Car, but did have a glass-sided variation of its Sedan Delivery. But there is no information to indicate that rear passenger seats were available for these models as they were in the past. Available only on special order, with the side conversion probably done by Brigg's LeBaron Division, the bodies were identical to the Sedan Delivery except for the fixed glass panels. These could be used as display boards, or could be left open. It is not certain whether these conversions were available on an individual basis, or whether they were produced only for fleet orders.

The well dressed Ford had a rather cluttered dash when fully equipped. Again, as in 1935, three distinct dash panels were used. The one illustrated here is from a Deluxe coupe or sedan model. The Convertible Sedan and Station Wagon used a similar dash but without the upper windshield knob, as windshields on these models would not open. And the Roadsters and Phaetons continued to use their own more narrow dash with slanting glove compartment door. This car wears an accessory clock and a locking latch on its glove compartment door, and has been fitted with the $45 accessory radio, which occupied the center dash spot otherwise used for the ash tray. Four knobs bracketed the radio. On top were the dash light switch on the left and the cigarette lighter on the right. Below were the choke on the left and the throttle. The far right knob adjacent to the glove box door is a heater control.

Certainly not a Ford item, but one that enjoyed moderate popularity in 1936 (and is quite sought after today) was the Pines front trim. The 10-piece kit consisted of three horizontal bars for each side, three wrap-around grille bars, and a small nose piece. Available only for the 1936 models, the Pines trim was not redesigned for the 1937 style. It was produced by the Pines Winterfront Co., whose specialty was manufacturing clip-on leatherette grille covers for various makes of cars. These were used in the winter to help keep the engine temperatures up and provide more hot water for the heater. Such fronts are still used on heavy trucks in the northern areas.

In its last automotive effort, the prestigious James Cunningham, Son & Co. of Rochester, N.Y., turned out this rather high but nicely styled limousine on the Deluxe Ford chassis. Available either in limousine style as seen here, or in open front town car style, all featured the large blank quarter panel, modified trunk with almost vertical rear panel, vertical spare, and immaculate workmanship throughout. It is not known how many of these beautiful machines were produced before all automotive body work ceased. Founded in 1838, the Cunningham firm had developed into one of America's best known builders of high quality and high priced funeral and professional cars, and had also produced a fine line of ultra-luxury cars under its own name from 1907 to 1930. It also built vehicles for the military, including half-track conversions, and even produced its own aircraft in the late 1920s. All of this activity was finished in 1936 when the last Ford chassied luxury cars and Cadillac chassied professional cars left the plant. The Cunningham company still survives in Rochester, however, as a manufacturer of electric components.

An unusual run of cars left Ford's plant this year. Under a special order from Allegheny Ludlum Co., a total of six stainless steel Deluxe Tudors were built by Ford and Briggs. Apparently construction problems were quite severe, as the stainless steel could neither be formed nor welded as could the regular steel. However, the six cars were completed, and sent on extensive promotional runs for both Ford and Allegheny during the year. Four of the cars still exist. Two are in Allegheny's ownership, one is in private hands, and one is in the Crawford Auto-Aviation Museum at Cleveland. The cars were never painted, and because of the strange, almost glowing appearance of the stainless steel, drew quite a bit of attention wherever they went. Ford had also built three 1931 Tudors of stainless steel, which also received quite some publicity, but not to the extent of the 1936 versions. None of the Model As survive.

Although it was gaining fame for its stretched sedans, the main business for the Shop of Siebert was still in the professional car field. Having been in business in Toledo since 1853, the company for years had a reputation as a producer of good mid to low-price funeral cars and ambulances on various chassis. In this era the company leaned very heavily on Ford chassis, yet did not market its products through Ford dealers. Instead, National Hearse & Ambulance Co. of Toledo acted as distributors for the line, supplying the cars to their own outlets throughout the country. The basic funeral coach in Siebert's fleet this year is shown here, priced at $1,420 complete with velvet drapes. Called the Aristocrat, it was also available in ambulance trim for $1,455, or as a combination car (convertible from ambulance to hearse and back) for $1,470. A similar service car with blank side panels was $1,350. In producing these vehicles, Siebert cut Ford Sedan Deliveries behind the B-pillar and added its own special inserts with doors on both sides. The chassis were available in either Standard trim, as shown here, or in Deluxe versions.

The Shop of Siebert in Toledo continued to do a fine business, stretching Ford passenger cars into 12-passenger vehicles for use by smaller bus lines, resort hotels, sightseeing companies, and even private owners. One such owner was Wallace Beery, famed actor of the time, who used his stretched job to carry friends on hunting trips and vacations between movies. Beery's version, shown here, carries a few more trim items than most of the stretches, but still these were not dull vehicles. Almost all were built in Deluxe trim, and featured extra lights, fancy paint jobs, and nice interiors. The 6-foot stretch by Siebert occurred at the B-pillar. Normal sedans were cut in half at this point, a 6-passenger 4-door section was inserted, and the whole thing was welded back together. All units now had a roof-top luggage rack which doubled as a cantilever brace to prevent the car from sagging in the middle. Some bus units had passenger doors on the left side only for both safety and economy. Because of the added weight, these cars had to have truck tires and vacuum assisted brakes.

Unlike Siebert, which converted Ford Sedan Deliveries into professional cars, the A.J. Miller Co. of Bellefontaine, Ohio, bought cowl-chassis units and added their own special designed bodies. This particular ambulance was ordered by a hospital in Long Beach, Cal. It uses the regular Miller body, with beaver tail rear styling, and has etched frosted glass in its rear quarter windows. When produced for funeral usage, these bodies would have different interiors, but otherwise were identical. Miller had a full line of professional cars, from luxury models on Packard chassis, to mid-range products on Chrysler and Hudson wheels, to the low cost models which used Ford and Chevrolet bases. The cars were available through Miller's own dealer network. Besides the stocked items, the company would install its bodies on whatever chassis a customer might prefer.

Although Ford was so embarrassed by its 1935 display at the Indianapolis 500 that it wouldn't even consider racing, the racers still considered Ford. As before, the fledgling stock car circuits were totally dominated by Ford products, and any racer other than a Ford was usually considered little more than a joke. Safety modifications were few in this era, as can be seen with this almost stock model participating in one of the events at Daytona Beach. Driven by Milt Marion, the car's lettering indicates it was entered as a "test car" by Permatex Form-A-Gasket. A heavy leather strap holds the hood in place, but aside from this and a lack of bumpers, the car appears stock. It is even equipped with a top boot, hub caps, beauty rings, and has the stock Roadster windshield with windshield wiper and rearview mirror still attached. Note the crowd control and protective fencing—none! In a promotional move, all of the car's gaskets were replaced with Permatex. It is believed Marion was declared the winner of this event.

Ford was expected to come out with some new styling in 1937. The move had been hinted at through most of the summer, and both dealers and the public awaited the new models which were to be introduced in early November.

But what was introduced surprised even the skeptics. Here was a totally new car. The streamlined styling was definitely Ford, but was also definitely new and modern. The engine was the V-8, but with so many changes that it essentially could be termed a new engine. And then there was a new engine! It was a 60 horsepower model for people who preferred economy to performance. Even the chassis was new. About all that remained of the old Ford was the 112-inch wheelbase and the mechanical brakes that Henry so insisted upon.

Right from the front bumper, the cars were all new. A sharp V-grille graced the nose. Flanking this were two teardrop headlights blended into the catwalks. These represented Ford's first use of headlamps molded into the sheet metal rather than standing alone. The fenders had a similarity to the previous model. But, with higher crown and larger skirts, they were definitely new. The hood no longer lifted from the sides, but was the new alligator type, opening from the latch at the hood ornament and swinging upward on hinges set against the cowl. The hood sides were removable panels fitted with full-length horizontal louvers with stainless bars.

At the cowl was a brand new V-shaped 2-piece windshield with a prominent center bar. As before, windshield frames and grilles were painted on Standard models, chromed or stainless on the Deluxe cars. Standard models continued to use only one windshield wiper, with the right one being an extra-cost item. All Deluxe models had two wipers. On the closed cars, these were set into the windshield header, while the open models and the station wagons had the wipers mounted on cowl pedestals.

The new rear fenders could give a body shop a royal set of fits. The new Fords used four distinct styles of rear fenders, even though all models used the same front fenders. But in the back, coupes and roadsters used one style; slant-back sedans used a different style; touring sedans used still a third kind, and station wagons and sedan deliveries continued to use the 1936 style rear fender which was still active in the commercial line.

In the body department, all type numbers remained the same but there was now an alphabetical differentiation between Standard and Deluxe models and between slant-back and touring designs.

Only one new model appeared this year. It was the Club Coupe, Type 720, which essentially was the coupe with a close-coupled rear seat within the body, rather than having a rumble seat. Built by Murray, it followed the same seating pattern set by the previous year's Club Cabriolet, and in a sense, set the stage for both the demise of the rumble seat and for the design of all the 5-passenger coupe styles that were to follow. Gone was the 3-window Coupe by Murray, and thus the number

of body styles available remained at 17.

All bodies were totally new, and though they retained the same type numbers of the previous models, the styling was completely different. In addition to the new windshields, the most striking change in the closed cars was the use of a full steel roof on all models. No longer would closed car roofs be constructed of an imitation leather or a rubber material surrounded by a metal frame. Huge new presses in the shops of both Murray and Briggs led to the ability of Ford to offer the same "Turret Top" styling that General Motors had crowed about since 1935.

As before, Murray Corp. continued to build all of the open styles and coupe models, plus assemble the station wagons, while Briggs Mfg. continued to build all of the Tudor and Fordor bodies, plus the Sedan Delivery. Budd continued to supply the pickup bodies and cabs to the commercial division. However, continuing labor problems at Briggs, plus that company's massive contracts to build bodies for both Chrysler Corp. and Packard, was putting a strain on the Ford/Briggs relationship.

Under the hood is where Ford came in with a few surprises. Foremost was a new V-8 of 60 horsepower, which was designed with economy in mind. Having a bore and stroke of 2.6x3.2 inches, the new engine displaced 136 cubic inches and could deliver up to 25 miles per gallon. Essentially a scaled down version of the larger V-8, the little unit went through none of the start-up problems associated with the big engine—at least not in this country. Production was started on this block in July of 1935, and all of the first 6,601 engines were sent to Europe for installation in foreign-built Fords. Production for U.S. use began with block 6602, and by December 31, 1937, had reached 468894, which was far more engines than was called for by car production. All 60 horse engines used the prefix "54" ahead of the block number.

Although the little V-8 looked like the big one, there were some major differences. The cylinder heads were aluminum and interchangeable; the water pumps and front engine mount were all contained in a 1-piece front cover, and the oil pump was a new design that was gear driven off the crankshaft. In all, approximately 300,000 of these blocks were installed this year, but many went into commercial vehicles. In the passenger car line, they supposedly were available only in the Standard models and the Station Wagon, though special order Deluxe models could also have them. But, as the year progressed and buyers noted the difference in performance between the two engines, interest in the small block began to decline.

On the big V-8 things were just the opposite. Still rated at 85 horsepower at 3800 rpm, and still having a 3-1/16x3.75 inch bore and stroke, the 221 cubic inch engine nevertheless underwent some strong modifications. These included a totally redesigned block which included longer water cooling jackets; self-lubricating water pumps; revised valve guides; a redesigned ignition system, and new engine mountings. Unlike the 60 horse model, the big V-8 no longer used aluminum heads. These were now of cast iron, while the new pistons were cast steel, as opposed to aluminum. At mid-year, the engine also received a redesigned and heavier crankshaft which utilized replaceable bearings. Also designed was a special high compression cast iron head for use in high altitudes, or for buyers who wished to use alcohol or natural gas in place of gasoline. This optional head was very rare and seen primarily in the Rocky Mountain area and in the far western states.

Other changes to the engine included a new cam shaft that appeared as a running change at mid-year; an improved design in the intake manifold; a redesigned thermostat (later one made by Detroit Lubricator Co.); new exhaust manifolds; new and larger A.C. fuel pump, and at mid-year, the inclusion of alternate carburetors made by the Chandler-Grove Co. Of all engines, about 75% of the 1937 cars used the Stromberg No. 97 carburetor, while the rest used Chandlers. Also new were the air cleaners. Of similar design, they were supplied by either A.C. or by the Burgess Co., and were the same as used on the small V-8.

Engine numbers of the big V-8 started with 3216675 on Jan. 1, 1937, and ended with 4438368 on Dec. 31, for a total of 1,221,693 blocks built within the calendar year.

Also changed this year was the chassis, with five different variations now being used. Of these, two were regarded as light frames, while three were rated as heavy. The first of the light frames was used strictly on the Standard models destined to receive the 60 horse engine, while the second light chassis was used for all

Tudor, Fordor, and coupe bodies with the big V-8. Of the heavy chassis, the first was used on all other car models, including the Sedan Delivery, while the other two were used on light commercial vehicles only. All of these chassis had redesigned engine supports and various other small modifications which differentiated them from previous chassis. Front axles were redesigned, and a mid-year, new connecting rod ends were introduced. Made by Thompson Products, these ends first became options, but later were phased in as old Ford stocks ran out.

Brakes remained the old mechanical type, since Henry mistrusted hydraulic units. However, the emergency brake was redesigned, and its handle moved from its central position next to the shift lever to a new under-dash location against the left kick panel.

Only two body styles exceeded the 100,000 mark, and both involved Briggs' Tudor body. Highest production was achieved by the ever popular Standard Tudor, which registered 308,446 sales, while the Standard Tudor Touring Sedan registered 130,227. The only other models coming close to these figures were the Deluxe Fordor Touring Sedan with 98,687 builds to its credit, and the Standard Coupe, with 90,347 sales. Total production reached 929,390, which was substantially up from 1936, but not enough to capture the first place title from Chevrolet.

(Note: for some reason, there are wide variations in this year's production tally, and some lists would show that Ford actually was first in sales, since Chevrolet showed only 825,220 cars moving off the floors for the model year. Included in this chapter are the figures that we felt were most correct, although we acknowledge that they are higher than the totals shown on one other accepted list).

Once again Ford's least popular model was the Roadster, of which only 1,250 were built. Produced by Murray, the Roadster this year was identical to the Cabriolet, except for the fact that it did not have roll-up windows in its doors. Probably because of its similarity to the Cabriolet, combined with its low sales, it was not continued into the 1938 year. Thus another chapter of Ford's sporty open cars was coming to an end. The Roadster this year used the same solid windshield framing as did the other open cars, but was equipped with wind wings, which were not used on the Cabriolet. The interior was done in genuine tan leather with matching artificial leather panels. A rumble seat was standard, and there were no trunk back versions. In basic form, the car listed for $695 and weighed 2,576 pounds. Yes, the model shown here is missing its running board trim.

Companion to the Roadster was the Cabriolet, priced at $720. Far more popular than the Roadster, this model drew 10,148 orders, proving that roll-up windows vs. side curtains did make a difference. As was the Roadster, the Cabriolet was available only in Deluxe trim and rumble seat style. The 2,616-pound car was available with a choice of interiors, either a leather version similar to the Roadster, or a gray bedford cord throughout. In all cases, the rumble seat was finished in 2-tone artificial leather seat with matching cardboard panels.

No, the Standard Coupe did not come complete with pickup bed, but such an attachment was available as a factory installed option. In regular form, with a trunk deck, the Standard Coupe was one of Ford's more popular styles, accounting for 90,347 sales, of which 43,866 had the 60 horse engine. With the 85 horses, it weighed 2,496 pounds and cost $585, while with the 60 it weighed 2,296 pounds and cost $545, thus being Ford's lightest and least expensive car. The pickup bed accessory shown here was a Ford offering to a similar attachment offered by Chevrolet. Although Chevrolet had success with this concept and carried it right up until World War II, Ford's sales were so poor that the idea was dropped before year-end. When wearing the factory installed bed, the car was considered a Type 770-C.

Galloping forward in popularity was Ford's year-old Club Cabriolet, the forerunner of the modern convertible. Sales of the Murray-built model were 8,001, which was almost double those of 1936. The car sold for $760 and featured two small (and relatively uncomfortable) rear seats within the main seating section. A full-size trunk occupied the rear. Appearance was quite similar to the Cabriolet, except that the top extended further back, resulting in a rather large blank quarter. The fender skirts shown on this model appeared for the first time this year as an accessory, and became very popular with that segment which was willing to spend a few extra dollars to improve the looks of their cars. The Club Cabriolet was available in the same interior combinations as the Cabriolet. In base form it weighed 2,636 pounds. The Cabriolet was designated the Model 760-A, while the Club Cabriolet was the Model 760-B. Although none of the open coupes were supposed to be available with the small engine, it appears that 35 Roadsters; 41 Cabriolets, and 66 Club Cabriolets had the 60 horse block.

An early production version of the Deluxe Coupe, this model lacks the bright running board trim associated with Deluxe jobs. Far less popular than the Standard offering, the Deluxe versions saw sales of only 26,738, all at a base price of $660. All of these Murray-built coupes were available in trunk-deck form only. The Deluxe models varied from the Standard versions only in the bright grilles and windshield frames, dual wipers, and more plush interiors. Standard models were finished in 2-tone taupe mohair or taupe bark cord, while the Deluxe versions were either in gray mohair or gray flat wale cord. An optional interior of genuine leather seat and artificial leather panels was available for both models. The 60 horse Standards were considered the Model 74-770, while all 85 horse coupes bore Model 78-770.

Totally new for the year was the Club Coupe, Ford's first modern 5-passenger coupe design. Designated the Type 720, it was available in Deluxe trim only. For some reason, the Murray-bodied car did not attract the attention one would expect from such a concept, and thus, only 16,992 were built this year. Because of the rear seat, doors on this model were wider than on the regular coupes, and the front seats had forward swinging backs. The rear quarter windows also differed from the regular coupes, in that they would swing outward for ventilation, while on the regular coupes they were set in place. The Club Coupe cost $720 and weighed 2,616 pounds, the same as the Club Cabriolet. Rear seat passengers did not find the leg room as great as in the old rumble seats, but the comfort index was much higher. The interiors were of the same material options as on the regular Deluxe Coupes. Of the two Deluxe coupe models, the 60 horse engine went into 70 Club Coupes and 33 5-window Coupes.

By far Ford's most popular model was the Standard Tudor Sedan, which saw sales of 308,446. Quickly identified by its single windshield wiper and painted grille and windshield frame, the car was available with the 60 horse engine for $570 or with the 85 for $610. In small block form, it weighed 2,416, while the big block was 200 pounds heavier. Despite the slant back, the Standard Tudor did have a trunk area and exterior trunk deck, though its storage capacity was not as large as that of the Touring Sedans. All models bore the designation 74-700 in small block form or 78-700 with the 85 horses, regardless of whether they were in Standard or Deluxe trim. Despite the most accepted list showing 309,446 Standard Tudors built, another list at Ford shows production of only 296,261, of which 147,794 had the big engine and 148,467 had the 60 horse unit.

Having a more plush interior and a more sparkling exterior, but way down in sales, was the Deluxe Tudor Sedan. One list credits production at 33,683, while another credits only 32,675 units, of which 24 had the 60 horse engine supposedly not available in Deluxe models. Since Briggs built all Tudor and Fordor bodies, the differences between Deluxe and Standard models was one of trim level only. Standard models used the same materials as found on the Standard Coupes, while Deluxe versions had the superior quality gray mohair or gray flat wale cloth. All models could be ordered with the optional leather interior.

Why the Standard Touring Sedan had less than half of the orders of the slant-back Standard model is a puzzle. Certainly the $25 additional cost for the model with the larger trunk could not have been that much of a factor—or was it? Regardless, sales were only 130,227, of which 78,895 had the large engine and 51,332 had the 60 horses. All of these models had an adjustable front seat, with split seat backs that would swing forward for access to the rear. Base priced at $635 for the large block or $595 for the small, the car weighed 2,648 or 2,448 pounds, depending on which engine was installed.

According to Ford advertising, feeding time for this model would have been a lot easier if it had been the Standard model with the small engine. But as a Deluxe Tudor Touring Sedan, it was supposedly available with the large block only. However, of the 69,902 that were built, records show that 62 did sneak by with the small block under the fancy interior. Priced at an even $700, the car weighed 2,679 pounds. Notice the grille. One of the bad things about the thin bars used in this year's grilles and side panels was that when the car was viewed from certain angles, the grilles presented a see-through attitude similar to an open venetian blind.

Although Briggs built all of the Tudor and Fordor bodies, Murray did get a crack at 4-door models with its two open cars, the Phaeton and Convertible Sedan. Blessed with a totally new body and top, the beautiful Phaeton still failed to attract buyers, and only 3,723 were built, all in Deluxe trim. The new style body, which was also shared by the Convertible Sedan, featured a downward curving beltline very similar to that used on the Lincoln phaetons and convertible sedans. Unlike the Briggs-built Fordors, the doors on the Murray cars all latched to the rear. Priced at $750 and weighing 2,691 pounds, the Phaeton came equipped with side curtains and wind wings. Both the round rearview mirrors and stainless steel hub and spoke "spiders" are genuine Ford accessories. Designated the type 78-750, the Phaeton was supposedly available only with the big block, but it appears that 175 were turned out with the 60 horse engine.

Radiator hose and air cleaner are quite visible through the hood panel bars when the car is viewed directly from the side. More substantial grille and panel treatment on the 1938 models would cure this illusion. Shown here is the Murray-built Convertible Sedan, which shared its body with the Phaeton, but wore type number 78-740. Ford's most expensive model, it was priced at $860. At 2,861 pounds, it also laid claim to being the heaviest Ford, not including the Station Wagon. A total of 4,378 were built, all in Deluxe trim, and all but 42 having the large engine. It is interesting to note that even though Ford said the small block would not be available in Deluxe models, numerous exceptions to this rule quickly occurred. On the interior, the Phaeton was finished only in genuine leather seats with imitation leather panels, while the Convertible Sedan could be ordered with a gray bedford cord interior in place of the leather.

Just as the Standard Tudor was highly favored among fleet buyers, so too was the Standard Fordor Sedan, which was base priced at $670. However, the Fordor had no where near the popularity of its 2-door cousin, and as a result, Briggs built only 49,062. Weighing 2,649 pounds with the large engine, the cars were available in both 85 and 60 horse versions. The larger engine was a bit more popular, with 30,521 being turned out in that form as opposed to 18,541 with the small block. The model shown here, owned by the U.S. Navy's Fleet Marine Force, probably had the small block, as did most versions sold to corporate or government fleets.

Enjoying less than half the sales of the Standard version was the Deluxe edition of the Fordor Sedan. Only 22,885 were turned loose, with all but 148 having the large engine. The base price of $735 did not include the whitewall tires. Interior selections for the Deluxe models were in gray mohair or gray flat wale cord, while the Standard models were in beige mohair or bark cord. Either version could be ordered with genuine leather seats and artificial leather panels. Gray floor mats were used in the front on all models, while the rear floor was finished in brown carpeting.

A catalog X-ray view shows the seating and luggage arrangement in the Standard Fordor Touring Sedan. The illustration shows six people happily traveling in the car, but by standards of the 1960s or 70s this would have been a tight squeeze. However, by the standards of the 80s or 90s, the car was quite spacious. The Standard version of the Touring Sedan bore the same type number 74-730 as did the regular sedan when fitted with the small block engine. When equipped with the large block, all Briggs-built 4-door models were considered type 78-730. Only half as popular as the Deluxe version, the Standard Touring Sedan drew only 45,531 orders, of which 13,976 had the small engine. In base form, it was priced at $695 with the large block.

For the first time, fender skirts were available as a dealer-supplied option, and they really did look good on all models. Also dressing up this Deluxe Fordor Touring Sedan are the large chrome hub caps and wheel spiders that were also a popular accessory. The skirts could be fitted to all models except the Station Wagon, because the wagon continued to use 1936 style rear fenders that were carried over for all commercial vehicles. Twice as popular as the Standard version, the Deluxe Fordor Touring drew 98,687 orders, and thus was the most popular 4-door model. Of these, 809 had the small engine. Priced at $760 and weighing 2,696 pounds, this was Ford's most expensive closed car. Interior selections for this model were the same as in all other Deluxe units. This was the final year for the rear window roller shades.

Still classed as part of the commercial line was the Station Wagon, priced at $755 and weighing 2,991 pounds with the large engine. The wood-bodied car continued to be Ford's heaviest passenger vehicle. Ford continued to ship the pre-cut components from its Iron Mountain plant to Murray's Detroit facility where they were trimmed and final assembly occurred. A total of 9,304 were produced this year, all using Deluxe trim on the front end, but the 1936 holdover rear fenders. Of the total, only 193 had the small engine. Designated Type 78-790, the car featured an interior of artificial brown leather, with varnished natural wood panels. Only two exterior colors were available. They were Autumn Brown or Sand Beige, but any commercial car color could be special ordered at an additional price. Standard passenger car colors were not available on the wagons.

The rear view of this wagon displays Ford's newest option—sliding glass in the rear door and rear quarter windows. Available for an extra $20, these glass panes replaced the side curtains that normally provided protection for all but the front door windows. On the front doors, roll-up windows were standard. The spare tire lived on the tailgate once again this year, thus giving the wagon the distinction of being the only Ford with an exterior spare. In 1938, the spare would move to a new interior location behind the front seat. Note the rear fenders. All commercial Fords used carry-over types from the 1935/36 era. The tail and signal lights on this model are not original. Ford wagons continued to use only one tail/brake light on the left rear.

1937

The nicely styled Sedan Delivery continued to be manufactured by Briggs. This year, buyers had a choice of an internally stored spare, or one mounted on the rear cargo door . The internal unit probably looked better, but the rear-mount provided easier access and gave more usable cargo space. Available in both Deluxe form or as the Standard model shown here, the truck could be ordered with the large engine or have the 60 horsepower unit at a $10 savings. The base price was $595 with the big block. A total of 7,841 were turned out in Standard form, of which 3,238 had the little engine and 4,603 had the 85 horses. All versions featured dual bucket seats upholstered in the same artificial brown leather as used in the station wagons.

Produced only in prototype form was this interesting Utility Coupe, which was planned for the light commercial line. Not of pickup style, the car would have featured a large cargo area, completely enclosed by a very large deck lid, probably counterbalanced for easy opening. The hinges of this deck are visible immediately behind the rear window, while the latch was at bumper level. The vehicle was to be priced at about $700 and was to be available in both Standard and Deluxe trim. Everything forward of the C-pillar was identical to the Murray-built Coupe, and therefore it is assumed that Murray was to have been the builder. Between some relatively extensive market queries, coupled with the dismal response to the pickup box attachment for the Standard Coupe, it appears that Ford officials came up with a negative feeling for this model, and it was quietly dropped from sight.

Certainly nice looking but probably just a bit too fancy for the average buyer was the Deluxe Sedan Delivery. Only 707 were built in this form, with 103 of these having the small block engine. Deluxe items matched those of the passenger car line, and included dual wipers and sun visors; bright grille and side panels, and dual horns. The spotlight and chrome hub caps and spiders on this model were extra-cost trim items. The Sedan Delivery bore the designation 74-780 with the 60 horse engine or 78-780 with the large block. As did the Station Wagon, the Sedan Delivery continued to use carry-over 1936 rear fenders and rear bumper. As before, the interior of the cargo area was paneled in masonite, with a steel cover for the spare.

The Deluxe version of the Siebert line included all of the exterior Deluxe brightwork including the dual windshield wipers, beauty rings on the wheels, and stainless steel rub strip on the running boards. Also included were the Ford supplied fender skirts. Priced at $1,495, this model used the same Sedan Delivery conversion base as did Siebert's low-price line. Also in the Siebert catalog was a combination ambulance/funeral car for $1,520; a straight ambulance for $1,500, and a service car for $1,350. All used the same basic body design as seen here except the service car, which had blanked quarters rather than glass sides.

The Shop of Siebert of Toledo, marketing its cars through National Hearse & Ambulance Co., introduced its new low priced line of professional cars based on extended Ford chassis and available in either Standard or Deluxe trim. Lowest priced funeral coach of the line was this Standard model, which sold for $1,470. The price included the tasseled draperies in the rear compartment, and the owner's identity plates in the rear door windows. Siebert used Standard Sedan Deliveries for the conversion base.

Funeral Coach	$1470.00
Combination	1520.00
Ambulance	1500.00
Service Car	1350.00

Fully equipped ready to drive.
F.O.B. Toledo, Ohio.

Ford entered 1938 with a totally restyled car line and a marketing concept that would be carried through for the next three years. Rather than have Deluxe and Standard models that varied only in trim level, Ford now made these two distinct car lines, with totally different sheet metal for each, and even different Tudor and Fordor bodies for the two lines.

The reasoning behind Ford's two car line of distinctive styling is unclear. Chevrolet had tried this in 1933 with its Mercury Series and again in 1935 with its Standard and Deluxe Series, and apparently had not been overjoyed at the result. Possibly Ford's idea was to have a very low price and a slightly higher price Ford on the market, to compliment its medium price Mercury when that car was introduced in 1939. Whatever the reason, there was no mistaking a Deluxe Ford for a Standard.

The Deluxe line was characterized by totally new front end sheet metal which featured teardrop styling of the grille, and a down-turn of the hood which blended into the "V" caused by the grille halves. Unlike the separate grilles used previously, the 1938 grille was part of the overall front sheet metal and thus, along with the hood louvers, was painted in body color. Headlights remained a blended part of the catwalks, but the fenders were now more fully crowned and bulbous in styling. The Standard models, meanwhile, retained the 1937 styling, modified so that the upper grille bars formed a continuous louver design with the hood panels. Gone from both series were the free-standing taillights. These units were now incorporated into the new rear fenders, hiding behind small red lenses blended into the fender tips just above the bumper level. As before, Deluxe models used dual taillights, Standard models only a left one. However, it was now virtually impossible for a Standard owner to add an extra taillight to the right side, because doing so would entail ordering an entire rear fender.

With the Roadster gone, the Convertible Coupe or Cabriolet, Type 81A-760A, became the only Ford to still have a rumble seat. Built by Murray, the sporty car drew a total of 4,702 orders, of which all but 22 had the large engine. Priced at $770 in basic Deluxe trim, it weighed 2,679 pounds. Unlike the sedan line, neither the convertibles or regular coupes had any changes made to their body designs this year, but instead accepted the new front end sheet metal with a few minor cowl modifications.

Open bodies and the coupe line changed very little, but the Deluxe Tudors and Fordors had totally new sedan bodies with a streamlined rear design that encompassed trunk and trunk deck into one smooth sweep. The Standard Tudors and Fordors, meanwhile, continued to use the bustle back bodies that were used on the 1937 Touring Sedans. Briggs continued to be the sole supplier of these bodies, but was unable to handle orders for all of the new designs. Therefore, a combination of Briggs, Murray, and Budd participated in the Deluxe sedan bodies. Some reports would also indicate that Murray and Budd also shared in the production of the Standard sedan bodies, but this cannot be ascertained. As before, Murray supplied all of the coupe and open car bodies, while Budd supplied the pickup bodies and cabs. Also totally changed was the Station Wagon, still considered part of the Deluxe line. Although following the same basic design and measurements of previous wagons, it now featured sliding glass panes in the rear door and rear quarter windows. Last year this glass had been a $20 accessory.

Also changed was the wood design on doors and sides. These panels now contained three horizontal double strips, one each at top and bottom and one in the center. Before a total of six strips were used on the doors, while five braced the rear panel. In addition, the spare tire on the wagon was moved from the tailgate and now lived in its own compartment behind the driver's seat. The bad thing about this position was the fact that over the years the spare tire cover would get lost or wear out, and the tire would tend to rattle around loose in back, in all of its dirt and grit carrying splendor.

Along with the changes to the wagon was a change of assembly points. Up until now, all wood parts for the

More popular than the Convertible Coupe with rumble seat was the Convertible Club Coupe, with its 5-passenger seating capacity. Murray built 6,080, of which 38 were sent out with the small but supposedly unavailable 60 horse engine. The same gray taupe bedford cord or antique-grain brown leather was used in both convertibles as had been used in 1937. The top was in drab canvas interlined with rubber. Designated the Type 81A-760B, the car cost $800 and weighed 2,719 pounds. Notice that this year the hubcaps were no longer finished in body color, but were stainless steel units with an embossed "V-8" pattern in the center. Oddly, this model would be dropped for 1939, but the less popular rumble seat version would be continued.

wagons had been cut and trimmed at Ford's own plant at Iron Mountain, Mich. Then the components were shipped to the Murray plant in Detroit for final assembly. This year, Iron Mountain took over the entire production, and completed bodies were shipped direct from there to the various assembly plants.

Mechanically, the cars were virtually unchanged. Both the 85 and 60 horsepower engines continued to be offered, but orders for the smaller block were down drastically from the previous year. As before, the small block was supposedly available only in the three Standard models, and not in any of the Deluxe vehicles. However, records show that a handful of these underpowered blocks still managed to sneak into every Deluxe style on the books, as special factory orders, probably to suit the whims of good customers.

Because of a severe dip in the country's financial conditions, all car sales were down substantially this year, with Ford's probably dipping a shade more than most. As a result, Chevrolet firmly took over the first sales spot, and would continue to hold that position for the next 30 years.

Due to this economic downturn, Ford wound up with only two styles that exceeded the 100,000 mark. They were the Standard Tudor with the old bustle back body, whose production reached 106,117, and the new Deluxe Tudor, with sales of 101,647. The next highest production was the Deluxe Fordor, with sales of 92,020, while the lowest production was achieved by the Deluxe Phaeton, with only 1,169 sales. Incidentally, this would be the last year for the Phaeton, as dwindling sales of these beautiful but impractical cars made it financially unfeasible to keep them on the roles. Already off the books was the Deluxe Roadster, which saw its last example roll from the line during the 1937 run. The demise of this car left only one style Ford still equipped with a rumble seat. That was the Deluxe Convertible Coupe, which was still drawing its share of interest despite the

sales inroads made by the 5-passenger Club variation.

During the year, the 26-millionth Ford rolled from the line in November, while the 5-millionth V-8 engine was produced in May. In January, sagging sales in the Standard line caused Ford to add a series of chrome bars to the grille, instal;l bright metal windshield frames, and add a bright stainless steel belt molding strip to all Standard models, including the Sedan Delivery. Whether or not this move resulted in any upsurge of sales is unknown, but it certainly did help to make these rather drab vehicles look a bit better.

Surprisingly, the Deluxe Club Coupe did not come close to the sales popularity of the 3-passenger model. In fact, its sales of 7,171 were less than half of those achieved in 1937. As with other coupes and convertibles, the Club Coupe also used a carry-over Murray body, with the same interior materials as on the 3-passenger Deluxe model. The Club Coupe was not available in Standard trim, but only as a Deluxe Type 81A-720. It cost $745 and weighed 2,688 pounds. Surprisingly, there were only four 3-passenger coupes fitted with the 60 horse engine, yet a total of 57 small blocks were installed in this model. Probably the reason for the low interest was that people who had need for extra passenger space would go with the Tudor Sedans, which offered much more passenger room in the rear. Probably due to low sales, this model was not continued in 1939.

Ford's most popular Deluxe model was the Tudor Sedan, which offered a brand new body with fast-back styling. A total of 101,647 were built, with production shared by Briggs, Murray, and Budd. Priced at $725, the car weighed 2,742 pounds with the large engine, or 2,542 with the odd 119 which received the small block. Like the coupes, which retained the same upholstery and panel material as used in 1937, the sedans also made use of the 1937 style gray mohair or gray flat wale cord. One interior change involved the roll-up rear shade, which was no longer used. This year only a driver's side arm rest was used in the front, and a right front arm rest had to be purchased as an option.

Available only with a trunk deck and wearing a carry-over body by Murray was the Deluxe Coupe. The car was sometimes referred to as the 5-window Coupe, which was correct but unnecessary as there was no 3-window variation. A popular car with salesmen and small families, the Coupe drew 22,225 orders, all priced at $685. Weighing 2,606 pounds, this was Ford's lightest and least expensive Deluxe model. It shared its body with the Standard version, which appears later in this chapter. Interiors were the same gray wale cord or gray mohair which had been used in 1937. Unlike the Club Coupe, the rear quarter windows on this model would not open. Despite its popularity as a business car, this model had only four small blocks installed during its entire run.

Appearing for the last time this year was the beautiful but unpopular Phaeton. Ford's least popular model, it drew just 1,1690 orders, with a basic price of $820. Still using its unchanged Murray body, the Phaeton was finished with genuine leather seats in an antique brown finish, with artificial leather panels. The wind wings were still standard fare, and weather protection was still by side curtains. Available in Deluxe trim only, the car here sports the very attractive fender skirts which were available from Ford dealers. Of those built, a total of 67 were fitted with the 60 horse engine.

Ford's most expensive model, and the only one to break the $900 mark was the Convertible Sedan, available only in deluxe trim. Priced at an even $900 in base form, the car was designated Type 81A-740. It used the same basic carry-over Murray body as did the Phaeton, but was equipped with roll-up windows in the doors rather than side curtains. When top and windows were up, a removable post was placed in the B-pillar position to both brace the top and provide a rattle-resistant guide for the windows. Production of this model was down considerably this year, with only 2,743 being built, of which 42 had the small engine. Unlike the closed cars, the windshields of the convertible models would not open. This was due to the fact that all open models (and the Station Wagon) had their windshield wipers located in the cowl, while the closed cars had them in the header.

Graced with a totally new body was the Deluxe Fordor Sedan, now available in only one style. Essentially this was a totally new car, except for the mechanics, as virtually no sheet metal or trim from the 1937 issue would fit this model. Most striking in the design was the new streamlined rear end treatment, which incorporated rear window and trunk deck into one sweeping line from windshield header to rear bumper. This was similar to the earlier fast-back styling, but with a more pronounced rearward angle, giving a much more modern appearance. Also new were the rear fenders which now contained the taillights in flush mounted lenses just above the bumpers. Sales of this model reached 92,020, with 674 being fitted with the small block engine. Because of recurring production difficulties at Briggs, manufacturing of the new Tudor and Fordor Sedan bodies was divided among Briggs, Murray, and Budd. The base price of $770 did not include the dealer-supplied extra equipment on this model. Visible special equipment includes fog lights, spotlight, radio and header-mounted antenna, wind deflectors, fender skirts, and special hubcaps and chrome wheel spiders.

The Station Wagon also received a new body this year, with the side panel bracing totally different than used on the 1937 issue. Also new on this model were the sliding glass in the rear door and quarter windows. This glass had been a $20 accessory in 1937. Priced at $825, the wagon saw its production fall to 6,944, of which only four had the small block engine. In addition to the side trim, a major change involved the spare tire, which moved from the tailgate to a special storage area behind the driver's seat. This meant that Ford no longer had any passenger vehicles with outside spares. Murray no longer assembled the wagons. This year all of the production work was done at Ford's own plant at Iron Mountain, Mich.

There was absolutely no way to confuse this year's Standard and Deluxe models. Looking exactly like the re-hashed 1937 model that it was, the Standard Coupe led the entire Ford list as the economy special, with its base price being $625. Available only in trunk form, the car used the same Murray-built body as did the Deluxe model, but continued to wear the base 1937 sheet metal. However, rear fenders were the new issue, with the Standard's single taillight on the left side only. This is a late model, built after January, which has stainless steel trim on the grille, a bright windshield molding, and stainless beltline trim. These items were added to help boost sagging sales by brightening up an otherwise drab car. Still, sales lagged, with only 34,059 being produced. Of these, only 13,712 had the 60 horse engine. Of rather odd note are records that show a total of 446 Standard Coupes being built with pickup beds, even though there is no other indication that the pickup unit was still available in 1938 as a factory installation. Most records indicate that the pickup addition was only available in 1937, despite a body type number of 770C being shown for this style in 1938.

Least popular of the three Standard models was the Fordor Sedan, which also used a carry-over bustle back body from the 1937 Touring Sedan. Only 30,287 of this model were built, with 5,878 of these having the 60 horse engine. Priced at $665, the rather drab car was only $105 less than the much brighter Deluxe version, which had three time the appeal. This is one of the early models, with no brightwork at all on the nose or the windshield frame, and no beltline trim. Even the beauty rings on the wheels would have been an extra-cost accessory. Briggs appears to have built all of these bodies, though some information would indicate that Budd or Murray also had a hand in production. Unlike the Deluxe models, which used the same interior materials as in 1937, the new Standard models received new and less expensive materials. Buyers had a choice of 2-tone taupe boucle cloth or brown stripe mohair. As before, an interior of natural leather seats with artificial leather panels could be ordered at extra cost.

Perched on a auto transporter on its way to some midwestern dealership is this Standard Tudor, Ford's most popular model of the year. Priced at $665 and weighing 2,674 pounds, the car achieved 106,117 sales, of which 30,850 used the small engine. This view gives a look at the carry-over bustle-back body that was used on all Standard models this year. Note the new taillight treatment on the new style fenders, and the fact that only a left hand taillight was used on Standard models. This matched the left hand only windshield wiper, sun visor, and arm rest. This is an early model, lacking the brightwork at the beltline and in the grille bars. The bodies were produced by Briggs. Some records indicate that both Murray and Budd also shared in this production, but this cannot be ascertained for the Standard models, even though it is known that both of these companies built a good portion of the new Deluxe styles.

Available only in Standard trim was the Sedan Delivery, with its Briggs-built body. As did the passenger cars, the Sedan Delivery also benefitted from the brightwork added after January. This particular example, owned by Ford, is a veritable rolling display of dealer supplied accessories. In base form, the truck cost about $700. Sales were way down, and only 2,672 were built, with 1,120 having the small engine. Records also indicate that an additional 28 were built with Deluxe front sheet metal, though there is no indication that such a variation was available. Possibly these were for a special fleet order. Buyers still had a choice of having the spare mounted in an inside compartment, or on an optional outside hanger on the rear door.

Finally—Fords now had hydraulic brakes. After fighting these units for over 10 years on the grounds that he considered them unsafe, Henry Ford finally bowed to the will of his corporate advisors. He allowed his engineers to go ahead with a Lockheed designed hydraulic system to replace the now archaic mechanicals which had been in use since 1903—albeit in succeedingly improved form.

The brakes in themselves should have been the big Ford news of the year, coupled to the new and even more modern sheet metal changes on the cars. But this was not to be. Overshadowing everything that Ford had done under its own banner was the brood's newest chick, the Mercury. Introduced as a type of "Super Ford," the new make this year stole all of the publicity from its parent. It was four inches longer, had a 116-inch wheelbase rather than a 112-inch; used a 95 horsepower version of the V-8 rather than Ford's 85 horses; had a more plush interior, and simply looked like "Super Ford." Designed to compete head on with such makes as Studebaker, Pontiac, Oldsmobile, and Dodge, the new baby got all the attention while the "good ole boy" Fords shuffled along in the shadows.

Yet, had not Mercury come along, Ford's claim to fame would simply have been some new and pleasing sheet metal on the front ends, a shuffling of some models, and, of course, the new hydraulic brakes.

In a pattern established in 1938, Ford continued to use two distinct series, with Deluxe models receiving a totally new face while the Standard models received the sheet metal made over from the previous year's Deluxe designs.

On the Deluxe models, again there was no confusing the cars with previous models or the Standard series. A new grille composed of vertical chromed bars came only to headlight level, where it was met by a large hood, devoid of separate side panels. The hood itself was trimmed with an upper stainless horizontal rib which continued rearward as the belt molding, and a lower bar which terminated at the cowl. Totally new fenders appeared, carrying the headlights at the leading edges rather than in the catwalks, while the headlights themselves were located behind large teardrop shaped lenses framed by chrome bezels.

In the Standard line, the cars picked up a slightly modified version of the 1938 Deluxe sheet metal, including the sharply pointed hood and the pressed steel grille in body color. Also carried over were the distinct hood panels with louver bars at the cowl end, and the old front fenders with the headlights mounted in the catwalks. In an attempt to differentiate this year's Standard from last year's Deluxe models, the hood side was given a pointed forward edge which protruded into the grille area, while three bright bars added a bit of sparkle to the grille itself. All models now had bright windshield frames.

In the body department, there was quite a bit of movement, much of which went unnoticed by the public.

The cause of this action was Ford's intention to produce its own bodies from now on, rather than to rely on its former independent body builders such as Briggs, Murray, and Budd. Although these three companies would continue to supply a few bodies to Ford during the year, and would build components in the coming years, the major portion of body construction was now going to be handled by Ford within its own plants.

In line with this, the number of body styles was reduced to 10, with four being in the Standard line and six in the Deluxe. The lone gain in the Standard division occurred when the Station Wagon was offered in both Deluxe and Standard sheet metal. The remaining three Standard models, Coupe, Tudor, and Fordor, retained the carry-over bodies of the 1938 Deluxe models, although the Coupe body was slightly redesigned. Despite the redesign of the Coupe, Murray remained the producer of this style until later in the year when Ford took over. Ford meanwhile took over total production of the Tudor and Fordor styles in both Standard and Deluxe versions. In the Deluxe realm, the available model list shrunk from nine to six, with the Phaeton, Convertible Club Coupe, and Club Coupe gone from the books. As before, Murray continued to build both the Convertible Coupe and Convertible Sedan bodies, and also built the early Coupe bodies until Ford was able to schedule that production into its own shops. The puzzle here is why Ford had Murray drop the Convertible Club Coupe with its 5-passenger interior, yet continue with its Convertible Coupe with the now archaic rumble seat.

As before, the 60 horse engine was available only in the Standard models, along with the 85 horse version, while the Deluxe models were equipped only with the larger block. At least this year it appears that either no or very few 60 horse engines went into the Deluxe models, and one list would indicate that less than 2,000 of the small engines went into Standard models. As occurred in 1937 and 1938, the Standard models told which engine was installed. This year the designation plaque was nestled in the sharp "V" at the end of the hood.

Once again, production figures tend to be muddles, possibly because of Ford's taking over much of the body business. Officially, the lists show 532,152 cars built for the model year, yet a tally of the most accepted production listing by body style shows only 492,454 cars turned out between the November introduction and the October model closing. Using this latter list, once again the Tudor Sedan was the only model to break the 100,000 production mark. It did this with a tally of 124,866 for the Standard version, and 144,333 for the Deluxe model. The only other style to even come close to this record is the Deluxe Fordor, with 99,377 builds to its credit.

Also in the record box was the construction of the 27-millionth Ford on Feb. 15, at the Richmond, Cal., plant, while the 6-millionth V-8 engine was built at River Rouge on May 1.

1939

Ford's last remaining rumble seat appeared for the final time this year on the Convertible Coupe, Type 76. Using a slightly modified version of the 1938 body, the Murray-built car drew an amazing 10,422 orders. Priced at $790, it weighed 2,840 pounds. The puzzle remains why Ford dropped the 5-passenger Convertible Club Coupe and retained the rumble seat model when every indicator pointed to the end of the rumble seat era. Possibly the error of the ways was noticed, because in 1940 the club style would return and sales of this particular model would more than double. Among the accessories on this beautiful example are the fog and spot lights, rearview mirror, fender skirts, and beauty rings and oversized hubcaps on the wheels.

With the demise of the 5-passenger Club Coupe, Ford this year had only one basic coupe body, available in both series. This is the Deluxe version, which sold for $700 and weighed 2,752 pounds. Of 3-passenger configuration, it had a large rear cargo area accessible via a rear deck lid of totally new design, and another small storage area in the front, accessible by pulling forward on the 1-piece seat back. In addition, there was a large parcel shelf behind the seat back. Although bearing a similar shape to the previous 3-window coupes, the new model was of smoother design and was one inch longer from cowl to the tip of its sloping back. A favorite with salesmen and single people, the car drew 33,326 orders. Production was first started by Murray, but during the year Ford came into the act and the Murray bodies were slowly phased out.

By far the most popular Ford this year was the Deluxe Tudor, which enjoyed a run of 144,333, all built by Ford. Priced at $745, the car weighed 2,867 pounds. The body design was a direct carry-over from 1938 with the one exception being that the spare tire now stood upright against the trunk wall. In 1938 it lived flat in its own compartment under a special trunk floor. Windshields on all closed models except the Station Wagon could still be opened via a knob on top of the dash. However, this was the final year for this innovation. Beginning with the 1940 models, front ventilation would be by a cowl vent and the windshield wipers would move from the header to the cowl top.

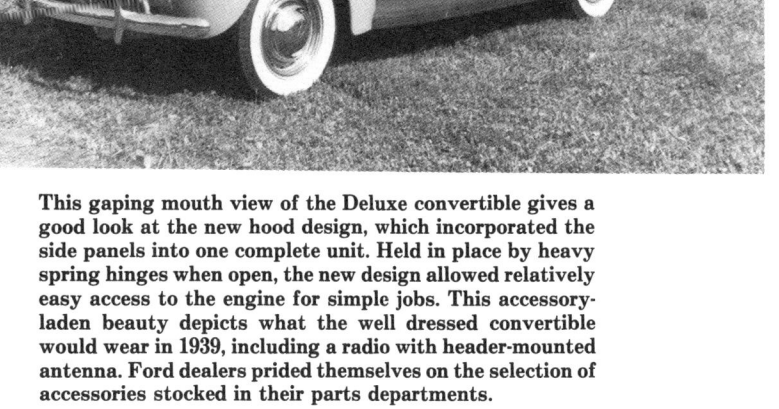

This gaping mouth view of the Deluxe convertible gives a good look at the new hood design, which incorporated the side panels into one complete unit. Held in place by heavy spring hinges when open, the new design allowed relatively easy access to the engine for simple jobs. This accessory-laden beauty depicts what the well dressed convertible would wear in 1939, including a radio with header-mounted antenna. Ford dealers prided themselves on the selection of accessories stocked in their parts departments.

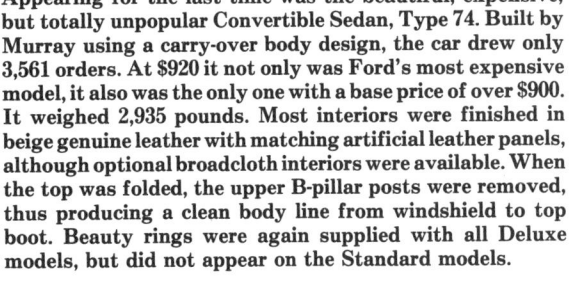

Appearing for the last time was the beautiful, expensive, but totally unpopular Convertible Sedan, Type 74. Built by Murray using a carry-over body design, the car drew only 3,561 orders. At $920 it not only was Ford's most expensive model, it also was the only one with a base price of over $900. It weighed 2,935 pounds. Most interiors were finished in beige genuine leather with matching artificial leather panels, although optional broadcloth interiors were available. When the top was folded, the upper B-pillar posts were removed, thus producing a clean body line from windshield to top boot. Beauty rings were again supplied with all Deluxe models, but did not appear on the Standard models.

Almost breaking the 100,000 production figure was the Deluxe Fordor, which registered 99,377 builds. Priced at $790 and weighing 2,898 pounds, the car probably would have enjoyed a wider acceptance had it not been for the introduction of "Super Ford," better known as the new Mercury. Production of this model is listed as being by Ford exclusively and by Ford and Briggs. Possibly, as was the case with Murray and the coupes, Briggs began production early in the year, then slid out of the picture as Ford took over later in the season. Or, it is possible that Briggs supplied many of the components, with Ford doing the final assembly. As with the Tudor, the spare this year moved from a horizontal plane on the trunk floor to an upright position against the trunk back.

After a major change of design and assembly point last year, it stood to reason that the Station Wagon would retain its carry-over body shell this year. Priced at $920, it could have tied with the Convertible Sedan as the most expensive Ford passenger car. Except, even in the Deluxe package shown here, the wagon was still considered part of Ford's commercial line. At 3,095 pounds, it was Ford's heaviest passenger vehicle. Production of the Deluxe version was 6,155, which wasn't bad, considering the model now had competition from the Standard version. Once again the spare tire nested behind the driver's seat, but this year an optional hanger was available which allowed the spare to ride on the exterior of the tailgate.

Despite its slightly modified carry-over front sheet metal, the new Standard 5-window Coupe availed itself of the new body with redesigned trunk deck and more flowing line. New for the Standard series this year were the dual windshield wipers and chromed windshield frame, both of which items had formerly been restricted to Deluxe models only. Actually, the bright frame came out at mid-year in 1938 in an overall sprucing of the Standard line. Priced at $640 and weighing 2,710 pounds, the Standard Coupe continued to be Ford's lightest and least expensive car. Both price and vast cargo area made it popular with salesmen and fleet owners. Production reached 38,197, with the early models coming from Murray's plant, while later ones were built by Ford. On the Coupes too, the spare tire was relocated, going from a horizontal spot under its own floor on the 1938 models, to a slanted upright position against the trunk back this year.

Ford's second most popular car was the Standard Tudor, which saw a run of 124,866, all coming from within Ford's own confines. Priced at $680, the car weighed 2,830 pounds. Although the 1938 front sheet metal is very obvious, subtle changes helped to clarify the year. These included the pointed forward edges of the hood panels which ran into the former grille curve; half-length horizontal louver slits on the side panels, and three stainless bars on the grille itself. As before, buyers of Standard models had their choice of either the 60 or the 85 horse engine, but this year sales of the 60 horse unit were so low that they really weren't a factor in Ford's overall finances.

Sales of the Standard Fordor were again far below that of its Deluxe counterpart. In fact, percentagewise, they were even lower than in 1937. The reason for this possibly could be placed on the notable styling difference between the two cars. Most buyers probably preferred to pay the extra $60 to get a car that looked like a new model, not one from the previous year. Priced at $730 and weighing 2,850 pounds, the Fordor drew a total of 28,940 orders, with all bodies built by Ford. The Standard Fordor was designated the Type 73-A, while the Deluxe model was the 73-B.

Expanding the Standard series was the new Standard Station Wagon, which used the same body as the Deluxe version, but differed only in the front sheet metal. Priced at $840, the 3,080-pound car was by far the most expensive in the Standard series. Yet it gave budget-minded wagon buyers a chance to get into the car for $80 less than they would have paid for the Deluxe model. And, 3,277 buyer took advantage of this, resulting in total wagon sales of 9,432 which was a record for this body style. Favored by tradesmen, especially the numerous house painters of this era, the wagon provided a good working vehicle that could easily be converted to passenger car status for weekend use. The wagon was the Type 79-A in Standard form, 79-B in Deluxe.

Although snowmobile conversions were not all that unusual in the 1920s, improved road and plowing conditions across the northern states resulted in a rapidly decreasing need for such vehicles. Still, the Michigan State Police probably felt such a unit might be necessary, especially to act as an emergency ambulance in a snow-bound rural area. It is not known if this was the only such conversion or one of a small fleet produced by the police or state garages. The conversion entailed removal of all four fenders and the addition of skis to the front axles. Model A wheels were used on the rear, together with a set of idler wheels for the track. The skis were set above the front tire line, so that on hard surfaces the tires would touch the ground first. Presumably, the advent of spring would cause this vehicle to revert to its normal station wagon appearance.

Although 4-wheel drive vehicles are commonplace today, they were quite a novelty in the 1930s. Such conversions usually involved off-road trucks, yet a number of 4-wheel drive units were placed under station wagons and even some sedans. In the Ford line, the Marmon-Herrington Co. of Indianapolis was the leading converter, advertising its station wagon and sedan products as All-Wheel-Drive Ford Commercial Cars. When sold under this guise, all Ford emblems were removed and replaced with "M-H" emblems. Designed for off-road field crews, such as surveyors, M-H found an excellent market with the newly organized Arabian-American Oil Co. ARAMCO purchased a large fleet of these wagons for seismographic work in the Middle Eastern deserts. In order to fit the 4-wheel drive components under the standard chassis, the vehicle had to be raised several inches from its normal road clearance, as can be seen in this view of the M-H Standard Wagon.

Ford had dropped its Coupe-Pickup idea after only one or two years on the market (depending on which records are used) but that didn't mean that the idea had died. Other aftermarket companies, probably seeing the success that Chevrolet had with this style, and mindful of Ford's dismal experience, introduced their own conversion kits. One such manufacturer was American Body & Equipment Co. of Dallas, Texas, which offered this unit made of metal-covered oak. When installed, it offered a cargo area 63.5 inches long by 34 inches wide by 12 inches deep. The new and much larger trunk deck on the redesigned coupes made this box more practical than the ones on previous models. This view also gives a good look at the new rear design of the coupes, and the nicely rounded rear fenders that were used on all models.

Once again, the Sedan Delivery, Type 78, was available only in the Standard series trim. Briggs continued to build the bodies for these nice little trucks, and turned out 2,809, all base priced at $685 with the 85 horse engine. As was the case with all Standard models, dual windshield wipers were used. Unlike other light commercial vehicles, the Sedan Delivery continued to use the old style rear fenders from the 1937 issue. All other light trucks used tear-drop fenders styled similar to those on the current passenger cars. The spare tire now lived inside only, as the exterior hanger on the rear door was no longer available.

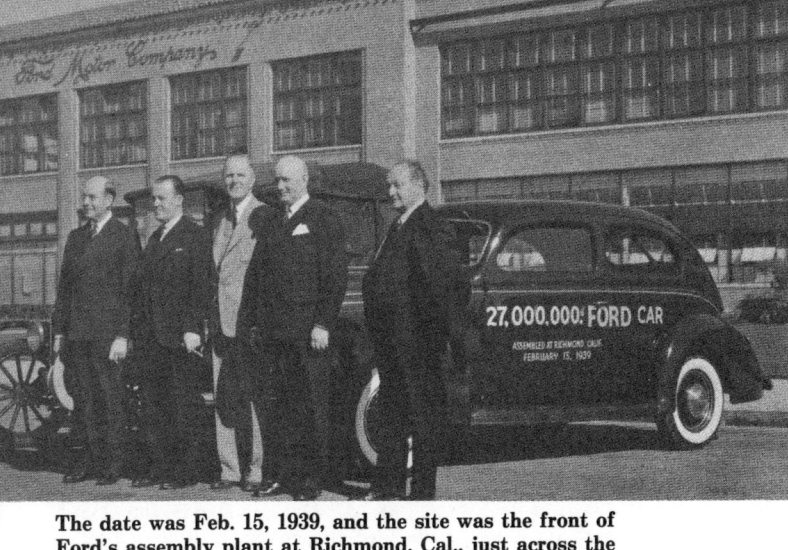

The date was Feb. 15, 1939, and the site was the front of Ford's assembly plant at Richmond, Cal., just across the bay from San Francisco. The event was the production of the 27-millionth Ford car, scheduled to occur on the West Coast this time rather than in Dearborn. Honoring the event were several of the top management from the company and the branch, standing rather stiffly in front of both a brass-era Model T and the honored Deluxe Tudor. From here the car was driven to San Francisco's Golden Gate Exposition, from where it began a coast-to-coast and return promotional trip.

Appearing at the New York World's Fair for promotional display was part of the schedule of the 27-millionth Ford. Driven from the Golden Gate Exposition in San Francisco, the car appeared at select dealerships enroute, and collected special honorary license plates in most of the states that it drove through. After a stay at the New York fair, it returned to California over a different route, again repeating its one and two day stops at selected dealers, and collecting even more license plates on the back swing. Upon reaching California, it once again went on display at the Exposition.

Another one of the many unusual automobile-based rail cars appeared in 1939, this one the work of the shops of the Kansas City Southern Railway. A relatively simple conversion, the Deluxe Fordor was equipped with Hy-Rail wheels manufactured by Fairmont Railway Motors of Fairmont, Minn. The custom wheels consisted of flanges behind the tires to keep the car on the rails. The narrow tires were mounted on demountable rims, and were for traction on the rails only, as the car was not easily converted to street driving. The bars jutting out from under the running board were to allow a relatively large crew to insert iron rods and physically lift the car and turn it around in places where no turntable or "Y" was available.

The Shop of Siebert of Toledo was now building all of its professional cars exclusively on Ford chassis. Except for the changing front sheet metal, the line continued to resemble those variations shown in earlier chapters, and continued to use extended sedan or Sedan Delivery bodies as the base. One of Siebert's later offerings, called the Aristocrat Service Car, utilized the Sedan Delivery. The center section between the B and C-pillar was fabricated in Siebert's own shops. The quarter panel was decorated with a carved relief, and the rear side doors were covered with heavy drapes. Designed primarily as a service car to move needed funeral equipment from one location to another, the vehicle could also be used as a hearse when necessary. Siebert continued to market its products through National Hearse & Ambulance Co. of Toledo, but unlike other manufacturers, it used the Ford name on the chassis, and did not switch emblems to "Siebert."

Siebert wasn't the only professional car builder to avail itself of the Ford chassis. This unusual limousine hearse was turned out by the J.C. Little Co. of Ontario, using a Deluxe Tudor as its base. Little built the door section between the B and C-pillars, and converted the tonneau area into casket-carrying capabilities. Otherwise, no modifications were made to the car except to add aftermarket sealed beam headlights to the fenders. Once sealed beams were introduced on the 1940 Fords, several aftermarket firms began to produce conversion kits for the 1939 models also. This vehicle apparently could be loaded either through the standard trunk deck opening, or from either of the side doors.

Once again Ford carried over its "Teardrop" styling, this time for the final year. Yet some very handsome restyling at the hands of Eugene Gregorie, probably assisted by Edsel Ford himself, gave the cars a refreshingly new look. Many have described this model as the best looking of the traditional Ford design.

In addition to its new appearance, two main items highlighted Ford's brag list this year. These were the new sealed beam headlights and a new column-mounted shift lever. The headlights were prominently mounted in large chromed bezels on the Deluxe fenders, but painted in body color on the Standards. In both cases, the parking lights lived behind small lenses set into the upper edge of the bezels.

A totally new innovation for Ford was the column-mounted shift lever. Gone forever was the old floor mounted shift. The new shifter used the same "H" pattern as found on the former floor shift, but for some reason this transposition proved to be almost incomprehensible to many drivers, and a traumatic irritant to many others. It is pretty certain that most readers of this book who are over 60 years of age will have some memories of a friend or relatively hopelessly grouping around the center of the floor for a shift lever that was no longer there. Then, finally remembering the column location, slamming the car into some unlikely gear in a move best described as one of total frustration.

Despite the fact that styling was carried over from the previous year, this was the first time that all bodies were produced within Ford's own confines. True, the new convertible body was produced in Lincoln's plant, and the station wagon bodies still came from Iron Mountain, but both of these facilities were under Fords ownership. Thus, for the first time, no outside body builders were supplying completed units to Ford, although several were still manufacturing components.

Besides the sealed beam headlights, there were several other styling innovations. Foremost among these, of course, were the new grilles that decked both the Deluxe and Standard models. Once again there was a distinct difference between the two series, with the Deluxe versions having a totally new face while the Standard models used a reworking of the previous year's styling. However, this time Standard fronts were more akin to the new truck grilles than to the previous Deluxe styles.

Also new on the bodies was an innovation that Chrysler had installed in 1934—vent windows. Now all Ford owners could also crack the vent for improved ventilation in cold or inclement weather, plus smokers now had a convenient self-cleaning ash tray right at the leading edge of the door. Balancing the vent pane concept was the fact that closed car windshields no longer could be opened as in the past. With all windshields being set firmly in place, the wipers moved down from their header location to new places under the cowl, in the same locations as they had been all along on the wagons and convertibles.

Inside the cars was a totally new dash, with distinct differences between the Deluxe and Standard versions. The Deluxe models were finished in 2-tone maroon and sand, and fitted with Deluxe-faced instruments, while the Standard version had a brown panel with totally different gauge faces. Also, the steering wheel and control knobs varied between the two series. Standard buyers had their choice of mohair or broadcloth interiors, while Deluxe customers had choices of the same two materials but in Deluxe versions. Although this would be the final year for wide exterior styling differences between Standard and Deluxe cars, the future would show a definite continuation of interior variations between the series.

In all, the sales listing contained 12 body styles, of which seven fell into the Deluxe realm and five into the Standard. Of these styles, four were coupes, all using the same basic body shell. But now there were Standard and Deluxe 3-passenger Coupes, and Standard and Deluxe 5-passenger Business Coupes. The latter contained a split pull-down front seat back and two small jump seats in the area behind the front seat. On the regular Coupe, this area was occupied by a large parcel shelf above and a covered luggage area underneath. Although a return was made to the 1938 Club Coupe concept, the new version was not nearly as spacious in the rear as was the previous model, and for a full-size person, the jump seats were downright uncomfortable.

Also new this year was a Deluxe version of the Sedan Delivery. Sporting a totally new body built in Ford's own shops, the pretty little truck was not available in Standard trim, but only with all Deluxe fittings. The only variation from this was in the fact that it could be ordered with the 60 horse engine, while no other Deluxe models had this dubious distinction. Also, on its wheels, the stainless steel beauty rings were an added-cost option, whereas they were part of the Deluxe package on all other models.

The one car body that was totally new this year was the Convertible Coupe. With both the Convertible Sedan and the old rumble seat coupe versions gone, the new 5-passenger Convertible Coupe was Ford's only open car. Of big new to rag top lovers was Ford's first automatic top which appeared on this model. The unit used two vacuum cylinders, one on each side of the rear seat, connected to the engine manifold. When raising or lowering the top, vacuum from the manifold caused the cylinders to actuate either up or down. Obviously, the engine had to be running when the top was activated—and, the faster the better, especially after the mechanism got older and leaks developed.

As was the case with the 1938 Club Convertible Coupe, the new style used a rather long top with blank quarters, which was very attractive from a styling standpoint, but provided poor visibility to the rear seat passengers. As in previous open models, standard upholstery was in genuine beige leather, but for the first time, buyers had a choice, and could order an interior in red genuine leather.

Ford's only totally new body this year, not counting the Sedan Delivery, was the Convertible Coupe, Type 66. The car featured a 5-passenger body, built at the Lincoln plant. Also totally new for the year was Ford's first automatic top. This vacuum operated unit consisted of two large cylinders flanking the rear seat, with arms extending to the redesigned top irons. Manifold vacuum would activate the cylinders causing the top to raise or lower. The engine had to be running to work the system, and as leaks developed with age or usage, the engine sometimes had to be running quite fast to create enough vacuum to move the pistons. Priced at $850, the 2,956-pound convertible had an impressive sales of 23,704 units.

The new rear seats within the body of the Convertible Coupe meant that the rear roofline had to be extended . When the top was raised, the large blank canvas panels created a very attractive style, but provided rather poor visibility for rear seat passengers. All convertibles were now finished in genuine leather only, with no cloth interiors being available. However, new for the year was a choice of leathers, with either natural beige or bright red being available. Gone for good was the rumble seat concept formerly found on this model. Ford would not have another rumble seat until an aftermarket firm began producing "bird nests" for the first generation Thunderbirds.

Probably one of Ford's all-time best looking styles was the 1940 5-window Coupe, which appeared in four different variations. This is the 3-passenger style, Type 77-B, which offered vast trunk space in the rear, a substantial package shelf behind the front seat, and an enclosed and partially hidden luggage area under the package shelf. The sleek styling of these coupe bodies made them a favorite with dirt track stock car racers of the 1940s and 50s, and led to their scarcity today. When new, this model sold for $721 and attracted 27,919 orders. In base form, the car weighed 2,791 pounds.

1940

For the first time in years, some rather significant changes were made to the chassis and running gear. One of the more important of the collection of small changes was in the wheel design, which affected all passenger car and light truck models. The new wheels used a 5.5-inch bolt circle and smaller hub caps, though tires continued to be 6.00x16 on all cars except those few Standard models with the 60 horse engine. Here 5.50x16 tires were again used. Also, the front suspension of all models was revised slightly, as was the length of the springs. All models now used the same 9-inch semi-centrifugal clutch, regardless of engine. Apparently so few 60 horse blocks were sold that it was felt infeasible to continue the smaller clutch for the little block. Also, Standard models now used many of the same components that previously had been reserved for the Deluxe cars only. These included the 2-brush generator with voltage regulator, a crankshaft-mounted fan, and lower but wider radiator.

In the world of production figures, once again only the two Tudor styles broke the 100,000 mark. The Deluxe Tudor hit a very presentable 171,368, while the Standard version saw 150,933 builds. Once again, the only model to come close to these figures was the Deluxe Fordor, of which 91,756 were built. No models except the Station Wagons were under the 10,000 figure, but here a total of 13,199 bodies were built, divided between 8,730 Deluxe and 4,469 Standards.

One of Ford's new styles for the year has always caused confusion because of its name. Engineers redesigned the 5-window Coupe interior so that two small folding seats could be located behind the driver's seat in what was the storage area on the 3-passenger model. Similar to the older Club Coupe in concept, the rear area however was far more cramped than on the earlier version, and was downright uncomfortable for tall people. Public acceptance was relatively good and 20,183 were sold at a base price of $745. Public terminology for this car usually was "Opera Coupe." However, for some odd reason, Ford called it the Business Coupe, Type 67-B. But, since "Business Coupe" usually referred to a 3-passenger car, such as Ford's Type 77-B, the reference to this model as a Business Coupe often causes confusion as to which car is actually being discussed. The same confusion holds true in the Standard series, where both models also appeared, with the true "business" version being referred to simply as the 5-window Coupe, and the "opera" style being designated the Business Coupe.

By far Ford's most popular car was the Deluxe Tudor, of which a total of 171,368 were built. Priced at $765, and weighing 2,927 pounds, the very popular family-oriented car offered both style and performance at a relatively low price. New on all two and 4-door sedans this year was the fitted windshield. Which would no longer open. This allowed the wipers to be moved from the header bar to under the cowl, as had been the location of wipers on all open cars and wagons. Also new were the front vent panes, which provided excellent ventilation in all weather. Oddly, Chevrolet picked up these vent panes in 1933, and Chrysler added them in 1934, but Ford waited another half-dozen years before incorporating them onto their closed cars.

The flagship of the Ford line poses with a flagship of American Airlines. In the days when aircraft bore names just as ships still do, this DC-3 was christened the Flagship Louisville. Selling for $810, the 2,966-pound Fordor drew 91,756 orders, thus becoming the third most popular model on Ford's list, after the two Tudors. On April 8, a car similar to this left the lines at Edgewater, N.J., and was designated the 28-millionth Ford. As was the case with the 27-millionth model, this car was also sent on a transcontinental trip, stopping at selected dealerships and collecting license plates as it made its way across the country and back.

Almost twice as popular in Deluxe form as in Standard version was the Station Wagon. Of the 13,199 wagons built this year, 8,730 went on Deluxe chassis. Priced at $950 and weighing 3,262 pounds, this was both Ford's most expensive and heaviest car of the year. All bodies were built at the Ford plant at Iron Mountain, Mich. Roll-up windows were used in the front doors, but rear doors and quarters still used sliding glass panes. In addition to the exterior differences and the dash board, a major improvement in the Deluxe wagon models was the use of tan genuine leather for the seats as opposed to the artificial leather seats used in the Standard wagon. Once again on these models, the spare moved to the outside of the tailgate, where it lived inside of a special metal covering. Once more, Ford had an exterior spare.

In an unusual move, the totally new Sedan Delivery became part of the Deluxe line, rather than being in the Standard series where one would expect to find a delivery vehicle. Designated the Type 78, the new body was both longer and wider, offering 76.5 by 52 inches of cargo floor space. Ford also took over production of this body, which for years had been a Briggs staple. Styling was very smooth and appealing, being marred only by the protruding gas filler which led to the 17-gallon tank beneath the floor. A total of 4,886 were built. Finally, the spare tire moved away from the right cargo wall. It was now located in a special compartment under the floor, just ahead of the rear or cargo door. This year only a driver's seat was included. It was upholstered in black imitation leather. A matching passenger's seat had to be purchased as an accessory. This well restored model wears dealer-issue fog lights and rearview mirrors and bumper wing tips. In base form, it cost $690 and weighed 2,638 pounds with the 60 horse engine.

As was the case with the Deluxe Coupes, the 3-passenger Standard model was called a 5-window Coupe while the 5-passenger version was called the Business Coupe. Most popular of all four coupe variations was the 3-passenger Type 77-A, which drew 33,693 orders. At $660 it was Ford's least expensive car, and many of these orders probably were from fleet customers. At 2,763 pounds, it was also Ford's lightest car of the year. The cowl-mounted antenna would indicate that this car probably has an aftermarket Motorola radio rather than a Ford unit. The Ford radios had their antennas mounted on the header, just above the windshield divider. Wide whites were coming into popularity in this era, but it is doubtful if too many were installed on Standard Coupes.

The small face peering out of the quarter window identifies this car as the Standard Business Coupe, Type 67-A. Equipped with two small and very uncomfortable folding seats in the area behind the front seat, this model and its Deluxe counterpart represented Ford's newest coupe design. Least popular of all four coupe variations, the Standard Business Coupe drew only 16,785 orders. Priced at $680, it weighed 2,801 pounds. All Standard models this year offered buyers a choice of broadcloth or mohair upholstery. This was the last year for the 60 horse small V-8. Though it was optional in any Standard model, very few were ordered.

Far less popular in Standard form than in Deluxe was the Fordor. Designated the Type 73-A, the car drew only 25,545 orders, which was slightly more than one-quarter that of the Deluxe Type 73-B. In plain trim, it cost $750 and weighed 2,936 pounds. Regardless of body color, Standard models were fitted with black wheels, unless colored ones were ordered at extra cost. Beginning on May 3, 2-tone color combinations were available on both Standard and Deluxe models at extra cost. These featured a body and hood in one shade, with the fenders in a compatible hue. However, such combinations were definitely unpopular and virtually never seen.

Ford's second most popular car, and the only other model to record over 100,000 sales was the Standard Tudor, Type 70-A. It drew 150,933 orders, with a base price of $700 even. Note that the front end sheet metal used on the Standard models is a variation of the Deluxe styling of 1939. Yet it really looks more akin the grille styling used on this year's Ford light trucks. This would be the last year that there would be substantial appearance differences between the Deluxe and Standard series. Beginning in 1941, Ford would revert to the established practice of having the different series vary only in the detail of upholstery and appointments. In true form, this Tudor should have had painted headlight bezels rather than the chromed units shown here. The chromed variety was strictly for the Deluxe models, though any Standard owner who wanted to pay the price, could have switched the bezels quite easily.

Ford's least popular style passenger car was the Standard Station Wagon, Type 79-A. Only 4,4690 were turned out in this form, all bearing a base price of $875. The Standard versions used the same body as did the Deluxe, but of course, used Standard front sheet metal, and could have been equipped with the small V-8 had anybody wanted the underpowered little block. Unlike the Deluxe versions which used brown genuine leather on its seats, the Standard model seats were covered in artificial leather of a medium brown shade. As before, both the rear and center seats could be removed with relative ease, thus making these wagons fairly popular with those tradesmen who could afford them.

One would expect most fleet car sales to be of the Standard variety, and most police car sales to be of the Fordor model. Yet the city of Detroit did just the opposite on both counts. When it restocked part of its police fleet, it went with the Deluxe series and the Tudor models. Twin spotlights and siren with red flasher give this car quite an official look, while the big V-8 probably gave it all the speed it needed within city limits. Although the engine was unchanged from previous 85 horsepower design, many of this year's Ford catalogs refer to it as a 90 horse block, not 85. Still, no evidence could be found to substantiate this increase.

The shop of Siebert of Toledo continued to offer its line of Ford-based professional cars, blending into the new Sedan Delivery style with ease. Still marketed through National Hearse & Ambulance Co. of Toledo, the top line cars were considered to be in Siebert's Aristocrat Series. These included the Funeral Coach seen here, and both ambulance and service car variations using the Deluxe front end. It also appears that Siebert built a few similar vehicles using Mercury chassis this year.

The budget end of the Siebert line was filled by bodies utilizing the Standard chassis. However, the large dummy landau bars and functional coach lights on this Service Car helped to offset the stark appearance usually associated with low-cost funeral vehicles. Stainless steel belt line and running board trim added a bright touch also, as did the cast owner's name on the door—in this case, an A.A. Collins. Rather than calling this a service car, Siebert refereed to it as a "general purpose car," contending that it could be used for both service work and also double as a first-line hearse when needed.

1941

A totally new design and a totally new engine were spread out before the public this year. Gone was the "triangular" or "teardrop" styling that had been in effect since 1937. Replacing it was a new "square box" school of design that would continue until the "slab side" appearance arrived in 1949.

Gone too were the major appearance differences between Special or Standard and Deluxe cars. Now only trim levels would determine the series. Gone too was the never appreciated and always underpowered 60 horsepower small V-8. And, of all things, replacing it was the first 6-cylinder engine since the Model K. Also gone was the old chassis of 112-inch wheelbase, this being replaced by a similar but new chassis of 114 inches, complete with a revised suspension system. And, though a late comer in the field of hydraulic brakes, Ford played catch-up with a vengeance and now offered the largest brakes of any low priced car.

The totally new bodies offered squared-off front and rear fenders, slightly rounded but still rectangular body styling, and a sharply sloping back without the bustle on the Tudor and Fordor models. The grille consisted of a full-length centerpiece of vertical chrome bars, flanked by two air-scoop grilles of matching vertical bars, chromed on the fancy models, and painted on the plain. The headlamps were mounted relatively far out on the massive front fenders and were topped by nicely styled independent parking lights. For this year only, the fenders themselves were stamped in two pieces, of upper and lower sections.

Within the body, passengers found seven inches of extra hip room, accomplished by widening the body beyond the normal inside fender line. The increased width drastically reduced the space allowed for the running board, and only a thin vestige of grooved rubber running between the fender edges gave hint that there was any running board at all.

Gone were the old Standard and Deluxe faces, being replaced by three series containing a total of 15 model varieties. Of these, seven styles occurred in the new Super Deluxe range, five were in the Deluxe series, and three were in the Special series, which was the new low-buck line for stripped models with the new 6-cylinder engine.

All bodies were new this year, but all reflected previous styling concepts of Coupe, Tudor, Fordor, Convertible, and Station Wagon. The only exception to this was the new Sedan Coupe, a 6-passenger close-coupled model similar in concept to the Club coupe of 1938. It was available only as a Super Deluxe. In the regular coupe field, the 3-passenger models still offered vast luggage space, while the 4-passenger variety continued the concept of placing a long folding seat behind the main seat of the 3-passenger model.

All bodies except the Convertible Coupe and the Station Wagon were built at Ford's plant. The convertible continued to be constructed at the near-by Lincoln plant, while the wagon continued to come from Ford's facility at Iron Mountain. This year all basic body shells were shared with the relatively new Mercury, which facilitated body production by having one less line to build.

Although there were no marked sheet metal differences between the Super Deluxe and the lower series Fords, there still were quick visual differences. The Super Deluxe range had all three grille sections of cast chrome, and the wheels were painted in body color. Also, after January, Super Deluxe cars had a stainless bright molding between the fender halves. The Deluxe models had only the center grille section chromed, while the flanking sections were painted body color and the wheels were black, regardless of the body hue. The three Special or Standard models came only in black, or light or dark gray, had only a single taillight, and reverted back to the single windshield wiper. As mentioned, these cars were equipped only with the 6-cylinder engine, while in the other two series, the V-8 was standard while the Six was a $15 delete option.

The new six was an historic occasion for Ford, in that Henry had resisted the 6-cylinder engineering concept since the Model K was built. Insofar as originality went, the new Six had none. It was a standard L-head configuration, of 3.3x4.4 inch bore and stroke, displacing 224.8 cubic inches and developing 90 horsepower at 3300 rpm. It compared closely to a contemporary Continental (not Lincoln Continental) engine of just about the same size and power. The Ford version consisted of a cast iron block and head, and contained a cast iron crankshaft with a viscous-type vibration damper, running in four main bearings. A Ford carburetor was used.

In order not to have the new engine overrun the V-8 in power, the old standard was slightly modified to produce the 90 horsepower that it had been rated for in 1934/35. The rating, at 3800 rpm, was made by a slight increase in compression ratio and carburetor adjustment. The engine retained its bore and stroke of 3-1/16x3.75 inches and its displacement of 221 cubic inches, and thus was actually a bit smaller in volume than was the new Six.

Acceptance of the new styled Ford was very good, and calendar year production moved up to 600,814 units. As in years past, only the Tudor models cracked the 100,000 mark, with the Super Deluxe Tudor recording 185,788 sales, while the Deluxe version recorded 177,018. Only the Super Deluxe Fordor came close to these sales, with 88,053 being registered. Also of note was the production of the 29-millionth Ford on April 29. Built at the River Rouge plant, it was a Super Deluxe Station Wagon, which Edsel Ford immediately donated to the American Red Cross.

Of minor interest is the fact that the Special models were not shown at Ford's introductory party at Dearborn in September, 1940. Only the Super Deluxe and the Deluxe models were available and only with the V-8

1941

engine. The Six wasn't even mentioned, but was used as a secondary headline grabber later in the year, after its production start-up on Nov. 20.

Of more interest nationwide was Ford's new activities in the "defense" field. With Europe fully engaged in World War II and Japan busy invading China and whatever islands it could reach, most major sectors of American industry were turning at least part of their attention to producing military items. Ford was no exception, and was in the process of breaking ground for a giant aircraft plant to be built at Ypsilanti, Mich. Later to be known as the Willow Run Plant, this facility became famous for producing 8,685 B-24 Liberator bombers. Ford also received a contract this year for its first 1,500 4-wheel drive reconnaissance cars, later to be known as Jeeps, and 300 field kitchens to be built on its modified 1-ton truck chassis. Interestingly, Ford could not fit production of the Jeep bodies into its plants, and thus these were contracted out to the former Auburn Automobile Co., which had until the mid-1930s, been part of the famous Auburn-Cord-Duesenberg complex.

Of lasting importance to American agriculture overall was Henry Ford's experimenting with soybeans, which had begun in the late 1920s. Now, with certain types of oils being curtailed by the war, the importance of soybean oil was being recognized. Thus, the oil was being produced in ever increasing quantities by both Ford's own soybean processing plant, and other such upstart factories. Ford's efforts in the soybean area caused so much interest that when a new experimental plastic car was shown at Dearborn in August, the press assumed it was made of a type of soybean fiber resin. Actually, the strange little car was made of a type of fibrous formaldehyde plastic, also produced in Ford's own factory. Unveiled on Aug. 13, 1941, the car was heralded as a look into the future, when low cost plastics could be used to turn out virtually damage-proof cars for about $400. The irony was that steel cost Ford about eight or nine cents a pound, while the plastic used on the 2,300-pound experimental car cost well over $1 per pound. Still, the car is historically interesting in that it marked the first time that a running vehicle had its entire skin made of a plastic material—but not of soybeans.

New for the year and available only in the Super Deluxe series was the Sedan coupe, Type 72, which Ford rated as a 6-passenger car. However nice and practical its styling, a full compliment of six people would have put quite a strain on interior dimensions. Priced at $850, the car achieved 45,977 sales. Also available in the Super Deluxe range were two other coupe models looking quite similar to the version shown in the Deluxe section. These were the 3-passenger Type 77-B, which cost $775 and drew 22,878 orders, and the 4-passenger Type 67-B, which cost $800 and saw production of 10,796. These two latter models differed only in interior layout, with the 4-passenger model having a single pull-down seat behind the front seat, while the 3-passenger version occupied this area with luggage space. Neither coupe offered operating rear quarter windows, while on the Sedan Coupe these windows would swing outward.

Available only in Super Deluxe Style was the new Convertible coupe, Type 76. The car shared the distinction with the Station Wagon of having the only body not built within Ford's own plants. In this case, the body was sourced from the nearby Lincoln facility. Weighing 3,187 pounds and costing $950, the convertible enjoyed excellent sales this year, with 30,240 being produced. Interiors were done in natural leather, as in past years. However, this year buyers had a choice of leather color to match the exterior, with both red and tan being carried over from 1940, and blue natural leather being added to the list. Available, but not popular were 2-tone paint combinations with the body in light gray, and the fenders, wheels, and door flares in either dark gray, green, maroon, or blue.

As before, the Convertible Coupe did not use rear quarter windows, but had a "caravan" type of top with large blank quarters. This certainly made an appealing looking car when the top was raised, but did little for rear seat passenger visibility, nor did it help when backing into a tight parking space. The large chrome wheel covers were a moderately popular accessory this year, as were the fender skirts which cost $12.50 per set. Buyers had a choice of top colors this year, either a black canvas as shown here, or the standard taupe. New for this model were twin electric motors to operate the top mechanism. These replaced the year-old vacuum system, and marked a major improvement, in that the engine did not need to be running to operate the top, and vacuum leaks did not develop in the lines, making the top difficult to operate.

Most popular of all Fords this year was the Super Deluxe Tudor, which recorded a total of 185,788 sales. Shown here is an early model, without the stainless molding between the upper and lower fender halves. This is the only time that Ford used 2-piece fenders of this type. Selling for $820 and weighing 3,110 pounds, the Super Deluxe Tudor continued to provide young families with a practical yet attractive car in a moderate price range. The header mounted antenna indicates that a Ford radio was installed on this model, while the white wall tires add a nice touch. The front bumper guards, shown on virtually all models, were actually a $3.50 accessory.

The 29-millionth Ford was built on April 29 of this year. Produced at Dearborn, it was this Super Deluxe Station Wagon. In a show of patriotism, Edsel Ford donated the car to a local chapter of the American Red Cross, which was already active in civil defense preparations. As before, all station wagon bodies were built at the Iron Mountain plant in northern Michigan. Ford's heaviest and most expensive passenger vehicle, the Station Wagon in Super Deluxe trim weighed 3,419 pounds and cost $1,015, thus being the first V-8 to break the $1,000 barrier. Despite its price tag, it was more popular than the Deluxe version, and as a result, 9,485 were sold. Designated the Type 79-B, the car used beige/brown genuine leather seats. The totally redesigned body now featured rear door hinges rather than the former piano hinge, but still used sliding glass windows in the rear doors and the rear quarters. Also new were the flared door sills. The interior cargo space now measured 82.5 inches long by 54 inches wide by 46 inches high when the center and rear seats were removed. This special model, possibly converted for ambulance work, has been fitted with stationary panels in the rear doors and quarters.

Well up in sales, though not breaking the 100,000 mark was the Super Deluxe Fordor, which recorded 88,053 builds. Priced at $860 and weighing 3,146 pounds, the car was designated the Type 73-B. This year, all Super Deluxe models were upholstered in either of two exclusive materials —a taupe chevron-pattern mohair, or a combination bedford and broadcloth weave. Little known is the fact that an all-leather interior could still be ordered at extra cost. In addition to exclusive upholstery materials, the Super Deluxe models had their own instrument panel done in what was called a "Kelobra Grain" pattern. Another difference, not often noted, between the Super Deluxe models and the lower priced series was in the bumper design, with the Super Deluxe cars having a much heavier looking, rigid bumper, while the other series used plain bumpers.

Replacing the old Standard Series was the new Deluxe Series, which formed a middle ground between the high-trim Super Deluxe and the low-buck Specials. All bodies were basically the same, but varied only in trim level. As mentioned in the Super Deluxe caption for the Sedan Coupe, the Deluxe series carried both the 3-passenger 5-window Coupe, Type 77-A, and the 4-passenger version, Type 67-A. Except for trim level, both were identical to the Super Deluxe offerings. Only a $20 price separated the two Deluxe models, the 3-seat version being $730, while the jump-seat type cost $750. However, there was a big difference in production, with the 3-passenger version drawing 33,598 sales, while the auxiliary seat variety saw only 12,844 leave the showrooms. The 6-passenger Sedan Coupe was not available in the Deluxe series.

As could be expected, Ford's second most popular car was the Deluxe Tudor, Type 70-A, which saw sales of 177,018. This and its Super Deluxe version were the only two models to break the 100,000 sales mark. Priced at $775, the car weighed 3,095 pounds. Unlike the Super Deluxe models, which received stainless steel welting between the fender halves in January, the Deluxe series kept the plain fender appearance. Also, the two flanking grille sections were painted in body color, while the wheels were black, regardless of the body color. Buyers who desired the new 6-cylinder engine in the Deluxe series received a $15 discount from the stated V-8 price. The same option was available in the Super Deluxe range, but was seldom utilized.

Far less popular in Deluxe trim than in the Super Deluxe range was the Fordor Sedan. In the middle bracket, the car sold only 25,928 units, all base priced at $815 and weighing 3,121 pounds. This model is shown wearing the stainless wheel rings, which were standard on the Super Deluxe models, but were optional on the Deluxe cars. All cars in this series were upholstered in their own exclusive material. These were either a patterned mohair in gray taupe, or a striped tan broadcloth. Dashboards in this and the Special series were finished in an ebony grain design.

Showing off its new body is the Deluxe Station Wagon, Type 79-A. Identical to the body used on the Super Deluxe version, the car varied only in its use of artificial leather seats, and its dash trim. On the exterior, painted lower grilles, plain bumpers, black wheels, and lack of bright fender separators quickly identified the Deluxe series. In this form, the wagon was priced at $965, weighed 3,412 pounds, and drew 6,116 orders. The spare tire continued to be mounted on the lower half of the tailgate, and was supplied with its own special metal covering.

Not appearing until December was Ford's new low-buck line, the Special series. Designed primarily as an economy line to house the new 6-cylinder engine, the cars in this series were totally devoid of most trim items, even to the point of having only one taillight on the right side only, and just one windshield wiper for the driver. The lowest priced Ford this year, naturally, was the Special Coupe, available only in 3-passenger form, and not in an auxiliary seat variation. Selling for $706 and weighing 2,878 pounds, it drew 9,823 orders, probably many for fleet sales. It was designated the Type 77-C.

The only model in the Special series to achieve any popularity was the Tudor Sedan, Type 70-C, which drew 27,189 orders. Powered with the 6-cylinder engine, the car cost $735 and weighed 2,983 pounds. Special models were available only in black, light gray or dark gray. Upholstery was in a boucle cloth, with an imitation leather interior being available at extra cost, probably for taxi work, on the 4-door models. The wheel rims shown in this catalog drawing would have been extra cost items, but the plain bumper, chromed central grille, and bright hub caps were the car's own claim to being pretty.

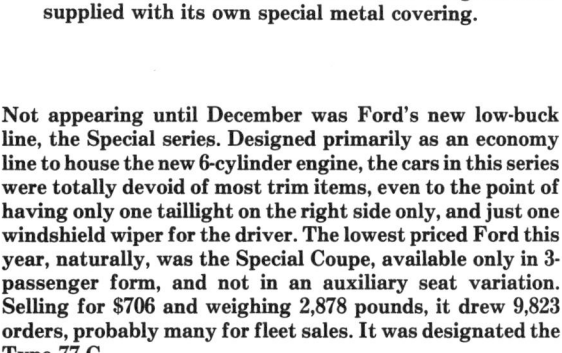
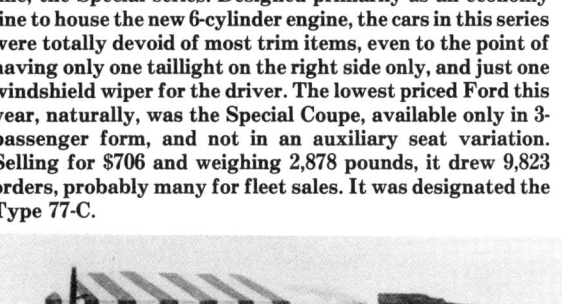

Despite some rather nice purchases by various arms of the U.S. military, production of the Special Fordor Sedan, Type 73-C, reached only 3,838. Sprayed over with an olive drab paint job, this version has even managed to hide what little chrome trim it once had. Snapped up by some army headquarters company, it appears to be in totally stock form except that its normal parking lights have been replaced by military black-out lamps. It is interesting to note that Fords were still supplied with a crank hole in the grille, and a crank was part of the tool kit. Yet, it is doubtful if too many drivers were still able to spin the engine by hand.

1941

A real unusual move this year involved the Sedan delivery. Although it would revert back to passenger car styling in 1942, this year it held onto the old 1940 design, but with a revised grille similar to that used on the rest of the commercial line. Designated the Type 78, the truck was now totally akin to the Pickup and 1/2-ton Panel in appearance, and as a result, had no real connection to the passenger car line. Sales were 4,846 or 6,881, depending upon which list is used, putting orders roughly in the neighborhood of 1940 figures. Did this indicate that buyers of Sedan Deliveries really didn't worry that much about styling, just as long as the vehicle looked presentable? On paper at least, the Sedan Delivery was considered part of the Deluxe series, and carried the identification "Ford Deluxe" on the hood panel just ahead of the cowl. It cost $730 and weighed 2,763 pounds as a V-8, or $710 and 2,593 with the 4-cylinder tractor engine, which was an odd option for this model.

In August, 1941, about 9 months after Henry's trunk banging spree, the company introduced its all-plastic car. Shown here with Lowell Overley, the designer, the car consisted of a multitude of plastic panels set onto a light tubular steel frame, and powered by the old 60 horse V-8. Because Ford was heavily engaged in experimentation with and manufacturing of soybean related products, the car is often erroneously referred to as being made of soybean derivatives. Actually, the panels were of a phenol-formaldehyde plastic strengthened by the addition of straw and hemp. Even the windows were of plexiglass rather than plate glass. Although early promotion predicted the car could be sold for under $400, company sources showed that the relatively new plastic material would cost over $1 per pound for the 2,300-pound car, as opposed to eight or nine cents a pound raw material cost for steel. Still, the little experimental vehicle was the first American automobile to have a body made completely of plastic, which back in the early 1940s was still a very novel material.

One of the more dramatic action photos of Henry Ford shows the old man swinging an ax full force at the trunk of a new Fordor. No, Henry wasn't mad at the car. He was demonstrating for the press a new plastic material with which the Ford company was experimenting. And what better way to show the strength than to make a virtually damage-proof trunk deck out of the material. Despite the publicity gained from the photo, such trunk decks never materialized on production models. It proved far too difficult to bind the metal latches and hinges with the plastic, and though dent resistant at first, the material tended to become quite brittle after a period of time.

Just because Ford came up with a totally new style was no reason for railroads to stop using them as inspection and official cars. But finally a way had to be found to make them easily convertible from rail to road use. Evans Products of Plymouth, Mich., designed these retractable guide wheels which could be lowered to the rail level when the car was to run on tracks. The wheels supported no weight, but simply held the vehicle on the rails. When road use was necessary, the iron wheels were simply raised to bumper level, and the car driven away in a normal manner. The company converted both Fordor Sedans and Station Wagons to this use, reworking the grille so that the front guide wheels could fit between the grille and bumper. In addition to adding the wheels, Evans also strengthened the suspension and the frame to help compensate for the rigors of railroad use. This particular wagon served on the Burlington Northern R.R. Evans marketed the conversions under the trade name Auto-Railer.

Although some major parts of the 1942 Fords received extensive reworking, overall the 1942 models were quite similar in appearance to the previous issue. Having a year-old basic body design, the company was not about to make major structural or skin changes at this point. And, for Ford, the move turned out to be a wise one, though at the start of the model year no one could realize just how wise was this conservatism.

That answer was supplied on Dec. 7, 1941, when the Japanese pulled off their surprise attack on Pearl Harbor, and thus threw America into a world war that had been edging ever closer anyway. Even before Pearl Harbor, most major industries in the country were in some way or another involved in manufacturing military supplies, either for American "defense," or for sale to the European allies.

In addition, much raw material had become labeled "war material," and was not available to companies manufacturing civilian products, but only to those building military items. After the Japanese attack, almost all raw materials were curtailed for civilian use, and on Feb. 10, 1942, all automobile manufacturers had to cease passenger car production to make way for exclusive manufacture of military items. Thus, between curtailed regular production during the year because of lack of materials, coupled to the Feb. 10 shut-off, the 1942 model year turned out to be the smallest ever for passenger car production since 1911.

As mentioned, the Fords that did emerge this year were similar, but not identical to the previous models. For one thing, all were 1-inch lower than the 1941 models. This was the result of a new and lower frame, with lower and wider leaf springs. The design also incorporated dual lateral stabilizer bars, while the axles now had a 2-inch wider tread, being 58 inches in the front and 60 in the rear as opposed to the 55.75 front and 58.25-inch rear tread of 1941. Tire size remained the same 6:00x16, and the wheelbase remained 114 inches.

On the exterior, the two most obvious changes involved the grille and the fenders. The grille was now a low, massive stamping, rather than the vertical cast unit. The use of stamped metal in the grille was again part of the war conservation effort. Ford claimed the use of stamped metal for trim and many mechanical parts released large quantities of zinc and aluminum for war materials.

The same argument was made for greatly downsizing the parking lights and moving them to new inboard locations in the catwalk area, and in greatly reducing the size of the hood ornamentation and eliminating the beauty rings from Super Deluxe wheels.

The new 1-piece fenders were not the result of material savings, but simply of cost savings by Ford, which occurred when new 1-piece dies were cut for the fenders. Eliminating the upper and lower halves of all four fenders saved a substantial amount of assembly time. New for Ford were stone shields located between the bumper and the fenders and grille shell on the front, and

between the bumper and fenders and body sill on the rear. On the sides, a major modification involved the body and door sills themselves. These now swept down and outward on the bottom, totally concealing the running boards and providing an attractive rocker line. On the rear fenders, new painted taillights of horizontal design were located in approximately the same area as the vertical chrome units of 1941.

Within the cars, no great changes occurred, but the dash was revised slightly, and now made wide use of plastic trim in place of former chromed castings. The upholstery materials also changed, with the Super Deluxe cars now being finished in superior grades of mohair or broadcloth, while the Deluxe models had a more plain variation of these materials and the Special models used a basic broadcloth. Appearing for the first time were two items that all drivers now take for granted. These were turn signals hooked to the parking and taillights, and windshield washers. Both came in kit form as accessories, and had to be installed at the dealership level.

As before, three different series were available. The Super Deluxe and Deluxe series varied only in trim and upholstery level, while the Special models not only had the bare basics of trim, but also were available only with the 6-cylinder engine and could not be ordered in V-8 form.

In the Special series, all three models remained the same, but in the Deluxe and Super Deluxe series a few switches were made. For one, the 4-passenger Coupe, which was really the 3-passenger Coupe with a jump seat in place of the parcel shelf, was now gone. Nothing replaced it in the Super Deluxe range, but in the Deluxe series a lower level Sedan Coupe was added to the line. Also, a totally new Sedan Delivery was put into the Deluxe series for trim level. It featured all passenger car styling, even though it was still considered part of the commercial car line.

As a result, with the Sedan Delivery included in the Deluxe series, both that grouping and the Super Deluxe lines each now offered six different models.

Mechanically, the horsepower was raised on the V-8 to 96 at 3800 rpm. This was primarily the result of again increasing the compression ratio, with the new figure now being 6.2:1. The relatively new Six was left almost unchanged, and was still rated at 90 horses at 3300 rpm. As a result of material restrictions, many mechanical parts were modified, not in shape, but in the materials used. Both starters and generators now had pressed steel end plates to conserve cast metal. And, within the engine and transmission, such items as valves, gears, and cam and crank shafts were now made of steel alloyed with chromium and molybdenum rather than nickel as a hardening alloy. Ford claimed that these parts were as good or better than the nickel hardened metal, but years of wear showed that this was really not true.

Because of the mandated end of passenger car production on Feb. 10, plus the earlier production slow downs caused by material shortages, this year's production figures are far below those of previous years. Still, the Tudor Sedans led the pack, with 37,199 coming out in Super Deluxe trim, and 27,302 in Deluxe form. The surprise figure occurred in the Fordor Sedan line, where the Special model accounted for 27,189 sales, while the Super Deluxe drew only 24,846 orders. The reason for this can probably be found in large orders placed by the military for the Special models to be used as garrison cars.

Following the Feb. 10 plant change-over (to Jeeps, in Ford's case) all civilian cars and trucks were impounded at either dealership or factory sites. During the succeeding four years, these vehicles would be closely watched by the war rationing boards, and would be doled out only to those people who could prove an extreme need for a new car.

Most of these high priority cars were the so-called "black-out" models that were produced after a Dec. 19th mandate by the government that no chrome or brightwork could be used on passenger cars. Those companies which had stocks of brightwork left were required to paint the trim in body or trim color, so as not to compete unfairly with makes that had no chrome to display. Since production was very limited by this time, few of these black-out models appeared, and once rationing began, only very select persons were allowed to purchase such a car.

Note: Because Ford's military production has been so well documented in three previous Crestline books, it was felt that duplication of this material would be superfluous within these pages. Therefore, the section from 1943 to 1945 will be omitted, using as a base of reason the fact that no passenger car production occurred within the war years, and that commercial vehicles, airplanes, and war materials are outside the scope of this book.

Suffice to say, Ford was the leading producer of B-24 Liberator bombers, and was the second largest producer of Jeeps (after Willys Overland) turning out 277,896 under license from Willys. Also in production were military versions of the regular Ford commercial line, plus such things as tank destroyers; universal gun carriers; Sherman tanks; command cars; anti-aircraft detectors; anti-aircraft gun directors, and components for a multitude of other products being produced by other manufacturers, not to mention being the exclusive producer of all Amphibious Jeeps.

Detailed histories of this period and many of its products may be found in three other Crestline/Motorbooks titles: *FORD TRUCKS SINCE 1905*, by James K. Wagner, and *U.S. WHEELED MILITARY VEHICLES* and *U.S. TRACKED MILITARY VEHICLES*, both by Fred W. Crismon.

Meanwhile, on the Axis side, the Ford plants at Cologne, Germany, and in France, Holland and Copenhagen, Denmark, had been taken over by the Nazi forces and were being utilized to produce their own particular forms of military hardware. Obviously, Ford was decidedly unhappy about this turn of events.

One very sad note to occur during this time was the death of Edsel Ford on May 26, 1943, of stomach cancer. With his death, Ford lost its president, and the world lost a truly brilliant automotive designer. Not completely comfortable in the limelight, Edsel more often than not was content to work behind the scenes and oversee the final product that had been developed either under his direction or with his full approval. Among these designs were the Lincoln Continental; many of the custom bodies that graced the Series K Lincolns; full participation in most of Ford's Model A and V-8 styles, and both the Lincoln Zephyr and Mercury projects. Sadly, the genius of Edsel Ford has never received the acclaim that it really deserves.

Ford's first passenger vehicle since the Model A Town Car to break the $1,000 price barrier was the new Convertible Coupe, Type 76. Available only in the Super Deluxe series, it bore a base price of $1,080. At 3,238 pounds, it was also Ford's heaviest passenger car. True, the 1941 Super Deluxe Station Wagon also exceeded $1,000, but the wagons were still officially classed as commercial vehicles, despite their appearance in the Super Deluxe and Deluxe series. Among the rarest of Fords, the convertible had a run of only 2,920. It continued to share its Lincoln-built body with the equally rare Mercury model. The interior was done in genuine leather, with buyers having a color choice or red, blue, or tan leather and a choice of black or beige tops. With the concealed running boards came another new innovation—black rubber stone shields on the leading edges of the rear fenders. These were to ward off flying gravel that normally would have been deflected by the running boards.

This year the 5-window Super Deluxe Coupe, Type 77-B, came only in one form. It was this 3-passenger style with a large parcel shelf and concealed luggage area behind the front seat. No longer available was the 4-passenger model with the cramped and uncomfortable jump seats behind the main seat. Priced at $850, this was the most economical Super Deluxe vehicle. Because of curtailed production, only 5,411 were built. As before, the quarter windows were set in place. Despite the fact that the $39 factory radio was a very popular option, no official Ford publicity photos this year show the antenna that would indicate radio installation. Also, few of these photos show white wall tires, which were put out of production in August, 1941, by government mandate.

A slightly hump-backed look to the rear quarter identifies this as the 5-passenger Super Deluxe Sedan Coupe, Type 72-B. Priced at $910, the car had 13,543 models built before production was turned off. It weighed 3,120 pounds, which was 70 pounds more than the 3-passenger model. On this style, the quarter windows would swing outward, with the hinges at the top and bottom of the frame, about one-quarter way back from the leading edge. The latch is barely visible here at the trailing edge of the frame. To conserve chrome, these frames were now painted black. For the same reason, trim rings were no longer included on Super Deluxe wheels.

One of Ford's most widely distributed promotional pictures of the year is the one of the Super Deluxe Tudor Sedan, which was Ford's most widely sold car of the year. Designated the Type 70-B, its production reached 37,199 before the February shut-down. Base priced at $885, it weighed 3,159 pounds. This is a very early model, shown with white wall tires, which were a $15 additional cost, if they could be found. To conserve white natural rubber for "defense" efforts, the government had called for a halt to white wall tire production in August, 1941. However, those tires already in stock could be used, and therefore some lucky cars did get to wear white shoes (at least for the first set). During the war years, tires became so scarce that they were one of the highest priority items on the civilian ration list.

This view of the Super Deluxe Fordor Sedan gives a nice look at the new 1942 grille and front end styling. Although it looks cast, the grille is actually of pressed steel, again to save certain metals for the war effort. Directly above the center vertical bars, a small wing-like emblem gives a perch to the Ford script and also contains the figures "8" or "6" to designate which engine was living under the hood. Note that the parking lights, which had been in large cast pods atop the fenders, were now behind rather small bezels in the catwalk area. This, plus a reduction in the size of the hood ornament, was another metal-saving move. The Super Deluxe Fordor had a run of 24,846 before closing time. It cost $920 and weighed an even 3,200 pounds.

Ford's most expensive model officially wasn't even on the passenger car list. It was the Super Deluxe Station Wagon, Type 79-B, which technically was still considered part of the commercial line. It was base priced at $1,100 and weighed 3,468 pounds, thus also qualifying as Ford's heaviest passenger car. Production managed to reach 5,483 this year, with all bodies coming from Iron Mountain. New for the year were the roll-up windows in the rear doors. However, because of the door curve over the rear fender, these windows could not be lowered to sill level, but only went about half-way down. The rear quarter windows were still of the sliding variety, and the two rear windows were still set firm in the swing-up lift gate. As before, the spare lived on the lower tailgate section, and was fitted with its own metal covering, painted to match the fenders and hood. Natural tan genuine leather was still used in the interior, but the red or blue dyed leather of the convertibles was not available in the wagon.

Described as having one of the best looking rear end designs on the American car scene this year were the Ford 3-passenger 5-window Coupes. This is the Deluxe version, Type 77-A, which was priced at $810 and weighed 2,978 pounds. On the exterior, the only significant difference between the Super Deluxe and Deluxe models was that the Super Deluxe had their own unique bumpers, while the Deluxe cars use the Super Deluxe bumpers from the 1941 models. Also, the lower series had "Deluxe" spelled out in the grille center, rather than having script on the left front fender. As with the Super Deluxe Coupes, the Deluxe models were available only as 3-passenger vehicles, with the jump-seat model gone forever. Production of this model was cut short, and only 5,936 were built.

A very poor catalog rendering is the only illustration that could be found of the Deluxe Sedan Coupe, Type 72-A. Priced at $875 and weighing 3,065 pounds, the car had slightly higher headroom in the rear, and a slightly larger greenhouse to accommodate the additional rear full bench seat. Listed as a 5-passenger vehicle, it did not enjoy the production of its counterpart in the Super Deluxe range, and thus, only 5,419 were built. The main difference between the Super Deluxe and the Deluxe ranges was found inside the car. It consisted mainly of a higher quality fabric upholstery in the Super Deluxe series, and a dashboard finished in Sequoia Grain pattern as opposed to Crackle Mahogany Grain in the Deluxe. In both series, buyers had a choice between mohair and broadcloth.

Beauty trim rings on the wheels identify this Deluxe Tudor sedan as a very early model. These rings disappeared from the Super Deluxe models very early in the year, and from the dealers' accessory shelves as stocks ran out. Ford's second most popular model this year, the Deluxe Tudor had a run of 27,302. It was base priced at $840 and weighed 3,141 pounds. With all sorts of rationing looming on the horizon, a new Ford accessory was catching on rapidly. That was a locking gas cap. These had been available in prior years, but until gas shortages and long fill-up lines occurred, they had not drawn much interest. Now they not only drew interest, they were almost a necessity.

Suffering from the short production year was the Deluxe Fordor Sedan, Type 73-A, of which only 5,127 were built. Priced at $875, it weighed 3,161 pounds. Apparently photographed on a hot day, before automotive air conditioning, the car is shown with all its windows down and vents open. Note that the rear door windows would not go all of the way down because of the curve for the fender line. Operational vent windows both front and rear were especially helpful for ventilation, particularly when there were smokers in the car. On the opposite end of the ventilation scene were the heaters. Ford continued to offer both water and air heaters, with the water types drawing heat from the engine's cooling system, while the air types drew hot air from the exhaust manifold. The air heater cost $23, while the hot water type cost $20 installed.

The Station Wagon appeared also in the Deluxe range, but its rear door windows are a puzzle. Some sources indicate that the roll-up windows appeared only on the Super Deluxe models while other say that both trim levels received the new mechanisms. Possibly this was a running change. The main difference between the two series in the wagon line was that the Super Deluxe used natural leather seats, while the Deluxe had imitation tan leather with canvas lower backing. Notice that with the rear seat in place, there was scarcely any luggage room once the tailgate was raised. Bearing 1944 Michigan plates, this particular example has seen some wear. It has been fitted with the optional wheel rings, but lacks the metal spare tire cover. This might have been lost over the years, or possibly was never supplied if this was a late model produced after materials began to get scarce. In Deluxe trim, the wagon was priced at $1,055 and weighed 3,460 pounds. Only 567 were produced in this form, making this vehicle the most rare of all 1942 Fords.

Wearing all new sheet metal of the passenger car variety, the Sedan Delivery once again joined the ranks of the automobile line in appearance, even though it was technically in the commercial line. In addition to passenger car sheet metal, it used the new passenger car chassis, and was designated the Type 78 for body style. It was slotted into the Deluxe range, where it could be ordered with either the V-8 or the Six. It was base priced at $825 and weighed 3,075 pounds. A total of 1,274 were built. This model was part of a fleet ordered by American Tobacco Co. The trucks were finished in black fenders while the body was in "Lucky Strike Green." Shortly after Pearl Harbor, Lucky Strike came out in white packaging, in order to conserve green ink for military use. This resulted in one of the most famous advertising slogans of the day—"Lucky Strike Green Has Gone To War."

Ford's lowest price car, and the only one with a base price of under $800 was the Special 5-window 3-passenger Coupe, Type 77-C. It was priced at only $780 and was available only with the 6-cylinder engine. Devoid of all trim, even to the extent of having just one taillight on the left side, the car weighed 2,910 pounds and thus was also Ford's lightest model. Designed primarily for fleet and business use, the coupe had a run of only 1,606. All Special models were upholstered in a basic broadcloth, and had their own dashboard finish called Kelobra Wood Grain. A quick identification of this series was in the grille, which had the entire framing painted in body color, with only the vertical bars in stainless steel.

The advertising art for the Special Tudor Sedan showed a happy couple loading the rather spacious trunk. Though a few families might have purchased such a car, most special models went into business use, and a salesman loading samples might have been a more appropriate illustration. Designated the Type 70-C, the low-line Tudor was base priced at $815 and weighed 3,053 pounds. Production was very much on the low side, with only 3,187 being built. In addition to painted grille framing and single taillights, Specials had no bright trim on the fenders as did other series, only an embossed line. The open trunk gives a look at the upright mounting of the spare against the trunk wall. This was the standard mounting for all sedan spares in all lines this year.

The only Special model to enjoy any popularity this year was the Fordor Sedan, Type 73-C. It had a production run of 27,189. The reason for this popularity is obvious in this photo. The military services procured large numbers for garrison duty at bases all across the U.S. This model wears the unusual World War II blackout lamps above the headlights, and is lacking inboard parking lights. Since there is no evidence that the parking lights were ever on this car, the switch was probably made at the factory at the request of the Army. In civilian form the Special Fordor was priced at $850 and weighed 3,093 pounds. This army model had all of its brightwork painted in olive drab. Actually, after Dec. 19, 1941, all cars were supposed to have all brightwork painted over, and these vehicles were known as "blackout" models. Most were impounded by the government, and slowly released only to top priority users. The lack of chrome and stainless trim affected General Motors more than Ford, as Ford had substantial reserves of bright trim and grilles. But to keep bright cars from having an unfair sales advantage over "blackout" models, the government mandated that all trim on all cars be painted.

Will the real last Ford please make itself known? These two pictures, taken at identical spots at Ford's assembly line at Dearborn, supposedly show the last car turned out on Feb. 10, before the line was switched over the assembly of Jeeps. But either the car was finished in chameleon-acting paint that could change colors, or more than one model was selected to be the "official" last car. The light colored car appears to be a Super Deluxe Fordor, while the dark one looks like one of the rare convertibles, which certainly would have made a more attractive subject for the "last car" publicity pictures. Regardless of which was which, the lines did shut down on Feb. 10, and civilian passenger car production would not resume again until July 3, 1945, when the government relaxed its mandates and allowed the companies to return to peace time production once more.

1942

During this era, the Marmon-Herrington Co. was working closely with Ford in producing a series of 4-wheel-drive conversions for virtually any model that the customer might want. Although these conversion packages could have been installed on coupes or sedans, most wound up on station wagon models, and even a few graced the undersides of the new Sedan Delivery. Here a Super Deluxe version of the wagon wears the M-H unit. When producing such conversions, Marmon-Herrington applied its own signature plaque to the hood sides, but otherwise left the Ford script in place. Surveying companies, oil and mineral prospectors, and heavy construction companies were the primary customers for the wagon conversions, and it is probable that some did wind up in the military also. The use of the Super Deluxe version is not that unusual when one considers the better wearing qualities of the natural leather seats, and the roll-up rear door windows on this series.

The Sedan Delivery version of the Marmon-Herrington 4-wheel-drive conversion produced a rather nice looking panel truck, albeit one that sat quite high in the air. This one, illustrated in a M-H catalog, has been fitted with mud tires all around, a feature not uncommon on these vehicles. This particular conversion was listed as Marmon-Herrington's Model LD6P-4. The new body offered a cargo area 79 inches long by 60 inches wide and 44 inches high. The spare tire continued to live in its own well under the floor boards, but it is doubtful if this space could accommodate oversized tires such as the ones used here. The lack of fender trim was common on the Sedan Deliveries. Despite their being in the Deluxe series, the fenders bore the same lack of trim as found in the Special line.

The Shop of Siebert of Toledo continued to convert Ford and Mercury cars into professional vehicles, but this year the advertising emphasis appeared to be on ambulances rather than funeral equipment. The base body used for these conversions was the Sedan Delivery. This body lent itself to such conversions, since large quarter windows could be easily installed, while the rear service door was already in place on a nicely squared-off back panel. The extension section between the B and C-pillars was manufactured by Siebert. This ambulance is all decked out with flashing lights and siren. Siebert referred to this as its Aristocrat Ambulance, listing it among the 18 professional vehicles offered on either Ford or Mercury chassis. Later Siebert ads stressed that those customers who wanted a new vehicle should get their orders in as soon as possible, while there were still chassis available.

Finally, after four torturous years, World War II began to draw to a close. The destruction, waste, and stupidity of this conflict had devastated most of Europe and many parts of the Orient, but had left the U.S. mainland unscathed. Thus, while people in many other parts of the world were concerned with rebuilding their entire lives, Americans for the most part were only looking toward the creature comforts that had been denied them for the duration. And, one of the prime items that was longed for was a new car.

Finally, on July 3, 1945, Ford Motor Co. was given permission by the government to resume automotive production. Thus, Ford began building its first "postwar" vehicles. And, as was the case with every other American auto maker, its new postwar production was simply a rehash of what had been offered in 1942. Faced with the need to get cars on the market just as quickly as possible, the American automotive industry in unison did little more than make a few cosmetic changes to their 1942 offerings, and put these out as 1946 "postwar" cars. And even with the minor changes, material shortages still loomed, and it was not unusual to find cars in the show rooms with wooden "temporary" bumpers, or plastic "temporary" rear windows, let alone holes in the dash board for missing instruments, radios, etc.

Still, when the new "postwar" models were introduced by Ford on Oct. 22, 1945, each Ford dealer had at least one complete Super Deluxe model on the showroom floor for the car-hungry public to gawk at. And gawk is just about all that most people could do. The rather strict rationing system remained in effect, and only high-priority buyers could get new vehicles. Others

had to go on long waiting lists, and then be content to take whatever happened to be on the floor when the buyer's number came up. (The Author, then 13 years old, well remembers his own father—a pragmatic Dutch dairy farmer—being offered a bright green Buick Super Convertible when his name came up. It was take it or go back to the bottom of the list! To the Author's delight, Fred Dammann took the car and kept it until 1952, but never really seemed comfortable driving it, and only once put the top down!)

More pragmatic than the Sportsman was the conventional Convertible Coupe, Model 76, which was available only in the Super Deluxe series and only with the V-8 engine. Weighing 3,240 pounds, the attractive car cost $1,488, which included an electric "Motor-Lift" top, but not hydraulic window lifts. The same genuine leather interior choices were available here as in the Sportsman, but in addition, buyers could select a bedford cord interior at no extra cost. The Station Wagons and both convertibles all shared their own exclusive dash pattern, done in a Sequoia Grain applique. A total of 16,359 rag tops were built this year.

Even with the top up, the new Ford Convertible was a very attractive car, able to hold its own in styling against most other vehicles of the era. This attractive example sports two popular bumper accessories—the end wings and the rectangular grille guard. A left hand spot light was also a popular item, which was often seen but seldom used. Notice the "Super Deluxe" emblem resides directly under the left headlight, on the fender face panel. Beauty rings were used only on Super Deluxe wheels, while Deluxe models had three paint stripes on each wheel.

One of the most widely published publicity photos of the decade was this illustration of the new Ford Sportsman Convertible, Model 71. Introduced after the initial Ford announcement, the car drew quite a bit of attention, but its sales were somewhat dampened by its $1,982 price tag, and only 723 were sold. Designed by Bob Gregorie, the car was the first model approved by Henry Ford II in his new role as president. The wood was not just an applique, but a fully structured body built over a metal frame. This raised the car's weight to 3,340 pounds. Automatic "Motor-Lift" top and Ford's new hydraulic window risers were standard, as was the V-8 engine. This model probably would have created more of a sensation had not Chrysler brought out its whole line of wood bodied Town & Country cars this year. It was upholstered in genuine leather, in either tan, gray, or red.

In the Ford camp, only two series were available. They were the Deluxe, which was now the base line, and the Super Deluxe, which was simply a higher trim level. The old Special series was dropped, but its 6-cylinder engine was now available in either of the two remaining series. A small "6" or "8" embossed into the hood ornament quickly told which engine powered the car.

Mechanically, the cars were almost identical to the 1942 offerings, except that the V-8 was now rated at 100 horsepower at 3800 rpm. This was primarily due to the compression ratio being raised to 6.8:1 from the previous 6.2:1. The V-8 used a Holley 2-barrel carburetor, while the Six used a Holley single barrel.

On the exterior, both series featured a totally new grille consisting of a massive upper horizontal bar, with four lesser bars underneath. Less complicated than the 1942 style, the new grille was an attractive piece of design, and gave the cars a lower and wider look from the front.

Both series shared the Tudor, Fordor, and Coupe body shells, with these respective bodies differing only in trim. For example, the Deluxe cars had rubber windshield moldings, single sun visor, arm rest on the driver's side only, and a horn button. Super Deluxe cars had chromed windshield moldings; dual sun visors and arm rests; a horn ring, and an electric dashboard clock. Super Deluxe models were identified by a chrome signature on the left front fender face panel, while Deluxe models had that nameplate attached to the top grille bar.

Initially, a total of 10 models were available in the two series. Appearing in both series were the 2 and 4-door sedans and the Business Coupe. Exclusive to the Deluxe series was the Sedan Delivery, while the Station Wagon, 5-passenger Sedan Coupe, and Convertible Coupe were exclusive to the Super Deluxe series. The Convertible was the only Ford which could not be ordered with a 6-cylinder engine.

In late fall, Ford introduced its only totally new body style. This was the Sportsman Convertible, a wood-bodied version of the convertible, in the same concept as Chrysler's new Town & Country line. Designed by Bob Gregorie during the war years, the model was the first totally new style approved by Henry Ford II in his new role as president of Ford Motor Co. The revolutionary car had a structural wood body similar in construction to the Station Wagon. All of the wood came from Ford's Iron Mountain facility. Available in both Ford Super Deluxe and Mercury variations, it was the only model to have hydraulic windows as standard equipment. Also, because of the exclusive curve of the rear body, it was the only Ford passenger car to use Sedan Delivery rear fenders. Certainly not an economy model, the Sportsman listed at $1,982, which was almost $500 more than the regular convertible, and $850 above the plain business coupe,. In the price structure, all models reflected the inflationary spiral which had occurred during and immediately after World War II. Whereas in 1942, only the Super Deluxe Convertible and the Station Wagon broke the $1,000 mark, in 1946 there were no Fords under that figure. The lowest price model on the lot was the Deluxe 3-passenger Coupe in 6-cylinder form, which listed for $1,074. The same car was $1,123 with a V-8, while in Super Deluxe trim it listed at $1,148 as a Six or $1,197 with the V-8.

Not surprisingly, the most popular model of the year turned out to be the Super Deluxe Tudor, which cost $1,260 in V-8 form. A total of 163,370 were built. Its companion in the Deluxe series came in third, with 74,954 rolling off the line. The Super Deluxe Fordor was second, with 92,056 being built. As could be expected, the ultra-high priced Sportsman had the lowest production, with only 723 being built in Ford form, while another 200 went onto Mercury chassis. In all, a total of 372,543 Fords left the plants this year in Super Deluxe trim, while another 94,870 were built in Deluxe trim, giving a total production level of 467,413 for the year, which was 64,432 more than later-starting Chevrolet.

The chrome framed rear quarter windows point out that this is the 6-passenger Sedan Coupe, which was available only in the Super Deluxe Series. On 3-passenger Coupes, the rear quarter windows were fixed into place, while on the 6-passenger models these windows could be swung open. Designated the Model 72B, the Sedan Coupe weighed 3,140 pounds and cost $1,307 with the V-8 or $50 less with the Six. Wide whites, such as worn by this car, were a popular item in years following the war, but were almost impossible to find immediately after World War II. When new, virtually all of these cars were supplied with black wall tires. Tire size remained the same 6.00x16s as used in 1942.

Available in both the Super Deluxe and Deluxe series was the 3-passenger Coupe, often referred to as a Business Coupe. Designated the Model 77B in the Super Deluxe series, the car cost $1,197 as a V-8 or $1,148 as a Six. Not a very popular model, production in the Super Deluxe series totalled only 12,249. The car was the lightest of the Super Deluxe models, weighing only 3,040 pounds.

Ford's most popular car by a wide margin was the Super Deluxe Tudor, of which 163,370 were turned out. Weighing 3,190 pounds, the Model 70B cost $1,260 with the V-8. A model similar to this was the first Ford to roll off the Dearborn assembly line on July 3, 1945. It was personally delivered to President Harry Truman by Henry Ford II, now president of Ford Motor Co. All closed Super Deluxe Fords were upholstered in a gray material, either a striped broadcloth or a striped mohair. Buyers were supposed to have their choice of interiors, but in this era the car hungry public would take whatever it could get.

The second most popular model in Ford's overall picture was the Super Deluxe Fordor, Model 73B. Production reached 92,056, and probably would have been much greater had not the company been hit by several crippling strikes early in the fall. Priced at $1,322, the Fordor weighed 3,240 with the V-8, and was 33 pounds lighter with the Six. All Fords wore the black rubber stone guards on the leading edges of the rear fenders, but these guards were far more noticeable on light colored cars than on dark ones. Often overlooked in identification is the fact that only the 1946 Fords had red striping on the grille bars, while the similar grilles of the 1947/48 cars did not have this paint trim.

When all three seats were in place, cargo space in the Ford station Wagon was definitely limited. However, the rear and center seats were relatively easy to remove, and with these gone, the cargo area was truly spacious. Designated the Model 79B, the wagon was available only in the Super Deluxe series. Priced at $1,553, it was Ford's second most expensive style, after the other wood bodied car, the Sportsman. Like the Sportsman, its bodies also were built at Iron Mountain, but differed in that these were of all wood framing, whereas the Sportsman bodies were constructed over a metal frame. Production reached 16,960, possibly indicating a growing awareness of wagon models by the American public. Notice that only a single swing-down left taillight was used. A right light, also of the swing-down type, could be ordered as an accessory. Wagons used their own exclusive rear fenders, similar but not identical to those used on the Sedan Delivery and Sportsman. Upholstery was in tan artificial leather or bedford cord.

Ford's lowest price model continued to be the 3-passenger Deluxe Coupe, often referred to as a "Business Coupe." It sold for $1,074 with the Six or $1,123 with a V-8. Designated the Model 77A, the 3,040-pound car drew only 10,670 orders, making it a relatively rare vehicle. Lack of the series insignia on the left front fender face is quick identification of Deluxe Series cars. This one, however, wears such trim items as wide whites and wheel trim rings. Its dual radiator hoses clearly indicate that the 100 horse V-8 lives under the hood.

As could be expected, the best selling car in the Deluxe series was the Tudor Sedan, Model 70A. Sales of the 3,190-pound vehicle reached 745,954, which was enough to put the car into third place overall on this year's list. Priced at $1,185 with the V-8, the car offered a nice package for the dollar. Upholstery in the Deluxe series was either in tan striped broadcloth or tan striped mohair, as opposed to the gray materials used in the Super Deluxe models.

Except for the ultra-high priced Sportsman Convertible, the lowest production vehicle in the entire Ford line turned out to be the Deluxe Fordor. Only 9,246 of this model were built, leading one to speculate that with the demand for cars at such a high peak, the company did not have to turn out its low-trim models to entice buyers. Priced at $1,248, the 3,220-pound car bore model number 73A. This view gives a good look at the rear design shared by all Tudor and Fordor models this year. The twin stainless steel horizontal bars on the trunk deck were standard on all models, but disappeared from the 1947/48 cars. Triple paint stripes in contrasting tones graced all wheels, but the beauty rings were an added-cost item on deluxe models.

Technically part of the commercial line, the Sedan Delivery qualifies for inclusion here simply because of its use of all passenger car components for its front end styling. Designated the Model 78, the Sedan Delivery also used a 1942 carry-over body, and was fitted in Deluxe series trim. It could be ordered with either the V-8 or the Six. Production was far from exciting, with only 3,187 leaving the plant this year. In 1947 the picture was no different, and only 3,484 were built, leading Ford to drop this model for several years. Its surprising that, despite Ford's excellent truck sales, its Sedan Delivery model should do so poorly. Chevrolet, on the other hand, was very content with the sedan delivery concept, and continued to offer this style through the later 1950s. In basic form, with the Six, it sold for $1,186 and weighed 2,978 pounds.

The interior of the Sportsman Convertible was similar to that of the regular convertible, except that in the Sportsman, the hydraulic window units were standard, whereas they were an accessory on the regular model. Genuine leather was used for both the seats and the panels, and the buyers had a choice of tan, red, or gray. Horn rings and right hand sun visor and arm rest were standard on all Super Deluxe models, but were extra-cost options on Deluxe vehicles. Immediately after the war, virtually all car manufacturers experimented with wood bodied or wood trimmed vehicles, with Chrysler having the widest selection in its Town & Country line. But despite their beauty, continuous maintenance was a headache that most buyers did not want, and by 1949 virtually all natural wood had disappeared from the automotive scene.

As soon as Ford got back into production with its new models, Siebert devised a way to convert them into professional cars. The Toledo, Ohio, company quickly came out with a line of hearses, ambulances, and service cars, all based on a stretched version of the Deluxe Tudor. This is the hearse version, which could be loaded either via the normal trunk opening, or by either of the extra-large custom side doors. A sliding glass partition between the compartments was standard, as was leather upholstery for the driver's seat and velvet curtains for the rear windows. Siebert also made similar conversions to Mercury sedans, and continued with this style through the 1948 model year. However, the new 1949 styling proved to be incompatible to such conversions, and Siebert then began to use light Ford panel trucks for its products.

It looked good, it provided occupants with unlimited visibility, it was not too expensive—but on a warm day, it literally cooked the passengers. That in a nutshell is the total story of the rise and fall of an interesting accessory brought out in 1946 for the Ford and Mercury convertibles. Called the Plexi-Top, and manufactured by the Plexi-Top Co. of Detroit, these 50-pound auxiliary tops cost approximately $200. Installation was relatively easy, and only a couple of minutes were required to transform the car back to its normal rag top status. The tops would fit all Ford and Mercury convertibles from 1942 to 1948, and plans were underway to make similar tops for General Motors and Chrysler products. Whether the latter ever materialized is not known. The sun's rays were the undoing of these tops, and the company tried tinted plexiglas and even roller shades, but to no avail—on a warm sunny day, the heat was terrible. By 1948, orders had dropped to almost zero, and by 1949 the tops were off the market. Because plexiglas of that era was very prone to age-crazing, it is doubtful if any of these tops survive today.

Siebert wasn't the only company to convert Ford sedans into stretched professional cars. In Canada, the John Little Co. of Ingersol, Ontario, produced this line of funeral cars on both Ford and Monarch chassis through the 1948 model year. Very similar to the Siebert conversions, the Little vehicles used Tudor bodies, fitted with a center stretch-section. The use of Tudors as opposed to Fordors gave a wider front door and a much longer rear quarter section. On the Siebert model, only one rear hinge was exposed, while the Little version used three relatively large exposed hinges for the rear door.

A specialized California bus route was the one operated by Lassen National Park Co. between its ski resort in the park and the city of Redding. In 1946 its main vehicles were several of these stretched Fords, which could carry 10 or 11 passengers, in addition to the driver and plenty of luggage. The latter would ride on the rooftop rack, which also served as a cantilever brace to keep the unit from sagging in the middle. Luggage access was via an external ladder up the C-pillar. The cars (this is No. 15) were stretched Super Deluxe Fordors, cut at the B-pillar, and fitted with a new 6-passenger mid-section. It is not known for certain who did these conversions, but the work looks like that done by the Stageway Co. of Ft. Smith, Ark.

Granted, Ford cars changed very little this year. But even if they had become totally new vehicles, the cars would have taken second place to the company's major news story—one that not only filled the front pages of virtually every daily newspaper in America, but was told in major headlines world wide. That news concerned the death of Henry Ford, who passed away on April 7, 1947, at the age of 83. A fantastically complicated man of genuine engineering and business genius, Ford had risen from being an obscure farm boy to heading one of the largest private owned corporations in the world. And, he had done this during an era when folk heros were still venerated, when the shining example was a man who through sheer hard work and intelligence could rise to unbelievable heights, without having to feel embarrassed or self conscious about the feat.

True, as the years wore on, Ford's reputation became tarnished by a variety of "unusual" actions. But these must be weighed against his underdog fight against the Selden patent, which freed the entire American automotive industry from the grasp of a large eastern investment syndicate; against his development of the Model T as a low-cost automobile for the working man; against his foresight in adapting the assembly line and modern machine methods to all American industry, and even to his unheard of high wages of $5 a day minimum so the average factory worker could enjoy a somewhat comfortable life.

On the actual automotive side, the 1946 line was quite similar to the 1942 line, and the 1947 line was almost identical to 1946. With the demand for new cars continuing at a pace that was almost impossible to meet, all three of the giant auto manufacturers saw little reason to waste time and money making styling changes that were not needed to induce sales in the first place. Even two of the major independents, Nash and Hudson, continued with their warmed over 1942 styles. The only real excitement in the automotive world, save for the short lived Tucker and only slightly better faring Frazer, was the totally new postwar styles brought out by both Studebaker and Packard.

Although Ford did not change much, it did change, and at least one could tell a 1947 Ford from a 1946, which is more than could be said for Chrysler products. Most obvious of the changes was the movement of the parking lamps from rectangular units on the catwalks above the grille to simpler (and cheaper) round units below the headlamps. Also changed slightly was the grille, which no longer carried the red highlighted embossing, but now consisted of plain horizontal bars of the same size and style as in 1946. Also loosing their groves were the headlight bezels, while the side trim began the year with an indented grove, but was smoothed as old stocks ran out and new trim was ordered.

Once again, the line was divided into Deluxe and Super Deluxe series, with both the V-8 and Six available in all models except the Sportsman and the regular convertibles, which could be had only with the V-8. The difference between the two series was almost exclusively on the interior, with the Deluxe models having only one sun visor, one arm rest, one interior light, no electric clock on the dash, and only a horn button rather than a ring.

Under the hood, virtually nothing changed on the V-8 engines, but the 6-cylinder units were now rated at 95 horsepower, or only five horses less than the V-8. Apparently this boost in horsepower was a running change, as early references to the Six continue to list it as 90 HP. Where the new horses came from is a bit of a mystery, as the engines continued with all specifications unchanged, and even the carburetor remained the same single-barrel Holley that was used in 1946. Likewise, the compression on both the V-8 and the Six remained a constant 6.8:1, and the Six continued to use a bore and stroke of 3.3x4.4 inches, which displaced 226 cubic inches, as compared with the 239 cubic inch displacement of the V-8.

Within the two series, all models remained the same. The Deluxe line had only three styles, the 3-passenger Business Coupe, and the Tudor and Fordor Sedans. The Super Deluxe range had these three styles plus the 5-passenger Sedan Coupe, the Convertible Coupe, Sportsman Convertible, and Station Wagon.

Of all these models, the Super Deluxe Tudor was the most popular, accounting for 136,126 orders, while the Super Deluxe Fordor came in second with 116,744. Also high on the list was the Super Deluxe Sedan Coupe, with production at 80,830. In the Deluxe series, production was split almost evenly between the Fordor, with 44,563 orders, and the Tudor, with 44,523 builds. Lowest production of all was recorded by the Sportsman Convertible, whose 2,274 were far below what even the most pessimistic dealer could imagine. Both Ford and Chrysler were finding out that most people would admire the beautiful wood bodies, but few wanted the high initial cost or the continuing maintenance of these termite tenements.

In all, Ford produced 99,958 Deluxe models and 385,108 Super Deluxe cars, for a grand total of 485,067 vehicles during the model year. This was only slightly more than the entire Fleetmaster range of Chevrolet, whose total production reached 684,145 for the model year.

If anything changed during the year, it was the price index. For the first time since the 1908 Model K, Ford had a production model with a base list price over the $2,000 mark. That was the Sportsman, whose list of $2,282 certainly did not help to enhance its sales, especially when compared with the regular convertible at $1,740. Not far behind the Sportsman was the Station Wagon, now listing at $1,972. Even Ford's lowest priced Deluxe Business Coupe was up by $80, with its new list at $1,154.

If anything, World War II had created another monster-creeping inflation!

1947

Far more popular than the Sportsman version was Ford's conventional Convertible Coupe, or Club Convertible, Model 76B. A total of 22,159 were sold, which placed this car well ahead of either business coupe and just ahead of the Station Wagon. Priced at $1,740, it weighed 3,266 pounds, or just 100 pounds less than the Sportsman. For the first time, genuine leather was not used for the seats. Instead seat material was a combination of tan or red artificial leather with bedford cord inserts, or in some cases, simply all artificial leather.

There's no denying that the Sportsman Convertible, Model 71B, was a very attractive car. But high initial cost plus buyers' fears of constant and costly body maintenance, resulted in sales of only 2,274 this year, thus making this model by far the most rare 1947 Ford. Its base price was $2,282, marking the first time since the 1908 Model K that a Ford had broken the $2,000 figure. Once again, hydraulic window risers were standard equipment, as was an interior of genuine leather. Buyers had a choice of tan or red pebble-grain cowhide. Weighing 3,366 pounds, this was the second heaviest model after the Station Wagon. Like the wagon, its body was built at Ford's Iron Mountain plant. The left hand antenna on this model might be an aftermarket unit, as most Ford antennas were mounted on the right side of the cowl.

Well battered when photographed in the late 1960s was this Super Deluxe 3-passenger Coupe, often referred to as the Business Coupe. Designated the Model 77B, the car was identical to the Sedan Coupe except that it offered a relatively large storage area behind the front seat, rather than rear seating. Priced at $1,330, the 3,066-pound car drew only 10,872 orders, according to Ford's list. Oddly, this is the same figure shown for the Deluxe version of this car, which seems to be a very unbelievable coincidence. The small metal tab on the leading edge of the hood is the only identification that this is a Super Deluxe model.

As always, Ford's most popular model was the Super Deluxe Tudor Sedan, Model 70B. This year its production reached 136,126. Priced at $1,382, it weighed 3,216 pounds. Buyers had a choice of blue or gray broadcloth or gray mohair. The small plate on the leading edge of the hood signified the model was a Super Deluxe. Within the emblem, a "6" or an "8" signified which engine was under the hood. As an early 1947 model, this car lacks the low-set hood ornament that would appear on all except the very early models. Parking light location is the quickest way to tell a 1946 from a 1947/48 model. The grilles on both years are similar, but not interchangeable, as the 1946 cars had embossed bars trimmed in red, while the later models had smooth bars.

Far more popular than the 3-passenger version was the Super Deluxe Sedan Coupe, which was listed as a 6-passenger model in some references and as a 5-passenger in others. Priced at $1,409, the 3,166-pound car was designated the Model 72B. The chrome edging to the rear quarter window, and barely visible latch, were unique to this model, as it was the only coupe on which the rear quarter windows would swing open. On the 3-passenger versions, these windows were fixed in place and were simply edged in black rubber. By far the most popular coupe design, this model saw its production top out at 80,830 units. Unlike the two convertible coupes, which were available only with the V-8, these models could be ordered with either the Six or the V-8.

The second most popular model this year was the Super Deluxe Fordor, Model 73B, which had a run of 116,744. Priced at $1,440, it was only $58 more than the Tudor. It weighed 3,266 pounds. New for the year was the chrome trim at the lower edge of the front fenders, in effect carrying the rocker panel trim right up to the wheel well. Notice that this model uses the header-mounted antenna rather than the cowl-mounted type. Actually, both types were used, but the header type more often was installed on the sedans, while the cowl-mounts (of several different types) more often graced the coupes.

1947

Holding a relatively popular spot on the sales list, the Station Wagon drew 16,104 orders this year, which was only 850 less than last year. Designated Model 79B, it cost $1,972. At 3,520 pounds it was once again Ford's heaviest model. As was the case with the Sportsman, its body was provided by Ford's plant at Iron Mountain, Mich. Unlike the Sportsman, the wagon used a fully wood framed body with a composite roof, while the Sportsman had a metal shell. Buyers had a choice of tan vinyl or extra-cost beige genuine leather upholstery. The wagon was available only in the Super Deluxe series, but could be ordered with either engine.

Lowest priced of all models was the Deluxe 3-passenger Coupe, Model 77A, also known as the 5-window Coupe or the Business Coupe. It was priced at $1,154 with the Six. It offered spacious cargo areas, both in the trunk and behind the front seat. A puzzle exists over production figures on this model. Most sheets list production at 10,872 for the Deluxe and another 10,872 for the Super Deluxe version, which would have been quite a coincidence. It is possible that the same number were produced in each series, but it is also possible that the 10,872 represents the TOTAL of all 3-passenger coupes produced in both series. If that is the case, then the model year total must be decreased by 10,872, as this double figure was used in computing the grand total. Whatever the figure, the car is one of the more rare of the 1947 styles.

Although the Tudor was by far the overall sales leader in the Super Deluxe range, it enjoyed no such popularity in the Deluxe division, where it came in second place with 44,523 units. Priced at $1,288 with the V-8 or $1,212 with the Six, it was only $94 cheaper than the Super Deluxe model. For this savings, buyers received only one sun visor and door arm rest, no electric clock, only one interior light, and a lesser grade of mohair or broadcloth upholstery. Probably many individuals felt the savings did not warrant the drop in series. Unlike previous years when the lower lines received just one taillight and one windshield wiper, all Fords this year had dual wipers and taillights. On all models, the centrally located rear deck latch contained a small lamp which illuminated the license plate.

The entire story of the Deluxe Fordor seems to be in mystery. The most accepted production lists show this car as being the most popular of the three Deluxe models, with 44,563 being built. Yet, another list would indicate that only 20 were built before the model was dropped in favor of Super Deluxe versions. Also, the car illustrated was credited with being the 1-millionth something, but what? Certainly 1-million cars were not built in 1947. Was it the 1-millionth postwar model, or 1-millionth Six, or possibly 1-millionth from some unnamed assembly plant? Ford shot the picture, but apparently made very little use of the publicity. Selling for $1,270 as a Six or $75 more as a V-8, the car weighed 3,246 pounds. Only interior fittings distinguished the Deluxe from the Super Deluxe models. Also in the Deluxe series was the Sedan Delivery, not illustrated here simply because no photos of a 1947 version could be found. Sales of this model remained so low that Ford decided to drop it before year end, by which time production had reached only 3,484. This was still almost 300 more than had been built in 1946, but Ford apparently felt it was not worth carrying the truck into 1948, and it had no designs for it in the 1949 line. This year it cost $1,302 and weighed 3,164 pounds, for some reason becoming both heavier and more expensive than the 1946 version.

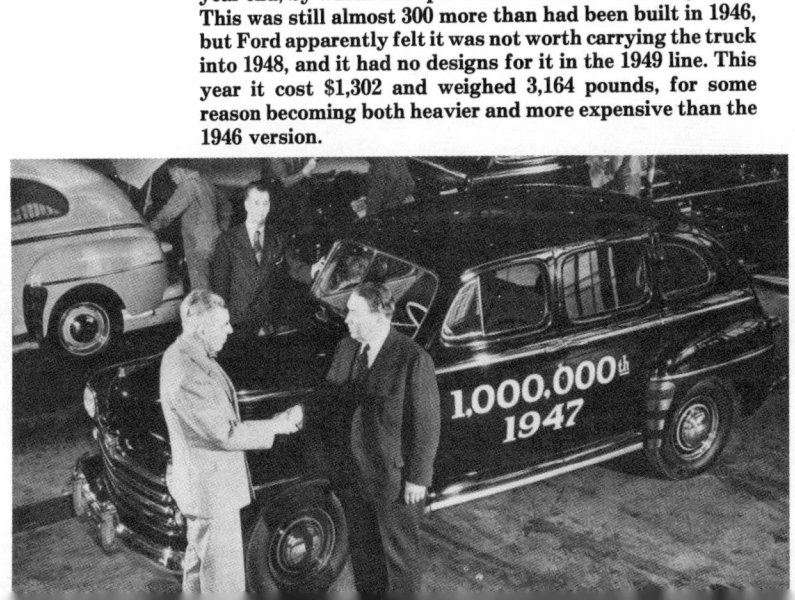

If 1947 was a year of minimal change, then 1948 was the year of no change. The reason for this was two-fold. First, the cars were still selling at a high level, and only now was production beginning to catch up with demand. And secondly, Ford was still working on its new postwar models, which would finally be introduced as 1949 cars. In this respect, the company was right in step with both General Motors and Chrysler. The Big Three finally would introduce their "Postwar" cars in unison, three years after World War II ended and almost in time to get involved in the Korean War.

Since by design 1948 was to be a short year for production, Ford could really not justify any changes. The new Fords, which had cost about $75 million in retooling, were to be introduced in June. This meant that production of the old models would end in mid-spring. With both high tooling costs for the new models, plus a short production year facing the company, it is doubtful if anyone could have seriously argued for a change on the 1948 models. And, this same story held just as true for General Motors and Chrysler.

To differentiate between the new and old models, Ford decreed that all cars built after Nov. 1, 1947, were to be titled as 1948 cars. Titles and some very minor running changes were about all that could be used to tell one model from the next.

As the 1948 model year began, all styles that had appeared in 1947 were continued, except for the Sedan Delivery. That nicely styled little truck had been dropped late in the summer, with the company citing poor sales as the reason. Actually, 1947 had been bet-

ter for the truck than had 1946, with sales at 3,484 as opposed to 3,187. However, there were no designs for a sedan delivery type in the 1949 line, and the company probably felt that the short 1948 year would not justify its continuation.

The same story seems to hold true for the Sportsman Convertible. Although all information would indicate that Ford planned to run this style throughout the 1948 year, the model was dropped before the end of November. Production lists show that only 28 Sportsmans were built as 1948 cars, but these very well may have been 1947 models retitled for the new year.

Also confusing are the lack of production figures for the Deluxe Fordor and the Super Deluxe 3-passenger Coupe. Both of these models are listed in Ford's books, but there is little to indicate that any of these cars were actually built.

The prices too cause confusion. Some sources indicate that all models received an average price increase of about $100, yet dealer price books from the era would indicate a surprising price stability during the year.

In all, because of the short year, production was down, with only 28,040 Deluxe models being accounted for, and 219,320 Super Deluxe cars. At the top of the list again was the Super Deluxe Tudor Sedan, which accounted for 82,161 sales, and the Super Deluxe Fordor, with 71,358. Obviously, this was not a banner year for Ford, but better days were right around the corner.

Ford used a photograph of a 1947 Sportsman to illustrate its 1948 model in its official publications. But no one could tell the difference, and in addition, it is very likely that the 28 Sportsman models turned out as 1948 cars were really retitled 1947 vehicles. Continuing buyer resistance to the interesting but pricey car, plus no replacement model in the coming 1949 line, caused Ford to drop the Sportsman soon after the year began, even though initial plans had been to keep the style through the 1948 model year. Designated Model 71B, the Sportsman retained its price of $2,282 and its weight of 3,366, and thus remained Ford's most expensive model. All such wood bodied cars were fighting for their lives in this era, as buyers were reluctant to take on the maintenance required by these attractive bodies. Remember, this was the time before epoxy finishes, and these bodies had to be revarnished about every two years, and protected from strong sunlight at all times.

Far more popular than the Sportsman Convertible ever thought of being was the conventional Club Convertible. Sales registered 12,033, which can be considered excellent, inasmuch as this was a relatively short production year. Bearing Model 76B, the 5-passenger car sold for $1,704 and weighed 3,266 pounds. Upholstery continued to be in tan or red artificial leather seat edges with matching bedford cord interior panels. The door and side panels were in the same artificial leather as used on the seat edges. The convertible and the station wagon continued to use a wood-grained dashboard finish with beige plastic, while all of the other passenger cars used a metallic gray finish with gray plastic. This photo or variations thereof were the most widely publicized Ford promotional illustrations of the year.

Was this car ever built? Ford publications list the Super Deluxe 5-window 3-passenger Coupe (Business Coupe) as the Model 77B, and give it a price of $1,330 and a weight of 3,066 pounds. Yet, production records indicate that this style was built only in Deluxe version, while the Super Deluxe models were all done in 6-passenger Sedan Coupe style (both models used the same body shell). Still, the nose emblem on the hood identifies this as a Super Deluxe, while the rubber trimmed non-opening rear quarter windows identify it as a 3-passenger Coupe. With the low interest in this model, Ford probably made a last minute decision to drop it from the Super Deluxe line and offer it only in the business-like Deluxe series where it really belonged in the first place. If any of these Super Deluxe Coupes did materialize as 1948 cars, they were probably retitled 1947s.

Apparently the only coupe style in the Super Deluxe series was the 6-passenger Sedan Coupe, Model 72B. A surprisingly popular style, considering how crowded it was with six full-size people aboard, the car drew 44,828 orders. Although both the Sedan Coupe and the Business Coupe used the same body shell, the Sedan Coupe can be quickly identified by the chrome molding around the rear quarter window, which signified that this glass could be swung open. The Sedan Coupe cost $1,409 and weighed 3,166 pounds.

As always, Ford's most popular model was the Super Deluxe Tudor, which this year claimed 82,161 sales. Designated the Model 70B, it cost $1,382 with the V-8 or $1,309 with the Six. Its V-8 weight was 3,216 pounds. Interiors of all closed Super Deluxe models continued to be finished in a choice of blue or gray broadcloth or gray mohair, with matching panels and headliner. B-pillars on these models were fitted with small interior lights, with a manual switch being located on the right lamp only. Assist straps were provided for rear seat passengers on both the Tudor and Fordor models.

Only slightly less popular than the Tudor was the Super Deluxe Fordor, which drew 71,358 orders. Listed as Model 73B, the car cost $1,440 and weighed 3,266 with the V-8. The header-mounted antenna was usually used on Tudor and Fordor Sedans, while coupes often appeared with cowl-mounts. Of course, convertibles and wagons almost exclusively favored the cowl-mounted types. This would be the last year for Ford's use of transverse springs, a now-archaic suspension system that had been used on all Fords since the Model N of 1906.

Although natural wood panels were listed as part of the buyer resistance of the Sportsman, no such resistance was found regarding the all-wood station Wagon, Model 79B. Here, a total of 8,912 were sold this year, with the drop in sales more attributable to the short model year than to buyer indifference. Priced at $1,972 and weighing 3,520 pounds, it remained Ford's heaviest car. It could be ordered with the Six, but because of its weight, most dealers discouraged such a selection and recommended the slightly higher horsepower V-8. This beautiful example wears a rare roof-top luggage rack in addition to dual fog lights and beauty rings on the wheels. Rear quarter windows were still of the sliding type.

Ford's lowest price model was the Deluxe 3-passenger Coupe, Model 77A, which cost $1,154 as a Six or $1,230 as a V-8. At 3,066 V-8 pounds, it was also the lightest Ford. Despite the fact that the 3-passenger model had apparently been dropped from the Super Deluxe series, sales of this version only reached 5,048. A practical car for business use, since it offered huge cargo or luggage area, a 3-passenger vehicle really wasn't practical in the family-oriented car marketing philosophy of the era. This model is also referred to as a 5-window Coupe, or a Business Coupe, the latter being where it saw its greatest application.

If production records are indeed accurate, then the only two cars in this year's Deluxe series are the Business Coupe and this Deluxe Tudor Sedan, Model 70A. By far the most popular Deluxe vehicle, the low-trim car recorded 23,356 sales, which was still only one-third of those registered by the Super Deluxe version. Often equipped with the 6-cylinder engine, the car was priced at $1,212 and weighed 3,183 in that form, while as a V-8 it cost $1,288 and weighed 3,216 pounds. Upholstery was in a gray broadcloth or mohair, similar to but of lesser quality than that used in the Super Deluxe models. As before, only single sun visors, arm rests, and interior lights were used on these cars.

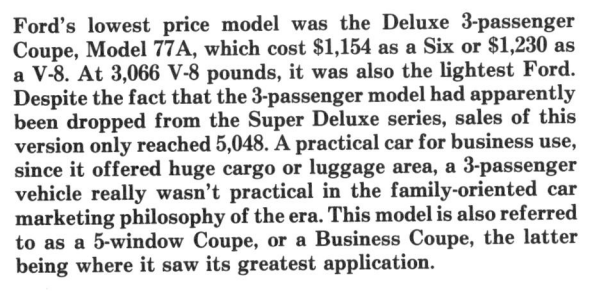

Another car that appears to have been dropped in a last minute decision was the Deluxe Fordor, Ford's low-trim version of its popular Super Deluxe model. Listed as the Model 73A and given a V-8 price of $1,346 in early Ford material, the production lists would indicate that no such vehicles were actually produced. Possibly Ford recognized that buyers preferred to spend a few more dollars to get the higher trim level found in the Super Deluxe models, and felt it wasn't worth the bother of producing the low level car for the few customers that might want the savings. Actually, this same model also caused confusion in 1947, with some production lists showing that 44,563 were produced, and other lists indicating that only 20 were made!

Finally the big day arrived. Ford would at last show off its "Postwar" creations. Hyped by scores of planted "secret" press releases, bolstered by both real and created rumors, and carried by genuine interest on the part of the public, the announcement of the new models was the largest publicity event staged by the company since the unveiling of the Model A. And so far as public and consumer interest went, the event was probably the largest in Ford history, either past or in the future.

The big day was kicked off on June 10, 1948, at the Waldorf-Astoria Hotel in New York City. Young Henry had selected (in fact, rushed into) the early showing in order to beat both General Motors and Chrysler, which were keying their postwar vehicles to a more conventional early fall schedule. The move worked perfectly. With little other automotive news on the scene at the time, Ford received the dominant place in just about every publication that even remotely thought about printing automobile articles. The "top secrecy" attitude of the company in prior months had whetted the interest of every automotive journalist in the country, and now the plan was paying off in thousands upon thousands of printed columns—virtually all good!

Most obvious to the public was the totally new style body for Ford. It had the modern slab-side design, with front fenders, body sides, and rear quarters forming one continuous line from head to taillights. A substantial squared trunk area provided 50% more luggage space while at the same time giving a balanced profile to the car—the new "Can't tell back from front" look. A simple yet attractive grille and a well balanced green house completed the appearance of a totally modern car, in effect telling the public that this really had been worth waiting for.

Responsible for the final approval, of course, was Henry Ford II. The approval marked the new president's first major decision as head of the Ford empire. And, approving a $72 million retooling project plus another $10-plus million for promotion and advertising certainly qualified as a major decision in anyone's book.

Actual credit for the cars goes to a design team headed by engineering vice-president Harold Youngren, and a styling team headed by George Walker. Walker later became vice-president and director of styling at Ford. The overall styling was so good that it not only won the Fashion Academy Award for 1949, it turned around and won it again for 1950.

Although the cars appeared longer and lower, they actually retained the same wheelbase of the previous models, and actually were 1.5 inches shorter than the 1946/48 models. The only exception to this was the totally new 2-door Station Wagon, which grew to 208 inches. Inside the new bodies, the story was completely different. Front seat passenger room was over 6 inches wider, going from 55.3 to 61.5 inches, while the rear seat room expanded 8.5 inches, going from 51.5 inches to an even five feet.

Not only was the body a totally new design, but the complete underside was also new, and totally radical to Ford. For the first time since the 1906 Model N, Ford did not have solid front axles and transverse leaf springs. Nor did it have the old X-type frame (except on the Convertible and Station Wagon, where the extra strength of the X-type was needed).

Instead, the cars were built on a lighter ladder-type or box frame, sometimes referred to as a K-type. The front wheels no longer lived on a single I-beam axle, but were supported by two independent A-frame units. These in turn were supported by coil springs and tubular shock absorbers. At the rear, independent longitudinal leaf springs replaced the single transverse spring, while an open Hotchkiss drive replaced the torque tube. Even the brakes were changed, going from 12x1.75 inches, which had 162 square inches of lining area, to 10x2.25 inches, which offered 177 square inches of lining. Since the curb weight on all cars had dropped an average of 250 pounds, the brakes offered greatly improved stopping power. Although the wheels remained 16-inches (except on the Station Wagon where they were 15-inch), an extra cost option would give all models 6.70x15 wheels with low pressure tires. These would effectively lower the overall height of the car about 1.5 to 2 inches when on the road.

While the exterior, interior, and chassis were totally new, the under-hood view was not all that different. However, changes did take place to both the Six and the V-8, and even though their basic dimensions and power ratings remained the same, those who derided Ford for keeping the same old horses in the barn were not quite telling the truth.

For example, both the Six and V-8 received new combustion chambers to provide better burning and more power on regular grades of gasoline. Both engines also received new intake manifolds and redesigned cooling systems and lubrication systems. The ignition system was also changed slightly on the V-8, and the distributor now stood upright. Likewise, the transmission was redesigned, and could be fitted with an optional automatic overdrive. All this, coupled with the overall reduction in weight, gave the new models a good bit more pep and speed than the previous cars, even though the basic power rating remained at 100 horses for the V-8 and 95 for the Six.

This year the line-up once again consisted of a high and low-trim series, with both the V-8 and Six available to all models, even the convertibles and station wagons. The old terminology was gone, and the low-level lines were simply referred to as Fords, while the high-trim batch was called the Custom series. Four different models were available as plain Fords. They were the 2-door and 4-door Sedans, the 6-passenger Club Coupe, and the 3-passenger Business Coupe. In the Custom line were found three of the above styles, as the Business Coupe did not enter this series. Apparently Ford felt this car was as its name implied, a business vehicle, and as such did not need a higher trim level. Also in the 5-model Custom series was the Convertible and the new wood-bodied, metal framed 2-door Station Wagon, which was a totally different concept from the old work-type former wagon design.

Ford gambled on its new designs and won. Thanks in part to the new styling and in part to the 18-month model year, Ford finally produced over 1-million cars and once again unseated Chevrolet as the top producer. In fact, production totaled 1,118,740 before a switch was made to the 1950 models. Of these, 204,449 were in the plain Ford series, while 914,291 were Customs. As always, the high-trim custom 2-door Sedan was the overall sales leader, with 433,316 units being sold. The Custom 4-door came in second, with 248,176 units, while the Custom 6-passenger Coupe was third with 150,254 sales.

As could be expected, all prices were up slightly, with the top line 2-door going from $1,382 in 1948 to $1,590 for the new model. The highest priced car in the line was the Station Wagon, which listed for over $2,000, being $2,119 for a Six or $2,246 for the V-8.

As mentioned, Ford had gambled and won. Had it not, this book and Ford history might very well have ended in the early or mid-1950s. In actuality, Ford was in terrible shape at the end of World War II. Henry II had no bed of roses to fall into when he took over from the old man, and it was only through some very daring moves, some hard handed personnel changes, and some modern engineering and styling, that the company moved from its $10-million a month loss factor in the late 1940s to a similar profit factor in the 1950s. Essentially, all of the changes and innovations made to this year's Ford were radical in terms of previous models. But to the industry overall, these were simply refinements of what had been in effect all along. What really happened was that Ford finally left the early 1930s behind, and in one jump, made up almost 15 years. It was a big gamble, but it worked.

Running third on Ford's sales chart was the Custom Club Coupe, Model 72B, which enjoyed 150,254 sales. The car shared its body with the two plain coupe models, but was the only version to enter the Custom series. From the exterior, only the small "Custom" plaque at the leading edge of the side molding told the plain from the fancy. On the interior, the story was the same as in the 1946/48 models. Plain Fords had a less expensive interior, a horn button, and single sun visor, while the Customs had more deluxe fittings. The Club Coupe was regarded as a 6-passenger car, though seating was tight for six adults. It cost $1,596 as a V-8 and weighed 2,968 pounds. In the plain Ford series, which is not shown here, the style was available as the Club Coupe, Model 72A, or the Business Coupe, Model 72C. The plain Club Coupe, at $1,523, drew only 4,170 orders, and differed from the Custom only in trim level. The Business Coupe, at $1,420, was a relatively popular commercial-type, and drew 28,946 sales. It had a single front bench seat, and a large cargo space where the rear seat resided in the Club Coupe. Outwardly the cars looked the same, but the rear quarter window of the Business Coupe was lined in black rubber and would not open, while those on the Club Coupes were chrome edged and would swing open in vent-pane fashion. The Business Coupe was not available in the Custom series.

Epitomizing the totally new 1949 Ford was the Convertible, Model 76. Available only in the new Custom series, the car still could be ordered with either the Six or the V-8, though few actually were delivered with the Six. With the V-8 it was priced at $1,949, the price matching its year! Weight was 3,234 pounds. The convertible and the wagon were the only models not to use the new ladder frame. Ford felt both of these models should continue with the old X-frame since that offered more support. The Convertible turned out to be surprisingly popular, with 51,133 being sold. Red was its most popular color. Once again genuine leather was used in the seat upholstery, in combination with bedford cord inserts. Buyers had a choice of red or tan leather with beige cord, or green leather with green bedford cord. Tops were in gray-tan; black, or green to harmonize with the interior schemes.

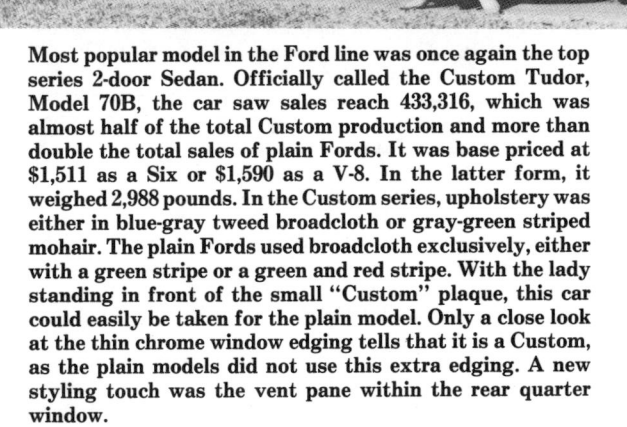

Most popular model in the Ford line was once again the top series 2-door Sedan. Officially called the Custom Tudor, Model 70B, the car saw sales reach 433,316, which was almost half of the total Custom production and more than double the total sales of plain Fords. It was base priced at $1,511 as a Six or $1,590 as a V-8. In the latter form, it weighed 2,988 pounds. In the Custom series, upholstery was either in blue-gray tweed broadcloth or gray-green striped mohair. The plain Fords used broadcloth exclusively, either with a green stripe or a green and red stripe. With the lady standing in front of the small "Custom" plaque, this car could easily be taken for the plain model. Only a close look at the thin chrome window edging tells that it is a Custom, as the plain models did not use this extra edging. A new styling touch was the vent pane within the rear quarter window.

The style most changed in concept was the Station Wagon, Model 79, which went from a 4-door work-a-day philosophy to a 2-door family transporter. Unlike previous models which were framed in wood, the new wagon had an all-steel top and steel subframing, with the wood panels playing primarily a decorative role. As before, all wood work and assembly was done at Ford's Iron Mountain plant. Ford's most expensive and heaviest model, the wagon sold for $2,264 and weighed 3,563 pounds with the V-8. It could also be ordered with the Six for $145 less. Still, the price seemed to be no detractor, and 31,412 were sold, marking a definite high point for the wagon style within Ford's ranks. An unusual styling touch was found in the huge rear quarter windows, which were of the sliding type. The spare continued to be attached to the exterior of the tailgate, residing in its own metal cover. The driver's seat was upholstered in genuine tan leather, but the two rear seats were in a matching vinyl. Because of the all-metal roof, Ford wagons had headliners for the first time in their history.

The overall changes in body design are probably more evident in the 4-door Sedan and the wagon than in other models. Here the rear quarters came under a completely new concept. On the Fordor, Model 73B, these involved a large squared trunk with 50% more capacity, a completely independent superstructure, and the end of rear quarter windows. To compensate for the latter, vent panes were designed into the door windows. These were functional vents, and could be swung open for flow-through ventilation. The Custom Fordor was Ford's second most popular model, having a run of 2248,176. It sold for a base $1,559 as a Six, and $1,638 as a V-8, in which form it weighed 3,033 pounds. Once again, an all-vinyl/leather interior could be ordered for any Custom or plain series closed car. The material was a tan vinyl similar to that used on the passenger seats of the wagons. No longer a popular option, it was not carried into the 1950 model year.

Probably because all of the hype concerning the new Fords centered on the fancier Custom models, very little promotional material was put out on the plain series. If fact, factory photos of the plain series have been impossible to find. This is the most popular of the plain styles. It is the Ford Tudor, Model 70A, which had a run of 126,770. Wearing accessory fog lights and a spotlight, this hard-driving salesman's special sold for $1,425 as a Six or $1,499 as a V-8. Its companion, the Ford Fordor, Model 73A, listed for $1,472 as a Six or $1,546 as a V-8. It had a run of 44,563. The two models used the same bodies as the Custom series, and differed only in the level of interior trim and comfort items. From the exterior, it took a very sharp eye to distinguish one from the other. Also in the plain Ford line were the Club Coupe and the Business Coupe, described in the caption accompanying the Custom Club Coupe.

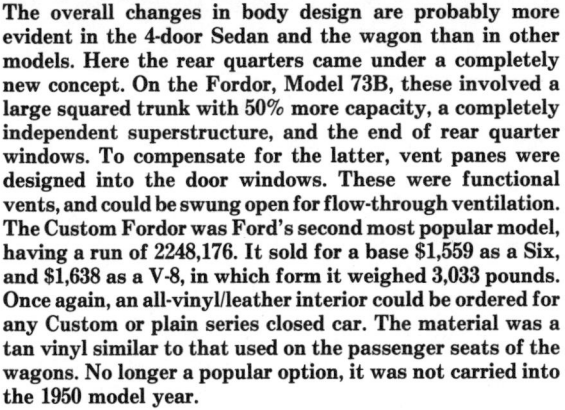

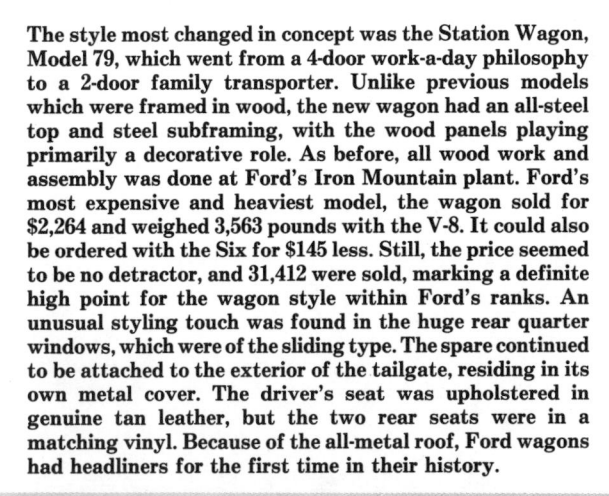

Those who wanted 4-door Ford station wagons could still get them, but they had to be specially ordered from the Shop of Siebert in Toledo, Ohio. Once again this company was busy stretching Fords into various types of professional and transporter cars, and this year it included the new wagon in its list of available models. The added section gave the car an 11-passenger capacity. Its intended use was probably for airport transport, hotel livery, and the like. A roof-top ventilator has been added to this unit.

The typical Shop of Siebert stretch involved two and 4-door sedans, more often than station wagons. This version is based on the Custom Fordor, and probably utilizes the V-8, although Siebert did offer the model as a Six. In the professional field, the primary market for this vehicle was as a 9-passenger pallbearer's car. As an airport transporter, it could hold 12 passengers. Siebert would also produce the model with a luxury private limousine interior, and claimed its ride was comfortable as that of limousines costing thousands of dollars more. Siebert was still building a multitude of professional cars on Ford chassis, but the vast majority of these were based on Ford light truck units, and not on passenger cars.

The traveling auto thrill show, which had originated in the mid-1930s, reached its zenith during the decade spanning the late 1940s to the late 1950s. Literally dozens of these shows rode the county fair circuit, crisscrossing America with their feats of automotive daring and destruction. Many tried to get auto company backing to help ease the financial load, but few succeeded. One of the best known troupes, and one that had the full backing of Ford, was the Joie Chitwood Auto Daredevils. Chitwood actually had five shows traveling the country, all using new Custom models—no low-buck cars were going to be shown to these auto fans. Here one does a high wheel stand, as an unconcerned clown sits on a corner of the ramp. In order to perform in the shows, suspensions were modified, exhaust systems removed, and the gas tank relocated to the trunk for safety. About 50 shows was the maximum that a car could take.

One of several Fordillacs to come out during this era is this interesting 2-seater. Built at Briggs Cunningham's shops by Alfred Momo, Cunningham's chief engineer and race team coordinator, it is not known if this was a one-off experiment, or one of what was to be a limited production run. A few other firms played with the Fordillac concept—that of combining the new Ford's excellent handling with the power of the 348 cubic inch Cadillac engine. On this particular example, the chassis and frame have been left untouched, but the hood and fenders have been stretched about two feet, and a 2-seat cockpit occupies the area normally reserved for rear seat passengers. Bill Frick of Long Island, N.Y., was another converter, turning out a multitude of Fordillacs, Studillacs, and Cadillac-Allards, although Frick's creations were not as radical as this Cunningham creation.

The manufacturers of the Plexi-Top clear hardtops for convertibles had pretty much come to the conclusion that the clear bubbles were interesting, but buyers found them just too hot to be bearable in the summer. In a final effort to stay in the market, the company came out with these Add-A-Top units, and marketed them through local Ford dealers. Available for the 1949 and 1950 models, the tops could be easily installed in place of the lowered convertible top. The all-plastic units were far more heat resistant than the clear tops, and contained a headliner which provided further insulation. Cadillac Plastic Co., of Detroit was the actual manufacturer. In 1951 the whole idea came to a screeching halt when Ford brought out its own Custom Victoria Hardtop.

As the 1949 Ford had been a complete break with tradition, in both engineering and styling, it was no surprise to anyone that the 1950 models would undergo only minimal change. And Ford was not alone in this marketing situation. Chrysler and General Motors also made major changes in 1949, and only a few changes in 1950. The only exception to this in the major leagues was found in Buick, which underwent a transitional styl-

Ford's headline catcher of the year was the Crestliner, designed to offset the new hardtop coupe styles that were being offered by both General Motors and Chrysler. However, the Crestliner almost didn't make it in 1950, not being introduced until July, almost in time to be considered a 1951 model. Essentially the car was simply a gussied-up Tudor, with its own exclusive side trim; stainless steel rocker plates; special interior; vinyl top; and fancy wheel covers and fender skirts. It came in only two colors: a lime green and a deep maroon, both having black side inserts and black vinyl tops. Considered part of the Custom Deluxe Series, it was available only with the V-8 engine. Its base price was $1,711, which was only $121 above the Custom Deluxe Tudor. Designated the Model C70C, it weighed 3,050 pounds. Probably due to its late introduction, production reached only 17,601 before the style was switched to the 1951 sheet metal.

Once again the Convertible enjoyed excellent sales among those seeking a sporty car, and production totalled 50,299 units. Again Ford switched its policies, and deleted the 6-cylinder engine from the Convertible's options. Although separate production figures were not kept, it can be assumed that very few 6-cylinder convertibles were ever sold anyway. Designated the Model C76, and available only in the Custom Deluxe series, the car cost $1,948 and weighed 3,263 pounds.

ing into a very attractive car in 1949, and then went through a major and perplexing styling change in 1950, coming out as the ugly-ugly of the year.

Meanwhile, in the Ford camp, only a few refinements were made. Ford advertised "50 changes for 1950," but included among those changes such things as extending the gas filler; changing door latches to a push-button type; redesigning a new horn ring, and such other mind-shattering innovations. When one got down to serious differences, the major outward change involved moving the parking lamps from the ends of the grille bar to a new chrome-surrounded location below the grille bar. Also, on the deluxe models, the identification plaque was still at the leading edge of the side trim, but now was above the trim rather than below.

During the year, Ford management was taking a serious look at the "new" hardtop "convertible" designs which were coming on the scene, especially from General Motors. The concept wasn't new-going back into the early teens—but stylists had ignored the idea of a solid roofed convertible throughout most of the 1930s and 40s. Yet, when one thinks about it, one wonders why the concept took so long to re-emerge. Regardless, other car makers had hardtops and Ford did not!

As a result, a crash design program was set up with Wettlaufer Engineering Corp. to design an all-metal roof that could be grafted onto the coming 1951 convertible shells. The result was the 1951 Victoria, but that didn't help the 1950 models.

In a second crash program, both Ford and Lincoln-

The rear view of the new Convertible shows little change from the 1949 models. Even with the top raised, the car promoted a sporty flair, and continued its reputation as America's most popular convertible, outselling the comparable Chevrolet version by almost 20,000 units. Tops were available in tan, black, or green, all with a glass window in the removable rear panel. A wide variety of interiors were available this year, including genuine leather in light tan; 2-tone tan; chartreuse and black; red and black; or in combinations of natural or dyed leather and bedford cord panels. The metal interior areas, including the dash areas, were painted either lime green, red, or tan, depending on the interior and exterior color selections.

Mercury division set about to come up with an eye-catcher that would take some of the steam from the General Motors hardtops. Lincoln-Mercury reached the line first, coming out in June with the Mercury Monterey and the Lincoln Lido and Capri (well documented in Crestline's *THE CARS OF LINCOLN MERCURY*, by James K. Wagner and George H. Dammann.

In July, the Ford offering finally arrived, almost in time to wear 1951 styling. Called the Crestliner, the car was simply a Custom Tudor outfitted with a special high-grade trim level. Only two body colors were available, either a lime green or a maroon red, both set off by large black side panels outlines in exclusive stainless steel trim. A black vinyl top graced the roof, while special rocker trim and special wheel covers and rear skirts took care of the lower portion. Twin side mirrors, a special steering wheel and interior decor, and special matching finish on the dash completed the picture.

Despite the fact that the Crestliner was priced at $1,710, which was only $120 more than the regular Custom Deluxe Tudor, sales were not really astonishing. Probably a combination of late entry coupled with the fact that sporty car buyers had already made their move by July resulted in comparatively low sales for the car. Production figures are confusing inasmuch as the Crestliner was carried over to 1951, but was dropped at mid-year when the Victoria came along. Still, figures tend to show that a total of 17,601 Crestliners were produced in 1950 garb, despite the short sales slot.

Incidentally, the name "Crestliner" has no connection with Crestline Publishing Co., now a part of Motorbooks International. The publishing company's name was taken from the family farm on which the author was raised, and refers to the crest of the nearest hills as being the original property line of the farm-hence Crestline.

And in line with crests, all Fords sported one this year on the hoods and rear deck. This was the first introduction of what has now become the famous and well recognized Ford Crest, and has appeared on cars, advertising, and publications, with an on-again-off-again basis right up to present day.

Beside the Crestliner, the Ford line was marked by the disappearance of one model. The Club Coupe was now available only in the high-trim series, while the low-buck line had only the 3-passenger business interior built into the coupe body shell. Very poor sales of the plain Club Coupe in 1949 had certainly been responsible for this decision.

Once again, two forms of "Deluxe" were used to designate the trim levels. Replacing the plain Ford name was the low-trim Deluxe series, while the high-trim cars were called Custom Deluxe models. The Deluxe series held only the Tudor and Fordor Sedans and the Business Coupe. Some information would indicate that a Club Coupe version was indeed available here, but no production information can be found for such a car.

In the Custom Deluxe line were found the Tudor and Fordor Sedans, the Club Coupe, 2-door Station Wagon, Convertible, and the new Crestliner. Once again Ford put engine restrictions on some models, and the Convertible and Crestliner could only be ordered with the V-8. All other models in both series could have either engine, and could be ordered with the optional automatic overdrive.

Production for the year again topped 1-million, reaching 1,198,036. Of these, 388,368 were in the Deluxe series, while 809,668 were in the Custom Deluxe range. As before, the Custom Deluxe Tudor drew the most orders, with its 398,060 topping all of the production of the entire Deluxe run. Second in popularity was the plain Deluxe Tudor with a surprising sales count of 275,360, representing almost two-thirds of the total Deluxe production. The Custom Deluxe Fordor Sedan came in third with 247,181 sales, which was just about the same as 1949. But this was not enough to hold off the plain Tudor, which enjoyed an unexplained one-year peak of popularity, possibly attributable to some very large fleet orders.

On the cost scene, everything remained the same as in 1949 or even edged downward slightly. Thus, while the V-8 and Six versions of the Custom Deluxe models remained steady, the Station Wagon actually went down to $2,107, which was a $157 drop from the 1949 list.

Available only in the Custom Deluxe series was the 6-passenger Club Coupe, Model C72. Although the car shared its basic body with the 3-passenger Business Coupe, it was not available in 3-passenger form in the Custom Deluxe series. Beside the side trim differences, the Club Coupe could be quickly identified by the swing-out rear quarter windows, edged in stainless steel. Retaining its limited popularity, the car drew 85,111 orders. It was priced at $1,595 as a V-8, or $84 less with the Six. As a V-8 it weighed 3,003 pounds. Notice this year that the "Custom" designation is above the side spear, while in 1949 it was below the trim. Although Ford referred to its top line models as "Custom Deluxe," the word "Deluxe" did not appear on the car.

As always, Ford's most popular car was the Custom Deluxe Tudor, Model C70. This year the car drew 398,060 orders, which was more than all of the orders for the total Deluxe series. Priced at $1,590 as a V-8, it was the lowest cost car in the Custom Deluxe line. It weighed 3,031 pounds. Quick identification between 1949 and 1950 models can be made by the parking lights, which this year were located in rather large bright casings below the center grille bar. The Tudor differed from the Club Coupe in that it had a longer upper structure and passenger compartment, and its rear quarter held both a roll-down window and a swing-out vent.

Still a pretty, if not impractical car, was the 2-door Ford Station Wagon, Model C79. Continuing to be Ford's most expensive and heaviest model, it weighed 3,531 pounds and cost $2,107 as a V-8. Thus, despite a slight reduction in price from the 1949 mark, it was still the only Ford to exceed a $2,000 base price. Upholstery continued to be in tan genuine leather for the front seat, with matching artificial leather used for the rear seats and tan vinyl used on the headliner. As before, the body was of wood, constructed within a metal frame. All wagon production continued to be done at the Iron Mountain plant in northern Michigan.

Falling to third place in overall production was the Custom Deluxe Fordor Sedan, which slipped behind the Deluxe Tudor this year. Still, its sales held at 247,181, which was less than 1,000 off the 1949 tally. Priced at $1,637, it weighed 3,093 as a V-8. It was designated Model C73. This year all Custom Deluxe closed cars were upholstered either in gray mohair with gray and red stripes or in gray broadcloth with gray and blue stripes. All metal within the bodies, including the dash panel, was finished in metallic gray, regardless of the exterior color.

The Ford wagons continued to have a rather unique rear design. Most obvious, of course, was the continued use of an outside spare, encased in its own metal cover and usually fitted with a standard wheel cover, though that is missing from this example. The upper gate consisted of two separate glass panes, within an all-metal frame. The lower swing-down gate had a metal frame, but was built of wood. A special bumper had to be used, with a cut-out to allow space for the spare when the gate was lowered. Still, only one taillight was supplied, but the extra-cost right hand unit was a popular accessory. Note the rods extending from the taillight to the lower body. These were hinged and insured that the light would be facing rearward, not downward, when the gate was lowered. Rear quarter windows were still of the slider type.

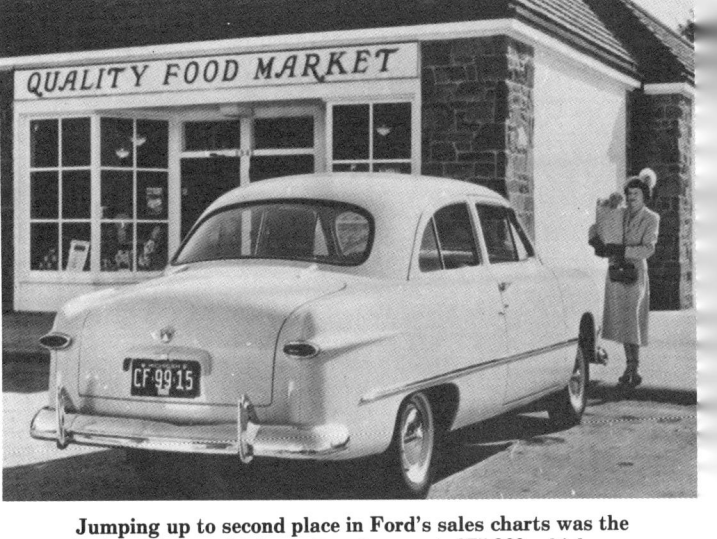

From this angle it is difficult to tell whether this is the Deluxe Business Coupe or the Deluxe Tudor. For the sake of illustration, it will be considered the 3-passenger Business Coupe, Model D72C. Priced at $1,333 with the Six or $1,419 with the V-8, this was Ford's lowest price model. At 2,965 pounds as a V-8, it was also the lightest. Production reached 35,120, all in 3-passenger business form, as the 6-passenger Club Coupe was no longer available in the low priced series. However, some early information would indicate that a club coupe model was considered for this series, but never materialized. The lack of chrome trim around the windshield quickly identifies this model as a Deluxe version. Otherwise, there was no frontal difference between the Deluxe and Custom Deluxe series.

Jumping up to second place in Ford's sales charts was the Deluxe Tudor, which saw its sales soar to 275,360, which was more than double those of 1949. No explanation can be found for this sudden surge in popularity, except to note that the differences between the Deluxe and Custom Deluxe models were so small that many buyers might have figured they would save the $92 and go with the plainer model. Base priced at $1,424 for the Six, it was also available with the V-8 for $1,498. Designated the Model D70, it weighed 2,988 as a Six. Interiors of all Deluxe models were finished in either gray mohair with rust stripes or in a tan broadcloth with blue and rust stripes. All interior metal was finished in either a light tan metallic or in the same gray metallic as used in the Custom Deluxe cars. Only the lack of stainless trim around the rear window differentiated the Deluxe model from the Custom Deluxe when seen from the rear.

Far less popular in the Deluxe series than in the Custom Deluxe was the Fordor Sedan, Model D73. Sales reached only 77,888, which was only one-third of those of the Custom Deluxe counterpart. Side trim gave quick identity of Deluxe models, as forward trim consisted of only a plain spear point, whereas the more expensive models carried the "Custom" name at the leading edge of the trim. Some information would indicate that stainless window trim was not used in the Deluxe series, but numerous photos of these cars show them with bright window edging, but lacking the stainless trim around the windshield and rear window. The Deluxe Fordor sold for $1,472 as a Six, or $73 less as a V-8. It weighed 3,050 pounds as a Six. As before, in this series, only one sun visor and one arm rest were provided, and a horn button took the place of the horn ring found on Custom Deluxe models.

Once again Ford sponsored the Joie Chitwood auto thrill shows, and supplied them with Custom Deluxe models. Here a slightly battered Fordor participates in a stunt called the "slide for life." In this act, a stuntman dropped from the rear of the speeding car and slid through a blazing pool of gasoline. Stunts like this were much harder on the stuntman's padded pants than they were on the cars. Only minor modifications to the suspension and exhaust and fuel system differentiated these vehicles from regular passenger cars.

Despite the fact that it continued its 1949 body styles into their third unchanged year, Ford managed to come up with two headline grabbers this year. And, this was in addition to redesigning the car's face to give it a totally new and more attractive frontal appearance.

The first big news from Ford was announcement of the cars' first automatic transmission. A late-comer in the field of automatics, Ford made up for the delay with a unit that almost every automotive writer of the day praised to the sky. Designed jointly by Ford and Borg-Warner, the new automatic was built exclusively in a new plant in Cincinnati. Featuring planetary gears (shades of the old Model T) and three speeds forward, the new unit was available on Fords as a Fordomatic (sometimes spelled Ford-O-Matic) and on Mercurys as a Merc-O-Matic. In normal operation, the "Drive" mode was selected. Here the car would start off in the intermediate range, and shift into drive at about 2000 rpm. In the "Low" range, the transmission was locked into a low-speed power gear, and had to be up-shifted manually.

Surprisingly, no additional horsepower was given to either engine when the new automatic was ordered. A slight concession was made to the cooling system, and a different fan and slightly larger radiator were included with automatics, but otherwise the engines remained the same in all models. And, just like the bodies, they were essentially 1949 models. The new automatic could be ordered on any body style and with either V-8 or 6-cylinder power for an additional $159. Also available was the 3-speed manual transmission with automatic overdrive, introduced in 1949, which now listed at $92 above the standard manual 3-speed.

The other big news of the year had to wait until the snow fell. This involved Ford's first true hardtop, called the Victoria. Finally, after falling behind General Motors for two years and Chrysler for one year, Ford also had a hardtop. And, so well received was the new style that it outsold both the established Chevrolet Bel Aire and the Plymouth Belvidere, having an excellent run of 110,286 for its 9-month production period.

Birthing efforts for the new Victoria did not come easy. Ford's own design staff was tied up with a multitude of new ideas, and when the crash program for the Victoria began, it was obvious that Ford could not do it alone. This was to be no "add-a-top" design for the convertible. Ford wanted a totally new design engineered to be a complete hardtop, not a compromised ragtop. Thus, a design team was formed, headed by Gordon Buehrig (of Auburn-Cord-Duesenberg fame) and consisting of designers and engineers from both Ford and Wettlaufer Engineering Corp. The development couldn't be made in time for the 1951 introduction, but when it did occur a few months later, it created a whole new flurry of publicity for Ford.

At the main line introduction itself, the new Fords received glowing reports in the automotive press, despite the fact that the bodies, chassis, and engines were virtually unchanged. What did impress most people was the new frontal treatment, consisting of a new grille with two torpedoes; new taillight treatment with large chrome pods extending halfway forward on the quarter panel; new headlight rims; new hood ornament, and new identity emblems. Inside, a totally new dash faced the driver, and put all controls within easy reach and sight. Taken individually, only the new grille gave any real visual impact, but overall the entire package was one of quiet refinement that resulted in

Ford finally got its hardtop. Two years behind General Motors and one year behind Chrysler, the Ford hardtop, called the Victoria Model 60, finally emerged in mid-winter. Still, the car drew rave reviews from the automotive press, and almost windfall acceptance by the buying public. A total of 110,286 were sold in the short remaining year, beating even the sales of the established Chevrolet Bel Aire. Priced at $1,925 and weighing 3,188 pounds, the car was essentially in the same dollar category as the true convertible. Oddly, the new Victoria was not simply the convertible with an added hardtop. It was a totally new body style, with exclusive styling designed by a team headed by Gordon Buehrig and consisting of personnel from both Ford and Wettlaufer Engineering Corp. Though introduction came late in the year, this too proved to be plus for Ford, as the new model grabbed headlines in virtually every automotive journal of that era. The Victoria was available only with the V-8 engine.

The real Convertible, Model 76, was still one of the best selling soft tops in the country, even though this year its sales slipped to 40,934, a drop of almost 10,000. Priced at $1,949 and weighing 3,268 pounds, the car came with a variety of top options. There were: black; black with red binding; tan, or green. Interiors could be ordered in 2-tone tan leather; or chartreuse, red, or blue-green, all with black leather, or any of the leather combinations with matching panels in a new craftcord material. Interior metal was finished in a metallic paint of either blue-green, red, lime green, or tan, to match the interior color combination. Once again, the Convertible came only with V-8 power.

a very nice looking vehicle.

Once again, the available models were divided into a high and low trim series. The low price line retained its name "Deluxe," but the former Custom Deluxe series was now once again simply called the "Custom" line. Within the Deluxe series was the Tudor and Fordor Sedans, which shared spaces in the Custom line, and the 3-passenger Business Coupe, which was exclusive to the Deluxe series only, even though the basic body appeared in the Custom series as the 6-passenger Club Coupe.

In the Custom series were the same three closed bodies as found in the Deluxe range, plus the Crestliner, the Convertible, the Victoria, and the Station Wagon. Of these exclusive models, only the Station Wagon could be ordered with the 6-cylinder engine as an option, while the other three "sport" models came with the V-8 only. This year, for the first time, Ford used the name "Country Squire" on its wagon, a name that would continue to grace the top line wagons seemingly forever.

At introduction, as mentioned, Ford still did not have its hardtop, so the Crestliner once again had to carry the flag as the sporty Ford. As in the previous year, the Crestliner was simply a variation of the Tudor Sedan, fitted with exclusive exterior trim and paint combinations, and a unique interior. The model this year came in four special paint colors: Greenbriar Metallic; lime green, and a light tan, all having a black insert and black vinyl top, or Hawaiian Bronze with a brown insert. The former maroon with black was no longer available. The interiors were in black artificial leather with chartreuse

or blue-green craftcord inserts, or brown artificial leather with tan craftcord panels.

Despite its rather exotic looks, the Crestliner was not drawing customers this year, and production of the model was halted shortly after the new Victoria appeared. As a result, only 8,703 were built before the run was ended.

Total production was down slightly this year, despite the new Victoria, but still was over the 1-million mark. Of the 1,013,381 Ford cars produced this year, only 220,618 were in the Deluxe range, while 792,763 were in the Custom series. As usual, the most popular model was the Custom Tudor Sedan, which had a run of 317,869, down almost 80,000 from 1950. Second place was once again filled by the Custom Fordor Sedan, which recorded 232,691 sales, which was almost on par with 1950. The big drop was felt by the Deluxe Tudor, which, while still holding third place, had only 146,010 sales, a drop of almost 129,000 from the previous year. Surprisingly, the only other model to record over 100,000 units was the new Victoria, with its 110,286 examples rolling out the door.

On the price scene, everything remained relatively static, with only the Custom Station Wagon breaking the $2,000 mark. The Crestliner was the only model to go into a price decrease, beginning the year at the $1,700 figure as of 1950, but winding up during the winter priced at just about the same as the Custom Tudor.

Toward the middle of the model year, rumors began to circulate that Ford had some new tricks up its sleeve for 1952, and many potential buyers began the typical "let's wait" game. Those who waited probably were not disappointed, as 1952 once again ushered in a totally new Ford. Still, those who did buy 1951 models had no cause to cry either, as this year marked the third refinement of what initially was an excellent car to begin with.

The new Crestliner sported revised and definitely improved side trim and paint, but even this didn't seem to help sales. The car limped along until mid-winter, when the new Victoria was introduced, and after that production apparently dribbled to a close. As a result, only 8,703 were built as 1951 models. Prices began in the $1,700 range, but it appears that by mid-year, the Crestliner was selling for little more than the Custom Tudor, on which it was based. Exotic touches continued to include a black vinyl roof, exclusive side trim, black or brown paint insert, special wheel covers, and custom interiors similar to those of the convertible but using artificial leather rather than the genuine leather used on the convertibles. New colors included two shades of green and a light tan, all with black inserts, and a Hawaiian Bronze with brown inserts. The maroon version was no longer available. Unlike the Custom Tudor which could be ordered with a Six, the Crestliner came only in V-8 form.

Available only in the Custom series was the 6-passenger Club Coupe, which used the same body shell as the 3-passenger Business Coupe in the Deluxe series. This year the Custom version could be quickly identified by the full-length side trim, which was similar to that used in former years. However, the plain Deluxe models did not use this stainless molding. On the Club Coupe, the rear quarter windows continued to be of the swing-out type, outlined in stainless steel. Priced at $1,590, the car weighed 3,034 pounds as a V-8, and thus was the lightest and least expensive of the Custom models. Designated the Model 72C, it had a run of 53,263. The lack of V-8 emblem on the front fender, just above the "Custom" designation, indicates that this model was equipped with the 6-cylinder engine. As such, it would have been $85 less than the V-8.

A lake-side picnic seems just the thing for a young family to enjoy with their new Custom Tudor. Still Ford's most popular style, the Model 70B drew a total of 317,869 orders this year. The figure, though good, still represented a drop of over 80,000 from 1950. Priced at $1,585, the Tudor weighed 3,062, these being V-8 figures. When equipped with the new Fordomatic automatic transmission, this price would go up another $159. The small V-8 emblem just above the leading edge of the side trim indicates that this car has the big engine. If it also had the automatic, a "Fordomatic" plaque would be attached on the lower edge of the trunk deck.

Displaying Ford's new grille is this Station Wagon, Model 79, which was the first to bear the "Country Squire" designation. Written in chrome script, the Country Squire emblem appeared at the leading edge of the doors. This would be Ford's last true wagon. Even though it was constructed on a metal frame, the wood panels and posts on this model were still functional, as opposed to a wood veneer which was being used by most other car manufacturers. Since Ford closed its Iron Mountain plant during the 1950 model year, it could no longer produce its own wagon bodies. Thus, it had to contract with Iona Body Co. to construct the 1951 wagon bodies, to specifications identical to the 1949/50 Ford units. Iona built a total of 29,017 before a switch was made to the all-steel 1952 version. Priced at $2,110 and weighing 3,550 pounds, the Country Squire continued to be the only Ford beyond the $2,000 mark. The 2-piece tailgate remained, with the swing-up top portion being of all steel with two rear window panes, while the lower swing-down portion continued to support the external spare tire and the swing-out taillights. Despite being in the Custom series, the wagon had no side chrome on the front fenders, except for the small V-8 emblem seen here when the large engine was installed.

Well representing the Custom Fordor is this V-8 equipped model, which sold for $1,633 and weighed 3,144 pounds. Probably it has the new Fordomatic transmission, or at least the $92 optional overdrive. Once again Ford's second most popular car, the Fordor accounted for 232,691 sales, which was almost on par with the 1950 production. This year interiors were either in tan craftloom with a rust stripe; gray or green craftweave, or 2-tone brown craftcord, all being brand new fabric types for Ford. Interior metal parts were finished in brown, green, or blue-gray metallic paint. Ford's taillights were now set off by large chrome pods which went forward halfway into the rear quarter panel.

Appearing only in the low-price Deluxe series was the 3-passenger Business Coupe, Model 72C. Priced at $1,324 with the Six, it was Ford's lowest price car of the year. The small V-8 emblem behind the front fender spear indicates that this car had the larger engine, which was an $87 upgrade. All Deluxe models now had stainless steel around all side windows, but continued to use just plain rubber molding around the windshield and rear glass. The Business Coupe used the same body as the Club Coupe, but was fitted with only a single front bench seat and a large luggage or cargo area in the rear section. Except for the Crestliner, this was Ford's least popular model, drawing only 20,343 orders. It weighed 2,960 pounds with the Six.

Slipping back to third sales spot was the Deluxe Tudor, Model 70, which recorded only 146,010 units built this year. This was a drop of almost 130,000 from 1950. Priced at $1,492 with the V-8 as shown here, it weighed 3,062 pounds. The lack of side trim gave these cars a terribly stark appearance and did nothing to protect the doors from parking lot dings. The small spear on the front fender carried the word "Deluxe" but really did little to prevent the tub-like appearance caused by the lack of beltline brightwork. Whereas in previous years the difference between the high and low series had been primarily in interior fittings, this year the visual distinction was immediately apparent.

Apparently demonstrating the pulling power of the 6-cylinder engine, this Deluxe Fordor is navigating some pretty sticky gumbo—or is it stuck? Designated the Model 73, the Deluxe Fordor weighed 3,089 pounds and cost $1,465 with the Six as shown here, or $75 more with the V-8. Sales topped out at 54,265, which was less than one-quarter than that of the comparable Custom model. Deluxe cars carried the same chrome taillight pods as found on the Custom series, but suffered greatly in appearance from the decision to remove the side molding. An interesting note here is the rear deck which sports a "Fordomatic Drive" plaque between the deck handle and the Ford crest. Although Fordomatics could be ordered with the 6-cylinder engines, such a combination was relatively rare in this first year of the automatic, and most of these transmissions were hooked to V-8 blocks.

The Shop of Siebert of Toledo, Ohio, continued with its line of professional cars this year. Based on the Ford passenger car chassis, rather than the light truck line, these cars were called the Aristocrat Series. This is the hearse version, built in limousine style and mounted on an extended and reinforced frame. Although Siebert closely followed the Ford sheet metal lines, and utilized portions of the original Tudor bodies, virtually everything from the cowl rearward was constructed in Siebert's shop. The company even modified the forward chrome trim to read "Siebert" rather than "Custom."

The other primary professional vehicle in Siebert's Aristocrat Series was the ambulance. Both hearse and ambulance used the same body shell and differed only in interior design and superficial items such as siren and etched rear quarter glass for the ambulance. Siebert used only V-8 equipped cars, but it is not known if the company availed itself of the new Fordomatic transmission, which it seems, would have been a natural for these vehicles. Although Siebert added its own stainless side trim and decorative louvers on the rear quarters, it appears that the chrome taillight pods were removed—or at least Siebert's catalog drawings do not show these pods being chromed.

It appears that this was the final year of Ford's sponsorship of the Joie Chitwood thrill shows. Here four new Deluxe Fordors are performing Chitwood's precision low ramp jump while traveling at about 50 MPH. This year Chitwood got low-level Deluxe models rather than the Custom versions he had received in the past. Though still moderately popular, thrill shows such as this were just beginning their downhill slide, which would terminate with the virtual disappearance of these shows by the mid-1960s. A few shows did survive, and a few are still around, but overall, TV and movie stunts of spectacular proportions made such things as ramp jumps on a local fairgrounds track seem pretty tame. Note the lack of V-8 emblems on the front fenders. These cars were all equipped with 6-cylinder engines.

A third variation in Siebert's Aristocrat line of professional cars was the Landau style, which was available in hearse, service car, or combination ambulance/hearse forms. The Landau used the same basic Siebert body shell as did the other models, but had a large blank quarter panel rather than the large quarter windows in the limousine hearse or ambulance styles. The hearse version drew its name from the large chrome decorative landau bars on each side of the rear quarters. However, these bars were omitted when the vehicle was produced in service car form, and were optional when the order was for a combination car. Combination cars were rather common in small towns where the one vehicle could do double duty as either an ambulance or a hearse. In most such cases, the car would wear the interior of a basically equipped ambulance, but this interior could be removed with little trouble, and a basic hearse table and curtains installed for funeral car use. When the funeral was over, the vehicle could be quickly returned to its ambulance guise. The only problem was that no one dared get sick or injured while a funeral was in progress.

Although the year is often overlooked by historians, 1952 was probably as large if not larger a milestone for Ford as was 1949. Determined not only to catch up with its competitors, but to move ahead of them, Ford launched one of its biggest change years in 1952, with new body structures, new sheet metal, new chassis, a new engine, dozens of lesser engineering and design innovations, and even its first experimental car for the show circuit.

Yet, for some reason, 1952 has never been recognized as the banner year that it actually was. Possibly much of this has to do with the Korean War and its resultant stifling of new car sales. Or possibly the country was more preoccupied with the war and other matters to take the interest in automobiles that it had in the past. Whatever the case, despite a totally new line of cars, sales were down and a ho-hum attitude seemed to prevail throughout the industry. Possibly too, this might have been due to the late Feb. 1, 1952, introduction of the line, a delay caused in part by war events.

Still, as General Motors had little new to offer, one would have expected the new Ford line to draw more attention than it did receive. Here were totally new body shells, with new slab-sided sheet metal; new grilles with the basic theme reverting back to 1949; new one-piece windshields and rear windows; new superstructures, and even a totally new body style in the form of a return to the 4-door station wagon. The overall styling utilized a higher front fender line, a rear quarter panel with an embossed "fender" design incorporating a diagonal slash highlighted by stainless steel trim, and new taillights located in pods which actually were an extension of the upper body line. Also new for Ford was the gas filler pipe located at mid-point behind the rear bumper and concealed by the swing-down license plate bracket.

All models were about one inch longer than previous models, and all were built on a brand new K-bar frame with a 115-inch wheelbase, as opposed to the 114-inch of last year. Attached to this frame was a newly designed steering system, new suspension with the springs more tuned to the various body weights, and larger brakes on the station wagon models. Within the bodies were found the industry's first use of suspended brake and clutch pedals. The latter gave greater leverage to these controls, and did away with the usual openings in the floor board. Eventually the entire auto industry would accept the concept of suspended pedals.

What publicity Ford did receive this year seemed to be preoccupied with its totally new engine. Possibly this was because Ford for 20 years had been associated with the flat-head V-8. And the new engine was—of all things—an overhead valve Six! Didn't the Chevy buffs have a field day with this one! Actually, it appears that Ford had planned a whole new series of overhead valve engines, both in the 6-cylinder and V-8 lines, but retooling problems caused by the Korean War restricted

engine changeover. As a result, only the new OHV Six came out for Ford, while Lincoln got the other extreme, a new OHV V-8 of 317 cubic inches.

But the new Six was nothing to sneer about. In fact, several automotive magazines claimed that it could outrun the conventional V-8, and do so with greater gas savings and smoother acceleration. This, despite the fact that the V-8 was upgraded somewhat so that it would now develop 110 horses 3800 rpm. Mainly, this was done by designing a new compression chamber and raising the compression ratio from 6.8:1 to 7.2:1. The bore and stroke remained 3.19x3.75, and displacement remained 239 cubic inches.

The new Six replaced the old model, and in fact had as much in common with the former L-head version as Model A did with the current model. Using the OHV design, it had an almost square bore and stroke of 3.56x3.6 inches, and displaced 215 cubic inches, which was 11 cubic inches less than the flat-head Six. Yet, with a compression ratio of 7:1, it developed 101 horsepower at 3500 rpm, using a single barrel Holley carburetor. Among the features of the new engine were four main bearings; wedge-type combustion chambers; integrally cast valve guides; cast nodular iron crankshaft; left-side manifolding, and integral full-flow oil filter. as before, the new engine could be fitted with any of the three available transmissions—the standard 3-speed manual; the manual with automatic overdrive, or the fully automatic Fordomatic.

The new Six was available in two of the three new car series, but could not be ordered in the top of the line Crestline series. Yes, three series! This year Ford began its march toward what would result in today's chaotic mess of innumerable series and sub-series and cars which range from microscopic minis to luxury limousines, all gathered under the Ford name rather than under the individual makes, which they actually seem to be.

But for this year there were three distinct series: The top-line Crestline; the mid-range Customline, and the low-price Mainline. The new Crestline series, which took its name from the former Crestliner (not from Crestline Farm!), contained Ford's Victoria hardtop, the Sunliner convertible, and the totally new all-metal 4-door station wagon, the Country Squire. The wagon version was the only Ford to have any natural wood, being coated with a wood veneer trim. But gone for good was the wood-structured wagon of the past.

The Customline series, which accounted for the bulk of Ford's sales, consisted of the Tudor and Fordor Sedans, a Club Coupe, and its own version of the new 4-door Station Wagon. The wagon was the only Customline style that could not be ordered with the new Six, coming only in V-8 form. It used the same body as the Country Squire, but lacked the wood veneer trim. In this guise, it bore the name Country Sedan.

The Mainline series utilized three of the Customline

bodies, but had its own exclusive wagon. The utilized bodies were the Tudor and Fordor, plus a 3-passenger Business Coupe version of the Customline's Club Coupe. Oddly, however, its station wagon was a brand new all-steel 2-door model called the Ranch Wagon. The totally new body also provided a base for Ford's return to the Sedan Delivery field. Called the Courier and featuring Mainline trim, the new truck used the Ranch Wagon's basic shell, but with blank sides as opposed to the single large window in the side of the wagon. It also used a vertically hinged rear door as opposed to the wagon's split lift and tail gate.

As mentioned earlier, the Korean War was causing both material shortages and a slowdown in automotive production. As a result, 1952 was one of the less attractive sales years for the automotive industry overall, even though Ford's market percentage rose slightly. Still, production reached only 671,733, which was a tremendous drop of 341,648 below 1951's million-plus figure. Of course, the late introduction and short model year didn't help anything either.

Of this amount, only 105,280 were in the top-line Crestline series, and only 163,911 were in the low-line Mainline series. The bulk of the sales, all 402,542, were in the mid-range Customline series. Surprisingly, this year the 4-door Customline Sedan was the top seller, with 188,303 units moving out. The usual top-place Tudor came in second, with 175,762 Customline sales. However, in the Mainline range, these figures were reversed, and the popular Tudor accounted for 79,931 sales, while the Fordor lagged with only 41,277. In the Crestline series, the Victoria was the best selling model, with a nice run of 77,320. The new 4-door station wagon did not prove to be as popular as expected, with only 11,927 sales recorded in Country Sedan trim and only

5,426 in Country Squire form. Oddly, the 2-door Ranch wagon drew 32,566 orders.

As could be expected in a quasi-war economy, prices were up, but not quite as much as might have been expected. Ford now had three models base-priced over the $2,000 mark. These were the Country Squire at $2,186; the Country Sedan at $2,060, and the Sunliner at $2,027. Even some of the options were up in price. For example, the Fordomatic, which this year went in over 30% of the cars, was now up to $170, while the automatic overdrive was up to $102.

And finally, the age of X-Cars, those exotic experimental show cars that would tour the world's auto show circuit, began to dawn. Ford's first entry emerged in February of 1952, but initially it was tagged as a Lincoln, not a Ford. First called the Continental X, it was quickly decided that the name was too similar to the yet-to-be introduced Continental Mark II. Its name was changed to the Lincoln XL-100, and then, for some reason, it quickly became the Ford XL-100. The car was a fully operational 5-passenger hardtop with a removable roof section. It utilized a hand-built aluminum and steel body, and rode on a special frame of 123-inch wheelbase. It was powered by a highly modified version of Lincoln's new V-8 which could produce over 300 horsepower. After traveling the show circuit for a coupe of years, the car was loaned to MGM and apparently was used in some 1956/57 movies. It was subsequently returned to Ford and exists today.

The best selling style in the Crestline series was the Victoria, or Victoria Hardtop, as it was often called. Designated the Model 60B, it saw sales go up to 77,320, which made it the fourth best selling Ford style of the year. Priced at $1,925, it was the only Crestline model under $2,000. Both the convertible and the Victoria carried a chrome "Crestline" signature on the front fender, just behind the V-8 emblem. Crestline Publishing has no relation to Ford's use of the name. Its derivation is Crestline Farm in upstate New York, a name that pre-dated Ford's use by many years. Upholstery of the Victorias was in craftweave material with vinyl panels. Three color options were available: tan cloth with a brown stripe and mahogany vinyl; gray with a blue stripe and blue vinyl, and gray with a green stripe and green vinyl panels. The exteriors were done in a choice of 14 2-tone combinations.

With Ford now breaking into three series, the top-line cars fell into the new Crestline category. Flagship of this line was the Convertible, Model 76B, which now bore the name Sunliner. Except for two wagons, it was the only Ford base priced at over $2,000, with its ticket reading $2,027. It weighed 3,339 pounds and saw production peak at 22,534. Four top colors were available: black; black with red binding; tan, or green with dark green binding. Likewise, four interior schemes were also available: red natural leather with black vinyl panels; tan leather with mahogany vinyl panels; ivory leather with green vinyl panels, and light blue leather with dark blue vinyl panels. All interior metal surfaces were painted in metallic tones to match the interior color selections.

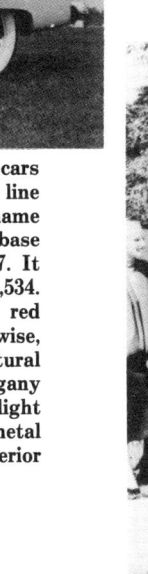

A new mid-range was created this year. Called the Customline series, it consisted of four models, of which the Club Coupe was an exclusive style. Designated the Model 72B, the car shared its body shell with the Mainline Business Coupe, but had an exclusive full 6-passenger interior. Sales continued surprisingly well, with 26,550 leaving the factories. It was base priced at $1,649 and weighed 3,153 pounds.

Totally new for the year was Ford's first 4-door wagon since 1948, and Ford's first ever all-steel wagon. It appeared in both the Crestline and the Customline series, but there was no chance of mistaking one for the other. The Crestline version, known as the Country Squire, was the only Ford to use any wood trim. The body bore a wood grained area outlined in natural birch, while the inner panels were in wood-grained decal. Ford's most expensive model, the Country Squire had a base price of $2,186. At 3,640 pounds it was also the heaviest model. Despite its practical applications coupled with top-line trim, buyers were scarce, and only 5,426 were turned loose. Unlike the cars in this series which bore Crestline plaques, the wagon wore "Country Squire" emblems on its front doors. As with all Crestline series, the wagon was available only with the V-8 engine.

In a surprising turn of events, the top level Tudor was no longer the top selling Ford. It now ranked in second spot, with sales of 175,762. Although placed in the new mid-range Customline series, the car was still the top-trim Tudor available. Designated the Model 70B, it was priced at $1,640 and weighed 3,151 pounds. All Customline cars wore their signature on the front fender, just above the chrome side trim. Lack of V-8 emblem ahead of this signature signifies that this car is equipped with the new overhead valve Six. Both the Tudor and Fordor now featured relatively expensive 1-piece wrap around windshields and rear windows.

Ford's best selling car of the year turned out to be the Customline Fordor Sedan, which saw production reach 188,303. As was the case with the Customline Tudor, this was Ford's top of the line 4-door, even though it resided in the mid-rage Customline series. With the new body design, the cars lost some of their tub-like appearance. Vent windows were used in the rear doors, but on the Tudor these were removed from the rear windows. This model is equipped with the V-8, as told by the fender emblem; and probably has the $170 optional Fordomatic transmission. A total of five interior combinations were available in the Customline series, while interior metal came in six different metallic colors to match the overall scheme. In this series, the car was known as the Model 73B.

Ford's low-buck special continued to be the 3-passenger Business Coupe, Model 72C. Found only in the low-price Mainline series, it sold for $1,459 and weighed 3,085 pounds, thus being again the lightest as well as the least expensive Ford of the year. As before, it shared its body with the Club Coupe, now in the Customline, but differed in interior layout and in the level of exterior trim and interior upholstery. It still used the same split-back front seat as did the Club Coupe, but its rear compartment was fitted for storage. Primarily a fleet car, it saw sales top off at 10,137.

The new all-steel 4-door wagon body was shared by both the Crestline and Customline series. However, in the Customline range it lacked the wood and wood-grain applique trim, and probably looked better for it. As was the case with the Country Squire, the Custom version wore its own name plaque of "Country Sedan," rather than the series signature. Unlike other Customline cars which could be ordered with the new Six, the wagon was available only in V-8 form. More than twice as popular as the Country Squire, the Country Sedan had sales of 11,927. It was base priced at $2,060, and was the only Customline car to break the $2,000 mark. Designated the Model 79C, it weighed 3,617 pounds. With the new body style, the spare tire finally moved back inside. The tailgate was still of the 2-piece type, with upper and lower gates. This model wears the optional full wheel covers, usually found on the Crestline models, but not restricted to any particular style. The interior was finished in mahogany and straw colored vinyl.

Although in the Customline series the Fordor far outsold the Tudor, such was not the case in the new Mainline series. Here the Tudor Sedan took top place, and in fact, became Ford's third best selling model, with 79,931 going out the door. Known as the Model 70A, the car was base priced at $1,555 and weighed 3,151 pounds. All Mainline cars suffered greatly in appearance from lack of side trim. Even the rear fender embossing trim was reduced to a ribbed black rubber stone guard, while the only concession to series was the chrome "Mainline" signature on the front fender. If this car had the V-8, that plaque would have appeared ahead of the Mainline designation. Since it carried the Six, it would have sold for $1,485 base price, or $70 less than a V-8. Notice that Tudor models no longer had vent windows in the rear quarters.

1952

The Mainline Fordor, Model 73A, was the economy sedan, and as this model shows, was often found equipped with the new 6-cylinder OHV engine. In 6-cylinder form it was priced at $1,630, with the V-8 costing $70 more. Not nearly as popular as its Customline cousin, it drew only 41,277 orders. All Mainline closed cars still offered buyers a choice of four interior options. However, the interior furnishings were spartan, and still included only one sun visor, an arm rest for the driver only, and a horn button rather than a ring. Such things as assist straps; dual visors; arm rests, and chrome windshield molding were left to the Customline series.

Exclusive to the Mainline series was Ford's totally new 2-door wagon, Model 59A. Known as the Ranch Wagon, it outsold the 4-door wagon by almost 2-to-1, having 32,566 sales to its credit by year-end. The body was distinguished by a huge glass upper quarter panel, consisting of two sliding panes running full-length from the B-pillar to the tailgate. As with other Mainliners the car carried no side trim except for the "Ranch Wagon" signature on the front fender. Unlike 4-door wagons, this one could be ordered as a Six, as seen here, or as a V-8. With the Six, it cost $1,832 and weighed 3,377 pounds. Its interior was finished in all vinyl, with a combination of mahogany and tan being used. Although all of the car styles now had their gas fillers hidden behind the rear license plate, the wagons had the fillers located under a small door at the top edge of the rear fender, just ahead of the left taillight.

After an absence of five years, Ford finally came out with another sedan delivery. Known as the Courier, the neat little truck used the basic body of the new 2-door wagon, but with the sides blanked in rather than equipped with windows. Also, it used a vertically hinged rear door, rather than the lift and tail gates. The exterior trim level was the same as used on the Mainline series, and on some lists the truck is considered part of the Mainline family. The interior was finished in a brown vinyl driver's seat with gray headlining and gray masonite body panels. A single driver's seat was standard, but a passenger's seat could be ordered. The Courier was available with either the Six or the V-8 as seen here, and could be equipped with the Fordomatic transmission. A relatively slow starter in the sales field, it drew only 6,225 orders this year. In 6-cylinder basic form it weighed 3,109 pounds and cost $1,539.

The Lincoln that became a Ford. That's the best way to describe Ford's first radical show/experimental car. Built during 1951, the car was first introduced in February as the Continental X. Fearing confusion with the in-progress Continental Mark II, Ford quickly changed its name to Lincoln XL-100, but shortly thereafter renamed the car the Ford XL-100. Actually, since it sported a 300 horsepower highly modified version of the new Lincoln OHV V-8, the car probably should have retained its Lincoln nomenclature, as few Ford production parts could be found on the vehicle. A fully functional car, the XL-100 had 5-passenger seating capacity. Its body was handcrafted of steel and aluminum and sat on a special frame of 123-inch wheelbase. The 2-part top consisted of a fixed tonneau portion with a removable panel between the windshield header and the B-pillar. Headlight and side sculpturing would appear on the 1956 Lincoln, while the rear treatment is quite similar to the 1961 Thunderbird. After traveling the show circuit for a couple of years, the car was loaned to MGM and appeared in at least one major movie. Subsequently it was returned to Ford Motor Co. and still exists as a usable vehicle.

Ford was getting set to celebrate its 50th anniversary in 1953. Starting from mid-1952 on, the public was led to believe there would be a marvelous new series of Fords unveiled for the big event. Even though a totally new Ford had reached the market in 1952, even automotive writers who should have known better, were led to believe that another totally new Ford would appear in 1953.

What a disappointment!

When the new models were finally unveiled on Dec. 12, many people could not tell them from the 1952 stock. True, there was a new and more refined grille, with attractive parking lights beneath the central bar. And, the taillights were changed somewhat, as was the side trim, but still, the cars looked just like the 1952 models that they were. There was no new engine as promised; no radical new styling, and no exotic new models—just more of 1952.

True, the chassis was designed for a new suspension and an overhead valve V-8 that would have one more year to wait before introduction. And there was an emblem on the steering wheel that read "50TH ANNIVERSARY 1903-1953." And the dash was a bit different. But that was about all. As one automotive writer of the era put it, the new Ford was "A chassis of the future with a body of today powered by an engine of yesterday."

And still, the public loved the cars. Production soared, and sales did likewise, despite an overall price increase brought about by inflation due to the Korean War. Ford totalled out the model year with sales of 1,244,540 cars, which was close to double the previous year's production. Styling alone was not the answer to this sales surge. For the most part, the entire automotive industry was experiencing one of its best years since 1950. In addition, Ford became very competitive in the market place. Despite its price increases, the overall Ford prices were not up as much in percentage as were those of other makes, especially the independents such as Studebaker, Nash, and Hudson.

The one factor that Ford did have to brag about in its 1953 models was the new and more stable ride, the result of a re-engineering of the basically good 1952 suspension system. Among the improvements were new rubber compression bumpers at the front, coupled with new support plates to allow greater up and down movement of the front wheels. In addition, both front and rear shocks were re-valved to give a softer reaction to sudden road bumps. And, even the rear springs, new in 1952, were once more redesigned to harmonize with the new front end components. Part of the suspension revisions were in answer to numerous complaints that the 1952 Fords would bottom out on rough roads. The 1953 models would not.

Aside from the suspension, engineering changes were minimal, with the major move being the reduction in wheel size. Tires went from the standard 6.00x16 of 1952 to the new 6.70x15 units which had been optional last year. Station wagons now used 7.10x15 tires.

Within the styling framework, the same three series still held the same 11 body styles (12 if the Courier is counted as part of the Mainline series). Within this list, the only change occurred with the Mainline Ranch Wagon, which could no longer be ordered with the 6-cylinder engine. That meant that all Ford station wagons now had V-8 power only.

As occurred in 1952, the Customline Fordor once again was the sales leader, with 374,487 being sold. In second place again was the Customline Tudor with 305,433 sales, while the Mainline Tudor came in third with 152,995. Even the sporty Crestline Victoria was up substantially, and registered 128,302 units.

On the national price index, everything was up, and Fords were no exception. For example, the popular Customline Fordor now had a base factory price of $1,858, as compared to $1,685 in 1952. The higher priced models fared even worse, with the Country Squire going from $2,186 in 1952 to $2,403 this year. In line with this, the difference between the Six and the V-8 was now $75 as opposed to $70, while the Fordomatic was a $184 option as compared with $170 in 1952. The increases were not huge, but they did represent an escalation that still continues today.

The fact that Ford had virtually nothing new with which to celebrate its 50th anniversary seems not to have hampered the publicity writers, though it probably resulted in some severe strain to their imaginations. Among the celebrations events were the opening of a new Research & Engineering Center at Dearborn, with non-other than President Dwight D. Eisenhower participating in the ceremonies; the opening of a new Technical Service Laboratory at Livonia, Mich.; the dedication of the Ford Archives at Greenfield Village; a reopening of the Dearborn Rotunda showplace after 10 years of being closed, and the nomination of a Ford convertible as the Official Pace Car for the 1953 Indianapolis Race.

On the more artistic side, Ford commissioned the publication of two "official" history books; Norman Rockwell was commissioned to create six unique paintings for a special 50th anniversary calendar; a historical movie was produced, and finally, a 2-hour TV extravaganza was aired on both CBS and NBC simultaneously. This production, featuring some of the top stars of the day, cost $500,000, and was one of the most expensive TV productions staged up until that time. In all, the anniversary party went well, even if the cars did look like the previous year's models.

Ford's style leader continued to be the top-line convertible, officially known as the Crestline Sunliner, Model 76B. Often seen with a red paint job, the popular rag top this year drew 40,861 orders, almost double that of last year. This was despite the retention of the old flathead V-8, a second-year body style, and a new base price of $2,230. Except for the wagons, it was Ford's most expensive car and also its heaviest, at 3,334 pounds. Interior selections changed, with only red and ivory vinyl complimenting four different colors of natural leather. The combinations were black leather with red vinyl panels, or blue, green, or brown leather with ivory vinyl panels. Tops were either black or gray with similar binding, black with red binding, or green with dark green binding, all with matching boots.

1953

Even with the top raised, the Crestline Sunliner was an attractive car, especially when fitted with one of the aftermarket continental spare kits that were starting to become very popular. Although Ford this year offered its own kits through its dealers, this is not one of the official units. The Ford variety blended into the trunk deck and lifted with the deck. This unit is a free-standing affair, which would swing backward slightly in order to gain access to the trunk. The model shown here required bumper bracket extensions and a new splash apron, but looked much more realistic than the Ford version. Notice the "Fordomatic" signature on the trunk deck, just to the right of the spare. All Fords equipped with Fordomatic received the chromed signature when the automatic was installed.

The best selling Crestline model was the Victoria, Model 60B, which topped the 100,000 mark with sales of 128,302. Available in a variety of optional 2-tone paint combinations, the popular hardtop was base priced at $2,120. As before, all Crestline cars were available only with the V-8, but could be equipped with the manual, overdrive, or Fordomatic transmission. All Victorias used a combination of vinyl and nylon interiors, in three different combinations. These were green and green; blue and blue, or mahogany vinyl with brown nylon. This year, the name "Victoria" was embossed in the stainless lower window trim on the doors. Similarly, the name "Sunliner" was embossed in this trim on the convertibles.

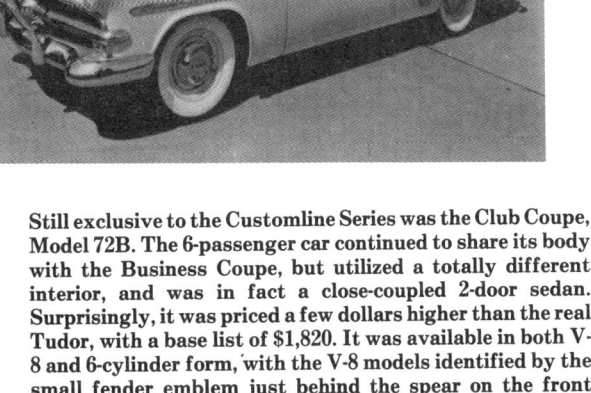

Ford's top wagon was technically in the Crestline Series, but the Crestline name did not appear on the car. Instead, the "Country Squire" signature in chrome appeared at the leading edge of the front doors. Ford still used real maple for the outer trim, and in fact, was the only auto manufacturer still using decorative wood on any model. The mahogany inner panels were a heavy grained paper, glued over the metal. Ford's most expensive style, the Model 79C Country Squire had a base price of $2,403 and weighed 3,609 pounds. Sales reached 11,001 by year end. Unlike the cars, which now used 6.70x15 tires, the wagons used 7.10x15. The white walls were optional at $27 extra per set. Unlike other Crestline models, the Country Squire did not use the chromed spear on the front fender.

Still exclusive to the Customline Series was the Club Coupe, Model 72B. The 6-passenger car continued to share its body with the Business Coupe, but utilized a totally different interior, and was in fact a close-coupled 2-door sedan. Surprisingly, it was priced a few dollars higher than the real Tudor, with a base list of $1,820. It was available in both V-8 and 6-cylinder form, with the V-8 models identified by the small fender emblem just behind the spear on the front fender. The spear end was embossed with the "Customline" signature. For some reason, this model retained its following, and 43,999 were sold this year. Its big advantage over the Tudor was greatly increased luggage space in the trunk.

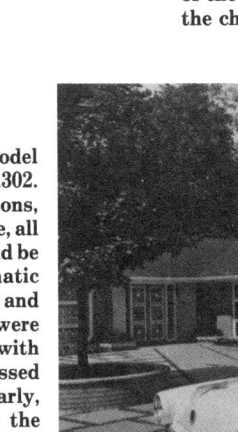

Ford's second most popular car for the second year in a row was the Customline Tudor, Model 70B, which saw its sales rise to 305,433 this year. It was priced at $1,809 with the V-8 as shown here, or $75 less as a Six. New options for the year included power steering at $125 and power brakes at $35. The Fordomatic was now up to $184 extra, while the automatic overdrive was $108. Of all the options, only the Fordomatic had its own exterior identity plaque, located on the right corner of the trunk deck.

Backing into a tight parking space was supposed to be much easier with Ford's new power steering unit, which was a $125 option this year. Setting the example is Ford's best selling car, the Customline Fordor, Model 73B. Sales reached 374,87. Called Master Guide, the new power steering unit was introduced in mid-June, barely in time to make the 1953 model run. It appears that it was only available on V-8 engines this year. In base form, with the V-8, the Customline Fordor sold for $1,858 and weighed 3,193 pounds. Interior selections included three cloth patterns plus a blue or a mahogany vinyl with ivory vinyl panels.

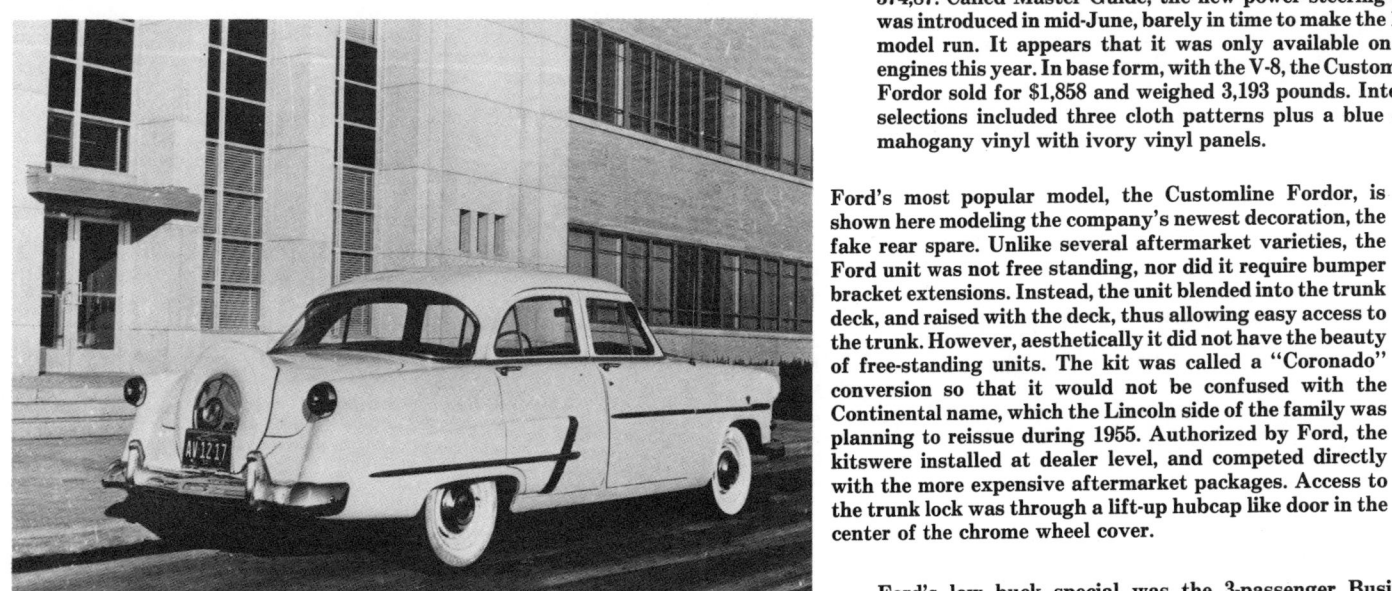

Ford's most popular model, the Customline Fordor, is shown here modeling the company's newest decoration, the fake rear spare. Unlike several aftermarket varieties, the Ford unit was not free standing, nor did it require bumper bracket extensions. Instead, the unit blended into the trunk deck, and raised with the deck, thus allowing easy access to the trunk. However, aesthetically it did not have the beauty of free-standing units. The kit was called a "Coronado" conversion so that it would not be confused with the Continental name, which the Lincoln side of the family was planning to reissue during 1955. Authorized by Ford, the kitswere installed at dealer level, and competed directly with the more expensive aftermarket packages. Access to the trunk lock was through a lift-up hubcap like door in the center of the chrome wheel cover.

Ford's low price 4-door station wagon was the Model 79B Country Sedan, found in the Customline Series. Essentially, it was the Country Squire without the hang and paste-on wood trim. Possibly more buyers felt the wagon looked much better without the wood, or maybe the $136 saving tempted them. Whatever the reason, a total of 37,734 Country Sedans were sold, or more than three times as many as Country Squires. Available only as a V-8, the car cost $2,267 and weighed 3,539 pounds. The 2-tone paint scheme here was a popular option on this particular style, and did much to enhance its good looks. The rear doors were fitted with roll-up windows in the forward section, but the back section was fixed in place, and was not a swing-out vent. The rear quarter window was of the sliding type, with the forward section sliding rearward for additional ventilation.

Ford's low buck special was the 3-passenger Business Coupe, Model 72C, which sold for $1,539 as a Six in basic form. Exclusive only to the Mainline series, the car utilized the same body as the Customline Club Coupe, but had its rear portion fitted for luggage or parcel storage rather than for passengers. At 3,068 pounds, it was also Ford's lightest car. And, except for the Country Squire, it was also the company's least popular model, with only 16,280 being sold, many going for fleet use. The V-8 had a $1,614 base price, but it is doubtful that too many left the factory in that form. Certainly companies or salesmen who were trying to economize on this car in the first place would have gone for the Six.

1953

The only Mainline style to break the 100,000 sales mark was the Tudor Sedan, model 70A, which registered 152,995 sales. As shown here, equipped with the 6-cylinder engine, it had a base price of $1,642 and a curb weight of 3,067 pounds. The Mainline series continued to be devoid of side trim. The only concession to trim was the chrome "Mainline" signature just ahead of the A-pillar, and a small stainless stone guard on the rear fender embossing. Mainline interiors came in craftcord of gray and gold stripe, or in either blue or mahogany vinyl with ivory vinyl panels. The fender antenna indicates either the $88 6-tube radio or the $100 8-tube Custom radio, either of which could be dealer or factory installed.

This year's Mobilgas Economy Run went from Los Angeles to Sun Valley, Idaho. Winning in its class was the Mainline Fordor Sedan, Model 73A, equipped with the gas-saving 6-cylinder engine. In this form, the car cost $1,690 and weighed 3,115 pounds. When wearing the V-8, it would have cost $75 more. It is pretty certain that this car was also equipped with the optional automatic overdrive transmission, which added an extra cruising gear to the drive train and an extra $108 to the price. Still, when engaged in high-mileage usage, the overdrive would eventually pay for itself, even at the 25-cent a gallon gas prices. Least popular of all the Customline and Mainline Tudor and Fordor Sedans, the Mainline model drew only 66,463 orders. On this model, the front vent windows would open, but those on the rear doors were fixed in place.

Ford's most popular wagon by far continued to be the 2-door all-steel Ranch Wagon, Model 59A. A total of 66,976 were sold, which was more than 18,000 above the combined sales of both 4-door models. Exclusive to the Mainline series, the vehicle followed the lead of the other two wagons, and did not have a series name on its side, only the "Ranch Wagon" signature on the front fender. It also followed the lead of the other wagons, in that it was available in V-8 form only, and could not be ordered as a Six. This meant that for 1953, Ford had no 6-cylinder wagons on the market. In basic form, as shown here, it had a base price of $2,095 and thus was the only Mainline vehicle above the $2,000 mark. The Ranch Wagon was highlighted by a huge glass rear quarter, with no pillar between the B and C-pillars. The rear pane of glass was fixed in place, but the forward pane could be slid about two-thirds of the way back for ventilation.

A catalog rear view of the popular Ranch Wagon shows that the 1-piece tailgate concept had not yet been developed. Instead, the vehicle used the traditional rear design, with a solid swing-down tailgate and a framed glass swing-up liftgate. Both the Country Sedan and Country Squire used the same rear treatment. Unlike the 4-door wagons which were of 9-passenger style, the Ranch Wagon was strictly a 6-passenger vehicle, with no rearmost seat. The seats were no longer removable, but folded down, with the rear portion of the seat backs creating a solid cargo floor. The interior was all in vinyl. All wagon bodies were now being built at Ford's plant at Wayne, Mich.

Utilizing the basic body shell of the Ranch Wagon was the Courier Sedan Delivery. Technically part of the Mainline series, the pretty little package truck was fitted in Mainline trim—or lack of it. Unlike the Ranch Wagon, however, it could be ordered in either V-8 or 6-cylinder power. The basic body was the same as the Ranch Wagon's, but fitted with steel panels in place of the large quarter windows. The interior was covered in masonite body panels, with a vinyl seat. Note that all wagons and the Courier continued to have their gas fillers ahead of the taillight, rather than behind the license plate as on the passenger cars. The Courier's rear panel was fitted with a vertically hinged single rear door, with the hinges on the left side, so the opening faced curbside. Following the trail of all other Fords this year, the Courier saw a substantial upswing in sales, and 10,575 were produced. All weighed 3,109 pounds and were base priced at $1,515 or $24 less than the 1952 version.

Making good use of the Courier was the Shop of Siebert. This well known Toledo, Ohio, builder of low-priced professional cars used the standard Courier as a base for its lowest price hearse model. In observance of Siebert's 100 years in the business, this vehicle was called its Centennial model. Surprisingly for Siebert, it also carried the "Courier" signature on the front fender. Although this 6-cylinder model uses the standard wheelbase, Siebert also produced extended wheelbase models based on both Ford and Mercury passenger car components. The Centennial could also be ordered in ambulance or combination car trim, or as a service car. In the latter role, it looked just about like a standard Courier, except for a more plush interior.

As part of its 50th anniversary celebration, Ford sponsored the official pace car at this year's Indianapolis 500 mile race. The Sunliner, painted "Pace Car White," was driven by William Clay Ford, Henry's youngest grandson. Following the race, the car was presented to winner Bill Vukocvich, who pushed his Offenhauser powered Fuel Injection Engineering Special through the 200 laps at an average speed of 128.74 MPH. Following this, Ford built 2,000 copies of the Pace Car, complete with lettering and AAA emblems. These were shipped to select dealers who first displayed them and then subsequently sold them to the general public. One such replica was used as the pace car for the Pikes Peak Hill Climb the following September. All of the cars wore Ford's new Coronado rear tire kit.

Ford was one of the innovators in the crash testing program—an activity that would become common among all car manufacturers a decade later, and finally become mandatory under government regulations. But in this era, few companies were willing to demolish their cars simply to study structural soundness. Here a brand new remotely controlled Victoria is shown at the Dearborn test track, hitting a solid barrier at 30 MPH. An electronically wired anatomically correct dummy is in the passenger's seat. The left door has been removed so that high speed cameras can record the dummy's movements throughout the entire spectrum of the crash. From such tests came Ford's poorly received 1956 program to sell safety features. Still, many safety features that are taken for granted today were developed during such crash programs. Among these are seat belts; concaved or heavily padded steering wheels; pop-out windshields; air bags, and double door latches.

Ford was so proud of its new front suspension system that it used cut-away views of the mechanics in its major advertising. Or did it do this because there was virtually nothing else new on the cars? Among the new components were compression bumpers; support plates, and re-valved shock absorbers. Ford bragged that its front tread was a full two inches wider than the rear tread, thus giving the car greater stability in turns. The car had 58-inch front tread and 56-inch rear, which was a carry-over from 1952—but little was said about the tread in '52. Prior to this, Fords had a 56-inch tread fore and aft.

Was this really the first Thunderbird? This cobbled mess, looking like something from a third world high school body shop class, is reputed to be the vehicle on which chassis and suspension tests were made during the development for the forthcoming T-bird. The car is a regular Customline Fordor, sectioned to a wheelbase of 102 inches, with the body hacked away to fit the new frame length. The 13-inch space that was omitted meant that the body had to be sectioned even more in order to match the new frame. Apparently the interim section was filled in with whatever sheet metal could be found in the scrap bin. Since the dual exhaust is evident at the rear, it is probable that the car also is fitted with the new OHV V-8 that would come out in 1954. No, there were no plans to market this particular model.

To many people, it seemed that Ford's clock was running one year late. The big 50th anniversary celebration occurred in 1953, but the cars were almost identical to the 1952 models. Now, one year after the celebration, Ford came out with a new engine, new suspension, new power options, and three new models. Where were all of these last year?

With the basic styling carried over for yet another year, the major news turned out to be Ford's new overhead valve Y-block V-8. This, of course, was the first real replacement for the old flathead that had been introduced in 1932. It also represented a total departure from Henry Ford's concept of engine construction. For some reason, but possibly because of Chevrolet's success with its now world famous OHV Six, the elder Henry seemed to despise the overhead valve design.

Actually, the new engine was the third in a series of new OHV V-8 engines that Ford had developed. The first ones appeared in 1952 in the Lincoln line and Ford's heavy truck series. But mainly because of restrictions caused by the Korean war, the mid-sized Ford and Mercury models could not be introduced until this year.

Both the Ford and Mercury versions were virtually identical, with the Mercury being a bit larger at 244.4 cubic inch displacement, compared with Ford's 239.4 cubic inches. Those who expected a much larger engine did not get their wish. The new Ford block was less than one cubic inch larger than the flathead model in total displacement. The bore and stroke however, measured an almost square 3.5x3.1 inches, as opposed to the longer stroke 3.19x3.75 bore and stroke of the old flathead.

But in every other respect, the new Y-block was a totally new engine. Of deep block construction (the block extended well below the crankshaft) it utilized five main bearings and a precision-ground crankshaft with eight counterweights. The pistons were solid skirted aluminum alloy units of three ring design, which terminated in a new wedge-shaped combustion chamber that produced a 7.5:1 compression ratio. A chain-drive camshaft with mechanical lifters operated the large adjustable valves, which included integral guides. Feeding the new block was a 2-barrel Holley carburetor set on top of a double-deck intake manifold. The combination resulted in an engine now rated at 130 horsepower at 4200 rpm, while the Mercury version gave out 161 horsepower at 4400 rpm. Not surprisingly, there were a multitude of parts that were interchangeable with both the big Y-block V-8 of Lincoln and truck use, and also with the modified I-block Six.

Not just satisfied to come out with a totally new V-8, Ford also made some changes to the Mileage-Maker Six, and these turned out to be all for the better. Foremost was an increase in bore from 3.56 to 3.62 inches. Although the stroke remained 3.6 inches, the new "Square" B&S resulted in the displacement going from 215 cubic inches to 223. In addition, the compression was raised from 7.0:1 to 7.2:1. All of this resulted in the horsepower going up to 115 at 3900 rpm. Other modifications included a new lower block casting, relocation of the fuel pump, distributor, and oil filler, and new engine mounts. A Holley single barrel carburetor was still used. Nevertheless, test reports of the day show that the new Six, when hooked to a standard transmission, could outperform the new V-8 when coupled to the Fordomatic transmission.

In another move which was rather astounding, considering all of the publicity given to Ford's new front end suspension system in 1953, Ford this year received a totally new front end suspension. Patterned after the unit used on Lincolns, and totally interchangeable with that used on the Mercury, the new Ford system was of ball-joint design, and appears to have been a first in the low-price market. The concept consisted of a very uncomplicated design, in which each wheel steered via ball-joints rather than the conventional kingpin, which went back to the turn of the century. Spring loaded to compensate for wear, the new joints were supposed to be self-aligning and eliminated 12 of the 16 wear points found in the old suspension system.

In order to utilize the new suspension system, Ford once again had to redesign the frame, shocks, front and rear springs, and stabilizer mounts. Among the frame modifications, which took place forward of the K-bar, were two new cross members and new frame ends.

Along with the new engine and chassis was a whole list of power options, some of which had actually begun to appear in the summer of 1953 on the later built 1953 models. However, all were advertised as being new for 1954. Among these were Master-Guide power steering at $134; Swift-Sure power brakes at $41; power-lift windows at $102, and a power-operated front seat at $64. The power windows and seat were available only on the Crestline and Customline series, but the other units could be ordered in all three series.

Facing the driver was a new dashboard, which included a relocation of the radio speaker to the top of the dash, and a new instrument cluster with warning lights instead of gauges for both oil pressure and engine temperature. The speaker could be fitted to either of two radio options, priced at $88 and $99 respectively.

Aside from the mechanical and optional features and the new engine, buyers still had a bit of trouble telling the 1954 from the 1953 from the 1952 models. Once again a new grille appeared, but this almost seemed a minor variation of the 1952 style, with a split center bar, and a large central torpedo or spinner, flanked by two similar but smaller units on either end of the bar. Side trim was changed somewhat, and a wider stainless belt bar now ran full-length from fender edge to fender edge on both the Crestline and Customline cars. The Mainline Series was still devoid of side trim. On the rear, the taillights changed only slightly, and now had a 3-pronged chromed insert on the lens, while the trunk handles seemed to spread their wings a bit more.

What was new and what did grab the headlines, was

Ford's totally new style called the Skyliner. Available only in the Crestline series, this model was essentially the Victoria with a Plexiglas panel inserted into the roof. The quarter-inch thick plastic was tinted a moderate green in an attempt to ward off the sun's summer rays, which had been the downfall of the aftermarket bubble tops of the late 1940s and early 50s. The car used all other trim found in the Crestline series, but had its own "Skyliner" embossed window edging. It also had a slightly different rear roof treatment than did the Victoria. The Skyliner was priced at $2,241, the same as the Sunliner Convertible.

Also new on the car lists was a Crestline 4-door Sedan. Known simply as the Crestline Fordor, the car utilized the same body as did the Customline and Mainline Fordors, but had a trim level comparable with the Crestline series, including the exclusive wheel covers. With the introduction of the Fordor into the Crestline series came another innovation—the first 6-cylinder usage in this series. Before, the Six was not available in any of the Crestline models, but now it could be ordered in any of the five body styles in the series, including the Sunliner and the Country Squire.

The third new model on the list was the introduction of the 2-door station wagon into the Customline series. The car was in addition to the 4-door Country Sedan wagon, and in fact was simply an up-trimmed variation of the Mainline Ranch Wagon. It too bore the name Ranch Wagon, and was intended to offer 2-door wagon

Ford's totally new model for the year was the Crestline Skyliner, Model 60F. Essentially, the car was the Crestline Victoria with a large green-tinted Plexiglas are inserted over the front seat position. Apparently Ford was influenced in this model by the bubble-top attachments that had been offered for Ford convertibles in the 1940s. The demise of those tops was caused by the sun's rays, which would literally cook the occupants on a hot day. The tinted glass was supposed to nullify this condition, but owners reported that the Skyliners were still overly hot on sunny days. Priced the same as the Sunliner ($2,241), the car could be ordered with the Six or the V-8, though it is doubtful if many had the Six. The small emblem just below the leading edge of the belt trim signified the V-8. Initial buyer interest in the car was relatively high, and a total of 13,144 were sold. However, this was the high point in sales for the design, and orders would fall off rapidly, with the 1956 models not even breaking the 2,000 mark.

buyers a slightly higher trim level than the basic Mainline unit. Considering the $92 difference in price between the two wagons as compared with the much better appearance of the up-trimmed Customline version, the added cost was well worth the investment.

Because of the rather late introduction date this year (Jan. 6, 1954) coupled with the Oct. 25, 1954 introduction of the 1955 models, this was a relatively short production year. Still, a total of 1,165,942 cars were built, which was only 75,000 less than last year, in round numbers.

Of this amount, the mid-range Customline series once again had the most sales, recording 674,295. The Crestline and the Mainline series were almost equal in sales, with the Crestline models accounting for 254,768, while the Mainline drew 233,680. The remaining 3,200 models appear to have been the Courier Sedan Delivery, which was in a sort of gray area between truck and car, and unofficially was part of the Mainline trim package. Of the totals, the same three models again took the top position, and in fact were the only ones to exceed 100,000 in production. Only this year a switch was again made, and the Customline Tudor was once again the most popular, with sales of 293,375, while the Customline Fordor was second with sales of 262,499. In third place was the Mainline Tudor with 123.329 sales. Almost reaching the 100,000 mark, but falling short by only a few sales was the new Crestline Fordor, which drew 99,677 orders. The other top Crestline model was the Victoria, with 96,464 sales.

And finally, in what had to be one of the longest of long-range publicity previews ever for Ford, the company showed off its new Thunderbird. The initial introduction occurred on Feb. 20, 1954, at the Detroit Auto Show, followed by subsequent showings at Kansas City and Chicago. First hailed as Ford's "new kind of sports car," the Thunderbird apparently was slated to go into production as a 1954 vehicle. In fact, initial catalogs show the car with air-brushed 1954 license plates, and early publicity pieces issued in the spring hinted at consumer availability by mid-summer.

Except for the headlight bezels, the catalog cars looked pretty much like the actual Thunderbirds. But then, on Aug. 20, 1954, a different version appeared, wearing a variation of what would be the 1955 Fairlane trim. This publicity or experimental model has led to the erroneous belief by some that there actually was a 1954 production model, with heavy stainless side trim.

The "real" Thunderbird finally went into production on Sept. 9, 1954, but did not go on sale until Oct. 22, and then as a 1955 model. And, as such, it will be treated in the following chapter. Suffice to say here that the spring and summer of 1954 witnessed a substantial amount of publicity and rumor about Ford's answer to the hotshot Corvette. At least this time, the fans were not to be disappointed. The real Thunderbird turned out to be all that was expected, and then some.

Still Ford's style leader, the attractive Sunliner Convertible graced the Crestline series. Designated the Model 76B, the car was now up in price to $2,241, not a tremendous increase, but still a creeping up of all prices. Although the vast majority of buyers went for the new OHV V-8, this year for the first time, the improved Six could be ordered for the convertible. In that form, it cost $2,164, or $77 less. A total of 33,685 convertibles left the showrooms this year, many with the new power-lift window option, which cost an additional $102, or $166 when coupled to the power seat. All Crestline models had three small slashes behind the small chrome stone guard on the rear fender. The Crestline signature appeared on the rear fender, just behind the V-dash in the beltline trim.

The new kid on the block in the Crestline Series was the Fordor, Model 73C. Using the same body shell as the Customline and Mainline Fordors, the car varied only in trim level. The Fordor proved to be the most popular Crestline model, with sales reaching 99,677. It was the only Crestline model priced under $2,000, with its base list in V-8 form being $1,975. The three chrome slashed behind the stone shield, stainless A-pillar coverings, and the Crestline signature on the rear fender identify this as the top Fordor. This was the last year that the Crestline name would be used.

Far more popular than the Skyliner was the Crestline Victoria, Ford's major entry into the hardtop field. Production reached 95,464, which might have been down substantially from 1953, but still was no small amount. Designated the Model 60B, the Victoria listed for $2,131 with the V-8. As before, all Crestline 2-doors had their model name embossed in the stainless window sill, midway between the door handle and the vent window. Thus, the trim pieces were not interchangeable, as the convertible's would say "Sunliner," the hardtop's would say "Victoria,' and the see-through would say "Skyliner." All of the Crestline 2-doors were about the same weight, ranging from 3,305 for the Victoria to 3,352 for the convertible.

Ford Motor Co. had a rather interesting distinction with the Country Squire. It was the only wagon left on the market that still used real wood pieces for its trim outline. However, the dark center portion was a high-grade wood-grained paper. Also, this would be the last year for the natural wood. Beginning in 1956, the outer trim pieces would be of wood-grained metal. Wearing model number 76C, the 8-passenger Squire represented the top of the wagon line, and was considered part of the Crestline series, even though the Crestline signature did not appear on the exterior. Ford's least popular wagon, it had sales of only 12,797. Possibly part of this was due to its $2,415 price tag, and part might have been due to the nuisance of keeping the wood trim in good shape. As with other Crestline models, it could be ordered with the 6-cylinder engine for the first time this year. It was the heaviest of all Fords, weighing 3,684 pounds as a V-8 or 3,536 as a Six.

Still exclusive only to the Customline Series was the 6-passenger Club Coupe, Model 72B. Although the least popular of all Customline models, it still drew a healthy 33,951 orders. As a V-8, as shown here, it cost $1,830 and weighed 3,201 pounds. Customline cars had stainless steel edging around both the windshield and the rear windows, but did not have the stainless wrapped A-pillar as did the Crestline models. Interior fittings on the Club Coupe included a rear seat central armrest and assist cords on the B-pillar.

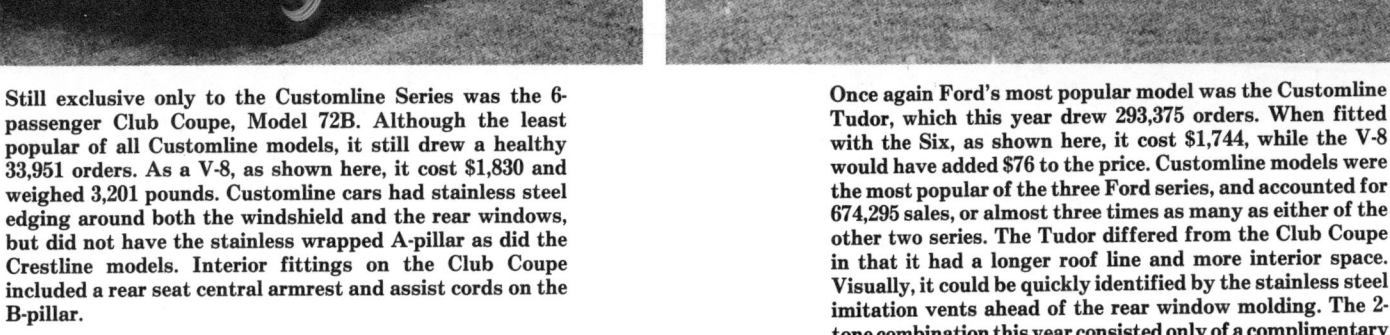

Once again Ford's most popular model was the Customline Tudor, which this year drew 293,375 orders. When fitted with the Six, as shown here, it cost $1,744, while the V-8 would have added $76 to the price. Customline models were the most popular of the three Ford series, and accounted for 674,295 sales, or almost three times as many as either of the other two series. The Tudor differed from the Club Coupe in that it had a longer roof line and more interior space. Visually, it could be quickly identified by the stainless steel imitation vents ahead of the rear window molding. The 2-tone combination this year consisted only of a complimentary colored top. As a Six, the car weighed 3,009 pounds.

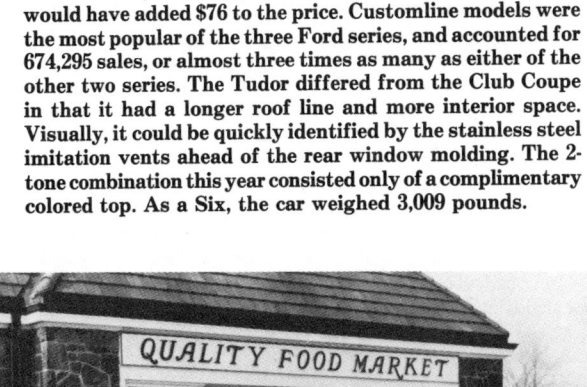

The Customline Fordor had a little less chrome and a slightly lower level of interior fittings than did the new Crestline version, but it had 2.5-times as many sales. With orders peaking at 2,62,499, however, the model slipped from 1st to 2nd place in overall sales, once again relinquishing the top spot to the companion Tudor. Known as the Model 73B, the car was available with the new V-8 or the modified Six as shown here. In this form, it sold for $1,793 and weighed 3,155 pounds. Even with the Six, it could have been equipped with the new Master-Guide power steering for $134, the new Swift-Sure power brakes for $41, or the well-tested and excellent Fordomatic at $184, though these options were usually placed on V-8 powered cars. More often the Six got the automatic overdrive for $110.

The third new model on this year's list was the Customline 2-door Station Wagon, Model 59B, better known as the Customline Ranch Wagon. However, as was the case with other Ford wagons, the series designation did not appear on the exterior of the car. As could be expected, the Customline version was simply the Mainline Ranch Wagon, but with a higher trim level. Its main outward differentiation was the full-length stainless steel belt molding, which improved the appearance tremendously. Available in both Six and V-8 versions, it is shown here equipped with the Six. In this form, it was base priced at $2,122 and weighed 3,344 pounds. Not quite as popular as either the 4-door Customline wagon or the Mainline version of the Ranch Wagon, this edition drew 36,086 orders. Look close and note the interesting scissors hinge arrangement on the lift gate.

Now sharing station wagon space in the Customline series was the Country Sedan, the series 4-door wagon offering. Designated the Model 79B, it used the same body as the Crestline version, but lacked the exterior wood trim and some minor interior items. The most expensive car in the Customline series, the Country Sedan had a base price of $2,279 and weighed 3,634 pounds in V-8 form as shown here. The 2-tone scheme was optional on all wagons, and consisted of a complimentary colored band around the entire window area. Both top and lower body were in the same color, as were the wheels. The gas filler on all wagons still was located at the upper trailing edge of the left rear fender. The Country Sedan could be ordered in either Six or V-8 form, and as a six or 8-passenger vehicle. The forward portions of the rear quarter windows slid rearward, but the small rear panes on the back doors were not moveable vents, but were set permanently in place.

Once again the 3-passenger Mainline Business Coupe, Model 72C, was the lowest priced Ford, base priced at $1,548 in the 6-cylinder form shown here. At 3,021 pounds, it was also the lightest model. Built primarily for salesmen and fleet use, the car had a large storage area behind the front seat, and spacious trunk area. The only brightwork consisted of a small stainless steel molding running completely around the car at window sill level, and a small stainless stone guard on the rear fender embossing. As before, the car used the same body as did the Customline Club Coupe. As on the Club Coupe, the rear quarter windows could be lowered about 3/4-way down. Despite its low sales of 10,665, Ford deemed the car a necessary part of its low-price line, and would continue it into the new 1955 bodies.

When Crestline and Customline models were equipped with the V-8, the special emblem was located at the leading edge of the front fender. In the Mainline series, however, this emblem was placed just above the trailing edge of the front wheel well. When so equipped, the Mainline Fordor sold for $1,777 and weighed 3,263 pounds. The least popular of all of the 4-door offerings, the Mainline version drew only 55,371 orders. On this model, the rear vent windows could not be opened. The new embossed trim behind the rear door adds a bit of brightness, as does the new stainless stone shield, but a bit of side trim sure would have helped.

As always, the Mainline Tudor was the most popular car in the low-price series, accounting for 123,329 sales. This was more than the rest of the series combined. This is the 6-cylinder version, which was base priced at $1,651 and weighed 3,086 pounds. When equipped with the V-8, it would have worn a small "V-8" emblem at the mid-point of the front fenders. A slight concession toward trim was made on both the Mainline Tudor and Fordor this year. It consisted of a small embossed stainless panel on the trailing edge of the C-pillar, between the drip molding and the black rubber window molding. The Business Coupe did not get this trim. As before, only the driver received a sun visor and a door-panel arm rest in the Mainline series.

Once found exclusively in the Mainline series, the Ranch Wagon this year shared its body with the Customline version. Still, the handy little work horse was more popular in the low-price field, and drew 44,315 orders. Designated the Model 59A, it is shown here in V-8 form and with the optional 2-tone paint. In this rather rare form, it would have cost $2,106 and weighed 3,459 pounds, with the paint being extra. As before, the forward half of the huge rear quarter window would slide rearward, but the back portion was fixed in place. The Mainline Ranch Wagon came in 6-passenger style only. Those wanting an 8-passenger version had to go to the Customline offering.

Based on the 2-door Ranch Wagon body shell, the Courier sedan Delivery fit into a gray area between car and truck. It used all passenger car parts and sheet metal, yet was considered part of the truck fleet. Its trim level was strictly Mainline, even to the stainless band around the sill, but it bore the name "Courier" on its fender sides, just as the wagons bore their own names rather than that of the series in which were fitted. The rear door was hinged on the left so that it would open on the curb side—except in cases such as this when the driver parked on the wrong side of the road. The small emblem on the lower door corner shows that this particular model is equipped with the $184 extra Fordomatic unit, while lack of any emblem on the front fender says that the $76-delete 6-cylinder engine lived under the hood. The fender mounted antenna indicates the optional radio, which was priced at $88 for the standard set or $99 for the deluxe. As far as can be ascertained, about 3,200 Couriers left the plant this year. All would have been base priced at $1,515 and weighed 3,109 pounds with the 6-cylinder engine. Yes, this was the same price and weight as listed for the 1953 model.

The argument continues over whether or not the Thunderbird was supposed to be a 1954 car that was delayed too long, or if Ford had all along planned it to be a 1955 model. Adding weight to the "delayed" theory is that catalog, issued in 1954, which shows the car in not quite introductory form. The following page in this brochure shows the back view, with "1954" plainly displayed in the license plate area. Only the headlight bezels differ from the real model. And, if the car wasn't planned for 1954, why were the initial showings made as early as Feb. 20, 1954? Ford apparently did have a scheduling squeeze in its body plants, and for that reason, production of the Thunderbird body was contracted to the Budd Co. Whether that held up production, or whether the car had been scheduled for 1955 all along is still open to discussion.

A Ford was once again entered in this year's Mobilgas Economy Run, and managed 22.33 miles per gallon over the 1,335-mile course. The car used was the Customline Fordor, equipped with the Six with automatic overdrive, which was a $110 option. Set up in this manner, the vehicle was said to outperform the V-8 version in both gas mileage and in overall handling. Despite the preference of the V-8 by most performance-oriented buyers, the new Six was no engine to ignore. Its upgrade of 14 horses made it a mill to be reckoned with in normal operating circumstances.

Built in 1954 and scheduled for the January, 1955, auto shows was the Mystere, Ford's newest show car. Designed by Ford stylist Bill Boyer, the car featured styling so close to the planned 1957 trim (also designed by Boyer) that its introduction was held back until 1956. The car featured a lift-up plexiglas top with no windows; half doors; four pivoting bucket seats, and a radio-TV console for the rear passengers. It also marked Ford's first use of quad headlights. It was designed for a gas turbine rear engine, but it appears that no engine was ever installed in this model.

The Distinctively New

FORD

Thunderbird

Introducing a completely new kind of sports car... a truly fine car... with low-silhouette styling... road-hugging stability... and high performance... plus the conveniences and all-weather protection of today's modern automobile

One wonders if a crystal ball at the start of the 1955 year could have foreseen the tremendous success that Ford would enjoy during the next few months. In fact, by the close of the 1955 model year, Ford had built 1,451,157 cars, winding up with the second best year in its entire history, second only to the thoroughly mixed-up calendar year 1923 production.

And why shouldn't the company have a banner year. On the showroom floors was the brand new Thunderbird; a new and very attractive top line called the Fairlane Series; cars with new overall body styling, and new horsepower ratings under the hood. So what if Chevrolet could beat Fords hands down in any drag race—the Fords looked good, were priced right, and the American public loved them.

The big news of the year, of course, was the new Thunderbird, which finally was introduced on Oct. 22, 1954. As predicted, it had a 2-passenger body with a removable hardtop, and in general, followed the lines of the show version that came out in February, 1954. It utilized a 102-inch wheelbase chassis and was 175.3 inches long overall. Power was by the Mercury 292 cubic inch V-8, which was rated at 198 horsepower when hooked to the automatic transmission, or 193 with the manual 3-speed or the automatic overdrive. The difference in horsepower was due to the 8.1:1 compression ratio of the lesser power engine and the 8.5:1 of the higher. Both engines used the same 3.75x3.3 inch bore and stroke and the same Holley 4-barrel carburetor. This engine was exclusive only to the Thunderbird, and was not available in the regular Ford line until mid-year, when it appears that it was released as an option through select Ford dealers.

In outward appearance, the new Thunderbird was a real knock-out. Long and sleek, it had an aircraft-type wrap-around windshield; oval grille opening with a fine-mesh egg-crate grille; hooded headlights; forward hinged hood with functional air scoop, and a row of small chrome slash marks on the front fenders. Oddly, the car came with a removable fiberglass top as standard equipment. The rayon convertible top was available as an option, for $290 if bought in addition to the standard top, or for $75 if bought in exchange for the solid unit.

The side trim on the initial model continues to cause confusion even today. What had happened was that somewhere between the car's long range introduction in February, 1954, and the actual start-up of production on Sept. 5, 1954, some of the top management at Ford decided that the Thunderbirds should wear a flashy side trim piece similar in appearance to what would appear on the new Fairlane series. The idea was to bring the Thunderbird into closer union with the top-line Ford car, rather than have it stand as a separate entity. But, however good the side spear looked on the Fairlanes, the concept was lost on the shorter Thunderbirds. Finally the stylists in charge convinced top management of the beauty of the plain-sided bird, and

the side spears never did appear on production models.

What confuses the issue, though, is the fact that a couple of pre-production models with these spears were widely shown to the public, beginning in August, 1954. Also, Ford sent out numerous publicity pictures of the bird with the spears, and even authorized ads in the leading magazines showing the car with spears. In fact, the entire back page of the November, 1954, issue of *MOTOR TREND* is a 4-color ad showing a red, a black, and a turquoise Thunderbird, all three wearing the side spears—and this was over a month after the actual car was on the market.

With all of the fuss over the Thunderbird, one would think that the rest of the Ford line would be ignored. It certainly was not. The line was exemplified by the new Fairlane series, which replaced the former Crestline series. Wearing totally new skin over the old inner body shell, the new lines were much prettier vehicles than the 1954 offerings, and the Fairlanes were by far the prettiest of all.

Highlighting the Fairlane line was the new Crown Victoria, which looked somewhat like the regular Victoria hardtop, but had a heavy chrome band looped over the greenhouse in the place occupied by the B-pillars on a normal 2-door. The new model came in two variations: The plain Crown Victoria and the Crown Victoria Skyliner, which featured a Plexiglas bubble between the windshield header and the B-pillar. The bubble-top featured an aluminized nylon headliner that could be snapped and zippered into place to prevent cooking the occupants when the car was used on hot sunny days.

All Fairlanes were quickly identified by the wide swash molding which ran from the top of the headlight bezels to the outer mid-point of the taillight bezels. This generous use of stainless steel swept downward on the front fender, V-ed at the center of the front door, and then ran horizontally to the taillight. This trim concept, in various forms, would signify the top-line Fords through the 1959 model year.

In addition to the Crown and plain Victorias, the Fairlane series also contained the convertible and 4-door sedan that had been in the old Crestline series, and also acquired a new 2-door model. This was a revision of the former 2-door sedan body that had appeared in the 1954 model line, and in fact, bore the same Model 70 designation. Meanwhile, the old 2-door coupe body, model 72, had been dropped completely.

Causing confusion here was the fact that when this basic body appeared in the Fairlane family, it was called the Club Sedan, Model 70C, but when it appeared in the Customline series, it was known as the 2-door Sedan, Model 70B, while in the Mainline series it was both the 3-passenger Business Coupe, Model 70D, and the 2-door Sedan, Model 70A. With the dropping of the Model 72 Club Coupe, the Customline series was reduced to just two models, the 4-door and 2-door sedans. In the Mainline series, however, the number of car models was not changed because the Business Coupe simply became a 3-passenger version of the 2-door sedan. Causing a rather drastic reduction in models within all series was the creation of a new Station Wagon series, which encompassed all wagons of all trim levels, and called them by their own names rather than by the former series names. This, in effect, had been going on before, as the wagons never bore the names of their trim level series. But now with the new series for station wagons, the move became official. As before, the Ranch Wagon and Courier retained the Mainline trim level, while the Country Squire used Fairlane appointments. However, the Country Squire did not use the swash molding of the Fairlanes, but instead was trimmed in imitation wood paneling with wood-grain fiberglass framing. The last use of natural wood went out with the 1954 models.

Between the Ranch Wagon and the Country Squire were three mid-range wagons. The 2-door version was called the Custom Ranch Wagon. It used Customline features, including the single horizontal bar of side trim. In the 4-door models, however, Ford came up with a funny that has caused moderate confusion ever since. Called the Country Sedans, the 4-door mid-range wagons

After first being introduced in February, 1954, the new Thunderbird finally reached the dealers on Oct. 22, 1954, about three weeks ahead of the new 1955 Ford line. Despite the fact that it had been "previewed" for months, acceptance of the little bird was still overwhelming, and Ford knew for sure that it had a winner on its hands—if not in sales, at least in positive publicity. Weighing 2,980 pounds, the car was built on a chassis of 102-inch wheelbase and was 175.3 inches long overall. Oddly, or possibly as a cost saving measure, it used the same 6.70x15 tires as did the rest of the Fords, a factor which seemed to make the wheels look too large for the rest of the car. Production reached 16,155, which was a big step above the 700 Corvettes sold this year. The car was base priced at $2,944, which made it the first Ford to come close to the $1 per pound ratio. The base price included the removable fiberglass top, but not the convertible rag-top.

were available in 6-passenger and 8-passenger forms. But not only was the seating different, the side trim also varied greatly. The 6-passenger model used the same single bar as did other Customline models, but the 8-passenger unit used the same swash molding as did the Fairlane series.

Under all hoods, a few changes had taken place as Ford engaged in the start of the now-famous horsepower race. In line with this, the Six was now rated at 120 HP at 4000 rpm, the result of raising the compression to 7.5:1 from the former 7.2:1. But totally new was the modified OHV V-8, which now sported 272 cubic inches, and had a bore and stroke of 3.62x3.3 inches. Running a compression of 7.6:1, the engine was now rated at 162 HP at 4400 rpm. In all Fairlane and station wagon models, this engine was equipped with a dual exhaust system for even greater horsepower. And finally, a "Special" V-8 was added. This was a 182 HP version, which was the regular 272 cubic inch model, but having 8.5:1 compression and a Holley 4-barrel Power Pack carburetor rather than the Holley 2-barrel used on the regular engine. The 182 HP version was only supposed to be available in Fairlane of station wagon models equipped with Fordomatic.

In line with the larger engines, there were some chassis modifications, which resulted in the cars gaining a half-inch in wheelbase length, going from 115 to 115.5 inches. Overall length grew also a half-inch, going up to 198.5 for the cars, and 197.6 for the wagons.

As noted earlier, the Customline series was now down to two models, the 4-door sedan and a 2-door sedan. Although sales of the two models were just about even, and ranked in 2nd and 3rd place, the series did not own the top selling car. That honor went to the new Fairlane series, where the 4-door Town Sedan outsold all other Fords with a total of 254,437. The Customline 2-door Sedan came in 2nd with 236,575 sales, while the Customline 4-door Sedan was 3rd with 235,417 units. also accounting for production of more than 100,000 were the new Fairlane Club Sedan with 173,311 leaving the lines, and the Fairlane Victoria, with 113,372 sales. Within the four series, the new Fairlane was the sales leader with 626,250 units; the Customline was next with its two models producing 471,992 sales; the new Station Wagon series was 3rd with 209,459 sold, and the Mainline low-buck cars came in last with 127,301 orders. And, if one counts the Thunderbird as a Ford model (at this point this was uncertain) then another 16,155 cars had to be added to the list, bringing the year's total of 1,451,157.

Throughout all of this production activity, Ford's corporate side was also occupied, and three new factories were opened. They were a new one at Mahwah, N.J., replacing an old one at Edgewater, N.J.; a new plant at San Jose, Cal., replacing an old one at Richmond, Cal., and a new plant at Louisville, Ky., replacing an older one in that city.

One of Ford's most often published publicity pictures shows the new Thunderbird with its fiberglass top removed. From this angle, there were few people who could argue about the beautiful sporty lines of the car. Power was by a special Mercury block of 292 cubic inches, which was identified by "Thunderbird" embossing on the rocker covers. When fitted with the standard 3-speed or automatic overdrive transmission, this engine was provided with an 8.1:1 compression ratio and produced 193 horses at 4400 rpm. When the Fordomatic was ordered, the compression was raised to 8.5:1 and the engine was now capable of 198 HP at 4400 rpm. Wisely, Ford did not promote the car as an all-out sports machine. Only one or two of the very early ads referred to the new T-Bird as a "sports car," while all later ads referred to it as a "personal car."

Surprisingly, Ford did not include the nylon convertible top with the basic Thunderbird. One would have expected the soft top to be standard and the hard top to be the accessory. Yet just the opposite occurred, and the convertible unit was the extra-cost item. It could be ordered along with the fiberglass top for an extra $290, or in place of the hard top for $75. When folded, it lived in its own hidden compartment behind the seat, and could be left there when the hard top was installed. Maybe Ford had the right idea in its top provisions. Had the hard top been the extra item, probably only a few people would have bought it. But, with the convertible top being necessary protection when the hard unit was left in the garage, almost all buyers went for the extra-cost soft unit.

Just as the exterior was a prime example of beautiful automotive design, the interior of the new Thunderbird was also extremely attractive, with just enough carry-over so that one knew it was a Ford product. Facing the driver was a large domed speedometer, with a clear glass rear panel to shed light onto the speedometer face during daylight hours. On the left is Ford's first standard tachometer, reading up to 5000 rpm, while on the right is a standard electric clock. Directly below the speedometer are heat and fuel gauges, while two small lamps bracketing the lower bar are generator and oil pressure warning lights. A floor shifter was used, regardless of whether the car had the standard 3-speed or the optional Fordomatic at $178 extra. The radio was another $99, while the heater-defroster added still another $71, even though it almost always came installed in the car.

No sooner did the Birds appear, than the aftermarket companies got busy designing accessories for them. One of the first on the market was the Town Car conversion, designed for those owners who did not want to spring $290 for the soft top, yet wanted the joys of open air driving without the risk of leaving the hardtop at home. Built by the Sanco Co. of Atlanta, Ga., the kit retailed for $89.50. It consisted of runners and tie-down straps to allow the top to be slid rearward and rest over the trunk area. It could be pulled back over the driver's head in 15 seconds, the company claimed. The company reported that even at maximum speed, the top would stay in place because the windshield would carry the slipstream over the top of the car and prevent all wind buffeting.

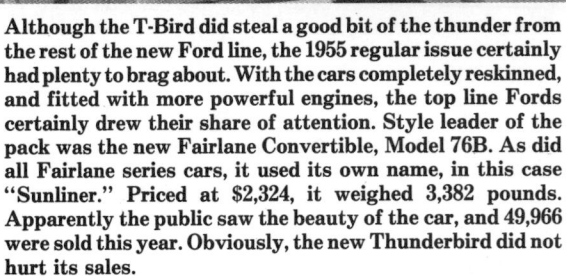

The T-Bird that never was. Still causing confusion today are Ford publicity photos such as this, which show the Thunderbird wearing Fairlane-like side trim. Initially the car was proposed without such trim, but later in its development, top Ford management wanted to bring the Thunderbird closer to the rest of the Ford family in looks, and thus the side swash was contemplated. Thus, many Thunderbird ads from August on show the cars with this trim. Even as late as November, 1954, the back page of *MOTOR TREND* carried a T-Bird ad showing three different colored cars, all with the swash. However, the stylists hated the trim, fought against it, and eventually won, apparently only weeks before production actually started. One thing the trim would have accomplished—it would have prevented the side dings and scrapes so common on Thunderbirds that had to park in head-in situations.

Although the T-Bird did steal a good bit of the thunder from the rest of the new Ford line, the 1955 regular issue certainly had plenty to brag about. With the cars completely reskinned, and fitted with more powerful engines, the top line Fords certainly drew their share of attention. Style leader of the pack was the new Fairlane Convertible, Model 76B. As did all Fairlane series cars, it used its own name, in this case "Sunliner." Priced at $2,324, it weighed 3,382 pounds. Apparently the public saw the beauty of the car, and 49,966 were sold this year. Obviously, the new Thunderbird did not hurt its sales.

Totally new for the year were the two Crown Victoria models, which were exclusive to the Fairlane series. Most exotic of the pair was the Crown Victoria Skyliner, Model 64B. The car was virtually the same as the regular Crown Victoria, but had a green tinted Plexiglas bubble between the stainless tiara and the windshield header. Priced at $2,372, it was the most expensive Fairlane, while at 3,388 pounds, it was also the heaviest. Far from popular, the style drew only 1,999 orders. A headliner of aluminized nylon could be zippered into place to keep from cooking the occupants when the car was used on hot sunny days.

Ford's headline grabber for the year was the new Crown Victoria, which appeared in the Fairlane series only. The 2-style model consisted of the bubble-top Skyliner and the plain Crown Victoria, Model 64A. Though built with the Victoria's roof line, the car was not a true hardtop, in that its large stainless crown or tiara acted as B-pillars, thus turning the car from a hardtop into a coupe style. Priced at $2,302, the style did not prove to be as popular as hoped. Therefore, despite its very attractive appearance, it drew only 33,165 orders. For this model, Ford created a special crowned crest which nested in the V-portion of the swash and on the hoods of all Fairlane models. Mainline and Customline cars and the Station Wagon series continued to use the old style crest without the crown.

Far outselling its brighter trimmed Crown cousins, the plain Victoria drew 113,372 orders this year. Designated the Model 60B, the car was the only true hardtop in Ford's entire line. Exclusive to the Fairlane series, it cost $2,195 and weighed 3,318 pounds. The Fairlane series this year replaced the former Crestline series as the top of the line. The name Fairlane was derived from Henry Ford's Dearborn mansion, Fair Lane, and seemed a fitting tribute to the elder Ford. This view gives a good look at the new concaved grille, flanked by the large parking lights. Fairlane models were the only ones to use chrome trim pieces under the headlight eyebrows.

Another new style for the year was the Club sedan, Model 70C, which appeared in the Fairlane series. The car used the same pillared 2-door sedan body as found in both the Customline and Mainline series, but for some reason was called a coupe in Fairlane trim while it went by the name 2-door sedan in the other series. Thus, Ford's top line had four different 6-passenger coupe models. Priced at $2,014, the car was the least expensive of the Fairlanes. It was also one of the most popular, with 173,311 being sold. Upholstery and trim were identical to that of the Fairlane 4-door Sedan. With the upgrading in power of all engines, this year any Ford could be ordered with the 120 horsepower Six or the 162 horse V-8. The "special" high compression V-8 of 182 HP was available only to Fairlanes and station wagons equipped with automatic transmissions.

With the movement of its station wagon models to the new Station Wagon series, and the demise of the former Club Coupe (body No. 72), the Customline series was left with only two models. Nevertheless, these two were the second and third most popular cars in the Ford line. Ranking in second place was this Customline 2-door Sedan, Model 70B, which attained sales of 236,575. Base priced at $1,901, it weighed 3,194 pounds. The small round insignia on the front fender, between the grille and wheel opening, indicates that this car is equipped with the 120 horse Six, rather than the V-8. In this guise, it would have cost $1,801 in base form. Customline models had their series signature on the trailing edge of the front fender, just above the trim bar.

Ford's best selling model this year was the Fairlane 4-door Sedan, Model 73C. Base priced at $2,060, it saw orders reach an amazing 254,437, which was a big bunch of cars for the top of the line model to attain. It weighed 3,268 pound, and shared its body with similar sedans in both the Mainline and Customline series. Barely visible on this example is Ford's new 2-tone paint scheme. With this option, both top and body sections below the swash were painted in one color, while the hood, trunk deck, inner fender sections, and area between the swash and greenhouse were in a second color. Headlight bezels retained the color of the lower body, even on the inside portion where the secondary color was used on the fender. This year, all Fairlane models were equipped with dual exhaust systems. A miniature repeat of the grille decorated the trunk deck, which also carried the Fairlane and Fordomatic signatures.

In an impromptu drag race, a 1955 Customline 4-door Sedan pits itself against a 1956 Fairlane Victoria. The outcome is not known, but with the new higher horsepower in the standard V-8 of 1956, it is probable that the newer model won. Ford's third most popular car, the Customline 4-door drew 235,417 orders. Priced at $1,945 as a V-8, it weighed 3,236 pounds in that form. Customline cars could be quickly identified by the single bar of full-length belt trim. The cars could be ordered with Fordomatic, but supposedly could not be fitted with the special 182 horse engine that was available to Fairlanes. All 4-door sedans shared the same body and differed only in upholstery and trim levels.

Of all three Mainline cars, only the 4-door Sedan, Model 73A, made any concession to trim. It sported a tiny stainless stone guard at the leading edge of the rear wheel opening. Base priced at $1,853 in the V-8 form shown here, the car weighed 3,216 pounds. The rear windows were equipped with vent panes, but these would not open. The white sidewalls on this model would have been a $27 exchange. Removing all side trim might have saved a few dollars on the basic car, but it almost seems like foolish economy. Within a short period of time, parking lot dings would thoroughly spoil the side panels, thus giving the car a shop-worn appearance long before its time. Still, the Mainline 4-door drew 41,749 orders, so there certainly were plenty of people who put price ahead of brightwork.

The Business Coupe was continued in the Mainline series, but the 3-passenger car was now wearing a new body. Ford discontinued the former coupe body, Model 72, and as a result, the Business Coupe had to utilize the Model 70 2-door Sedan body. In this form, it was known as the Model 70D. The rear compartment was upholstered in tough vinyl and intended only for carrying luggage or packages. In 6-cylinder form as shown here, it weighed 3,026 pounds and cost $1,606, thus being Ford's lightest and least expensive car. In V-8 form, it would have cost $100 more and been 110 pounds heavier. Never a popular model, the Business coupe drew only 8,809 orders this year, most for commercial and industrial fleet usage.

The top of the line in Ford's new Station Wagon series was the Country Squire, Model 79C. Using Fairlane trim levels, the 8-passenger car was fitted with glue-on paper planking outlined by wood-gained fiberglass framing. This was the first year that no natural wood was used in the wagon's top of the line trim package. Unlike the cars, where the 2-tone paint combination included the hood and upper door frames in the secondary color, the primary color on the wagons covered everything but the area surrounding the windows. Least popular and most expensive of all the wagons, the pretentious Country Squire drew only 19,011 orders with its $2,492 price tag. The Country Squire signature appeared on the rear fender, just above the fiberglass framing. New was the location of the gas filler, which now was found behind its own small door just ahead of and below the taillight bulge on the left side. The decorative framing wrapped around the outside corner of this door.

Utilizing the same body as the Business Coupe was the Mainline 2-door Sedan. In this form it was called the Model 70A. It was priced at $1,707 with the 6-cylinder engine, as shown here. The Mainline series continued to be devoid of all side trim, and did not even have a series identification plate. As before, all window molding was in black rubber, and inside only one sun visor and one door panel arm rest was provided—for the driver, of course. Still, the 2-door drew a total of 76,698 orders, again, with much of the production going into municipal or industrial fleets.

Appearing in a scene from some long forgotten movie is this 8-passenger Country Sedan. Despite the fact that 53,209 copies of this model were produced, factory photos of the car are very difficult to find. The fooler on this model is the fact that it was trimmed with the Fairlane side swash, while in 6-passenger form it wore the single horizontal trim bar of the Customline series. Designated the Model 79B in this form, the 8-passenger vehicle cost $2,387 and weighed 3,603 pounds with the V-8, as indicated here by the V-8 emblem on the front fender. In addition to the Fairlane side trim, the 8-passenger model also wore the Fairlane wheel covers while the 6-passenger example wore Customline hub caps.

Why the difference of a rear seat should create such a difference in exterior trim is not known. However, the 6-passenger Country Sedan, Model 79D, wore the exterior trim of the Customline series. On the 6-passenger version, the rear seat was a single unit, straight across, while the 8-passenger model had this seat split with a folding portion allowing access to the rearmost seat. In 6-passenger form, with the V-8, the Country Sedan cost $2,256 and weighed 3,527 pounds. Ford's wagons still used the swing-down tailgate and upward hinged liftgate, as did the rest of the industry. The one-piece gate with disappearing rear window had not yet come into use. Rear quarter windows continued to feature a forward half that would slide across the rear portion. Rear door windows could be lowered to sill level, but the vent panes within these windows would not open. The upper gate was held open by spring-loaded scissor-type hinges. A total of 53,075 6-passenger models were sold this year.

Of the two 2-door wagon variations, the Custom Ranch Wagon reflected the higher trim level. It used the same exterior appointments as did the Customline series and the 6-passenger Country Sedan. Designated the Model 59B, it was available in 6-passenger form only. Its base price as a V-8 was $2,209, while its weight was 3,461 pounds. Relatively popular, it enjoyed sales of 43,671. On all wagons, the rear seats would fold down for additional cargo space. When folded, the cushion rested against the front seat, with its underside providing a hard protective bulkhead against which cargo could ride. The seat back then folded forward, and its backside became an integral part of the floor.

Once again the Courier Sedan Delivery was based on the Model 29 basic body shell. Only in Courier form, the large rear windows were filled in with metal panels, and the interior walls were covered in masonite, while the headliner and seat upholstery was in copper vinyl. The neat little package truck continued to adopt the Mainline exterior trim level, but did not have the wrap-around stainless molding found on the Ranch Wagon. Its only side trim was the "Courier" signature on the front fender and, in this case, the V-8 emblem on the leading edge of the front fender. Apparently all power options, including the "special" V-8 and accompanying Fordomatic, could be ordered for this model. The Courier was in sort of a gray area between car and truck, and its production figures were not tallied with the car lines. In 6-cylinder form it had a base price of $1,725 and weighed 3,141 pounds.

The plain Ranch Wagon, Model 59A, differed from the Mainline trim scheme in that it had stainless molding completely encircling the car between the greenhouse and the body proper. Otherwise, it was as devoid of brightwork as was the low-line series in the passenger car line. Priced at $2,143 as a V-8, it was $100 less when fitted with the Six as shown here. Despite its plain looks, it enjoyed sales of 40,493. As before, the forward halves of the huge rear windows would slide backward for ventilation. All wagons were upholstered in vinyl, with the quality of material varying by trim level.

Although the Shop of Siebert of Toledo probably built more professional cars on Ford chassis than did any other such builder, the company was not alone in the field. Another firm starting to produce such specialized vehicles with Ford components was the Memphis Coach Co. Utilizing the base Courier, this Tennessee firm added a window center section and frame extension to produce this rather attractive ambulance. The car, which still bears the Courier signature on its fenders, gained a totally new roof with tunneled roof lights, large red flasher, and front fender combination light and siren. A nice touch involved the small functional vent windows in the rear of the etched glass panes. Although painted in red and white, this unit could have used a bit of trim to break the huge expanse of side metal.

Siebert of Toledo, Ohio, continued its traditional role as a builder of fine, low priced professional vehicles using the new Ford bodies. Most often used was the Courier, shown here in two extremes. As a Service Car (top) it was basically the stock Courier treated to a new and more plush interior, and fitted with exterior coach lamps on the B-pillars and a large cast and chromed winged wreath on the side panel. Below is an ambulance, version, which featured a rather long frame extension, and a double-doored addition between the two parts. The rear part of the Courier has been left intact, but has been fitted with etched glass panels in the normally blank side walls. Also available on the stretched wheelbase were limousine and landau hearses, with all models featuring the center doors. Siebert was still the major producer of Ford-based professional cars.

Whether or not the Futura should be considered a Ford or a Lincoln is open to discussion. Designed in Dearborn, and built in Italy by Ghia in 1954, the car was first presented as the Lincoln Futura, but in 1955 toured the show circuit as the Ford Futura. The car was powered by a modified Lincoln 341 cubic inch engine, coupled to Lincoln's new Turbo-Matic automatic transmission. Besides the unique body, the car's most startling innovation was the double-bubble cockpit, featuring twin windshield pods, and an enveloping Plexiglas canopy that slid rearward for entry or exit. Standard swing-out doors were used for access. Built on a 126-inch wheelbase, the car was 19 feet long, but only 53 inches high. Ford claimed that in addition to being a show stopper, the car was a functional rolling laboratory, and would be used to road test new innovations. Whether or not this ever occurred is not known.

Another Memphis, Tenn., professional car firm that started to work on Fords this year was the Weller Brothers Co. This particular unit, shown under construction, was probably slated to be an ambulance, judging by the large functional vent windows in the rear. Based on the Courier body, according to the front fender signature, the car has been fitted with side trim from an 8-passenger Country Sedan. The extension section ranges from the B-pillar to the C-pillar, while the vent windows have been cut into the Courier's side panels. Since no side doors have been provided for the rear compartment, this ambulance would have been rear-loading only. The Weller Brothers firm had been in business since 1922, but up to now had done most of their professional car work on Chevrolet chassis.

Decked out in full equipment, and sporting what appears to be a red and white paint job, this unit by the Weller Brothers Co. of Memphis would have been the pride of any ambulance service. Despite the use of the Country Sedan side trim, Weller left the Courier name on the front fenders, and added its own small signature just below that plaque. Except for the stretch unit between the B and C-pillars, little change was made to the Courier's basic sheet metal, save for the large triangular vent window in the rear quarter. Weller also had a larger 4-door ambulance available, but built this on extended Pontiac wagon bases.

As could be expected after the significant changes of 1955, the 1956 Fords entered their second year of a proposed 3-year cycle of major body changes. This meant that there would be new grilles and side trim, movement and redesign of such things as parking lamps and series signatures, some new interior trim and fabric, but overall no major changes. The 1955 Ford had been a darned good looking car, and the 1956 was slated to be better yet. Why make any radical changes?

The one thing that Ford did do, was to add materially to the selection of available styles. A buyer now had 19 different models to choose from, including six station wagons. And, this did not count the Thunderbird, which was living its own life independent of the other Fords.

What was irking Ford officials, however, was the inroad being made by Chevrolet, which not only had a very well accepted body style, but also was consistently leaving Ford in the dust in the performance areas. Ford's reaction to this was two-fold. It brought in more power, and in an odd turn, attempted to steer away from the Chevrolet/Plymouth performance results by selling a series of safety features. As could be expected, the public went for the new power plants, and virtually ignored the safety program.

In the styling area, the Fairlane side trim followed the concept of 1955, but was now heavier, with the rearward half of the swash being of fluted design. The Customline series also picked up a variation of the "V" side trim, which was certainly an improvement over the old straight trim. And, even the usually super-plain Mainline models received rear quarter trim, which essentially was the rearward half of the Mainline trim. As could be expected, a new grille was provided, and the parking lights were now oval in shape, and nested in large chromed bezels at the outer corners of the front fenders, just above the bumper tips.

Within the car there were some new fabric choices, a new deep-dished steering wheel, new safety door-latches, and two new major options—the first Ford factory installed air conditioning units, and the first 9-tube signal-seeking radio. Called Polar-air, the new air conditioner units included tinted window glass, and carried a $275 price tag. Also on the option list was a safety package which included Ford's first seat belt; a padded dash, and padded sun visors.

Wearing all of these innovations were the 19 body styles, which included seven Fairlane models, three models each for the Customline and Mainline series, and six wagons. Totally new for the year was the Fairlane Fordor Victoria, which was Ford's first 4-door hardtop. Exclusive only to the Fairlane series, it was priced at $2,349, or $200 more than the regular Fairlane Town Sedan. Another new model was the Customline Victoria, but this was simply a trim downgrade of the Fairlane victoria. Still, the move brought the Customline series back to three models, and provided buyers with a lower trim level and lower priced hardtop model. The opposite

movement occurred in the station wagon family. Here a new Parklane Ranch Wagon appeared. This was simply the 2-door wagon upgraded to wear what essentially was Fairlane trim. Formerly, this model had been found only in the Customline and Mainline trim levels.

Despite the changes to the sheet metal and a new body design, it was under the hood where the majority of the interest was taking place. Essentially, to stave off the performance embarrassment being caused by Chevrolet, Ford upgraded the horsepower of all its engines. It also made the former Mercury-based Thunderbird engine standard in the Fairlane and Station Wagon series; made this engine optional in the Customline and Mainline series at mid-year, and finally made the new Thunderbird Special engine available in the Fairlane and wagons. Thus, what had been Ford's largest V-8 in 1955 was now its smallest V-block at the end of 1956.

In its standard form, the 272 cubic inch basic engine was now rated at 173 horses at 4400 rpm, or 176 HP when coupled to the Fordomatic transmission. Much of this added horsepower came about by raising the compression ratio to 8:1 from its former 7.6:1.

The Fairlane and wagon series now used the 292 cubic inch block, which had been exclusive to the Mercury and Thunderbird models in 1955, but had also shown up in Police Interceptor models and was offered by some dealers as a mid-1955 option. However, here too, more horses were added, and the engine was now rated at 200 HP at 4500 rpm, or 202 with Fordomatic. Again, this was achieved primarily by raising the compression from 8.1:1 to 8.4:1, and recommending the use of high octane gas only. At first this engine was not available to the Customline or Mainline cars, but at mid-year this block became available on any model.

The above mentioned 292 cubic inch block was also standard in the Thunderbirds, but to give that car a boost, a new engine was devised. Called the Thunderbird Special, it was a 312 cubic inch Y-block OHV model, running a bore and stroke of 3.8x3.44 inches. With a compression ratio of 8.4:1, it developed 215 HP at 4600 rpm, or 225 when hooked to the automatic. In the latter form, it used a 9:1 compression ratio and mandated high octane gas. Both engines used Holley Double Twin-Jet carburetors, and had new heads with high-turbulence combustion chambers. The success of the Thunderbird Special engine was so great that by mid-year Ford made it an option for all Fairlane and wagon models equipped with Fordomatic. At this time also, Ford made available through its dealers several different performance packages, which included such speed products as dual 4-barrel manifolds; high-compression heads, and performance cams and valve lifters.

In the world of power increases, even the pragmatic Six was not ignored. Here too, horsepower was raised to 137 at 4200 rpm, primarily by boosting the compression from 7.5:1 to 8:1. What is surprising, with all of the interest in performance and increased horsepower, Ford still left the Six as a optional engine in all models, it being approximately $100 less than the base 272 cubic inch V-8. Conversely, the 292 T-Bird engine was approximately $125 more than the 272 version, while the Thunderbird Special was about $125 more than the regular Thunderbird 292 block.

Regarding the Thunderbird, the car remained basically unchanged, but what few changes did occur made the 1956 model impossible to mistake for any other year. Foremost among the innovations was the relocation of the spare tire from the trunk to a new exterior position above the now-extended rear bumper. Complete with metal covering, the new spare location caused very mixed feelings. Some people, including the author, loved the design, while others hated it.

The move apparently was an attempt to gain more usable luggage space in the tiny T-Bird trunk. In this respect, the move was successful. But, since the car was engineered along very tight lines, with little margin for modification, the addition of approximately 350 pounds of dead weight aft of the trunk deck had a very adverse effect on steering and handling. Although changes were made to both the steering and the rear suspension to compensate for this weight, few Thunderbird buffs will claim that the 1956 model handles as well at high speed as do the 1955 or 1957 versions.

Other main differences between the 1955 and 1956 Birds included the addition of air vents on the cowls, ahead of the leading door edges. This was a move that was greatly appreciated by those who used their cars in hot climates. But the most noticeable change occurred in the fiberglass tops. As an option, a buyer now could have a solid-sided top or one with a porthole on the rear quarter. The portholes were added to appease those who felt the blank tops made it difficult to back into tight parking spaces, while the plain tops were kept in stock to appease those who didn't like the portholes. In a reversal of 1955, either hardtop was now a $290 option, while the soft top was considered standard.

All Fords, including the Thunderbird, received one other major change. That was the permanent switch from a 6 volt to a 12 volt electrical system. The new system, which probably didn't receive as much publicity as due, involved a complete re-engineering of the entire electrical system, and meant that few electrical components would be interchangeable between 1955 and earlier cars and the 1956 and later models. It also meant that the cars would now start much easier, having both a hotter spark and a higher rate of cranking.

Introduction of the new models began in mid-September for the Fords and late October for the new Thunderbirds. Sales, though not as good as record-breaking 1955, were not too bad either, and Ford wound up the model year with 1,408,478 cars sold, including 15,631 T-Birds.

Of these, 665,306 were in the Fairlane series, which provided a home to three of Ford's most popular models. There were the 1st place Town Sedan, with 224,872 sales; the 2nd place Club Victoria or plain Victoria, with a tremendous jump to 177,735 sales, and the Club Sedan, which ranked in 5th place with 142,629 units. The 3rd and 4th sales spot were taken up by two Customline models. These were the 3rd place Customline 4-door Sedan, with production of 170,695, and the Customline 2-door Sedan, with 164,828 sales. The only other model to top the 100,000 figure was the Mainline 2-door Sedan, with 106,974 registered units.

Lowest sales were recorded by the "bubble top" Crown Victoria Skyliner, whose production was terminated early in the season. All told, only 603 of the Plexiglas Victorias left the plant, making the car quite rare today, if one can be found with the Plexiglas still in good shape.

In a reversal of 1955 policy, the Thunderbird now came with the convertible top as standard equipment, and the hardtops were considered accessories. Totally new for the year is the rear mounted spare, which certainly increased usable storage space in the trunk. Feelings on the outside spare were mixed—many liked it, many did not. However, adding 350 pounds of weight that far beyond the rear axle caused handling problems that suspension revisions were unable to correct completely. Primarily for that reason, the spares appeared only this year. The price of the new T-Bird was up this year, to $3,151, and likewise, the weight climbed to 3,088 pounds. Despite rave reviews in virtually all of the automotive press, sales were still down, ending the model year at 15,631. Still, that was more than four times what Corvette was doing, and 1956 was one of the Corvette's better years to date. Soft tops were available in either a light beige or in the black shown here.

Besides the rear spare, 1956 Thunderbirds can be quickly identified by two other less conspicuous points. Those are the new vent windows and the air vents located on either cowl side. Both of these items were well received, as the cockpits of the 1955 Birds tended to become quite hot in warm weather. In redesigning the rear bumper to make room for the outside spare, engineers came up with the idea of routing the exhaust tips through the bumper ends. This tended to be rather nice when the cars were new, but prolonged mileage would stain and blacken the bumpers. This model is shown with its plain hardtop. Weighing about 65 pounds, the top cost an additional $290.

Convertibles and Fords always seemed to be synonymous, and 1956 was no exception. The new Fairlane Sunliner proved its good looks by being one of the few models to exceed its 1955 sales. A total of 58,147 were sold, which was 8,181 more than the 1955 record year. Priced at $2,459, the car had a base weight of 3,455 pounds, and thus was the heaviest Ford outside of the wagon series. Designated the Model 76B, the car could be ordered with either a V-8 or a Six, though one wonders how many 6-cylinder Sunliners left the plant. When fitted with the V-8, the car would also be equipped with a dual exhaust system and a special slotted rear bumper with the exhaust pipes terminating through the bumper tips.

Posed with one of the most beautiful cars of the year—the new Lincoln Premier—this snappy little T-Bird shows off its new porthole top, which was devised in answer to complaints that the blank sided top cut visibility when parallel parking or merging into heavy traffic. Priced at the same $290 as the plain version, the portholes quickly gained acceptance, and became far more popular than the plain models. Under the hood, another option was available. This was the new Thunderbird Special engine of 312 cubic inches, which developed 215 horses with the manual transmission or 225 when coupled to the $215 optional Fordomatic. The Thunderbird Special cost $123 more than the standard T-Bird 292 cubic inch V-8. Another popular option on the T-Bird was power windows, which added $70 to the cost; power brakes at $40, and power steering at $65.

Ranking just behind the Victoria in Fairlane sales, and in 5th place in Ford's overall picture, was the Fairlane Club Sedan, Model 70C. A total of 142,629 were sold. Priced at $2,147, the car weighed 3,250 pounds. A solid B-pillar, fully-framed doors, and a more vertical rear window were the main differences between this model and the Victoria. When ordered with a V-8, all Fairlane models automatically received the new 292 cubic inch block, which had been used in the 1955 Thunderbirds, and then became a limited option about the middle of the 1955 season. The 272 cubic inch block was reserved strictly for Customline and Mainline installations.

A sudden surge in popularity boosted the Fairlane Victoria up to the second sales spot. This year a total of 177,735 Victorias left the plant, an increase of over 64,000 from 1955. All Fairlanes with a V-8 engine were fitted with a stylized eagle on the front fender, just above the massive new parking light casings. Those few Fairlanes that had the 6-cylinder engine did not get this emblem. Designated the Model 64C, the Victoria cost $2,294 and weighed 3,345 pounds. Some literature refers to this car as the Club Victoria, apparently to differentiate it from the far less popular Crown Victoria.

Dropping drastically in popularity was the Fairlane Crown Victoria, Model 64A, which this year had only 9,209 sales. This was less than one-third of the previous year's orders. Billed as a hardtop, the car was really a coupe or 2-door sedan, with heavy B-pillars. Still, it used the frameless doors of the Victoria. The rear quarter windows would roll down flush with the sill line. The stainless steel "crown" which ran over the top from sill to shining sill, contained decorative embossed rectangles to imitate exhaust or vent ports. But these were strictly decorations, as the crown was of solid metal. A similar stainless bar went across the inside of the top. Oddly, the Crown Victorias were the only Fords to have a folding center arm rest in the rear seat back. In basic form, with the Thunderbird 292 V-8, the Crown Victoria sold for $2,438 and weighed 3,217 pounds.

Drawing such little interest that it was dropped from the production rolls by mid-year was the Crown Victoria Skyliner. Part of the Fairlane series, this car drew only 603 orders in 1956, thus making it by far the most rare of all of the year's Fords. Essentially, it was the Crown Victoria with a tinted Plexiglas insert between the windshield header and the B-pillar crown. To cut down on interior temperatures, a cloth headliner could be zippered across the Plexiglas. Designated the Model 64B, the car used the same basic body as did the plain Victoria and the Crown version.

Ford's totally new style for the year was the Fairlane 4-door Town Victoria, Model 57A. Exclusive to the Fairlane series, the car marked Ford's first 4-door hardtop design. All four windows could be lowered to sill level, and none of the doors used framing. Likewise, no B-pillar was used above the sill line, and the car could be opened completely for warm weather driving. Possibly because it was a new concept for Ford, buyers were a bit shy, and only 32,111 were sold. The car was base priced at $2,349 and weighed 3,440 pounds. Popular options on all Fairlanes were the Fordomatic automatic transmission at $178, power steering at $51, and power brakes at $32. Front and rear power windows were another $100, while a power front seat added still $60 more to the package.

Ford's best selling car by a good margin was the Fairlane Town Sedan, Model 73C. The car used the same body as did 4-door sedans in the Customline and Mainline series, but the higher trim level both inside and out attracted a total of 224,872 buyers this year. Priced at $2,194 with the 292 V-8, the car weighed 3,290 pounds. With "safety" being used as a sales theme, all Fords had a redesigned dash, with dash and sun visor padding being available. The steering wheel also was of the safety type, and had a hub recessed 2.5 inches from the rim. For the first time, seat belts could be ordered in any model. Notice the eagle-shaped "Thunderbird" insignia on the front fender which signifies that this car has the 292 cubic inch V-8, which was the standard V-8 power in all Fairlanes and wagons. The Town Sedan differed from the Town Victoria in that it had a solid B-pillar and all four doors were fully framed. In addition, vent windows were provided on the rear doors of this model, but not on the Victoria version.

Far more popular than the pillar-less Victoria was the Customline 2-door Sedan, Model 70B. In this form, the 2-door body drew 164,828 orders, and thus ranked 4th on Ford's sales charts. Lack of front fender emblem points out that this model is fitted with the revised 6-cylinder engine, which now boasted 137 horsepower at 4200 rpm. In this form, it would have been base priced at $1,939 and weighed 3,107 pounds. Notice the difference in 2-tone design. On the Fairlane models, the lower body color continued around the headlight bezels, while on the Customline, these bezels were finished in the same color as the upper part of the body. The roof always followed the same color as did the lower body.

New for the year but not drawing much interest was the Customline Victoria, Model 64D. The car was simply a down-trimmed version of the super-popular Fairlane Victoria. Probably buyers who wanted all the flash and style of the Fairlane series were not too intrigued by the measly $100 savings offered by the Customline version, especially since that savings also involved dropping to the 272 cubic inch V-8 as the main power source. In all, only 33,130 of the Customline Victorias were sold, all with a base price of $2,193 in V-8 form or $2,093 with the Six. Note the small V-8 emblem on this model, which is a carry-over from 1955. This signified the 272 cubic inch engine, as opposed to the Thunderbird shaped emblem for the 292 block.

Ford's low buck car continued to be the 3-passenger business model, found exclusively in the Mainline series. Still using the basic Model 70 body, the car was now called a 3-passenger Business Sedan, rather than Business Coupe, as it had been in the past. Designated the Model 70D, the car was priced at $1,748 in 6-cylinder form as shown here, or at $1,848 with the 272 V-8. Besides the base price, the main attraction of this model for salesmen was the vast amount of storage space for sample cases, luggage, etc. Note that the Mainline series finally received some badly needed side trim. This stainless swash was the same trim as used on the rear half of the Customline models. Interestingly, early catalogs do not show this trim, but portray the cars with the blank sides for which the Mainline Series had been known. Not a popular model, the Business Sedan drew only 8,020 orders.

Ford's most popular Customline model, and its 3rd most popular car overall was the Customline 4-door Sedan, Model 73B. Production totaled 170,695. Again, lack of V-8 emblem shows that this car has the 6-cylinder engine, in which case it would have been priced at $1,985, with the complimentary colored top and the rear fender skirts being extra, as were the full wheel covers. If ordered in V-8 form, the car would have used the 272 cubic inch model with a single exhaust. After mid-year, the 292 cubic inch V-8 with dual exhaust was also available to Mainline cars for an additional $123 above the basic V-8 price, which in this case would have been $2,086. Notice the new side molding, which now follows the basic theme of the Fairlane trim. The Customline signature appeared in the V-section on the rear door.

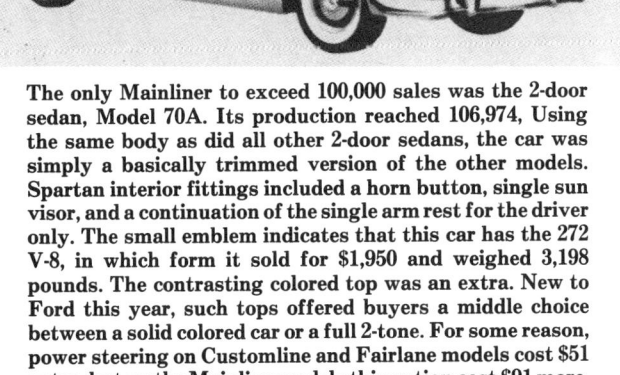

This 4-door Sedan, Model 73A, shows the unusual 2-tone paint scheme which was available on Mainline models for the first time this year. The scheme includes an extra stainless lower trim bar, with the space between the two bars finished in the same complimentary color as the top. The lower trim bar was only used with the extra-cost 2-tone paint job, while solid color cars had only the upper bar running rearward from the V-swash. The Mainline 4-door was priced at $1,995 in the V-8 form as seen here. A fairly popular car, it drew a total of 49,448 orders. The car used the same basic 4-door body as did all other pillared sedans, but differed in trim and in the fact that the rear vent windows were non-operational. This was the final year for the Mainline series.

The only Mainliner to exceed 100,000 sales was the 2-door sedan, Model 70A. Its production reached 106,974, Using the same body as did all other 2-door sedans, the car was simply a basically trimmed version of the other models. Spartan interior fittings included a horn button, single sun visor, and a continuation of the single arm rest for the driver only. The small emblem indicates that this car has the 272 V-8, in which form it sold for $1,950 and weighed 3,198 pounds. The contrasting colored top was an extra. New to Ford this year, such tops offered buyers a middle choice between a solid colored car or a full 2-tone. For some reason, power steering on Customline and Fairlane models cost $51 extra, but on the Mainline models this option cost $91 more.

The style leader of Ford's Station wagon series continued to be the Country Squire, Model 79E. It was the only wagon to have the wood-type trim, although no real wood was used. The inner panels, of imitation dark mahogany, were a type of heavy paper stick-on, while the outer framing was of wood-grained fiberglass. Priced at $2,633 and weighing 3,638 in V-8 form, it was Ford's most expensive and heaviest passenger vehicle, not counting the Thunderbird. It was also one of the least popular wagons, with sales reaching only 23,221. It was available only in 8-passenger form, but could be ordered with either the Six or the Thunderbird 292 V-8.

The Country Sedan wagons continued the odd practice of using different trim to signify the 8-passenger and 6-passenger models. This is the 8-passenger variation, designated Model 79B. Shown here in its most usual form, with 2-tone paint, it used side trim identical to that of the Fairlane series. This and the Country Squire constituted Ford's only 8-passenger wagons. In both models, the rear and center seats would fold flush with the floor to provide a flat cargo area. The 8-passenger model was priced at $2,528 and weighed 3,628 pounds in V-8 form. The V-8 was the 292 Thunderbird, as the 272 V-8 was not available in the Station Wagon series. However, any wagon could be ordered with the 6-cylinder engine.

When built in 6-passenger form, the Country Sedan was designated the Model 79D, and was fitted with Customline side trim. In this form, with the V-8, it cost $2,397 and weighed 3,536 pounds. A popular model, the Country Sedan in both six and 8-passenger forms drew a total of 85,374 orders, thus being Ford's best selling wagon. As before, the rear quarter windows were of the slider type, with the forward section moving rearward across the back pane. The rear seat back and cushion were backed with a heavy vinyl that matched the cargo area flooring, so that when folded, a clear and flush cargo floor was provided right up to the front seat.

New for the year was the Parklane, which was an up-grade of the 2-door Ranch Wagon. Designed to compete against the sporty Chevrolet Nomad, the car used Fairlane side trim and an interior upgraded to match Fairlane standards. Designated the Model 59C, it used the same body as did the other two 2-door wagons. It was priced at $2,528 and weighed 3,503 pounds with the V-8. Not particularly popular, it still drew 15,186 orders, which was about double the Nomad's sales. Part of its exclusive equipment included a vinyl cargo or luggage cover, which snapped over the entire cargo area just below the sill line, fitting like a large convertible top boot. Although this cover could not protect the luggage from theft, it did hide what was in the rear, and helped make the cargo area look much neater.

The mid-range of the 2-door wagon line was the Custom Ranch Wagon, Model 59B. As could be expected, it took its trim level from the Customline series and used the Customline exterior side molding. With the V-8 it cost $2,350 and weighed 3,488 pounds in base form. All wagons could be fitted with Fordomatic for $178 extra, or the automatic overdrive transmission for $110 extra. With the latter unit, the overdrive gear would automatically cut in at about 27 MPH, and on slowing, would cut out at about 20 MPH. A kick-down unit operated when the transmission was in overdrive. With this, full pressure on the gas pedal would drop the car back to third gear for passing or other instant power needs. The Custom Ranch Wagon turned out to be a relatively popular car, with 42,317 being sold.

Lowest priced and most popular of all the 2-door wagons was the plain Ranch Wagon, Model 59A. The car benefitted greatly from the new Mainline-type side trim, especially when the 2-tone paint scheme was ordered, as shown here. Lack of fender emblem shows that this version has the 6-cylinder engine. In this form, it would have cost $2,185 and weighed 3,330 pounds. If ordered with the V-8, it would have received the 292 cubic inch Thunderbird model, because even in the lowest trim form, the 272 V-8 was not available to station wagons. Ford turned out 48,348 of this model.

As always, the Courier delivery truck was based on the Model 59 2-door station wagon shell. It varied, of course, from the wagon models in that its rear quarters were of solid metal, while inside it was furnished with Masonite side panels. The rear too was different, being fitted with a full rear door, hinged on the left. The Courier also used its own special trim, which consisted of a stainless band completely encircling the greenhouse at sill level. The Courier could be ordered with the 6-cylinder engine for $1,738 or with the V-8 for $1,838. However, unlike the Station Wagon series, where the 292 V-8 was considered the standard block, the Courier received the 272 cubic inch V-8 as standard fare, with the 292 cubic inch model being available only at $125 extra cost. As with the car models, both automatic overdrive and Fordomatic transmissions were available, as was power steering and power brakes.

Automotive Conversion Corp. of Birmingham, Mich., came onto the scene this year with its Ford-based Amblewagons. Using the 8-passenger Country Sedan as a base, the company modified the interiors for basic ambulance usage, but left the rear seats in place, folded of course, so that the vehicle could still be used as an 8-passenger wagon. Among the modifications were a full-length rear door, from the Courier, plus a split front and center seat. The right side of the front seat could be folded forward, with the seat back forming a solid wall against the dash board, while either side of the center seat could be folded independent of the other. On the center seat, when the right half was folded, it formed a flat floor when the front seat was also folded. Otherwise, it formed a bulkhead against the front seat back. Etched glass quarter windows; flashing red roof light; siren, and ambulance equipment were all part of the package. Amblewagons were sold and serviced through all Ford and Lincoln-Mercury dealers. The fully equipped price was about $5,000, including the 292 Thunderbird Special engine and Fordomatic transmission.

The Courier heritage of this little ambulance is quite evident. Constructed by the Welles Corp. in Windsor, Ontario, the vehicle was sold in both the U.S. and Canada. Most obvious in the conversion was the cutting of large windows into the rear panels. These etched glass windows were fixed permanently in place and could not be opened. Tunneled red lights were molded into the roof, complimented by a central flasher. In true Courier style, the vehicle is powered by the 272 cubic inch V-8 rather than the Thunderbird version, as evidenced by the relocated V-8 emblem behind the front wheel opening. The major modifications were to the interior, where complete ambulance equipment has been installed, along with vinyl upholstered walls and headliner in place of the normal Masonite panels.

Appearing on the show circuits this year was Ford's latest experimental and show car, the XL-100, or X-100 as it is sometimes called. Built in Coupe DeVille style, the car used many styling and engineering innovations that would appear in the near future on various Ford products. These included the Lincoln-type front fenders and hooded headlights, and the torpedo shaped Thunderbird rear styling of 1961. Packed with every sort of electric gadget imaginable at the time, the car contained a collection of 44 electronic tubes; 24 electric motors; 92 separate switches, both automatic and manual, and 50 light bulbs. The sliding roof panels contained their own automatic brain, and moisture sensitive electric cells, so that the first drop of rain would automatically close the top when the car was unattended. The sliding portion of the top nested in the solid section, while door windows were of the conventional type. The car also appeared under Lincoln sponsorship, bearing the names Continental and Continental 195X.

Ford completed its proposed 3-year cycle of the 1954-56 cars and as planned, came out with a totally new line of cars this year. And what a line! Side trim let the buyers know that the cars were definitely Fords. But aside from that, virtually everything else was either totally new, or at least revised or modified. In fact, as a result of a $246-million engineering and design program, the cars wound up being the most extensively changed Fords since the 1949 models appeared.

Included in the program were totally new bodies, heavily revised engines, new series nomenclature, and for the first time since 1908, the use of two different size wheelbases. Only the Thunderbird remained almost untouched on the exterior, but even here, there were some startling innovations under the hood.

The headline grabber of the year was a new concept that Ford engineers had been playing with for years in an experimental vein. Known officially as a Fairlane 500 Skyliner, the car was a retractable hardtop. This meant that it took the guise of a normal hardtop when the roof was raised. But, at the touch of a button, a bank of solenoids activated an army of electric motors. These would simultaneously elevate the top from its mountings while raising the rear deck from the forward edge. Then the top would move backward and downward into what normally would be the trunk compartment. With the top properly nested in its compartment, the rear deck would lower into place, and be secured by more electric motors.

Despite the high-tech action of the total mechanism, the tops overall worked quite well. But price and buyer doubts held deliveries down, and the car did far better as a publicity magnet than it did as a money maker. Still, considering its mid-year introduction and the fact that it was by far the most expensive Ford, its sales of over 20,000 were nothing to sneeze at.

The Skyliner resided in the new Fairlane 500 series, which was now Ford's top bracket. It shared some of its bodies with the old Fairlane series, which was a slightly lower trim level than the 500 series. Both of these series used the new chassis of 118-inch wheelbase, which was 2.5 inches longer than the previous Fords. Their bodies were 207.7 inches overall, except for the Convertible and the Retractable, which were 210.8 inches long.

At the lower end of the scale were two new series which replaced the old Mainline and Customline series. These were called the Custom and the Custom 300. They used bodies built on a new chassis of 116-inch wheelbase, which was still a half-inch longer than the previous models. These chassis were also used on the Station Wagon series, and for the Courier Sedan Delivery and the new Ranchero Pickup. In the lower two series, only two basic passenger car shells were used. They were the Style 70 2-door sedan, which also was used for the

Business Coupe, and the Style 73 4-door sedan. These bodies both provided 201.6 inches in overall length, which was three inches longer than the 198.5 inches of all 1956 models.

The Fairlane and Fairlane 500 series also had their own totally new bodies. Four styles were shared between the two Fairlanes. These were the Style 58 4-door Town Sedan; the 64 2-door Club Sedan (both of which had B-pillars); and the Styles 57 4-door Victoria and 63 2-door Victoria, both of which were built in hardtop style. Exclusive to the Fairlane 500 series were the two open cars, the convertible and the Retractable.

The Station Wagon series, which also used the 116-inch wheelbase of the low-line series, lost one model from the previous year. This occurred when the former Custom Ranch Wagon and Parklane Wagon were combined into one upper trim level 2-door station wagon called the Del Rio. Like the former Parklane, the new Del Rio was conceived as competition for the Chevrolet Nomad. It did an excellent job of competing, selling 46,105 as compared to the Nomad's sales of only 6,103. The Del Rio and the Ranch Wagon used the new Style 59 body, while the other three wagons used the new Style 79 4-door body. All wagons were 203.5 inches long, as compared with 197.6 inches in 1956.

Also new for the year, and based on the Style 59 shell, was the Ranchero Pickup, which joined the Courier in Ford's passenger car/light truck family. As did the Courier, the Ranchero used all passenger car sheet metal and components, but from the B-pillar rearward, it contained a pickup bed. The concept was similar to the Ute Pickups that Ford and others had been building in Australia for years, and in effect, harkened back to the old Roadster Pickup concept of Model T days.

On the technical side, all vehicles used the new chassis which were not only longer, but also wider, with the side rails now curving outward to the body compartments, and meeting the body sills. This allowed the bodies to settle within the frame rails, and the cars were reduced up to four inches in height without any reduction in head room. Other chassis revisions included new one-piece arms on the front end, and longer asymmetrical leaf springs on the rear, these being 55 inches in length. Attached to these chassis were totally new exhaust systems and fuel tanks, and new 14-inch wheels, which also helped to reduce the overall height of the cars.

All bodies were characterized by new wraparound windshields fitted to dog-legged A-pillars. The latter proved to be great "knee-knockers" for tall people such as the author. Other new innovations on the body were cowl-top vents; a front-hinged hood; flat-topped fenders a continuation of the tube taillight concept; a continuation of the swash theme for top level side molding; rather bug-eye type headlight bezels, and nicely styled tear drop design wheel cutouts. All told, the design was a very graceful and good looking package, and probably was the most attractive Ford to come out since the 1930s. Sadly, the cars were very prone to rust, and by a decade later, they had a tendency to show their age.

Just as the exteriors and chassis were totally new, there were some rather startling innovations made under the hoods also. Even though the three basic engines remained the 223 cubic inch Six and the 272 and 292 cubic inch V-8s, these were all increased in horsepower. Totally new for the year was the 312 cubic inch Thunderbird Special, which had a bore and stroke of 3.8x3.44 inches, used a 4-barrel Holley carburetor, and in "normal" form developed 245 horses at 4500 rpm, with a 9.7:1 compression ratio.

But it was not the normal form that got people excited about the 312 engine. Shortly after introduction, a dual 4-barrel model was introduced, which would develop 270 horses at 4800 rpm. This was followed by the availability of a "Racing Special" version, sold either complete or in kit form. With this setup, the engine had a 10:1 compression, dual Holley 4-barrels, and would produce 285 horses at 5000 rpm. Then finally, the Thunderbird Special Supercharged models came out. Using a lower compression ratio of 8.5:1 and single Holley 4-barrel carburetors, these mills were equipped with either Paxton centrifugal or McCulloch superchargers. With this setup, they would develop 300 horsepower at 4800 rpm, or in the NASCAR version, would come up with 340 horses at 5300 rpm.

Designed to return Ford's reputation as the car of speed and sport, the latter engines were very short lived, and today are a very rare piece of engineering. Designed primarily for recognized racing teams, and not generally available to the public, the supercharged engines were banned by NASCAR in the late spring of 1957. NASCAR correctly feared that the horsepower race was going to lead to nothing but chaos, and thus restricted all engines to only a single 4-barrel stock carburetor. Meanwhile, the Automobile Manufacturers Assn. also was taking a dim view of the horsepower race among the various makes, and issued its own ban on factory promoted racing teams and optional performance engines such as the blown 312 Fords or the fuel injected Chevrolets.

But even for the average buyer, all horsepowers in all stock engines were now raised. The 292 cubic inch block was now rated at 212 horsepower at 4500 rpm with its new 9.1:1 compression ratio; the standard 272 cubic inch block ran 190 horses at 4500 rpm with a compression of 8.6:1, and even the 223 cubic inch Six now had 144 horses to its credit at 4200 rpm with an 8.6:1 compression ratio. All engines were available in all models, except that the Skyliner could not be ordered with a Six. The 272 cubic inch V-8 was $100 extra above the basic Six price, while the 292 cubic inch Thunder-

bird engine was another $43 extra. Prices could not be ascertained for the Thunderbird special variations.

In the Thunderbird itself, a moderate restyling of the rear end took place, but otherwise the car was little different from the 55/56 versions. The major change involved doing away with the outside spare and once again placing the extra tire in the trunk. As expected, this greatly enhanced the handling characteristics of the car. Also in keeping with the rear end treatment of the big Fords, the Thunderbirds received a minor flared fin and the new 14-inch wheels. The latter move was a definite improvement, as the earlier Birds always looked as if their wheels were too big for the car. As could be expected, the Supercharged Thunderbird Special engine was available in the Thunderbird. However, the high-priced, high-tech, gas guzzling blower was not a particularly big seller, and of the 21,380 Thunderbirds sold this year, only 208 had the 330/34-0 horse engine.

In the world of numbers, Ford's performance this year was absolutely sensational, with the model year topping out with 1,674,448 vehicles leaving the plant, including the 21,380 Thunderbirds. By series, the most popular was the Fairlane 500 bracket, which recorded sales of 637,161. Surprisingly, this was followed by the two-model Custom 300 series, which had sales of 355,237. The Station Wagon series was third, with 319,170, while the plain Custom series drew 192,775. Also a surprise, the worst sales were recorded in the new Fairlane series, whose four models drew only 148,725 orders combined.

By model, the most popular style of all was the Custom 300 4-door Sedan, which recorded 194,877 orders. Following close behind was the Fairlane 500 version of the same model, with 193,162 sales. Third spot was picked up by the Fairlane 500 Club Victoria, with a run of 183,202. Other models breaking the 100,000 sales barrier were the Custom 300 2-door Sedan, with 160,360 sales; the 6-passenger Country Sedan, with 135,251 sales, and the Custom 2-door Sedan, with 116,963 units sold.

Helping somewhat with these sales figures was the fact that the 1957 Fords ran a 13-month model year. Introduced on Oct. 1, 1956, they remained on the market until the late arriving 1958 fare came out in November, 1957. Still, even discounting the extra month of sales, the 1957 Fords were exceedingly well received by the public—so well in fact that for the first time in years, Ford took the top spot from Chevrolet in *Model Year* production. However, in calendar year production, Chevrolet came up with 1,522,536 cars built, while Ford showed only 1,522,406, or just 131 vehicles short of ousting Chevrolet from both model and calendar year figures. The result, of course, is that both Ford and Chevrolet claim to have been the Number One producer in 1957.

Sporting the cleanest face ever, the new Thunderbird was appearing for the last time ever as a 2-passenger car. Gone from its nose were the large spinner-like grille guards, and the fender mounted parking lamps. Instead, a new front bumper dipped gracefully in the center to allow more open grille space, while the bumper tips now contained the relocated parking lights. Standard with the car this year was the solid top, with the convertible top once again being considered an extra-cost option. Both "porthole" and blank-side tops were available, but the porthole model shown here was most popular. Base priced at $3,151, the Thunderbird weighed 3,088 pounds. Production figures conflict. The most accepted list from Ford shows a total of 15,631 T-Birds built during the model year. Yet another often-accepted figure credits the model year with 21,380. Regardless of how many, it is known that the last Bird left the factory on Dec. 13, 1957, thus bringing to a close the chapter on Ford's 2-passenger Early Birds.

The major change between the 1956 and 1957 Thunderbirds occurred on the rear section, where a new longer and larger trunk once again contained the spare tire, and where new finned rear fenders followed the overall design theme of the Ford passenger car line. Also new for this year were the 14-inch wheels, which made the Birds lower and better looking, as the earlier 15-inch wheels had always seemed too large for the car. Under the hood things also changed. Available engines included a revised copy of the former 292 cubic inch block, or a new 312 variation, available at first as the 245 horsepower Special or 270 horse Super Thunderbird model. Later, this model was also issued as a 285 HP racing Special, and later still in two supercharged versions of 300 and 340 horsepower.

Seemingly to be too little too late was the unique Birdnest that appeared this year. Designed by William Colgan of Burbank, Cal., and marketed through his own Birdnest Co., the kit converted the T-Bird into a 4-passenger car via a rumble seat adaptation of the trunk deck. Priced at $298 in base form, the kit contained a reworked rear deck encompassing a cut-out center section which would flip up in rumble seat fashion. The kit included a naugahyde seat and seat back and matching side panels. However, the curved Plexiglas windshield was another $60, while a matching floor mat was $25 extra. Installed, the entire package ran about $500. Plans were apparently under way to design similar nests for the 1955 and 56 Birds, but poor sales of this kit seemed to have cancelled that idea.

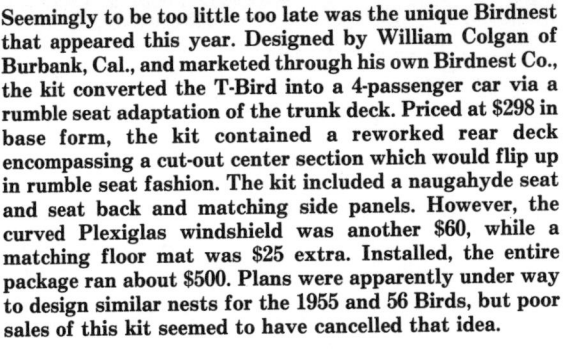

Way back in the mid-1960s, Gloria Dammann, wife of the author, posed with her pride and joy—a canary yellow Thunderbird with a white plain-side top, and a black interior with a black convertible top. Both the author and wife felt the car looked better without the fender skirts, and thus these attachments usually stayed in the barn. Although the car looked beautiful and handled nice, fuel and carburetion problems plagued the 270 horse Super Thunderbird engine. Obviously dubbed the "Yellow Bird," the car remained in the Dammann fleet for several years before being traded for—horror of horrors—a modified 1957 Corvette.

Ford's headline grabber of the year did not appear until mid-winter. It was the Fairlane 500 Skyliner Retractable Hardtop, the first full hardtop produced by a major American builder to be convertible into an open car. (Playboy had such a model in 1947, but that Buffalo, N.Y., manufacturer certainly cannot be considered a major producer.) Priced at $2,942 and weighing 3,916 pounds, the high-tech vehicle was both Ford's most expensive and heaviest car. Despite initial buyer wariness and the high price tag, the season ended with 20,766 units being sold. Visually, the car differed greatly from the Victoria, having a totally different roof line, much higher rear quarters, squared rear deck, and the gas filler located ahead of the left rear wheel opening. It bore style designation 51A.

The Fairlane 500 Skyliner is shown here with its top at the mid-point of retracting. The author, who over the years owned 1957, 58, and 59 variations of this model, always held his breath at this stage of the retraction. Yet never once did the mechanism fail on any model. A single switch to the left of the steering column activated the entire mechanism, which consisted of five individual electric motors; a relay bank of 13 switches located behind the rear seat; nine independent circuit breakers, and over 600 feet of special wire. Because of the nesting requirements of the top, luggage space in the trunk was relegated to a tub-like affair in the center of what normally would have been a very spacious rear compartment. Experimentation on the retractable idea began in 1953, and the concept was first considered for the Lincoln Continental. Ford received the design after Lincoln decided that it did not need the flip-top package. However, later Lincoln and Thunderbird models used essentially the same mechanism on their convertible models, but with a soft top instead of the solid unit.

Ford's "normal" convertible was the Fairlane 500 Sunliner, Model 76B. A fantastically popular car, it saw sales peak at 77,728 by the end of the model year. Priced at $2,605 with the small V-8, it weighed 3,497 pounds. Unlike the Skyliner, which was only available in V-8 power, the Sunliner followed the general rule of all other Fords, and could be equipped with whatever engine the buyer was willing to pay for, from the 144 horsepower Six to the 340 horse supercharged NASCAR Special V-8. However, very few of the latter engines were sold to the average buyer.

With the top down, the Fairlane 500 Sunliner was a mighty attractive vehicle, and sales records show that buyers felt the same way. In fact, Ford's record breaking rag top sales were over 30,000 more than the 47,562 Bel Air Convertibles recorded by Chevrolet this year. Sadly, on today's collector market, it is the Bel Air models that draw the high bucks, while the Fords are seldom seen. The Fairlane 500 series used its own unique side trim, which swept upward from the V and traveled along the new outwardly canted fins. This looked good from certain angles, but from others gave the rear an overly massive appearance.

Ford had the new Skyliner, which was a hardtop with retractable capabilities, and it also had one with a non-retractable top. This was the Fairlane 500 Club Victoria, Model 63A. The car, as before, turned out to be a super popular style, and drew 183,202 orders by year-end. Priced at $2,439, it weighed 3,442 pounds. Note how this top differs from that of the Skyliner. Whereas the latter model used a squared-off top design, soon to be found on next year's Thunderbird, the Club Victoria's top swooped rearward in a gentle curve, accented by stainless steel rain gutters, and stainless windshield and rear window molding. For the first time this year, there were no outward emblems to signify which engine resided under the hood.

With the rear door handles almost hidden by the stainless side trim, the Fairlane 500 Town Victoria almost looked like a 2-door model at quick glance. One of the less popular styles in the top line, it drew only 68,550 orders. With the basic 272 cubic inch V-8, it was priced at $2,504 and weighed 3,487 pounds. Designated the Model 57A, the pillarless sedan was distinguished by its unique rear doors with the upswept trailing edges. The radically swept-back A-pillars on the new Fords were aesthetically attractive, but proved to be real knee-knockers for tall people.

Both the Club Victoria and the Club Sedan used the same top styling, but the Club Sedan used solid B-pillars while the Victoria was a true hardtop. Shown in Fairlane 500 trim, the Club Sedan was the Model 64B, which weighed 3,407 pounds and cost $2,381 with the small V-8. It was the lightest and least expensive car in the Fairlane 500 series. Despite its close appearance with the Victoria, it drew only half of the hardtop's orders, and finished the year with a run of only 93,753. Both models also appeared in the plain Fairlane series. The trunk deck was a popular spot to mount radio antennas this year, especially on 2-door models. The radio cost about $100 extra, while a heater/defroster unit added another $85. Gaining popularity were pedal operated windshield washer kits which cost about $10 plus installation.

The most popular car in the Fairlane 500 series, and Ford's second most popular car overall, was the Town Sedan, Model 58B. It saw production reach 193,162 units. Using the 118-inch wheelbase chassis, as did all Fairlane and Fairlane 500 cars, the attractive 4-door was 210.8 inches long overall, and thus was the longest Ford ever built until this time. Normal power was the Six or the 272 cubic inch V-8. As a Six, it cost $2,403 and weighed 3,380 pounds. The V-8 form cost $125 more for the 272 cubic inch model and $175 more for the 312 cubic inch version.

In a rather unusual move, the plain Fairlane models were devoid of side chrome when ordered in single colors. When ordered as a 2-tone combination, they used a very distinctive trim and paint combination not unlike that found on the Oldsmobile, of all things. Lowest price of all of the 118-inch wheelbase models was the Fairlane Club Sedan, Model 64A, which was a pillared version of the Victoria. Priced at $2,235 as a Six, it weighed 3,270 pounds. Popularity was not its strong suite, and only 38,843 were sold.

In addition to the two 2-door styles, the Fairlane series contained two 4-door models. They were the Town Sedan, Model 58A, shown here, and the Town Victoria, Model 57B. The main difference between the two was that the Town Sedan had permanent B-pillars and rear doors with vent windows, while the Town Victoria was a true hardtop and had ventless rear doors with a prominent upsweep on the trailing portion of the sill. Except for upholstery and exterior trim, the bodies were identical to those in the Fairlane 500 series. With the 272 cubic inch V-8, the Town Sedan cost $2,386 and weighed 3,437 pounds, while the Town Victoria cost $2,457 and weighed 3,427 pounds. Sales were no match for the brighter 500 series, and the Fairlane Town Sedan drew only 52,060 orders, while the Town Victoria could only draw 12,695 buyers. The entire Fairlane series drew only 148,725 sales, compared with 637,161 in the Fairlane 500 series. Apparently those buyers who wanted "big" Fords also wanted fancy Fords.

When ordered with the optional 2-tone paint scheme, the Fairlane models received this rather unique side trim/color combination package. It certainly produced a huge improvement over mono-colored Fairlanes, which were totally devoid of side chrome except for the "Fairlane" signature on the front fender. Shown here is the Club Victoria, Model 63B, which sold for $2,393 and weighed 3,427 pounds with the basic V-8. Production only reached 33,127. The car shared the same body with the comparable Fairlane 500 model, but lacked the high level of trim. Beside the side trim, the plain Fairlane models also did not use the stainless trim on the C-pillars.

The top of the line cars using the "short" 116-inch wheelbase chassis was the new Custom 300 series. The line consisted only of a 4-door sedan and this 2-door Sedan, Model 70B. Both cars used an attractive type of side trim similar to that of the Fairlane 500 series, but with the rear portion of the trim running along the mid-section of the taillight tunnel, rather than on top of the fins. Actually, this produced a better looking effect, as the break made the rear section look both longer and lower. Available only as a pillared model, the 2-door Sedan with the 272 cubic inch V-8 sold for $2,205 and weighed 3,289 pounds. Certainly a popular car, it saw sales rise to 160,360.

Ford's most popular car of the year turned out to be the Custom 300 4-door Sedan, which had sales of 194,877. Carrying the most attractive side trim of any 1957 Ford (in the author's estimation) the car always appeared longer than the comparable Fairlane or 500 models. This was despite the fact that it was 9.2 inches shorter than the larger car, and was built on a 166-inch wheelbase rather than the Fairlane's 118-inch chassis. Besides being shorter overall, the body of this model varied from the comparable Fairlane's in that the rear section had a sharper slope, and the rear doors ended ahead of the C-pillar. The small rear vent windows were in the body proper, and not in the door. They were fixed in place and would not open. In the Custom 300 series, with the basic V-8, the 4-door sold for $2,257 and weighed 3,334 pounds. It could be ordered with any V-8, including the basic 312 Thunderbird Special, in which case its base price climbed to about $2,600.

The lowest priced of all Fords was the Custom Business Coupe, a 3-passenger model which in 6-cylinder form sold for $1,889. Designated the Model 70D, the car used the same body as did all other Custom and Custom 300 2-door sedans. But, as before, the rear section was built with padded sides and no rear seat, so that the entire space could be utilized for stowage of packages, luggage, samples, or whatever. Besides being the lowest price model, the car also had the distinction of being the lowest production, with only 6,888 being turned out. Unlike the Fairlane series, the Custom series still used rear fender side trim even when painted in a single color. The "Custom" identification did not appear anywhere on the car.

When dressed up in its optional 2-tone paint scheme, the Custom models belied the fact that they were Ford's lowest price series. Within the series was Ford's last 6-passenger car to be base priced at under $2,000. When fitted with the Six, the 2-door Sedan had a base price of $1,991. Possibly this was an aid to sales, as a total of 116,963 were sold, with all types of engines being available. With a weight of 3,154 pounds, it was the lightest Ford, and therefore lent itself to some pretty heavy racing action, especially on the NASCAR and USAC circuits. Here it was often fitted with the 340 horsepower supercharged NASCAR 312 cubic inch engine. No, in that form it did not sell for under $2,000.

Low price and good performance made the Custom 4-door Sedan, Model 73A, a popular garrison vehicle with the military. This particular unit, wearing Air Force blue, was part of a relatively large fleet bought up by all three of the armed services. As a result, a total of 68,924 were produced. With a base price of $2,142 as a V-8, the car represented good value for the money, whether in civilian garb or in uniform. Despite the fact that they were more than nine inches shorter than comparable Fairlane models, the Custom and Custom 300 cars really did not look smaller unless they were placed side by side.

Complete with artificial wood trim, the Country Squire remained Ford's top of the line station wagon. Available only in 9-passenger form, the wagon was base priced at $2,784, which made it the most expensive Ford until the new Skyliner came along. It was also Ford's least popular wagon model, having sales of only 27,690. It used the same basic Style 79 body as did all other Ford 4-door wagons, but as Model 79E, it had its own exclusive fiberglass wood trim. The "Country Squire" signature was carried in an embossed panel on the front door. Surprisingly, the wagons did not use the 118-inch chassis, but instead were set on the 116-inch unit.

In a move consistent with previous year's styling, the 9-passenger Country Sedan continued to use side trim similar to that of the top-line Ford. But this year, the trim was from the top-line short wheelbase model, the Custom 300, rather than the long wheelbase Fairlane 500. The car is shown here with both the rear and the center seat folded, in which form it offered plenty of carrying space. When folded, the seat backs and undersides provided a heavy-duty yet attractive floor for the cargo area. A new sliding latch arrangement was installed on the lift gate, replacing the rather complicated scissor-types used on the previous models. Notice how this year the lift gate cuts into the body sides and is wider than the tailgate. Unlike previous models, the rear windows could no longer be opened. They were now of one-piece glass, with no sliding section. Also of interest is the fact that on the 2-tone models, the taillight bezels took the color of the lower portion of the body even though over 3/4 of the bezel was in the upper color area. Again, on the wagons, the tops always matched the lower sections in color.

Using its own distinctive side trim was the 6-passenger Country Sedan, Model 79D. Not only Ford's best selling wagon, it was the only wagon model to have sales in excess of 100,000. A total of 135,251 were sold. Note the wide difference in trim between the 6-passenger and the 9-passenger models. Not only was the trim different, but the 2-tone paint option also varied greatly. On the 9-passenger model, the center color ran from the trim to the roof drip line, whereas on this model it essentially only occupied the area immediately around the windows, from sill to drip line. Whenever possible, interior colors harmonized with the exterior. The 6-passenger Country Sedan cost $2,551 and weighed 3,590 pounds with the small V-8.

Ford's low buck work horse was the 2-door Ranch Wagon, which overall reflected Custom trim, but used its own unique side piece. Also, this model had its "Ranch Wagon" signature on the trailing edge of the front fender, whereas all other wagons had their name plaques on the taillight tunnel. Using the same body as the Del Rio, the Ranch Wagon was the Model 59A. With the small V-8, it was base priced at $2,401 and weighed 3,520 pounds. All Fords this year had a forward-hinged hood, which opened from the cowl. This was supposed to be a safety factor, but it did make it more difficult to service the engine.

Designed to compete against the Chevrolet Nomad, and doing an excellent job of it, was the new Del Rio. Essentially it was a high trim level 6-passenger 2-door station wagon, designated Model 59B. The car was priced at $2,497 with the 272 cubic inch block, and weighed 3,527 pounds. Sales topped out at 46,105, compared with only 6,103 Nomad deliveries. However, on today's collector scene, the Nomad is a hot item, whereas the Del Rio is virtually unheard of. The nicely styled wagon used the side swash of the Custom 300 series and was fitted with an interior comparable to that trim level. Unlike the 4-door wagons, which had one-piece fixed rear quarter windows, the 2-door models still had sliding forward sections in their huge rear quarters.

Totally new for the year was the Ranchero, a station wagon-based pickup, available in both plain and the Custom version shown here. As did the Courier Sedan Delivery, the Ranchero used a body based on the Style 59 2-door station wagon, with the rear section modified for pickup use. The concept was similar to the Australian Utes (for utility) which had been around since the early 1930s, but which had never caught on in the U.S. In Custom form, the Rancheros used the side molding quite similar to that of the lower bar of the Custom 300 Ranch Wagon, and had the bed outlined in stainless steel trim. It featured a deluxe interior, including the high-level steering wheel with horn ring, and a choice of four 2-tone vinyl interiors. A total of 10 2-tone exterior color combinations were also available. Base priced at $2,149, the Custom Ranchero weighed 3,276 pounds. Buyers liked the fancy little truck, and a total of 15,277 were sold. The wheel covers on this example were aftermarket wires.

Far less popular than the Custom Ranchero was the plain Ranchero, which had its sides and bed totally devoid of trim, and used an interior level comparable to the Courier or the plain Ranch Wagon. Only 6,428 were built in the plain form, apparently because buyers who wanted a true work truck went with the half-ton F-100 pickups rather than the car-based Ranchero. In plain form, it cost $2,098 and weighed 3,251 pounds. Despite being based on the Style 59 body shell, the Ranchero carried model designation 66A in plain form and 66B as a Custom Ranchero. Also using the Style 59 shell as a base was the Courier, of which no photos could be found for the 1957 example. It listed for $1,989, and had a run of 6,178 for the year.

Hospital Pick-Up . . . Vault Service . . . Flower Car . . . Hearse

a low initial investment eliminates supplemental vehicles

The Pickway

Now . . . at Last! . . .

CUSTOM-MADE by MILLER-PICKING CORPORATION

Recognizing a good thing when they saw it, the Miller-Picking Corp. of Johnstown, Pa., began offering this unique flower car based on the Custom Ranchero. The car uses the side trim from the Custom 300 series, a beefed suspension, and a unique double door on the rear rather than a tailgate. Otherwise, it is pretty much stock Ranchero. This side trim is also found on several Ford early release photos of the Custom Ranchero. However, it cannot be ascertained whether this was used on early production models, or if the side trim changed to the single bar variety before production started. The stainless steel and chrome flower tray shown here was easily removable, so the vehicle could be used for a pickup when needed. With the tray in place, the casket could be carried in the bed, thus allowing the vehicle to be used as both a hearse and a flower car.

In an era when stock cars really were "stock" cars, Ford decided to do battle with both Chevrolet and Dodge, and Ford came out pretty good. With its new supercharged 312 cubic inch block, Ford was able to produce 300 horses, which was more than the 283 horsepower that Chevrolet could coax out of its 283 cubic inch fuel injected block. Here Fireball Roberts takes the lead during the NASCAR National at Daytona. He is using an almost stock Custom Business Coupe with the McCulloch modified mill. Shortly after the February Daytona Beach race, NASCAR banned the supercharged models, but USAC permitted them on its tracks. A combination of high cost, Automobile Manufacturer Assn.'s disapproval of the horsepower race, and the introduction of the new 352 cubic inch block all helped to spell the end of the supercharged 312 mills by the end of the model year. During September, 1956, just before the new models were to appear, Ford also showed up at Bonneville with a special racing team of supercharged 1957 cars, and broke 458 national and international land speed records in a wide variety of classes.

Overall, the 1958 model year was a poor one for the automotive industry. For Ford, it marked a rather unhappy time. The troubles began on Sept. 4, 1957, when Ford's new kin was born. Known as the Edsel, it received mixed reviews in the general press, equally mixed blessings from the automotive press, and a general "ho-hum" from the public. This tale of woe is aptly described in Crestline's *THE CARS OF LIN-COLN MERCURY* by the author and James K. Wagner, and will not be treated here. Suffice to say, the "different" looking Edsel caused many to wonder what the new Fords would look like.

Finally, on Nov. 7, 1957, the public was introduced to Ford's 1958 models. Many people, including the author, felt that someone had accidentally turned on the ugly machine at Dearborn. After the excellent and well balanced styling of 1957, the 1958 styling seemed heavy handed, bulgy, and far out of step with the previous design. And, this was despite the fact that the basic body lines were unchanged. Granted, it did not look like the Edsel, and that was probably the best that could be said.

Ford explained the style changes by saying that a totally new front end had to be devised to accept the new quad headlights. But that didn't explain the vacuum cleaner look of the grille, the overly massive bumper, or the funny air scoop on the hood. From the back or side the car was in excellent taste, but it just lacked something in the front. Apparently many people felt the same way, as sales were down quite noticeably from 1957.

Then, on Feb. 13, Ford came out with a real winner. The new 4-passenger Thunderbird was finally unveiled,

and was an instant success. By this time, Ford needed a bright spot, and the new T-Bird was it. Sales soared, considering the price and exclusiveness of the car, and finally peaked at 37,892, which was almost double the production of the 2-seater. The press and the public loved the car, to the extent that *MOTOR TREND MAGAZINE* named it "Car of the Year." However, over the years, the popularity of the Early Birds has soared on the collector market, while the "Square Birds" remain more of a curiosity than enjoying the collectible status that they deserve. But, in 1958, it was the new 4-seaters that drew all the attention.

To compare the 2-seater and the 4-seater is impossible. They are two distinctly different cars, sharing only a common name. The new Bird was TOTALLY NEW! It exceeded the old model's length by two feet, being 205.4 inches long, as compared with 181.4. It was given a new wheelbase of 113 inches, compared with 102 inches, and gained almost 600 pounds in weight, now going at 3,708 pounds.

Radically new was the body construction. Thunderbird shared with the new Lincoln the concept of a single unit body which incorporated body, frame, front and rear fenders, bulkhead and dash, and floor into one piece of sculptured steel. Excellent rectangular lines, coupled to an attractive hardtop similar to the styling of the Retractable Ford, quickly gave the new Thunderbird the nickname "Square Bird." Setting off the front was a massive chromed bumper surrounding a honeycomb grille not unlike that used on the regular Fords. At the rear, this grille theme was duplicated around the four

Although the convertible edition of the new Thunderbird had initially been planned, production of this model didn't begin until mid-June of 1958, almost at the close of the model year. And even then, production was slowed by a few design problems, especially in the very complicated top operating mechanism. Still, 2,134 were sold in the few remaining months before the 1959 models appeared. They were priced at $3,914 and weighed 3,903 pounds, marking the first time that a Ford ever exceeded the $1-per-pound ratio. For those wanting a bit more luxury than provided by an all-vinyl interior, Thunderbird this year offered seats upholstered in natural leather for an additional $106. Also additional was the new 3-speed Cruise-O-Matic transmission. Costing just about $200 extra, the unit proved to be one of the better automatic designs, and ranks with the 2-speed Ford-O-Matic as one of the longer lived and most dependable automatics.

Not appearing until Feb. 13, the new Thunderbird was an instant success, and provided one huge bright spot in an otherwise dismal year for both Ford and the auto industry in general. A totally new concept in automotive design, the personal luxury type of vehicle used a unitized body which combined frame, inner shell, fenders and outer skin, bulkheads, floor, and roof into one integral structure. Under the hood was Ford's newest and largest engine to date, the 352 cubic inch Interceptor block of 300 horsepower. The 4-passenger interior was done in all vinyl, in colors harmonizing with the 12 single or 34 two-tone paint combinations. Coil springs were used all around, and this proved to be the car's only real deficiency. The public was impressed, and a total of 35,758 Thunderbirds were sold. Each was base priced at $3,630 and weighed 3,708 pounds. The overall rectangular styling soon earned this model the nickname "Square Bird."

circular taillights which nested horizontally (two to a side) between the rear bumper and the trunk deck. Completing the design was an embossed rocket motif that began at the forward portion of the door, and blended into the rear bumper ends.

Within the car, all was also changed. Upholstery was in 2-tone vinyl, color keyed to the exterior, with the seats having four panels in a pleated tone, complimentary to the solid main color scheme. For the first time, the front seats were of the bucket type, separated by a wide console that ran from the fire wall to the rear seat. This not only hid the rather high driveline tunnel, but also gave berth to the radio speaker, ash trays, and electric window controls when installed.

Under the hood, there also occurred several changes. Namely, the old 312 cubic inch Thunderbird Specials were gone, being replaced by a new 300 horsepower V-8 of 352 cubic inches. The new engine, which was standard in the Thunderbird, ran a bore and stroke of 4.0x3.5 inches, had a 10.2:1 compression ratio, and used a Holley 4-barrel carburetor. This engine also became an option in all station wagons and Fairlane 500 models for an extra $150. Attached to this engine was a new 3-speed automatic transmission called Cruise-O-Matic, which was approximately a $200 option over the Thunderbird's standard 3-speed manual transmission. The new Cruise-O-Matic could also be ordered in place of the 2-speed Fordomatic, which cost $180 above the standard unit.

New engines also appeared in the regular Ford range. These were two variations of the "FE" big block that appeared in the T-Bird, but trimmed down to 332 cubic inches. The basic form was known as the Interceptor, while a higher horsepower version was the Interceptor Special. The engines used the same 4.0x3.3 inch bore and stroke and 9.5:1 compression ratio. However, the

Interceptor used a Holley 2-barrel carburetor and developed 240 horses at 4600 rpm, while the Interceptor special used a 4-barrel Holley and developed 265 horses at 4600 rpm. On both the 332 and the 352 cubic inch blocks, most parts were interchangeable, and all used the same basic block structure.

Also remaining were the two basic engines, the 223 cubic inch Six which was now rated at 145 horsepower at 4200 rpm, and the former Thunderbird 292 cubic inch engine, which was now down-rated to 205 horsepower at 4500 rpm as a result of switching carburetion from a Holley 4-barrel to a Holley 2-barrel. Gone from the available engine list was the old standard 272 cubic inch model, and the entire family of 312 cubic inch blocks.

All engines could be ordered for any model, but in regular factory production, the normal upgrade put the 332 Interceptor Special in the Custom models for $195 extra, and in the Fairlanes for $180, while the 352 blocks went into the Fairlane 500 for an additional $160, and into any wagon for $150 extra. All blocks could be coupled to the new 3-speed Cruise-O-Matic transmission for approximately $200 extra, or to the old 2-speed Fordomatic (Ford-O-Matic) for $180 more. Also still available was the automatic overdrive for $108.

As mentioned, the regular Ford line gained a new front and rear, and new side trim. The basic body shell remained the same. Side trim was moved around a bit, but still in keeping with the overall Ford theme. Again, two different chassis were used, with the lower price models and station wagons using the 116-inch wheelbase unit, and the Fairlane and Fairlane 500 models using the 118-inch version. In the Fairlane and Fairlane 500 series, all models remained the same, but were marked

In the real Ford line, the Fairlane 500 series remained the top of the line for this one final year. Style leader of the pack was the Fairlane 500 Sunliner, Model 51A. Priced at $2,749 with the 292 cubic inch V-8, it could be ordered with either of the 332 cubic inch engines at the start, and later in the year could also have the 352 engine for an additional $160. On the other end of the line, it could be ordered with the Six for $2,625. With the 292, it weighed 3,637 pounds.

Front or back, the new Thunderbird was a fine looking car, displaying styling exercises that seemed to blend into an excellent total unit. The same concept was used on the regular Ford line this year, but here the front appeared to be like something that didn't quite belong. On the Thunderbird, the honeycomb grille design was repeated in the taillight nests. The trunk was quite shallow, but made up for vertical space in both length and width. This year's convertibles had a very complicated top operating arrangement, and the driver had to activate the trunk deck from inside the car, manually lift the deck lid, operate the top from the trunk body, and then reset the whole thing into place. A one-button operation it was not.

by a wide difference in side trim. The 500 models used a sweeping beltline molding which divided at the start of the leading door edge and came together just before the rear bumper tip. Filling in the area between the divided strips was a new anodized gold section. The plain Fairlane models used two plain stainless moldings which came to a point just before the rear wheel opening.

In the lower price range there was some action and confusion. The former Custom and Custom 300 series were now combined into one series which sometimes was referred to as Custom 300 and other times just bore the plain Custom name. Confusing the issue, though, was the fact that three different trim options were available, each with its own exterior scheme. There was the basic Custom trim, which consisted of an upper molding which began at the front fender and swept down to meet the lower molding just behind the B-pillar; there was the Custom Special trim which began at the front fender and, almost like that of the 1957 Ranch Wagon, swept upward just after the B-pillar, and finally there was the Custom Styletone package which had molding similar in concept to the standard Custom trim, but used a double lower bar, with the center filled in with an anodized gold section.

These same trim level variations appeared in the Station Wagon series, where the Courier and the 2-door and new 4-door Ranch Wagons used the Custom Special trim or the plain Custom molding, and the Del Rio and Country Sedan models used the Styletone trim. Both the standard and Styletone trim appear to have been used on the Ranchero, while the Country Squire used its own special wood-grain trim package. The new 4-door Ranch Wagon, incidentally, was the only new model to appear this year. As expected, it was simply the Country Sedan with a slightly lower trim level. It was available only in 6-passenger form.

In Ford's world of sales receipts, everything was down this year except for the Thunderbird. The T-Bird, incidentally, joined Rambler as being the only American cars to show a sales gain over 1957. All others showed losses, and Ford was no exception, with total model year sales dropping to 987,945, including the Thunderbirds, but excluding the Rancheros and Couriers. Thus, once again, Ford fell behind Chevrolet.

Of the total, the top two selling models were the Custom 2-door Sedan with 173,441 units sold, and the Custom 4-door Sedan, with 163,368. The only other model to top 100,000 was the Fairlane 500 4-door Town Sedan, with 105,698 units. Lowest sales were recorded by the new Thunderbird Convertible, which had a run of only 2,134. However, this was not all because of buyer resistance. The car did not reach the market until June of 1958, and even then production was slowed by a few design problems.

In other Ford activities, three of the older assembly plants were closed. These were at Buffalo, N.Y., Memphis, Tenn., and Somerville, N.J. Meanwhile, a new plant opened at Loraine, Ohio, reportedly with an assembly capability in excess of all three of the closed units combined.

The rectangular angle of the top says that this is the Fairlane 500 Skyliner, Ford's unique retractable hardtop. The styling of the top was exclusive to this model, and appears to have set the pace for the Thunderbird's hardtop roof line. This view also gives a good look at Ford's version of the honeycomb grille and quad headlights, both of which were new for the year. On the T-Bird, this styling looked good. On the Ford, the whole front end looks like it had been stuck on in a hurry—which, according to some reports, was exactly what had happened. People continue to be awed by the retractable's top mechanism, which was surprisingly well designed and trouble free. However, a combination of high price and high-tech unfamiliarity kept buyers away, and sales this year dropped to 14,713. At $3,138 in base price, it not only was Ford's most expensive car, it was the only one to retail for over $3,000 in basic form.

A higher sweep of the rear fins, squared trunk deck, and gas filler ahead of the rear wheel well all state that this is the Fairlane 500 Skyliner retractable, and not the Sunliner convertible. This was the only Ford to come in V-8 form only, with the Six not being an option. The 292 cubic inch block was standard, while the 332 Interceptor was a $55 recommended upgrade. After December, the 352 Interceptor of 300 horses was available for an additional $160. Not only was the Skyliner Ford's most expensive model, it was also the heaviest, at 4,094 pounds. One bad factor about the Skyliner was in its luggage space. When the top was raised, plenty of luggage could be carried, packed into the area reserved for the roof. But when the roof was retracted, luggage had to be relegated to a rather small and tub-like space in the center of the trunk. Also, neither luggage, tools, nor the spare tire were accessible when the top was down.

The 2-door models in both the Fairlane 500 and plain Fairlane series used a nicely swept-back roof line rather than the squared back of the retractable model. Second most popular of all Fairlane 500 models was this Club Victoria, Model 63A, which saw sales reach 80,439. The true hardtop listed at $2,534 and weighed 3,446 pounds with the 292 cubic inch V-8. The large swash of side trim was of stainless steel, with the center filled in with anodized gold. This year, almost 75% of all Fords had V-8 engines, while 68% had one of the two available automatic transmissions. In the Fairlane 500 series, these numbers came close to 100%.

The lack of vent windows on the rear doors says that this is the Fairlane 500 Town Victoria, Ford's 4-door hardtop style leader. Designated Model 57A, it sold for $2,598 and weighed 3,549 pounds. Production was far from that of the Town Sedan, and reached only 36,509. The car sports the attractive Fairlane 500 2-tone paint job, which was a $25 addition. New for this year was Ford's Ford-Aire suspension systems at $156 extra. Introduced on many different makes during this era, such suspension systems used air-filled rubber bags to augment the regular suspension. The theory was that the air suspension would give a smoother ride and allow the car to level itself no matter what the load. The system did not prove successful in any of its forms, and Ford's was no exception. It was taken off the option list before year end.

Most popular of all the Fairlane 500 models, and the only one to exceed 100,000 in production was the Town Sedan, Model 58B. Priced at $2,527 and weighing 3,510 pounds, it saw its sales peak at 105,698. The car differed from the Town Victoria in that it had fixed window frames in the doors, a solid B-pillar, and used small vent windows in the rear doors, whereas the Victoria model had stainless steel triangles in this area. This particular model is shown in India, where it was participating in an "Around the World" promotion staged by the company. The drive took the cars from Detroit to England, through Europe, across Iran and the Khyber Pass, through India and Thailand to Saigon, and then by ship back to the U.S., with stops in Manila, Guam, and Hawaii. From San Francisco the return to Detroit was via Salt Lake City, Kansas City, and Chicago.

Wearing a selection of factory accessories is this Fairlane 500 Club Sedan, Model 64B. It differed from the Club Victoria only in the fact that it had a fixed B-pillar, and its door and window frames remained in place when the windows were lowered. Priced at $2,473 and weighing 3,443 pounds with the small V-8, it drew 34,041 orders. Among the accessories on this version are the fender mounted combination spotlight and rearview mirror; rear fender skirts, and continental kit which included an extended bumper. The antenna on the rear deck would be for the $77 standard radio or the $99 9-tube signal seeking radio. The turbine-type wheel covers were standard on the Fairlane 500 models, and a $20 accessory on all other models.

Totally different side trim differentiated the lower ranked Fairlane series from the Fairlane 500s. The Fairlanes did not use the full-length swash, but instead had a rearward pointing spear or rocket formed by stainless steel molding. When a 2-tone paint combination was ordered, as on most Fairlanes, the inside of the spear and the top would carry the secondary color, while the remainder of the car had the primary tone. Shown here is the Fairlane Club Victoria, Model 63B, which was that series' 2-door hardtop. It sold for $2,453 and weighed 3,420 pounds with the small V-8. Not nearly as popular as the Fairlane 500 version, it drew only 16,416 orders.

From the rear, the 1958 Fords offered a nice appearance, with the twin taillight pods each carrying twin lenses within an oval stainless steel bezel. When the optional back-up lights were ordered, they were set between the two red lenses. Only the outer lamps were set in the body proper. The inner lenses and parking lamp were part of the trunk deck, and would raise with that deck. The gas filler continued to live behind the license plate bracket on all but the station wagons and retractable. This is the Fairlane Club Sedan, the 2-door pillared model that sold for $2,320 and weighed 3,399 pounds. Designated the Model 64A, it had a run of 38,366.

The Fairlane series contained only four models, a pillared and hardtop 2-door, and a pillared and hardtop 4-door. In the case of the 4-doors, the pillared Town Sedan, Model 58A, shown here, was by far the most popular, accounting for 57,490 sales. It was priced at $2,374 and weighed 3,468 pounds with the small V-8. In hardtop form it was known as the Town Victoria, Model 57B. Here it cost $2,517 and weighed 3,499 pounds. However, the hardtop version was definitely not a popular model in the Fairlane series, and only 5,868 were produced. Both models used the same bodies as the Fairlane 500 counterparts, and differed only in trim. As in the upper level, the Town Sedan used small vent windows in the rear doors, while the Victoria version had stainless inserts in this area. The Fairlane 500 and Fairlane models continued to use the 188-inch wheelbase chassis, while all other Ford models were built on a 116-inch chassis.

The Custom or Custom 300 series (Ford used both names interchangeably this year) was now a single series with three different side trim options. These options were the regular Custom trim; the Custom Special, and the Custom Styletone. Use of the different side trim often confuses the fact that only one base series was issued, and all trim levels were simply add-on extras, and not considered a different series or sub-series. In the Custom line was found Ford's most popular model, the 2-door Sedan, model 70A, which drew 173,441 orders. It is shown here with the popular Styletone trim package, which included special side molding with an anodized gold stripe between the bars of the spear, and a 2-tone paint scheme. In base form, the 2-door Sedan sold for $2,202 and weighed 3,289 pounds with the 292 V-8.

Ford's second most popular car in 1958 was also in the Custom series. It was the 4-door Sedan, Model 73A, which drew 163,368 orders. It too is shown here with the Styletone trim package. In standard Custom form, it cost $2,256 and weighed 3,319 pounds with the small V-8. Notice that this body differed materially from that of the Fairlane series, in that there were four distinct pillars, and the rear vent window was part of the body, not an insert into the rear door frame. Fairlane 500 wheel covers were available on all Custom models, but were a $20 option. Popular in the south this year were the two varieties of air conditioning offered by Ford. They were Polar Aire at $270 or Select Air at $395. Both units were factory installed and included tinted glass in all windows.

The 3-model Custom series contained Ford's two best selling vehicles, but it also held another record—its third vehicle was Ford's poorest selling model. It was the Custom Business Coupe, sometimes called Business Sedan, Model 70D. The car had only 4,062 sales to its credit. In 6-cylinder form, it sold for $1,977, and thus also had the distinction of being the only Ford with a base price of under $2,000. The car used the Model 70 2-door Sedan body, but contained only a front seat, with the rear or tonneau area being fitted for carrying luggage, sample cases, or other business-type cargo. It is shown here wearing the Custom Special trim package, which was a mid-range option between the plain Custom trim and the Styletone package.

The Custom Special trim package is shown here on the 2-door Sedan. Whereas the Styletone packages almost always included a 2-tone paint job, the Special package could be ordered with either a mono or a 2-tone color scheme. Shown on this model are the standard Custom hub caps. Popular as a 6-cylinder model, the Custom 2-door cost $2,065 and weighed 3,197 with the Six.

Still another variation of Custom trim is seen on this 4-door Sedan. The package here is the Custom Special, with a 2-tone paint job. The Fairlane 500 wheel covers were a $20 extra. With this package, the primary color covered the roof, lower sides, and complete rear of the vehicle, while the secondary color was used on the entire front end, hood, upper fenders and door portions, and completely surrounded the window area between drip rail and window sill. All Custom models used the 116-inch wheelbase chassis, as opposed to the 118-inch wheelbase that was exclusive to the Fairlane models.

The "true" Custom side trim is seen on this 2-door Sedan. When neither the extra cost Special or Styletone packages were ordered, Custom models were turned out with a relatively attractive two bar side piece similar in concept to that of the Styletone package, but lacking the anodized gold section on the rear portion. In plain form, the Custom models were usually turned out with a single color, rather than a 2-tone paint job.

Among Ford's most popular station wagons were the Ranch Wagons, Model 59A. The 2-door, 6-passenger vehicles lent themselves nicely to either work, as seen on the right, or passenger car use, as seen on the left. Production totalled 34,578. With the small V-8, the cars sold for $2,479 and weighed 3,607 pounds. The Ranch Wagons used a trim scheme similar to the Special trim package of the Custom series, and could be ordered in either single or 2-color schemes. The same taillight pods were used on the wagons as on the passenger cars, but on the wagons the inner lenses dropped with the tailgate rather than rising with the trunk deck. The outer lenses were part of the rear fender. Notice how the lift gate portion was substantially wider than the tailgate unit, allowing a large rear glass area.

Ford's only new model this year was the 4-door Ranch Wagon, Model 79A. Essentially a down-trimmed version of the Country Sedan, it was available only as a 6-passenger vehicle. With the small V-8 it was priced at $2,533 and weighed 3,670 pounds. Certainly a popular model, it had a run of 32,854. As did the 2-door Ranch Wagon, the 4-door model used a side trim similar to the Custom Special package, with the 2-tone paint and Fairlane wheel covers being extra. The primary color covered the lower portion of the car, tailgate, and roof, while the secondary color was used on the forward area, hood, and window surrounds. Once again, all wagons used the same 116-inch wheelbase chassis as used on the Custom series.

Ford's answer to the Nomad continued to be the Del Rio, but this year the Nomad was dead while the Del Rio happily sold 12,687 copies. Bearing Model 59B, the $2,478 car was simply an up-trimmed version of the popular 2-door Ranch Wagon, and in fact, wore Ranch Wagon emblems on its rear fenders. Side trim was similar to that of the optional Styletone package found in the Custom series, and included the anodized gold filler between the upper and lower bars of the spear. Interior trim level was similar to that found on the Fairlane series, and included 2-tone door panels and seat coverings in a leather-grained vinyl. In this model, the window surrounds took the color of the lower portion of the car.

1958

Once again, Ford's most popular wagon was the 6-passenger Country Sedan, Model 79D. However, this year production reached only 68,772, as compared with over 135,000 in 1957. Most often equipped with the V-8, the car was base priced at $2,639 and weighed 3,682 pounds. As with the Del Rio, side trim followed that of the Custom Styletone package. The interior was done in leather-grained vinyl, with 2-tone door panels and seats matching the exterior colors.

With both rear and middle seats down, the 9-passenger Country Sedan could double as a small cargo handler or a large passenger car. Seatbacks and undersides of the seat cushions were finished in a heavy vinyl that provided a hard and durable flat floor space when one or both seats were down. Listed as the Model 79C, the 9-passenger Country Sedan was priced at $2,746 and weighed 3,752 pounds with the small V-8. It could be fitted with the 300 horsepower Interceptor engine for an extra $150. Production of the 9-passenger model reached 20,702.

Ford's premier station wagon continued to be the Country Squire, Model 79E. It was available in 9-passenger form only, and was the only Ford to use the wood-like fiberglass trim and wood-grained side applique. Priced at $2,876, it was Ford's second most expensive vehicle, after the Skyliner retractable. Its weight was 3,799 pounds. As did all other Fords, this model too had a production slump, and only 15,020 units were turned loose. Fairlane wheel covers, and the little front-fender gunsights were standard on this model only. But despite all of its Fairlane trim items, it still used the 116-inch wheelbase and base Model 79 body of all other wagons.

Once again the Ranchero pickup came in two different trim levels, though both versions were considered part of the Custom series. In plain form, the cute little truck used the seldom-seen side trim of the standard Custom models and a rather stark interior which included horn button, single visor, and single armrest. When ordered with the Styletone package, as seen here, the exterior utilized the stainless molding with gold anodized insert; steering wheel with horn ring, and a deluxe type of interior. In plain form, the Ranchero was Model 66A and listed at $2,170, while the Styletone package changed its designation to Model 66B, and raised its price to $2,236. It also raised its weight 10 pounds to a total of 3,275 pounds. Obviously buyers of this type of vehicle liked the flashiness of the passenger car sourced styling, and thus 8,479 were bought with the Styletone package, but only 1,471 went out in plain form. There is no indication that the Custom Special trim was available on the Ranchero, even though it was standard on the Courier. Although the 6-cylinder engine was considered standard, both the 292 and 352 cubic inch V-8s could be ordered, and the 352 was mandatory if the new 3-speed Cruise-O-Matic transmission was ordered at an extra $200.

Unlike the Ranchero, which came in two trim levels, it appears that the Courier this year appeared in only one form, wearing the Custom Special side trim bars. As it did in 1957, the Courier once again had a one-piece swing-up lift gate rather than a side opening rear door. As seen here, this lift gate was essentially the upper and lower gates of the station wagon, welded together into one unit. However, unlike the wagons, the Courier had only single lens taillights of 1957 styling built into the body, and did not have inner lenses on the lift gate. Designated the Model 78A, the Courier was base priced with the 6-cylinder engine at $2,062. A total of 3,352 were sold. This was the last year that the Courier would appear with blanked sides. Although the little panel truck had always been based on the 2-door station wagon shell, it at least had given the appearance of a panel truck. Beginning with the 1959 models, it would simply be a station wagon variation, with full windows but no seats. Once again, both the Ranchero and the Courier were based almost entirely on Custom series passenger car components, and thus used the 116-inch wheelbase chassis of that series.

On Oct. 17, 1958, one of the best looking lines of Fords ever produced was unveiled to the public. And the public, after a year of semi-recession and disinterest in the 1958 Ford styling, responded with enthusiasm, shooting sales up in a welcomed surge.

Overall, the new Ford design was so good looking that later in the year it took the Gold Medal for Exceptional Automotive Styling at the Worlds Fair in Brussels, Belgium. Basically, the new Fords almost seemed to be a logical extension of the 1957 styling. In fact, they appeared to be what the 1958 models should have been in the first place.

Once again, the styling was well balanced, with a star-filled grille topped by a flat hood and fender line. The quad headlights remained, but now were definitely part of the styling, and did not look like some sort of pods that had been plopped atop the fenders. The silly false airscoop was also gone, but the little gunsights on top of the front fenders remained. But on this model they seemed to appear natural.

The beltline was raised on all models, which enhanced the appearance, but also would contribute to many side dings in parking lots, as there was little protection from neighboring doors being carelessly swung too wide. Adding both protection and beauty to the top two series was a large stainless stone shield on the rear quarters, extending from the rear wheel well to the rear bumper.

Rear styling was also handled nicely, with a return to round taillights nested under the brows of a large stainless "V" that swept across the entire rear deck edge and rear quarters. Above the extreme tips of this "V" were the twin back-up lights, while below its reversed apex was located the gas filler.

Initially, the Fairlane 500 series was the top of the line. However, shortly before the start of the year, a new series appeared called the Galaxie. This new series offered the same two and 4-door sedans and hardtops as appeared in the other series, plus it absorbed the Sunliner Convertible and the Skyliner Retractable from the Fairlane 500 series. Over the years, this has caused some confusion, because very few convertibles and retractables were produced in Fairlane 500 form, and production records of these two models were included with the records for the Galaxie versions. Still, in the early weeks, these two models did appear in Fairlane 500 nomenclature. It appears that the only difference between the Fairlane 500 and Galaxie versions of these two models was found in the signatures attached to the rear fenders.

On the two and 4-door models, however, the situation was completely different. Here the Galaxie models had a completely new roofline and different back window than did the Fairlane 500 models. Whereas the Fairlanes and Custom models used a top similar to the 1958 design, with a large rounded back window, the new Galaxies had an exclusive top, similar in styling to that of the Thunderbird. This top, which included a larger blank rear quarter panel and a flat rear window, was highlighted by ribbed chrome panels at the base of the rear pillar, and had a stylized Ford crest floating above this trim.

The Town Victoria models also carried this theme into a small ribbed triangle at the trailing edge of the rear door glass. In addition to the roof lines, only minor trim upgrading differentiated the Galaxie models from the Fairlane 500 units. Still, the public decided that the new roof line was reason enough to switch preference to the Galaxie models. As a result, sales of Fairlane 500 variations dropped substantially, as buyers of premium Fords headed for the new top model.

When the Galaxie series absorbed the Sunliner and the Skyliner, the Fairlane 500 series was left with just a two and 4-door sedan and a two and 4-door hardtop. As before, the hardtop models bore the designation "Victoria." The plain Fairlane series lost two models, as both of its hardtop styles were gone, and only the pillared versions of the two and 4-door sedans remained. These same two body styles also appeared in the Custom 300 series, but this low-buck line also had a third model. That was the 2-door Business Coupe, a 3-passenger variation of the Club Sedan, available only in the Custom 300 series and only as a 6-cylinder model. It was Ford's lowest price car, selling at a base of $2,132, which meant that for the first time in its history, Ford had no car under the $2,000 mark.

Throughout the entire line, only one basic series of bodies was used, as all models were now built on the same size wheelbase of 118 inches. This made the Custom 300 models six inches longer than in 1958, while the wagons grew about 5.5 inches and the Fairlane models grew one inch. Surprisingly, though, the Skyliner Retractable shrunk by three inches.

In the Station Wagon series, a new model appeared, but this was simply a name change. Appearing this year was the 2-door Country Sedan, which was essentially a slightly down-trimmed version of the former Del Rio 2-door wagon. The Del Rio (Of The River) name was now gone. Actually, it had had no real meaning, and possibly was considered too close to Chevrolet's Delray (Of The Sun) series. By adopting the new name, the 2-door wagon was brought into line with the trim levels of the other two Country Sedan models. Also remaining in the wagon series were the two low-trim Ranch Wagons and the luxury level Country Squire.

In the world of Thunderbird, there was little change. This, of course, was to be expected, as the car was brand new in 1958. Still, the new models could be easily identified by the new grille consisting of thin horizontal bars, duplicated in effect by similar treatment on the taillight pods. The family of five barred decorative plates on the doors was now gone. Side trim now consisted of a large chromed spear-tip at the leading edge of the side embossing, with the name "Thunderbird" almost appearing as a spear shaft in the center of this point. Mechanically, the Thunderbirds received a new leaf spring suspension in the rear, replacing the somewhat bouncy coil spring units of 1958.

Late in the year, the Thunderbird Convertible finally got a fully automatic top. The top mechanisms of 1958 and the first half of 1959 appeared to be needlessly complicated, and required some manual work and the operator getting out of the car to engage switches located in the trunk. Now, a single switch on the dash activated the entire operation. It might be noted that the rear deck on the Thunderbird Convertibles still opened from the leading edge, in a manner similar to the rotractable's deck, while the deck on the hardtop version opened in a conventional manner.

For the power-hungry, Lincoln's 430 cubic inch engine was made available in the Thunderbird this year. Not available in other Ford models, this engine cost only $177 extra, but could only be installed if the $242 extra 3-speed Cruise-O-Matic transmission was also ordered. Rated at 350 horsepower at 4400 rpm, this engine had a bore and stroke of 4.3x4.7 inches, a compression ratio of 10:1, and used a Holley 4-barrel carburetor. This turned out to be the only new engine offering in Ford's entire line this year. However, due to this block, Thunderbird enjoyed a famous year in the NASCAR spotlight, taking many of the season's most important races. However, the time of glory was a short one, and by the 1960 season new engines, including Ford's own 352 of 360 horsepower, put the heavier Thunderbird back into the luxury car class and off of the major race circuits.

For those who did not opt for the extra horses, the normal Thunderbird engine was the 352 cubic inch block, still rated at 300 HP at 4600 rpm, but now having a lowered compression ratio of 9.6:1. Formerly known as the Interceptor 352 Special, this year the engine was referred to as the Thunderbird 352 Special.

Bearing the Thunderbird name, but not available in the Thunderbird cars, was the Thunderbird 332 Special, which had been known as the Interceptor in 1958. The block was the same as the previous model, but a lowering of the compression ratio to 8.9:1 plus other modifications resulted in a horsepower downgrade to 225 at 4400 rpm, as opposed to the 240 horses of 1958.

Also downgraded was the tried and true 292 cubic inch basic block, which now had an 8.8:1 compression ratio and developed only 200 horses at 4400 rpm. The only engine not changed was the old faithful Six with its 223 cubic inches, 145 horses, and 8.6:1 compression.

Appearing this year was a totally new Ford-built 2-speed automatic transmission. Bearing the name Ford-O-Matic or Fordomatic (spelled both ways) it is often confused with its predecessor. Yet, the new transmission was 50 pounds lighter, had an aluminum casing, and contained 25% fewer parts than the old Borg-Warner unit that it replaced. It was available for both six and 8-cylinder engines, while the unchanged Cruise-O-Matic 3-speed could only be coupled to V-8 blocks. Among the other mechanical changes or additions was Ford's first limited-slip differential, called Equa-Lock; a new foot-operated parking brake; aluminized mufflers, and a new oil filter which promised 4,000 miles between oil changes.

Ford reported that this year, 78.1% of its cars (about 1,142,000 vehicles) had V-8 engines, while 71.7% (about 1,048,380) had automatic transmissions.

As a result of both the new styling and the new Galaxie series, Ford's model year production soared back over the 1-million mark once again, with 1,394,724 Fords rolling off the line, accompanied by 67,456 Thunderbirds, for a grand total of 1,462,180 passenger cars. Surprisingly, of this amount, the low-buck Custom 300 series proved to be the most popular, with 482,210 total sales. The most popular model was the Custom 300 4-door Sedan, with 249,553 leaving the plant, while the Custom 300 2-door Sedan came in 2nd with 228,573 sales. The only other models to break the 100,000 mark were the third place Galaxie 4-door Town Sedan (pillared) with 183,108 sales, and the Galaxie 2-door Club Victoria (hardtop) with 121,869 sales. Coming in 5th with a good try was the 6-passenger 4-door Country Sedan, with 94,601 builds.

All told, Ford produced 15 different car models in four different series, plus six different station wagons in their own exclusive wagon series, and the 2-model Thunderbirds. All except four were available with either the Six or the V-8. The exceptions were the Custom 300 Business Coupe, which came only with the Six, and the Thunderbirds and the Galaxie Skyliner which came only with the V-8s. Also on the list were two gray-area car/truck variations, the Courier and the Ranchero, both of which were based on the 2-door wagon shell.

While Ford was certainly happy enough with its total of 1,462,180 passenger cars, Chevrolet managed to produce 1,481,071 cars during the model year, and thus continued to claim number one sales spot. However, Ford later countered with the contention that its 1959 calendar year production was 1,528,592 cars, as opposed to Chevrolet's 1,428,962. Thus, Ford self-named itself the number one producer for 1959. Take your choice.

Showing off its new horizontal bar grille is this Thunderbird Convertible, Style 76A. Priced at $3,979, it weighed 3,903 pounds, thus marking the first time that a Ford had exceeded the "over $1 per pound" ratio. Despite being the highest priced car to wear a Ford emblem, sales still reached 10,261. For the first time, Thunderbird buyers could order Lincoln's 430 cubic inch engine for their cars. The big block was not available to other Fords, and could be installed only if the Cruise-O-Matic 3-speed transmission was also ordered. This package cost $419 more than the base price mentioned above.

With everyone standing outside the car looking at the top, one wonders if it had just become stuck in its half-way position. This appears to be the second generation Thunderbird top, which did not appear on the cars until mid-season. The 1958 and early 1959 models had what appeared to be a needlessly complicated mechanism, which required the operator to put the top halfway down from inside the car, then complete the operation with a switch located in the trunk. The new top was fully automatic from the driver's seat, with one switch activating a series of solenoids and motors that controlled both the top and the rear deck. Despite its high degree of complexity, these tops were pretty fool-proof. Note that the Convertible's rear deck is hinged at the rear section to accommodate the top, while the Coupe's deck was hinged in the normal way.

During the late 1950s, Ford engineers were playing with flip-top roof panels above the doors to ease entry and exit for passengers and especially for tall drivers. Possibly inspired by the new on the market flip-top cigarette boxes, these panels would swing upward automatically when the door was opened, and would snap back into place when the door was shut. The panels first appeared on a Mercury show car in 1956, went away, and then reappeared on the Thunderbird. However, the T-Bird was not a show car, but an engineering vehicle never intended for display. Apparently Ford felt these swing-up flaps were not worth the effort or the cost, and except for a few further experiments in the mid-1960s, the idea was left to die.

Totally new this year, and not even appearing until after the first of the year, was the Galaxie series, which took over as Ford's top line. Flagship of the series was the attractive Sunliner Convertible, Style 76B. Priced at $2,957, it weighed 3,628 pounds with the base V-8. Records indicate a total of 45,868 having been built, but this figure also includes those models built early in the year, which wore the Fairlane 500 crest. Once the Galaxie series was introduced, production of the Fairlane 500 Sunliner ceased. Convertible tops this year were in a shiny woven vinyl material, with a heavy metal header bar bracing against the upper windshield frame. The twin fender-mounted rearview mirrors on this model have been popular for years in Europe, mandatory in Japan, but never gained favor in this country.

By far the most popular of the two Thunderbird models was the Tudor Hardtop or Coupe, Style 63A, which saw production climb to 57,195. Priced at $3,696, the car weighed 3,813 pounds in basic form. Among this year's mechanical innovations was the replacement of the somewhat bouncy rear coil springs with conventional leaf springs. The 1959 Birds were easy to identify by the large chromed spear tip at the leading edge of the embossed side trim. Despite the availability of Lincoln's 430 cubic inch block, most Thunderbirds were equipped with the regular 352 cubic inch engine.

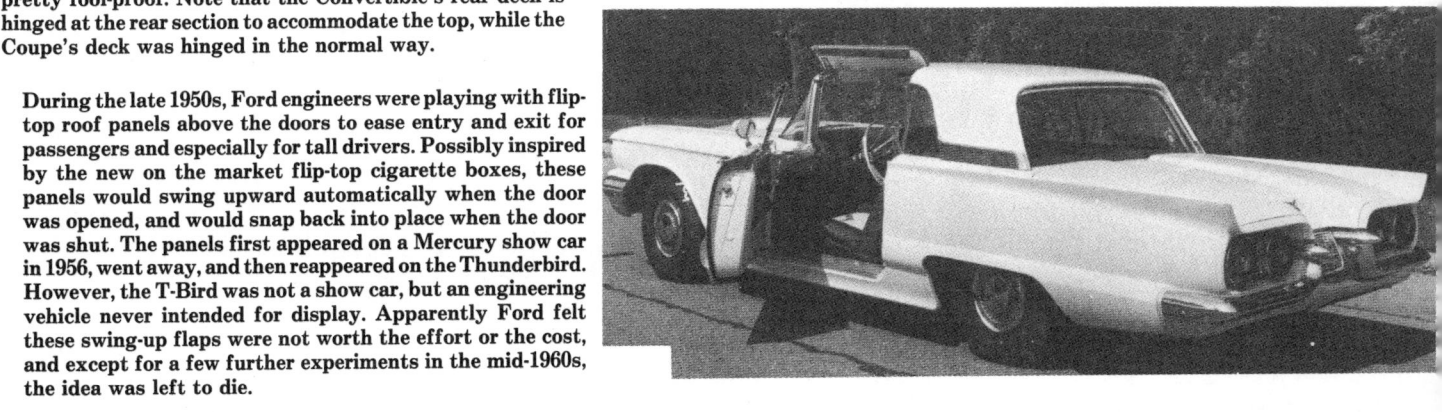

One of two 1959 Skyliner Retractables owned by the author over the years was this bright red model, shown here ready for a top-down summer drive. Designated Style 51A, the Skyliner was the only Ford this year which could not be ordered with a 6-cylinder engine. Its basic power was the 292 cubic inch V-8, but most were turned out with either the 332 Thunderbird Special or the 352 Thunderbird Special. Ford's heaviest and most expensive car, the Skyliner weighed 4,064 pounds and sold for $3,346 in basic form. It was the only Ford to have a base list price in excess of $3,000.

Shown with its top in half-up position is the author's red Skyliner. Although all owners of this model had a terrifying fear that the top would lock in this position during operation, the highly complicated units proved to be relatively trouble free overall. The main complaint was that the seals between the top and windshield header and the ones between the forward flip-down section and the main top tended to leak in heavy rains, making the cars far from weather tight in torrential storms. The Skyliners used the same type of trunk deck latching as did the Thunderbird Convertible. In both cars, the deck was hinged at the rear and contained a full metal panel that would meet the rear seat back when the top was lowered, thus doing away with the top boot usually associated with convertibles. All operations of the top and deck lid were automatic, controlled by a single switch on the dash. In the event of automatic failure, a manual operation was possible, but quite time consuming.

The author's second Skyliner was this pink and white model, shown here on a cold but sunny Illinois winter day. Slightly more dressed than the red version, this model wears chromed fender skirts, fender-mounted spotlight, and small running lights just behind the eyebrows. As with the Sunliner, the Skyliner first came out as a Fairlane 500 model, but was absorbed by the new Galaxie series after the first of the year. Thus, of the total of 12,915 produced this year, an unknown number wore the Fairlane 500 designation, while the rest became Galaxies. This was the final year for the Retractable. Continuing poor sales were attributed to the high list price, poor luggage space, and a general fear of the very complicated top mechanism. Of the author's two 1959 models, both are fully restored and living happy lives in Sweden, where they were shipped in the mid-1970s.

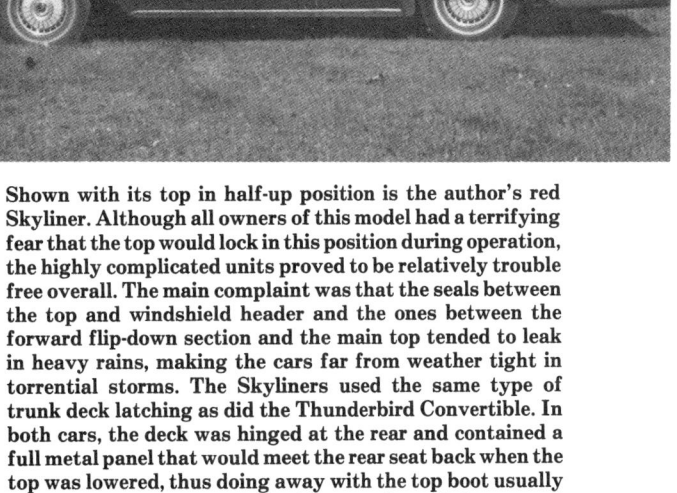

When the new Galaxie line appeared in January, it used the base body of the Fairlane 500s, but had its own exclusive tops with a style similar to that of the Thunderbird coupes or the Retractable. Two 2-door models were available, the hardtop Club Victoria, Style 65A, shown here, and the pillared Club Sedan, Style 64H. The Club Victoria proved to be the second most popular Galaxie, with 121,869 being produced, while the Club Sedan had only 52,848 sales. The hardtop model weighed 3,439 pounds and cost $2,707, while the pillared version weighed 3,478 pounds and cost $2,646 in base V-8 form. When viewed from this angle, the Club Victoria looked quite similar to the Skyliner. However, the winged crest on the rear top panel and lack of fuel filler door above the rear wheel well quickly said that this was the hardtop model, not a Retractable.

One of the best looking 4-door models this year was the Galaxie Town Victoria, introduced after Jan. 1 as an upgraded version of the Fairlane 500 model. As with other Galaxie models, the main difference between this car and its Fairlane counterpart was in the new top design, which followed the basic lines of the Thunderbird. Even with the windows up, the car could be differentiated from the Town Sedan version by the bright kick-up panels at the rear window sills. These triangular panels, which formed a continuation of the ribbed rear top trim, were exclusive to the Galaxie Town Victoria, and appeared on no other Ford. Not nearly as popular as the Town Sedan, the Town Victoria drew only 47,728 orders, all base priced at $2,772. With the small V-8, it weighed 3,595 pounds.

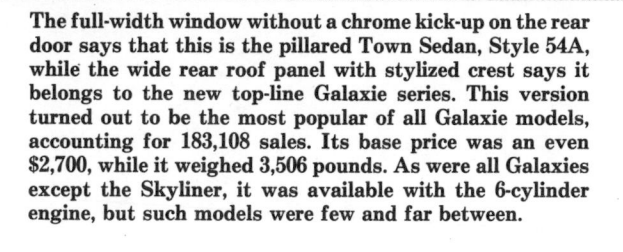

The full-width window without a chrome kick-up on the rear door says that this is the pillared Town Sedan, Style 54A, while the wide rear roof panel with stylized crest says it belongs to the new top-line Galaxie series. This version turned out to be the most popular of all Galaxie models, accounting for 183,108 sales. Its base price was an even $2,700, while it weighed 3,506 pounds. As were all Galaxies except the Skyliner, it was available with the 6-cylinder engine, but such models were few and far between.

Once the new Galaxie series arrived in January, sales of the Fairlane 500 models went into a tremendous slump. Thus, the attractive Fairlane 500 Club Victoria tallied only 23,892 builds. The large curving rear window marked the main difference between this and the new Galaxie models. Designated the Style 63A, the car weighed 3,446 pounds, and cost $2,655. Apparently most buyers felt it was worth the additional $52 to get the higher styled Galaxie version with its squared Thunderbird inspired top treatment.

From model introduction date on Oct. 17, 1958, until January, 1959, all Ford Convertibles wore the Fairlane 500 designation. Once the new Galaxie line appeared, the Fairlane 500 Convertible ceased to exist, and all further soft tops became part of the Galaxie series. Unlike the hard-top models, which differed substantially from the Galaxies because of top treatment, the only real change in the convertibles was in the name. The early models had "Fairlane 500" signatures on the trailing edges of the rear fenders, while the late models had "Galaxie" signatures in this place. Because the difference was simply a name switch, separate production figures were not kept, and thus the number of Fairlane 500 convertibles produced this year is lost in the 45,868 total Sunliners turned loose during the 1959 season.

The Fairlane 500 signature on the rear fender, instead of a Galaxie, is the only thing that differentiates this early version of the Skyliner from a later model. As was the case with the Sunliner Convertible, the Skyliner Retractable also was absorbed by the new Galaxie series after Jan. 1, 1959. But unlike the two and 4-door sedans, there was no change of style number, price, or weight when the new series came about. As with the Sunliner, the Skyliner's Fairlane 500 production is lost in the total 1959 production of 12,915 retractables.

Shown on the display floor of Ford's styling studio is the final version of the Fairlane 500 Club Sedan. This is the version that was soon to go into production. Designated the Style 64B, the car differed from the Club Victoria only in the fact that it had a solid B-pillar behind the door, and used different rear window edging. Priced at $2,594, it weighed 3,439 pounds. Production was nothing to brag about, with sales reaching only 10,141.

The Fairlane 500 model least affected by the new Galaxie series was the Town Sedan, Model 58B. Production reached 35,670, indicating perhaps that buyers of this family oriented sedan were not as impressed by the new Galaxie styling as were buyers of the more sporty models. The car was priced at $2,648 and weighed 3,518 pounds. It differed from the Town Victoria in that it had solid frames around the windows and a full floor to roof B-pillar between the front and rear doors.

Double rear side tunnels ended in rounded taillights on the new Fairlane 500 models. The lower and larger tunnels terminated in the nicely styled lenses surrounded by ribbed bezels somewhat resembling the wheel cover design. The upper and smaller tunnels ended in the back-up lights, which sported their own distinctive bezels. Connecting the back-up lights was a full-width shallow "V" which also provided the color break line on 2-tone models, while at the same time providing a perch for the "500" numerals. The gas filler had its own separate door between the rear deck and the license plate section of the pressed steel bumper. This is the Fairlane 500 Town Victoria, Style 57A, which was the lowest priced 4-door hardtop in Ford's list. It was priced at $2,720 and weighed 3,552 pounds. As was the case with other sporty Fairlane 500s, production fell rapidly once the new Galaxie series appeared, and as a result, only 9,308 of this model were built.

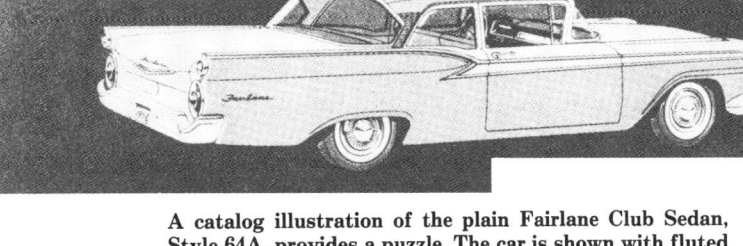

A catalog illustration of the plain Fairlane Club Sedan, Style 64A, provides a puzzle. The car is shown with fluted stainless trim on the C-pillar, but conflicting information would indicate that this trim was used only on the Fairlane 500 models. Possibly the deletion of this trim was made after the catalogs were printed. The Fairlane line consisted of only two models, this Club Sedan, and the 4-door Town Sedan. Both were pillared styles, as hardtop versions did not filter this low on the trim level scene. Priced at $2,475 and weighing 3,332 pounds, the Fairlane Club Sedan drew 35,126 orders.

The only Ford not available with a V-8 engine this year was also the lowest price vehicle in the entire line. It was the Custom 300 Business Coupe, Style 64G. It was also the only Ford available only in 3-passenger configuration, as the area behind the front seat was fitted strictly for parcel use, and had no seating facilities. Designed primarily for fleet purchasers, the car listed at $2,132 and weighed 3,283 pounds. This year marked the first time that Ford did not have a car priced under $2,000. The base body was a variation of the Style 64 2-door sedan, and all production figures were combined in the total of the regular Custom 300 Coupe.

Both of the two plain Fairlane models carried their series signature on the lower rear tunnel, as opposed to the Fairlane 500 models, which had this signature on the upper tunnels. Also, the bright trim on the C-pillar was omitted on the plain models, as were the large stainless rear fender outlines and stone guards found on the Fairlane 500 models. Otherwise there was not too much difference between the two Fairlane versions. This is the Town Sedan, a pillared model noted as Style 58A. It cost $2,529 and weighed 3,516 pounds. It turned out to be the most popular in both the Fairlane and Fairlane 500 series combined, drawing 64,663 orders.

The most popular model in this year's Ford line was the Custom 300 4-door sedan, Style 58E, which saw production reach 249,553. Priced at $2,391, it had a weight of 3,486 pounds as a V-8. With the Six, it was 100 pounds lighter and $118 cheaper. The car is shown here in strictly stock form, which included only a single sun visor and arm rest for the driver only. However, in actuality, few models left the dealerships in this form, as most buyers spent a few extra dollars to get the added interior fittings. This model also sports a radio, which could be the basic $59 unit or the signal seeker model for $83. Rocker panel trim at $11 installed was also a popular option in this series.

The Custom 300 series may have been Ford's low-buck range, but it was also by far its most popular, with sales far outstripping the other series. This is the Club Sedan, Style 64F, in Custom 300 trim. It did not carry a "Custom" signature on the sides, but rather was fitted with four small accessory chrome rear fender ornaments which resembled a formation of jet fighters viewed from above. The side trim also differed substantially from the Fairlane and Galaxie models, in that only a single stainless piece ran from headlight to back-up light bezel and provided the color break on 2-tone models. Priced at $2,337 and weighing 3,411 pounds with the basic V-8, the Club Sedan was Ford's second most popular car, with sales totalling 228,573.

Ford's lowest priced wagon continued to be the 2-door Ranch Wagon, Style 59C. It sold for $2,685 and weighed 3,691 pounds. Production reached an impressive 45,558. All wagons, regardless of trim level, sported the same pattern when ordered with 2-color paint combinations. Essentially this consisted of the lower body and roof being painted in the primary color, and the hood, fender tops, door sills, and window frames being in the complimentary second color. Since Ranch Wagons followed the trim level of the Custom 300 models, they were equipped with hub caps rather than wheel covers.

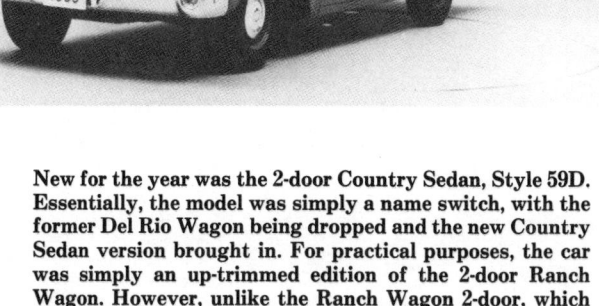

Also high on the popularity scale was the 4-door Ranch Wagon, Style 71H. It recorded production of 67,339. In fact, the two Ranch Wagon models accounted for almost half of Ford's total wagon production. A nicely styled work/play vehicle, the 4-door version sold for $2,752 and weighed 3,786 pounds as a V-8. Its trim level followed that of the Custom 300 series, as attested to by the small "jet planes" on the rear quarter. However, unlike the cars which wore a formation of four "planes," the Ranch Wagons sported only three. The reason for this probably was the fact that the fourth plane would have wound up on top of the gas filler door.

New for the year was the 2-door Country Sedan, Style 59D. Essentially, the model was simply a name switch, with the former Del Rio Wagon being dropped and the new Country Sedan version brought in. For practical purposes, the car was simply an up-trimmed edition of the 2-door Ranch Wagon. However, unlike the Ranch Wagon 2-door, which enjoyed a high level of acceptance, the Country Sedan model turned out to be Ford's poorest selling wagon, with only 8,663 being sold. Available only in 6-passenger form, the car sold for $2,796 and weighed 3,714 pounds as a V-8.

The only Ford wagon to exceed the $3,000 mark was the pretentious Country Squire. It was base priced at $3,076 and weighed 3,859 pounds as a V-8. Available only in 9-passenger form, it was the only wagon to be fitted with the artificial wood side trim. A pretty vehicle, it probably lacked popularity because of its price. Still, sales did reach 24,336, which was a nice improvement over 1958. The Country Squire was available with any option, but it is doubtful if many left the factory with the 6-cylinder block. The trim level of the Squire was on par with the Galaxie or Fairlane 500 models.

Ford's most popular wagon by a wide margin was the 6-passenger 4-door Country Sedan, Style 71F, which accounted for 94,601 sales. It was priced at $2,863 and weighed 3,819 pounds. Its 9-passenger counterpart, Style 71E, looked identical from the outside, but was fitted with a rear seat and a few other interior modifications. Not near as popular as the 6-passenger model, the 9-passenger wagon had a run of 28,881. Its base price was $2,947, while it weighed 3,868 pounds. All Country Sedans wore a trim level comparable to that of the Fairlane 500 models.

No longer did the Courier Sedan Delivery resemble a nicely styled small panel truck. Now it was simply a down-trimmed version of the 2-door Ranch Wagon. This had been the case in prior years, but then the sides were blanked in to give delivery truck appearance. Now the wagon parentage was obvious, with non-operable windows occupying the side panels, and the standard wagon tail and lift gates being used instead of the Courier's one-piece swing-up rear door. Economies consisted of a total lack of side trim except for the "Courier" signature on the rear quarter, and an interior fitted with a single driver's seat, which was in effect the left portion of the folding middle seat of the 9-passenger wagons. Priced at $2,424, the Courier drew 5,141 orders this year.

As was the Courier Sedan Delivery, the Custom Ranchero Pickup was also based on the Style 59 2-door Station Wagon body. Thus, as the new Fords grew with the 2-inch increase in wheelbase, the Ranchero was now able to offer a 7-inch longer cargo bed. The increased length resulted in an even better looking and more practical pickup. This year, only the Custom Ranchero was available, as the former basic Ranchero had been dropped. As was the case with the Courier, the 6-cylinder engine was considered standard, but any V-8 could be ordered as an option. With the Six, the Custom Ranchero sold for $2,313. Production reached 14,169. An interesting feature was a split back seat. When folded forward, the back revealed the spare tire on the passenger's side or a small storage compartment on the driver's side.

The attractiveness of the 1959 Ford was appreciated world-wide, and even extended to the overseas professional car industry. Even one of Europe's top professional car builders, the Pollmann Karosseriefabrik of Bremen, Germany, turned to Ford chassis for some of their beautiful coach work. It appears that a Custom Ranchero provided the working foundation for this high-headroom hearse, which features a single large frosted pane of etched glass in the rear compartment. A combination of Fairlane 500 and Galaxie trim has been used in overall beautification, while the slanting B-pillar of the Ranchero is still obvious. Because of their size and strength, American car chassis were popular with European professional car builders.

Ford let loose with a double barrel blast this year, not only coming up with one of the most radically styled cars in its postwar career, but also answering the low-price buyer by coming out with a totally new compact model.

In the big car line, the totally new Ford was built on the longest wheelbase chassis that had ever carried the Ford name. The new chassis of 119 inches wheelbase gave the brand new sheet metal and body components an overall length of 213.7 inches, an increase of almost six inches over previous models.

Styling was totally different for Ford, and provided much controversy in both the press and with the buying public. Many people loved it from the start, but just as many disliked it immensely. A great many, including the author, disliked it at first, but later came to really appreciate the smooth lines, spacious interior and luggage room, and nice handling characteristics. In fact, the author later bought a plain Fairlane 4-door Sedan as a workhorse car, and put over 100,000 virtually trouble-free miles on it in just about every state east of the Rockies.

With the new bodies came a shuffling of series. The old Custom 300 series was now gone, except for a limited run of special fleet cars. The series was replaced by the plain Fairlane as the low-buck range. With that move, the Fairlane 500 series became the intermediate range. The year-old Galaxie series retained its position at the top of the line, but the Galaxie Special sub-series was

The only Fords not to receive radical styling changes were the Thunderbirds. But their turn would come in 1961. For this year, a new grid-pattern grille with a main horizontal bar bisected by three vertical bars contributed to the frontal change. Gone was the large chrome spear point on the door embossing, but the Thunderbird signature remained. By far the best selling T-Bird yet, the 2-door Hardtop Coupe, Style 71, accounted for 80,938 sales. Its base price of $3,755 could easily be exceeded by the $177 optional 430 cubic inch engine, the $242 Cruise-O-Matic, or the $144 overdrive. The car weighed 3,799 pounds with the basic 300 horsepower 352 cubic inch engine.

concocted to take on the Starliner 2-door Hardtop and the Sunliner Convertible. Oddly, though the 2-door hardtop went into the new sub-series, the 4-door hardtop remained in the plain Galaxie series. As mentioned in the previous chapter, the unique Skyliner Retractable Hardtop died with the 1959 line.

Also in the totally new department was the Falcon. Representing Ford's answer to the popular Nash Ramblers and Studebaker Larks, the Falcon was hatched just in time to bump heads with Chevrolet's very radical new Corvair and Plymouth's nicely styled and nice handling Valiant. However, unlike the rear engined air-cooled Corvair, the Falcon was part of the very conventional pack, and in effect, looked quite a bit like a scaled down Ford.

Built on the unit construction principle, the car had a frameless combined chassis, floor pan, and body metal which resulted in structural rigidity but with light weight. The only vestige of a true frame occurred at the front, and provided a nesting for the engine and attachment for the frame members. Also, the frontal design incorporated easily detachable front fenders, for economical minor bump repairs.

The car sat on a wheelbase of 109.5 inches, and the cars were 181.2 inches long overall. When the two wagon designs finally appeared, they were 189 inches overall. At first only two body styles were offered in only one series. These were a two and a 4-door sedan. In January, a two and a 4-door station wagon joined the line, but for practical purposes, these didn't begin to reach buyers until early March. For a change, the Falcon line followed the T-Bird concept, and was offered in one series or trim level only, even though there was a moderate $66 trim and interior option package available.

Power for the new Falcon was by a new 6-cylinder engine of 144 cubic inches which developed 85 horsepower at 4200 rpm. Later, this figure was uprated to 90 horsepower. Designed specifically for the Falcon, the little block had a bore and stroke of 3.5x2.5 inches and had an 8.7:1 compression ratio. Buyers had a choice of a 3-speed manual transmission or an optional specially redesigned 2-speed Fordomatic at $180 extra. Tires on the Falcon were 6.00x13 as opposed to the 7.50x14 tires used on full-size Fords.

With a totally new "real" Ford and a brand new Falcon line, it was no wonder that the Thunderbird entered the year with virtually no changes. The car retained its 113-inch wheelbase, and for the third straight year made use of the attractive "Square Bird" styling. One totally new Thunderbird option was the Sliding Roof Hardtop. Often considered a separate model, this facility was simply a $220 option on the standard hardtop which drew the attention of 2,536 buyers.

With a new top secret Bird awaiting the 1961 season, only the expected cosmetic changes were made on this year's model. They included a new grille, removal of the large chrome spear tip on the doors, and the addition of three sets of triple chromed bars on the trailing edge of the rear fender. The "three is better" concept was also carried to the taillights, which now consisted of three round lenses per side, each nested in a pod whose background design resembled the new grille pattern.

Thunderbirds were again powered by the 352 cubic inch engine which developed 300 horsepower at 4600 rpm. The engine was unchanged from the previous year, but somewhere along the line a name switch occurred, with the earlier versions carrying the Thunderbird Special name, while later information refers to the block as the Interceptor Special. Also available to Thunderbird buyers was the Lincoln-sourced 430 cubic inch Thunderbird Special. This $177 option still ran a bore and stroke of 4.3x3.5 inches and developed 350 horses at 4400 rpm, but its compression was now raised to 10.2:1. As ever, a 3-speed standard transmission came with the car, but overdrive could be ordered for $144 extra, while Cruise-O-Matic (mandatory with the 430 block) was $242 extra. Ford-O-matic (or Fordomatic) was not available in the Thunderbird line.

In the regular Ford line, the Interceptor Special was available also as a $177 option, but the 430 cubic inch block was not available through normal dealer sources. Once again, the base Ford engine was either the 223 cubic inch Six of 145 horses, or the 292 cubic inch V-8, now downgraded to 185 horsepower. The Six was slightly changed, in that it dropped to 8.4:1 compression, from the previous 8.6:1. The Six was a $113 delete option from the prices shown in this book.

At the start of the year, only two engine options were available. They were the Interceptor Special mentioned above, and a new version of the 352 cubic inch block, which replaced the now-discontinued 332 cubic inch model. Simply called the Interceptor, the new version ran the same 4x3.5 inch bore and stroke as the other 352s, but had a compression ratio of 8.9:1, used a Holley 2-barrel carburetor, and was only rated at 235 horsepower at 4400 rpm. It was priced at $148 extra.

At mid-year, buyers were given another 352 block to choose from. This newly designed model also used the same 4x3.5 inch bore and stroke, but boasted a 10.6:1 compression ratio and a Holley 4-barrel. It was rated at 360 horses at 6000 rpm. It bore the same "Interceptor Special" name as did the 300 horse unit.

In the world of numbers, Thunderbird's production was way up, despite the fact that the car really had little to offer that was new. Still, production of the hardtop reached 80,938, while the convertible went up slightly to 11,860, giving the line a total production of 92,798 which was the highest in its history.

Taking top honors in sales, and probably surprising everyone in the process, was the new Falcon 2-door Sedan, which had a production run of 193,470. It was closely followed by its 4-door version, with a run of 167,896. It is interesting to note that none of the full-size Fords even came close to these sales marks. Finishing just the opposite were the two Falcon wagons, but these did not reach the market until March, 1960, as opposed to the early October introduction of the Falcon cars, or the rest of the Ford line. Total Falcon production at year end was 435,676.

In the full-size line, the most popular model was the Fairlane 500 4-door Town Sedan, which had sales of 153,234. This was followed in 2nd place by the plain Fairlane Town Sedan, with sales of 110,373. The plain 3-model Fairlane series accounted for 205,667 sales, which included 874 two and 4-door sedans put out strictly for fleet sales under the old Custom 300 designation. These latter cars were ultra-stripped Fairlanes (if that were possible) and were built with 6-cylinder engines and standard transmissions only.

Of the fancy Fords, the Fairlane 500 series accounted for 244,275 sales, which included the best selling 4-door sedan. The top line Galaxie series had 289,268 sales, with the 4-door Town Sedan also being the most popular here. It had a run of 103,784.

In the final category, the Station Wagon series, production tallied 171,824, which was quite a drop from 1959. Accounting for only 27,136 units was the 2-door Ranch Wagon, which should have done much better since the 2-door Country Sedan had been dropped. Once more, the best selling wagon was the 6-passenger 4-door Country Sedan.

Sporting a set of non-standard wheels, but otherwise strictly stock, is this beautiful Thunderbird Convertible, owned by Clarence Engborg of Bodafors, Sweden. The all-white car has a red and white stock leather interior, which was $106 extra. One of 11,860 built this year, it had a base price of $4,222 and a weight of 3,897 pounds. Among its other options are a padded instrument panel and sun visors, the $83 fresh air heater, and a $113 radio. The $466 air conditioning unit was not necessary in Sweden.

New for both Ford and the industry was the manually operated sunroof, which could be ordered on any Thunderbird Hardtop for $212, factory installed. Because of the novelty of this unit, it is sometimes thought that the cars equipped with the sunroof were a separate model. In addition, this car wears the accessory aftermarket continental spare and rear bumper extension. A total of 2,536 sunroofs were installed, but it is not known how many continental kits were produced, as these were not Ford-supplied items. This year Thunderbirds sported six taillight lenses, three to each side nested in a bezel whose background was similar to the grid pattern of the grille. Also new for the year were the three groupings of three chromed bars on the trailing edge of the rear fenders.

Operation of the new Thunderbird sliding sunroof was relatively simple. One crank retracted the panel. Turn it the other way, and the panel went back in place. This model wears the panel console, which houses radio speakers, ash trays, and controls for the $466 air conditioner and the $102 power windows. A power-operated driver's seat would have cost another $92, while the leather interior shown here was an additional $106. Obviously, it did not take long to run a Thunderbird into the $6,000 range.

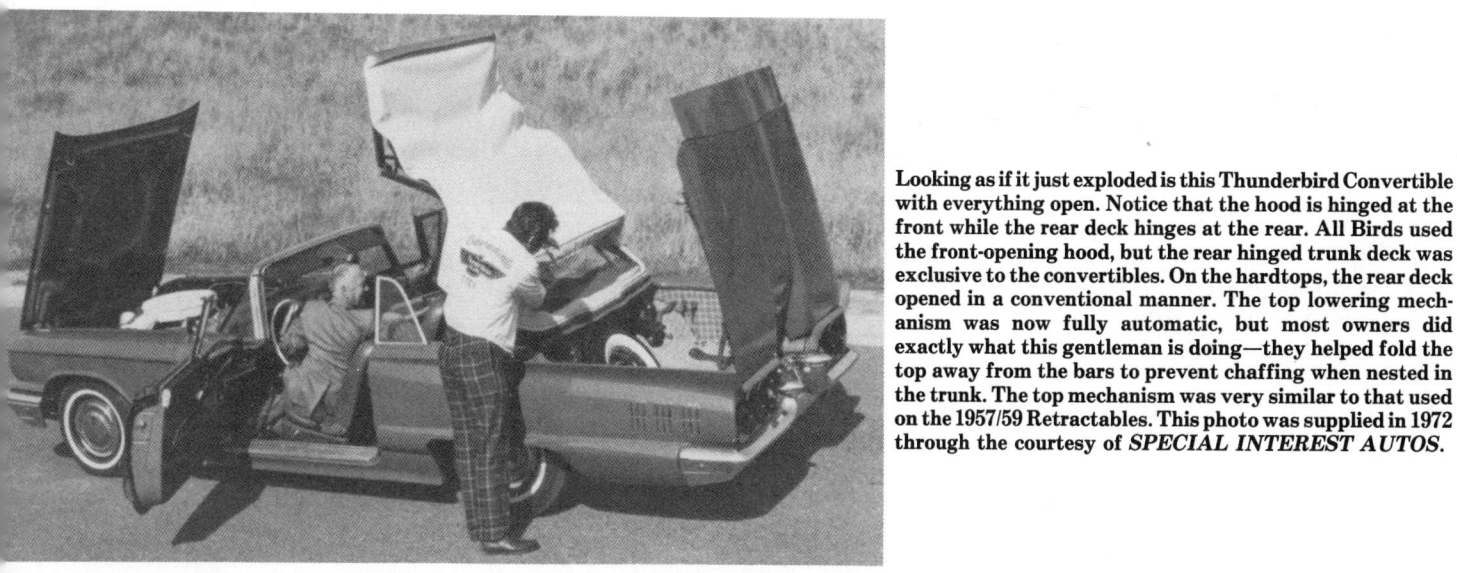

Looking as if it just exploded is this Thunderbird Convertible with everything open. Notice that the hood is hinged at the front while the rear deck hinges at the rear. All Birds used the front-opening hood, but the rear hinged trunk deck was exclusive to the convertibles. On the hardtops, the rear deck opened in a conventional manner. The top lowering mechanism was now fully automatic, but most owners did exactly what this gentleman is doing—they helped fold the top away from the bars to prevent chaffing when nested in the trunk. The top mechanism was very similar to that used on the 1957/59 Retractables. This photo was supplied in 1972 through the courtesy of *SPECIAL INTEREST AUTOS*.

Sure it looks like a Thunderbird, but should it be called an Allegheny? Actually, this car is one of two built almost exclusively of stainless steel by Allegheny Ludlum Corp. of Pennsylvania. The bodies were specially pressed of satin finish stainless sheets, while the bright parts and grille were pressed of a bright finish stainless metal. In addition to the exterior panels and trim parts, more than 300 other stainless components were manufactured especially for these two vehicles. The cars complimented the six stainless steel Fords built by Allegheny Ludlum in 1936. Both models were unveiled on July 11, 1960, not too far from the cut-off date for the last of the Square Birds.

While several other manufacturers designed upright fins on their cars, Ford went the other way, and had fins on a horizontal plane. The chrome edged fender extensions blended nicely with the trunk deck, providing a flat and uncluttered rear. Once again, Ford got away from round taillights, and used two arched lenses on the extreme ends of a full-width chromed panel which housed both the twin back-up lights and the gas filler door. This trim appeared on the Galaxie models only. Fairlanes had the same layout, but without the bright insert. Both the Sunliner Convertible shown here and the Starliner 2-door Hardtop were considered to comprise the Galaxie Special sub-series of the top line Galaxie series. Designated Style 55, the Sunliner cost $2,973 and weighed 3,841 pounds. Production totalled a nice 44,762. The convertible did not wear the Galaxie signature, but instead had "Sunliner" plaques for identity.

One hopes that the driver of this aquatic Starliner is not playing in salt water. Sadly, the 1960 Fords rusted quickly enough without the added assistance of a salt water bath. This view gives a good look at the exclusive hardtop used on the Starliner. To carry through with the name, three chrome and gold star-shaped emblems were located on the curving rear pillar, between the twin stainless steel top molding pieces. The rear bumpers on the 1960 Fords have always fascinated the author. The embossed recesses just below the arched taillights would indicate that originally this space had been considered for exhaust ports, back-up lights, or even additional taillights, yet apparently nothing was ever designed to fit into these spaces.

This is the attractive Starliner, the other model in the 2-style Galaxie Special sub-series. With the demise of the Skyliner Retractable Hardtop, the former Club Victoria model was given a status boost and elevated to the sporty top of the line position. With a suitable name change to Starliner, and an exclusive hardtop roof line, the car drew 68,641 orders. Designated Style 53, it sold for $2,723 and weighed 3,667 pounds. A 2-tone paint option was available but not often seen on 1960 Fords.

With the Starliner being the only 2-door hardtop in Ford's line, the plain Galaxie series had to contend with the pillared Club Sedan, Style 51, as its only 2-door model. The top on this car, in addition to having a solid B-pillar, also uses a much larger C-pillar panel than found on the Starliner. As with all Galaxie models, the car wears large ribbed stainless steel stone guards on its rear quarters, and matches this design in the space sandwiched between the trunk deck and rear bumper. The Club Sedan cost $2,662 and weighed 3,653 pounds. The least popular of all Galaxie models, it had sales of only 31,866.

Although the sporty 2-door hardtop was given the name Starliner and placed in the unique Galaxie Special sub-series, the equally sporty 4-door hardtop retained its old Town Victoria title and remained in the plain Galaxie series. This nice looking model, like the Starliner, was an exclusive design, and did not appear in any of the lesser series. Designated Style 54, it attracted 40,215 orders with its $2,901 price tag. It weighed 3,853 pounds and thus was the heaviest of all non-wagon Fords. A design carry-over was the small triangular trim piece at the rear door edge, which blended with the trim piece on the rear top panel. These pieces, in addition to being decorative, helped to brace the rear windows when they were in the raised position. The pushbutton radio on this model cost $59 extra.

The most popular car in the entire Galaxie series, and the only one to exceed 100,000 sales was the 4-door Town Sedan, Style 52. The pillared sedan looked quite similar to its hardtop counterpart, but had fully framed door windows and a solid B-pillar. Its attractiveness was attested to by its 103,784 sales. In base V-8 form it cost $2,716 and weighed 3,734 pounds. All Galaxie models wore the series script on the front fenders ahead of the wheel wells and again on the trunk deck. All also had a bright metal spear molding extending forward from the fluted stone guard or accent panel on the trailing ends of the rear fenders.

Ford's most popular full-size car was the Fairlane 500 4-door Town Sedan, Style 42. It accounted for 153,234 sales, all with a base V-8 price of $2,501 and a weight of 3,710 pounds. Note that the Fairlane 500 sedan carried its signature on the trailing edge of the rear quarter. This series did not use the fluted stone guards, side trim, nor rear trim plate found on the Galaxie models. According to some sources, the Fairlane 500 signature was located at the front and five "delta wing" bars were located on the rear quarter, as on the 2-door sedan. The name "Fairlane" also appeared in block letters on the trunk lid, while the "500" identity decorated the gas filler door.

Apparently the only Ford to wear a set of five "delta wing" ornaments on the rear fenders was the Fairlane 500 2-door Club Sedan, Style 41. Some references indicate that the Fairlane 500 4-door Sedans were also equipped with these wings, but no photographic evidence supports this. When the Fairlane 500 series was downgraded this year to the mid-range level, its available models were reduced to just the 2-door and 4-door pillared sedans, with the former hardtop styles being dropped. Still, the series was a popular one, accounting for 244,275 sales. Of these, 91,041 were the Club Sedan. It was base priced at $2,447 and weighed 3,636 pounds.

Ford still felt there was an adequate market for its 3-passenger Business Coupe, Style 33, and thus kept the car on the market. Outwardly it looked identical to the Fairlane 2-door Sedan, except that the rear passenger compartment contained no seat, but instead was fitted for carrying parcels, salesmen's samples, etc. As part of the low price Fairlane line, the car carried no series identification at all. Both hood and rear deck carried only the word "FORD" in block letters. Priced at $2,283 and weighing 3,605 pounds with the V-8, the car drew only 1,733 orders, and thus qualifies as the most rare (but probably least desirable) of all 1960 Fords.

With the Custom 300 series relegated to "fleet sales only" status, the plain Fairlane series became Ford's low-buck line. Besides the 2-door Business Coupe variation, it contained the same two models as did the Fairlane 500 series. These were the 4-door Town Sedan, Style 32, and the 2-door Club Sedan, Style 31, shown here. The 4-door was one of only three full-size models to exceed the 100,000 sales mark this year. Its production peaked at 110,373. With the Six, which was more popular in this series, the car was priced at $2,311 and weighed 3,605 pounds. The car illustrated, the Club Sedan, was more popular in plain form than in its Fairlane 500 guise. As a plain Fairlane, it drew 93,561 orders. It had a V-8 base price of $2,370, and weighed 3,632 pounds.

Still on the books but no longer available to the general public was the Custom 300 series. Now relegated to fleet sales only, the series consisted of two models, the 2-door Club Sedan shown here and the 4-door Town Sedan. In outward appearance they were identical to the Fairlane models, but their major exception was that they could only be ordered with the 6-cylinder engine and the standard 3-speed transmission. The interiors were also of a slightly lower trim level than the plain Fairlane series. Seemingly hardly worth the effort of keeping a separate series, sales amounted to only 572 for the 4-door and 302 for the 2-door models. The Six turned out to be fairly popular in the low-level cars, and 297,400 Fords this year were turned loose with the small engine.

Actually considered part of Ford's commercial fleet, despite being totally based on the 2-door Ranch Wagon, was this year's Courier Sedan Delivery, Style 69. The car differed from its wagon counterpart in that it was fitted with a solid cargo floor, and had only a single driver's seat, although a passenger's front seat could be ordered. This year even the tailgate was the same as used on the wagons, and not the one-piece door that had been used when the vehicle resembled a true panel truck. Despite the fact that the same working features could be found with the more practical Ranch Wagon, the Courier still managed to draw 2,374 orders, at its $2,456 base price. However, with the differences between the Courier and the Ranch Wagon becoming less and less, the decision was made to drop this model at year-end.

Only the addition of full passenger seating made the 2-door Ranch Wagon different from the Courier Sedan Delivery. Designated Style 61, the car had a 6-cylinder price of $2,586, which was $130 more than the Courier. For this, buyers received two full-width seats, with the rear seat able to fold to provide almost the same cargo space as found in the Courier. Not the most popular of wagons, this model drew only 27,136 orders, most with the 6-cylinder engine and standard transmission. This was Ford's only full-size 2-door wagon this year.

No, they did not come without hubcaps. But for some reason, both photos of Ford's new Ranch Wagons are shown without and wheel coverings. They are parked near the docking area of the River Rouge plant. In 4-door form, known as Style 62, the Ranch Wagon proved to be more popular than the 2-door and consequently 43,872 were sold. Its V-8 price was $2,769, though most buyers probably opted for the Six at $113 less. In trim level, the Ranch Wagons were comparable to the Fairlane series. This angle shows the interesting curved "wrap-around" of the lift gate. All four door windows were operational, but the large rear quarter windows were stationary.

Ford's most popular wagons continued to be the Country Sedans, available as the 6-passenger Style 64 or the 9 passenger Style 66. Outwardly the two variations were the same, differing only in interior seating. The 6-passenger model was Ford's best selling wagon, drawing 59,302 orders. Priced at $2,865, it weighed 4,062 pounds. The 9-passenger variety was far less popular, drawing only 19,277 orders. It listed at $2,950 and weighed 4,108 pounds. In trim level, the Country Sedans were in the Galaxie range, even to the use of the rear quarter bright accent panels (stone guards) and side trim spear. All wagons except the Country Squire carried their signature on the rear quarter, just ahead of the wrap-around bumper tip.

As before, Ford's top of the line wagon was the Country Squire, decorated in its own exclusive imitation wood paneling. This year the mahogany center part resembled the caulked decking of a sailing ship. The light birch-like framing was fastened with functional chrome-headed carriage bolts. Built only in 9-passenger form, the Style 68 Country Squire had a base price of $3,080, and thus was the only Ford model to exceed the $3,000 mark. Weighing 4,122 pounds, it was also the heaviest model of the year. Sales leveled off at 22,237. Finally in this year, the "knee-knocker" dog-leg windshield design was eliminated on all Fords and a much more sensible curved windshield was installed.

Introduced to the public in early October, 1959, the Falcon line initially consisted of only two vehicles in one series. Besides the 2-door sedan there was this 4-door Sedan, Style 58A. Priced at $1,974 and weighing 2,317 pounds, it was only slightly less popular than the 2-door model, drawing 167,896 orders. Built on a wheelbase of 109.5 inches, it was 181.2 inches long overall. Power was from its own exclusive 90 horsepower engine, though early models had engines rated at 85 HP. The standard transmission was a 3-speed manual, but an exclusive redesigned Ford-O-Matic was available for $180 extra. Although a gray interior was standard, a blue, green, or gray nylon tweed interior could be ordered.

Appearing in January, but not really reaching the public until late February or early March was the new Falcon wagon line. It consisted of two models, this 2-door Style 59A, and a 4-door version. Priced at $2,225 and weighing 2,540 pounds, the 2-door model drew 27,552 orders. The wagons were almost eight inches longer than the Falcon cars, being 189 inches overall. Both versions were available only in 6-passenger form. The Falcon wagon marked the first time that Ford used a single-piece tailgate with a retractable rear window rather than a rear window framed in a lift gate.

Roaring onto the American automotive scene with an acceptance that even the most optimistic Ford officials found hard to believe, was the totally new Falcon. Designed to compete with Chevrolet's novel Corvair and Plymouth's more pragmatic Valiant, the nicely styled Falcon came in only two forms at first, a 2-door and a 4-door sedan. Lowest priced of all the compacts, the 2-door Sedan, Style 64A, drew an astounding 193,470 orders. As a result of this, it became Ford's best selling vehicle of the year. Its base price of $1,912 included a gray vinyl and nylon interior with dual armrests and sun visors. The small 6-cylinder engine and 2,282-pound weight provided up to 30 miles per gallon, a figure almost unheard of in this era.

More popular than the 2-door model was the 4-door Falcon Wagon, Style 71A. It drew 46,758 orders with its $2,287 base price. Both wagons suffered in sales because of their late introduction and subsequent production delays. However, both proved to be very popular styles, and this popularity carried over into the 1961 sales year. As with the 2-door versions, this model offered a folding rear seat with vinyl back that became part of the cargo floor.

1960

A cut-away drawing shows Falcon's new unit construction, which was similar to that being used on both the Lincoln and Thunderbird models. The floor pan, interior framing, and rear exterior sheet metal all formed one basic solid unit, braced by the roof and roof pillars. The front section was part of the overall unit, but consisted of more frame-like components in order to provide for the engine and front end mountings. Only the front fenders were bolt-on pieces. Ford reported that the front fenders and grille assembly were kept separate in order to keep down repair costs on relatively minor front end damage.

Ford began the year without a Ranchero model, that cute little half truck-half car vehicle originally inspired by the Australian Utes. But in January, after the Falcon wagons made their appearance, a new Ranchero was introduced. Based on the Falcon 2-door wagon, rather than on a full-size Ford, the Ranchero billed itself as "America's Lowest Priced Pickup." At that, it had a base cost of $1,882 and weighed 2,345 pounds. The public really went for the little hauler, and sales peaked at 21,027, which was far more than the full-size Ranchero had ever drawn. The cargo box measured six feet long and gave 31 cubic feet of load area. The payload was rated at 800 pounds, which gave a G.V.W. rating of 3,200 pounds.

Still very active in the professional car trade was the Shop of Siebert of Toledo, Ohio. As before, the company specialized in converting Ford vehicles into very well designed ambulances and hearses. This is the new ambulance offering, which incorporated a substantial stretch rearward from the B-pillar to the rear wheel well. It provided high headroom via a fiberglass pod which also acted as a base for the built-in warning and signal lights. The ambulance had 3-stretcher capacity, with one stretcher being uniquely suspended from the roof. A similar high-headroom pod was used on the Siebert Landau funeral car. A basic vehicle used in these conversions was the Country Sedan, while similar conversions were also made on Mercury chassis.

Automotive Conversions Corp. of Birmingham, Mich., was another company which happily converted Ford and Mercury station wagons into practical professional vehicles. However, unlike Siebert, Automotive Conversions did not extend the wheelbases or raise the roof lines. Instead, they worked within the confines of the stock wagon body. Marketed under the trade name "Amblewagon," the company came out with this attractive and low-price ambulance utilizing a very stock Country Sedan as its base. The interior may have been more cramped than in the stretched ambulances, but such vehicles found a ready market with small municipalities and ambulance corps that could not afford the more luxurious equipment.

Automotive Conversions Corp. also produced a landau hearse within the confines of the standard Country Sedan body. The company also came up with this interesting Combination Car, which could be quickly switched from hearse to ambulance and back again. On this model, the side panels with the large landau irons were quickly removable, and the interior velvet drapes detached easily. Naturally, the ambulance equipment was rather basic, but probably was sufficient for most calls of that time. On the true hearse versions, casket rollers were installed in the tailgate and the floor itself, while these rollers were deleted from the combination car models.

For the third time in as many years, Ford introduced a totally restyled car in its primary line. Haunted by buyer resistance to its 1960 style theme, it brought in a model line which was totally new from the beltline down, and which was four inches shorter and two inches wider than the previous series, even though its wheelbase remained 119 inches.

But despite the acceptance of the new Fords, the company's headline grabber for the year was the totally new Thunderbird. Although keeping the same basic dimensions as previous models (113-inch wheelbase and 205-inch overall length) the car was blessed by new "space ship" styling that bore no resemblance to anything ever issued from Ford or any other car maker.

All of the former angular lines were removed, and the front end now bore a rounded, almost torpedo shape, highlighted even more by the rounded but plain sides. These blended into tube-type rear quarters culminating in rocket-like taillights topped by small fins and complimented by four horizontal bars. The greenhouse was extended 10 inches, giving more interior room. Shoulder room was expanded by two inches and hip room by four. The same two models, a hardtop coupe and a convertible, were still offered. The convertible had a fully automatic top, which nested in the rear deck, and continued to have a rear hinged lid. Once again, the main problem was that when the convertible's top was down, there was no room for luggage.

On the mechanical side, the new Thunderbird featured a "swing-away" steering column for easy entrance. Since most buyers ordered all of the automatic features anyway, all T-Birds now came with automatic transmissions, power steering, and power brakes as standard equipment. Also, the line received a totally new family of engines, which will be discussed later.

Although the new Ford line was shorter, the car's interior dimensions remained the same. This was the result of using the same basic body structure as had been used in 1960, with the result being a totally new looking car with far less tooling expense than one might expect. Highlighting the front was a new and very attractive concave grille of anodized aluminum, with the quad headlights nicely nested at the outer extremes. Once again the taillights became large round affairs topped by small canted fins, in the same style concept as found on the new T-Birds. Both the hood and trunk deck were higher, allowing slightly more room in each compartment. Galaxie models continued to use large bright stone shields behind the rear wheel openings, while Fairlane models continued to use the same basic body but devoid of most frills. On the mechanical side, Ford touted its first use of self-adjusting brakes.

About the only car not changed was the Falcon, which set a multitude of sales records during its first year and wisely was left alone in its second go-round. The major change to the Falcon was, as expected, a new grille. This one was convex as opposed to the slightly concave grille of 1960. Also, sometime after the official Sept. 29 introduction date, a new model was added to the four regular Falcons. This was the Futura, which was simply a fancy version of the 2-door sedan, but fitted with a vinyl interior with bucket seats and central console, and sporting special hubcaps and decorative darts on the rear fenders.

In other Falcon news, the car now had an optional 170 cubic inch 6-cylinder engine, at about $40 extra. The block was the same as the year-old untouched 144 cubic inch Falcon mill, but had a stroke of 2.94 inches, compared to the old 2.5 inches. Both engines had a 3.5-inch bore and both had an 8.7:1 compression ratio. The new engine produced 101 horsepower at 4400 rpm, while the standard block was again downrated to its original 85 horses at 4200 rpm. A standard transmission was still used, but the 2-speed automatic remained available for $163 extra.

In other engine news, about as much activity occurred under the hoods as did to the exteriors of both Thunderbirds and Fords. As mentioned, the new Thunderbirds received a whole new family of 390 cubic inch engines, which replaced the now-discontinued 430 cubic inch Lincoln derivative and the 352 cubic inch Interceptor Specials. The new 390 line eventually would consist of four variations, all based on a re-engineered 352 block which had a bore and stroke of 4.05x3.78 inches. All would eventually be available in the Ford line also.

The standard Thunderbird engine used a 9.6:1 compression ratio, a Holley 4-barrel carburetor, and developed 300 horses at 4600 rpm. Also available was the Thunderbird Special, which was essentially the same as the standard Thunderbird engine, but with a 10.6:1 compression ratio. This engine was rated at 375 horsepower at 6000 rpm. Falling between these two models was the seldom seen Thunderbird Police Special. This engine used the same 9.6:1 compression as the standard Thunderbird, but was rated at 330 horsepower at 5000 rpm.

Finally, a mid-year offering, known as the 3-Carb Thunderbird Special took over the top horsepower bracket. This engine used the same 10.6:1 compression ratio as the other Special, but was fitted with three Holley 2-barrel carburetors. It could turn an amazing 401 horsepower at 6000 rpm, and marked the first time that a stock dealer-installed Ford engine topped the 400 horsepower mark. Arriving with this engine was Ford's first dealer installed 4-speed manual transmission, or Floor-4.

In the regular Ford line, both the 300 and the 360 horsepower Interceptor Specials were gone, but the plain 352 cubic inch Interceptor remained as an option in any model. However, this engine was reduced in horsepower to 220 at 4400 rpm. Likewise, the standard 292 cubic inch Ford V-8 also was given a horsepower reduction, going down to 175 at 4200 rpm, while the standard Six of 223 cubic inches was down-rated to 135 horses at 4000 rpm. Compression ratios remained the same as in 1960, with the Six being 8.4:1, the standard V-8 being 8.8:1, and the optional 352 being 8.9:1. In the price structure, the base V-8 cost $116 more than the Six; the Interceptor cost $148 more, and the 390 cubic inch Thunderbird engine cost an additional $197. Fordomatic listed at $190 on a V-8 or $180 on a Six, while Cruise-O-Matic, available only on the V-8, was an additional $212.

Within the Ford line, all series remained basically the same, although the former 2-model Galaxie Special sub-series was dropped and its convertible and sleek hardtop became part of the regular Galaxie series. In the plain Fairlane line, the never-popular Business Coupe was dropped, thus reducing that series to the same two models found in the Fairlane 500 series.

Also in the low-buck models, it appears that 303 4-door sedans and 49 2-door sedans were produced in ultra-stripped form. Although they bore no official designations other than "Ford," some information would indicate that these special-order fleet-only vehicles were listed as part of the old and unused Custom or Custom 300 series. On the other end of the price scale, the Station Wagon series gained one more model as the 6-passenger Country Squire was finally offered. Prior to this, Country Squires had been available in 9-passenger form only. The move brought to six the number of different wagon models offered.

Overall, 1961 was not as good a year as 1960, with only 1,339,043 model year sales, as opposed to 1960's tally of 1,439,553. Oddly, only one big Ford broke the 100,000 mark. That was the Galaxie 4-door Town Sedan, with 141,823 orders. The only other two models in this league were both Falcons. The 4-door Sedan with 159,761 sales was Ford's most popular model, while its 2-door counterpart came in second with 149,982 sales.

In the odd neitherland of car/truck things, the Falcon based Ranchero Pickup this year was joined by the Courier Sedan Delivery. Once again based on the 2-door station wagon shell, the little truck again looked like a true delivery truck, with blank sides, rather than having the station wagon appearance of the 1960 model. In another move, more akin to the truck field, Ford introduced its series of Econoline vehicles. These forward controlled "pie wagons" were heavily based on Falcon components, but were considered part of Ford's commercial vehicle line. They came in pickup and van forms, and in the passenger carrying category, appeared as an 8-passenger Station Bus accompanied by an 8-passenger School Bus variation. Since this series has been well covered in James K. Wagner's *FORD TRUCKS SINCE 1905*, published by Crestline/Motorbooks International, it will only be touched on lightly here.

Ford's headline grabber was the totally new Thunderbird, which in its third styling generation, exhibited its sleekest lines ever. Often described as coming from the rocket ship school of design, the car looked much longer and lower than the previous model. However, its dimensions remained basically the same, with its length still being 205 inches and its wheelbase being 113 inches. The only drawback to the new styling was the trimless sides, which were very prone to parking lot dings. Exemplifying all that was beautiful in these cars was the Convertible, Style 73. At $4,637, it was the most expensive Ford. Far less popular than the hardtop version, the Convertible drew only 10,516 orders. At 4,130 pounds, it was also the heaviest car to bear the Ford name.

Taking the automotive spotlight this year was the new Thunderbird Hardtop Coupe, Style 71. However, despite rave reviews throughout the automotive press, buyers were a bit wary of the new design, and only 62,535 units were sold. This was a 20,000 drop from the 1960 Square Bird. Since Ford saw that almost all T-Bird buyers wanted the car fully equipped, this year's base price of $4,170 included Cruise-O-Matic transmission, and power steering and brakes, plus the new 390 cubic inch Thunderbird engine. All of this pushed the base weight up to 3,958 pounds.

Top honors were accorded the new Thunderbird when it was selected to pace the Indianapolis 500 race on May 30, 1961. The honors were heightened to a degree by the fact that this was the 50th or Golden Anniversary race, and as such, seemed to draw even more attention than ever. In honor of the anniversary, the official Thunderbird pace car was painted gold. Notice how sleek the convertible appears with the top lowered. This is due to the fact that the top disappeared completely into the trunk space, allowing the rear deck to run right up to the rear seat back. The drawback to this design is that when the top was down, there was no space left in the trunk for luggage.

Many people, including the author, feel that the new Thunderbird was even more beautiful from the back than from the front. Among the styling highlights were the nicely rounded rear quarters, which culminated in large jet-like round taillights with attractive bezels blending into the massive rear bumper. The rear quarters were topped by small canted fins, which complimented the design without overpowering. Rear wheel skirts were standard, as were the four arrow-like trim bars. On the hardtop, the trunk deck was hinged in a conventional manner, and the trunk offered a fair amount of luggage space. On the convertible, the trunk deck continued to be hinged at the trailing edge, and opened from the front to swallow the top. When the top was lowered, luggage space on this model was virtually non-existent.

Posed alongside the fountain wall at the famed Kapock Tree Restaurant in Clearwater, Florida, is the new Galaxie Convertible, Style 55. Still bearing the name "Sunliner" on the front fenders, the model was no longer in its own sub-series, but was considered part of the total Galaxie series. Still holding its popularity, it drew 44,614 orders, which was almost identical to the 1960 sales. In V-8 form it cost $2,963 and weighed 3,792 pounds, thus being both the most expensive and heaviest of all Ford cars, not counting the wagon models.

Still fitted with its own exclusive top design was the sporty Ford Starliner Coupe. Although the car bore the name "Starliner" on its front fenders, it followed the Sunliner in now being part of the Galaxie series, and was no longer in a special sub-series. Not a particularly popular model, the Starliner drew only 29,669 orders this year. As a result, the sleek hardtop styling would not reappear as a 1962 model. Priced at $2,713, it shared the same dollar figure with the new and much more popular 2-door Victoria. Designated Style 53, the Starliner weighed 3,615 pounds. Among its exclusive styling features were heavy chromed rain gutters and three star-like emblems on the curving rear pillar.

New for the year and stealing a great many sales from the Starliner was the Galaxie Club Victoria. The car used the same squared-off Thunderbird-type top treatment as did the Club Sedan, but was built in hardtop style, with no upper B-pillar. It could also be differentiated from the plain Club Sedan by its heavier chrome trim on the rear top panel, and a bright aluminum rain guard running from the windshield to the rear window trim. Designated Style 57, the Club Victoria bore the same $2,713 price tag as did the Starliner. It was slightly heavier, coming in at 3,643 pounds. In popularity, it was way out in front, with 75,437 being sold. Notice the attractive rear treatment of all 1961 Galaxies, with a duplication of the grille pattern filling the space between the large round taillights. Attractive canted fins were topped by a chromed runner, while a large bright aluminum gravel shield occupied the trailing edge of the rear quarter, blending into the heavy side spear.

The 4-door beauty in the Galaxie series continued to be the Town Victoria, Style 54. Exclusive only to the Galaxie series, this model did not appear in the lesser Fairlane range. Of true hardtop style, it was quickly identified by the triangular wedges on the rear doors, and by the exclusive squared-off roofline with heavy rear panels. Far less popular than its pillared Town Sedan counterpart, the Victoria drew only 30,342 orders at $2,778 in base form. It weighed 3,686 pounds. Air conditioning was becoming a popular accessory on Galaxie models. Polar Air was available for $271, while the more sophisticated Select-Air cost $436. Both units were factory installed and both included tinted glass in all windows.

Strangely, in the 2-door field, the most popular model was the hardtop while in the 4-door range, the pillared model was the most popular. Thus, the pillared Galaxie Club Sedan, Style 51, drew only 27,270 orders. Base priced at $2,652, it was the least expensive Galaxie. It weighed 3,586 pounds. Power steering would add another $82 to this cost, while power brakes were $43 extra. The 3-speed Cruise-O-Matic automatic transmission of $212 was also a popular option.

Despite the fact that it was Ford's most popular model, no decent photos of the Galaxie Town Sedan could be found. With sales hitting 141,823, this was not only Ford's most popular car, but also the only full-size Ford to have sales above the 100,000 mark. Designated Style 52, it was priced at $2,706 and weighed 3,668 pounds with the basic 292 cubic inch V-8. The basic V-8 raised the price $116 above the 223 cubic inch Six, which was still considered the standard engine, though very few Galaxie models left the factory so equipped. Despite the fact that the cars looked totally different from the 1960 models, the basic body structure remained the same, and the upper portions (greenhouse) were identical to 1960 models.

Ford's intermediate series continued to be the Fairlane 500, appearing in full-size form for the last time this year. Beginning with the 1962 models, the Fairlanes would become an intermediate size car. Nicest looking of the lot was the Fairlane 500 Club Sedan, Style 41. It sold for $2,492 and weighed an even 3,600 pounds with the small V-8. Production of this model slipped drastically, and only 42,468 were built. Its rear roofline and rear window treatment differed substantially from that of the Galaxie models, but from the beltline downward, the basic bodies were identical. Fairlane 500 models used the chrome side and fin trim of the Galaxies, but were not fitted with the aluminum stone guards on the rear quarters.

In the 2-model Fairlane 500 series, the 4-door Town Sedan sold more than twice as well as the 2-door, with 98,197 sales recorded. But this was still 54,000 less than recorded in 1960. Known as Style 42, the car in base V-8 form sold for $2,546 and weighed 3,691 pounds. Like all full-size Fords, the car had a 119-inch wheelbase, used the same frame as in 1960, but was four inches shorter in length, ending up at just shy of 210 inches overall. Ford's full-width concave grille was made of anodized aluminum with a heavy chromed horizontal center bar. The parking lights were located in the lower bumper tips, where they were prone to easy damage.

The plain Fairlane series continued to be Ford's lowest price full-size line. However, this year the series was down to the same two models as found in the Fairlane 500 series. Its former third model, the Business Coupe, had been dropped for lack of sales. Fairlanes lacked the full-length side trim of the other series, but did have a short piece of stainless brightwork running full-length on the front fenders, above the wheel well. Unlike the Fairlane 500 models, which carried their series signature on the front fenders just behind the headlight bezel, the Fairlanes used no series identification. Most popular of all Fairlanes was the 2-door Club Sedan, Style 31, which drew 97,208 orders. It weighed 2,685 pounds with the small V-8, though many of these cars were turned out with 6-cylinder engines. The 2-tone paint on this model was $22 extra.

Although the 4-door sedan was by far the most popular car in both the Fairlane 500 and Galaxie series, in the 2-model Fairlane series the roles were reversed. Here the Town Sedan, Style 32, took second place to the Club Sedan, with production reaching only 66,924. Priced at $2,431 and weighing 3,585 pounds as a base V-8, it too saw much of its production equipped with 6-cylinder blocks. In addition to exterior differences, the Fairlanes also had a less costly interior material, and were fitted with a horn button rather than a horn ring.

Shown in U.S. Army uniform is this 4-door sedan, which may still be classed as a Custom or Custom 300 model, even though that series designation had not been officially used since 1959. However, records indicate that Ford turned out 49 Club Sedans and 303 of the 4-door Town Sedans in ultra-stripped form, and classed these beneath the Fairlane series. Some sources would indicate that the Custom or Custom 300 series designation was continued exclusively for these fleet-only vehicles. Besides the military, it appears that a few of these spartan models found their way into taxi and municipal fleets. Judging by the limited production, today these would be very rare vehicles, though not very desirable ones.

For the first time, the wood-trimmed Country Squire was available in two different variations. Buyers had a choice of six or 9-passenger configurations, whereas formerly the Squire was strictly a 9-passenger vehicle. Surprisingly, the interior configuration was not simply considered plus-or-minus an additional seat. Instead, each was considered a separate style, thereby bringing to six the available models in the Station Wagon series. In 9-passenger form, the car was Style 68, with a list price of $3,127 and a V-8 weight of 4,064 pounds. In 6-passenger form, the Squire was Style 67, with a base V-8 price of $3,057 and a weight of 4,036 pounds. Industry-wide, a swing was being made to shorter and more streamlined wagons, with rear-facing third seats. Yet, because the previous base structure was still being used, both Ford and Mercury 9-passenger wagons continued to have forward-facing third seats. The new 6-passenger Squire claimed 16,961 sales, while the 9-passenger drew only 14,657.

Comparable to the Galaxie series in trim level was the Country Sedan, Ford's intermediate line of wagons. As before, the Country Sedans were available in six or 9-passenger form, with each variation being considered a distinct model within the Station Wagon series. In 9-passenger form, the Country Sedan was the Style 66. As such, it cost $2,972 and weighed 4,060 pounds. In 6-passenger form it was the Style 64, which sold for $2,868 and weighed 4,032 pounds. As with the Squire, the Country Sedan's 6-passenger model was the most popular, with 46,311 orders as opposed to 16,356 for the 9-passenger model.

With its trim level falling somewhere between the Fairlane 500 and the plain Fairlane series, the 4-door Ranch Wagon, Style 62, still proved to be popular model, with 30,292 being sold. Available in 6-passenger form only, it sold for $2,772 and weighed 4,009 pounds with the base V-8. Side trim on this model was similar to that of the plain Fairlane series, and consisted only of a stainless bar on the front fender. Also, even though the more expensive models bore the signature of "Country Squire," or "Country Sedan," the Ranch Wagons had no identification other than the Ford block letters.

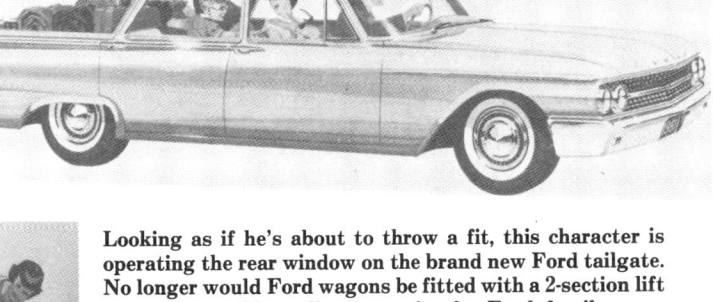

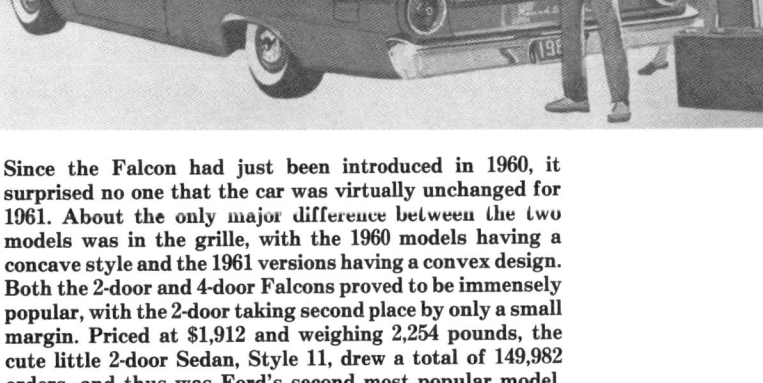

Looking as if he's about to throw a fit, this character is operating the rear window on the brand new Ford tailgate. No longer would Ford wagons be fitted with a 2-section lift and tailgate. Now all wagons in the Ford family were equipped with single unit gates, with roll-up rear windows operable from a locked exterior regulator. In order to lower the tailgate, the rear window had to be cranked all the way down, or the gate would not release. The car shown here is Ford's least expensive wagon, the 2-door Ranch Wagon, Style 61. Available only in 6-passenger form, it cost $2,702 and weighed 3,914 pounds as a V-8. On all Ford wagons, the rear seats could be folded flat to form a continuous cargo floor. Ford's lowest production wagon, the 2-door Ranch drew only 12,042 orders.

Since the Falcon had just been introduced in 1960, it surprised no one that the car was virtually unchanged for 1961. About the only major difference between the two models was in the grille, with the 1960 models having a concave style and the 1961 versions having a convex design. Both the 2-door and 4-door Falcons proved to be immensely popular, with the 2-door taking second place by only a small margin. Priced at $1,912 and weighing 2,254 pounds, the cute little 2-door Sedan, Style 11, drew a total of 149,982 orders, and thus was Ford's second most popular model. But at mid-year, the Falcon Futura was introduced. Designated Style 17 and priced at $2,160, the Futura was really the 2-door sedan fitted with bucket seats and a central console, and wearing different side medallions, three small darts on the rear fenders, and fancy hub caps. The move to sportiness was enough to attract 44,470 customers, and when this total is added to the overall sales of the 2-door, then the model easily becomes Ford's most popular style of the year.

Ford's most popular single style was the Falcon 4-door Sedan, Style 12. It had a run of 159,761. Available only in one series for the last time this year—in 1962 there would be Standard and Deluxe Falcons—the sedan cost $1,974 and weighed 2,289 pounds. For those who wanted something a bit better, there was a Deluxe interior trim package for $78, and the new 170 cubic inch 6-cylinder engine for $37. Also, the 2-speed Fordomatic transmission could be purchased for an extra $163. The Deluxe wheel covers shown here cost another $16 a set.

Most popular of the two Falcon wagons was the 4-door variation, Style 22. It had sales of 87,933, was priced at $2,268 and weighed 2,558 pounds. This particular version is wearing the optional side trim package, which consisted of the special wheel covers and a double strip of stainless steel side molding which encircled the embossed side panels of the entire car. It also sports the $54 manual radio, and probably has the $73 heater/defroster unit. Air conditioning was not available factory direct, but many dealers could install aftermarket units. However, an owner would certainly have wanted to new 101 horsepower Six if he decided to go that route. As in other wagons, the Falcon's rear seat could be folded down to make a flat cargo floor.

The lowest priced and least popular of the two Falcon wagons was the 2-door model, Style 21. It sold for $2,225 and with only 32,045 sales, was the least popular of all Falcons. These little wagons had led the entire Ford wagon line in the introduction of the one-piece tailgate with its retractable rear window, gaining this design with their inception in 1960. Although most units came with the manually operated rear window, an electric control was available for $30. This allowed the driver to raise or lower the window without leaving his seat.

Since it was totally based on the Falcon car line, the new Ranchero pickup changed very little except for the new grille. A handy small truck, it had a cargo bed of 31.5 cubic feet, with a 42-inch long cargo floor and a swing-down tailgate. Interiors were all the same, with a brown vinyl seat with beige vinyl facings. The spare tire was carried behind the seat back. Its payload was considered to be 800 pounds. Priced at $1,887 and weighing 2,338 pounds, the cute little truck attracted 20,937 buyers. Options included the 101 horsepower Six and Fordomatic automatic transmission.

Totally new on Ford's scene was the new line of mini-trucks called Econolines. The initial family, as shown here, consisted of a Pickup, Panel Delivery (often called a pie wagon), and a Station Wagon. All were based on Falcon components, and in fact, early models were often referred to as Falcon trucks rather than Econolines. Since these vehicles have been well covered in Crestline/Motorbook's *FORD TRUCKS SINCE 1905*—by James K. Wagner, only the passenger versions will be included in this book. Suffice to say, the popular little van versions became quite popular very quickly, while the pickup and bus versions followed along as expected.

Once again Ford's Sedan Delivery became a true panel truck rather than a variation of the station wagon. But this year, like the Ranchero, the Sedan Delivery came out as a Falcon. Using the 2-door station wagon as a body structural base, the Sedan Delivery had blanked sides and a true truck-type cargo area complete with linoleum covered plywood floor. Its only concession to its wagon heritage was the fact that it used the same one-piece tailgate with retractable window as did the wagons. There was no provision for a side-opening rear door. Priced at $2,109 and weighing 2,463 pounds, the Sedan Delivery drew only 1,988 orders. As was the Ranchero's, its load capacity was rated at 800 pounds.

To make sure there was no confusion between the Falcon station wagons and the new Econoline passenger carriers, the Econolines were called Station Buses. The stubbiness of the little 90-inch wheelbase vehicle car be seen here. Still, it offered full 9-passenger capacity, and aftermarket companies quickly started converting examples into mini-campers. The front compartment had a door on each side, but access to the rear compartment was via two swinging doors on the left side only. Double swinging doors were also fitted at the rear. Priced at $2,092, the Station Bus drew 15,082 buyers this year. Power was only by the 85 horse Six. The new 101 horsepower Falcon Six was not available in this vehicle, nor was an automatic transmission included as an option.

The Shop of Siebert also based a high-headroom ambulance, known as the Aristocrat 1045, on the new Ford Country Sedan. Below the roofline, the vehicle was reworked in the same method as was the Combination Car. But above the drip rail, the original roof was replaced with a molded fiberglass pod which not only provided needed inches of headroom on the inside, but also gave nesting places to the various emergency and signal lights. As with the Combination Car, the rear section was widened to allow for a larger right-hinged access door. Ambulances of this type could carry a wide range of emergency medical supplies and were usually equipped with hot and cold running water, air conditioning, and other service-type units.

It didn't take Ford fans long to realize the potential of the new 401 horsepower 3-carburetor Thunderbird engine. Especially appealing to the hot rod and race set was the fact that the new engine set-up need not be factory installed, but could be built right at dealer level, using the 375 horse Thunderbird Special as the starting point. Here a New York based Starliner, running as a B Gas contender, prepares to leave the line. First appearing in February, 1961, the new 401-horse conversions quickly provided headaches for owners of 409 Chevrolets. Surprisingly, however, neither the new Ford nor Chevrolet engines did that good on the 1961 NASCAR circuit. There the field was being dominated by Pontiacs and Dodges. Yet on drag strips across the country, the 3-carb Ford set-up was the car to try to beat.

When the new Fords came out, the Shop of Siebert of Toledo, Ohio, quickly designed their funeral car and ambulance conversions to fit the new sheet metal. The result was a very attractive professional car. Shown here is the Combination Car, designed for small town operations, where the ambulance could be quickly converted to funeral duties, and just as quickly be returned to an ambulance. Based on the Country Sedan, these units were extended behind the C-pillar, leaving all four doors intact. However, in order to accommodate a larger side-opening rear door, the aft section had to be widened. This resulted in the rear quarters being equipped with pods ahead of the rear wheels to fill in for the slightly wider rear area. The trim level was on par with the Country Sedan, and included the attractive ribbed aluminum stone guards on the rear fenders.

Running for a record time on the salt flats at Bonneville, Utah, was this Galaxie Club Victoria, wearing oversized mag wheels and having the new 3-carb set-up under the hood. The car reportedly reached 155.85 MPH, but failed to set any records. The 3-carb set-up, with its special aluminum manifold was essentially a bolt-on item, even though Ford considered it a separate engine. The unit could also be installed on the older 332 and 352 cubic inch engines, but when this was done, all racing rules required that the cars run in the modified classes. If the 3-carbs were to be considered stock, they had to be used on the 1961 block of 360 cubic inches only.

The story was almost getting old. For the fourth time in as many years, the primary Ford line went through a total restyling. In addition, a brand new line of intermediate size cars was born, two new big blocks appeared on the performance stage, the Galaxie Series enjoyed the re-addition of a special sport sub-series, and two new Thunderbird models were hatched.

Probably drawing the greatest interest was the new intermediate size line, bearing the Fairlane signature. Not making its bow until almost 45 days after the rest of the line—coming out on Nov. 16—the new Fairlane models left no doubt as to their parentage. Styling was definitely Ford, though hinting more at the 1961 models than at the new Galaxies. Built on an exclusive wheelbase of 115.5 inches, the Fairlanes came in two styles, a 2-door and a 4-door sedan, and in two series, the plain Fairlane and the Fairlane 500. The 500 series also had a 2-door Sport Coupe model, based on the 2-door Sedan.

Not only did the Fairlanes have their own exclusive chassis and bodies, they also were provided with a brand new 221 cubic inch thin-wall V-8 which developed 145 horsepower at 4400 rpm. It had a bore and stroke of 3.62x2.87 inches and a compression ratio of 8.7:1. The new small block weighed a little over 400 pounds complete, and was the lightest of all small block V-8s on the market, despite the fact that it used cast iron, not aluminum castings. Also available in the Fairlanes as a standard basic block was the 170 cubic inch Six of 101 horses. This engine also was available as an option in the Falcon line, and was unchanged from its 1961 Falcon option role.

The Fairlanes were expected to fill the gap between the economy sized Falcons and the big-car Galaxie series. Whereas the former Fairlanes had simply relied on lack of trim to keep the price down, but used full-size models as their base, the new line created a class which totally fit between the big and small cars in both price and size—a true intermediate.

The big car line retained the Galaxie name, but now expanded into three sub-series, based on price and trim level. All used the brand new big Ford body with its slab sides, smooth hood and deck styling, four eyes, and the traditional round taillights and bright escutcheon plate. Lowest priced of the big cars were the two plain Galaxie models, a 2-door and a 4-door sedan. Containing all of the available models was the Galaxie 500 sub-series, which consisted of hardtop and pillared coupes and sedans and the convertible. Once again a return was made to a sport-type series, with the creation of the Galaxie 500 XL models. This sub-series consisted solely of the Sunliner Convertible and the Club Victoria. The XL models used distinctive emblems. had bucket seats and a floor-mounted shifter in a central console. All Galaxies were available with V-8 power or the unchanged 223 cubic inch Six, except that the Six was not available in either the 500 Convertible or in either of the two XL models.

Interestingly, the Galaxies lost one model when the Starliner Hardtop was discontinued. With sales low, Ford felt that the sleek-roofed Starliner was not worth continuing, and thus the more formal roofed Club Victoria became Ford's only big 2-door hardtop style.

As could be expected, Galaxies retained their 119-inch wheelbase chassis, but dropped one-half inch in overall length to 209.3 inches. In comparison, the new Fairlanes were 197.6 inches overall, while the Falcons remained 181 inches for the cars and 189 for the wagons.

In line with previous Ford construction, the full-size wagons continued to use a variation of the big car styling. However, this year for the first time since 1954, there was no 2-door station wagon. Wagon sub-series were the 4-door Ranch Wagon, available only as a 6-passenger model, which used a trim level comparable to the basic Galaxie, and the six and 9-passenger Country Sedans and wood-trimmed Country Squires, which used a Galaxie 500 form of trim.

In the land of little cars, the Falcon family now divided itself into two series, the Standard and the Deluxe. The Standard consisted of a two and 4-door pillared sedan, and a two and 4-door station wagon. The Deluxe series contained the same four models, but in addition had a Country Squire style wagon with imitation wood trim, and also continued to house the Futura Sport Coupe. Essentially, the Deluxe series now provided the trim level that had formerly been available in the optional deluxe appearance package of 1960-61. Only now it was an official series, and not an accessory book order.

Once again, the entire Falcon line remained basically unchanged. New for dating purposes were the grille, again a convex unit, but now of plain vertical bar design, and the rear trim and emblem design. The Futura Coupe now had its own distinctive roof, similar in design to that of the Galaxie hardtops. Again, only 6-cylinder power was available in the Falcon line, with the 144 cubic inch block being standard and the 170 cubic inch model being an added cost option of $38 extra charge. Both engines were unchanged from 1961.

In the Thunderbird nest, things were getting crowded, with two new Birds hatching this year. They were the Landau Hardtop, which was essentially the hardtop T-Bird fitted with a vinyl roof and a few extra luxury items, and the Sports Roadster. Not really a true roadster, since it had very weather-tight roll-up windows, the Sports Roadster nevertheless was a beautiful albeit very expensive personal car. Essentially, it was the convertible fitted with a removable fiberglass tonneau cover, with molded headrests, which fit over the rear seat portion and made the car into a super-sleek 2-passenger model. Adding to the overall appeal were Kelsey-Hayes chromed wire wheels with knock-off spinner hubcaps, and special rear fenders which would not accept the normal fender skirts. These skirts were omitted on the Roadster in order to give the wire wheels as much exposure as possible. Not a bargain basement model, the new

Roadster marked the first time that a T-Bird broke the $5,000 base price.

With the exception of the new models, only minor changes were made to the year-old third generation Thunderbird. Quickly identifying the car as a 1962 model were the new grille and the new side trim, the latter this year consisting of three sets of horizontal bars on the rear fender pod, as opposed to the single flag of such bars on the previous models.

Under the hoods, there was also some activity. The 6-cylinder blocks, described earlier, provided the base power in their respective vehicles, while the afore mentioned 221 V-8 was as totally new as was the Fairlane in which it resided. The basic V-8 in the full-size line remained the 292 cubic inch model, but once again its horsepower was reduced, now being rated at 170 at 4200 rpm. This engine listed at $109 over the base Six.

Remaining unchanged was the optional 352 cubic inch block of 220 horses, called the Interceptor, and the 390 cubic inch block of 300 horses. However, this latter engine bore a new name of "Interceptor 390." These options cost $160 and $246 respectively over the base price. Also available, but supposedly for police use only was the 390 which developed 330 horses at 5000 rpm.

Also starting the rear were two Thunderbird 390s. These were the 4-barrel carburetor unit which developed 375 horses at 6000 rpm, and the year-old special which used three 2-barrel carburetors and developed 401 horses at 6000 rpm. However, at mid-year both of these engines were dropped with the introduction of the new big block 406 cubic inch mill. This engine ran a bore and stroke of 4.13x3.78 inches. Not just a rebored 390, the 406 engine had its own exclusive thick-walled block. The engine came in two versions, a 4-barrel model which developed 385 horses at 5800 rpm using an 11.4:1 compression ratio, and a triple 2-barrel "Special" unit which developed 405 horses at 5800 rpm, with an 11.3:1 compression ratio. Prices for these engine options were $430 for the 4-barrel unit and $488 for the 3-carb model.

Both engines bore the Thunderbird name, but oddly, neither was available in the Thunderbird car. There the top engine was a new mid-year 390 which developed 340 horsepower at 5000 rpm. This Thunderbird exclusive used triple 2-barrel carbs and had a 10.5:1 compression ratio. It cost $242 more than the standard Thunderbird 390 of 300 horses.

Finally, Ford came out with one more mid-year engine. This was the 260 cubic inch V-8, which despite its relatively small size, was destined to show some impressive performance. Introduced along with the sporty Falcon Futura and Fairlane Sport Coupe, the new 260 used a bore and stroke of 3.8x2.87 inches, an 8.7:1 compression ratio, and developed 164 horses at 4400 rpm. This year it was available only in the Fairlane line as a $140 option.

For the year, production was up nicely, reaching 1,459,877. Of this, 297,116 was in the new Fairlane line,

while 575,124 was in the Galaxie line. Probably because of the new Fairlanes, the Falcon family dropped by a fair amount, ending up with 396,129 sold, despite now having two series. As had occurred in the past, both the wagons and Thunderbirds held relatively steady, with 113,537 wagons and 77,971 T-Birds being produced.

In individual sales, it was a big Ford that once again took top honors. The Galaxie 500 4-door Town Sedan was Ford's most popular single model, with 174,195 being built. Coming in 2nd spot was the Falcon 2-door Sedan with 143,650 sales, while the new Fairlane 500 4-door Sedan ranked 3rd with 129,258 sales. Two other models to top the 100,000 mark were the Falcon 4-door Sedan with 126,041 being built and the plain Galaxie 4-door Sedan, with 115,594.

Ford also remained in the car/truck line with its Ranchero Pickup and Falcon Sedan Delivery, and its Falcon-based forward-control Econolines. But totally opposite these vehicles, the company would soon find itself playing with a new toy, thanks to the inventive mind of one Carroll Shelby.

A man in and out of sport and performance cars for years, Shelby took one look at the new light-weight 260 cubic inch V-8, took a second look at the rather underpowered British AC Ace, put the two together, and promptly blew the doors off of some factory sponsored Corvettes. Ford immediately realized that it had an instant competitor against the Corvette, with none of the design and tooling necessary to produce a low-production series of high performance sports cars. A deal was quickly drawn up between Shelby, Ford, and the AC Company, a factory was procured near Los Angeles, and the first of what would be about 75 total AC Cobra 260s began to leave the plant.

After the drastic change in 1961, it was not surprising that the 1962 Thunderbird received only dating cosmetics this year. The most pronounced identity marks were the three groupings of horizontal bars on the rear fender pods. Also new was a slightly altered grille. Most popular of the Birds was the Hardtop Coupe, Style 83, which drew 68,127 orders. Weighing 4,132 pounds, it sold for $4,321, with air conditioning being an additional $415. The year started with the 300 horse 390 V-8 being the only available engine, but shortly after the first of January the triple carburetor 340 horsepower 390 was made an option at $242. Four-way power front seats cost $92 for each side.

A new variation of the Thunderbird was the Landau. It was considered a separate model, even though it bore style designation 83 and its production was listed with the regular hardtop. Priced at $4,398, the car was simply the hardtop with an exclusive vinyl top and decorative landau irons. A possible, but not very popular option this year was a set of chromed Kelsey-Hayes wire wheels at $373 for five. The wheels included knock-off hubs with spinners. Installation required the deletion of the rear fender skirts to clear the hub spinners.

One of the better looking convertibles on the road was the new Thunderbird. Known as Style 85, the car weighed 4,370 pounds and cost $4,788 f.o.b. its factory at Wixom, Mich. Far less popular than the hardtop version, it saw production reach only 8,417. As before, the trunk deck was hinged at the rear, and opened automatically in order to swallow the top as it was lowered. A major fault of these cars was the fact that virtually no luggage could be carried in the trunk when the top was down. In addition, the spare tire nested against the forward trunk panel, making it quite difficult to reach and remove the spare when it was needed. Still, this was one of the most beautiful convertibles on the road!

Grabbing all kinds of attention, but few orders, was Ford's other new Thunderbird offering for 1962. It was called the Sports Roadster, Style 85. Essentially it was the convertible, fitted with a fiberglass tonneau cover which included molded headrests. The Kelsey-Hayes chrome wire wheels were standard. Marking the first time that a Thunderbird had broken the $5,000 base price mark, the Sports Roadster was priced at $5,439 at the factory. The tonneau cover could be removed, thus converting the car back to a 4-passenger model, as seats, carpets, and all tonneau fittings came with the car. Although production only reached 1,427 this year, several aftermarket companies began producing their own variations of these tonneau covers, and probably far more examples of this styling were dealer installed than were actually factory built. Still, this model is considered one of the most desirable of the later T-Birds from a collector's standpoint. When photographed, this car was owned by Warren Banes of Houston, Texas.

Not appearing until mid-year was the new Galaxie XL sub-series. This series consisted of the Galaxie Convertible and the Hardtop Coupe, fitted with bucket seats and a full console with central shifter. Special emblems designated the series, and many of the cars were fitted with the new 406 cubic inch engines which were introduced about the same time. Style leader of the new XL series was the Convertible, Style 65, which was also known as the XL Sunliner. Weighing 3,804 pounds, it was base priced at $3,358, but the 406 engine would have added another $430 to $488 to the price, while a floor-four was still another $188. A total of 13,183 XL Sunliners left the factory in the car's half-year on the market.

Companion to the XL Sunliner was the Galaxie XL Club Victoria. The car used the same body as the Style 63 Galaxie Club Victoria, but had bucket seats and central console in its all-vinyl interior. It too could be ordered with the new 406 cubic inch engine with triple carburetors. In basic form it cost $3,108 and weighed 3,625 pounds. A total of 28,412 were built during the short half-year of production.

A car that many claim was not really built was the Galaxie 500 Starlift Convertible. Due to poor sales, Ford had dropped its swept-back Starliner after the 1961 season, leaving the formal top Club Victoria as the only 2-door hardtop. However, the NASCAR circuit was running both convertibles and hardtop races as separate classes. Most Ford owners and drivers used Starliner tops that could be unbolted to allow the cars to run as convertibles. The Starliner tops, because of their sleekness and lower wind resistance, were preferred over the squared Victoria tops. At the start of the 1962 season, several Ford racers continued to use 1961 tops on their 1962 cars, until NASCAR officials stepped in and demanded that only 1962 style tops be used on 1962 cars. Rather than force the racers to use the squared tops, Ford at mid-year came out with a very limited production Starlift Convertible in an attempt to force NASCAR to accept the sleek tops as production models. The base car was the Sunliner Convertible, and the Starlift top simply bolted into special holes drilled into the convertible's body. The top was light and quickly removable, but it is reported that its fit left much to be desired. Once the point was made with NASCAR, it is very likely most Starlifts were converted back to convertibles. As far as can be ascertained, few of these cars were sold outside of the Atlanta and Daytona Beach areas, and their price is unknown.

The true Galaxie 500 hardtop was called the Club Victoria, Style 63. It used the squared formal-style top and differed from the Club Sedan only in its lack of B-pillars. The second most popular car in the Galaxie 500 series, it saw sales reach 87,562. Production probably would have gone higher had not the XL version appeared at mid-year. Base priced at $2,783, the car weighed 3,616 pounds. It was available as a Six, but it is doubtful if many were sold in that form. All Galaxies used a ribbed stainless steel escutcheon plate below the trunk deck. This plate was outlined by bright molding which carried around the taillights. Nice rear bumper design provided cutouts for the taillight lenses. The gas filler was centered in the escutcheon plate, immediately above the license.

Until the sporty Galaxie XL series was conceived, the Galaxie 500 series was Ford's top category. Flagship of the series was the Sunliner Convertible, Style 65, which was the only Galaxie to have a base price over $3,000. It sold for $3,033 in basic form with the small V-8. This was also the only Galaxie not available in 6-cylinder form. It weighed 3,782 pounds. Relatively popular for a rag top, it drew 42,644 orders, and probably would have seen more sales had not its XL variations come along at mid-year.

The pillared version of the Galaxie 500 2-door was called the Club Sedan, Style 61. Far less popular than the hardtop model, it drew only 27,824 orders. It weighed 3,587 pounds and had a base V-8 factory price of $2,722. All Galaxie 500 and XL models were fitted with a medallion in the center of the grille. The 500 models also used a triple bar of side trim, and had bright outlines on the wheel openings. Two popular accessories in the south were Polar Aire and Select Aire air conditioning. These cost $271 and $361 respectively, but required at least the basic V-8 engine.

Ford continued to use the bright metal triangle on the rear doors of its 4-door Town Victoria, making it easy to tell the hardtop model from the pillared Town Sedan when the windows were up. Of course, with the windows down there was no mistaking the Style 64. Priced at $2,848, the attractive Town Victoria weighed 3,688 pounds. Sales reached 30,778. This model could be ordered with an all-vinyl interior for an extra $26. All Galaxie 500 models had the small chrome "gunsights" on top of the front fenders and were fitted with stainless rockers and rear fender stone guards.

A nice styling feature of the Galaxie 500 Town Sedan was the recessed rear window, highlighted by its bright surround. The Town Sedan was the most popular Ford of all this year, accounting for 174,195 sales. Designated Style 62, it cost $2,776 and weighed 3,679 pounds. Throughout the year, Ford made available nine different engine choices for Galaxie 500 cars, ranging from the 223 cubic inch Six to the 406 cubic inch triple carburetor Thunderbird Special.

The base Galaxie 2-door Sedan, Style 51, was half of the 2-model plain Galaxie series. The 2-door drew 54,930 orders. It was priced at $2,562 and weighed 3,589 pounds. Despite being the basic big car, the Galaxie models were far more luxurious than had been their Fairlane counterparts in 1961.

Most popular of the plain Galaxie series was the 4-door Sedan, Style 52. A total of 115,594 were sold, with basic V-8 prices starting at $2,616. The car weighed 3,684 pounds. Many of these cars came out with the 6-cylinder engine, which represented a savings of $109 over the basic 292 cubic inch V-8. For a six, the Galaxies used the 223 cubic inch engine, which was not available in any other Ford-built cars. All plain Galaxies used a single bright bar of side molding, and lacked bright rockers or wheel opening molding. Also, they did not get the nose medallion, which actually provided them with a cleaner grille style.

Ford made its first entry into what would become known as the "intermediate" size car market this year. But rather than coin a new name for the car, it simply moved the Fairlane designation to the new vehicle. The nicely styled Fairlanes rode on a wheelbase of 115.5 inches and had an appearance that definitely said "I am a Ford." Divided into two sub-series, the top of the line models were called Fairlane 500s. Sitting here in Dearborn's shipping facility is the Fairlane 500 2-door Sedan, Style 41. The car weighed 2,932 pounds and had a base V-8 price of $2,345. It drew 68,624 orders.

Most popular of the new Fairlanes was the 500 4-door Sedan, Style 42, which saw production reach 129,258. Priced at $2,407, the car weighed 2,966 pounds. Fairlane 500 models were quickly identified from the plain Fairlanes by their wide belt trim, small "gunsights" on the front fenders, and three elongated dashes on the rear fender pods. As did the Galaxies, the Fairlanes used a full-width bright escutcheon plate on the rear, with the gas filler located in the center of this plate.

Not appearing until mid-year was the Fairlane 500 Sport Coupe, Style 47. Initially, Fairlanes were powered by either the 170 cubic inch Six, which was also optional in the Falcons, or by a totally new 221 cubic inch V-8, which was exclusive only to Fairlanes. At mid-year, both the Sport Coupe and a totally new 260 cubic inch V-8 were made available in the Fairlane 500 line. The new 260 was a $140 option, and carried its own special emblem, shown here on the lower portion of the front fender, just aft of the wheel cutout. Designed for the buyer who wanted a sporty car without the size or expense of a Galaxie XL, the new Sport Coupe with the 260 offered relatively good performance in addition to bucket seats and a central console similar to that used in the Falcon Futura. Priced at $2,607, the 3,002-pound Sport Coupe drew 19,628 orders in its half-year on the market.

Lowest priced of the new Fairlanes was the plain 2-door Sedan, Style 31, which sold for $2,154 as a Six or $2,257 with the 221 cubic inch V-8. Although lack of side trim did not seem to detract too much from this model, most buyers seemed to feel that the $88 difference in cost between this and the 500 version made it clear that the 500 was a better buy. Thus, sales of the plain Fairlane Coupe were only 34,264. The wheel covers shown on this model were a $19 option. Standard fare on the Fairlanes were plain hubcaps, such as seen on the accompanying 4-door Sedan.

In Ford's world of wagons, the wood-trimmed Country Squire continued to be the style and price leader. Once again, this model was available only as the Style 78 9-passenger version, with the former 6-passenger version having been dropped at the end of 1961. A styling innovation this year involved carrying the light imitation wood trim down on the trailing edge of the rear fender to act as a type of stone guard. The Country Squire was not only the most expensive, but also the least popular of all Ford wagons, with sales topping out at 15,666. As was the case with all wagons, the Squire could be equipped with a 6-cylinder engine, though it is doubtful if many such examples left the factory. With the basic V-8, it cost $3,197 and weighed 4,062 pounds.

Although the Fairlane was designed primarily as a lower level form of transportation, sandwiched between the full-size Galaxies and the small Falcons, the public showed a decided lack of interest in the lower level Fairlane models. Thus, the plain Fairlane 4-door Sedan, Style 32, drew only 45,342 orders as opposed to the 129,258 sales of the similar model in Fairlane 500 trim. The 4-door was priced at $2,319 as a V-8, or $103 less with the 170 cubic inch Six. After mid-year, an additional $140 would have the car powered by the new 260 cubic inch V-8, but it is doubtful if too many plain Fairlane sedans were given this option. With the small V-8, the car weighed 2,949 pounds, which was 34 pounds more than the 2-door Sedan.

Identical to the Country Squire in every way except for the exterior wood trim was the 9-passenger Country Sedan, Style 74. The 4,057-pound wagon sold for $3,042, meaning that the wood trim on the Squire added $155 to the overall cost. Only slightly more popular than the Squire, the Country Sedan in 9-passenger form drew only 16,562 orders. Trim level on this and the Squire followed that of the Galaxie 500 cars and included the wide anodized aluminum backing to the side trim, the "gunsight" fender ornaments, and the grille medallion. Far more popular in the Country Sedan book was the 6-passenger version, which looked identical from the exterior. Known as Style 72, it drew 47,635 orders with a base V-8 price of $2,938. It turned out to be Ford's best selling wagon of the year.

With the 2-door Ranch Wagon having been discontinued at the end of 1961, the 4-door 6-passenger Ranch Wagon became Ford's lowest price full-size wagon. Designated Style 71, and priced at $2,842, it drew a total of 33,674 orders. It weighed 4,016 with the V-8 or 3,905 with the big Six. In trim level, the Ranch Wagon followed the theme of the plain Galaxie series, using a single bar of side trim and no fender ornamentation. However, the wheel covers shown here were a $29 accessory, with plain hubcaps being the stock fare.

At mid-year, the Falcon Futura received a drastic change in appearance, even though its designation remained Style 17 and its price remained $2,232. But adding to its attractiveness was a new formal-type top with less wrap-around to the rear window and much heavier C-pillars. In addition, new spoke-type wheel covers replaced the former drilled type. Both wheel cover styles were exclusive to the Futuras, as was the side trim. Also coming out as an option to Futuras only was the 4-speed manual transmission as used in the British Fords. Still, the top engine remained the 170 cubic inch Six of 101 horsepower.

Seen in the styling studio is a pre-production version of the new Falcon Deluxe 2-door Sedan, Style 11. Interestingly, this car wears the word "FALCON" in block letters on its hood, just above the grille. This was later changed to "FORD." This view gives a good look at the new vertical bar Falcon grille, which probably was the most noticeable change in the car this year. In the Deluxe series, the 2-door Sedan sold for $2,071 and weighed 2,282 pounds. It turned out to be Ford's second most popular model, with 143,650 sales.

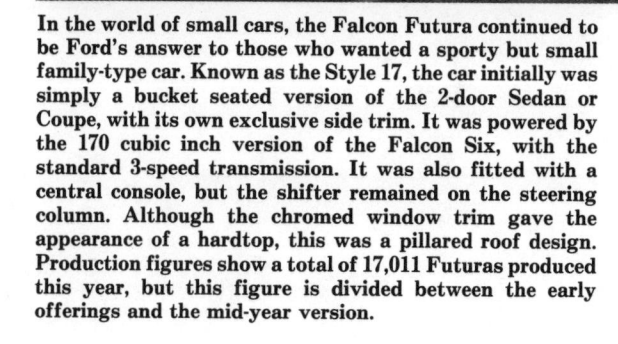

In the world of small cars, the Falcon Futura continued to be Ford's answer to those who wanted a sporty but small family-type car. Known as the Style 17, the car initially was simply a bucket seated version of the 2-door Sedan or Coupe, with its own exclusive side trim. It was powered by the 170 cubic inch version of the Falcon Six, with the standard 3-speed transmission. It was also fitted with a central console, but the shifter remained on the steering column. Although the chromed window trim gave the appearance of a hardtop, this was a pillared roof design. Production figures show a total of 17,011 Futuras produced this year, but this figure is divided between the early offerings and the mid-year version.

In 1961 Ford had offered a "Deluxe" appearance package for Falcons as an extra cost option. This year the Deluxe package became a separate Falcon sub-series, known, of course, as Falcon Deluxe. These models differed from the plain versions primarily in exterior trim, which included bright window surrounds, an exclusive emblem on the front fender side, and bright side trim ending in an anodized rear fender stone guard. Interior trim included padded sun visors, arm rests, and other luxury touches. In Deluxe form, the 4-door Sedan was Style 12, priced at $2,133. It drew a total of 126,041 orders, but some of these were in the plain series, as separate production records were not kept between plain and Deluxe Falcons.

Ford's only 2-door wagons this year appeared in the Falcon line, in both plain and Deluxe trim. This is the Deluxe version, which wears such exterior identity marks as the front fender "gunsights," wing-like side trim, and bright rear fender stone guards. The least popular of all Falcon wagons, the 2-door model drew only 20,025 orders in both plain and Deluxe versions. In the Deluxe form, it sold for $2,384 and weighed 2,584 pounds. Normally powered with the 144 cubic inch Six, it could be equipped with the 170 cubic inch model for an extra $38.

Falcon's most popular wagon was the 4-door version, available in both plain or Deluxe versions, but apparently far more popular in Deluxe guise as seen here. In this form, it sold for $2,427 and weighed 2,621 pounds. A total of 66,819 were built in both plain and fancy versions. All Falcon wagons were of 6-passenger capacity. All used a single tailgate with disappearing rear window. The small panes in the rear doors would not open, but the front door vent panes were functional. For an extra $30, the tailgate window could be electrically operated from the driver's position.

The plain Falcon line consisted of 2-door and 4-door Sedans and 2-door and 4-door wagons, but lacked the Futura Sport Coupes and the Squire Wagons. Side trim in this sub-series was relegated strictly to the Falcon crest on the front fenders and bright molding around the windshield and rear window. In plain form, the 2-door Sedan shown here cost $1,985 and thus was not only Ford's least expensive car, it was the only one with a base price of under $2,000. In this sub-series, the 4-door Sedan listed at $2,047. All Falcons, whether plain or Deluxe, bore the same style numbers, and as such, the 2-door was Style 11 while the 4-door was Style 12. As mentioned, production figures were not separated between plain and Deluxe Falcons.

Totally new for the year, and available only in the Falcon Deluxe series was the Falcon Squire Wagon, Style 26. This was simply the Style 22 4-door wagon, but fitted with imitation wood trim. In this form, the car cost $2,603 and was by far the most expensive Falcon. Still, this did not deter buyers, and sales reached 22,583, which was a far better record than that set by the full-size Country Squire. Available only on this model was the Squire Sport package, which consisted of bucket seats and a mini-console in the front. The rear seat remained stock. This package added $120 more to the base price, while the chromed roof rack shown here put on another $39.

In the plain Falcon sub-series there were two wagons, the 2-door and the 4-door version. The 4-door model, shown here, had a base price of $2,341, while the 2-door went out at $2,298 in base form. The 170 cubic inch engine would have added another $38 to the cost, while an automatic transmission upped the bill by an additional $163. The wheel covers shown here were another $16.

The first of what would become the famed AC Cobras, or Shelby Cobras, were conceived this year. Carrroll Shelby, a well-known race driver and Texas chicken farmer, got the brain storm of putting the new light-weight Ford 260 cubic inch engine into the well-handling but under-powered British A.C. Ace sports car. The results were far better than expected, and Ford, which had been looking for something with which to compete against Corvette, took quick notice. With Ford's total backing, Shelby set up a plant near Los Angeles, signed a contract with A.C. Cars Ltd., of Surrey, England, to supply a constant source of chassis and bodies, and began to install the 260 engines into the light sports cars. Between the end of 1962 and 1963, approximately 75 Cobras with 260 engines came out of California. Later in 1963 a switch was made to the 289 engine, but that is for the next chapter to deal with. The bodies of all Cobras were of hand-formed aluminum, while the 90-inch wheelbase chassis was of steel tubing. Disc brakes were standard. The 260 Cobras were priced at about an even $6,000.

Despite its very low production, Ford continued to offer its Sedan Delivery, based on the body shell of the 2-door Falcon station wagon. But with sales down to 1,568, one wonders why the little truck was continued. Priced at $2,111, it weighed 2,463 pounds. The Sedan Delivery did not use a swing-out rear door, but instead was fitted with the same tailgate with disappearing glass as found on all Falcon wagons. The side emblem simply said "Falcon" in script, but was not the same emblem used on the car models. The new Falcon hood design gave the impression of an air scoop at the leading edge. However, this was strictly decorative.

Still holding its own in the sales race was the cute little Falcon-based Ranchero Pickup. This year a total of 20,842 were sold, which was just about the same as in 1961. Priced at $1,889 and weighing 2,348 pounds, the truck was considered Falcon Style 27. It followed the interior and exterior trim level of the plain Falcons, but had its own "Ranchero" signature on the front fenders. The 144 cubic inch Six with a 3-speed transmission was considered standard, but options included the 170 cubic inch engine, a 2-speed automatic transmission, or a 4-speed manual floor-shifter transmission.

Not only did Ford's Falcon line split into plain and Deluxe versions, the Falcon-based Econoline Wagons now also came in plain and fancy variations. Now bearing the name "Club Wagon," these 8-passenger forward-control wagons were drawing a fair amount of interest, and a total of 18,153 were built in the three available forms. In the plain variety were the Station Bus, with four sets of seats, and the Club Wagon shown here with three sets of seats. Less fancy of the two was the Station Bus, Model E-11, which listed at $2,287. The Club Wagon, Model E-12, listed for $2,436. Interior trim variations were the main difference, with the bus using vinyl upholstery and the wagon using a woven vinyl seat covering and slightly more plush interior.

The Falcon Deluxe Club Wagon was the fanciest of the three passenger-carrying Econoline models. It sported bright trim on the sides, with the center portion of this trim filled in a complimenting color. Inside it had a padded dash and all-vinyl pleated upholstery over foam cushions, and a full-length floor mat and headliner. Bumpers, wheel covers, and grille were all finished in bright metal. In addition, the 170 cubic inch Six was standard in the Deluxe Club Wagon, while the 144 cubic inch Six was standard in the Station Bus and the plain Club Wagon. The Deluxe variety cost $2,673 and weighed 2,796 pounds. Club Wagons used a 90-inch wheelbase and were 168.3 inches overall.

Five years and five major styling changes. That was one of the main highlights for Ford this year. Other early year news included a new line of low-buck full-size cars to replace the pre-1962 Fairlane range; a whole flock of new Falcons flying under the Futura banner, and a total of 77 separate models crossing the price scale from the $1,985 Falcon Six to the 45,800 Thunderbird Sport Roadster with the big engine.

Once again Ford played the waiting game with its big guns. The range of Galaxies, Falcons, and Thunderbirds was introduced in late September, with the little-changed Fairlanes following by a few weeks. But the cars of real interest did not make their debut until after the calendar year had changed, in what can best be described as a mid-1963 introduction date. These cars included a beautiful new Galaxie hardtop with a swept-back convertible-like top, and a brace of sporty Falcons with the name Sprint. But it was under the hoods that the big new occurred at mid-year. It was there that one found Ford's fabulous 427 cubic inch mill, available in three variations; Fairlane's new 289 cubic inch model, and Falcon's new 260 representing that line's first V-8 power. Again, it seemed that Ford saved the best for last.

In the big car line, all new sheetmetal once again graced the sides from the beltline downward. Front and rear styling was totally new but followed previous Ford concepts in that the grille design was repeated on a rear escutcheon plate set between the two round taillights. Inside, drivers looked at a new dash, and were surrounded by newly designed seats and panels. Under the hood, the 292 cubic inch engine was dropped in favor

of the new small block 260 as the base V-8, but this selection lasted only until mid-year. Then a brand new 289 cubic inch engine took over as the basic V-8 power plant. It had a bore and stroke of 4x2.78 inches, a compression ratio of 8.7:1, and developed 195 horses at 4400 rpm. This was opposed to the 164 horses offered by the 260 block. The 260 did not go away, but remained a popular option in both the Fairlane and Falcon ranks.

Other changes in the big car field included a new low-buck line, simply called the 300 series; and after mid-year, the aforementioned Sport Hardtop; an XL Sedan with bucket seats; a new 3-speed manual transmission; a continuation of the floor-four manual for serious performance driving, and a swing-away steering wheel, which did not turn out to be very popular. Late in the year both the six and 9-passenger Squire Wagons were included in the XL ranks and drew 758 orders.

All Galaxie models retained their 119-inch wheelbases, but grew about a half-inch to 209.9 inches overall. The chassis received a new front end, quite similar in design to that used on the Thunderbirds. The optional 427 cubic inch engine will be discussed later.

As could be expected for a virtually new car, the Fairlanes did not change too much in appearance, but their ranks were beginning to grow. Adding to the availability list were a new hardtop coupe, and a 4-door wagon that came in both plain and wood-trimmed variations. The Sport Coupes featured bucket seats and full-length console. Also new for the year was a 4-speed manual transmission by Borg-Warner, available only on the V-8s.

Although the car remained basically the same, the new Thunderbird did receive a noticeable styling change. It was in the form of an embossed body line, extending horizontally from the forward fender point until it dipped into a blend with the door at about the 3/4 mark. The group of three bar panels was once again used, but these were now of diagonal bars and located on the doors, bordered by the down-sweeping ridge. T-Bird sales suffered this year, and as such the beautiful Convertible, Style 85, drew only 5,913 orders. It cost $4,912 and weighed 4,395 pounds. As before, the rear deck was hinged at the rear to allow the top to disappear when lowered. However, this design made it very difficult to load luggage in the trunk when the top was up, and made it impossible to use the trunk for storage when the top was lowered.

It was probably one of the most beautiful cars of this era, but it just did not attract buyers, That was the story of the Thunderbird Sports Roadster, which only drew 455 orders this year. Despite the low projected sales, the car was given its own identification this year, and was known as Style 89. At 4,395 pounds, it was the heaviest Thunderbird. At $5,563 it was the most expensive of all Fords, and the only one to be base priced at over $5,000. As before, the attractive Kelsey-Hayes wire wheels were standard with this model. On other T-Birds, they were available for $373 for a set of five. The fiberglass tonneau cover could be removed when a 5-passenger capacity was needed.

Under the Fairlane hood, the 170 cubic inch Six of 101 HP started out as basic power, but was replaced at mid-year by the new Six of 200 cubic inches, which developed 116 horses at 4400 rpm. This engine had a bore and stroke of 3.68x3.13 and an 8.7:1 compression ratio. In the V-8 models, the 221 cubic inch block of 145 horses was standard, while the 260 cubic inch model of 164 HP was a $155 option.

Then at mid-year the performance buffs were treated to a new option. That was the 289 cubic inch plant of 4x2.78 inch bore and stroke, which developed 271 horses at 6000 rpm. Priced at $425 additional, the new performance mill was given an 11.1 compression ratio, used performance-type heads and headers, and was fed through a Holley 4-barrel. A derivative of the 260, it shared its parent's name of "Challenger," but was known as the HP Challenger." The "HP" stood for High Performance.

The Falcons also received a face lift, and a strong pull out of the economy class and a shove into the performance light. The standard Falcons still remained for the low-buck contingent, but a new Futura series was conceived to replace the Deluxe series of 1962. In this bracket were found Falcon's first convertible and even a sporty Squire wagon with bucket seats and a console. And, at mid-year, the Futura series provided the base for the new super sporty Sprint sub-series, plus a new hardtop coupe in both Futura and Sprint versions.

Initially the Falcons started out with the 144 cubic inch Six being standard, and the 170 cubic inch Six being a $37 option. Then, at mid-year, Falcons received their first V-8. This was the 164-horse 260 that was also available in the Fairlane models. Along with this came the optional 4-speed Borg-Warner transmission. The 260 cost an additional $196, while the floor-four added another $188 to the tab.

Virtually the only car that didn't receive a mid-year performance boost was the Thunderbird, which again had only cosmetic changes, plus a new horizontal embossed ridge running from the point of the front fender to a downward disappearance just aft of door's mid-point. Once again, three decorative bar groupings were used, but these now consisted of diagonal bars located on the doors, rather than horizontal bars on the rear fenders. The interesting Sports Roadster was again offered, but not promoted heavily, and as a result, sales were way down. The car still used the beautiful chromed Kelsey-Hayes wire wheels as standard fare, while these remained a $373 accessory for other Birds.

As before, the 300 HP 390 cubic inch V-8 was standard in the Thunderbirds while the 340 horse "six-pack" version of this engine was a $242 option. Then, sometime between introduction and mid-year, the Thunderbirds received another exclusive engine. This was a single 4-barrel version of the triple carburetor Special, that developed 330 horses at 5000 rpm. Called the "Police Special," this engine formerly had been available only in special-order police cars, but was now released for T-Bird use.

But when one thinks of Ford engines of this era, the highlight has to be the mid-year introduction of the 427 cubic inch block. Developed in answer to the on-going Big Three horsepower race, encouraged in large part by NASCAR, the new block used a bore and stroke of

The most popular Thunderbird was still the plain Hardtop Coupe, Style 83, which this year accounted for 42,806 sales. Base priced at $4,445, it weighed 4,195 pounds. Rear fender skirts were available on all Thunderbirds except the Sport Roadster. However, when a bird was ordered with the Kelsey-Hayes wire wheels, the skirts had to be omitted in order to allow room for the spinner hubs. On all Thunderbirds, the 300 horsepower version of the 390 cubic inch engine was standard. However, the 340 horse version with triple 2-barrel carburetors was available for an additional $242. And late in the year, the 330 horsepower 4-barrel carburetor version of this engine was also made available.

Having its own designation of Style 87 was the year-old Landau Hardtop. Essentially, this was simply the plain hardtop fitted with an all-vinyl, pebble-grained top and large decorative landau irons. Achieving moderate popularity, it drew 14,139 orders, with a base price of $4,548. It weighed 4,320 pounds. Although Thunderbirds were pretty complete when they left the factory, power windows and seats were still extra cost items. The windows cost an additional $106, while the seats were $92 for each front unit. A buyer could order simply a powered driver's seat, or just a power passenger's seat, or both.

4.23x3.78 inches and ran a compression of 11.6:1. It was available in two production forms, with the most sedate being a 410 horsepower version (5600 rpm) that went for $515. The second version was a 425 horse unit (6000 rpm) which sold for $570 extra. The main difference between the two was that the higher horse unit used dual 4-barrel carburetors, while the other used a single 4-barrel. Not easily available, but sold primarily to select professional drag racers, was a special version with 12:1 compression, special dual 4-barrels, and a special cam.

When ordering the 427 block, a buyer received a Galaxie that was not the same as one with a smaller engine. Included in the package were 7:10x15 nylon tires, as opposed to stock 7.00x14 tires; heavy duty suspension; a heavier frame; stronger driveline, and larger brakes. The floor-four was a mandatory item also, and cost an additional $188. The 427s were available in all Galaxie models except the wagons, but were most often seen in the Club Victoria or the new Sport Coupe.

As might be expected, with the introduction of the 427, the 406 cubic inch blocks were discontinued. These year-old engines had been the big blocks at the start of the year, but were felt unnecessary in the face of the 427s. Unchanged from 1962, they were initially offered as a single 4-barrel of 385 horsepower, or with the triple 2-barrel "six-pack" set-up giving 405 horsepower. In the half year that they were available, the single carb model was a $430 option while the 405 horse went for $477, with either block requiring the $188 4-speed.

In the world of numbers, production was once again up nicely, with the model year tally being 1,580,831. Of this, 845,292 were big Fords, including 127,130 full-size station wagons. Fairlanes accounted for 343,887, which included 61,601 of the new wagons; and Falcon accounted for another 328,339 which included 61,821 of its popular wagons, including 1,461 wearing the Squire

designation. Not included in these figures are 17,633 Econoline wagons, which on some lists this year were included in the Falcon figures. Lastly, Thunderbird was down, with total production reaching only 63,313.

Ironically, though overall production was up, the profusion of models being offered resulted in only three specific styles breaking the 100,000 mark. Also surprising was the fact that two of these were in the Galaxie 500 series. The year's top seller, and the only Ford to top the 200,000 mark, was the Galaxie 500 Town Sedan, with 205,722 sales. Third on the list was the Galaxie 500 Sport Coupe, Ford's newest offering, which in its short half-year on the market still managed to attract 100,500 buyers. The second place model was the Fairlane 500 4-door Sedan. Surprisingly, no Falcon models made the 100,000 list this year, as in contrast to 1962 when both the two and 4-door Deluxe Falcon sedans were in the top bracket.

And finally, out in California, Carroll Shelby started the year continuing production of his 260-powered Cobras. By the time a total of 75 of these had been completed, the new 289 cubic inch block was available, and these were installed in the succeeding cars. Production records of the 289 Cobras are not available on an individual year basis. But, between the 1963 half-year and the end of the 1965 season, a total of 580 were produced. In 1963 and 1964 the cars used a 90-inch wheelbase, while this was stretched to 108 inches in the 1965 versions.

At the start of the year, only two models were available in the Galaxie 500 XL series. They were the Sunliner and this 5-passenger Victoria, or Club Victoria as it was sometimes known. The car was priced at $3,268, which was a $485 increase over the regular Galaxie 500 Club Victoria. For this, buyers received twin bucket seats in the front, a floor shifter for whatever transmission was selected, and a multitude of bright fittings throughout the interior. Oddly, the only external difference between this and the Galaxie 500 model was the small front fender plaque containing the letters "XL." More popular than the Sunliner, the Club Victoria drew 29,713 orders. Designated Style 67, it weighed 3,670 pounds. At the start of the year, all XL models used the 260 cubic inch engine as the basic power plant, but after mid-year the 289 block became standard. People usually think of XL models as having huge engines, but any increase in engine size was the same extra-cost option that was available to the buyer of any Galaxie.

Front bucket seats, a console with floor shifter, and a very plush interior set the Galaxie 500 XL models off from the rest of the line. These appointments really stood out on the Convertible, Style 69, when the top was down. Priced at $3,518, it was the most expensive Ford on the list, outside of the Thunderbird family. Also known as the Sunliner, the car weighed 3,820 pounds. It enjoyed relatively good sales considering its price tag, and a total of 18,551 were sold.

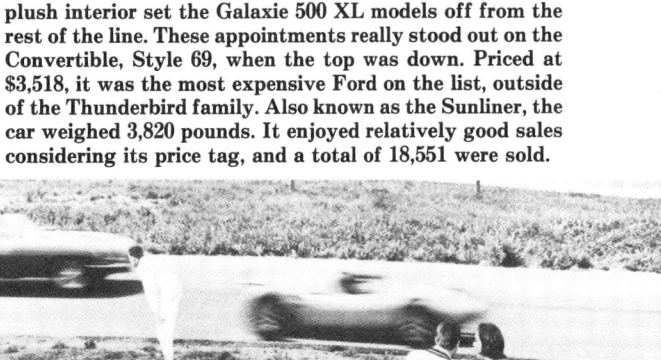

At mid-year, the Galaxie 500 XL series was joined by one of Ford's best looking models. It was the Fastback Coupe, Style 68, which came out in answer to buyers (and NASCAR drivers) who wanted a hardtop with less wind resistance than provided by the formal-topped Club Victoria. The new coupe was not a fastback in the true sense, since it still had a definite notch between the rear posts and the rear deck. But it was sleek enough to attract sufficient buyers to make it the number one car in the XL sub-series. A total of 33,870 were sold, with a base price of $3,268, the same as the Club Victoria. An unusual yet very attractive styling touch involved the imitation ribs embossed into the top metal, giving the appearance of a convertible top. At 54.5 inches high, this car was a full inch lower than the Club Victoria.

A split-back 3-passenger front seat and column mounted shifter show that this is the plain Galaxie 500 Sunliner, and not the XL version. The car was far more popular in this form, possibly because of the $485 difference in price. As a plain Galaxie 500, it cost $3,033 and drew 36,876 orders, which was almost twice that the XL model. Designated Style 65, it weighed 3,770 pounds. Notice that for the first time in several years, the top of the line Fords did not use the large stone guards on the rear fenders. These units were quite attractive and certainly helpful in rural areas where gravel roads were still commonplace. Yet, with this year's models, they were gone for good.

Outside of the Kelsey-Hayes wheels on the Thunderbird, one of the most attractive accessories this year was the vinyl top option for the new Galaxie 500 and XL versions of the Fastback Coupe. Selling for $75 and usually done in black canvas-grain vinyl, this top contained all of the ribs and seams found on the true convertible, and at a quick glance looked just like a top-up rag-top. This view of the XL version gives a good look at the rear window of the Fastback, which was a good bit smaller than that found on the Club Victoria. Also notice that Ford continued its traditional rear styling, with large round taillights, and a bright escutcheon plate repeating the design theme of the grille.

At the same time that Ford brought out the highly successful Fastback Coupe, it also added another model to the Galaxie 500 XL line. This was the 4-door Town Victoria, priced in XL form at $3,333. As in the other models, the package included bucket front seats and console, but the rear seat remained the same as in the Galaxie 500 line. Unlike other XL models, this car did not get its own style number, but retained Style 64 from the Galaxie 500 series. More popular than one would expect, the sporty 4-door drew 12,596 orders. The XL interior added 70 pounds to the weight of this car, bringing it up to 3,750 pounds.

The lowest priced, the lightest, and the least popular of all Galaxie 500 models. That was the description of the 2-door Club Sedan, Style 61. It cost $2,722 in base form, weighed 3,600 pounds, and had sales of only 21,137. This and the Town sedan were the only Galaxie 500 models not available in XL form. Still, with the windows raised, this car looked almost identical to the Club Victoria, differing only in the use of a B-pillar on this model. The seven small vertical bars on the rear fenders were known as "vent bars," but they were strictly decorative and served only to differentiate the 500 and XL models from the plain Galaxies.

Until mid-year, Ford's only 2-door hardtop in the Galaxie 500 series was the formal-roof Club Victoria, Style 63. Certainly an attractive enough model, it was priced at $2,783 and weighed 3,615 pounds. The front fender emblem, consisting of an eagle in front of two checkered racing flags, indicates that this particular model has been fitted with the new 427 cubic inch block, probably the 410 horsepower version, which added $515 to the base price. That engine also would have mandated the 4-speed manual transmission, which was still another $188 extra. Fast Fords were getting expensive.

At mid-year, this beauty appeared in both Galaxie 500 and XL variations. Despite the short selling season, in sales alone it blew the doors off of every other 500 model except the 4-door sedan. Known as the Fastback Coupe, Style 66, the car was met with a phenomenal acceptance, and 100,500 were sold in the 6-months of remaining sales time. The car was priced at the same $2,783 as the Club Victoria, and weighed the same 3,615 pounds. Because of its success, the 1964 Club Victoria would wear this roof line, and the formal style would be dropped. This model wears the attractive deluxe wheel covers which simulated wire wheels. Both these or the all-chrome full disc types were available. Both used attractive center spinners which were strictly decorative, and both listed for about $45 a set above the standard Galaxie wheel covers.

A straight-back bench seat indicates that this is the regular Galaxie 500 4-door Town Victoria, and not the XL version. Not a particularly popular model, it drew only 26,558 orders. Known officially as Style 64, the same as its XL counterpart, it was priced at $2,848 and weighed 3,695 pounds. Once again, Ford Galaxie 4-door hardtops retained the small triangular piece between the rear door sill and the rear pillar. This helped to brace the glass when the rear windows were raised. As could be expected, power windows were a popular option on this model, costing about $100 extra.

The most popular car in Ford's entire fleet was the Galaxie 500 4-door Town Sedan, Style 62, which saw its sales rise to 205,722. This marked the first time that an individual Ford style had broken the 200,000 sales mark since the old Custom 300 series of 1959. Priced at $2,766 and weighing 3,680 pounds, the attractive model used a solid B-pillar, but hidden behind the chromed window surrounds. Thus, except for the rear door flare, it looked almost like the Town Victoria with its windows raised. New side trim this year began at the headlights, ran full-length to the taillights, then made a wide "U-turn" and returned to the forward edge of the front door. The trim was not only very attractive, but did much to protect the car's sides from parking lot dings.

The most popular model in the 2-style plain Galaxie series was the 4-door Sedan, Style 52. Base priced at $2,616, it weighed 3,660 pounds and drew a total of 82,419 orders. The body and running gear were the same as in the 500 or XL series, but trim and interior appointments were of a lesser level. However, virtually all accessories available to the upper level cars could be ordered for this model, including the full wheel covers shown here. Notice that the plain Galaxie series did not use the rear escutcheon plate between the taillights, but simply had this area painted in body color. One usually thinks of these models as always having the small engines, but actually all blocks right up to the 427 with 4-speed were available in these cars.

Those wanting a full-size car, but not desiring the luxury trim of the Galaxie 500 range, could look into the plain Galaxie series. Here two available models offered all of the mechanical refinement, space, and ride of the full-size Fords, but lacked the exterior trim, interior luxury touches, and of course, did not offer any sporty models. Lowest priced of the two models was the 2-door Sedan, Style 51, which booked at $2,562 with the small V-8, or $109 cheaper with the Six. Certainly not ignored by buyers, the 3,850-pound car drew 30,335 orders. All models had the Galaxie signature on the back half of the front fender, with a single chrome strip running from this emblem to the taillights. Standard hubcaps were provided, but almost surprisingly, the bright front fender "gunsights" of the 500 and XL models were also used here.

New for the year was a return to the stripped low-buck big car. Called the 300 series and available in the same two models of the plain Galaxie series, these cars were primarily intended for fleet sales, though anyone could order one from a dealership. Lowest priced of the series, and lowest priced of all full-size Fords was the 300 2-door Sedan, Style 53. It was base priced at $2,433 with the small V-8 or $2,324 with the Six. As a V-8 it weighed 3,560 pounds. A total absence of side trim greatly detracted from this year's otherwise very nice styling. Still, sales reached 26,010, proving that a market did exist for these low-buck specials.

Companion to the 2-door Sedan was the new 300 series 4-door Sedan. Known as Style 54, it weighed 3,640 pounds with the V-8 and cost $2,387. Sales hit 44,142. Trim on this model consisted of a Ford signature on the front fender panel, a small bright bar at the base of the C-pillar, and bright metal around both the windshield and rear window. Despite the rather spartan exterior, the cars were fitted with dual sun visors, and each door had its own arm rest. Many of these cars went into police work, being fitted with special suspension and handling packages, and large engines, right up to the mid-year 427s.

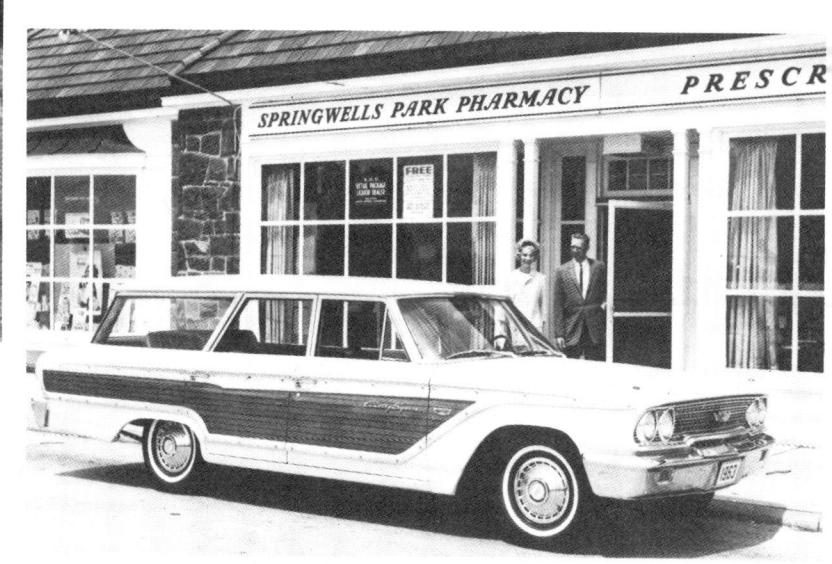

Ford reduced its large wagon offerings this year to just two basic models, each available in either six or 9-passenger form. Both used the Galaxie 500 trim level, and the Country Sedan went so far as to use Galaxie 500 side trim. In 6-passenger form, the Country Sedan was known as Style 72. Here it weighed 3,990 pounds, cost $2,938, and drew 64,954 orders. In this form it was the only V-8 wagon base priced under $3,000, and also was Ford's most popular full-size wagon. As a 9-passenger it was style 74, which cost $3,042 and weighed an even two tons. In this guise it drew 22,250 orders. The lower level Ranch Wagon was now gone from the full-size ranks, but its name was transferred to the Fairlane series.

Ford's premium wagon continued to be the artificial wood-trimmed Country Squire, also available in both six and 9-passenger variations. The 6-passenger was Style 76, which was base priced at $3,127 and weighed two tons even. A total of 19,922 were sold. The 9-passenger Style 78 weighed 4,010 pounds, cost $3,197, and drew 19,246 orders. At mid-year, the Squires apparently were introduced to the XL series. Some records would indicate that they actually came out as XL models, while others show them having all of the XL fittings, including bucket seats in the front and full consoles, but not officially being part of the XL line. Whatever, in this form, 437 bucket-seat 5-passenger Squires were sold, while another 321 went out in 8-passenger form. None had the 427 engines, as the wagon models were the only full-size Fords excluded from the big blocks.

Coming up with shades of the old Buicks, Ford this year also found triple portholes for the front fenders. However, this unusual styling touch appeared on only one model and lasted only this one year. The model was the new Fairlane 500 Sport Coupe, Style 47, which used its own exclusive side trim and nameplates; had a full console with front bucket seats and bucket-styled rear seats, and came with full wheel covers with spinners. The small emblem on the front fender tells people that the car is powered with the 260 horse V-8, or, if it was a post mid-year model, that the 289 lurked under the hood. Priced at $2,607 and weighing 3,002 pounds, the sport Coupe attracted 28,268 buyers. Because of the rear seat styling, the car was essentially a 4-passenger model, even though it is listed as a 5-passenger.

More sedate and better received than the Sport Coupe was Fairlane's other new hardtop, the 500 Hardtop Coupe, Style 43. Essentially the same car as the Sport Coupe, it used Fairlane 500 side trim, had a full rear bench seat and full split front seat for 6-passenger capacity, and had a column shifter. All power options were available for all 500s. This model wears the front fender emblem signifying the larger Fairlane V-8. Whether it was because of the 6-passenger capacity or the $180 lower price tag is not known, but the Hardtop Coupe enjoyed almost twice the sales of the Sport Coupe, registering 41,641 sold. It was base priced at $2,427 and weighed 2,982 pounds.

The third coupe style in the Fairlane 500 range was the pillared 2-door Sedan, Style 41. The car used the same squared or formal top styling as did the hardtop models, but had thinner rear pillars. As before, the car was available in both Fairlane 500 and plain Fairlane trim, with the 500 models being quickly identified by the small bright "gunsight" ornaments on top of the front fenders, and also by the wider side trim. In 500 form, the 2-door sedan sold for $2,345 and weighed 2,962 pounds. Its popularity rating fell mid-way between the two hardtops, with 34,764 being turned out.

Ford's second most popular car of the year was the Fairlane 500 4-door Sedan, Style 42, which registered 104,175 sales. It was priced at $2,407 and weighed 2,870 pounds. The lack of front fender emblem indicates that this model is powered by a Six, either the 170 cubic inch unit, or the new 200 cubic inch version if the car was built after mid-year. Fairlane 500 models followed the lead of their top of the line big brothers, and came with bright rear escutcheon plates, running full-length between the round taillights. The gas filler was centered in this plate, just above the license and just behind the Ford emblem. The Fairlanes were also the only Fords to continue the use of small tail fins on the rear fenders.

New to the Fairlane family were the station wagon models. All of 4-door styling, the wagons appeared in two variations in the 500 series and in just one form in the plain Fairlane series. In both series, the plain side version took the Ranch Wagon name from the big car line. Fanciest of the two available Ranch Wagons was the 500 series Style 48. It cost $2,716, weighed 3,342 pounds, and drew 29,612 orders. It used the same side trim and interior level as did other 500 models. Shown here as a Six, it could be equipped with the 260 cubic inch V-8, but not with the 289 cubic inch version.

Least popular of the three new Fairlane station wagons was the Squire, available only in the 500 series. Designated Style 49, it attracted only 7,983 buyers, even though its $2,884 price was only $168 higher than the plain 500 version. Possibly buyers who wanted a fancy wagon trimmed in imitation wood wanted a full-size vehicle. Whatever the reason, the Squire idea appeared only briefly at the start of the 1964 season (some sources indicate that it never appeared at all in production form) before being dropped. All Fairlane wagons were of the 6-passenger variety. After mid-year, Ford attempted to boost Squire acceptance by offering a fancy model, ala the Galaxie 500 XL concept. Thus, Fairlane Squires were offered in 5-passenger style, with front bucket seats and a full console. Not a popular concept, only 277 were built in this form.

Was it strictly a show car, or did a limited run reach selected buyers? Possibly it was both. Called the "Starburst," this modified Fairlane 500 first appeared on the show circuit at mid-year. It used the interior of the Fairlane 500 Sport Coupe; Kelsey-Hayes wire wheels; a coupe-de-ville top styling with a removable center section; and modified rear wheel wells, in addition to its own exclusive side trim and ornamentation. Some information would indicate that a small run was produced for select dealers, and that these cars were later sold to the public by the dealers once the 1964 models arrived. This cannot be substantiated, but if true, one of these models would make an interesting collector's piece today. Nothing can be found as to the supposed price, weight, or number actually built.

The plain Fairlane line consisted of two 4-door models, a sedan and a wagon, and this 2-door Sedan, Style 31. Plain Fairlanes looked the part, having but a single piece of bright trim running full-length from the headlights to the taillights. Deleted on these models were the front fender trim pieces and the rear escutcheon plate. Although the 260 V-8 was available in this series, it is safe to assume that the majority of cars went away with the 6-cylinder engine. The 2-door was base priced at $2,257 with the V-8 or $2,154 with the small Six. It weighed 2,924 pounds with the V-8 or 2,815 pounds with the Six. Production totalled 28,984 units.

Most popular of the plain Fairlanes was the 4-door Sedan, style 32, which drew 44,454 orders, with a base V-8 price of $2,319 and weight of 2,987 pounds. Hubcaps were standard on this model, but wheel covers were a popular option. A fordomatic 2-speed automatic transmission could be ordered for an extra $189, while a push-button radio was a $58 option.

Fairlane's least expensive wagon was the plain Ranch Wagon, Style 38, which used the plain Fairlane single-bar side trim and Fairlane interior level. Built in 6-passenger form only, it sold for $2,628 and weighed 3,327 pounds as a V-8. It attracted 24,006 orders. All Ford wagons used the single swing-down tailgate with disappearing rear window. A popular option was an electric rear window control which cost $32. Also popular but not shown here was the roof-top luggage carrier at $45. The interior was all vinyl.

Not appearing until mid-year was the Falcon Sprint sub-series. Sometimes referred to simply as the Sprint option for the Futura models, this package included a heavier frame, more firm suspension, and the 260 cubic inch V-8. Obvious exterior touches included wire wheel covers, chromed rocker covers, special emblems, and a dashboard-mounted tachometer. Most attractive of the two Sprint models was the Convertible, which used the same Style 15 designation as did the Futura version. Priced at $2,837, the pretty and peppy car drew only 4,602 orders in its short half-year of life. This model is posed in front of a Monaco back-drop, not unusual since beefed-up Falcons proved to be fierce competitors on several European rally courses this year, including the famed Monte Carlo course at Monaco.

The other model in the mid-year Falcon Sprint package was the 2-door Hardtop, which was a variation of the Style 18 Falcon Hardtop. Priced at $2,603, the hardtop version was much more popular than the convertible, drawing a total of 19,479 sales in its half-year of life. The interiors on these cars had the same 4-passenger bucket seat styling as found on the Futura Sports models. Under the hood, the 260 cubic inch V-8 received a less restrictive chrome air cleaner, chrome valve covers and oil filler, flow-through mufflers, and special engine decals. Later in the year, under contract to Ford, Holman & Moody shipped three highly modified Sprint Hardtops to Europe, where they were used by three different teams on the European Rally circuit. All of the cars showed admirable performance, while the one driven by a Swedish team won its class in all six races on the circuit.

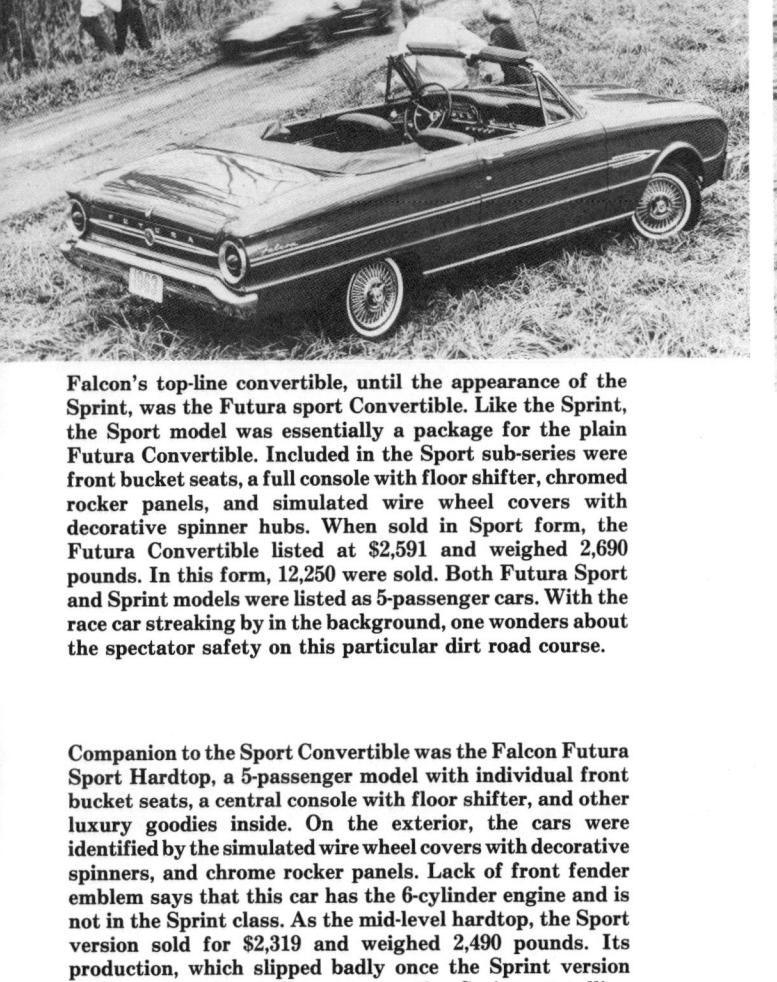

Falcon's top-line convertible, until the appearance of the Sprint, was the Futura sport Convertible. Like the Sprint, the Sport model was essentially a package for the plain Futura Convertible. Included in the Sport sub-series were front bucket seats, a full console with floor shifter, chromed rocker panels, and simulated wire wheel covers with decorative spinner hubs. When sold in Sport form, the Futura Convertible listed at $2,591 and weighed 2,690 pounds. In this form, 12,250 were sold. Both Futura Sport and Sprint models were listed as 5-passenger cars. With the race car streaking by in the background, one wonders about the spectator safety on this particular dirt road course.

When the Falcon line finally got a convertible it seemed to go hog wild. The new model was immediately listed in not one but three variations, the Futura Style 15, shown here, the Sport version, and the mid-year Sprint. As attested to by this photo, the basic Futura model was classed as a 6-passenger car, and was fitted with a split full-length seat in front and a bench seat in back. It also used a column shifter, and was fitted with standard wheel covers. In Futura form, it cost $2,470 and weighed 2,655 pounds. In this version it turned out to be the most popular of the trio, with 18,942 being sold. Unlike the top-line Galaxies and Fairlanes, the Futura Falcons did not use rear escutcheon plates, but instead had a full-width double sword-like bar extending outward from the center-mounted emblem below the trunk.

Companion to the Sport Convertible was the Falcon Futura Sport Hardtop, a 5-passenger model with individual front bucket seats, a central console with floor shifter, and other luxury goodies inside. On the exterior, the cars were identified by the simulated wire wheel covers with decorative spinners, and chrome rocker panels. Lack of front fender emblem says that this car has the 6-cylinder engine and is not in the Sprint class. As the mid-level hardtop, the Sport version sold for $2,319 and weighed 2,490 pounds. Its production, which slipped badly once the Sprint version arrived, was almost the same as the Sprints, totalling 10,972. In plain Futura form, the car looked identical to the Sport model, but had no rocker trim, used plain full wheel covers, had bench seats and a column shifter, and was considered a 6-passenger car. Designated Style 18 in any form, the basic Futura Hardtop Coupe sold for $2,198, weighed 2,455 pounds, and had 17,524 sales.

Until the new Style 18 Falcon Hardtops appeared, the sportiest car in the Falcon's nest was the Futura 5-passenger Sport Sedan, Style 17. A pillared model, it had larger and more upright rear roof panels, but otherwise came close to the hardtops in appearance. The car used the same bucket seats and full console interior as did the later hardtop Sport and Sprint models, but wore plain wheel covers and lacked the bright rocker molding. In basic 6-cylinder form, the Sport Sedan cost $2,237 and weighed 2,350 pounds. Sales only reached 10,344, as the new hardtop models virtually knocked this style out of the ring. The car is shown with the optional vinyl roof treatment, which cost an extra $75.

Companion to the Futura Sport Sedan was the plain Futura 2-door Sedan, Style 19, which sold for $2,116 and weighed 2,315 pounds. When fitted with the $75 optional vinyl top, as seen here, the car did not look that much different than the Sport Sedan. The main difference was in the interior, with this model having 6-passenger capacity, via bench seats front and aft (the front one split, of course) and a column shifter. Both models used bright window frames all around. Slightly more popular than the sport version, the 2-door Sedan drew 16,674 sales.

As could be expected, the most popular model in the Falcon Futura series was the 4-door Sedan, Style 16, which drew 31,736 orders. Priced at $2,165, it weighed 2,355 pounds. All windows were surrounded by bright metal, as was the upper B-pillar. The vent windows in the front doors were functional, but the triangular windows in the rear were set in place. Once again the Falcon line made use of the basic body introduced in 1960, distinguished by periodic dating changes. However, this would be the last usage of the old body style, as a totally new Falcon would hatch in 1964.

Although the Futuras represented the top-line Falcons in the car line, the concept did not carry over to the wagons. In this field, the top line was the Deluxe sub-series. Some contend that this was not a true sub-series, but simply the standard Falcon line treated with a deluxe trim package. However, Ford usually did not keep separate production figures on trim packages. Yet it did set the Deluxe Falcon wagons apart from the plain versions on the production rolls. Thus, this book will consider these as separate models. Least popular of all Deluxe wagons was the 2-door Style 21, which drew only 4,269 orders with its base price of $2,434.

Since the Falcon's top wagon line followed the deluxe concept rather than Futura trim level, it did not get the Futura's distinctive side trim. Instead, it used the single side-bar strip of chrome, and wore rather plain hub caps rather than wheel covers. Full wheel covers, however, were a popular option, and probably more Deluxe wagons went out the door with the covers than with the hub caps. Most popular of the Deluxe wagons was the 4-door Style 22. Priced at $2,477, it saw production reach 23,477. As before, the front door vent windows were functional, but those on the rear door were fixed in place. All windows were surrounded by bright metal.

Falcon's luxury liner wagon was the Squire, Style 26, which offered simulated wood trim and full wheel covers as part of its package. There is some question as to whether the Squire fell into the Deluxe Falcon sub-series, or whether it should be considered part of the Futura line. This was the only Falcon this year to use the three decorative vertical bars on the rear fender, retaining this styling touch from the 1962 season. More popular that the 2-door model, the 6-passenger Squire drew 6,808 orders at a base price of $2,703. At mid-year, this model followed the lead of the larger Squires, and also was offered in 5-passenger Sport Style, with individual bucket seats and a full console on the front. In this form it cost $2,738 and drew a surprisingly high sales tally of 1,461 units.

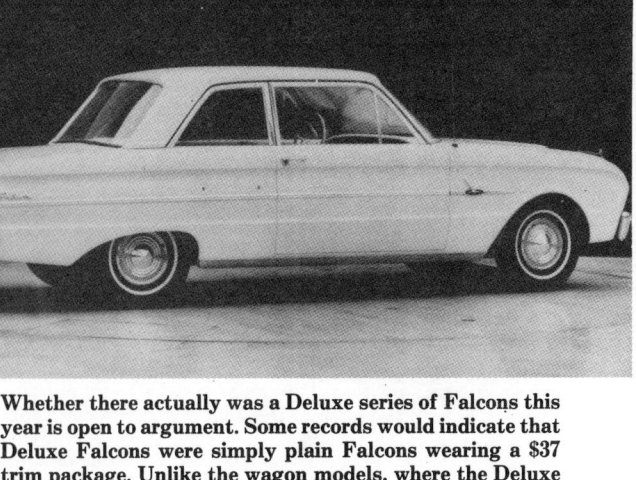

Whether there actually was a Deluxe series of Falcons this year is open to argument. Some records would indicate that Deluxe Falcons were simply plain Falcons wearing a $37 trim package. Unlike the wagon models, where the Deluxe versions were on separate production roles, Deluxe passenger cars were lumped in with the plain Falcon production. Regardless, in Deluxe form, the Falcon 2-door Sedan cost $2,022, sported a single bar of side trim, and wore full wheel covers. Surprisingly, in the low-buck category, the Falcon 2-door Sedan was more popular than the 4-door, and drew 70,630 buyers.

Shown in Deluxe trim is the Falcon 4-door Sedan, which was priced at $2,084. It too used the full wheel covers and single side trim, and inside was fitted with a horn ring and rear arm rests, as opposed to the plain model, which did not have these features. As on the other Falcons, the base engine was the 144 cubic inch Six, with the 170 cubic inch model being available for an extra $37. Even though the 4-door Sedan was not as popular as the 2-door version, the plain Falcons were far more popular than the Futura models. Thus, a total of 62,365 Falcon 4-door Sedans were sold, almost twice the number of Futura models. Whether or not dressed in Deluxe trim, the Falcon 4-doors were designated Style 02.

Without the Deluxe package, the Falcon 2-door was a very plain car. It's amazing what a couple pieces of chrome and full wheel covers will do for a car's appearance. In basic form, the Style 01 Falcon 2-door Sedan cost $1,985, and was the only Ford automobile with a base price under the $2,000 mark. The plain 4-door Falcon went out the door at $2,047 with the small Six. Falcon's new grille and simulated air scoop gave the car a nice frontal appearance, but after four years, the overall style was becoming dated. In 1964 a totally new Falcon family would hatch.

This view of the base Falcon 4-door Station Wagon shows why 18,484 were sold. The car provided a goodly amount of cargo space when the rear seat was folded, nice family transportation when the rear seat was up, and all at a base price of only $2,341. Designated Style 22, the Falcon wagons used a manually operated disappearing rear window in the tailgate. However, this could be replaced by a power-operated window for $29 extra. All Ford wagons used a hard vinyl composition for the flooring, and used a variation of this material on the rear seat back and underside. A very tough and protective material, it came in the same basic shades as did the interior.

Falcon's lowest price wagon was the Style 21 2-door model, which was base priced at $2,298 with the small Six. Devoid of virtually all trim, it nevertheless provided good basic utility transportation, and as a result, drew 7,322 orders. This basic shell also provided the foundation for both the Ranchero Pickup and the Falcon Sedan Delivery.

The popular little Falcon Ranchero Pickup, Model 27, continued to attract customers, though not as many in 1962. This year only 18,533 were sold, despite the fact that the Ranchero once again returned to a plain and Deluxe concept. In plain version it sold for $1,898 and drew 12,218 orders. The Deluxe version, shown here, drew 6,315 customers. Oddly, the Deluxe unit did not include the Deluxe side trim of the car line. Instead it consisted of bright metal around all windows, and a bright metal molding around the top of the cargo bed and on the tailgate. Inside, it included a Deluxe steering wheel with a horn ring, and a choice of red or black vinyl upholstery rather than the standard brown used in all Rancheros and Sedan Deliveries.

As before, both the Ranchero and the Falcon Sedan Delivery used bodies based on the 2-door station wagon sub-structure. Despite its low sales of only 1,038 this year, Ford not only felt it wise to continue the truck in production, but to offer it in plain form or with a Deluxe package. In plain form, the Sedan Delivery cost $2,111 and weighed 2,463 pounds. As before, it did not have a rear cargo door, but utilized a station wagon tailgate with disappearing rear window, manually operated from the outside.

Unchanged was the Falcon-based Station Bus, Ford's low-buck version of the pie-wagon shaped Club Wagon. Designed primarily for livery and small school bus applications, the Station Bus featured removable rear seats, plain gray vinyl upholstery, and no headliner from the driver's seat rearward. The signal lights mounted above the headlight pods were accessories. Virtually no brightwork was used on this model, with even the grille and the bumpers being painted in body color. Priced at $2,287 and weighing 2,712 pounds, the Station Bus drew 10,332 orders.

The mid-model in the Falcon-based Econoline wagon series was the Club Wagon, Model E12. Both this and the Model E11 Station Bus used the 144 cubic inch Six. All used a 90-inch wheelbase and were 168.3 inches long. The Club Wagon used woven vinyl upholstery and had full-length headliners and floor mats. Occasionally referred to as the Custom Station Bus, this model cost $2,436 and weighed 2,770 pounds. Orders only reached 4,378. Oddly, though in base concept these vehicles were part of the Econoline truck range, Ford called them by their Falcon name, and often listed them with the passenger car models.

The top of the line of the forward-control vehicles was the Falcon Deluxe Club Wagon, Model E13. Besides having bright bumpers, grille, and wheel covers, the principal difference between this and the two lesser versions was the fact that this unit used the 170 cubic inch Six as basic power, not the 144 incher. It was priced at $2,673 and weighed 2,796 pounds. Inside it had pleated all-vinyl upholstery, a padded dash and padded sun visors, and a vinyl spare tire cover. Still, customers were scarce, and only 2,923 were sold in this form.

Out near Los Angeles, Carroll Shelby, shown here, was happily stuffing 260 cubic inch Ford engines into British-built AC chassis and bodies, and calling them AC Cobras. Then about mid-year, after 75 such Cobras had been released, Ford came out with its new 289 cubic inch V-8. So ended the 260 blocks in the Cobras. An immediate switch was made to the new mills, and the Cobras, which had been excellent performers on the sports car circuits, became even more of a threat to competing machines. Still using the Ford 4-speed manual transmission, the new power house fit nicely into the unchanged tubular frame with its light aluminum skin. The wheelbase remained 90 inches, the overall length 151.5 inches, and the weight 2,020 pounds. Even the $5,995 price remained unchanged, though street-type extras such as the windshield and grille shown on this model would have been at added expense. Between mid-1963 and the end of production in mid-1965, a total of 580 Cobras came out in 289 cubic inch form. An annual production schedule has been impossible to find.

Introduced on Oct. 7, 1962, and thus considered a 1963 show vehicle, was the Mustang I. Bearing little in common with the soon-to-arrive production Mustang, this mid-engine sports car possibly would have been a competitor of the AC Cobra, had it gone into production. The car used a special steel tube chassis and light aluminum body like the Cobra. It was built by Trautman & Barnes of Los Angeles. Both the steering and V-4 engine were modifications of the British Ford Cardinal or German Taunus. The engine developed 90 horses with dual 2-barrel Weber carburetors. The car was extensively track tested in addition to being widely displayed—including a demonstration drive by Dan Gurney around the circuit during the Watkins Glen Grand Prix. For a short time it looked like the sleek 2-seater might even go into limited production, but after much consideration, Ford decided to stay out of the very demanding sports car field, probably feeling that building cars for that market was better left to the likes of Carroll Shelby, who already was taking the Ford name to many circuit victories.

Also entering the Ford show ring this year was the Italien. Attempting to promote the idea of a sleek 4-passenger sports salon, the Italien hinted strongly of current Thunderbird styling with some innovative flairs. In fact, it looked much like what an excellent California custom house could have done with a stock Thunderbird had it been given the contract. Rear styling was semi-fastback, with a slight but definite notch between the rear window area and the trunk deck. Front bucket seats were upholstered in genuine leather, while the central console held the shifter and other controls. The rear seats swept around the sides in "cocktail lounge" style, which would appear later in production Birds. Engine, chassis, and wheels were stock Thunderbird.

Not entering the show circuit until late in 1963 and gaining most of its promotional impact during the early 1964 season was the beautiful Mustang II. The vehicle came very close to what would be the actual mid-1964 Mustang, and in fact, looked very much like a real Mustang that had just made an expensive run through an excellent customizing shop. Built in 4-passenger form, it was fitted with a removable hardtop, ala the first Thunderbirds. It was powered by the High Performance Challenger 289 cubic inch engine, which developed 217 HP. Interesting is the fact that all of the emblems appearing on the Mustang II later appeared on the production versions.

Not content with a major restyling of one line and facelifts for the others, Ford this year came up with a total restyling of the entire line. Among the changes were a totally new body for the Thunderbird and a brand new skin for the big Ford, which in the author's estimation produced two of the best looking Ford products to come down the pike in a long time.

But it was not the restyling that produced Ford's big news bomb of the year. That explosion occurred on April 17, 1964, when the new and oft-rumored Mustang was born. Considered by some to be an early 1965 car, and by others to be a mid-1964 model, the sporty little vehicle really was what the Thunderbird could have been had it not grown up so fast. Catching the American public like few cars have ever done, the super-popular Mustang recorded 97,705 Hardtop and 28,883 Convertible sales for a total of 121,538 examples sold in just its first five months of production.

Not a particularly fast car, and certainly not a sports car in the true sense, the Mustang nevertheless offered the public what it apparently wanted. That was a nicely styled sporty vehicle, with a long hood and short back, standard bucket seats and console, cramped but usable rear seating, brisk performance with either the Six or V-8, dependability, and finally, a reasonable price. Mustang managed to wrap it all in one very attractive package, and the public went for it in a big way—to the extent that the Mustang must be considered among the world's most successful cars.

Built on a 108-inch wheelbase chassis, the cars were 181.5 inches long overall. Engines included the basic 170 cubic inch Fairlane/Falcon Six, and a brand new 200 cubic inch Mustang Six which used a 3.68x3.13 bore and stroke, a 8.7:1 compression ratio, and developed 116 horsepower at 4200 rpm. In V-8 form, a buyer could have the standard 260 cubic inch model, or any of three variations of the Challenger 289 cubic inch engine, with the top end being the High Performance Challenger, which was introduced in 1964. This block ran a bore and stroke of 4X2.87 inches, had a 10.5:1 compression ratio, and developed 271 HP at 6000 rpm with a single Holley 4-barrel. It was available to Mustangs only when the manual 4-speed transmission was ordered.

In the big Ford line, the same basic body shell was used as had been introduced on the 1960 models, but totally new sculptured sheet metal gave the car the look of a brand new vehicle. Still, the wheelbase remained 119 inches and the overall length stayed at 209.9 inches. Once again, round taillights graced the rear, separated by a large full-width escutcheon plate. Only this time, the plate did not imitate the grille design. The grille itself was a new and very attractive affair of horizontal bars bent at three separate positions to create a vertical bar motif with four recessed panels. The quad headlights resided in the outermost of these recesses.

Within the line some name shuffling occurred. The old low-buck 2-model 300 series was now again called the Custom series. What had been the 2-model mid-range Galaxie series was now the Custom 500 series. Both the Galaxie 500 and the Galaxie 500 XL series remained intact, but their model lists dropped by one with the demise of the formal-roof Club Victoria. This year all 2-door hardtops took the roofline of the mid-1963 Fastback, but retained the former name of Club Victoria. The big wagon line also remained unchanged, with six and 9-passenger models of both the Country Sedan and Country Squire being available.

The mid-size Fairlanes received a very nice styling treatment which included shaving off the rear fins, rounding out many of the severe lines, and adding a grille quite similar to that of the big Fords. The plain Fairlane series retained its three low-buck models, but the Fairlane 500 series lost one model when it was decided not to carry the Country Squire wagon into 1964.

In the world of little cars, the Falcon received its first major styling overhaul. All lower sheet metal was new, the width was increased one inch (as was also true for the Fairlanes) and the new length of 181.5 inches was one-half inch longer than in 1963. The wheelbase remained 109.5 inches, but the station wagons grew to a new overall length of 189 inches. Once again the line consisted of the 2-model plain Falcon series, and the 9-model Futura series which included the Deluxe, Futura, and Sprint variations. In addition, there were the Falcon wagons, now trimmed down to four available models with the discontinuance of the Deluxe 2-door and the Sprint Squire (or bucket-seat Squire).

And finally, the Thunderbird also received its scheduled redesign. Virtually a new car, the Thunderbird had a new wheelbase length of 113.2 inches and a new length of 205.4 inches. The all-new body featured a longer hood, sculptured side panels, sculptured rear deck, shorter roof lines, and new rear ends dominated by huge rectangular taillights. Insides were also new and were highlighted by central consoles, wrap-around rear seat backs, reclining passenger seat, and a heavy-handed use of chrome trim. Model selection returned to three models, two hardtops and a convertible. The very attractive but not-popular Sports Convertible was officially dropped. However, the molded tonneau covers were available from Ford dealers for $269, and the Kelsey-Hayes chrome wire wheels were available for $345, so any dealer could supply a Sports Convertible right out of his accessories stores—and several did just that.

For a change, there was not too much action under the hoods this year. Aside from the aforementioned Mustang Six, the 6-cylinder range remained the same, with the 144 cubic inch model being the base in the Falcons, the 170 cubic incher being the base in the Fairlanes and Mustangs, and the new model being a $62 upgrade when it became available after mid-year. The large 223 cubic inch Six was still the unchanged base in the large Ford line.

In the V-8 world, the 221 cubic inch model was gone

for good, and the 260 cubic inch model remained unchanged but was now the smallest V-8 available. New on the list were two "tamed" versions of the 289 cubic inch High Performance Challenger. These were a 195 horse version using a Holley 2-barrel, and the 225 horse model using a 4-barrel. The first used a 9:1 compression ratio, while the 225 horse unit used a 9.8:1 ratio. All used the same 4X2.87 inch bore and stroke of the High Performance Challenger described earlier, and both ran under the Challenger name.

In the field of big engines, the 352 cubic inch Interceptor was still around, but its horsepower was now raised to 250 at 4400 rpm through the addition of a new Holley 4-barrel. The two Thunderbird 390 cubic inch blocks remained, having 300 and 330 horsepower respectively, but the 390 horse version with the 6-pack carburetor set-up was gone. Ford's two biggest blocks remained the unchanged 427 cubic inch models. The less powerful developed 410 HP at 5600 rpm, with a single Holley 4-barrel, while the top engine hit 425 HP at 6000 rpm, using an 11.5:1 compression ratio and twin Holley 4-barrels.

With the phenomenal acceptance of Mustang, Ford's sales swept to 1,715,591 this year, reflecting a substantial gain over 1963. Even when Mustang's 121,538 units are subtracted, production still was 1,594,053, which was 13,222 more sales than enjoyed in 1963. And these figures do not include the Falcon car/truck vehicles such as the Econoline buses, the Rancheros, or the Sedan Deliveries. But, as before, the profusion of models mean that only two individuals topped the 100,000 sales mark. Both of these were Galaxie 500 models, with the Club Victoria being the most popular Ford of the year, with 206,998 sales, and the Town Sedan being the second most popular with 198,805 sales. In total, large Fords accounted for the most sales, with 923,232 leaving the showrooms. Fairlane production reached 277,586, while 300,770 Falcons flew away. As could be expected, Thunderbirds ranked last with 92,465 sales, which still represented a nice gain over 1963, and a new high in T-Bird sales, indicating that the new styling was appreciated.

Finally, at mid-year, Ford introduced its lowest production and least-known model. This was the Thunderbolt, designed specifically to meet NHRA standards and hit Dodge and Plymouth right between their drag racing eyes. Resembling stock Fairlane 2-door Sedans, the cars were almost totally modified and reconstructed by Dearborn Steel Tubing. Chassis, suspension, and running gear was totally modified, while the engine was the 427 High Riser, which developed 425 horses.

In order to conform to NHRA's requirements, Ford listed the Thunderbolt as a production vehicle, at dealer special order. Priced at $3,900 ready-to-race, the car was available to anyone who walked into a dealership with check in hand. A total of 54 were sold, almost all going to serious drag racers. Although Ford reportedly lost substantial amounts of dollars on each Thunderbolt sold, the cars' awe-inspiring performance on drag strips across the country provided more than enough pay-back in publicity. By season's end, the Thunderbolt had contributed greatly to Ford being awarded the NHRA Manufacturer's Cup, while the NHRA Top Stock point champion was Gas Ronda, driving a Thunderbolt.

Sporting a totally new body, and probably being able to claim the title of best looking car of 1964 was the new Thunderbird. In fact, the style was so well received that the T-Bird broke all of its sales records, with a total of 92,465 being sold. The styling also won T-Bird the prestigious *MOTOR TREND* "Car of the Year" award for engineering advancement and total performance. With the beautiful but not successful Sports Roadster officially gone, Ford's most expensive car once again was the Thunderbird Convertible, Style 85, which was base priced at $4,853. It weighed 4,441 pounds. Sadly, the car was not particularly popular, and only 9,198 were sold. This model is shown without its rear fender skirts.

Most popular of the Thunderbirds was the Hardtop Coupe, Style 83, which drew 60,552 orders. Base priced at $4,486, it weighed 4,431 pounds. Popular extras included air conditioning at $415; power windows and seats at $290, and leather seats at $160. The wheel covers shown on all models were $16 extra, which really seems like a cheap shot on a car that usually listed out at over $5,000 in 1964 dollars. The cars were well identified with the "Thunderbird" script appearing on the front fenders, while "Thunderbird" in block letters appeared on the hood and on the small escutcheon plate between the taillights.

A vinyl top option was not available for this year's Birds. Those buyers wanting the formal look of a vinyl top had to order the Thunderbird Landau, Style 87. Priced at $4,589, or $100 above the standard hardtop, the Landau version featured the vinyl top and large decorative landau irons. A relatively popular model, it drew 22,715 orders. This year's T-Birds were all powered by the 390 cubic inch block of 330 horses, which used a single Holley 4-barrel carburetor. Since the 3-carb 390 engine was no longer offered, T-Bird buyers had no engine options available. Still, the completely new sculptured sheet metal did far more to attract customers than did the previous performance packages, showing again that most Bird buyers were more interested in beauty and comfort than they were in speed.

Although the beautiful Thunderbird Sports Roadster was no longer officially being produced, the fiberglass tonneau sections were still available from the Ford accessory list for $269. The Kelsey-Hayes wire wheels also could be purchased for another $345 for a set of four. This view not only gives a good look at the formed tonneau cover, but also at Thunderbird's new rectangular taillights which dominated the car's rear end. Stylized Thunderbirds occupied the center of each lens, while "Thunderbird" in block letters appeared on the escutcheon plate between the taillights. Since the K-H wire wheels were an accessory and not part of the former roadster package, it is probably that many cars fitted with the tonneau covers went away with no more than the $16 deluxe wheel covers shown here.

Showing off its top-down mode is the new Mustang Convertible, Style 08. Not introduced until April 17, and considered by some to be 1965 models, the mid-1964 Mustangs took the automotive world by storm. Seldom has a single new model created the stir or produced the sales that were achieved by Mustang between introduction and the official start of the 1965 model year on Oct. 15. Least popular of the two available models, the Convertible achieved only 28,833 sales. It was base priced at $2,614 and weighed 2,615 pounds, working out to $1 per pound. The automatic top mechanism was a $54 option, as the standard convertible was listed with a manual top.

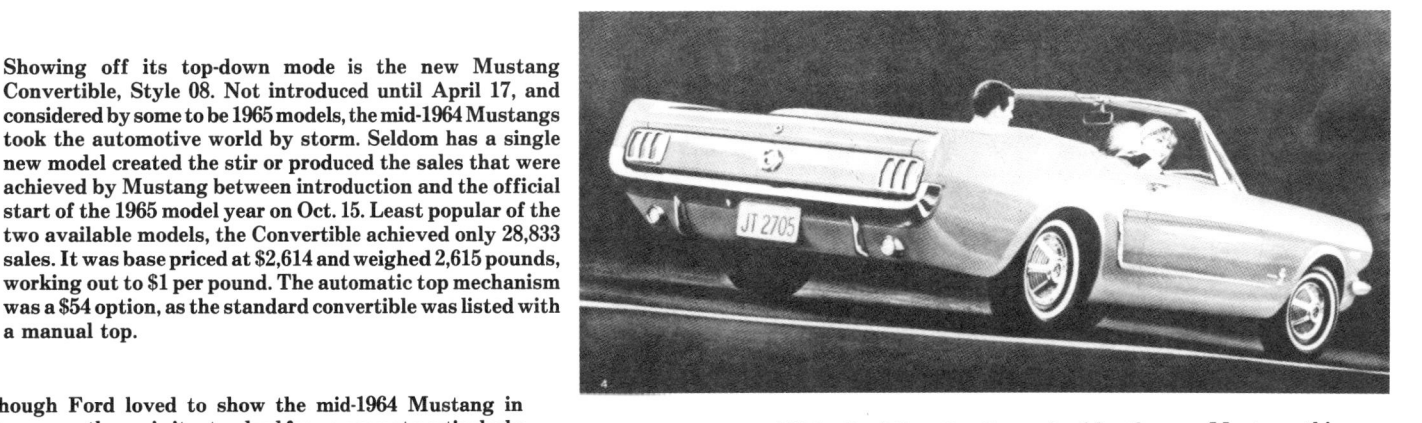

Although Ford loved to show the mid-1964 Mustang in racing poses, the car in its standard forms was not particularly fast—it was simply a lot of fun to drive and just looked as if it was fast. Buyers had engine options of two 6-cylinder variations and four V-8 varieties, ranging up to the 271 horse 289 cubic inch Challenger block. The big engine was a $442 extra and required the $188 extra 4-speed manual transmission. Surprisingly, of the 121,538 total Mustangs sold, 32,780 were fitted with 6-cylinder blocks. By far the most popular model, the Hardtop shown here resulted in 97,705 sales in its 5-month sales period. Designated Style 07, it sold for $2,368 as a Six and weighed 2,449 pounds.

With all of the attention gained by the new Mustang this year, it is no wonder that the car was selected to pace the Indianapolis 500. Appearing as part of a huge fleet of Mustang and Ford cars that participated as support vehicles at this year's race, the Pace Car Mustang was driven by Benson Ford. This year, there were seven rear-engine Fords entered in the race, with the best coming in 2nd place. That was the Kaiser Aluminum Special driven by Roger Ward, which finished at an average speed of 146.33 MPH. Sadly, the other six Ford-powered racers were out before the finish due to a variety of engine, chassis, and accident problems. The scene was not nearly as good as in 1963, when only two Ford-powered Lotus racers were entered and Jim Clark placed 2nd while Dan Gurney took 7th place.

One of the best looking Fords ever, in the author's estimation, came out this year in the form of the Galaxie 500 XL models. Flagship of the 3-car series was the Convertible, Style 69, which at $3,484 was the most expensive model to wear the Ford name. XL models were available only in V-8 form, and only with a bucket seat interior with central console. Rear seating was of the semi-bucket design, meaning that although rated as 5-passenger cars, they really seated only four in comfort. Special XL identification on these models included exclusive spinner wheel covers; special side molding ending in "XL" plaques, and the special signature on the escutcheon plates. Weighing 3,787 pounds, the Convertible drew 15,169 orders this year.

A beauty mark of the Galaxie 500 XL Hardtop was the convertible-like vinyl top with stainless window surrounds, drip moldings, and rear accent bar. Not a standard item, this top treatment was a $75 option over the plain steel top, which also contained two embossed rib designs. Officially called the Club Victoria, Style 68, the hardtop sold for $3,222 in basic form, and weighed 3,622 pounds. Production reached 58,306, all equipped with V-8 engines ranging from the 289 to the 425 horse 427 cubic incher. The latter engine was a $570 extra and required the $188 manual floor-four. In addition to its exterior items, the XL models also had exclusive interiors, which included heavy use of bright Mylar trim, special door-mounted courtesy lights, a deep-dish steering wheel, and even exclusive foot pedals.

Least popular of the three XL models was the Town Victoria, Style 60, which listed only 14,661 sales. Weighing 3,722 pounds, the car had a base price of $3,287. Exclusive features included chromed rockers and individual reading lights for the rear seat passengers. Power windows at $102 extra were a popular option on all XL models. Available but not often seen were factory installed Kelsey-Hayes wire wheels, which went for $412 for a set of five. This was the last year these wheels would fit on Fords, as the 1965 brake design would not accept the old wheel design.

The Galaxie 500 series contained two hardtop models, including Ford's runaway best seller, the Club Victoria, Style 66. Sales hit a phenomenal 206,998. The car sold for $2,783 in basic V-8 form, which would have included a plain steel roof with two embossed ribs. The much more attractive vinyl roof shown here was a $75 accessory, and was identical to the one used on the XL models. Not only did these roofs appear to have the convertible's side seams, but the rear trim also imitated the cross-bar of the real soft top. Note the attractive rear treatment on this year's big Fords.

Lack of rear fender emblem and non-spinner deluxe wheel covers identify this convertible as the plain Galaxie 500, Style 65, and not the XL version. Far more popular than the XL Convertible, the regular model drew 37,311 orders, with its base V-8 price being $3,045. It weighed 3,757 pounds. Unlike the XL cars, the regular Galaxie 500 models could be ordered with the 223 cubic inch Six as well as any of the V-8 blocks. The Six was $109 less than the V-8 prices shown here. All Galaxie 500 models used bench seats front and rear and were full 6-passenger cars. The "500" designation on these models stood for the 500 mile NASCAR races, which saw Ford as a dominant force in this era.

While the Club Victoria turned out to be Ford's top selling model, its 4-door companion, the Town Victoria, Style 64, was one of the less popular Galaxies, with only 49,242 sales. Priced at $2,848 in basic form, the car used full bench seating front and rear. With the windows lowered such as here, there was no mistaking the Victoria version for the pillared Town Sedan. However, with the windows raised, the cars looked quite similar. A quick point of distinction on this model is the small kick-up at the trailing edge of the rear door window. The Town sedans had straight sills.

The Galaxie 500 series also included two pillared models. They were the 2-door Club Sedan, Style 61, and the 4-door Town Sedan, Style 62, shown here. Just opposite of the Club Victoria, which was Ford's most popular car, the Club Sedan turned out to be the least popular of all big Fords, with sales reaching only 13,041. However, the 4-door Town Sedan came out as Ford's second most popular model, with its sales tally reaching 198,805. The 2-door had a base price of $2,722 and weighed 3,572 pounds, while the 4-door cost $2,776 and weighed 3,672 pounds. Note the difference between the rear door lines on this Town Sedan and the accompanying Town Victoria.

Under the new name switch, the old plain Galaxie was now the Custom 500 series. Consisting of only two models, the two and 4-door pillared sedans, this series provided a mid-range in price and trim between the low price Customs and the fancier Galaxies. Lowest priced and least popular of the two models was the 2-door Sedan, Style 51, which cost $2,562. It attracted only 20,619 buyers. Weighing 3,557 pounds, it used the same body as did the Galaxie 500 Club Sedan, but differed in its lack of fancy side trim and in its interior fittings. Interior touches included arm rests with ashtrays for all doors and rear panels, nylon floor carpeting, and twin padded sun visors.

Most popular of the two models in the newly renamed mid-price Custom 500 range was the 4-door Sedan, Style 51. It drew 68,828 orders with a base price of $2,626 in V-8 form. Its weight was 3,657 pounds. Custom 500 models used only a single side trim strip, which extended from the headlight bezel to just before the trailing edge of the front door. The small emblem on the trailing edge of the rear fender read "Custom 500" in script. Among Ford's advertising claims this year was that the cars could go 36,000 miles between chassis lubrication and fuel filter changes, and 6,000 miles between oil changes.

No, the plain Custom 2-door Sedan, Style 53, did not normally look like this when driving down the street. But English Motors of High Point, N.C., took advantage of the car's 3,527-pound weight and $2,459 price tag. It converted this into one of the many Ford contenders competing on the "new car" stock car circuits, both within NASCAR's jurisdiction and without. When fitted with the fantastic 427 engine and whatever chassis modifications they could get away with, these cars kept Ford a dominant factor on the race tracks across the country. In plain street form, the Custom 2-door Sedan drew 41,359 orders. It was the lightest and least expensive of all the big Fords.

Dressed in military uniform, but otherwise unchanged from its stock appearance is this Custom 4-door Sedan, Style 54, which was Ford's lowest price full-size 4-door. It cost $2,513 and weighed 3,617 with the basic V-8. Designed primarily for salesmen's fleets, the military, and taxi work, the cars sported no side trim, rubber mats rather than carpets, and had a primary grade of upholstery material. Still, they did boast of arm rests on all four doors, twin sun visors, and chromed horn rings, all of which were unheard of in the low-buck models of only a few years earlier. Exterior identification on the Custom models consisted of the signature on the trailing edge of the rear fender, and the three cast chevrons on the leading edge of the front fender—does that mean that this example held the rank of sergeant? Note the heavy rear antenna necessary for the 2-way radios of the day. A total of 57,964 Custom 4-doors were sold.

In the big Ford line only four station wagons were available, and all were classed in the Galaxie 500 range of trim. All used the same body, and differed only between being six and 9-passenger models, and having plain or wood trimmed sides. As before, the plain sided model was the Country Sedan. Most popular of all the wagons, the 6-passenger Style 72 drew 68,578 orders. Base priced at $2,938, it was the only full-size Ford wagon under $3,000. Its 9-passenger version, Style 74, cost $3,042 and drew 25,661 orders. Both models weighed about 3,975 pounds.

Just the thing for a day at the beach was the new Fairlane 500 Sport Coupe, Style 47. Essentially the Fairlane 500 answer to the XL models, the Sport Coupe featured bucket seats and an exclusive interior in addition to standard spinner hubcaps and exclusive "Sport Coupe" script on the roof panel. Unlike the big XL models, the car could be ordered with either the Six or a V-8. In the latter form, it sold for $2,591 and weighed 3,012 pounds. Since the Fairlane family did not have a convertible, this was the sportiest of all the models in this mid-size range. The least popular of all Fairlane 500 models, it saw only 21,431 examples leave the factory.

Ford's big fancy wagon continued to be the Country Squire, available as the 9-passenger Style 78 or the 6-passenger Style 76. For a change, there was little difference in sales between the two, with the 6-passenger model drawing 23,570 orders and the 9-passenger drawing 23,120. The 6-passenger sold for $3,127 and weighed 3,986 pounds, while the 9-passenger version was $70 more and 10 pounds heavier. Not really designed for herding these sheep, the top line wagon could be fitted with any engine from the Six to the 427 big block. The emblem just aft of the front wheel well signifies that this car has either the 390 or the 427 engine. The emblem consisted of crossed racing flags with the cubic inch numbers set between them.

Less sporty but almost twice as popular as the Sport Coupe was the Fairlane 500 Hardtop Coupe, Style 47. It drew a total of 42,733 orders with its base V-8 price of $2,430. It weighed 2,992 pounds. All Fairlane 500 models used the dual body side molding with a painted accent insert, which ran through the simulated body side air scoop and terminated at the taillight bezel. As with the big Fords, the top line Fairlanes used little "gunsights" at the leading edges of the front fenders. Plain Fairlanes did not have this trim.

The pillared 2-door in the Fairlane 500 series was the Club sedan, Style 41. It differed from the other 2-doors in that it had a crest on the roof side panel, while the hardtop version had its crest on the chrome trim of this panel and the Sport Coupe had its signature in this place. Fairlanes also continued to use the round taillights, with the 500 models having a bright escutcheon plate between the lenses. The spinner wheel covers on this model were standard on the Sport Coupe, but cost $18 extra on any other models. A vinyl roof for this car cost an extra $75. In plain form, the Club Sedan cost $2,365 and weighed 2,913 pounds. Sales reached 23,447.

The only 4-door sedan in the Fairlane 500 series was the pillared Town Sedan, Style 42. Most popular of all the Fairlane 500s, it drew 86,919 orders. Priced at $2,406, it weighed 3,051 pounds. All Fairlane 500 models carried their signature at the trailing edge of the front fenders, just above the side trim. The signature also appeared in a rectangular plate on the right side of the rear escutcheon plate. The gas filler still lived within this cove area, having its own door just above the license recess on the rear bumper.

It appears that the Fairlane 500 series had only one station wagon model this year. Called the Custom Wagon and available in 6-passenger form only, it was designated Style 48. It listed a base price of $2,701 and a base weight of 3,377 pounds. A total of 24,962 were sold. Body trim was the same concept as used on the car models, except that the left rear trim ran through the circular gas cap, which was located on the rear fender panel and not above the rear bumper as it was on the passenger car models. All Fairlane hoods contained an embossed hump at the leading edge, which might have been considered for a simulated decorative air scoop.

Whether or not the Fairlane Squire Wagon ever went into production is open to question. Shown here on the styling department floor, the car would have been the Style 49. Early sources credit it with a price of $2,869 and a weight of 3,387 pounds. Some sources would indicate that the car was dropped before production, while others contend that a limited number were built very early in the year, but that the style was discontinued in late fall. Since the Squire concept did very poorly in the 1963 Fairlane roster, it is no surprise that the model was discontinued. The only question is when?

The lower-price level of the mid size Ford range was the plain Fairlane series, which used three basic models from the Fairlane 500 series, but lacked a hardtop coupe style. Lowest priced and least popular of all Fairlanes was the 2-door Sedan, Style 31. It cost $2,283, but only 20,421 examples were sold. It weighed 2,922 pounds. All plain Fairlanes had a single trim strip which ran the full length of the car. Exterior trim also included the simulated air scoop on the rear panel, bright bar applique on the rear roof panels, the "Fairlane" script on the trailing edge of the front fenders, and a "Fairlane" crest on the roof panels.

As could be expected, the most popular model in the plain Fairlane series was the 4-door Sedan, Style 32. Priced at $2,324 and weighing 2,962 pounds, the car drew 36,693 orders. The hubcaps shown here were standard, but a $12 set of full wheel covers was a common investment. The front vent windows were functional, but the small vent-like windows in the rear doors were fixed in place. Unlike the Fairlane 500 models which had full carpeting, the plain Fairlanes used rubber floor mats.

The plain Fairlane Station Wagon, Style 38, was a nice 4-door model, not too far removed in trim level from its counterpart in the Fairlane 500 series. Buyers apparently thought the same, and a total of 20,980 were sold at a base V-8 price of $2,620. Available only in 6-passenger form, the wagon had a folding rear seat, allowing a cargo space from tailgate to front seat-back. The tailgate latched from the exterior, and the rear window was manual. However, an electric rear window was available for $32. A chromed roof rack was also available for an additional $45. These looked nice, but were a real nuisance when washing the car.

Until the Mustang came along, Ford's small car hotshots were the two Falcon Sprint models, the Convertible shown here, and the hardtop. Not really a sub-series, the Sprints were technically Falcon Futuras with the Sprint option. This package included the 260 cubic inch V-8, bucket seats, central console, dash-mounted tachometer, heavy-duty suspension, and wire wheel covers. Wearing its "Sprint" signature on the front fender panel, this Convertible, Style 14, was base priced at $2,660. A total of 3,652 were built in full Sprint fashion, while another 626 were built with plain bench seats and no console, apparently for those who wanted a full 6-passenger car rather than a 4-passenger model.

The more popular Sprint was the 2-door Hardtop. Officially known as the Falcon Futura Sport Hardtop with Sprint package, Style 13, the car drew 10,001 orders with the expected bucket seat interior, and another 3,829 orders in 6-passenger form with bench seats and no console. The dash-mounted tachometer is plainly visible in this photo. Also evident is the nicely sculptured hood design on this year's Falcons. When purchased in full Sprint form, this car listed at $2,425 and weighed 2,813 pounds.

Despite the Sprint wheel covers, the lack of fender signature and dash mounted tachometer shows that this is the Falcon Futura Convertible, Style 15. This was a full 6-passenger car with bench seats fore and aft. It could also be ordered as the Sports Convertible, Style 11, in which case it would have had front bucket seats and a central console, but not be considered a Sprint. As shown, the regular Futura Convertible sold for $2,470 and weighed 2,710 pounds. In this form it attracted 13,220 buyers. As the 5-passenger Sports Convertible it listed at $2,586, weighed 2,735 pounds, and attracted 2,980 buyers. In either style, it could be ordered with either the Six or V-8 engine, while in Sprint form it was available only with the 260 cubic inch V-8.

If the Falcon Futura Hardtop could appear in three variations, there seemed no reason why the Futura 2-door Sedan shouldn't arrive in both regular and sport variations. Shown here with bench seats is the plain Futura 2-door, Model 62B. In this form, the pillared 2-door sold for $2,116 and weighed 2,350 pounds. Not as popular as the new hardtop, it still was no slouch on the market, and attracted 16,621 sales. However, in Sport form, with bucket seats and console, it did miserably, with only 212 examples being sold. In that style, it cost $2,237 and weighed 2,375 pounds. All Falcon Futuras were quickly identifiable by the double full-length trim bars that occupied the sculptured ridges on the cars' sides.

The most popular Futura, in fact the most popular Falcon, was the 4-door Sedan, which drew 38,032 orders. It appears that this was the only Futura which was not available in Sport version with bucket seats. As a V-8, it was base priced at $2,165 and weighed 2,410 pounds. As did the larger Fords, the Falcon Futuras used a bright escutcheon plate across the full width of the rear. The gas filler was centered in this plate, while the "Futura" signature was in the rectangular plate on the right side. The completely restyled body was a definite improvement for the Falcon line.

As before, Ford's least expensive and lightest car was the plain Falcon 2-door sedan, Style 01. In base form, it sold for $1,985, and thus remained the only Ford model under $2,000. This example is shown with the basic Six. For another $170 it could have been equipped with the 260 cubic inch V-8. In basic form, with either engine, it was also known as the Model 62A. In this mode it drew a total of 36,441 orders. When equipped with the $43 optional Deluxe trim package, it changed to the Model 62D. In the latter form, it attracted 28,411 buyers, for a grand total of 64,852 examples. In plain form, the car had no side trim whatever, except for the "Falcon" script on the front fender.

Just as the Falcon Futura Convertible was available in standard or sports form, so too was the hardtop. But here Falcon went one step further and offered the car as a standard 6-passenger model with bench seats, as a Sports Hardtop with bucket seats and central console, and as an unnamed variation with bucket seats but no console. In plain Futura Hardtop form the car listed as Model 63B, which cost $2,198, weighed 2,515 pounds, and attracted 32,608 buyers. With the bucket/console full sports interior, the car was listed as Model 63C, which cost $2,314 and weighed 2,545 pounds. In this form, a total of 8,322 were sold. Then, as Model 63H, with bucket seats but no console, it attracted 285 buyers at an undisclosed price.

All plain Falcons were available either in regular trim or, for $43 extra, in the Deluxe mode as displayed by this 4-door Sedan, Style 02. Surprisingly, in plain form they were considered Model 54A, but when the Deluxe package was added, they became the Model 54D. And even more surprising, separate production figures were kept for those released in standard form and those with the Deluxe package. Thus, a total of 54,254 Falcon 4-door Sedans left the nest, 27,722 in standard trim and 26,532 in Deluxe trim. In standard guise, the car weighed 2,400 pounds and cost $2,040. With the Deluxe package, it cost $2,083. On the exterior, Deluxe trim included a single bright side molding running full-length down the center ridge of the side sculpture.

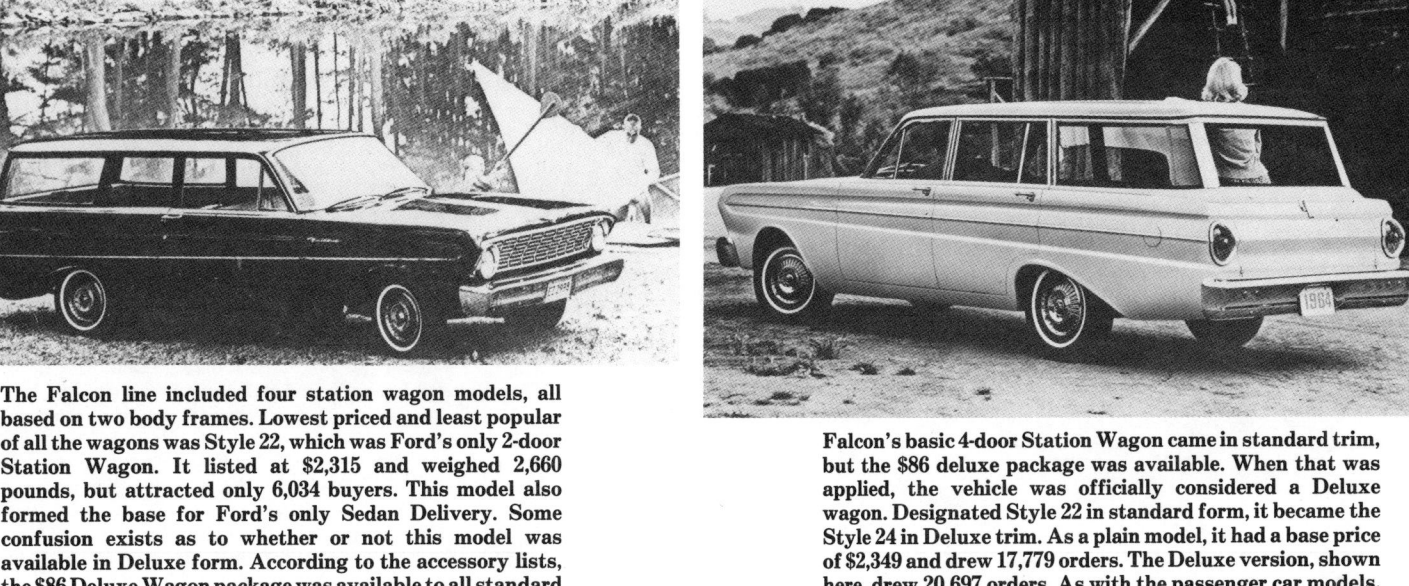

The Falcon line included four station wagon models, all based on two body frames. Lowest priced and least popular of all the wagons was Style 22, which was Ford's only 2-door Station Wagon. It listed at $2,315 and weighed 2,660 pounds, but attracted only 6,034 buyers. This model also formed the base for Ford's only Sedan Delivery. Some confusion exists as to whether or not this model was available in Deluxe form. According to the accessory lists, the $86 Deluxe Wagon package was available to all standard Falcons. However, Ford did keep separate production records of cars with or without the Deluxe package, and these lists do not indicate any of the 2-door wagons having the Deluxe trim. In this photo, what looks like a strip of side trim is simply light reflecting from the sculptured sides.

Falcon's basic 4-door Station Wagon came in standard trim, but the $86 deluxe package was available. When that was applied, the vehicle was officially considered a Deluxe wagon. Designated Style 22 in standard form, it became the Style 24 in Deluxe trim. As a plain model, it had a base price of $2,349 and drew 17,779 orders. The Deluxe version, shown here, drew 20,697 orders. As with the passenger car models, the Deluxe versions could be quickly spotted by the single bar of bright metal running from fender tip to taillight along the central ridge of the side embossing. Wheel covers and a slightly more plush interior completed the deluxe package. In plain form the Falcon 4-door Wagon weighed 2,695 pounds, and 20 pounds more as a Deluxe.

Falcon's prestige wagon was the Squire, Style 26. Not nearly as popular as the work-a-day models, it attracted only 6,766 buyers. It weighed 2,720 pounds and had a base price of $2,611 which did not include $180 extra for the 260 cubic inch V-8. Evidence of V-8 engines was via a small emblem on the front fender panel, while the "Falcon Squire" signature appeared just above the engine emblem, but within the dark simulated wood area, and not on the body-color portion. A popular option on this model was a power operated tailgate window, which cost an additional $30, but allowed the driver to raise or lower the gate window from his seat.

Ford's Ranchero, based almost totally on Falcon components, continued to attract its share of buyers, with 9,916 being sold this year. In basic form, it sold for $2,047 and weighed 2,748 pounds. Its engine was the 144 cubic inch Six, but both the 170 cubic inch and the 200 cubic inch Mustang Six could be ordered, as could the 260 cubic inch V-8. Of the 9,916 Rancheros sold, 2,516 were in the plain form seen here, while 7,400 were equipped with the Deluxe package. Of the Deluxe models, 235 were ordered with bucket seats. The deluxe package consisted of bright molding around the box top and tailgate, black or red pleated vinyl upholstery with matching color steering wheel and dash, and bright window frames, plus other minor niceties. The wheel covers were extra, and side trim was not available.

Although none of the three Falcons based on this common body structure achieved any great production, the same skeleton provided the foundation for the three different vehicles. They were the 2-door Falcon Station Wagon; the Ranchero, and the Falcon Sedan Delivery shown here. Least popular of the three, the Sedan Delivery, Model 78A, drew only 776 orders, with a base price of $2,260 and a weight of 2,858 pounds. Of these, only 98 had the deluxe package, which included a red or black pleated vinyl full bench seat with color-matching steering wheel, dual sun visors and arm rests, and chrome molding on the tailgate. Unlike the standard Falcon passenger cars, the deluxe package for the Rancheros and Sedan Deliveries did not include any side trim. Unlike the Ranchero, the Sedan Delivery did not have its own signatures. Instead, the fender-side signature simply said "Falcon." The bright window moldings show that this version has the deluxe treatment.

Ford offered four variations of its forward-control Falcon-based Econoline Van. They were the standard Station Bus; Custom Station Bus; Club Wagon, and the Deluxe Club Wagon shown here. Prices ranged from $2,318 for the standard Station Bus to $2,684 for the Deluxe model. The plain Station Bus turned out to be the most popular, with 9,249 being sold. This was followed by the Custom Station Bus, with 4,729 leaving the factory. The fancier Club and Deluxe Club Wagons accounted for only 2,687 sales combined. The main difference between the two Club Wagons seems to be that the Deluxe model had a higher level of interior fittings, prominent side spear with the center filled in a complimentary paint shade, and the 170 cubic inch Six, while all of the other models used no side trim, had progressively less plush interiors, and used the 144 cubic inch Six.

While the American race fans were enjoying the antics of the Thunderbolts, in Europe a totally different Ford was creating awe. These were the Ford GTs, designed for one purpose only—to win at LeMans. Americans got their first view of the cars at the New York Auto Show in April, 1964. With body and chassis built by Lola of England, and engine and drive train conversions created by Carroll Shelby, the new GTs were far less Ford than anything that had yet left Dearborn. Still, they carried the Ford name to victory at both Daytona and Sebring; they had been designed primarily by Ford personnel and exclusively with Ford's finances, and theoretically, they could be purchased through select Ford dealers for about $20,000 each. Ford finally won at LeMans in 1967, and terminated the GT program in 1968. By that time, approximately 123 GT models of varying type had been built. Part of the reason for cancelling the project was that Ford had achieved its aim—it had won at LeMans. The other reasons were linked to the run-away costs of the project, and the impending emissions and safety standards mandated by the federal government for 1968 cars. These would have made the GT impossible to sell as "production" cars without huge and harmful modifications.

For this year only, anyone with $3,900 in his pocket could walk into any Ford dealership, and theoretically order a ready-to-race Thunderbolt. He could then have it dealer prepped and deliverer—right to the closest NHRA drag strip if he so desired. Produced through a cooperative effort between Andy Hotton's Dearborn Steel Tubing Co. and Ford, the cars had to be available through the dealer network in order to satisfy NHRA's requirement for the "stock" classes. Designed to hit both Chevrolet and Plymouth right between their drag racing eyes, the Thunderbolts proved to be sheer terror for those who had to compete against them. Only 54 were sold, almost all to serious drag racers, and Ford reportedly lost a fortune on the project. Still, these cars delivered such awe-inspiring performance across the country that Ford's investment was well paid back in publicity. By season's end, Ford claimed both the NHRA Manufacturer's Cup and the Top Stock Point Championship, both feats due entirely to the Thunderbolt's performance.

One of Ford's most attractive show cars this year was the Golden Palomino. Not some way-out creation, this car looked as if it could be driven right out onto the street. It wears a set of gold plated Kelsey-Hayes wire wheels, with modifications (possibly narrowing the rear axle?) made to allow the spinner hubs to fit under the fender skirts. Prominent in this view are the flip-top roof panels which raised when the doors were opened, allowing easier entrance and egress. After touring the show circuit, the car was sent to select dealers for display periods ranging from a few days to a week or more. Finally, in mid-1965, it was retired.

Despite becoming involved in the new Ford GT project, Carroll Shelby continued to produce the Shelby Cobras at his Los Angeles facility, with Ford's blessing. Little changed from the original concept, the cars were now all powered by the 289 cubic inch block. The 2-seat performance sport car continued to be priced at about $6,000. Its weight remained 2,100 pounds. Shown here in competition form, with flared fenders, this car was one of 580 produced from 1962 through 1965.

which complimented the 500 XL series. Now the XL series consisted only of sporty versions of the 2-door hardtop and convertible, while the LTD series consisted of luxuriously appointed variations of both the 2-door and 4-door hardtops. Dropped from the Galaxie series was the pillared 2-door sedan, although this model remained an active part of the Custom and Custom 500 series.

Also new on the scene, but not built directly Ford was the LTD 7-passenger Limousine. These specialty cars were stretched by the Lehmann-Petersen Co. of Chicago, upon special order from select Ford dealers. Similar to the stretched Lincolns that Lehmann-Petersen was building under contract, the Galaxie LTD versions were based on the 4-door hardtop, and thus were probably the longest hardtops ever built. Unlike the Lincoln versions, the Ford models were not well received and it appears that very few were constructed.

Just as the big Fords received a major appearance change, so too did the Fairlanes. However, in the case of the Fairlanes, this change involved a lengthened body and chassis, and resulted in one of the greatest styling moves that had ever occurred to the Fairlane line. Now the new models had a half-inch longer wheelbase, measuring an even 116 inches, while the overall length grew to 198.4 inches for the cars and 203 inches for the wagons, an increase of one inch on the cars and two for the wagons.

Within the Fairlane line, all models remained intact, but the former "ready-to-race" Thunderbolt of 1965 was doomed by the car's new weight and size and by rule changes within the NHRA ranks which now demanded a production minimum of 100 models before a car could qualify as a Super Stock. It appears that a Thunderbolt racer was initially planned, and a few may even have been built and sold, but by mid-winter the car was completely gone.

Having received a new body shell last year, the Falcons got only trim and cosmetic changes, including the mandatory grille switch. Within the ranks, all models remained as before, but far less emphasis was being put on the sporty Falcons—that was now left to the Mustangs. In fact, the Sprint models were no longer considered a sub-series, but now were simply an option package, selling for $222 on the hardtop and $273 on the convertible. Also, the front bucket seats, which had been an important part of the sporty-type Falcons, could now be ordered on any Falcon model for an additional $69.

As could be expected, the Thunderbirds were given only a few cosmetic changes to identify them as 1965 models. Among the trim items was an interesting reversed scoop just aft of the front wheel well and a Thunderbird crest on the leading edge of the hood. A new feature on the car was disc brakes, which resulted

Despite an almost total restyling of the Ford and Fairlane lines, it was the sensational new Mustang which captured the vast amount of automotive attention this year. All of the other Ford products were lucky to get even a glance by the automotive press, as the young Mustang galloped through the spotlights and took both automotive interest and sales by storm.

The acceptance was so great that by year end Mustang had recorded a total of 559,451 sales, which was more than recorded by any other Ford nameplate. Also, its Hardtop Coupe version registered 409,206 sales, which was over 2.5 times more than its next closest competitor. The secret of its success, of course, was that Mustang offered a car for just about every budget. It looked like a sporty and fun car to drive, and it backed its image by offering an options list which allowed a buyer to create whatever kind of car he or she wanted, from a docile yet sporty looking primary car for the young family, to an all-out race machine heavily refitted by Carroll Shelby and crew.

New for the year in the Mustang stable was the 2+2 Fastback, which appeared on Oct. 1, 1964, when the mid-1964 cars officially became 1965 models. Then, in April of 1965, the Shelby GT350 appeared in two variations, both using the new Fastback body. The cars both used the 289 cubic inch engine, but the plain GT350 developed 306 horsepower while the GT350"R" (the "R" stood for "Race") provided an advertised 350 horsepower. The 350"R" also showed a curb weight of 2,550 pounds, as opposed to 2,800 pounds for the GT350. Pricewise, the "R" version listed at $5,995, the "plain" GT350 listed at $4,547, while the plain Fastback went at $2,589, all in basic form. The 350"R", which advertised a top speed of 165 MPH, actually earned far more of a reputation than its limited production would suggest. In all, 562 Shelby GT350 Mustangs were built, but of these no more than 30 bore the "R" designation of all-out racing machines.

And for all of this, what did a buyer receive in the GT350? Really, the package offered quite a list of goodies, including a competition reworked Cobra 289 engine; computerized suspension, 130-MPH Goodyear tires; power disc brakes; limited slip rear end, and a rather spartan race-type interior.

Just opposite of the Mustang, which did not change, the big Ford line once again changed dramatically, but not necessarily appealingly in the author's estimation. Billed as being the "Newest Since 1949," the cars had a totally new body shell and skin, a new interior, new front and rear design, and for the first time, a new suspension consisting of coil springs on the rear as well as on the front. Despite the new styling, the wheelbase remained at 119 inches, and the overall length increased but a hair to 210 inches even.

New for the year was the Galaxie 500 LTD series,

in quicker and smoother stopping ability, but also had an adverse effect. They made it impossible to use the attractive Kelsey-Hayes wire wheels, as these would not clear the new rotors. Since the convertible body was unchanged, it was still possible to use the attractive Sport Roadster tonneau cover, but it seems that this accessory was fast falling from favor on the dealer's accessory lists. Late in the year, a "Special Landau" model was made available. This model had an interior of a special parchment-colored vinyl; either a white or "Emberglo" special paint job, and a parchment-colored long-grain vinyl top among its major differences.

In the engine rooms, a new monster mill appeared, but with far less fanfare than could be expected for a major racing engine. Ford's answer to the 1964 Chrysler Hemi, the new block was the 427 SOHC (Single Over Head Camshaft). Based on the 427 block, the new engine employed special heads with hemispherical combustion chambers. Single overhead cams rode atop of each head, operated by a rather complicated combination of chain drive and gearing. The bore and stroke remained the same 4.23x3.78 inches as found in all 427s, but the compression was 12.1:1. Horsepower was rated at 616 at 7000 rpm in the plain version, or 657 at 7500 rpm in its hottest style. Apparently the engine appeared late enough in 1964 to end up in a few of the Fairlane Thunderbolt drag cars, but aside from this, it was strictly an over-the-counter item priced upward from $2,500, and was not an official option on any production Ford.

Initially, its intended realm was the NASCAR circuit, but here it was disallowed because of low production and no evidence of "stock" usage. Where it did make its mark was in the drag racing field, where such notables as Don Prudhomme and Connie Kalitta used it with some success. Ford would keep the engine on tap through 1968, when it would disappear in the face of the new Boss 429. However good it might have been, the 427 SOHC never came close to attaining the reputation or sales of the Chrysler Hemi, and today what few remain are considered more of a curiosity than a viable racing engine.

Aside from the 427 SOHC, there were no changes in any of the big block families, but there was a welter of movement among the small units. In the 6-cylinder line, both the 144 and the 223 cubic inch engines were dropped. Now the smallest 6-cylinder, and the base engine in the Falcon, Fairlane, and Mustang Six models, was the 170 cubic inch block. This now sported a new compression ratio of 9.1:1 and a new rating of 105 horsepower at 4400 rpm. Likewise, the middle ground Six of 200 cubic inches now had a ratio of 9.2:1 and sported 120 HP at 4400 rpm. Replacing the 223 as the big Six was a new 240 cubic inch block with a bore and stroke of 4x3.18 inches; a 9.2:1 compression ratio, and

a rating of 150 horses at 4000 rpm.

In the V-8 world, the 260 cubic inch model was gone, leaving the Challenger 289 variations as Ford's smallest Eight. Here too, changes were made, with the basic model having a 9.3:1 compression and developing 200 horses at 4400 rpm, while the middle block had a 10:1 ratio and gave 225 horses at 4800 rpm. Everything from the High Performance 289 upward remained untouched.

Once again Ford's model year production soared upward, this time breaking the 2-million mark. With 559,451 Mustangs being born, and 1,463,372 other Ford models being turned out, total sales hit 2,022,823. As mentioned earlier, the Mustang Hardtop Coupe was the most popular model with 409,206 sales. Two other models broke the 100,000 mark. They were the Galaxie 500 4-door Sedan, with 181,183 sales, and the Galaxie 500 2-door Hardtop, with production reaching 157,284.

Sales of the large Fords went up to 978,519 (including the wagons), but despite its totally new styling, Fairlane production slumped to 223,954. And, with the new Mustang cutting heavily into small and sporty car sales, Falcon found its production sliding way down to 185,927 units. Even Thunderbird found itself on the down side, with only 74,972 units leaving the plant, although it is doubtful if many of these sales were lost to Mustangs. In all, it was an excellent year for Ford, even though a few individual models wound up with Mustang hoof prints on their production ledgers.

Back in the mid-1970s, when the author thought he could not survive unless he was surrounded by a covey of Thunderbirds, this Convertible fluttered into the flock. Designated Style 76A, the car was the least popular T-Bird of the year, accounting for only 6,846 sales. In basic form, it cost $4,851 and weighed 4,588 pounds. The author's version came with many extras, including the $106 black leather seats; $290 power seat and window package, and the $425 air conditioning unit. It is seen here parked behind the Dammann's barn, in back of a 1965 Landau model that was also part of the collection.

Once again, the most popular Thunderbird by a wide margin was the plain Hardtop Coupe, Style 63A. However, sales this year slipped to 42,652. It was base priced at $4,394 and weighed 4,470 pounds. Thunderbirds changed very little this year, with the most pronounced difference between these and the 1964 models being the chrome simulated vent on the front fenders and the movement of the Thunderbird signature from the front fender to the trailing edge of the rear fender pod. New front disc brakes aided in smoother and quicker stopping power, but made it impossible to use the Kelsey-Hayes wire wheels, as these would not clear the new rotor design.

This view of the Thunderbird Landau Hardtop shows the new taillight design, with the lenses divided into five separate units by the chrome grid frame. The escutcheon plate between the lenses contained a newly designed Thunderbird emblem. Also shown on this model were the new deluxe wheel covers which cost an additional $16, while the fender-mounted antenna shows the car had the $84 AM/FM radio, which was installed in all Thunderbirds unless a delete order was issued by the dealer. In base form the Landau cost $4,495 and weighed 4,478 pounds. Designated Style 63B, it had a run of 25,474, including 4,500 which were turned out in Special Limited Edition form. These cars were finished in either a special white or a new "Emberglo" paint, had a white parchment vinyl interior and a long-grained parchment vinyl roof. Not expensive, the Limited Edition package cost only $49.60 more than the base Landau price.

Entering its first full year and still taking the country by storm was the new Mustang, which had been introduced as a mid-1964 model. On Oct. 1, 1964, the Mustangs officially went from 1964 to 1965 models, with virtually no change. Prettiest of the lot, though the least popular, was the Convertible, Style 76A. In 6-cylinder form, it sold for $2,614 and weighed 2,650 pounds. A total of 73,112 were sold. This figure includes 2,111 models equipped with bench seats and considered 6-passenger cars, and another 5,338 fitted with the "Luxury" package which included bright accents inside and out, chromed rocker moldings, and fancy wheel covers. A power unit for the top cost an extra $54.

Ford's most popular car of the year—of the decade really— was the Mustang Hardtop Coupe, Style 65A, which saw sales rocket to a total of 409,250! Of these, 22,232 had the Luxury package shown here, while another 14,905 were equipped with front bench seats and were rated as 6-passenger cars. In base form, with a Six, this model cost $2,372 and weighed 2,465 pounds. The vinyl top would have added $76 to the price. Engine options ranged from the Challenger 200 V-8 at $108 extra to the Challenger 271 with the mandatory special handling package at $443. A 4-speed manual transmission was another $188 on the V-8s or $116 on the Six.

Totally new for the 1965 season was the Mustang Fastback Coupe, Style 63A. Not nearly as popular as the Hardtop Coupe, this model drew only 77,079 sales. Advertised as a 2+2 model, meaning two seats forward and two in the back, it was not available with a bench seat in front as were the other two models. However, 5,776 models went out with the Luxury trim package, while many more had the low racing stripe and grille-mounted driving lights, which were part of the GT package. In base form, this model cost $2,589 and weighed 2,515 pounds. A running change between the mid-1964 and 1965 models was the switch from a generator to an alternator, and the dropping of the 170 cubic inch Six in favor of the 200 cubic inch Six as the basic block. Also dropped was the 260 cubic inch V-8 in favor of the new 289 as the basic V-8. Also popular on this model was the $71 Rally-Pac, which included tachometer and clock.

1965

Ford was actively involved in all sorts of racing this year, and it didn't take long for the company to want a hot version of the Mustang for competition. Quickly aiding in this endeavor was Carroll Shelby, who designed the Shelby Mustang or Mustang GT350, using the new Fastback Coupe as a base. The cars were delivered to Shelby's Los Angeles plant, where they were fitted with a heavy suspension package; race-tuned 289 cubic inch block rated at 306 horses at 6000 rpm; 2-seat racing interiors, and special fiberglass hoods with scoops. All were finished in white with blue racing stripes. Not appearing until April, 1965, the cars drew a fair amount of interest in sports car circles. In "tame" form, the GT350 drew about 530 orders with a base price of $4,547, while about 30 more went out as GT350 "R" models, in full race trim for $5,995. It was in one of these that Jerry Titus won the SCCA National Title for this class of cars in 1965.

Sales leader of the new 2-model Galaxie 500 LTD sub-series was the 4-door Hardtop Sedan, which drew 68,038 sales. Known as Style 57F, the car had a base price of $3,245 and weighed 3,588 pounds. A vinyl top with distinctive trim and chrome rocker molding and stone guards quickly set the car apart from other 4-doors. In addition to the trim and luxury interiors, all LTDs were fitted with the 200 horsepower 289 cubic inch V-8 and Cruise-O-Matic transmission as standard fare. Of course, larger V-8 engines could be ordered, but the Six was not available.

A brand new sub-series for the year was the Galaxie 500 LTD line, which consisted of the 2-door Hardtop shown here and the 4-door Hardtop. The series was conceived as a companion to the Galaxie 500 XL sub-series. Now the XL models would be considered Ford's top sporty styles while the LTD versions would be the top luxury liners. Highlighting these models were deeply padded seats with special Pinseal upholstery; walnut applique; door-mounted courtesy/safety lights; gabardine headliner, and vinyl tops styled to look like convertible tops. The round medallion on the quarter panel signified LTD models. Least popular of the two models was this 2-door, Style 63F, which drew 37,691 orders. It cost $3,167 and weighed 3,469 pounds.

With the Lincoln Division having great success marketing 7-passenger limousines stretched by the Lehmann-Petersen Co. of Chicago, Ford felt sure that there might be a market for a lower-priced companion based on the new LTD 4-door. Thus, a contract was signed, and L-P designed a stretch version for the Ford. Essentially, this involved adding a section between the front and rear doors. Some reports show this to be a 7-inch section, others say 12 inches. Included in the package was a totally new interior fitted to the customer's order, which could have a disappearing glass partition between the front seat and rear compartment. This model, shown parked in front of the Detroit Free Public Library, appears to be one of the few manufactured this year. The car was not particularly popular, was not highly promoted, and neither price nor production figures could be found.

Providing a contrast to Ford's top wagon, the Country Squire in the background, is Ford's top convertible, the Galaxie 500 XL, shown here with its top lowered and its boot neatly in place. The sportiest of all Ford cars, the XL sub-series featured front bucket seats with console and floor-mounted shift lever; special door trim set off by lower carpeting and bright work, and full chrome rocker panels and stone guards. Both LTD and XL models carried the stylized star on the rear quarter panels, and both lines were considered the top sub-series of the Galaxie 500 category. The XL Convertible, Style 76B, was Ford's most expensive model, selling for a base of $3,426. At 3,675 pounds it was also the heaviest model, not counting the wagons. Only 9,849 were sold this year.

Companion to the Galaxie 500 XL Convertible was the more popular 2-door Hardtop, Style 63C. The two cars constituted the total XL sub-series. The hardtop shared its body and trim level with the LTD version, but differed in its use of an all-steel top; bucket front seats; central console with floor shifter, and bright interior trim. Both variations came with the 200 horse 289 V-8 and Cruise-O-Matic as the basic power train. In base form the XL 2-door sold for $3,167 and weighed 3,507 pounds. Relatively popular, it drew a total of 28,141 orders. The "Galaxie 500 XL" signature appeared on the front fender.

Though the beautiful styled vinyl top gracing this Galaxie 500 4-door Hardtop gives it a very regal look, the top was considered an extra cost item at $76 additional, whereas in the LTD sub-series the top was included. Unlike the Galaxie 500 2-door, which fared far better than its more expensive variations, the Galaxie 500 4-door Hardtop did not do nearly as well as its LTD counterpart. As a result, only 49,982 were sold. Designated Style 57B, the car cost $2,815 and weighed 3,502 pounds.

The Galaxie 500 range this year contained two sporty 2-door models. They were the 2-door Hardtop, Style 63B shown here, and the Convertible, Style 76A, which looked identical to the XL version shown in an adjacent photo. Both models came very close to looking like their XL or LTD counterparts, but lacked such exclusive trim items as the respective medallions and the rocker and rear fender trim. However, an optional convertible-like vinyl roof was available for this 2-door at $75, while the full wheel covers shown here cost another $26. Also, these cars used a bench front seat and column shifter. The Convertible cost $2,996 and weighed 3,616 pounds while the Hardtop cost $2,737 and weighed 3,402 pounds when in V-8 form. With the Six they were $107 cheaper. Both models were far more popular in plain Galaxie 500 form than in XL or LTD dress. Thus, the Convertible drew 31,930 sales in this series while the 2-door Hardtop turned out to be Ford's third best selling model, with 157,284 sales.

Ford's most popular car, not counting the Mustang, once again was the Galaxie 500 4-door Sedan, Style 54A. This year a total of 181,183 were sold, a slight reduction from 1964. This year Ford dropped its designation of "Town Sedan" for pillared models and "Victoria" for hardtop versions, and called the styles simply sedans or hardtops. In Galaxie 500 form, the 4-door Sedan cost $2,730 and weighed 3,462 as a V-8. In was not available in the LTD sub-series, but instead shared its body with the lower priced Custom and Custom 500 versions. All Galaxie 500 models were upholstered in 2-tone vinyl on both seats and doors.

Ford's premium wagon continued to be the Country Squire, available as the 6-passenger Style 71E or the brand new 10-passenger Style 71A. This year Ford changed its rear seating arrangement. Rather than have a rear-facing third seat as did other manufacturers, Ford used two smaller rearmost seats, running lengthwise between the rear seat back and the tailgate and facing the center of the car. It claimed these seats could each hold two passengers, and thus rated their maximum capacity wagons as 10-passenger vehicles. The Country Squires experienced a slight overall rise in sales this year, with the 6-passenger model drawing only 24,308 sales, but this drop being made up in the 10-passenger line, which saw 30,502 orders. The 6-passenger cost $3,147 and weighed 3,945 pounds, while the 10-passenger cost $3,216 and weighed 3,959 pounds.

Just as the Country Squire changed its seating pattern from nine to 10-passengers via double center-facing rearmost seats, so too did the Country Sedan. In 6-passenger form, this wood-less wagon was the Style 71B which sold for $2,904 and weighed 3,901 pounds. In 10-passenger style it was the 71C, which sold for $3,005 and weighed 3,915 pounds. Unlike the Country Squire variations, Country Sedan sales were down slightly, with the 6-passenger drawing 59,693 orders and the 10-passenger model drawing 32,344.

Once again returning to the Ford lineup was the Ranch Wagon. Ford's lowest price wagon, this model had been dropped from the lists at the end of the 1962 season. Now it once again returned, available only in 6-passenger form, and wearing the interior trim level of the Custom 500 series. Designated Style 71D, the workhorse vehicle is shown here wearing the $26 optional wheel covers. In base V-8 form it was priced at $2,813 and weighed 3,891 pounds. Sales were a healthy 30,817. A powered tailgate window would have added another $32, while a roof rack was available for $45.

Just as was the case with the 2-door Sedan, the Custom 500 4-door Sedan, Style 54B, did not sell as good as did its lower priced counterpart. Costing $2,573 and weighing 3,430 pounds as a basic V-8, it saw only 71,727 orders. This was a fair upswing from 1964, but was beaten by the basic Custom model. Custom 500 cars could be differentiated from other Fords by the unique side trim, and from other Custom models by the brightwork around the windshield and rear windows and the emblems on the rear fenders.

Ford's only full-size pillared 2-door sedan appeared exclusively in the Custom and Custom 500 series. The more expensive but less popular of the two was the Custom 500 variation, Style 62B. It cost $2,520, weighed 3,358 pounds, and drew 19,603 orders. Custom 500 models were the only Fords to use a chrome side strip with four fluted indentations. The Custom 500 signature appeared on the rear fenders. Inside, the series was fitted with nylon carpeting, and had arm rests with ashtrays on all doors and side panels.

Ford's lowest price full-size car was the Custom 2-door Sedan, which shared its unique pillared body with the Custom 500 model. Often seen as a Six, in this form it cost $2,313 and weighed 3,278 pounds. With the basic 289 V-8, it was $106 more. Relatively popular despite its spartan appearances, it drew 49,034 orders, probably more with the 240 cubic inch basic Six than with the V-8. Still, it could be equipped with any V-8 engine, right up to the 425 horse 427 block, which was a $571 option favored by serious drag and stock car racers.

Custom & Custom 500 Sedans

Often going into taxi or police work was the Custom 4-door Sedan, Style 54, which was Ford's basic large sedan. Wearing no series identification or side trim, the car was plain looking indeed. Still, its base price of $2,366 and weight of 3,350 pounds in 6-cylinder form made it a favorite with fleet buyers and those who wanted the most economical big-car transportation possible. As a result, a total of 96,393 were sold. When used for police work, these cars often were equipped with the special 390 cubic inch block that developed 330 horses at 5000 rpm. This $334 option usually was combined with the heavy-duty brake and suspension package which called for another $23 expenditure. Cars destined for city taxi work often got the $11 heavy duty radiator.

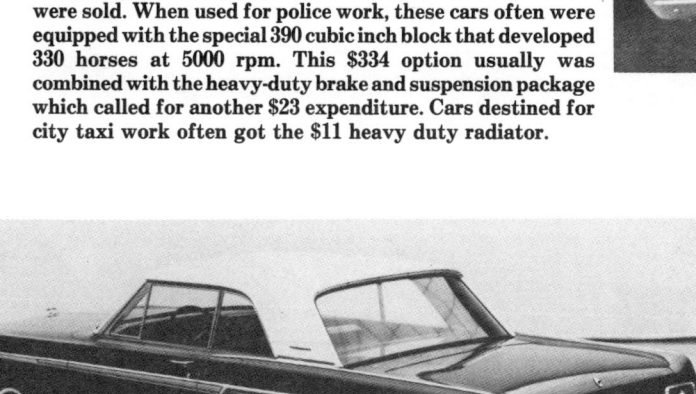

Companion to the Sport Coupe, but far more popular, was the Fairlane 500 2-door Hardtop, Style 65A. This model used a plain bench front seat and column shifter, and was considered a 6-passenger car. Only a simple stylized Ford crest graced its roof side panel. Second most popular of the Fairlane 500 models, it saw sales of 41,405. On this model, the deluxe wheel covers were a $22 option, while the white painted roof was another $22. A vinyl roof could have been added for $76 more. In V-8 form, the car had a base price of $2,432 and weighed 3,069 pounds. As a Six it would have been $108 cheaper. An expensive option was the High Performance 289 engine which delivered 271 horses at 6000 rpm. Not available in the big Ford line, this engine was a $430 option on Fairlanes.

Hotshot of the Fairlane 500 family was the Sport Coupe, Style 65B. The car used the same body as did the 2-door Hardtop, but had its own "Sport Coupe" signature on the rear top panel and used the deluxe wheel covers as standard fare. Inside was where the major difference was found, as the car had front bucket seats, floor shifter and central console, and unique trim items. It was available as both a Six or a V-8, though it is doubtful if many came out with the Six. In basic V-8 form it cost $2,590 and weighed 3,080 pounds. It drew a total of 15,1412 orders.

The Fairlane 500 series contained two 2-door hardtops, and also had a 2-door pillared sedan. Called Style 62B, the car looked almost like the hardtop with the windows raised. As did all Fairlanes this year, it benefitted from the new sheet metal in some ways, lost some looks in other ways. The lowest price model in the Fairlane 500 series, the 2-door listed for $2,369 and weighed 2,997 pounds, thus being the only V-8 Fairlane to be under the 3,000 pound mark. Not particularly popular, it drew only 16,092 orders. All Fairlane 500 models had the series identification marked plainly on the rear quarter panel, just above the trim line.

The most popular model in the entire Fairlane family was the 4-door Sedan, Style 54B, in the Fairlane 500 Series. A total of 77,836 were built. Since the Fairlane group had no 4-door hardtops, this and the wagon were the only models having more than two doors. The body moldings this year contained a center section done in argent and black. Both two and 4-door sedans used bright molding around all windows and covering the center B-pillar. A bright bar ran between the taillights on the escutcheon plate, but this plate was in body color. Above the bright bar, "Ford" appeared in block letters, while the fuel filler lived behind its own door between the trim bar and the bumper. The Sedan cost $2,409 and weighed 3,055 pounds as a V-8.

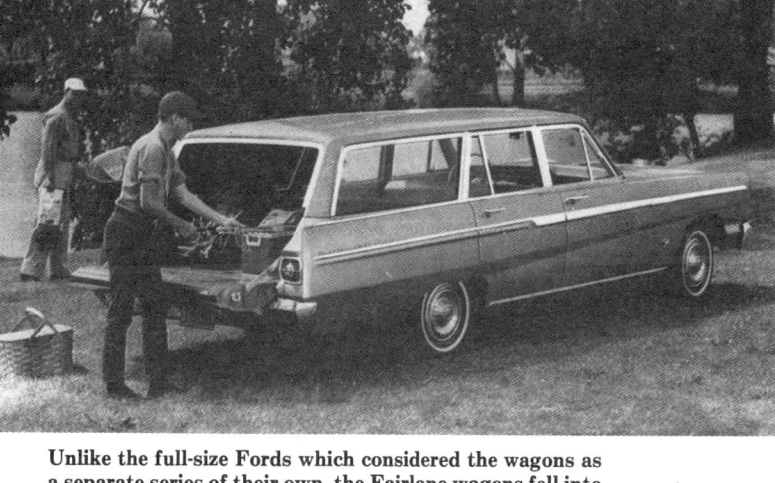

Unlike the full-size Fords which considered the wagons as a separate series of their own, the Fairlane wagons fell into either the plain series or the better trimmed Fairlane 500 series. This is the fancy version, Style 71B, which not only used Fairlane 500 interior trim levels, but also used that series' side trim and signatures. In this form, it cost $2,697 and weighed 3,412 pounds, and thus was the heaviest of all Fairlanes. Production reached a comfortable 20,506. The Fairlane wagons were built in 6-passenger form only, with no third seat options being available.

Ford's low-buck intermediates were the plain Fairlanes, which consisted of a wagon, a 4-door sedan, and this 2-door Sedan, Style 62A. It listed for $2,288 with the basic 289 V-8 or $2,183 with the new 200 cubic inch Six. Least popular of all Fairlanes, this model drew only 13,685 orders. The Sedan, Style 54A, fared better, but even this was no great feat. Drawing only 25,378 sales, the car sold for $2,329 and weighed 3,055 pounds. Except for a thin strip of bright rocker molding and the "Fairlane" script on the front fenders, Fairlanes were devoid of any side trim. What appears to be trim on this rear fender is simply a reflection from the fender embossing. Inside, the cars used plain vinyl upholstery and had vinyl-coated rubber floor mats.

Ford's lowest price intermediate wagon was the Fairlane 4-door, Style 71D. Priced at $2,618 and weighing 3,375 pounds, it drew only 13,911 orders. Apparently in the Fairlane line, buyers felt the few extra dollars were well worth it to step up from the low level to the much brighter Fairlane 500s. Unlike the big Fords, which changed their appearance but not their size, the Fairlane wagons not only looked different than the 1964 models, they were also two inches longer, now being 203 inches in total length.

The Falcon Futura Convertible still had companion Sprint and Sport models, but these were now considered option packages for the basic car, and not sub-series. Thus, in base form, the Futura Convertible was the Style 76A, shown here. Selling for $2,428 it was a 6-passenger car fitted with vinyl-covered bench seats and a column shifter. In this form, it was the most popular, accounting for 6,191 sales. In Sport version, it became the Style 76B, which cost $2,481. Decidedly unpopular, this variation accounted for only 124 sales. Finally, with the Sprint package, it became the Style 76D, which cost $2,660 and drew only 300 orders. The Sprint package used the same bucket seat and central console interior as did the Sport package, but also added the 289 V-8 as standard equipment. The Sprint models had their own identity insignias, but the Sport models used Futura trim and differed only in the interior.

Just as was the case with the convertible, the Falcon Futura Hardtop was the basic car, while this Sport model and the Sprint were considered option packages, not sub-series or separate models, even though they did each have their own style numbers. Thus, the Sport Coupe shown here was Style 63B. It was of 5-passenger configuration, with bucket seats in the front, but did not use the central console as did the convertible. In this form it cost $2,226, weighed 2,380 pounds, and drew 1,303 orders. In Sprint form, it had its own special emblems and wire-type wheel covers, and came with the 289 V-8 as standard. Here it was the Style 63D which cost $2,425. With only 2,806 Sprint Hardtops going out of dealerships, Ford decided those who wanted sporty cars could buy Mustangs, and the Falcon Sprint became a thing of the past before year end.

In addition to a bevy of 2-door hardtop and convertible selections, the Falcon Futura flock also included a 2-door Sedan, Style 62B. Of pillared style, it was base priced at $2,099 and weighed 2,375 pounds. With the Six, it drew 11,670 orders. It could also be ordered with the 289 cubic inch V-8 for an extra $153, and have the Cruise-O-Matic installed for another $182.

Shown living a long and happy life in Sweden is this Falcon Futura Hardtop, Style 63B. This plain base version of the Falcon hardtops had the greatest drawing, with 24,451 being sold, many with the V-8 at $2,179. The 2,396-pound car had bench seats, 6-passenger capacity, and a column shifter. The 2-tone paint job was a $19 option. Sprints this year were given a total trim reworking, plus a new grille and rear design. The mud flaps were a genuine Ford accessory, but the reflectors are strictly Swedish aftermarket.

Most popular of all the Falcon Futura models was the 4-door Sedan, Style 54B. Priced at $2,146 and weighing 2,410 pounds with the Six, it had a run of 33,985. Side trim on all Futuras consisted of spear-type dual body side moldings with a contrasting painted insert and the word "Falcon" spelled out at the rear between these moldings. This year any Falcon model could be equipped with front bucket seats for an extra $69.

Information differs on whether the Falcon wagons were considered a separate series, or whether they were included within the Futura and plain Falcon series. For simplicity, this book will treat them as part of their respective series. Thus, the mid-priced wagon was the Falcon Futura 4-door, Style 71B. Priced at $2,453, it weighed 2,670 pounds. A relatively popular model in a family of relatively unpopular wagons, it nevertheless drew 12,548 orders. This model used the same full-length double bar side spear as did the Futura automobiles. It was available in 6-passenger form only unless the front bucket seats were ordered, in which case it became a 5-passenger car. There was, however, no third rear seat available.

The most expensive Falcon Futura wagon was the Squire, which wore imitation wood side trim. This trim was similar to that used on the Country Squire, but was more spear-like in keeping with the side trim of all the other Futura models. In base 6-cylinder form, the Futura Squire cost $2,608 and weighed 2,695 pounds. The roof rack was a $45 option, while a power tailgate window would have been another $30. Possibly because of its price, the Falcon Squire was not particularly popular, and only 6,703 were sold.

Lowest priced of all Ford cars, and the only one still with a base tag under $2,000 was the plain Falcon 2-door Sedan, Style 62A. It listed at $1,977 and weighed 2,370 pounds. Most popular model in the plain Falcon series, it drew 35,858 orders in regular form, as seen here, and another 13,850 with the deluxe trim package. The 170 cubic inch Six was still the basic engine for all Falcons, but many of those with 6-cylinder power had the optional 200 cubic inch model which cost an extra $53.

Total lack of side trim and a Falcon signature on the trailing end of the front fender says that this is the plain Falcon 4-door Sedan, Style 54A. As such, it had a base price of $2,038 and weighed 2,410 pounds with the small Six. Certainly an economical car, if not particularly sporty, it drew 30,186 orders in plain form, as seen here in Ford's styling studio, and another 13,824 with the deluxe trim package. The deluxe package consisted of bright front fender molding which extended into the front doors, a hood ornament, and bright drip rail moldings. The molding at the base of the roof pillars was standard on all models.

Wearing the deluxe trim package available to all plain Falcon vehicles is the Falcon 4-door Station Wagon, Style 71A. Compared with the plain sides of the regular Falcon line, the inexpensive deluxe package added immensely to the overall appearance. Most popular of all Falcon wagons, the plain 4-door drew 14,911 orders. Its base price was $2,317, and its weight 2,680 pounds. the full wheel covers shown here were not part of the deluxe package, but were a $22 option, while the whitewall tires were another $30 extra. Falcon wagons were 190 inches long, compared with 181.5 inches for the cars.

Based on the same shell used for the 2-door Falcon Wagon was the cute little Ranchero Pickup, which used all Falcon parts in its construction. In base for the truck cost $2,095 and weighed 2,713 pounds. It is shown here in the styling studio, with the deluxe trim package which included the double side moldings with contrasting paint in the center and the five chevron-like bars at the trailing edge. Also in the package was a special red or black pleated vinyl interior, matching carpeting, and bright trim around the box top. Production records show 1,799 built in plain form and another 16 plain jobs with bucket seats, and 7,734 with the deluxe package and bench seats and 990 in deluxe form with bucket seats. The Courier Sedan Delivery also used the same shell, but interest was disappearing, and only 537 were turned out in plain form while another 112 had the deluxe package. The Courier sold for $2,309 and weighed 2,798 pounds. This would be the last year for the Courier.

Ford's lowest priced and by far least popular wagon was the Falcon 2-door, Style 59A. Available only in the plain Falcon series, it drew only 4,891 orders. However, its basic shell also provided the foundation for the relatively popular Ranchero Pickup and the totally unwanted Courier Sedan Delivery. Thus, with three different body styles hinged to this one shell, Ford probably figured it was worth carrying the car for this one last year. The style would not reappear in 1966.

Appearing for the last time this year was the Shelby Cobra 289. No, the interesting car would not go away. But beginning with this year's late models, it would sport the newly styled body shown here and be powered with the terrific 427 engine. These cars would be known as Shelby Cobra 427s. Meanwhile, the early hatch were virtually unchanged from previous models, and a small but steady run of Cobras continued to leave Los Angeles in the former form. Later in the year, the new models did appear with the 427 engine, but whether these were considered late 1965 models or early 1966 in unknown. These later models apparently had the flared wheel openings and louvered front fenders of the true 1966 editions, and for all purposes can be considered 1966 stock, released early. Owners of these early models, however, tend to regard them as true 1965 vehicles.

Virtually identical to the 1964 varieties was the 3-model line of Falcon Econoline wagons. Shown here in school bus livery is the least expensive of the three, the Station Bus, Model E-11. It was base priced at $2,293 and lacked such refinements as side trim, wheel covers, and bright bumpers. The middle ground of this van family was occupied by the Club Wagon, based at $2,438, while the Deluxe Club Wagon occupied the top spot. Its base price was $2,635, and included such things as a right hand chrome mirror, spare tire cover, pleated vinyl upholstery, and padded dash and sun visors. All wagons weighed about 2,800 pounds. New for the year was an extended version of the Station Bus. This model drew 573 orders, as opposed to the 7,116 for the regular version shown here. The regular Club Wagon drew 3,813 sales, while the Deluxe version accounted for only 2,259.

Gas Ronda, the 1964 NHRA Top Stock Champion, this year switched to a Mustang Fastback. Running in NHRA's Factory Stock Class, the car was sponsored by Russ Davis Ford of Covina, Cal., and was modified to the very limits of the Factory Stock regulations by Performance Associates. Despite Ronda's searing performances, he was not able to duplicate his 1964 record, coming in second at the Winter Nationals at Pomona and repeating this performance at the NHRA Nationals at Indianapolis. In both cases, Ronda was beaten by other finely tuned Mustangs.

Although the vast majority of professional cars this year came out on Cadillac and Oldsmobile chassis, a few companies continued to build economical models with Fords as the base. One such firm was Automotive Conversions Corp. of Birmingham, Mich. and Port Credit, Ontario. Known as Amblewagons, these vehicles were based on stock Country Sedan wagons, and were available in either hearse or ambulance form. The hearse model, shown here, had casket rollers in the tailgate, and was equipped with blind quarter panels with large landau irons, and velvet curtains on the rear door windows. The roof was covered in grained black vinyl. Curtains and side panels were quickly removable so that the vehicle could easily be converted back to station wagon configuration. On the ambulance version, the rear quarter windows were of frosted glass. Destined more as a transport vehicle than an emergency ambulance, the Amblewagon carried only minimum first aid equipment.

No, Mustang had no idea of coming out with a station wagon model, but if it did, this might have been the result. The unique car was designed by Robert Cumberford and custom built by Carrozzeria Intermeccancia of Italy. Not unlike similar wagon modifications that were appearing on Corvette bodies, the Mustang wagon model provided fairly ample rear seat and luggage space while still holding to a relatively sporty concept. Though this one-off model never drew any further orders, one must admit that it was a pretty nice looking little car, despite the fact that as a working wagon, it left much to be desired.

1965   **AMBLEWAGON**   1965

Once again, the full Ford line received a total restyling, but once again it was the virtually unchanged Mustang that grabbed both the headlines and the order forms. Mustang sales climbed to a new and almost unbelievable height, totalling out at 607,568, which was almost 50,000 more than the previous record year. And, surprisingly, all of this increase was found in the bread-and-butter Hardtop Coupe, which saw sales go up to 499,751, a jump of well over 90,000 sales. This model, of course, was Ford's best selling car of the year by a wide margin.

Losing ground, surprisingly, was the sleek 2+2 Fastback Coupe, where sales fell to 35,698. This was less than half of the 1965 record. The Convertible managed to hold its own with a virtual consistent 72,119.

Although all of the other Fords underwent complete or major restyling, the cars received little recognition for the effort. Probably this was caused by the fact that in appearance they were not that far removed from the 1965 issue, even though the sheet metal was totally new.

In the large Ford line, most interest was given to the new Galaxie 500 7-Litre Series. Consisting of the same two sport models as found in the Galaxie 500 XL series, the 7-Litre models held Ford's newest engine offering, the 428 cubic inch model that developed 345 horses. Considered standard in this series, the engine was coupled to either the Cruise-O-Matic or manual 4-speed as a no-cost item. Other standard items included dual exhaust, front power disc brakes, bucket seats, and floor shifter.

But it was the 428 engine more than the new 7-Litre models that drew the interest. Having no relation to the old 427 cubic inch models, the new blocks were derived from the 410 Mercury mills, and used a bore and stroke of 4.13x3.98 inches and a compression of 10.5:1. Hydraulic lifters and single 4-barrel carburetor were standard, and a welter of power equipment could be added at extra cost. The 428 was produced in only one version for retail sales, but later a Police Interceptor model with aluminum intake manifolds became available. It developed 360 horses at 5400 rpm.

Although the new 428 blocks were drawing all the attention, the famed 427 was still available in 410, 425, and 650 horsepower SOHC versions. Still, except for the serious racing fraternity, little interest was displayed regarding the 427, and only 237 such blocks were installed this year. Price was a major factor here, with the basic 427 being a $1,075 option while the 428 was only $325 extra.

Also changed in the engine department was the good old 390, which now came in three variations. The most basic of the three was now rated at a moderate 275 horses at 4400 rpm, using a 9.5:1 compression ratio and a 2-barrel carburetor. The middle ground was occupied by a new 4-barrel version which developed 315 horses at 4600 rpm, while the "hot" version, called the GT 390, produced 335 horses, using an 11:1 compression ratio, a higher lift cam, and redesigned cast iron manifolds.

Making good use of the new family of 390 engines was the greatly restyled Fairlane line. Not only were the cars totally different in appearance, with stacked headlights, and rectangular taillights, they were also wider, longer, lower, and had a larger engine compartment to accommodate even the hottest version of the 390. In addition, the line was expanded by a new series and a new model. The model was a return of the Squire Wagon, available in the Fairlane 500 series. The new series was the Fairlane 500 XL, which consisted of a hardtop coupe and a convertible. Among the special features of this series were bucket seats, central console, special wheel covers, and special identification. Shortly after introduction, two more models were added to this series. These were the same two body styles, but were called Fairlane 500 XL GT models. They were essentially the same as the regular 500 XL versions, but used the large 390 cubic inch block as standard power.

Not to be outdone, the Falcons also received a total restyling, being given a longer hood, non-embossed sides, rounded edges, a shorter rear deck, and a more attractive and substantial looking front end design. However, the line received a reduction in models, with the 2-door wagon going away, the entire wagon series being divided into a plain 4-door in the Falcon series and the Squire in the Futura line, and all sporty versions being deleted from the Futura block. Now the 2-door Sport Coupe was as fancy as one could get in the Falcon line—and don't even think of a performance model.

In line with the Falcon's new styling was a lengthening of the car, due in large part to the fact that the line no longer used its own chassis, but was built on a shortened version of the Fairlane frame. This gave the cars a new wheelbase length of 110.9 inches (1.5 inches longer) and 113 inches on the wagons. The new overall length was now 184.3 inches for the cars and 198.7 inches for the wagons.

And, of course, there were the Thunderbirds, which this year were probably the most attractive of the three generations that used the old body shell. But a totally new grille design, new body sculpturing, and a rear filled by a single taillight complex that stretched full-width across the car, made the 1966 Birds among the best looking of the lot. Also in the nest was a new Bird. Called the Hardtop Town Sedan, it was a combination of the plain Hardtop and the Landau. It turned out to be not especially popular, and the concept was not carried over when the line was completely redesigned for 1967. Also new for the Thunderbirds was a power boost, with the new 428 cubic inch engine being available, along with the standard 390.

As mentioned, the Mustang Hardtop Coupe stole the sales show with its incredible run of 499,751. However, three other models joined the ranks of cars with sales over 100,000. They were the Galaxie 500 2-door Hardtop, with 198,532 sales; the Galaxie 500 4-door Sedan with 171,886 units, and the Custom 500 4-door Sedan, with

109,449 sales. Orders for large Fords were up again, with production reaching 1,104,104. Fairlanes also recorded a nice increase, with sales reaching 317,274. However, the two birds suffered losses. Falcon's sales slumped to 195,589, which included the funny little Club Wagons, while Thunderbird dipped down to 69,176, despite the addition of a new model and the 428 engine option. Still, overall, this was once more an excellent year for Ford.

And, totally new for Ford was another horse to keep the Mustang company. This was the Bronco, Ford's first entry into the "Jeep-like" light utility field since it completed its government contract for the real Jeep following World War II. Although actually more of a truck than a car, the Bronco was a 4-passenger vehicle, and for that purpose its birth will be covered. However,

Appearing for the last time this year was the beautiful Thunderbird Convertible, Style 76A. Sales had dropped to 5,049, and with a totally new Thunderbird about to appear in 1967, Ford felt that it wasn't worth the effort to design a convertible model in its top luxury car. Still available for this car, but seldom seen, was the beautiful aftermarket tonneau cover with molded headrests, which transformed the car into a 2-passenger roadster. In plain form, as seen here, the Convertible weighed 4,496 pounds and sold for $4,845.

Of the three hardtop coupes available in this year's Thunderbird line, only one had the small opera windows in the rear quarter. That was the basic Hardtop Coupe, Style 63A, which at $4,395 was also Thunderbird's least expensive car. Least popular of the three hardtops, this model drew only 13,389 orders. A new option this year was the 428 cubic inch engine, which cost only $65 more than the basic 390.

successive models will not be traced here, since this line is well documented in James K. Wagner's excellent book *FORD TRUCKS SINCE 1905*. Suffice to say, the Bronco was initially offered as a door-less and topless little off-road vehicle, with a utility body built by the Budd Co. Soon after introduction, this was followed by two more models, a Sport Utility with a 2-man bolt-on steel top and small cargo area, and a Wagon, with rear seat, removable 4-passenger top, and full front doors. The Wagon turned out to be the most popular, with 12,756 sold, while the Sport Utility registered 6,930 units and the "Roadster" ran 4,090. All used the 170 cubic inch Six for power, with the new 289 V-8 also being available.

And finally, on the race circuit, Ford impressed the European community by winning the 24-hour Gran Prix at LeMans, France, with a Ford GT-40 Mark II designed especially to compete in this race. Also continued was the interesting Shelby Mustang, which this year entered into a strange companionship. That occurred when Hertz Rent-A-Car ordered 936 black Shelby GT350s and entered them in select rental fleets. The idea was to provide business customers with a sporty change of pace to the average sedan—and to one-up Budget Rent-A-Car, which had been offering Mustangs ever since their inception. However, the idea had reverse merit. True, the cars rented well, but too often came back to Hertz with evidence of drag strip numbers on their sides. Hertz did not repeat the project in 1967, but this year its 936 orders helped boost Shelby's Mustang conversions to 2,378 for the year. This figure also includes six Shelby GT350 convertibles which were produced as special promotional vehicles.

The all-time favorite car of Gloria Dammann, wife of the author, was this Thunderbird Landau, which was totally rebuilt and given to her as a Christmas present in 1974. Finished in deep maroon, with a maroon interior and black vinyl top, the car is shown here sporting aftermarket wire wheel covers and wide whites. Notice that this model does not have the opera windows in the rear quarter. The most popular Bird of the year, the Landau accounted for 35,105 sales, all with a base price of $4,552. Designated the Style 63D, it weighed 4,367 pounds. This particular model had the 428 engine, the $413 air conditioning system; power windows and seats for $296, and the AM/FM radio at $82.

A new Thunderbird style for the year, and one that would appear in 1966 only, was the 2-door Hardtop Town Sedan, Style 63B. Essentially, the car was the Hardtop Coupe, but fitted with an uncovered top used on the Landau. It lacked the opera windows of the Hardtop Coupe, but also lacked the vinyl top and landau bars found on the Landau model. As did its styling, both its price and its sales fell between the other two hardtops, and thus it was base priced at $4,552 and accounted for 15,633 sales. Although the attractive fender skirts were a dealer supplied accessory, the majority of the 1966 Birds seem to have left the nests with open rear wheel cutouts. When the skirts were installed, the stainless trim around the rear wheel opening had to be removed.

Proving that it was strong enough to tow and launch a small boat was this Mustang Hardtop Coupe, Style 65A. Ford's all around best selling car this year, this model accounted for 499,751 sales, which was about a 90,000 increase over the 1965 production. Of this amount, 55,938 had the luxury interior at $100 extra while another 21,397 opted for a plain front bench seat at $25 extra in place of the buckets. The Hardtop had a base price of $2,416 and weighed 2,488 pounds. The rocker moldings shown on this model and the convertible were not stock items, but were a $16 option. Popular on this car was a vinyl roof at $76 extra. New for the year was the grille design which featured a "floating" horse outline (Mustang, of course) within a central rectangle (corral?) with no horizontal bars. All Mustangs still used a 108-inch wheelbase chassis and were 181.5 inches overall.

Although its sales slipped slightly, the perky little Mustang Convertible, Style 76A, still saw production reach 72,119, which was better than all Thunderbird sales combined. The car was base priced at $2,653 and weighed 2,650 pounds, thus coming in at just about $1 per pound. As before, numerous options could be added, including the 225 horsepower V-8 package for $162 or the Challenger 271 High Performance package for $444. The wheel covers shown here, with small central spinners, were a $20 dealer accessory. Included in the production figures were 12,520 models which had the $100 luxury interior which included wood-grained steering wheel, rear and door courtesy lights, and special door handles. Also, 3,190 convertibles had bench seats rather than the standard bucket seats.

Wearing the $152 GT package is this 2+2 Fastback, Mustang's least popular car. In fact, this model suffered a decided slump in sales, with production reaching only 35,698, which was less than half of the 1965 sales. Of this, 7,889 had the luxury interior, but the records indicate none built with bench seats. In base form, the Fastback sold for $2,607 and weighed 2,519 pounds. It was considered Style 63A. The GT package consisted of special side stripe, grille-mounted fog lights, dual exhaust, disc brakes, and the special suspension handling package. Engine choices were optional.

Hertz Rent-A-Car unwittingly got into the "Rent-A-Racer" business this year when it contracted with Carroll Shelby for 936 Shelby GT 350s. All were to be painted black with gold trim, and the cars differed from the regular Shelby Mustangs only in carrying the side designation GT 350H, with the "H" standing for Hertz. Early delivery models were fitted with the 4-speed manual transmission, but later models used the Cruise-O-Matic. Hertz hoped to provide a sporty car for its up-scale business customers, but too often found the cars being returned with evidence of drag race numbers on the sides. The rental program was not continued in 1967. In addition to the Hertz order, Shelby built 1,442 Mustang 350s this year, for a total production of 2,378. One of these took the National "B" Production title for SCCA, shutting out an amazed Corvette contingent. In addition to the above production, Shelby built six Convertible GT 350s, but not for sale. These were promotional vehicles, and were presented to close associates.

Ford's luxury 2-door was the Galaxie 500 LTD Fastback Coupe, Style 63F. This year the stylized Galaxie emblem moved from the rear quarter to the front fender space just aft of the headlights. The "Galaxie 500" signature which had occupied this spot was deleted. Base priced at $3,201, the car weighed 3,601 pounds. Production dropped slightly to 31,696. All LTD models used the 200 horse 289 cubic inch engine as basic power. Almost all LTDs went out the door with vinyl tops, but technically this was not a stock item this year. Rather, it was a $75 extra on the 2-doors and $85 on the 4-doors.

Ford's most luxurious 4-door, and the foundation of the Lehmann-Petersen Limousines, was the Galaxie 500 LTD Hardtop Sedan, Style 57F. What has always seemed unusual was that Ford based its most luxurious sedan on the hardtop styling, rather than on the pillared sedan base, which in plain Galaxie form was a far better selling model than was the hardtop version. Base priced at $3,278, it weighed 3,649 pounds. Production was over twice that of the 2-door, peaking at 69,400. The interiors were done in "Pinseal" vinyl seats and panels, gabardine headliner and visors, and walnut applique on the dash and door panel inserts. As with the 2-door, the vinyl top was an extra cost item, though very few LTD models were ever seen without this attractive option.

Appearing for the last time was the Ford LTD stretch limousine, probably the longest hardtop sedan ever built on a semi-production basis. Sanctioned by Ford and available on special order from Ford dealers, the car was actually built by the Lehmann-Petersen Co. of Chicago. This firm was having great success stretching Lincolns into 7-passenger luxury limousines, and felt that the Ford LTD would lend itself to a slightly less expensive example of the same concept. However, buyers were scarce and the project was dropped before year end. Probably those who wanted a luxury limousine also wanted a luxury chassis for its base.

Hotshot of the year was the new Galaxie 500 7-Litre series. The models were the same two as found in the 500 XL series, and in fact, were totally dressed in XL trim. The big difference between the 7-Liter and XL versions was that the 7-Liters used as standard power the new 345 horse 428 engine and power disc brakes on the front. The transmission was the same Cruise-O-Matic as found in the XL series, but the manual 4-speed with floor shifter was available as a no-cost option. Sportiest of the two models was the convertible, Style 76D, which cost $3,844 and was the most expensive Ford of the year. It weighed 4,059 pounds, and thus was also the only non-station wagon Ford to top two tons. Not particularly popular, the "super car" drew only 2,368 orders.

The "7-Litre" emblem on the front fenders indicates that this hardtop is not the one to challenge to a traffic light drag race. Companion to the convertible in the new 2-model Galaxie 500 XL 7-Litre series, the Hardtop or Fastback Coupe (both names were used) was considered Style 63D. The car used the same body as did the XL, LTD, and 500 variations, but differed in trim and, of course, standard power. Priced at $3,596 and weighing 3,914 pounds, this power house drew 8,705 orders. Helping advertise the fact that this car had plenty of guts was the standard dual exhaust system with low restriction (Hollywood) mufflers, and a non-silenced air cleaner. Straight pipes, which were still legal or quasi-legal in some states, provided a real healthy rumble! This was the only year the 7-Litre would appear in series form. In 1967 it would become an option package.

A bit more sedate than the 7-Litre model was the Galaxie 500 XL Convertible, which came with the 289 cubic inch block and Cruise-O-Matic as standard fare—though more powerful engines surely could be ordered and often were. Being to the Galaxie 500 line what the LTD was in luxury, the XL series was one step up in sportiness. Standard equipment included bucket seats, central console with shifter, polished upper door panels, and heavy carpeting running half way up the side and door panels. Designated Style 76B, the XL Convertible cost $3,456 and weighed 3,761 pounds. It enjoyed a run of 6,360 units.

Whereas the LTD Fastback Coupe was usually seen with a vinyl roof, the XL versions were usually born with a plain steel top set off by three small stainless simulated air scoops. Fluted rocker panels and rear fender stone guards were standard on all Galaxie models, as were stainless wheel cutout moldings. Far more popular than its soft-top companion, the Fastback XL Coupe drew 25,715 orders. Designated Style 63C, it had a base price of $3,208 and weighed 3,616 pounds. The "XL" designation followed the Galaxie signature on the rear fenders. Special lighting on these models included warning and courtesy lights in the door panel, with dual lenses displaying a white light downward and a red light rearward when the door was opened. In addition, hardtop models had dual rear reading lights.

Photographed while relaxing at a Pacific Coast beach is this Galaxie 500 convertible, Style 76A. Far more popular than either the XL or the 7-Litre models, this variation saw its sales top at 27,454 orders. The car could be ordered with either the six or the base V-8, though the vast majority probably went out with the larger V-8 engines. In basic V-8 form, it weighed 3,677 pounds, and at $3,041, was the only Galaxie 500 to top the $3,000 mark. This model wears the optional bucket seats, which were standard in the XL models but had to be special ordered in the plain 500 series.

Ford's second most popular model, after the Mustang Hardtop, was the Galaxie 500 Fastback Coupe. Designated Style 63B, this car had a run of 198,532, mainly with V-8 engines, though a few came out with the available Six. Oddly, this was the only model to appear in all of the four Galaxie series. Often called the Hardtop Coupe, it showed up as a 500, an LTD, XL and 7-Litre model. In its base 500 form, where it proved most popular, it had a V-8 price of $2,791 and weighed 3,481 pounds. The "500" plate appeared at the leading edge of the Galaxie signature on the rear fender.

Appearing in both the Galaxie 500 and LTD series was the Fastback Sedan. Usually called a 4-door Hardtop, the car was designated Style 57B in Galaxie 500 trim. In this form it sold for $2,869 with the base V-8 or $2,743 with the Six, as seen here. In this form, it weighed 3,526 pounds, while the basic V-8 added another 45 pounds. A total of 54,886 of this model were sold, showing that with this style at least, more buyers were willing to go the extra bucks and get the LTD version—a trait that certainly didn't hold true with the Fastback Coupe.

Ford's third most popular car of the year also was in the Galaxie 500 series. It was the 4-door Sedan, Style 54A, which drew 171,886 orders. It was available as either a V-8 or a Six. The front fender emblem on this model shows that a V-8 lives under the hood, giving the car a base price of $2,784 and a weight of 3,500 pounds even. Split grilles were new for the year and housed the parking/signal lights in their outer ends, adjacent to the stacked headlights. All Galaxie 500 models had interiors done in 2-tone vinyl seats and doors.

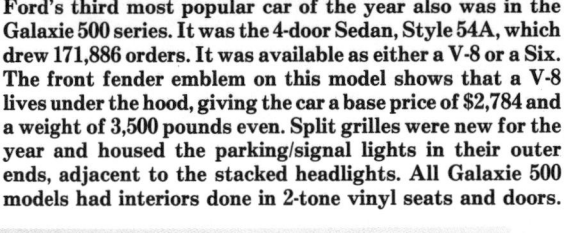

The full-size pillared 2-door Sedan was found only in the Custom 500 and Custom series, and was not available in Galaxie trim. In the upper level Custom 500 series, shown here, the car was designated Style 62B. Sporting a front fender emblem indicating it is a V-8, this car would have had a base price of $2,588, weighed 3,419 pounds, and drew 28,789 orders. The vinyl top shown here was an extra $75, while the wheel covers cost $22 a set. Unlike the Galaxies, the Custom signature on the trailing edge of the rear quarter provided identification.

Besides the two Galaxies, the only other Ford to top the 100,000 sales mark was the Custom 500 4-door Sedan, Style 54B. Its sales reached 109,449. Shown here in taxi form, this car sports the V-8 engine and the $85 vinyl top. Without the top, it would have had a base price of $2,639 and weighed 3,488 pounds. Custom 500 models used full carpeting, and had arm rests with ashtrays on all four doors. Outwardly, the cars used a horizontal aluminum strip running along the body line from the leading edge to the trailing end of the rear door. Though not much, it provided a lot more parking lot protection than the lack of side trim on the Galaxie models.

Ford's lowest priced full-size car was the Custom 2-door Sedan, shown here in police trim but with 6-cylinder power. In this form, it cost $2,363 and weighed 3,333 pounds. Adding the 289 cubic inch V-8 would have upped the price $106 (some lists show $125) while the popular automatic transmission would have been another $184. Designated Style 62, the "salesman's special" drew 32,292 orders. Custom models were devoid of all trim, except for a small signature at the trailing edge of the rear quarter.

Often used for taxi or municipal fleet work was the Custom 4-door Sedan, Style 54, which was Ford's lowest price full-size 4-door. Certainly popular in its low-buck field, the car drew 72,245 orders. Most were probably fitted with the Six, as is this example. In this case, it would have sold for $2,415 and weighed 3,433 pounds. All Custom models used rubber floor mats rather than carpeting, while the interiors were done in solid vinyl. Arm rests were used on all four doors, but these were not equipped with ashtrays. This year the backup lights on all full-size Fords appeared as white square lenses in the center of the square taillights. All custom and Galaxie models used the same chassis with a 119-inch wheelbase and were 210 inches long overall.

Once again Ford continued to list its large station wagons as a series unto themselves. The top of the line continued to be the wood-trimmed Country Squire models, while the plain-side Country Sedans were in the mid-range. As were the Squires, the Country Sedans were divided into 10-passenger models, shown here, and 6-passenger. The 10-passenger Style 71C sold for $3,105, weighed 4,019 pounds, and drew 36,633 orders. Most popular of all full-size wagons was the 6-passenger Country Sedan, Style 71B. This model cost $2,989 and drew 55,615 buyers.

New for the year, and revolutionary in the wagon field, was Ford's new dual-action "Magic Doorgate." This, the newest thing in wagon design since the self-storing tailgate window came along in the 1950s, allowed the tailgate to be opened either like a door, as shown here, or as a normal fold-down tailgate. Standard on all Ford and Fairlane wagons, the new gate could be equipped with a power window for another $30. Center-facing rear seats show that this is the 10-passenger Country Squire, Style 71A, which was Ford's heaviest and most expensive wagon. In this form, it weighed 4,062 pounds, cost $3,372, and drew 41,953 orders. In 6-passenger form, it was the Style 71E, which sold for $3,289 and drew 27,645 orders. Oddly, Chrysler products would not get this type of gate until 1968, and GM cars would not have it until 1969!

The lowest price full-size Ford wagon was the Ranch Wagon, Style 71D. It was priced at $2,900 with the V-8, and weighed 3,963 pounds. Not particularly popular, it drew 33,306 orders. Devoid of all side trim, it followed the Custom 500 line in interior fittings. Usually seen with the 150 horsepower Six, this was the only wagon that could not be ordered with the dual facing rear seats.

Totally new for the year was a hotshot Fairlane called the 500XL GT when fitted with a standard transmission, or 500XL GTA with an automatic. Considered a sub-series of the new Fairlane 500 XL series, the cars came with the 335 horse 390 cubic inch engine as standard power. They were quickly identified by chrome simulated hood louvers which contained the engine size numbers. Bucket seats and console with floor shifter, and a black-out grille with a special "GT" center badge were also included. Best looking and least popular of the mid-size hot ones was the Convertible, Style 76D. It drew only 4,327 orders. Its base price was $3,068, thus making it the only Fairlane to top the $3,000 mark. It weighed 3,070 pounds.

Conversely, just as the new Fairlane 500XL GT Convertible was the poorest selling model in the 500 XL Series, the Hardtop, Style 63D, was the best mover. A total of 33,015 went out the door, all base priced at $2,843 and weighing 3,493 pounds. In addition to the special louvered hoods, the 500XL GT sub-series cars had their own special racing stripes in place of the rocker moldings found on the regular 500XL models. The interiors were identical to those of the XL models, but the signature block on the rear fender would say either "GT" or "GTA."

The top-down view shows the bucket seat interior which distinguished all models in the new Fairlane 500XL series. Designated Style 76C, the Convertible looked especially good with the exclusive rocker molding and wheel opening surrounds found in this series. Surprisingly, these cars could be ordered with the basic 6-cylinder engine as well as the basic 289 cubic inch block but it is doubtful if many went out the door so equipped. Numerous engine options were available, including four variations of the 390 block, and both of the 427 styles, including the mid-year released 425 horsepower model. With the basic V-8, the 500XL Convertible cost $2,874 and weighed 3,268 pounds. Only slightly more popular than the 500XL GT model, it drew 4,560 orders.

The new Fairlane 500XL Hardtop Coupe was a more formal looking car than its GT cousin, and its sales suffered in the sport oriented market for which these cars were aimed. Thus, sales reached only 23,942, which was more than 9,000 less than that enjoyed by the GT version. Called Style 63C, it had a base V-8 cost of $2,649 and weighed 3,053 pounds. The "XL" badges appeared in the center of the grille medallion, on the rear quarters, and on the trunk lid. The fancy wheel covers were standard equipment. Small crossed flags on the front fenders just aft of the wheel opening shows the car has some form of 390 engine under the hood. These engines could add between $200 and $250 to the base cost of the car, while Cruise-O-Matic or a manual 4-speed would jump the price another $200 approximately.

Oddly, in the plain Fairlane 500 series, both the Hardtop Coupe, shown here, and the Convertible sold better than they did in the sport-oriented XL or XL GT series. In plain form, the Convertible was Style 76B, which drew 9,299 orders and had a price of $2,709. The Hardtop Coupe, Style 63A, saw sales reach 75,947, making this car the most popular model in the entire Fairlane range. It sold for a base V-8 price of $2,484 and weighed 3,025 pounds. Again, the small crossed flags just behind the front wheel opening show that this car has the 390 cubic inch block.

Not appearing in either XL or GT guise was the Fairlane 500 2-door Sedan, Style 62B. Not really a pillared version of the hardtop, the 2-door used its own distinctive top with a more formal rear roof line. Not a particularly popular style, it drew only 14,118 sales, many of them with the Six, as seen in this example. In this form, it cost $2,317 and weighed 2,754 pounds. With the base 289 V-8 it would have cost $106 more and been 154 pounds heavier. Note that on the Fairlanes, the parking/signal lights nested in the bumper ends, where they were very subject to dirt and breakage.

The Fairlane 500 4-door Sedan, Style 54B, was a nicely styled car that found 68,635 buyers this year. It could be ordered with either the 200 cubic inch Six, as shown here, for $2,357, or with any of the six available V-8 engines. As a Six, it weighed 2,798 pounds. Interiors of all Fairlane 500 models included full carpeting, colored keyed to the vinyl seats. On the 4-door Sedan, all window surrounds and the B-pillar were done in stainless steel. The front vent windows were operational, but the rear ones were not.

Unlike the large Ford line, where the wagons were considered a separate series, the Fairlane wagons were classed with their respective car series. Thus, the intermediate wagon fell into the Fairlane 500 series, where it was designated Style 71B. As did other 500 models, the car used aluminum rocker trim, but did not get the fancy rear quarter stone guards reserved for the XL models. Most popular of the three Fairlane wagons, this model listed at $2,770 with a V-8, and weighed 3,361 pounds. Available only in 6-passenger form it drew 19,826 orders. As did other 500s, it had stainless window edging and pillars. All Fairlane wagons were built on a 113-inch wheelbase, as opposed to the cars, which used a 116-inch chassis. Yet the wagons were 199.8 inches overall, while the cars were only 197 inches.

New for the year was the Fairlane 500 Squire Wagon, shown here showing off its new "Magic Doorgate." Fairlane's top wagon, the wood-trimmed beauty was to this series what the Country Squire was to the full-size family. Priced at $2,901 and weighing 3,369 pounds, it was the heaviest of all Fairlanes. It was available only as a 6-passenger vehicle, there being no rear seat options in the book. Sales were a nice 11,558. But really, this car was not built for hauling cord wood!

The plain Fairlane series consisted of three models, a 2-door Sedan, a Station Wagon, and this 4-door Sedan, Style 54A, shown here in taxi trim. Outwardly, the main difference between the up-scale 500 models and the plain Fairlanes was a lack of rocker panel trim on the plain models. These, in turn, had a full-length beltline molding, with the Fairlane signature at the leading edge of the front fenders. Window surrounds were in body color, but the windshield and rear window were surrounded by stainless steel. Inside, the cars used rubber floor mats rather than carpeting, and had a lower grade of vinyl for the upholstery. Least popular of the three models was the Station Wagon, Style 71D. Selling for $2,694, it drew 12,379 orders. The 2-door Sedan, Style 62A, at $2,345 for a V-8, didn't do much better, with only 13,498 sales. Even the 4-door Sedan drew only 26,170 orders, with its V-8 tag of $2,386.

With the Mustang eating up the market for small sporty cars, the days of the hotshot Falcon were all but gone. Only one model remained for those Falcon fans who wanted a spiffy looking vehicle, and for some reason did not want to go the Mustang route. That car was the Falcon Futura Sport Coupe, Style 62C, shown here posed at the top of Lombard St. in San Francisco. Priced at $2,328, the 2,587-pound car featured a bucket seat interior, special wheel covers, and "Sport Coupe" script on the rear roof panel. Its standard power was the 120 horse Six of 200 cubic inches, while other Falcons had the 170 cubic inch Six as standard power. In addition, the Sports Coupe used distinctive pin striping on the sides and rocker panels. Considering the competition from Mustang, sales were not all that bad, and 20,289 were sold.

A cute little car, but not as sporty as the Sport Coupe, was the Falcon Futura 2-door Club Coupe, Style 62B. Although both this and the Sport Coupe were pillared models, the Sport Coupe appeared to be a hardtop style, while this model looked like a 2-door sedan. Priced at $2,183, it weighed 2,527 pounds. Orders were just about the same as for the Sport Coupe, with 21,997 leaving the nest. This year Falcon no longer had its own exclusive chassis, but used a 110.9-inch wheelbase version of the Fairlane frame.

Most popular of the Falcon Futura models was the 4-door Sedan, Style 54B, shown here accompanying a California St. cable car up one of San Francisco's many hills. Selling for $2,237 and weighing 2,567 pounds, the car drew 34,039 orders. As with the Fairlane 4-doors, the front vent windows were functional, while the rear ones were not. All Futura models except the Sport Coupe used the aluminum trim on the rocker panels, which bled front and rear into the stainless steel surrounding the wheel openings. Although most Falcons flew with either of the two available 6-cylinder engines, the 289 cubic inch V-8 was available for another $131, while Cruise-O-Matic could be added for $167.

Falcon's best wagon fell into the Futura series, where it was Style 71B. As did the cars, it used lower rocker trim, and had the Falcon signature on the front fender panel. Unlike the cars, it had its own special Fairlane-derived chassis of 133-inch wheelbase and was 198.7 inches long overall, which was only one inch shorter than the Fairlane wagons. Priced at $2,553 and weighing 3,045 pounds, the Futura Wagon was the most expensive and heaviest of the Falcons. But the big bird wasn't all that popular, and sales levelled at 13,574. The Falcon wagons did not get the "Magic Doorgate" but had to rely on a standard tailgate. The luggage rack shown here was a $45 accessory, while the wheel covers shown on all Futuras were $21 extra.

With costs rising, this year for the first time, Ford had no car base priced at under $2,000. The lowest price vehicle, the Falcon 2-door Sedan, now listed in basic form for $2,060. For this, buyers received the 170 cubic inch Six, a manual 3-speed transmission, and blackwall tires rather than the white striped ones shown here. Designated Style 62A, the car shared its new body with both the Futura 2-door and the Sport Coupe. It weighed 2,519 pounds. Production reached a healthy 41,432, making it the most popular of the three models in the plain Falcon series.

Despite its rather attractive appearance here, lack of rocker molding and bright wheel well surrounds proves that this is the plain Falcon 4-door Sedan, Style 54A. All series used the "Falcon" signature on the front fender panels, and had "Falcon" in block letters across the trunk deck. The new styling gave Falcon cars an overall length of 184.3 inches, which was almost three inches longer than last year's models. The 4-door Sedan was base priced at $2,114 and weighed 2,559 pounds. Probably because of its new styling, sales were up by over 4,000, totaling out at 34,685.

Add deluxe wheel covers at about $20 a set, a roof rack for another $45, and white walls for a $32 replacement charge, and even the plain Falcon Wagon, Style 71A, came out a moderately attractive car. Only the lack of rocker molding gives quick proof that this is the plain Jane, and not the Futura example. In this form, the Falcon Wagon had a base price of $2,442 and weighed 3,037 pounds. This model was totally new for the year insofar as the series went, as Falcon wagons had previously been in their own special series, as was the case with the larger Fords. This year, however, the reduction of available Falcon styles put the wagons into the two trim series, and thus, the plain Falcons and the Futura each got their own example. In plain form, the wagon did better than its Futura counterpart, and 16,653 were sold.

Although it was now called simply the Ranchero, there was no doubt that this cute little truck was closely related to the Falcons. With the Courier Sedan Delivery gone, the Ranchero was now Ford's only small truck based on automobile components. It came in two versions, the Deluxe form shown here, Model 66B, or the plain Model 66A. Besides exterior trim, the Deluxe version used full carpeting rather than rubber mats, and had crinkle-grain vinyl upholstery and full-vinyl rear panel and door panels. The 200 cubic inch Six was standard, but the 289 V-8 could be ordered. The Deluxe version was base priced at $2,411. Sales totalled 11,038 in regular form and another 1,242 with bucket seats. The plain Ranchero sold for $2,330 and drew 9,480 orders.

The Falcon-derived Club Wagons continued virtually unchanged, and were still available in their three trim categories. The top of the line, shown here, was the Deluxe Club wagon, Model E-13. It used side trim molding, bright bumpers, hub caps, dual mirrors, and an all-vinyl interior with pleated seats. Selling for $2,779, it drew 2,195 orders. The middle ground was occupied by the Custom Club Wagon, which cost $2,91 and drew 3,875 orders. Most practical of the batch was the bus-like plain Club Wagon, Model E-11, which was priced at $2,462. It reached 6,850 sales. All versions used the 170 cubic inch Six as standard power, but could be ordered with the 240 cubic inch Six.

1966

Ford made headlines this year when it entered the 4-wheel-drive utility vehicle market with its cute little Bronco. More truck than car, the vehicle is well documented in Crestline's *FORD TRUCKS SINCE 1905*, and thus, only its initial birthday will be covered here. The vehicle came in three styles, an open Roadster sans roof and doors for $2,404; a pickup-like Sports Utility with a 2-passenger bolt-on cab and small cargo area, for $2,480, and this Bronco Wagon, which was the most car-like of the herd. Priced at $2,625, it had a full-length removable steel top and seating for four. The body was built by Budd. Not particularly successful in its first year, the Wagon drew only 12,756 orders, while the Utility drew 6,930 and the Roadster 4,090.

Ford took world wide honors this year by having the first, second and third place winners at the famed Le Mans Gran Prix in France. These were the first American cars ever to win this prestigious event. Using 13 vehicles built by Carroll Shelby, the team set a blistering pace around the rain-soaked circuit, and easily beat the Ferrari team, which was its closest competitor. Far removed from everyday Fords, the racers used bodies and chassis built in England, but powered by the excellent 427 cubic inch engines of 425 horsepower. The cars were known as GT-40 Mark IIs to differentiate them from the earlier GT-40s which used the 289 cubic inch engines. These cars also won the Daytona Continental race, and finished the year by again beating Ferrari in the Manufacturer's Championship prototype division.

Once again Ford totally restyled its full-size line, and compared with the rather plain 1966 models, came up with a real beauty. But, insofar as publicity went, the move was virtually unnoticed. The reason for this was Thunderbird, which this year gave up all pretension of being a sporty car. Instead, the new Bird dripped with luxury and aimed its sights at the lower level of the Lincoln/Cadillac/Imperial market. Mustang could now take care of the sport set.

With the exception of engine and transmission, the new Thunderbirds carried over little from the previous flock. The cars set on two new chassis with different lengths for the 4-door and 2-door models. The new 4-doors had 117-inch wheelbases, while the 2-doors grew two inches to a 115-inch length. Overall, the 4-doors measured almost 210 inches, while the 2-doors were just shy of 207 inches. This was only 1.5 inches longer than the previous models, but the new rounded styling made the cars look much larger and longer than their predecessors.

Along with the new styling was a deep set grille which resembled the open mouth of a jet engine. Enhancing this concept was Ford's first use of hidden or retractable headlights. All 4-door models carried decorative landau bars, as did the 2-door Landau model. In an unusual touch, the new 4-door featured rear doors that opened from the B-pillar. Ford's last use of these center-opening doors was with the 1948 models, although both Lincoln and Mercury had carried the design right into this era. Another unusual styling feature occurred with the 2-door models, where the small "opera" window behind the door retraced horizontally into the roof panel rather than vertically into the body.

As mentioned in the previous chapter, the 1966 Thunderbird convertible was the last soft-top that the breed would have. With sales for luxury convertibles being on the low side, and T-Bird no longer looking at the sport market, the decision to drop the open model probably was a wise one. Also, despite the anguish of the Thunderbird lovers who still worshipped the 2-seat models, the decision to add a 4-door was probably not all that bad. Sales of the sedan reached 24,967 and helped boost total Bird sales to 77,956, which was better than the past two years, despite an overall turndown in the car market this year.

Also receiving new styling was the Mustang. However, whereas the Thunderbird changed totally, the new Mustang still looked like its older stable mate. Only the new horse was slightly larger, growing two inches to a new overall length of 183.6 inches, even though its wheelbase remained 108 inches. Also, it was a mite heavier, and sported new styling that just made it look larger. Heavy sculpturing on the sides led to a large simulated air scoop, while the grille was both higher, wider, and more deep-set. It also featured a horizontal bar leading from the galloping horse, which visually made the car wider. Under the hood, everything remained the same, but a new addition was the availability of the 390 cubic inch block, which in this case was rated at 320 horsepower at 4600 rpm.

On the disquieting side, Mustang sales dropped by almost 135,000, beginning a slide that would continue until the totally different Mustang II was introduced in 1974. For the little horse, the honeymoon was over. Although the Hardtop Sport Coupe was still Ford's best selling model, with 356,271 leaving the barn, other sporty products from GMC, Chrysler, and even American Motors were starting to nibble at Mustang's territory. Thus, what was America's runaway best seller only two years ago, was now just another competitive model on the total market. Also, the Mustang-sourced

Taking most of the attention this year was the totally new Thunderbird, which contained virtually no carryover from previous models except for the drivetrain components. Built on a new chassis of 115 and 117-inch wheelbase lengths, the cars were 206.9 inches in 2-door form and 209.9 in the 4-door configuration. All new body styling graced the exterior while the new interior was the epitome of luxury. No pretext whatsoever was made toward the sport contingent—this was a personal luxury car! Base vehicle in the 3-model line was the 2-door Hardtop, Style 65A, which was priced at $4,603 and weighed 4,348 pounds. Least popular of the three models, its sales stopped at 15,567. It was finished with a plain steel top, graced by stylized Thunderbirds on the panels. A vinyl top was not available as that trim item was reserved strictly for the Landau model.

Even with the new styling, Thunderbird's premium 2-door continued to be the Landau, Style 65B. This car was basically the same as the Hardtop, but was distinguished by a vinyl covered top with large decorative landau irons. Most popular of the Birds, it saw 37,422 leave the nest, all base priced at $4,704. Both the Hardtop and the Landau featured small opera windows in panel behind the doors. In an unusual styling move, these windows would recess horizontally into the roof panel rather than vertically in a normal fashion. The new grille was compared to a jet intake. Composed of a small blackout grid, it held Ford's first use of concealed headlights. In the rear, a full-width taillight complex was surrounded by a stainless bezel which also formed the rear fender tips.

Mercury Cougar did little to help this sales picture.

In the large Ford line, the cars were also completely restyled, using little except the drivetrain from the 1966 models. The new bodies were three inches longer than the former models, now measuring 213 inches overall for the cars and 213.9 for the wagons. The 2-door models were particularly attractive, having a severely swept-back rear roofline on the hardtops, and a pleasing but more formal line on the pillared coupes. The sides were nicely designed with an embossed beltline that ran from the stacked but staggered headlights to the new rectangular vertical taillights. Particularly attractive was the stamped aluminum grille, which consisted of two major horizontal pieces with vertical intersecting bars. All models remained the same, but the former 7-Litre sub-series simply became a sports package for the Galaxie 500 XL models, while the LTD became a series of its own.

With these major changes being made to three of its nameplates, it was no wonder that neither the Fairlanes nor the Falcons received much styling attention. Both makes used the bodies introduced in 1966, with the expected cosmetic changes to tell one year from the other. The Fairlanes received new grilles with three vertical bars intersecting the single horizontal bar, while the Falcon's main claim to fame was a set of simulated louvers on the front fender panel, just behind the wheel cutouts. In both cars, all series and models remained the same, except that the Fairlane 500 GT models became a separate sub-series, and were not part of the Fairlane 500 XL series. The models still bore the "GT" designations when equipped with manual transmissions or the "GTA" when fitted with automatics.

In the engine compartments, everything remained the same. For once there were no new blocks, and virtually no modifications to the existing plants. As mentioned, Mustang now had the 390 V-8 available, and a special super-performance kit became available for the very limited production 427 cubic inch block, but aside from that, everything was quiet in the engine department.

On the sales scene, things were not that good this year, as a depressed economy and lower car sales combined with a giant 57-day U.A.W. strike against all Ford plants. As a result, total sales, including 472,121 Mustangs, reached only 1,730,236. This compared rather dismally with the 2,211,617 cars sold in 1966. In fact, it represented a drop of almost a half-million cars.

Within this sales structure, the Mustang 2-door Hardtop, now referred to as the Sports Coupe, was once again the leading model, with 356,271 sales. Two other models also broke the 100,000 mark. They were the Galaxie 500 2-door Fastback Coupe, which had 197,338 units produced, and the third place Galaxie 500 4-door sedan with 130,063 orders.

And, the year saw the final production of the famed Shelby Cobras. With federal emission and safety regulations lurking in the shadows, Carroll Shelby could see little future for his limited production fire-breathing all-out sports cars. The formidable task of redesigning the car to meet the safety standards and the reengineering needed to meet the emission codes would have been far too costly for the low volume of Cobras leaving the plant. Also, such changes would certainly have been detrimental to the car's notable handling and performance, and that in itself was something that neither Shelby nor his devoted followers wanted. Better to let the famous snake die in honor than to limp along as a shadow of itself. In all, the doors closed after approximately 630 of the 260 cubic inch and 510 of the 427 cubic inch Cobras had streaked off for the tracks and by-ways of America. And, quite a few of these blistering beauties are still running today.

Although sales dropped substantially this year, Ford's best selling model continued to be the Mustang Sport Coupe, Style 07. Priced at $2,461, it saw its sales reach 356,271, which was more than recorded by some total series. Wearing a completely new body, the car was now 183.5 inches long overall, even though its wheelbase remained 108 inches. More rounded styling and deep sculpturing on the sides simply made the car look bigger. The side vents were strictly decorative. Also known as the Hardtop Coupe, this model was usually fitted with bucket seats and console, but for an additional $25, could be equipped with a full bench seat with folding arm rest. A total of 8,190 were so equipped, while another 22,228 had the luxury interior, a decor package which sold for an additional $108 or $140 with comfort-weave vinyl seats.

Creating the most interest, and causing the most anguish among those who would rather have had the Thunderbird revert to its sports car status, was the brand new 4-door Landau, Style 57B. Using its own exclusive chassis of 117-inch wheelbase, the luxury-level car was hailed as a "personal luxury sedan," with comfort seating for four passengers only. At $4,825 it was the most expensive vehicle on Ford's list. At 4,348 pounds, it was also the heaviest Ford. Sales reached 24,967. Note how the rear door styling reached into the vinyl roof area. This was the first Ford since 1948 to use centrally opening doors.

Regaining much of its popularity this year was the Mustang Fastback or 2+2 Coupe, Style 09. A total of 71,042 were built. The car had a base price of $2,592 and weighed 2,605 pounds. The bench seat option was not available on this model, but the luxury interior was, and 17,391 were turned out in this form. This model carries the somewhat rare dual exhaust system, found on only 25,000 Mustangs, and probably has been fitted with the 390 cubic inch engine which was available to Mustangs for the first time this year. It was offered only in 320 horsepower form for an additional $263.

Dropping quite a bit in popularity was the Mustang convertible, Style 08. This year only 44,808 were sold, as compared with over 73,000 in 1966. Base priced at $2,698, it weighed 2,738 pounds. It too could be ordered with a bench seat in front rather than the buckets, and a total of 1,209 were built in this form. Also, 4,848 had the interior decor group. All Mustangs this year used bright rocker moldings except when the GT package was ordered. Despite the fact that Mustangs were designed primarily for the sporty set, almost one-third of all the little horses left the barn with 6-cylinder engines.

Take one Mustang, select any one of four V-8 engines ranging from the 289 cubic inch Challenger to the 390 Thunderbird Special, add the GT equipment group, and the result is one sporty little car. Included in the GT package were 4-inch fog lamps inserted into a special grille bar; Wide-Oval Sport tires with thin stripes; competition rated springs and shocks, and a stronger front stabilizer. For those who wanted even more road readiness, a $62 competition handling package could be ordered, which included adjustable shocks; 3.25 rear axle, and limited-slip differential. Here the GT package has been added to both the Sport Coupe and the Convertible.

The "GT" option was not a model, but an extra-cost package available on any Mustang. Still, the package was most often seen on the 2+2 Fastback, which was a very sporty car to begin with. Included in the $435 GT set was a special hood with simulated scoops; the fog lights and grille bar; dual exhaust with bright tips, and a special racing stripe in place of the chrome rocker moldings. Also included as a base was the 271 horse version of the 289 cubic inch V-8, and power front disc brakes. When the car was equipped with an automatic transmission, the nomenclature read "GTA."

Far removed from the conventional Mustang GTs were the Shelby Mustang conversions, available this year as GT350s and GT500s. Both models were based on the Mustang Fastback and looked quite similar. However, the GT350, priced at $3,995, used the 289 cubic inch engine boosted to 306 HP, while the new GT500 was base priced at $4,195 and used the 428 cubic inch block of 355 HP. Both cars had a rated top speed of about 130 MPH. The Shelby Mustangs used their own fiberglass nose and louvered hood, and also had a fiberglass rear deck spoiler and used Cougar taillamps. Functional rear fender scoops led fresh air to the rear brakes, while upper functional scoops helped to ventilate the cabin. The cars were built in 2-passenger form only, and the interiors incorporated functional rollbars capable of withstanding several complete roll-overs. Conversions were made by both the Shelby Co. in Los Angeles, or under contract by the A.O. Smith Co. of Iona, Mich. As far as can be ascertained, a total of 1,175 GT350 models were built this year, while another 2,050 of the new GT500s left the plants. It is also known that about 50 GT500s were built using the relatively rare 427 cubic inch block, in either 410 or 425 horse version. However, it appears that none of the models were turned out in full-race form, but all were street legal.

Most popular of the new LTD series was the 4-door Hardtop, Style 57F. It recorded sales of 51,978, all with a base price of $3,363. Totally new styling and a very handsome grille once again made the big Fords among the best looking cars on the road. Although usually fitted with a vinyl top, this item was standard only on the 2-door models, and was a $85 option on both 4-doors. Standard power for the LTD series was the 200 horse 289 V-8 with Cruise-O-Matic. More powerful V-8 options could be ordered, but 6-cylinder engines were not available.

Although the car was directly derived from the Galaxie models, this year the LTDs became a series unto their own, and were no longer identified with Galaxie name plates. Most handsome of the batch was the 2-door Hardtop, which featured a sweeping rear top treatment with relatively large blind quarters and small quarter windows. The vinyl-covered top was standard on the LTD 2-door Hardtops, but was an option on the 4-door models. Wide lower side trim and wheel opening surrounds was a style feature of both LTD and XL models, while the small round crest on the rear roof panel was an LTD exclusive. Designated Style 63F, the 2-door LTD was base priced at $3,362 and weighed 3,626 pounds. Quite popular, it saw sales go up to 46,036.

A new model in a new series. That was the case of the LTD 4-door Sedan, Style 54F. Least popular of the three LTD models, this car utilized the same 4-door pillared sedan body as found in the Galaxie and Custom lines. Although usually seen with the extra-cost vinyl roof, some LTD Sedans did come off the lines with plain steel tops. With either roof, the round LTD emblem on the rear panel provided series identification. The LTD Sedan was the least expensive of the three models, being base priced at $3,298. Still, it drew only 12,491 orders. All LTDs used special wheel covers. Inside they used simulated wood on the instrument and door panels, and had seats deeply upholstered in foam cushions and equipped with pull-down arm rests both front and rear. For $116 more, all LTDs could be equipped with "Twin Comfort Lounge Seats," which were similar to oversized buckets.

Although the LTD became a series of its own, the XL models remained a sub-series of the Galaxie 500 line. Here they were considered the top sport models, and were known officially as Galaxie 500 XLs. Sportiest of the two models was the Convertible, Style 76b, which had a base price of $3,493, and as such was the most expensive of the large Fords. It weighed 3,704 pounds. Sales were not particularly good, and only 5,161 left the plant. Side trim was the same as used on the LTD models, except that "XL" plaques were used and wheel covers were of a different design. All interiors were done with bucket seats in front, and with a central console containing a floor shifter, regardless of whether the car had an automatic or manual shift. No 6-cylinder engines were available in this series. Base power was the same 200 horse 289 V-8 as found in the LTD line.

The 7-Litre models were no longer a sub-series of the Galaxie 500 line, but were now simply an option package on the Galaxie 500XL models. Priced $516 above the base XL, the package included a special louvered hood under which resided the 428 cubic inch block with 4-barrel carburetor, rated at 345 horsepower. For those who wanted even more go, the package was available with the 410 or 425 horse 427 engine for $1,165 over the base XL price. Besides the hood, special "7-Litre" ornamentation behind the front wheel cutout said that this car could move. Power front disc brakes also came with the package, as did dual exhaust with low-resistance mufflers. Since the 7-Litre was an option package, no production breakouts were made, but all were part of the XL numbers.

Despite all of the hype about speed and power, it was the plain Galaxie 500 models that received the most sales, not the XL or 7-Litre variations. Thus, the beautiful Galaxie 500 Convertible, Style 76A, drew a total of 19,068 orders, or almost four times that of the XL variations. Priced at $3,110, the car weighed 3,704 pounds. Unlike the XL models, the regular Galaxie convertibles used bench seats front and rear. These were finished in ribbed vinyl, color keyed to the car's finish. Exterior trim was similar to the LTD or XL models, but without the signatures.

More than three times as popular as the convertible was the 2-door Hardtop Galaxie 500XL, Style 63C. Often refereed to as the Fastback Coupe, the car used the same top as found in the regular Galaxie 500 line. This was similar to the top used on the LTD models, but the LTD had more formal side panels and much smaller quarter windows. Sales of this model reached 18,174, which was only one-tenth that of the comparable model in plain Galaxie 500 form. It was priced at $3,243 and weighed 3,594 pounds. The side plate just behind the front wheel cutout shows that this model has some form of the 390 V-8 under the hood, rather than the stock 289.

Ford's second most popular model, after the Mustang Hardtop, was the Galaxie 500 Fastback Coupe, Style 63B. A total of 197,388 were sold, all with a V-8 base of $2,861. Although the roof lines of this model looked better with a painted top, a vinyl top was available for an extra $75. However, this did not make the car look like an LTD. Even though the same basic top was used on both models, the LTD was exclusively modified to have larger side panels and smaller quarter windows. An option growing in popularity was air conditioning, which cost an extra $356.

Galaxie 500 2-Door Hardtop

1967

Ford's third most popular car, and the only other model to have over 100,000 sales was the Galaxie 500 4-door Sedan, Style 54A. This pillared model drew a total of 130,063 orders. It had a base 6-cylinder price of $2,732 and weight of 3,481 pounds. The small emblem behind the front wheel opening shows that this model has a 390 cubic inch engine under the hood, which would have been $185 more if it was the 270 horse, or $265 more if the 315 horse version. It might also have had the 345 horse 428 for $352 more. Deluxe wheel covers were standard on all Galaxie 500 models, but whitewalls were $44 more.

Using the same body as the LTD 4-door Hardtop was the Style 57B 4-door Hardtop in the Galaxie 500 series. Sometimes called the Fastback Sedan, the car was base priced at $2,808 with the standard 240 cubic inch Six, and $107 more when the basic 200 horse V-8 was installed. With the Six, it weighed 3,552 pounds, while the V-8 was 26 pounds heavier. All Galaxie 500 models were quickly identified by the name in block letters on the trailing edge of the rear fenders. Far less popular than the pillared sedan in the Galaxie 500 series, the hardtop drew 57,087 orders.

As it had for years, the Custom line encompassed Ford's middle and low price section of the large car field. The middle ground was occupied by the Custom 500 series, a 2-model bracket consisting of this 2-door Sedan, Style 62B, and a 4-door Sedan, Style 54B. Least popular of the two was the 2-door, which sold for $2,659 in V-8 form, but accounted for only 18,146 sales. The 4-door, which was priced at $2,701 with the basic V-8, drew 83,260 orders. Of these, it is very likely that a good number were fitted with the Six, which would have reduced the price by $150. Conversely, the model shown here has a fender plaque indicating that a 390 engine lurks under the hood. Custom 500 models were identified by the signature and "500" emblem at the leading edge of the front fender, and by a full-length bright trim piece along the embossed beltline, which ran from headlight to taillight.

Once again Ford's lowest price full-size car was the Custom 2-door Sedan, Style 62E, which this year was up to $2,548 as a V-8 or $2,441 with the Six. Oddly, sales of this model were almost identical to those of the same model in the Custom 500 series, totalling 18,107. With the Six, it weighed 3,411 pounds, and thus was Ford's lightest full-size car. Unlike the Galaxie models, the Custom lines did not use the rear applique plate, but simply had the word "Ford" in block letters on the rear deck. The "Custom" signature appeared on the leading edge of the front fender, but no side trim was used along the beltline. What appears to be bright metal in this picture is simply an airbrushed highlight of the embossed ridge.

Something new was added to the base-level Custom series this year. For the first time, the cars were fitted with nylon carpeting like all other large Fords, rather than the rubber floor mats that had been exclusive to the plain Custom series for years. Still relatively popular as a business vehicle, and often found in taxi trim, was the Custom 4-door Sedan, Style 54E, which weighed 3,507 pounds and sold for $2,602 in plain V-8 form. A total of 41,417 were sold. As could all large Fords, the Custom line could be fitted with any Ford engine that the buyer wished to pay for, as evidenced by the 390 V-8 plaque on the front fender of this model. For the first time this year, all Fords used a dual master cylinder on the brake system, which was designed to prevent total brake failure should one unit of the cylinder give out suddenly.

Once again, Ford's large wagons were considered a series unto themselves. As it had for years, the Country Squire occupied the top shelf in this line. The wood-trimmed beauty continued to be available in two variations, both of which looked identical from the outside. The Style 71E was the 6-passenger model, which sold for $3,340, while the Style 71A was the 10-passenger version, with dual center-facing rear seats. This variation cost $3,466. Once again the 10-passenger model was the most popular, with 44,024 orders as opposed to the 6-passenger with 25,600 sales. On all 10-passenger models, power front disc brakes were standard.

Available only in 6-passenger form was Ford's lowest price full-size wagon, the Ranch Wagon. Priced at $2,943 with the V-8, it was also the only wagon with V-8 power to be based at under $3,000. Called the Style 71D, it differed from the other 6-passenger models only in exterior side trim and interior appointments. For the most part, its trim level was somewhere between the Custom and Custom 500 models. Often delivered with 6-cylinder power, it sold for $2,836 and weighed 3,911 pounds in that form. A total of 23,932 were sold. This year all full-size wagons were 213.9 inches long overall, or one inch longer than the car models. All big Fords continued to use the 199-inch wheelbase which had first appeared with the 1960 models.

The sporty bracket of the Fairlane family became a series of its own—though some of the early material still shows the cars as part of the Fairlane 500XL series. Called Fairlane GTs when equipped with manual transmissions, or GTAs when fitted with automatics, the series consisted of two models, this Convertible and the accompanying hardtop. Known as Style 76D, the GT Convertible cost $3,064 and weighed 3,6078 pounds. A rare find today, the car accounted for only 2,117 sales. GT models had their own exclusive hoods with twin vent strips, racing stripe side trim with the GT or GTA designation, bucket seats and console, and used the 200 horse 289 cubic inch engine as a base.

Shown in Ford's styling studio while undergoing side trim experiments was the Country Sedan, Ford's mid-level wagon. The vehicle was identical to the Country Squire, but lacked the latter's simulated wood trim. As with the Squire, the Country Sedan was available as the 6-passenger Style 71B, which sold for $3,042 with the base V-8, or the 10-passenger Style 71C, which cost $3,168. All models were also available with the basic Six, at $107 less. The sales pattern of the Country Sedan was just the reverse of the Squire. Here the 6-passenger model was the most popular, selling 50,818 units, while the 10-seat model sold 34,377. All Ford wagons now used the "Magic Doorgate," which could fold down like a tailgate or swing open like a door.

Companion to the Convertible in the new Fairlane GT or GTA series was the Hardtop Coupe, Style 63D. Priced at $2,839 and weighing 3,301 pounds, the car drew 18,670 orders and was the best selling of the four Fairlane special sport models. In addition to the bucket seat interior as found in the XL models and the items listed in the convertible's caption, GT and GTA cars had their own dark gray black-out grille, deluxe wheel covers, power front disc brakes, special emblems, and special door panels with red and white safety/courtesy lights in the doors. Interesting were the turn signal indicators located at the ends of each vent strip on the hoods.

Fairlane GTA Convertible

Companion to the sporty Fairlane GT series was the Fairlane 500XL series, which consisted of the same convertible and hardtop models, but with more luxury trim and less emphasis on speed or racing. Even more rare than the GT Convertibles, the XL Convertible drew only 1,943 orders. The car was designated Style 76C, cost $2,950, and weighed 3,356 pounds. An option gaining in popularity with the youth set was the new multi-speaker Stereo Tape System, which might not have shaken down the walls like today's rolling boom-boxes, but certainly could be heard for a country mile.

More popular than its convertible mate was the Fairlane 500XL Hardtop Coupe, Style 63C, which had a run of 14,871, cost $2,724 and weighed 3,0389 pounds. XL models had their own special plaques on the rear fenders and a special "XL" grille bar. Exterior trim was similar to the Fairlane 500 series, but the interior contained special bucket seats in the front, console, and special door panels with the same red and white safety/courtesy lights as on the GT models. Oddly, the deluxe wheel covers shown here were not standard, but represented a $20 investment, while the vinyl top was another $75 extra.

Unless one read the rear fender plaques or looked inside, there was not too much to differentiate this year's Fairlane 500 Convertible from the XL version. Designated Style 76B, the car featured full-width bench seats in the front, and had a column-mounted shifter. There was no console. On all Fairlane Convertibles, a power operated top was not standard, but was a $53 add-on. All Fairlane 500 and 500XL models considered the 200 cubic inch Six as the base power, though it is doubtful if too many convertibles left with a Six under the hood. More popular than either of the sport styles, the Fairlane 500 Convertible drew 5,428 orders.

The Fairlane 500 Hardtop Coupe almost looked better in this form than it did as an XL or GT model. Far more popular as the Style 63B, the car drew 70,545 sales and thus was the most popular of all Fairlane models. It cost $2,545 and weighed 3,011 pounds with the basic 289 V-8. It could be ordered with any of the available Fairlane engines, including the two limited production 427 models. However, the 428 block was not available to Fairlanes.

The only 4-door model in the Fairlane 500 line, except for the wagons, was the Style 54B 4-door Sedan. Of pillared design, it proved to be a nicely styled intermediate car which attracted a total of 51,552 buyers. Its base price in V-8 form was $2,522, and its weight was 2,971 pounds. Buyers were treated to color-keyed nylon carpeting and a choice of four different vinyl interiors. As with other Fairlane 500 models, all window surrounds were in bright metal, but on the 4-door the B-pillar was not hidden as it was on the 2-door.

Although the Fairlane 500 2-door Hardtop was the series' most popular model, the same cannot be said for the 2-door Sedan, Style 62B. This model drew only 8,473 sales, all starting with a base V-8 price of $2,482. Built in pillared style, the car used a more formal roof line than did the hardtop. However, the chromed window surrounds hid the B-pillar and made the car look like a hardtop with the windows rolled up. The deluxe wheel covers shown here were a $20 extra on the XL models, but cost $40 more on other Fairlanes.

Unlike the large Ford line, where the station wagons were in their own series, the Fairlane wagons were grouped into their two major trim classes. Thus, both the prestige and the middle level wagons were placed in the Fairlane 500 camp, and shared interior trim levels with that category. Prestige leader of the wagons was the Fairlane 500 Squire, which featured a nice swath of imitation wood decoration running from headlights to taillights. Priced at $3,007 and weighing 3,386 in V-8 form, it was not a particularly well appreciated vehicle and only 8,348 were sold. A power window for the tailgate cost $32, while the rooftop luggage rack shown here was another $44.

Though setting no sales records, the mid-level Fairlane 500 Station Wagon, Style 71B, was still the most popular of all three Fairlane wagons, even though its sales stopped at 15,902. It had a base price of $2,824 and weighed 3,375 as a V-8. Both this and the Squire Wagon used brightwork around all windows and on the B and C-pillars. All Fairlane wagons were of 6-passenger style, but additional seating was now available via a rear-facing third seat priced at only $30. All used the "Magic Doorgate," which allowed the tailgate to open like a door or drop like a true tailgate. Fairlane wagons were built on a 113-inch wheelbase, which was 3-inches shorter than that of the cars, but were almost 200 inches long overall, which was three inches longer than the cars.

The plain Fairlane line this year was graced by a single run of side trim which went from the taillight bezel to a point just above the front wheel opening. In addition to providing a welcome bit of relief for the blank sides, this piece helped immensely in protecting the cars from parking lot dings. Lowest priced of all Fairlanes was the 2-door Sedan, Style 62A, which sold for $2,402 as a V-8. A pillared model, it weighed 2,916 pounds. Total sales were 10,628. Unlike the 500 models, the plain Fairlanes put the block letters "Ford" directly on the trunk deck rather than nesting them in a full-width escutcheon plate. A single trim bar ran between the white lenses of the back-up lights.

Despite its low-buck status, the plain Fairlane 4-door Sedan, Style 62A, was a rather attractive car for its class. The "Fairlane" signature appeared in the speartip at the forward end of the molding, while "Ford" in block letters duplicated on the hood the letters on the trunk deck. Priced at $2,445 with the small V-8, it weighed 2,951 pounds. Of all plain Fairlanes, it was the best selling of the lot, with 19,740 moving out. The cars still used rubber/vinyl floor mats instead of carpeting. The deluxe wheel covers shown here were a $40 accessory.

The plain Fairlane Station Wagon, Style 71D, was Ford's low price mid-size wagon. Often seen in 6-cylinder form, it sold for $2,643 and weighed 3,198 pounds. It drew 10,881 orders, probably very few with more than the basic Six and V-8 blocks. This year the Fairlane grille was a single aluminum stamping that helped to hold costs, both on the manufacturing end, and in the repair shops in the event of an accident.

Once again the hotshot of the Falcon line was the Futura Sports Coupe, Style 62C. Although sometimes referred to as a "Hardtop," the car utilized the same pillared body as the 2-door sedan. Besides some outward differences in emblems, the main attraction of the Sport Coupe was its bucket seat interior. The base engine in this model was the 120 horse Six of 200 cubic inches. The wheel covers shown here were standard equipment, but the vinyl top, almost always shown on Sport Coupes, was actually a $75 option. The special emblem and "Sport Coupe" signature appeared on the rear roof panel. Selling for $2,437, the car weighed 2,556 pounds. Production drooped to a low 7,053.

Utilizing the same body as the Sport Coupe was the Falcon 2-door Sedan, Style 62B. The car was priced at $2,280 with the basic 105 horse Six of 170 cubic inches, but could be equipped with the larger Six for another $26. Or, it could be fitted with either the 200 or 225 horse 289 V-8. In base form, it weighed 2,528 pounds. Sales were even worse than those of the Sport Coupe, and only 6,287 were sold. The side panel on the $75-extra vinyl top read "Futura" in script. This and the Sport Coupe were the only two Falcons on which a vinyl top could be installed. Power front disc brakes were available on Falcons this year, but only on those models equipped with a 289 V-8. These brakes were not available on 6-cylinder models.

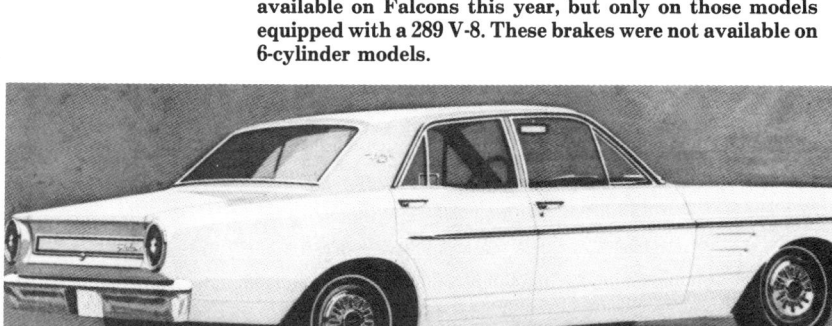

Futura 4-Door Sed

Falcon wagons came in two varieties, the Futura Style 71B shown here, and the plain Falcon Style 71A. Both were identical except for their trim level and the fact that the Futura version had a full-length bright molding running along the beltline. In addition, the Futura wagon used the 120 HP Six as its base power, while the plain Falcon Wagon used the 105 horse Six of 170 cubic inches. New to both models this year was the "Magic Doorgate," shown here opening in door fashion. Classed as a $45 option on all Falcon wagons, it could be closed and reopened as a drop-down tailgate. Two other options obvious here are the $45 roof rack and the $21 wheel covers. Available only in 6-passenger form, with no rear seat options, the Futura Wagon sold for $2,609, weighed 3,062 pounds, and had sales of only 4,552. Faring a bit better was the plain Falcon Wagon, which cost $2,497, weighed 3,030 pounds and had sales of 5,553.

Sales leader of the Falcon Futura series was the 4-door Sedan, Style 54B. However, with sales at such a low point, the car wasn't that much of a leader, and only 11,254 were sold. In base form, it cost $2,322 and weighed 2,559 pounds. All Futura models featured bright metal around the wheel wells, and had a spear running from the headlight bezels to the rear wheel openings. The new vent-like embossing on the front fender panels was attractive, but it is very surprising that Ford designers didn't come up with some form of bright trim to call attention to these indentations—at least on the Futura or Sport Coupe models. Possibly that was in the offing, but new styling in 1968 meant that this was the only year that Falcon would sport these pseudo-vents.

Once more, Ford's lowest price car was the Falcon 2-door Sedan, Style 62A, which now sold for $2,118. Devoid of virtually all trim except for the "Falcon" signature on the rear fender, the little car still attracted enough fleet interest to push production to the 16,082 mark, meaning that this plain Jane was the best selling of the entire Falcon and Futura line. It is interesting to note that after years of using round taillights as its mark, the only Fords left with these round lenses were the Falcon car models.

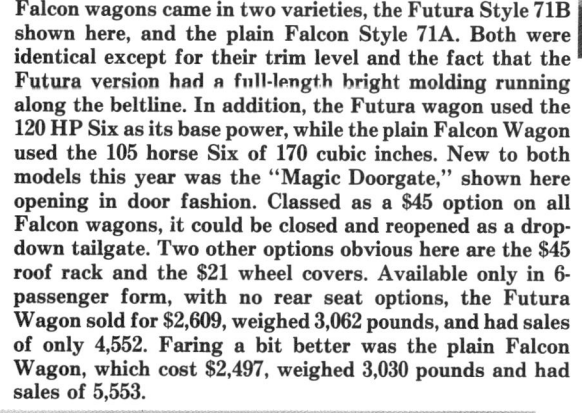

Designed primarily for fleet use was the Falcon 4-door Sedan, Style 54A. Ford's lowest price 4-door, the car sold for $2,167 and weighed 2,551 pounds. A total of 13,554 were sold. All Falcon cars this year used an 111-inch wheelbase, while the wagon models used a modified Fairlane unit of 113 inches. The cars were just a shade over 184 inches long, while the wagons jumped 14.5 inches over the cars to a new length of 198.7 inches. Standard transmission was the 3-speed manual, while a 4-speed manual was available only on cars with the V-8, but was not available in the wagons. Cruise-O-Matic was optional at $168 on 6-cylinder Falcons, or $187 on those with V-8 engines.

Once again the Club Wagon family was virtually unchanged. About its biggest news was the installation of dual master cylinders on the brake system. Three variations continued to be available. They were the basic Club Wagon at $2,532, which was the most popular with 4,233 sold; the mid-range Custom Club Wagon, shown here, for $2,668, with 1,538 sold, and the Deluxe Club Wagon, at $2,841 with only 741 sold. All used three rows of seats and varied only in the level of interior vinyl and exterior trim.

Ford's little Bronco changed very little, as was to be expected for a year-old vehicle. Except for the new dual master cylinder and a new variable speed windshield wiper, the little horse was the same as in 1966. It came in three variations, with the Wagon, Model U-150, shown here being about a close to a car as it could get. Priced at $2,633, it was the most popular model, with 10,930 sold. The pickup-like Utility of 1966 was renamed "Pickup Model U-140." It sold for $2,546 and saw 2,602 leave the barn. Least popular was the open and doorless Roadster, Model U-130. Priced at $2,417, it saw only 698 turned out to pasture. All were in 4-wheel-drive configuration.

After one year in limbo with no family designation to call its own, the Ranchero once again had a home. Through a new nose clip and other sheet metal marvels, the cute little car/truck was now known as the Fairlane Ranchero, available in either plain or Fairlane 500 trim, with the latter being available in regular or 500XL versions. The Ranchero retained its 113-inch Falcon-sourced wheelbase, but the new nose gave it an overall length of just about 200 inches even, which was a 2.5-inch jump over 1966. Most popular of the three varieties was the Fairlane 500 version, shown here, which sold for $2,611 and saw 9,504 examples go out the door. The plain Fairlane Ranchero, in workday clothes, went for $2,514 and had sales of 5,8589. Sportiest of the set was the Fairlane 500XL Ranchero, which featured an interior with bucket seats and console and used the 500XL identity plaques. This sold for $2,768 but only drew 1,881 orders. All used the 200 cubic inch Six as basic power, but could be fitted with any 289 or 390 cubic inch V-8.

For a change, it was not the big Fords or the sporty or luxury models that took the spotlight this year. Instead, it was the Fairlane division, which not only had a totally new body, and new overall length, but also sprouted a new series that would eventually gobble up its parent Fairlane in 1971.

Called the Fairlane Torino series, but usually referred to simply as Torinos, the series was divided into two sub-series of three models each, which for all practical purposes replaced the old Fairlane 500 XL and XLGT sub-series. These were the luxury-type Torino models and the more sporty Torino GT styles. All used basic Fairlane bodies, but represented the highest trim level of that family of cars. However, though based on Fairlane bodies and considered part of the overall Fairlane series, the name "Fairlane" did not appear on the cars.

Included in the totally restyled Fairlane line was one of the nicer looking Ford models to come along in years. This was the Fastback Coupe, with a sleek roofline blending directly into the rear deck, with no "notch" division separating roof from deck. Very similar to the styling of the Mustang 2+2 Fastback, the new design appeared only in the Fairlane 500 and the Torino GT series. In the latter, it wound up being the best selling of all Fairlane models.

Along with the new styling was an overall increase in length, with the cars now being 201 inches overall (up from 197) and the wagons being 203.9 inches, up from 199.8. However, the chassis remained the same, with the cars using a 116-inch wheelbase, while the wagons had a 113-inch wheelbase.

Although the changes were minimal on the large Fords, all new sheet metal forward of the windshield gave the cars a totally new look. Included in the appearance change was a very attractive grille containing concealed headlamps on the XL and LTD series. The grille contained flip-up doors on the outer ends that would automatically raise when the headlights were turned on. Also in the lighting department were the front and rear side marker lights mandated under the new federal highway safety regulations.

Within the large Ford line, the Galaxie 500 series received two new 2-door hardtop models to replace the single 2-door hardtop of 1967. These models were the "Formal" Hardtop Coupe, with its notch-back roofline, and the totally new Fastback Coupe, which bore the same styling as the smaller models in the Fairlane and Mustang families. The Formal Hardtop was also available in the LTD series, while the Fastback appeared in the XL series.

In other big Ford switching, the Station Wagon series received two new models. These were the Custom Wagons, available as six or 9-passenger cars. They all used the same basic wagon body, fit between the mid-priced Country Sedan and the low-buck Ranch Wagon, and were on a trim level comparable to the Custom 500 series.

Changing virtually not at all were the three remaining Ford nameplates—Thunderbird, Mustang, and Falcon. All retained the same number of models as appeared in 1967, all retained the previous year's bodies and chassis, and all received slightly different grilles and trim items to visually differentiate one year from the next. Only the Falcon line was divided into two-sub-series, the Standard Falcon, and the upper bracket Falcon Futura. As with the Torinos, most references simply go with the name "Futura" rather than "Falcon Futura."

Directly related to the Mustangs was the Shelby Mustang, which this year reached a starburst of glory by having both convertible and hardtop models available in three different engine and equipment categories. They were designated the GT-350; GT-500, and GT-500KR. The GT-350 came with a modified 302 cubic inch block, with a supercharged version being available. The GT-500 used the 428 cubic inch block, but a highly modified 4267 engine was an option. At mid-year, when the former Police Interceptor 428 reappeared as the new Super Cobra Jet 428, this was added to the Shelby line, and called the GT-500KR. The "KR" stood for "King of the Road," and was slapped on the cars in a hurry after information leaked to Ford that Chevrolet was planning a hot Camero called the "King of the Road."

Despite the profusion of Shelby Mustang models, things were not going all that well with the car's creator. Carroll Shelby, who loved ultra-fast racing-type cars, was becoming disenchanted with the new Ford/Mustang arrangement. Too many orders were being handed down from Dearborn; too many government regulations were being applied to the cars, and even on the buyer side, too many "luxury" items were being purchased, such as air conditioners and power steering as opposed to superchargers and quick-change rear ends! And, to top it all off, in mid-fall, as the last of the 1967 models rolled from Shelby's Los Angeles plant, all Shelby Mustang production was moved to the Detroit area, where the A.O. Smith Co. was given the contract to convert the 1968 line of Mustangs into Shelbys. The days of the muscle cars were far from over, but a few people in Detroit were already beginning to see markings on the wall.

Evidence of this could be found under the hoods, where a bunch of activity occurred this year. And, this activity did not necessarily pertain only to the big blocks. In the little world, even the 170 cubic inch Falcon/Fairlane basic Six had its compression reduced 8.7:1 from 9.2:1, resulting in a horsepower drop to 100, while the Mustang 200 cubic inch basic Six had its horses drop to 115 via compression reduction to 8.8:1.

The small block Challenger 289 was reduced to 195 horsepower, with compression down to 8.7:1, while the High Performance 289 was dropped completely. New on the scene were two variations of a 302 cubic inch V-8 with a 4x3 inch bore and stroke. The low-power version had a 9.5:1 ratio and a 210 horsepower rating, while the hot one had a 10.5:1 ratio, a 4-barrel carburetor, and a rating of 230 horses.

The old Interceptor 352 was also discarded, but in its place were a pair of new 390 variations added to the previous unchanged Thunderbird 390. However, both of these blocks were meant for the economy set, not the performance group. The first, with a 9.5:1 compression delivered 265 horses, while the second, with a 10.5:1 compression was rated at 280 HP. The regular T-Bird 390 remained unchanged, but the GT 390 version was decreased to 325 horses and a 10.5:1 ratio.

The old standard 427 cubic inch block, long a favorite of the racing fraternity, was now downed to 390 horses with a 10.9:1 compression ratio in stock form, but could still be ordered with a whole spectrum of speed parts, including the super expensive SOHC conversion. However, the new, cheaper, and simpler 428 was making itself known, and by year end production of the 427 quietly slipped from the picture.

Even the touted 428 received some downgrading, as its horsepower slipped to 335 in the Cobra Jet variation and 340 in the Thunderbird model. The only bright spot here was the availability of the new Super Cobra Jet 428, which last year had been the somewhat restricted Police Interceptor Special. And, totally new but not arriving until the year was almost over, was the 429 cubic inch V-8. Far from being a bored-out 428, this was a totally new block with a bore and stroke of 4.36x3.59 as opposed to the 428's 4.13x3.98 bore and stroke. Using a Motorcraft 4-barrel carburetor, the Thunder Jet 429 could produce 360 horses at 4600 rpm.

As diluted as some of the horsepower figures seem, that did not tell the whole story. For example, Ford's powerhouse 427 was now hooked to the C-6 Cruise-O-Matic transmission, and no longer could be ordered with a manual transmission. New federal emissions laws cut down on compression ratios. And even accusations of over-rating horsepowers caused Ford to downgrade both its performance and its high power claims.

Ford's best selling car once again was the Mustang Hardtop. However, this year's sales stopped at 249,447, which was a whopping 106,824 down from 1967! Other models also noted production slippage, and the only other model to break the 100,000 mark was the Galaxie 500 4-door Sedan, which registered 117,877 sales. Surprisingly, despite some models being lower in sales than in 1967, the year as a whole was a mite better than the previous one, with a total of 1,752,502 Fords being sold, not counting another 17,243 Fairlane Ranchero pickups and 13,230 Broncos, both of which figures were listed with truck production.

And finally, on the racing scene, after little to brag about in 1967, Ford came back strong in the 1968 season, with the new Torino Fastback being the principal race vehicle. In NASCAR alone, Ford captured 20 major races, while in USAC and ARCA an equally impressive record brought Ford back into the spotlight. Top drivers racing Fords this year included LeRoy Yarborough; A.J. Foyt; Benny Parsons; David Pearson; Art Pollard; Dan Gurney; Parnelli Jones; Bobby Allison, and Cale Yarborough, who later switched to the slightly faster Mercury Cyclones. And, in addition to these wins, Ford was selected as the official Pace Car for the 1968 Indianapolis 500. The car selected was the new Torino GT Convertible, driven around the pace laps by William Clay Ford, long an enthusiast of the Indy 500.

Least popular of all Thunderbirds was the plain Hardtop, Style 65A, which registered only 9,977 sales. Known as the 5th generation models, the cars sported little more than a revised grille and some very minor trim variations to differentiate them from the 1967 offerings. Apparently these changes did not impress the public, and Thunderbird's overall sales dropped to 64,931, which was the lowest in years. Weighing 4,366 pounds, the plain hardtop cost $4,716 with a front bench seat as opposed to buckets. A total of 4,557 were built in basic configuration.

Best seller of the three Thunderbird variations continued to be the Landau. Basically the hardtop with an exclusive alligator-grain roof and chrome decorative landau bars, the car accounted for 33,029 sales. A popular option on this model was the 429 cubic inch Thunderjet engine, which supposedly was not available until mid-year or later, despite its appearing in promotional material at the start of the season. Often spelled "Thunder Jet," the engine featured its own specially designed emission control system. In base form, with bench seats, the Landau cost $4,845 and weighed 4,372 pounds. Of the total sales, 13,924 were equipped with bench seats, while the remainder had buckets and a central console.

Still being billed as a 4-door sport sedan was the Thunderbird 4-door Landau, Style 57B. The car used the same alligator-grain roof vinyl as did the 2-door version, and also had stylized chrome landau bars on the rear quarters. Priced at $4,924, it was the most expensive Bird in the nest, and at 4,458 pounds, it was also the heaviest. The front bucket seat and console option was also available in this model, but not surprisingly, the majority of sales were for the bench seat version. Thus, out of 21,925 sold, 17,251 had bench seats.

Playing hard on election campaign slogans was this advertising picture for the new Mustang GT Convertible, Style 76A. The Mustangs, like Thunderbirds, got only a mild restyling treatment on the front, and slightly modified simulated air scoops ahead of the rear wheels. The GT models were quickly identified by a very attractive side decal, sometimes referred to as a "C stripe" which ran rearward from the top of the headlight surround to embrace the rear air scop, and then continue forward to mid-point on the doors. Similar to last year's GT package, the option continued to be primarily an exterior visual grouping with the 230 or 325 horse engine being optional. The package added $147 to the Convertible price, not counting the engine cost.

In regular form, the Mustang Convertible lost some of the pizazz of the GT model, but still was a very attractive small car. Still, production slipped dramatically, and only 25,376 of the rag tops left the corral, which was only slightly more than half of the 1967 production. Both this and the GT version are shown with headrests on the front seatbacks. These were options, as were the wheel discs shown on this model. Although most Mustang convertibles had power tops, a manual top was considered standard, while the power version was a $53 option. In base form, the Convertible cost $2,814 and weighed 2,745 pounds.

Once again Ford's most popular car overall was the Mustang Hardtop, shown here wearing the GT trim package. However, this year sales were down to 249,447, a drop of almost 110,000 from last year's 356,271. In base form, the car cost $2,602 and weighed 2,635 pounds. New to the GT package were chromed quad exhaust outlets, heavy-duty rear springs, and a more firm front sway bar and front shocks.

Showing off its striking rear treatment is the Mustang Fastback Coupe, Style 63A. This model also has the special GT option package, and probably has either of the two new engine options, the 302 cubic incher of 230 horses, or the mighty 427 of 390 horses. The latter block was a $775 addition to the price. Although it made a real screamer of the car, its initial cost and fuel hoggishness resulted in its going in only a very few models. With the unlikely basic Six, the Fastback Coupe sold for $2,712 and weighed 2,659 pounds. A total of 42,325 were turned loose. Standard equipment included bucket seats and console, but a bench seat was a no-cost option.

Functional hood and rear brake air scoops and a totally different face quickly identify this as being a Shelby Mustang, while the lower racing stripe broadcasts that it is the GT 500 model (some models said G.T. 500, others said GT 500). Occupying about one-third of Shelby's total production was this new convertible model, which included a sculptured but also very functional roll bar. Both the special hood and nose were of fiberglass, as was the front gravel pan. The car was also available in GT 350 style. All Shelbys were now being converted by the A.O. Smith Co. near Detroit, and were based on Mustangs built at the Metuchen, N.J., assembly plant.

Showing its stuff on a gravel road was the hardtop version of the Shelby Mustang, in this case being of the GT 500 variety. The quarter roof scoops on this model were fully functional and assisted greatly in interior ventilation. The lower scoops directed cooling air to the rear brakes. The rear spoiler was part of the overall Shelby exclusive rear configuration of molded fiberglass. The GT 500 used the 428 cubic inch block, while the GT 350 was powered by the 302 cubic inch mill. Both engines were equipped with "Cobra" aluminum valve covers and special aluminum intake manifolds.

At mid-year, the old Shelby GT 500 was replaced by the new Shelby GTKR models. Available in both soft top and fastback versions, the car was most often seen in this Fastback form. The primary change in this model, aside from the "KR" addition, was the use of the new Super Cobra Jet 428 engine. The "KR" stood for "King of the Road," and was added to head off a reported Camero intention to use a similar designation. The King of the Road title was probably prompted by this year's hit song of that name by the late Roger Miller. Apparently Shelby production reached its high point this year, with 4,450 being produced. Of these, Fastbacks accounted for the largest share with 1,253 in GT 350 form; 1,140 in GT 500 form, and 933 as GT 500 KRs. As soft tops, the numbers ran 404 for the GT 350; 402 with the GT 500 designation, and 318 as GT 500 KRs.

Style leader of the full-size Fords was the very attractive LTD 2-door Hardtop Coupe, Style 65A. Greatly benefitting from all new sheet metal forward of the windshield, the LTD line also had a nice upsurge in popularity, with sales of this model climbing to 54,163. The base engine was the 302 cubic inch small block V-8 of 210 horsepower, while the Six was not available. In basic form, the Hardtop Coupe sold for $3,153 and weighed 3,679 pounds. On this model only, the vinyl top was standard.

Showing off its totally new grille with the interesting hidden headlights covered by flip-up doors, is the new LTD 4-door Hardtop, Ford's most elegant model outside of the Thunderbird realm. Although seldom seen with a metal roof, the very attractive vinyl roof was actually an $83 option on the 4-door models. Select-Shift Cruise-O-Matic was standard on all LTDs, as was the exterior trim/ identification package and special wheel covers. LTD's most popular model, the 4-door Hardtop accounted for 61,755 sales, all base priced at $3,206. The car weighed 3,642 pounds.

Rarely seen in this strictly basic form is the LTD 4-door Sedan, a pillared version of the 4-door Hardtop. Least popular of all LTD models, the 3,596-pound car drew only 22,834 orders with its $3,135 base price. When the $83 optional vinyl top was not installed, the LTD identity emblem was still placed on the rear quarter panel. Notice that the Sedan had a more rectangular rear door window than did the 4-door Hardtop, which had a rounded rear door line. New side marker lights both fore and aft were part of a government mandated safety package.

Owned by Clarence Engborg of Bodafors, Sweden, is this Galaxie 500 XL Convertible. Ford's top line convertible, the car approximated the LTD models in trim level, but stressed sportiness rather than luxury in its interior. Thus, bucket seats and a console were standard equipment, along with the Cruise-O-Matic transmission and basic 302 engine. The Galaxie 500 XL models could not be ordered with the Six, though it is unlikely that anyone would want to do so. Priced at $3,321 and weighing 3,765 pounds, this model was relatively rare, drawing only 6,066 orders. Yes, it is wearing later model wheel covers.

Just as the LTD 2-door Hardtop was Ford's big luxury cruiser, the Galaxie 500 XL Fastback Coupe was the premium sporty big car. Designated Style 63C, the interesting model used a totally new body with rear styling similar to that found on the popular Mustang Fastback, and noted by its lack of break between the rear window line and the trunk deck area. Costing $3,092 in basic form, and weighing 3,608 pounds, the model proved itself quite popular and drew 50,048 orders. Several of these had the large 427 cubic inch block, though this engine was now detuned to 390 horses. Later the mid-year 429 would also be available in this model.

Drawing almost twice the orders as it did in its exclusive 500 XL form, the plain Galaxie 500 Convertible saw 11,832 units leave the factories. In this guise, the car cost $3,215 and weighed 3,699 pounds. Unlike the XL models, these convertibles used a plain bench seat in the front, although the interior was still in vinyl throughout. Also unlike the XL models, the "GT" packages of heavy suspension, tuned exhaust, and other minor features found in the former 7-Litre package were not available on the plain convertible.

1968

The Ford Galaxie 500 Formal Hardtop Coupe, Style 65C, stood apart from its LTD counterpart in two major areas: It did not have the exclusive grille with hidden headlights, and it did not come with a standard vinyl top. On this model, if a vinyl top were to be added, it would have cost another $74 over the basic price of $3,023. Weighing 3,560 pounds, the car was the second most popular Galaxie, with 84,332 being built. Among the styling features was the rakish slope of the rear panel, ending in a relatively short deck which enhanced the long-hood look for which Ford was famous this year.

Ford's newest style of the year was the big fastback, a style formerly available only on the smaller models. Included in the styling was a slightly recessed rear window of rather gigantic proportions, nested between rear quarters that blended effortlessly into the deck lid area. Not quite as sloping as the styling found on the Mustang, the design nevertheless provided a nice alternative to the formal 2-door design. It accounted for 69,760 sales in the Galaxie 500 range alone. In basic V-8 form, these sold for $2,988 and weighed 3,554 pounds. All Galaxie 500 models had their signatures on the rear fender, just ahead of the taillights.

More popular in LTD style than in plain Galaxie 500 form was the 4-door Hardtop, Style 57B, shown here with the optional $83 vinyl top. With the top and accessory wheel covers, only the LTD medallion on the rear and lack of hidden headlights said that this was not the premium model. In plain form, the car came with a manual transmission, and could be ordered with either a Six or small block V-8, or any of the larger engines. As a basic V-8, it cost $3,043 and weighed 3,582 pounds. The Galaxie 500 version accounted for 55,461 sales.

The most popular model in the entire Galaxie series, and the only one to have sales in excess of 100,000 was the Galaxie 500 4-door Sedan, which accounted for 117,877 production units. It is shown here as an almost basic V-8, except for the radio ($57 AM only, or $134 AM/FM) and the deluxe wheel covers. The side plaque, just behind the front wheel opening, says that the engine is the $184 extra 390 cubic inch block, which probably indicates that the car also has the $220 optional Cruise-O-Matic. In base form, it cost $2,971 with the 302 V-8, and weighed 3,536 pounds.

The Custom 500 series still provided a trim level mid-way between the ultra-stark Custom and the upper class Galaxie 500 range. The series consisted of two models. This is the 2-door Sedan, a model that was exclusive only to the Custom and Custom 500 ranges, and not found in the Galaxie or higher classes. A pillared coupe, the style was definitely not at the top of the popularity ratings, and accounted for only 8,938 units. As a small block V-8, it cost $2,806 and weighed 3,480 pounds. Only a single aluminum bar decorated the rear panel, as opposed to the egg-crate design used on the Galaxie models.

Full length side trim and the "Custom 500" signature on the rear fender says that this is 4-door model one step above the Custom stripper and one below the Galaxie 500. Using the same body as the very popular Galaxie 500 pillared sedan, the Custom 500 Sedan was designated Style 54B. Lack of identity plaque on the front fender would indicate that this pre-production model has the 6-cylinder engine of 240 cubic inches. In this form, it cost $2,741 as opposed to $2,848 for a V-8. Most popular of all Custom class models, it drew 49,398 sales. All Custom 500 cars offered buyers a choice of four interior selections.

Devoid of all exterior trim, but wearing the extra-cost wheel covers, is this Custom 2-door Sedan, Style 62E. Lowest price of all full-size Fords, it cost $2,584 as a Six or $2,691 as a V-8. Using the pillared body style that was exclusive to the Custom line, the car was more popular than its "500" counterpart, and drew 18,485 orders. This popularity also rubbed off onto its companion, the Custom 4-door Sedan, Style 54E. Ford's basic 4-door model, it was priced at $2,691 and weighed 3,518 pounds as a V-8. It accounted for 45,980 sales, many for fleet or taxi use. All Custom models were fitted with nylon carpeting and vinyl or nylon interiors.

Ford's big wagons were kept as a class unto themselves, despite the fact that their trim levels matched those of the companion car lines. Thus, the top wagon, the Country Squire, had a trim level on par with the LTD class, and even went so far as to use the beautiful new LTD grille with its flip-up headlight doors. Ford's most expensive wagon, the simulated wood trimmed beauty cost $3,539 and weighed 4,059 pounds. Thus, it was Ford's heaviest passenger car. By far the most popular wagon, the Country Squire accounted for 33,994 sales as a 6-passenger model and 57,776 as a 9-passenger. The 9-passenger was the best selling of all wagons.

Not very far removed from the Country Sedan class of wagons was the Custom Wagon series, which followed the Custom 500 series in trim level. Also available in six or 9-passenger form, it was designated Styles 71H and 71J respectively. The 6-passenger unit cost $3,170 and weighed 3,995 pounds, drawing 18,181 orders, while the 9-passenger cost $3,283, weighed 4,001 pounds, and accounted for only 13,421 sales, thus being Ford's least popular large wagon. On this model, the roof rack was a $44 accessory, while the adjustable rack shown on the Country Squire cost $63.

Following the Country Squire in trim level was Ford's Country Sedan, available as the 6-passenger Style 71B shown here or as the 9-passenger style 71C. Having a trim level comparable to the Galaxie 500 series, it utilized that line's open-eyed grille. Unlike the Country Squire, which was available only as a V-8, the Country Sedan could be ordered in 6-cylinder form. As a 9-passenger, it cost $3,402 and weighed 4,021 pounds as a V-8. Here it drew 29,374 orders. As the more popular 6-passenger model it cost $3,288 and weighed 3,964 pounds, with sales reaching 39,335.

The rear fender signature says "Ranch Wagon," but the fancy wheel covers and side molding say that this model is playing dress-up for the camera. Ford's least expensive wagon, the Ranch Wagon was comparable to the plain Custom series in trim. Available only in 6-passenger form, and usually found with the 6-cylinder engine, it listed for $3,000 even, or $107 more for the small V-8. Designated Style 71D, it weighed 3,945 pounds. Production, only slightly more than the Custom Wagon, stood at 18,237.

Using the Ranch Wagon as its base, Automotive Conversions Corp. of Troy, Mich., built these Amblewagons for facilities that needed an inexpensive yet functional basic ambulance or transporter. Unlike much earlier Siebert conversions which involved cutting the body and adding lengthening sections, the Amblewagons made use of the existing structure, and simply fitted its facilities within the given confines. The major alteration involved removing the rear seat and adding frosted glass panels to the rear quarters. The vehicles could be fitted as the ambulance shown here, or as funeral cars, or even private invalid transports.

Officially known as the Fairlane Torino, but usually referred to simply as the Torino, Ford's newest offering came in six flavors, including this 4-door Sedan, made even more attractive by its optional $83 vinyl roof. Known as Style 54C, the car priced out at $2,776 and weighed 3,514 pounds with the small V-8. It drew 17,962 orders. The V-8 was a $107 option over the line's base 240 cubic inch Six, which was rated at 150 horsepower, as opposed to the 210 horses of the 302 cubic inch V-8. Not a hardtop, the Torino Sedan was of pillared style.

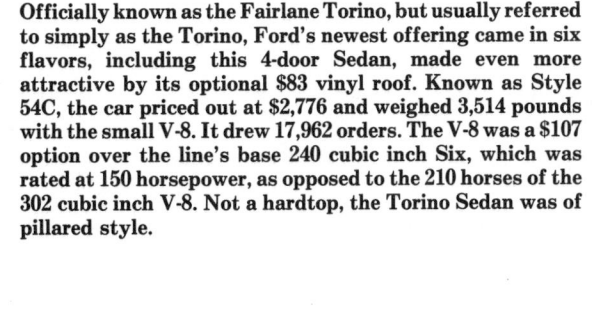

The cockpit of the new Torino line was nicely done, placing all gauges in four pods directly in front of the driver. This is the GT interior, in a model fitted with the 4-speed manual transmission, which was a $184 option when hooked to the 390 cubic inch engine. That engine was also an option, costing $184 extra when equipped with a 2-barrel carburetor or $264 when fitted with the 4-barrel unit. Surprisingly one would expect the $134 AM/FM stereo radio in this car rather than the $54 AM version shown here.

The luxury 2-door of the new Torino line was the Style 65C Hardtop with an LTD-like vinyl top, complete with side identity plaque. In addition to the higher interior trim level, all Torino models used a very low side molding as opposed to the beltline molding found on the Fairlane models. Priced at $2,798, and weighing 3,195 pounds, the Torino Hardtop was the most popular of the line, accounting for 35,964 orders.

Hotshot of the mid-size wagon line was the Torino Country Squire, still officially part of the overall Fairlane line. Available only in 6-passenger form, it had a trim level almost on par with its full-size counterpart, the Country Squire. It was V-8 priced at $3,119 and weighed 3,514 pounds. Not particularly popular, it drew only 14,773 orders. Although the Fairlane name did not appear on the cars, all Torinos were based on Fairlane bodies and chassis.

The official pace car for the 52nd annual running of the Indianapolis 500 turned out to be this Torino GT, shown with William Clay Ford at the wheel. Ironically, though Ford powered racers won in 1965, 66 and 67, and would win again in 1969, it was an Offenhauser engine which brought in the honors at this year's event. In less famous stock form, the Torino GT Convertible, Style 76D, listed at $3,001 and weighed 3,352 pounds. Only 5,310 were built, making it the most rare of all Torinos. Since it appears that the name "Torino" came late in the planning stages, some early references to this car call it the Fairlane GT.

By far the most popular and best known of all the new Torino models was the Fastback Coupe, Style 63B. Quickly grabbing the attention of those who liked sporty or speedy looking cars, the totally new style saw production run up to 74,135. All had some form of V-8, since the Six was not available in the Torino GT sub-series. Priced at $2,747, it weighed 3,208 pounds. The rear was a virtual copy of the Mustang Fastback, and featured a vast expanse of glass for the rear window. Quarter panel louvers were functional and aided in ventilation. Almost a bit too formal for the Torino GT class was the 2-door Hardtop, Style 65D. Yet the car was given a place both in this sub-series and in the admittedly formal Torino sub-series. Still, this model drew 23,939 orders in GT form, where it sold for $2,772 and weighed 3,194 pounds.

A rather cute little blob of a convertible is the how the author describes his Fairlane 500 Convertible, shown parked in the driveway of a former home. Designated Style 76B, the car used the same body and running gear as the Torino version, but this one had a full bench seat, Cruise-O-Matic transmission, and the small block V-8. Still, it was a pleasant, if not inspiring car to drive. Priced at $2,910 and weighing 3,323 pounds, it was the least popular of the entire Fairlane/Torino line, drawing just 3,761 orders.

The new Fastback Coupe design was the sales leader in the Torino GT Series, while the formal Hardtop Coupe took second place. In the Fairlane 500 series, however, the roles were reversed. In this series, the 2-door Hardtop Coupe shown here took the lead in the 2-door race, with 33,282 orders, while the Fastback came in a close second with 32,452 units. The formal top model sold for $2,679, while the sleek Fastback was priced at $2,653. Respectively, their weights were 3,136 and 3,177 pounds. All Fairlane buyers had a choice of four nylon or vinyl interiors.

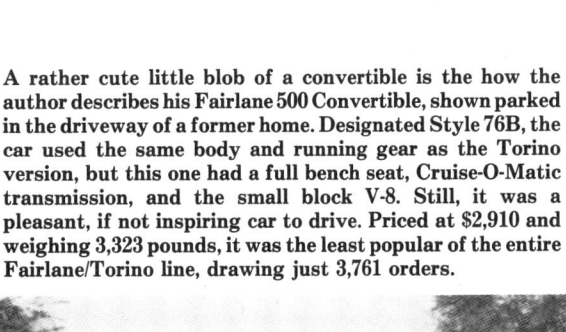

The most popular Fairlane 500, yet the most difficult of which to find an illustration, is the 4-door Sedan, Style 54B. Shown here with an optional $83 white vinyl top, the car was built in pillared form, and sat on a 116-inch wheelbase. Priced at $2,631, it drew a total of 42,390 orders. All Fairlane 500 models used color keyed carpeting both front and rear. The Fairlane 500 identification script rode on the rear fender, just above the side molding.

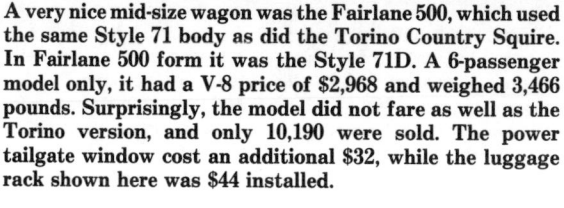

Fairlane 500 Wagon

A very nice mid-size wagon was the Fairlane 500, which used the same Style 71 body as did the Torino Country Squire. In Fairlane 500 form it was the Style 71D. A 6-passenger model only, it had a V-8 price of $2,968 and weighed 3,466 pounds. Surprisingly, the model did not fare as well as the Torino version, and only 10,190 were sold. The power tailgate window cost an additional $32, while the luggage rack shown here was $44 installed.

The lowest trim level in the mid-size line was the plain Fairlane sub-series, comprised of three models. The only 2-door in the pack was the Hardtop Coupe, Style 65A, which in V-8 form sold for $2,544 and weighed 3,125 pounds. All Fairlanes this year were totally restyled, resulting in even the lowest level being very attractive vehicles. However, a couple dollars worth of side trim could have done wonders for this car, without affecting the sales price one degree. Still, the Hardtop was the most popular Fairlane, credited with 44,683 units.

Still relatively good looking despite its austere lack of brightwork, the Fairlane 4-door Sedan bore Style 54A. The car is shown here in totally stock form, with the small hubcaps, but the $34 extra set of white wall tires, of the thin band style. Priced at $2,551, it weighed 3,083 pounds. Not nearly as popular as its 2-door stable mate, it drew only 18,146 orders. All Fairlanes were now 201 inches long, except the wagons, which measured 203.9 inches.

The lowest price wagon in the mid-size line was the Fairlane version, Style 71B. As a Six, it sold for $2,770, while in small block V-8 form it was $2,858. It weighed 3,244 as a Six, 3,422 as a V-8. Production totaled 14,800, which put it right in line with the Fairlane Squire in popularity. A workaday vehicle, the no-frills model was available only as a 6-passenger car.

Still the hotshot of the virtually unchanged Falcon line was the Futura Sports Coupe, with its vinyl top and medallion on the quarter panel. Among the special features on this model were standard bucket seats, interior toys such as map light, lighted glove box, deluxe seat belts, and a remote outside driver's rearview mirror. Available either with a Six or V-8, the base V-8 price was $2,541, while its weight was 2,713. A total of 10,077 were sold.

Quite similar to the Futura Sports Coupe, but utilizing a full bench seat rather than front buckets, was the Futura 2-door Sedan. Sporting a B-pillar between the front and rear seating areas, the car was not available in Hardtop form. Designated Style 62B as opposed to the Sport Coupe's Style 62C, the car was priced at $2,415 and weighed 2,685 pounds. One of three Falcon Futura models in the 10,000 sales bracket, this car drew 10,633 orders. The vinyl top shown here was a $74 add-on.

Falcon Futura Wagon

Looking quite attractive in this catalog illustration is the Falcon Futura Wagon, Style 71B. Falcon's heaviest and most expensive vehicle, as a base V-8 it cost $2,728 and weighed 3,132 pounds. It was one of three Futura models to be in the 10,000 sales area, with its production topping at 10,761. The basic engine for all Falcons was the 170 cubic inch Six, while the 200 inch Six and both the 289 and 302 cubic inch V-8s were optional. The latter engine was a $183 upgrade, but was usually installed when the $187 Cruise-O-Matic transmission was ordered.

The lowest priced and lightest of all Ford cars this year was the Falcon 2-door Sedan, Style 62A. It sold for $2,252 and weighed 2,659 pounds. Most popular of all the plain Falcons, it drew 36,443 orders. Although officially it was called the 2-door Sedan, some advertising refers to the car as the Falcon Club Coupe, a name closer to its styling than the "sedan" tag. All Falcons used a 3-speed fully synchronized manual transmission as standard fare, but could be equipped with Cruise-O-Matic if any engine above the base 170 block was ordered.

Shown in its pre-production stage in one of Ford's engineering or styling laboratories is this Falcon Futura 4-door Sedan, Style 54B. Most popular of the Futura models, it drew 18,733 orders, with a basic V-8 price of $2,456. It weighed 2,719 pounds. Although the body was unchanged, its new grille was made of stamped sheet aluminum. On the backside, taillights were now rectangular, in line with other Fords, rather than the round units that Falcons had used since their inception.

Dressed up with its $44 optional roof rack and wearing a $21 set of optional wheel covers, the Falcon Wagon belies the fact that it was the lowest price and most stripped of all Ford wagons. Of 6-passenger variety, the Style 71A cost $2,617 and weighed 3,132 pounds. It had quarter windows in the rear doors, but these could not be opened. Still, the rear door windows could be lowered to sill level. More popular than the Futura version, it drew 15,576 orders.

Ford's lowest price 4-door was the Falcon Sedan. Devoid of brightwork, it was still able to deliver dependable transportation for $2,301. Designated Style 54A, it weighed 2,714 pounds and drew 29,166 orders. Definitely an economy model, the plain Falcon line was home to the only Fords to have a horn button instead of a horn ring, and were the only 4-doors not to have arm rests for the rear seats, providing these to front seat passengers only. Still, the interiors were nicely done in an attractive combination of 2-tone vinyl and nylon seating, with vinyl door panels.

Reflecting its Fairlane heritage was the Ranchero pickup, available this year in three distinct versions. They were the plain Ranchero, priced at $2,632, which had a run of 5,014; the most popular mid-level Ranchero 500, priced at $2,731, which had a run of 10,029, and the very rare Ranchero GT shown here, which with its $2,964 price tag drew only 1,669 orders. The 200 cubic inch Six was standard in the plain model, while the 500 and GT versions came in V-8 form only, with the 289 as the basic block. Among the features of the GT models were bucket seats finished in pleated vinyl, exclusive "C-stripe" side trim, and special GT wheel covers. All models weighed about 3,150 pounds.

Shown in an unlikely section of Central Park while on duty with the New York City Police Department is this Bronco Wagon, Ford's answer to passenger-carrying 4-wheel drive vehicles of Jeep-like design. Once again the Bronco was available as a full open Roadster, a Pickup with 2-man cab, and this Wagon form. In order to provide full 4-passenger seating, the spare was moved to outside the cab. Continued this year for the Wagon and Pickup was the Sports Package, which included all sorts of minor interior goodies, plus a chrome grille and front bumper and fancy wheel covers similar to the ones on the rear of this example. Prices ranged from $2,650 to $2,850. The only engine offered was the 170 cubic inch Six. Weights ranged from 2,800 to 3,100 pounds.

Ford's experimental efforts this year looked into the world of mid-ship engines, and the result was the Mach II. The unique sports car featured a rather squared rear fitted with large functional louvers in its flat rear deck/hood. The cab, only 47 inches from roof to ground, was set off by a very sloping windshield, but an almost vertical rear window set deeply into a pronounced roof tunnel. The front was radically sloped, and carried concealed headlights, and a large air scoop under a rather thin front bumper. A functional vehicle built on a Mustang chassis, the car is reported to have had excellent performance and handling characteristics.

New styles, new models, new series, and finally—a totally new car! That was the Ford story for 1969, and a complicated and busy story it was. With the exception of the slowly diminishing Falcon line and the top-level Thunderbirds, everything else was either changed dramatically or was brand new.

Newest of all, of course, was Ford's brand new car, the Maverick. Introduced on April 17, 1969, exactly five years to the day of the Mustang's introduction, the new animal received a healthy bit of interest, but nowhere the acclaim that the Mustang had drawn. Of course, the cars were totally different. Whereas the Mustang was definitely aimed for the sporty car set, and attracted a wide range of buyers from the speed hungry to those who simply wanted a sporty personal car, the Maverick was aimed specifically at the economy car market. The only Ford to be priced at under $2,000, it used the Falcon frame, shortened to a 103-inch wheelbase, and was powered by the basic Falcon 170 cubic inch Six. Available only as a 2-door Fastback, it had about as much style and appeal as could be found in a basic economy car.

Its name fit into the Ford zoo, already populated by Thunderbirds, Mustangs, Broncos, Cobras and Cougars, but the Maverick was not another horse. In fact, a Maverick is simply a young unbranded head of beef cattle, but the word is often used to describe someone or something that is unconventional or non-conforming. Actually, the Maverick fit neither definition.

In the big Ford line, the cars were all totally new. True, their basic overall lines made certain that one knew they were Fords, but aside from basic looks and running gear, they shared nothing with the 1968 models. Wearing more rounded lines, the cars were both larger and larger looking. Built on a new chassis of 121 inches (2 inches longer) the cars were 213.9 inches overall, while the wagons grew three inches to a new length of 216.9 inches.

In the top LTD series, a new and exclusive grille, again with hidden headlights, set the styling theme, while standard vinyl tops and velour and vinyl interiors gave a rich note of luxury. Topping off the changes was Ford's attention to sound proofing, and the author will attest to the fact that at high speed, the new LTDs were among the most quiet cars on the road in 1969. Also, the LTDs came only with the 302 cubic inch V-8 as the basic model, with no 6-cylinder power available, while surprisingly, the sporty 500 XL series could be ordered with a new 250 cubic inch Six in addition to all of the optional V-8s.

The Fairlane line also was changed dramatically, but here the emphasis was put on performance and speed rather than styling, and only a mildly revised issue of the 1968 bodies graced the 1969 chassis. But within the line, a new Fairlane Torino GT Cobra sub-series and a less brutal plain Torino GT sub-series were the headliners. The series consisted of formal, fastback, and convertible styles, powered by any selection of engines,

right up to the new Super Cobra Jet 428 cubic inch block that delivered 360 horses at 5400 rpm. And, at mid-year, to appease the production rules for NASCAR qualifications, the GT Talladega Fastback was introduced. Equipped with the 428 Super Cobra Jet as standard power, the Talladega had its own exclusive extended front end, grille and front bumper, and could be ordered with either the 4-speed manual of the Select-Shift Cruise-O-Matic transmission. The car drew its name, of course, from the famous Alabama race track.

Not to be outdone in the sport scene, the Mustang line came up with two new models in addition to some rather significant styling changes. Though the basic body remained the same, a totally new and longer front end contained the line's first quad headlights. The outboard lights were set in deeply recessed coves at the fender edges, while the inboard ones were mounted within the grille unit. Interestingly, the decorative side scoop still appeared, but for this year it was reversed, with its opening pointing toward the rear. And, to make the luxury contingent happy, the new Grande formal hardtop was introduced. This model had all the features of the Deluxe Hardtop, and included a vinyl roof, special steering wheel, luxury bucket seats, and exclusive wheel covers and side trim.

But it wasn't the luxury contingent that Mustang impressed this year—it was the speed set. The first hot horse was the new Mach I, which came with the 2-barrel 351 cubic inch mill as standard fare, but was more often seen with the 4-barrel carburetor if the "small" 351 was used. However, with the 390 GT or the Cobra Jet or Super Cobra Jet 428 engines being available, the car quickly became a speed-set favorite. Built only in fastback styling, the Mach I was soon impressing other competitors at tracks across the country.

Late in the season, primarily to thwart heavy competition from Dodge and Chevrolet on the Trans-Am circuit, the awesome Boss 302 and Boss 429 Mustangs were born. Virtually all-out racing machines, these latter cars when properly tuned, could come up with over 500 horsepower, though their factory rating was a "modest" 375 at 5600 rpm. Along with the special competition engines, the Boss models featured special suspension; a heavy-duty 4-speed transmission; power front disc brakes and oversized rear drums; special ignition; and exclusive exterior details. In order to meet SCCA production requirements, the cars had to be offered on a dealership basis, and so great was the interest that a total of 1,934 were snapped up. Some references list all of these models as mid-1969 vehicles, while others list them as early 1970s. Still, the cars won the 1969 Trans-Am Championship, and thus probably should quality as 1969 models.

The new Boss Mustangs did little too enhance the appeal of the far costlier Shelby Mustangs, nor did they sweeten the relationship at this time between Carroll Shelby and Ford. The Shelby versions were still being converted by the A.O. Smith Co. in Dearborn, however, and would finish out the 1969 year, with approximately 600 more being re-registered as 1970 models, though in fact they were built of 1969 components within the time frame of the 1969 model year. Once again the Shelbys used exclusive fiberglass front and rear deck components. Available only in fastback or convertible styles, the Shelbys were again divided into the GT 350 and GT 500 versions, but the GT 500KR was gone. This year, though, the 350 used Ford's new 351 cubic inch block rather than the old 302, while the GT 500 was given a more tame 335 horsepower version of the 428 cubic inch block, as opposed to the 360 horse model that was standard in 1968. Production rested at 1,536 fast-back models and 335 convertibles.

From the excitement of the hot Mustangs to the world of the dying Falcons was almost a step in backwardness. As could be expected for a car that was soon to be discarded, the Falcon line received very little attention, save for some very minor trim changes. Even the grille remained unchanged, leaving it very difficult to tell a 1968 Falcon from a 1969 model. "Major" changes included a redesign of the front marker lights and a redesign and relocation of the rear lights, and the substitution of rocker molding in place of side molding on the Futura models.

Also changing very little was the Thunderbird, but here the line was waiting for major revisions scheduled for 1970. Still, the Bird did have a new grille in its jet-shaped mouth, and again featured hidden headlights within the grille. In the rear, the taillight and backup light configuration also changed, with the backup lights now being a long single unit centrally mounted in the escutcheon plate. The same three models appeared—hardtop and 2-door and 4-door Landau models—but the optional electrically operated sun roof is sometimes regarded as a separate "Sun Roof Landau" model. However, this was simply a new $450 option available only on the 2-door Landau.

Under the hoods, things were quiet for the small blocks, with only a new 250 cubic inch Six showing up. Having a bore and stroke of 3.68x3.91 inches, it developed 155 horsepower at 4000 rpm. It had a 9:1 compression ratio. In effect, it slid into the slot formerly occupied by the old Challenger 289 V-8, which was discontinued this year.

In the 302 cubic inch family, the basic block had its horsepower raised to 220 from 210, via an increase in the compression ratio to 9.5:1. The 4-barrel carburetor version of the 302, which had been rated at 230 horses, was now gone, but it was replaced by the "Boss 302" sporting a 10.5:1 compression and a 290 horsepower rating.

New on the block were two 351 cubic inch engines, both having a 4x3.5 inch bore and stroke. The quiet one had a 2-barrel carburetor, 9.5:1 compression, and developed 250 horsepower at 4600 rpm. The wild one used a 4-barrel carb, had a 10.7:1 compression, and was listed at 290 horses at 4800 rpm.

The old Thunderbird 390 of 265 horses was now called the Interceptor 390, but otherwise was unchanged, as were the 280 horse Thunderbird 390 and the GT 390. However, the 4-barrel Thunderbird 390 of 315 horsepower was dropped, as was the excellent but high priced and low volume High Performance 427 that had been so loved for so long by the speed set.

In addition, the Thunderbird 428 was dropped, leaving only the plain 428 Cobra Jet of 335 horses and the Super Cobra Jet of 360 horses. New on the scene was the aforementioned 429 cubic inch block, which came in awesome "Boss" set-up, or in a more tame 320 horse version.

In an unusual and virtually unexpected sales race, the Mustang hardtop almost lost its sales lead, as a surprising number of buyers apparently opted for the little Maverick. Thus, the Mustang Hardtop was still first in sales, but with only 127,954 cars, while the Maverick pulled in a close second, with 127,833 sales. Oddly, though the two lower priced cars took sales spots one and two, it was the upper priced cars that stole the rest of the show, with three models being above the 100,000 sales mark. These were the third place LTD 4-door Sedan, with 113,168 sales; the fourth place LTD Formal Top Coupe, with 111,565 sales, and the fifth place Galaxie 500 4-door Sedan, with 104,606.

With the Mustangs included, this year's sales figures reached 1,937,607, or a nice increase of 185,105 over 1968. However, much of this sales increase had to be credited to the new Maverick, though an upsurge in interest in the larger cars was also noted. Oddly, it was the more sporty models that seemed to fare the worst this year, while the pragmatic family vehicles carried the major load. Incidentally, the production figures this year seem to vary to a wide degree, with some reports showing the large Fords reaching 1,014,750, while the figures used in this book tally only 998,796. Also, other reports list total production without the Mustangs as 1,637,783 or 1,937,607. This chapter uses the figures thought most correct, but does not guarantee their accuracy.

Showing off its new horizontal louvered texture grille with the three vertical dividers is the new Thunderbird 2-door Hardtop, Style 65C. Having the lowest trim level in the well-trimmed Thunderbird line, this model was base priced at $4,807 and weighed 4,348 pounds. Least popular of all the Birds, it drew only 5,913 orders, indicating that if buyers were going to throw out the big bucks for a Thunderbird, they weren't going to quibble at going the whole route, rather than trying save a bit with a simple plain model.

Most popular of all three Thunderbird models was the 2-door Landau, which saw its sales reach 27,664. Possibly the fact that the Thunderbird retained its old body shell and varied from 1968 only in grille and minor trim and rear changes kept buyers at a low edge this year. Also not helping sales were continuing rumors of a totally new Bird that would hatch in 1970. The Landau cost $4,947 and weighed 4,360 pounds. It differed from the plain Hardtop in that it had a vinyl top with decorative landau irons, which came right up to the door windows, thus eliminating the small quarter windows found in the lower price model.

Ford's only model to top the $5,000 mark in basic form was the Thunderbird 4-door Landau, Style 57C, which listed at $5,026. However, this was for the basic car, and such things as an air conditioner would add $499; AM/FM radio, $150, and power windows and seat, $207. All Birds were powered with the 429 cubic inch 4-barrel block of 360 horsepower. The 4-door weighed 4,460 pounds in base trim. As was the case with all Birds, production slipped substantially, and only 15,650 were built. Note how the rear door cut into the vinyl side panel. This opening was bracketed by the decorative landau bar which has its upper point at the rear edge of the rain gutter.

Mustang's new hot horse this year was the Mach I, designed specifically to impress the speed set. In base form it was powered by the 2-barrel 351 cubic inch mill, but even if this small block was used, it often sported a 4-barrel carb. More often, however, the car was turned loose with either the 390 GT or the Cobra Jet or Super Cobra Jet 428 engines. Available only as a Fastback Coupe, and wearing its own exclusive hood, the car was designated the Style 63C, wearing a base sticker price of only $3,122. Somebody at Ford guessed right with this combination, and the Mach I turned out to be the second best selling Mustang in the herd, with 72,458 coming out of the corral.

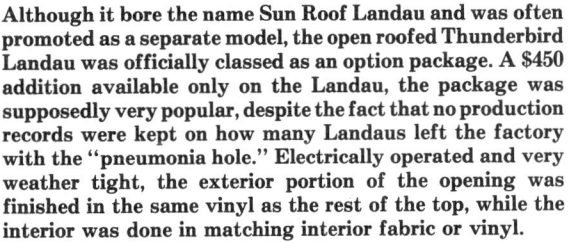

Although it bore the name Sun Roof Landau and was often promoted as a separate model, the open roofed Thunderbird Landau was officially classed as an option package. A $450 addition available only on the Landau, the package was supposedly very popular, despite the fact that no production records were kept on how many Landaus left the factory with the "pneumonia hole." Electrically operated and very weather tight, the exterior portion of the opening was finished in the same vinyl as the rest of the top, while the interior was done in matching interior fabric or vinyl.

Not content with the Mach I, at mid-year Mustang spun off the Boss 302 as an answer to the small block Camero Z-28. Priced at about $3,450, the car was powered by a 290 horse variation of the solid 302 cubic inch block. Front spoiler and blackout hood and head and taillight surrounds were standard. However, the rear window slats, chrome Magnum 500 wheels, and rear deck spoiler were options. the Boss 302 proved to be a formidable competitor on this year's Trans-Am circuit, taking a good number of wins in its class from both Cameros and Chargers. Buyer interest was relatively high for an almost all-out race machine, and 1,934 were sold.

Following the Boss 302 onto the mid-year scene was Mustang's virtual all-out race machine, the Boss 429. Designed for serious competition only, the car was the most expensive Mustang in the barn, listing at $4,798 in base form. Too competitive to really be popular, the awesome vehicle saw only 504 copies leave the dealerships. However, these figures were more than enough to meet SCCA production requirements and the cars not only competed in, but would up winning the 1969 Trans-Am championship. Reports credit the engine with being capable of well over 500 horsepower when well tuned, even though Ford rated them at a "modest" 375 horses. Functional hood scoop, front spoiler, chrome Magnum 500 wheels, functional rear brake air duct, and lack of side trim give these cars a unique appearance. Competition-tuned engines, special suspension, heavy-duty 4-speed transmission, and special large brakes were among the unseen goodies.

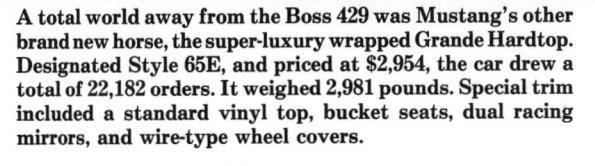

A total world away from the Boss 429 was Mustang's other brand new horse, the super-luxury wrapped Grande Hardtop. Designated Style 65E, and priced at $2,954, the car drew a total of 22,182 orders. It weighed 2,981 pounds. Special trim included a standard vinyl top, bucket seats, dual racing mirrors, and wire-type wheel covers.

Least popular of the Mustangs, not counting the limited-interest Boss models, was the Convertible, Style 76A. Priced at $2,937, the pretty soft top drew only 14,746 buyers. It weighed an even 2,800 pounds with the base V-8. New frontal length and overall styling changes made the car seem much longer and lower than previous models. This view gives a good look at the reversal of the simulated rear air scoop. Last year this scoop faced forward, while this year the opening faced toward the rear. Not shown, but relatively popular this year was the $147 GT package, which included a special racing stripe; argent styled steel wheels; non-functional hood scoop, and pin-type exposed hood latches.

Still by far Mustang's most popular model, the Hardtop Coupe this year drew a total of 127,954 orders. Wearing Style 65A, the car was priced at $2,723 in basic V-8 style, which included the 320 cubic inch block. Six cylinder models began at $2,618 for the basic 200 cubic inch block, or $25 more for the 250 cubic inch Six. This view gives a good look at the totally new Mustang front end, with its first use of quad headlamps. However, unlike matched quads, the outboard lights were located well back and to the far outside in deep fender coves, while the inboard ones were set into the outer ends of the new grille. The wire wheel covers on this model were an $80 option.

Providing the base body for the red hot Mach I and mid-year Boss models was the Fastback Coupe, Style 63A. This year, the model was officially called the "SportsRoof." In basic stock form it was simply a rather tame but sleek looking 2+2 model which sold for $2,723 as a V-8 or $2,618 with the basic Six, the same price as the Hardtop. Relatively popular, but not nearly to the degree of the Hardtop, the SportsRoof drew 61,980 orders. Dual rear exhausts with double tips indicate that this model houses at least a 351 cubic inch engine, and might even have the 428 Cobra Jet V-8, which would have been a $421 option, not counting the mandatory heavy-duty transmission or recommended heavier suspension.

Still available and still being modified by the A.O. Smith Co. of Dearborn, Mich., were the fabulous Shelby Mustangs. They were available as the GT 350 or GT 500 Sportsroof, but the GT 500 KR was gone. The GT 500 model shown here drew 1,536 orders, while the GT 350 drew 1,085. Once again, exclusive fiberglass noses, front fenders, hoods, and rear sections were fitted. However, the new Boss models cut deeply into the interest in the Shelbys, and by mid-1970 the last versions were gone.

The first car that the author ever bought new off a showroom floor was this LTD 2-door Formal Coupe, Style 65A. It was bought in Dearborn, Mich., with the purchase based on "love at first sight," while the author was working on the initial version of *ILLUSTRATED HISTORY OF FORD.* The car proved to be an exceptionally good vehicle, that provided thousands of trouble free miles through virtually every state east of the Mississippi. Base priced at $3,234, and weighing 3,745 pounds, this example was one of 111,565 turned out by Ford this year. Done in white with a black top and interior, it was powered by the new 390 Interceptor engine of 265 horsepower, which was a $60 addition.

Companion to the 2-door coupe was the 4-door LTD Hardtop Sedan, which turned out to be the most popular model of this upscale big Ford series. A total of 113,168 were built. Priced at $3,261, it weighed 3,840 pounds. All LTDs came with Cruise-O-Matic transmissions as standard fare, but the vinyl tops so often associated with this sub-series were actually an add-on, costing approximately $100 above the base price. Ford liked to brag that its 1969 LTD models were the "world's quietest road cars," and the author will attest to that claim—the cars were super quiet at all speeds.

Barely holding its place on the dealership floor was the convertible version of the Shelby Cobra. Also available in GT 350 and GT 500 form, the car drew only 194 orders with the small block and 335 in GT 500 form. New this year was the exhaust system, which now exited in dual combined outlets located at the center of the rear bumper. Special fiberglass rear decks with spoiler flare, and functional rear brake air scoops gave a heavy appearance to the back end. The styled roll bar was both functional and standard. Special 5-spoke aluminum wheels were a new addition, as were the design of the side stripes and taillights. The GT 500 continued to carry the 428 Cobra Jet block.

Looking naked without its $100 optional vinyl roof covering is the LTD 4-door Sedan, a pillared model that had a base price of $3,192 and weighed 3,745 pounds. Designated Style 54C, it was far less popular than the 4-door hardtop version, and accounted for only 63,709 orders. The very attractive cast aluminum grille hid its headlights behind flip-up doors on the outer edges. On the rear, a lattice-work of bright metal was superimposed on a red applique. The upper side molding seen on the author's car but not on this version was an added cost item.

Returning to their own trim level series were the station wagons, now no longer considered a series onto themselves. Thus, the LTD series received Ford's top of the line wagon, the country Squire. Complete with imitation wood trim on the sides, the wagon was available as the 6-passenger Style 71E shown here, or the 10-passenger Style 71A. It was priced at $3,644 as a 6-passenger or $3,721 in 10-passenger form, with the weights running 4,202 and 4,227 pounds. Far more popular in 10-passenger style, it drew 82,790 orders in that form, but only 46,445 with seating for six. The luggage rack, which included a wind deflector for the rear window, was a $63 accessory.

Another excellent Ford owned by the author for a couple of years was this bright red Galaxie 500 XL Convertible, Style 76B. Shown here with a good coating of rural Illinois dust, the car provided many miles of trouble free service during the early 1970s. It was base priced at $3,385 and weighed 3,975 pounds. Far from being a popular model, the XL Convertible drew only 7,402 orders. The XL sub-series was the sporty division of the overall Galaxie line, and used the same basic trim level as was found on the LTDs. However, the series used the basic Galaxie 500 grille, unless the cast LTD grille with its hidden headlights was ordered as an extra cost option.

As did the LTD series, cars in the 2-model Galaxie 500 XL sub-series carried a stamped metal lattice bar over a red applique across the entire stern. The bar, in effect, matched the grille texture. This is the new XL 2-door Fastback, Style 63C, which was base priced at $3,157 and weighed 3,825 pounds. An interesting and very attractive design feature of this model was the sweeping rear panel, which blended into the body almost at the rear fender tip. Well recessed between these sail-like panels was the rear window. On the sides, an interesting kick-up in the lower line of the quarter windows emphasized the swept-back design features. All XL models were fitted with standard bucket seats, an all-vinyl interior, and grille and wheel covers identical to those of the LTD. A relatively popular car, the XL Fastback (sometimes called SportsRoof) drew 54,557 orders.

Less fancy and less desired than the XL Convertible was the Galaxie 500 Convertible, Ford's only other large soft top. Priced at $3,247, the 3,880-pound car drew only 6,910 orders, and thus accounted for the lowest production of the entire large Ford line. It differed from the XL version in that it used a bench seat in front, had the standard Galaxie 500 grille, and was fitted with rather dull hubcaps unless one of the more attractive sets of wheel covers was ordered for $21 extra. Surprisingly, though the related LTD sub-series came in V-8 form only, all of the sporty Galaxie 500 models, including the XL versions, could be ordered with the 240 cubic inch Six.

Shown in almost basic trim is the best selling of all Galaxie 500 models, the 4-door Sedan, Style 54A. Of pillared design, the car accounted for 104,606 sales, and thus was the only Galaxie 500 model to exceed the 100,000 production mark. It was base priced at $3,002 and weighed 3,710 pounds. All of these models had the "Galaxie 500" signature on the trailing edge of the rear fenders, just ahead of the new rectangular taillights. The full-length lower body side molding was integral with the wheel opening moldings, and was similar to that found on the LTD models. XL models were noted for their lack of upper side trim, a factor which made them quite vulnerable to parking lot dings.

Well trimmed with vinyl roof and deluxe wheel covers is this Galaxie 500 4-door Hardtop Sedan, Style 57B. Companion to the LTD version, this lesser trimmed model used the stamped aluminum Galaxie grille and exposed headlights. At the rear, a black applique was covered with a series of four full-length bars rather than a lattice-stamped panel. Priced at $3,071, the car weighed 3,745 pounds. Far less popular than the slightly more expensive LTD version, it drew only 64,031 orders.

Just as the Country Squire moved into the LTD series, the all-new Country Sedan moved into the Galaxie 500 range. Here it was the Style 71B in 6-passenger form, or the 71C in 10-passenger style. As a 6-passenger, it cost $3,362 and weighed 4,107 pounds, while the 10-passenger went for $3,487 and weighed 4,132 pounds, thus being the heaviest and most expensive of all Galaxie 500 models. Far more popular in 6-passenger style, it drew 36,287 orders in that form, but only 11,563 as a 10-passenger. All big Fords used quad headlights this year, nicely seated near the outward ends of the extruded aluminum grilles.

Beautiful in the XL version, the new SportsRoof or Fastback Coupe model was still a mighty attractive vehicle in plain Galaxie trim. Here the car wore a split front bench seat with twin head rests and center arm rests. Priced at $3,018 and weighing 3,720 pounds, it was designated Style 63B. It drew 63,921 orders. This view gives a good look at the sweeping roof pillars and the tunnel effect of the rear window design.

Shown here in absolutely basic form is the Galaxie 500 Formal Hardtop Coupe, Style 65C. This is the way the car would look at its $3,070 price tag and 3,675-pound weight. Obviously, few of this model ever left dealerships looking like this, and most would quickly be fitted with the $100 vinyl top; $21 wheel covers; $181 AM/FM Stereo, and $388 air conditioner. The base 6-cylinder engine was also seldom seen, and any engine option right up to the 429 Thunder Jet with 4-barrel carburetor could be added. This latter engine cost an extra $237 but required the $222 Cruise-O-Matic or $194 manual 4-speed. One of the more popular Galaxie 500 models, the Formal Top Coupe accounted for 71,920 units.

Appearing for the last time was the pillared coupe design found only in the Custom and Custom 500 series. This is the basic Custom 500 model, known as the 2-door Sedan, Style 62B. Priced at $2,836 and weighing 3,610 pounds, it was 40 pounds lighter and $105 cheaper when carrying the Six rather than a V-8. Not at all popular, it drew only 7,585 orders. Custom 500 models had no rear panel applique, but instead spelled "FORD" in block letters below the trunk deck drip rail.

A single side bar running full length at the belt line division and a signature on the trailing edge of the rear fender marks this as the 4-door Sedan version of the Custom 500 line. The most popular car in the series, it accounted for 45,761 units. Designated Style 54B, it was priced at $2,878 and weighed 3,660 pounds in V-8 form, with the wheel covers being a $21 add on. All Custom 500 models used bright drip rail moldings and had bright body trim outlining the greenhouse area. Buyers had a choice of four different upholsteries and interior combinations.

Not surprisingly, the Custom 500 series also received its station wagon. This was the Ranch Wagon, available as both the 6-passenger Style 71H or the 10-passenger Style 71J. In 6-passenger form it cost $3,243 and weighed 4,122 pounds, while the 10-seater was $3,556 and 50 pounds heavier. Again, the 6-passenger was the more popular of the two, with 16,432 being produced as opposed to 11,563 for the larger capacity unit. All 10-passenger models used dual facing rear seats and were provided with electric powered rear windows. On 6-passenger models, the powered tailgate window was a $35 extra,

Soon to be dropped was the lowest priced of all large Fords, the Custom 2-door Sedan, Style 62B. Really a pillared coupe, the model sold for $2,632 as a Six or $2,737 as a V-8, where it weighed 3,625 pounds. Designed mainly for fleet use, the rather basic car is shown here with the $21 extra wheel covers rather than the dull hubcaps. Devoid of most trim, it still kept the "Custom" signature on the rear fender. Orders totalled 15,439. The rear treatment was identical to that of the Custom 500 models. The rear quarter trim on this model was for photographic purposes only, and did not appear on the real cars.

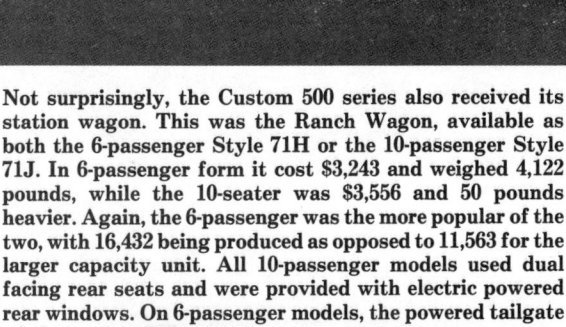

Most often seen in taxi or fleet service was the Custom 4-door Sedan, Style 54E. The basic car sold for $2,674 as a Six, where it weighed 3,608 pounds. Most popular of the three Custom models, it attracted 45,653 buyers. All Galaxie 500, Custom 500, and Custom models used the same grille, while inside the same "Flight Cockpit" instrument panel surrounded the driving area and placed recessed controls within fingertip reach.

Appearing this year only was the Fairlane Torino GT Cobra 2-door Hardtop, Style 65A, which featured a formal roof. Coming out of the factory wearing the 428 cubic inch engine of 335 horses and the 4-speed manual transmission as standard equipment, the quick car was priced at a relatively reasonable $3,208 and weighed 3,490 pounds. Sadly, its production figures were mixed in with the Torino GT models and therefore cannot be counted separately. A large Cobra emblem on the front fender panels quickly identified these cars. Despite Carroll Shelby's use of the "Cobra" name, Ford did not hesitate to apply a similar designation to its top running Torinos.

Available only in 6-passenger form was Ford's least expensive full-size wagon, the Custom Style 71D Ranch Wagon. Priced at $3,179 as a V-8, it weighed 4,109 pounds and attracted 17,489 buyers. Shown here while in the design studio, this model wears the wrong wheel covers and has been fitted with slats for a roof-top luggage rack. All Ford wagons this year used a swing-away doorgate, which opened as a door without lowering the rear window.

Appearing only this year was the Fairlane Torino GT Talladega Special, shown here in street form. Named for the famous Alabama race track, it was built primarily as a race car. However, it had to be offered at dealership level to satisfy the NASCAR requirement for a "production" vehicle, and thus at least 500 had to be sold. In all, 754 left the lots, all with the 428 Super Cobra Jet and either a manual 4-speed or modified Select-Shift Cruise-O-Matic transmission. All used an exclusive front end of special hood, grille, and bumper. A mid-year model, it was also fitted with the 429 block in some cases. All were built at Ford's plant at Atlanta, Ga., and most were sold in the southern states.

Although production figures are mixed with other Torino GTs, probably the most popular of the two new Torino GT Cobra models was the Fastback or SportsRoof version, which sold for $3,183. A "fast snake" and the word "COBRA" on the rear panel warned other drivers that this was a car that could move out. Besides the heavy power, other exclusive items included a rather sparse interior, heavy-duty suspension, 6-inch wide wheels, blackout grille, and special hood with exterior locking pins. The rear window slats were at extra cost, but the dual exhaust pipes were standard fare.

Shown in racing trim and taking the 1969 Daytona 500 is a more common example of the new Torino GT Talladega Special. Piloted by Lee Roy Yarborough, the car was running the old 427 Ford engine at this point. Driving similar Talladega models were Donnie Allison, who placed 3rd; A.J. Foyt, 4th; David Pearson, 6th; Benny Parsons, 7th, and Richard Petty, 8th. The main competitor for Ford on the NASCAR circuit this year was the new Dodge Charger Daytonas, also named for a famous NASCAR track.

Appearing for the last time this year was the Fairlane Torino GT 2-door Hardtop, a formal-topped luxury-style car that promised some hot performance when properly outfitted. As did all Torino models, it carried a non-functional air scoop on the hood, and had the argent-colored egg crate grille exclusive to the series. The vinyl roof was not included, but came as a $90 option. Designated Style 65D, the car carried a $2,848 base price and 3,173 pound weight sticker when equipped with the basic 302 cubic inch V-8. Although always referred to simply as "Torino" models, the line was still officially part of the overall Fairlane series, and thus the official name is Fairlane Torino GT.

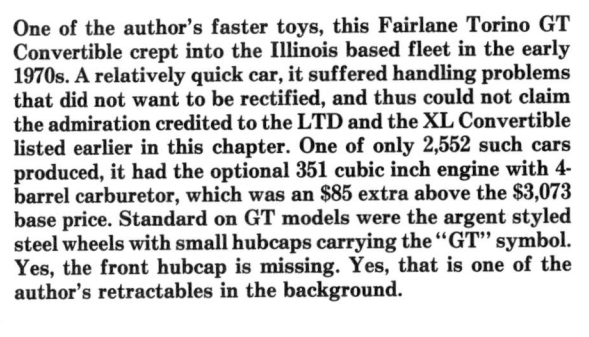

One of the author's faster toys, this Fairlane Torino GT Convertible crept into the Illinois based fleet in the early 1970s. A relatively quick car, it suffered handling problems that did not want to be rectified, and thus could not claim the admiration credited to the LTD and the XL Convertible listed earlier in this chapter. One of only 2,552 such cars produced, it had the optional 351 cubic inch engine with 4-barrel carburetor, which was an $85 extra above the $3,073 base price. Standard on GT models were the argent styled steel wheels with small hubcaps carrying the "GT" symbol. Yes, the front hubcap is missing. Yes, that is one of the author's retractables in the background.

Sleekest looking and most popular of the Fairlane Torino GT series was the Fastback or SportsRoof Coupe, Style 63D. Production was 61,319 with all sorts of engines ranging from the base 302 to the 335 horse 428 with 4-barrel carburetor and Ram Air induction, which cost $420 extra and mandated the $222 Cruise-O-Matic or the $194 manual 4-speed. The "428" noted on the hood scoop shows that this model is ready for some serious track work. In basic form, the SportsRoof Coupe cost $2,823 and weighed 3,220 pounds. The race-type side decal was a popular item used on this model only. It was known as a "C-stripe."

Less hot and less costly than the Torino GT models was the plain Fairlane Torino 2-door Hardtop Coupe, Style 65B. The car differed from the GT version primarily in its lack of simulated hood scoop and in its wheels, which were standard Fairlane rather than the exclusive argent-style of the GT models. Priced at $2,827 in V-8 form, it weighed 3,195 pounds. Plain Fairlane Torinos were also available in 6-cylinder form. The most popular of this three style class, the 2-door drew 20,789 orders.

The top Fairlane wagon bore the official name of Fairlane Torino Squire, though it was usually referred to as the Torino Squire or simply Squire. The only wagon in the series to be fitted with decorative simulated wood panels and molding, it was designated Style 71E. Available only in 6-passenger form, it cost $3,180 as a V-8 and weighed 3,556 pounds. It turned out to be the most popular of all of the mid-size wagons, drawing 14,472 orders.

Appearing for the last time this year was the plain Fairlane 500 Convertible, Style 76B. Less popular even than the Torino GT model, it saw its production top out at 2,264 units, and thus is the most rare of all Fairlane models. Classed as a mid-level trim series between the plain Fairlanes and the Torino models, the Fairlane 500 series was facing a dubious future in view of the new Tornio class. The convertible used a bench-type front seat and an all-vinyl interior with color-keyed carpeting front and rear. In base form, the convertible sold for $2,924 and weighed 3,336 pounds with the V-8.

In basic form, the Fairlane 500 2-door Hardtop Coupe sold for $2,699 and weighed 3,143 pounds as a V-8. It used a split bench seat, with dual individual headrests, and had side molding so low on the body that it almost could be considered rocker molding. Its grille housed quad headlights, and though similar to that of the Torino models, was enough different to identify the series. Also for identification was the "Fairlane 500" signature on the rear fender. One of the more popular Fairlane 500 models, it saw production reach 28,179. The hub caps shown here were standard.

Attempting to be Fairlane's answer to the LTD was the Fairlane Torino 4-door Sedan, Style 54C. The top of the line sedan cost $2,806 and weighed 3,180 pounds. However, buyers apparently were not impressed, and only 11,971 were sold. Nice stamped grillework nested over a full-length applique at the rear, carrying the grille theme to the rear. Full-length bright rocker molding was used, as were the deluxe wheelcovers. The vinyl roof, installed on virtually all models, added $90 to the cost.

In its final year in the Fairlane 500 series was the Fastback or SportsRoof Coupe, Style 63B, which shared its body with the sleek Torino versions. Fast looking, but sometimes wearing even the 6-cylinder engine, the car gave the impression of speed and sport without the high initial cost or gas-gobbling habits of the larger engine versions. Apparently this idea sat well with many buyers, and they made this car reach the 29,849 mark in sales. As a V-8 it cost $2,674 and weighed 3,190 pounds. This was the only Fairlane 500 style to use the simulated air intakes on the roof.

Shown in basic form is the best selling of all Fairlane 500 models, the 4-door Sedan, Style 54B. A total of 40,888 left the plants, all with a price of $2,641 and a weight of 3,135 pounds. Unlike the Torino models, which used a decorative panel across the rear section, the Fairlanes had only a series signature on the right side of the painted panel. Although the SportsRoof model used high side trim, all other models including the Sedan used the very low molding which integrated into the bright wheel well surrounds. Hubcaps were standard, but the fancier wheel covers were usually applied at $21 a set.

Showing off Ford's "Magic Doorgate" rear end is this Fairlane 500 Station Wagon, Style 71B. Available only as a 6-passenger wagon, it was essentially the Torino Squire without the decorative wood trim. The doorgate could be opened as shown here, or dropped like a regular tailgate. When opening as a door, the rear window could remain raised, but when dropped as a tailgate, it had to be lowered. Priced at $2,934 as a Six, it weighed 3,415 pounds. The base V-8 was $90 more. Production reached a rather uninspiring 12,869. Although listed as 6-passenger wagons, a rear facing back seat could be ordered for all Fairlane wagons for an extra $53, thus turning these cars into 9-passenger vehicles.

Very surprisingly, the lowest level Fairlane was also the most popular of all models in the entire Fairlane/Torino series. It was the plain Fairlane 2-door Hardtop, which listed at $2,482 as a Six. It had a total production run of 85,630. Shown here wearing the extra-cost wheel covers, the rather plain car used vinyl covered rubber floor mats rather than carpeting, and was devoid of virtually all trim except for a bright aluminum grille and bright side window frames, rain gutters, and windshield and rear window surrounds.

Despite its being the lowest priced model, the plain Fairlane 4-door Sedan, Style 54A, drew a surprising 27,296 orders, probably many going for fleet use. Shown here in absolute standard form, with hub caps gracing the extra-cost white walls, the car went out the door for $2,471 as a Six. This was one of the few times that a 4-door sedan would take honors as the lowest price car in a line, as this title usually went to a 2-door model. Despite being the austerity offering, the Sedan still had arm rests front and rear and was fitted with a chrome horn ring and a cigarette lighter in the ash tray.

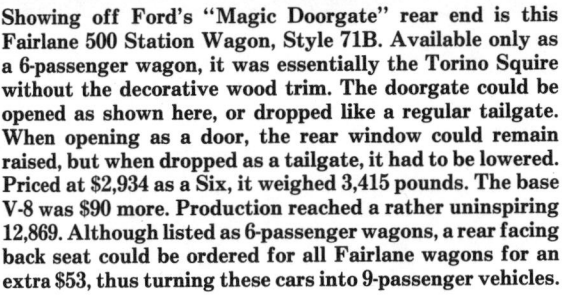

Ford's economy mid-size wagon was the 6-passenger Fairlane Style 71D. It was priced at $2,824 as a Six, in which form it weighed 3,387 pounds. Stressing convenience and value, the car could be fitted with a rear-facing back seat for three extra passengers. Production was not all that bad, and 10,882 left the plants. As were other plain Fairlanes, the wagon was also devoid of any side trim except for the "Fairlane" signature on the rear fender.

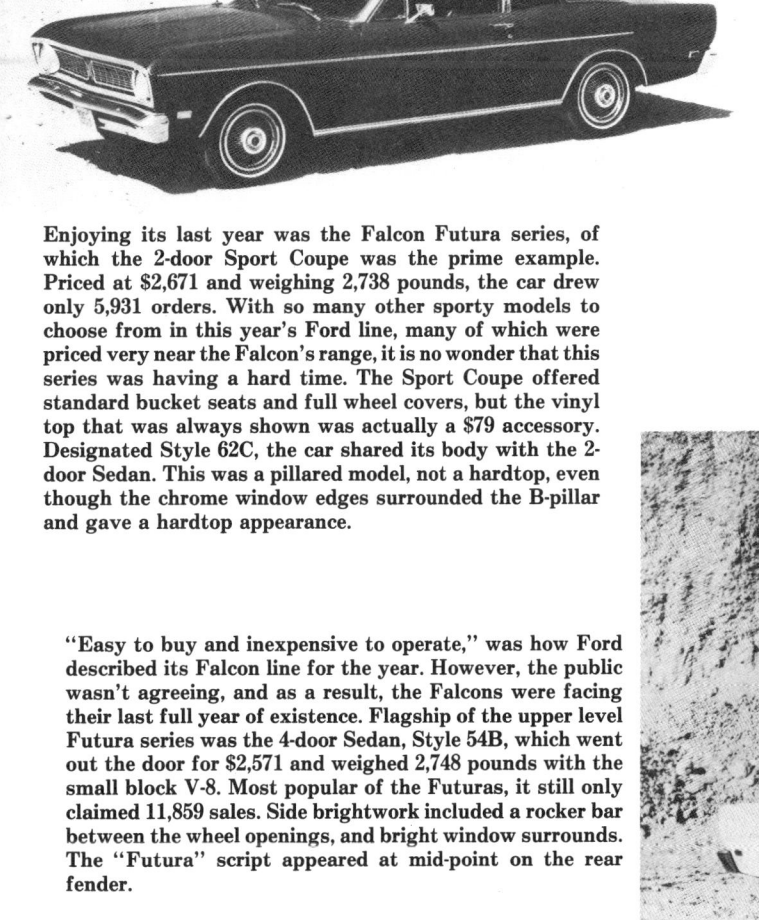

Enjoying its last year was the Falcon Futura series, of which the 2-door Sport Coupe was the prime example. Priced at $2,671 and weighing 2,738 pounds, the car drew only 5,931 orders. With so many other sporty models to choose from in this year's Ford line, many of which were priced very near the Falcon's range, it is no wonder that this series was having a hard time. The Sport Coupe offered standard bucket seats and full wheel covers, but the vinyl top that was always shown was actually a $79 accessory. Designated Style 62C, the car shared its body with the 2-door Sedan. This was a pillared model, not a hardtop, even though the chrome window edges surrounded the B-pillar and gave a hardtop appearance.

"Easy to buy and inexpensive to operate," was how Ford described its Falcon line for the year. However, the public wasn't agreeing, and as a result, the Falcons were facing their last full year of existence. Flagship of the upper level Futura series was the 4-door Sedan, Style 54B, which went out the door for $2,571 and weighed 2,748 pounds with the small block V-8. Most popular of the Futuras, it still only claimed 11,859 sales. Side brightwork included a rocker bar between the wheel openings, and bright window surrounds. The "Futura" script appeared at mid-point on the rear fender.

Offering a load space of 85.2 cubic feet, the Falcon Futura wagon provided a practical alternative for those who could use a smaller size vehicle. As did other Ford wagons, the Futura and plain Falcon wagons both offered as a $45 option, the 2-way "Magic Doorgate." It is shown here in the downward or traditional tailgate mode. In the Futura range, the wagon sold for 2,844 with the V-8 and weighed 3,120 pounds. A total of 7,203 were built.

Looking very dowdy from the rear is the Falcon 2-door Sedan, Style 62B. When seen in basic form, such as here, these cars lost much of their appeal. Priced at $2,534 with the 302 cubic inch V-8, it weighed 2,738 pounds. Surprisingly, the 2-door Sedan sold better than did its fancier Sport Coupe cousin, and a total of 6,482 went out the door. Possibly this was because people liked the bench seats of the sedan better than the buckets of the Sport Coupe, which restricted seating capacity.

Least expensive of any car with a Ford name tag, prior to the Maverick, was the plain Falcon 2-door Sedan, Style 62A. Priced at $2,226 with the small Six, it weighed 2,700 pounds even. Plain Falcons this year fared much better in the sales race than did their fancier Futura running mates. Probably this was because most of the large fleet sales were for the stripped, not the deluxe, models, thus boosting greatly the sales of the low-buck cars. In all, a total of 29,263 2-door plain Falcons were hatched, making this model the most popular of all the little birds. Power in these cars ranged from the fuel-saving 170 cubic inch Six of 100 horses to the 2-barrel carburetor 302 cubic inch V-8 of 220 horses.

Unlike all other cars in the Ford lineup, Falcons retained the dual headlamps, and did not go to quad units. It is not known whether this was an economy decision or one based on long-range knowledge that the line was soon to be cancelled. Lowest priced of all 4-door Fords was the plain Falcon Sedan, Style 54A. With a 6-cylinder base price of $2,316, it drew 22,719 orders, or approximately twice that of its Futura version. Note that the rear door windows could be lowered to sill level, but the small quarter windows were fixed in place. A Cruise-O-Matic transmission could be ordered for any Falcon engine for $175, while power steering cost $89.

The plain Falcon Wagon, Style 71A, could also avail itself of the "Magic Doorgate" for an extra $45, and for another $35 could have a powered tailgate window. The roof rack on this model cost another $45, while the wheel covers were $21, the whitewalls $33 for the set, and the AM radio another $61. And, if this buyer went all out for the Select Aire Conditioner which mandated the V-8, it cost another $368. With so many extras, one wonders who would go for the stripper wagon in the first place, unless the $2,733 base V-8 price was a big incentive. More popular than the Futura version, this wagon accounted for 11,568 sales.

Ford's big news car of the year comes at the end of the chapter. Why? Because it is the smallest vehicle in the Ford line and as such runs at the end of the list. Not introduced until April 17, and sometimes classed as an early 1970 model, the miniature car was the only Ford priced at under $2,000, having its list price pegged at $1,995. Weighing 2,411 pounds and rated as a 6-passenger car (albeit very tight for six passengers) it drew quite a bit of interest. Its 127,833 orders made it a very close second to the Mustang Hardtop in the sales race. Only one model was available, and all were powered by the 170 cubic inch Six. It rode on a shortened Falcon chassis of 103-inch wheelbase, and was 179.4 inches long overall.

Virtually unchanged was the Bronco, Ford's little 4-wheel-drive vehicle that couldn't decide whether it was truck or car. This year its available models were reduced by one, as the open roadster was deleted from the list. Most popular of the remaining styles was the Wagon version, which offered 4-passenger seating capacity for $2,945. A total of 18,639 slipped out of the corral. The 2-passenger Pickup, with its stubby little cab, cost $2,834, and accounted for only 2,317 orders. With the open roadster gone, all models now had non-removable tops and the windshield could no longer be lowered. The wheelbase was still 90 inches, and the basic power was still the 170 cubic inch Six.

Once again the now-independent Ranchero was available in three distinct levels, the plain Ranchero; the Ranchero 500, and the Ranchero GT seen here. Though based on Fairlane components, the little trucks had been divorced from the parent line at the end of the 1967 season. Prices and production ran amazingly close to the 1968 figures, with the plain model selling for $2,623 and issuing 5,856; the mid-level 500 costing $2,740 and resulting in 11,214 sales, and the top-buck GT model costing $2,954 and accounting for only 1,658 orders. As before, The GT models sported bucket seats; a unique air-scoop hood; deluxe wheel covers; special grille, and the exclusive C-Stripe decal on the body. The argent styled-steel wheels shown here were extra. Also available this year was a 428 Ram Air Cobra Jet package, which included the big engine and a special suspension package.

After a very busy 1969, Ford almost seemed to take a breather this year. True, there was the expected model switching name changing, and horsepower additions, but all of these were more evolutionary than revolutionary. The list of available models remained at 54, although some heavy handed name switching would make it look as if some new models had actually crept into the pack.

Most changed of all, both in name, size, and styling, were the new Torino models, which had been called Fairlane Torinos in 1969. Sporting all new bodies, including a sleek SportsRoof version, the cars now had a 1-inch longer wheelbase, being 117 inches, while the wagon and Ranchero models likewise grew an inch to 114. Overall length grew by four inches to 206 for the cars. Much more sleek than previous models, the Torinos were billed as being "Shaped by the Wind." In addition to fine styling, a variety of grilles were used, with the top of the line model having optional disappearing headlights.

Coming into their own, the Torinos now appeared in four distinct sub-series. They were the blistering one-model GT Cobra Fastback; the GT sport set of convertible and fastback; the luxury Brougham line which had two hardtops and the Squire wagon, and the plain Torino sub-series, consisting of a low-buck version of each model except the convertible, which was exclusive to the GT grouping.

Also changing quite a bit was the Thunderbird, which received some heavy sheet metal work, and now sported a protruding grille, which preceded the car by an almost ridiculous length. In fact, the grille protruded so far out, that many insurance companies tacked a hefty price increase on the collision portion of the 1790 Thunderbird coverage. In addition to the "snout," the grille featured the first open headlights since 1966, a feature which may or may not have been a step in the right direction. As before, the Thunderbird line consisted of two basic styles, spread over three models—two 2-doors and one 4-door.

If nothing else, the new Mustangs provided almost instant identification from the 1969 models, through the use of single headlights as opposed to the double units that had been used on the 69-ers. The single lights were mounted inside the new and larger grille opening and were flanked by functional air scoops. Not counting the last of the Shelbys, the Mustang line consisted of seven distinct models, counting the limited production Boss 429.

Once again, the most popular of the Mustangs was the Hardtop Coupe, but here only 82,569 were turned out, as opposed to 127,954 in 1969. In fact, total 1970 Mustang production amounted to only 197,045 counting the two Boss versions, which was a drop of 102,779 from 1969, or almost a one-third cut in sales. Ford, for the most part, saw this as due to competition not only from its own little Maverick on the low-buck side, but also from the Plymouth Barracuda; Pontiac Firebird; Dodge Challenger, and Chevrolet Camero, all of which now had hot and sporty cars in the same market corral as was the Mustang.

In the world of big cars, little was changed except some names. New for the year was the LTD Brougham series, which was now the top line of the big car grouping. The former plain LTD series, which had been the top trim models, now replaced the Galaxie 500 series as the mid-price range, although this category continued to contain the Squire Wagon. Two sporty models, the convertible and the fastback 2-door, which had been in the Galaxie 500 XL sub-series, for this year only bore simply the title "XL." The Galaxie 500 series continued as a lower mid-price range, but lost its convertible model, and thus was reduced to four automobile and two wagon offerings.

At the lower end of the scale, the Custom 500 and Custom sub-series remained for those wanting big car transportation at small car cost. However, each series was now reduced by one, as their 2-door sedans were taken away.

Since the new style large cars had been introduced last year, only minor styling changes took place this year. These included new taillights and a new and more attractive grille on all models. As before, the LTD series came with hidden headlights, but now the XL models also had the same grille, whereas in 1969 the sporty models used the Galaxie 500 grille unless the LTD grille was ordered as an option.

As mentioned previously, both the Fairlanes and the Falcons were destined to be dropped during the year, and thus received the least attention of the pack. The Fairlane remained a two sub-series line, consisting of Fairlane 500 and plain Fairlane classes, each containing the same three Torino-based models. The Falcon line also consisted of two sub-series, but these were completely different. The early Falcons were simply run-off 1969 models with virtually no changes whatsoever. Then, when this line was dropped for good, the Falcon name was carried over to a super-stripped trio of Fairlane models, which appeared only in the last half of the 1970 sales year.

And finally there was the Maverick. Introduced in April, 1969, as a mid-1969 or early 1970 model, it now entered its first full year of sales. Available only in a single model, a fastback 2-door, the little car was drawing a tremendous amount of both attention and sales. In fact, with 451,081 units leaving the dealerships, the car was proving to be one of the best selling items that Ford had come up with in a long time. Maybe it was hitting some Mustangs where it hurt, but it was also knocking a bunch of Volkswagen sales out of the ring, and that was exactly what Ford had hoped it would do.

Under the hoods, a few changes took place, with two new offerings in the super-high horsepower ranges, and a couple of minor horsepower raises in the very low end of the market and in the mid-range blocks. Also, two 390 cubic inch blocks disappeared. They were the Thunderbird 390 of 280 horsepower, and the GT 390 of 320 horses.

New in the high-power market was a Police Interceptor 429, which developed 370 horses at 5400 rpm, and a new Ram Air Boss 429 which was identical to the regular Boss 429 but fitted with a ram induction system. At mid-year, two new 429 blocks of 375 horses were introduced, but though these monsters did get into some 1970 cars, they are primarily considered 1971 engines.

On the low-power side, the old Falcon Six was now renamed the Maverick Six, and had its horsepower upped to 105 for the 170 cubic inch version and 120 for the 200 cubic inch model. The only other increases occurred in the 351 4-barrel, which now produced 300 horses at 5400 rpm, and in the lone remaining 390, where the horses went up to 270 at 4400 rpm.

Once again production figures were a bit muddled, but not quite as bad as last year. According to the Ford-supplied figures used in this book, a total of 1,956,307 Fords left the various plants. Of this number, the big Fords accounted for 850,315, while the new Maverick drew a whooping 451,081, to be the second most popular series in the entire Ford line. Loosing by a landslide this year was Mustang, whose total sales reached only 197,045.

On a body-style basis, it was obvious that the single-model Maverick series took top honors, since its total production was credited to a single style. But on the over-100,000 list, there was not a Mustang to be found—marking the first time that this had happened since the first half-year mid-1964 introductory models. In fact, the only other model to break the 100,000 mark was the Galaxie 500 4-door sedan. All other units suffered sales setbacks ranging from minor to major, making one wonder what Ford's sales picture might have been had not the little Maverick jumped into the picture.

Preceding the rest of the car by almost a ridiculous length was the new snout attached to an otherwise very attractive new Thunderbird. In fact, the new frontal length was so great that many insurance companies, fearing numerous and costly collision claims, tacked surcharges on the vehicles. Once again the base T-Bird was the 2-door Hardtop, Style 65C, which was the only Bird under the $5,000 mark. In base form it cost $4,961 and weighed 4,354 pounds. Reflecting the fact that buyers in this category would rather pay a bit more to get more was the fact that this was the poorest selling Thunderbird, with only 5,116 being built.

Although the 2-door Landau lost its decorative bars, these attractive trim pieces still graced the 4-door Thunderbird Landau. The most expensive car in the entire Ford line, this Style 57C sold for $5,182 and weighed 4,464 pounds. A total of 8,401 left the nest. Once again, despite a new body, Thunderbird sedans had their doors latching at the B-pillar. The new 4-doors were 215 inches overall, while the 2-doors were 212.5 inches. Other new features included exposed quad headlights, hidden radio antennas, and concealed windshield wipers. The vinyl top was standard on this model.

Taking top sales honors in the brand new Thunderbird line was the 2-door Landau, which continued to feature a vinyl top but no longer used the decorative landau bars. Its sales of 36,847 were almost triple the other two models combined. It was priced at $5,104, weighed 4,630 pounds, and was listed as Style 65D. Available only on this car was the power operated Sunroof option which cost $453. The high-back bucket seats visible on this model indicate that it also wears the Brougham leather and vinyl interior package, which cost $227. The base engine on all Thunderbirds was the 429 cubic inch 4-barrel V-8 which produced 360 horsepower. There were no engine options.

Powerhouses of the new Mustang line were again the Boss models, consisting of the Boss 429 and the far more popular Boss 302, shown here. However, because of very limited sales, few of the Boss 429 models were actually produced this year. Such was not the case with the Boss 302, where production was up five times over 1969, to reach 6,318. Available only in Fastback (SportsRoof) style, the car listed at a hefty $3,720. It made exclusive use of a modified version of the 302 cubic inch engine with a 4-barrel carburetor, which produced 290 horses. Exclusive suspension, racing stripes, quick ratio steering, and functional spoilers also came with the package. Listed as Style 63, it ran a weight of 3,227 pounds. For practical purposes, the Boss models sealed the fate of the Shelby Mustangs, and thus only 315 Shelby GT 350 models and 286 of the Shelby GT 500 models were sold before the A.O. Smith Co. closed the contract. And, indications are that these were actually 1969 models re-registered as 1970 stock.

Although the Boss models had the reputation for speed, those who liked big engines went with the new Mustang Mach I, which could be ordered with any block up to the 428 cubic inch Cobra Jet Ram Air engine, which produced 335 horsepower and added $376 to the tab. In base form, with the stock new 351 cubic inch V-8, it sold for $3,271 and weighed 3,240 pounds. One of the most popular Mustangs, the Mach I drew 40,970 orders. Among its features were a low-gloss grille with running lamps, blackout hood center with functional air scoop, dark accented rocker panel moldings, racing mirrors, deep-dish sport wheel covers, vinyl bucket seats, and console-mounted shifter.

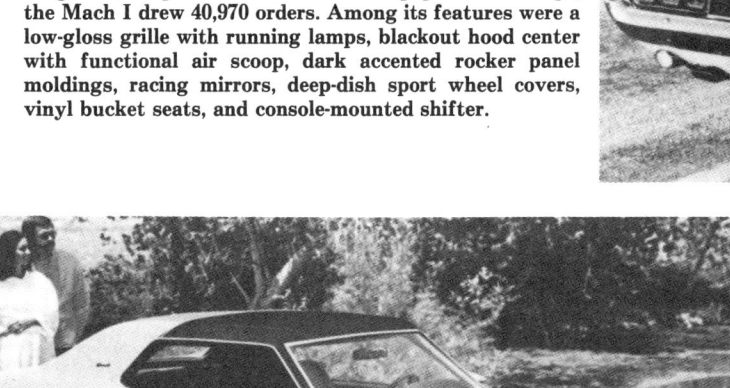

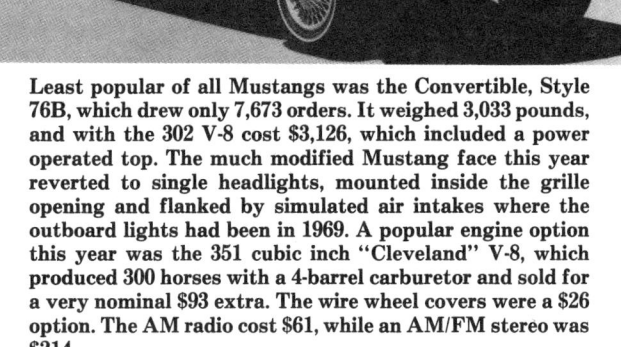

Just as the Mach I was available only in SportsRoof form, the Mustang Grande was available only as a formal hardtop. Designed for luxury, not speed, it could be ordered with a Six or any V-8. In base 302 V-8 form it cost $3,028 and weighed 3,008 pounds. Here luxury took a back seat to performance, and only 13,581 were sold. Among its features were the half vinyl roof, wheel covers, luxury-trim bucket seats, color keyed racing mirrors, and 2-spoke steering wheel. A full vinyl top could be added for $26 extra.

Least popular of all Mustangs was the Convertible, Style 76B, which drew only 7,673 orders. It weighed 3,033 pounds, and with the 302 V-8 cost $3,126, which included a power operated top. The much modified Mustang face this year reverted to single headlights, mounted inside the grille opening and flanked by simulated air intakes where the outboard lights had been in 1969. A popular engine option this year was the 351 cubic inch "Cleveland" V-8, which produced 300 horses with a 4-barrel carburetor and sold for a very nominal $93 extra. The wire wheel covers were a $26 option. The AM radio cost $61, while an AM/FM stereo was $214.

This year's Fastback Mustang was called the SportsRoof (capital R in Roof), Style 63B. Available as a Six or V-8, it was V-8 based at $2,872 and weighed 2,947 pounds. A very popular model, it saw 45,934 leave the corral. This year all Mustangs had new high-back bucket seats in the front, and bench rear seats in all but the Boss models, which were built as 2-passenger cars. Interior upholstery was in stripes, houndstooth fabric, or vinyl. In the 6-cylinder family, the old 200 cubic inch model of 120 horses was given a new head and carburetor which increased displacement to 250 cubic inches and produced 155 horsepower.

By far the most popular Mustang was the basic Hardtop Coupe, Style 65B, which saw its production reach 82,569. Though high, this was a disappointing figure for a model that just a year before had sold over 127,000. Priced at $2,822 with the 302 V-8, it weighed 2,923 pounds. Except for the optional wire-type wheel covers shown here, this car appears to be in basic form. A vinyl top would have improved its looks, and would have cost only $84 more. Cruise-O-Matic was a popular transmission choice, and cost $201 extra with any engine up to the 351 V-8, and $222 for any of the larger engines. A 4-speed manual with a Hurst shifter, as was standard on the Boss models, could be ordered for $205.

Some people, such as the author, felt that the new frontal design of the 1969 LTDs just couldn't get any better. Then along came the 1970 models, with their new 3-section grilles and disappearing headlamps. Now divided into two sub-series, the LTD line sprouted a Brougham category for cars with the most lavish interiors. Best looking of the new LTD Broughams was the 2-door Hardtop Coupe, Style 65, which sold for $3,537 and weighed 3,855 pounds. Surprisingly, the new LTD lines did not include the vinyl roof, which cost an extra $105.

Since the LTD Brougham sub-series was simply an interior trim level of the main LTD series, no specific production data could be found on these models. Thus, we know that the LTD Brougham 4-door Hardtop cost $3,579 and weighed 4,029 pounds, but we simply have to guess at its production. With the windows down, the 4-door Hardtop resembled an elongated version of the 2-door Hardtop, even to the curve of the rear roof line. The attractive vinyl roofs were available in six different colors, but they cost an additional $105, the price being the same for both the coupe and sedan models. Also available in the LTD Brougham line was a pillared 4-door Sedan which sold for $3,502.

Mounted on hydraulic rams on the Ford ride simulator in Dearborn's engineering laboratories is this LTD 2-door Hardtop Coupe. Most popular of all LTD models, the ultra-quiet car drew 96,324 orders, all base priced at $3,356. Weighing 3,727 pounds, the cars came standard with steel tops, as seen on this model, but rarely seen on the street. In the pictured test, cars were taken off the line at impulse, and were placed on the simulator, which could duplicate any type of road condition and speed. Strobe lights indicated all motions of the body and frame as various road shocks were fed into the wheels. Through machines such as these, Ford developed its vibration-voiding butyl body mounts used on its top lines.

As was the case with the LTD Brougham sub-series, the LTD series also offered two 4-door sedans. Most popular was this 4-door Hardtop, Style 57F, which drew 90,390 orders. It cost $3,385 and weighed 3,771 pounds. Slightly less popular was the pillared 4-door Sedan, which looked similar to the hardtop version but had a full-length B-pillar. It drew 78,306 orders with a base price of $3,307 and a weight of 3,701 pounds. All LTD and LTD Brougham models used the 2-barrel 351 cubic inch V-8 of 250 horsepower as the base engine. No 6-cylinder options were available in this series.

As before, the Country Squire remained an official part of the LTD series. Available as the 6-passenger Style 71E or the 10-passenger Style 71A, it was the only full-size Ford wagon to use the simulated wood trim. New this year was the optional vinyl top shown here, which cost $142, and was often combined with the $46 luggage rack. The 6-passenger model cost $3,832 and weighed 4,139 pounds. It drew a total of 39,837 orders. Far more popular was the 10-passenger style, which saw sales reach 69,077. It cost $3,909 and weighed 4,185 pounds, and thus was the heaviest and most expensive full-size Ford.

The Galaxie 500 line offered two 2-door hardtops, this SportsRoof Style 63B, and the formal Hardtop, Style 65C. Of the two, the latter was the more popular, drawing 57,059 orders with its $3,205 price and 3,671 pound weight. Not far behind was this SportsRoof, which saw 50,825 orders flow in. It was base priced at $3,154 and weighed 3,670 pounds. Notice that the Galaxie 500 models did not use a stamped lattice applique at the rear, but instead had a single panel with the word "FORD" spelled on an argent panel in widely spaced block letters.

Double or nothing! That's what the author played with red XL Convertibles. After having had excellent experience with the 1969 Galaxie 500 XL Convertible shown in the previous chapter, he bought this 1970 model in 1974, and experienced the same kind of excellent performance that had accompanied the 1969 model. No longer considered an official part of the Galaxie line, this year's top sport styles were now called Ford XL or just plain XL models. Designated Style 76B, it listed for $3,501 and weighed 3,983 pounds. Most rare of all big Fords, it drew only 6,348 orders. The 2-model XL series now used V-8 engines exclusively, with the never-popular Six being unavailable. The 351 cubic inch block of 250 horses was the standard unit. This model had the high-back bucket seats and console, a $188 option. With the demise of the Galaxie 500 convertible, this was the sole remaining large Ford soft top.

Second car in the newly named Ford XL sub-series was the 2-door SportsRoof, Style 63C. Priced at $3,293 and weighing 3,750 pounds, it drew a total of 27,251 orders. Once more the car featured the sweptback roof line with the tunneled rear window. The car used the same grille with hidden headlights as was used on the LTD models, and could be ordered with any V-8 from the 351 to the 429 of 360 horsepower. The latter engine cost $242 over list, but also required the $222 Cruise-O-Matic transmission. The newly located side marker lights now flashed when the turn signals were used. Unlike the LTD models, which measured 216 inches overall, all other big Fords, including the XL models, were 2134.9 inches in length.

Also in the Galaxie 500 series were two 4-door sedans, a Hardtop Style 57B and this pillared Style 54A. The pillared model not only was the best selling Galaxie 500, but was the only large Ford to attain sales of over 100,000, with a total of 101,784 being recorded. It cost $3,137 and weighed 3,661 pounds with the basic 302 cubic inch V-8. Meanwhile, the 4-door Hardtop Sedan fared only half as well, drawing 53,817 orders. It cost $3,208 and weighed 3,732 pounds. Galaxie 500 models could also be ordered with the 200 cubic inch Six of 150 horsepower. A full-length strip of vinyl-filled bright molding graced the sides of all Galaxie 500 models, and apparently could be special ordered for XL models as well.

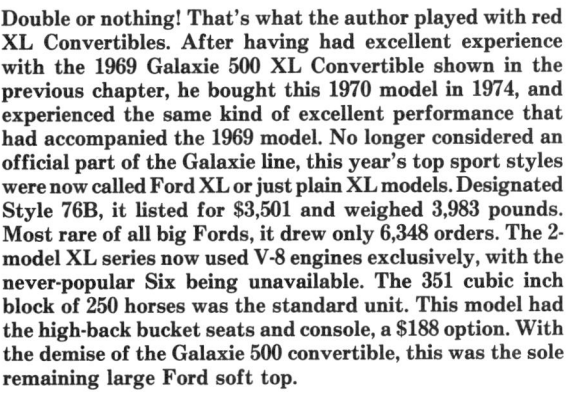

Two versions of the Country Sedan lived within the Galaxie 500 ranks, but neither looked like this conversion. They were the 6-passenger Style 71B and 10-passenger 71C. Both bore approximately the same interior trim level as did the Country Squire, but lacked that model's imitation wood trim. The 6-passenger cost $3,488 and weighed 4,112 pounds, and was the most popular of the two, drawing 32,209 orders. Recording 22,645 sales was the 10-passenger model, which sold for $3,600 even. Automotive Conversion Corp. of Troy, Mich., continued to convert large wagons into attractive ambulances and hearses. Its top line hearse used the Country Sedan as its base. It filled in the rear quarter windows and covered the entire top and side quarters with a vinyl roof. Decorative landau bars and velvet curtains in the rear door windows gave a luxury touch. Neither the wheelbase nor the body was extended in this conversion.

With the 2-door pillared Sedan dropped from the large Ford lines, the Custom 500 series was reduced to three models, this 4-door Sedan and two variations of the Ranch Wagon. Designated Style 54B, and being of pillared design, the car filled a minor trim level between the stark Custom series and the more upscale Galaxie 500. With the base 302 V-8 it was priced at $2,951 and weighed 3,603 pounds. Production reached 41,261. Custom 500 models used a single side molding similar to that used on the Galaxie 500, except that it did not have the soft vinyl center.

Two variations of the Ranch Wagon were available in the Custom 500 series. They were the 6-passenger Style 71H and the 10-passenger Style 71J. Neither was particularly popular, with the 6-passenger model drawing 15,304 orders, while the 10-passenger only accounted for 9,943. The 6-seat went for $3,368, and weighed 4,049 pounds, while the unit with the dual facing rear seats cost $3,481, and was 4,137 pounds. Both versions featured Ford's practical "Doorgate."

Lowest trim level of all full-size Fords continued to be occupied by the plain Custom series, now reduced to only two models. They were the 6-passenger Ranch Wagon, Style 71D, and this 4-door Sedan, Style 54E. Devoid of almost all exterior trim, the Custom models were designed primarily for fleet or taxi work, though some were sold to the general public. The sedan cost $2,850 and thus was the lowest price large Ford. It weighed 3,563 pounds and attracted 42,849 buyers. The Ranch Wagon meanwhile, available only in 6-passenger form, cost $3,305 and weighed 4,079 pounds, with sales reaching 15,086.

With the Fairlane name dropped as a prefix, the Torino line now became a full series unto its own. Hottest of the cars was the Torino GT Cobra, available only in the SportsRoof style shown here. This year a much more subtle Cobra cartoon graced the front fenders and rear panel, but the performance of the red hot car was not diminished. Exterior identification now included the slatted rear window, and blackout hood and grille. Running gear included the 429 cubic inch V-8 Cobra Jet with ram air induction to its 4-barrel carburetor, and a 4-speed manual transmission with Hurst shifter. With all this in the package and a $3,270 price tag, it is surprising that production reached only 7,657.

The only soft-top in the Torino line was the GT Convertible, Style 76F. Despite its good looks and reported nice handling, the car was suffering the fate of all convertibles on the American market—buyers were turning away in droves, preferring the comfort of an air conditioned closed car to the wind battered joys of open motoring. Thus, only 3,939 examples of this pretty car were turned out, making it by far the most rare of all Torinos. It cost $3,212 with the 351 V-8 and weighed 3,490 pounds, which was 124 pounds heavier than the SportsRoof. This view gives a good look at the interesting full-width lattice work stamping over the taillamps and rear panel. The car is shown with its stock wheels with small hubcaps and beauty rims, rather than the extra cost competition wheels on the SportsRoof.

Far more popular than the Cobra was the plain Torino GT SportsRoof Coupe, Style 63F. The more luxurious and less performance minded car drew 56,819 orders. Its base price of $3,366 included only the 351 cubic inch V-8 and manual 3-speed, with all other performance items being at extra cost. Featured was a very appealing egg crate grille with hidden headlights, a non-functional air scoop on the hood, non-functional decorative louvers on the rear quarters, and twin high-back bucket seats in vinyl. Often seen on this model was a "Blazer Stripe" side decal, which was a $32 trim option. Dual racing mirrors were part of the package.

Just as the large Fords had sporty XL and luxury LTD models, so too did the new Torino line. Only here the sporty cars were called "GTs," while the luxury models were called "Broughams." Leader of this series was the 2-door Hardtop Coupe, with its formal roof line. Designated Style 65E, it drew 16,911 orders to become the most popular of the 3-model line. It cost $3,006 and weighed 3,293 pounds. Virtually always shown with vinyl roofs, the Broughams actually came with steel tops, with the vinyl being $95 extra regardless of model. The mag-style or turbine-type wheel covers shown here were also an added cost item.

Wearing the almost mandatory added-cost vinyl top is the Torino Brougham 4-door Hardtop, the only 4-door in this series. Although there was a pillared 4-door in the plain Torino line, it did not receive the Brougham trim treatment. Known as Style 57E, the hardtop cost $3,078 and weighed 3,309 pounds. Slightly less popular than the 2-door, it drew 14,543 orders. It is shown here with its standard wheels, with hubcaps and beauty rings. Unlike the GT models, the Brougham's rear panel was composed of two distinct taillights with a textured center section. All Brougham models used a bright version of the egg crate grille with hidden headlights.

Following the lead of the big Fords, the new Torino line also had an upscale wagon, known as the Torino Brougham Squire, Style 71E. The only Torino wagon to use imitation wood siding, it scaled in at 3,673 pounds and cost $3,379, thus being the heaviest and most expensive of all Torinos. A total of 13,166 were produced. All Broughams used the 302 cubic inch V-8 as power, but only the Squire had front disc brakes as standard equipment.

Coming into the plain Torino line at mid-year was the SportsRoof Hardtop, Style 63C. Earlier in the year this body had been reserved only for the GT and Cobra models, but a growing interest in the well balanced design led to a decision to enter it into the lower trim and power series as well. Even as a late entry, a total of 12,490 were sold with a V-8 price of $2,899 and a weight of 3,311 pounds. Prior to the introduction of this model, the only 2-door in the plain Torino series was the formal Hardtop, Style 65C. Having a good lead on sales, it drew 49,826 orders, priced at $2,812 and weighing 3,273 pounds. All Torinos could be ordered with either the 250 cubic inch Six or the 302 V-8 as basic power, with all larger engines being available.

Wearing its $95 optional vinyl top is the Torino 4-door Hardtop, Style 57C. A new model to the Torino line, this very attractive car proved to be not as popular as expected, and only 14,312 were built. Its base price was $2,885, while its weight was 3,289 pounds. This view shows the lattice work rear panel, which was centered between the horizontal taillights, with their 5-section lenses. All Torinos this year had concealed windshield wipers. The full-length body molding had a soft vinyl center strip for both looks and better protection against parking lot dings.

Attracting over twice the sales as the 4-door Hardtop was the Torino 4-door Sedan, a pillared model known as Style 54C. Production went up to 30,117. In base form it sold for $2,778 and weighed 3,258 pounds, and thus was the lightest and least expensive of all Torinos. This model is wearing the optional vinyl roof and wheel covers, but is fitted with the stock Torino grille. This unit was very similar to the egg crate grilles used in the Brougham and GT series, but had exposed quad headlights rather than the hidden variety.

Even standing still, the new Fairlane 500 Style 65B 2-door Hardtop gave the impression of performance. Of course, it took a great number of options to make it live up to its looks, and with the standard 250 cubic inch Six it was a rather docile car. With the base 302 V-8 it cost $2,750 and weighed 3,228 pounds. It drew 70,636 orders and thus was the most popular model in the Fairlane/Falcon roster. Also in the early Fairlane 500 list were the 4-door Sedan for $2,716, which drew 25,780 orders, and the 4-door Station Wagon, which listed at $3,047 and attracted 13,613 buyers. The Fairlane 500 used the same frontal design as the Torino, but had a much finer mesh grille divided by a center bar which embraced the exposed quad headlights.

Essentially the Squire model minus the exterior wood trim, the plain Torino 4-door Wagon utilized an interior level of luxury comparable to other Torino models. Still, it fell behind the Squire in interest, and drew only 10,613 orders. With a base price of $3,164, it weighed 3,653 pounds. This version is shown with a host of extras, including the optional grille with concealed headlights, the turbine wheel covers, functional roof rack, and trailer-towing package with heavy suspension. All Torino wagons were built on a 114-inch wheelbase while the car models were stretched out to 117 inches. Still, the wagons measured 209 inches overall, while the cars were 206.2 inches.

Essentially the old Fairlane 500 with a new name, the mid-1970 Falcons appeared as an interim car between the Torinos and the little Maverick. With the real Falcon line essentially killed off by the Maverick, Ford decided to switch the slow-selling Fairlane 500 name to Falcon in an attempt to boost sales. This caused the virtual demise of the Fairlane 500, and continued the Falcon's nest for only a few months. Why the Falcon wasn't simply dropped at mid-year is anybody's guess. Most popular of the three new Falcons, the 4-door Sedan, Style 54A, drew 30,443 orders, all with a basic Six price of $2,500 and a weight of 3,116 pounds. A 302 V-8 cost $28 more and weighed 100 pounds additional.

Yes, it looks like the old Fairlane 500 or Torino wagon, but its identity plaque on the rear fender says "Falcon." It is the mid-1970 Falcon 4-door Station Wagon, Style 71D, which replaced the more square style original Falcon. Priced at $2,856 in Falcon form, with the V-8, it weighed 3,225 pounds. Production reached 10,539. When the switch was made from Fairlane 500 to Falcon designations, it is not certain whether the Fairlane 500 line was continued to a trickle-off point, or if it was terminated at the time of the changeover. By year end, both name plates were gone.

At mid-year, sales of the real Falcon had dropped so low that the line was cancelled, and cars that had been listed as Fairlane 500 models now took on the name of Falcon. Once again the style leader of the 3-model pack was the 2-door Sedan, Style 62A, which sold for $2,479 and weighed an even 3,200 pounds. Sales were 26,071. Unlike the Style 65B which had occupied the 2-door slot in the earlier 1970 Fairlane 500 series, this was a pillared model with a definite B-pillar, as opposed to the Fairlane version which was a hardtop style.

The "real" Falcon appeared only for the first six months of the 1970 model year, and then only at relatively rare intervals. With the line trimmed drastically, the Futura Sport Coupe found itself a forgotten item, and the only 2-door in the line was the Futura 2-door Sedan, Style 62B. It was priced at about $2,530, and featured bright rockers and wheel cutouts, but the wheel covers shown here were an extra. Total production for the old Falcon line amounted to 15,700, but it has been impossible to find a definitive breakout on a per-body basis.

The Falcon Futura 4-door Sedan, Style 54B was a virtual carbon copy of the 1969 models, and was priced at a similar $2,600 (approximately) with the 302 V-8. Although all early Falcons bore the Futura signature and 1969 Futura side trim, it does not appear that any were turned out in plain Falcon form. As before, the rear door windows would lower to sill level, while the door quarter windows were fixed in place. Making no bones about the car's demise, Ford early in the year explained that the old style Falcon would only be produced until December, 1969. After that date, its manufacturing facilities would be converted to production of the new hot-selling Maverick.

Utilizing the large cargo capacity of the Falcon Futura Station Wagon, Style 71B, this lady is finding that a lot of flowers can be carried, especially if the rear seat is folded down. Built in 6-passenger form only, the early Falcon wagon was identical to the 1969 line. With Ford making promises of a new Falcon at mid-year, though not indicating that it would simply be a Fairlane with a name switch, dealers found that interest in the old style Falcons was almost non-existent. Despite the listing of a plain Falcon series in some early literature, it appears that all Falcons bore the Futura name this year. The early wagon was priced about $2,850 with the small V-8. Falcon wagons were not available in California this year.

Ford's best selling car by a tremendous margin was the little Maverick, available only in one style, and totally unchanged from the mid-1969 model. A total of 451,081 units were produced, all being rather cute little 2-door fastback sedans. Offering much more pep and room than the smaller Volkswagen Beetle that it was intended to slap down, the Maverick was built on a 103-inch wheelbase version of the old Falcon chassis, and was powered by the old Falcon Six of 170 cubic inches. In basic form it was still priced at $1,995.

Ranchero took a hint from the wood-trimmed wagons and this year came out with the Ranchero Squire Pickup. The new model brought four trim levels to the Torino-based car-type pickups, and gave top-buck buyers a really distinctive model to sport around in. Priced at $2,965, it was slightly cheaper than the GT version, but its sales were slightly better, topping out at 3,943. In addition to the exterior imitation wood trim, the dash was also done in a wood grain applique. However, the high-back bucket seats shown here were at added cost.

Although the Maverick was basically a take-it or leave-it car insofar as body styles went, it did offer a hatful of options, including the $52 accent group seen on this model. This included bright drip moldings and window frames, color keyed carpets, and full wheel covers. The radio, in AM form only, cost $61, while those who wanted to go whole hog could also order the Select Aire air conditioning system for another $380, which also required the $48 tinted window package. Cars going into California also had to have the $37 emissions control system. This view gives a look at the nice frontal styling, with its egg crate grille centered with a Maverick emblem having a long horn steer in the middle portion.

Most expensive of the four available Torino-based Rancheros was the GT model, which at $3,010 was the only Ranchero with a base above $3,000. It featured its own exclusive side "laser stripe," color coordinated with the body shade, used a deluxe carpeted interior with soft vinyl upholstery, and was fitted with the deluxe grille and wheel covers. However, the bucket seats in black or white knitted vinyl were now an extra cost option, as was the deluxe grille with hidden headlights. Not quite as popular as the new Squire, the GT version accounted for 3,905 units, which still was a substantial climb over 1969.

The workaday Rancheros still came in two forms, the basic Ranchero and the better trimmed Ranchero 500 shown here. The trimmed version was by far the more popular, accounting for 8,976 sales, as opposed to 4,816 for the stripper. Its price difference of less than $200 probably accounted for the preference, with the plain model going for $2,646 while the trimmed model cost $2,860. Its interior trim level was almost that of the GT or the Squire, and it too used the deluxe grille and full wheel covers. The Rancheros used the Torino's 117-inch car chassis, not the 114-inch wagon wheelbase. The 250 cubic inch Six was the basic power in the plain models, while the 302 V-8 was basic in the other three. But all engine options right through the 429 Cobra models could be ordered.

Still virtually unchanged was the nimble little horse called Bronco, available only in 4-wheel-drive form with either the 170 cubic inch Six or the 302 V-8. It was still offered in 2-passenger pickup style, or as the 4-passenger Wagon, Model U150 shown here. The wagon was by far the most popular, with sales of 16,750 as opposed to the 1,700 of the pickup. It was priced at $3,145, or about $100 more than the pickup, while its weight of 3,090 was exactly 100 pounds more than the pickup. Surprisingly, the rear seat was an added-cost option. The rear quarter and liftgate windows were set in place and would not open.

Flushed with the success of its little Maverick, Ford this year brought out an even smaller animal—though when it first appeared on Sept. 11, 1970, many thought the name connotation to pinto bean would have been more appropriate.

Named Pinto, which is a small, multi-colored horse in addition to a bean, the little car was again aimed directly at the Volkswagen market. Styling had a definite European flair, with high-back bucket seats, limited rear seating, 4-speed manual transmission, peppy little 4-cylinder engines in choices of single or dual barrel carburetion (75 or 100 horsepower), and optional front disc brakes.

Parking it next to a common Volkswagen Beetle really made the Pinto look attractive. Its wheelbase of 94 inches was a half-inch shorter than the VW, but its overall length was 163 inches, or almost 4.5 inches longer. In height, the Pinto was 50 inches, or 7.7 inches lower than the VW, making the puffy German look like something left over from before the war—which is exactly what it was.

Initially offered as a single model 2-door sedan, the Pinto quickly grew into a 2-model family with the mid-season introduction of the Runabout, a 3-door or hatchback version. The initial sedan was the lowest priced of all Fords this year, with a stripped sticker of $1,962, thus making it the only Ford under the $2,000 mark. However, this was still $120 higher than the stripped Volkswagen.

Sales of the little horse were certainly up to expectations, with 352,402 leaving the corral. Of course, some of these sales bit into the Maverick market, which sagged almost 180,000 units to record 271,897 sales. Still, between the two compacts, Ford recorded well over a half-million sales that it probably would not have enjoyed had not some of its top people started to "think small."

Apparently with the new Pinto keyed to the small European car buyer, Ford felt it was time for the Maverick to start growing. Hence, this series witnessed its first major change. That came in the form of a 4-door sedan. Also, it received its first V-8, gaining the 302 cubic inch block in a special sport version of the 2-door called the "Grabber." The Grabber, which turned out to be a surprisingly quick little animal, featured a special hood with blackout panel and twin air scoops. The 2-door Mavericks retained the 103-inch wheelbase and basic body of the previous year, but the all-new 4-door was built on a 109.9-inch wheelbase, though its overall length was only 180 inches, or just a half-inch longer than the 2-door models.

Since the little Grabber would now be referred to as "the poor man's Mustang," the real Mustang needed something to brighten up its life. And it got it via a totally new styling package that left no doubt about the car being a 1971 model. The new Mustangs were now 190 inches long and had a wheelbase of 109 inches, as opposed to 187.5 and 108 inches of the previous year. A new hood with concealed windshield wipers led down to a totally new front end with a full-width grille opening encompassing the headlights, while the parking lights nested in the grille itself on the Boss and Mach I models. The new horses looked larger and heavier than the previous herd, and they were, averaging 50 to 100 pounds more per model than the 1971 designs.

The same six body styles remained, but the choice of engines was reduced from 10 to seven. Gone were two of the small 6-cylinder blocks, the excellent Boss 302, and both 428 variations. Reports show the Boss 429 was also gone, but it seems that this was simply due to a name switch, with the engine reappearing as the Super Cobra Jet 429. New for the year was the Boss 351 of 330 horses, and the Cobra Jet 429 of 370 horses. On the remaining engines, all ratings were dropped from five to 10 horsepower.

Also enjoying a total restyling was the big Ford line, which now had all new sheet metal, but in overall appearance was still very much "Big Ford." Although the wheelbase remained at 121 inches, the cars grew in size, going from 213.9 inches to 216.2 inches overall, while the wagon models went from 216.9 inches to 219.2 inches. Most prominent features of the new styling were the hood with its attractively raised center section, and a totally new front with a massive pointed central grille flanked by dual exposed headlights, with no retractable options. As could be expected, the Galaxie models were a direct reflection of the top-line LTD series, differing only in interior detailing and minor exterior trim pieces.

One major change was the dropping of the year-old XL series, which had broken out of the Galaxie ranks just last year. The two models of this series, the Fastback Coupe and the Convertible, were now gone, though the Convertible did appear in the LTD sub-series as a new model. Now the only 2-door hardtop model in the big Ford line was the formal top style.

In the Torino series there was a bit of movement, but little appearance change in the cars themselves. The movement occurred within the series, where the Fairlane, Fairlane 500, and Falcon names were gone for good. Actually, the "real" Falcon had disappeared in mid-1970, but the name was carried onto a sub-series of three stripped Fairlane models. With the Fairlanes gone, the total Ford offerings this year dropped to 46 models, down 10 from the 1970 offerings. However, the growth of option packages more than made up for the decrease in models, and diversity was still the main game in town.

Insofar as styling went, the Torinos were essentially the same cars as the year before. A few minor changes in the grille and side trim and some new color choices in the interior fabric and vinyl constituted what was new for 1971. Both the Torino and the Torino Brougham and GT series used chrome grilles, while the one-model Cobra sub-series had a black-finish grille and blackout panels on the hood. The Cobra also had its own exclusive polished aluminum wheels.

Also virtually unchanged was the Thunderbird, which continued to have its protruding nose, despite dire predictions from the insurance industry of astronomical collision claims. Actually, records will show that the Thunderbird's noses were not that much more vulnerable to collision damage, and if high claims did occur, it was because of the cost of parts, not because of any particular accident proneness. As before, the Thunderbirds were still available in two and 4-door models, but this would be the final year for the 4-door. Next year a totally new bird would be hatched, based on the Lincoln Mark IV body.

In the engine rooms, there were still 16 available power plants, but a good bit of shuffling made this scene quite different from last year. Gone were the Boss 302 of 220 HP; the "old" 351 4-barrel of 300 HP; the Cobra Jet and Super Cobra Jet 428s of 335 and 360 HP respectively; the Thunderjet 429 of 320 HP, and the Ram Air Boss 429 of 375 HP.

New on the scene were two little 4-cylinder mills for the Pinto. The smallest, which promised 25 miles per gallon city driving, was a 98 cubic inch model of 75 HP, while the larger one developed 100 horses from 122 cubic inches. Also new was the Cleveland 351, in 2-barrel and 4-barrel configurations. The 2-barrel developed 240 HP, while the 4-hole ran 285 HP. Also in this family, but not bearing the "Cleveland" name was the new Boss 351 which developed 330 HP and had an 11.1:1 compression ratio. Also bearing the "Cleveland" name was the new 400 model, which only used a 2-barrel carburetor and 9:1 compression to develop a lazy 90 horses.

Not really new, but bearing new names, were two of the 429 blocks. The Police Interceptor of 370 HP was now known as the Cobra Jet 429, while the old Boss 429 of 375 HP was now called the Super Cobra Jet 429. The Thunder Jet 429 of 360 HP remained untouched, and in fact was the only engine that had no revision to its name or output. All other carry-over blocks faced a reduction in horsepower ranging from five to 15.

Once again Model year figures vary, with some lists showing a tally of 1,910,924 models. Yet, when production records by individual model are totaled, the figure becomes 1,904,673. Either figure shows a slight decrease in sales, but certainly not enough to cause anyone any concern.

The top seller, of course, was the new Pinto Sedan, which drew 288,606 orders. Still selling over 100,000 vehicles, but falling drastically from last year's figure of 451,081 was the Maverick. In total, the now 3-car series sold only 271,897 vehicles, while its single most popular mode, the 2-door Sedan, came in far behind the Pinto with only 159,726 sales.

Ford loved to advertise that its line of station wagons constituted the most popular wagons in America. This year they proved it, as the LTD Country Squire became the company's third best selling car, with 130,644 units leaving the plant. Two other models, both big Fords, also broke the 100,000 mark. They were the 4th place Galaxie 500 2-door Hardtop Coupe, with 117,139 sales, and the 5th place LTD 2-door Formal Top Coupe, with 103,896 orders. By comparison, the lowest ranking of all models was the Torino Brougham GT Convertible, which is a rare car today, as only 1,613 were built.

And, as a final note, this was the year that Lee Iacocca became president of Ford Motor Co.

Still classed as a personal luxury car, and still wearing its protruding snout, was the virtually unchanged Thunderbird. Once again, the line found itself substantially down in production. Lowest priced of the three Birds was the 2-door Hardtop, Style 65A, which was priced at $5,295. The car differed materially from the Landau model in that it used retractable rear quarter windows while the Landaus filled in this area with a solid quarter panel. Both models used the same Thunderbird emblem on the quarter panel. Not especially popular, the 4,399-pound car drew only 9,146 orders.

By far the most popular Thunderbird was the 2-door Landau, Style 65B, with its large blind quarter. Though attractive, this style top was of little help when backing into a tight parking space, and offered no visibility to rear seat passengers. Drawing 20,356 orders, the Landau cost $5,438 and weighed 4,370 pounds. Also remaining in the nest was the 4-door Landau Sedan, Style 57C. This seldom, seen model cost $5,516, weighed 4,590 pounds, and drew only 6,553 orders. Vinyl tops were standard on both of the Landau models, but were extra cost options on the Hardtop. The 2-door models utilized a 114.7-inch wheelbase and were 212.5 inches overall, while the 4-door had a 117.2-inch wheelbase and was 215 inches long.

The only Convertible in the Mustang line appeared in the plain form, as Style 76D. Although greatly enhancing many of the other models, the new "cut-off" rear styling seemed to give the top-down convertible an over-abrupt look from the rear. Priced at $3,322, the 3,145-pound car drew only 6,121 orders, which some seers at Ford used to predict the demise of both the convertible and the entire pony car market. High-back bucket seats were standard on all Mustangs this year, but a center console with shifter was a $60 option.

Appearing this year only was the new Boss 351, shown here with its racing stripes and blackout, non-scooped hood. Essentially a replacement for both the Boss 429 and Boss 302 models, both of which died with the discontinuation of their exotic engines, the Boss 351 used the 330 horsepower High-Output V-8 with 4-barrel carburetor. Hottest of all this year's Mustangs, it was base priced at $4,124, but with the options, usually went well over the $5,000 mark. Equipped with a 4-speed manual transmission with Hurst shifter, competition suspension, functional front and rear spoilers, blackout grille, and a host of other high-priced toys, this model was as close to an all-out race machine as Ford would get this year. Of rather limited appeal, the car drew approximately 1,800 orders.

More tame, though just as formidable looking was the new Mustang Mach I, which certainly benefitted from the totally new styling package accorded the line this year. Built with the basic 302 V-8 with 2-barrel carburetor, the car was normally seen with the 351 Cleveland under the hood. Reports indicate that a few of these cars managed to sneak out with the new 429 Cobra Jet and even the Super Cobra Jet engine, but with this option going at $375 or more, it appears that the orders were few. This model wears the optional hood with NASA functional dual air scoops, which was a no-cost feature. With the 302, it was base priced at $3,268 and weighed 3,202 pounds. Mustang's second most popular model, it drew 36,449 orders.

Just as the Mach I was Mustang's performance machine, the totally new Grande was the luxury liner. Available only with the formal hardtop roof, set off by its attractive tunneled rear window treatment, the car offered a deluxe ride for $3,212 with the small V-8. Of mediocre appeal, sales reached only 17,406. For this, buyers received a vinyl top, deluxe high-back bucket seats in a combination of cloth and vinyl upholstery, deluxe instrument panel and steering wheel, fancy wheel covers, and bright wheel openings.

Using the same body as the Mach I and Boss 351 was the new Mustang SportsRoof, Style 63D. Ford described this new Shelby-inspired Mustang design as having a unique "flat roof" styling with a much thinner actual roof line over the doors. High-back Bucket seats virtually fill the interior and made visibility poor for rear seat passengers. Available in base form with either the 250 cubic inch Six or the $302 V-8, it cost $3,068 with the 302 and weighed 2,993 pounds, thus being the lightest of all Mustangs. Production tallied 23,956. This year's Mustangs were wider, heavier, lower, and more streamlined than any previous models, being over 2-inches longer than the 1970 versions. They now had a 109-inch wheelbase and were 190 inches overall.

Most popular of all the new styled Mustangs was the Hardtop Coupe, which used a formal roofline with a tunneled rear window treatment. Style 65D, as it was officially known, drew a total of 65,696 orders, with most having the plain steel top shown here, though some did get the $26 optional vinyl treatment. Priced at $3,066 as a 302 V-8, it was Mustang's least expensive model. It weighed 3,026 pounds. All Mustangs used an all-vinyl interior with color-keyed carpeting, had flush-mounted exterior door handles and concealed windshield wipers.

Sporting a totally restyled body was the entire large Ford line. Leading the flock in the luxury category was the LTD Brougham series, which this year lost its very attractive grille with hidden headlights. But, despite this year's exposed quad units, no one could say the front end was ugly—in fact, it was downright pretty, but probably could have been enhanced by headlight doors. Based at $3,959 (later raised to $4,097) the 2-door Hardtop Coupe, Style 65K, was the most popular of all Brougham models, with 43,303 leaving the floor. Included in this price were such extras as the vinyl top, double stripe whitewall tires, and body-side accent stripes. Stock wheel covers are seen on this model, though the deluxe variety were usually worn.

As before, a pair of 4-doors were included in the LTD Brougham series. Most attractive and most popular by a small margin, was the 4-door Hardtop Sedan, Style 57K, which saw 27,820 leave the floors. It cost $4,140, weighed 3,944 pounds, and had its own exclusive roof treatment. Also on the list was the lowest price LTD Brougham, the 4-door Sedan, Style 53K. Built with a full B-pillar, this model sold for $4,094 and weighed 3,949 pounds. It drew 26,186 orders. Included in these prices are the vinyl tops and deluxe wheel covers, which technically were add-on extras.

With the XL series gone, the full-size Convertible had to move into the base LTD line. Thoroughly enhanced by the new styling, the beautiful Ford suffered from the nationwide apathy toward open cars, and only 5,750 were built. All featured V-8 engines only, with the 351 block being the base. New for the year was the full-width taillight bar, with three rectangular units raked forward, with the upper edge nested beneath the overhanging trunk deck. Known as Style 76H, the LTD Convertible was priced at $4,094 and weighed 4,091 pounds, thus costing $1 per pound.

Shown with the optional vinyl top, the LTD 2-door Hardtop turned out to be the second best seller in the LTD line and the 5th best selling of all Ford models. A total of 103,869 left the plants. Called Style 65H, the car sold for $3,923 and weighed 3,853 pounds, and thus was also the lightest and least expensive of all LTD models. All large Fords had newly designed body shells in addition to exterior sheet metal, and carried steel guard rails within the doors. Also found on all models was a power ventilation system. Standard fare on all LTD models included power front disc brakes.

The same two 4-door models that appeared in the LTD Brougham series also were found in the base LTD series. They were the 4-door Sedan, Style 53H, and the 4-door Hardtop, Style 57H. Only whereas in the Brougham series the hardtop was the best seller, in the base line the pillared sedan outsold the hardtop by almost a two-to-one margin. Here the sedan accounted for 92,260 sales, all listing a base price of $3,931 and a weight of 3,913. The hardtop, meanwhile, listed only 48,166 sales, with a list of $3,969 and a weight of 3,908. The vinyl roof on this model was a $113 extra. On the sedan, the vinyl ran down the exposed B-pillar.

As before, the Country Squire was located in the LTD series, and was available as the 10-passenger Style 71, or the 6-passenger Style 71H. As a 6-passenger, it cost $4,308 and weighed 4,308 ($1 per pound) while in 10-passenger form it cost $4,496 and weighed 4,358 pounds. Since no breakout was made in production figures between the two models, the combined Country Squire sales of 130,644 was enough to rank the car in third place in total Ford sales. New on the option list was a doorgate washer and wiper. The roof rack with its built-in wind deflector also assisted in helping keep dirt and road splash from sticking to the rear window. Included with the Squire, in addition to the imitation wood trim, was pleated vinyl upholstery, power doorgate window, and deluxe wheel covers.

The middle trim range of the large Ford line was occupied by the Galaxie 500 series. With the convertible exclusive to the LTD series, the only 2-door model in this line was the 2-door Hardtop, shown here in completely stock form. Priced at $3,749 and weighing 3,826 pounds with the 315 cubic inch V-8, it turned out to be Ford's 4th best selling car overall, with 117,139 being sold. Hubcaps and steel top were standard fare on all Galaxie 500 models. This year's Fords not only received totally new bodies, they also grew. Though the wheelbase still measured 121 inches, the new models were now 216.2 inches overall for the cars, and 219.2 for the wagons.

A Ford Galaxie 500 4-Door Sedan.

Far more popular in the Galaxie 500 series than the hardtop was the 4-door Sedan, Style 54F. It drew 98,130 orders, many with the extra cost vinyl top and deluxe wheel covers shown here. In base V-8 form, it cost $3,307 and weighed 3,826 pounds. Ford this year was noted for its exceptionally quiet and smooth riding qualities, while comfort was enhanced via the use of thick carpeting throughout. On all Galaxie 500 models, the 3-speed manual transmission was considered standard, while most cars left the floor with the Cruise-O-Matic transmission, which cost $217 to $238 depending on engine choice.

Wearing its $113 vinyl roof is the Galaxie 500 4-door Hardtop Sedan, Style 57F. Base priced at $3,786 with the 315 V-8, it was also available with the 250 cubic inch Six (truck engine) for $3,665. With the V-8, it registered 3,881 pounds. Moderately popular for the series, it saw 46,595 go out the door. All wore the rather plain hub caps shown here unless deluxe wheel covers were ordered. Full length side trim and bright wheel openings were part of the series, as was wood grain appliques on the instrument panel and the inside door panels.

Again, the Country Sedan was the Galaxie 500 answer to station wagon customers. Probably because of its size, weight, and carrying capacity, this was the only Galaxie 500 that could not be ordered with the Six, but had to avail itself of one of the V-8 blocks, beginning with the 351 cubic inch model. As did the Country Squire, the Country Sedan came in 6-passenger form as Style 71F, or in 10-passenger form as Style 71D. The 6-passenger cost $4,074 and weighed 4,241 pounds, while the 10-passenger was $4,188 and 50 pounds heavier. No production breakdown was made this year between six and 10-passenger models, but records do show that a total of 60,487 Country Sedans in total left the factory. Probably many had the roof rack and trailer towing package shown here, but probably very few had the $142 vinyl roof option offered this year.

The low-buck lines of the big Fords continued to be the Custom 500 and the totally stark Custom series. Each line consisted of a 4-door Sedan and a 6-passenger Ranch Wagon. Occupying the Custom 500 popularity seat was the 4-door Sedan, Style 54D, which cost $3,426 with the 250 Six. It sold 33,765 copies. Despite using the same grille as the Galaxie 500 models, its only bright work was found on the wheel openings and drip molding. Style 54B was the plain Custom version which did not even have this trim. It cost $3,288 as a Six, and sold 41,062 copies, thus being the most popular of all Custom and Custom 500 models.

Shown while still in Ford's styling studio is this example of the Custom 500 6-passenger Ranch Wagon, Style 71D. At this point, the car is wearing experimental side trim that did not make it to final approval. Unlike the sedans which could be ordered with the Six, the Custom and Custom 500 wagons followed the lead of the Galaxie 500 wagons, and were available only with a V-8, which could range right up to the new 400 cubic inch model if one wanted to pay the price. The Custom 500 wagon sold for $3,982 and weighed 4,215 pounds. It drew 25,957 sales. In the base Custom line, Style 71B cost $3,890, weighed 4,190 pounds, and accounted for only 16,696 orders.

Wearing a coiled chrome cobra on the center bar of its grille, and cartoon cobras on the trailing edge of its rear fenders, Torino's hot shot performance car left no doubt about its name. Designated Style 63H, the car came in stock form with the 351 Cleveland V-8 of 285 horsepower, and ran this through a 4-speed manual transmission with Hurst shifter. Base priced at $3,295 and weighing 3,594 pounds, the muscle-bound car saw a substantial drop in popularity, and only 3,054 were built. Among its other exclusive features were a blackout grille with indented panels, argent wheels with bright hubcaps, dual exhausts, and pleated vinyl upholstery on the high-back bucket seats.

Displaying the optional Blazer Stripe side trim is the Torino GT Convertible, Style 76F. Despite being the only soft-top in the entire Torino line, it still fared very poorly, and only 1,613 were produced. It had a base price of $3,408 and weighed 3,486 pounds. A power operated top was standard, as was an all-vinyl interior and high-back bucket seats. Basically, except for the grille and a few trim items, the car was unchanged from the 1970 fare. GT models were identified by the initials on the leading edges of the heavy rocker panel trim, and by the nonfunctional air scoop on the hood.

Except for the new 2-piece grille with a pronounced central bar, one might think that this was the 1970 Torino Squire Wagon, and not the 1971 model. Style 71E was available only in 6-passenger form and only with the V-8. Weighing 3,663 pounds, it had a production run of 15,805. All dressed up, this version wears turbine wheel covers, a $52 roof top luggage rack with wind deflector, and probably also has the $35 power tailgate window. On the front it wears the optional grille with hidden headlights, which was used fairly frequently in 1970, but for some reason became quite scarce in 1971. Once more, the Torino Squire was considered part of the Torino Brougham series.

Just as the Torino GT Convertible was the line's poorest selling car, its companion GT SportsRoof came in as one of the best selling. As Style 63F, it accounted for 31,641 sales, all with a base price of $3,150 and a weight of 3,346 pounds. This view shows the exclusive GT rear treatment, which consisted of a full-length horizontal lattice running across the entire lower panel, even acting as a covering for the taillights. Dual color keyed racing mirrors were part of the GT package. Those wanting blistering performance could have the 429 Cobra Jet installed for $378, and a manual 4-speed transmission for another $250.

The Torino Brougham line consisted of the Squire Wagon and two hardtop models, the 2-door Coupe, Style 65E, and the 4-door Sedan, Style 57E. Both could be quickly identified by the Brougham plaque on the rear quarters of the vinyl tops. The 2-door sold for $3,175 and weighed 3,390 pounds, while the 4-door sold for $3,248 and weighed 3,345 pounds. Both were available only with V-8 engines. Surprisingly, neither was a popular model, and the 2-door drew 8,593 orders while the 4-door shown here fared far less, with only 4,408 produced. Although virtually never seen with a steel top, Torino Broughams did not consider the vinyl top as standard, but classed it as a $95 option.

Wearing a full trim compliment of extra-cost vinyl top and fancy wheel covers is the Torino 500 4-door Hardtop Sedan, Style 57C. All that is lacking is the rare optional grille with hidden headlights. Priced at $3,054 with the V-8, it weighed 3,289 pounds. Sales were soft, however, and only 12,724 left the factories. All Torino car models were built on the 117-inch wheelbase chassis, but the wagons used a 114-inch base. The cars remained 206.2 inches overall, while wagons were 209 inches.

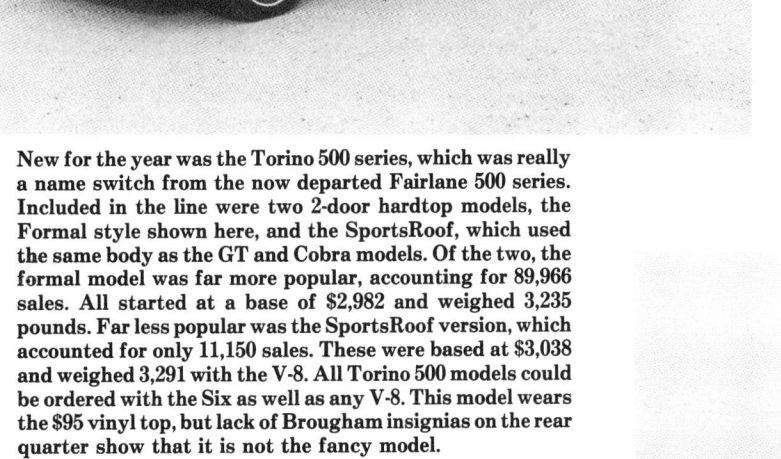

New for the year was the Torino 500 series, which was really a name switch from the now departed Fairlane 500 series. Included in the line were two 2-door hardtop models, the Formal style shown here, and the SportsRoof, which used the same body as the GT and Cobra models. Of the two, the formal model was far more popular, accounting for 89,966 sales. All started at a base of $2,982 and weighed 3,235 pounds. Far less popular was the SportsRoof version, which accounted for only 11,150 sales. These were based at $3,038 and weighed 3,291 with the V-8. All Torino 500 models could be ordered with the Six as well as any V-8. This model wears the $95 vinyl top, but lack of Brougham insignias on the rear quarter show that it is not the fancy model.

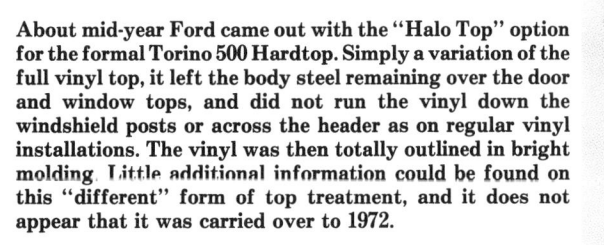

About mid-year Ford came out with the "Halo Top" option for the formal Torino 500 Hardtop. Simply a variation of the full vinyl top, it left the body steel remaining over the door and window tops, and did not run the vinyl down the windshield posts or across the header as on regular vinyl installations. The vinyl was then totally outlined in bright molding. Little additional information could be found on this "different" form of top treatment, and it does not appear that it was carried over to 1972.

The Torino 500 series used a totally different rear panel design than did the upper series. Here the taillights stood totally alone, each within a 5-lens pod. Separating these was a body-color panel with "FORD" spelled out in block letters. This is the Torino 500 4-door Sedan, which was almost three times as popular as the Hardtop model. It drew a total of 35,650 orders. All were V-8 based at $2,950 and weighed 3,225 pounds. All models in the Torino 500 series used grooved rocker panel trim and bright wheel well moldings.

Hauling its heart out is this Torino 500 Station Wagon, Style 71C. Available only as a 6-passenger model, it could be ordered as either a Six or a V-8. However, for heavy work such as this, it is doubtful if a Six lived under the hood. In base V-8 form it sold for $3,265 and weighed 3,639 pounds. In all, 23,270 were turned out. A variety of trailer towing packages were offered, keyed to both the engine and anticipated towing needs. Most included such items as power front disc brakes, heavy duty suspension, extra cooling package, and heavy duty alternator and battery. Not restricted to wagons, the towing packages could be installed on any model Ford.

The base line in the mid-series was the plain Torino, a 3-style line of virtually untrimmed models. Yet, the promotional picture of the 2-door Hardtop, Style 62A, shows the car wearing an added cost set of turbine wheel covers and a $34 set of whitewalls, plus the $95 vinyl top. This was not the treatment one would normally accord to a low-buck special. In basic 6-cylinder form, it sold for $2,706 and weighed 3,1512 pounds. Relatively popular, it drew 37,518 orders. Also in this series was the 4-door Sedan, style 54A. Of pillared design, it cost only $2,672 as a basic Six, and thus was the lowest price model in the entire Torino line. It weighed 3,141 pounds with the Six. Not as popular as the 2-door, it still drew 29,501 sales.

The lowest price mid-size wagon was the Torino, Style 71D. Devoid of all side trim except for the Torino signature directly under the gas filler door, the 6-passenger 6-cylinder model was priced at $3,023, not counting the white walls shown here. Plain hubcaps were standard on all lower line Torinos, but often were replaced with any of several styles of wheel covers. Despite their low trim level, Torino 4-door models featured arm rests on all four doors. Weighing 3,498 pounds as a Six, the wagon drew 21,570 orders.

After the tremendous acceptance received by the Maverick in 1970, Ford quickly decided to expand the line, bringing in two totally new little animals. The hottest of these was the Maverick Grabber, Style 62D, which could be ordered with any one of the three 6-cylinder engines, or could have the 302 cubic inch V-8 of 210 horses installed. Priced at $2,523 and weighing 2,763 pounds with the V-8, the surprisingly quick little car drew 38,963 orders. Among its exclusive items were deep dished steel wheels with wide aluminum beauty rings; a special hood with blackout panel and twin functional air scoops; special blackout grille with twin running lights; blackout rear panel, and special racing stripes.

Virtually unchanged from the 1970 line was the plain Maverick, Style 62A. Still built on a 103-inch wheelbase, the surprisingly popular little car could have any of the engine options of the Grabber, but usually was seen with some form of Six. At its most basic, with its exclusive 170 cubic inch Six of 100 horses, the Maverick sold for $2,175, representing an increase of $180 over 1970. It weighed 2,478 pounds. Booted from its previous No. One sales spot by the new Pinto, this year it had to settle for 2nd place ranking overall, with 159,726 leaving the yards.

Totally new this year was the Maverick 4-door Sedan, Style 54A. The decision to produce this car was reached only after the initial success of the 2-door version was noted during its first six months. Using standard Maverick sheet metal for the forward half, the car was built on a stretched chassis of 109.9 inches, and was 186.3 inches long overall, or 6.9 inches larger than the 2-door model. With the basic Six, it cost $2,235 and weighed 2,610 pounds. Nobody made a mistake on this decision, and there were many smiles at Ford when 73,208 orders rolled in, giving the total Maverick line a sales tally of 271,897 units.

Pinto meets pinto, or as some would quip, horse meets bean. Ford's totally new car this year went even one step further than the Maverick in downgrading, and the result was a truly diminutive car with its own exclusive foreign-built engines. Power was by a 4-cylinder unit, either a British-built 98 cubic inch model of 75 horses, or a German-sourced 122 cubic inch mill of 100 horses (or Pintos). At first available only as a stripped 4-passenger model for $1,191, it soon developed an accent group option which, with the white wall tires shown here, boosted the price to $2,007. The rear quarter windows were functional and would open from the trailing edge. As expected, the car was tremendously successful, to the point of being Ford's Number One sales leader this year, with 288,606 going out of the corral.

1971

With the Pinto prancing happily across the sales charts, it was understandable that someone somewhere would think up an addition to the line. Such a move occurred at mid-year, when the new Pinto Runabout was introduced. Designated Style 64B, it featured a fold-down rear seat which greatly enhanced the cargo space, plus it had a large swing-up rear panel which led to its being termed a 3-door model. It was priced at $2,062 and weighed 1,994 pounds, with its roof rack shown here being an extra cost option, as was the exterior decor group. Considering its late entry, sales were not bad, reaching 63,796 for the remainder of the model year. Considered a sub-compact, Pintos were built on a 94-inch wheelbase and were 163 inches long overall. The main competition for the car, aside from foreign models, was the AMC Gremlin and the Chevrolet Vega.

Once again the cute little Torino-based Ranchero pickup came in four flavors, raging from ultra stripped to real fancy, to sports car hot. For the speed set, there was this Ranchero GT, the most expensive of the lot with a base price of $3,273. For this, buyers received the 302 V-8 with 2-barrel carburetor; exclusive grille and argent rocker moldings, both with GT lettering; exclusive "Sport-Scoop" hood; sport wheel covers with beauty rims, and a deluxe interior including full carpeting and pleated vinyl seats. A total of 3,632 were ordered in this form. Although the 302 was considered standard power, any larger engine right up to the 429 Cobra Jet could be ordered, along with a manual 4-speed with Hurst shifter.

Fanciest of all Rancheros was the Squire, shown here with the optional grille with hidden headlights. Using imitation wood trim similar to that used on the Torino Squire wagon, the pretty little truck proved to be the least popular of all Rancheros, and drew only 2,595 orders. It was priced at $3,192, which included the 302 V-8 with single barrel carburetor. Most popular of the Torino-type trucks was the Ranchero 500, which saw sales of 12,678. With a trim level based on the Torino 500 series, the truck also used the 302 V-8 as basic power, and had a base price of $2,983. The workaday version was the plain Ranchero, which at $2,851 came with the 250 cubic inch Six as basic power. It enjoyed a run of 6,041, which Ford must have felt was unsatisfactory, as this model did not reappear in 1972. All Rancheros ranged in weight from 3,285 to 3,445 pounds, with the difference mainly determined by what lived under the hood.

Once again the Bronco entered a new year with virtually no changes to the exterior. It was still available with the 170 cubic inch Six as basic power and the 302 V-8 as an option. Also, it still came in two styles, the popular Wagon model shown here, which enjoyed 18,281 sales, or the 2-passenger Pickup, which drew only 1,503 orders. Also on the boards was a special Baja Bronco, customized for off-road racing by Bill Stroppe & Associates, while Ford offered a Sport Package, which was more of an appearance group than a competition package. In basic form, the Wagon sold for $3,570 with the Six, while the Pickup was $3,466. On the wagon, the rear seat was still an extra cost option.

For a change, no new animals entered the Ford fold this year. And, several of those who were there went through no major changes whatsoever. But that didn't mean that Ford was without new models this year. On the contrary, both Thunderbird and Galaxie became totally new cars, bearing virtually no resemblance to previous models.

Most changed of all was Thunderbird, which went from its own exclusive 3-style body line to a single style utilizing the Lincoln Continental body and chassis, modified of course for positive identification. The new one-style Bird appeared to be the largest ever to leave the nest, being built on a wheelbase of 120.4 inches. But, being 214 inches long overall, it was actually one inch shorter than the previous 4-door sedan. Only one model was available, the 2-door Hardtop. However, a host of options insured that there would be a wide diversity between a stripped model (if there ever was such a thing) and the most loaded offering. Included in the list were a power sun roof, and a vinyl roof with landau irons.

Also totally new from top to bottom was the Torino series. Starting with the jet intake style grille, running down the slightly bulging sides, and ending with the massive rear bumpers which included homes for the taillights, the new Torinos bore virtually no resemblance to any of the previous models. On the 4-doors, the wheelbase was extended one inch to a new length of 118 inches, while the other models retained the old 114-inch length. Overall, the cars now had three new distinct lengths, with the 2-door models being 203.7 inches, the 4-doors being 207.3 inches, and the wagons stretching to 211.6 inches.

The plain Torino line was increased by one model, now having available a 4-door hardtop sedan as well as the previous 2-door hardtop, 4-door sedan, and wagon. However, above the base models, the series were completely changed. Gone were the Brougham, the GT, and the Cobra names, while in their place was simply a top-line series called the Gran Torino. Although the line did make a concession to sportiness with a Sport Hardtop, the true sports styles of GT Sport Coupe, GT Convertible, and Cobra were now gone. In fact, with the Torino Convertible gone, the only sporty soft top left was in the Mustang line, while LTD carried the luxury convertible for the final time this year.

In the Mustang line, the major change might have been the deletion of the Boss 351 Fastback as an available model, and the dropping of the two 429 cubic inch engines as power options. This year the Cleveland 351 was the biggest powerplant in the corral, but even this was a far cry from the previous year. Now the hottest engine available was a 275 horse version with 4-barrel carburetion. Called the "High-Output V-8" (HO V-8), this engine was a special-order option costing $870. The normal high-power V-8 was the 4-barrel 351 Cleveland of 266 horses, which was a $115 option.

New government mandates regarding the use of unleaded gas plus various pollution controls resulted in all engines going down substantially in both compression ratios and horsepower. With the exception of the above, little was changed on this year's Mustangs, except that Ford advertising now referred to them as "Sport Compacts."

Of the little cars, the new Pinto series was the only one to gain a new model. Here a 2-door Station Wagon joined the previous 2-door Sedan and 3-door Runabout, making Pinto a 3-car series. The Runabout also received a slightly larger rear window, but aside from that, no changes were made to the year-old model. The wheelbase remained 94 inches, the overall length 163 inches, and the power was one of two fours, either the 98 cubic inch Britisher or the 122 cubic inch German model. The latter produced 86 horses and cost $50 extra. As before, Cruise-O-Matic was available for an additional $177.

Ford's other little car, the Maverick, was almost totally unchanged from 1971. It continued with its 3-car line, having a 2-door Sedan, a 4-door Sedan, and the sporty-type Grabber. Sales of the little animal remained almost consistent with the previous year, but it was evident that the Pinto had taken some of the appeal from its slightly larger corral mate.

Similar to the small cars, the large Fords also changed very little. Except for a new and heavier front bumper to meet anticipated safety standards, and a new set of grilles for model-year identification, the Custom, Galaxie 500, and LTD series were carbon copies of the 1971 models. The Custom line continued to be divided into base Custom and Custom 500 series, each offering a 4-door Sedan and a 4-door Ranch Wagon. Both the Galaxie 500 and LTD series appeared to have lost one model each, but this was only because the 10-passenger station wagon was no longer considered a separate model. Now it was simply an option to the 6-passenger wagon. As before, the LTD wagon was the imitation wood trimmed Country Squire, while the Galaxie 500 version was the plain-sided Country Sedan.

Under the hoods, a few changes were evident, none of which were particularly thrilling to the speed set or the power lovers. For one thing, all compressions were reduced to meet the aforementioned government mandate that all cars be able to run on lower octane nonleaded gas. Also, a switch from the old brake horsepower ratings to the new SAE ratings made the horsepowers appear substantially lower than previous classes.

The SAE ratings were based on theoretical power outputs, taking into consideration losses produced by such units as air conditioners, automatic transmissions, alternators, hydraulic power steering pumps, etc. Besides the federal emissions mandates and even more stringent requirements by California, one other factor hastened the end of the super car age. That was an across the board levy by the auto insurance companies of surcharges on high horsepower engines and recognized muscle cars. Hitting the car owner where it hurt the most, these levies probably did as much to discourage the production and sale of powerhouse engines than did all the compression and emissions regulations.

As a result, both the Cobra Jet and Super Cobra Jet 429 engines were dropped. The only remaining 429 was the new Thunderbird version which was rated at 205 SAE horsepower. Essentially, this engine replaced the former Thunder Jet 429. Also dropped was the 390 V-8, which was not replaced in any form, and the little 200 cubic inch Maverick Six, which likewise was not replaced.

New under the hoods, besides the Thunderbird 429, were the 351 Windsor engines which replaced the former base 351 cubic inch block, the 351 High Output Cleveland engine of 266 horses (and its special performance variation of 275 horsepower) and a totally new 460 cubic inch Thunderbird 460 of 224 SAE horsepower. These changes brought to 15 engines (including the 275 horse 351) available this year, as opposed to 16 last year.

Still, these changes did not seem to hurt production. This year Ford recorded a fantastic 2,247,193 sales for the model year. Accounting for a major share of these were the new Torino models, which registered a total of 496,644 models produced. Coming in a close second

was the Pinto line, with 480,405 sales. The LTD line ran a very close third, with 475,292 units, while the Galaxie 500 line strayed to a more distant fourth with 269,199. Both Mustang and Maverick sales slipped, however. Mustang shipped only 125,093 cars, while Maverick did 254,964. Only two series shipped under 100,000. They were the Custom lines with sales of 87,782, and the new Thunderbird, which increased its sales substantially by recording 57,814 orders.

As could be expected with a total such as this, a number of body styles exceeded the 100,000 sales mark. In fact, an amazing tally of nine models went above this figure.

Best selling of all Ford products was the Pinto Runabout, with 197,920 orders. Pinto also took 2nd place, as its 2-door Sedan accounted for 181,002. Third spot went to the Maverick 2-door Sedan, with 145,931 orders, while the new Gran Torino 2-door Hardtop came in 4th with 132,284. Ford's now-favorite wagon, the LTD Country Squire, scored 121,419 sales to account for 5th place, while 6th and 7th spots were shared equally by the basic LTD 4-door Sedan and the Galaxie 500 4-door Sedan, each registering 104,167 sales. The basic Torino 4-door Sedan came in 8th with 102,300 sales, while the new Pinto Station Wagon completed the 100,000-plus list with 101,483.

Totally new for the year was the Thunderbird. No longer using its own exclusive body, the car now shared its basic metal with the Lincoln Continental. That meant that the 4-door had to be dropped, as there was no such animal in the Continental line. The result was an amazingly good looking car, available in 2-door form, powered by the new version of the 429 cubic inch block, called the "Thunderbird 429" and rated at 212 horses. Only one model was offered. It was this Style 65K, which bore a base price of $5,293 and weighed 4,420 pounds. Public acceptance was good, and sales rose to 57,841. The largest Thunderbird ever offered, the new model had a 120.4-inch wheelbase and was 214 inches long overall.

Although only one Thunderbird model was offered, a host of options could transform the basic car (and basic price) to one of the most luxurious vehicles on the road. The car is shown here with its Landau option, which included decorative chrome landau bars on a special vinyl top. Other popular options were the vinyl top for the $137; a sunroof for $505; air conditioning for another $505, and power windows and seat for $331. Cruise-O-Matic was standard. Although styling would indicate a hidden headlight feature could easily be installed, no such option was available.

After a total restyling in 1971, it stands to reason that the Mustang line would be virtually unchanged this year. Providing a sporty car to the few rag-top fans still left was the Mustang Convertible, Style 76D. Almost identical to the 1971 issue, its sales also were almost identical, with 6,401 leaving the corral as compared with last year's 6,121. It sold for $3,101 and weighed 3,147 pounds with the basic 302 cubic inch V-8. However, the base engine was still the 250 cubic inch Six, now bearing a SAE horsepower rating of 98 as opposed to the 145 brake horses listed in 1971.

1972

The hottest horse in the Mustang corral was the Mach I SportsRoof, Style 63R. The only Mustang not available with a Six, it used as its base power the 302 V-8. Only three hotter engines were available, and they were all variations of the Cleveland 351 V-8, as the 429 was no longer available in the Mustang line. In basic form the Mach I cost $3,246, which included competition suspension, hood with functional twin NASA-type scoops, blackout grille with built-in Sportlamps, special decals, and deep dished steel wheels with trim rings and special hub caps. Possibly the taming of the model resulted in loss of interest in the speed set, as only 27,675 were sold. And, this number probably included those purchased because the Boss models were no longer on the list.

Although the hottest Mustang this year was a relatively cool horse with not too much performance strength, a quick run through the options book could produce a real screamer. Such a creation is this Mach I with the 351 Cleveland High Output V-8 with Holley 4-barrel and Ram Air Induction. Rated now at 266 SAE horsepower, and probably capable of producing well beyond this figure, the HO V-8 cost an additional $870 and required the 4-speed manual at another $193. The special Ram Air hood with blackout panel, functional air scoops, and locking pins, was included in the price, but Magnum 500 chrome wheels were another $139.

Luxury liner of the Mustang herd was the Grande, Style 65F, which was based on the formal top coupe. Priced at $3,002 and weighing 3,051 pounds, it featured a deluxe interior done in a combination of Lambeth cloth and vinyl; vinyl top with "Grande" signatures; special wheel covers; exclusive instrument panel appliques, and carpeted trunk. Interest in this car went up slightly, and a total of 18,045 were sold.

Almost as sleek as the Mach I, since they shared the same body, was the Mustang SportsRoof, Style 63D. Available with either the Six or V-8 options, the car used the standard Mustang grille and hood. It was priced at $2,873 and weighed 3,025 pounds. As did all Mustangs, it featured high-back bucket seats and a mini-console in the front. Side brightwork included wheel opening trim, a side strip running to just behind the door, and rocker moldings. All Mustangs used full wheel covers, except for the Mach I which had competition-type wheels. Oddly, the rear quarter windows on this model were now fixed in place and could not be opened. Interest in this model did a downturn, and only 15,622 were sold.

As always, the most popular Mustang was the basic 2-door Hardtop Coupe, Style 65D. But this year, sales dropped to 57,350. The cute little car cost $2,816 and weighed 3,025 pounds with the basic V-8, but the vinyl top shown here was a $79 option. All Mustangs used concealed windshield wipers and dual color-keyed racing mirrors as standard equipment. A 3-speed manual floor shift was considered standard, but a 4-speed could be ordered for $193, while Cruise-O-Matic cost $204.

1972

After last year's total restyling, no one expected the large Ford line to change very much—and that is exactly what happened. Flagships of the line continued to be the LTD Brougham series, of which the most attractive and most popular was the 2-door Hardtop, Style 65K. Once again, however, despite the fact that the LTD Broughams were virtually never seen without vinyl tops, these were actually a $110 add-on. Available only as a V-8, using the 351 engine as basic power, the car listed at $4,050 without options. It weighed 3,883 pounds, and drew a total of 50,409 orders. The deluxe wheel covers shown here were part of the Brougham package.

Most automakers have the nasty habit of adding a few pieces of chrome or a slightly different grille to a car and considering it a separate model. Yet when Ford gave the Power Sunroof to the LTD Brougham line, it was simply a $505 option to the regular 2-door Hardtop. Among the standard features of the Brougham line was a new front seat described as "high-backed flight-bench seating." Also included in the interior were center arm rests; cut-pile carpeting, and special door side panels.

As before, the LTD Brougham line contained two 4-door models, a pillared Sedan, Style 53K, and this Hardtop Sedan, Style 57K. In a switch this year, the pillared model drew the most sales, recording 36,909, while the hardtop saw only 23,364 leave the floors. The pillared model sold for $4,047 and weighed 3,949 pounds, while the hardtop was $4,090 and 3,944 pounds. On both models, all four windows could be lowered to sill level, but this facility provided both looks and ventilation in the hardtop, an open appearance that was lost by the fixed B-pillar in the Sedan. All LTD Broughams had bright rocker molding.

Appearing for the last time this year was the beautiful LTD Convertible, Ford's only soft-top outside of the Mustang line. Detroit often attempted to blame the demise of convertibles on restrictive government safety standards, but in truth, buyer apathy to the attractive but somewhat impractical styles was the main reason. For example, though this was announced as the last year for Ford's soft tops, only 4,2324 customers took one off the floor. High expressway speeds and lower cost dependable air conditioning were the major contributing factors in the convertible's loss of favor. This model, available only with the 351 V-8 or larger option, was base priced at $4,073 and weighed 4,091 pounds.

Only a slight difference in side trim and lack of the Brougham plaque on the rear roof panel differentiated the plain LTD 2-door Hardtop, Style 65H, from its fancier kin. The main difference between the two models was the interior fittings, which were more luxurious on the Brougham. On all models, the vinyl top was a $110 option, but usually had to be ordered as a delete, since most high level cars automatically came with this feature. As did the LTD Brougham series, the LTD series was also available only with V-8 engines, with the basic power being the 351 V-8. Priced at $3,893, the 2-door Hardtop weighed 3,853 pounds. A very popular car, its sales totalled 101,048.

Not far removed from the Brougham model in looks and trim level was the plain LTD 4-door Hardtop, Style 57H. It cost $3,941 and weighed 3,908 pounds. However, for some unexplained reason, it was the poorest selling of all LTD models, excepting the convertible, and only 33,742 were sold. Horsepower ratings on all engines became confused this year as most manufacturers switched to the lower rated SAE (Society of Automotive Engineers) system instead of the old familiar brake horsepower system. This caused all engines to seem reduced in power, when in effect they were little changed from the previous ratings. However, the increase in emissions standards, plus requirements to run on lower octane gas, did lower the overall power output of all engines to a varying degree.

Ford's 6th best selling car this year turned out to be the LTD 4-door Sedan, now officially called a "Pillared Hardtop." It saw 104,167 leave the factories. Known as Style 53H, it had a base price of $3,906 and weighed 3,913 pounds. The price did not include the vinyl top, deluxe wheel covers, or thin white wall tires shown here, nor did it include the $486 air conditioning system that was probably added. Power front disc brakes were standard on all LTD models.

No longer did Ford consider the 6-passenger and 10-passenger wagons separate models, and thus in the Country Squire, the Style 71H designation stood for both cars. Now the 10-passenger wagon was simply the station wagon with optional dual facing rear seats. Still an official part of LTD line, the Country Squire not only turned out to be the best selling model in that series, it was Ford's 5th best selling style overall. A total of 121,419 left the plants, helping to make Ford the undisputed King of the Wagons. In basic 6-passenger form, the Country Squire this year cost $4,318 and weighed 4,308 pounds. The deluxe wheel covers and roof rack on this model were extras. Also available on full-size wagons this year, but seldom seen, was the vinyl top option for $148. New for the year was a semi-transparent wood-tone siding, which allowed a hint of the body color to show through, especially in bright sunlight.

The mid-range of the large or full-size Ford line continued to be the Galaxie 500 series. The only 2-door in the line was the Style 65F Hardtop, shown here with an optional color-keyed vinyl top, but wearing the standard wheel covers. As did all full-size Fords, the series used the 351 V-8 and Cruise-O-Matic as standard running gear. Priced at $3,572 and weighing 3,826 pounds, this model contributed 80,855 sales to the Galaxie line.

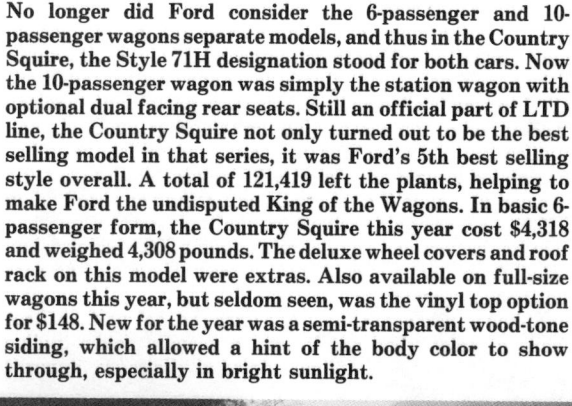

When fitted with the very popular deluxe wheel covers and color-keyed vinyl top, the Galaxie 500 4-door Hardtop, Style 57F, was difficult to distinguish from the LTD or Brougham models. Only the lack of distinctive side trim spelled the difference, with the Galaxie 500 having only a medium width rocker molding and wheel opening surrounds, in addition to the bright work around the window area. Priced at $3,720 and weighing 3,881 pounds, the car turned out to be the least popular of all Galaxies, and drew only 28,939 orders.

Best selling of all Galaxie 500 models was the 4-door Sedan, now known as a "Pillared Hardtop." Style 54F was base priced at $3,685, which would deliver a car just about as shown here, with a steel top, standard wheel covers, and basic outside mirror. Topping the sales list, it attracted 104,167 buyers, and thus ranked in 7th spot on Ford's overall high-flying sales chart this year. All Galaxie models used a grille that was similar to the LTD, but had a wider mesh in the side panels.

The Country Sedan continued to live in the mid-level Galaxie 500 series, and use the basic interior trim level of that line. Essentially a wood-less version of the Country Squire, the model was still a good step above the Ranch Wagon in plushness. Known as Style 71F, it weighed 4,308 pounds, and cost $4,028, not counting the practical roof-top luggage rack. This rack had a wind deflector at the rear which would force air down over the rear window, thus helping to keep normal turbulence from kicking dust and spray against the doorgate. A popular model, the Country Sedan accounted for 55,238 orders. This wagon also wears the now-optional dual facing rear seats, and thus last year would have been classed as a separate 10-passenger model.

The low-level full-size Ford line was still divided between the stripped Custom 500 models and the super stripped Custom offerings. This is the Custom 500 4-door Sedan in basic form. Known as Style 54D, it cost $3,418 and weighed 3,764 pounds. Sales reached 24,807, probably all with the basic 351 V-8, as larger engine options would be relatively rare in this series. Despite the low level, power steering and Cruise-O-Matic transmissions were still considered standard items on both the Custom 500 and Custom lines.

Shown with one of several custom-fitted trailer towing packages is the Custom 500 Ranch Wagon, also containing the optional dual facing rear seats, which in 1971 would have classed this vehicle as a 10-passenger model. Now it was simply the Ranch Wagon, Style 71D, with 10-passenger option. It also wears the very popular roof rack. All full-size wagons except those in the plain Custom series were fitted with powered doorgate windows, which had been extra-cost items up to this year in all but the Country Squire models. The Custom 500 wagon sold for $3,895 and weighed 4,327 pounds without the extra seats. Far less popular than the better trimmed versions, it accounted for only 16,834 sales.

The only large Fords that could be ordered with the 240 cubic inch Six as base power were the plain Custom models bought in fleet lots. Individual buyers of Custom models still received the 351 V-8 under the hood. An example of the lowest trim level Ford is this Custom model in Army garb, fitted with a removable red light bar and used as a Military Police patrol unit. Known as Style 54B, it would have sold to an individual for $3,288, but probably went for less in a fleet purchase. A total of 33,014 were delivered. Also in the Custom series was the lowest level Ranch Wagon, which was priced at $3,806. Not faring nearly as well as the sedan, it attracted only 13,064 buyers.

Going through a total restyling this year was the entire Torino line. Besides all new sheet metal and frontal appearance, the old nomenclatures were changed, and the top level cars were now called Gran Torinos. One of the most attractive and best selling of this new line was the Gran Torino SportsRoof, Style 63R. Of fastback design, it attracted 60,794 customers. Available only with a V-8, it used the 302 cubic inch model as basic power. In this form, it cost $3,094 and weighed 3,496 pounds. It is shown here with the special GT hood, which was part of the new Torino Sport package.

A new model for the year was the Torino Sport Hardtop Coupe, which surprisingly used the formal-top Style 65R as its body, rather than the SportsRoof model. The car featured the GT hood with simulated air scoops, had a unique recessed oval grille finished in two-tone argent, and featured a heavier suspension than plain Gran Torinos. Basic power was the 302 V-8, but heavier engines, especially the Cleveland 351 models, could be ordered. Also in the package were the high-back bucket seats and center console. The car had a base price of $3,094 and weighed 3,474 pounds. Not nearly as popular as the SportsRoof, it drew only 31,239 orders.

All Gran Torinos used a grille distinctive from the plain Torino line. Though similar to the basic grille, the Gran models used a double egg-crate texture, and the upper half was framed by a wide piece of bright molding. This is the 2-door Hardtop Coupe, Style 65D, which differed from the Sport model in not having the scooped hood, and which used the 250 cubic inch Six as its base. The high-back bucket seats, vinyl top, and heavy side molding were all from the option book, which was delved into by many buyers of the upscale Torinos. In basic form, with the 302 V-8, it cost $2,967 and weighed 3,548 pounds. A very popular model, it not only ranked first in all Torino sales, but came in 4th in all Ford sales overall, with a total of 132,248 leaving the factories.

This year bearing the name of 4-door Pillared Hardtop, the Style 53D was formerly known simply as the 4-door Sedan. Available with either the Six or V-8, it sold in basic V-8 form for $2,947. As a Six it was $91 less. Weighing 3,555 pounds, it was the second most popular car in the Gran Torino line, accounting for 102,300 sales. This also made it the 8th best selling Ford overall. As expected, the vinyl top was a $93 option. This car also has the high-back bucket seats in the front, and a center console, an option package rare in a 4-door sedan.

1972

With the mid-range Torino 500 series gone, the mid-level wagon was upscaled into the Gran Torino series. Here it could be ordered with either a Six or V-8, though the Six was probably the lesser choice. As a small block V-8 it cost $3,186 and weighed 3,960 pounds. All Gran Torinos this year had front disc brakes as standard equipment, though power brakes were still extra cost. Also on all Gran Torino wagons this year was the "Magic Doorgate" as standard fare, whereas up to now it had been an extra-cost option on all but the Squire models. Most popular of all the Torino wagons, the Gran model drew 45,212 orders. The roof rack and turbine wheel covers were added cost accessories.

The top wagon of the Torino line was the Gran Torino Squire, Style 71K, which featured a simulated wood side trim very similar to that used on the full-size Country Squire. All wagons now shared the new Torino frame, with its 118-inch wheelbase, as used on the 4-door models. Two-door models had a 114-inch wheelbase version. Relatively long, the Torino wagons all shared the same body of 211.6 inches overall. Gran Torino Squires were available only in V-8 form, with the 302 cubic inch model being basic, but all options right up to the 429 being available. The Squires also had their own exclusive wagon interior of deluxe pleated vinyl. Wheel covers were standard on all Gran Torinos. Priced at $3,486, this was the most expensive Torino, while at 4,042 pounds, it was the only one to exceed two tons. Not quite as popular as the plain model, it still drew 35,595 orders.

The base mid-size wagon was the Torino, Style 71B, shown here with accessory roof rack and wheel covers. Although disc brakes were standard on all Torinos, all wagons in the two series had power front discs as standard equipment. High-back front bench seats were also standard on all Torinos, as were all-vinyl interiors. The plain wagon had a 6-cylinder price of $2,955 and weighed 3,879 pounds. The V-8 was $90 extra and weighed 80 pounds more. Least popular of all Torino wagons, this model drew only 22,204 orders. Although the doorgate was standard, a power rear window cost an extra $35, while the luggage rack with wind deflector cost $77.

A single full-width egg-crate grille without bright molding quickly identifies this pretty car as the plain Torino 2-door Hardtop, Style 65B. Available with either Six or V-8, it seems logical that this unit had both the trailer towing package and the 351 V-8 option. Also included is the $93 vinyl top, which left a strip of body-color metal behind the quarter windows. It sold for $2,762 and weighed 3,448 pounds. Not nearly as popular as the Gran version, it drew only 33,530 orders.

Among the new Torinos was this 4-door Pillared Hardtop, which formerly would have been called a 4-door sedan. Style 53B was available in either Six or V-8 form, and was the basic model of the line. At $2,731 as a small V-8, it was also the least expensive Torino. It weighed 3,548 pounds, and drew 33,486 orders, which was almost 100,000 less than its comparable Gran model. For the first time in Torino history, these cars did not have a unit frame body, but were built with an independent body installed on a totally new flexible frame or chassis.

Sporting a special hood with twin air scoops and a 2-tone color-keyed panel is the new Maverick Grabber, Style 62D. Utilizing the regular 2-door sedan body, the Grabber could be ordered with either the 170, 200, or 250 cubic inch engine, or the 302 V-8. With the V-8, it cost $2,519 and weighed 2,786 pounds. Sales went to 35,347, making this the least popular Maverick in the herd, despite the sprightly performance given by the V-8. High-back bucket seats and a console were part of the Grabber package, as was the exclusive side paint stripe.

All gussied up in a host of luxury items, the Maverick 4-door Sedan, Style 54A, certainly left the ranks of the stripped economy car behind. Among its options are a vinyl top; wheel covers; side trim or decor group package, and probably the deluxe interior. With such extras on the outside, it certainly must have had the Cruise-O-Matic transmission; $92 power steering, and $59 AM radio on the inside. Without all of the toys, it would have had a base V-8 price of $2,406, or have been even $161 less with the basic Six. It weighed 2,826 pounds. Production wasn't bad, with 73,686 being sold, though probably very few were as dressed as this example.

No one was in a hurry to change a winner, so this year's Pintos were virtual carbon copies of the 1971 models. The base car was the little 2-door Sedan, Style 62B, which at $1,960 was the only car in Ford's entire line to be priced at under $2,000. However, this model is all dressed for its picture, and wears the Luxury Decor Group, a $137 package that included chrome window moldings and a vinyl top. It also sports a set of $23 wheel covers and $42 extra white walls. With sales of 181,002, it was the second best selling car in the entire Ford line. At 1,968 pounds, it was also the only Ford model to weigh less than one ton.

Turning out to be Ford's 3rd best selling model overall was the plain Maverick 2-door Sedan, Style 62A. It drew a total of 145,931 orders. Essentially an untrimmed version of the Grabber, it could still be ordered with the same engine options as the supposedly "hot" Grabber. Thus, as a V-8, it cost $2,350 and weighed 2,731 pounds, with the lesser weight technically giving it slightly more performance than the Grabber. Cruise-O-Matic was a popular option costing $177.

The little Pinto Runabout turned out to be the best selling Ford of all this year, recording sales of 197,920. Priced at $2,078, it weighed 2,012 pounds. Runabouts differed from the sedans in that they had a folding rear seat and larger swing-up rear panels. Because of this, they were often referred to as 3-door cars. New on the Runabouts this year was the much larger back window, that now occupied almost the entire rear deck. This model wears the Accent Group that included side trim and chrome window edging and rain gutters, and has the optional rear quarter flipper windows.

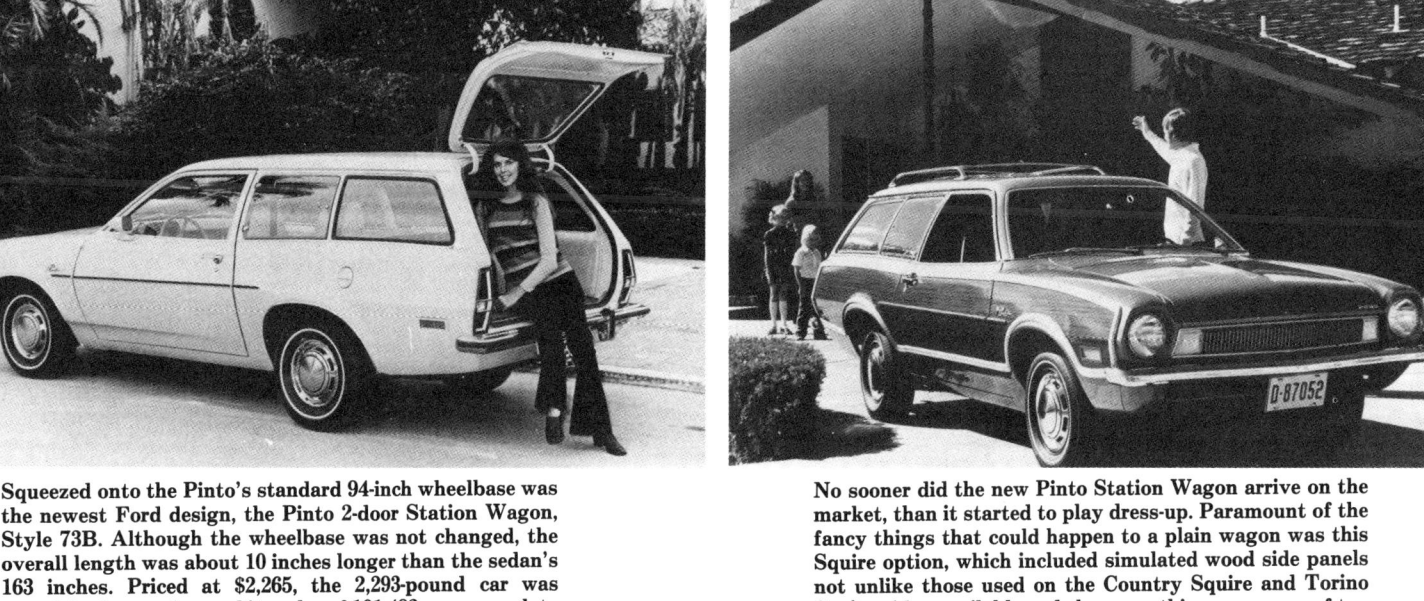

Squeezed onto the Pinto's standard 94-inch wheelbase was the newest Ford design, the Pinto 2-door Station Wagon, Style 73B. Although the wheelbase was not changed, the overall length was about 10 inches longer than the sedan's 163 inches. Priced at $2,265, the 2,293-pound car was surprisingly popular, and its sales of 101,483 was enough to rank it in 9th place overall on Ford's sales chart. As did the Runabout, it featured a folding rear seat, and a flip-up rear. However, the rear quarters were well extended, and the rear gate was almost vertical, and had a distinct lower panel. The center window was of the flip-out type, hinged at the leading edge, but the rear quarter window was fixed in place.

No sooner did the new Pinto Station Wagon arrive on the market, than it started to play dress-up. Paramount of the fancy things that could happen to a plain wagon was this Squire option, which included simulated wood side panels not unlike those used on the Country Squire and Torino Squire. Also available and shown on this car was a roof-top luggage rack and the wheel covers. Although the 98 cubic inch Four was standard on Pintos, it is a good bet that this little bean had the optional 122 cubic inch German sourced overhead cam Four that cost $50 more. It might even have had the $175 Cruise-O-Matic transmission.

Just as the Pinto wagon models could be ultra-trimmed in Squire dresses, the 2-door sedans also were treated to a host of extras that far exceeded their basic concept as economy cars. Most ostentatious of these options was the new manually operated Sun Roof, seen here with the equally optional vinyl top. The car also includes the Luxury Decor Group, wheel covers, white wall tires, and appears to have the deluxe all-vinyl interior on its high-back bucket seats. One wonders why someone would order a basic economy car, and then add all of the trimmings, unless total fuel economy was an overriding factor. But with gas still around 30 to 35-cents a gallon maximum in this era, it seems unlikely that someone who wanted all of the toys would worry about fuel economy.

With the plain Ranchero now gone, only three flavors of the Torino-based truck were available. They were the most popular Ranchero 500, the unpopular but pretty Ranchero Squire, and this Ranchero GT. The GT filled the middle-line in sales, with 12,620 going to market, but it hit the high point in price, being based at $3,201 with the 302 V-8. The 500 model, meanwhile, was the lowest priced Ranchero at $2,850 with the 250 cubic inch Six, but was also the best selling with 23,431 going out the door. The GT models featured an exclusive racing stripe on the sides and tailgate, had their own hood with twin air scoops. and used deep dished wheels with bright beauty rings and hubcaps.

Least popular of the three Torino-based Ranchero models was the Squire, which accounted for only 4,283 sales. Priced at $3,088, it weighed 3,330 pounds, while the 500 model was 3,295 pounds and the GT was the heavy at 3,445 pounds. Standard items on the Squire included the imitation wood on the sides and tailgate, bright wheel covers, and the 302 V-8. Both the Squire and 500 used single barrel carburetors, while the GT had a 2-barrel unit. New on all Squire trim this year was a semi-transparent type of wood-tone paneling, which allowed a hint of the body color to show through.

After giving full styling treatments to Torino and Thunderbird last year, Ford this year turned its attention to the big car lines. Thus, large scale Custom 500, Galaxie 500, LTD and LTD Brougham lines all received their share of newness, with the overall differentiation being strictly in trim level of the four sub-series. Enhancing the new big cars was an overall smoothing of lines, giving a more rounded effect to the sides. A new and "European" type of grille (ala Mercedes) graced the front, while only slight styling modifications were made to the rear.

And, spoiling the whole concept to a degree, were the massive "safety" bumpers mandated by the government. Designed to withstand a 5 MPH impact with no damage to the vehicle, these large and protruding bumpers did little to enhance the frontal appearance of any American car this year, and the new and otherwise very good looking Ford was no exception.

The new styling was surface only. Underneath, except for engine changes to be detailed later, the running gear remained the same, the chassis continued to have a 121-inch wheelbase, and the overall length continued to be 216.2 inches for the cars and 219.2 inches for the station wagons, plus about one inch for the new bumpers.

Missing from the big car list was the 2-model basic Custom series. Now the Custom 500 series, consisting only of a 4-door sedan and the Ranch Wagon, was the base trim level for large Fords. Also missing was Ford's only big convertible. The LTD convertible, which in 1972 had drawn only 4,234 orders, was this year sent into oblivion. Many sources tend to blame federally mandated safety standards for the demise, noting that a convertible could not meet roll-over tests. True, but the main reason for dropping soft tops industry-wide seems to be the low sales figures generated by these cars over the past half decade.

The demise of the LTD convertible left the Mustang with Ford's only soft top. In fact, industry-wide, the convertible was virtually a thing of the past, and Mustang would carry this model only until the end of 1973. The totally new bodies of the 1974 Mustangs would have no provisions for a convertible model. Oddly, after being off the market for almost 15 years, convertibles began to enjoy a revival during the late 1980s, and are now once again a viable part of the overall automotive scene.

Aside from carrying Ford's only convertible, Mustang's main claim to fame this year was a growth of four inches, to a new overall length of 194 inches. The new length was mainly forward of the front wheels, and was mandated primarily by the new bumper set-up, which resulted in a new frontal restyling of only moderate change. With a totally new Mustang ready to be born in 1974, Ford obviously was not going to go to any great styling efforts on the car this year. Once again, the line offered the same five basic models. Total Mustang sales

were up slightly from the 1972 figures, but still, Ford knew very well that something new was needed in the barn.

In the world of little cars, both Pinto and Maverick remained unchanged but both grew slightly in length due to their new front bumpers. Oddly, a change in buyer preference this year made the year-old Pinto Station Wagon Ford's number one selling vehicle, and the first in years to exceed the 200,000 mark. With sales of 217,763, the car accounted for almost 10% of Ford's total production.

A good part of this interest might have been due to a bunch of friendly Arabs who instigated an oil embargo against the U.S., causing widespread gas shortages across the country. Along with the shortages was a rapid and steady increase in gas prices, going from 28/32-cents a gallon to over $1 per gallon before prices leveled off—if they ever have. Along with government threats of needless gas rationing came a new public awareness of gas guzzling engines and the alternative of smaller, less powerful, more fuel efficient cars—with the Pinto and Maverick sitting nicely in the front row.

On the other end of the scale was the Thunderbird. A totally new car in 1972, this year's Bird received only the expected embellishments to differentiate one year from the other. Telling people that the T-Bird at hand was a 1973 model was a new egg-crate grille, and an opera window in the large C-pillar or rear quarter. The small opera window was supposed to assist in backing up by giving more vision than the former blind quarter, but in reality its purpose seems to have been more cosmetic than functional. Running at a tangent to the public's interest in small cars, the new T-Bird was still available with both the 429 or the 460 cubic inch engine—and was anything but fuel efficient. Still, its sales went up almost 30,000 to a nice tally of 87,269 for the year.

With Torino sporting a totally new appearance last year, it stood to reason that few changes would be forthcoming this year. Stylewise that was true, but suddenly more models appeared, there now being 11 to choose from, as opposed to nine in 1972. In the model shake-up, the base Torino line lost one car, as the 4-door Hardtop Sedan was removed from its ranks. Meanwhile, a new Gran Torino Brougham sub-series contained both a 4-door Sedan and a 2-door Hardtop Coupe.

In a rather pronounced engine shake-up, Ford reduced the number of blocks available from 14 to 11. Gone was the little Pinto Four of 98 cubic inches; the Maverick Six of 170 cubic inches; the Ford Six of 240 cubic inches, and the 4-barrel Cleveland 351 of 8.6:1 compression ratio that developed 248 SAE horsepower at 5400 RPM.

New on the scene was only one small block. That was a Maverick Six of 200 cubic inches, which had an 8.3:1 compression. With a bore and stroke of 3.68x3.13 inches, it developed 84 SAE horses at 3200 rpm using a single-barrel Motorcraft carburetor. Also new, but in name only, was the 351 Cobra Jet Cleveland of 266 horses. However, this was simply a new title for the old 351 HO (High Output) Cleveland. It does not appear that the 275 horsepower optional version of this engine was available. Still available, but waiting to be phased out in 1974, was the powerful Thunderbird 460 that ran 219 horses at 4400 rpm, a reduction of five horsepower due to a compression reduction from 8.5:1 to 8.0:1.

Production once again soared, and probably brought broad smiles to most of Ford's executive staff. With model year sales closing at 2,349,367, the company saw production swell 102,174 over the previous year, which in itself was an excellent time to be a Ford dealer.

As in 1972, a grand tally of nine separate models exceeded the 100,000 mark. As mentioned earlier, the leader of this pack was the Pinto Station Wagon, with its tally of 217,763. Second in line was another Pinto, the 2-door Runabout, with 150,603 sales. The Maverick 2-door Sedan came in 3rd with 148,493, while the super popular LTD Country Squire was 4th with 142,933.

Only one Torino made the list. That was the Gran Torino 2-door Hardtop, with 138,962 sales, which placed it in 5th spot. Places six and seven were both occupied by LTD models, with the 4-door Sedan taking 6th with 122,851, and the 2-door Hardtop Coupe coming in 7th at 120,864. Pinto, which had every model in the 100,000-plus bracket, was 8th with its 2-door Sedan selling 116,146 units, while Maverick crept in with a close 9th with its 4-door Sedan posting 110,382 sales. Meanwhile, Mustang was the only major line not to show a substantial increase. Its total sales were 134,817, which was 9,724 above the 1972 figures, but still on the low side when compared with Ford's other lines.

Showing off its optional "Opera Window' treatment, along with its $137 vinyl roof, is the new Thunderbird. This view gives a good look at the rear design, with a single light bar stretching full-width across the back. Again available on these cars was the power-operated Sun Roof for $505 and a Climate Control air conditioning system, also for $505. Other pricey options included the AM/FM stereo radio for $146, and power seats and windows for $331. Despite a minimum of changes this year, the Thunderbird was almost $300 more expensive than in 1972.

Sporting a brand new face with an egg-crate grille and independently mounted quad headlights, the new Thunderbirds helped Ford celebrate its 70th anniversary this year. The name "Thunderbird" was now spelled out in block letters across the leading edge of the hood, while a stand-up ornament graced the top. Power was by the Thunderbird 429, but the year-old optional 460 cubic inch engine of 219 SAE horses was available as an option. Only one model was offered, but again, a multitude of options gave the car a wide range of appearance differences. In base form, the Bird was considered Style 65K, had a price of $5,577, and weighed 4,572 pounds. Sales were up substantially, and 87,269 were sold.

Still Mustang's hot horse, the Mach I this year drew 35,440 orders to show a healthy increase over 1972. This model is also wearing the NASA-type hood with twin scoops, but not in competition or blackout style. Among the special features of the Mach I were a heavy suspension system, blackout grille and rear panel, deep-dish steel wheels with bright beauty rings, high-back bucket seats, and an all-vinyl interior. The wheels shown on this model, however, are the forged aluminum type which cost $120 per set extra. Based on the SportsRoof body, the Mach I, Style 63R, was the only Mustang not available as a Six. Its base power was the 302 V-8, but either the Windsor or the Cleveland 351 could be ordered. With the 302 it cost $3,088 and weighed 3,090 pounds.

Appearing for the last time was Ford's last remaining soft-top, the Mustang convertible, Style 76D. Shown here with its optional NASA-type hood with functional scoops in the blackout panel, the car was fitted with a power-operated vinyl top. Standard equipment included vinyl-knit seats and an all-vinyl interior, and power front disc brakes. Although it was available with a Six, the scooped hood would indicate one of the hotter V-8s was under the hood. As a base V-8, it cost $3,189 and weighed 3,198 pounds. Being the last convertible, sales went up substantially, and the 11,853 sold marked the highest convertible production since 1969.

A long hood and short rear deck were the hallmarks of the Mustang Grande, Style 65F, which was still the line's luxury leader. Except for a new grille, this year's Mustangs were little changed from last year's, probably in anticipation of the all-new models that would appear in 1974. Among the features of the Grande was the standard vinyl top; dual color-keyed racing mirrors; seats in a combination of vinyl and Lambeth cloth; special wheel covers, and a carpeted trunk. For all of this, a buyer had to shell out $3,033 for the basic V-8, which weighed 3,074 pounds. As was the case with most other Mustangs, sales were up, and a total of 25,274 galloped out of the corral.

The only Mustang to suffer a severe drop in sales was the unique SportsRoof, Style 63D. Still often referred to as a Fastback, the car saw only 10,820 leave the dealerships. It is shown here in strictly stock form, The rear window was tinted and the quarter windows were fixed in place and would not open. The rear treatment, including the taillights, was virtually identical to that of the previous year. With the base V-8, it cost $2,907, with the 250 cubic inch Six it was $87 less. Its weight was 3,083 pounds.

Showing off its new grille is Mustang's top selling model, the 2-door Hardtop Coupe, Style 65D. Built in formal-top fashion, the pretty car drew 51,430 orders, which was down from last year, but still the top of the Mustang roster. This model is wearing the $80 vinyl top, which included a tri-color ornament on the corners and a body-color vertical bar on the C-pillar section. This is the same top that was standard on the Grande. Inside it appears to have the $115 Sport Group, which included 2-tone knitted vinyl high-back bucket seats, molded vinyl door panels, and deep deluxe carpeting. Although base priced at $2,847 for the small V-8, the option list for Mustangs was virtually endless this year, and with a handful of dollars, any model could be transformed to whatever a buyer desired.

The LTD Brougham series was still the top line of all Ford cars, excepting the Thunderbird, of course. This year the vinyl top was finally made a standard item rather than a virtually mandatory extra. All models had a newly designed grille of tight mesh, with the headlights noticeably recessed. Deluxe wheel covers and heavy rocker panel trim set the appearance theme, while protection was by a full-length belt molding of color-keyed vinyl. Again the most popular LTD Brougham was the 2-door Hardtop, Style 65K, which sold for $4,107. It drew a total of 68,901 orders, which was a nice increase from 1972.

The only one of the three LTD Brougham models to go down in sales was the 4-door Hardtop, Style 57K. This year sales reached only 22,268. With the basic 351 engine, this model sold for $4,103 and weighed 4,189 pounds. All big Fords this year had their front marker lights set very low on the front fenders, with heavy chrome surrounds. All LTD Brougham models were known primarily for the luxury interiors, which included color-coded deep-cut pile carpeting.

The LTD Brougham 4-door Pillared Hardtop continued to gain in popularity, and sales reached 49,553. Known as Style 53K, it utilized the high-back Flight Bench seats with center armrests, for which the series was known. The rear treatment was very similar to last year's, with LTD spelled out in block letters atop of the red applique between the taillights. Brougham signatures appeared only at the forward corners of the upper quarter panels. Priced at $4,113 and weighing 4,179 pounds, it was the most expensive of the Broughams.

Wearing its optional $110 vinyl top, this model represents the 4-door Hardtop in the plain LTD line. As it did on all vinyl-top Fords, the vinyl stopped short of the leading edge of the C-pillar, and left a kick-up section of body colored metal. On the sedan, this section was part of the door frame, but on the hardtops it was part of the top's rear quarter, and the door nested below. As unpopular here as it was in the Brougham series, the Style 57H drew only 28,608 orders, which was very low when compared with other LTD models. It sold for a basic $4,001 and weighed 4,160 pounds. All large Fords benefitted this year from slightly revised sheet metal, which gave a more rounded effect to almost all of the lines.

With the optional vinyl top and deluxe wheel covers, there was little exterior difference between the plain LTD 2-door and the Brougham variety. The major differences occurred inside, where the plain model used deep-cushion low-back bench seats rather than the high-back Flight Benches of the Brougham series. Priced at $3,950 and weighing 4,100 pounds even, Style 65H was a relatively popular car. It accounted for 120,864 orders, which put it in 7th place on Ford's overall sales charts. With the 351 V-8 as standard fare, all other larger Ford engines were available, right up to the 460 Thunderbird V-8 of 202 SAE horses, which cost an additional $222.

Ranking 6th in Ford's overall sales roster was the LTD 4-door Pillared Hardtop, Style 53H, which recorded 122,851 orders this year. This model, with its optional vinyl top, is showing off its new "Mercedes-style" grille, so-called because it bore somewhat of a resemblance to the face of the luxurious Mercedes Benz. Also very visible here are the huge bumpers that were mandated under the growing federal safety standards. The huge units were supposed to absorb a 5 MPH direct hit with no damage. Priced at $3,958, the pillared model weighed 4,150 pounds.

A mid-year issue was the LTD Station Wagon, which used all of the LTD features including the 400 cubic inch V-8, but did not have the imitation wood trim. First introduced at the Chicago Auto Show on Feb. 23, the wagon's acceptance is not known as all production figures were combined into those of the Country Squire. With a base price of $4,296, it was available, as was the Squire, in 6-passenger standard form, or with optional dual facing rear seats, which would give it 10-passenger capacity. It is not certain if on this model the roof rack was standard, or if it remained an added cost accessory.

Top selling of all LTD models, and ranking the 4th best selling Ford overall, was the attractive Country Squire. Its sales tallied 142,933. Called Style 71H, it continued to be trimmed with imitation wood applique, and used as its base the 400 cubic inch V-8 rather than the 351. In addition to the roof rack with rear wind deflector, this example carries the seldom seen vinyl roof package which added $148 to the cost. Other standard features included the doorgate with power window, and power disc brakes. Prices began at $4,401. It weighed 4,642 pounds.

Wearing an egg-crate grille of similar but different styling than that found on the LTD models was the new Galaxie 500 series. Still Ford's mid-level of large cars, these models sported their own brand of wheel covers, and normally came with a steel top, though the $110 vinyl roof was a popular accessory. Known as Style 65F, the 2-door Hardtop was priced at $3,778 and weighed 4,059 pounds. Second most popular of the Galaxies, it recorded 70,808 units. Interiors were nicely finished in bench seat styling, upholstered in a combination of cloth and vinyl.

As expected, the Galaxie 500 series also contained two 4-door models. They were the 4-door Hardtop, and this far more popular 4-door Pillared Hardtop. The true Hardtop, Style 57F, turned out to be the least popular Galaxie, with only 25,802 being produced. It cost $3,833 and weighed 4,120 pounds. The pillared model, shown here in absolutely stock form, enjoyed a run of 85,654, and thus was the most popular Galaxie 500. It had a base price of $3,771, and thus was also the lowest priced Galaxie. This view gives a good idea of the massiveness of the required high-impact bumpers. These were often referred to as "park bench" bumpers because they protruded so far out that they almost provided the same seating capacity as the average park bench.

The Country Sedan continued to be the mid-level wagon, and as such was in the mid-level Galaxie 500 series. Here it was slightly less trimmed than the Squire model, but still featured an all-vinyl interior with wood applique on the door panels and dash. All big wagons used a special sound deadening insulation, with the degree of soundproofing based on the car's trim level. Called Style 71F, this model featured full wheel covers and side molding of color-keyed vinyl. It weighed 4,581 pounds, and was priced at $4,164, which was not that far away from the mid-year de-wooded LTD Wagon. Possibly because of this, sales slipped to 51,290. This model has both the vinyl top and roof rack option.

Ford's lowest level full-size cars were now grouped into just one series known as the Custom 500. The plain Custom line of super-stripped models was now gone. Despite lack of trim, all Custom 500 cars came with the 351 V-8, Cruise-O-Matic transmission, and power steering as standard features. Only two models were offered, a 4-door Sedan based on the Pillared Hardtop body, and this Ranch Wagon. The Sedan, Style 53D, had a base price of $3,606 and weighed 4,078 pounds, and thus qualified as the lightest of all full-size Fords. It drew 42,549 orders. The Ranch Wagon, Style 71D, was priced at $4,050 and weighed 4,550 pounds. Least popular of all the wagons, it accounted for only 22,432 units. It is shown here with optional wheel covers, roof rack, and side molding.

Hot shots of the mid-size line were the Gran Torino Sport models, which came in two variations. They were available as the formal roof 2-door Hardtop, Style 65R, or as this SportsRoof model, Style 63R. All came only in V-8 power, with the 302 V-8 as a base, but all other engine options were available. Interiors were finished in pleated vinyl high-back bucket seats, while the exteriors had small "Sport" decals under the Gran Torino signatures, and were fitted with dual racing mirrors. Yet the Magnum 500 competition wheels shown here, or the often-seen full-length laser racing stripe were added cost options. Least popular of the two Sport models was the formal top version, which drew only 17,090 orders. The SportsRoof version, meanwhile, accounted for 51,853. Prices were the same, with each going for $3,154 in basic trim, but the formal model weighed 3,652 pounds, while the SportsRoof came in at 3,670.

Since the big Fords had their top line Brougham models, someone decided that the mid-size models should also be blessed with super-trim variations. Thus, the new Gran Torino Brougham series arrived on the scene this year. It consisted of two models, the Style 65K 2-door Hardtop Coupe, and this Style 53K 4-door Pillared Hardtop. Both were available with either the Six or the V-8, though undoubtedly the V-8s were the more popular. The 2-door model was priced at $3,160 while the 4-door came in at a slightly lower $3,140. Since these were basically trim options of the Gran Torino series, their production was not separated from that series' comparable models. Features included high-back Flight Bench seats, vinyl tops with special emblems, and special turbine-type wheel covers.

The last true Ford (not counting Lincolns) owned by the author was this Gran Torino Hardtop Coupe, Style 65D. It wore a $93 optional vinyl top and had the $44 Cleveland 351 option, along with the $211 Cruise-O-Matic transmission and $112 power steering. Bought in 1978 for second car duty, it was one of the author's lesser used vehicles, and never left the state of Florida. Base priced at $3,015, its actual new car sales figure was closer to the $4,000 mark. Best selling of all Torinos, it was also Ford's 5th most popular car overall, with sales of 138,962. It weighed 3,656 pounds.

The only 4-door model in the Gran Torino line was the 4-door Sedan, or Pillared Hardtop, Style 53D. Frontal treatment of the Gran Torinos this year was similar to 19782, but the grilles were double egg-crate design, with wide bright rectangles superimposed over an inner grille of finer mesh. The only Gran Torino with a base V-8 price under $3,000, the 4-door model came in at $2,984 and weighed 3,719 pounds. Relatively popular, it drew 98,404 orders.

The top-line mid-size wagon was the Gran Torino Squire, which essentially was the regular Gran Torino with imitation wood side trim. It also featured deluxe wheel covers and pleated vinyl upholstery on the seats, but the roof rack was extra. Production reached 40,023, all with a base price of $3,559 and a weight of 4,124 pounds. Torino wagons and 4-door sedans continued to use a 118-inch wheelbase, while the 2-door models utilized a 114-inch base. The wagons were 211.6 inches long overall, compared with the 4-doors, which were 207.3 inches.

The Gran Torino Station Wagon was a nice looking model, wearing all of the trim upgrades of the Gran Torino line. Here is a good comparison of the distinctive grilles on the Gran Torinos, foreground, and the plain Torino line in the background. Gran Torino wagons were only available in V-8 form, with the 302 cubic inch engine being the base. Power front disc brakes and 3-way doorgate were standard, but the luggage rack was a $77 accessory. Priced at $3,344 and weighing 4,124 pounds, the plain-sided wagon was the most popular, with 60,738 being sold.

Having a totally different grille and side trim than the Gran Torino models, the plain Torinos represented the lowest trim level in the mid-size line. Three models made up the series: Style 65B 2-door Hardtop Coupe, selling for $2,826 as a V-8; Style 53B 4-door Sedan, selling for $2,701 as a Six, and this Station Wagon, Style 71B, which was available only as a V-8 and sold for $3,198. The 4-door Sedan was the most popular of the bunch, drawing 37,5245 orders, while the 2-door accounted for 28,005. Least popular was the wagon, with production of 23,982. All used plain hub caps and were devoid of side trim. All Torino wagons offered 84 cubic feet of cargo space when the rear seat was folded.

Still making a bid to be the "poor man's Mustang," the Maverick Grabber continued its pretension of being a hot number. This year the Grabber offered a new paint and tape treatment and had the 5-MPH mandatory bumpers, but little else was new. Among the exclusives on this car were dual racing mirrors and raised white-letter wide oval tires. The cast mag wheels shown here were added cost items, as was the vinyl roof, but the blackout grille and headlight bezels were standard. Maverick's least popular model by a country mile, the Grabber only attracted 32,350 customers. Available with either a Six or the 302 V-8, it cost $2,541 with the V-8 and had a shipping weight of 2,855 pounds.

Far less sporty looking, but theoretically a better performer than the Grabber when equipped with comparable engines and gear ratios, was the Maverick 2-door Sedan, Style 62A. With the Arab oil embargo in full swing, the 6-cylinder versions of this little car drew renewed interest. As a result, a total of 148,943 2-door sedans were sold, making this not only the best selling Maverick, but also Ford's 3rd best selling car overall. With the new 200 cubic inch Six, the car cost $2,240 and weighed 2,642 pounds. The V-8 was $122 more, while Cruise-O-Matic added another $177.

Continuing in popularity was the little Maverick 4-door Sedan, Style 62B, shown here with the extra-cost vinyl top and deluxe wheel covers. Sales of this car shot up to 110,382, making it the 9th most popular car in the Ford listing. With the basic Six it sold for $2,297 and weighed 2,737 pounds. All Maverick 2-doors continued to use the 103-inch wheelbase chassis, while the sedans had a base of 109.9 inches. In addition, the 2-doors were 187 inches long, while the 4-door models stretched out to 194 inches.

Virtually unchanged except for the design of the front and rear bumpers, the little Pinto remained Ford's top selling line. In fact, all three of its models topped the 100,000 sales mark, and wound up on the top 10 of Ford's overall best seller list. Least popular of the entire range was the 2-door Sedan, which drew only 116,146 orders to be Ford's 8th best selling car. Priced at $1,997 with the basic 122 cubic inch engine, it was the only Ford automobile to come in under $2,000. With the British-sourced 98 cubic inch block gone, Pinto had no engine options this year.

Slipping from 1st to 2nd sales spot this year was the Pinto Runabout, Style 64B, which was also referred to as the 3-door Sedan or Hatchback. A total of 150,603 were sold, all base priced at $2,120 and weighing 2,162 pounds. The car is shown here with the $137 Luxury Decor Group, which included full wheel covers, chrome window edging, and deluxe interior. The rear quarter windows were of the flip-out type, with hinges at the leading edges.

Actually introduced as a mid-year item in 1972, but not gaining any popularity until this year was the Sports Accent Option for the Pinto two and 3-door models. Included in the package were a vinyl top, special side trim, and special paint schemes below the trim. The Runabout models, as shown here, retained the folding rear seat and gas-operated cylinders to raise and hold the rear hatch. The forged aluminum wheels on this car were not part of the sports package, but were a $154 option. No longer standard on this model was the tinted rear window. This was still available, but as an extra-cost option.

Surprisingly, Ford's overall best selling car this year was not a 2-door Sedan, but was the 2-door Station Wagon in the Pinto series. Called Style 73B, it drew a total of 217,763 orders. Priced at $2,319, it was the most expensive Pinto, and at 2,397 pounds, was also the heaviest. This model wears the Luxury Decor Group, which included the bright rocker panel moldings and bright window trim. The center windows continued to be the flip-out type, hinged at the leading edge, while the rear quarter windows were fixed in place.

Most expensive of all Pintos was the Station Wagon with the $241 Squire option package. This trim group included imitation wood paneling similar to that used on the Country Squire, and full wheel covers. The roof rack may or may not have been part of the package. A very large swing-up lift gate provided easy loading access, but probably resulted in a multitude of bumped heads. Another popular but costly addition to the base Pinto was the Cruise-O-Matic transmission, which added another $170. When the wagon's rear seat was folded, the interior cargo area was surprisingly spacious.

A show car that easily could have been put into production was the Pinto Sportiva. Built on the standard Pinto chassis with its 94-inch wheelbase, the car used the standard 122 cubic inch Four and conventional running gear. Of 2-passenger configuration, it used a rather impractical large fixed rear window. Removable top panels inserted between the frames provided coupe styling. The forged aluminum wheels were similar to what were being offered as a Pinto option. The car was developed and built at the Ford Design Center in Dearborn.

All full-size Ford wagons stored their spare tires in a covered well on the right rear quarter. However, removing this spare when in the hole could be a mean chore for a small person. This year Ford tried to solve the problem with this Spare Extractor, which fit under the tire, with its handles sticking upward. Theoretically, all one had to do was pull on the handles and the spare would rise from its well and tip over onto the floor, from where it could be easily removed. Sure!

Once again available on the Pinto sedans was the manually operated Sun Roof option, usually seen with the optional vinyl top. Among the other added cost items on this over-dressed (and probably over-priced) Pinto are the Sports Accent Option with the lower paint matching the roof vinyl, bright window frames, and an interior of cut-pile carpeting and seats upholstered in "super soft" vinyl with cloth insert panels.

New for this year and available only for large Ford wagons with the dual facing rear seat option was this removable game table. The folding, easily installed unit helped keep the kids busy on long trips, or at least it would provide them with a space to fight over. When not in use, the dual facing rear seats folded into a lower compartment, and provided a level cargo floor. As can be seen here, their padding was on the thin side, and though rated at four adult capacity, they were mighty uncomfortable for full-size people on a trip of any length.

Ford's big news this year again concerned one of its animal-named cars. This time it was the original animal, the Mustang, which came in for a complete change. No revisions were in order on this move. From bumper to bumper, the Mustang was a totally new horse, albeit a bit smaller than its parents, measuring a full 19 inches shorter than the 1973 version. In fact, since it was a totally new car, Ford decided to give it a new name, calling it the "Mustang II," and promoting it as "The right car at the right time."

Styling leaned heavily on designs from Ford's recent acquisition, the famed Italian coachbuilding and design firm of Ghia. In fact, one model even was called the Ghia Coupe. Coupled to the Italian firm's work was Ford's own engineering and design teams, necessary to translate artistic Italian designs into practical American products that could stand the heat of mass production.

Offered were two basic 2-door bodies, a fastback and a notch-back style, with each style having two distinct models created through deft use of trim and minor revisions. All cars were built on a new chassis of 96.2 inches wheelbase, which was 12.8 inches shorter than previous models. Overall length was only 175 inches, while the tread was 55.6 inches at the front and 55.8 inches at the rear.

Power was by three new engines, two of which were kept exclusively for Mustang use this year. The basic plant was a 140 cubic inch Four, which developed 85 horsepower. With a bore and stroke of 3.78x3.13 inches, it used a compression of 8.3:1. This engine quickly found popularity in the Pinto line as well as the base Mustang.

The big power news, however, were two versions of Ford's first V-6, which were for Mustang use only. The new basic block had a bore and stroke of 3.66x2.7 inches, displacing 169 cubic inches. With a 2-barrel carburetor and a compression ratio of 8.0:1, it developed 105 SAE horsepower. A variation of this engine, sometimes considered a separate model in itself, was the 2.8-liter V-6, which displaced 171 cubic inches, using the same bore and stroke of the basic engine. Having a SAE horsepower rating of 105, the 2.8-liter block was standard in the Mach 1 models, and cost $299 above the basic V-6 in all other models.

Available styles were the basic 2-door Hardtop Coupe, the basic 3-door Fastback or Hatchback Coupe, the luxury trimmed Ghia Coupe, and the performance oriented Mach 1 Fastback. Often seen were Rallye models, but the Rallye option was a trim package, not a separate model. It was available for $328 on the basic coupe, $284 on the hatchback (also referred to as the 2+2) and $150 extra on the Mach 1. However, it could not be installed on the Ghia models.

Did all of this new design work help the sagging Mustang sales? You bet it did! For the first time since 1969, a single Mustang model exceeded the 100,000 mark. This occurred when the basic coupe sold 177,671 copies, which was 42,854 more than the total Mustang sales for 1973. When sales of the other three models were included, Mustang wrapped up a picture of 385,993, which is a big herd of horses.

Obviously, Mustang grabbed all of the headlines this year, which was a good thing, as the rest of the Ford line had very little new to brag about. In the big cars, only minor revisions of the front and rear ends spelled the difference between the 1973 and 1974 issue. New parking lamps, revised grille and headlight surrounds, and a smoother bending of the front bumper with the rest of the car were the main claims of the front end, while new wheel covers and a revised side trim graced the side view. Unknown at this time was the fact that the Galaxie 500 line was in its last years. Its models would continue, but under the LTD banner.

In the Torino line, a grille with a smaller egg-crate design combined with a new front bumper to give the

ion: Medium Ivy Yellow (Code 6N) tfully paired with a Gold Odense roof

* See Color Code reference on inside back cover.

Showing very little change overall was the Thunderbird, Style 65K. The major movement in this model was under the hood, where the 429 V-8 was no longer available. This left the car with only the 460 cubic inch mill of 220 horsepower, and no engine options. The car was subject to a severe price increase of almost $1,650, with its base price now being $7,221, as opposed to the $5,577 base of 1973. Probably this had a good bit to do with its production, which slumped substantially, with only 58,443 Birds leaving the nest. All weighed about 4,825 pounds, untrimmed.

Showing off its Sunroof option, now priced at $525, is this decked out Thunderbird. New for the year, but not pictured here, was a powered operated Moonroof at $800. Thunderbird's most expensive option, the Moonroof was basically the same concept of glass roofed 1955/56 Skyliners, only now fitted with an electrically operated inner liner. Also seen on some Birds was another pricey option, the $411 Burgundy Luxury Group package. Not only did this year's Birds go up substantially in price, the list of options also included some mighty expensive toys.

car a 1974 appearance. The big news here was a new model called the Gran Torino Elite, an option-loaded 2-door Hardtop Coupe with a new opera window treatment in the C-pillar. Introduced at mid-year, this model also featured a different grille variation, full-length side molding with vinyl inserts, and special headlights and parking lights and surrounds.

The other major Torino news concerned the demise of all 6-cylinder power for this line. Now the smallest Torino engine was the 302 V-8, with the 351, 400, and 460 blocks being available as options. Similarly, the smallest engine available in the large Ford lines was the 351 Windsor or Cleveland.

In the little car world, both the Pinto and Maverick received their total energy-absorbing bumpers this year, as opposed to the reinforced bumpers that had been installed last year. The new bumpers mandated minor revisions to the front ends of both cars, but aside from this, absolutely no changes were made to either line. Right now, Ford had a list of absolute winners with these two cars, and was not about to change its luck.

Also not changing its luck, but slipping substantially in sales was the Thunderbird. Going into its third year with virtually no change, the car slipped from 87,259 sales in 1973 to only 58,443 this year. Possibly hurting more than helping in this line was the demise of the 429 cubic inch block. With their long-time "standard" blocks gone, the only engine available to the line was the Thunderbird 460, rated at 220 horsepower in its namesake cars, but only 215 when installed as an option in full-size or Torino models. With gas prices rising and shortages looming, the public was getting a bit leery of the big-engine cars.

In that respect, Ford's attention in the engine room concerned the aforementioned new V-6 in the Mustangs and the new Four in both the Pinto and Mustang II lines. With the 429 blocks gone, some horsepower increases were made in the other lines. Here, both the Cleveland and the Windsor 351 blocks received slight

boosts in power, with the Cleveland now being rated at 162 SAE, while the Windsor was listed at 163 SAE horsepower. Conversely, the old 351 Cobra Jet was now simply termed the 351 Cleveland 4-barrel, and had its rating drop to 255 horses. Finally, the Cleveland 400 was now simply called the "400" although its power was raised to 170 at 3400 rpm.

Hurting all engine performance even more this year were the federally mandated emission controls. These anti-pollution devices still hadn't reached the level of proficiency found today, and combined with the still relatively heavy weights of the cars, caused truly terrible performance when compared to the cars of only a few years previous. Also, the car's sizes still hadn't begun their drastic reductions. For example, the Pinto was a midget of a vehicle in 1974, but looks pretty big when parked next to many of today's mid-size models.

On the production side, the major surprise was that absolutely no full-size or Torino models passed the 100,000 sales mark this year. Production was down only slightly, dropping by 169,576 to 2,179,791 for the model year. However, though the numbers weren't shockingly low, the fact was that the little cars were the ones that were selling, while the big ones had to search for buyers.

As a result, only six models topped 100,000 in sales. The leader was once again the Pinto Station Wagon, with 237,394 sales. Number two was the aforementioned Mustang Coupe, with a tally of 177,671, while 3rd place was another Pinto, the 3-door Hatchback which registered 174,754 sales. The 4th and 5th place spots were occupied by Mavericks, with the 2-door Sedan coming in 4th with 139,818, and the 4-door Sedan placing 5th with 137,728. Last on the exclusive sales list was the Pinto 2-door Sedan with 132,061 sales.

In the big car lines, the brand new Gran Torino Elite was the only model to come close to the 100,000 mark. It sold a total of 96,604 copies, which was not too bad for a mid-year introduction.

Hot horse of the totally new Mustang herd was the Mach I, which used the Hatchback or Fastback body as its base. Fitted with the new 2.8-liter V-6 engine, the car came complete with dual exhaust; competition styled steel wheels with bright beauty rims; blackout rocker panel and rear panel finish, and special Mach I lettering. The interior used the 2+2 style seating, with a fold-down rear seat. Priced at $3,621, it was the most expensive Mustang, while its sales of 44,046 made it the lowest production style. Designated Style 69R, it weighed 2,778 pounds.

Since the new Mustang II models were styled by Ford's affiliated Italian design and coachbuilding firm of Ghia, it seemed fitting that the most luxurious of the new breed be called the Ghia Coupe. Based on the notch-back body, Style 60H was fitted for luxury, not sportiness. Refinements included a super sound-proofed body, shag carpeting, an upholstery choice of super-soft pleated vinyl or Westminster cloth, and wood-grain dash and door appliques. Among the standard exterior items were remote controlled color-keyed exterior door mirrors, a color-keyed vinyl top, and special wheel covers. Priced at $3,427, the 2,866-pound car drew a total of 89,477 orders.

Showing off its new rear styling is the Style 69F Mustang II. It was known under the names Fastback Coupe; Hatchback Coupe, or 2+2 Coupe. The car appears here with a set of competition mag wheels that probably would have looked more at home on the Mach I, which used the same body. Available with either the new 140 cubic inch Four or the 169 cubic inch V-6, the car could also be equipped with the new 2.8-liter V-6 for an extra $230. In base trim it cost $3,275 and weighed 2,699 pounds. Not as popular as either of the notch-back styles, the Fastback drew 74,799 orders in its basic form.

Most popular of all the new Mustang II models was the Hardtop Coupe, Style 60F, which saw an amazing total of 177,671 enter the highways. This was the highest run of Mustangs recorded since the comparable model came out in 1968. Priced at $3,081 and weighing 2,620 pounds, the new and much smaller Mustang II benefitted from the on-going Arab oil embargo and the resultant gas crunch and price escalation. A full 13 inches shorter than the previous models, the cars seemed to cater to the same audience that was making both the Maverick and Pinto such a success, and hence emphasis was more on economy and economical luxury than it was on performance.

Still the flagships of the large Ford line, the LTD Broughams continued to be offered in 2-door Hardtop form, Style 65K, and as two variations of 4-doors. Again the most popular of the Brougham line, the 2-door Hardtop still suffered an agonizing decline in orders, with sales dropping almost 30,000 to rest at 39,084. Part of this may have been due to a $500 increase in price, with the new base being $4,598, and part might have been to an overall disinterest in large cars this year by the general public. High-back Flight-Bench seats with central arm rests were still a hallmark of the LTD Brougham line, as was a standard color-keyed vinyl roof and special Brougham signatures.

Sliding way down in popularity was the LTD Brougham 4-door Hardtop Sedan, Style 57K. This year's sales ended at 11,371, which was barely half that of 1973. As a result, the model would be dropped at the end of this season. Most expensive of the three Brougham styles, the car sold for $4,646 and weighed 4,310 pounds. Interiors continued to feature cut-pile carpeting on floors and lower door panels and wood-grain appliques on the dash and upper door panels. Full deluxe wheel covers were standard, as was the vinyl top. The 351 cubic inch V-8 was standard, but the 400 and 460 cubic inch V-8s could be ordered for $95 and $305 respectively.

Almost three times as popular as the 4-door Hardtop was the LTD Brougham 4-door Pillared Hardtop, or Sedan, as both names were used. Production reached 30,203, all with a base price of $4,576. As before, except for the medallions on the rear quarter panels, there was little to differentiate the exterior of the Brougham line from the plain LTD models. On all Broughams, the sound deadening insulation was supposedly on par with or better than any other car on the road, as Ford continued to pride itself on its totally quiet ride.

Appearing for the last time was the LTD 4-door Hardtop Sedan, Style 57H. Faring no better in the plain series than in Brougham trim, the car accounted for only 12,375 sales. It was base priced at $4,166, but this did not include the $115 vinyl top shown here. Also in the plain LTD line was the 2-door Hardtop, which turned out to be the best seller of the lot, with 73,296 being turned out. It too was the victim of a hefty price increase, with its base going up $365 to a new high of $4,318. Both hardtops were in the 4,250-pound range.

Showing off its new parking lamps and slightly revised grille is the popular LTD 4-door Sedan, or Pillared Hardtop. A modified design of the impact-absorbing bumper gave a better overall look to the front. The parking lights still resided in an extension of the full-length bright rocker trim, which was also continued on the rear fenders as a type of stone shield. As did other LTD models, the Style 53H Sedan also had a $350 price increase, now being based at $4,299. These across the board price increases meant that except for a Custom 4-door, there was no large Ford on the lot with a base price under $4,000.

Suffering an almost unbelievable drop in sales of almost 80,000 units was the attractive Country Squire, Style 71H. Still Ford's most expensive full-size car, this year its production dropped from the record 142,933 of last year to a miserable (for this model) 64,047. Part of the buyer resistance might have been due to the $425 price increase, with the base tag now being $4,827. Also, probably hurting sales was the fact that the smallest engine available in this car was the relatively gas hungry 400 cubic inch V-8, with the 460 V-8 being the only other option. With gas supplies low and prices high, a strong public awareness of fuel economy was sweeping the nation. Certainly the sales resistance was not due to the looks of the car, which was as finely styled as anything on the road. This view gives a good look at the division between the three parts of the exclusive LTD grilles.

Essentially a Country Squire minus the wood trim, the LTD wagon entered its first full year of production. Introduced as a mid-year 1973 model, the wood-less luxury wagon apparently found enough favor for Ford to continue the model. Priced about $125 less than the Squire, the LTD Wagon utilized the unique grille of that series, plus the deluxe interior of the Squire. It is shown here with a color-keyed vinyl roof, which still was a $148 option. However, the 400 cubic inch engine was standard on this model, as it was on the Country Squire. As before, production figures of this model were combined with the Country Squire.

Essentially, the full-size Ford line had two middle grounds, the LTD series representing the upper level and the Galaxie 500 series representing the lower mid-level. This is the Galaxie 500 2-door, which in basic form cost $4,140 and weighed 4,690 pounds. As with the LTD models, sales were down here too, and this Style 65F recorded only 34,214 units, which was about half of the 1973 production. The car is shown here in virtual basic trim, with a steel roof with the Galaxie signature on the upper rear quarter. Galaxie models used a rear design quite similar to the LTD models, except that the escutcheon plate was fitted with a grid-like covering that matched the grille texture.

Not only would the 4-door Hardtop, Style 57F, disappear at the end of this model run, but the entire Galaxie 500 series was now facing its final year. Having descended from Ford's top of the line cars to its lower mid-level range over the years, the proud name was to be retired permanently at the close of the 1974 season. But, with only 11,526 sales to its credit this year, the 4-door Hardtop was not going to make much difference in Ford's overall production line. Priced at $4,166, this model weighed 4,212 pounds. What appears to be B-pillars in this model are the new seat belts, suspended from the upper door sills. Although the Galaxie 500 models were well insulated, a sound package was available which provided additional fiberglass lining under the hood, on the firewall, under the roof, under the floor carpets, and in the trunk.

Ford's mid-level wagon continued to be the Country Sedan, which essentially was fitted with Galaxie 500 interior trim, and used the Galaxie grille. This frontal unit differed slightly from that of the LTD, primarily in the fact that its egg-crate texture was divided by three heavy horizontal bars, and there was no vertical body-color divider between the center and outer sections. Designated Style 71F, the Country Sedan saw sales top off at a relatively poor 22,400, again less than half of the 1973 figure. Its price of $4,513 and weight of 4,690 was based on the 351 cubic inch V-8. Standard on this model was the special sound insulation package, full loop-pile nylon carpeting, and exclusive all-vinyl seats. The dash had wood-grain applique.

Most popular of all Galaxie 500 models was the 4-door Pillared Hardtop, Style 53F. It drew a total of 49.661 orders with its base price of $4,093, which was a $322 increase over last year. Adding to the cost of this model is the $115 vinyl roof. Inside, such accessories as $426 standard air conditioning; $243 AM/FM radio, and $240 power windows and seats could run the price up substantially. For those who really wanted to spend the bucks, there was also the Brougham Luxury interior package at $380; AM/FM stereo with a tape player for $378, and the 460 V-8 of 215 horsepower for $304. All Galaxie 500 models used the 351 V-8 as base power, but had the 400 and 460 engines available as options.

Certainly not Ford's most popular nor most photo-graphed series, the Custom 500 line remained home to the lowest priced full-size cars. In fact, this was the only illustration that could be found of this year's Custom 500 range. The 2-model line consisted of this 4-door Pillared Hardtop, Style 53D, and the Ranch Wagon, Style 71D. At $3,911, the sedan represented the only full-size Ford to be base priced at under $4,000. It drew a total of 128,941 orders. The Ranch Wagon, meanwhile, was priced at $4,417 and sold 12,104 copies. Despite their low trim level, the Custom 500 models still used the Galaxie 500 grille, and were powered by the 351 V-8 with Cruise-O-Matic as standard. Why Ford chose to keep this line in stock while retiring the Galaxie 500 name is unknown.

Chevrolet's super-popular Monte Carlo models sold a grand total exceeding 300,000 in 1973. And don't think Ford didn't take notice of this, especially since it had no models that could compete head-on with the high-flying Chevy. Finally, at mid-1974, a new Gran Torino Elite was released in hopes of out Monteing the Carlo. Though it did not succeed in overriding Chevrolet's figures, the car did manage to gain 96,604 orders in its short market year. Priced at $4,374, the Style 65M Elite included a vinyl roof with twin opera windows, its own exclusive front end with special grille and single headlights in square chrome bezels, special side trim, and deep dished chrome disc wheels. Its engine was the 351 Cleveland V-8 with 2-barrel, with Cruise-O-Matic, power steering, and power front disc brakes all being standard. The Elite was promoted as a "personal luxury car" or "poor man's Thunderbird" and was not considered a sport model.

Until the appearance of the Elite, the top luxury models in the mid-size range were the Gran Torino Broughams. Available in both two and 4-door Hardtop styles, they were designated 4-door Style 53K and this 2-door, Style 65K. Neither car was particularly popular, and the 2-door drew only 26,402 orders with its $3,912 price tag, while the 4-door sold only 11,464 at $3,903. Standard equipment in the Brougham series included padded vinyl tops, vinyl and cloth upholstery, and special trim molding. However, the opera window shown in the rear roof panel was an extra-cost factory-order option that usually was included in the package. Also available on all Torino 2-door models was a Sunroof for an additional $490.

Totally different grilles still differentiated the Gran Torino series shown here from the lower-level base Torino. Most popular of all Torinos until the Elite came along, the Gran Torino class held two models. They were this 4-door Pillared Hardtop, Style 53D, which sold for $3,391, and the 2-door Hardtop, Style 65D, which sold for $3,485. The 2-door was the more popular of the two by a narrow margin, drawing 76,290 orders as opposed to the sedan's 72,728. Both the deluxe wheel covers and the vinyl top on this model were at added cost. Power steering added another $117, while power disc brakes were $71 extra.

GRAN TORINO SPORT:
2-Door Hardtop. Bright Red (Code 2B).

Representing the sporty side of the field was the Gran Torino Sport, which utilized the 2-door Hardtop body, but had its own exclusive grille and hood with functional air scoop, was fitted with color-keyed dual racing mirrors, deluxe wheel covers, and had a special all-vinyl interior. Still the vinyl roof shown here was a $96 option, and the 302 cubic inch V-8 was considered standard, with the Cleveland 351 and other hot engines being at optional extra cost.

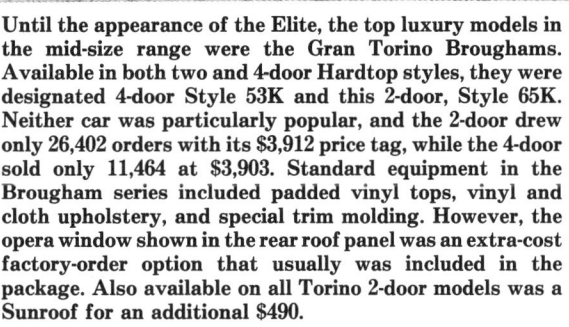

The Gran Torino Station Wagon, Style 71D, utilized that series' bright rocker panel molding with rear stone guard extension, and had bright wheel cutout trim. However, side trim was part of a luxury decor package. Power front disc brakes were standard on this model, as was the 3-way doorgate. However, a power tailgate window was an extra $35, while a rear-facing third seat was $67. In basic trim, as shown here with plain hubcaps, the wagon cost $3,954 and weighed 4,209 pounds. Most popular of all the mid-size wagons, the Gran Torino model drew 29,866 orders.

A totally different grille and frontal appearance differentiated the low-level plain Torino series from the more upscale Gran Torino models. The series contained three styles, with the most popular being the 4-door Pillared Hardtop, Style 53B, shown here. Base priced at $3,176, it drew 31,161 orders. Also available was a 2-door Hardtop, Style 65B, which cost $3,310 and drew 22,738 customers, and the plain Station Wagon, Style 71B, which sold 15,393 copies at $3,755 base price. The interiors featured all-vinyl upholstery and high-back bench seats, but used vinyl floor mats rather than carpeting. New to this series was the basic 302 V-8, which formerly had been an option, but now was considered standard power, as 6-cylinder engines were no longer available in the overall Torino line.

Until the Elite came along, the only Torino to have a base price over $4,000 was the Gran Torino Squire, Style 71K, which listed at $4,237. Not as popular as the plain Gran Torino wagon, it drew 22,837 orders. The wood-grain applique was similar to that used on the Country Squire, and was of a semi-transparent type, which allowed a hint of the body color to show through in strong sunlight. Deluxe wheel covers were part of the package, but the roof rack shown here was an extra $80. The interior was in soft pleated vinyl of a trim level similar to the Torino Brougham or Sport series. Despite the fact that most Torino models were fitted with the Cruise-O-Matic transmission, this was still considered a $219 option.

The only small Ford not to break into the 100,000-plus sales figure was the Maverick Grabber, Style 62D, still described as a "poor man's Mustang." Sales only reached 23,502, with a base price of $2,923 for the Six. When fitted with the 302 cubic inch V-8, it was the only small Ford to break the $3,000 mark, here having a base price of $3,081. With the small Six it weighed 2,787 pounds, while the V-8 added 163 pounds to the total. Blackout lower body sides and rear panel, and exclusive side tape were standard, but the vinyl top shown here was an $83 option.

Most popular of all Mavericks and 4th most popular Ford overall was the 2-door Sedan, Style 62A, which drew 139,818 customers. Shown here in total stock form, with no visible trimming except for the white walls, it would have been priced at $2,742 with the 200 cubic inch Six, $2,784 with the 250 cubic inch Six, or $2,902 with the V-8. A Cruise-O-Matic transmission would have added another $212 to the price, while power steering was $106. Relatively spacious for its size, the trunk offered 11.3 cubic feet of usable luggage space.

Ford's 5th most popular was the Maverick 4-door Sedan, Style 54A, which saw its orders go up to 137,728. In basic form, with the V-8, it cost $2,982. At 3,014 pounds with the V-8, it was the only Maverick to exceed 3,000 pounds base weight. All gussied up for its picture, this model wears the $332 Luxury Decor package; $33 white sidewall tires; $83 vinyl top, and $61 AM radio. If dollars were not a consideration, it might even have the $383 air conditioner. Oddly, this year a catalytic converter was mandatory on the 200 cubic inch Six, but was not necessary with either of the two larger engines.

Least popular of the 3-model Pinto family, but still selling enough to rank 6th spot on Ford's sales roster was the little 2-door Sedan, Style 62B. It drew 132,061 orders. Fitted with the basic 122 cubic inch Four, it cost $2,527 and weighed 2,372 pounds. With the optional 90 horse engine of 139 cubic inches, it was $52 more. The vinyl top on this model would have been an additional $83, while the wheel covers were $23 and the white sidewalls were a $44 trade. The car registered 169 inches in overall length, and was 50.3 inches high. The standard transmission was a manual 4-speed, but Cruise-O-Matic was available for $212 extra.

Wearing the $137 Luxury Decor package is this Pinto 3-door Hatchback or Runabout. Similar in styling to the 2-door Sedan, the car featured a larger rear panel and a folding rear seat which would provide substantially more luggage or package room. Priced at $2,631, Style 64B drew a total of 174,754 orders, and thus was the 3rd best selling car on Ford's total roster. Shown here is the new federally mandated front bumper which supposedly could absorb a 5 MPH head on crash with no damage. On the base Pintos this bumper was in plain chrome, but when the Luxury package was purchased, rubber horizontal strips and vertical guards were added.

Ford's best selling car of the year was the Pinto Station Wagon, which registered 237,394 sales. It is shown here with the optional Squire package, which cost $241 extra. However, the Squire trim was simply considered an option in the Pinto line, whereas it was a full model in all other lines. In base form, with plain sides, the wagon sold for $2,771 and weighed 2,576 pounds. As before, three different types of windows were used. The door windows rolled down, the center ones flipped out from forward hinges, and the rear quarter ones were fixed in place. Among the highest priced options on this year's Pintos were air conditioning at $383, and an AM/FM stereo radio at $222.

Definitely not a Ford product was the Pinto Electric Runabout, produced this year by Lyman Electric Products of Norwalk, Conn. The car was based on the standard Pinto Runabout, minus engine and transmission. In place of the running gear was a 20 horsepower 96-volt DC electric motor operating from a bank of batteries stored under the hood. Not a cheap vehicle, the total package as shown cost $10,000, which was a far cry from the price of the Pinto, which without engine or transmission probably was well under $2,000. Also available from Lyman was a conversion kit at $2,750, for those who wanted to set up an existing Pinto for electric operation; electronic controls for the package at another $750, and the electric motor itself for $1,800. Probably the Arab oil embargo had much to do with this company's dreams of success, while the returned availability of plentiful gas supplies put a severe crimp in the sales potential.

After building a veritable farm containing Pintos, Mavericks, Mustangs, and even Thunderbirds and Falcons, Ford this year came out with a brand new car that didn't bear the name of some sort of animal. Instead, the new vehicle carried the title of Granada, named no doubt for the famous city in southeastern Spain.

Initially planned to replace the Maverick, the new Granada carried styling more akin to the large Fords than to the sleeker Mavericks or Pintos. The car used the same chassis as did the 4-door Maverick, with a 109.9-inch wheelbase, but its styling gave it an overall length of 198 inches in the plain models and 200 inches in the higher-trimmed Ghia series. This was opposed to Maverick's overall length of 194 inches. The total new body was also wider than the Maverick, being 74 inches as opposed to 71 inches.

Two basic bodies were offered, a 2-door and a 4-door sedan. These were split into Granada and Ghia sub-series, giving a total of four model options. Basic styling was referred to as "European" in concept (Mercedes), but the car bore an unmistakable Ford look, which certainly must have helped to enhance its sales. The 200 cubic inch Maverick Six was the basic power in the plain models, while the Ghia versions received the 250 cubic inch Six. In addition, either the 302 V-8 or the 351 Windsor V-8 could be ordered as an option. Reception to the car was very good, but probably at the expense of Ford's other three small car lines, which all were down this year. Still, in a relatively poor sales year, the two basic Granada models were two of the only three models overall to reach over 100,000 sales.

In the big car line, the Galaxie 500 was now gone for good, and the Custom 500 was in its final year as a model for the general public. It would still be around next year, but supposedly for fleet sales only. Not only were the Galaxies dropped, but Ford made another important change, as this year it dropped all hardtop models. The 4-door and 2-door hardtops were now in the class with the convertible—available on used car lots only. All 4-door models were now of the pillared (sedan) variety, while all 2-door styling carried a B-pillar and opera windows in the C-pillar or sail panel.

Left in the full-size line were three basic models spread over four series, with the Custom 500 being the basic trim level, while the new LTD Landau series offered top-luxury two and 4-door models. Essentially, the old Galaxie 500 series now became the LTD, with the LTD trim level dropping slightly from 1975. Also in this series was the Country Sedan, which had been the plain-sided Galaxie 500 wagon. Replacing the former LTD series in trim level was the downgraded LTD Brougham series, which now provided a home to the imitation wood-trimmed Country Squire wagon, formerly in the LTD series.

With the exception of the name and series switching, little was changed in the large Ford line. Most different was the new LTD Landau styling, which enjoyed a return to hidden headlights, and used a distinctive front end design. The car also was the only one fitted with Ford's redesigned high-back "Flight Bench" seats with center arm rests and automatic seat back releases on the 2-door models.

Similar to what happened with the large Fords, in the Torino line more model switching occurred, while virtually no physical changes were made on the cars. The three basic trim groups were still the Torino, Gran Torino, and Torino Brougham, with the new Elite sub-series and the Torino Sport being one-model sub-series.

The Thunderbird also went through a virtual no-change program, befitting of its role as Ford's top luxury car (exclusive of Lincoln/Mercury). Its main claim this year were two optional decor packages. These were the Silver or the Copper Luxury Groups, which included special color-keyed wheel covers, special seats of leather or velour, a heavy-grained half-roof or silver or copper vinyl, and a special deluxe trunk lining and spare tire cover. As always, all power units except power seats were standard, as was the 460 cubic inch Thunderbird engine.

As could be expected, the year old Mustang II went through virtually no exterior changes, though new options and models were added. Still consisting of two basic body styles, the Mustang II line now contained the plain Coupe, the 3-door Hatchback or Fastback Coupe, and the Ghia Coupe. New in name only was the Mach I, now considered a separate sub-series of its own. In the option department, there was a Moonroof for the body and a V-8 for the engine room. The latter was the 302 cubic inch block, but rated at 122 horsepower rather than the 129 that was listed for the rest of the Ford line. In addition to the Rallye Package, a top luxury option called the Ghia Silver Luxury Group was available on

Once again up in price over $500, the new Thunderbird continued to be Ford's top model for sheer elegance. Now base priced at $7,701, the 4,893-pound car was once more down in sales, with only 42,685 leaving the nest. All power except front seats was provided, including the new anti-locking power disc brakes on all four wheels. A power Moonroof was still available for $800, and two new option packages were added to the list. They were the Silver Luxury group, or the Copper Luxury group shown here. Both consisted of the named color theme being carried throughout the car. In the case of the copper unit, this meant Copper Starfire paint; fully padded copper-colored vinyl half roof; color-keyed side molding and full wheel covers; special pin striping, and a choice of copper velour or leather seating and matching carpeting and trunk upholstery.

special order. This $150 option included exclusive silver metallic paint, a silver vinyl roof in Normandie grain, special cranberry color velour interior, center console, and special side trim.

Going the other direction on the Mustang II were two mid-year models. One was a down-trimming of the Ghia Coupe, with resulting lower prices, while the other was known as the Mustang II MPG model. This was a stripped version of the basic coupe, fitted with the 140 cubic inch Four, a Mustang exclusive using a bore and stroke of 3.78x3.12 inches, as opposed to the Pinto Four of 144 cubic inches with its bore and stroke of 3.78x3.13 inches. Keyed to the national interest in fuel shortages and prices, the Mustang II MPG promised 26 to 28 miles per gallon on the highway.

Also living directly on the fuel concerns were the Maverick and the Pinto, both of which were virtually unchanged this year. For the Maverick especially, the fuel crunch meant a new lease on life, as this line had been scheduled for dismissal this year as the new Granada came into being. Instead, Ford wisely decided to continue the popular car as part of its "little car" fleet. The basic Maverick engine continued to be the 200 cubic inch Six, while the 250 cubic inch Six or the 302 V-8 were options. The base Pinto engine was the 144 cubic inch Four, while the 2.8-litre Mustang V-6 was the only engine option. Late in the year, an ultra-stripped Pinto Pony appeared as a super-economy car both in price and fuel savings.

In other engine news, Ford this year offered nine blocks for its main lines, plus two exclusive Mustang mills. Of the latter, the smallest was the basic 140 cubic inch Four of 83 horses, while the other was a revised version of the 302 V-8, now called a 5-litre. The former 2.8-litre V-6 was rated at 97 horsepower as opposed to the old rating of 85 horses. Also enjoying a slight horsepower boost was the little Pinto Four, now rated at 83 SAE horses. Going the other direction were the 351

Cleveland of 162 horses, which was now called the 351 Modified and rated at 148 HP; the 400 cubic inch block previously with 170 horses, now rated at 158, and the Thunderbird 460, formerly a 220 horse engine in the Bird or 215 HP unit when installed in the large Fords, which now was changed to a constant 218 horses regardless of what vehicle gave it a home.

Gone were the little Pinto block of 122 cubic inches, which had turned out a surprising 86 horsepower, and the 4-barrel version of the Cleveland 351, which had been rated as a 255 horsepower unit. Part of the reason for the demise of the latter engine were the increasingly stringent pollution controls, plus the mandate that all engines be required to run on unleaded gas.

This year, for the first time, the majority of models came with catalytic converters on the exhaust systems, an installation heartily disliked by many car owners. Still, the catalytic units provided many an independent muffler shop with an unexpected income, as scores of new car and truck buyers hastened to their local pipe shops to have the unwanted converters removed. It would still be several years before the removal of these converters would void the vehicle's warranty.

This year was not a good one for Ford overall, as sales for the model year fell to only 1,569,607, a reduction of 610,184 from the 1974 figure. The drop appeared across the board, with no lines except the new Granada showing the strength of the previous season. So low were the figures, that only three models achieved sales of over 100,000. And, of this list, two of the cars were Granadas. The best seller of the year turned out to be the relatively new Torino Elite, a luxury-type coupe aimed at the Chevrolet Monte Carlo. The Elite drew 123,372 orders. The other two were the base Granada 4-door Sedan with 118,168 sales, and the base Granada 2-door Sedan with 100,810 orders. Even last year's winning Pinto Station Wagon, with almost a quarter-million sales, this year did not even make the list, but came in at 90,763.

Most popular of the Mustang II models was the 2-door Coupe, which this year accounted for 85,155 sales. With the basic Four it sold for $3,529 and thus was the lowest priced of all the little horses. With the V-6 it was $272 higher while the 302 V-8 would add $470 to the base price. Later in the year this model served as a base for the Mustang II MPG, a super-stripped model with only the basic Four under the hood and the 4-speed manual transmission. The car is shown here in its basic form, with hubcaps and total lack of extra trim items.

Now considered its own one-model sub-series was the Mustang II Mach I. Available only with the 2.8-litre V-6 or the optional 5-litre V-8 (302 V-8), the car was equipped with a manual 4-speed. Priced at $4,188 with the V-6, it weighed 2,879 pounds. Least popular of all Mustang II models, its production reached only 21,062. The cast mag wheels shown here were from the option book. In regular trim, the Mach I wore very attractive styled steel wheels with wide beauty rims, and came with raised white letter steel-belted tires. The lower body blackout paint was standard, as were the dual color-keyed remote racing mirrors.

Using the same basic body as the regular coupe was the Mustang II Ghia Coupe. Only this model sported its luxury with a flair. Among its standard items were the vinyl half roof colored-keyed to the interior; special semi-spoke wheel covers; special color-keyed side molding; a choice of Westminster cloth or super-soft vinyl; shag carpeting, and the Super Sound package. Priced at $4,210 with the V-6, it was the most expensive of the Mustang II line. Not a bad performer in the sales race, it drew 52,320 orders, which was a far cry from 1974, but not bad considering the poor sales year.

Taking a lead from Thunderbird, the Mustang II line also came up with a special luxury package. Priced at only $151 above the base Ghia Coupe, the package was known as the Silver Ghia Luxury Group. It included metallic silver paint; silver Normande-grain padded half-roof; matching special side molding, and an all-cranberry interior with the seats in Media crushed velour and the remainder in matching vinyl, including the central console. Also promoted for this model was the $422 manual Moonroof, Mustang's most expensive accessory.

Wearing its Swedish license plates is this Mustang II Fastback. Also known by the names 2+2 Coupe or Hatchback Coupe. The car provided the base for the Mach I, but in plain form could be ordered with either the Four or the V-6. As a V-6, it sold for $4,090 and weighed 2,812 pounds. A total of 30,038 were built. Standard equipment on this model included the styled steel wheels with beauty rings and a fold-down back seat, with the rear of the seat back providing a cargo floor for increased luggage space. The rear quarter windows were normally fixed in place, but flip-out units could be ordered for an extra $31. The mud flaps were a Ford accessory, but the back-up lights below the bumper were not.

New for the year was the LTD Landau series, which became the top line of full-size Fords, and put the Brougham series down one space. The 2-model series consisted of a 2-door Coupe and this 4-door Sedan, Style 53L. The Coupe, Style 60L, cost $5,401, and was the most expensive of all Fords, except the Thunderbird. It drew 26,919 orders. Less expensive but more popular was the Sedan, which cost $5,370 and drew 32,506 orders. Both models weighed about 4,450 pounds. All Landau models used high-back Flight-Bench seats with center arm rests; full cut-pile carpeting including carpeted lower door panels; vinyl tops, full wheel covers; and bright rocker moldings with rear fender extensions.

Showing off its new opera window top is the LTD Brougham Coupe, Style 60K. This top was used on all LTD 2-door models this year, as the former hardtop styling was no longer available. This car sports the vinyl top, which was no longer standard in the Brougham series, but now was a $115 option. Rated as a 6-passenger car, the Brougham series used low-back bench seats of a combination cloth and vinyl upholstery, and full carpeting. Full wheel covers were also standard, but the bright rocker molding shown here was an extra on all but the Landau models. The Coupe cost $5,050 in base form, weighed 4,391 pounds, and drew 24,005 orders.

Ford once again had a front with hidden headlights, but it was relegated strictly to the LTD Brougham and Landau models. The attractive new face made identification relatively easy, and at the same time lent a definite air of luxury to these upscale models. Shown here is the LTD Brougham 4-door Sedan, Style 53K, which filled in the mid-range between the Landau and plain LTD models. The wide side molding and wheel cutout trim was standard, but the rather odd looking rear fender skirts were a seldom seen accessory. Power for these cars was from the 351 Windsor V-8, but both the 400 and 460 blocks could be installed. Cruise-O-Matic was standard.

With the Galaxie 500 gone, Ford's two lowest trim series were now the plain LTD line and the soon to disappear Custom 500 series. The LTD series consisted of two body styles, this 4-door Sedan, Style 53H, and a 2-door Coupe, Style 60H, while the Custom 500 had only the 4-door model, Style 53D, as its non-wagon offering. The plain LTD coupe utilized the same body as did the rest of the total LTD series, complete with opera windows, and could be fitted with the optional vinyl top and all other trim and engine options. It sold for $4,656 and weighed 4,359 pounds. Orders totalled 47,432. In the 4-door family, the LTD version was a 4,408-pound car that cost $4,615 and turned out to be the best selling of all LTD models overall, with 82,382 leaving the floors. In down-trimmed Custom 500 form, it sold for $4,380 and drew 31,043 orders.

Ford continued the country Sedan and Ranch Wagon trim levels for its full-size station wagon, but with the Galaxie 500s gone, the Country Sedan now utilized the plain LTD trim and was considered part of that series. The Ranch Wagon meanwhile, remained in the Custom 500 series for one more year. Far more popular of the two models was the Country Sedan, Style 71H. It drew 22,935 orders with a base price of $5,061. The Ranch Wagon, meanwhile, drew only 6,930 orders, with its base price of $4,970. Both models weighed about 4,800 pounds. Considering the differences between the two wagons, the Country Sedan offered much more in both looks and sound proofing than did the Ranch Wagon, and for the dollar, provided a far better buy, unless total utility was the only consideration.

Now considered part of the LTD Brougham series was Ford's upscale full-size wagon, the Country Squire, Style 71K. As part of the top level line, the wood-grained beauty wore the hidden headlight face of the top cars. On this model only, the 400 cubic inch engine of 158 horsepower was standard, whereas it was a $95 option on all other top models. Priced at $5,340, the Squire scaled in at 4,845 pounds, and thus was the heaviest of all large Fords. A total of 41,550 were sold.

Ford's best selling car of the year turned out to be the relatively new Elite, brought in at mid-year in 1974 to compete against the Chevrolet Monte Carlo. It registered a total sales tally of 123,372, all base priced at $4,721. Although utilizing all Torino components, the car was no longer was considered part of the Torino series, and stood alone as its own one-model series. Visible here is its unique rear treatment with a special 3-panel escutcheon plate between the exclusive taillights with their triple division. The center panel of the escutcheon bore the "Elite" signature, and also was the flip-down door behind which lived the gas filler. Also unique to the Elite was the dual opera windows in the standard vinyl top.

From the front, the Elite definitely disclaimed its Torino parentage. Differences included the single headlamps set in large chromed bezels, a double egg-crate grille with the finer mesh superimposed by a heavy grille of three horizontal and six vertical crossbars, and the large vertical parking lamps set at the leading edges of the fenders. Also exclusive was the heavy color-keyed body side molding, and the deep dished aluminum wheels. These wheels, though seen on virtually all Elites, are sometimes listed as an option. Definitely an option was the tinted glass Moonroof shown on this model, which added over $500 to the base price. Ford described the Elite as offering all of the price and operating economy of a mid-size car combined with all of the top luxury of the Thunderbird. The Elite was listed as Style 65M.

In the true Torino series, an attempt was again made to capture the sport set with a special one-model sub-series known as the Torino Sport, Style 65R. Priced at $4,744, it utilized the 351 cubic inch V-8 as standard fare, and could be ordered with either the 400 V-8 with 2-barrel or the 460 V-8 with 4-barrel. Other optional performance items included a special handling suspension package, and various axle ratios. The interior utilized super-soft vinyl bucket seats, and special full instrumentation, including a tachometer, while the exterior was graced by special Sport striping, vinyl top with blanked quarters, dual color-keyed racing mirrors, and the turbine styled wheel covers shown here. Still, buyers were scarce, and only 5,126 Sport models left the floor. This model also wears the optional $492 Sunroof.

Except for the technically non-Torino Elite, the top luxury cruiser in the mid-size range was the Gran Torino Brougham 2-door Opera Window Coupe, Style 65K. The car turned out to be the most expensive 2-door, yet the least popular of all Torinos. It cost $4,759 and drew only 4,849 orders. As in the Sport and Elite models, the 351 cubic inch engine was standard, and both the 400 or 460 V-8s could be ordered. Also standard were power front disc brakes; power steering; the padded vinyl top, special thin side molding with a vinyl insert color-keyed to the top, and special wheel covers.

Faring little better than its 2-door counterpart in the Gran Torino Brougham series was the 4-door Sedan, Style 53K. With a base price of $4,791, it was the most expensive of all Torino models, yet its sales were only 5,929. This gives a good look at the Torino face, as compared with the Elite frontal treatment. Here were quad headlights set in chrome bezels that extended into the inner leading edges of the front fenders. The grille was a single unit consisting of fine egg-crate mesh divided by seven heavy vertical bars. The parking lights lived behind the outer most of these grille divisions. As a Gran Torino Brougham, this car came equipped with a padded vinyl top and combination cloth and vinyl bench seats as standard fare.

Wearing the $96 optional padded vinyl top is this Gran Torino Opera Window Coupe, Style 65D. Far more popular than the Brougham version, the $4,234 car drew 35,324 orders. All Gran Torinos used the 302 cubic inch engine, had manual front disc brakes, but wore the bright wheel well surrounds and the heavy chrome rocker trim and rear fender trim extension (stone guard). As before, the 2-door Torino models used the 114-inch wheelbase chassis, while the 4-door and wagon versions utilized the 118-inch model.

Most popular of all Torinos this year was the 4-door Gran Torino Sedan, which saw its sales top out at 53,161. When fitted with the optional $96 vinyl top, the $4,258 Sedan, Style 53D, looked little different than the Brougham version. As in the Broughams, a combination of cloth and vinyl was used on all seats, while the doors were in vinyl and carpeting. An interior of super-soft all vinyl could be ordered at extra cost, as could the 351 or larger V-8 engines. The most expensive option in the Torino line was air conditioning at $426. Torino 4-doors weighed in the neighborhood of 4,100 pounds, while the 2-door models were about 100 pounds less.

Ford's top line mid-size wagon again was the Gran Torino Squire, which followed other Squire models in having its sides trimmed in imitation wood. Priced at $4,593, it was the more popular of the two Torino wagons, and drew 23,951 orders. Known as Style 71D, it weighed 4,456 pounds. Standard on this model, besides the wood trim, was an all-vinyl interior of deluxe pleated seats; the 351 V-8 engine; power front disc brakes, and full wheel covers. However, these cars did not use the bright rockers and wheel trim moldings of the automotive lines. Also, a powered doorgate window was a $35 extra, while the roof-top luggage rack was $80

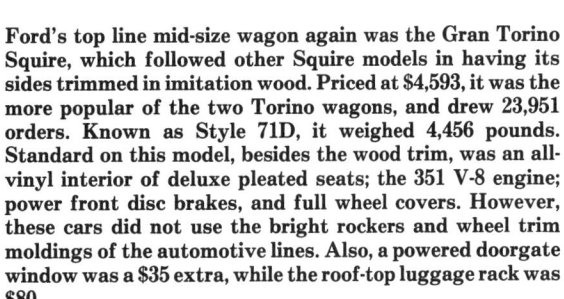

Small quarter windows rather than the cut-in opera windows quickly differentiate the plain Torino 2-door from its fancier Gran Torino and Brougham kin. Also not used on these cars was the rear escutcheon plate, but instead a body-color panel ran downward from the trunk deck. Its central door gave access to the gas filler. Known as Style 65B, this was the lowest priced of all Torinos, coming in with a base of $3,954. At 3,987 pounds, it was the only Torino to weigh less than two tons. Not particularly popular, it drew only 13,394 orders. Interiors were in all-vinyl, in a choice of three colors, with full matching cut-pile carpeting. However, the wheel covers shown here were extra.

Most popular of the plain Torinos was the 4-door Sedan, Style 53B, which saw sales of 22,928. With a base price of $3,957, it was the only other Torino besides the coupe to be under the $4,000 mark. It is shown here in totally stock form, with a steel top and standard hub caps. Often referred to as a Pillared Hardtop, the car lacked the bright rocker and wheel lip molding, but did have a length of color-keyed vinyl-insert body side molding. In plain form, the car had the 302 V-8 and 3-speed manual transmission.

The plain Torino Station Wagon, Style 71B, offered plenty of styling and convenience for a base price of $4,336. However, unlike the Squire version, its base engine was the 302 V-8. Still, it did offer power front disc brakes and the 3-way doorgate as special features, but the roof rack shown here was an $80 extra, while an AM/FM radio would have been $217 more. An all-vinyl interior was standard. Not nearly as popular as the Squire version, this model saw its sales stop at 13,291. The wagons were the longest Torinos, being 223 inches overall, as compared to 218 inches for the sedans and 214 for the coupes.

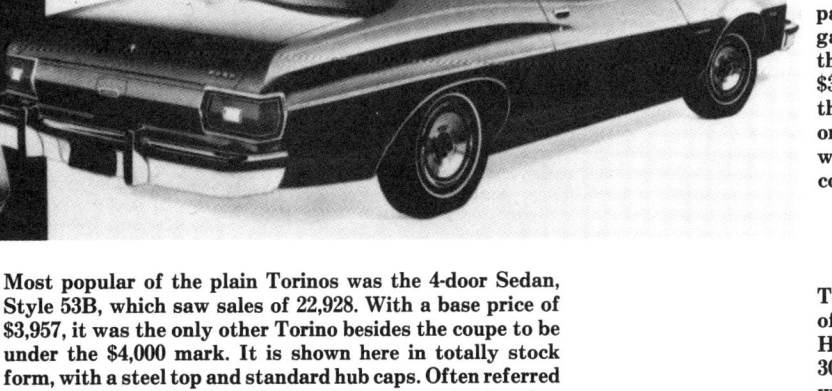

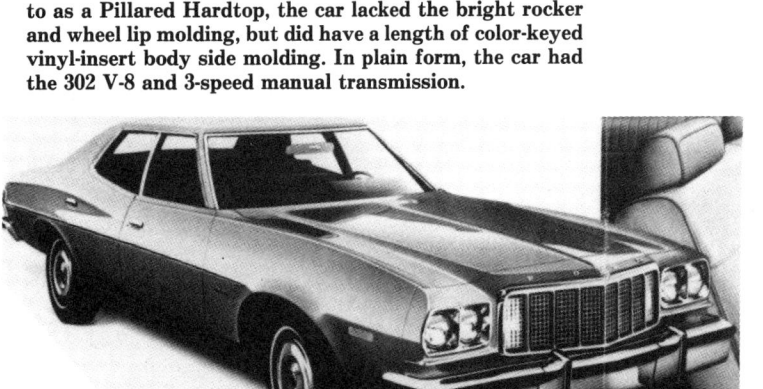

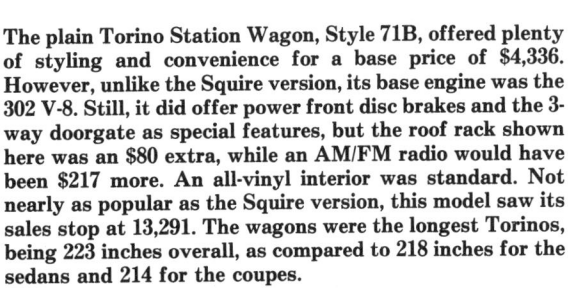

Showing off its standard vinyl top, deluxe wheel covers, and wide side molding with its vinyl insert color-keyed to the top is the Granada Ghia 4-door sedan, Style 54K. Built on the Maverick 4-door sedan chassis with its 109.9-inch wheelbase, the new Granadas were described as being of distinctively European compact style, with a luxurious flavor and the precision of American engineering. Not cheap, the 4-door Ghia sold for $4,240 with the 250 Six. It weighed 3,361 pounds. Sales reached 43,652.

Totally new on the scene this year were the Ford Granadas, divided into upscale Ghia and plain models. This is the Ghia Coupe, Style 66K, sometimes referred to as the 2-Door Sedan. It cost $4,182 with the 250 cubic inch Six which was standard in this series. With the 302 V-8, it was $85 more. It could also be ordered with the Windsor 351 V-8. A 3-speed manual transmission was standard, but Cruise-O-Matic could be ordered for an extra $212. Also standard on Ghias were the padded vinyl tops, wide side molding, and full-width wheel covers. Least popular of all Granadas, the Ghia Coupe drew only 40,028 orders.

Definitely hammering at Maverick's sales was the new Granada 2-door Sedan or Coupe, Style 66H. This car turned out to be Ford's third best selling model overall, with 100,810 sales. Unlike the Ghias, which used the 250 cubic inch Six as a base, the plain Granadas were equipped with the 200 cubic inch block of 75 horsepower that was also standard in the Maverick. Often described as a Maverick with a new body, the Granada was much nicer stylewise than the Maverick, but also quite a bit more expensive. In basic form, the Coupe cost $3,698 with the small engine. It is shown here with the standard trim package, which included bright rocker and wheel lip moldings, body side molding, and deluxe wheel covers. A vinyl top would have added another $83 to the price.

Most popular of all the new Granadas, and Ford's second best selling car, was the 4-door Sedan, Style 54H, which drew 118,168 orders. Although built on the large Maverick base, the cars bore definite Ford styling, with a "European" overtone. Priced at $3,756, the car was probably one of the most luxurious compacts on the market, and was a far cry from the stripper models that one usually associated with economy compacts in this era. Some of the design work was done at Ford's affiliated Ghia studios in Italy, and thus the top level cars carried that name.

Saved by the on-going fuel shortage was the Maverick line, which originally had been scheduled to be discontinued once the new Granada hit the streets. However, with the public's interest in fuel economy still high, it was decided to give the Maverick one final year of life. Still trying to be a "poor man's Mustang" was the Grabber, Style 62D. Once again it was the least popular Maverick, but this year only 8,437 were sold, all with a base price of $3,346 for the model with the 302 V-8. Among the Grabber's features were a special non-scooped hood with racing stripes; special 2-tone body striping; dual outside racing mirrors, and styled steel wheels with raised-letter wide oval tires. Blackout body sides and a blackout grille were also special features.

In tame or "non-Grabber" trim, the little Maverick 2-door Sedan, Style 62A, was still a cute little car. However, its unchanged styling bore no relation to Ford's overall lines, but (horrors) was actually more akin to Chevrolet's Vegas. Utilizing a wheelbase of 103 inches, the 2-door was 187 inches overall, as opposed to the new Granada 2-door, which was 198 inches in length. In base form, the 2-door cost $3,061 with the 200 cubic inch Six, and weighed 2,943 pounds. Sales reached only 63,404, a drop of 85,539 from last year. This was due in part to both the competition from the new Granada, plus an overall poor economic climate. The car is shown with the $392 Luxury Decor Package.

Although the Maverick provided the platform and basic running gear for the new Granada, that was where the similarity ended. Actually, the Granada was supposed to be the next generation Maverick, but with a new name. However the nation's overall interest in fuel economy convinced Ford that the Maverick should have one more year of life, despite the anticipated competition from the new Granada. Virtually unchanged and still Maverick's best selling car was the 4-door Sedan, Style 54A. However, this year its sales did not even hit the 100,000 mark, stopping at 90,695. The car sold for $3,025 with the small Six, but was $122 more with the 302 V-8. Some information would indicate that the 250 horse Six was the standard power, but other pieces show this as an option. This model has the Exterior Decor Group, which included vinyl-filled side molding, full wheel covers, and bright window molding.

Shown in military trim while serving with the U.S. Army in Heidelberg, Germany, is this Pinto 2-door Sedan, Style 62B. Basically unchanged, the little horse still used the 144 cubic inch Four as basic power, with some information indicating that the V-6 was not available in this model, but only in the Hatchback and Station Wagon. With the Four, it sold for $2,769, and shared with its Hatchback kin the distinction of being the only two Fords priced under $3,000. It is shown here in absolute basic form. Due to overall poor automotive sales nationally, only 64,081 were sold, which was less than half that of 1974.

Approximately $200 more expensive than the sedan, but certainly far more handy for carting materials was the Pinto 3-door Runabout, often called the Hatchback. With a fold-down rear seat as standard equipment, and a larger flip-up rear hatch, the car offered a five-foot long cargo deck. It was base priced at $2,967 with the Four, or $3,220 with the Mustang V-6 of 159 cubic inches. However, the V-6 was not a popular option, and less than 20% of all Pintos had this plant. The overall sales slip was even more drastic with this model. Its sales stopped at 68,919, which was a drop of 105,835 from last year. It is shown here with the Luxury Decor Group, which added $137 to the price. This package included full wheel covers; body side molding, and bright window surrounds.

Ford's top selling car in 1974 didn't even break the 100,000 mark this year. The little Pinto Station Wagon, Style 73B, drew only 90,763 orders. This in itself wasn't bad until one considers that in 1974 this model accounted for 273,394 units. Priced at $3,347 with the V-6, it weighed 2,874 pounds. It is shown here with the popular Squire option, an imitation wood-trim package that put a $241 addition on the sticker price. Also adding to the cost was the $80 roof rack, and the radio, which would have been $60 extra if a plain AM, or $222 if an AM/FM stereo.

PINTO

After bringing out the new Granada in 1975, Ford once again entered a new sales year with only minimal changes to its overall line, both in appearance and in the engine department. If anybody even notice, the main change seemed to involve the Custom 500 series becoming a fleet-sales-only line, not available to the general public. This, plus a bunch of option packages in most lines this year accounted for Ford's major moves in 1976. The one thing that was expected—the disappearance of the Maverick—did not occur, and again the little animal was given a reprieve based on continuing fuel saving awareness by the public. Of course, it was unknown at this time that there would be some tremendous activity in 1977, with the introduction of a new line of cars, a totally new Thunderbird, the demise of the Torino, and again, the continuation of the Maverick, but for 1976, things remained on the mild side.

As mentioned, the Custom 500 line was now available only for fleet sales. But, to increase its appeal in this area, a 2-door coupe model was reintroduced. Many of these vehicles would eventually work their way into private usage via the used car market, and thus were not particularly unusual on the road, but for 1976 they were unavailable to the general public. With this move, the LTD now became the base trim level for the full-size Ford line. The base sub-series was enhanced by the addition of the Squire Wagon, which was demoted from the luxury LTD Brougham sub-series. Still, the Squire continued to carry the special frontal styling of the Landau and Brougham models, even though its interior was on the trim level with the base cars.

The Torino line, destined to be phased out at the end of the year, already saw one model go away. That was the Torino Sport Hardtop, which had made a very poor showing in 1975, and was deemed unnecessary this year. Replacing the car in the list of total models available was a plain wagon in the Gran Torino series, in addition to that line's Squire Wagon.

Although it would reappear as a totally different and smaller car in 1977, this year's Thunderbird shared the

same fate as the Torino line. With its demise in sight, virtually no changes were made from the previous year. The car's major claim this year were three new option packages distinctly different than the 1975 options. This year the offerings included a Creme/Gold Luxury group, which consisted of two-tone gold and cream paint scheme, a gold padded vinyl half roof, deep-dish aluminum wheels, and an interior of gold and cream leather or gold velour. The second offering was called the Bordeaux Luxury Group and consisted of a deep maroon special paint, a padded vinyl half-roof in either silver or red with matching body side molding, and simulated wire wheel covers. Last on the list was the Lipstick Luxury Group, which included a white paint job with red interior. Pricing on these luxury packages ran from about $800 extra for the Creme/Gold package to $550 for the Lipstick treatment.

In the little car world, the Maverick remained virtually unchanged, but lost one model when the never-popular Grabber was taken away. Still, this model's place was filled in effect by a new option package called the Stallion, which featured special silver paint, special

Showing off its hatchback design is the Mustang II Mach I, Model 05, which was hottest thing that Ford had to offer in the sport realm. Available only as a V-6 or a V-8, the car cost $4,209 with the German-built V-6, while at $4,154 with the 302 V-8 it represented the most expensive Mustang in the barn. Least popular of the herd, it drew only 9,232 orders. Features still included competition styled steel wheels with bright trim; blackout lower body sides, blackout grille and escutcheon panel; 4-speed manual transmission, and front disc brakes.

Thunderbird this year offered virtually no changes from the 1975 models, but it did have three new option packages with which to play dress-up. These were the luxurious Creme/Gold group at $800, which featured a special cream and gold exterior; the Bordeaux group shown here, which at $700 featured an exclusive burgundy and maroon based treatment, and the Lipstick package at $550, which essentially was an all white car with a bright red special interior. The deep-dished chromed aluminum wheels shown here were standard on the Creme/Gold package, a $163 option on the other two, and $263 extra on the plain models. In basic form, the Thunderbird, Model 87, sold for $7,790 and weighed 4,808 pounds. Production hit 52,935. The 460 cubic inch engine with 4-barrel carburetor continued to be standard.

body moldings, horse decals on the front fenders, styled wheels, dual racing mirrors, and a few minor changes to the suspension. The package was supposed to give the impression of high performance, but in reality was for appearance only. It cost $330 extra.

While Maverick did virtually nothing except create a few new options, the Pinto family had a virtual explosion this year, with a total of six models being offered. These included a basic 2-door Sedan; the ultra-stripped Pony 2-door; a base 3-door Hatchback; a Squire Hatchback; a plain 2-door Station Wagon, and the top of the line Squire Wagon, now considered a distinct model and not an option package. In addition, the Stallion option, similar to that of the Maverick, was available on both two and 3-door Pintos, while for the more mature set, a luxury package dressed up the inside, while the half roof of padded vinyl did wonders for the exterior.

Obviously, with the year-old Granada being a super-successful car, Ford was not about to make any changes. Resting on the fact that the number one and two model sales spots were occupied by Granadas, Ford was content to make only a few minor changes, such as improving the fuel economy slightly. Ford claimed that the car was "the most successful new car of the year," which most certainly was true.

But, advertising people liked to compare the Granada to both the Cadillac Seville (probably because both were named after Spanish cities) and the Mercedes, which certainly was stretching a point.

In the so-called sporty field, Mustang retained its two basic body styles, and continued to offer these in plain fastback and notch back versions, or as the more luxurious Ghia or more sporty Mach I. In addition, Mustang buyers gained two new sport packages this year. One was the Stallion unit, similar to that of the Maverick or Pinto, while the other was the Cobra II

package. This latter option included a blackout grille with a cobra emblem, cobra side decals, simulated hood scoop, rear spoiler, front air dam, louvered covers for the rear quarter windows, special interior, and special white paint with blue racing stripes. Besides this, the Rallye package still remained an available favorite, as did the Ghia luxury group.

New for Mustang was a 2.8-litre V-6 built by Ford's German factories at Cologne. Having a bore and stroke of 3.66x2.7, the engine had an 8.7:1 compression ratio and developed 103 horsepower. Still optional was the 302 V-8, while the base engine was considered the 140 cubic inch Four.

In addition to Mustang, the 2.8-litre engine was also made an option for the Pinto line. with this exception, the engine list received no new plants, but lost three former models. Gone was the year-old 144 cubic inch Four which had been the base for the Pinto line, and the year-old 159 cubic inch V-6 which had been an option in both the Pinto and Mustang lines. Also off the list, probably due to emission problems, was the 351 Modified, which had replaced the 351 Cleveland during 1975.

Despite the fact that no totally new vehicles arrived on the market, this year proved to be better for Ford than did 1975. Total model year production reached 1,753,369, which was an increase of 183,762 cars. And, of this number, five individual models exceeded the 100,000 sales figure. As mentioned, Granada models took the number one and two sales spots, with the basic 4-door Sedan being first with 187,927 copies, while the 2-door Sedan ranked 2nd with 161,618. Coming in 3rd was the Elite, which drew 146,475 orders, and must have given some second thoughts to those responsible for curtailing its production in 1977. The 4th spot was occupied by the LTD 4-door Sedan (also called a Pillared Hardtop), while the little Pinto Station Wagon again made the list with sales of 105,328.

The 3-door Hatchback, Fastback, or 2+2 Coupe (all three names were used) Model 03, was a style unto itself, and also provided the base for the Mach I, and for two new sport options available this year. It is shown here with the highly touted but very inexpensive Stallion package. This decorative trim option included special 2-tone paint and striping, Stallion decals on the front fender, dual racing mirrors, competition suspension, and styled steel wheels. The entire package cost only $74 extra. However, the cast aluminum wheels shown here were a $180 option. In basic form, the Model 03 cost $3,781 with the Four, and $266 more with the V-6. Production 62,312 including those cars with the option packages.

Luxury liner of the little-changed 1976 Mustang II line was the Ghia, Model 04, built only in notchback style. Not particularly keyed for performance, the car came only with the Four or the V-6. With the basic 140 cubic inch Four it cost $3,859, while with the V-6 it was up to $4,125. Among its features were a standard vinyl top, exclusive opera window treatment, and the deluxe wire-spoke aluminum wheels seen here. Also, the cars had a central console and seats done in an exclusive crushed velour. Buyers had their choice of the padded half roof seen here or a full vinyl top an no extra charge. Despite its rather high price, the Ghia drew a nice sales run of 37,515.

Mustang II Hardtop

Lowest priced and most popular of all Mustang II styles was the Coupe, Model 02, which came in notchback style, and was produced with the Four or the V-6. In strictly stock form, as shown here with steel roof, plain hub caps, and no side trim, it sold for $3,525 as a four. The car also provided a base for the unpopular MPG model (Miles Per Gallon), a super stripper available only with the Four, and having a very bare interior. On the exterior, the MPG resembled the plain Coupe. For an additional $75, a buyer could have the Stallion option installed on this car also, although most went onto Fastback models. Most popular of all Mustang IIs, the Coupe saw 78,508 copies leave the corral.

The highest priced package in the Mustang II line was the new Cobra II treatment. Costing $325, the package included a special white and blue paint job with exclusive lower body side decals; dual racing mirrors; a rear spoiler and a front air dam; non-functional hood scoops; white letter tires; rear quarter window louvers, and special black grille with Cobra emblems. However the cast mag wheels were another $180 option. Standard power in this model was the German-built V-6 with a 4-speed, but the V-8 option could be ordered. With the V-8, the car reportedly could hit 0-60 in under 9 seconds.

The luxury liners of the Ford line, excluding Thunderbird, continued to be the two LTD Landau models. Here, showing off the exclusive face used only by the Landau sub-series, is the Landau 2-door Pillared Hardtop, model 65. Most expensive of all non-wagon styles, it was base priced at $5,613 with the 315 V-8. It could also be ordered with the 400 or 460 engines, which would have increased both price, and weight from the 4,346 base pounds. Appreciated on the market, the high-styled Ford drew 29,673 orders.

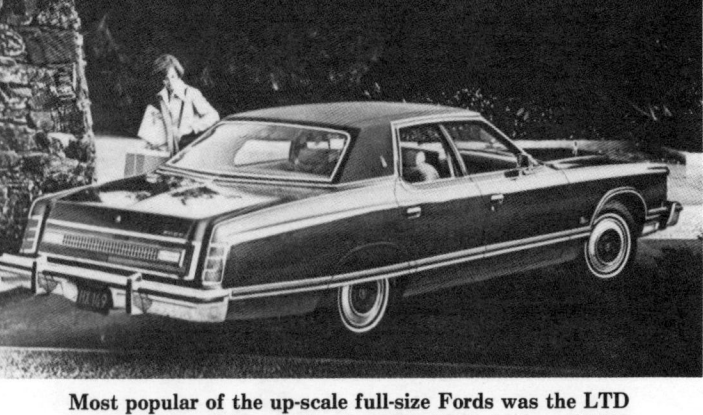

Most popular of the up-scale full-size Fords was the LTD Landau 4-door Pillared Hardtop, Model 64. It drew 35,663 buyers, offering them a base price of $5,560. The rear escutcheon plate was covered with an egg-crate grid which ran between the back-up lights and duplicated the grid pattern used on the grille. Interior luxury was stressed on these cars, with the passenger seat reclining manually, a lighted vanity mirror in the right visor; woodtone appliques on the dash and door panels; a fold-down center arm rest for the rear seat; deluxe steering wheel, and thick cut-pile shag carpeting throughout. All Landaus came equipped with standard vinyl tops and exclusive side trim.

In addition to the Landau models, Ford's big 2-door Pillared Hardtop came in Brougham, (Model 68); plain LTD, (Model 62), and Custom 500, (Model 52), styles. The Brougham, shown here, was very similar to the Landau, but lacked the distinctive side trim and the frontal unit with hidden headlights. As a Brougham, it cost $5,299 and drew 20,863 orders. In basic LTD style it was far more popular. Here it accounted for 62,844 sales, with a base price of $4,780. It also appeared in Custom 500 form, but these were for fleet sales only, and not available to the general public. Fairly stripped, the low-buck line drew 7,037 sales at $4,520 each.

Displaying its front end with the conventional headlights is this LTD Brougham 4-door Sedan, Model 66. As did the Landau, it wore a standard vinyl top and full wheel covers, but lacked the heavy side trim and premium face. Priced at $5,245, it drew 32,917 orders. Its companion, the plain LTD 4-door Pillared Hardtop, Model 63, turned out to be the most popular of all large Fords, and the 4th most popular of the overall Ford line, with sales of 108,168. Here it cost $4,752 and weighed 4,298 pounds. In its lowest form, as the fleet-sales only Custom 500, it drew 23,447 orders with a base price of $4,493.

In an odd move, the Country Squire this year was taken from the up-scale line, and dropped to the base-level plain LTD series. However, it still retained the hidden-headlight frontal treatment of the Landau sub-series, and in fact, was the only non-Landau model to have this face. Most expensive of all Fords, except the Thunderbird, the Squire cost $5,523 in 6-passenger form, or $5,649 with the optional dual-facing rear seats. Ford's heaviest car overall, it weighed 4,837 pounds. Most popular of the three wagon models, it accounted for 47,379 sales. As before, all wagons came equipped with the 400 cubic inch engine, rather than the 351 V-8 that was the basic power in all car models.

As did the Squire, the Country Sedan now also resided in the basic LTD series. Here it was Model 74, which sold for $5,207 in 6-passenger form. It drew 30,237 orders. Some information would indicate that the name "Country Sedan" was either dropped or being phased out this year, and the models were simply called station wagons. However, in the fleet-only Custom 500 series, the remaining wagon was still called the Ranch Wagon, Model 72. Here it sold for $4,918, but attracted only 4,633 customers. In jobs such as boat hauling, the 400 cubic inch V-8 certainly must have been appreciated. The 460 V-8 with dual exhaust was also available. This year, in addition to standard power brakes, all wagons were fitted with hydro-boost rear brakes. Power steering and auto-matic transmissions remained standard on all large Fords.

Now considered a one-model line onto itself was the beautiful Elite, Model 21. Sadly, this was the only year the car would appear as a free-standing model. Despite the fact that it drew 146,475 orders and was Ford's third best selling model, Ford decided to drop the entire Torino series at the end of this year. And since the Elite was essentially just an up-scale Torino, it too would disappear when the 1977 models hit the scene. For this year, however, it was a very well accepted car base priced at $4,879 with the 351 V-8 being standard, and both the 400 and 460 V-8s being available to make the 4,169-pound car a real screamer. Standard equipment included power steering and power front disc brakes, steel-belted radial tires, solid state ignition, and the distinctive front end, with single headlights and large vertical parking lights at the leading edges of the front fenders. The special side trim and vinyl top with its exclusive double opera windows were also standard, but a powered sunroof would have added another $550 to the price. The turbine spoke cast aluminum wheels shown here were a $226 option exclusive to the Elite.

With the Elite now considered a series of its own, the top 2-door in the mid-size line was the Gran Torino Brougham 2-door Hardtop, Model 32. Considered a pillared hardtop because of its opera window, the car nevertheless still shared its small hardtop-like quarter windows with the Elite, but used a single opera window rather than the double units of the Elite. And, of course its front and rear were different than that of the Elite. With its $4,883 price tag, this was certainly not a popular car, and only 3,183 were ordered, making it the poorest selling of all Fords overall.

Only slightly more popular than its 2-door kin was the Gran Torino Brougham 4-door Pillared Hardtop, Model 33. Its sales stopped at 4,473. It was base priced at $4,915 and weighed 4,144 pounds. As before, the Torino 4-doors and wagons continued to use the 118-inch wheelbase foundation, while the 2-doors, including the Elite, used a 114-inch version. The full wheel covers and vinyl roof were standard on Torino Brougham models, but the funny little rear skirts on this model were a $41 option.

Available as a Gran Torino (Model 30) or a plain Torino (Model 25), was the 2-door Hardtop. It is shown here with optional competition styled steel wheels with bright trim, but otherwise is in totally stock form. This included a steel top without opera windows. However, a vinyl roof could be added for $120 and the opera windows were another $50, and that would have brought the exterior appearance almost up to that of the Brougham version. Note that the plain Torinos used an untrimmed body color rear panel, while the upper levels used bright escutcheon plates in this area. As a Gran Torino, the 2-door cost $4,461 and drew 23,939 orders, while its plain Torino counterpart cost $4,172 and drew 34,518 buyers. All 2-doors now had automatic front seatback releases that locked the backs when the doors were closed, and opened them automatically when the doors were opened.

The addition of a $120 vinyl top and $100 deluxe wheel covers sure brightens up the standard Gran Torino 4-door Pillared Hardtop, Model 31. Most popular of all the Gran Torino models, the $4,495 car drew 40,568 orders. All Torinos continued to use the attractive front design with its egg-crate grille divided by seven heavy vertical bars and its parking lights hidden behind the outermost grille sections. Also showing on this car is the deluxe bumper group which consisted of rubber faced vertical bars and a rubber/vinyl facing strip on the horizontal portions.

Torino wagons came in three flavors this year, a plain Torino (Model 40); a Gran Torino (Model 42), and the Gran Torino Squire (Model 43) shown here. Obviously the Squire was the top of the line, and was the only Torino to be base priced at over $5,000. Its base tag was $5,083, which didn't prevent it from attracting 21,144 orders. The luxury wheel covers shown here were $95 a set, while the luggage rack was $90. More popular was the plain sided Gran Torino Wagon, which cost $4,769 and drew 30,596 buyers. The plain Torino Wagon, however, was the least popular with only 17,281 sales going out with a base price of $4,520. All of the wagons averaged about 4,420 pounds, and all were 222.6 inches long overall.

The lowest priced mid-size 4-door appeared in the plain Torino sub-series, where it was the Model 27. Devoid of all side chrome, this version nevertheless wears a set of optional full wheel covers and has the rubber/vinyl faced front vertical bumper guards. In basic form, the car cost $4,206 and drew 17,394 orders. Despite being the base mid-size level, plain Torinos were still powered by the 351 cubic inch V-8 with SelectShift automatic transmission.

Exuding luxury not thought of in a small car, the new Granada Ghia models set the pace for Ford's little car world. Called Model 84, the attractive 2-door Sedan came complete with heavy body side molding, wire type wheel covers, and a vinyl top with opera windows. Under the hood could be the 250 cubic inch Six, which would base the car at $4,265, or the 302 cubic inch (5 litre) V-8, which would base it at $88 more. The 200 horse Six, which was the base power in the plain Granada line, was not available in the Ghia series. This year, Ghias had a new "floating pillow" design on their all-vinyl seats, Map pockets and assist handles were also standard on the backs of the front seats, whether the full bench or the reclining split bench type. A total of 46,786 Ghia 2-doors found homes.

Appearing shortly after new model introduction was the Sports Sedan option for the 2-door Granada Sedan only. This $482 package included a half-vinyl roof with heavy opera window treatment. The heavy body side molding and wheel lip trim of the Ghia was deleted, and as a substitute the cars received bright rocker trim and thin wheel well edging similar to that used on the plain Granada lines. Also in the package was special striping and styled color-keyed steel wheels with bright trim. Inside there was a floor shifter and a leather wrapped steering wheel. As could be expected of a popular car, this year Granada's accessory book fairly exploded, and virtually any type of custom fitting could be accomplished beyond the available trim packages.

Even in its plain form, the new Granada Ghia 4-door Sedan, Model 83, was a nice looking car. But when dressed up in its Luxury Decor Option for an extra $642, it became a real good looker. In regular form, the Ghia Sedan sold for $4,355 with the large (250 cubic inch) Six, or $4,443 with the V-8, and drew 52,457 orders. The Luxury Decor package included the spoked cast aluminum wheels shown here; a mandatory 2-tone black and tan paint job; front and rear bumper strips; 4-wheel disc brakes; and a special interior of soft vinyl and velour upholstery. With this model, Ford attempted to claim that the Granada would rival the Mercedes.

Although the upscale Granada Ghia models were selling nicely, it was the plain Granada family that really boosted Ford's sales figures this year. Second most popular car of the entire line was the Granada 2-door Sedan, Model 82, which had 161,618 units leave the floors. Base priced at $3,707 with the 200 cubic inch Six, it was the least expensive of all Granada models. Nicely dressed for its picture, this model wears the extra-cost body side molding; accent stripes on the body and deck lid; rocker panel molding; full wheel covers, and deluxe bumpers. Without the optional trim pieces, it was a rather plain car. Upholstery was in all vinyl, but an optional interior of vinyl and velour could be ordered.

Best selling model in the entire Ford line turned out to be the Granada 4-door Sedan, Model 81. Its sales reached 187,923. These had a base price of $3,798 with the small Six, or 3,952 with the V-8. The car is shown here with optional body side molding, full wheel covers, and deluxe bumpers, but otherwise appears to be in basic form. Little changed from the introductory models, the cars did sport a slightly revised front bench seat and some new interior trim. Fine design of the "precision" compact gave little hint that it was derived from the Maverick platform and drive train, and used the same 109.9-inch wheelbase as the Maverick 4-door sedan. However, the Maverick was only 193.9 inches overall, while the Granada ran 197.7 inches.

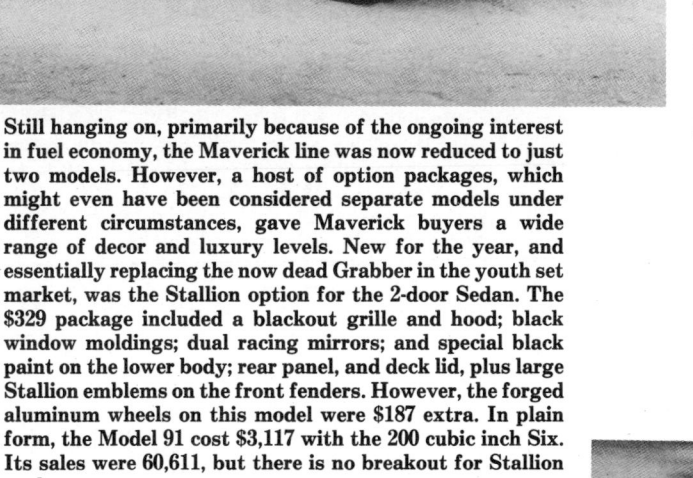

Still hanging on, primarily because of the ongoing interest in fuel economy, the Maverick line was now reduced to just two models. However, a host of option packages, which might even have been considered separate models under different circumstances, gave Maverick buyers a wide range of decor and luxury levels. New for the year, and essentially replacing the now dead Grabber in the youth set market, was the Stallion option for the 2-door Sedan. The $329 package included a blackout grille and hood; black window moldings; dual racing mirrors; and special black paint on the lower body; rear panel, and deck lid, plus large Stallion emblems on the front fenders. However, the forged aluminum wheels on this model were $187 extra. In plain form, the Model 91 cost $3,117 with the 200 cubic inch Six. Its sales were 60,611, but there is no breakout for Stallion packages.

Shown with the $510 Luxury Decor package is the Maverick 4-door Sedan, Model 92. Without this package, the car cost $3,189 with the small Six. More popular than the 2-door, its sales reached 79,076, a drop of about 14,000 from 1975. Optional engines in the Maverick remained the 250 cubic inch Six or the 302 V-8. The Luxury decor package included a vinyl top; heavy side molding with a vinyl insert matching the top; deluxe bumpers; full wheel covers, and door edge moldings. Often accompanying this package was the Luxury Interior Decor group, a $217 option including special vinyl and cloth seats with center arm rests and other deluxe trim items.

Enjoying a nice upswing in sales was the entire Pinto family, which recorded 290,132 total units. Not quite breaking the 100,000 mark was the Pinto 2-door Sedan, Model 10, which came close with 92,264 coming onto the track. It was priced at $3,025 with the 140 cubic inch Four, or $450 more with the German-based V-6 of 171 cubic inches. The wheel covers were a $28 option.

New for the year in the expanded Pinto series was the Pony, sometimes called the Pony MPG or just MPG (Miles Per Gallon). The ultra-stripped car was the only Ford with a base price under $3,000, listing out at $2,895 with the 4-cylinder engine, and no engine options available. It used a 3.00 axle ratio, and all manual operations, with no power options such as air conditioning, power steering, or automatic transmission. However, decor packages could be added, but one wonders who would decorate a basic car designed for total economy. The car used the Pinto 2-door sedan as its base, and its production figures are included in that model's 290,132 total.

Surprisingly, sales of the 3-door Hatchback were just about the same as those of the 2-door Sedan, settling in at 92,540. Priced at an even $3,200 with the Four, the car still featured a fold-down rear seat, carpeted luggage area, and a large swing-up rear deck, and thus provided far more cargo space than the sedan. it is shown here with a $175 set of forged aluminum wheels and the $240 Luxury Decor group which included a full vinyl top; wheel lip moldings; deluxe rubber-trimmed bumpers; dual outside mirrors, and other trim goodies.

Aimed at the youth market, was the Stallion option, which was strictly an appearance package and not a performance option, despite its insuation of such. Priced at $283, the package included a blackout grille, hood, and lower rear panel, special silver body paint, stallion medallions, and black tape on the wheel cutouts, lower body sides, and rocker panels. Also included were styled steel wheels, black window surrounds, dual racing mirrors, and deluxe bumpers, but the forged aluminum wheels shown here were not included. Separate production figures were not kept on this model.

Pinto's most popular model and Ford's 5th best selling car overall was the Station Wagon, Model 12, shown here with the exterior trim package. A total of 105,328 were sold, all with a base price of $3,365 for the Four. Offering basically the same seating as the hatchback, the wagon had a longer and more squared body which added greatly to the available cargo area. Its overall length was 178.8 inches, as opposed to 169 inches even for the other Pintos. Also, its wheelbase was slightly longer, being 94.8 inches, as opposed to 94.5 inches on the car models. As before, the center windows would flip out from the trailing edge, but the rearmost windows were fixed in place.

New for the year in the expanded Pinto series was the Squire Hatchback, which bore the same Model 11 designation as did its base Hatchback. Essentially the plain Hatchback with imitation wood exterior trim and a special deluxe interior, the pretty but not necessarily popular car had a $3,505 base price, not counting the forged aluminum wheels on this example. As was the case with the Pony, production figures reverted back to the base vehicle.

Also new in the Pinto herd was the Squire Station Wagon. Emulating its big brothers, this model also represented the top priced Pinto, and with the optional V-6 was the only Pinto to break the $4,000 mark in basic form. As a Six, its tag read $4,171, with the roof rack still being another $75. As was the case with both the Pony and the Squire Hatchback, production figures were included with those of the plain station wagon. Still, from the number of Squires seen on the streets, this apparently was a popular little model.

Ford made the automotive headlines this year with two new cars, both of which were destined to register some nice sales and raise Ford slightly above its 1976 figures. Although billed as totally new, the smaller and less expensive Thunderbird continued to use its traditional nameplate, while the all-new LTD II was in effect a continuation of the old Torino line, which was phased out at the end of the season.

Drawing the most interest and contributing to an amazing 324,603 sales was the totally changed Thunderbird. No longer in the Continental luxury class, the new T-Bird now used the old 114-inch wheelbase of the Torino, coupled to a substantially modified basic 2-door body of the all-new LTD II Coupe. Essentially, it was what the former Elite would have been had it stayed on the market. Helping to disguise its LTD II roots was a vastly different front end with hidden headlamps, and a variation of the distinctive egg-crate grille that this year marked all large and mid-size Fords. The body sides were changed via a distinct wrap-around roof molding and large quarter windows, again referred to as "opera windows." Under the hood was a 302 cubic inch block in all states but California, where the 351 block was mandated. The 351 and 400 cubic inch blocks were optional in all parts of the country, but the 460 was no longer available, since that powerhouse was now reserved strictly for the LTD series.

Available in only two models, the new Bird found itself in a market slot almost $3,000 lower than the former luxury liners. Thus it was able to compete with such cars as Chevrolet's Monte Carlo rather than the

Taking top honors as the best selling Ford in over a decade was the totally new and downsized Thunderbird, at first available only in a single style. Now on a 114-inch wheelbase and down-priced to $5,063 in base form, the car drew an amazing 318,140 orders. No longer sporting the big block, basic Birds used the 302 V-8, except in California where the otherwise optional 351 V-8 was mandatory. Also available was the 400 cubic inch block, but the 460 V-8 was no longer seen in the Thunderbird nest. Essentially, the new Bird was an upscale version of the old Torino or the new LTD II, and as such had a relatively long option list and few items that were considered standard. This changed at mid-year, when the new upscale Town Landau model was introduced at $7,990. This model featured a unique frontal treatment; aluminum top, turbine spoke aluminum wheels, and a host of other items that were on the extra list of the plain Thunderbird.

high-dollar luxury vehicles. Part of this price down-grading was due to downsizing, but a good part was also due to the fact that many former stock items were now on the extra-cost option list. The two available models, each considered its own sub-series, were the base Thunderbird, which turned out to be the best selling Ford by far of anything in the past decade, and the Thunderbird Town Landau, which was simply a higher trim level of the base model. Among the Town Landau's attractions were an aluminum roof wrapover, slightly altered frontal styling and trim, dual sport mirrors, and special turbine-spoke cast aluminum wheels. For those who desired an even higher trim level there were interior and exterior decor packages. And, at mid-year, two other feature packages were offered. These were a Silver and a Lipstick package. Each featured a choice of special silver metallic paint and silver vinyl top, or lipstick red paint with matching vinyl top. Both packages used a dove gray all-vinyl interior trimmed in lipstick red, and with matching red carpeting.

The other new car, the LTD II, was in effect a carry-over of the Torino, but with totally new (albeit similar) styling. Using the same Torino wheelbase of 114 inches for the 2-door models and 118 inches for the 4-door and wagon varieties, the cars were 215.5 inches overall for the two-doors and 223.1 for the wagons. Styling features included the relatively long hood (a carryover from Torino styling) and a unique grille flanked by square quad headlights, set vertically rather than horizontally. Basic power was the 302 cubic inch V-8, except in California where the 351 was mandated. Optional were the same two higher-power 351 engines and the 400 cubic inch block that were available for the closely-related Thunderbird.

Although the cars were totally dissimilar, the similarities of the named "LTD" and "LTD II" has caused so much confusion over the years that many buyers and dealers wished Ford had found a different title for its new series, or better yet, simply continued with the perfectly acceptable Torino handle. Adding to this confusion was the fact that the base LTD II was not the basic model. That role belonged to the LTD II "S" series. At the other end was the LTD II Brougham series. Ford never identified what the "S" stood for, but since the cars were ultra-basic, a fair assumption is that the "S" equated "stripped." Each of the three sub-series contained a 2-door and a 4-door sedan, while the base and the "S" sub-series also had a wagon model.

At mid-year, Brougham Creme or Blue Special packages were made available. These featured cream or metallic blue paint with a cream or blue vinyl roof, and a cream color vinyl interior with blue trim.

In the real LTD series, the mid-level Brougham series was dropped, leaving just the base LTD and the LTD Landau versions. The Custom 500 series was continued for fleet sales only, but since many of these cars would later find their way onto the used car markets, it was not unusual to find Custom 500 models owned by private individuals. Overall, the LTD changed very little from 1976, remaining a true full-size car of almost luxury proportions. As before, the Custom 500 and base LTD models shared the same frontal styling, while the LTD Landau versions had their own unique front, with concealed headlamps and special trim on the flip-up doors. Once again, the base power in the cars was the 161 high performance 351, while the wagons had the 173 horsepower 400 cubic inch block as their base. Optional only in LTD models this year was the 460 cubic inch block, available only in 197 horsepower form, though some reports show a higher horsepower "Police" version could be ordered by the public.

As before, the Landau series contained only the top trim level 2 and 4-door sedans, while the Country Squire and Country Sedan wagons were in the base LTD range, and the Ranch Wagon was for fleet sales only. At mid-year, Landau Blue or Creme trim packages, similar to those described for the LTD II Broughams, were made available in the LTD Landau line.

In the sporty Mustang line, once again there were few changes. The base engine was still the 140 cubic inch Four, with a V-6 and the 302 cubic inch V-8 being available as options,. The German-built V-6 dropped from 103 to 93 horsepower, but the V-8 climbed from 134 to 139 horses. The same two body styles remained, divided between basic, Ghia, and Mach I sub-series. An extensive option list still included the Cobra II package (really a sub-series, but not considered such) and a Sports Performance package. The Stallion package was dropped, but replaced at mid-year with a "2+2 Rallye" appearance package.

The still popular Granada line was wisely left virtually untouched in the styling department, but mechanically the car became Ford's first standard model to receive a 4-speed manual transmission, with the 4th speed being an overdrive. The base engine was still the 200 cubic inch Six, with the 250 cubic inch Six and the 302 and

351 V-8s being optional. The same two body styles appeared in base and Ghia versions, while at mid-year a Sport Coupe trim package became available. This consisted of a special vinyl half-top, exclusive interior and exterior trim, and special steel wheels. Wire-wheel covers or spoked cast aluminum wheels were available for all Granadas, as they were for all other Fords.

Maverick, finally being in its last year, after super good sales because of the gas crunch, was virtually unchanged. Pinto, however, got both a new face and tail in one of the first restyling efforts ever directed at this popular little car. Styling included a sloping hood ending in a rearward slanting plastic grille, with heavy headlight surrounds of soft urethane and a pronounced front bumper. The rear received new dual-lens taillights, and heavier aluminum bumpers. The 140 cubic inch Four remained the base engine, while all Pintos except the Pony could have the 170.8 cubic inch (2.8 litre) V-6 of 103 horses. This block, exclusive to the Pinto and Mustang lines, had a bore and stroke of 2.66x2.7 inches. In addition to a Sports Rallye package, Ford came up with another idea to attract the youth set to the Pinto. That was the "Cruising Wagon" package, available only on the station wagon. It included blanked rear quarters with small portholes, a front spoiler, special styled wheels, and the Sports Rallye package.

Sales for the year were up slightly, rising to 1,804,427, an increase of 51,058 over 1976. Of these, the aforementioned Thunderbird was the runaway best seller of the decade, accounting for 318,149 sales, divided between the two trim levels. In addition, three other models boasted of sales in excess of 100,000. They were the 2nd place Granada 4-door Sedan, with 163,071 sales; the 3rd place LTD 4-door Sedan, with 160,255 sales, and the 4th place Granada 2-door Sedan, with 157,612 orders. The new LTD II line accounted for 232,324 sales, but these were spread over nine models, with the top sales of only 57,449 going to the LTD II 2-door Sedan.

Wearing a set of official newspaper reporter's license plates (NYP stood for New York Press—the author had them for years) the Mustang II Fastback also went by the names of 2+2 Hatchback, 3-door Hatchback, or Model 03. Priced at $3,900 with the Four, the car also felt this year's slump in Mustang sales, and recorded only 49,161 sales. The car is shown here with such extras as the styled steel wheels with beauty rings; body side striping, and the aluminum spoke sports steering wheel. It may also have had the 302 V-8 which was a $230 option. On the 2+2, those who wanted a front spoiler could have one installed at no extra cost. Last year the car provided the base for the Stallion option, but that rather unpopular package disappeared at year end. It was replaced by the Sports Rallye package and the Cobra II option, both not appearing until mid-year.

Most popular of all the little horses was the Mustang II Hardtop, also called the Notchback Coupe, Model 02. Production reached 67,783, but this was more than 10,700 below last year's total. The car is shown here in pretty much stock form, with a steel roof and hub caps, but the rocker molding would have been extra. In this form, with the Four, it was $3,702, and represented the lowest price Mustang in the barn. Normally the car would have a manual 4-speed transmission, but in California, if the car had a V-6 or V-8 engine, an automatic transmission was required. There the 4-speed could only be had with the 4-cylinder mill.

1977

The luxury liner of the Mustang II family continued to be the Ghia, Model 04, produced in notchback style only. Available as a Four or a V-6, it was base priced at $4,119 with the 140 cubic inch Four, or $280 more with the V-6. Production dropped down to 29,510, with some of these sales probably being swallowed by the new Thunderbird. Standard items on the Ghia were the vinyl half roof; wire-type wheel covers; heavy body molding with vinyl inserts matching the top, and an interior done in Media Velour cloth. Available for an extra $422 was the Ghia Sports package, which included a special black or beige paint job, full vinyl top; cast aluminum wheels with body-color inserts, and a rear deck luggage rack.

Still occupying honors as Mustang's muscle offering was the Mach I, Model 05, available only in fastback style. Available only with the V-6 or V-8, the car could not be ordered with the basic Four. Surprisingly, with the V-6 the car cost $4,332, but with the V-8 it was only $4,284. Still the least popular Mustang, the Mach I accounted for only 6,719 sales. Features included black lower body side and rear treatment; styled steel wheels with heavy beauty rings; twin racing mirrors, and raised white-letter tires.

Coming in just after the other Mustangs, but often thought of as a mid-year package, was the $535 Cobra II option for the 2+2 Hatchback. Apparently a successful package in 1976, the option was basically an appearance unit, and any engine options had to be purchased over and above the Cobra price. Included in the list were new racing stripes running the entire length of the car, across hood and top and rear deck; body side decal with "Cobra II" in outstanding size; the snake cartoon on the front fender; special functional scooped hood; blackout grille; quarter window louvers, and front and rear spoilers. For another $607 the Sports Performance package could be added, which included the 302 V-8, special suspension, power steering and brakes, and a heavy-duty 4-speed manual transmission, except in California where the automatic was mandated. The forged aluminum wheels shown here were another $193 extra.

Showing off its unique front with the flip-up headlight doors is the LTD Landau 2-door Pillared Hardtop, Model 65. Priced at $5,717, it drew a total of 44,396 orders. Power was by the 351 cubic inch V-8, but the 400 V-8 was available for $100 extra, while the 460 V-8 was a $300 option. The LTD series was the only Ford line that still had the 460 as an option. The interesting vinyl half roof was standard, as was the heavy side trim. The interior was of a combination of Ardmor cloth and vinyl. The deep-dish aluminum wheels shown here were a $283 option.

With the LTD Brougham series gone, the plain LTD line was the only other big-car Ford series besides the fleet only Custom 500. Sporting the $135 vinyl half roof is the 2-door Pillared Hardtop, Model 62. More popular than its Landau kin, it sold 73,637 copies, all with a base price of $5,128. In addition, another 4,139 were sold in stripped form as fleet-only Custom 500 models. The car is shown here in relatively stock form, and sports the regular hub caps, rather than the more often seen wheel covers.

Once again the flagship of the entire Ford line was the full-size LTD Landau 4-door Pillared Hardtop, Model 64. Ford's most expensive car, not counting the wagons or Town Landau, it had a base price of $5,742. Retaining the 121-inch wheelbase, LTD models were truly big cars, being 224 inches long overall. More popular than the 2-door variety, the 4-door drew 65,030 orders. At mid-year, Landau Creme and Landau Blue option packages became available at approximately $500. These option units carried a special paint and vinyl matching their noted colors, and also utilized an even higher level of interior trim than did the plain Landau models.

Ford's most popular big car, and the third best selling of all Ford lines was the LTD 4-door Pillared Hardtop, Model 63. It saw a total of 160,255 go out the door. All were base priced, with the 351 V-8 and automatic transmission, at $5,152. The 4-door weighed 4,240 pounds, while the 2-door scaled in at 4,190. The full vinyl top shown here was a $135 option, while the deluxe wheel covers were another $100. In addition to these models, another 5,582 cars were built as Custom 500s, for fleet sales only, probably mostly as taxis or police cars.

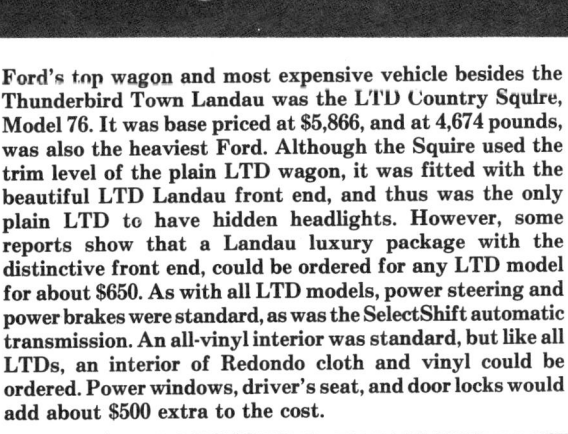

Ford's plain full-size wagon was the LTD Station Wagon, Model 74. The car was sometimes referred to as the Country Sedan, although it doesn't appear that Ford used this title officially for its mid-range wagon. As before, the 400 cubic inch V-8 was standard in the wagons, but the 460 was a $187 option. Dual facing rear seats were an additional $135, while the roof rack was $100. In base form, the LTD Wagon sold for $5,415. A total of 90,711 LTD wagons were sold, but there is no breakout of how many were in plain form, or how many were in Country Squire style. However, another 1,406 were built with the Ranch Wagon designation, as part of the fleet-only Custom 500 range. The body molding was an extra $43.

Ford's top wagon and most expensive vehicle besides the Thunderbird Town Landau was the LTD Country Squire, Model 76. It was base priced at $5,866, and at 4,674 pounds, was also the heaviest Ford. Although the Squire used the trim level of the plain LTD wagon, it was fitted with the beautiful LTD Landau front end, and thus was the only plain LTD to have hidden headlights. However, some reports show that a Landau luxury package with the distinctive front end, could be ordered for any LTD model for about $650. As with all LTD models, power steering and power brakes were standard, as was the SelectShift automatic transmission. An all-vinyl interior was standard, but like all LTDs, an interior of Redondo cloth and vinyl could be ordered. Power windows, driver's seat, and door locks would add about $500 extra to the cost.

New in town was Ford's LTD II line, which technically was a replacement for or continuation of the old discarded Torino line. Serving as the top sport-type model, and also being the base for the new Thunderbird, was the LTD II Brougham 2-door Hardtop, Model 32, which sold for $5,121. Not quite as popular as expected, especially considering its close relation to the Thunderbird, the car drew only 20,979 orders. Actually, its base price was higher than the basic T-bird, and most buyers probably felt they would rather sport around in a known name like Thunderbird than in something wearing an LTD II badge.

Luxury liner of the new LTD II line was the Brougham 4-door Pillared Hardtop, Model 33. Designed with what Ford described as a "trim and lean sculptured look" the car featured the long hood and short rear design of the former Torino. Priced at $5,206, this model weighed 3,930 pounds. Even less popular than the 2-door version, it drew only 18,851 orders. At mid-year, Brougham Creme and a Brougham Blue packages became available for both the two and 4-door Broughams. These featured special blue or cream paint jobs, with matching vinyl tops and matching interiors.

More popular in plain LTD II style than in the Brougham version was the 2-door Hardtop, Model 30. It drew 57,449 orders, and thus was the most popular of all the new LTD II models. Its base price of $4,785 did not include the $100 deluxe wheel covers or the $135 vinyl half roof shown here. This year, optional vinyl roofs came in the style shown here; the rear half roof which extended back from the B-pillar line, or the full vinyl roof. All were priced at $135 installed. All LTD II models used the 302 V-8 as base power, except in California where the 351 was mandated.

LTD II wagons came in two flavors, plain and Country Squire. Both offered a load floor of over 7 feet long and 4 feet wide between wheelhouses with the rear seat folded. This translated into 85 cubic feet of cargo space for those who used this form of vehicle for both work and general transportation. Shown here with full wheel covers, extra side trim, and optional luggage rack, the plain LTD II wagon sold for $5,064 in basic form, and weighed 4,404 pounds. A total of 23,237 were sold. A factor that the author has never been able to comprehend is why Ford chose a confusing name such as LTD II for its mid-size rage, when other names were available and even the old Torino handle was perfectly acceptable.

Shown with the optional $135 full vinyl roof is the LTD II 4-door Pillared Hardtop, Model 31, which sold for $4,870 in base form. This example also wears a set of the beautiful cast aluminum turbine spoke wheels that were priced at $270 per set. Attractive frontal styling included stacked quad headlights set in large rectangular bezels, and an egg-crate grille very similar to the real LTD design. Despite its nice looks, the 4-door Hardtop accounted for only 56,704 sales, which was up somewhat from the old comparable Gran Torino model, but not in the amount that Ford had expected.

Most expensive of all LTD II models was the Country Squire Wagon, which was base priced at $5,335. At 4,430 pounds, it was also the heaviest LTD II. Sales reached 17,162. For some reason, it remained part of the plain LTD II series, and was not installed in the upscale Brougham line. It was known as Model 43, as opposed to the plain version, which was Model 42. Of all Ford frontal designs this year, the new LTD II was probably the most attractive, and was the only one to feature quad headlights stacked atop of each other. All wagons and 4-door LTD II models used a 118-inch wheelbase and were 223 inches overall, while the 2-doors used a 114 inch base and were 215.5 inches in length. Yes, the base was the same as used on the old Torino.

The mid-size low-buck line was not the plain LTD II models, but was now called the LTD II "S" sub-series. Although Ford never mentioned what the "S" stood for, "stripped" might be a good guess. Not particularly popular, the best selling of the "S" models was this 4-door Pillared Hardtop, Model 27, which saw its sales go up to 18,775. It cost $4,579 in base form. Also in the series was a plain station wagon, Model 40, which listed at $4,806 and drew 9,636 orders, and the 2-door Hardtop, Model 25, which drew 9,531 orders. At $4,528, the 2-door was the lowest priced LTD II on the books. The example shown here has full wheel covers and rocker trim, which were options.

A bit of confusion exists over whether the Granada Sports Coupe was an actual model, or simply a $515 option package placed on the 2-door Sedan. The car did not have a separate model number in the books, but was usually advertised as if it stood alone. Arriving later in the year, the package carried a special vinyl half roof; styled steel wheels with beauty rings; special rear design with exclusive taillight lenses, and dual sport mirrors. Inside, it had dual reclining bucket seats in the front, with upholstery in a special perforated soft vinyl. Since it technically was an option package, no separate production figures were kept for the Sport Coupe. However, the very similar Granada Ghia 2-door Sedan, Model 84, base priced at $4,452 did draw 34,166 orders.

The Granada signature on the front fender and lack of Ghia medallion on the C-pillar indicates that this is the plain Granada 2-door with a heavy list of options, and not the Ghia model. In this form, it was the Model 82, which turned out to be Ford's 4th best selling car, with sales of 157,612. With the 200 cubic inch basic Six it cost $4,022 and weighed 3,124 pounds, thus being both the lightest and least expensive of all Granadas. New for this year was a 4-speed manual transmission, which was considered standard. Essentially the old 3-speed with an overdrive gear, it helped in the mileage department

Big luxury in a small car was one way to describe the Granada Ghia 4-door Sedan, Model 83. The upscale car was base priced at $4,735 with the optional V-8. It weighed 3,324 pounds and accounted for 35,730 orders. Standard trim included the heavy body side molding with matching color-keyed insert; wheel lip moldings, and a vinyl top. However, the attractive lacy spoke cast aluminum wheels shown here were a $120 option on the Ghia models, or $220 on plain Granadas.

Ford's second best selling car, with 163,071 units to its credit, was the Granada 4-door Sedan. With the basic 200 cubic inch Six and 4-speed it sold for $4,118, but did not sport the wheel covers or side trim seen here. Besides the basic Six, three other engine options were available to Granada buyers. They were the 250 cubic inch Six at $102; the 302 V-8 at $165, and the 351 cubic inch V-8 at $212. The 400 cubic inch V-8 was not available in Granadas.

Using the same 109.9 inch wheelbase and running gear as the Granada, the Maverick 4-door Sedan was base priced at $3,395 for the Six, which was more than $700 lower than the upscale Granada. More popular than the 2-door, the 2,887-pound Model 92 drew 58,420 orders. New for the year on the virtually unchanged car were the wide vinyl-filled moldings and the addition of an optional reclining bucket seat for the driver as well as for the passenger. The side molding was part of a $105 exterior decor group, while the vinyl roof shown here was a $110 option.

Lowest priced of all Fords was the Pinto Pony 2-door Sedan. Essentially a stripped version of the regular Pinto Sedan, the car listed at $3,099 with the small Four. It had no other engine options, nor could it be ordered with any of the power units such as brakes or steering. However, buyers had a choice of a combination cloth/vinyl or all vinyl upholstery on the standard high-back bucket seats. The car also featured color-keyed carpeting and a mini-console. The rear quarter windows would not open. The hubcaps shown here were considered standard on all Pintos, and give a good indication why wheel covers were so popular.

Now in its final year was the Maverick series. With the end in sight, no changes were made to the 2-model line. As before, the car used much of the Granada's running gear, including optional 250 Six and the 302 V-8, with the 200 cubic inch Six being the base engine. However, the 351 was not available in this line. Still using the 103-inch wheelbase was the little Maverick 2-door, which this year drew 40,086 orders. At $3,322 base price, it was Ford's least expensive 6-cylinder car. With the 302 V-8, it cost $160 more. The optional "pie plate" wheel covers were new this year.

Dropping drastically in sales was the Pinto 2-door Sedan, Model 10. It reached a total of only 48,863 units, which included those models marketed under the Pony name. Although it is shown here with a host of options, in its basic form it looked more akin to the Pony than to this example. In base trim, with the 140 cubic inch Four, it sold for $3,237, while as a V-6 it hit $3,519. This version wears the $128 Exterior Decor group, a $120 set of wire wheel covers, and the $133 vinyl half roof. Wheel lip and rocker moldings were part of the decor package, as was the body strip and special striping.

An all-glass third door was a new option for the Pinto Hatchback, costing all of $13 extra. However, it does not appear that it was a highly popular option, probably because most people didn't want that much visibility from behind. The Model 11 Hatchback was also known as the Runabout. Costing $3,353 with the small Four, it weighed 2,350 pounds. Production was down, settling at 74,237. Other options shown on this model are the flip-out quarter windows, the wire wheel covers, and the Exterior Decor package. As before, the rear seat of the runabout would fold down to make a full cargo floor right up to the front seatback.

Most popular of all Pintos was the 2-door Station Wagon, Model 12, which drew a total of 79,449 orders. It is shown here with the Exterior Decor package, wire wheel covers, and the $80 roof luggage rack. This, of course, upped the $3,548 base price with the Four or the $3,830 price with the V-6. As before, the Pinto wagons used a wheelbase slightly longer than that of the cars, being 94.8 inches as opposed to the car's 94.5 inches. However, the overall length was almost 10 inches longer, being 178.8 inches as opposed to 169 inches.

The most expensive Pinto, and the only one to have a base price of over $4,000 was the Pinto Squire Wagon, which with a V-6 listed at $4,172. At 2,675 pounds, it was also the heaviest Pinto. Since the Squire model was often listed as an option package, production figures for this little car are combined in the overall figures for the plain Pinto wagon. On this model, the roof rack was an $80 option, while the standard wheel covers were $30 extra. As before, the middle windows would flip out from the trailing edges, but the rear side windows were set in place. The rear seat folded to provide a continuous cargo floor, and a carpeted cargo compartment could be ordered for an extra $55, including a cargo cover.

New for the year was the Cruising Wagon option for the Pinto Station Wagon. Aimed at the youth set, this $415 package included full-length blank quarters that fit over the wagon's two rearmost windows. Providing some light was a round porthole of either clear or tinted glass. Exclusive (wild) vinyl tape striping and styled steel wheels were a part of the package, as was a fully carpeted rear section and front air dam. Also included in the Cruising Wagon group was the Sports Rallye package, a $90 kit that included tachometer, temperature gauge, ammeter, sport steering wheel, stiffer springing, and a front stabilizer bar.

Definitely a Ford, but technically beyond the scope of this book is the Fiesta, which Ford dealers began to handle starting in August, 1977. Despite the fact that they were definitely 1977 European production, it seems that the initial batch of Fiestas were still titled in the U.S. as 1978 cars. Designed primarily at Dearborn for Ford's German subsidiary, the Fiesta was built in Germany starting in 1976. The little car had front wheel drive, a 90-inch wheelbase, and derived its power from a 97.6 cubic inch Four, mounted transversely. No engine options were offered. Initially priced at $3,680, it sold 40,549 copies during the remainder of the 1977 model year. Rather plain in base form, it had several decor options available, right up to a $725 Ghia trim package.

Rightfully, Ford made a big promotion out of its 75th or Diamond Anniversary. Among the big productions were announcement of a totally new car, a new sport series for the Granada, and some special Thunderbird editions. Along with these were smaller Diamond Jubilee activities, sales promotions, and displays, not to mention an entire year's ad campaign heavily geared to the fact that Ford had been in business far longer than most Americans had been on the face of the earth. The program turned out to be a success, with sales once again up over the previous year and buyer acceptance of the new models on a level expected for a new car.

On the negative side, however, the celebrations were marred somewhat by publicity surrounding over 4-million recalls, plus the ousting of Lee Iacocca as president. The recalls included two major allegations—that of safety standards (or lack of them) regarding the Pinto gas tank location and construction, and the annoying and dangerous trick of some automatic transmissions to suddenly jump from "Park" to "Reverse" when the engine was left running while the car was in Park. The flamboyant Lee Iacocca did not leave Ford on the best of terms, and rumors abounded in Detroit over the real cause of the ouster. He was replaced by Phillip Caldwell. Within months, however, the indomitable Iacocca would emerge as head of the then-ailing Chrysler Corp., and eventually bring semi-stability to that automotive giant.

But on the bright side, Ford had a brand new car wearing an old name. Replacing the now-gone Maverick in sales position, the new car bore the name Fairmont. Styling was similar to the large Fords, thus leaving only the Pinto and Mustang as having the "non-ford" look. Built on an exclusive chassis having a 105.5-inch wheelbase, the new Fairmont was 193.8 inches long overall, making it larger than the old Maverick but still smaller than the Granada. Base power was the same 140 cubic inch Four as found in the Pinto and Mustang, while engine options were the 200 and the 250 cubic inch Six blocks and the 302 cubic inch V-8.

With its design heavily influenced by Ford's European styling studio, Ghia of Italy, the new Fairmont came in four distinct body styles. These were a 2-door Sedan; a 4-door Sedan; a Station Wagon, and a Sport Coupe. However, the latter did not arrive until the start of the calendar year, and thus could be considered a mid-year model.

When it did finally show up, it was given another old Ford name—that of Futura Sport Coupe. With the initial three models closely following other Ford styling, it was no surprise that the new Futura would emulate the Thunderbird, being equipped with a unique front end with quad headlights (which made the car two inches longer than the rest of its family) and having a unique roof with a large decorative wrapover. Good looks, sensible small styling, and an active promotional campaign gave the new Fairmont an excellent sales start, with three of its models being in the above 100,000 sales ranking.

Although the year-old Thunderbird was essentially unchanged, a heavy share of Ford's anniversary promotion was levelled at this top line model. The result was that once again Thunderbird was not only the company's best selling model, it also broke its own record of 1977, with sales of 333,757, not counting another 18,994 for the mid-year Diamond Jubilee Edition, for total sales of 352,751.

Among the major changes was the addition of the Diamond Jubilee Edition a special model which marked the first time that a "Ford" had exceeded the $10,000 sales figure, with a base price of $10,105.

Considered a separate sub-series, the Diamond Jubilee was not simply a trim package. Available only in special metallic colors of Diamond Blue or Ember, the car was fitted with an exclusive padded vinyl roof in matching shade, and used a color-keyed special grille, flanked by flip-up concealed headlamps. Color accented turbine-style cast aluminum wheels were also standard, as was unique side trim. The interiors were keyed to the exterior color, with the Ember cars having a chamois (light yellow-beige) type of vinyl, while the blue models had blue Luxury Cloth.

Also continued was the Town Landau version of the Thunderbird, with its unique roof trim, including a wrapover bar of brushed aluminum, and its special cast wheels with color-coordinated inserts. A Sports Decor group, available on the base models, included a blackout grille, spoke-style wheels, and imitation rear deck straps. The Sports Decor group was considered a trim package, while the Town Landau version was considered a separate model. Once again, the 302 V-8 was the standard power, with options including the modified 351 of 152 horsepower, or the 400 cubic inch V-8, but not the 460, which again was only available in LTD models.

Also gaining models was the Granada line. It kept its same two basic styles, but now spread them over three series, the base, the Ghia, and the new "ESS" line. Also heavily influenced by the Ghia studios, the new series letters referred to "European Sport Sedan." Some information would indicate that the ESS was simply a trim package, while others indicate that it was considered a separate upper-level sub-series. Whichever, the ESS cars carried their own exclusive blackout grilles, special wheel covers, black rocker panels, and exclusive interior and exterior trim units.

All Granadas this year received new grilles with modified headlight surrounds, rectangular headlamps rather than the round units, new rear styling, twin opera windows in the 2-door models, and other new trim that definitely made them 1978 cars. Also changed were the engines, with the base now being the 250 cubic inch Six rather than the former 200 cubic inch model. On the other hand, the 351 V-8 option was dropped and the only V-8 available was the 302 cubic inch model.

Ford's big car line remained virtually unchanged as could be expected for a series that was to be drastically revised in 1979. Gone was the Custom 500 line, even for fleet sales, but about 5,500 Custom 500 models were produced strictly for Canadian sales. Some of these may later have entered the American market as used cars, but the numbers would be very low.

As before, the base LTD series continued both the two and 4-door sedans, and both the plain station wagon and the imitation wood-trimmed Country Squire. The LTD Landau series listed only the cars, not the wagon models, and was Ford's highest price line, not counting the Thunderbirds. The base engine remained the 302 cubic inch V-8, but the 351, 400, and 460 V-8 blocks were still available as options.

With the Maverick gone, Mustang and Pinto were the only two Fords that did not carry the "Ford look." Mustang this year was again virtually unchanged, since, like the LTD line, it was destined for total revision in 1979. Again coming in both notchback and fastback (other names were 2+2 or hatchback) styling, the car continued to be available in base, Ghia, or Mach I series, with a vast array of options. Among these were the Cobra II package, a new King Cobra package, a Rallye package, a Fashion accessory group, and a Ghia Sports group. The two Cobra packages were aimed strictly at the speed set, while the other three were primarily dress-up packages. The King Cobra package came with the 302 cubic inch V-8 and 4-speed manual transmission as standard fare, while all other models had the 140 cubic inch Four as the base power, with the German-built 2.8 litre V-6 being a mid-range option.

Similar to Mustang, the little Pinto was scheduled for a rather full revision in 1979, and thus it too received only minor changes. Its five main models were continued, as was its Sports Option package, and its interesting Cruising Wagon option. New was a Rallye Appearance package consisting of special blackout moldings, dual racing mirrors, and other exclusive trim

items. As with the Mustang, the Four was the base engine, with the V-6 being the only other option.

Within the engine department, all blocks remained, with the exception that one version of the 351 was dropped, leaving just the base 351 and the modified 351 available. Both were optional in the LTD II line, while the base 351 of 144 horses was optional in the real LTD, and the modified version of 152 horsepower was an option in the Thunderbird.

The year-old LTD II line was virtually unchanged, as could be expected, but the unexpected happened when the station wagon models were dropped from the series. Faced with disappointing LTD II wagon sales, and a nicely styled wagon appearing in the brand new Fairmont line, it appeared that the LTD II version was not really needed. In fact, it appears that Ford officials were taking another long look at the misnamed car, probably wondering if the entire line was really needed. The answer would be forthcoming at the end of 1979. Again, the line was divided into three sub-series, the stripped "S" models, the base trim level, and the upper trim level Broughams. The basic engine was again the 302 V-8, with both 351 blocks and the 400 cubic inch V-8 being available options.

As mentioned, Ford's anniversary year promotion and new models combined to give the company a sales increase over the previous year, with a tally of 1,944,777 sales being recorded. This was an increase of 140,350 over 1977. In addition, a total of seven models exceeded 100,000 sales. Foremost of these, of course, was the super-popular year-old Thunderbird, with the base model accounting for 333,757 builds. Second place was taken by the Granada 4-door Sedan, with 139,305, while the new Fairmont 4-door Sedan took 3rd with 136,849. Fairmont also took the 4th and 5th places, with its station wagon recording 128,390 sales for 4th spot, and its late-introduction Futura Sport Coupe recording 116,966 for 5th. The large LTD 4-door Sedan came in the 6th place with 112,392 sales, while the list was finished off by another Granada, the 2-door Sedan with 110,481 units built.

By far the most expensive Ford was the Thunderbird Diamond Jubilee edition, put out this year only in honor of Ford's 75th anniversary. With a base price of $10,105, the car could quickly top the $11,000 mark if the buyer was let loose in the options book. Essentially, this was twice what the regular T-Bird cost. Standard features on the car included a thickly padded vinyl half roof; exclusive opera windows in the B-pillar; a special color-keyed grille with styled flip-up door lights; special side trim with color-keyed vinyl inserts, and turbine type cast aluminum wheels. Inside was a leather-trimmed instrument panel; power windows and seat; AM/FM stereo, and exclusive upholstery. The cars came only in a special Diamond Blue or Ember metallic finish. This model is shown with the powered moon roof, which was a $700 addition. Despite its price, the Model 87-603 drew a fair amount of interest with the result being 18,994 sales—a figure which must have surprised even the most optimistic of Ford's officials.

Providing plenty of "back pooch" space was the new Mustang II Mach I, Model 05, which used the standard Hatchback as its base. Still the least popular of all of the little horses, it accounted for only 7,968 sales. Available only with the V-6 or the 302 V-8, it was priced at $4,253 with the basic engine, or $150 higher with the V-8. Among the goodies on the Mach I were the styled color-keyed steel wheels; black lower panels and rear panel, and distinctive grille. No, the dog was not an accessory.

With the Diamond Jubilee edition occupying Ford's top spot, the upscale Thunderbird Town Landau now became the mid-level Bird. Priced at $8,420, which was $3,000 above the plain version, the car continued to use an exclusive roof wrapover and a half roof of brushed aluminum; color-keyed cast aluminum heavy-spoke wheels, and special ornamentation and side molding. Inside was the Interior Luxury group, plus power windows and seats. Despite the fact that the Town Landau was considered a separate sub-series, and not a trim option, all of its production figures were included in those of the basic Thunderbird.

Continuing as the luxury liner of the Mustang II herd was the Ghia, Model 04, which used the Notchback Coupe as its base. It was available with both the 140 cubic inch Four or the V-6, in which case it cost $4,185. With the 302 V-8, it was $360 higher. Relatively popular, it drew 34,730 orders. Standard on this model were the spoke-type wheel covers, vinyl half roof, and the side trim shown here. There was also a Ghia Sport group available this year for $360. This consisted of a special metallic paint, black or beige vinyl half roof, color-keyed lace-spoke aluminum wheels, and special trim and striping.

Once again the most popular of all Fords, the plain Thunderbird, Model 87, registered an amazing 352,751 sales, including the Diamond Jubilee contribution, or 333,757 as the plain and Landau models. Certainly not dowdy in plain form, the basic Thunderbird became even more attractive when fitted with the $450 Sport Decor group. For those who wanted to go even higher on the ladder without buying the Town Landau, the Interior Luxury group of crushed velour seats and power everything could be added for another $785. Base priced at $5,411, the car weighed 3,907 pounds. The Sport package included a special blackout grille; cast aluminum heavy-spoke wheels, imitation chromed trunk straps; twin remote mirrors, and distinctive striping and trim items.

Apparently the Cobra II package for the Mustang II Hatchback was so well received that this year there were two such packages. They were the plain Cobra II grouping shown here, and the new King Cobra package. The plain Cobra group cost $700 extra, while the King Cobra went for $1,250 above the base Hatchback. The King package did not use the side striping shown here, but instead had a huge cobra cartoon on the hood, and lead with a rather large frontal air dam under the special blackout grille. Under the hood was the 302 V-8 with 4-speed manual transmission and power brakes and steering. The plain Cobra II package included front and rear spoilers; the striping treatment shown here; small cartoon snakes; black rear and rear quarter window louvers, and blackout trim around the window areas and on the grille. Although Ford often advertised both Cobras as separate models, in reality they were simply packages added to the basic Fastback. As such, their production is included in that of the 2 + 2.

Although Mustang no longer had a convertible, this year it did have an open-air vehicle. That was the new T-Bar roof option, a $630 installation available only on the Fastback style. Actually a mid-1977 addition which drew little interest, the T-Roof was now coming into its own in popularity. Shown here on the plain Hatchback, it was also available on the Mach I. But it is not clear whether or not it could be ordered in conjunction with the Cobra options. The removable tinted glass panels stored in the rear when not in place. The model shown here also has the $245 Exterior Accent group with front spoiler or air dam. In plain form the Hatchback, 2+2, or Fastback (all three names were used) cost $4,011 with the V-6, and weighed 2,751 pounds. A total of 68,408 were sold, but it is not known how many had the fancy tops.

With all Mustangs up in sales this year, the ever-popular plain Notchback Coupe, Model 02, recorded 81,304 sales. The car is shown here with the $170 flip-up open air roof, which was a lower cost alternative for the new T-Bar top for those still liking a windblown feel. Also shown here are the very attractive wire spoke wheel covers. Otherwise, the car appears in basic trim, as it would when purchased at $3,555 with the Four. In this form, it would have weighed approximately 2,600 pounds.

The LTD Landau series continued to be Ford's top flight line of full-size cars. Consisting of this 2-door model and a 4-door, both wore the designations of Pillared Hardtops, which was simply fancy terminology for the old coupe and sedan designations. Of the two, the Model 65 4-door was the most popular, with 39,836 going out the door at a base price of $5,973. The 2-door version, Model 64, drew 27,305 orders at $5,898. As before, the Landau sub-series used its own exclusive frontal treatment with flip-up headlight doors. On the rear, its escutcheon plate carried an egg crate grid similar to the grille design. The deep dish aluminum wheels shown here were a $300 option.

Noting the exposed quad headlights is the easiest way to tell that this is the plain LTD 2-door Pillared Hardtop, Model 62, and not the Landau version. Available only in V-8 form, this example is shown with the $140 vinyl half roof. In base form, with the wheel covers shown here, it would have cost $5,335 and weighed 3,972 pounds. Production reached 57,466. Since the LTD line was destined to be totally redesigned for 1979, there were virtually no changes between these and the 1977 models.

Most popular of the full-size Fords, and Ford's sixth most popular model overall, was the LTD 4-door Pillared Hardtop, Model 53H. It drew a total of 112,392 orders. Unlike the Landau versions, which carried the theme of the grille design across the escutcheon plate, the plain LTD models had a vinyl inserted center band, carrying the "LTD" signature. This band was flanked by the backup lights. The entire unit was part of the trunk deck, and would rise with the deck when it was opened. Without the $140 full vinyl top or the deluxe wheel covers, this model would have sold for $5,410 in basic form. Those desiring a fancy interior could order the Landau Luxury group for an additional $580.

The only non-Thunderbird Ford to be base priced at over $6,000 was the Country Squire Wagon, which saw its tag go up almost $350 to a base of $6,207. Still considered part of the LTD series, it nevertheless wore the hidden-headlight front that was exclusive to the LTD Landau series, and thus again was the only non-Landau to have these interesting covered lights. Even on this model, the roof rack was an $80 option, while the full wheel covers were $40. The 320 V-8 was still the base engine, but both the 351; 400 and 460 V-8s could be ordered, with the 460 being a $425 addition.

Featuring plain sides and exposed quad headlights was the LTD Wagon, Model 74. It was still available in 10 passenger form with dual facing rear seats, with these seats being a $145 option. On this example, the roof rack was an $80 option, while the deluxe wheel covers were $100 for the set. Priced at $5,797, the 4,532-pound wagon had a total production run of 71,285, but no breakout was made as to how many looked like this, or how many were in Country Squire trim.

Interestingly, Ford claimed that this year's LTD II Brougham 2-door Hardtop, Model 30, was a "Trimmer, sportier, mid-size LTD at a trimmer price." However, the car was virtually unchanged from last year, and thus was no sportier, while its base price was now $5,405, which was actually $285 fatter than the 1977 model. An attractive car, the Brougham version included the vinyl top and rocker trim with attached wheel lip moldings, but the luxury wheel covers shown here were a $100 accessory. For some reason, Ford did not separate the LTD II and the LTD II Brougham production figures, and therefore no definite figures exist for this model.

Combining the luxury of the LTD with the sporty handling and flair of the Mustang II, the LTD Brougham 4-door Pillared Hardtop, Model 31, was supposed to exemplify the best of both worlds. However, its base price of $5,505 was so close to that of the full-size LTD, that it is probable most buyers preferred the larger car for the approximately $200 difference. Brougham models were equipped with the full vinyl top and wheel covers seen here, while the side molding with vinyl insert was an optional variation. As with the 2-door, production figures of this model are included with the base LTD II.

The plain LTD II 2-door Pillared Hardtop bore the same Model 30 designation as did the Brougham version. This would lead to the belief that the Broughams were simply trim packages on the base model (technically they were) rather than being independent models. However, all of Ford's material classed them as independent though no separate production breakouts were made between Broughams and plain LTD IIs. Thus, between the two subseries a total of 76,285 2-door units were turned out. As the base LTD II, this car sold for $5,069 and weighed 3,773 pounds. The vinyl half roof was a $112 extra.

New for the year was the Sports Touring package for both the LTD II and LTD II "S" 2-door models. Shown here on the plain LTD II, the package consisted of blank quarter panels with the signature "II" on the sides; styled steel wheels, and exclusive two tone paint design. The package cost $435 above the plain LTD II, and was often coupled to the $138 Sports Instrumentation package.

The 4-door Pillared Hardtop in the base LTD II series really was a nicely styled car, with a long hood and relatively short rear deck. It is shown here with the $115 full vinyl roof and the $300 set of cast aluminum turbine-type wheels. In base form it sold for $5,169. Designated Model 31, just like the Brougham, it saw a total of 64,133 units go out the door, divided between the two sub-series. All LTD II models used the 302 V-8 as base power, but could also be fitted with the 351 or the 400 cubic inch V-8 blocks, but not the 460, which was reserved solely for the full-size LTD.

Again, the base LTD II was not the basic model. That slot was filled by the LTD II "S" sub-series, which unlike the Broughams, was treated as a separate line of models. Thus, the LTD II "S" 2-door Pillared Hardtop was the Model 25, which had a base price of $4,814. A definitely unpopular car, it had a run of only 9,004. It is shown with the vinyl half roof, and the $145 set of wire wheel covers. Also shown are the body side moldings, which cost $45, while the antenna indicates that it might have the $200 AM/FM stereo radio. This gives a good view of the very attractive frontal design achieved by stacking the rectangular headlamps in their own separate pods set back from the leading fender edge.

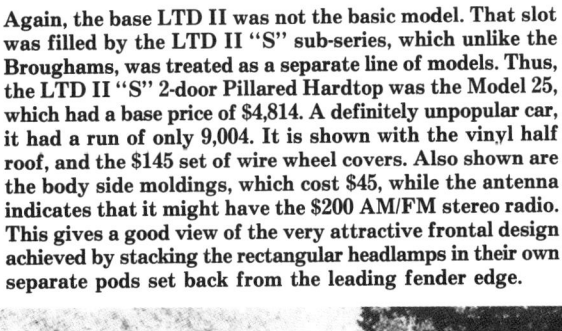

In addition to the Sport Touring package, the LTD II line also had the Sport Appearance package. This $363 grouping, shown here on the LTD II "S" 2-door, was available on all LTD II coupe models. Basically a slightly lower key version of the Sport Touring package, it too consisted of solid rear quarters covered by a distinctive trim wrapover with "II" prominently installed on the lower leading edges. Also included was the special wide body stripe, and lower trim molding. The color-keyed wheels were an optional part of the package, whereas the wire-spoke wheel covers shown on the "S" coupe were standard with this package.

The lowest price 4-door of the line was the LTD II "S" Pillared Hardtop, Model 31. Except for the deluxe bumpers and the $35 deluxe wheel covers, it is shown here in pretty much standard form. In this mode, it would have cost $4,889 and weighed 3,836 pounds. Less popular than its upscale team mates, it drew only 21,122 orders. With the wagon models now gone, the 4-door LTDs were the sole users of the 118-inch wheelbase chassis. The 2-door models still used the 114-inch version, as did the Thunderbird.

If imitation is a form of flattery, then Mercedes must have been highly pleased at the styling of the new Granada ESS 4-door Sedan. Though not identical with the German sedans, the new ESS models carried enough overtones to make one think of the Mercedes upon quick glance. Included with these models were the color-keyed wheel covers, blackout grille sections, side moldings, window area surrounds and rockers, and blackwall tires. Inside were individually reclining bucket seats in the front, a leather-wrapped steering wheel, and heavy sound insulation, while underneath was a heavy-duty suspension. In V-8 form, the 4-door Model 82 sold for $5,095 and was the most expensive Granada. As a straight Six it was $4,915.

New for the Granada series was the "ESS" sub-series, which was shared by this 2-door Sedan, Model 81, and the 4-door. The "ESS" stood for European Sport Sedan, and now represented the highest trim level in the little Granada line. Not all that much over the regular Granada prices, the V-8 versions of these cars still were the only Granadas to be based at over $5,000. Thus, the 2-door shown here had a V-8 base of $5,017, while the 250 cubic inch in-line Six was $4,914. Attractive wheel covers, ala Mercedes, and blanked in quarter windows with non-functional air inlets were part of the "ESS" package.

The Granada Ghia 4-door Sedan still was a luxurious little car, despite the appearance of the ESS models. Filling the middle ground for 4-doors, it was priced at $4,909 with the 302 V-8, which now was the largest engine that could be installed since the 351 was dropped from this line. Those wanting a more upscale car could order the luxury interior package at $475, which included power everything plus a high quality velour-type upholstery and individual front bucket seats.

Making good use of its new styling innovations was the Granada Ghia 2-door Sedan. This upscale car now filled the space between the base Granada and the new ESS models. Among its new features were a redesigned grille, large rectangular headlamps set above large rectangular parking lights (not unlike the style of the LTD II), one piece wraparound taillamps, and redesigned side molding. On the 2-door models, new double opera windows filled in the rear quarter panels. With the 200 cubic inch Six now gone, the 250 in-line Six was the basic engine. With this unit, the Ghia 2-door was priced at $4,650, or $180 more with the V-8.

A rear view of the basic Granada 2-door Sedan, Model 81, gives a good look at the unique double opera windows that were new to these and the Ghia models this year. Called "Twindows," they were highlighted by a bright surrounds and a central divider. This view also shows the new rear styling with its wrap-around taillights. In basic form, the 2-door sold for $4,264 with the Six and weighed 3,124 pounds. It turned out to be Ford's seventh best selling car, with 110,481 sold. This total was divided among plain, Ghia, and ESS versions, since no sub-series breakdown was made of Granadas this year. The wire-type wheel covers were a $100 option.

Most popular of the two Granada styles was the 4-door Sedan, model 82, shown here in plain Granada trim. It was also ford's second best selling car, with 139,305 going out the door. However, these figures are a bit clouded, because this year Ford did not keep separate records of plain, Ghia, and ESS production. Thus, though the figures look good, one has to remember that the total 4-door Granada production in 1977 was almost 199,000, so the line actually reflected a drop of 60,000 4-doors. As a Six, this model sold for $4,324 and weighed 3,122 pounds.

Ford borrowed the old name of Fairmont for its new line that replaced the Maverick. Also, for its top sport model, it borrowed another previous name, this time from Falcon, and called the car the Fairmont Futura Sport Coupe, Model 93. Most often just called the Futura Coupe, the car used some unique styling touches, most obvious being the smaller rear quarter (opera) windows and the full vinyl top divided by a heavy wrapover at the B-pillar. This wrapover was covered by a brushed aluminum sheath, edged front and rear by bright trim that formed the roof edging. Not considered a performance model, the car was available with either the 140 cubic inch Four, or the optional 250 inline Six or 302 V-8. Fairmont's most expensive model, it cost $4,044 with the Four. The pretty car turned out to be Ford's fifth most popular model, with 116,966 sold.

Far less striking than the Futura Sport Coupe was the plain Fairmont 2-door Sedan, Model 91. At $3,589 with the basic Four, it was Fairmont's lowest price model, but its sales of 78,776 also made it the least popular. Fairmonts were built on their own exclusive chassis of 105.5-inch wheelbase, and were 193.8 inches long overall, except for the Futura, which was two inches longer. Unlike the Maverick which had its own unique styling, the Fairmont's lines definitely said "I am a Ford."

Essentially taking the place of the now-gone LTD II wagons were the new Fairmont 4-door Wagons, which used the same 105.5-inch wheelbase as did the cars. The wagons came in the plain form shown here, or with the Squire option. In total, the combined wagon production represented Fiord's fourth best selling car, with 128,390 being turned out. In base form, with the Four, the plain wagon sold for $4,031 and weighed 2,718 pounds. The Straight Six would have added $120 to the price, while the 302 V-8 would have cost another $320. This example wears the $96 Exterior Accent group and the $75 luggage rack.

Most popular of the new Fairmonts and Ford's third most popular car overall was the 4-door Sedan, Model 92. It drew a total of 136,849 orders, with a base price of $3,663. Considered a 5-passenger vehicle, the Fairmonts were said to combine fuel efficiency, space efficiency, and cost efficiency into one lean, trim appearing vehicle. The wire wheel covers shown here were a $115 option on Fairmonts, even though they were $100 a set for most other cars. This car also has been fitted with the $215 Exterior Decor group, and might also have the $300 Interior Decor group. The new 140 cubic inch Four was a domestically produced 4-cylinder engine, being built at the Lima, Ohio, plant. It is sometimes referred to as the "Lima Four."

Although considered a separate model in other series, the Squire imitation wood treatment was simply an option package in the new Fairmont line. Priced at $365 above the base wagon tag, the attractive package could be applied to any Fairmont wagon. But, being a package, no separate production figures were kept, and therefore it is not known how many Fairmont Squires were turned loose.

Up in sales this year were the Pinto 2-door Sedans, divided between regular and Pony models. Production hit 62,317, which was a gain of 14,000 from last year. Engines remained the 140 cubic inch Four as used in the new Fairmont, or the V-6 of 171 cubic inches. With the Four, the 2-door Sedan sold for $3,336, while the V-6 was $275 more. This model sports the $40 Exterior Decor group and has the $250 set of forged aluminum wheels. Basically the decor group consisted of rocker trim, vinyl-filled side molding, and dual mirrors.

Ford's lowest priced car, and the only one under the $3,000 mark, was the Pinto Pony, which was based on the 2-door Sedan body. Priced at $2,995, it was available only with the 4-cylinder engine and 4-speed manual transmission. No engine or power options were allowed on this model, but apparently trim groupings could be ordered, if one wanted to brighten up the rather plain little car. Pinto cars continued to use the 94.5-inch wheelbase chassis and were 169.3 inches long overall.

The Pinto Station Wagon dropped in sales again this year, probably as a result of competition from the new Fairmont wagon. Production settled at 52,269, divided between plain, Squire, and Cruising wagons. The plain wagon wore a base sticker of $4,067 with the V-6 and weighed 2,637 pounds. The Pinto wagons used their own exclusive chassis of 94,8 inches and were 179 inches long overall. As in the hatchback, the rear seat of the wagon would fold down, thereby providing 57 cubic feet of cargo space. Loaded with options, this model sports the exterior Decor package; $60 roof luggage rack; $90 wire wheel covers, and may have the $180 Interior Decor group.

Shown with the Rallye Appearance package and the all-glass rear hatch is the Pinto 3-door Hatchback, Model 11. More popular than the 2-door Sedan, the Hatchback this year drew 74,313 orders, using a base price of $3,450. The Rallye package would have added another $200 to the price, but would have provided exclusive body striping, dual racing mirrors, front spoiler, and blackout trim. The white forged aluminum wheels were another $265, while the all-glass third door was $25 extra. The rear seat could still be folded to provide additional cargo space.

Listed as a variation of the Model 12 Station Wagon was the Pinto Squire, which was the most expensive horse in the herd. It had a base V-6 price of $4,382. As before, all Pinto wagons featured a center window that would flip open from the C-pillar, while the rearmost window was fixed in place. The wagons continued to have a lift-up rear gate, similar in operation to that of the hatchback. Also available was the Cruising Wagon, which was a $400 option above the basic wagon price. It was similar to that shown in the 1977 chapter, and featured blanked in sides with a large porthole at the rear and some pretty wild paint and stripe treatment.

Entering its second year on the American market was the Ford Fiesta, produced in Germany and sold on both sides of the Atlantic. Based at $3,680 it technically was the lowest priced vehicle sold by Ford dealers, but was not a domestically sourced item. A total of 76,145 left their ships, but most did not wear the $180 cast aluminum wheels shown on this model. Using a 97.6 cubic inch four transversely mounted, this was Ford's first U.S. experience with front wheel drive. New for this year were a $555 Sport group (shown here) and a $722 Ghia package, which made short work of any economy expected from this model. Going that route, why not add the $430 air conditioning, $200 flip-up sun roof, and $160 AM/FM stereo unit.

After its big 75th Diamond Jubilee celebration, Ford had to do something to keep the public's attention. It did, and it did it to both ends of its sales scale. On the upper part was a totally new LTD line of slightly down-sized full-size cars, while on the other end was a totally new and slightly larger Mustang with a very new and exclusive power plant.

Following GMC by two years, Ford felt it finally had to down-size its big cars to meet the new government fuel economy standards. Giving credit where it is due, at least the company held out for two extra years in keeping decent size vehicles around, and with its Town Car, even today produces a car of the size and comfort that many people, including the author, prefer.

Despite the down-sizing, deft engineering and more frugal use of space allowed Ford to actually increase interior space, even though the body's overall dimensions shrunk 17.8 inches to a new length of 209 inches for the cars and 212.9 inches for the wagons. Also more narrow, the width went down from 79.5 inches to 77.5 inches. Likewise, the new chassis was a full seven inches shorter, now being 114.4 for all models.

Styling was still unmistakably Ford, and except for size, the cars were not that much different than the 1978 models, even though the metal was totally new. As before, two different fronts were used for base LTD and Landau models, with the plain versions having single rectangular headlamps, while the Landau models and the Country Squire (considered part of the base series) used quad rectangular headlamps nested horizontally above long rectangular parking lamps. The old flip-up hidden headlights were discontinued, though they continued to appear on all Thunderbirds.

As before, the plain and imitation wood-trimmed Country Squire wagons appeared in the base LTD series, along with a 2-door and a 4-door sedan, while the Landau series simply carried the two sedan models. In addition to their exclusive fronts, Landaus were quickly identified by coach lamps on the rear quarters. The base engine was still the 302 V-8, while a pair of optional 351 blocks would produce 135 or 155 horsepower respectively. With all big blocks discontinued this year, the modified 351 was the best that one could get in the down-size full-size line.

Also taking top billing this year was the brand new Mustang, which once again bore the respected name of "Mustang" without the "II" suffix. However, unlike the LTD which went down in both size and power, the new Mustangs actually grew in size and wound up with a new and exclusive performance engine.

The Mustang's totally new sheet metal was built on a new chassis of 100.4-inch wheelbase. Using a modified Fairmont chassis, the new base was 4.2 inches longer than the Mustang II. Also, its new overall length was 179.1 inches, an increase of 4.1 inches over the old horse. The new model featured a sloping front with a sharply slanted egg-crate grille, overall not too unlike the Pin-

to styling concept. Quad rectangular headlights were used in place of the old round models, and soft urethane bumpers enhanced the styling continuity and gave an illusion of even greater length.

As before, the Mustang came in notchback and hatchback style, though the hatchback was not as pronounced a slope as before, and could no longer qualify for the term "fastback." Only base and Ghia models were offered, but several option packages and a world of individual options were again available. The base engine was the 140 cubic inch Four, but this year a new option was there for the speed set. Exclusive to Mustang, this engine was the Turbo Four. Essentially it was the same as the base engine, but fitted with a 2-barrel Holley carburetor and a Turbocharger. The additions were reported to boost performance to about the same level as a well-tuned 302 V-8, while still providing the economy of a Four. Not cheap, it was a $542 option, placing it about $35 above the optional 302 V-8. The German V-6 was also available for about $275 extra, but the not too popular engine was now it its final year on the U.S. market.

Despite the promotion given to the new Turbo Four, when a Mustang was named to pace the Indianapolis 500 race, it was a V-8 version that was selected. Following this event, Ford turned out 6,000 Indy Pace Car Replicas. Other packages available were the $1,175 Cobra, which included the Turbo Four and a special scooped hood, and the usual Sport options.

Also getting a face lift was Ford's other little horse, the Pinto. Foremost in its styling changes was a new grille, and a switch from round to rectangular single headlamps separated from the grille by rectangular parking lamps set vertically. New style aluminum bumpers had black bump strips front and rear, while new wheel covers graced the upper trim cars. Although the new bumpers and slat-type grille helped give the car a longer appearance, this year's Pinto was actually one-half inch shorter than in 1978, being 168.8 inches for the cars and 178.6 inches for the wagons.

As before, Pintos came in sedan, hatchback, and station wagon models. This year in addition to the ultra-stripped Pony Hatchback, there was a stripper Pony Station Wagon. Under options, the interesting Cruising Package was now available on the hatchback as well as the wagon. It continued to feature blanked out quarter windows and louvered rear windows, as well as special bright paint and trim. Also available was an ESS (European Sport Sedan) option for sedans and hatchbacks, which featured a blackout grille, dark rear glass, and special body molding. New cast aluminum wheels were also featured, but were not part of any package. Engines were unchanged from the previous year, and the Turbo Four was not available even though the base engine was the foundation of the new powerhouse.

Obviously a highly successful car was not going to

change, and thus the Thunderbird received only minor year-dating modifications. Most prominent, of course, was a new grille, of wider spaced horizontal and vertical bars, flanked again by hidden headlamps, with a slightly different design on the flip-up doors. Again, the plain Thunderbird was the base model, while the Thunderbird Landau occupied center stage. At the top end was the new Heritage Edition, replacing the former Diamond Jubilee Edition, whose name obviously allowed only one-year usage. The new Heritage models came in two monochromatic colors, the choice being light blue or maroon, with corresponding vinyl tops and a choice of velour or leather seats. They had the distinction of being the only Fords to top the $10,000 base price mark. As with the LTD, the basic engine was the 302 V-8, with the plain and modified 351 V-8s being the only options.

Also as could be expected, a year-old super-successful car was not going to be changed. That was the story of the Fairmont line, which was still available in four models and several options. Included in the list this year was a continuation of the ES package (Euro Styled) which included a black-out grille, black and bright trim, and special turbine-type wheel covers. Also available for all models were two-tone paint schemes formerly offered only on the Futura Sport Coupe, and the optional Sport Group which included a gray argent grille, special trim, and turbine wheel covers. Both Ghia and Futura trim levels were still offered as options, as was the Squire wagon package.

In its final year, the LTD II continued with virtually no change. The sad note here was that it was a relatively nice looking car, burdened by a confusing name, in a class where it just really never caught on.

Still offered was the basic "S" series, the regular line, and the Brougham series. A Sports Appearance package or a Sports Touring package could be ordered.

As mentioned, the basic engine changes involved the dropping of both the 400 and the 460 cubic inch blocks, and the addition of a turbocharger to the base Four in the Mustang line. Efforts were still being made to bring fuel economy up while lowering emission pollutants, but these efforts again resulted in lower horsepower.

Production was down slightly this year, dropping 135,590 units to a total of 1,809,187, this despite Mustang's excellent rebound. However, the Thunderbird line, though still Ford's best selling car, saw its figures drop a total of 68,610, to finish at 284,141 this year, as opposed to 352,751 total Birds in 1978.

Still, eight cars, including the Number One Thunderbird, were on the list of models with sales of over 100,000. In 2nd place was the new Mustang Notchback, with 156,666 sales. Third place went again to the Fairmont 4-door Sedan, which this year registered 133,813 builds. Mustang came back on the list in 4th spot with 120,535 units for its Hatchback model. The new LTD 4-door Sedan managed to get into 5th spot with 117,730 sales, while the Fairmont Sport Coupe occupied 6th with 106,065. Even Granada got ionto the act, with the 4-door sedan ranking 7th with 105,526, but these included ESS and Ghia versions as well as the base models. Finally, the Fairmont Station Wagon came in 8th, having 100,691 units.

Replacing the Diamond Jubilee Edition as Ford's top of the line car was the new Thunderbird Heritage Edition, Model 87/603. Priced at almost twice the cost of a basic Thunderbird, the Heritage model came in with a tag of $10,678. Thus it qualified as the only Ford to break the $10,000 mark. Among the inducements on the Heritage were an exclusive formal padded vinyl roof; exclusive monochromatic paint in either maroon or light blue, and cast aluminum turbine-type wheels. Inside was a color coded interior with leather trim and 36-ounce cut-pile carpeting front and rear; speed control; AM/FM stereo-search radio; power windows, door locks, and 6-way driver's seat; air conditioning, and adjustable tilt steering wheel. Unlike last year when the Diamond Jubilee was considered a separate model, this year's Heritage had its production included with that of all Thunderbirds.

Showing off its new taillights and rear end design is the Thunderbird Town Landau, Model 87/607, which occupied a middle trim level between the Heritage and the plain Bird. This model is shown with a new option, a T-Bar Roof which was a $750 extra. Also still available was a powered Moon Roof at $700. The Town Landau and plain models differed from the Heritage in that they offered huge rear quarter windows, while the Heritage had these panels blanked in by the exclusive roof cover. Buyers had their choice of eight body colors and four vinyl top shades, but were not offered the two exclusive Heritage finishes. The 302 V-8 was the basic block, but either of the 351 engines could be ordered optionally. Priced mid-way between the plain Bird and the Heritage, the Town Landau models carried a sticker of $8,866.

Showing off the Sports Decor group, a $520 option, is the plain Thunderbird. The popular option included cast aluminum spoke wheels, with the heavy spokes painted in a color-keyed finish; a vinyl half roof, and chrome imitation hold-down straps on the trunk deck. Often combined with this package was the Interior Luxury group, an $815 option which included power everything. This model also appears to have the $700 powered Moon Roof, which, when all tallied up, would bring the car well above its base price, and almost in line with the Town Landau model.

Totally new in style was the Mustang Hatchback, shown here in its new Ghia trim. In this form, it was the only Mustang to exceed the $5,000 base price, with a tag of $5,097 with the V-6. It came under that mark with the Four, as its price there was $4,824. No longer fitted with a radically sloping rear, the car was well named Hatchback because of its lift-up rear door, but could not qualify as a true "fastback" since the slope of its rear was broken by a slight hump. Least popular of all the Mustang styles, the Model 05 drew only 36,384 orders. Technically, this version replaced the old Mach I in the sales roster, as the Mach I was not carried into the new line.

Even in plain form, the new Thunderbird was a very nice looking vehicle, which explains why it was also Ford's best second selling car for yet another straight year. Including the Heritage and Town Landau models, a total of 284,141 Birds flew out of the 1979 nest. The base model is shown here in just about stock form, in which guise it would have sold for $5,877—of course, few ever went out of the door in this form. The new frontal design shows off very well here, with the heavy rectangular bars of the outer grille providing a nice setting for the much finer egg-crate secondary grille. Also slightly changed were the Thunderbird emblems on the flip-up headlight doors.

The Ghia sub-series continued to offer the top trim level of the totally new Mustang line. However, Ghias were now available in both the notchback version shown here, or as a hatchback. The car was available with either the basic Four or the V-6, with the 302 V-8 being a $240 charge above the V-6. As a V-6, the Ghia Notchback, Model 04, cost $4,915. Standard equipment included turbine-style wheel covers, heavy body side molding, dual outside mirrors, and low-back bucket seats with European-style headrests. However, the vinyl roof was now a $102 accessory. A total of 56,351 Ghia Notchbacks were turned loose.

Despite the fact that the Mach I did not appear in this year's Mustang herd, the Cobra model was continued as an option package. Priced at $1,175 above the base hatchback, the Cobra offered as standard equipment the new Turbo Four engine and a special Turbo hood with functional air scoop. However, the 302 V-8 and plain hood could be ordered as a no cost option in the package. Exterior goodies included black lower panels all around; blackout grille; black window edging and racing mirrors; forged aluminum wheels, and special "Cobra" decals. Inside was an engine-turned dash, and an 8000 rpm tachometer. However, the hood graphics shown here were an $80 addition.

Best selling of all of the new Mustangs was the Notchback Coupe, Model 02, shown here in just about basic form. It accounted for 156,666 sales, thus becoming Ford's 2nd best selling car. Its base price with the Four was $4,071. Despite the fact that almost all other cars were down-sizing this year, the Mustangs grew. Built on a modified Fairmont chassis, their wheelbase was now 100.4 inches as opposed to 96.2, while the overall length was 179.1 inches, an increase of over four inches from the old 175 inches. As mentioned in the text, all sheet metal was brand new, with no carryover at all from the previous line.

Ford's newest power plant turned out to be a Mustang exclusive this year. It was the Turbo Four, which used as its foundation the standard 140 cubic inch Four, but added a turbocharger and two barrel Holley carburetor. The engine was a $542 extra above the base price, with the installation including a "Turbo" hood with functional air scoop. The example shown here also wears the $175 sport option, which included black lower panels all around, black side molding, and a blackout grille. At mid-year, the old German-built V-6 was discontinued, and was replaced by the 250 cubic inch inline Six. Despite the change from a V-6 to an inline model, it appears the price addition of $275 remained.

Mustang this year was selected to be the Pace Car for the Indianapolis 500 Race. Shortly after that Memorial Day event, Ford issued a series of 6,000 Hatchback models done up as Indy Pace Car Replicas. They were part of the 120,535 plain Hatchback sales recorded this year. With the 302 V-8, as used in the Replica, the plain Hatchback would have sold for $45,950, but it is not known how much extra the Replica package ran—however, it was expensive. Included in the grouping was a T-Bar Roof; special silver and black paint with orange and red accent stripes and lettering; black lower panels; blackout grille; special hood with functional reversed air scoop; black window surrounds and quarter louvers; front and rear spoilers, and a black leather interior. The T-Roof was non-production item. A similar roof had been a $625 option in 1978, but was not available on 1979 models, except for this Replica. However, possibly because of its use here, the T-Bar would be reintroduced on the 1980 models.

Totally new in size and style was the LTD line of full-size Fords. Still commanding the top spot in luxury and price was the LTD Landau sub-series, consisting of this 4-door Sedan, Model 65, and a 2-door Sedan, Model 64. Marking the first time that a top level Ford had broken the $6,000 base (exclusive of Thunderbird), the 4-door Landau priced out at $6,474, while the 2-door version hit $6,349. Still, sales were brisk, and the 4-door model accounted for 74,599 units while the less popular 2-door reached 42,314. Nicely squared rear lines provided a huge rear window and a rather formal trunk deck. Space accountability was a factor in the design, and the trunk now offered 23.3 cubic feet of storage space, which was more than in the 1978 models.

The plain LTD line consisted of the same two car models as did the Landau sub-series, plus had two wagon models. In the car line, there was this Model 63 4-door sedan and the Model 62 2-door Sedan. Most popular of all LTDs, the 4-door accounted for 117,730 sales, and thus also became Ford's fifth most popular model overall. It was base priced at $5,913, while the 2-door version was $100 cheaper, and drew less than half as many orders, ending with production of 54,005. All LTDs used the 302 V-8 as their base power, with both 351 models being available as options. However, all larger blocks had now been discontinued. This example is shown with the optional vinyl top, a $116 extra.

Despite its down-sizing, Ford claimed that its LTD Station Wagon, Model 74, would still hold as many passengers or as much cargo as did the former models. Once again, the dual facing rear seats were available at $150 for those wanting 10-passenger capacity. Priced at $6,122, the wagon drew 37,955 orders in base form. The luggage rack was a $115 option. The LTD models now used a 114.4 inch wheelbase chassis, as opposed to 121 inches in 1978. Also, the wagons were now 212.9 inches overall, as opposed to 225.7, while the cars were 209 inches as opposed to 224.1 inches. Ford was proud of the fact that its full-size wagons offered 91.7 cubic feet of cargo space, and that they could carry a standard 4x8 sheet of plywood flat on the cargo floor.

Buyers who wanted four-eyed LTDs had to go with the Landau models in the cars or with the Country Squire in the wagon field. Only the top level full-size Fords used the quad headlights, set horizontally on top of long rectangular parking lights. Plain LTD models used single rectangular headlights set in large chrome bezels, and had the parking lights set into the grille. Although the Country Squire was officially part of the plain LTD line, it once again used the exclusive frontal design of the Landau sub-series. Ford's highest priced model, outside of the Thunderbirds, the Squire listed at $6,615, with the wire type wheel covers being another $145 for the set. Oddly, though the Squire is usually thought of as a separate model, Ford also listed it as an option package at $760 above the base wagon price. Still separate production figures were kept on the Squire (seldom done with an option package), showing that 29,932 went out the door this year.

Entering its final year was the nice looking, misnamed, and never popular LTD II series of cars. Representing the highest trim level was the Brougham sub-series, with probably the most stylish being the 2-door Hardtop Coupe, Model 30. It was base priced at $5,780, which included the 302 basic engine used in all LTD II models. Broughams this year had new interior fabrics, and used a full bench seat with pull-down center arm rests. The vinyl half roof was standard, but the wire-type wheel covers shown here were an option at $160 a set. Apparently because of low sales, all Brougham production figures were included with those of the standard LTD II models.

The other style in the 2-model LTD II Brougham sub-series was the 4-door Sedan, Model 31. Still officially referred to as a Pillared Hardtop, the car is shown here with its standard full vinyl roof, deluxe wheel covers, and wide side trim with color-keyed vinyl inserts. In this form it was priced at $5,905 and represented the highest priced LTD II. At 3,889 pounds, it was also the heaviest. The LTD 4-doors still used a 118-inch wheelbase, while the 2-door models were on a 114-inch base.

The plain LTD II 2-door Hardtop was a mighty pretty car when fitted with the $450 Sports Appearance package shown here. the grouping included a color-keyed full-length tape stripe with matching C-pillar wrapover and blanked opera windows. Also included were the magnum styled steel wheels with chromed beauty rings and bright spoke faces. Often sold in conjunction with this package was the $150 Sports Instrumentation group, which included a tachometer and real oil pressure and ammeter gauges. For another $210, buyers could have an interior with vinyl front bucket seats and central console.

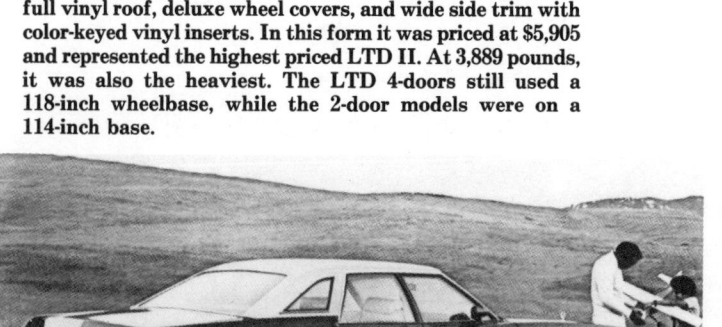

The LTD II still offered one of the most unique and classic type front end designs to come about in years. The sad part is that it appeared on a car with little buyer interest. Shown without the Sports package is the standard 2-door Hardtop, which bore the same Model 30 as the Brougham. Total production of this model, in both Brougham and standard form was only 18,300. In standard form it had a base price of $5,445. Though usually seen with opera windows as shown here and on the Brougham version, these actually were $55 factory-installed accessories. The standard rear quarter would have had blank sides, as in the sports packages. The car shown here has the optional 2-tone paint treatment ($80); vinyl-filled side trim ($40); vinyl half roof ($115); luxury wheel covers $110), and dual racing mirrors ($70), plus whatever interior options do not show.

Although the LTD "S" models represented the lowest trim level in that series, the addition of a $525 Sports Touring package made the car look like anything but a stripper. The Sports Touring package offered a unique 2-tone paint treatment, exclusive side trim, special argent grille, and the same Magnum 500 styled-steel wheels with brightwork and white lettered tires as found on the Sports appearance package. The 2-door Hardtop is shown here without the addition of the opera windows, most often seen on the Broughams and standard LTD IIs. In the "S" series, the 2-door was the lowest priced of all LTD II models, based at $5,198. It also was the least popular, with only 834 sold. Faring better, but still very low was the "S" 4-door, priced at $5,569. It drew all of 9,649 sales.

Displaying all of the European influence that their name implied were the two Granada "ESS" models, the 4-door Sedan, Model 82/433 shown here, or the 2-door version, Model 81/433. Standing for "European Sport Sedan," the ESS sub-series represented the top of the Granada line. Detailing was heavily influenced by the Mercedes, including the color-keyed wheel covers, blackout center grille, and black window surrounds and trim. Inside were individually reclining front seats with European-type head rests, and a leather wrapped steering wheels. Most expensive of all Granadas, the 4-door sold for $5,273 as a V-8, while a similar powered 2-door was $5,161 with the 302 block. Production figures were not separated in the Granada line this year.

Though looking even better than the Brougham version, information shows that this is simply a well-dressed standard version of the LTD II 4-door Pillared Hardtop. Without all of the goodies, such as the $360 set of cast aluminum turbine wheels or the $115 vinyl full roof, the car had a base price of $5,569. Despite its good looks, sales were lacking, and only 19,781 were turned out in both the plain and Brougham versions. All LTD II models could avail themselves of either of the two optional 351 V-8 engines with the 2-barrel model being a $265 addition. Thus, the car shown was well over the $6,000 mark and very much into what a full-size LTD would cost. This, plus lack of the promised gas economy of the LTD II probably hastened the demise of an otherwise very good and nice looking vehicle.

The Ghia sub-series was the middle ground of the Granada line. It consisted of the same two models as did each sub-series, with this example being the 2-door Sedan, Model 81/602. As a V-8 it sold for $5,011, while with the 250 straight Six it was $285 less. A 4-speed manual transmission was standard, with 4th being an overdrive gear. Ghia interiors were more plush than those of the plain Granada, and the vinyl half roof was standard. However, the wire-type wheel covers shown here were a $65 option on the Ghia and ESS models, but $120 extra on the plain Granadas. Ghias also used heavy side molding and had bright trim on the escutcheon plate.

Shown with the attractive 2-tone paint option and cast aluminum wheels is the Granada 4-door Sedan, Model 82/602. Without the fancy work, the car was base priced at $5,113 and weighed 3,203 pounds with the 302 V-8. The 2-tone treatment was another $165, while the cast aluminum wheels were $250 a set in the Granada and ESS sub-series. A view through the windshield shows that this model might have the $270 optional leather seat trim, and the $100 console, not inappropriate for a well-dressed Ghia. A $900 powered Moonroof would have really sent the price upward.

Also wearing cast aluminum wheels, which in the plain Granada models cost $290 extra, is this 2-door Sedan, Model 81. Less popular than the 4-door, the car drew 76,850 total orders, including ESS and Ghia versions. In basic form it was priced at $4,342 with the straight Six. Granada 2-doors were noted for their unique double opera windows. The 4-door variation was by far the more popular having 105,526 sales to account for 7th place in Ford's overall sales picture. The 4-door had a base price of $4,445 and weighed 3,098 pounds with the Six.

Fairmont's style leader was the Futura Sport Coupe, Model 93. Most often seen with the basic Six for $4,312, it was also popular with the 302 V-8, a $525 option. Least popular was with the basic Four, in which form it sold for $4,071. All totalled, Futura's sales accounted for 106,065, making it the 2nd most popular Fairmont and the 6th most popular Ford overall. The Futura Sport Coupe used its own distinctive front, being the only Fairmont to have the dual rectangular headlamps stacked over the dual rectangular parking/signal lamps. It also had front disc brakes and a deluxe sound deadening package.

All dressed up in the popular Sport Group package, a $100 option, is this Fairmont Futura Sport Coupe, Model 93. Essentially the Sport Group included the unique rear tape striping, an argent grille in dark gray, and color-keyed turbine-styled wheel covers. Though keyed to the youth set, the sport Group in some ways detracted from the very good overall looks of the regular Futura.

At mid-year, the Futura Sport Coupe received a new addition in the form of the Luxury Futura. Sometimes called the Futura Ghia, this model featured three exclusive paint treatments, with color-coordinated interiors and unique luxury-cloth seats and trim. Also part of the package were the color-keyed turbine-type wheel covers shown here, bright dual remote control mirrors, and the Futura's exclusive face. The Ghia treatment was considered an option package priced at $500. It was often combined with the $310 Interior Accent Group, which included flight-bench seats; luxury steering wheel; woodgrained instrument panel; deluxe interior trim; 18-ounce cut pile carpeting, and a carpeted luggage compartment.

Most popular of the Fairmont line, and Ford's 3rd most popular model overall, was the Fairmont 4-door Sedan, Model 92, which drew 133,813 orders. As a basic car, it cost $3,810 with the Four, or $4,051 with the Six. Of course, that did not include the dress-up package shown on this model, which included a $125 set of wire-type wheel covers; the $72 installation of side trim; or the $115 full vinyl roof. Other popular options this year included tilt steering wheel at $75; Cruise control at $125; power windows and seat at $350, and air conditioning at $610.

The plain Fairmont 2-door sedan, Model 91, differed substantially from the Futura model, in that it used large quarter windows, had no B-pillar wrapover, and was fitted with the standard Fairmont front, which had single rectangular headlamps, flanked by the parking/signal lamps. Least popular of all Fairmonts, it drew only 54,798 orders, despite its 4-cylinder base price of $3,710 being the lowest in the Fairmont line. The car is shown here with the $330 ES (Euro Sport) package, which included a blackout grille; black window surrounds; special bright and black side molding; black remote sport mirrors; a handling/suspension package; rear stabilizer bar, and the turbine wheel covers shown here.

The Fairmont wagon line also included a Squire model, but it was considered a $400 trim package, and not a distinct model. Essentially the Squire Option offered the vinyl wood-grained trim, and a slightly upgrade of interior trim. The wire-type wheel covers shown here were still a $125 addition, while the roof rack was another $75. Popular options on this model were a lockable rear storage box and a rear window wiper/washer. Unlike the Pinto wagon which used a lift gate, the Fairmont wagons used a conventional tailgate and roll-down window.

The top ranking station wagon in Ford's entire line was the Fairmont, Model 94, which drew 100,691 orders to place in 8th spot overall. With the 6-cylinder engine it was the most expensive Fairmont, costing $4,398 in the basic trim shown here. However, this example does have the $40 deluxe wheel covers and the $75 luggage rack. As before, Fairmont wagons used the same chassis of 105.5 inches wheelbase as used on the passenger cars while its overall length was the same 193.8 inches. This meant that the wagon was actually shorter than the Futura Sport Coupe, which measured 195.8 inches overall.

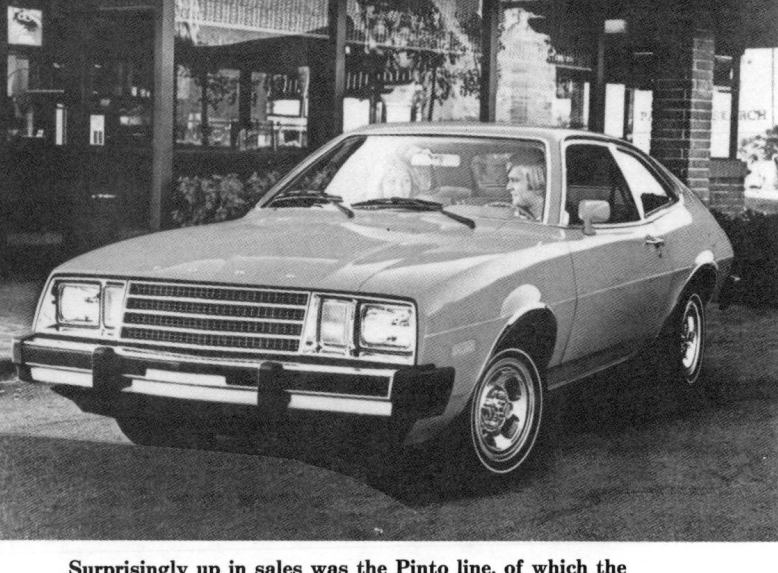

Surprisingly up in sales was the Pinto line, of which the 2-door Sedan was still the best selling. Named the Mode 10, it accounted for 75,789 sales. With a base price of $3,629 with the 140 cubic inch Four, the car was also available with the V-6 for $275 more. This view shows off the new grille, Pinto's main claim to fame this year. Also shown are the attractive forged aluminum wheels, which sold for $290 a set, and really were beyond the pockets of most Pinto buyers. The new frontal concept was similar to that found on the Fairmonts, with large rectangular headlights being separated from the grille by vertical rectangular parking lights.

With the 1979 base price of the Pinto Pony up to $3,199, Ford left forever the under $3,000 base tag. Continuing to be the only Pinto with no engine option, Pony buyers took only the 140 cubic inch four and 4-speed manual transmission. Still, the cars offered front disc brakes and rack-and-pinion steering as standard equipment. Since the Pony's production was mixed in with that of the 2-door Sedan, it is impossible to tell how many of the 75,789 sales went to this model, or how many were for higher trim versions.

Showing off its $30 extra all-glass third door is the Pinto Hatchback, Model 11. Often referred to as the 3-door Hatchback, the sprightly little car is shown here with the $40 exterior decor group, a $100 set of wire-type wheel covers, and defroster strips in the rear glass, which cost another $85. Without the trim, the car would have sold for $3,744 with the Four, or 4,017 with the V-6. It weighed about 2,500 pounds. Barely visible on this model is another popular Pinto option, the $200 flip-up open air roof. Still equipped with a fold-down rear seat, the Hatchback dropped in popularity, and registered only 69,383 units.

New for the Pinto line was the ESS Option, which attempted to give the little horse a look of European sportiness. Available on both the 2-door and 3-door models, the $260 package included a special black grille and window surrounds; special dark glass on the back door; black wheel lip moldings and side trim; dual black racing mirrors, and styled steel wheels with beauty rings and bright spokes. New on all Pintos was a revised instrument cluster.

Another of Ford's mid-year toys was the Rallye package for Pintos. Coming out in May, 1979, this trim grouping was a $370 option available only on the Hatchback and Station Wagon models, but not on the Sedan. The package included an all-glass rear door; front and rear spoilers; white styled steel wheels with trim rings but painted spokes; dual sports mirrors; heavier suspension; performance instrumentation, and of course the heavy Rallye trim on the lower body. When added to the Station Wagon, the package also included steel side panels with port hole windows for the rear section, carpeted load floor, and a black luggage rack. On the wagon, the Rallye Pack cost $625.

The Pinto Wagon was now the basis for three different major trim packages (Cruising Wagon; Rallye; and Squire). But in its plain form, as Model 12, it provided a nice low-buck vehicle for those needing more room than provided by the Pinto cars. Prices began at $4,157 for the Four, or $4,398 for the V-6. A total of 53,846 were built. Pinto Wagons continued to use an exclusive foundation with a 94.8-inch wheelbase, as opposed to the 94.5 inches for the cars. They were substantially longer than the cars, however, being 178.6 inches overall as opposed to 168.8 inches for the cars.

Providing what Ford called a "country club look" was the Squire Package for the Pinto Station Wagon. The popular wood grain addition gave the car a luxury look for about $300. Not included was the $65 luggage rack or the $100 set of wire wheel covers. As before, the center windows would flip open from the trailing edge. All Pinto wagons used a full lift gate, hinged at the roof.

Pinto's unusual "Cruising Wagon" package this year was available on both the wagons and the hatchback models, though it was probably most often seen on the wagons, as shown here. This year the package had an entirely new set of multi-color graphics, running full length along the belt line, and streaming from the B-pillar to the porthole. On the hatchback, the package cost $330 while on the wagon it was $565. Included in the box were white cast aluminum wheels; blackout front similar to that of the Rallye, dual racing mirrors, and on the wagon, a chromed roof rack. The interior was fully carpeted in both versions.

Continued to be offered by Ford dealers was the little German-built Fiesta, Ford's first front-wheel-drive offering. Now base priced at $4,198, the car continued to use a transverse-mounted 4-cylinder engine of 97.6 cubic inches. It was built on a 90 inch wheelbase, and measured 147.1 inches overall. Surprisingly, interest in the little car continued to grow, and a total of 78,109 were sold. This marked the high-point for Fiesta sales in the U.S. This year the car featured front bucket seats with higher backs and integral headrests, but otherwise was unchanged from the 1978 models.

Appearing for the last time was the Ranchero, based on the LTD II chassis, and using the attractive front sheet metal from that line. Virtually unchanged for the past three years, the very attractive truck came in plain 500 form for $5,866; as a Squire with imitation wood sides for $6,014, or as the most expensive unit, the GT model shown here for $6,289. Both the plain and GT models enjoyed about the same popularity, with the plain model drawing 12,093 sales while the slightly more popular GT drew 12,159. The Squire, meanwhile, barely survived with only 758 going out the door. The GT package included styled steel wheels with beauty rings; special exterior graphics; dual sport mirrors, and a flight-bench front seat in cloth and vinyl. It was available with either the 302 or the 351 V-8, with the 351 engines being the most popular. With the demise of the LTD II, the Ranchero also went away.

After only three years on the market, the Thunderbird was once again given a total revision. Now once again a smaller car than offered previously, it also suffered from being fitted with Ford's smallest V-8 engine as standard power. But to point out that sales suffered tremendously from the downsizing would be unfair.

True, Thunderbird sales dropped substantially, but so too did Mustangs', and the big LTD line took a whooping 43% drop from 1979. In fact, production reached such a low level that it forced the closing of two major Ford plants, the one at Mahwah, N.J., and the other at Los Angeles. But Ford was not alone in the sales crunch. Throughout the industry, severe buyer resistance was the norm this year. Also not helping Ford sales was the discontinuance of the LTD II line. Though never popular, the LTD II series still accounted for over 50,000 units in 1979.

Regarding the Thunderbird, the car was still billed as Ford's top luxury model. However, it now utilized a 108.4-inch wheelbase, a 5.6-inch reduction, while its overall length decreased to 200.4 inches from 217.2 inches, a big reduction of 16.8 inches. The car had a new unitized body, with deft styling to hide the fact that for all practical purposes it was built on a somewhat modiied Fairmont coupe body. Because of the smaller size, Ford could no longer claim 6-passenger capacity, and thus advertising stressed the Thunderbird as being a luxury vehicle for four passengers.

Styling features included a rather unusual frontal treatment, which still hinted strongly of previous Thunderbirds, including the retention of concealed headlamps. The basic Thunderbird and Town Landau models entered the scene first, closely followed by the Thunderbird Silver Anniversary Model, which replaced last year's Heritage Edition. Silver Anniversary

Totally new and greatly downsized was the new Thunderbird, Model 87. Base priced at $6,432, the 3,118-pound car is shown here dressed up with the Exterior Decor Group. This $360 package included a rear vinyl half-roof, wire-type wheel covers, dual remote control outside mirrors, and special side trim. The package was usually accompanied by the Interior Decor group, a $350 option. Whether it was economics or the car itself, or the $500 increase in price, or a combination of all three, the end result was the same. Total T-Bird production was down to 156,803. This was enough to make Thunderbird the best selling of all Fords, but still represented a decrease of 127,338 sales from the 1979 figures.

models came in a variety of colors, but all shared the same Dove Gray interior. All base and Landau Thunderbirds also used as standard power a new 255 cubic inch V-8, which will be described later, while the Silver Anniversary models had the 302 cubic inch engine and automatic transmission as standard equipment. This combination was the only engine option available to the rest of the T-Bird line this year.

In the big Ford line, the major news concerned a name switch, with the old Crown Victoria title being resurrected to replace the former Landau designation as the top line. Included with the switch was the Country Squire being moved from the mid-series to the top line category for this year only. The super-basic LTD "S" series, comparable to the old Custom line, also received a wagon this year, in addition to its coupe and sedan models. The 302 cubic inch block remained the basic engine, while the 351 V-8 was the only option. Once again, a high-output 351 was available for police use only, but probably found its way to the general public as well.

In the Fairmont line, a new series emerged, known as the Futura. Available first only as a Sport Coupe, the series was similar to the Futura package offered as an option previously. Later in the year, the Futura designation was extended to the sedan. Futura models had a unique grille fitted with halogen headlamps, special moldings on the body sides, wheel cutouts, and door edges, and a more luxurious interior. In addition, a Futura Sports Group package could be ordered, which

Hotshot of the new Thunderbird line, at least at the start of the year, was the Town Landau version, which initially was the only Ford to break the $10,000 mark. It had a base price of $10,036. Among the extras provided on this model were the vinyl half-roof, wrapover roof applique, and unique quarter windows about half the size found on the regular Bird. Wire-type wheel covers, remote exterior mirrors, and a plush interior were also in the package, but the two-tone paint job shown here was $165 extra. Over 16 inches shorter than the previous T-Birds, the new models were built with a unitized body which essentially was a stretched version of the Fairmont coupe. Even though Ford claimed that the new Birds had more interior space than the previous models, they were still listed as 4-passenger cars, rather than the 5/6-passenger capacity rating held by last year's models.

included turbine-type wheel covers. Those wishing a different sedan could order the $380 Euro-Styled (ES) Package, which included a unique blackout grille, turbine wheel covers, and exclusive moldings.

Early in the year, it was announced that Mustang's turbocharged 4-cylinder engine would be available in the Fairmont line, but this never materialized. Instead, the basic engine was the 140 cubic inch four, with the 200 cubic inch Six being an option along with the new 225 V-8. The old 302 V-8 was no longer offered in the Fairmont line.

In the Mustang barn, engines also made big news. Both the Four and its turbocharged variation were again offered, but the German-built V-6 was no longer in use. Instead, Mustang reverted back to Ford's in-line Six of 200 cubic inches, while it also accepted the new 255 cubic inch V-8 as its top power option. As with Fairmont, the 302 V-8 was no longer available. Stylewise, the major changes occurred on a package, not on the line itself. This was the result of the $1,480 Cobra option receiving a new slat-type grille similar to the previous Indy Replicar version. Also similar to that design were the new rear spoilers, frontal air dams with fog lights built-in, hood scoop, and tape graphics. Less speed oriented buyers had package choices such as Ghia trim, Sport Option, Carriage Roof, and Exterior Trim packages.

Virtually unchanged was the Granada, still available in base, Ghia, and "ESS" series. The basic engine remained the 250 cubic inch Six, with the 302 V-8 being the only option. However, California required the new 255 V-8 as the base power package, and this too became available on all Granadas.

Entering its last year, the Pinto also received few changes. Its main claim was the availability of the 140 cubic inch Four as the only engine, as the German V-6 was no longer being imported. The car was still available in three body styles, in both basic and Pony (stripped) trim levels. In addition, there was a Rallye Pack and an ESS Edition package available, the latter carrying a gray argent grille and headlight surrounds, and black moldings as its primary points.

As mentioned, one of Ford's largest items this year was the new 255 cubic inch V-8, which was a basic block in Thunderbirds, and appeared on the option list of both Fairmont and Granada, but did not enter the LTD ranks. Essentially a rework of the old 302 which it replaced in those models, the engine had a bore and stroke of 3.68x3 inches and a compression ratio of 8.8:1. Surprisingly, optional Fairmont and Granada models were rated at 119 horsepower, while Thunderbird versions were rated at only 115 horses, both ratings being made at 3800 rpm. In other engine news, the modified 351 of 151 horsepower was discontinued, and only the 140 horse 351 was available, and was used only in LTDs.

As mentioned, production slumped dramatically, dropping down to 1,167,581, a loss of 641,606 sales from 1979. In addition, only three models topped the 100,000 list. They were the new Thunderbird with only 156,803 sales, the Fairmont 4-door Sedan with 1453,118, and the Mustang Notchback with 128,893 units produced.

Virtually unchanged was the year-old Mustang styling. Once again the top series was the Ghia, which consisted of the Model 04 2-door Notchback and this 3-door Hatchback, Model 05. Least popular of all Mustangs, the Ghia Hatchback drew only 20,285 orders. It was base priced at $5,512 with the Four or $5,731 with the In-line Six, which though an old Ford engine, was a new block for Mustang. The German-built V-6 was no longer available, but the new 255 cubic inch V-8 became a popular option at $340. Ghia's other model, the Notchback, drew 23,647 orders, with a base price of $2,565 for the Four.

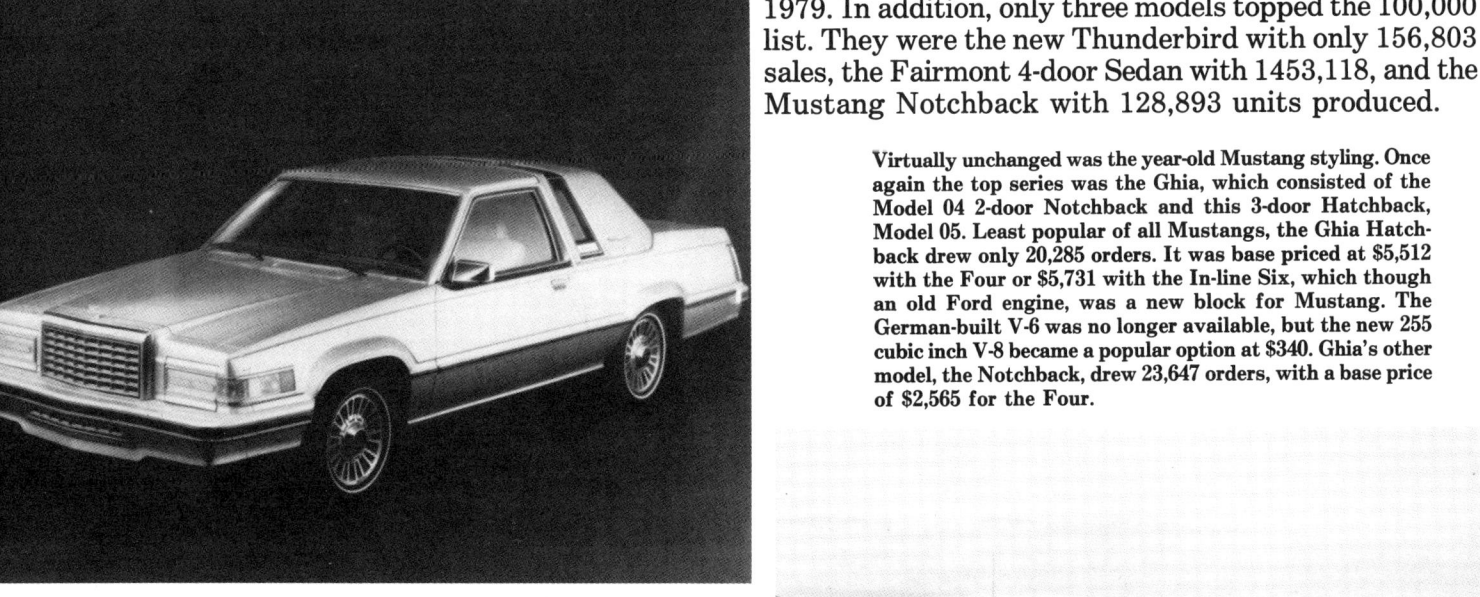

Popping up with the tulips in the spring was Ford's most expensive car to date. It was the Silver Anniversary Thunderbird, priced at $11,679. Named in honor of the 25 years that Thunderbird had been on the market, the Silver Anniversary edition had a special luxury interior done in Dove Gray, were fitted with special cast aluminum wheels, wore a slightly different front end, and had a standard 4-speed overdrive automatic that was a $140 option on regular Birds. The standard engine was the new 255 cubic inch V-8, but the 302 was used in the Silver Anniversary model. Ford kept no separate breakout figures on the Town Landau or the Anniversary edition.

Most popular Mustang, and in fact Ford's third most popular car, was the plain Notchback, Model 02. It drew a total of 128,893 orders. Also in the plain Mustang family was the Model 03 3-door Hatchback, which attracted 98,497 buyers. As a Six, the Notchback cost $5,103, while the Hatchback version was $410 more expensive. This example sports the new diamond-grain vinyl Carriage roof, which was supposed to provide a convertible-like look. It was priced at $625, as opposed to the plain full vinyl roof, which was only a $120 option. Also apparent in this view are the high-back Recaro bucket seats, which cost an additional $535. The low-back regular buckets, which were standard in Ghia models, cost an additional $345 in the plain Mustangs.

When fitted with the Turbo option, the Ghia Hatchback took on a different appearance. In addition to the standard Ghia low-back bucket seats and Euro-style trim, the Turbo models sported a unique hood with "Turbo" signatures. Under this hood lived the turbo-charged 140 cubic inch Four which developed 150 horses at 4800 rpm, as opposed to the 88 horses developed by the regular 140 cubic inch Four. Not cheap, the Turbo package could be installed on any Mustang for $480 extra.

The Mustang Cobra, often thought of as a separate model, was actually a $1,485 package on the plain Hatchback. Included in the treatment were a new front end featuring a blackout grille with two horizontal slats and encompassing the quad headlights; a special bumper with air dam which incorporated high-intensity driving/fog lights; special hood with rear-facing non-functional scoop, and a rear spoiler. New graphics included the black lower panels and molding, and revised striping. Forged aluminum wheels, a 4-speed floor shifter, special suspension system, and 8000 rpm tachometer were also part of the package. Buyers had a choice of the Turbo Four or the new 255 cubic inch (4.2 litre) engine, and a 3-speed automatic could be substituted for the floor-four. But the hood graphics shown here were a $90 extra.

The LTD Crown Victoria was not a new model, it was simply a new name for the old LTD Landau models. Best looking and least popular of the new Crown line was the 2 door Sedan, Model 64, which drew only 7,725 orders. The $7,070 car is shown here with the two-tone paint and trim option, which cost an additional $75. However, the vinyl half-roof and wrapover top trim were standard Crown items. The 302 cubic inch V-8 was standard this year, but the 351 was still a popular option at $150. The new 255 V-8 was not available in LTD models, nor was the High-Output V-8, which was now Ford's most powerful engine and restricted to police use only...at least in theory.

Most popular of the new Crown Victoria models was the 4-door Sedan, Model 65, which drew 21,962 orders. It was base priced at $7,201 and weighed 3,524 pounds. In addition to the vinyl half-roof and distinctive trim, Crown Victorias included 18-ounce cut pile carpeting, luxury instrument panel, a "flight bench" front seat with pull-down center arm rest, and deluxe door panel trim. However, the beautiful cast aluminum wheels so often seen on these cars were a $310 option. Another popular option was the new 4-speed overdrive automatic transmission, which cost $140 extra. Despite a design which would have easily accommodated them, there were no hidden headlight models available this year, except for the Thunderbirds.

For this year only, the Country Squire returned to the top ranks and was considered part of the new Crown Victoria sub-series. However, the car suffered a substantial drop in popularity, and only 9,868 were sold. These went for a base price of $7,426, making the 3,743-pound wagon both the most expensive and heaviest model Ford outside of the Thunderbird ranks. The car is shown with the standard Crown Victoria full wheel covers. As always, the roof-top luggage rack was an accessory, this year priced at $115. Again, dual facing rear seats were available for $150 a set, factory ordered.

For those not liking the wood body sides or high trim level of the Country Squire, there was the Country Sedan, which remained in the plain LTD ranks. Designated Model 74, it had a base price of $6,741 (almost $700 less than the Squire) and weighed 3,717 pounds. A bit more popular than the woodie, it drew 11,718 orders. It is shown here with wire-type wheel covers at $140 a set, optional roof rack, and $75 two-tone paint job. All LTD's sold in California were base priced $235 above other similar units due to that state's mandatory emissions systems.

Playing policeman is this LTD 4-door Sedan, Model 63. It is shown here in strictly stock form (except for the police light bar) with the standard hub caps, black wall tires, and single side molding. Even in this form, the car turned out to be the most popular of the large Fords, with 51,630 sold. They were based priced at $6,302 with the 302 V-8. However, in police guise, the car probably had the High-Output 351 V-8 and heavy-duty suspension package. Also in the plain LTD ranks was the Model 62 2-door Sedan, which sold for $6,549. Far less popular than the 4-door version, it saw only 15,333 go to market.

The lowest priced full-size Fords were those in the LTD "S" line. Not simply an interior trim reduction, the "S" cars wore a completely different face, more akin to the Fairmonts than to the other LTD members. The "S" line was divided into three models, with this 4-door Sedan, Model 61, being the most popular with 19,283 sold. It was base priced at $6,320. New to this sub-series was a Station Wagon, Model 72, which sold for $6,741 and drew 3,490 models. Having the lowest production of any large Ford was the third LTD "S" model, the 2-door Sedan, which saw only 553 leave the plant. However, these 2-doors might all have been on special order, as little information on them is carried in any of Ford's literature. The 2-door model did not appear in the 1981 line.

The top of the Granada line remained the "ESS" sub-series, which included both a 2-door and a 4-door version. This is the 2-door, which sold for $5,477 with the In-line Six or $5,515 with the 302 V-8, except in California where the new 255 cubic inch V-8 was a mandatory replacement for the 302. Standing for "European Sports Sedan," ESS models were distinguished by black rocker panels and black side molding with bright inserts. The 2-door also had a louvered applique on the opera window, while inside resided bucket seats with special vinyl upholstery and trim. ESS production was included with that of all Granadas.

Trying to look as close to a European (Mercedes) sedan as an American car could get was the Granada ESS 4-door Sedan, which was priced at $5,598 with the Six. Among the identifying features of this model was the unique blackout grille and the special wheel covers, painted in matching color to the body (again ala Mercedes). Also unique to the ESS models were the wide wheel opening moldings, leather wrapped steering wheel, and dual remote control outside mirrors, painted in body color.

Only slightly lower in trim than the ESS sub-series was the Granada Ghia line, which also consisted of a two and a 4-door Sedan. These models used a bright grille rather than the ESS blackout variety, and had plain wheel covers, rather than the Mercedes-type. However, this example wears the beautiful cast aluminum wheels at $350 a set, and also sports the $120 vinyl roof and what appears to be the indentations for the $998 power moon roof. In standard form, the Ghia 4-door sold for $5,509 with the basic Six, while the 2-door went for $5,388. The 302 V-8 was $188 more, but the 255 V-8 was only $38 extra.

As did the two upper trim level series, the plain Granada series also consisted to a two and a 4-door sedan. Surprisingly, in the total Granada line, the 2-door models were far more popular than the 4-doors, with 60,872 being sold, as opposed to only 29,557 4-door models. In plain form, the Granada 2-door sold for $4,987 as a Six, and thus was the only Granada under the $5,000 mark. The 4-door version, meanwhile, sold for $5,108. All Granadas averaged about 3,200 pounds in weight, with 2-doors ranging around 3,100 and 4-doors up to 3,300 pounds. This example is wearing the optional vinyl top and the $120 set of wire-type wheel covers.

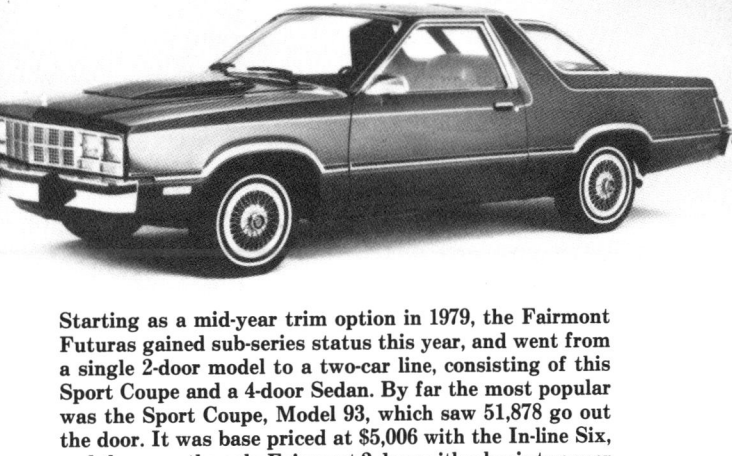

Starting as a mid-year trim option in 1979, the Fairmont Futuras gained sub-series status this year, and went from a single 2-door model to a two-car line, consisting of this Sport Coupe and a 4-door Sedan. By far the most popular was the Sport Coupe, Model 93, which saw 51,878 go out the door. It was base priced at $5,006 with the In-line Six, and thus was the only Fairmont 2-door with a basic tag over $5,000. It is shown here in 4-cylinder Turbo form, which was a $480 option above the $4,873 basic price for the plain 140 cubic inch Four. The distinguishing feature of this example, obviously, is the Turbo hood, which left no doubt about what was powering the neat little car.

For those who wanted to show that their Fairmont Futura Coupe really had it all, Ford offered the Sport Option, available with or without the Turbo engine. The package, shown here on the Futura Turbo Coupe, cost $115, and consisted of turbine-style wheel covers, a blackout grille, black aluminum steering wheel spokes, and the obvious rear quarter graphics. This model also has the $55 two-tone paint scheme, which put the lower panels in a contrasting color to the primary shade.

Although the main stress of the Fairmont Futura Coupes was its sporty air, the model also had its luxury package. This came in the form of the Ghia package, which was only a $195 option on the Sport Coupe, but ran up to $565 when applied to the 4-door Sedan. Included in this package were the quad halogen headlamps, exclusive Futura grille, and the exclusive Futura Coupe rear quarter treatment, all involved in a special paint scheme with its own striping. The Ghia option could be applied to all Futura 2-door models, including the Turbo, as seen here.

Appearing at mid-year was the Futura 4-door Sedan, Model 92. Priced at $5,070 with the standard Four, it was the only Fairmont to have an absolute base price over $5,000. Only one-tenth as popular as the 2-door Futura Sport Coupe, it drew 5,306 orders. The price included the turbine-styled wheel covers shown here, the heavy body side and wheel cutout moldings, and the exclusive Futura grille in bright chrome, but the vinyl top shown here was $120 extra. Bright window trim was another feature of the Futura sub-series.

The plain Fairmont 2-door Sedan used a totally different rear quarter than did the Futura models, with the aft section being of rather plain conventional styling as opposed to the unique Futura treatment. In absolutely basic form, the Fairmont 2-door Sedan, Model 91, was priced at $4,435 with the small Four, or $170 more with the In-line Six. However, this example wears the $95 Exterior Accent Group, which included bright rocker panel, body side and wheel lip moldings, bright window surrounds, and full wheel covers. Least popular of the plain Fairmonts, the 2-door Sedan drew 45,074 orders.

Those who wanted an ultimate Fairmont sport machine without going to the Futura Sport Coupe could settle for the Turbocharged Fairmont Coupe with the ES (Euro Styled) grouping. This package, costing approximately $375 above the base car, not counting the extra $480 for the Turbocharged Four and its exclusive Turbo hood and 4-speed manual floor shifter transmission. The package provided front disc and rear drum brakes; a special handling package; dual rectangular halogen headlights (except in states where prohibited); blackout grille; special molding, striping, and rear quarter vent louvers; turbine-type wheel covers; black sport mirrors, and black sport steering wheel.

The plain-Jane Fairmont 4-door Sedan, Model 92, is shown here without wheel covers while navigating Ford's Dearborn test track. This model turned out to be Ford's second best selling model overall, with 143,118 leaving the factories. As shown, in absolute basic form, it sold for $4,552 with the small Four. This view gives a look at the regular Fairmont grille, which consisted of an egg crate mesh superimposed by one central vertical and two thin horizontal bars, rather than the double egg crate design of the Futura models. In addition to the Four and Six, a popular option in Fairmonts was the new 255 cubic inch V-8, which cost $290 above the basic price.

The ultimate Fairmont 4-door Sedan was not the Futura version, but was the plain Fairmont with the Ghia option. Here the package has been combined with the Turbo engine grouping. By itself, the Ghia application cost $565 when applied to the 4-door, and added another $480 for the Turbo. Included in the package was the unique two-tone paint scheme and a choice of wire-type or turbine-styled wheel covers. Surprisingly, the package did not pick up the Futura's attractive grille, but utilized the more plain standard Fairmont face.

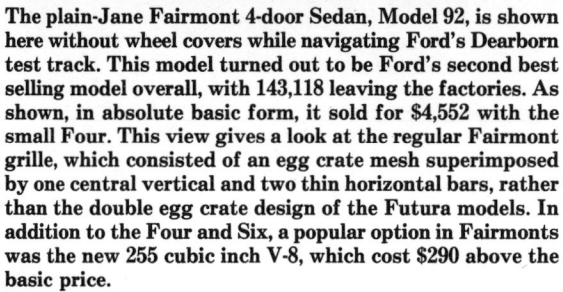

Although the Fairmont station wagons were considered part of the regular line, they did pick up the Futura's unique double egg crate grille and quad halogen headlamps, which made a very attractive unit. More popular than the large wagons, the Model 94 Fairmont variety drew 77,035 orders, all with a basic 6-cylinder price of $4,890. Heaviest of all Fairmonts, it weighed about 2,750 pounds. It was also available with either the plain or Turbo Four, or the 255 cubic inch V-8. This model is wearing the $160 set of wire-type wheel covers.

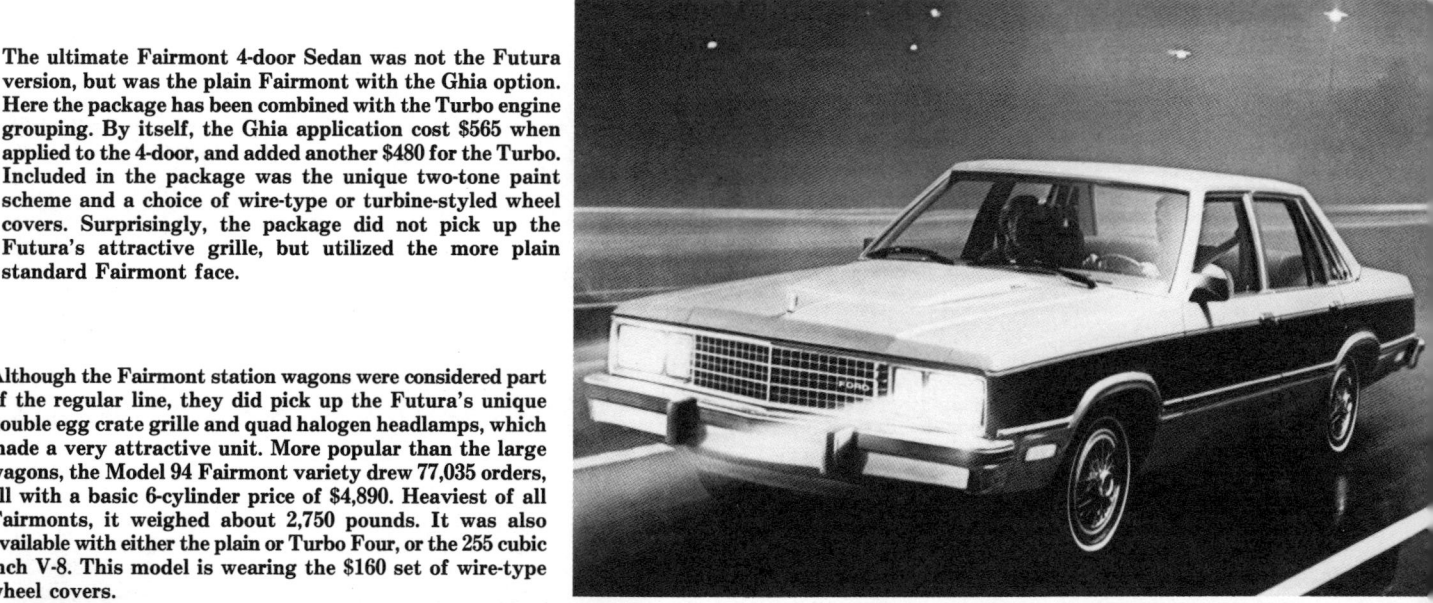

Although application of Squire trim often set a wagon apart as a separate model, in the Fairmont line it was simply another option package. Not cheap, the wood trim added $460 to the basic wagon price, not including the roof luggage rack which was another $90. The full lift-gate was standard, but the rear windshield wiper was a relatively new idea that was becoming quite popular on wagons of all types.

Even the little Pinto received dress-up packages this year. Here the 2-door Sedan, Model 10, is shown with the $315 ESS package, which boosted its $4,223 basic price a fair amount. Most popular of all Pintos, the 2-door Sedan registered a total of 84,053 sales. The ESS grouping included a blackout grille with black headlight bezels; black window moldings; black dual racing mirrors, and styled steel wheels with black centers.

Ford's lowest price car, and the only one to have a sticker reading under $4,000 was the Pinto Pony Sedan, which listed at $3,781. Essentially a stripped version of the Pinto Sedan, the car was available only with the barest of essentials, and all options, including the full wheel covers shown here, had to be purchased extra. This year Pintos had no engine choices, with the 140 cubic inch Four being the only available power. The former German V-6 was no longer being imported and the Turbo Four was not available in the little car line. Production figures of the Pony are included with those of the regular sedan.

All dressed up in a $120 Sport Grouping is this Pinto 3-door Hatchback. In standard form, the Model 11 was priced at $4,335. Not as popular as the sedan, it drew only 61,842 orders. The Sport Package included the all-glass third door, heavy black bumper strips, and unique graphics. The forged white aluminum wheels were $330 extra. This being Pinto's final year, few changes were made to the overall line.

Wearing the year-old Rally Option is this Pinto Hatchback. Costing $370, this package included a special blackout grille with three horizontal slats; special headlight bezels; black window surrounds; "Rally" graphics on the lower panels; dual black racing mirrors; full glass third door, and styled steel wheels. The flip-up roof panel was not part of the package, but was another $220. The Rally package was also supposed to be available on the wagon models, where it cost an extra $625.

Pinto's little 2-door Station Wagon, Model 12, continued to be a rather popular little horse, and 39,159 were sold. In basic form it cost $4,622 and weighed 2,553 pounds. This model is wearing the Exterior Decor Group, a $45 trim option which provided bright rocker panel and wheel lip moldings. It also wears the $70 rooftop luggage rack and the $56 set of styled steel wheels.

Ford's lowest price wagon was the Pinto Pony, shown here with extra cost full wheel covers. Priced at $4,284, it provided basic service at a relatively low price, though only a half-dozen years earlier no one would have thought of a basic car being in the $4,000 range. Pony models did not use tinted glass, body molding, or rear window defrosters. Pony production was part of the total Pinto wagon figure.

Most upscale of all the Pintos was the Squire Wagon, which sometimes is listed as an option package to the regular wagon, and other times is listed as a separate model priced at $4,937. Obviously, the roof rack alone would put this example into the $5,000 category. The wire-type wheel covers were $104 extra. On all Pinto wagons, the windows between the B and C-pillars would flip open, being hinged at the leading edge and latching at the trailing side.

Still aimed at the youth set was the Cruising Wagon option for the Pinto wagon. Priced at $610, the package included exclusive graphics, styled steel wheels, and a blackout panel with porthole covering the two rear quarter windows. Producing an effect similar to the old sedan delivery models, the Cruising Package was primarily popular on the West Coast, though a few were seen in eastern states. The same blackout type of grille and headlight surrounds that was used on the Rally package appeared here. Those not wanting the bright side graphics could opt for a $70 lower price, but in that case, the Cruise wagon really did look like a sedan delivery.

With the arrival of Ford's new front wheel drive Escort planned for 1981, the German-built Fiesta was facing its last year of life. Now priced at $4,493, the peppy little car still managed to draw 68,595 orders. It is shown here with the $560 Sport Package, which included the ubiquitous blackout grille and headlight bezels; black window surrounds; body side tape ending in the letter "S"; heavy duty shock absorbers and rear stabilizer bar; special cloth trim for the low-back reclining bucket seats, and a tachometer. However, the cast aluminum wheels shown here were a $180 option. The Fiesta still used its 97.6 cubic inch transverse-mounted Four, which produced 66 horsepower at 5000 rpm.

It had long been hinted, but now it was a reality. Ford this year introduced its ultra-small car, the Escort. Using Ford's first domestic front wheel drive, and hosting the smallest engine in Ford's domestic history, the little car essentially replaced the Pinto in the sales slotting. However, comparing the two models was impossible, as they were worlds apart in looks, size, and performance. If fact, when parked side by side, the Pinto actually looked large and sleek (if one can imagine a sleek Pinto) while the Escort looked small and boxy, and not too far removed from the German Fiesta. About all that was retained to hint of Pinto was the slanted egg-crate grille and headlamp surround theme. Everything else was Escort exclusively.

The car was issued in a whooping 10 models, all based on two body styles. These were a 2-door with hatchback (also called a 3-door hatchback) and a 4-door sedan with rear liftgate, which possibly could have qualified it for station wagon status. Both models utilized a 94.2-inch wheelbase, which was almost the same as Pinto's, but at 163.9 inches overall length, the hatchback was just about seven inches shorter than the comparable Pinto, while the 4-door at 165 inches overall was 15.6 inches shorter than the Pinto wagon. Both models were 65.9 inches wide.

Ford pointed with pride to the claim that the Escort was a totally new car, with no carry-over components. In fact, Ford boasted that over $3-billion had been spent in its development, of which over $1-billion went into engine design alone. The engine, which offered no options, was an in-line 4-cylinder block of only 97.6 cubic inch displacement, which was the same displacement as the German-built Fiesta. However, the bore and stroke was different than used on the Fiesta, being 3.15x3.13 and the compression ratio was 8.8:1. The smallest domestic Ford engine ever, the little unit turned out 65 horsepower at 5200 rpm as opposed to 66 at 5000 rpm for the Fiesta. The head and intake manifold were aluminum, but the block was cast iron. Being front wheel drive, it utilized a 4-speed manual transaxle as standard fare, but offered a 3-speed automatic as an option. Due to the welter of models issued, and the fact that these really were trim options rather than true models, production information became impossible to decipher. Suffice to say that a total of 320,727 Escorts reached the market, which certainly was a help, in view of Ford's otherwise sagging sales.

Also changed substantially, but almost unnoticed in the light of the new Escort was the Granada line. This was a surprise, as it had been hinted that Ford was thinking of dropping the line, and seldom are major changes made to a series that is about to be abandoned. As occurred with the LTD when that model was down-sized in 1979, the Granada became bigger on the inside but smaller on the outside. Its overall length was cut to 196.5 inches, a reduction of over three inches, while its wheelbase decreased 4.4 inches through the use of

the Fairmont platform for the fully unitized body. Ford said the car was the most changed American sedan of the year, weighing approximately 400 pounds less than previous models, while supposedly offering more shoulder, hip, and leg room and also more usable luggage capacity.

In styling, the car was typically Ford, with its grille flanked by dual rectangular halogen headlamps. The trim levels of L, GL and GLX replaced the former series of Granada, Ghia, and ESS designations. Under the hood, the base engine was the same 140 cubic inch Four as used in the Fairmont, while the 200 cubic inch Six and 255 cubic inch V-8 were the only options.

With the Granada almost becoming a super-Fairmont, the Fairmont itself did very little in the way of changes. Its Futura series was expanded through the addition of a station wagon, but this was a plain-sided model, with the Squire imitation wood trim still being a $200 option. New to the line was an "S" (stripped) model 2-door sedan. The same engine options available to the Granada line were carried by the Fairmonts. Despite the similarity of the cars, their looks were separated by totally different frontal designs, both of which were unmistakably Ford. A totally different checkered grille theme was used, flanked by large parking lights situated between the grille and the single rectangular headlamps. The sedans had six side windows, with the rear window separated from the door by a thin

Replacing the Silver Anniversary model as the top Ford and top Thunderbird was the new Heritage Edition. The pricey car had the distinction of being the most expensive Ford; being the only Ford with a base price of over $10,000 (excluding the special order McLaren Mustang), and being the only Thunderbird to come with a V-8 engine as standard equipment . . . even though that engine was the 255 cubic inch model, and not the optional 302. The car was quite similar to the Anniversary model, and included its own exclusive interior and wore the cast aluminum wheels as standard fare. On other Birds, these wheels were a $565 option. By far the most expensive model, the Heritage had a base price of $11,355.

C-pillar. This was opposed to the Granada models which simply used door windows, with fixed rear corner windows resembling vent panes.

In the land of Mustang, once again change was minimal to the regular line, but headlines were achieved by a special model. Only unlike last year's Cobra changes, this year's big news Mustang was a super-hot limited production model known as the McLaren Mustang. Looking very much like the IMSA Special, the much-modified Mustang's entire front end was taken up by a large air dam which eliminated the grille, had bulging fender flares, functional hood scoops, rear spoiler, and special alloy wheels. The much modified 140 cubic inch Four was fitted with a variable speed turbocharger and produced 175 horsepower. Not cheap, the car appeared at mid-season with a $25,000 price tag. By the end of the model year it had run up a production of 250, some of which were reportedly sold in 1982.

As to the standard Mustang, a new 5-speed manual overdrive transmission was offered for the 4-cylinder engine, a new T-bar roof option was made available for either body style, the Ghia models continued to be the top of the luxury line, and the Cobra package was up to $1,590 in price. All engines remained the same as in 1980.

The big news in the LTD line was the downsizing of the base engine to the 255 cubic inch version, thus making both the 302 and the 351 V-8s extra-cost options. Little changed in appearance, the LTD's year was marked by having the Country Squire once again move back into the base LTD series from the Crown Victoria, and having the "S" series trimmed to two models through the loss of the 2-door sedan...though some information would indicate that this actually occurred

in the 1980 model year.

Just as the LTDs lost power, so too did the year-old downsized Thunderbird. But here the move was even more drastic, and the line found itself housing the old 200 cubic inch Six rather than a familiar V-8. Those who wanted V-8 power had to go for the optional 255 or 302 blocks, or order the new Heritage Edition, in which the 255 cubic inch block was considered standard. The Heritage name was brought back to replace the top-line Silver Anniversary Edition, which of course was a name that could be used for one year only.

In the engine department, the 250 cubic inch Six was gone, but the number of engines being produced remained the same due to the new aforementioned Escort Four. The special Turbocharged Four used on the McLaren Mustangs was an exclusive edition, not available for any other car. Also supposedly exclusive for police use only but apparently finding its way onto the market was a High-Output 351 block that produced 165 horses as opposed to the standard 351 rating of 145 horses.

Once again, despite the new Escort, Ford's model year production slipped, this time by 112,605 units to dip down to 1,054,976. As in 1980, only three models made the list of over 100,000, and two of these were the new Escort. This little car registered 192,554 sales in all trim levels of its hatchback models, and 128,173 sales in its 4-door style. The only other model to come close to these figures was the Fairmont 4-door sedan, which listed 104,883 sales. For some reason, a substantial amount of this decrease was found in Mustang sales, which reached only 182,552 this year, representing a drop of 88,770. And, sadly, 1982 would prove to be even worse for the little horse.

Mid-range in the Thunderbird nest continued to be occupied by the Town Landau models, which shared their unique top styling with the Heritage models. This involved a vinyl half-roof with small opera windows, led by a wrap-over applique of brushed metal. Rather shocking to Bird lovers this year was the decision to use the in-line 200 cubic inch Six as basic power in plain and Town Landau models, and make the 255 V-8 optional for only $50 more (a very wise choice) or the 302 available at $90 more. The wire-type wheel covers shown here were $135 extra. In basic form, the Town Landau cost $8,689 with the Six. All Thunderbird production, regardless of model, was lumped into one figure this year, and no breakouts were made for Landaus or Heritage models.

Plain Thunderbirds could be quickly spotted by their own form of rear quarter treatment, which included an opera window approximately twice the size of that on the Heritage or Landau. In addition, the wrap-over B-pillar trim was not used on the plain models. Costing $7,551 with the Six, the car was suffering from escalating prices and lowering sales. Total production this year reached only 86,693, which was roughly half of the rather poor 1980 showing. This model is shown with the convertible-like carriage roof, which was a $900 option, and it also wears the $100 set of luxury wheel covers.

Continuing to lead the luxury parade of the Mustang family was the Ghia 2-door Notchback, Model 12. Priced at $6,645 with the Six, it was the most fancy and least popular of all Mustangs, with only 13,422 being built. All Mustangs this year weighed approximately 2,600 pounds. For some reason Ford tried to apply the name 2-door Sedan to this model this year, but common terminology of "Notchback" prevailed.

Companion to the Ghia Notchback was the Ghia 3-door Hatchback Coupe, Model 13. Slightly more popular and more expensive than the Notchback, the car drew 14,273 orders with its base 4-cylinder price of $6,729. This model sports the flip-up roof panel which was a $225 option. Engine choices included both the plain and Turbo Four, the 200 cubic inch in-line Six, and the 255 cubic inch V-8. The V-8 added $263 to the price.

Showing off its new $875 T-bar roof is this Mustang 2-door Sedan, or Notchback Coupe. In plain form, this most popular little horse sold for $6,171 with the plain Four, and drew 77,458 orders. The 3-door Hatchback version was almost as popular, drawing 77,399 orders with its base price of $6,408. Judging by the performance shown here, this car might also have the $610 Turbo Four and the brand new $150 5-speed manual transmission with 5th being an overdrive. As noted, Mustang production also took a sever downturn this year.

The hottest Mustang was not a model, but continued to be a $1,600 option package available for either the Notchback or Hatchback models. Included in the well-known Cobra grouping were a distinctive front bumper with integral air dam housing halogen running lights; special slatted blackout grille and black headlight surrounds; black lower body paint and body molding, and black window surrounds. The Turbo Four was standard, but the 255 V-8 could be substituted for a $350 credit. The forged aluminum wheels were also standard, as was the special Turbo hood and rear spoiler. However, the Cobra hood decal shown here was still an $85 addition.

With the Country Squire no longer in the Crown Victoria sub-series, the only other body in that line was the 4-door Sedan, Model 35. Far more popular than the 2-door, the 4-door drew 39,139 orders, which made it the best selling of all the large fords. Its base price was $8,384 while its weight registered 3,538 pounds. Both Crown Victorias are shown here with the beautiful cast aluminum wheels, but these actually were a $340 addition. Also, the vinyl half-roof on this example cost $140, which included the bright wrap-over B-pillar trim.

After the Thunderbird, Ford's most luxurious 2-door was the LTD Crown Victoria Coupe, or 2-door Sedan as Ford termed the car. However, as was the case with Thunderbird, Ford attempted to improve its EPA gas mileage rating by reducing the size of the base engine, and thus the 255 cubic inch V-8 was now considered standard power. However, both the 302 and 351 V-8 engines were still available as rather low-cost options, and information would indicate that the former "police only" High Output 351 was now available for an extra $180. In plain form the 2-door Crown Victoria cost $8,251. A total of 11,061 were sold.

Seldom seen without some form of vinyl roof was the LTD 2-door Sedan, Model 32. This year the plain LTD line and the Crown Victorias were quite similar in exterior appearance when in stock form. Of course, additions of a virtually endless assortment of options could create just about any appearance on any model. Shown here with standard wheel covers, the LTD 2-door had a base price of $7,607. Production was on the low side, with only 6,279 being built.

With the Country Squire back in the plain LTD sub-series, that trim category now provided a home to two full-size wagons. They were the Squire shown here, Model 39, which was base priced at $8,640, and the plain sided LTD wagon, Model 38, which had a tag of $8,180. As it turned out, the plain wagon was the sales leader, drawing 10,554 customers, while the Squire had only 9,443 sales. As before, the Squire was both the most expensive of all full-size Fords, and at 3,737 pounds, was also the heaviest. For people who still liked operational vent windows in the front, Ford offered these units, as shown here, for an additional $55 on any LTD model.

Only slightly less popular than the crown Victoria version was the plain LTD 4-door Sedan, Model 33. It accounted for 35,8932 sales, all at a base price of $7,718. This version is shown with the $140 full vinyl roof. The interesting vent-like windows in the rear doors would not open, but were in place to allow the main glass to lower unimpeded by the wheel housing cutout. The rather strange looking wire-type wheel covers cost $135 extra.

With the unpopular 2-door sedan gone, the LTD "S" sub-series was reduced to two "stripped" models. They were the 4-door Sedan, Model 31, which had a base price of $7,522, and the Station Wagon, Model 37, which cost $7,942. The sedan, often bought for taxi or police work, accounted for 17,490 sales, while the wagon proved decidedly unpopular and drew only 2,465 orders. New for the "S" models this year were the same quad halogen headlights that were used in other LTDs. Dual facing rear seats with removable seat cushions were still available for all full-size wagons for an extra $150. However, Ford now said that these seats increased passenger capacity to eight people, whereas just a few years earlier it had claimed 10-passenger capacity when the rear seats were added.

Rolling through California's grape country is this Granada "L" 2-door sedan, Model 26. The entire Granada line went through a complete renovation this year, becoming in effect "Super-Fairmonts." This move surprised many, who assumed that the relatively slow moving Granada line would soon be abandoned. Lowest of three new trim level groupings, the "L" model cars were the least expensive of all Granadas, and the 2-door was the least expensive of all, with a base 4-cylinder price of $6,474. It weighed 2,707 pounds.

Showing off its distinctive Granada face, with its bright grille and quad halogen headlights, is this "L" series 4-door Sedan, Model 27. The lowest price 4-door in the line, it sold for $6,633 with the Four. Using a variation of the Fairmont body, the Granada was now 3 inches shorter than previous models, with an overall length of 196.5 inches as opposed to last year's 199.7 inches. Likewise, its wheelbase decreased 4.4 inches, since it now used Fairmont's platform of 195.5 inches.

Playing the role of "Super Fairmont" is this "GL" model Granada, the line's middle ground 4-door Sedan. Classed as Model 27/602, it cost $7,035 with the Four. However, it seems that most buyers opted for the Six at $213 additional, or went for the 255 cubic inch V-8, which added $263. The 302 V-8 was not normally available in the Granada line. Production of 4-door Granadas was more than double the 2-door variety, and 86,284 left the factories. Again, no divisions were made as to how many were in each trim level.

Granada's middle ground was now occupied by the "GL" designation. This category offered slightly a higher trim level than found on the "L" models, but did not include the full vinyl top shown here. This was a $115 option. However, the full wheel covers were standard, while "L" models used large hubcaps. The "GL" 2-door wore a 4-cylinder price of $6,875, while the 200 cubic inch Six went for $7,088. The Six also increased the overall weight by 90 pounds. Since Ford did not break production down into the three trim levels, it is known only that 35,057 Granada 2-door Sedans were produced, but it is not known how many were in each level.

The top 2-door in the newly designed Granada line was the "GLX" version, which had a 4-cylinder price of $6,988. This sub-series offered a host of luxury items, but the cast aluminum wheels shown here were still a $500 option. Essentially, this trim level replaced the former "ESS" or European Sports Styling designation used in 1980. Granada's standard transmission was the 4-speed manual mounted on the column, but a floor-shift unit could be ordered for $45. Also, the Select-Shift automatic was a popular option at $350 extra.

Described by Ford as "America's most changed car," the totally new Granada lost out in the publicity race to the newly introduced Escort, and for the most part its total transformation went virtually unnoticed by the public. This, plus the fact that it was essentially a dressed up Fairmont, did little to help its sales. Most dressed of the batch was the "GLX" 4-door Sedan, Model 27/933, which was the only Granada to have a 4-cylinder base price in excess of $7,000, tagging in at $7,148. All Granada 4-cylinder models weighed in the 2,700-pound category, while the 6-cylinder versions went 90 pounds more.

The Fairmont Futura sub-series now gave a home to the upper trim levels of that line, but it no longer was the sport oriented grouping that it once was. Essentially being upscale pragmatic, it consisted of three models, this 4-door Sedan, Model 21/605; a 2-door Coupe, Model 22, and a Station Wagon. The Coupe, for some reason, was the only Futura model to have its own exclusive model number, and the only one which registered separate production figures. The other Futuras were lumped in the overall listings. Thus, the 2-door drew 24,197 orders. It had a base 4-cylinder price of $6,347. Meanwhile, the 4-door shown here had a base price of $6,361.

Often thought of as a separate model, the Fairmont Futura Squire wagon was simply a $200 trim option available on the regular Futura wagon. It is shown here with $90 roof luggage rack and the $120 set of wire-type wheel covers. All Fairmonts and Granadas had their fuel filler door on the right rear quarter The large rear quarter windows could not be opened, nor could the small rear door windows which resembled vent panes. All Fairmont wagons were the same 195.5 inches overall as were the car models. The only variation to this figure was the Futura 2-door Sedan, which still stretched to 197.4 inches overall.

New to the Fairmont Futura sub-series was the Station Wagon, Model 23/605. Simply an upscale version of the regular Fairmont wagon, the Futura version was distinguished by wide vinyl-filled body molding and bright wheel opening cutouts. As before, Fairmont wagons used a one-piece lift gate, hinged at the upper cross bar, rather than a conventional tailgate or door gate. Futura models also used a distinctive grille of heavy rectangles superimposed over a finer mesh inner grille, and were equipped with quad rectangular halogen headlamps with the parking and signal lights located underneath. The Futura wagon was base priced at $6,616 and weighed 2,755 pounds.

1981

This view of the plain Fairmont Station Wagon, Model 23, gives a good look at the differences between the lower level face and the fancier Futura grille treatment in the background. The plain models used a grille similar to 1980, with the cross-hatch divided by two heavier horizontal bars and one heavy vertical central bar. Also, it used regular rectangular headlamps rather than the halogen variety, and its parking/signal lights were located in one unit between grille and headlight, rather than being separate units under the quad lights. This model also sports a nice but seldom ordered option...that being the functional front vent pane windows which cost $55 extra. In basic form, the Fairmont wagon listed at $6,384 with the Four. It is not clear whether the Squire package was available in the plain series.

The plain Fairmont 2-door Sedan was the Model 20. It was available in regular form, as shown here, or as a new "S" model, which was devoid of all trim whatsoever. The "S" models were the only Fairmonts base priced below $6,000, having as 4-cylinder tags of $5,701, and 6-cylinder prices of $5,914. The regular models were base priced at $6,032 in 4-cylinder form, and $213 higher with the Six. Not particularly popular, the Fairmont 2-door Sedans registered a total of 23,066 sales in both forms. Oddly in the plain Fairmont range, the 2-door was called a "sedan," while in the larger Futura form it was called a "coupe."

The plain Fairmont line lacked both the attractive body side trim and distinctive grille and headlight treatment of the Futura sub-series. Still, the cars were quite popular, and represented Ford's third best selling model, with 104,883 leaving the showrooms. However, it is not known how many of these were in plain form as shown here, or how many bore the Futura designation. Note that while the Granada 4-door models used the same body as the Fairmont, they had solid rear roof quarters, while the Fairmonts inserted a triangular fixed window into this area. Both lines used the fixed rear pane in the rear doors. The plain Fairmont 4-door was priced at $6,151 as a Four. It had no "S" model option as did the 2-door.

Taking virtually all of ford's publicity and attention this year was the new Escort, Ford's first domestic-built front wheel drive little car. Amazingly, Ford did not do as it had in the past and issue the new baby in one or two variations, and then subsequently add trim levels. This time it came out directly with five trim levels spread over two basic models, thus giving the car an immediate range of 10 recognized model designations, plus other option packages such as Squire options. The top of the line was occupied by the "GLX" sub-series, of which this is the 3-door Hatchback, Model 05/602. Highest priced of all the 3-doors, it came in at a base of $6,476.

For some reason Ford did not officially term this new Escort a station wagon, but instead referred to it as 4-door with Liftgate. Shown here in "GLX" guise, the practical little car was the highest priced of all Escorts, having a basic tag of $6,799. At 2,137 pounds, it was also the heaviest Escort. Styled steel wheels and vinyl-filled side trim were standard on "GLX" models, as were a multitude of interior luxuries, such as reclining low-back bucket seats, dual remote control mirrors, and a console.

Keyed to the sport set was the Escort "SS" sub-series. As did all sub-series, it consisted of the same two models, with the 3-door going for $6,139 and this 4-door being pegged at $6,464. "SS" models received an exclusive black grille and headlight surrounds; black bumpers with argent stripe; black mirrors, body molding, and rocker panels; reclining high-back bucket seats, and heavier suspension package. Since there were no power options available, the engine was the same as found in any other Escort.

The "GL" sub-series represented the upper mid-level of the new Escort line. Its bragging points included deluxe bumper strips; vinyl-filled side molding; high-back reclining bucket seats; 4-spoke sport steering wheel, and mini-console. However, the cast aluminum wheels shown here were a $330 extra. Normally, the car came with steel wheels and hubcaps. Less popular than the 4-door versions, the 3-door Hatchbacks were still Ford's second best selling model, with overall sales reaching 128,173. Best selling of all Fords this year was the 4-door Escort, which had combined sales of 192,554. In the "GL" sub-series, the 3-door sold for $5,838.

The lower level Escorts were in the slightly trimmed "L" sub-series and the totally plain Escort category. Both sub-series offered the two models, with the 3-door hatchback in "L" form shown here. In this guise, it cost $5,494, but the price did not include the $100 2-tone paint treatment. In "L" form, the 4-door cost $5,814, while the price for the basic models was 45,731 for the 4-door and $5,158 for the most stripped 3-door. On these models, pressed steel wheels without hubcaps were the norm. All Escorts used the relatively new halogen lamps as standard lighting, and all had a folding-back rear seat.

Not content with 10 individually listed models, Ford also added Squire option packages to the 4-door line, resulting in a total of five more unique looking Escorts on the road. Here the $260 Squire package has been added to the "GL" 4-door. This plus the $75 roof luggage rack certainly gave a station wagon appearance to the little car, though Ford was reluctant to class the car as a wagon. without the imitation wood trim, the "GL" 4-door listed at a base of $6,178. The Squire package was the third most expensive Escort option, with the most expensive being air conditioning at $530, followed by an automatic transaxle at $345.

Appearing in April, and sometimes considered an early 1982 model rather than a mid-1981, was the unique little Ford EXP. Built on the Escort's platform of 94.2-inch wheelbase and powered by the Escort's 97.6 4-cylinder engine and front-wheel-drive, the little 2-seater drew a high degree of attention when first shown at the spring Chicago Auto Show. Ford pointed out that it was the first 2-seater the company had produced since the Thunderbird 25 years earlier, and predicted a great future for the car. Sadly, a Thunderbird it was not, and its 1981 sales were combined with the 1982 figure to show a total of 98,256. Not particularly cheap for such a basic car, it rolled off the floor at $7,387 without options.

Trying to come back into the sporty field in force, Ford this year launched a brand new sport-type car, and gave a big power and speed boost to the Mustang's option list. The new car worked, at least for this year only, but the Mustang's performance image drew little attention and very disappointing sales.

The new car was the EXP, a 2-door, 2-seat model using the Escort's platform and 94.2-inch wheelbase. Being the first 2-seat Ford since the last 1957 Thunderbird, the car used its own exclusive sheet metal on its notchback body. The rear was equipped with a fairly large liftback hatch, similar to a hatchback. Yet the references were to a notchback, probably in regard to the sloping rear glass and almost horizontal rear deck. The front end featured a sharply sloped hood bracketed by sloping fenders which terminated at the front in large and unusual notched headlamp surrounds, housing the large single-type headlamps. Overall, the car was 170.3 inches long, as opposed to 163.9 for the Escort hatchback or 165 inches for the 4-door. Also, it was only 50.5 inches high, as opposed to 53.3 for the Escort, while its width was 63 inches as opposed to Escort's 65.9 inches. However, it weighed 2,047 pounds, as opposed to 1,920 for the lightest Escort.

Actually introduced as a mid-1981 car, as described in the previous chapter, the EXP came on the market following the Chicago Auto Show. However, despite the early release date, some reports show that all models were titled as 1982 vehicles, and all production data was registered into the 1982 model year. Initial response was good, but once buyers found that the performance-oriented car offered no performance, a noticeable slump in interest developed. The reason, of course, was that the EXP was totally powered and operated by an unchanged Escort Four front-wheel-drive unit of 70 horsepower. Rectifying the situation somewhat was a new modified version of the Four. Available for both the Escort and EXP, this model did not come out until March, almost 11 months after the first EXPs left the showrooms. This new engine version offered 80 horsepower and gave a bit more snap to both lines. EXP sales, though not bad, were still not as high as hoped for, with 98,256 units leaving the factory. Sadly, this would turn out to be EXP's banner year, with future interest being far down on the list.

Also experiencing a disappointing year was Mustang, this despite a welter of promotion billing the car's high performance capabilities. Creating this claim was the reintroduction of the High-Output 302 V-8 with a 4-speed transmission.

Essentially the same unit as offered up to 1979, the 302 V-8 replaced the Turbo Four, which for technical reasons was discontinued this year but would return in 1983. The new V-8 option was a more peppy setup than used in 1979, due to a larger diameter exhaust system, larger 2-barrel carburetor, and less restrictive air cleaner. Better breathing meant better performance, and Mustang claimed less than 8 seconds to go from 0 to 60 MPH. It also was rated at 157 horsepower at 4200 rpm.

Aside from the new $450 V-8 option, little else was new in the Mustang barn. The base engine remained the 140 cubic inch Four, while the in-line Six and 225 cubic inch V-8 remained non-performance options. Styling was essentially the same as 1981, but the Cobra option was a thing of the past. A totally revised system of identifying trim level did away with the old base, Ghia, and Mach I series, while instigating a trim identification based on L, GL, GLX, and GT, which sometimes was listed as a separate series. Appearance options included a flip-up "air roof" probably so called because it was too small to be a sunroof, a $735 convertible-like carriage roof, and a full vinyl roof, in addition to various appearance packages. But, despite the new engine option, sales were very disappointing, and represented a drop of over one third of last year's miserable figures. Final Mustang production rested at only 130,418.

In the non-sporty little car field, the Escort was treated to a new body style which proved to be a very marketable car. The new model was the 4-door sedan, with styling based heavily on the former 4-door liftback, which now was officially termed a station wagon. With the total revision occurring aft of the C-pillar, the new 4-door sedan used a hatchback rear entry for its exposed cargo area. This was in the same manner as the hatchback on the 3-door (now officially called a 2-door) and the liftgate on the wagon. The new body gave Escort a total of three distinct models spread over five trim level sub-series, resulting in 12 distinct model classifications. All of this might have caused a welter of confusion, but it also helped Escort continue its role as Ford's sales leader.

In a rather surprising move, the Granada line received a new station wagon style...the first ever for this line. What was so strange about this move was the fact that it had already been foretold that the Granada line would be dropped at the end of the 1982 model year. Usually, very few changes are made to a model scheduled for abandonment, let alone giving it a totally new model. Still, the new wagon style appeared in both the L and GL trim levels, while the Squire trim, which probably should have been a GLX model, was considered an option package. The base engine in the wagon was the 200 cubic inch in-line Six, while all other Granadas used the 140 cubic inch Four as the base. Aside from the new wagon body, little was changed in the Granada line, with the cars still looking like a downsized version of the large Fords.

Just as it seemed surprising to give the soon-to-disappear Granada a new wagon, it seems equally strange that the continuing Fairmont line should loose not only its wagon model, but its entire series of low-price models. Now all three remaining Fairmonts... Sport Coupe, 2-door, and 4-door sedans...were under the Futura designation. Also surprising, considering

Ford's interest in performance, was the dropping of the 255 V-8 from the Fairmont option list. The base engine was the 140 cubic inch Four, with the in-line Six being the only option. The V-8 was still available, but only in conjunction with police or taxi packages. In the styling department, Fairmonts received a slightly revised face, with the quad headlights continuing to set above long and narrow horizontal parking and signal lights. A new grille with a pronounced center bar featured 12 rectangular openings in line with the expected Ford styling.

Again, just as performance was stressed in small cars, it was dropped in both the LTD and Thunderbird lines. Gone was the old reliable and well-liked 351 V-8. The engine was still in production, but now relegated only to LTD's police package and available only in High-Output form. LTD's base engine remained the 255 cubic inch V-8, while the 302 remained the only option. As before, no 6-cylinder blocks were used in the LTD line. Styling was little changed in the LTD ranks.

Just as the 351 was gone from the LTD ranks, the 302 was dropped from the Thunderbird line. Now the biggest block available to the Birds was the 255 cubic inch V-8. Stressed for Thunderbirds was a brand new V-6 of 232 cubic inches. Also available as a Granada option, this new engine featured a bore and stroke of 3.8x3.4 inches and produced 112 horsepower at 4000 rpm. It used a cast iron block but had aluminum heads. The base T-Bird block was still the in-line Six.

Aside from engine switching, Thunderbirds changed little. Base, Town Landau, and Heritage series were still offered, with a vinyl top being available on all models, though standard on the Town Landaus. The interesting frontal treatment still utilized concealed headlamps set behind huge wrap-around clear plastic panels. Sales were very disappointing for the Birds, with an almost 50% drop for the year.

Except for the new Mustang 302; mid-year High-Output Four, and the new V-6 described above, engine changes were minimal this year. The biggest disappointment for Ford fans probably was the dropping of the 351 for all but special police packages.

Production figures for the model year were confusing this time, with quite a dissimilarity between the total figures shown by Ford, and the figures obtained by tallying individual model production. Tabulating the individual models shows total production of 1,035,063, down only 19,913 from 1981. However, Ford claimed sales of only 888,633 for the model year. Of the tabulated production, 904,645 was in the Ford line, while Mustang came in with the aforementioned disappointing 130,418 total.

Best selling of all the lines was Escort, with total production of 385,132, while the worst was Thunderbird with only 45,142. Again, only three models made the 100,000-plus production list. Escorts led the list with the 2-door coming in first with 165,660 while the new 4-door sedan ran second with 130,473. Third place went to the Fairmont Futura 4-door sedan once again, with 101,666, while the new EXP just missed the list with production of 98,256, including those released in the last half of the 1981 model year.

Only the small "Heritage" signature on the trailing edge of the upper front fender identifies this car from its less upscale Town Landau model. However, the price difference was apparent, with Heritage being the only Ford to ever break the $12,000 mark in basic form. It sold for $12,742 with buyers having a no-cost choice of either the 255 cubic inch V-8 or the new 232 cubic inch V-6. The in-line Six, basic in other Birds, did not appear in the Heritage model. Other high priced options, such as the interior trim group, a $1,200 option on the plain birds, were also standard on the Heritage, but the Ricaro bucket seats were still a $220 option here, while in the plain Birds they cost $525 more. Heritage production once again is combined into the total T-Bird figure.

Looking almost identical to the Heritage edition is the Thunderbird Town Landau. Only the identifying script on the upper rear portion of the front fender says that this car is the Model 42/60T Landau and not the top of the line variety. Here the in-line Six was considered standard power, providing a base price of $9,970. The 255 V-8 brought the price to $9,944. All Birds weighed between 3,000 and 3,300 pounds. In both the Heritage and the Town Landau, the vinyl half-roof with its bright wrap-over was standard. The vinyl top could be ordered for the plain Bird, but the wrap-over was exclusive to the two top models. A new option was the wire-type wheel covers, which were standard on the Heritage, $45 on the Landau, and $150 on the plain Bird.

1982

Showing off its $320 optional vinyl half-roof is the plain Thunderbird, Model 42. Note that this roof differs substantially from that on the Landau and Heritage models, and includes a rather large opera window but only a thin wrap-over. This view gives a good look at the huge taillights exclusive to all Birds. The central portion contained clear lenses for the back-up lights. With the in-line Six, the base Thunderbird listed at $8,492. Production of all T-Birds was down substantially this year, with only 45,124 total being built. Being stressed for the plain Thunderbird models was the new V-6, which cost $240 extra, the same as the 255 cubic inch V-8.

This year the old Mustang trim levels were discarded, and a new listing of L; GL, and GLX designations was employed. Essentially replacing the former Ghia series was the new GLX series, Mustang's highest trim level. As with the Ghia models, the two models in this series proved to be the least popular of all Mustangs, though with the introduction of the new GT as a model and not a package, they were no longer the most expensive. The Notchback, Model 12, was listed at $6,980 with the Four, while the base price of the GLX Hatchback shown here was $7,101 with the Four. The 200 cubic inch in-line Six added $215 to the price. The Hatchback, Model 13, was most popular in the GLX line, accounting for 9,926 sales, while the Notchback drew only 5,828 orders, and thus was the least popular of all Mustangs.

The new Mustang GL sub-series was the line's middle ground. It too consisted of the two models, the Notchback which sold for $6,844 and the Hatchback shown here, which listed out at $6,979, both prices being with the base Four. Most popular of the Mustangs, the GL category drew 69,348 sales for the Hatchback and 45,316 for the Notchback. These models could be fitted with the new 302, but when this was added, it was recommended that the $585 TR performance suspension package also be included. This package included a set of forged aluminum wheels, as seen on the illustrated GT model, stiff springs and shocks, and a rear stabilizer bar.

Totally new in the corral was the Mustang GT, Model 10, a hot horse blessed with a return to the old 302 V-8. Only now the 302 was rated at 157 horses at 4200 rpm, which was slightly higher than the rating of the previous High-Output 302 that disappeared at the end of 1979. Available only with the new 302 engine, the new Mustang GT model was a distinctive car was aimed strictly at the speed set. The most expensive of all the horses, its base price was $8,308. Essentially a replacement of the old Cobra package, the new GT was able to go from 0 to 60 in under 8 seconds, using the manual 4-speed transmission. Interest in the car was high, but probably because of the high price, sales were 23,447, which certainly was not bad, but was less than expected. Although the GT could only be ordered with the 302, the 302 engine could be ordered for other Mustangs at a cost of $450.

Available only in Notchback form was the plain Mustang or "L" series model. Priced at $6,345 with the Four, it offered Mustang sportiness at a lower price than the better trimmed models. Production of the stripper is not known, as its figures were combined with those of the GL Notchback, but it is assumed that the demand for this car was not all that great. As can be seen, the Notchback differed substantially from the Hatchback in that it had a conventional trunk deck and trunk area, while the Hatchback used a flip-up rear access door and had extensive storage space due to a fold-down rear seat.

Except for a major deletion under the hood, there was little difference between this year's full-size Fords and those of 1981. The big move, of course, involved the abandonment of the 351 cubic inch V-8 for all use except in special order police vehicles. Now Ford's top big car engine was the 302 V-8, while the 255 cubic inch V-8 was considered standard. There were no 6-cylinder options. As before, the top of the line 2-door was the Crown Victoria, Model 34. Base priced at $9,149, the 3,523-pound car saw sales of only 9,287.

Ford's most popular big car was the Crown Victoria 4-door Sedan, Model 35, which drew 41,405 orders. This was an increase of over 2,000 from the 1981 figures. Priced at $9,294 the car was often seen with one of the most attractive wheel designs ever produced by an American car maker. These were the cast aluminum turbine-type wheels seen here, which actually were a $385 addition, but well worth the money in both beauty and longevity. The car is seen here with the vinyl half-roof, but could also be ordered with a full vinyl top.

The wandering LTD Country Squire once more was on the move, this year again settling back into the Crown Victoria sub-series after spending the previous year in the plain LTD line. The most expensive and heaviest large Ford, it had a base price of $9,580 and weighed 3,740 pounds. It is shown here with the $150 set of wire-type wheel covers, and has been fitted with the $65 front vent panes. If this picture looks familiar, it is because it appears in the 1981 section also. Ford made so few changes on its large cars that it didn't even bother to change the catalog art work, but simply made note of the fact that the Squire was now part of the Crown Victoria line. Also on this model is the trailer towing package, which in 1981 was a $175 "heavy-duty" option. Now, because the 351 V-8 was no longer available, the trailer package was rated as "medium-duty," but its price was up to $250.

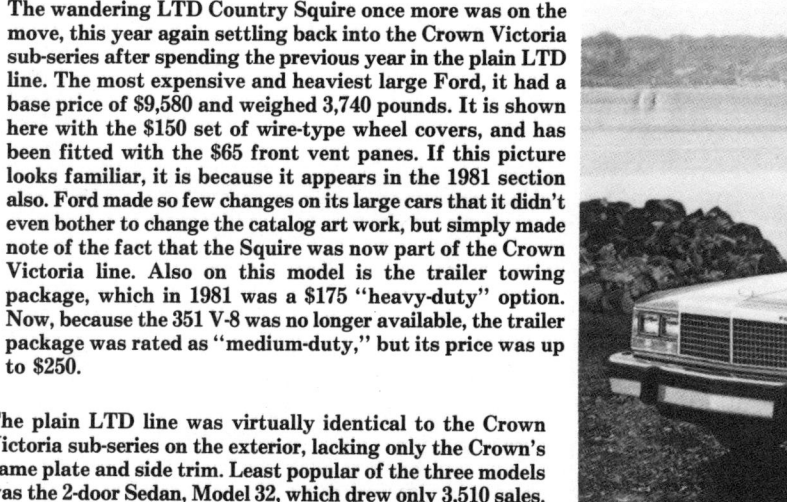

The plain LTD line was virtually identical to the Crown Victoria sub-series on the exterior, lacking only the Crown's name plate and side trim. Least popular of the three models was the 2-door Sedan, Model 32, which drew only 3,510 sales. Base priced at $8,455, it weighed 3,496 pounds, and thus was the lightest of the large Fords. This model wears the $80 set of deluxe wheel covers, and also has been fitted with the $165 vinyl half-roof, and the optional bright rocker panel and lower door moldings.

Not quite as popular in the plain LTD line as in the Crown Victoria sub-series was the 4-door Sedan, Model 33. Here sales reached only 29,776. Slightly dressed, this example wears the relatively inexpensive exterior trim option of vinyl-filled side molding, but shows off the standard steel top. In basic form, this car cost $8,574, but the 302 engine would have pushed this up by $60. This definitely was a good investment as the available power was greater and the touted gas savings of the 255 V-8 was virtually nonexistent in the large Fords. This same model could be purchased in stripped LTD "S" guise for $8,312, where it was listed as the least expensive full-size Ford. Popular for taxi and police work in this form, it drew 22,182 orders.

Although the upscale Country Squire moved to the Crown Victoria nest, the plain-side wagon, once called the Country Sedan, remained in the lower categories. As a plain LTD it was the Model 38, where it cost $9,073 and drew 9,294 orders. Those looking for economy could order the wagon as the Model 37, where it was part of the LTD "S" sub-series and cost $8,783. Apparently not too many buyers were interested in the stripped form, as only 2,973 were sold, making that version the poorest selling of all large Fords. The luggage rack was now $105. Dual facing rear seats were still available at $165 a set.

Continuing to take top honors in the soon-to-disappear Granada line was the GLX 2-door Sedan, Model 26. It was base priced at $7,666 for the 4-cylinder version, but was $8,290 with the more popular in-line six. Although the Six was only $213 above the Four, buyers who wanted the Six also had to take the automatic transmission at $411, as the manual 4-speed was not available on 6-cylinder Granadas. Those who wanted a bit more power could add another $70 to the price and receive the 232 cubic inch V-6.

Continuing to imitate the "European" look of the former Granada ESS models was the GLX 4-door Sedan, Model 27. It is shown here with its optional wide bright side trim and the standard luxury wheel covers with their painted centers. Extending the European tradition, this year's signal light levers had a pull-up high beam flasher for use in passing or warning. European cars had this facility for years, but it was only now gaining popularity in the U.S. All Granada production this year was lumped into one base figure, and no breakouts were made by trim level.

Center stage of the Granada line was the GL sub-series, of which this was the 4-door Sedan, Model 27. In 4-cylinder form, it cost $7,718 and weighed 2,735 pounds. Its companion was the GL 2-door Sedan, Model 26, which had a base price of $7,543. In total, 4-door Granadas accounted for 62,339 sales, while the 2-door models drew only 12,802 orders. In effect, Granadas were simply super Fairmonts, with both using the same engines and 105.5-inch wheelbases. However, Granadas were one-inch longer than Fairmonts, being 196.5 inches overall.

In a very surprising switch, Ford moved its station wagon models from the Fairmont line to the Granada line. The move was unusual on two counts: Granadas had never had a wagon style before this, while Fairmonts had always had wagons, and also the Granada line was scheduled to disappear at the end of the year, whereas the Fairmonts would continue (without a wagon) for still another year. Granada wagons were only available in 6-cylinder form, with automatic transmissions, and could not be purchased with the Four or with a manual shift. Two variations were available, the GL Model 28 seen here, and the "L" version, which also bore Model 28. In the well-trimmed GL form, it cost $8,399, while the "L" cost $7,983. A total of 45,182 were sold.

1982

The lowest trim level in the Granada line was the "L" sub-series. It consisted of the same three models as the GL division, with its most popular style being the 4-door Sedan. In plain form, without the optional side trim or luxury wheel covers shown here, the car cost $7,301 with the Four. Its companion was the 2-door Sedan, Model 26, which was Granada's lowest price vehicle, with a basic tag of $7,126.

Not content with two plain sided models for the new Granada station wagon line, Ford also came out with a Country Squire version. However, the Squire trim was simply an option package, and not part of the GLX line, despite the fact that this example is seen with the standard GLX Euro-type wheel covers. The $280 wood trim package was usually combined with the $115 luggage rack. Since it used the old Fairmont Wagon body, the car availed itself of the old liftgate arrangement at the rear. Apparently this type of gate was more acceptable than the old drop-type tailgate or the doorgate, both of which used disappearing rear windows. The window on the liftgate was fixed in place and could not be lowered.

A welter of difference in styling, length, price, and popularity separated the regular Fairmont Futura 2-door Sedan, Model 20, from the Sport Coupe. This car used the standard Fairmont/Granada 2-door body with its large quarter window and small B-pillar; was the typical Fairmont 195.5 inches in overall length, and drew only 8,222 orders. In addition, at $5,985 for the Four, it was not only the least expensive Fairmont, but the only one to have a base price under $6,000. It is shown here in completely stock form.

The Fairmont Futura Sport Coupe, Model 22, continued to offer its unique top treatment and elongated rear quarters. The car measured 197.4 inches overall, which was two inches more than other Fairmonts and one inch more than the Granadas. Surprisingly, despite its sporty lines that would have been a natural for the Granada trim level, the style was never picked up by that division. Relatively popular, it drew 17,851 customers. It could be ordered with the Four and manual transmission for $6,517, but probably most went out with the in-line Six or V-6 with the mandatory automatic transmission. With the in-line engine, it cost $7,141 and weighed 2,682 pounds.

Showing how the $150 set of wire-type wheel covers would brighten a 4-door sedan is this Fairmont Futura Model 21. It also sports the $140 full vinyl top. In base form, with the Four and manual shift, it listed at $6,419, while the Six was 7,043. Fairmont sedans continued to use the unusual triangular window in the rear quarter panel, in addition to the fixed pane in the doors. Granadas, which used the same body, did not use the quarter panel window. With 101,666 orders to its credit, the Futura 4-door not only was the best selling of all Fairmont/Granada models, it was also Ford's third best selling style and the only non-Escort to break the 100,000 mark.

Entering its first full year of production was the unique little EXP. It was Ford's first 2-door sport-type model since the initial Thunderbird was introduced. Built on the Escort's platform, and using all Escort running gear, the car was aimed at the sport set. However, its performance was anything but sporty, and though it could cruise comfortably, it certainly was no contender in an impromptu drag race. Actually introduced as a mid-1981 model, the little car was always considered an early-release 1982, and thus enjoyed an elongated model year for its first time around. This put its production at a healthy 98,256, which wasn't bad, but was still disappointing to those at Ford, who had hoped for another Mustang stampede. It was base priced at $7,387 and weighed 2,047 pounds. It is shown here with the $120 2-tone paint job, and $230 set of cast aluminum wheels.

Now officially termed a station wagon was the Escort Model 08, which had simply been called a 4-door with liftgate in 1981. The introduction of the new 4-door Sedan made it clear that this vehicle was indeed a wagon, while the optional Squire trim left no doubt that it was also the top of the line version. As part of the GLX sub-series, the wagon was priced at $7,475 and thus was the most expensive Escort. Add to this the $300 Squire package, the approximately $300 aluminum wheels, $95 luggage rack, $100 basic radio, and $615 air conditioner, and the car quickly reached for $9,000 mark.

New for the year in the popular Escort line was the 4-door Sedan, Model 06. Last year, what appeared to be an Escort wagon was actually the only 4-door available. But this year, a true 4-door Sedan was created, primarily by reworking the former 4-door's rear body section. Officially called a 4-door Hatchback, the car's top level version was this GLX model, which sold for $7,302, not counting the $275 flip-up roof; the $60 front window vent panes, or the $110 remote operable rear quarter windows. Companion to this model was the 2-door GLX Hatchback which sold for $7,086, and the sport-oriented 2-door GT Hatchback, priced at $6,706.

Unchanged was the Escort 2-door, Model 05. Shown here in the mid-level GL form, it was also available as an "L" model, and for the remainder of this year as a base Escort model. However, the base line would not be carried into 1983. Ford's most popular style, the 2-door accounted for 165,660 sales in all trim levels. Definitely less expensive than the GLX version, the GL model sold for $6,406, which included high-back reclining bucket seats in the front. In "L" form it was $6,046, while the base level was the least expensive Escort, with a starting price of $5,462. The 2-door was also the base for the GT version, a sport oriented model with blackout grille and black trim; heavier suspension, and front air dam.

Ford's second most popular car turned out to be the new Escort 4-door Hatchback, Model 06, seen here in GL form. All told, 130,473 of the little sedans entered the highway system. In GL form, it sold for $6,622, while as an "L" model it was priced at $6,263. The car, for this year only, also appeared in the base Escort sub-series, where it sold for $5,668. The base Escorts were the only ones not exceeding the $6,000 figure. Notice that the rear gate of the new sedan was similar in concept to that of both the 2-door hatchback and the wagon, but was of substantially smaller size and included a short horizontal panel that approximated a trunk deck.

In addition to the GLX models, the 4-door Escort Station Wagon, Model 08, also appeared in GL form, as seen here, and as an "L" model. However, it did not appear in the base Escort level this year. As a GL, it cost $6,841, while the "L" designation was $6,461. A popular little vehicle overall, the wagons still took a distant third spot away from the two hatchbacks, and only 88,999 were built. Still, the baby Fords were definitely keeping the public happy, and helped to turn an otherwise dismal sales year into one that was at least bearable.

If 1982 was a busy year with the new EXP, then 1983 should have been a relatively quiet time. It wasn't. In fact, a more busy and exciting year had not been seen in quite awhile. Not only was a brand new car introduced, but an old-line series bit the dust, a new convertible model was reborn, and a totally new Thunderbird appeared in the nest.

The new car was the LTD, which replaced the Granada in sales slot only, even though it was built on the same 105.5-inch platform used by both Fairmont and the former Granada. Though it was only one inch longer than the Fairmont sedan, being 196.5 inches overall (the same as the old Granada), its styling was totally new and fresh, and more akin to Mustang or Escort in concept than to Fairmont or former Ford designs. Among the advanced features was a sharply sloping front in keeping with aerodynamic design, housing a slanted grille of thin horizontal bars, again of the Escort concept. Flanking the grille were rectangular quad halogen headlights set deeply into housings matching the slant of the grille, while the parking lights occupied cutouts in the front bumper.

Unlike the former Granada, the LTD was available only as a 4-door sedan and a wagon, with no 2-door bodies in stock. The sedan was available in plain or Brougham models, while the wagon had the availability of the Squire wood-trim option. Buyers had their choice of three engines, with the 140 cubic inch Four being the basic package in the sedan, while the in-line Six was standard in the wagons. Both models could have the V-6 of 232 cubic inches (3.8 litres) as an option, while later in the season, a propane fueled version of the Four was made available. This was probably more with an eye toward large fleet sales, primarily in the midwest, than for individual sales.

The new LTD turned out to be a very nice and very well received car, despite being hampered by a return to a very confusing name, inasmuch as the vehicle had nothing at all in common with the real full-size LTD. At least the last time Ford glopped up the proud LTD title, it added the suffix "II" to the name to differentiate it from the real McCoy. This time it didn't even bother to do that, apparently assuming that the size and price differences alone would tell one series from the other. Also, the old full-size LTD was now officially known as the LTD Crown Victoria, while the new version simply took the name of LTD. Still, in the author's estimation, a better or at least less confusing name could certainly have been conceived, or even the old Granada title could have been left in place.

Offering no confusion in name, but certainly in appearance to those who were looking for a conventional model, was the new Thunderbird. Totally restyled and again downsized, the new Bird was built on a 104-inch wheelbase platform, a reduction of four inches from 1982. Overall, it was 197.6 inches long, which was only 2.8 inches shorter than the previous models. Styling was definitely a preview of things to come, with full aerodynamic curves throughout, including sloping hood, sharply slanted windshield and rear window, spoiler-styled decklid, and rounded front bumpers with built-in air dam. The grille was a relatively small rectangular affair, flanked by deeply recessed rectangular quad headlamps in surrounds with sidemarker lamps built into the outer edges.

Initially the car was issued in plain and Heritage editions, with the Town Landau being dropped. The upscale Heritage models had unique quarter windows and carriage lamps to identify them from the plain versions. Later in the season, a new Turbo Coupe was issued, which answered those who still thought Thunderbird should offer performance as well as luxury. Utilizing a multitude of exclusive items, the Turbo's main claim to fame was its totally new Turbocharged Four of 140 cubic inches (2.3 litre). Used exclusively on the Turbo Coupe, the engine offered fuel injection, an 8.0:1 compression ratio, and developed 142 horsepower at 5000 rpm. Regular and Heritage Thunderbirds used the V-6 of 232 cubic inches as base power, while the 302 cubic inch V-8 with new electronic fuel injection was an option. With an 8.4:1 compression ratio, this block offered 130 horsepower at 3200 rpm. Gone from Thunderbird usage was the old in-line Six.

Not quite as exciting as the totally new Thunderbird, but nevertheless gathering its share of automotive news this year was Ford's return to the ragtop realm. This total change of concept in the sporty car field occurred only in the Mustang corral, and only on Mustangs of the top GLX trim level or the V-8 powered GT machines. The open style was not available in the lower trim levels, nor in the Turbo model. Not really a true Ford product, the convertible actually was a conversion of the notchback coupe, with the cars being shipped from Ford's Dearborn assembly point to Cars & Concepts of Brighton, Mich. There the steel tops were removed, and the convertible tops and equipment installed. Not a cheap conversion, the soft-tops were from $4,150 to $4,600 more expensive than the comparable notchback. Still, a total of 23,438 such conversions were produced this year.

In the regular Mustang line, a few changes were also noted. A new facelift gave more aerodynamic lines to the cars and differentiated them from previous models. Also, a new V-6 of 232 cubic inches was offered for the first time, replacing the old in-line Six. This was similar to the V-6 used in the Thunderbird and LTD Ford line, but had an 8.7:1 compression ratio rather than 8.65:1, and developed 112 horses rather than the 110 in the larger cars.

The High-Output V-8 of 302 cubic inches gained a new 4-barrel carburetor, which boosted horsepower from 157 to a new rating of 175. Conversely, the base Four now had a single barrel carburetor rather than the old 2-barrel. And finally, after an absence of over a year, a new Turbo Four arrived. Still of 140 cubic inches, the new Turbo used multi-port fuel injection, and was essentially the same 142-horse unit as used in the new Thunderbird Turbo Coupe. Along with the in-line Six, the 255 cubic inch V-8 block was also not available to Mustangs this year.

In the small car field, the year-old EXP experienced horrible sales, with less than 20,000 cars being sold. This was about one-fifth the number of EXPs moved in the initial year, despite the fact that the high-output Four of 80 horses had been available since mid-year 1982. Performance continued to be stressed with such options as a new 5-speed manual transmission, and a fuel injected version of the Escort's 97.6 cubic inch block. Styling remained virtually unchanged, but the line was expanded to four distinct models (trim levels), possibly in anticipation of the declining sales. Yet, despite these moves and the excellent reception in 1982, buyers for the little front-wheel-drive two-seater were super scarce this year.

A loss of about 80,000 sales was also noted in the Escort line, even though the tiny vehicle was still credited with being America's best selling car. Styling was virtually unchanged, but the plain Escort sub-series was dropped, making the "L" models the new base. This reduced to 10 the available Escort models, but since the trim levels were so easily mixed via options, it really was difficult to tell one model from the other without reading badges. Still available were the three basic styles of two and 4-door hatchbacks, and a 4-door station wagon.

Lastly, the full-size car line was now officially called the LTD Crown Victoria. It was available in standard form, or as the less fancy "S" models. The latter trim level (or lack of such) was available only on 4-door sedans and the wagon, while the 2-door sedan was available only in the upper Crown Victoria form. In the upper form also were found the two upscale wagons, the plain Crown Victoria, and the wood-trimmed Country Squire. In styl-

ing, the line had a new grille and some minor trim changes, but essentially was the same offerings as made in 1982 and previous years.

In the engine department, the Crown Victorias now had an electronically fuel-injected 302 V-8 as standard power. It produced 130 horsepower at 3200 rpm, and was soon joined by an optional High-Output version that ran 145 horses at 3600 rpm. Both engines were optional in the Thunderbird and LTD models. Unclear was whether the 351 cubic inch High-Output Police Special of 165 horsepower was available as an option in Crown Victorias sold to the general public. Also new from the engine department were the aforementioned Turbocharged Four as used on the Thunderbird Turbo Coupe and later in the Mustang Turbo GT, and the fuel injected Four of the EXP and Escort lines.

Production figures varied again this year, with Ford claiming only 914,666 cars produced, while a tally of individual model or series production shows 928,146 vehicles coming off the lines during the model year. At the top of the list, of course, was Escort, which retained its claim as "America's Best Selling Car," with total sales of 315,370. Once again, three models made the over 100,000 list. They were the number one Escort 2-door sedan with 151,386 units; the new Thunderbird with a very nice second place 121,999 spread over all three models, and in third place the new LTD 4-door sedan, with production of 111,813.

The tail of the new Thunderbird was also like nothing ever seen before. Styling included a small built-in rear deck spoiler, and heavy body-color bumpers which continued as part of the side protection. Shown in plain form, this Thunderbird nevertheless wears the $350 exterior accent group and the $220 two-tone paint treatment. If the owner really wanted to splurge, the $1,175 interior luxury group could have been installed along with the $800 air conditioner and $400 AM/FM radio with cassette player. However, a vinyl top was not available. In basic form, the plain Bird was up from last year's price, now going for $9,197 with the V-6. Still, the public apparently loved the new model, and made it Ford's second best selling car overall, with total sales of 121,999.

Drawing all kinds of attention from the press and the public was the new downsized and aerodynamically correct Thunderbird. Slightly smaller and slightly lighter than the previous models, the car now rode on an exclusive platform of 104-inches wheelbase, but was 197.6 inches long, which was a reduction of only 2.8 inches shorter than the previous model. Once again, the top model was the Heritage, which sold for $12,228 with the V-6, or $288 more with the new fuel-injected 302 V-8. Among the Heritage features were a special velour interior, electronic everything, and special rear quarter windows. The new front featured a greatly reduced grille of typical Ford egg crate design, quad headlights recessed into deep bezels, and a combined front bumper and air dam with built in parking and side marker lights.

Not arriving until April, and considered a mid-1983 model was Thunderbird's answer to the performance contingent. Called the Thunderbird Turbo Coupe, the car was equipped with a re-engineered version of the old Mustang overhead cam 140 cubic inch Turbocharged Four, coupled to a new Borg-Warner manual 5-speed transmission, with an overdrive 5th. The engine, which was equipped with Bosch multi-port fuel injection, now put the turbo unit ahead of the throttle control, thus effectively eliminating the step-down lag that had often bothered drivers of turbocharged cars. Rated at 145 horses, the new Turbo Four claimed better performance than could be obtained from most V-8s on the market. Falling mid-way between the plain and the Heritage Thunderbirds in price, the new Turbo Coupe had a base tag of $11,790. The cast aluminum wheels were $155 extra on the Turbo models, $470 additional on the Heritage, and a $650 option on the plain Bird.

Mustang owners who wanted open air but not the $4,000-plus extra cost of the convertible could opt for the T-Bar installation, with removable roof panels. This $1,055 factory option is shown here on the new GT Hatchback. The "5.0" emblem below the "GT" plaque on the front fender refers to the 302 V-8, which was the only engine choice in the GT line. Actually, the new Turbo was also a choice, but Ford regarded it as a separate GT model, and not an option. Large triangular quarter windows with slotted non-functional vents were standard on all hatchback models, but on the GT were finished in the same racing black as used on all GT special trim.

Totally new for Ford was a return to the convertible. The style was available only on the performance-oriented GT sub-series, or on the luxury-oriented GLX models as shown here. Priced at $12,467 in the GLX series, it could be ordered with only the V-6 or optional V-8 engine, but was not available with the Four. The powered top was not of Ford manufacturer. Ford shipped finished notchbacks in either GLX or GT guise to Cars & Concepts of Bright, Mich., where the steel tops were removed and the convertible units added. Oddly, though GT notchbacks were sent out for convertible conversion, a GT notchback was not an available model at dealer level. Quite popular considering its price and the fact that Chrysler had also re-introduced its own convertibles, the Mustang soft tops nevertheless accounted for 23,438 sales.

Designed with the sport or competitive driver in mind was the Mustang GT, now available in three variations. It could be ordered as a basic GT model shown here for $9,328 with the V-8; as the new convertible model for $13,479, or as the equally-new Turbo edition, which included the re-engineered Turbo Four. In Turbo form it cost $9,714 and promised to outperform almost any other stock machine on the market. Produced in hatchback style only, the GT models were not available as notchbacks or with 6-cylinder engines. The convertible was the most expensive Mustang in the corral. GT models were the only Mustangs to use the blackout version of the new grill, and had an exclusive hood with a black central panel encompassing a pronounced bulge panel.

Mustang's luxury liners lived in the GLX series, where they were available in both notchback and hatchback form. The hatchback, shown here, was the more expensive of the two, listing a base price of $7,557 with the plain Four. The notchback, with similar power, listed at $7,398. The V-6 option would have added $309 to the price, while the 302 V-8 would have been a rather heavy $1,343 addition, except in the convertible, where the extra cylinders cost only $595. Hatchbacks proved to be the most popular Mustangs again this year, with production of 64,234 spread over all of the series. And, despite its high cost, the V-8 option was definitely more popular than the Four, with 32,847 units having the 302 as compared with 27,825 with the Four.

The mid-level of the Mustang line was the "GL" series, which consisted of this notchback, Model 26, and a hatchback, Model 28. These same model designations were used through all series. The notchback was the less expensive of the two, listing for $7,264 with the Four, while the 4-cylinder hatchback went for $7,439. All notchbacks had large rectangular quarter windows as opposed to the triangular quarter panes in the hatchbacks. This model is wearing the new cast aluminum wheels, which were a $404 option. The GL models used vinyl low-back bucket seats. On all Mustangs, the heavy body side molding wrapped completely around the car as a continuation of the front and rear bumpers. Not quite as popular as the hatchbacks, total notchback production reached only 33,201.

Least expensive of all the new style Mustangs was the "L" series, available only in notchback form. With the 4-cylinder engine, the car proved to be the only little horse to have a base price of under $7,000, listing out at $6,727. Unlike the higher series, which used low-back bucket seats, the "L" models used a high-back version. Although flip-up air roofs, T-bar roof, and convertible tops were now optional in the Mustang line, the one item that no longer was available turned out to be the vinyl top option. As was the case with Thunderbird, the new styling apparently did not lend itself to vinyl coverings.

Ford's big car line continued to be the LTD Crown Victoria series, consisting of two cars and one wagon. Prices this year continued to creep upward, and now there were no Crown Victoria models under $10,000. Both the 2-door, Model 42, and this 4-door, Model 43, were base priced at $10,094, and both weighed approximately 3,600 pounds. There were no engine options, with the new fuel injected 302 V-8 being the only power plant allowed. By far the most popular, the 4-door drew 81,859 orders, while the 2-door accounted for only 11,414. Also in the big car ranks were the LTD Crown Victoria "S" 4-door sedans, designed primarily for fleet use in police and taxi operations. Costing $9,130 in base form, these cars were not available in 2-door configuration. Production figures of the "S" models are included with those of the 4-door sedan.

Totally new for the year was the LTD, a very attractive mid-size car that in effect replaced the Granada in Ford's sales roster. Built on the same 105.5-inch wheelbase platform of the Fairmont and the former Granada, the line consisted of two 4-door sedans and a wagon. Styling included a frontal appearance more akin to a big Escort than to the other Fords, with a sharply sloping grille of unmistakable Ford design centered between deep-set quad halogen headlights. The body itself was based on the existing Fairmont, and in fact, used Fairmont's unusual triangular quarter window. The lowest price model, and the only one with a base under $8,000, was the 4-door Sedan, Model 39, which went for $7,777 with the 140 cubic inch Four. Apparently the public liked the new baby, and it turned out to be Ford's third most popular car, with 111,813 leaving the show rooms. This figure covered both plain and Brougham versions.

For practical purposes, Ford's only full-size wagon was now the Country Squire, a member of the LTD Crown Victoria series. Costing $10,253, and weighing 3,773 pounds, it continued to be the heaviest Ford and the most expensive outside of the Thunderbird family. For those not wanting the wood trim, the wagon could be ordered as an "S" model with plain sides and a basic interior. In that form it cost $9,444, but apparently very few such models were ordered. In fact, wagon production was barely holding its own, and only 20,343 went out the door. As before, the attractive cast aluminum wheels were a $390 option.

From the exterior, there was nothing to distinguish a new LTD Brougham Sedan from the plain LTD 4-door. The Brougham differences were strictly internal, and essentially consisted of more upscale color-keyed carpeting, premium upholstery, deluxe dash trim, etc. With the Four, the Brougham cost $8,165. LTD buyers had their choice of the basic 4-cylinder engine; the in-line Six of 200 cubic inches, and the V-6 of 232 cubic inches. Later, an additional $890 would place the new Turbo Four under the hood. Some references also show the 302 V-8 available in the LTD, but because of the confusion of names, this may have pertained to the LTD Crown Victoria rather than the small model.

The new LTD Wagon, Model 40, was a nice looking vehicle, especially when trimmed with the $200 set of wire-type wheel covers. Available only with the in-line or V-6, the wagon could not be ordered with a 4-cylinder engine. With the 200 cubic inch Six, it cost $8,577, while the V-6 would have added another $70 to the price. Quite popular for a wagon, it saw its sales rise to 43,945. All LTD wagons contained a separate lockable side stowage compartment, designed for cameras and other small valuables that an owner might want to keep out of sight when locking up the car.

The new LTD line also had a Squire Wagon, but it was considered an option package to the standard wagon, and not an independent model. Priced at $280, the wood trim could be combined with a Brougham Wagon luxury interior package for another $365 to produce a really plush little vehicle. Regardless of the interior packages, all LTD wagons were fully carpeted throughout, even including the load floor. However, unlike the Country Squires which could be ordered with dual-facing rear seats, the LTD wagons provided only maximum seating for six, and comfortable seating for four.

Once one of Ford's best selling models, this year's Fairmont Futura 4-door sedan, Model 36, saw its sales drop to 69,287. With the Fairmont line destined to be dropped at the end of the season, dealers were placing total emphasis on the new LTD, which in effect was simply a more modern super-Fairmont. Both cars used the same platform, drive train, and basic bodies, but the LTD was revised into a far more aerodynamic shape. Both 4-doors used the interesting 4th window in the rear quarter sail panel. Base priced at $6,590 with the Four, the car could also be ordered as a stripped "S" model for $6,125. In that form it was available only with the 4-cylinder engine, but in Futura trim it could have the optional in-line Six and mandatory automatic transmission for an additional $678.

Appearing for the last time this year was the Fairmont Futura line, which consisted of a 4-door sedan and these two 2-doors, the upper one being the sedan and the lower being the Sport Coupe. However, Ford seldom used the "Sport" reference for the coupe this year. The difference in styling between the two 2-doors is very evident here, with the coupe having its own unique rear quarter treatment, relatively small quarter window, and huge slanted B-pillar. The coupe was slightly more expensive, being $6,666 as opposed to the $6,444 for the 2-door sedan, with both prices being for the basic Four. Neither car was particularly popular, and the coupe drew only 7,882 orders while the 2-door sedan drew 3,664. The lowest priced Fairmont was the "S" model 2-door sedan, which at $5,985 was the only Fairmont under the $6,000 mark. Its production is included in the above figure.

The year-old EXP might have taken off like a little rocket, but by the end of its first sales year Ford knew that the car was in trouble. In order to boost sagging sales, a whole flock of EXP variations were conceived. In addition, though all used the basic 97.6 cubic inch Four, there were two new engine options, plus a more refined and quicker version of the basic block. The options were a High-Output Four that produced 80 horses and had a new Borg-Warner 5-speed transaxle, and a multi-port fuel injected version of the same block, with a Bosch injector system. Most basic of all models, and the only one under $7,000 was the plain EXP 3-door Hatchback, Model 01. With the plain engine, it sold for $6,426.

Ford lists both a HO (High Output) Coupe and a HO Sport Coupe on its roster. The plain HO model was very similar to the regular EXP, while the Sport Coupe edition shown here used its own rear quarter graphics, had black exterior trim, color-keyed styled steel wheels, and low-back sports performance bucket seats. Both models used the new High Output engine. The plain HO model was priced at $7,004, while the fancy model went for $7,795. Since all EXP production was lumped in one pot, there is no way to tell the popularity of individual models. Suffice to say, with total sales of only 19,697, no one model could be called popular.

At the top of the 2-passenger front-wheel drive EXP line, and priced above the $8,000 mark, were two prestige models that probably had the lowest overall popularity. They were the very well dressed EXP Luxury Coupe, shown here, and the supposedly red hot EXP GT Coupe. The Luxury Coupe came with a set of cast aluminum wheels, outside racing mirrors, and a deluxe interior. It used the High Output Four. The GT version used the new fuel injected block, also had cast aluminum wheels, and benefitted from a more competitive suspension system. The Luxury model cost $8,225, while the GT Coupe reached for the $9,000 mark with a base price of $8,739.

The supposed hot shot of the Escort line was the GT 2-door Hatchback, which at a base price of $7,339, was also the most expensive of the line. For this, buyers received the new electronic fuel injected engine with Borg-Warner 5-speed transmission, the TRX heavy suspension package, unique front bumper with built-in running lights in the attached air dam, special exhaust system, blackout trim, reclining sport bucket seats, and the cast sport aluminum wheels shown here, among the items.

Appearing for the last time was the GLX series of Escorts, which represented the top of the line in trim and accessory items. The 4-door cars would remain in production, but the designations would be changed to "LX" and the 2-door model would be dropped. This year the 2-door GLX sold for $6,771. Ford did not separate the models on its production lists, but simply went by body style. Therefore, the 2-door Escort in total was the best selling of all Fords, with 151,386 being sold. It was also the only Escort to exceed the 100,000 mark, which in view of 1982 sales, must have been disappointing to Dearborn's officials.

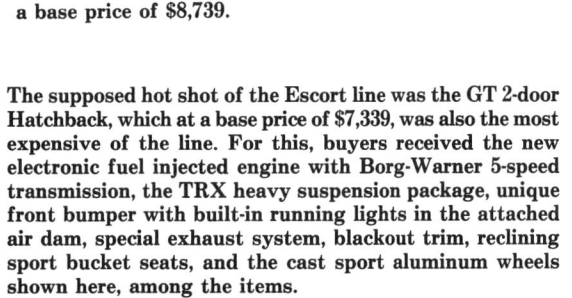

The 4-door GLX Escort Sedan would be called the LX in 1984. This year it represented the top of the 4-door line, and was priced at $6,988 with the basic transverse-mounted 4-cylinder engine. New for the GLX category this year were the wide body side moldings of black vinyl, and new seat material of a woven vinyl. The argent styled steel wheels with beauty rings were also standard. Sales of the 4-door sedan dropped substantially, going down to 84,649, a loss of 45,824 sales. If this photo looks familiar, it's because Ford used the same GLX publicity shot in both 1982 and 1983.

Buyers of the GLX 4-door Station Wagon could have a plain sided car with wide black vinyl body molding, or for an extra $350, could have the Squire wood-trim option. In plain form, Escort's top wagon was the only model beside the GT to break the $7,000 mark, with a base price of $7,150. Add one of the new engine options to this, plus a $625 air conditioner, $200 radio, and a few other toys, and one was getting into the $9,000 range. As did the 4-door sedan, the wagons also took a tumble, dropping to combined sales of 79,335, or a loss of 9,664. This was not good, but at least it wasn't as bad as that suffered by the sedan.

The GL series marked Escort's mid-ground, with there really being very little difference between the GL and GLX models. In this category, the 2-door Hatchback cost $6,384. New for this series were the low-back reclining bucket seats as standard equipment. All Escort and EXP models this year received a 13 gallon gas tank to extend their cruising range. The 4-door sedan in GL trim was priced at $6,601. This year Ford interchanged the title 4-door sedan and 4-door Hatchback.

Ford's two lowest price station wagons occurred in the "GL" and "L" levels, with the GL being slightly more upscale. As a GL, the wagon cost $6,779, while the plain L version was $6,052. The GL models featured a knit vinyl seat upholstery while the L models were in plain vinyl. Also, all GL and higher models had a self-locking gas filler door with inside release, while the L models simply used a plain swing-out fuel door.

Ford's only two models to be priced under $6,000 were the two L series Escort sedan styles. The 2-door hatchback, shown here, was Ford's lowest priced vehicle, costing $5,639, while the 4-door sedan came in at $5,846. This, of course, was for the basic car, with no trim or convenience options whatsoever, and very few if any were ever sold in this form. Most had at least enough basic options, plus dealer set-up and tax charges to bring the price easily into the $6,000 range. Now turn back to Pg. 104, where a basically equipped Model T sold for $260 right off the dealership floor!

Ford entered the 1984 selling season early this year, with the introduction of a brand new front-drive car called the Tempo. Replacing the now-departed Fairmont in the sales roster, the new compact turned out to be Ford's best selling line for 1984, chalking up a hefty tally of 402,214 units by the end of the model year.

Totally different than the Fairmont, the Tempo availed itself of the latest aerodynamic styling, and from some angles, looked like a miniature Thunderbird. Built on a pan of exclusive 99.9-inch (don't ask why it wasn't an even 100 inches) wheelbase, it used its own exclusive body of 176.2 inches overall length. Actually, the body was exclusive only in the Ford line, as the same basic shell and sheet metal was also used by the new Mercury Topaz. The car was available only in two styles, a 2-door and a 4-door sedan, but these were divided into L, GL, and GLX trim-level models.

Powering the new car was a totally new 4-cylinder engine developed especially for the Tempo. Confusing the issue was the fact that the new block had the same 140 cubic inch displacement as did the old Fairmont Four, but there the similarity ended. Built in both the U.S. and Mexico, the new mill featured what Ford called HSC heads (High Swirl Combustion) and a bore and stroke of 3.7x3.3 inches, as opposed to the 3.78x13 bore and stroke of the old Fairmont Four. Still, its base horsepower was listed as only 84, as opposed to the 90 rating of the old model. The old Four, incidentally, still appeared as the base engine in the LTD line, being available in both gasoline and propane versions, and bearing an 88 horsepower rating in either form.

Attached to the new mill was a front-drive transaxle with either a standard 4-speed manual or optional automatic or a 5-speed manual transmissions. Although the pan appeared to be simply a stretched version of the 94.2-inch wheelbase Escort chassis, the suspension differed greatly, with quadra-link rear suspension with MacPherson struts, and a front suspension using both a stabilizer bar and MacPherson struts.

One would think that with such heavy sales going to the new compact Tempo, its smaller kin would suffer. But such was not the case, and Escort actually saw a healthy jump, with production going from 315,370 for the 1983 model year to a nice 372,523 for this year. Although the car was virtually unchanged from the previous models, it did receive two new engines. One, for the sport set, was the Turbo Four, which was a fuel injected, turbocharged version of the standard 97.6 cubic inch (1.6 liter) engine. Rated at 120 horsepower, the block as standard in LX models and an option in all other Escort and EXP models.

The other block was a new Diesel four, initially produced by Mazda. Bearing no relation to the gasoline fours, the new diesel engine displaced 2 liters (121 cubic inches) and had a square bore and stroke of 3.39 inches. With fuel injection and a 22.5:1 compression ratio, the diesels were rated at 52 horsepower. The engines were initially optional only in the base-level L and GL Escort series, but later became available in the Tempo line as well. They turned out to be popular in neither, possibly because of their $560 cost above the standard gasoline Four.

Closely aligned with Escort, though certainly not sharing its popularity, was the rather different little EXP, Ford's 2-passenger mini-sport car. Aiming even more at the sport set this year, the car dropped its old exterior and received totally new sheet metal complete with a new bulging liftgate and different though familiar frontal styling. Gone were the old HO and GT models, while in their place was a new Turbo Coupe, which featured the new Turbo Four described above. Along with the new engine, the Turbo Coupe models sported a rear deck spoiler and a front air dam (more for aesthetics than ground effects) and prominent "TURBO" decals on the sides. The new models helped a bit, and sales crept up to 23,016, which was not a large jump in actual numbers, but represented almost a 20% increase in acceptance.

Ford's real sporty-type car, the Mustang, also received some treatment aimed directly as the speed set. The package was in the form of the new SVO (Special Vehicle Operations) Tubo Four Coupe, which replaced the former Turbo GT. Heartbeat of the SVO was the same 140 cubic inch Turbo Four as used previously, but now fitted with an air-to-air intercooler that pushed 175 horses from the fuel injected block. Attached to the SVO engine was a new Borg-Warner 5-speed transmission with a Hurst shifter. Other toys in the box were adjustable bucket seats in real leather, 4-wheel disc brakes, a special suspension package, and a totally different front end featuring a hood scoop, an air scoop below the bumper, and a hood that swept downward to the bumper, with no hint of grille. Not a cheap toy, the new SVO Coupe sold for $15,596, which was more than $6,000 above the similar GT Coupe with the 302 V-8. As has been the rule all along, performance comes with a price tag.

The Turbo Four engine was also available in the GT series, priced at approximately $1,775 above the basic Four, or $200 above the V-8. Within the line, the GL and GLX labels were now known simply as the L and LX trim levels. These models used the 140 cubic inch carbureted Four as base power, or could be ordered with the optional V-6 of 232 cubic inches for an additional $410. The V-8 could also be installed in these models at special order and for the aforementioned $1,575. Also available was a fuel injected version of the 302 V-8 which produced 165 horsepower. As with other models, Mustang finally saw a nice production increase, with 141,480 galloping onto the field during the model year.

Mustang's far distant cousin, the Thunderbird, dropped its Heritage model but picked up two new trim designations, the Flia and the Elan (often, "elan" was spelled without a capital). Along with the plain version and the Turbo Coupe, this gave the Bird four varieties in its nest. The Fila derived its name from Fila Sports Inc., an Italian manufacturer of skiing and tennis apparel and equipment. It came only in an exclusive 2-tone gray paint job, with exclusive red and blue striping, and an exclusive gray interior. It came only with the fuel injected 302 V-8, while plain and Elan (elan) models used the 232 cubic inch V-6, now fuel injected, while the Turbo Coupe used its own version of the 140 cubic inch fuel injected turbocharged Four of 145 horsepower. Again, acceptance of the new models made Ford folks smile widely, as sales went up almost 50,000 to tally out at 170,553.

Also having good acceptance was the year-old LTD, which now added formal roof styling to its Brougham, but otherwise changed very little. Its basic engine was still the 140 cubic inch Four available in either gasoline or an exclusive propane fueled version, but the High Output Four was no longer available to the line. The new fuel injected 232 cubic inch V-6 was still standard on wagons, and was a popular option on many sedans. Also available was a propane fueled version of the Four, but this engine never proved popular, probably because of a combination of low power and its almost $900 cost above the basic Four.

Ford's remaining "real" car, the LTD Crown Victoria, received a new grille this year, while the 4-door sedans received a newly styled padded Brougham roof. However, the padded top was considered an option, and not part of a separate trim level. Available were the highly trimmed standard Crown Victorias, and the stripped "S" models designed primarily for fleet use. The only engine was the 302 cubic inch V-8, but the 315 cubic inch High Output V-8 was available but only with the special police package.

Engine selections, most of which have been detailed, reached almost silly proportions, with nine variations of 4-cylinder blocks being offered, along with one V-6 and two V-8s, and this does not include the Mustang exclusives. Missing from the list however was the old in-line Six of 200 cubic inches, which disappeared along with the Fairmont.

As mentioned throughout, production was up substantially for the model year, rising to a total of 1,466,194, which represented an increase of more than 500,000 units. In addition, six models broke the 100,000 list, but some of these may have made the list only because Ford no longer differentiated between trim-level series when compiling its production.

The number one seller was the new Tempo 4-door sedan, with 295,149 models. Coming in second was the Escort 2-door hatchback with 184,323. Third place was taken by all Thunderbirds in total, with production of 170,533 not broken down into the four models. Fourth place went to the LTD 4-door sedan with 154,173, while the LTD Crown Victoria 4-door sedan came in fifth with 130,164. Last on the list was the new Tempo 2-door sedan with 107,065, while the Escort 4-door hatchback sedan just missed with 99,444. In all, Ford had a happy year in 1984.

Returning as Thunderbird's hot one was the Turbo Coupe, Model 46/934. Priced at $12,330, the car could be now ordered with either the standard 5-speed manual gearbox or a special automatic for an additional $315. Exclusive to the Turbo was the special bumper with integral air dam and built-in high intensity running lights. The engine was still the 140 cubic inch turbocharged Four. Window moldings were now in a charcoal finish. On standard shift cars, a clutch/starter interlock system prevented engaging the starter while the car was in gear without the clutch being depressed.

The most expensive Ford until the SVO Mustang came along was the new Thunderbird Fila Coupe, which had a V-8 price of $14,855. Named for an Italian sportswear manufacturer, the car came only with an exclusive 2-tone light and dark gray paint job with red and blue striping. Wheels and grille were in body color, while window moldings and headlight bezels were in charcoal finish. Inside, it had an exclusive Oxford gray interior with the articulated seats trimmed in white Oxford leather or Oxford gray luxury cloth. It came only with the fuel injected 302 V-8. The pivoting front vent panes were an $80 option.

The Thunderbird Heritage model was now gone, but its place was taken by both the expensive Fila, Model 46/606 and the slightly less expensive Elan model shown here. This version, which actually was a brighter looking vehicle than the Fila through its use of chromed front and bright window surrounds, bore a base V-8 price of $13,281, or $12,661 with the V-6. Elan, which can be construed to mean dash, intensity, or even passion, was often not capitalized by Ford. In trim level, the car was situated between the plain Thunderbird and the Fila, but had none of the exclusive appointments for which the Fila was known.

Although Ford did not break down Thunderbird's production by trim level, it is safe to assume that the major portion of the 170,533 Birds that left the nest this year were of the plain Model 46 variety as seen here. In this form, the car sold for $9,633 with the V-6, and thus was not only the lowest price T-Bird, but also the only one listing under the $10,000 mark. Power steering, power brakes and automatic transmission were standard items, but the list of options still remained as long as the car. New for the V-6 this year was a fuel injection set-up similar to that used on the V-8.

Ford's most expensive car this year was not a Thunderbird or upscale Crown Victoria, but a new hot shot Mustang called the SVO Coupe, Model 28/939. Priced at a blazing $15,596, the car featured the 140 cubic inch turbocharged 4-cylinder engine, but fitted with an intercooler, which helped boost horsepower to 175 while providing quick low-speed response. Standing for "Special Vehicle Operations," the SVO featured an exclusive front with single halogen headlights bracketed by signal and parking lights; an air dam integral with the front bumper and including halogen running lights, and an aerodynamic scooped hood which swept down across the front and completely eliminated the grille. Among the other toys on this model were articulated bucket seats in real leather, multiple-setting struts and shocks, 4-wheel disc brakes, and a Borg-Warner 5-speed manual transmission. Ford claimed the car had a top speed in excess of 130 MPH.

Part two of the Mustang GT series was the convertible, Model 27/932. Almost reaching the SVO in price, it had a base of $13,245 with the turbocharged Four or $13,050 with the V-8. The GT used a front bumper similar to that of the SVO. This unit contained an integral air dam and provided space for the optional driving lamps shown here. Relatively popular, the Mustang convertible in total saw production of 17,600.

Now downgraded slightly by the new SVO Coupe was Mustang's former hot shot, the GT Coupe. Like the SVO, the car came only in 3-door hatchback style, with the notchback not available. It could be ordered with either the Turbo Four (without intercooler) for $9,762, or with the 302 V-8 for $9,578. Special features of the GT models were the blackout hood and grille, and heavy black molding which completely surrounded the car from bumper to bumper. This example wears the special order T-Roof with twin removable panels, which was a $1,075 extra. Also available was the flip-up air roof, for $315. GT production was not kept separate, but was part of the 86,200 hatchbacks Mustang built this year.

A mid-year issue was the 20th Anniversary Package that could be added to the GT models. When applied, the V-8 cars were known as GT 350 models. Surprisingly inexpensive, the anniversary package added only $145 to the basic price of the car. Included in the grouping was an exclusive all-white exterior, which included white grille, headlight surrounds and body and bumper molding; special red rocker stripe with "GT 350" signature; red interior, and articulated front bucket seats in red vinyl. GT buyers had a choice of two V-8 engines, a normally aspirated model or a new fuel injected 302 which developed 165 horsepower.

Soft-top lovers who did not want the expense of a GT model could opt for the LX Mustang convertible, model 27/602. Available only with a V-6 or V-8, the car had a base V-6 price of $11,849, with the V-8 in this case being only $727 more. Ranked as America's best-selling convertible, the car featured roll-down quarter windows, and a full-width rear seat. It was rated as a 4-passenger car. Even though the convertible work was done by Cars & Concepts on basic notchback bodies, the cars being earmarked for convertible conversion were now stiffened at the factory with a new structural reinforcement package. The LX convertible was essentially in the same slot that had been occupied by the GLX last year, but that trim level designation was no longer used.

Mustang 2-door notchback coupes came in two flavors, the Model 26/602 LX version, shown here at speed, and the basic Model 26 "L" variation. As the basic "L" model, it was the lowest price Mustang, with a tag of $7,098 for the 4-cylinder model. The "LX" version was not that much more, with its base being $7,290. Between the two models, a total of 37,680 examples left the barn. Production was probably evenly split between the 4-cylinder engine and the V-6 which cost an additional $410. However, the basic 302 V-8 upped the price another $1,575, and therefore probably wasn't as popular in the lower ranking models as were the two smaller blocks.

The former trim levels of L, GL, and GLX were now reduced to just two designations, the low-level "L" series and the mid-level LX. Most popular of all models in both series was the 3-door hatchback, seen here as the plain "L" Model 28. In this form, with the Four, it cost $7,269 and weighed 2,584 pounds. Slightly more plush as an LX model, it cost $7,496 in that form. The cast aluminum wheels shown here were a $350 option in all trim levels. Hatchbacks continued to use a triangular quarter window, while a slanted rectangular type was used on the notchbacks. With a folding rear seat and large rear opening, the hatchback offered substantially more luggage room than did the notchback.

Least popular of all the full-size Fords was the LTD Crown Victoria 2-door Sedan, Model 42. It accounted for only 12,522 sales in the Crown line, and none as an "S" model because it wasn't available in the lower trim level. It was base priced at $10,954, the same as the 4-door sedan. It is shown here with the wide lower body trim, which was a $40 option, and the new Brougham decor option, a $365 package consisting primarily of the vinyl half-roof with bright wrapover. Although these items were almost always included on Crown Victorias, they were still considered option packages.

A large slab of imitation wood trim occupied the sides of this year's Country Squire wagon, Model 44. Continuing to be the most expensive of all Crown Victorias, the Squire had a base of $11,111, and thus was the only full-size Ford over the $11,000 mark. And, that price did not include the cast aluminum wheels, rooftop luggage rack, or $167 set of dual facing rear seats. Wagon production in total was 30,803, which included both plain and Squire models, and the few "S" versions that might have been turned out. The "S" wagons followed the sedan's lead in being totally stripped, and designed primarily for fleet or livery work. They were priced at $10,136.

The new LTD Crown Victoria 4-door sedan, Model 43, is also shown with the optional Brougham roof treatment and the wide lower body trim. In addition, this version wears the cast aluminum turbine-type wheels, which were another $390 per set. Adding to the vehicle's class was a lengthy lighted "coach lamp" running down the B-pillar. This gave an attractive glow when the lights were on. For those who wanted total luxury, a plush interior luxury group was available for another $1,035. Conversely, the car was available in "S" form, where it was base priced at $9,826, thus being the only Crown Victoria under $10,000. Available only to "S" sedans was a police package for $400.

Ford's fourth most popular car overall was the LTD 4-door sedan, Model 39, which in 1983 had been the third most popular model. Despite its sales being up nicely, rounding out at 154,173 this year, the hot selling Thunderbird still nudged the sedan from third spot. As could be expected, the year-old car was virtually unchanged. Standard power was the 140 cubic inch Four, with both gasoline and propane versions being available. The only engine option was the 232 cubic inch V-6, though the 302 V-8 was an option for the police package only. However, though it is reported that a few of these V-8 models did sneak out to select non-police buyers. In basic 4-cylinder form, the car sold for $8,605, and was the only LTD under the $9,000 mark. As a Six, its price jumped to $9,014.

Showing off its new grille is the plain LTD Crown Victoria station wagon, Model 44/41E. The new grille this year featured a double mesh, with the outer one being of bright metal, while the inner one had an argent finish. As before, the only engine in the Crown Victoria line was the fuel injected 302 with automatic transmission. However, the wagons used a high-output variation of this engine, rated at 155 horses, as opposed to the 140 horses found in the sedans. The plain wagon was priced at $10,861.

New for the year was the LTD Brougham Sedan, Model 39/60H. Priced at $10,389 with the V-6, it was the only LTD to break the $10,000 base mark. Its claim to fame was a new and very attractive convertible-like woven vinyl top, with large sail panels that blocked the normal rear quarter opera window on the sedans. Not a new stamping, the Brougham roof was simply an application over the standard LTD sedan top. In addition to the new roof, the car also featured a more deluxe interior and a set of luxury wheel covers. Its production was blended in with that of the regular sedan, and thus it is impossible to tell how many of these attractive mid-size cars entered the highways. LTD sedans weighed in at 2,800 pounds with the Fours, and about 80 pounds more for the V-6. The vent windows shown on both sedans were an $80 extra.

Displaying a rather plain backside is the LTD Station Wagon, Model 40. Available only with the V-6, it sold for $9,102 and weighed 2,990 pounds. The rear door vent panes were similar to those used on the sedans, and like those of the sedans, would not open, but were there primarily to narrow the main window enough to clear the door's doglegs. As did the smaller Fords, the LTD wagon had a full liftgate, hinged at the window header, rather than the doorgate with disappearing window as used on the full-size wagons. Neither the rear nor the rear quarter windows could be opened on this model. Only about one-third as popular as the sedan, the wagon drew 59,569 orders.

When the Squire option was added to the plain LTD wagon, the result was a really attractive mid-size vehicle. The imitation wood trim, which also covered the liftgate, added $280 to the price, while the luxury wheel covers shown here were another $55 and the rooftop luggage rack was $125 more. Those who really wanted to splurge could also add the Brougham interior trim package for $365, which brought the wagon's interior trim up to a level approximating that found on the new Brougham models.

The top of the Tempo 4-door field was also the GLX, Model 23, which was priced at $7,621, the same as the 2-door. Rated as a 5-passenger sport sedan, the car featured bright window surrounds, and deluxe wheel covers in addition to a more plush interior and fancier trim on the low-back cloth-covered front bucket seats and rear bench seat. All Tempos used a stretched version of the Escort body pan, with revised suspension and an exclusive wheelbase of 99.9 inches.

Playing in the water is Ford's newest kid, the front-wheel-drive Tempo. This is the GLX 2-door, Model 20, the top of the line model with the top of the line price of $7,621. Powering the new Tempos was a totally new 140 cubic inch 4-cylinder engine built in both Mexico and the U.S. Not bearing any relation to the previous 140 cubic inch Four, which was still the base engine in the LTD line, the new block was an exclusive Tempo unit and not available in other models.

The mid-range of the new Tempo line was called the GL series. It also contained the two basic models, both priced at the same $7,159. Ford this year did not differentiate between the trim series in its production, instead lumping all Tempo cars into a 2-door and a 4-door list. Thus, overall 2-door Tempo sales reached 107,065, which was enough to place the car in 6th place on Ford's overall sales chart. The standard transmission was a 4-speed manual, but for an extra $75, a 5-speed manual with overdrive could be installed. And, for another $440, an automatic transaxle unit was available.

Showing off its full-width taillight bar with a centrally located license plate housing is this Tempo GL 4-door, Model 22. Tempo's mid-range sedan, it sold for the same $7,159 as the 2-door. Lack of bright window surrounds was the main exterior difference between this car and the GLX version. All Tempo 4-doors used a relatively large non-opening window in the rear sail panel. Far more popular than the 2-door models, the 4-door Tempos took Ford's number one sales spot this year, with a total of 295,149 being built in all three trim levels.

Without opening the hood, one would never suspect that this basic Tempo "L" sedan, Model 21, held Ford's newest engine option...a 4-cylinder overhead cam 121 cubic inch diesel. Produced in Japan by Mazda, the new diesel was available in both Escort and Tempo models for an additional $560, but mandated the $75 manual 5-speed transmission. The introduction of the Mazda diesel gave Tempo its only engine option. All Tempos used a body-color plastic grille consisting primarily of three horizontal bars. Deep-set single rectangular halogen headlights nested between the grille and the outer parking lights.

Most basic of the Tempos were those found in the "L" series, such as this 2-door which sold for $6,936. All Tempos weighed in the 2,300-pound range. "L" models lacked the basic side trim found on other series, and were fairly plain inside. Ford claimed the Tempo had aircraft designed doors, which wrapped slightly into the roof area to make for easier entry or exit. This was the same door design as found on the new Thunderbird. To eliminate wind drag, the normal exterior drip moldings were removed, and redesigned as interior rain channels, located behind the outer door skin. "L" models did not use the full-width taillight bar as found on other Tempos. Instead, they had a body-color valence panel between the taillight units and the license plate holder.

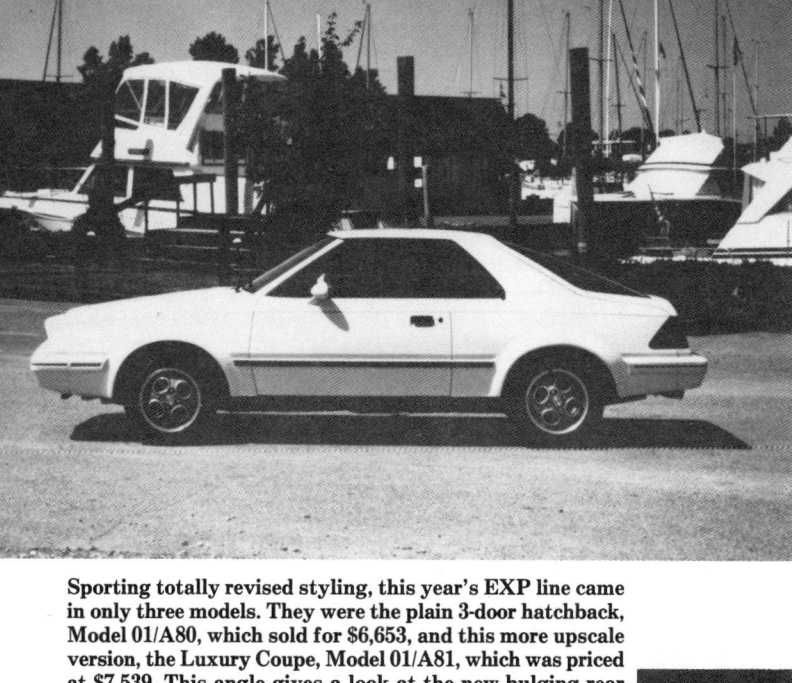

Putting some sport in the EXP's sport concept was the new Turbo High Output Four, which could produce 120 horsepower. Whereas the fuel injected turbocharged block was listed as an option in the related Escort line, the EXP used the engine as the basis for a separate Model. Called the Turbo Coupe, Model 01/A82, the new baby was based priced at a hefty $9,942. In addition to the new engine, it used an exclusive rear deck with integral spoiler, and a special front air dam. The greenhouse featured all black trim and window surrounds, cast aluminum wheels, special suspension, and the manual 5-speed transaxle. Production was impossible to ascertain because it was included with that of all EXP models.

Sporting totally revised styling, this year's EXP line came in only three models. They were the plain 3-door hatchback, Model 01/A80, which sold for $6,653, and this more upscale version, the Luxury Coupe, Model 01/A81, which was priced at $7,539. This angle gives a look at the new bulging rear glass, which was among the new design features. Other changes included a new but similar front treatment, new air dam, and the use of new taillights from the 1983 Mercury LN7, which had been discontinued. The EXP was still a 2-seater, and still billed as a low-price sports-type car. Possibly the new styling helped a bit, as sales crept upward slightly, with a total of 23,016 EXPs of all models being sold.

Besides the Escort-based sport-type 2-passenger EXP, the "real" Escort line also had a sport version. It was this "GT" model, available only as a 2-door hatchback. Known as the Model 07, the car cost $7,593 in basic form, which included the rather ugly "TR" style aluminum wheels that were introduced this year. Besides a few exterior differences such as black polycarbonate bumpers and side trim, rear spoiler, and exclusive window trimming, the GT models main feature was its standard fuel-injected Four. This was a modified version of the 97.6 cubic inch (1.6 liters) which produced 85 horsepower at 5200 rpm.

The small front fender plaque says that this is the new Turbo version of the Escort GT 2-door. It arrived late enough to almost be considered a mid-year model. Its claim to fame was the same turbocharged fuel-injected Four as used on the EXP Turbo. Only this car offered 4-passenger seating rather than two, and utilized the standard Escort 2-door hatchback body along with the standard "GT" trim. The turbo Four offered 120 horsepower at 5200 rpm, a real boost considering its block was still the same basic 97.6 cubic inch unit found in all Escorts. Turbo models also used the 5-speed manual transmission (transaxle), with no automatic option, and had stiffer suspension than other Escorts. Its price was close to the $9,000 mark.

The top-trim Escort models were in the "LX" series. This line was home only to the two 4-doors, the sedan shown here and the station wagon. The cars utilized the same fuel-injected Four as did the GT model, but emphasis was on luxury rather than sportiness. Exterior variations included the polycarbonate front and rear bumpers with attached fog lamps, exclusive side striping, and blackout body trim, essentially making it a luxury version of the 2-door GT. Inside was an overhead console with a bright digital clock, a tachometer, and full instrumentation. The running gear included the same 5-speed manual transmission and stiff "TR" suspension found on the GT. Relatively pricey for its size, the LX listed out at $7,848.

Escort's most expensive model was the LX Station Wagon, Model 15, which had a base price of $7,939. Essentially taking the place of the former GLX models, the new LX wagon used the same electronically fuel-injected Four as found in the LX sedan and the GT hatchback. Ford claimed that this was the most powerful and efficient small engine ever built on a production basis in America. The wagons had a new split rear seat, which folded down to form a more even cargo floor. Its split design allowed either the total seat to be folded, or either half left in the up position while the other half was folded.

Probably the major portion of Escort's 88,756 station wagon sales this year were in the popular mid-level GL series. In this form, the car sold for $6,773, and like all Escorts, weighed right around the 2,000 pound mark. GL models used the basic 70 horse Four, but a popular option was the HO (High Output) version, which delivered 80 horses at 5400 rpm. Popular in this series was the $440 optional automatic transaxle. Those interested in a bit more exterior flair could order the imitation wood Squire trim package for $375.

The mid-trim level of the Escort line was occupied by the "GL" models. In the car field, these were the 2-door hatchback, Model 05, which sold for $6,382, and this 4-door hatchback sedan, Model 14, which was base priced at $6,595. Since all Escort production was combined into body style totals, it is impossible to determine how many of each trim level were sold. However, it is safe to assume that the GL series accounted for the major portion of the 99,444 4-door Escort sedans and the 184,323 2-door hatchback models produced this year. In fact, the 2-door Escort hatchback in total came in as Ford's second best selling vehicle.

In 1983 the basic Escort line was dropped, and the "L" model cars became the basic trim level. This year however, the base level was put back into play. Thus on the lower levels, there was the "L" 2-door Model 04 shown here, which sold for $5,885, and the basic 2-door, also called Model 04, which was Ford's lowest price car, coming in at $5,629. Also in this series were two 4-door hatchback sedans, both called the Model 13. In "L" trim, the slightly fancier one was a $6,099 car, while the basic model was $5,835.

The lowest price station wagon on Ford's books was the Escort, selling for $6,313 in "L" trim. Unlike the two car models, it was not available as a basic model. This version is shown with the $65 set of functional front door vent panes; $45 body side molding kit; $55 set of front and rear deluxe bumpers and guards, and $100 roof luggage rack. It might also have Escort's newest optional power unit, the 2-liter Mazda-built 4-cylinder diesel that was a $560 option in both Escorts and the new Tempos. Note that the lower level Escorts used bright grilles and headlight surrounds, while the up-scale variations used blackout trim.

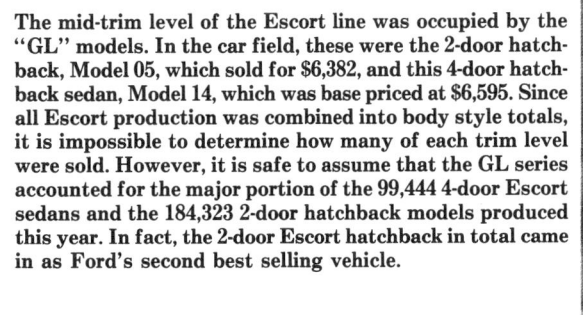

After a rather exciting 1984, Ford almost could have been accused of taking a nap this year, as there were virtually no major changes in any of the car lines. True, there were some increased production figures, which probably made the accountants and sales managers smile, and there were some welcomed increases in horsepowers, but overall, things just went on in a "business as usual" mode, on a nice healthy level.

Probably the most changes of any line occurred in the Mustang corral. Here all of the little horses got new noses, in the form of a more aerodynamic sloping front and a below-bumper air dam with airflow slots. Now the only hint of a grille was a single air slot running horizontally between the sloped and covered headlight/marker light units. This really was quite similar to the grille on the previous SVO coupe.

Although the 4-cylinder 140 cubic inch block remained basic, those who live on the other side of the spectrum were treated to horsepower increases in both the fuel injected and 4-barrel versions of the 302 cubic inch (5 liter) V-8. Accomplished primarily through a new cam and roller tappets, the fuel injected version now gave out 180 horses, while the carburetor mill belted out 210. The V-6 and the two Fours (plain and Turbo) were unchanged. Available models were reduced by two as the two low-buck "L" models were dropped. Now the LX series of three models was the base line. These were available only with the base Four or the optional V-6. Available only with a V-8 were the GT hatchback and the convertible, while the Turbo Four went only in the SVO hatchback. Despite a drop in models, the public

apparently liked what it saw, and sales went up to 156,514, an increase of over 15,000 from 1984.

Just the opposite happened with Thunderbird, Ford's other sporty type car. Here too some minor changes occurred, but the new items were mainly on the tail, not the beak. There, new full-width taillamps graced the stern and provided a home to both the backup lights and a new Thunderbird emblem. The same four models appeared as in 1984, but to celebrate Thunderbird's 30th birthday, a special edition Elan (elan) was introduced at mid-year. Painted a Medium Regatta Blue, the car was neither outstanding nor desirable, and production reportedly was halted after only a few thousand were built.

Under the Thunderbird hood, the same base V-6, optional V-8, and exclusive Turbo four appeared. However, the Turbo was now rated at 155 horsepower, an increase of 10. The V-6 remained at 120 horses while the V-8 remained at 140. But unlike the Mustang, T-Bird had nothing to smile about, as its sales slumped 18,682, dropping to 151,851.

As if to perplex the sales people even more, the Crown Victorias offered no changes at all, yet here production was up over 30%. The new total reached 199,110, an increase of 56,424. The same line-up remained, with two fleet-oriented stripped "S" models, two wagon variations, and a 2-door and 4-door sedan. The only engines were the 302 V-8, in base 140 horsepower, and an optional high output (HO) 165 horse version. The 351 cubic inch block was still around, but again supposedly for police car use only. It was rated at 180 horsepower, but was not available to the general public.

Initially the LTD line had only a minor grille and taillamp change to brag about. But at mid-season, a new LX Brougham 4-door Euro-sedan joined the pack. Having its own exclusive styling with body-color grille and black trim and highlights, it was in fact considered a one-model series of its own. The new LX Brougham

Definitely not for the economy minded was the Thunderbird Turbo Coupe, Model 46/934. Its base price of $13,365 represented an increase of $1,035 above 1984, and made it relatively easy to push the actual sales tag to over the $15,000 mark. New water-cooled turbocharger bearings and new full-flow electronic fuel injector design helped improved the Turbo's performance. Horsepower was now up ten, with the rating being 155 at 4600 rpm. The basic block remained the fuel injected 140 cubic inch Four. This year's Turbos appeared less flashy, due primarily to the switch to body-color grilles rather than the former chromed frontal units. Headlight surrounds were either in body color or in charcoal argent. Standard on the Turbo Coupe were all-electronic instruments, whereas these digital panels were optional on other models.

Ford's highest price car again was the Thunderbird Fila Coupe, which posted a hefty base price of $15,609 when fitted with the optional 302 V-8. Even with the 232 V-6, it still was tagged at $14,974. Apparently the price kept buyers away, as the model did not reappear in 1986. Features were a special "Fila-designed" interior, painted cast aluminum wheels of a new "Swiss cheese" pattern, charcoal lower bodysides and bumpers, body-color grilles, automatic transmission, and electronic everything. However, the front window vent panes were an $80 extra.

Euro was described by Ford as "A performance touring sedan." It came with its own exclusive fuel injected 302 cubic inch V-8 that produced 165 horsepower at 3800 rpm. This was the most powerful engine in the entire Ford list, not counting the three Mustang power plants. Coupled to a 4-speed automatic and having a special suspension package in addition to other performance toys, the new LX drew quite a bit of interest. Sadly, its production figures were not kept separate, and thus it is not known if the interest followed through to the sales floors. However, one indication might lie in the fact that the model did not reappear in 1986. Not cheap, the car was priced over $2,000 above the regular LTD Brougham.

Also getting a horsepower boost was the year-old Tempo High Swirl Combustion (HSC) engine, which ran with Holley carburetion in 1984, but now had its own fuel injection set-up. Still exclusive to the Tempo line, the 140 cubic inch Four was now rated at 86 horsepower in base form, or 100 horses in its optional high output version. Also available in the line was the Mazda-built diesel engine at almost $500 extra, but as far as can be ascertained, there were few takers for this unit either in the Tempo or the Escort. Otherwise, the Tempo changed almost not at all, but its sales appeal slipped by a noticeable degree, going from 402,214 in 1984 to 339,087 this year, a dip of over 63,000 units.

Once again the strange little 2-seat EXP came out in its three versions, with hardly any change to differentiate the new models from the old.

Probably the most activity for the year occurred to the least car. The little Escort began the year just like all the other Fords, virtually unchanged from the previous models. But then, at mid-season, a whole flock of new Escorts arrived. Called mid-1985 models, the new vehicles not only had a noticeable appearance change, but came in with a new Four of 1.9 liters (113 cubic inches) as the base block.

This plant delivered 86 horsepower at 4800 rpm, as opposed to the 70 horses of the former 1.6 liter Four, and the difference was quite noticeable. Once the mid-season models appeared, the smaller block was phased out, along with the two high output versions of that engine. Bringing in more power at the end of the season, and carried over into 1986, was a fuel injected version of the 1.9 liter block, which could turn out 108 horses at 5200 rpm. This block became standard in the Escort GT model, and optional in all other Escorts. Along with the new models came a reduction in available trim levels, with the LX models being shelved and only the 2-door hatchback being available in the basic series. Still, the Escort field remained crowded with base, L, GL, and GT models all competing for attention.

But apparently Escort was doing something right, as it again led the sales race. Production was up by 34,560, not as much as that experienced by the Crown Victorias, but certainly a healthy amount. Total Escort sales were 407,083.

In all, Ford's production reached 1,485,633, for a moderate increase of 19,439 units for the model year. As few breakouts were now being made for individual body styles or trim levels, it is impossible to ascertain which particular models led the pack. Suffice to say that in order of sales, the series were ranked as Escort; Tempo; LTD; LTD Crown Victoria; Mustang; Thunderbird, and EXP.

The mid-level in the Thunderbird nest continued to be occupied by the elan (Ford did not capitalize the name) Coupe, Model 46/607. Unlike the Fila and the Turbo, the elan continued to use a chromed grille, and had its lower body sides in the same color as the upper body. The elan differed from the plain Thunderbird mainly in interior fittings, with such items as power windows, AM/FM stereo and cassette player, and remote electrically powered outside mirrors being part of the standard package. With the V-8, it sold for $12,551, while the V-6 was $635 less. This model provided a base for the 30th Anniversary Edition Thunderbird. This was an all-blue model with silver body molding and bumpers, marketed in honor of Thunderbird's 30th birthday. Not too popular, the car was withdrawn after only a couple thousand had been produced.

Providing a foundation for all of the upscale Birds was the basic Thunderbird, Model 46. Priced at $10,249 with the V-6, it is shown here with a $345 set of the new cast aluminum wheels. Thunderbird's production was down this year, dropping to 151,851, for a loss of 18,628. A fully electronic digital instrument cluster was available at $330 this year. Still available was the flip-up open air roof for $315. The Birds continued to be built on a platform of 104-inch wheelbase and were 197.6 inches long overall. All weighed approximately 3,000 pounds with the V-6, or 200 pounds more with the V-8.

Not reappearing until mid-1985 was Mustang's hotshot, the SVO Coupe, Model 28/939. Named for Special Vehicle Operations, the SVO was powered by a revised Turbo Four, now producing 175 horses. Among the under hood changes was a new turbocharger intercooler and other minor modifications. On the outside, totally new frontal styling and an exclusive scooped hood made sure no one confused the car with any other Mustang. Despite an unheard-of price decrease, dropping $1,075 to a new base of $14,521, the new SVO apparently wasn't all that popular. Although its official production figures were wrapped in the 84,623 hatchbacks turned out this year, other reports tend to show that only between 1,950 and 1,970 SVO models were actually built. The price decrease, incidentally, came via the deletion of such high-buck items as air conditioning and stereo AM/FM.

Those wanting brute Mustang power did not look to the SVO, but instead turned their attention to the GT hatchback. Here the standard power was the 302 V-8, now rated at 210 horsepower for GT use, despite the fact that it was only rated at 140 horses in the Thunderbird, and 165 in the LTD Euro Sedan. Among the block's major changes were a new high performance cam, roller tappets, and some carburetor modifications. Normally, it drove through the 5-speed manual gearbox. This view gives a good look at the new "grille" which consisted simply of an open air slot between the headlights, and another in the air dam between the fog/running lights. Available to all Mustangs, but not to any other Fords, the High Output V-8 was about a $1,000 addition to other models, unavailable in the SVO, and standard in the two GT styles. The hatchback shown here now had a base price of $9,885.

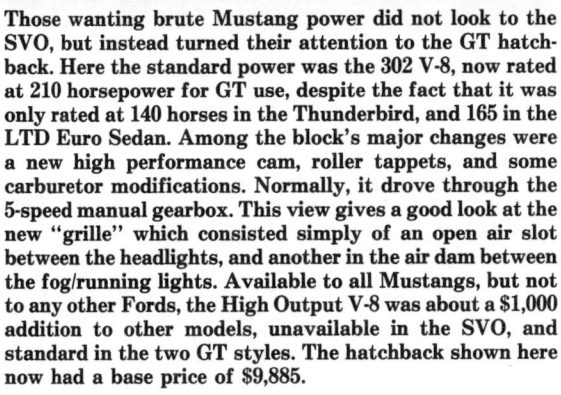

After the SVO, the most expensive Mustang was the GT convertible, Model 27/932, which retailed for a base of $13,585. As was the case with the hatchback, the convertible used the High Output 302 V-8 and 5-speed manual transmission, but could be fitted with a 4-speed overdrive automatic for another $550. Convertible production dropped substantially this year, with only 15,110 being produced in both GT and LX form. In addition to the exclusive blackout hood centers and black window surrounds and trim, GT models featured a luxury interior with articulated sport seats. Also changed was the interior rear quarter panel design, which now accommodated a revised seat belt system.

Those not wanting the price or performance of the GT convertible could opt for the Mustang LX convertible, Model 27/602. Here, with the standard V-6, the car sold for $11,958. Unlike other LX models, which used the 140 cubic inch Four as basic power, the LX convertible came only with a V-6 or the extra-cost V-8. Exterior differences between the LX and GT models was minimal, and consisted primarily of deletion of the blackout hood panel, a less costly air dam, and low back bucket seats rather than the articulated sport models of the GT.

With the dropping of the "L" models, the base Mustangs were now in the "LX" range. This series consisted of the accompanying Mustang convertible, a 3-door hatchback coupe, and this 2-door notchback. While the more expensive hatchback used the same basic body as the GT and SVO models, the notchback was an exclusive possession of the LX line. Here, in 4-cylinder form, it was the least expensive Mustang, going for a base $6,885, whereas a comparable LX hatchback cost $7,345. However, when the V-6 was stuffed under the hood, the prices of both models increased by $1,130. Fairly popular, the LX notchback drew 56,781 orders.

1985

The still-popular LTD Crown Victoria line of full-size cars was still a major factor in Ford's total sales picture, though that really didn't hold true for the 2-door sedan, Model 42. It accounted for only 13,673 sales. In base trim it cost $11,627. The car was not available in stripped "S" form. The cast aluminum turbine wheels were $390 extra. About the only major changes from the previous year were gas-filled shock absorbers, and a high beam flasher on the signal light control.

Once again, Ford's most expensive full-size car was the Crown Victoria Country Squire. It cost $11,809 and was not available in the "S" level. All Crown Victorias were powered by the 302 V-8, which was rated at 140 horsepower. This was hooked to a 4-speed automatic as the standard transmission. An optional High Output 302 was available which raised the horsepower to 155. Last year, this engine had been standard in the wagons, but now was an extra cost option in all models.

Worlds more popular than the 2-door was the 4-door LTD Crown Victoria, Model 43. Available in two forms, it saw production reach 154,612. It offered a regular model and could also be ordered in "S" form for fleet or business use, and now could also be purchased as a special police model. Most expensive, of course, was the standard version, which cost $11,627, the same as the 2-door. The "S" model was $10,609. With the new special police trim, the car sold for $10,929 with the 302 V-8, or $11,049 with the 351 V-8 which was not available to any other Ford model.

Ford pointed out that its LTD Crown Victoria models could still pull trailers up to 5,000 pounds in weight, when equipped with the special $390 trailer towing package. Or, with the rear seats folded, the full-size wagons could still offer 89.5 cubic feet of cargo area. And, of course, dual-facing rear seats were still available for $170, making the wagons full 8-passenger vehicles (It had been years since Ford credited them with 10-passenger capacity). In regular Crown Victoria form, the plain wagon sold for $11,559, while a stripper "S" version was $10,956. All Crown Victorias weighed in the neighborhood of 3,600 pounds, with the wagons being about 200 pounds more.

Appearing only this year was a true sport sedan in the European tradition, and with a European price tag. The car was the LTD "LX" Brougham Euro-Sedan, Model 39/938. Based on the standard LTD sedan body, the car was powered by a 105 horse fuel injected version of the 302 V-8 coupled to the 4-speed overdrive automatic. This meant that for sheer power, it was the most powerful Ford, being exceeded in horses only by the exclusive Mustang SVO and GT models, and the unavailable 351 police special of 180 horsepower. The car arrived at mid-year 1984, but was considered an early-release 1985 model. It featured a body-color grille, and all black or charcoal argent trim, along with the new cast aluminum wheels. The only exterior chrome was on the bumpers. Priced at $11,421, the car drew quite a bit of interest, but few sales, and reportedly only 3,260 were built.

Except for the LX Euro-Sedan, the top LTD luxury liner was the Brougham. It is featured here with a full convertible-like Brougham top that included blanked in quarters. Not included in the price, the top cost an extra $850. Inside was a luxury type interior with special door panels and high grade cloth upholstery. Since the brougham was priced only $388 above the standard LTD sedan, the difference in cost as opposed to the quality received seems like a very good purchase. In 4-cylinder form it cost $9,262, while the V-6 pumped it up to $9,680. The V-8 option was not available, but a propane version of the Four could be ordered.

In much more docile form than the LTD "LX" was the plain LTD 4-door sedan, Model 39. It also was far less expensive, hitting the register at $8,874 when blessed with the standard 140 cubic inch Four. New for the year on the LTD sedans were the taillights shown here. The lights consisted of three separate lenses divided horizontally into six rectangles, with the outer marker/signal lights wrapping around the fender edge. The central units were the backup lights. The unchanging roof line continued to feature the odd little triangular quarter window. A total of 162,884 LTD 4-door sedans were produced, including the 3,260 LX Euro-Sedans mentioned here.

Since there were no 2-door models in the LTD line, the only other available style besides the sedan was the wagon. Unlike the sedans, LTD wagons were available with V-6 engines only, with no power options. Designated Model 40, the wagon sold for $9,384, not including the $110 roof rack. It weighed 2,990 pounds, while the sedan models were about 100 pounds less. Relatively popular, it drew a total of 42,642 orders.

In the LTD line the Country Squire treatment for the wagon was simply a $280 option package, and not considered a separate model. For those who wanted the ultimate LTD wagon, a luxury interior could be ordered for $385. On the commercial side, LTD sedans were now being offered with a taxi package for $860 additional, or with a fully equipped police package for $1,430 above the base price. It is not clear whether the 302 V-8 was included in the police package, or if the standard V-6 was used.

The top of the Tempo line was filled by the GLX models, quickly identified by the bright window trim. In 2-door version, the GLX 2-door sold for $8,253. Among its standard features were power steering, power windows and locks, and a tilt steering wheel inside, and spoked cast aluminum wheels and bright trim on the exterior. Under the hood was the 100 horse High Output version of the High Swirl combustion (HSC) 4-cylinder engine, now fitted with electronic fuel injection.

Far more popular than the 2-door Tempo GLX was the 4-door version, which sold for $8,302. It had the same features as described for the 2-door GLX, but almost four times the sales appeal. Supposedly built in very limited quantities was a "Euro-styled" Tempo GTX sedan, which listed at $9,870, complete with a tubocharged Four. Tempos continued to use their exclusive body pan of 99.9-inch wheelbase and were 176.2 inches long overall. New on the interior were side window demisters that worked in conjunction with any of the heater or defroster settings; individual shut offs for the air conditioning ducts, a new flat-faced AM/FM radio and cassette player, and new heater/air conditioner controls.

Shown here with the $900 Sport Performance package is the Tempo GL 2-door sedan, Model 19. The package's main items consisted of the 100 horsepower HSC 4-cylinder engine, 5-speed manual transaxle, the 7-spoke cast aluminum wheels, and blackout trim. In regular form, the 2-door Tempo GL cost $7,160. Appearing for the last time this year was the 2-door Tempo "L" model, a less dressed version which sold for $7,052. Total Tempo 2-door sales amounted to 72,311.

Far outselling the 2-door versions were the 4-door Tempos, illustrated here with the GL model. Total 4-door sales of the front-wheel drive sedan reached 266,766. When fitted with the standard 86 horsepower Four, the GL sedan cost $7,160, but this did not include the cast aluminum wheels shown here. Also in the Tempo lot was the basic "L" 4-door sedan, Model 21, which was in its final year. It was priced at $7,052, the same as the basic 2-door. Still available in the Tempo engine room was the Mazda-built diesel, which cost about $480 above the basic Four.

Aimed at the comfort conscious buyer who wanted a sporty type of car was the EXP Luxury Coupe, Model 01/A81. Part of the total of only 26,462 EXP models produced this year, it was priced at a mid-range $7,585. Among the tell-tales on the Luxury Coupe were standard aluminum styled wheels, AM/FM cassette, seats trimmed in high grade cloth, 4-way adjustable driver's seat, tinted glass, and automatic liftgate release. The EXP continued to use the Escort's 94.2-inch wheelbase foundation and front-drive 97.6 cubic inch Four, and essentially was an Escort in disguise.

Appearing for the last time as a separate model was the EXP Turbo Coupe, Model 01/A82. The little 2-seat quasi-sports car's claim to fame was its turbocharged Four, a 120 horsepower version of the 97.6 cubic inch Four. Also on this model were aluminum wheels with low profile tires; Koni shock absorbers; TR suspension; exclusive air dam and rear spoiler, and black rocker panel moldings. A rather expensive toy, the Turbo Coupe was base priced at $9,997.

In its plainest form, the EXP hatchback coupe was the Model 01/A80. In this form, it had a base price of $6,697, which included the styled steel wheels seen here. The rear continued to be occupied with a large liftgate dominated by a single bubble-shaped tinted glass panel. Only one body style was available, and all models were of 2-passenger configuration, with fairly substantial luggage room in the rear sector. EXP production ended in mid-1985, but the car would return in mid-1986, totally restyled and looking more like a scaled down Mustang than an Escort derivative.

For the first half of 1985, the Escorts remained virtual carbon copies of the previous year. Thus, the luxury series was the "LX" line, which consisted of a 4-door sedan, Model 15, and this 4-door wagon, Model 11. The sedan was priced at $7,840, while the wagon was the highest priced regular Escort, with a base of $7,931. There were no 2-door models in the LX line, as the top of the line 2-doors had their own separate sport-oriented GT series. In this grouping were the standard GT 2-door, Model 07, and the GT Turbo Hatchback, Model 07/935. The plain GT sold for $7,585, while the Turbo model was the highest priced Escort, billing out at a basic $7,931.

Most popular of the Escorts was the mid-level GL series, illustrated here by the first edition 4-door sedan, Model 14. The vehicle shared GL space with the 2-door hatchback and the 4-door wagon. The 2-door, Model 05, was priced at $6,374, while the 4-door was $6,588. During the first series, 2-door production reached 112,406, while the 4-doors accounted for 62,709. Sometimes the 2-doors are referred to as 3-door hatchbacks, while the 4-doors are called 5-door hatchbacks.

Escort's most popular wagon was in the GL series, where it sold for $6,765. For those who wanted to travel in style, the Squire Package continued as a $375 option. A major change on this year's Escorts was the relocation of reverse gear on both the 5-speed and the 4-speed transaxles. The reverse now was located at the lower far right of the shift pattern, rather than in the upper left corner. This was the same move that had taken place on the Thunderbird Turbo and Mustang SVO in 1984, and Ford claimed it was done to decrease the chances of a driver accidentally slipping into reverse when shifting into low. For those who wanted basic station wagon convenience, Escort maintained its "L" model, which was priced at $6,305. Total first series wagon production reached 45,740.

The lower end of the first series of Escort production consisted of four models, a 2-door in the "L" and "basic" categories, a 4-door "basic" and this 4-door "L" model. In "L" configuration, the 4-door was the Model 13, which sold for $6,091, while the basic 4-door Model 13/41P was priced at $5,827. In the 2-door realm, the "L" was the Model 04, priced at $5,876, while the basic Model 04/41P was the lowest priced Escort at $5,620. Escort still offered a diesel engine option, but this was available only in GL and L models. Not too popular, it cost $560 more than the standard engine. A $45 set of vinyl-insert body side molding certainly improves the looks of this rather basic car.

Showing off its new face with aerodynamically correct slanted headlight covers, and single bar grille is the new second series, or mid-1985 Escort. This is the GL 4-door sedan, Model 37, which was now Escort's luxury model, since the LX series did not appear in the new line up. It was priced at $6,855. Its companion was the 2-door hatchback, priced at $6,642. Along with the new styling came a new 113 cubic inch Four (1.9 liter) which developed 86 horsepower as opposed to the former 70 horses of the old basic block. During the last part of the 1985 model year, a total of 48,676 4-door Escorts were turned loose.

As before, the "L" series was one trim level below the GL. However, it now represented the middle ground of the second series Escort line. Showing off the new rear design, with the large triple bar taillights, is this "L" model 2-door hatchback. Priced at $6,127, the Model 31 was part of the 100,554 total second series 2-doors turned out in the last half of 1985. Its lower scale companion was the basic 2-door (3-door) hatchback, which at $5,856 was not only the lowest price Escort, but also the only one to come in at under $6,000.

Highest priced of all of the new Escorts, and the only one to have a basic tag above the $7,000 mark was the second series GL station Wagon, Model 35. It had a price of $7,137. Although the initial run of second series Escorts had only GL, L and basic models, at the very end of the season a new GT 2-door hatchback was introduced to accept a brand new fuel injected version of the 1.6 liter Four. This block could turn out 108 horses at 5200 rpm.

The second series Escort line did not have a basic station wagon, so the "L" series wagon was the buyer's only economy choice. Priced at $6,622, it was one of 36,998 second series wagons sold during the remainder of 1985. Lack of side trim and plain steel wheels mark this as the basic model. The new styling and engine did little to change the weight of the Escort line, and overall, the cars weighed in the vicinity of 2,100 pounds. Although the taillight design changed substantially on the car models, the rear of the new generation of wagons was just about the same as the previous models. Escort wagons continued to use a single large liftgate.

After a relatively uneventful but pleasing 1985, Ford grabbed all of the headlines this year by bringing out a brand new car. Not making the model year introductions, but hinted at throughout the fall, the new baby was the Taurus, which was introduced in December.

A front-drive, mid-size vehicle, available in either 4-door sedan or 4-door wagon styling, the new Taurus had nothing at all in common with anything else in the Ford showrooms. The finale of a $3-billion engineering and design project, the cars were divided into three trim levels of L, GL, and LX. These were then joined at mid-season by an MT5 performance sedan for the sport set.

Styling was totally aerodynamic and totally different. From its grille-less front and curving integral-appearing bumpers, through its continuing bumper side wraps, along its rounded body sides, and ending with the strange vertical taillamps on the wagon, the car fit no pattern ever before set by Ford. Actually, had it not been for the belly-button type of Ford emblem stuck in a hole at the front of the car, one certainly would have wondered who was producing the Taurus.

As could be expected with so radical a car, construction was on its own exclusive body pan, with a 106-inch wheelbase. The sedan was 188.4 inches long overall, and the wagon was 191.9 inches. Not only was the car totally new, but it was blessed with two equally new and totally exclusive engines. They were a 153 cubic inch (2.5 liter) Four and a 183 cubic inch (3 liter) V-6. The new Four had an almost square bore and stroke of 3.7X3.6 inches, used a 9.0:1 compression ratio, and developed 88 horsepower at 4600 rpm. This engine was used in the L and GL sedans only. The V-6, which was used in all wagons and in the LX sedans, and was optional in all other Taurus models, had a bore and stroke of 3.5X3.1 inches, used a 9.25:1 compression ratio and developed 140 horses at 4800 rpm. Both engines were fuel injected. Transmissions included a 5-speed manual, and 3 and 4-speed automatic transaxles.

Response to the new Taurus was excellent, with 236,362 being released during its first short year. As

A body-color grille and special integral front air dam with fog lights identifies this as the Thunderbird Turbo Coupe. With the high priced Fila now gone, the Turbo moved up to be the most expensive T-Bird, base priced at $14,143. This tag included the turbocharged 140 cubic inch Four of 155 horsepower with the 5-speed manual transmission. For an extra $315 the Turbo Coupe could be ordered with a 4-speed automatic, but then the horsepower was downrated to 145. Inside, front seat passengers were treated to high-back articulated sport seats, which could be adjusted in six directions. Although Turbo Coupes were almost always shown with the cast aluminum wheels shown here, it appears that these were a $390 option.

Ford had expected, and planned, most of these sales were at the expense of the LTD. But, with the new front-drive mid-size, the rear-drive LTD was scheduled to go away anyway. And that is exactly what happened. With virtually no changes whatsoever, the LTD entered its final year with only three models to choose from. They were the standard and Brougham sedans, and the station wagon. The pricey and sporty LX Brougham Euro-Sedan was dropped completely, as was any thought of a V-8 option. The only engine this year was the V-6 of 232 cubic inches, as used in the basic Thunderbird. Some references show the Tempo's 140 cubic inch Four being available as an option, but if this was so, it wasn't a very popular choice. With production ending shortly after the new Taurus appeared, it is no wonder that the LTD registered only 72,483 sales. With its demise, Ford lost its last mid-sized rear-drive car, unless one considers the Thunderbird as a mid-size car in the overall rankings.

Regarding the Thunderbird, one model less appeared this year, as the Fila was kicked from the nest. Now the two trim options were the base and the elan coupes, plus the Turbo Coupe with its own exclusive 4-cylinder engine. Still, despite the loss of one model, Thunderbird's sales soared up to 163,965, a nice rise of 12,114. The base T-Bird engine was the same V-6 as used in the LTD, but probably the most popular option was the Crown Victoria's 302 cubic inch V-8.

This year, the V-8's horsepower rating was up to 150 at 3200 rpm, due primarily to the addition of multi-port fuel injection and a new combustion chamber design. However, the High Output version of the 302 was no longer available, and only this lone model was used in all Crown Victoria and V-8 Thunderbird applications, except the police specials, where the 351 block was still available.

In the big car world, the Crown Victoria line was greatly expanded with a whole new LX series of super-trimmed cars. The line now had its two low-buck "S" models, two station wagon variations, two base sedans, and now had four more models bearing the LX designation. Primarily, the LX package involved standardization of the former optional luxury interior, which included individual adjustable front seats, power windows, and a multitude of minor luxury items. Still, all of this activity did not help Crown Victoria sales, and production slipped to 124,037, down a horrendous 75,073 vehicles. Of course what made the slip look so bad was the excellent 1985 sales, where production increased over 30%, only to topple even more when the slip did occur.

In the little car world, the mid-1985 Escort became the official 1986 Escort, with its new 113 cubic inch engine (1.9 liter). As mentioned in the previous chapter, the new block produced a marked improvement in the Escort's performance, a factor which many people felt was too long in coming. With a bore and stroke of 3.23X3.46 inches and a 9.0:1 compression ratio, the new engine came up with 86 horsepower at 4800 rpm, as opposed to the old 70 horses from the former mill. It used a Holley 2-barrel carburetor.

As could probably be expected, the new basic engine was soon joined by a High Output version. This unit used multi-port fuel injection, and gave out 108 horses at 5200 rpm. The new mill became standard in the Escort GT and the EXP Sport Coupe, and was an option in other Escorts and the EXP Luxury Coupe. Also available in the Escort (and Tempo also) was the 121 cubic inch diesel, but since so few cars were built with this engine it is hardly worth the mention.

Speaking of the strange little 2-passenger EXP pseudo-sports car, the vehicle was held back in introduction as designers attempted to give a more sexy look to the never-popular car. The Turbo Coupe was now dropped, and only a new Sport Coupe and a redressed Luxury Coupe bore the EXP banner. Both had a new aerodynamic front, and a new bubble-styled hatchback. Apparently some people thought the new lines were pleasing, and production actually crept up to 30,978. This, plus a nice rise in Escort production to 430,053 certainly must have ended any home office arguments against the wisdom of stressing the small car market.

Along that line the Tempo, Ford's bigger little car, received a new design treatment on the front and rear. Its front now consisted of a very simple grille of dual horizontal slots in a body-color panel. This panel was flanked by new halogen headlamps of sloping aerodynamic design integrated with the sloping wraparound parking and side marker lights. The basic engine remained the 140 cubic inch Four, with a High Output version available. The base engine was rated at 86 horses, while the HO model produced an even 100. Also available on request was the same little diesel that was

equally as unpopular here as it was in the Escort line.

Possibly because there was so little difference between the series, the L models were dropped, leaving the Tempo line with just the GL and GLX trim levels. The 2-door and the 4-door appeared in each of these series, resulting in four Tempo models to choose from.

Although the new Taurus was projected as a replacement for the LTD, it appears that it also bit a chunk off of the Tempo's sales potential. Production slipped by a hefty 61,416, with the end result that only 277,617 Tempos were turned out this year. The figure in itself was not bad, but certainly a far cry from the 1984 and 1985 figures.

And then there was Mustang. Since the car came up with a new face in 1985, it could be expected that few changes would be made this year. And that is exactly what did happen. There were some under-hood changes however. The super expensive super-horse, the SVO (Special Vehicle Operations) now had a more potent version of the 140 cubic inch block, this one producing 200 horsepower at 5000 rpm. Included in the package was a new intercooled turbocharger, multi-port electronic fuel injection, and a quick action Hurst shifter hooked to a 5-speed transmission. Also, the two GT models now had a new High Output 302 V-8 that turned its own 200 horses at 4000 rpm. Apparently all of this pleased many people, and Mustang production soared to 224,410, an increase of 67,896.

Although some lists tend to show that Ford was down in sales and production this year, a tabulation of production records indicates that a grand total of 1,528,981 cars left the plants. This would actually put Ford's total vehicles 43,348 ahead of the previous year, with much of the help being supplied by Taurus, Mustang, and Escort, in that order.

As before, plain and elan (no capitalization) Thunderbirds used a bright grille and light argent headlight surrounds. Mid-way in trim level, the elan came with the V-6 as standard power, unless the optional 302 V-8 was ordered for an extra $785. Power windows, interval wipers, dual electric exterior rearview mirrors, and a few minor extras were all part of the elan package. In base trim, the car cost $12,554 with the V-6 or $13,339 with the V-8. Production of all Thunderbirds was up nicely this year, going to a total of 163,965, and this despite the loss of the Fila model.

From the exterior it was almost impossible to tell the plain Thunderbird coupe, Model 46, from the more upscale elan. In standard form, the car cost $11,020 with the V-6 or $11,805 with the V-8. The V-6 models included a 3-speed Select-Shift automatic, while the V-8 cars included a 4-speed automatic with overdrive. Roller tappets and electronic multi-port fuel injection helped boost the V-8 performance to 150 horsepower. Only one 302 V-8 was available this year, as the HO (High Output) model was discontinued.

Appearing for the last time was the Mustang SVO Turbo Four. The SVO, which stood for Special Vehicle Operations, was Mustang's most expensive model, selling for $15,272. The car could be quickly identified by its exclusive frontal design and scooped hood. Underneath this hood was a computer controlled turbocharged Four of 140 cubic inches, which produced 200 horses. The engine used electronic multiport fuel injection. A Hurst quick-throw 5-speed gearbox was standard, as were 4-wheel disc brakes. Although described by Ford as being "the ultimate Mustang," the SVO was probably just too high on the price ladder for most enthusiasts, and reportedly only 3,382 were built before the program was terminated.

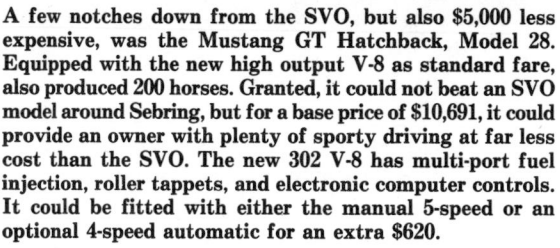

A few notches down from the SVO, but also $5,000 less expensive, was the Mustang GT Hatchback, Model 28. Equipped with the new high output V-8 as standard fare, also produced 200 horses. Granted, it could not beat an SVO model around Sebring, but for a base price of $10,691, it could provide an owner with plenty of sporty driving at far less cost than the SVO. The new 302 V-8 has multi-port fuel injection, roller tappets, and electronic computer controls. It could be fitted with either the manual 5-speed or an optional 4-speed automatic for an extra $620.

Companion to the GT Hatchback was the GT Convertible, Model 27. Mustang's second most expensive car, this one went out the door at a base price of $14,523. It featured all of the performance items of the GT Hatchback, which included exclusive rear spoilers with the now mandatory high visibility brake light built into the center brace. All GT models used articulated six-way front seats; special suspension, and quick-ratio power steering. Since the convertible was still essentially a modification of the 2-door notchback coupe, there were no separate production figures.

Mustang's base models continued to be termed LX models, a designation usually reserved for the top luxury versions of other lines. The cars were available with either the 140 cubic inch Four or 232 V-6 in standard form, or for an additional $1,120 could be ordered with the newly uprated 302 V-8. Lowest priced of all Mustangs continued to be the LX notchback coupe, which now listed at $7,189 with the Four or $8,153 with the V-6. This car, which also provided the base for all Mustang convertibles, had a very nice run of 106,720 this year. It was available only as an LX, and was not produced in either GT or SVO form. However, it could be ordered in convertible form, as a V-6 only, for $12,821.

In overall production, the 2-door hatchback coupe was the most popular, with 117,690 being turned out in LX, GT and SVO forms. By far the most popular guise was in the LX tradition, where the car had a base 4-cylinder price of $7,744, or $8,708 with the V-6. All LX Mustangs weighed about 2,800 pounds with the V-6, with V-8 models being about 200 pounds heavier, and 4-cylinder types about 100 pounds lighter. Showing in this photo is the new mandatory high-mounted brake light. Mustang mounted this new light in the center of its rear deck spoiler on the hatchback and convertible models. On the notchback, which did not use a rear spoiler, the lamp was centered on the package tray, shining out through the rear window (backlite).

The top of the line Fords again were the full-size LTD Crown Victoria models. But this year, a covey of even more lavish Crown Victorias were put on the road in the form of the LX models. Essentially the new series was the former luxury interior package, now standardized into a new sub-series of luxuriously outfitted models. All four Crown Victoria styles could be ordered in LX trim. The 4-door shown here cost $13,784 as an LX while its 2-door companion was priced at $13,752. In the wagon field, the plain model cost $13,567 as an LX, while the Country Squire LX was based at $13,817. All LX models had individual reclining front seats, with upholstery in a choice of luxury velour, vinyl, or extra-cost leather. Power windows and locks were part of the package, as were a multitude of less interior trim items. However, the operable front vent panes on this example were still an $80 option, while the wire-spoke wheel covers were $205 extra.

Except for interior trim and a small rear quarter emblem, there was no difference between the regular Crown Victorias and the LX models. As before, both 2-door and 4-door sedans were offered, with the Model 42 2-door shown here being by far the least popular. Its production reached only 6,559. It was base priced at $13,022, which included the fuel-injected 302 V-8 and 4-speed automatic. Its companion 4-door sedan, Model 43, saw a substantial drop in popularity, with only 97,314 units being spread over plain, LX, and "S" models. In plain form it sold for $12,562, while in the fleet-oriented "S" version it was the lowest price Ford sedan at $12,188.

Ford's plain Crown Victoria wagon appeared in all three forms…plain, LX, and "S" models, and also provided the foundation for the Country Squire models. In plain form, the car cost $12,405, while in the stripper "S" category it sold for $12,031, and thus was the lowest price large Ford available to the public. It's low price was beaten only by the Crown Victoria "S" Police Special, available only to municipalities and bona fide security organizations for $11,813 for the normal 302 V-8 or $120 more for the 351 cubic inch V-8 which also supposedly could not be ordered by the general public.

Appearing for the last time this year was the rear-drive LTD, whose sales slot and popularity had been taken over by the new Taurus line. Most popular of the two available styles was the 4-door sedan, Model 39, which drew 58,270 orders. These were divided between the plain sedan shown here and the more upscale Brougham version, but the expensive and performance oriented LX Euro-Sedan was not brought back for a second round. When ordered with the 140 cubic inch Four it was the lowest price LTD at $9,538. However, virtually all LTD models this year came with the V-6, which pushed the standard sedan's price to $10,032 and the brougham's to $10,420. The cars weighed about 2,900 pounds with the V-6 engine, or 100 pounds less with the seldom seen Four.

Far removed from the Police Specials in both cost and elegance was Ford's prestige wagon, the LTD Country Squire, Model 44. Most expensive of the large Fords, it sold for $12,655 in standard form, or $13,817 as an LX model. All Crown Victorias this year availed themselves of the new fuel injected 302 V-8 of 150 horsepower, and used the 4-speed automatic transmission. There were no engine or transmission options. Popular on the wagon models was the trailer towing package for $390 and the $170 set of dual facing rear seats. A total of 20,164 LTD Crown Victoria wagons of all types were turned loose this year.

Looking nice but selling poorly was the second LTD style, the 4-door station wagon, Model 40. It drew only 14,213 orders before production was terminated. Available only with the V-6, the wagon sold for $10,132. A wood-trim Squire package was available for $280, while a luxury interior could be ordered for another $390. LTD wagons continued to use a one-piece liftgate, hinged at the top. Neither the liftgate window nor the rear quarter windows could be opened. Likewise, the vent pane windows in the rear doors were also fixed in place.

Voted "Car of the Year" by *Motor Trend*, the new front wheel drive Taurus grabbed headlines and attention wherever it went. The end result of an engineering and design program reported to cost over $3-billion, the car was available in two styles spread over four sub-series. Most luxurious of the lot was the LX 4-door sedan, which was available only in V-6 form. Priced at $13,351, it actually exceeded covers were new this year, as was an optional driver's airbag, which cost a substantial $815. Gone from the line were the bright window surrounds, replaced by the European-type black surrounds. The 140 cubic inch Four was still the base engine, with both the 100 horsepower High Output version and the $510 4-cylinder diesel being available. The manual 5-speed transaxle was standard, but an automatic was available for another $450.

Also available only with the V-6 engine was the mid-level of the new Taurus. Designated the GL series, these cars came with a 4-speed automatic transmission, as did the LX models, but used front bucket seats and a lower trim level. A thinner band of body side molding identified the GL models. The sedan, shown here, wore an $11,322 price tag, while the wagon cost $11,790. Although all production figures were lumped together, with no sub-series breakout, it is fairly certain that the GL models were probably the most popular of the new line. The sedan far outsold the wagons, with 178,737 sedans being built as compared with 57,625 wagons.

Arriving a few months after the main Taurus line was the MT5 sub-series. With this grouping came Ford's introduction of a new 88 horsepower 4-cylinder engine of 153 cubic inches, featuring electronic multi-port fuel injection. Hooked to the 5-speed manual transaxle, the new four provided Taurus buyers with what Ford described as a "World Class Touring Car." The MT5 was available as a sedan, Model 29/934, which sold for $10,276, or as this station wagon, Model 30/934, which was priced at $10,741. The V-6 was not available in the MT5 series. Lowest rung on the ladder was occupied by the "L" series, which consisted of the station wagon, available only with the V-6 for $10,763, and the sedan, which was priced at $10,256 with the V-6, or with the new Four was the only Taurus under $10,000, having a base of $9,645.

The second style in the new Taurus line was the 4-door station wagon, which was also available in all four trim sub-series. Again, the most expensive and luxurious was the LX version, which cost a hefty $13,860 and thus qualified as the most expensive Ford outside of the Thunderbird or Mustang family. As did the Crown Victoria wagons, the Taurus models also offered an optional third seat, but this was a rear-facing unit instead of the dual facing seats of the big wagons. One item it did not offer, however, was a Country Squire package. The Taurus LX wagon was available only in 6-cylinder form. All LX models had power seats and door locks, air conditioning, and heavy black body side molding with a bright insert.

Sporting a new grille, consisting simply of two horizontal slots, was the Tempo series. Another change involved nomenclature, with the former GLX sub-series now being called the LX, while the GL division remained as the home of lower priced cars. The LX 2-door sedan, Model 20, shown here was one of 69,101 total Tempo 2-door models produced. No distinction was made between the LX and GL trim levels on the production tallies. As an LX, the car cost $8,578 and weighed 2,465 pounds. In addition to the new front, Tempo models also received a new tail revision, a new 4-spoke steering wheel, and other minor interior changes. Despite their relatively small size, Tempos were listed as 5-passenger cars.

The Tempo LX 4-door sedan, Model 23, was the most popular of the lot, with production of all 4-door Tempos reaching 208,570. It cost $8,777 and weighed 2,526 pounds. Halogen headlights with sloping covers were new this year, as was an optional driver's airbag, which cost a substantial $815. Gone from the line were the bright window surrounds, replaced by the European-type black surrounds. The 140 cubic inch Four was still the base engine, with both the 100 horsepower High Output version and the $510 4-cylinder diesel being available. The manual 5-speed transaxle was standard, but an automatic was available for another $450.

The Tempo GL sub-series differed very little on the exterior from the LX models, especially when one of the two trim packages were added. The packages were the Select, which cost $425 extra, or the Sport Package, shown here, which listed at $934. This was above the $7,358 base price for the Model 19 2-door. Included in the Sports Package was the High Output Four of 100 horses, a performance 5-speed manual transaxle, and special handling and suspension components. The styled wheels shown here added another $175 to the tag.

Plain hubcaps with "Ford" in the blue ovals marked this car as having the standard wheels rather than the more popular but extra cost styled wheels. Also wearing the $934 Sport Package was this GL 4-door sedan, Model 22. In base form, it cost $7,508. More popular than the Sports Package was the Select grouping, This $425 package added power steering; tinted glass all around; AM/FM stereo radio, and dual remote-controlled electric side mirrors. Fully reclining front bucket seats in cloth upholstery, power brakes, and interval wipers were all standard on GL cars.

As did the Tempo, the new late-arriving EXP also sported a new front end. But while the Tempo had twin horizontal slots in place of a grille, the EXP had only a single grille slot, but a large mouth in the below-bumper air dam. The car came in two forms, the Luxury Coupe, or the Model 01 Sport Coupe shown here. As a sport model, it cost $7,186. Under the hood was a new front-drive 1.9 liter Four, with multi-port fuel injection, rated at 108 horsepower. This was the same engine that was standard in the Escort GT models, and optional in other Escorts. Also in the Sport model were high-back "performance" bucket seats; a special handling package; built-in fog lights in the air dam; dual electric remote control mirrors, and a central console.

Ford's quaint little 2-seat EXP also had its Luxury Coupe version, the Model 01/931 shown here. Priced at $8,235, it was part of the total run of 30,978 EXP models turned out this year. Among the new styling features was a revised bubble glass for the hatchback, a built-in rear spoiler, and new style wheel covers. Luxury coupes used a carbureted version of the 1.9 liter Four, rather than the fuel injected version. Inside were low-back bucket seats in all vinyl (or optional cloth and vinyl); overhead console; tachometer; AM/FM stereo, and remote electric side mirrors. Initial reports showed the EXP as being discontinued in 1986, but the car finally returned as a mid-year offering, once again based on the Escort platform.

Essentially a 4-passenger version of the EXP was the Escort GT, Model 33. The car used the same new multi-port fuel injected 1.9 liter Four as the EXP, and essentially had the same suspension and control package. Most expensive of all Escort models, it was base priced at $8,112. This included the 8-spoke cast aluminum wheels shown here; front and rear stabilizer bars; rear spoiler; front air dam with built-in fog lamps; special front grille plate with twin airslots offset to the left; performance high-back bucket front seats, and other sport modifications.

New for the year was the Escort LX series, which contained the highest trim units of the Escort line. The series consisted of three models, the lowest priced of which was this 2-door hatchback, Model 32. It was priced at $7,284 and weighed 2,160 pounds. Since the Escort line had been heavily revised for the mid-year 1985 models, there was little change this year, except for the nomenclature switching. Again the Escort 2-door models were the most popular of the lot, with a total of 228,013 being produced in all four trim and performance levels.

The Escort 4-door came only in the high-trim LX sub-series or the more pragmatic L sub-series. As an LX, Model 37, shown here, it cost $7,448. LX models had their own unique blackout grilles, consisting of horizontal air slots divided by a single heavy center bar with the Ford oval at mid-point. LX models were identified by the wide body side molding; styled steel wheels, and remote releases on the liftgate and fuel filler door. Total 4-door production, divided between the LX and L models, was 117,300. This model was sometimes referred to as a 5-door sedan, in reference to the liftback being a fifth door.

As did the 4-door sedan, the wagon came only in LX and L trim. The heavy body side molding identifies this version as the LX Model 35, which cost $7,729. As the L Model 34 it would have cost $6,822. Least popular of the three Escort styles, the wagons drew a total of 84,740 sales. All Escort models used the 86 horsepower version of the 1.9 liter engine, but the HO unit was available as an option, as was the unpopular 121 cubic inch 4-cylinder diesel. Escort wagons followed the sedan's styling of having small non-functional vent windows in the rear doors, in addition to having a large rear quarter window.

At the low end of the Escort line were the three L models and a lone Pony 2-door. The Pony was the lowest priced Escort, going for $6,052, while the slightly upgraded L 2-door, Model 31, listed at $6,327. Lowest priced of the two 4-door sedan models was the L Model 36, which cost $6,541, while the L wagon rounded out that sub-series. L models were devoid of side trim, having instead an indented strip running lengthwise between the wheel wells. This indent provided a base for the side trim of the upper level cars. However, this side molding could also be applied to L models for an additional $45.

Not a year of changes, 1987 was more a year of numbers. There were big numbers, confusing numbers, conflicting numbers, good numbers, and bad numbers. According to many reports, this was the year that Ford once again surpassed Chevrolet in domestic production. It was also the year that Ford passed General Motors in net earnings. It was also the year that Ford's profits jumped 41% to hit $4.6-billion. And also, some reports show Escort remaining as the best selling American car and the year-old Taurus coming in as the second best selling American car, while other reports show just the opposite, with Taurus as Numero Uno and Escort in second place.

On the negative side, a tabulation of the model year production shows some mighty slides in the camps of Escort, Mustang, and the newly redesigned Thunderbird. These were offset by a huge increase in Taurus production, and minor increases by Tempo and the LTD Crown Victoria. The end result was a tabulated production total of 1,448,318, which was 80,6763 away from the 1986 figures, and about 26,000 away from the 1,474,116 model year production that Ford claimed.

In the Escort ranks, some sanity finally arrived, with the list of available models being cut from eight (there were 10 in 1985) to five. The L and LX series were both dropped. Remaining were the one stripper Pony model, one sporty GT, and three GL models. Also supposedly entering the official Escort family was its near kin, the EXP. However, the 2-model EXP line of 2-place sport-type cars was still ranked as a separate entity, and though some information would include it with its parent Escort, its production figures and overall identity were still kept separate. As ever, however, all EXP running rear and body pan were 100% Escort, with only the body sheet metal being different.

On the production scene, Escort tallied up 374,765 for the model year, which was only TWO cars more than the 374,763 production of Taurus. However, when the 25,888 EXPs were added into the Escort numbers, as some claim is only right, then Escort was the definite leader, with production of 400,653.

The relatively new Taurus, on the market only since December of the previous season, received virtually no change, nor did it need any to help its sales. Public acceptance of the very attractive and very logical front wheel drive car was as near to a peak as could be expected. Consumer reports and customer satisfaction were at a very high level, and certainly plaudits were in order for everyone in the Taurus development program. As before, the L and MT5 series and the GL sedan had the 2.5 liter Four as the base power, while the LX and GL wagon had the 3 liter V-6 as standard power. The V-6 was also an option in all but the supposedly sporty MT5, which was the only model to have a standard 5-speed gearbox.

In between the Escort and Taurus lived the big-little Tempo, which up to now had been available in front wheel drive only. This year an odd sort of bird appeared, in the form of an All Wheel-Drive Tempo model. The car used its normal front wheel drive for all practical road applications, but with the flip of a switch on the dashboard, could engage a live rear axle for those needed 4-wheel drive applications such as mud, heavy snow, slippery roads, or just plain rough going.

The All-Wheel-Drive vehicles were considered a series of their own, and were available in both two and 4-door versions. With a trim level about equal to the LX series, and using the High Output 2.3 liter (140 cubic inches) Four as standard power, the new AWD series was priced about $1,100 above the regular LX models. Also new to the Tempo line was the Sport GL series of two models, which used a variation of the GL trim level, but was equipped with the HO 2.3 liter engine as standard. All other Tempos used the regular 140 cubic inch Four of 86 horsepower. Both engines used a new throttle-body fuel injection set-up.

The only real styling changes of the year occurred on the sporty type cars, the Mustang and the Thunderbird. On the Mustang, a new face included aerodynamic headlamps and corner lights, plus a virtual grille-less front, with only horizontal air slots below the bumper. On the backs, a new taillight treatment was very evident, while new molding of heavier and wider vinyl-type material graced the sides. Under the hoods, cars with the base 2.3 liter Four now had multi-point fuel injection rather than a carburetor, which raised the horsepower slightly from 88 to 90. Also gaining horsepower was the 302 cubic inch V-8, which jumped from 200 to 225 this year. The V-6 was dropped as an engine option while the Turbo four was dropped both as an engine and as its part of the SVO (Special Vehicle Operations) series. Now there were just two breeds of horses to choose from . . . the LX series, with its basic Four or optional V-8, or the GT series, with its standard V-8. Only the two base engines were available this year, with no high output versions being offered. For some reason, model year production decreased significantly, dropping to 159,145, which was a reduction of 67,896 or 61,018, depending on which set of figures are used.

As did the Mustang, the Thunderbirds also were treated to a substantial revision. And, as was the case with Mustang, Thunderbird production also fell substantially, dropping to 128,878, for a loss of 35,087 vehicles. The drop was a blow to the Bird, which went through a rather total redesign, with all new skin being applied, and a new face and tail being devised. Overall, the car didn't look that much different from the previous model, but the intent had been to keep a continuity of appearance. But in actuality, it was a new Bird that greeted the public. Yet, the public was not impressed, even despite the fact that there were now four Birds in the nest. This year the elan was called the LX, while a new Sport Coupe was brought into the family. The base hardtop coupe and specialized Turbo Coupe remained

as before. In the engine department, the Turbo Coupe now took over the 140 cubic inch fuel injected, intercooled mill that had formerly been the exclusive property of the Mustang SVO. But with that car gone, the perfectly good and high performance Four was certainly not going to go to waste, and hence the Thunderbird Turbo now had its 190 horsepower all to itself. In all other Birds, the 232 cubic inch V-6 was standard, with the 302 V-8 being optional.

Ford's remaining big car, the LTD Crown Victoria remained virtually unchanged, but the $765 air conditioning unit was now standard in everything, with a subsequent increase in price of approximately $1,000 on each model. Once more, there were four LX models, four standard models, and two low-buck "S" models, if the "S" models' base price of almost $14,000 can be considered low-buck. Still, sales of the very attractive car were up by almost 5,000 to reach 1128,878. Incidentally, the old 351 cubic inch block was no longer available for police car use or any other passenger car application. Now Ford's 302 cubic inch V-8 (5 liter) was the largest passenger car engine being produced by Ford, and was used in every big block application, including the Lincoln Town Car.

Again, production figures vary widely, and one wonders if they are worth tabulating at all. A tally of the models produced by separate lines shows production reached 1,448,318 for the model year. Still, total production reports claim a model year tally of 1,585,881, which is a difference of 37,563 units. Using the individual model production figures would show that Ford was down 35,663 from its 1986 production, while Ford claims its total builds were over 101,000 above the 1986 figure. A remote explanation is that Ford this year might have included in car production such commercial-line vehicles as the Aerostar and Bronco. But this is simply speculation, and as to the difference in figures . . . no comment.

Finally, the automotive world suffered a loss with the death by pneumonia of Henry Ford II on Sept. 29. Mr. Ford, known for his flamboyant and often headstrong actions, had successfully guided the giant corporation from near financial ruin following World war II to the financially solid giant complex of today. Well respected, his funeral was one of the largest ever held in the city of Detroit.

A pair of plain Thunderbird Hardtop Coupes show off the new styling featured by the Birds this year. Though totally revised, the new skin and trim was so similar to the 1986 offering that to many, the changes went unnoticed. Among the 1987 features were a totally new grille of much smaller and lower configuration, aerodynamic single halogen headlamps, and a new bumper with twin air slots. Called the Model 60, the plain Thunderbird had a base V-6 price of $12,972 and a V-8 price of $13,611. A disappointing total of only 128,135 Birds left the nest this year.

A name switch took away the old uncapitalized name of elan, and replaced it with an LX designation. Otherwise, the Model 62 continued to be the most luxurious of all Thunderbirds. It continued the use of bright window surrounds; 6-way highback bucket seats; high quality AM/FM stereo, and other luxury items, including the "Swiss cheese" design cast aluminum wheels that differed from the spoke-type cast aluminum wheels of the Turbo Coupe. The car was available in V-6 form for $15,383, or as a V-8 for $16,022.

New for the year was the Thunderbird Sport Coupe, Model 61, which came in V-8 form only. Rated at 150 horsepower, the 302 V-8 was the largest engine in this year's Ford line, and offered no performance options. The Sport Coupe used the frontal styling of other Birds, but had the Turbo Coupe's suspension. The surrounds of the flush-fitting windows were in non-glare black, as was the heavy vinyl that completely surrounded the car. Except for the Turbo Coupe, all Birds including the Sport Coupe came with a 4-speed automatic transmission as standard equipment. In base form, the Sport Coupe listed at $15,079 and weighed 3,346 pounds.

As did the Thunderbird, the Mustang also went through a total revision. It came up with a new aerodynamic face similar to the Thunderbird's, even to the point of having its fog lamps integrated into the same slanted panels that covered the headlights. With the SVO discontinued, the hot horse now was the Mustang GT Hatchback, Model 42. It featured an exclusive grille-less front and below-bumper air dam with a large central air slot and integrated road lights. At the rear, the GT had exclusive trim, consisting of a louvered applique across the taillight lenses. Available only with the 302 (5-liter) V-8, the car cost $11,835 and weighed 3,080 pounds.

Most expensive of all Mustangs was the GT Convertible, Model 45, which listed at $15,724. Like its hatchback kin, it was available only in V-8 form. The engine was now rated at 225 horsepower. Drive was through a 5-speed manual transmission or a 4-speed automatic, both of which used an overdrive top gear. In addition to the V-8 and exclusive front and rear, GT models wore standard cast aluminum wheels, high-back multi-position bucket seats, and had a performance-tuned suspension system. Leather articulated sport seats could be ordered for another $415.

Not available as a GT model, but only in the LX division was the Notchback Coupe, Model 40. Mustang production figures vary on the car, with some lists showing a total of 44,376 being built, while other lists show a total of 58,100. The car was base priced at $8,043 with the fuel-injected Four or $9,928 with the V-8. With the larger engine it weighed an even 3,000 pounds. Notchback Coupes continued to provide the base for the Mustang convertible models. Being rear-drive, Mustangs could still avail themselves of the largest of Ford's passenger car engines.

A front panel with two horizontal grille or air slots identifies this as the Mustang LX Hatchback, Model 41, and not the GT version. The "5.0" medallion on the front fender panel says that this model has the more popular V-8, and thus went out the door with a base tag of $10,359. With the Four it would have been $8,474. Conflicting production figures show the total of all hatchbacks to be either 94,441 or 80,717, and this book will make no attempt at stating which is the correct amount. Although the V-8 cost an additional $1,885 over the fuel-injected Four, that did not include the automatic transmission, which pushed the price up another $515. The V-6 engine was no longer available, nor was the SVO Four.

The most expensive 4-cylinder Mustang was the LX Convertible, Model 44, which was based priced at $12,840. Unlike the closed cars, production of convertible models seems to be fairly well ascertained at 20,328, with the amount divided between LX and GT versions. Although Ford tried to downplay its increasing association with the Mazda company, the new Mustang dashboard was quite similar to that found in the Japanese sport models. However, Mustang referred to the interiors as European styled, possibly to counteract the comparisons made to Mazda by several automotive writers of the day.

Ford's luxury liners continued to be the Crown Victoria LX models. The full-size rear-drive cars were available as the 2-door Model 71, or as shown here, the 4-door Model 74. The 2-door, which was appearing for the last time this year, was priced at $15,421. The 4-door was only slightly more expensive, going for $15,454. This year, air conditioning was considered a standard item, which may help to explain the large price increase in these models as opposed to the 1986 stock. Despite the fact that LX models were seldom seen with steel tops, the "Brougham" vinyl half-roof was still a $665 accessory. Likewise, the beautiful cast aluminum turbine wheels added another $390.

The LTD Crown Victoria line included two station wagons, the Model 77 with plain sides, and the Model 79 Country Squire shown here. The Squire listed at $15,723, and thus was again the most expensive large Ford. With plain sides, the wagon cost $15,450. All Crown Victoria models used the 302 (5 liter) V-8 and 4-speed overdrive automatic as standard equipment, with no power or transmission options being available. Crown Victorias were also the only Fords remaining that used a separate body and frame. All other Ford lines now used unibody construction with frame horns attached to the body or floor pan.

As was the case in the Crown LX sub-series, the plain LTD Crown Victoria wagon also appeared as a wood-trimmed Country Squire, Model 78, or as this plain sided Model 76. As the Squire, it cost $14,507, while in plain form it had a base of $14,235. Dual facing rear seats at $175 would increase passenger capacity to eight people in all full-size wagons. Also available but disappearing at the end of the year was the Crown Victoria "S" wagon, Model 75, which was priced at $14,228. In comparison to the 4-door sedans, the Crown Victoria wagons were not all that popular, with only 17,562 being sold, with this figure including all five variations. As before, full-size Ford wagons continued to feature a rear doorgate, which could swing open door-like on side hinges, or be lowered like a conventional tailgate.

Also appearing for the last time this year was the plain LTD Crown Victoria 2-door, Model 70. No longer popular, 2-door Crowns drew only 5,527 orders, and were not available in the fleet-oriented "S" series. In plain form they cost $14,727 and thus were priced higher than the comparable 4-door models. Of course, this price did not include the $665 vinyl half-roof with its wrapover tiara of brushed aluminum, not did it include the cast aluminum turbine wheels.

All dressed up with an optional vinyl half-roof and a $215 set of wire wheel covers is this plan LTD Crown Victoria Sedan. Oddly, although the vinyl half-roof proved to be very popular, Ford did not offer a full roof in either vinyl or canvas. It left that accessory to the aftermarket contingent. In basic form, the 4-door sedan, Model 73, cost $14,355. In stripped "S" form it was the least expensive of all Crown Victorias, and the only one under $14,000, with a basic tag of $13,860. By far the most popular of all Crown Victoria styles, the 4-door accounted for 105,789 sales, divided across all three trim series.

The most expensive Taurus on the lot was the LX Station Wagon, Model 58, which had a base tag of $15,213. Available only with the 3 liter V-6, it also used the 4-speed overdrive automatic as standard fare. Other premium items on this car included a rear window wiper, automatic liftgate release, and the roof rack. Taurus wagons did not have the doorgate design of the large wagons, but instead used a one-piece liftgate. Taurus wagons proved to be relatively popular, and a total of 96,201 went out the door. However, no breakdown was made as to trim level or engine size.

Available only in 6-cylinder form was the luxury-oriented Taurus LX 4-door Sedan, Model 53. Priced at $14,613, the car featured 140 horsepower running through a standard 4-speed overdrive automatic. Although many lists show that the Taurus was now America's best selling car, followed by Escort, production listings show that overall, Escort nosed out Taurus by a total of TWO cars, with Escort's 374,765 beating Taurus tallies of 374,763.

The Taurus GL 4-door Sedan, Model 52, could be ordered with either the 2.5 liter Four or the 3 liter V-6. As a Four, it wore an $11,498 price tag, while it was base priced at $12,170 with the V-6. In either case, its standard transmission was the 3-speed automatic. Taurus sedans and wagons used the same body and basic drivetrain as did the Mercury Sable line, with the main difference being in trim level and front and rear decor. However, Sables came in V-6 form only, with no 4-cylinder options. Proving to be a very popular vehicle, the Taurus 4-doors accounted for 278,562 sales, but no differentiation was made regarding trim levels. However, this figure made the Taurus 4-door the single best selling style of any American car this year.

Showing off both its rear liftgate design and its supposed luggage holding capacity is this Taurus GL Station Wagon, Model 57. Unlike the GL sedan, the wagon came in 6-cylinder form only. The wagon weighed 3,242 pounds empty, as compared with 3,045 for a V-6 sedan, and Ford apparently felt that the difference in weight combined with the additional carrying capacity of the wagon would make that vehicle definitely underpowered if equipped with a 4-cylinder engine. In base form, the GL station wagon cost $12,688, but such options as air conditioning ($945); AM/FM cassette ($268); power windows and locks ($495); rear-facing third seat ($155), and cast aluminum wheels ($390) would quickly run the price close to the $15,000 mark.

Supposedly aimed at the sport set was the MT5 line of Taurus vehicles. This year the MT5 series contained the 4-door Sedan, Model 51, shown here, and the Model 56 Station Wagon. However, the wagon would be dropped at year end, probably due to the lack of interest in this type of vehicle among wagon buyers. Available only with the 2.5 liter Four of 90 horsepower, the MT5 line used a 5-speed manual transmission as standard fare....hence MT5 (Manual Transmission 5-speed). There were no engine or transmission options in this sub-series, and the line was the only one in the Taurus camp to have the 5-speed manual. Slightly more expensive that the GL sub-series, which used a similar trim level, the MT5 sedans were base priced at $11,966 while the wagons wore a base tag of $12,534.

The low-buck seats in the Taurus tent were occupied by the L series models, which consisted of the Model 55 Station Wagon and this Model 50 4-door Sedan. Similar to the GL series, the wagon came only in V-6 form, while the sedan could be ordered either as a Four or a V-6. All used the 3-speed automatic as standard transmission (transaxle). The wagon bore a base price of $11,722. As a Four, the sedan was the only Taurus to have a sticker price in the $10,000 range, with its base being $10,491. In V-6 form, it was based at $11,163.

As could be expected, the interior of the new Taurus showed ultra modern design compatible with the exterior. Shown here is the LX interior, which featured numerous luxury touches, but overall was not that different from the other sub-series. Split reclining front seats with individual folding armrests were a feature of the LX. Centered on the steering wheel, just below the horn button, are the two rocker switches for the cruise control, while the buttons for the electric windows are on the driver's door panel, just ahead of the pull bar. A nice feature of the Taurus models was the fact that heater and air ducts ran under the front seat for the comfort of rear seat passengers.

Totally new for the year were the All Wheel Drive (AWD) versions of the Tempo. Appearing this year only was the AWD 2-door Sedan, Model 34. Apparently strong interest in the 4-door AWD and little interest in the 2-door model prompted Ford to discontinue this particular model at year end. Considered a separate series, not an option package, the AWD models used the same trim level as the Tempo LX series. Obviously, 4-wheel drive does not come cheap, and thus the tag on the AWD 2-door was $9,984.

The only Tempo to break the $10,000 mark was the new All Wheel Drive 4-door Sedan, Model 39, which bore a base sticker of $10,138. All AWD models used the High Output Four of 94 horsepower and a 3-speed FLC automatic transmission which allowed shifting into or out of 4-wheel drive either while moving or while stopped. Also helping the car's ride and traction was the standard Tempo 4-wheel independent suspension system which utilized gas-pressurized shock absorbing struts. Inside trim was the same as the LX models and featured luxury weight carpeting in addition to other premium fittings.

Also new for the year was the Tempo Sport GL 2-door Sedan, Model 33. As did the AWD models, this creation also used the High Output 94 horsepower Four as standard fare, but had this coupled to the 5-speed manual transmission with fifth being overdrive. Power steering was now standard on all Tempos. The new Sport GL 2-door was priced at $8,888 and weighed 2,667 pounds. Sport GL models also used gas pressurized shock absorbing struts, but with a heavier road-tuned reaction. The styled road wheels were standard on this model, but cost $180 more on other Tempo series. The decklid luggage rack cost another $115.

1987

Showing off its blackout window surrounds is the new Sport GL 4-door Sedan, Model 38. Tempo's aerodynamically designed front end, with its slanted headlight covers actually provided an excellent slipstream at high speeds, not only for the sport models, but for all Tempos. The Sport GL series offered reclining performance bucket front seats along with a tuned suspension and High Output Four. The sedan was priced at $9,043.

Appearing for the last time this year was the luxury-oriented Tempo LX 2-door Sedan, Model 32. Among the exterior features on this model were the bright window surrounds; dual body side, hood, and decklid paint stripes; tinted glass all around, and dual electrically controlled outside rearview mirrors. Standard styled road wheels and performance radial blackwall tires completed the picture. The LX 2-door sold for $9,238. In the Tempo line, 2-door production was only one-third that of the 4-door sales, with only 70,164 total 2-door Tempos being built in all trim forms.

Outside of the AWD models, the most expensive Tempo was the LX 4-door Sedan, Model 37, which sold for $9,444. Among the standard toys found in LX cars were tilt steering wheels; power door locks; automatic decklid release; remote fuel filler door release; electronic AM/FM stereo; tachometer; trip odometer; actual temperature gauge instead of warning light; illuminated entry system, and a full compliment of interior lights. Still, the 86 horsepower 2.3 liter Four was considered standard. Total 4-door Tempo production reached 212,468. Those models equipped with automatic transmissions now had a new 3-speed FLC unit (Fluid Linked Converter) which negated the need for a lockup torque converter.

Still a rather attractive car was Tempo's economy-minded GL 4-door Sedan, Model 36. It had a base price of $8,198, not counting the Select GL Preferred Equipment Package on this example. Despite their supposed low trim level, GL models still were fitted with reclining front bucket seats upholstered in all cloth, and had fully padded door panels with a carpeted lower section. The body was fitted with a luxury-level sound insulation package, trimmed with a cloth headliner with coordinated visors with covered mirrors— just a tab more than one would expect in the lowest trim level series. All Tempos except the AWDs were front wheel drive.

Despite its low-buck nomenclature, the Tempo GL models still featured bright window surrounds and heavy body side molding, features once reserved for the more upscale versions. This is the GL 2-door Sedan, Model 31, which was the lowest price Tempo with a base tag of $8,043. Tempos were still classed as 5-passenger cars, as opposed to the 4-place rating given to Escorts. Heavily promoted on GL level Tempos, but apparently not on this example, was the Select GL Preferred Equipment Package. This $190 grouping included tinted glass all around; AM/FM stereo radio, and dual electrically operated remote outside mirrors, shown on the accompanying GL 4-door. This model wears the standard manually adjusted outside rearview mirror.

Appearing for the last time this year was the quaint little 2-passenger EXP Sport Coupe, Model 18. Oddly, even though the EXP was promoted as an Escort-based line of sport-type cars, it was the sport version that was dropped first, while the high-trimmed luxury version would continue. Although now officially considered part of the overall Escort series, the EXP line was still promoted as an individual vehicle. The sport version, which used the High Output 1.9 liter Four as standard fare, cost $8,831, and was the most expensive of the two EXP models. It was fitted with the manual 5-speed transmission. Total EXP production this year dropped to 25,888 divided between the two models.

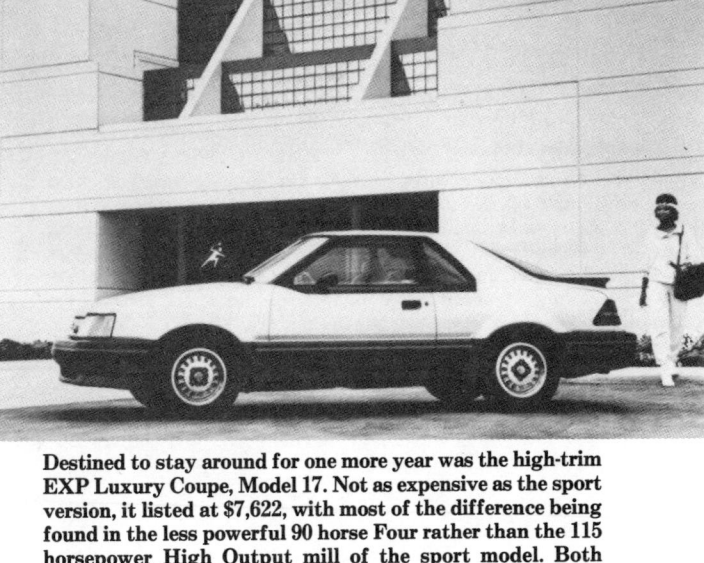

Destined to stay around for one more year was the high-trim EXP Luxury Coupe, Model 17. Not as expensive as the sport version, it listed at $7,622, with most of the difference being found in the less powerful 90 horse Four rather than the 115 horsepower High Output mill of the sport model. Both engines were fuel injected, with the 90 horse being through a throttle body while the 115 horse used a multi-port set-up. Also, the transaxle of the Luxury Coupe was a 4-speed version as opposed to the sport's 5-speed, and the suspension was more like the conventional Escort. Both front air dam and rear spoiler were standard on all EXPS, as was the black window surrounds.

Providing a base for the GT, the Pony, and the GL models was the 2-door hatchback body style. It is seen here as the Model 21 GL version, which had a base price of $6,801. As a stripped Pony, Model 20, it went for $6,436. Sometimes referred to as a 3-door Hatchback, the style was by far the most popular of all of the three Escort bodies, with 206,729 being produced in all three forms. New for the year on all Escorts were electrically motorized seat belts. Like those on many Japanese cars, these belts did not give the front seat occupants a choice of whether or not to wear the belt, but simply snapped into place once the door was closed.

Only one version of the Escort 4-door Sedan was available. It was this GL, Model 25, sometimes referred to as a 4-door or a 5-door Hatchback. The new GL sub-series was a combination of the former L and LX sub-series, with a trim level similar to that which had been found on the former LX models. In base form, the 4-door sold for $7,022 and weighed 2,222 pounds. Certainly not unpopular, it attracted 102,187 buyers. Those looking for even more economy could order any GL Escort with a 2 liter 4-cylinder 58-horse diesel engine as a no-cost option. Regardless of what engine was selected, the fuel tank remained at 13 gallons capacity.

In effect, the Escort GT 2-door Hatchback, Model 23, could be considered a 4-passenger competitor to the 2-seat EXP. It used the same pan and suspension set-up as the EXP Sport, and under the hood had the same 155 horsepower High Output 1.9 liter Four with multi-port fuel injection and 5-speed transaxle. Most expensive Escort on the books, it was the only model to base over the $8,000 mark, having a tag of $8,724. Distinctive frontal styling with offset air slots, special air dam with built-in road lights, and large GT emblem gave quick identity to the car. The cast aluminum wheels were also part of the package.

Escort's only wagon this year was the GL Station Wagon, Model 28, which incorporated the trim levels of the former L and LX versions. Priced at $7,312, the car was rated at the same 4-passenger seating as all other Escort models, but offered a bit of additional luggage space due to its more squared rear quarters. The liftgate was similar to that used on all Escorts, with the result that this was sometimes referred to as a 5-door vehicle. Least popular of all Escort styles, the wagon still drew 65,849 orders. A split fold-down rear seat meant that long luggage could be stored on one side, while a third person could ride in the remaining upright seat.

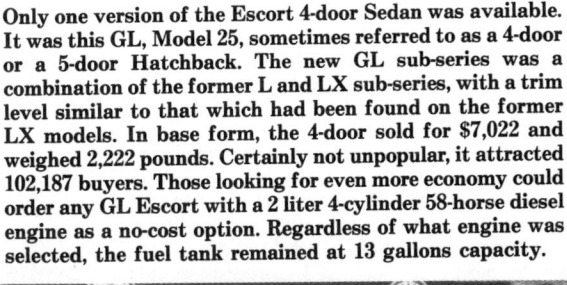

The luxury sedan in the popular Taurus line continued to be the LX Model 53, which was available only with the 3-liter V-6 engine and 4-speed automatic transmission. It had a base price of $15,295. For an additional $400, the car could be fitted with the 3.8 liter Thunderbird V-6. This block was rated at the same 140 horses as the standard 3-liter V-6, but had a much higher torque curve and resulting improved performance rating.

Easily closing in on the price range of the full-size Fords was the top-line Taurus LX Station Wagon, Model 58, which listed for $15,905 with the standard 3-liter V-6. All LX models came equipped with the automatic 4-speed transaxle with overdrive. All Taurus models were front wheel drive only. With the rear seat down, Taurus wagons offered 81 cubic feet of cargo room. On the LX models, the roof-top luggage rack was standard. A rear facing third seat could be ordered for $155. Relatively popular, Taurus wagon production reached 93,001, spread across L, GL, and LX trim levels.

The mid-level of the Taurus line was the GL series. The line consisted of both a 4-door Sedan, Model 52, (shown here) and a station wagon, Model 55. The sedan could be ordered with either the standard 3-liter V-6 or the 2.5-liter (152 cubic inches) Four, but the wagon came in 6-cylinder form only. As a Four, the sedan cost $12,200, while it booked at $12,872 with the V-6. The base wagon price was $13,380. The new 3.8 Thunderbird V-6 could be ordered for an additional $1,068 above the sedan's 4-cylinder price, or $400 above the wagon's base. Taurus 4-door sedan production this year climbed to 294,576, spread across all trim levels.

The basic trim level of the Taurus line was filled by the L series, of which this is the 4-door Sedan, Model 50. It could be ordered with either the Four or the V-6. The Four cost $11,699, and thus was the only Taurus based below the $12,000 mark. Another $670 added the 3-liter V-6, while $1,068 would have bought the Thunderbird V-6. The L series wagon was the Model 55. This was available only in 6-cylinder form, and cost $12,884.

A gearshift lever leading to a manual 5-speed transaxle shows that this is the interior of the unusual MT5 Taurus Sedan, Model 51. No longer available as a station wagon, the relatively unpopular MT5 sedan models were appearing for the last time this year. The only Taurus designs to use a manual transmission, the cars cost $12,835. They were available only with the 4-cylinder engine. MT5 stood for "Manual Transmission 5-speed." A nice car for drivers who liked the sporty feel of a manual 5-speed, the MT5 still suffered from lack of true performance due to its small engine, and lack of buyers due to its overall non-sporty appearance.

Most popular single model of all Mustangs was the LX Coupe, Model 40, sometimes called the Notchback Coupe. A total of 71,890 were sold. The only Mustang still in the $8,000 basic range, the 4-cylinder car had a tag of $8,726. However, in V-8 form, it jumped up to $10,611. Also in the LX series was the hatchback version, which was simply a downtrimmed GT. As a Four, it cost $9,211, but with the V-8 it ran up to $11,106. All Mustangs used the 5-speed manual transmission as standard, but a 4-speed automatic with overdrive could be ordered for another $515.

For those who wanted a sporty car, yet didn't need the performance or want the cost of a GT model, there was the LX Convertible, Model 44. It could be ordered with the basic 140 cubic inch Four of 90 horsepower for $13,702, or for another $1,885 could be fitted with the screaming new 302 V-8 of 225 horses. The V-8 packages also included a performance oriented suspension system. Mustang produced a total of 33,344 soft tops this year, spread between GT and LX series. Individual articulated sport seats in the front were standard in the GT, but were a $365 option in the LX convertibles.

Still the luxury liners of the large car field, the LTD Crown Victoria LX series was now cut to three models through the demise of the 2-door styles. Thus, the only non-station wagon available was the 4-door Sedan, Model 74. Among its new features were taillights with more wrap-around, intermittent windshield wipers, front door map pockets, and warning lights for low fuel and low oil. Luxurious and large, the LX models were again up in price, with the sedan going for $16,134. The companion LX Station Wagon, Model 77, went for $16,210, while the top-line LX Country Squire wagon (Model 79) crept up to $16,643. The LX Country Squire was the only Ford weighing over two tons, with its basic weight being 4,070 pounds.

Except for interior trim, there was little difference between the LTD Crown Victoria LX models and the plain versions. This is the regular LTD 4-door sedan, Model 73. It had a base sticker of $15,218, which did not include the $390 set of cast aluminum turbine-type wheels. Distinguishing the new Crown Victorias were a revised grille and hood, and new deck lids, in addition to the new taillight design. This model was also available in the stripped fleet-oriented "S" series, where it was the Model 72, costing $14,653. Due to the demise of the 2-door models and a loss of sales in the station wagon ranks, the 4-door Crown Victorias enjoyed an increase in sales, going up to 110,249. However, this was not enough to keep the overall line from being the only series of Fords to show a sales loss this year.

Showing off its new face and hood is the LTD Crown Victoria Country Squire, Model 78, which featured a wide expanse of imitation wood side trim. Costing $15,613 in standard form, the car was a companion to the plain sided Model 76, which sold for $15,180. Crown Victoria wagon production slipped this year, with a total of only 14,940 such units being built, and these spread across all four variations. All Crown Victorias continued to use the 302 V-8, this year sporting a new multi-port fuel injection system. However, in the Crown Victorias these engines were rated at 150 horsepower, as opposed to the 225 horses when set up for use in the Mustang line. Oddly, the higher horse version was not available to the full-size Fords. The full-size wagons continued to use the very handy rear doorgate design, and thus were sometimes referred to as 5-door vehicles.

Appearing for the last time this year was the Thunderbird Turbo Coupe. As before, the car had its own exclusive 140 cubic inch 4-cylinder intercooled fuel-injected turbocharged engine of 190 horsepower and 5-speed manual transmission. Its exterior was marked by an exclusive hood with twin scoops; a grille-less face, and a special air dam with built-in road lights. Inside it used power operated articulated sport seats, while underneath it had a special performance suspension with Automatic Ride control and 4-wheel anti-lock brakes. Designated the Model 64, the Turbo Coupe was the most expensive Thunderbird, and in fact, the most expensive of all Fords, with a base list of $17,250. For an extra $515 the 4-speed automatic could be ordered, but then the engine was downrated to 150 horsepower. There were no engine options in the Turbo Coupe.

1988

Luxury leader of the Thunderbird flock was the LX Coupe, Model 62. The car used all of the traditional T-Bird styling, and differed very little from other non-turbo models. However, on the inside owners were treated to electric everything; deluxe floor mats; luxury and convenience lighting groups; power antenna; dual power operated split reclining bench seats, and a premium sound system. It was priced at $15,585 with the V-6 or $16,606 with the V-8. The LX Coupe was among the 147,243 Thunderbirds which flew to customers this year.

Despite the hype surrounding the intercooled turbocharged engine, many buyers of performance-oriented T-Birds preferred the Sport Coupe, Model 61, which came only with the 302 cubic inch V-8, rated at 155 horsepower. New on this year's Sport Coupe were dual exhausts and the same articulated power-operated sport seats as found on the Turbo Coupe. A manual transmission was not available for this model, and as did all other Birds except the Turbo, it came with the 4-speed automatic as standard fare. Other extras included a tilt steering wheel, power windows, and styled road wheels. The car was base priced at $16,030, which actually put it below the LX Coupe's tag when that car carried the V-8.

The hot horses in the Mustang corral continued to be the GT models, available only in hatchback and convertible styles. At a base of $12,745, the GT Hatchback, Model 42, was the most expensive solid top. All GT models came with the 302 V-8 engine as standard fare, but in the Mustang version the mill produced 225 horses at 4200 rpm. As could be expected, it availed itself of the new multi-port fuel injection system developed for the 302 this year. Production was not broken down by series, but charts show a total of 74,331 hatchbacks produced, divided between GT and LX models.

Probably the most popular of the 147,243 Thunderbirds sold this year was the plain Hardtop Coupe, Model 60. It was available with the V-6 for $13,599, or with the newly redesigned 302 V-8 with multi-port fuel injection for $14,302. All Birds this year weighed between 3,200 and 3,400 pounds. Among the standard items on all Thunderbirds were tinted glass; air conditioning; a rear window defroster; interval wipers; power door locks; dual electric remote control sideview mirrors; electronic AM/FM stereo with cassette player; speed control, and styled road wheels.

The most expensive horse in the Mustang stable was the GT Convertible, Model 45, which had a base sticker of $16,610. For this, buyers got the V-8 engine, special interior, heavy suspension, special lower paint, and cast aluminum wheels. A Custom Equipment Group, which included Climate Control air conditioning and a premium sound system, added another $810 to the convertible's cost while the same system on closed cars was $910. Still, few GT models were let loose without this addition.

Ford came in with a new min-model this year, but despite some early attempts to "Americanize" the car, few people considered it anything but another Asian import. The new car was the Festiva, designed by Mazda and built by Ford's Korean factories. The new mini-mini really was as much a foreign car as were the British, German, or Australian Fords, and thus is outside the realm of this book.

In the real car world, Ford's big news this year was another nice increase in production, with every car line except the LTD Crown Victoria showing quite pleasant growth, and even the Crown slipping only slightly.

As probably could be expected, the ever-popular and affordable little Escort was once again the big leader. Now with the EXP series firmly tucked inside its lines, the Escort drew a total of 422,035 units out of the factories. Once more Ford did not follow the expected model year change with the little car. It began the 1988 season as a virtual carbon copy of the 1987 list.

But at mid-season, May to be exact, the second series Escorts arrived, including a newly styled EXP, and a host of new series. Now the Pony was a two-model grouping, with both a two and a 4-door, and the LX series returned. The GT model was the sport offering, as the EXP was now referred to as a 2-passenger luxury coupe. The new models availed themselves of almost all new sheet metal. But, as was the case with the 1987 Thunderbird, in the interests of appearance continuity, they did not look all that different than the previous line that they replaced. The engines remained untouched, with only the GT models getting the High Output Four. And finally, the never-popular diesel engine went away.

Visually, the well-accepted Taurus was no different this year than it was last year, but a few changes did take place. The MT5 Station Wagon was dropped, thus reducing the available models to seven. The MT5 Sedan remained as the only Taurus to exclusively use the 4-cylinder engine coupled to a 5-speed Manual Transmission (hence the MT5 name). The L and GL sedans used the Four as a base, but the 3 liter V-6 was optional in these models, while it was standard in all others. New for the year was the availability of the Thunderbird 3.8 liter V-6 as an option in all but the MT5. This 232 cubic inch engine provided 140 horsepower, which was the same as that of the standard Taurus V-6, but its torque and performance had a much higher rating.

In the production department, Taurus climbed steadily, reaching a year-end model-year figure of 387,577. However, Ford claimed that Taurus finally beat Escort in sales at the end of the 1987 calendar year. But, unless they were referring to a possible monthly sales surge, there is no indication that the mid-size model jumped over the little ones.

Happily occupying the middle ground between Escort and Taurus, the Tempo also experienced a nice sales gain,

going up to 313,262. Here part of the reason was attributable to the line receiving some substantial restyling, including a new "all Ford" face, new rear styling, new door skins, and other sheetmetal refinements. Available models were dropped to six, as both the AWD (All Wheel Drive) and the LX series became one-model lines, consisting solely of 4-door sedans. The 2-doors appeared only in the GL and GLS series. As before, all Tempos used their own exclusive fuel-injected Fours, with a High Output version being optional.

Despite no changes to speak of, Mustang production also went up this year, but where it went is open to discussion. When production is counted by model, the final figure is 179,565 for the model year. Yet Ford claimed model-year production of 211,225 and calendar year production of 200,089. As before, the LX series came with the 2.3 liter Four as standard and the V-8 as an $1,885 option. The GT models continued to have the V-8 as standard fare. All cars used the 5-speed manual transmission, unless the $515 4-speed automatic was ordered.

Going hand-in-hand with Mustang, Thunderbird also was unchanged this year, but saw a healthy increase in sales of almost 20,000, ending the model year with 147,243 units built. Under the hood, the Bird got the same revised V-6 as was given to the Taurus as an option, but here the result was a 20 unit jump in horsepower over the 1987 model V-6. Most of the jump was due to the new fuel injection system, which this year was multi-point, as opposed to the old throttle body system. The V-6 was standard on the hardtop and LX coupes, while the V-8 was optional on these models and standard on the Sport Coupe. Now all Thunderbirds with the V-8 were also equipped with dual exhausts. Again, the Turbo Coupe, now in its final year, had its own exclusive 4-cylinder intercooled turbocharged engine.

And finally the LTD Crown Victoria got a substantial revision. Among the changes were new grilles, hoods, taillights, and trunk decks. Happily, the cars still used their exclusive styling that proclaimed "Crown Victoria," and resisted all urges to become overgrown versions of the Taurus. However, the line did loose its 2-door models. Victorias now were available only as 4-door sedans or station wagons. Both standard and LX models were available, along with one lone "S" 4-door. Oddly, the Crown Victorias were the only Ford line to show a decrease in sales this year, dropping to 125,189 builds for the model year. Its only engine was the 302 V-8 with sequential fuel injection, which was essentially the same V-8 as found in the Thunderbird.

As mentioned earlier, Escort once again led the production list, followed by Taurus, with Tempo coming in third, Mustang fourth, Thunderbird fifth, and the Crown Victoria bringing up the parade in final place.

Showing off its new rear end design with the full-length wrap-around backup and taillight bar is this Tempo GLS 4-door Sedan, Model 38. Available both in this style and as the Model 33 2-door Sedan, the GLS models came only with the 100 horsepower High Output Four. The GLS (the "S" stood for "Sport") 4-door was base priced at $9,400, while the 2-door went for $9,249. Although the Tempo 4-door models enjoyed a nice surge in popularity, with production reaching 263,332, the 2-door models suffered a definite lack of sales, with production down to 49,930.

Ford described its new Tempo dash board as being "ergonomically" designed (whatever that was supposed to mean) and providing an eye-catching look. Full dial instrumentation, including a new temperature gauge, was clustered directly in front of the driver, while a swing down glove box occupied the right side. This example is fitted with the standard 5-speed manual transmission, but an automatic transaxle could be ordered for another $480. Also available, but costing 4815, was a driver's side air bag which nested in the steering wheel hub.

Playing in the snow, which probably is a good job for a 4-wheel drive vehicle, is the Tempo AWD 4-door Sedan, Model 39, This was Ford's only 4-wheel drive non-utility passenger car. With the 2-door AWD model discontinued, the All-Wheel-Drive (AWD) now became a one-style series. Priced at $10,413, it was not only the most expensive Tempo, but also the only one to break into the $10,000 range. Power was by the High Output Four, now enhanced by a new multiple-port electronic fuel injection system. Standard on all Tempos this year was a new motorized passive restraint system, in which the seat belts automatically ran into place when the door was closed. A driver-side air bag was also available for another $815.

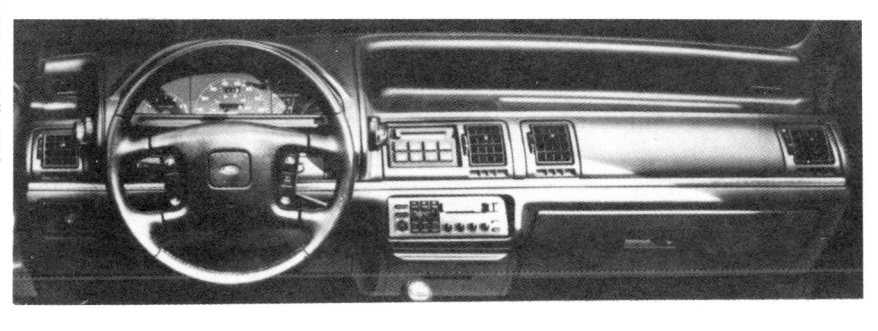

The new Tempo styling produced a more "Ford-like" face. Among the new features were the grille and slanted headlight units, new door skins, revised window designs, and new bumpers and air dams. Shown is the LX 4-door Sedan, Model 37, which represented the highest trim level of the Tempo line. No longer available as a 2-door, the LX came with the 98 horse Four as standard equipment, but the High Output version could be ordered as an option. In basic form, the LX sedan sold for $9,737. Also available were two more basic Tempos. They were the two GL series cars, the Model 31 2-door Sedan, which sold for $8,658, and the Model 36 4-door Sedan, which had a basic list of $8,808.

Appearing for the first half of the year was the old-style EXP 2-passenger sports-type car. Then in May a revised model appeared. But by the following October, the EXP was simply a memory. The initial model, totally unchanged from 1987, was priced at $8,037, while the revised second generation, with its new front fenders, bore a tag of $8,201. Since the EXP was now officially a part of the Escort line, no breakout production figures were kept for this unique little car. And, since the EXP was now considered a luxury 2-seater, rather than a sports type of vehicle, the 90 horse Four was the standard engine, with the High Output model apparently not being available.

The real performance vehicle in the Escort line was not the 2-place EXP, but instead was the 4-passenger GT 2-door Hatchback, Model 23. Sometimes called a 3-door hatchback, the car had an exclusive frontal treatment, with offset grille, large "GT" emblem, and special air dam with built-in road lights. Its engine was the electronically fuel injected High Output 1.9-liter Four (113 cubic inches) that produced 115 horsepower. Shown here in its early 1988 form, the car went through the same mid-season revision as did all other Escorts, and in the process received a new symmetrical grille, and special air dam with an egg-crate grid. Most expensive of the Escorts, the GT cost $9,055 in its first generation form, and crept up to $9,093 in its new guise as a Model 93, which appears in the 1989 section.

Attracting 113,470 buyers was the Escort 4-door Sedan, which first appeared as the Model 25 shown here, and then at mid-season became the LX Model 95. Sometimes referred to as a 5-door Sedan because of its large rear liftgate, the nice riding little car sold first for $7,355, but was up to $7,457 for the second generation. All Escorts used the 1.9 liter Four of 90 horsepower, with the High Output version now being for the exclusive use of GT models.

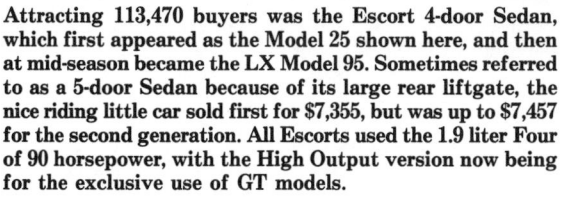

Least popular of all Escorts, despite being the most practical, was the GL Station Wagon, which drew a total of 56,654 orders during the total year. As did other Escorts, at mid-season it received new but similar front and rear styling, and change in nomenclature to the LX Station Wagon, Model 98. At this time also, its base price rose from $7,938 to $8,058. Since the wagon was basically a variation of the sedan's basic shell, it offered no more passenger room than did the 4-door sedan, but its large rear area was a great help when any amount of cargo had to be carried. All Escorts except the EXP were rated as 4-passenger cars.

Most popular of the Escort styles was the 2-door (3-door) Hatchback design, which accounted for 251,911 builds, shared between GT, GL, and Pony models. No slouch in sales, the Escort was credited as being the best selling line of cars worldwide for the past five years, an honor that Ford was only too happy to capitalize upon, and for good reason. The well-deigned little hatchback is shown here in GL form, where it was the Model 21, which cost $6,949. As the stripped Pony, Model 20, it listed at $6,632. At mid-year a new but very similar frontal design caused the GL to become the LX Model 91 at $7,127, while the Pony became the Model 90 at $6,747, a factor which resulted in the Pony being the only remaining Ford under $7,000 base price.

Not really belonging in this book, but included only because it was offered nationally by Ford dealers, is the Festiva. The minuscule car actually appeared on the West Coast during the 1987 selling season, then was offered nationally in 1988. Considered a sub-compact, the car was designed by Mazda of Japan, but produced in Ford's factories in Korea. Built on a front-wheel-drive pan of 90.2 inch wheelbase, the car used a 1.3-liter Four with plain carburetion, which developed 58 horsepower. It was available in basic style for $5,765, or in the LX version shown here for $6,868. Despite its tiny, rectangular styling, one look at the front immediately said "This is a Ford product!"

Ford's big news this year was another new car...and a sporty, performance oriented one at that. Essentially replacing the EXP in sales slotting, the new car was called the Probe, a name that still puzzles this author as to its intended meaning.

Initial reports had the car scheduled as a replacement for the Mustang, but this was obviously not to be. As different from the Mustang as the Taurus was from the Crown Victoria, the Japanese-American Probe was a front-wheel drive sport-type car built on a unibody pan of 99-inch wheelbase, and having an overall length of 177 inches, making it just slightly shorter than the 179-inch Mustang.

Its body styling, though done by Ford, seemed more modern and "Japanese" than did the Mustang. Setting off entire package was the front, which was fully curved from the air slot grille to the sharply raked windshield. Within the normal hood area lived the exclusive hidden headlights, with the doors on an almost horizontal plane, giving the car a definite frog-like look when the headlights popped up. Below the bumper, an integral air dam hosted a pair of running lights. Unlike the EXP, the Probe was a 4-passenger car, more rightfully called a 2+2 because of the very limited seating room or leg space for the rear passengers.

Power and drive train were strictly Japanese, and in effect were identical to the Mazda MX-6 Coupe. Making this a very logical move was the fact that production of both the Probe and the MX-6 Mazda emanated from the Ford plant at Flat Rock, Mich., (a few miles south of Dearborn). All power was from the Mazda 12-valve Four of 2.2-liter (3.39x3.7 inch bore and stroke) and 110 horsepower in the plain and GL versions. The performance-oriented GT model used an intercooled, turbocharged variation of this block, which produced 145 horses.

Introduced in May, 1988, the Probe still was considered an early 1989 model, and not an mid-1988 release. Production and sales acceptance was very respectable. However, for some reason Ford listed the Probe production on a calendar-year basis, showing 133,650 for the period. All other production was on an October/September model-year basis.

With the new Probe gaining a major portion of the attention, the total revision of the Thunderbird went almost unnoticed. Still, the new Bird was totally different from its previous kin. While it sported a new wheelbase of 113 inches, which was almost nine inches longer than the 1988 models, its overall length of 198.7 inches was actually 3.5 inches shorter than the previous models. However, the width was increased 1.5 inches, and the interior room seemed far more spacious than in earlier models.

Styling was akin to the Taurus-school, similar in effect to the former Turbo Coupe, with a sharply raked grilleless front divided by a single full-width air slot immediately above the bumper, and additional slots within the bumper and in the lower air dam. Unlike the Probe, the headlights continued to be housed in conventional pods, with sharply raked "slant-eye' exterior lenses.

Surprisingly, Thunderbird remained rear-wheel drive. Handling was improved through a new independent rear suspension and a speed-sensitive standard power steering unit. Under the hood there was only a V-6, with both the V-8 and Turbo Four options a thing of the past. The basic power, which was also available as a Taurus option, was the 3.8 liter (232 cubic inches) block of last year, still rated at 140 horses. However, new for the year and available only in the new Thunderbird Super Coupe, was a supercharged version of this block which produced 210 horses at 4000 rpm. This version could be hooked to a manual 5-speed or a 4-speed automatic in the Super Coupe, while the regular V-6 of the plain and LX coupes came only with the automatic.

Ford's other sporty car, the Mustang, defied the skeptics who expected it to disappear in the face of the new Probe. Not only alive and healthy, the virtually unchanged rear-wheel drive car saw its sales climb to 209,769, which was a nice and probably unexpected gain of over 30,000 sales above the 1988 figures.

Some confusion was created this year by Ford lists which show the V-8 powered LX models as being a separate sub-series from the 4-cylinder models. The result is that these lists show eight available models, while other lists tend to categorize only the conventional three LX and two GT models. As before, the Mustang played host to Ford's only convertible, still available in either LX or GT versions. However, power door locks and windows were now standard in both convertible models, whereas they had previously been extra-cost options on the LX cars.

Power was also a major selling point of this year's Taurus models. Not only did the car take Ford's top sales honors with a total of 395,261 sold, it also increased its production by almost 7,700 over last year. Part of the increase was due to the introduction of the new SHO Sedan, with SHO standing for "Super High Output." The car replaced the old MT5 as the line's sport/performance sedan, but the main difference was that the SHO had the performance that the MT5 had only hinted about.

Powering the SHO was a new and exclusive 220 horsepower variation of the 3-liter (182 cubic inch) V-6, but reengineered with dual overhead cams and 24 valves (four per cylinder). The engineering was done by Yamaha using Ford's basic blocks. Fitted to this block was a new 5-speed manual transmission which had been designed by Ford but was being built by Mazda. Driver egos were boosted by a standard 140 MPH speedometer and a tachometer that read up to 800 rpm. Four wheel disc brakes; aluminum alloy wheels; special air dams and ground effects panels, and power operated sports seats were among the other exclusive features that helped to explain why the new SHO tilted the cash register to over the $20,000 mark with little trouble.

As to the rest of the Taurus line, the two body styles were still divided into three trim levels of L, GL, and

LX, with the L and GL sedans being the only ones to avail themselves of the 153 cubic inch Four, while the LX wagon was the only one to use the new Thunderbird V-6 as standard power, though V-6 and Thunderbird V-6 engines were optional for any Taurus except the SHO.

In the world of little cars, the ever-popular Escort once again gave a happy face to Ford's sales lists, with 363,122 being built. However, this represented a drop of almost 60,000 cars, many of whose sales may have gone to the new Probe. Since the line had received a thorough revision and introduction with the mid-1988 models, there were no changes forthcoming for the 1989 offerings. The model line continued with the three LX, one GT, and one Pony of last year, but the aforementioned EXP 2-seater was gone for good, and little lamented. Mechanically, the cars also remained the same,

Enjoying the distinction of being named "Car of the Year" by *Motor Trend Magazine* was the new Thunderbird Super Coupe, or Thunderbird SC, Model 64. Using a 232 cubic inch V-6 engine redesigned by Ford and built by Yamaha, the car featured 24 valves and a supercharger, with horsepower rated at 210. Distinguishing the exterior were exclusive bumpers and air dams, with "SC" imprinted into the center and integral fog lights built into the outer ends. Under the car was a new Automatic Adjustable Suspension system which allowed shock absorber adjustment to any ride level from soft through extra firm. Power was through a 5-speed manual gearbox, but an automatic 4-speed could be ordered. Most expensive of all Fords, the Super Coupe sold for $19,823 in basic form. The performance-oriented car was reported to run 0 to 60 in 7.1 seconds with the manual transmission.

Totally new styling this year gave Thunderbird a wheelbase of 113 inches, which was almost nine inches longer than before. But, its overall length was now 198.7 inches, which was a reduction of 3.5 inches. Also, the wheels got larger, going back to 15 inches from the former 14-inch size. In addition to the super hot Super Coupe, the Bird family had two other offspring...the plain Model 60 and the more luxurious LX Model 62 shown here. From the exterior, the two coupes looked the same, with the LX differing in having power everything inside, plus a more luxurious interior. The LX sold for $16,817 while the plain coupe had a base of $14,612. Regular and LX coupes used the 12-valve non-supercharged version of the 232 cubic inch V-6. Total bird production this year was 114,868.

except that the suspension systems now included gas-filled struts. Engines were still the two variations of the 113.5 cubic inch Four, with the 90 horse unit being installed in all Escorts except the GT, which had exclusive use of the fuel-injected 115 horsepower version.

The Tempo, an interesting in-between front-drive model, also relied on its previous frontal revisions to carry it through the 1989 season. The same six models appeared, with the interesting and unusual AWD being Ford's only 4-wheel drive sedan. However, similar to the Escort's experience, Tempo also saw a drop in sales, slipping by over 20,000 to end the model year at 292,978. Again, Probe may have absorbed much of this market.

And finally there was the virtually unchanged LTD Crown Victoria line. Since it had gone through some major revisions last year, no one was surprised to see the 1989 models being virtual carbon copies of the 1988 line. The line was still divided into three plain LTD Crowns, three LX models, one of which was the Country Squire, and one stripped "S" model designed for fleet sales, mainly as taxi and police cars. The only engine was still the 150 horsepower 302 V-8 with its 4-speed automatic overdrive transmission. Air conditioning and tinted window glass continued to be standard equipment. Apparently the 351 V-8 may have been slid back into production (or maybe it never really left) but was only available on special order by bona fide police units or others demonstrating a definite need for a high performance block. For some reason, LTD Crown Victoria production went up almost 9,000 this year, cresting at 134,103 as opposed to 125,189 for 1988.

And finally, though it did not affect U.S. activities in any way, Ford bought the renown Jaguar Cars Ltd. of Coventry, England. Despite the prestige of the name, Ford has been very soft spoken about its Jaguar ownership, and has allowed the company to operate pretty much as an autonomous corporation.

Showing off its exclusive grille-less front and special bumper with slotted air dam and integral fog lights was the new Mustang GT Coupe, Model 42. Available only in V-8 form, Mustang's hot one continued to use the 302 cubic inch block, fitted with sequential fuel injection, and rated at 225 horses. Also in the GT package was a performance-oriented suspension system, articulated individual sport bucket seats, dual exhausts, and a manual 5-speed transmission. The 4-speed automatic could be ordered at $515 extra cost. So unchanged was the Mustang this year that Ford used some of its same promotional photos for both 1988 and 1989. Most expensive of the hardtop Mustangs, the GT version had a base price of $13,272.

1989

For those who preferred economy in a Mustang package, the basic LX models were still offered with the 90 horsepower 140 cubic inch (2.3 liter) Four as standard fare. When so equipped, this LX Notchback Coupe, Model 40, became the lowest price pony, leaving the barn for $9,050 in base form. For another $2,360 the optional 302 of the GT series could be installed, bringing the base price to $11,410. While some Ford lists show the V-8 models as simply being LX units with the optional engine, other lists this year consider the V-8 cars as a special sub-series, known as the "LX5.0L Sport" models. When V-8 equipped, LX Mustangs sported a small "5.0" emblem just aft of the front wheel well, as seen here.

Shown in comparison to a mid-1964 Mustang convertible, was this year's most expensive horse, the GT Convertible, Model 45. It wore a base price tag of $17,512, as compared to the original's price of $2,614, a difference of almost $15,000. As with the GT hatchback, the convertible was fitted with the V-8, wore exclusive cast aluminum wheels, used a performance suspension system and a Traction-Lock rear axle; had individually power operated articulated sports seats and power windows, and were fitted with the exclusive GT front and side ground effects panels, in addition to the rear spoiler. Power brakes and steering were standard on all Mustangs, as were tinted window glass and remote dual outside mirrors.

The small "5.0" emblem shows that this LX Hatchback, Model 41, is indeed considered the LX5.0L Sport model as opposed to the 4-cylinder plain LX version. In base 4-cylinder form, the car sold for $9,556, while the V-8 model had a base price of $12,265. The difference of $2,709 for a V-8 in hatchback form, as opposed to $2,360 in notchback, is because the hatchback package also included articulated front bucket seats, while on the notchback the package was basically an engine swap. This particular example is owned by John T. Wagner of Plymouth, Mich., son of James K. Wagner, Crestline/Motorbooks author and Ford engineer.

An unlikely car on a showroom floor is this Mustang LX Convertible, Model 44, with the 4-cylinder engine. Certainly the vast majority of LX convertibles would have gone out the door as LX5.0L Sport models with the 302 (5 liter) V-8 tucked nicely under the hood. This year's 4-cylinder convertibles cost $14,140, while the V-8 units were $17,001, putting them only about $500 away from the GT models, which offered a more sport oriented suspension and the exclusive GT look. New for all Mustang convertibles this year were power windows and door locks as standard equipment. Despite expected competition from the new front-drive Probe, Mustang's sales climbed nicely this year, reaching 209,769, an increase of over 30,000 above the 1988 figure. This was not bad for a totally unchanged car.

Essentially unchanged was the LTD Crown Victoria line of full-size Fords. Having gone through a full-scale redesign last year, it surprised no one when the 1989 models came out as virtual carbon copies of the 1988s. The most significant change appears to be the substitution of a "Check Engine" warning light for the "Low Oil Level" light on previous models. The top line of the Crown Victorias continued to be the LX series, which included this Model 74 4-door Sedan at $16,767; a Model 77 Station Wagon at $17,238, and the imitation wood-trimmed Model 79 Country Squire at $17,556. Most buyers of Crown Victoria models thought that they were getting an American-made car, but since all of Ford's big car production had been switched to Canada, in reality the cars were as foreign-built as anything from the Orient. This factor created a minor dilemma for the author, as this book was to be about U.S. built Fords only. Still, a total of 134,103 Crown Victorias were sold this year, and since the series had been Ford's top line for so long, its inclusion was assured.

Taking full advantage of its $400 heavy-duty trailer towing package is this LTD Crown Victoria Station Wagon, Model 76. Featuring a less luxurious interior than the LX models, the plain LTD Crown line included the same three styles as found in the upscale versions. Thus, this wagon had a base price of $16,209, while the related wood-trimmed Country Squire version, Model 78, sold for $16,527. The LTD Crown Victoria 4-door Sedan, Model 73, wore a price of $15,851, while the "S" version, still intended for taxi, fleet, and police work, was based at $15,434. Crown Victorias were still rear-wheel drive, and were based on a chassis of 1145.3 inches. All used the 302 cubic inch V-8 of 150 horsepower hooked to a 4-speed overdrive automatic transmission. There were no engine or transmission options.

1989

In its promotional pieces this year, Ford described its new Taurus SHO Model 54 as "a raging bull." Standing for "Super High Output," the SHO models were powered by a dual overhead cam, 24-valve 3-liter (182 cubic inch) V-6 of 220 horsepower, hooked to a manual 5-speed transaxle built by Mazda. Dual exhaust and sequential multiport electronic fuel injection completed the picture. Essentially, the car filled the sales slot deserted by the former MT5, only it was miles ahead of the rather docile 4-cylinder MT5 in performance. Most expensive of all Taurus models, the SHO Sedan had a base list of $19,739. This meant it was well into the $20,000 range when all of the additives were administered, and thus was the most expensive Ford 4-door this year, exceeding even the LTD Crown Victoria by several thousand dollars. An exclusive front bumper and ground effects side panels and wheel opening surrounds were part of the exterior package.

Luxury liner of the Taurus herd was the LX Sedan, Model 53. Overall, it was quite similar to the SHO, but used as power the "cool" version of the 182 cubic inch V-6, here rated at 140 horsepower. The 24-valve V-6 was a SHO exclusive not available to the rest of the Taurus line, but those wanting more power could order the Thunderbird V-6 of 232 cubic inches. This engine, in its Taurus modification, would also turn out only 140 horsepower, but would provide a much tighter torque curve and thus noticeably better performance. Except for the SHO, all Taurus models used an automatic transmission, with the V-6 cars having a 4-speed with overdrive, while the 4-cylinder cars had a 3-speed. The well dressed LX also had a well dressed price, with the base tag being $15,282.

The two lower level Taurus station wagons were, like the sedan models, divided into L and GL sub-series. They were available only with the standard 182 cubic inch V-6 or the optional Thunderbird 232 cubic inch variation. All used the 4-speed overdrive automatic transaxle as standard equipment. These were the largest front-drive wagons in Ford's inventory. The nicely styled GL version sold for $13,544, while the basic L model cost $13,143. All featured such standard touches as a roof-top luggage rack, mandatory brake light above the liftgate, and dual remote rearview outside mirrors. This view gives a look at the Taurus rear gate, which could swing upward in one section, or operate like the traditional old style gates, with the top portion lifting and the lower portion forming a dropable tailgate.

The lower levels of the Taurus line were filled by the lowest L trim series, and the mid-range GL division shown here. These models could be identified by the lack of cornering lights in the front bumpers, and by a lack of lower bodyside molding and the accompanying signatures on the leading edge of the front doors. Instead, these models simply said "Taurus" in the beltline door trim. Both models were available with either the 4-cylinder engine and 3-speed automatic transmission, or the V-6 with its related 4-speed automatic. These were the only Taurus models to still use the 4-cylinder block. In this form, the GL cost $12,202. The 4-cylinder L model was the lowest priced Taurus and the only one under $12,000, with a base of $11,778. The V-6 option (182 cubic inch) was $672 more.

The top Taurus Station Wagon was the Model 58 LX version, which had a list price of $16,524. It was the only Taurus to use the 232 cubic inch V-6 as standard power, and thus had no engine or transmission options. All Taurus wagons could be fitted with a rear-facing third seat, thus converting them to 8-passenger vehicles. Taurus production went up by almost 7,700 this year, with 395,261 of the well-accepted mid-size cars entering the market. This made Taurus by far the best selling of all Ford lines.

Ford's big news of the year was the Probe. A rather conglomerate car, it had a superbly styled body engineered by Ford, but in the "Japanese" school of design, was built on the Mazda body platform, used a special Mazda drivetrain, and emanated from the Ford/Mazda plant at Flat Rock, Mich. The hot shot of the new line was the GT model, which used an intercooled turbocharged 2.2-liter (133 cubic inches) Four of 145 horsepower. This model was available only with the 5-speed manual transmission, came equipped with 4-wheel disc brakes with an optional anti-lock unit, and had an automatically adjustable performance suspension system. For exterior identification, it used its own exclusive front and rear bumper styling, with the air dam having built in fog lamps. On the inside, dual adjustable performance bucket seats offered lumbar adjustment. Most expensive of the new Probes, the GT Model 22 went for a base of $13,593.

More pragmatic than the GT were the two less potent Probes, the luxury-oriented LX and the basic GL models. Shown here, the LX Model 21 sold for $11,443, while the GL Model 20 was $10,459 in basic form. The cars used the same lower structure, engine, and drive system of the Mazda MX-6 Coupe. The standard engine in the two lower levels was a 12-valve Four which produced 110 horses. Although rated as a 4-passenger car, some references to the Probe called it a 2+2 coupe, because of its rather limited rear seat space. The car used a 99-inch wheelbase and at 177 inches was just slightly shorter than the Mustang. Acceptance was excellent, and Ford reported 133,650 sold in the first year...however, this referred to a calendar year, so true model year production is not known.

Still up on the sales ladder was the Tempo line of two and 4-door sedans, but this year production slipped slightly, probably due to the new Probe. Still, a grand total of 292,978 were turned out, which is no figure to cry over. Restyled last year, the Tempos were virtual carbon copies of the 1988 line this year. Sportiest of the line was the GLS 2-door Sedan, Model 33, which came with a 100 horsepower High Output version of the 140 cubic inch Four. It was priced at $9,697.

Of the six available Tempo models, only two 4-door sedans were based above the $10,000 price. They were the LX Model 37, shown here, and the AWD Model 39. The LX was the luxury oriented version, with a premium interior, blanked rear quarters, and a $10,156 price tag. The AWD (All Wheel Drive) continued to be based on the GLS trim level and used the High Output Four of that series. It was the most expensive Tempo at $10,860. The LX used the 98 horse version of the 140 cubic inch Four. However, even though this engine was rated at only two less horsepower than the High Output model, its torque curve, response factor, and overall performance were noticeably less than that found in cars with the HO block.

Showing off its new $1,178 Sport Appearance Group option is the Model 38 Tempo GLS 4-door Sedan. Tempo's answer to the Taurus SHO, the sport-oriented GLS sedan also came with the High Output electronically fuel injected Four as standard power. Still under $10,000, the GLS Sedan wore a base tag of $9,697. Among the features of the new sport-group were blackout panels for the rear quarter windows, rocker-panel and wheel cutout ground effects flares, and white cast aluminum wheels. The package was only available for the 4-door models, not the 2-door GLS.

The GL series continued to be home to the two low-level Tempo styles. They were the Model 31 2-door Sedan, shown here, and the Model 36 4-door Sedan. The 2-door was the lowest priced Tempo, with a tag of $9,057, while the 4-door was only slightly higher at $9,207. Standard even on these models was an electronic AM/FM stereo radio with digital clock, a center consolette, and the ergonomically designed instrument panel. This model is shown with the optional Special Value package, which included bright window surrounds and styled wheel covers. A 5-speed manual was standard on all Tempos, but a 3-speed automatic transaxle could be ordered for $515 extra.

Still visually apart from the rest of the Escort line was the performance-oriented GT 2-door Hatchback, Model 93. Escort's answer to the low-buck performance fan, the hot little car was the most expensive Escort with a base price of $9,315. For this, buyers received a High Output version of the 133 cubic inch (1.9-liter) Four, rated at 115 horsepower. Exclusive to the GT, the engine featured multi-point fuel injection. Also in the package were high-backed sport seats, cast aluminum wheels, a modified suspension, rear spoiler, flared ground effect rockers, and a unique face.

Continuing to be one of the most popular Escorts was the Model 91 2-door Hatchback. Priced at $7,349, the car used the same basic body as did the GT, but was fitted with the standard Escort slotted grille and used the traditional Escort Four of 90 horsepower. Similar to this model but even less trimmed was the lowest priced of all Escorts and the only one under the $7,000 mark. That was the Model 90 Pony 2-door, priced at $6,964. This year all Escorts received gas-charged struts all around for better handling, especially at higher speeds. Despite its continuing popularity, Escort's sales took a substantial nose dive of almost 60,000 this year, with the model year tally ending at 363,122.

The only wagon in the Escort line was the LX Model 98. The unchanged little work horse was priced at $8,280. At 2,312 pounds, it was actually one pound lighter than the 4-door sedan upon which its body was based. Escorts continued to have a wheelbase of 94.2 inches. The cars were 166.9 inches overall, while the wagons were one inch longer. All Escorts except the GT used throttle body fuel injection.

The 4-door Escort was available only as the LX Model 95, with no engine options. It also came with the 4-speed manual transaxle, but the 5-speed version was available for another $75. For still another $490, buyers could have a 3-speed automatic transaxle installed, and many did just that. And, for still another $235, they could avail themselves of power steering. As a basic 4-door, the Escort was priced at $7,679.

Not really a Ford in the true sense of this book, the Korean-built Festiva was nevertheless in the U.S. dealer's showrooms. And, if the now Canadian-built LTD Crown Victoria still qualifies for inclusion, it would seem that the Festiva could also sneak in, as did the German-built Fiesta. Now available with both a $450 automatic transmission and $235 power steering, the Festiva came in one body style and three trim levels. These were the low-buck $6,319 L; the $7,111 L-Plus, and this $7,759 LX.

With the exception of a new V-6 engine for the Probe LX and a revised face for the Probe GT, the 1990 model year read like a review of 1989. Styling on everything remained virtually the same, all models stayed in their appointed sales slots, and the only real change was the fact that prices again escalated to an ever higher plateau.

In fact, in a move that was almost unthinkable a couple of years ago, a Taurus sedan was now the most expensive Ford on the basic price roles, topping the dollar sign of even the most costly Thunderbird. Moving into the top money slot was the Taurus SHO Sedan, which now had a basic price of $21,505 or $21,633, depending on which list is used. This exceeded even the Thunderbird Super Coupe, which gave its base as $20,390, and in fact, was the only other Ford with a foundation of over $20,000.

For the big bucks, Taurus SHO buyers received the Yamaha-built 220 horsepower 24-valve V-6 with dual overhead cams and dual exhausts; a Mazda-built 5-speed manual transaxle; special performance handling package; anti-lock braking; cruise control; a driver-side air bag, and the special slotted air dam and ground effects rocker panels which from the exterior said "SHO."

Other Taurus models remained similar to the 1989 stock, except all were up in price. The driver-side air bag became standard with the optional tilt steering wheel. The 153 cubic inch (2.5- liter) 4-cylinder engine remained available for the L and GL models, but virtually all Taurus cars went out the door with a V-6. These could be either the standard 3-liter or a 3.8-liter Thunderbird type which was available to all but the base L sedan.

New for the year was a Taurus police package which included the 3.8 liter V-6 and disc brakes on all four wheels. Standard equipment in all Taurus models included a 3-speed automatic on the 4-cylinder cars and a 4-speed automatic on all V-6 models. The SHO was the only Taurus to have a manual transmission, and this unit was not available to other Taurus models, though it was used in the Thunderbird Super Coupe. Other standard Taurus equipment included air conditioning and power steering.

As mentioned, the Probe LX received the 140 horsepower V-6. This resulted in each Probe model having its own exclusive engine, with no engine options available to buyers. Thus, the Probe GL used the 110 horsepower basic Four of 133 cubic inches, while the Probe GT used the turbocharged version of this block, rated at 145 horsepower. The GT was one of the few 1990 models to have a distinctive frontal change, now sporting a rectangular grid in its bumper/air dam, as opposed to the slotted mouth of 1989. In addition, the car's bodyside molding became less obvious, while new flared rocker panels gave a hint of ground effect skirts.

Mustang, which now could celebrate 12 years in its current basic rear-drive form, also received virtually no new treatments save for the deletion of a tilt steering wheel; a standard driver-side air bag; map pockets in the door panels, and shoulder belts for rear passengers. The line continued to offer Ford's only convertible, once more producing it in both GT and LX forms. As before, the GT came only with the 302 V-8, while LX buyers had their choice of the basic 3.2-liter Four or the optional V-8.

Thunderbird, Ford's rear-drive luxury-oriented sport-type machine, also saw no changes, despite the line entering its 35th year. However, the lack of change probably could have been anticipated since the car went through a total revision in 1989. Still, to commemorate the 35th, a run of 5,000 Super Coupes were turned out as anniversary models. These were completely finished in black titanium paint, with black wheels, thin blue pin

No longer taking honors as Ford's most expensive car, the Thunderbird Super Coupe, Model 64, had to step back a place for...of all things...the Taurus SHO. Still, its base tag of $20,390 ranked the Super Coupe as one of only two Fords with a monetary foundation of over $20,000. Super Coupes had their own frontal treatment, with an exclusive bumper/air dam housing dual fog lights. On the sides and rear, exclusive ground effects rocker panels and lower front and rear panels identified the car as being one hot Bird. Power was by a 210 horse supercharged version of the 232 cubic inch (3.8-liter) V-6, running through a Mazda-built 5-speed manual transmission.

Luxury liner of the Thunderbird family was the LX Coupe, Model 62, which sold for $17,283. From the exterior, it was difficult to tell the LX from the more plain Model 60, which was priced $2,300 less. All Thunderbirds except the Super Coupe used a 140 horsepower version of the 232 V-6, coupled to a 4-speed automatic transmission. Ford's Thunderbird advertising this year stressed the fact that the car had been on the market for 35 years, and called attention to its overall developments which lead to the contemporary aerodynamic styling, exceptional ride and handling, and interior roominess. Although all Ford production was down this year, Thunderbird sales suffered the least, allowing a total of 113,957 Birds to leave the nest.

striping and no trim whatsoever except for argent ground effect rocker moldings. In retrospect, the cars were disappointingly dull looking, with only a small fender plate stating they were "Anniversary Thunderbirds." As before, the Super Coupe used an exclusive intercooled and supercharged version of the 232 cubic inch V-6, giving it 210 horsepower.

In the big car world, the LTD Crown Victoria did not change visually from the previous year, but some minor changes were noted. As a disappointment for people who still liked operable front vent windows, these were no longer available as an option. However, power windows now became a standard item, as did the formerly optional tilt steering wheel. Inside, the straight-back bench seat was now a two-piece unit, while the handy map pockets in the door panels were eliminated. As occurred in the other lines, the driver-side air bag became standard, as did shoulder belts for rear seat passengers.

The two little car lines, Tempo and Escort, changed very little also. The biggest news was that the Escort could no longer claim to be America's best selling car, as the new Honda Accord took away that honor. Both lines continued with their former trim levels, and the interesting little 4-wheel drive Tempo (AWD) was still available. It was the only Tempo to have mandatory 3-speed automatic transaxles, with all others having 5-speed manuals as standard, with the automatic being extra-cost optional.

The largest jolt of the year occurred in the sales arenas, where all cars this year took a beating from buyer apathy. Total sales dropped 374,912, going from 1,643,751 reported in 1989 to this year's 1,268,839.

As noted, Escort lost its top billing, with its sales dropping the most, going down 166,812, from 363,122 to a new low of 196,310. Tempo slid to 265,893, while Probe recorded only 109,898 sales. However, the Probe figures are confusing, as the 1989 figures were based on calendar year production, with the 1990 figures being on the usual model year configuration. Therefore, it is not known how much overlap with 1990 figures occurred in the 1989 tally. Even the popular Taurus took a slide, reporting only 333,001 sales, a slide of 62,260.

Of the rear-drive cars, Mustang was down by 81,580 to a low of 128,189. The LTD Crown Victoria also slipped by 12,512 to record only 121,591 sales. The least drop was noticed by Thunderbird, where relatively new styling plus 35th anniversary billing may have combined to keep sales at 113,957, a drop of only 911. The fact that this was a year of little change probably was a financial asset to Ford. At least no large expenditures were made during a time of substantial market shrinkage.

The Mustang LX series continued to offer two hardtop styles. They were this Hatchback, Model 41, which sold for $9,962, and the Notchback Coupe, Model 40, which was the lowest price Mustang at $9,456 basic price. At these figures, the cars were fitted with the 140 cubic inch Four of 88 horsepower. When housing the 225 horsepower 302 V-8, the model numbers remained the same, but the names and prices changed to LX Sport Notchback Coupe at $12,164 and LX Sport Hatchback at $13,007. V-8 models could be quickly ascertained by the "5.0" plate on the trailing edge of the front fenders, and by the dual exhaust pipes.

Not arriving until January, 1990, was the official "Thunderbird Anniversary" model, which essentially was a special trim version of the Super Coupe. The car had a run of only 5,000, all identical. The car was finished in black titanium paint, with a fine blue pin strip. Black wheels and an all-black interior were offset by an argent silver lower body section and a thin brushed aluminum ring around the wheels' outer edges. A special anniversary plate was located just aft of the front wheel cutout. The cast aluminum wheels were standard on Super Coupes, but were a $820 option on other Birds. However, the black units shown here were exclusive only to the anniversary model.

The GT series continued to be home to the two hot Mustangs, the Hatchback, Model 42, shown here, and the Convertible, Model 45. All GT units used the 302 cubic inch V-8 as standard power, with either a 5-speed manual or 4-speed automatic transmission. Exclusive frontal styling, cast aluminum wheels, performance suspension package, and special ground effects lower panels were part of the package. The hatchback was base priced at $13,986, while the GT convertible went for $18,805. New on all Mustangs was a driver air bag and rear seat shoulder belts.

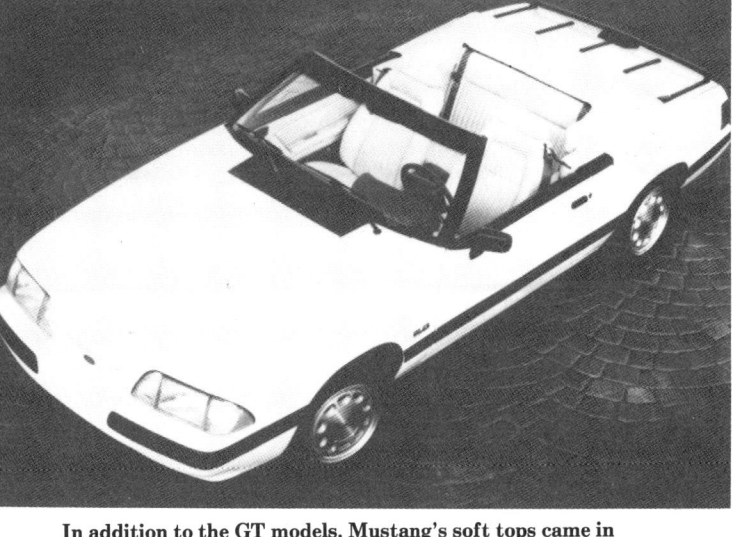

Little changed were Ford's big cars, the LTD Crown Victorias and the LX versions of these cars. Designated the Model 74 in LX trim the car sold for $17,894 as shown here, or for $17,257 in slightly more pragmatic Model 73 plain form. Also available was the fleet oriented S Model 72, which was based at $16,630. Though seldom seen without the vinyl brougham roof shown here, this feature remained a $665 option, while the often seen full leather seats were another $489, or $770 when power operated. LTDs were the only Fords rated at 6-passenger capacity.

In addition to the GT models, Mustang's soft tops came in two variations of the LX, Model 44. Seldom seen was the plain version with the 4-cylinder engine, which sold for $15,141. Far more popular was the LX Sport Convertible, seen here, with the 5-liter (302 cubic inch) V-8 engine, which sold for $18,183. This example is seen with the optional rear luggage rack, and the $500 optional natural leather seats. To keep pace with Thunderbird, Mustang also issued a special edition in January. Called the "25th Anniversary Model," the car was simply a 5-liter LX Convertible with a special green metallic finish; gold-finished cast aluminum wheels, and the white natural leather interior. Total Mustang production this year was 128,189, but no breakdown was made as to body styles or trim levels. However, Ford did announce that only 3,800 Anniversary Models were built.

Fitted with the heavy-duty trailer towing package, an option costing approximately $400, this LTD Crown Victoria could be found in either plain or LX fancy form. As the LX Model 77 it cost $18,418 with the dual facing rear seats, while as the plain LTD wagon, Model 76, it was priced at $17,841 as an 8-passenger or $17,668 as a 6-passenger wagon. The cast aluminum wheels shown on all LTDs in this section were a $440 extra, but were usually sold as part of a much larger package. In fact, few individual accessories or options were being marketed anymore, as most items were made part of large overall trim, performance, or convenience packages.

As always, the most expensive large Ford was the Country Squire Wagon, which was part of the LTD Crown Victoria line. It was available as the plain Model 78 for $17,921, or with the LX interior trim, as Model 58, for $18,805. The large Fords were the only models left to use an independent body set on top of a full, rear-drive conventional frame with coil springs all around. Power was by the 302 V-8 with a standard 4-speed automatic and 4-wheel power brakes. Power windows were now standard on all models, but the handy little front vent windows were no longer available as an option. Country Squires could be ordered as 8-passenger wagons, with dual facing rear seats for another $175.

Amazing a number of people was the fact that Ford's most expensive car of the year was not a hot Mustang or Thunderbird, or an ultra-luxurious LTD, but turned out to be a Taurus 4-door sedan. However, this was not just any Taurus. It was the SHO Model 54, powered by a dual overhead cam 24-valve V-6 built by Yamaha and running through a Mazda 5-speed manual transmission. Producing 220 horses, the engine and transmission combination was exclusive to the SHO, and was not available as an option on any other Ford product. Priced at $21,633 in basic form, the SHO was not only the most expensive Ford, but one of only two to break the $20,000 base mark. Dual exhausts, anti-lock braking, and special performance-oriented suspension aided in handling, while a new instrument cluster, special front and rear bumpers and air dams and lower body ground effects panels told the public that this was no ordinary Taurus.

The more pragmatic Taurus 4-door sedans came in three flavors. They were the basic L Model 50, the mid-level GL Model 52, and the luxury-oriented LX Model 53 shown here. All shared the same body, but the L and GL could be ordered with either the 2.5-liter Four and 3-speed automatic or the optional 3-liter V-6 and 4-speed automatic. The LX came only with the V-6, and was priced at $16,180. The GL cost $13,067 with the Four, while a similarly equipped L was the only Taurus under $13,000, with a base price of $12,594. With the V-6, both of these cars were about $700 more. Among the LX features not found on the other two sedans were power seats, windows, and door locks. A new accessory on all Ford cars this year was a compact disc player, listing at $500.

Luxury leader of the Taurus wagon family was the LX Model 53, which listed for $17,338. The 5-passenger wagon could be fitted with a rear facing third seat for three (tight squeeze) more passengers at $155 extra. The roof rack and dual outside mirrors were standard on this model, as were the cast aluminum wheels. However, these were a $280 option on GL wagons and supposedly not available on L models. All told, a total of 333,001 vehicles bearing the Taurus name were turned out this year, but no breakdown was made as to trim level or how many were wagons or sedans.

The hot one in the year-old Probe family of Japanese/American cars continued to be the GT Model 22. Powered by an exclusive turbocharged Four of 133 cubic inches, the sporty little car developed 145 horsepower. The standard transmission was the Mazda 5-speed manual, but this year the 4-speed automatic was also available. Revised front and rear styling and bodyside moldings helped identify the GT as a 1990 model. These included a new grille/air dam consisting of a very attractive grid pattern which encompassed the road lights, and movement of the parking lights to a spot near the outer ends of the bumper complex. Bodyside trim was simplified into a dual full-length embossed pattern, while a ground effects flare occupied the rocker area. Most expensive of the Probes, the GT sold for $14,726 and weighed 3,000 pounds even.

This GL Model 57 Taurus wagon has turned its back so that a good look can be taken of the vehicle's very practical rear design. Among its features are the vertical taillights, with backup lights forming the base of the lens; the high-mounted mandatory brake warning light, and the nicely handled two-piece gate. This unit could either be raised all in one section, or could be divided, with the all-glass upper portion swinging upward while the lower section dropped like a conventional tailgate. Taurus wagons were available only with the V-6 and 4-speed automatic, with the Four not being an option. As a GL, the wagon was base priced at $14,722, while the L version was $14,272. A powered sun roof was available on all Taurus models for an additional $750.

Because each Probe series had its own exclusive engine this year, there were no engine options in the Probe family, although buyers still had a choice of transmissions. Thus, the basic GL Model 20 used a fuel injected 133 cubic inch Four, which also served as the block for the GT's turbocharged unit, while the LX Model 21 shown here came in V-6 form only, running the same 182 cubic inch unit as found in the Taurus models. The GL was base priced at $11,470, while the LX, with its new 4-wheel powered disc brakes, was pegged at $13,008. Despite new frontal treatment, Probe sales slumped to 109,898. However, because this year's figures were on the traditional model year basis, while last year's Probe figures were on a rather meaningless calendar year, it is not known if this was a genuine slump or if the early 1990 Probe production had also been credited to 1989 figures. Probes continued to be built alongside Mazdas at that company's plant at Flat Rock, Mich.

Those interested in the 2-door compact Tempo had two versions to choose from. Snappiest of the duo was the GLS Model 33, shown here. Priced at $10,300, it was powered by the High Output 140 cubic inch Tempo Four which produced 100 horses. Similar in appearance, but powered by the standard Tempo 140 cubic inch Four of 98 horsepower was the GL Model 31, priced at $9,483. Both engines were Tempo exclusives, and not used in any other Ford. For those interested in a really sporty Tempo, either the two or 4-door GL could be ordered with the optional GLS Sport Package for an additional $1,178.

Dropping from its place as America's best selling car was the Escort, which this year had the sales honors taken away by the new Honda Accord. Ford officials were watching but not ready, and thus the 1990 Escorts followed the rest of the Ford field in being carbons of the 1989 offerings. However, Escort was being restyled, and new models would be issued in the spring, but not as late-90s . . . they would be titled as early 1991 styles. As before, the Escort GT, Model 93, remained the hottest of the little cars, and also the most expensive with a tag of $9,844. At the other end of the spectrum, but using the same basic body as the GT was the Pony Hatchback, priced at $7,402. As before, the GT had its own exclusive front styling, with slotted air dam and integral road lights. It also had its own High Output version of the 113 cubic inch Four, which developed 110 horsepower.

The Escort LX series continued to be the middle ground, and consisted of three separate styles. They were the 2-door Hatchback, Model 91, which used the same basic body as the Pony and GT; the 4-door Hatchback sedan, Model 95, and this Station Wagon, Model 98. Most expensive of the LX series, the wagon cost $8,737 while the sedan cost $8,136, and the 2-door was based at $7,806. All LX models and the Pony used the 90 horsepower version of the Escort's exclusive 1.9-liter block. The Pony and LX car models used a 4-speed manual transaxle, while the wagon and the GT used a 5-speed manual unit. An automatic transaxle remained available for an additional $515. Escort's overall sales slipped badly this year, dropping to 196,310.

Although the Tempo 2-door models came in only two levels, the 4-door sedans were available in four forms. Most luxurious was the LX Model 37 shown here, which booked at $10,605. Most expensive was the AWD (All Wheel Drive) Model 39, Ford's only 4-wheel drive passenger-type car, which had a base price of $11,331. More pragmatic were the GL Model 36 at $9,633 or the GLS Model 38 at $10,448. All used the manual 5-speed transmission except the AWD, whose 4-wheel drive configuration mandated the 3-speed automatic transaxle. In all other Tempos, the automatic was a $539 option. Both the GLS and the AWD used the High Output Four as standard power, while the LX and GL models were fitted with the standard Four. This year there were virtually no changes on the Tempo except for the addition of the new style wheels shown here.

Ford's little Korean-built Festiva received a new face this year, bringing it more into line with the rest of the Ford family. In addition to the frontal treatment, there were new taillight lenses on the rear, while under the hood an electronic fuel injection system and 5-speed manual transaxle appeared on all three models. Festivas used one base body, but were divided into three trim levels. These were the L Model 05 at $6,319; the L-Plus Model 06 at $7,111, and the LX Model 07 at $7,750. An automatic transaxle, similar to that used on the Escorts, was available for another $515, while power steering cost $235 extra.

A little car made the big news this year in Ford's camp, while in the animal barn, the Bird got more muscle while the horse got new shoes.

The main revision thrust was given to the Escort, which was due for a change, especially in the face of loosing its top sales billing to the Honda Accord and also slipping drastically in production. Actually appearing as a mid-1990 model, but titled as 1991 vehicles, the car was totally redone at a reported retooling cost of $600-million, and an overall cost including engineering of almost $2-billion. Still, the gamble paid off, and sales soared back to a comfortable 304,127, an increase of 107,817.

The new Escort remained at 170 inches overall length, but its wheelbase was now 98.4 inches, the result of the cars being built on a new Mazda body pan. However, production was not at Flat Rock, but remained at Wayne, Mich. On the exterior, subtle changes were made to the overall styling, while the new grille-less front definitely brought the car into the Taurus school of design. The exception to this was the GT model, which used asymmetrical slanted grille slots on the left side and a Ford emblem on the right side of the front panel.

Under the hoods, the main line of Escorts still retained the 113.5 cubic inch Four, but this was downrated to 88 horsepower from its previous 90. However, the engine now sported a new sequential multi-port fuel injection set up and computerized electronic ignition which did away with the conventional distributor.

Meanwhile, the GT model received a new and much smaller Four, produced by Mazda. This engine, had a bore and stroke of only 3.27x3.35 inches, resulting in a displacement of 109 cubic inches or 1.8-liter. Using 16 valves and dual overhead cams, the little screamer managed to turn out 127 horses. In the Ford family, the engine was exclusive only to the Escort GT, but it also appeared in Mazda's Protege. Along with the new mill, GT models could be ordered with a new automatic transaxle.

At the other end of the spectrum was the Thunderbird, which now had a new V-8 to crow about. After appearing only in V-6 form for the past two years, the additional cylinders were welcomed by those who still equated power, performance, and V-8 in the same thought. The engine was a variation of the standard 5-liter (302 cubic inches) that was used in Crown Victoria and the Mustang GT and LX5.0L models. However, in the Crown Victorias the block remained rated at 150 horsepower, while the Mustang's boosted the power up to 225 horses. Oddly, the new Thunderbird version fell between these two, and the Bird came out with 200 horses. The new V-8 was a $1,080 option in both the standard and LX Thunderbirds, but was not available in the Super Coupe which still used the supercharged 232 cubic inch V-6 of 210 horsepower. Aside from the engine addition, few changes were made in the overall Bird line.

The more sporty Mustang line received a set of new 16-inch 5-spoke alloy wheels, but little else was new in this barn despite the early hints of facial revision for the country's favorite horse. The car still came in coupe, hatchback, and convertible styles, and in GT, LX and LX5.0L Sport versions.

The Probe, Ford's poor-man's sports car based on Mazda pan and drive-train, still used three distinct engines for its three available versions. Since it had received a nice facelift in 1990, it was unchanged this year. The car still used a 99-inch wheelbase and was 177 inches long. Both the GT and LX models used 4-wheel disc brakes with anti-locking packages optional.

Also receiving new wheels was Ford's highest price car, the Taurus 4-door SHO (Super High Output) edition. Using an exclusive 24-valve Yamaha-built V-6 of 220 horsepower, the SHO listed at $22,071. It and the $20,999 Thunderbird Super Coupe were the only Fords in the $20,000 base range.

In the more tame Taurus models, a new 4-speed automatic transaxle was available for V-6 cars; the 4-cylinder engines of the L and GL series received a boost to 105 horsepower through a new sequential electronic fuel injection unit, and anti-lock braking was available on the wagons, as well as the sedans.

Just below the Taurus in size was the unchanged Tempo line, which still provided a home for the AWD, Ford's unique little 4-wheel drive sedan. Nicely accepted as it was, Ford saw no reason to change the Tempo in any way or form.

At the other end was the LTD Crown Victoria. These cars also were unchanged, but this time for good reason. After riding on the same basic 114.3-inch rear drive chassis since 1979, the big Ford's formal-styled body was finally due to be retired. In its place in 1992 would be a totally new Crown Victoria series, still using the 144.3-inch platform, but totally restyled in aerodynamic form. Also appearing for the last time were the LTD Crown Victoria wagons, which would not fit into the new styling mold. For this year, however, the cars remained as before, except that the LX wagons (regular and Squire) came only as 8-passenger vehicles with dual facing rear seats.

Although sales of the new vehicles should have been good, an overall poor economy led to substantial drop of 83,041 units, with model year sales ending at 1,185,798. Only the brand new Escort showed a market increase of 107,817, with the aforementioned 304,127 units going out the door. All other Ford lines suffered a decrease. These were: Thunderbird, 82,814, down 31,143; Crown Victoria, 85,532, down 36,059; Mustang, 98,737, down 29,452; Taurus, 302,197, down 30,424; Tempo, 218,197, down 47,696, and Probe, 93,814, down 16,084. Despite the poor figures, Ford managed to lead the country's automotive sales race, but on the dismal side was the fact that such things as expensive sales promotion, incentives, and overall cost increases caused the company to loose a record $2.3 billion this year. Happily, 1992 would show better results.

Exhibiting all of the traits of a performance car was the Thunderbird Super Coupe, Model 60. One of only two Fords with a base price over $20,000, the Super Coupe listed for $20,999 without extras. It had its own exclusive supercharged V-6 of 210 horsepower, and used a 5-speed manual transmission as standard. However, a 4-speed automatic was available for $595. Other special equipment on this model were 16-inch cast aluminum wheels; high performance tires; 4-wheel disc brakes with an anti-lock system; flared "ground effects" rocker panels, and special front and rear bumpers with integral air dams, containing embossed "SC" initials in the center.

A bit more tame than the Super Coupe were the other two Thunderbird offerings, the plain Coupe, Model 60, and the LX Model 62 shown here. Actually, outward appearances of the two models were just about the same. The base engine in both cars was a normally aspirated fuel-injected version of the 232 cubic inch V-6. However, either car could be equipped with the 5-liter V-8 of 200 horsepower for another $1,080. All Birds except the Super Coupes used a 4-speed automatic transmission. In base form, the plain coupe wore a $15,318 price tag, while the LX model was $17,334. The widely acclaimed anti-lock brake system cost another $700. Among the toys that differentiated the LX from the plain model were power everything inside, a tilt steering wheel, and an AM/FM stereo/tape system. Total Thunderbird production was down to 82,814 this year.

When it came to performance models, Mustang certainly ranked up there with its own GT models. Most expensive of all the hot horses was the GT Convertible, Model 45, which cost $19,864 in base form. Equipped only with the 5-liter V-8 (302 cubic inches) the car this year sported new 16-inch cast aluminum wheels of 5-spoke pattern, wearing Goodyear Eagle GT+4 high performance tires. The GT Mustangs continued to use their own exclusive frontal treatment, with a solid panel above the bumper and a wide 3-slot air dam below. Also new on the convertibles was a new electrically powered top design with a glass rear window, which allowed the top to settle more snugly into the body when in the down position.

Mustang's convertible models came in three versions, the aforementioned GT, the almost as hot LX 5.0L, and the plain LX. These latter two shared the same Model 44 designation, and differed only in the fact that the LX 5.0L was fitted with the same 225 horsepower V-8 as found in the GT, while the plain LX model ran with Ford's 2.3-liter (140 cubic inches) Four. No basic Four, the Mustang unit used twin spark plugs for each cylinder, was equipped with multi-port electronic fuel injection, and was rated at 105 horsepower. Despite the confusion caused by its 140 cubic inches being the same displacement as found in the Tempo Four, this engine was a Mustang exclusive, with a bore and stroke of 3.78X3.13 inches. As a Four, the convertible cost $16,222, while with the 5-liter it sold for $19,242. Dual exhausts and the "5.0" plaque ahead of the doors show that this model has the V-8.

More popular and less costly than the GT convertible was the companion Mustang GT Hatchback Coupe, Model 42. It sold for a base $15,034. All GT models wore the High Output 5-liter (302 cubic inches) sequential electronic fuel injected V-8 under the hood. This block put out 225 horsepower at 4200 rpm, and was rated at 300 lbs. ft/torque at only 3000 rpm. In addition to their distinctive faces, GT models were the only Mustangs to have flared rockers and ground effects styled lower panels with sculptured air vents ahead of the wheel wells. GT models also came with a standard performance suspension package and dual exhaust system.

Besides the GT, Mustang hardtops could be ordered in LX or LX 5.0L forms, and in either Hatchback or 2-door Sedan styles. Shown here is the 4-cylinder LX Hatchback, Model 41, which sold for $10,663. Its companion 2-door Sedan, Model 40, was the lowest price Mustang at $10,157. As LX 5.0L V-8 models, the sedan jumped in price to $13,270 while the hatchback rose to $14,055. LX and LX 5.0L models appeared virtually the same from the exterior, but the V-8s had the designation plaque on the rear section of the front fenders and ran a dual exhaust system. The standard Mustang wheels are shown here, but the new 5-spoke cast aluminum jobs on the GT and LX 5.0L models could be special ordered. Total Mustang production was only 98,737.

1991

Appearing for the last time in its classic "rectangular" design theme was the LTD Crown Victoria. Next year it would retain its 114.3-inch wheelbase and rear-drive chassis configuration, but its body would be a much more sleek aerodynamically designed unit, in keeping with the rest of the Ford line. For this year, however, the big Fords remained unchanged. The cars were still available as the fleet-oriented S Model 72 at $17,045; the mid-level Model 73 Sedan at $18,227, and the top-trim LX Model 74, shown here, with a base of $18,863. These cars were totally outfitted, with standard equipment including the 5-liter V-8; 4-speed automatic transmission; power steering and brakes; air conditioning; AM/FM stereo, and power windows. However, the brougham roof and turbine wheels seen here were still extra-cost options. With all Ford production except that of the Escort being down, The LTD Crown Victoria line could show only 85,532 sales overall, including wagons.

Exhibiting the potential of its 5,000-pound trailer towing package is this LTD Crown Victoria wagon. Despite the fact that dual electric remote control outside mirrors were standard on all big Fords, this owner has shown the wisdom of attaching wide fender-mounted mirrors in order to see around the trailer. The plain sided wagons came in two versions, the Model 76 at $18,083, or the LX Model 77, which at $18,833 was available only in 8-passenger form with dual facing rear seats. The extra rear seats could also be added to the plain wagon as a $215 option. Because of the new style Crown Victorias that would appear in 1992, this was the last year for the large Ford wagons. Thus another great but now slightly archaic automotive style was gone for good.

Once more holding claim to being the most expensive of all Fords (not counting L-M products) was the Taurus SHO Sedan, Model 54. Standing for Super High Output, the SHO models continued to use their exclusive 24-valve V-6 with dual overhead cams and six sequential injectors. The Yamaha-built engine was hooked to a Mazda-built 5-speed transaxle, and coupled to a performance-oriented suspension system to produce what can best be described as an "executive's sports car." There were no engine or transmission options on this model. The exterior was fitted with enough exclusive units (wheels, rockers, grille, air dam, and bumpers) to say that this was not the ordinary Taurus sedan. And to prove it, a basic price of $22,071 made it the top gun on Ford's price list.

After wearing the "Country Squire" designation since 1951, Ford's top of the line wagons ended their 41-year life span with hardly a notice. First used on the 1951 2-door wagon trimmed in real wood, the Country Squire title had always stood for Ford's prestige wagon, and probably was the best recognized of any wagon nomenclature ever devised. But, like the plain-sided wagon, the old rectangular shape had no place in the new and sleek Crown Victoria line that would appear in 1992. Again, the Country Squire was divided into the standard 6-passenger Model 78, at $18,335 base, or the LX Model 79, which came in 8-passenger form only. With its $19,085 base, it was the only Crown Victoria to reach into the $19,000 range. This year all LTD Crown Victorias were finished in a new clearcoat metallic paint.

Available only in V-6 form was the LX series of Taurus models. Most luxurious and costly of all Taurus sedans, not counting the SHO, of course, the Model 53 LX Sedan had a base price of $17,373. Its power came from a 182 cubic inch V-6, but a 140 horse version of the 232 cubic inch V-6 was optional. New this year and standard on all Taurus models except the SHO was a 4-speed automatic transaxle with electronic shifter and overdrive lockout. Anti-lock brakes were standard, as were power seats, windows, and door locks.

This year it was the luxury wagon of the Taurus line, but next year it would be the best that Ford had to offer in non-utility station wagon design. Most expensive of all non-SHO Taurus styles, the LX Model 58 wagon wore a base price of $18,963. For this, buyers received all of the standard equipment found on the LX sedan, in addition to having the 232 cubic inch V-8 as the only engine available. For the first time this year, an optional anti-locking brake system was available to Taurus wagons. The rear gate continued to consist of an upper all-glass lift portion, while the lower unit was a conventional tailgate.

1991

The GL series continued to be the middle ground for the Taurus insofar as trim level was concerned. Here demonstrating how easily it could squeeze out of a tight parking space, the GL Sedan, Model 52, could be ordered in 4-cylinder form for $13,582, or with the 182 cubic inch V-6 for $14,103. Its station wagon version, the Model 57, was available only in V-6 form, with the 182 being standard and the 232 cubic inch block being an option on both the sedan and wagon. With the base engine, the wagon cost $14,990.

A more simplified strip of side molding says that this is the Taurus L Sedan, Model 50, which represented the lowest trim level of the line. With a basic 4-cylinder price of $13,352, it also represented the lowest price Taurus on the list. When ordered with the small V-6, its price rose to $13,873. It too had its station wagon companion, Model 55, which like all Taurus wagons, could be obtained only with the V-6. Apparently Ford felt there was just not enough power in the Four to handle the extra weight of a fully loaded wagon, despite the fact that in bare form, the wagons weighed only about 200 pounds more than the 3,100 pounds recorded by the average Taurus sedan. The basic L wagon cost $14,784.

The lack of rectangular grille pattern beneath the slotted hood says that this is the Probe LX, and not the more powerful turbocharged GT. The LX could be considered the Probe's intermediate level. Available only with the 145 horse V-6 of 182 cubic inches (3-liter), the car registered a base price of $13,229. Despite costing over $1,500 less than the GT, it still offered many of the high-buck items of the more sporty car, such as 4-wheel independent suspension and 4-wheel power disc brakes. Those wanting a sporty appearance in a lower performance and price range could opt for the similar looking Probe GL. At $11,691 base price, this car offered the visual effects of the higher price Probes, but used a 110 horse 12-valve model of its 2.2-liter Mazda-built Four that turned out 110 horsepower. Thus, once more, there were three Probe models, each with its own exclusive engine.

It might have been touted as a poor man's answer to the Super Coupe, but with its base price of $14,964 the Probe GT was far from being an economy car. Still powered by a turbocharged version of the 133 cubic inch (2.2-liter) Four, the Probe continued to squeeze 145 horsepower from its Mazda-built engine. Built at Mazda's plant at Flat Rock, Mich., the Probe GT enjoyed a fine reputation among those who liked quick little cars. In fact, it was considered by many to be among the finest front-wheel drive performance cars in its price class. Four-wheel power disc brakes were standard on all GT and LX Probes, with an optional anti-lock braking system being about $700 more. A popular option on all Probes were the genuine leather seats, which added $490 to the cost. Total Probe production reached only 93,814 this year.

Appearing for the last time this year was the Tempo AWD, Ford's only 4-wheel drive non-utility sedan. Finding that most buyers of 4-wheel drive vehicles preferred the rugged construction and appearance of utility types such as the Bronco and Explorer to the civility of a somewhat plush sedan, Ford decided to discontinue the model at year-end. Never cheap, the Tempo AWD Model 39 had a base price of $11,390, making it the most expensive of the Tempo line. Available only in 4-door form, it was powered by the 100 horsepower HSO version of the 140 cubic inch Tempo Four.

Tempo's luxury liner continued to be the LX, available only as the 4-door Model 37, and priced at $10,663. Oriented toward comfort rather than performance, this car and the GL series used the basic 2.3-liter Four of 98 horsepower. The engine featured computer controlled multi-port electronic fuel injection and high-swirl combustion (HSC) head design. Because both this and the 100 horse Tempo block, and the 4-cylinder Mustang block all were of 140 cubic inch displacement, it is often thought that they were all variations of the same engine. Actually, they were quite different, with the Tempos having their own exclusive Four of 3.7x3.3 inch bore and stroke, while the Mustang had its own exclusive mill of 3.78x3.13 inch bore and stroke.

Beyond the AWD and LX Tempos lived the more popular series of GLS, GL and L models. In the 4-door family, the Model 38 GLS and the Model 36 GL shown here varied primarily in engine selection, with the GL and L models using the 98 horsepower Four while the GLS used the same 100 horse variation as found in the AWD. Both engines used multi-port electronic fuel injection. All Tempos used front wheel drive, a 4-wheel independent suspension system with gas pressurized struts, and rack-and-pinion steering. Of these three models, the GLS 4-door was the most expensive, at $10,506, while the L was the least expensive at $8,449. The GL fell between the two at $9,691.

Tempo 2-door sedans were not found in AWD or LX form, but only in the GLS, GL, and L sub-series. All were nice looking little 2-doors, sharing the same 5-passenger body, but varying only in trim, and a higher horsepower engine for the GLS. The GLS also had a stereo tapedeck as standard equipment. The GLS Model 33 was priced at $10,358; the GL Model 31 shown here had a base of $9,541, and the L Model 30 was the lowest price Tempo at $8,306. Essentially unchanged over the years, Tempos continued to use a 99.9 inch wheelbase and had an overall length of 177 inches.

Totally redesigned was the new Escort line which was now being produced on a Mazda-built bodypan. The performance number of the line continued to be the GT Model 12, available only in hatchback form. In addition to its exclusive looks, the car went through a total overhaul. Among its features were an all new independent front and rear suspension; 4-wheel disc brakes, and 15-inch cast aluminum wheels with all-season performance tires. Though keyed for the sport-type driver and normally fitted with a manual 5-speed transaxle, the GT for the first time this year could be ordered with an automatic transaxle. Priced at $11,484, under the hood was a brand new Mazda engine of only 109 cubic inches (1.8-liter). Still, this little screamer was fitted with dual overhead cams, had 16 valves, and managed to turnout 127 horses. Exclusive to the Escort GT in the Ford family, a variation of this engine was also found in the Mazda Protege.

Benefitting from its new total styling package was the Escort LX Station Wagon, Model 15. Although it used the same new Mazda-built floor pan with 98.4-inch wheelbase, the wagon was one inch longer than the Escort cars, stretching out to 171 inches. Despite the switch to Mazda drive and pan components, production of the Escorts remained at Wayne, Mich., and unlike the Probe, was not done at Mazda's Flat Rock plant. Despite its larger size, the wagon was not the heaviest Escort. That honor went to the GT, which weighed 2,458 pounds as opposed to the wagon's 2,411. In base form, the wagon cost $9,680. However, the roof rack and rear wipers shown here were extra-cost options.

A lower cowl, lower belt line, and larger glass area all were included in the new look being enjoyed by the Escort LX 4-door Sedan, Model 14. Also called the 4-door Hatchback or 5-door Sedan, the car continued to utilize the interesting little C-pillar window behind the rear door. However, neither this nor the rear door vent pane were operational. Although the Escort GT received a new and forceful engine from Mazda, the remainder of the family continued to use the line's exclusive 113.5 cubic inch Four, but this was now downrated to 88 horsepower from its former rating of 90 horses. Still, the engine now sported a new sequential multiport fuel injection unit with computerized electronic ignition.

Once again the 2-door hatchback style provided the base for the GT, LX, and Pony Escorts. Shown here in LX form, the car varied very little from the Pony, but could not be mistaken for the GT as that unit had an entirely different face. As an LX, the car was the Model 11, priced at $8,667. The Pony, Model 10, was the lowest priced Escort and the only one under $8,000, with a base tag of $7,976. Automatic transaxle, air conditioning, and power steering were among the items that could be added to all Escorts, but were seldom found on the Pony models.

In mid-1991, in order to boost Escort's performance image, a new Cayman GT was introduced. Available only for the remainder of the year, the Cayman was essentially a special trim package which included exclusive cast aluminum wheels, leather wrapped steering wheel, special floor mats, and other minor exclusive trim items. Its engine was the same 127 horsepower 16-valve Four as used in the regular GT.

After getting a slight facelift in 1990, the virtually unchanging Korean-built Festiva remained a carbon of last year. Once more the car was available in two models, the L and the GL, shown here. The GL, Model 06, was priced at $7,460. It featured a new monochromatic paint theme this year, while inside there were fully-reclining bucket seats. A 5-speed manual transaxle with overdrive was standard. Keyed only to the economy minded, the car offered gas ratings of 35 mpg city and 41 mpg highway.

The lowest price car in the Ford dealerships was the Korean-built Festiva L Model 05, which listed at $6,620 and was the only Ford item in the $6,000 range. However, if a buyer added such things as an automatic transaxle, air conditioning, power steering, a sun roof, and a stereo tape deck, he had a mini-car reaching easily for the $9,000 mark. Built on a platform of 90.2-inch wheelbase, the Festivas were 141 inches long overall. The 80.7 cubic inch (1.3-liter) engine was rated at 63 horsepower.

After being hinted at for well over a year, the new Crown Victoria appeared in mid-1991, but as a 1992 style. Before its arrival, two schools of prediction were evident. The first, including the author, thought (hoped) it would look like a slightly downsized Lincoln Town Car, or at least like the Continental. Others assumed it would simply be an overgrown Taurus. When the car made its early arrival debut in March, 1991, it proved both groups wrong or right. Actually, the car looked like a Taurus that had been sired by a Town car, or vice versa. Apparently Ford's designers had attempted to take the best of both designs and blend them into one sleek and good looking sedan...and they succeeded.

Overall, the car displayed obvious wedge-shaped styling and definitely said "I am a Ford." Its frontal treatment was in line with everything else in the Ford family. Gone was the distinctive grille and quad headlights, replaced by a sloping hood with a small center Ford emblem at its leading edge. Head, parking, and signal lights lived in elongated pods which wrapped around the edges of the very rounded fender areas. Just above the bumper rub strip, and actually a part of the bumper theme, was a small air slot divided into six sections by small vertical bars. Another much larger air intake lived under the bumper complex, in what could be considered an air dam position. The rub strip itself completely surrounded the car, becoming part of the side molding and continuing around the rear bumper.

At the rear, a large and nicely styled trunk section hinted strongly of Lincoln, while the taillight units wrapped around the softly curved rear fender edges in a simulation of the headlight lenses. The license was recessed deeply into the center of the lower bumper area. The greenhouse area was finished in black surrounds, and used the same interesting C-pillar window as found on the Taurus. Overall, the car continued its separate chassis and body concept, using a frame very similar to that of the former Crown Victoria. However, despite the industry-wide downsizing trend, the wheelbase grew a fraction, going from 114.3 inches to 114.4 inches, while the length grew by two inches, now being 213 inches overall.

Under the hood things also changed. Totally new for the car was a new V-8, down in size but up in horsepower. This was the 4.6-liter (281 cubic inches) block that had initially be introduced on the Lincoln Town Car in 1991, and now in the Ford family was the exclusive property of the Crown Victoria. Using dual overhead cams, electronic fuel injection, and other state of the art engineering, the smaller block turned out 190 horsepower in basic form and was later rated at 210 horses for the police special and the mid-season Touring Sedan. Still available was the former 302 cubic inch V-8, but this remained the property of the Thunderbird Sport Coupe and the Mustang GT and LX 5.0L models, where it was rated at 200 and 225 horsepower respectively. The 302

was not available in the new Crown Victoria.

Initially the Crown Victoria came out in standard and LX forms but at mid-season a new Touring Sedan was offered. This was a performance oriented 6-passenger car, with the usual automatic transmission, but having the 210 horse V-8; dual exhausts; heavy suspension; anti-lock brakes, and a special interior with power windows and seats and cruise control. In a strange bit of planning, especially since General Motors had just come up with a whole fleet of full-size wagons to spread across its spectrum, the new Crown Victoria line did not have any wagon models. The classic big Ford wagons of bygone years, which had once enjoyed the reputation of being America's most popular station wagons, had disappeared, and the famous old names of Country Squire, Country Sedan, and Ranch Wagon were gone from the scene.

Also going through an overall sheetmetal change, though just about unnoticed, was the Taurus. The reason for the lack of notice was that the change, though total, was so subtle that the cars almost looked the same as previous models. This was in keeping of Ford's "family resemblance" policy, but it did little to help differentiate one series from the previous models. Still, the Taurus got a new face with head/fog/signal light combinations now being in even more elongated pods. The bumpers received minor modifications, and the front and rear metal became even more rounded. Most interesting was the line's growth. Even though the wheelbase remained at 106 inches, the car's overall length went up three inches to a new measurement of 192 inches, while the wagons expanded five inches to a new total of 194. The width of both car and wagons also increased one inch, now being 72 inches.

In line with the new styling and growth, the 4-cylinder basic engine option was dropped. Now all Taurus models held V-6s, with all models using the basic plant of 140 or 145 horsepower, and the SHO having its own Super High Output version of 220 horses. Deleted was the electronic dashboard option, but in its place was the provision for a passenger-side air bag.

Escorts also received some recognition, this time in the form of a new body style. This was a 4-door Sedan, which sounds strange in light of the fact that there had been a 4-door in the Escort line for years. But this model was a true 4-door with a well defined trunk area rather than the 4-door hatchback sedan, which often was called a 5-door sedan. The hatchback style was also continued, while the new "real" sedan split into LX and LX-E models, with the latter having 4-wheel disc brakes, heavier suspension, and the same 127 horsepower Four with dual cams as was found in the GT models.

The Thunderbird nest began to get crowded again as a new Sport Coupe edition was created for this year only. Slotted in price between the LX and the standard models, the Sport Coupe essentially was the standard model fitted with a few extra goodies, including dual exhaust and the 210 horse version of the 302 cubic inch V-8 rather than the 140 horse V-6 worn by the plain and LX Birds. This engine was also available as a $1,080 option on the plain and LX models.

Also on the receiving end of new engines was the Tempo line, which for the first time could be ordered with a V-6. Formerly relegated only to its exclusive 140 cubic inch Fours, all Tempos could now avail themselves of the same 182 cubic inch V-6 as found in the Probe LX and plain Taurus models. However, in Tempo guise, this block was downrated to 135 horsepower. The new V-6 was standard in the two GLS models, but was a $685 option in the other three styles.

Ford's two semi-sport lines, the rear wheel drive Mustang and front wheel drive Probe, were essentially untouched except for a few new options and some switching and repackaging of option groups. The Mustang line still was the only Ford to carry a convertible style, while the Probe line was the only one to have an exclusive engine for each of its three distinct series.

The world of numbers came to a grinding halt this year, as production figures became conflicting and meaningless. A major part of this confusion came about from the sources attributed to the cars, with some models being built exclusively in Canada, Mexico, or Korea, and others being built in part in Japan, the U.S., and Europe. Thus, it not only became impossible to ascertain how many of a given model were built, it also became impossible to define an "American made" car simply because its components came from so many different sources.

Once more the Super Coupe could boast of being the hottest of the Thunderbirds and also the most expensive. Designated the Model 64, and base priced at $22,046, the Super coupe continued to use an intercooled supercharged 232 cubic inch V-6 of 210 horsepower as its exclusive engine. Not available to any other Ford, the 3.8-liter mill developed 315 lbs./ft. of torque at 2,600 rpm, giving the Super Coupe the performance to match its reputation. The transmission remained a 5-speed manual, while 4-wheel power disc anti-lock brakes and automatic ride control suspension helped in safety and handling. Also standard on this model were the 16-inch cast aluminum wheels shown here. However, these could be purchased as a $306 option on other Thunderbirds.

Luxury liner of the Thunderbird family was the LX Coupe, Model 62. Not oriented toward performance, the car used the same basic 140 horsepower 3.8-liter V-6 with sequential multi-port electronic fuel injection as found in the standard coupe. It also had the 4-speed automatic overdrive transmission, and the standard styled wheel covers shown here. New for the year was a front bumper complex that was very similar to the one used on the Super Coupe, thus bringing all Thunderbirds into an almost identical visual mold. Luxury features included 6-way powered bucket seats, powered windows and door locks, tilt steering wheel, cruise control, illuminated entry system and other interior luxury fittings. However, the AM/FM stereo system was no longer part of the package, but once more became an option.

Sitting in the rain-soaked parking lot of Motorbooks International of Osceola, Wis., is the latest Ford to come under the author's control. It is this leased Thunderbird Sport Coupe, Model 60, which was fitted with the 302 cubic inch V-8 of 200 horsepower. Appearing only this year, the Sport Coupe designation was a reincarnation of a V-8 title not used since 1988. Essentially the car was the same as the standard coupe, also Model 60, but with the V-8 rather than the 3.8-liter V-6. The car was base priced at $18,611 as opposed to the $16,345 base tag of the standard coupe. Surprisingly, for 1993, both the standard and Sport Coupe would disappear. Thoroughly impressed with the Sport Coupe, the author considers it an excellent handling and riding car.

Virtually unchanged, the Mustang continued its GT series as its top-line models. The series consisted of this Model 41 Hatchback and the Model 45 Convertible, which at $20,199 was not only the most expensive Mustang, but also the only one with a base price in the $20,000 range. The GT Hatchback was based at $15,243. Both GT models used the High Output 5-liter V-8 as standard power, and were fitted with the manual 5-speed transmission, with overdrive. An optional automatic could be fitted for $595. Special GT styling still included an exclusive front with integral fog/road lamps, a rear spoiler, and flared ground effects rockers and front and rear air dams.

When the new Crown Victorias first appeared in March, 1991, as early-release 1992 models, the LX Sedan, Model 74, was the top of the line. Priced at $20,87, it essentially was the regular LTD dressed in a luxury interior package which included all of the power and audio features expected on a top line car. The Crown Victorias all came with 4-speed automatics, power steering and brakes, and air conditioning, but under the hood was a new V-8 of 281 cubic inches (4.6-liter) which had been introduced on the Lincoln Town Car in 1991. Exclusive only to the Crown Victorias, this engine was first rated at 190 horsepower, but later issued in a 210 horse version when the Touring Sedan and the new police package appeared. The spoked cast aluminum wheels shown here were standard on both the LX and the Touring Sedan.

Appearing several months after the introduction date of the new Crown Victoria was the second most expensive model in the entire Ford line. It was the Crown Victoria Touring Sedan, Model 75, which was priced at 23,832 in basic form. Designed for those buyers who felt that driving should be more than simply getting from point A to point B, the Touring Sedan was equipped with a performance-oriented suspension; dual exhausts; anti-lock brakes; a special interior with power everything, and a new 210 horsepower version of the line's new 4.6-liter V-8. Essentially, this was the same performance and handling package used on the Police Specials, but coupled with an ultra-luxurious interior. Possibly because of its price, and apparently because it was not as popular as Ford would have liked, the Touring Sedan was not continued into the 1993 year.

Mustang's LX and LX 5.0L series continued to be identical except for the power train. The LX used its own exclusive 140 cubic inch Four of 105 horsepower while the LX 5.0L used the same 302 cubic inch V-8 (5-liter) and performance drivetrain as found in the GT models. In fact, with less weight to carry, the LX 5.0Ls actually were slightly better performers than were the hotter looking GT models. Both LX and LX 5.0L styles shared the same model numbers, with the same three styles appearing in 1992 as had in previous years. In the LX series, the base prices were $10,215 for the Model 40 Coupe; $10,721 for the Model 41 Hatchback, and $16,899 for the Model 44 Convertible. In LX 5.0L form the coupe was $13,422, the hatchback ran $14,207, and the convertible shown here was $19,644. LX 5.0L models were identified by the "5.0" plate on the front fender.

Showing off its nicely styled rear is this standard Crown Victoria, Model 73, which listed at $19,563. Although enjoying totally new styling, Crown Victorias (the LTD prefix was dropped) still were built with an independent body fastened to a conventional frame. Surprisingly, not only were the interior dimensions larger than on the previous models, the cars themselves grew two inches and now were 213 inches overall. The model shown here wears the conventional wheel covers, which were a far cry in appearance from the beautiful new spoked cast aluminum wheels which were a $440 accessory in the plain series. Despite a continuation of the rear-drive conventional chassis, Ford decided not to have a big wagon model available this year.

Once again the most expensive Ford of all was the Model 54 Taurus SHO (Super High Output) which sold for $23,839, or $7 more than the Crown Victoria Touring Sedan. The car was still powered by the Yamaha-built 24-valve dual overhead cam V-6 of 220 horses, hooked to a manual 5-speed Mazda-built transaxle. Also in the package were anti-locking 4-wheel powered disc brakes and a performance suspension and handling system. For the less sporty, a 4-speed automatic transaxle was available. Saying that this was not a car to entice into a drag race was an exclusive frontal design, similar to but still different than that of the regular Taurus.

Showing off its all-new sheetmetal and its new 194-inch total length (5 inches longer than in 1991) was the Taurus LX Station Wagon, Model 58. With the demise of the Crown Victoria wagons, this model became the top wagon, comparable to the old Country Squire but without the imitation wood trim. This was the only Taurus model to use the 232 cubic inch V-6 as standard equipment. Priced at $19,464, it came complete with the roof rack shown here, as well as a lockable under-floor compartment for carrying valuables such as cameras, etc. when traveling. The standard 60/40 rear seat allowed the major or minor portion of the back seat to be folded independently for carrying long cargo, while permitting the remainder of the seat to remain upright for passenger capacity. The rear glass could be raised independent of the rest of the gate, or the entire unit could be raised in one piece.

Essentially a SHO without the "go," the Taurus LX 4-door Sedan, Model 53, represented the luxury element of this mid-size front wheel drive line of super-popular cars. Standard equipment on this model included variable-assist power steering, bucket seats, a center console, 4-speed automatic transaxle, and optional anti-lock 4-wheel disc brakes. However, power was by the standard 140 horsepower V-6 used in all other Taurus models except when the $555 V-6 of 232 cubic inches was ordered. The all-new sheet metal also lengthened the sedans, but not as much as the wagons. They now measured 192 inches overall, an increase of three inches.

Appearing for the last time this year was the lowest series of Taurus models. This was the L Series, consisting of this Model 50 4-door Sedan and the companion Model 55 Station Wagon. Still holding claim to being one of the world's best selling families, the Taurus now offered an optional passenger-side air bag for $415 extra. Since the L and the GL models had come so close in trim level, and otherwise were identical to each other, Ford felt it wise to drop the L series at the end of 1992. For this year, the cars were base priced at $14,980 (the only Taurus below $15,000) while the wagons came in with a base of $16,013.

The GL series remained the mid trim level in the Taurus ranks for this final year. It consisted of the Model 52 4-door Sedan shown here, and the Model 57 Station Wagon, shown partially in the background. The wagon used the same divided rear seats and hidden storage compartment as the LX, but did not have the higher model's rear cargo net or remote fuel door. Benefitting from its new size, the wagon now offered 38 cubic feet of cargo space when the rear seat was raised, or 81 cubic feet with the rear seat completely folded. The sedan was base priced at $15,280 while the wagon went for $16,290.

Still wearing a distinctive frontal appearance, and still using its own exclusive turbocharged version of the 2.2-liter (133 cubic inch) Four was the Probe GT, Model 22, one of Ford's faster vehicles. Rated at 145 horsepower, the engine was hooked to a manual 5-speed transaxle, while power was through a tuned competition-type suspension, complete with 4-wheel disc brakes. Flared ground effects rocker panels and cast aluminum wheels also added to the unique package, which had a basic shelf price of $14,857.

Both the LX and GL Probes were destined to disappear at the end of the year, to be combined into one 1993 model simply called Probe. This year however, the cars looked quite similar, but were totally different under the hoods. The Model 21 LX, base priced at $13,257, was powered by the same 145 horsepower 182 cubic inch (3-liter) V-6 as found in the Taurus LX wagon. It also had a rear deck spoiler and was fitted with 15-inch cast aluminum wheels. The GL Model 20, meanwhile, retained the regularly aspirated 110 horsepower Four of 133 cubic inches (2.2-liter). It was the least expensive Probe at $12,257. All three Probe engines would be replaced in 1993.

Appearing for the last time this year was the Tempo GLS series, which now featured the 140 horsepower 3-liter V-6, marking the first time a Tempo had anything but a Four under the hood. Also included was an enhanced performance suspension system with a rear stabilizer. This combination would be available in 1993, but as an option package, not as a separate model. This year the GLS came in two styles, the 4-door Model 38 and this 2-door Model 33. The 4-door was the most expensive Tempo, based at $12,800, while the 2-door wasn't far behind at $12,652. This year's Tempos also came up with a new frontal unit, with twin slots set at the lower edge of the grille panel, and larger air slots above and below the redesigned bumper/air dam. On the GLS models, a special air dam held integral fog/road lights, while a special rear spoiler graced the trunk deck.

Once more the luxury liner of the Tempo family was the LX, available only as the Model 37 4-door Sedan. Priced at $11,115, the car featured dual powered side mirrors, power door locks, polycast wheels, and tilt steering wheel among its luxury features. New for the year was a sequential electronic fuel injection system for Tempo's exclusive 140 cubic inch (2.3-liter) Four. The new injectors supposedly gave better performance, but still the engine was downrated to 96 horsepower from its previous 98. New for the year were the taillight lenses, which now had more wrap-around. Tempos lost one model with the demise of the AWD (All Wheel Drive) sedan, which never had been a popular option.

Rounding out the Tempo line was the GL series, consisting of the 4-door Model 36 and this 2-door Model 31. The 4-door was priced at $10,137, while at $9,987, the 2-door was the lowest price Tempo and also the only one with a base under five figures. In regular form, the GL models used the High Swirl Combustion Four, now downrated to 96 horsepower despite the new electronic fuel injection. However, the new V-6 option could be ordered for an extra $685. The V-6 was the same 182 cubic inch model found in the Taurus family, but when used in the Tempo it was rated at only 135 horsepower.

Tempo GL 2-Door in Black.

Not to be outdone by the new Crown Victoria, the Escort line also got a new model, albeit one that looked quite similar to former styles. It was this 4-door Sedan, Model 16, which was a true sedan with separate trunk and deck, and not a hatchback. The new style was available in two flavors, the most exotic being the LX-E shown here. Priced at $11,933, this most expensive of all Escorts was distinguished by using the same dual overhead cam 1.8-liter 16-valve Mazda Four as found in the GT models. Also in the package was the competition suspension system and 4-wheel disc brakes of the GT. However, the sedan did not use the GT's exclusive frontal treatment.

More sedate than the LX-E was the plain LX Escort 4-door Sedan, Model 13. Although the new sedan was similar to the 4-door hatchback, it was 171 inches long, or one inch longer than the hatchback models and one inch shorter than the station wagon. Its new styling also put it above the 4-door hatchback in base price, with the sedan going for $9,795 while the Model 14 hatchback was tagged at $9,483. Unlike the 4-door hatchback, which used small triangular windows in the C-panel, the new sedan used a simple straight C-pillar at the rear. The vent panes in the rear doors were non-functional.

Continuing to provide the foundation for the GT, Pony and LX styles was the 3-door hatchback body. Shown here in Model 11 LX form, the car continued to offer a fully folding rear seat, converting the rear area into total cargo space. The car was priced at $9,055 as an LX model, but in Pony or standard form was tagged at $8,355 to be Ford's only domestic product under $9,000. Although the Pony name had been around since 1986 as a designator for the lowest price Escort, Ford began to phase out the title this year, referring to the car simply as an Escort. All 3-door models continued to use flip-out rear quarter windows.

The largest Escort in terms of size was the station wagon, available only in LX form. The wagon measured 172 inches overall. Priced at $10,067, it offered a split 6/40 folding rear seat similar to that found on Taurus wagons. With the rear seats up, the car offered 30.6 cubic feet of cargo space, while with the rear seats full folded, the usable stowage area increased to 66.9 cubic feet. A roller-type of cover ran from the tailgate to the rear seat backs to hide luggage. Both the roof rack and the rear window wiper shown here were part of the optional Wagon Convenience Group.

Despite its retention of an exclusive frontal area and rear spoiler, the Escort GT now had to share its 127 horsepower 1.8-liter 16-valve 4-cylinder Mazda engine with the new LX-E 4-door sedan. Still, both cars were surprisingly quick and responsive. Priced at $11,871, the car came with a 5-speed manual overdrive transaxle and competition suspension with both front and rear stabilizers. Four-wheel power disc brakes and styled cast aluminum wheels were part of the GT package, while an optional 4-speed automatic transaxle could be added. Oddly, a stereo tape deck was standard equipment on both the GT and the LX-E models.

Ford's little Korean offering, the Festiva continued to be available in standard (L) and GL versions. But this year it aimed for the youth market with six different sport options, each having their own unique tape-stripe designs. Also in the $366 sports package were a rear roof-edge spoiler and special seat fabrics in matching sporty colors. In plain form, the Festiva was base priced at $6,941, while the GL model went for $7,980. A popular sun roof option was another $243, while a 3-speed automatic transaxle added $515. The 141-inch long Festiva was still powered by a 1.3-liter (80.7 cubic inch) Four of 63 horsepower.

As of this writing...year-end, 1992...Ford has shown a definite continuing interest in sport types and small cars, and indicated an urge to downsize its inventory of available models.

Most noticeable on the floor was the brand new Probe, which actually was unveiled in early 1992 but was not scheduled for production until it could be titled as a 1993 vehicle. Wearing a greatly modified Ford-designed body and two Mazda-engineered high output engines, the Probe definitely entered the ranks of the sporty car set...a pleasure to look at and a thrill to drive.

The new body design had the cowl three inches lower and noticeably further forward than previous models, resulting in a windshield rake of 64 degrees. The fenders and hood line curved nicely into a low frontal area containing flip-up headlights, and broken only by slant-eyed parking/signal light pods and two low set air intakes which also provide a home to the fog/road lights on the GT model. On the sides, flush glass ran the full length from windshield to rear window and successfully hid both B and C-pillars, thereby greatly reducing body side air turbulence. The rear, which in true wedge shape was substantially higher than the nose, also was nicely rounded and provided space for a single wrap-around complex which housed taillights, back-up lights, and a centrally mounted license plate housing. And clinching the design were new covers for the 14-inch wheels on the Probe, and new 16-inch 5-spoke cast aluminum wheels for the GT models.

The former GL and LX models went away, and the Probe family now consisted of only a standard and a GT model, each with its own exclusive engine, wheels, and suspension. The standard model had a revised 16-valve 2-liter Four, with dual overhead belt-driven cams and multi-port fuel injection. Rated at 115 horsepower at 5500 rpm, the unit was hooked to a 5-speed manual overdrive transaxle. MacPherson strut 4-wheel independent suspension with stabilizer bars, power steering, and power brakes (rear drum, front disc) provided excellent handling. The screaming GT version had a new 24-valve V-6, of 2.5-liter (153 cubic inches) which was rated at 164 horsepower at 6000 rpm. This is more than one horse per cubic inch, an enginering feat once thought impossible. It too used dual overhead cams and multi-port electronic fuel injection. Its suspension was an exclusive upgrade of the standard Probe unit, while its brakes were powered 4-wheel discs. It too used a 5-speed manual transmission, but either model could be fitted with a 4-speed automatic for $732.

Ford's other sport-type car, the Mustang, changed very little, and retained its seven available models. As before, the LX series of three models used the 2.3-liter (140 cubic inch) Four with twin plugs for each cylinder and multi-port electronic fuel injection. The LX 5.0L and GT models continued to use the 5-liter (302 cubic inch) High Output V-8 with sequential fuel injection, dual exhausts, and Traction-Lok rear axle. As before, the GT models used their own exclusive front and flared rocker and side panels. The LX cars used stamped 14-inch steel wheels, while the others used 16-inch 5-spoke cast aluminum wheels.

Entering the Mustang corral this year and providing some confusion was the new Mustang Cobra. A project of Ford's Special Vehicles Team, the car had its own unique face, wheels, and Cobra plaque, but otherwise looked like a GT Hatchback. Power was by a modified 5-liter V-8, with special heads and roller rocker arms. Oddly, mention of the Mustang Cobra appears in a French/English 1992 catalog, with an accompanying photo which shows a car identical to the GT and makes no mention of special modifications. The new Mustang Cobra was projected as a limited-issue car, with neither price nor production figures announced at the time of this writing.

In the little car world, the Escort also received a face lift, but this occurred so early in 1992 that it was really old hat at the traditional fall announcement time. Still, the new-style Escorts were all registered as early-1993 models. Engines remained the same 1.9-liter Four of 88 horsepower in the standard and LX models, and the 1.8-liter 16-valve Four of 127 horsepower for the LX-E and GT models. Wheels became interesting, as all standard and LX models except the sedan used 13 inch wheels, the LX-E and LX sedans used 14 inch rims, and the GT used 15 inchers. In a minor name switch, the "Pony" no longer was around as a name, and its low-trim hatchback style was simply called the Escort.

At the other end of the spectrum were Ford's two traditional models, the beautiful Crown Victorias and Thunderbirds. The Victorias lost one model with the demise of the expensive and unpopular Touring Sedan. Now buyers had two trim choices, standard and LX. However, the Touring Sedan still existed in actuality if not name, via a $1,900 performance and handling package, which included the 210 horse version of the 4.6-liter overhead cam engine; dual exhaust; performance-revised shocks, stabilizers, and springs; rear air suspension; anti-lock brakes, cast aluminum wheels, and other goodies formerly found on the Touring Sedan.

Although visually the Thunderbirds hardly changed at all, the nest now held only two Birds. With both the V-8 Sport Coupe and the plain Thunderbird Coupe gone, the only Birds left were the LX and the Super Coupe, each with its own exclusive engine. In the LX was found the same 3.8-liter V-6 as appeared in the Taurus LX wagon, and as an option in other Taurus models. Rated at 140 horsepower, it used multi-port electronic fuel injection and was hooked to the 4-speed automatic transmission. Meanwhile the Super Coupe continued to use an intercooled supercharged version of this block, with sequential multi-port electronic fuel injection which built up 210 horsepower. This car continued to use a 5-speed manual transmission and special suspension. The former V-8 powered Sport Coupe was no longer available as a separate model, but the 5-liter V-8 engine and 4-speed automatic transmission could still be ordered as a package for the LX at a cost of $1,086.

With the L series of low-trim styles now gone, the

Taurus line was reduced to five models. This meant that the GL series of sedans and wagons were now the low-trim level, while the LX series of similar models represented the high-trim level. There was no mid-ground, as the SHO Sedan continued in a class by itself. Unchanged in appearance, the Taurus line continued to use the 3-liter V-6 with automatic transaxle as standard power in all but the SHO and LX. The LX had the Thunderbird 3.8-liter V-6 as standard power, and this engine was still a $555 option for all other Taurus models except the SHO. The SHO continued to use a special 24-valve dual overhead cam V-6 of 3-liters with a manual 5-speed transaxle, but at this writing there is anticipation of a new optional 3.2-liter version of this engine with a 4-speed automatic.

And last, but not least, was the Tempo line, which this year also saw a reduction of available styles. Gone were the two GLS models with their standard V-6 engines. Now the line consisted solely of the GL two and 4-door sedans, and the 4-door LX. All three models used the 2.3-liter Four with sequential electronic fuel injection and 5-speed manual transmission as standard power. The 3-liter V-6 was still available as a $685 option on all models, while the 3-speed automatic transaxle could be added to either engine for another $563.

All told, as this is being written, it appears that the remainder of the 1990s will be very kind to Ford, despite some huge financial losses at the beginning of the decade. Still, engineering and design are very strong, the company appears to have all of its programs in order, and its worldwide overall line is as good as any and better than many makes currently on the market. It appears today that the nationalistic tendency to categorize cars as American made, Japanese, Canadian, English, German, etc. is going to be a thing of the past.

More and more in the future we are going to be looking at multi-national cars, with components and even final assembly being made on all continents, and with decreasing regard to the origin of the parts. In this scene, Ford seems to be in an excellent position, with a vast network of semi-autonomous multi-national corporations ready to add whatever is necessary to produce a fine line of vehicles for world-wide consumption. Lets hope the coming decade proves this to be correct.

First seen in early 1992, but not entering the market until the 1993 season was the totally new Probe. Representing a design and engineering combination of Ford and Mazda, the sleek sports-type car had an all-new body and new engines. Once more, each model had its own exclusive engine. The GL and LX series were gone. Least expensive of the two new Probes was the Model 20, which had a base price of $12,845. Its power came from a newly revised 16-valve 2-liter Four with dual overhead cams and multi-port fuel injection. It was rated at 115 horsepower. All Probes used a 5-speed manual transaxle as standard fare, but could be equipped with 4-speed automatics for another $732. Four-wheel independent suspension and MacPherson struts and coil springs all around provided an excellent handling package.

Becoming a real screamer with its new body and 24-valve V-6 was the Probe GT, Model 22. Base priced at $15,174, the car carried a new dual overhead cam engine of 2.5-liters which produced 164 horses...or more than one for each of its 153 cubic inches. Among the design features were flush side glass which successfully hid both the B and C-pillars, new 16-inch 5-spoke cast aluminum wheels, and 4-wheel power disc brakes. The plain Probe used 14-inch pressed steel wheels unless the 15-inch optional cast aluminum 3-spoke wheels were ordered. The sleek lines hid the fact that the Probe was still built in hatchback style.

The most tame of only two remaining Thunderbirds was the Model 62 LX Coupe, priced at $15,797 in basic form. Gone were the very similar standard coupe and the V-8 powered Sport Coupe. Now the only standard engine in Bird's nest was the 3.8-liter V-6 in two forms. The plain block, which also was used in the Taurus LX wagon, provided 140 horsepower. No longer available in a separate Sport Coupe model, but obtainable as an option package was the 5-liter High Output V-8. Together with the mandatory 4-speed automatic, it cost $1,086. Although 16-inch cast aluminum wheels came with the Super Coupe, the LX had to contend with pressed steel wheels unless the 15-inch directional cast aluminum wheels shown here were ordered for $220 extra.

Ford's most potent performance vehicle was still the Thunderbird Super Coupe, Model 64, which used an intercooled supercharged version of the 3.8-liter V-6 with sequential multi-port electronic fuel injection and dual exhaust. Producing 210 horsepower, this engine was hooked to a manual 5-speed transmission, but a 4-speed automatic was available. In base form, the Super Coupe was posted at $22,030. Among the extras on this car were 4-wheel disc brakes with an anti-locking system; automatic adjustable ride control suspension; Traction-Lok rear axle; heavy-duty suspension package; articulated power-assisted seats, and 16-inch directional cast aluminum wheels.

1993

Continuing to promote its sports image was the Mustang GT series, available as a convertible, Model 45, for $20,950, or as this hatchback, Model 42, priced at $15,850. GT Mustangs continued to be powered only with the 5-liter High Output V-8 with sequential multi-port fuel injection. The cars continued to use their own fascia with integrated air dam, flared rockers, and dual exhausts, and were fitted with a unique rear spoiler. For sheer ego, the speedometer on these and the LX 5.0L models read up to 140 MPH. Traction-Lok rear axle, 16-inch cast aluminum wheels, and special heavy duty suspension with variable rate coil springs were also included in the package.

Basically the LX 5.0L models differed from the GT variety only in exterior decor, and since they were a bit lighter, they may have produced a slightly better performance record. In the LX 5.0L series were the Model 44 convertible shown here, at $20,390; the Model 41 hatchback at $14,810, and the Model 40 coupe (notchback) at $14,020. Using the same identical bodies and model numbers, but fitted with the 4-cylinder 2.3-liter engine, single exhaust, and 14-inch pressed steel wheels were the plain LX styles. Here the convertible was based at $15,839; the hatchback at $11,320, and the coupe at $10,810. All Mustang convertibles continued to be fitted with the rear deck luggage rack which incorporated the mandated high-position brake light.

The Crown Victoria line was now down to two models with the demise of the Touring Sedan. They were the plain Crown Victoria, Model 73 shown here, base priced at $20,115, and the Model 74 LX version, at $21,750. Externally the two models looked the same, with the LX treatment being strictly in interior level. The base engine was the 4.6-liter overhead cam V-8 of 190 horsepower. However, for $1,905, a special handling and performance package could be ordered. This included the 210 horse version of the V-8; dual exhausts; heavier springs, shocks, and stabilizers; 16-inch cast aluminum wheels; anti-lock braking; rear air suspension; electronic traction assist; a 120 MPH speedometer, and other deluxe toys which in effect returned the car to its 1992 Touring Sedan status.

Since the Country Squire no longer existed, Ford's most luxurious station wagon was the Model 58 LX Taurus. Base priced at $20,100, the wagon is shown here with the preferred equipment package, which added another $1,300 to the tab. The package added such items as rear window defroster and wiper; keyless entry system; AM/FM stereo with cassette and power antenna, speed control, cargo area cover, and load floor extension. Companion to this model was the GL Model 57 wagon, which was priced at $16,760. In addition to the multitude of differences between the LX and GL series listed in the sedan caption, the GL wagon used the 3-liter V-6, while the LX model had the 3.8-liter V-6.

The Taurus SHO Sedan, Model 54, still had the dubious honor of being Ford's most expensive model, with a base price of $24,829. For this, owners received the thrill of driving a performance-oriented sedan with a Yamaha-built 24-valve 3-liter V-6 with dual overhead cam; a 5-speed manual transaxle, and competition-type suspension. Additional items on the car included electronically controlled air conditioning; 4-wheel anti-lock disc brakes; leather trimmed power operated bucket seats; AM/FM stereo cassette with premium sound system; unique front with fog lamps integrated into the valence panel; a rear spoiler with brake light, and unidirectional sparkle spoke cast aluminum wheels. Later in the season, SHO buyers had the option of a similar Yamaha engine of 3.2-liters, hooked to an electronic 4-speed automatic transaxle.

With the demise of the L series, the Taurus had no middle ground trim level. The line was now divided into the lower trim GL series and the higher level LX grouping. Both series consisted of a 4-door sedan and a station wagon model. In the GL line, the sedan was the Model 52, based at $15,600, while the LX version, shown here, was the Model 53, base priced at $18,410. Both models used the 3-liter V-6 with 4-speed automatic transmission, with the 3.8 liter V-6 being available for another $555. A more plush interior, air conditioning, sparkle-cast aluminum spoke wheels, front power operated bucket seats, and power windows and door locks were among the extras found on the LX models.

1993

The Tempo line also received a cutback in models, with both GLS 6-cylinder cars going away. That meant that the only 2-door was the GL Model 31, which was base priced at $10,360. All Tempos were now powered by the High Swirl Combustion 2.3-liter Four, with no standard 6-cylinder series. However, the 3-liter V-6 was still available as a $685 option, with the price including special stabilizer bars. All models used a 5-speed manual transaxle, but again, the 3-speed automatic was available for $563 extra.

Although the Tempo 2-door now came in only one flavor, the 4-door styles were still divided between the GL Model 36 shown here and the LX Model 37. The GL was base priced at $10,360, the same as the 2-door, but the LX wore a $12,230 tag. For the extra bucks, LX buyers received the polycast wheels shown here as a GL option, plus a tuned suspension, deluxe interior, tilt steering wheel, dual electric remote side mirrors, special pin striping, power door locks, and a sport-type instrument cluster. LX models also wore a small identity plaque just behind the front wheel well. On the GL, the polycast wheels were a $193 option.

Topping the Escort price list was the LX-E 4-door Sedan, Model 16, which had a base price of $11,933. The car used the same 1.8-liter 16-valve dual overhead cam Four as found in the GT. In addition, it was fitted with power steering; 4-wheel disc brakes; reclining bucket seats; center console; AM/FM stereo with cassette and digital clock; remote releases for the decklid and fuel door; electric dual sideview mirrors, and 14-inch styled aluminum wheels, unique only to the LX-E. The car was built in true sedan form, with a definite rear cargo area accessible through a conventional deck lid rather than a hatch or 5th door. For families with small children, rear doors were equipped with child-safe locks to prevent opening from the inside.

The main line of the Escort field continued to be the LX series, which carried one of each available model. The Model 11 LX Hatchback shown here was priced at $9,364; the 4-door Hatchback, Model 14, was $9,797; the 4-door Sedan Model 13 was $10,041, and the Wagon, Model 15, was $10,367. The wagon and 4-door hatchback were exclusive LX models, while the 2-door hatchback was found in the plain Escort series and also used for the GT. Lowest priced of all Fords was the plain Escort Hatchback, formerly known as the Pony. This car was base priced at $8,355. The LX example illustrated here carries the newly introduced $757 sports appearance group, which included 14-inch bright cast aluminum wheels; a special opal gray interior with full cloth seats; GT steering wheel and tachometer; spoiler with integrated brake light, and special appliques.

Escort's little hot shot continued to be the GT Hatchback, Model 12, which listed for $11,871. Its 127 horsepower came from the same 1.8-liter 16-valve dual overhead cam Four as found in the LX-E, and all of the performance and luxury components found in the fancy sedan were also used on the GT. However, while the LX-E used its own 14-inch cast aluminum wheels, the GT used special cast 15-inch 5-spoke units. As before, the GT also had its own unique facia with conspicuous right-side slanted grille bars and fog lights installed in the valence panel. New rocker panel design and a special rear deck with spoiler and integrated brake light completed the 1993 changes. All hatchback models continued to use a fold-down rear seat which allowed a substantial amount of stowage space when folded. But rear seat leg room was still tight.

Back in 1968, when George Dammann had the initial idea for *Illustrated History of Ford*, no one could have convinced him that 25 years later he would finally be putting the finishing touches on that first book's sequel. And, within that time frame, he would be responsible for the formation and success of what was to become one of the country's best known and respected independent automotive and agricultural publishing companies; that he would author, co-author, or edit and design a total of 30 titles in the Crestline series, and finally, would see Crestline become part of Motorbooks International, the world's largest and best known distributor of specialty automotive books.

A 1933 model, George began his writing career with an upstate New York newspaper in 1956 following an army stint as a bulldozer and heavy equipment operator with a combat engineer unit. His life-time love of cars soon led to a weekend job as announcer, photographer and publicity manager in the then relatively new sport of organized drag racing. He filled this role for three years with NASCAR, and then three more years with NHRA after NASCAR left the northeastern drag racing scene.

In 1962 he left the newspaper field to take an assistant editor's job with the *National Underwriter*, the country's leading trade magazine for the insurance business. In this role, he specialized in all forms of automotive, transportation, and fire insurance, traveling extensively through the U.S., Canada, and Mexico writing investigative articles related to specialized insurance topics. By 1970, when his first free-lance book finally materialized, he was associate editor and Chicago manager for the National Underwriter Co.

Following *Illustrated History of Ford*, George next authored *50 Years of Lincoln Mercury* (which later became *The Cars of Lincoln Mercury*, co-authored with James K. Wagner) and *60 Years of Chevrolet* (which later became *75 Years of Chevrolet* and is credited with being one of the best selling automotive books ever compiled).

At this juncture, George left the rock-solid stability of the Underwriter Co. and took a wild gamble as general manager of Crestline Publishing (the name being derived from the Dammann's family farm, where the crest of the hills behind the barn formed the initial property line...hence, Crestline Farm). But the move paid off, and Crestline rose to become one of the better known publishers of quality automotive and agricultural history books.

During the formative years, the company was located in Glen Ellyn, Ill., about 35 miles west of Chicago. Here the Dammann's had the space to continue with their car collecting hobby, consisting of collector vehicles ranging from Model T Fords to hot rods, to modern-classic convertibles, muscle cars, and even exotic motorcycles. Not a static collection, enough vehicles were moved in and out of the confines each year to finally induce the State of Illinois to "request" that George take out a dealer's license.

That problem was solved in 1977, when Crestline began a move to Sarasota, Fla., completing the transfer and closing the Illinois office in 1978. With the change of locations, the car collection was trimmed to a couple of the beloved Model Ts, one hot rod truck, a couple of Cadillac convertibles, and George's overdressed Harley. Finally, over the years, these also disappeared, until now the Dammann's delight in old cars is fulfilled by admiring those of other owners at various car shows!

In 1992, Crestline became a part of Motorbooks International (Classic Motorbooks) of Osceola, Wis. This was a move that made utmost sense in that both companies had worked closely together since the early 1970s, and MBI had always been Crestline's largest distributor of its automotive line. Included in the acquisition was George's move to a consulting role, where he continues as an author, editor, and designer, still working from the old Sarasota office...no Wisconsin winters, thank you!

The move has allowed George and Gloria Dammann even more freedom to indulge in another of their true loves...world travel. In fact, a good part of the writing of this book was done in Oranjestad, on the island of Aruba, which has almost become a second home. In total, the Dammann's have now visited over three dozen different countries, on all continents except Antarctica.

The Dammanns have two grown children, and three grandchildren. Son Eric is owner of Eric's Auto Body and Towing, a major Sarasota collision repair shop which he founded in 1979. Daughter Carole Worthington, after five years of living in Japan, now resides in Silverdale, Wash., just across the bay from Seattle...still a ways away, and still a nice place to visit.